Using Quattro Pro® 4
Special Edition

PATRICK J. BURNS

que

Using Quattro Pro 4, Special Edition

Copyright © 1992 by Que® Corporation.

All rights reserved. Printed in the United States of America. No part of this book may be used or reproduced in any form or by any means, or stored in a database or retrieval system, without prior written permission of the publisher except in the case of brief quotations embodied in critical articles and reviews. Making copies of any part of this book for any purpose other than your own personal use is a violation of United States copyright laws. For information, address Que Corporation, 11711 N. College Ave., Carmel, IN 46032.

Library of Congress Catalog No: 91-68382

ISBN: 0-88022-931-4

This book is sold *as is*, without warranty of any kind, either express or implied, respecting the contents of this book, including but not limited to implied warranties for the book's quality, performance, merchantability, or fitness for any particular purpose. Neither Que Corporation nor its dealers or distributors shall be liable to the purchaser or any other person or entity with respect to any liability, loss, or damage caused or alleged to be caused directly or indirectly by this book.

95 94 93 92   4 3 2

Interpretation of the printing code: the rightmost double-digit number is the year of the book's printing; the rightmost single-digit number, the number of the book's printing. For example, a printing code of 92-1 shows that the first printing of the book occurred in 1992.

Using Quattro Pro 4, Special Edition is based on Quattro Pro through Version 4.0.

Publisher: Lloyd J. Short

Acquisitions Manager: Rick Ranucci

Project Development Manager: Thomas H. Bennett

Managing Editor: Paul Boger

Book Designer: Scott Cook

Production Team: Scott Boucher, Paula Carroll, Michelle Cleary, Mark Enochs, Brook Farling, Dennis Clay Hager, Audra Hershman, Carrie Keesling, Betty Kish, Phil Kitchel, Juli Pavey, Caroline Roop, Sandy Shay, M. Louise Shinault, Kevin Spear, Susan VandeWalle, Mary Beth Wakefield, Phil Worthington

DEDICATION

For Mom

Thanks for sitting me down in front of your typewriter all those years ago.

CREDITS

Product Director
Shelley O'Hara

Production Editor
Diane L. Steele

Editors
Susan M. Shaw
Robin Drake
Jeannine Freudenberger
Kelly D. Dobbs
Kelly Currie
Betty White

Technical Editors
Leslie Creach
Stacy Eggimann

Special Assistance
Lori A. Lyons

Composed in Cheltenham and MCPdigital by Que Corporation

ABOUT THE AUTHOR

Patrick J. Burns has a B.S. in finance and economics. A native of Pennsylvania, he is a worldwide traveler who has lived in Europe and Asia. A founder and principal of Burns & Associates, a San Diego-based professional consulting firm, he also is an established author and expert in spreadsheet development.

His work in the computer field includes Beta site testing, confidential review, and program development of software packages for major publishers. He also is an instructor at the University of California, San Diego, where he teaches courses about using Quattro Pro.

The coauthor of *Excel Business Applications: IBM Version*, published by Que Corporation, he has authored and contributed to fourteen other books about using Quattro Pro, Lotus 1-2-3, WordPerfect, Microsoft Excel, Microsoft Word, and Microsoft Windows.

TRADEMARK ACKNOWLEDGMENTS

Que Corporation has made every effort to supply trademark information about company names, products, and services mentioned in this book. Trademarks indicated below were derived from various sources. Que Corporation cannot attest to the accuracy of this information.

1-2-3, Freelance, Lotus, Symphony, and VisiCalc are registered trademarks of Lotus Development Corporation.

3Com is a registered trademark of 3Com Corporation.

Bitstream is a registered trademark and Fontware is a trademark of Bitstream, Inc.

Canon is a registered trademark of Canon, Inc.

Collage Plus is a trademark of Inner Media, Incorporated.

dBASE, dBASE II, dBASE III, and dBASE IV are registered trademarks and dBASE III Plus is a trademark of Ashton-Tate Corporation.

DESQview is a trademark of Quarterdeck Office Systems.

EPSON is a registered trademark of Epson Corporation.

IBM, IBM PC, IBM AT, and OS/2 are registered trademarks and IBM PC XT and PS/2 are trademarks of International Business Machines Corporation.

Intel is a registered trademark and Above Board is a trademark of Intel Corporation.

Microsoft, Microsoft Windows, MS-DOS, and Multiplan are registered trademarks of Microsoft Corporation.

Novell and NetWare are registered trademarks of Novell, Inc.

PC Paintbrush is a registered trademark of ZSoft Corporation.

PostScript is a registered trademark of Adobe Systems, Inc.

Rampage is a registered trademark of AST Research, Inc.

Quadram is a registered trademark of Quadram Corporation.

Quattro Pro, Paradox, and SideKick are registered trademarks and Reflex and VROOMM are trademarks of Borland International, Inc.

WordPerfect is a registered trademark of WordPerfect Corporation.

Trademarks of other products mentioned in this book are held by the companies producing them.

ACKNOWLEDGMENTS

To Shelley O'Hara and Diane Steele: My sincere thanks for your patience, considerate guidance, and consistently competent editing throughout the development of *Using Quattro Pro 4*, Special Edition.

To Meg Misenti: Thank you for your tireless work and unwavering professional attitude. You have succeeded in making this revision the smoothest one to date.

To David Maguiness: Thank you for contributing the Command Reference.

CONTENTS AT A GLANCE

Introduction 1

I Using Quattro Pro Spreadsheets 13
   1 Quick Start: Using Quattro Pro 15
   2 Getting Started 39
   3 Entering and Editing Data 83
   4 Manipulating Data 121
   5 Formatting Data 167
   6 Using Functions 225
   7 Analyzing Spreadsheets 295
   8 Managing Files and Windows 325

II Printing and Graphing 387
   9 Printing 389
  10 Creating Graphs 431
  11 Customizing Graphs 483
  12 Analyzing Graphs 541

III Advanced Spreadsheet Applications 571
  13 Managing Your Data 573
  14 Analyzing Data 611
  15 Creating Macros 649
  16 Customizing Quattro Pro 697

Command Reference 749

Appendix
   A Installing Quattro Pro 937
   B Macro Commands 959
   C Menu-Equivalent Commands 987
   D Using ASCII Characters 1021
   E Installing Quattro Pro on a Network 1029

     Index 1049

TABLE OF CONTENTS

Introduction 1
    The Evolution of Quattro Pro 2
    What's New in Version 4.0 4
    Who Should Read This Book 5
    How This Book Is Organized 5
        Part I: Using Quattro Pro Spreadsheets 7
        Part II: Printing and Graphing 8
        Part III: Advanced Spreadsheet Applications 9
        Command Reference 9
        Appendixes 10
        Conventions Used in This Book 10

I Using Quattro Pro Spreadsheets

1 Quick Start: Using Quattro Pro 15
    Beginning a Quattro Pro Work Session 16
    Executing a Command 17
    Entering and Editing Spreadsheet Data 18
        Entering Different Data Types 18
        Entering Formulas 22
        Copying Formulas 23
        Using @Functions 24
        Editing Data 26
    Improving Spreadsheet Style 27
        Moving Data 27
        Changing Column Widths 28
        Aligning Data in Cells 29
        Formatting Numbers 31
        Drawing Lines 32
        Inserting Rows and Columns 34
    Managing Documents 35
        Saving a Spreadsheet to a Hard Drive 35

  Saving a Spreadsheet to a Floppy Disk 35
  Ending a Work Session 35
 Summary 37

2 Getting Started 39

 Learning about Spreadsheets 40
  Understanding Columns and Rows 40
  Designing a Spreadsheet 42
  Asking What-If Questions 43
 Reviewing the Uses of a Spreadsheet 45
  Constructing a Spreadsheet 45
  Designing a Graph 46
  Building a Database 46
  Creating a Macro Program 47
 Starting and Ending a Work Session 48
  Starting Quattro Pro 48
  Returning to the Operating System 49
  Using Special Start-Up Parameters 49
 Working with a Keyboard 50
  Using the Alphanumeric Keyboard 51
  Using the Numeric Keypad 52
  Using the Arrow Keys 53
  Using the Function Keys 54
 Working with a Mouse 56
  Learning Basic Mouse-Movement Techniques 56
  Turbocharging Your Mouse 57
 Reviewing the Screen Display 57
  Pull-Down Menu Bar 58
  SpeedBars 58
  Input Line 61
  Spreadsheet Area 64
  Status Line 65
 Accessing Quattro Pro Menus 68
  Activating a Menu 68
  Choosing a Command 69
  Quitting a Menu Selection 70
  Reviewing Data on a Quattro Pro Menu 71
  Using Ctrl-Key Shortcuts 72
 Switching Display Modes 74
  The Zoom Icon 75
  The Resize Box 76
 Getting Help 76
 Questions & Answers 78
  Loading Quattro Pro 79
  Working with a Keyboard and Mouse 80

Using SpeedBars	80
Accessing Quattro Pro Menus	81
Getting Help	81
Summary	82

3 Entering and Editing Data 83

Learning Spreadsheet Terminology	83
Entering Data	84
Learning about Labels	86
Learning about Values	88
Entering Numbers	89
Entering Formulas	91
Entering Dates and Times	98
Entering @Function Commands	99
Working with Cell References and Blocks	101
Defining Relative Reference Format	101
Defining Absolute Reference Format	102
Defining Mixed Reference Format	102
Changing the Cell Reference Format	104
Working with Cell References	104
Working with Cell Blocks	107
Editing Data	109
Using the Alt-F5 Undo Key	111
Recalculating Your Spreadsheet Formulas	111
Viewing the Spreadsheet	112
Viewing the Basic Spreadsheet Window	112
Splitting the Screen Horizontally or Vertically	112
Displaying Tiled Spreadsheets	114
Selecting the Screen Display Mode	114
Questions & Answers	115
Entering Labels	116
Entering Values	117
Working with Cell References and Blocks	117
Editing Data	118
Viewing Data	118
Summary	118

4 Manipulating Data 121

Reviewing the Edit Menu	122
Copying, Moving, and Erasing Cell Data	124
Copying the Contents of a Cell	125
Using Copy Special	127
Moving the Contents of a Cell	128
Erasing a Cell's Contents	132

Working with Blocks 133
    Copying a Block 133
    Moving a Block 133
    Erasing a Block 134
Reversing Operations with Undo 134
Inserting and Deleting Rows and Columns 135
    Inserting a Row 136
    Deleting a Row 137
    Inserting a Column 138
    Deleting a Column 139
    Inserting and Deleting Row Blocks
      and Column Blocks 139
Naming a Block 142
    Creating Names 143
    Deleting Names 145
    Adding Notes to Named Blocks 147
    Using Labels To Create Names 149
    Resetting Cell Block Names 150
    Making a Table of Names 150
    Using Names in Formulas 152
Filling a Block with Numbers 153
Changing Formulas to Values 154
Transposing Data in a Cell Block 156
Searching for and Replacing Data 157
    Setting the Search Parameters 158
    Using Special Search Parameters 161
Questions & Answers 162
    Copying, Moving, and Erasing Cell Data 162
    Inserting and Deleting Columns and Rows 163
    Naming Cell Blocks 163
    Filling, Transposing, Searching for,
      and Replacing Data 164
Summary 165

5 Formatting Data 167

Using Style Menu Commands 168
    Undoing Style Menu Commands 170
    Changing the Default Global Settings 170
Controlling Data Display 172
    Aligning Data 172
    Formatting Values, Labels, Dates, and Times 175
    Protecting Important Data 185
Working with Columns and Rows 187
    Setting the Width of a Column 188
    Working with Multiple Columns 190

- Hiding a Column 193
- Setting the Height of a Row 195
- Working with Multiple Rows 197
- Selecting Presentation-Quality Options 199
  - Previewing Enhancements 199
  - Drawing Lines and Boxes 200
  - Shading Cell Data for Effect 203
  - Selecting Fonts 204
- Using Custom Spreadsheet Styles 208
  - Using Custom Styles 209
  - Creating a Custom Style 209
  - Applying Custom Styles 210
  - Creating a Custom Numeric Format 211
  - Erasing Custom Styles from a Block 215
  - Deleting Custom Styles from a Spreadsheet 215
  - Saving Custom Styles in Files 216
  - Retrieving a Style Sheet to the Active Spreadsheet 216
  - Editing a Custom Style 216
  - Editing the Default Style 217
- Customizing Predefined Fonts 217
- Using Page Breaks To Control Printing 219
  - Inserting a Page Break 219
  - Deleting a Page Break 220
- Questions & Answers 220
  - Controlling the Display of Your Data 220
  - Working with Columns and Rows 221
  - Selecting Presentation-Quality Options 222
- Summary 223

6 Using Functions 225

- Understanding Command Syntax 226
- Entering @Function Commands 227
- Using Mathematical @Functions 228
  - Using Arithmetic Commands in a Spreadsheet ... 229
  - Using Trigonometric Commands in a Spreadsheet 232
- Using Statistical @Functions 236
- Using String @Functions 240
- Using Miscellaneous @Functions 250
- Using Logical @Functions 263
- Using Financial @Functions 267
- Using Date and Time @Function Commands 282
- Using Database Statistical @Function Commands 287
- Questions & Answers 291
- Summary 293

7 Analyzing Spreadsheets 295

Using the Solve For Command 296
    Reviewing the Solve For Menu 296
    Understanding the Rules for Using Solve For 297
    Solving for a Depreciation Expense 298
    Solving for an Investment Return 301
    Solving for a Mortgage Interest Payment 302
    Solving for a What-If Analysis 305
Using the Audit Command 309
    Reviewing the Audit Menu 309
    Auditing Spreadsheet Formulas 310
Questions & Answers 322
    Solving Formulas 322
    Auditing Formulas 323
Summary 323

8 Managing Files and Windows 325

Reviewing the File Menu Commands 326
Working with Files 328
    Creating, Opening, and Retrieving Files 329
    Saving, Closing, and Erasing Files 331
    Password Protecting Your Files 333
    Setting the Directory Path Name 335
    Creating a Workspace File 336
Translating Spreadsheets 336
    Using dBASE File Formats 338
    Using Lotus 1-2-3 2.X File Formats 339
    Using Lotus 1-2-3 3.X File Formats 340
    Using Other File Formats 342
Setting the SQZ! File Compression Options 344
Using the DOS Shell 346
Using the File Manager 347
    Learning the File Manager Menus 347
    Maneuvering through the File Manager
        Window 348
    Using the Control Pane 350
    Using the File Pane 351
    Using the Tree Pane 352
    Manipulating Files with the File Manager 354
Working with Windows 356
    Organizing Windows On-Screen 357
    Creating Special Display Effects 361
Linking Spreadsheets 366
    Creating Linking Formulas 367
    Typing a Linking Formula 368

Typing a Linking Formula 368
Creating 3-D Consolidation Formulas 369
Creating Linking Formulas by Pointing
   and Clicking 371
Moving and Copying Linking Formulas 371
Opening and Updating Linked Spreadsheets 373
Using Advanced File Tools 377
Importing a File 377
Combining Two Files 378
Extracting Part of a File 381
Questions & Answers 382
Managing Files 382
Displaying Windows 383
Linking Worksheets 383
Summary 384

II Printing and Graphing

9 Printing 389

Reviewing the Print Menu 390
Printing Small Spreadsheet Reports 391
Printing Large Spreadsheet Reports 393
Choosing Layout Options 395
Using the Print Layout Dialog Box 395
Reviewing Layout Menu Settings 397
Adding Headers and Footers 397
Controlling Page Breaks 399
Scaling a Spreadsheet Printout 400
Setting Margins 400
Defining Dimensions 403
Choosing a Print Orientation 403
Using Setup Strings 404
Updating and Resetting the Layout Options 406
Using Other Print Commands 407
Choosing the Display Format 407
Specifying the Number of Copies 408
Adjusting the Printer 408
Printing a Spreadsheet That Fits 410
Choosing a Print Destination 410
Printing to a Text File 410
Printing to a Binary File 412
Printing to a Graphics Printer 413
Previewing a Printout On-Screen 414
Previewing Print Blocks 416

xv

Printing Graphs 417
    Choosing a Destination 418
    Creating the Layout of the Graph 418
    Creating a Special Graph File 421
Managing Multiple Print Jobs 422
    Printing in the Background 423
    Monitoring Multiple Print Jobs 424
    Changing the Status of Print Jobs 426
Questions & Answers 427
    Printing the Spreadsheet 427
    Printing a Graph 428
Summary 429

10 Creating Graphs 431

Reviewing the Graph Menu 432
Reviewing Hardware Requirements 434
Understanding Graphs 435
    Utility of Graphs 435
    Anatomy of Graphs 437
    Basic Graphs 439
Creating a Basic Graph 452
    Preselecting a Block 453
    Creating a Fast Graph 454
    Building a Customized Graph 456
Enhancing the Appearance of a Basic Graph 459
    Adding Titles 460
    Adding Legends 462
    Changing the Font 462
Managing Graph Files 468
    Naming and Saving a Graph 469
    Autosaving Edited Graphs 470
    Displaying a Saved Graph 470
    Erasing a Saved Graph 471
    Resetting the Current Graph Settings 471
    Copying a Saved Graph 471
Displaying a Graph 472
    Using Graph Zoom and Pan 473
    Creating a Slide Show 474
    Enhancing a Slide Show 475
    Inserting a Graph onto a Spreadsheet 476
Questions & Answers 478
    Creating a Graph 478
    Enhancing the Appearance of a Basic Graph 479
    Displaying Graphs 479
Summary 481

11 Customizing Graphs 483
Using the Graph Customize Dialog Box 484
Reviewing the Customize Series Menu Commands ... 486
Customizing a Graph Data Series 488
Changing Colors 489
Changing Fill Patterns 489
Changing Markers and Lines 491
Changing the Width of Bars 493
Adding Interior Labels 494
Creating Combination Graphs 496
Plotting a Second Y-Axis 497
Customizing Pie Graphs and Column Graphs 498
Customizing Bubble Graphs 502
Updating and Resetting Default Settings 504
Customizing the X-Axis and Y-Axis 504
Using the X-Axis and Y-Axis Dialog Boxes 504
Adjusting the Scale of an Axis 506
Adjusting Axis Ticks 508
Changing the Display of an Axis Scale 509
Customizing the Overall Graph 512
Using the Graph Overall Dialog Box 512
Using Grid Lines on a Graph 514
Adjusting Outlines 515
Changing the Background Color 515
Displaying a Graph in 3-D 516
Toggling On-Screen Color Display 517
Changing Drop Shadow Colors 517
Annotating Graphs 518
Reviewing the Annotator Screen 518
Learning Keyboard Assignments 521
Annotating a Graph 522
Managing Graphs with Graph Buttons 529
Annotating and Managing Multiple
Graph Elements 534
Questions & Answers 536
Summary 539

12 Analyzing Graphs 541
Defining Analytical Graphing 542
Reviewing the Analyze Menu Commands 544
Selecting the Analysis Option 545
Using Aggregation Analysis 546
Reviewing the Aggregation Options 546
Performing a Basic Aggregation Analysis 548

    Performing Aggregation Analysis
        with Multiple Series 552
    Creating a Table of Aggregation Values 554
    Resetting the Graph Series Analyze Settings 555
Using Moving Average Analysis 555
    Reviewing the Moving Average Options 556
    Performing a Basic Moving Average Analysis 557
    Performing Moving Average Analysis
        with Multiple Series 557
    Creating a Table of Moving Average Values 560
Using Linear Fit Analysis 561
    Performing a Basic Linear Fit Analysis 561
    Creating a Table of Linear Fit Regression
        Values 563
Using Exponential Fit Analysis 564
    Performing a Basic Exponential Fit Analysis 565
    Creating a Table of Exponential Fit
        Regression Values 566
Questions & Answers 568
    Using Aggregation 568
    Using Moving Averages 569
Summary 569

III Advanced Spreadsheet Applications

13 Managing Your Data 573

Turning a Spreadsheet into a Database 574
Reviewing the Database Menu 576
Entering Data 577
Sorting a Database 578
    Using One Sort Key 580
    Using Multiple Sort Keys 580
    Returning the Database to Its Original Order 583
    Fine-Tuning a Sort Operation 583
    Sorting Columns 584
Searching a Database 586
    Defining the Search Block 587
    Assigning Names to the Field Names Row 588
    Defining the Search Criteria...................................588
    Performing the Search 592
    Setting Up an Output Block 595
Using a Database as a Data-Entry Form 599
Controlling Data Entry 601
Using Paradox Access 601
    Reviewing the Requirements for Using
        Paradox Access 601

    Preparing To Use Paradox Access 602
    Running Paradox Access 604
  Questions & Answers 606
    Sorting a Database 607
    Searching a Database 607
    Accessing Paradox 608
  Summary 609

14 Analyzing Data 611

  Reviewing the Tools Menu 612
    Using Advanced Math Tools 613
    Using the Parse Command 618
    Using the What-If Function 628
    Creating Frequency Distributions 631
    Using the Optimizer 634
    Loading Add-In @Functions 644
  Questions & Answers 645
    Using Advanced Math Tools 645
    Parsing Data 645
    Using Sensitivity Analysis 646
    Using the Optimizer 646
  Summary 648

15 Creating Macros 649

  Learning about Macros 650
    Reviewing the Macro Menu 651
    Creating a Basic Macro Program 652
  Using the Macro Recorder 653
    Pasting the Recorded Macro into
      a Spreadsheet 654
    Interpreting the Macro 656
    Switching the Macro Recording Mode 658
    Viewing an Instant Replay 658
  Naming a Macro 659
    Using the Name Command 659
    Creating an Autoload Macro 660
  Managing Quattro Pro Macros 661
    Storing Macros on a Spreadsheet 661
    Documenting Macros 662
    Creating Macro Libraries 663
    Executing a Macro 665
    Editing a Macro 666
    Deleting Macros and Macro Names 667
    Interpreting Lotus 1-2-3 Macros 667

Using Advanced Macro Techniques 668
    Entering a Macro Manually 668
    Debugging a Macro 674
    Using the Transcript Facility 682
Questions & Answers 692
    Recording a Macro 693
    Executing a Macro 693
    Using the Transcript 694
Summary 695

16 Customizing Quattro Pro 697

Reviewing the Options Menu 698
Setting Hardware Options 701
    Choosing a New Screen 702
    Choosing Printers 705
    Reviewing Normal Memory, EMS,
      and Coprocessor Data 711
Using Quattro Pro's Coloring Palette 712
    Choosing Menu Colors 713
    Choosing Desktop Colors 714
    Choosing Spreadsheet Colors 714
    Choosing Conditional Colors 715
    Choosing Help Colors 716
    Choosing File Manager Colors 716
    Choosing Palettes Colors 716
Setting International Options 717
    Choosing a Currency Symbol 719
    Attaching Symbols to Negative Values 719
    Choosing the Punctuation 719
    Choosing Date Formats 720
    Choosing Time Formats 721
    Choosing New Sort Rules 721
    Choosing LICS Conversion 723
    Choosing Overstrike Print 723
Using WYSIWYG Zoom % 723
Setting Display Mode Options 724
Setting Startup Options 726
    Setting the Default Directory 726
    Using an Autoload File 727
    Choosing a Startup Macro 729
    Selecting a New Default File Extension 729
    Specifying Beep Tones 729
    Choosing a Menu Tree 730
    Using Dialog Boxes 730
Customizing the SpeedBar 731
Setting Graphics Quality Options 733

- Using Other Options 734
    - Undo 735
    - Macro Redraw 735
    - Expanded Memory 735
    - Clock Display 736
    - Paradox 737
- Setting Network Options 737
    - Drive Mappings 737
    - Print Job Banners 739
    - Refresh Interval 739
    - Queue Monitor 739
    - User Name 739
- Updating the Options 740
- Specifying Format Options 740
    - Numeric Format 741
    - Align Labels 741
    - Hide Zeros 741
    - Global Width 741
- Controlling Recalculation 742
    - Mode 742
    - Order of Recalculation 743
    - Number of Iterations 743
    - Circular Cell 743
- Setting Protection Options 744
- Questions & Answers 745
    - Hardware Options 745
    - Default Format Options 747
- Summary 747

Command Reference 749

- File Commands 750
- Edit Commands 772
- Style Commands 790
- Graph Commands 808
- Print Commands 851
- Database Commands 872
- Tools Commands 888
- Options Commands 910
- Window Commands 932

A Installing Quattro Pro 937

- Setting Up the Ideal System Configuration 938
    - Program Requirements 938
    - Microprocessor Clock Speed and Math
      Coprocessor Chip 939

       Random-Access Memory Management 940
       Hard Disk Drive Management 943
       Video Displays and Printers 943
       Mice 944
   Installing the Program 944
       Copying Files 945
       Selecting Your Equipment 948
       Selecting a Monitor Type 948
       Entering Your Name and Serial Number 949
       Selecting a Printer 949
       Selecting the Default Display Mode 951
       Installing for Use with Microsoft Windows 951
       Selecting the Character Set 952
       Completing the Installation 953
   After Installing Quattro Pro 954
       Loading and Quitting Quattro Pro 954
       Reconfiguring and Enhancing Quattro Pro 954
       Upgrading a Previous Version
          of Quattro Pro to 4.0 954
   Questions & Answers 956
       Ideal System Configuration 956
       Installation Utility 957

B Macro Commands 959
   Using Macro Commands in a Macro Program 959
       Using Subroutines in a Macro Program 962
       Using /x Commands 962
   Macro Command Glossary 963

C Menu-Equivalent Commands 987

D Using ASCII Characters 1021
   Entering ASCII Characters in Spreadsheet Cells 1021
   Entering ASCII Characters in Dialog Boxes 1025
   Converting ASCII Codes into Printer
      Setup Strings 1026

E Installing Quattro Pro on a Network 1029
   What You Need To Run Quattro Pro
      on a Network 1030
   Preinstallation Preparation 1031
   Installing the Program 1032

Choosing the Source Drive
    and Destination Directory 1032
Copying Files 1033
Entering the Personal Signature Data 1033
Specifying a Network Installation 1034
Selecting Your Equipment 1034
Recording Serial Numbers 1035
Preparing the Workstations 1037
Creating a Menu Preference File 1038
Creating a Default File 1039
Modifying the AUTOEXEC.BAT
    and CONFIG.SYS Files 1039
Assigning Access Rights to the Quattro Pro
    Directories 1041
Starting Quattro Pro from a Workstation 1042
Adding Users to the Network 1042
Upgrading a Network from Version 3.0 to
    Version 4.0 1043
What's Different about Using Quattro Pro on
    a Network? 1044
Questions & Answers 1046
    Installing the Program 1046
    Using Quattro Pro on a Network 1047
    Printing on a Network Printer 1047

Index 1049

xxiv

Introduction

Today's electronic spreadsheet programs replace the manual accounting worksheets of yesteryear. The electronic spreadsheet, in fact, combines the best features of the accountant's multicolumn worksheet with the number-crunching power of today's personal computers. Every spreadsheet program performs the same mathematical operations (addition, subtraction, multiplication, and division) easily and efficiently. The best spreadsheet programs, however, offer you much more than that.

Quattro Pro is one of the most powerful electronic spreadsheet programs available for personal computers. Version 4.0 is a crowning achievement in the ongoing development of Borland International's best-selling Quattro program. Version 4.0 demonstrates Borland International's continuing commitment to integrating the newest available technologies into the Quattro Pro spreadsheet environment.

With Quattro Pro, you can turn a spreadsheet into an income statement, a monthly calendar, a written paragraph, a database, or a pie graph. You can use Quattro Pro to record your personal financial budget, do regression analysis for economic forecasting, or store an inventory list of your favorite cassettes and CDs. With Quattro Pro Version 4.0, you can reach more ambitious spreadsheet goals faster and more easily.

Using Quattro Pro 4, Special Edition, teaches you how to install, operate, and master the operation of Quattro Professional (Pro) Version 4.0. The step-by-step instructions in each chapter clearly show you Version

4.0's potential for building elegant computer solutions to meet specific personal management and business reporting needs.

Using Quattro Pro 4, Special Edition, also teaches you how to install, operate, and master the operation of Version 4.0. Released in February, 1992, Version 4.0 offers a WYSIWYG (what-you-see-is-what-you-get) graphical user interface featuring a fully customizable SpeedBar for quick execution of common spreadsheet operations, enhanced spreadsheet analysis tools, custom formats and styles, faster fonts, interactive analytical graphing, background printing, improved network support, increased file support, and many other new spreadsheet features.

Using Quattro Pro 4, Special Edition, is a unique book for many reasons. In this book, you find 16 chapters of targeted, easy-to-follow tutorial text. Real-life examples sprinkled throughout each chapter help you envision your own uses for Quattro Pro.

Each chapter in this book offers a comprehensive look at one aspect of using Quattro Pro, such as enhancing spreadsheet style. Tips, Notes, and Cautions guide you through some of the more complex and interesting aspects of using the program.

A Questions & Answers section appears at the end of each chapter. These special troubleshooting sections cover many common problems and their solutions to help you maintain uninterrupted Quattro Pro work sessions.

The Command Reference is a quick, easy-to-use, and comprehensive guide to the procedures for using almost every command available on the Quattro Pro pull-down menus.

Five detailed appendixes provide you with invaluable coverage of additional user topics such as installing the program, using the macro command language, creating and using printer setup strings, and operating Quattro Pro in a network environment.

The tear-out menu map at the back of the book is an ideal reference source for quickly locating the main menu commands available in Quattro Pro.

Using Quattro Pro 4, Special Edition, will help you discover that Quattro Pro Version 4.0 does everything that Version 3.0 can do—and more.

The Evolution of Quattro Pro

When Borland released Quattro in November 1987, the company took the software industry by surprise. Quattro was the first functional, affordable, and fully 1-2-3-compatible spreadsheet program. With

INTRODUCTION

Quattro on the market, anyone could afford to enter the electronic number-crunching arena.

With the release of Quattro Pro Version 4.0, Borland demonstrates the company's commitment to keeping pace with changing hardware and software technologies. Throughout this evolution, each version of Quattro Pro still runs under the DOS 2.0 (or later) operating system and takes full advantage of the new 80486 hardware. Spreadsheet users who own older, slower computer systems, however, also can take advantage of Version 4.0's power.

Whether you are a beginning spreadsheet user or a dedicated "Quattrophile," you will appreciate Quattro Pro's power, professional look, compatibility, and functionality—qualities that make Quattro Pro the next premier spreadsheet.

Quattro Pro is powerful. With Version 4.0, you can link data between multiple spreadsheets, open and view up to 32 windows at the same time, transform a spreadsheet into a flat-file database, and permanently record repetitive spreadsheet formatting steps into macros for future use. Version 4.0 can operate on an IBM XT, a 486-class machine, and everything in between. With Borland's Virtual Real-time Object-Oriented Memory Manager (VROOMM), you also can load and run Quattro Pro with only 640K of RAM.

Quattro Pro is professional. Version 4.0 offers hundreds of screen fonts and an advanced WYSIWYG graphical user interface (GUI) that enables "real-time" development of original, professional-looking, presentation-quality reports. *Real-time spreadsheet development* means that what you create and see on-screen is what you get on a printed page, including customized fonts, shaded cells, drawn lines, and other stylistic enhancements. With Quattro Pro, you also can insert graphs directly onto your spreadsheets.

Quattro Pro is compatible. Quattro Pro automatically translates files created with earlier versions of Quattro. Version 4.0 also enables you to access the data stored in many popular program formats. Quattro Pro uses files created with 1-2-3, Releases 1A, 2.01, 2.2, 3.0, and the educational version; Lotus Allways and Impress files; Symphony, Versions 1.2 and 2.0; Surpass; Paradox; dBASE II, III, III Plus, and IV; Reflex, Versions 1 and 2; and files created with VisiCalc, Multiplan, and Harvard Graphics. With complete 1-2-3 (Release 2.01) macro, file, and keystroke compatibility, you know that your 1-2-3 data is preserved when you switch to Quattro Pro.

Quattro Pro is functional. You immediately feel at home with Quattro Pro. Version 4.0 offers pull-down menus, a SpeedBar, and keystroke shortcuts for command execution. Because Quattro Pro can use Logitech, Mouse Systems, PC Mouse, and Microsoft-compatible mice, operating a spreadsheet is easy.

Some of Quattro Pro's less conspicuous—but equally welcomed—enhancements include an installation program that automatically detects the hardware on your system, an Undo option, expanded printer controls, and a larger library of @functions and macro keywords. With Quattro Pro you also can create multiple hardware configurations, which you can invoke and cancel from the command menu, to hide spreadsheet borders and columns, to present spreadsheets and graphs on-screen, and to print a graph without leaving the program.

What's New in Version 4.0

The following paragraphs highlight some of the new features in Version 4.0:

- *A fully customizable SpeedBar.* Quattro Pro Version 4.0 enables you to reproduce many common spreadsheet operations by clicking the appropriate button on the SpeedBar, the sculpted horizontal panel appearing at the top of the screen display. You can toggle between WYSIWYG and text display mode, for example, by clicking a SpeedBar button, which enables you to develop applications more easily in either display mode. Look for the SpeedBar icons throughout this book to point out the quickest methods for using Quattro Pro.

- *Enhanced graph analysis capabilities.* Version 4.0 offers several new tools to assist in the analysis of your graph data. The **A**nalyze command enables you to graph data in aggregation, by moving average, and in a "best-fit" linear and exponential fashion. You also can zoom and pan graphs and display data using the new bubble graph type.

- *New printing features and improved printer management.* Version 4.0 offers new printing features and improved printer management. New features include displaying a border around the currently selected print block, and a Print Manager and Queue Monitor that help to track print jobs on both local and network printers. Printer management improvements include background printing that enables you to continue working with the current spreadsheet, and enhanced support for the HP LaserJet and Canon printer cartridges.

- *New spreadsheet commands and features.* Quattro Pro has several new commands and features to help you better manage your work sessions. The **C**opy Special command enables you to copy cell contents or cell formats, and the Row **B**lock and Column **B**lock commands enable you to insert and delete partial blocks of spreadsheet data without affecting an entire row or column. Version 4.0 enables you to create and name custom styles that contain all your favorite, most-used format combinations. You can use custom styles to format the current spreadsheet or other spreadsheets in memory.

- *Improved data analysis capabilities.* Version 4.0 contains improved versions of the popular **O**ptimizer and **S**olve For commands. The new A**u**dit command enables you to trace the path of calculations in spreadsheet formulas, quickly locate circular references, and monitor links to external files. Improved database capabilities include sorting records by columns or by rows.

Who Should Read This Book

This book is designed for beginning, intermediate, and advanced Quattro Pro users. This book teaches the beginner how to design and build spreadsheets and coaches more experienced users through the process of recording spreadsheet formatting steps and selecting macro language commands for use in macro programs. For the advanced user, this book shows how to handle many computational tasks at one time and how to control every operation to produce logical, well-organized, and up-to-the-minute reports.

Users at every level learn how to install and configure Quattro Pro so that they can delegate simple tasks (such as data input) to others without worrying about compromising the integrity of the business, the program, or the spreadsheet application.

How This Book Is Organized

Using Quattro Pro 4, Special Edition, shows the reader how to create and use spreadsheets from the first step to the last. All the important rules and programming procedures are emphasized throughout the book to create an efficient, self-paced curriculum leading to the successful creation of Quattro Pro spreadsheets. The book is divided into three major sections. Each section covers techniques that progress in difficulty.

Part I, "Using Quattro Pro Spreadsheets," includes Chapters 1 through 8 and covers basic Quattro Pro operations. Novices who selected Quattro Pro as their first spreadsheet program benefit from the Quick

Start material presented in Chapter 1. This tutorial chapter enables users of all levels to jump in and use Quattro Pro. If you want to create a spreadsheet quickly, see Chapter 1.

Beginners also benefit from the fundamental basics presented in Chapters 2 through 4. Detailed discussions show you how to get Quattro Pro up and running, and supporting examples show the best ways to design, create, edit, and improve your Quattro Pro spreadsheets.

Part I includes suggestions for using @function commands in your spreadsheets, improving the style of your spreadsheets, analyzing spreadsheet data, and effectively managing your spreadsheet files.

If you are an intermediate user who already knows how to use an electronic spreadsheet program, you can skip the initial chapters. Instead, you quickly can get up to speed by scanning Chapters 5 through 8 to get a feel for Version 4.0's new and different features. When you have the time for more detailed reading, begin reading Chapter 5 to learn about Quattro and specific ways to enhance your existing library of spreadsheets.

Part II, "Printing and Graphing," includes Chapters 9 through 12 and illustrates the two methods for presenting Quattro Pro spreadsheets: in graph form or on a printed page. These chapters include tips for placing live graphs on your spreadsheets, enhancing the look of your graphs, analyzing graph data, and preparing your printed output for use in other programs.

Part III, "Advanced Spreadsheet Applications," includes Chapters 13 through 16. Advanced Quattro Pro users and experienced programmers benefit from Part III's presentation of spreadsheet concepts you use to develop complicated applications. Chapters 13, 14, and 15 address the creation and management of databases, macro programs, and advanced macro applications. Chapter 16 offers complete coverage of how to set the Version 4.0 options.

The Command Reference is a quick, easy-to-use, and comprehensive guide to using almost every command available on the Quattro Pro pull-down menus.

Appendixes A through E address advanced user issues such as how to customize Quattro Pro so that the program uses your hardware in the most efficient manner, and how to use all the macro language commands. For advanced users, this material clearly illustrates how to build customized spreadsheet solutions with Quattro Pro. Users operating Quattro Pro on a local-area network (LAN) will find Appendix E particularly useful for learning about installing and managing the program in a LAN environment.

INTRODUCTION

Part I: Using Quattro Pro Spreadsheets

Chapter 1, "Quick Start: Using Quattro Pro," presents the basics for building and using Quattro Pro spreadsheets.

Chapter 2, "Getting Started," introduces the Version 4.0 spreadsheet and the proper way to begin and end a Quattro Pro work session. The next section shows how Quattro Pro interacts with a keyboard and mouse. The chapter progresses into specific discussions of the Version 4.0 screen display: the pull-down menu bar, the SpeedBar, the input and status lines, and the spreadsheet area. An overview of using the on-line help feature concludes the chapter.

Chapter 3, "Entering and Editing Data," shows how to enter, edit, move, and view data on the Quattro Pro spreadsheet. The discussion addresses the rules for entering numbers, formulas, and @function commands. The chapter also explains how to correct errors in formulas and use the Undo feature. This chapter concludes with a review of the different Quattro Pro display modes. These basics give you the logical and most ideal methods for consistently using Quattro Pro to build useful spreadsheet applications.

Chapter 4, "Manipulating Data," teaches you the methods for manipulating cell data to create the most logical, organized spreadsheet presentation. The first section shows how to copy, move, and delete cell data in the spreadsheet. The next section demonstrates techniques for extending the power of the menu commands by using blocks of spreadsheet data. The chapter concludes by showing you how to search for and replace data on a spreadsheet. These fundamental Quattro Pro commands are among the most used during every spreadsheet work session.

Chapter 5, "Formatting Data," presents a comprehensive review of the Quattro Pro Style menu. Use the commands found on this menu to enhance the look of a spreadsheet. The chapter shows how to change the way Quattro Pro displays data in a cell. The procedures for setting the numeric format and formatting text labels also are covered. This chapter also covers how to change and reset the width of columns and how to hide columns. The chapter concludes with directions for creating presentation-quality spreadsheets using fonts, line drawing, and shading.

Chapter 6, "Using Functions," defines and explains how to use Quattro Pro's built-in @function commands in your spreadsheets. From basic mathematical operations to applying logical and string functions, this chapter shows you how to turn spreadsheets into statistical, scientific, and financial analysis tools.

Chapter 7, "Analyzing Spreadsheets," shows how to monitor the construction of spreadsheet formulas using the Audit command. This material explains how to identify formula dependencies, how to locate circular, blank, label, and ERR references, and how to monitor external formula links to other spreadsheet files. The chapter concludes with a presentation of using the Version 4.0 Solve For command to solve formulas backwards.

Chapter 8, "Managing Files and Windows," covers multiple spreadsheet operations. Quattro Pro spreadsheets easily can consolidate information from several sources onto one spreadsheet. This chapter explains why, how, and when you should use multiple spreadsheets. Topics covered in this chapter include inserting text, moving between spreadsheets, and viewing multiple spreadsheets. Examples clearly illustrate several techniques for linking files with formulas.

Part II: Printing and Graphing

Chapter 9, "Printing," provides you with the tools, techniques, and instructions that you need to print spreadsheet reports and graphs in Quattro Pro. In this chapter, you generate an unformatted snapshot of data in the current window and examine your output on-screen before you print, using the Screen Preview feature. The chapter covers the procedures and rules for creating print files with a PRN extension, and you learn about printing draft-quality copy and final presentation-quality versions of your spreadsheet reports and graphs.

Chapter 10, "Creating Graphs," introduces you to one of the program's most appealing aspects: envisioning, designing, and displaying graphs. In this chapter, you learn about the utility and anatomy of the Quattro Pro graph, how to quick-create a basic graph, and how to build a custom graph from the ground up. Throughout this chapter, figures illustrate how to enhance the appearance of a basic graph. Finally, you learn how to manage graph files so that you can recall, update, and review these files during other work sessions.

Chapter 11, "Customizing Graphs," picks up where the preceding chapter leaves off. Although Chapter 10 offers many good suggestions for improving the appearance of a basic graph, this chapter introduces techniques for creating customized graphs that locate important trends and point out problem areas better than basic graphs. Customized graphs also leave a viewer with more than just a general feeling about spreadsheet data. Using the Graph Annotator tool, you learn how to add boxed text, geometric figures, and clip art to your graphs to create presentation-quality visual aids.

Chapter 12, "Analyzing Graphs," introduces the Version 4.0 **A**nalyze commands. With this group of commands, you can analyze a graph without altering the spreadsheet from which the graph derives. The material in this chapter illustrates advanced methods for analyzing graph data: in aggregate time periods, by moving averages, and in exponential and linear form.

Part III: Advanced Spreadsheet Applications

Chapter 13, "Managing Your Data," demonstrates that being an electronic spreadsheet program, Quattro Pro is a flat-file database manager. This chapter focuses on how to transform a spreadsheet into a database so that you can sort, extract, and delete records like you can with other database programs.

Chapter 14, "Analyzing Data," provides instructions for using Quattro Pro's data analysis tools. You learn how to perform regression analysis, do optimization modeling, build sensitivity tables, and conduct frequency distribution analysis.

Chapter 15, "Creating Macros," shows you how to record macro programs so that you can replicate keystrokes and menu command selections. These macros can assume many of the repetitive formatting steps that you perform each time you load a new, blank spreadsheet into Quattro Pro. Later chapter material familiarizes you with advanced macro topics such as macro program management, macro debugging, and manually writing macros to meet specific needs.

Chapter 16, "Customizing Quattro Pro," stresses the importance of mastering the commands found on the **O**ptions menu because these commands determine how Quattro Pro interacts with computer peripherals such as printers, expanded memory, and mice. Chapter 16 addresses how to create customized global spreadsheet settings to meet the unique needs of the user. Topics covered in this chapter include choosing the right printer and using display mode, fonts, colors, the date and time display, SpeedBar settings, and initial start-up options. With the **O**ption menu commands, you also determine how Quattro Pro recalculates, protects data, and interacts with data files from other programs.

Command Reference

The Command Reference is the ideal quick-glance reference source for using Quattro Pro menu commands. This section contains Purpose and

Procedure statements that describe exactly how to use each pull-down menu command. The Command Reference also includes numerous Reminders, Important Cues, and Cautions that greatly simplify and expedite your day-to-day use of Quattro Pro.

Appendixes

Appendix A, "Installing Quattro Pro," shows you how to build the ideal computer environment for Quattro Pro. This appendix presents a step-by-step review of the installation process and rules for reconfiguring and enhancing an installed copy of the program.

Appendix B, "Macro Commands," presents a comprehensive list of the Quattro Pro macro commands and an example of the appropriate syntax for use in written procedures.

Appendix C, "Menu-Equivalent Commands," presents a comprehensive list of the Quattro Pro menu-equivalent commands. This appendix is organized in chronological order by menu and within each menu by command name.

Appendix D, "Using ASCII Characters," contains a table of control characters and printable characters as presented by the American Standard Code for Information Interchange (ASCII). The table lists 255 characters and their decimal and hexadecimal equivalents.

Appendix E, "Using Quattro Pro on a Network," shows you how to install and manage Quattro Pro on a local area network (LAN). Because Version 4.0 arrives "network-ready," the discussion concentrates on the steps you take to prepare your network for program installation.

Conventions Used in This Book

The conventions used in this book have been established to help you learn to use the program quickly and easily. As much as possible, the conventions correspond with those used in the Quattro Pro documentation.

Italic type emphasizes an important point, introduces a new concept, and, in step-by-step instructions indicates a word or phrase that you should type.

Boldface type highlights the keyword that appears in a menu or command name. To execute the /**F**ile **S**ave **R**eplace command, for example, you type */FSR*.

INTRODUCTION

A special typeface like this example denotes on-screen messages or text.

Tips provide insider clues to many of the Quattro Pro features. The tips offer time-saving advice and suggestions that help you develop power-user skills.

Notes clarify topics and offer additional material about the use and application of a particular program feature.

Cautions warn you about the potential negative consequences of an operation or action.

is the icon used to point out spreadsheet operations that you can perform using a button on the Version 4.0 SpeedBar.

The following Quattro Pro elements appear in uppercase:

- Range names, such as PROFIT
- @Function commands, such as @SUM
- Mode and status indicators, such as POINT and READY
- Cell references, such as A1..D10

The following Quattro Pro conventions regarding macro programs also apply for this book:

- Macro names are formed with a backslash (\) followed by a lowercase letter, such as \a. This naming convention also indicates that you can execute this macro program by pressing Alt-a.
- All /x macro commands, such as /xc or /xl, appear in lowercase, and all other macro commands, such as {QUIT}, appear as uppercase characters embedded in braces.
- Quattro Pro menu keystrokes in a macro program, such as /fsr, are lowercase letters.
- Range names in a macro program, such as /ecPROFIT, are uppercase letters.
- The action of pressing the Enter key in a macro, such as /fsBUDGET~, is represented by the tilde (~).

All screen shots appearing throughout the book are in WYSIWYG display mode, except when noted otherwise.

PART I

Using Quattro Pro Spreadsheets

OUTLINE

1. Quick Start: Using Quattro Pro
2. Getting Started
3. Entering and Editing Data
4. Manipulating Data
5. Formatting Data
6. Using Functions
7. Analyzing Spreadsheets
8. Managing Files and Windows

CHAPTER 1

Quick Start: Using Quattro Pro

This chapter introduces you to the basic methods for using Quattro Pro Version 4.0. The material here covers five activities that are fundamental to using Quattro Pro.

The following topics correspond to a chapter in the first part of this book. When you come across a topic that you want to explore, refer to the corresponding chapter for complete coverage.

- Loading and exiting the program (Chapter 2)
- Creating and viewing a spreadsheet (Chapter 3)
- Using @function commands (Chapters 3 and 6)
- Improving spreadsheet style (Chapter 5)
- Saving a spreadsheet (Chapter 8)

This chapter also shows you how to build a sample spreadsheet from the ground up. Along the way, you will come across features that you have encountered in other programs as well as features that are new to you. In either case, after completing this hands-on exercise, you should be able to create spreadsheets that you can use to meet many personal management and business reporting needs.

Beginning a Quattro Pro Work Session

After you install your copy of Quattro Pro, you are ready to initiate a work session. (For information on installation, see Appendix A.) Perform the following steps to begin a new work session:

1. Type *cd \qpro* and press Enter.

    Unless you specified otherwise during the installation, the Quattro Pro program files are stored in a directory called QPRO.

2. Type *q* and press Enter to load Quattro Pro into your computer's memory.

    If you are operating in the Microsoft Windows environment, double-click the Quattro Pro icon to load the program.

Unless you specify otherwise, each time you load the program into your computer's memory, Quattro Pro displays a blank spreadsheet, SHEET1.WQ1, that is ready for input (see fig. 1.1).

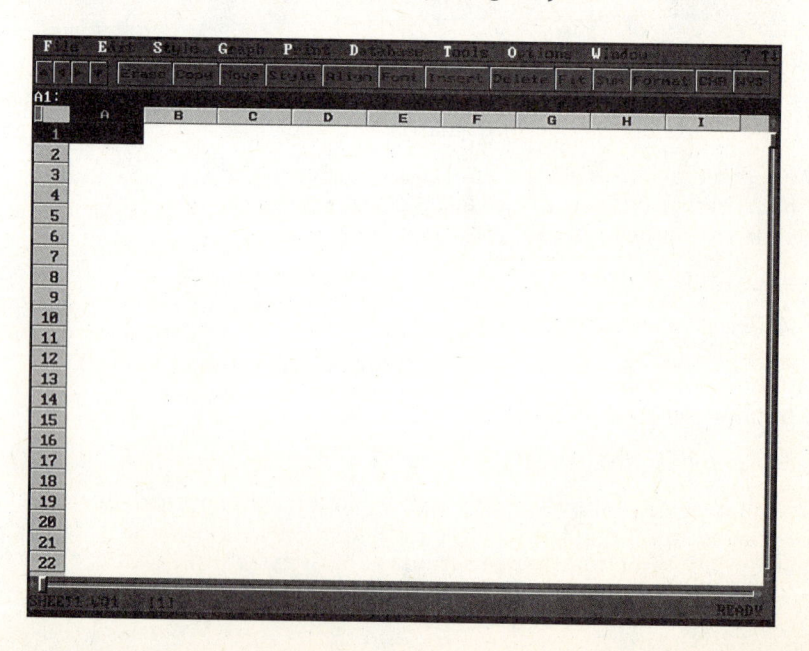

Fig. 1.1

The Quattro Pro screen display.

Executing a Command

After this spreadsheet is on-screen, you can enter data or execute commands. To execute a Quattro Pro command, you need to activate one of the nine pull-down menus. To activate a menu, press the forward slash (/) key to enter Quattro Pro's MENU mode. The word MENU replaces the word READY on the status line. Each menu contains a list of commands that perform various spreadsheet and file activities.

To open the File menu, for example, follow these steps:

1. Press the forward slash (/) key. By default, Quattro Pro highlights File in the menu bar.

2. Press Enter to pull down the File menu. You also can use the mouse to click File in the menu bar. Quattro Pro displays a list of commands that help you manage your spreadsheet files (see fig. 1.2).

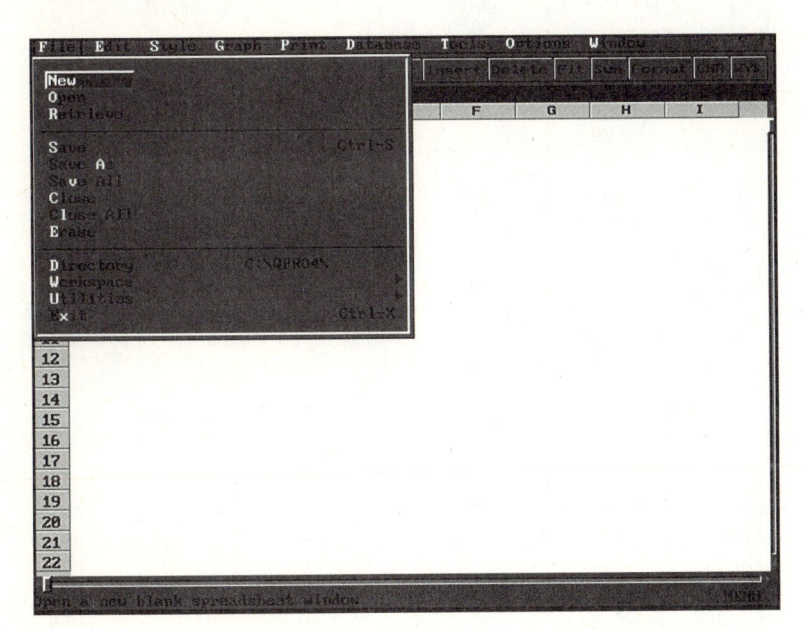

Fig. 1.2

The pull-down File menu.

Each command name appears at the left margin of the menu. Notice that one letter in each name appears in boldface. To choose a command when a menu is pulled down, press the letter that appears in boldface or click the command name.

3. To practice choosing a command, enter *D* to choose **D**irectory. You can use this command to change directories.

4. Press Esc to close the menu and return to READY mode.

PART I—USING QUATTRO PRO SPREADSHEETS

Entering and Editing Spreadsheet Data

With the remaining material in this chapter, you build a sample spreadsheet application for J. Dunn & Company, an industrial goods manufacturer. The finished application appears in figure 1.3.

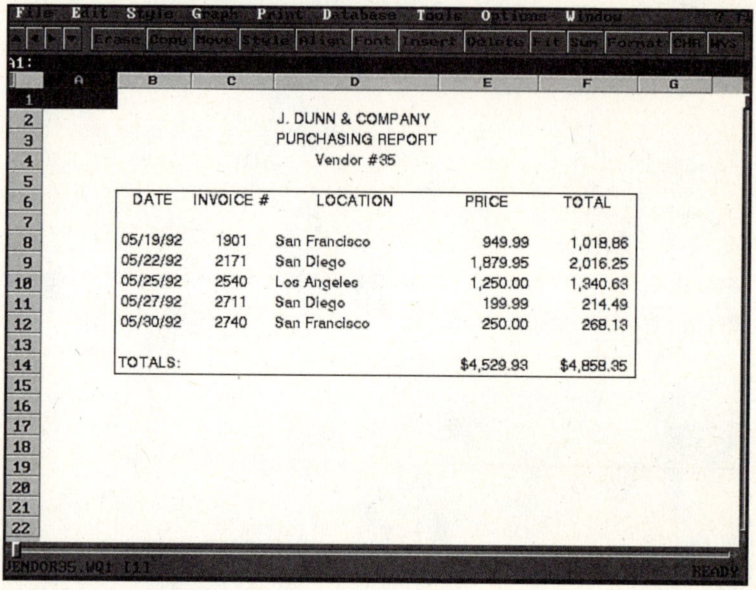

Fig. 1.3

The J. Dunn & Company purchasing report.

Entering Different Data Types

Quattro Pro accepts two types of data as valid entries: labels and values. A *label* is a text entry; a *value* can be a number, a formula, or a date-and-time entry.

Quattro Pro looks at the first character in an entry to decide whether that entry is a label or a value. When you enter a label into a cell, the mode indicator on the status line displays the word LABEL; when you enter a value, the mode indicator displays the word VALUE.

By default, Quattro Pro places an apostrophe in front of every label entry. A value entry must begin with a number (0 through 9) or with one of the following value symbols:

+ − . ($

Quattro Pro assumes that the value of all numbers is positive unless you specify otherwise.

Building the basic form of the spreadsheet shown in figure 1.3 is a three-step process as follows:

1. Enter the report titles.
2. Enter the column and row headings.
3. Enter data into the spreadsheet.

Entering the Report Titles

At the top of your spreadsheet, you want to add a title that explains what the spreadsheet contains. For the example, follow these steps to add a title:

1. Use the cursor-movement keys to move the cell selector to cell A1 or click cell A1 with the mouse.
2. Type *J. DUNN & COMPANY* and press Enter to record the main report title.

> **TIP**
> You also can press the down-arrow key or click cell A2 with the mouse to record the entry and move to cell A2.

3. Press the down-arrow key to move the cell selector to cell A2, type *PURCHASING REPORT*, and press Enter to record the secondary report title.
4. Press the down-arrow key to move the cell selector to cell A3, type *Vendor #35*, and press Enter to record the third and final report title.

Entering the Column and Row Headings

Each column in your spreadsheet contains a certain type of data. The DATE column, for example, contains dates. To enter descriptive headings for each of your columns, follow these steps:

1. Move the cell selector to cell A5, type *DATE*, and press Enter to record the column A heading.
2. Move the cell selector to cell B5, type *INVOICE #*, and press Enter to record the column B heading.

PART I—USING QUATTRO PRO SPREADSHEETS

3. Move the cell selector to cell C5, type *LOCATION*, and press Enter to record the column C heading.

4. Move the cell selector to cell D5, type *PRICE*, and press Enter to record the column D heading.

5. Move the cell selector to cell E5, type *TOTAL*, and press Enter to record the column E heading.

Add a row heading by following these steps:

1. Move the cell selector to cell A13.

2. Type *TOTALS:* and press Enter to record the row heading.

Your spreadsheet should look like figure 1.4.

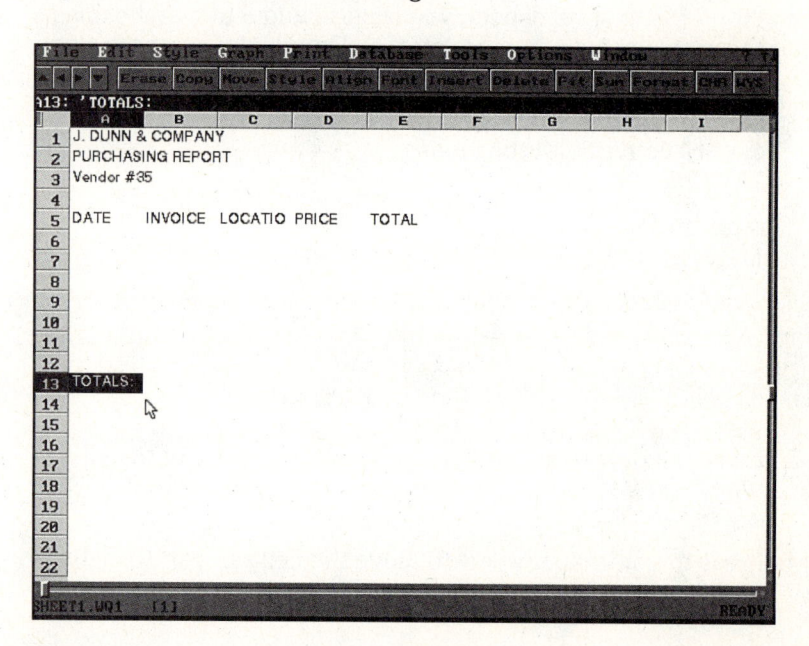

Fig. 1.4

The spreadsheet report with titles and column and row headings.

Notice that the INVOICE # and LOCATION descriptive headings shown in figure 1.4 may not display in full. Columns B and C are not wide enough to accommodate them. You will fix this display in an upcoming section titled "Changing Column Widths."

Entering Data

After you set up your column and row headings, you can begin to enter data. For the sample spreadsheet, you enter dates, invoice numbers, locations, prices, and totals. Follow these steps:

1 — QUICK START: USING QUATTRO PRO

1. Move the cell selector to cell A7 to begin entering the dates.
2. Press Ctrl-D to enter DATE mode. While in DATE mode, you can format cells to display numbers as dates.
3. Type *05/19/92* and press Enter to record the first date.
4. Move the cell selector to cell A8 to enter the second date.
5. Repeat steps 2 and 3 for the remaining four dates, incrementing one cell downward each time. Type the following dates: *05/22/92, 05/25/92, 05/27/92,* and *05/30/92.*

To enter the invoice numbers, follow these steps:

1. Move the cell selector to cell B7 to enter the first invoice number.
2. Type *1001* and press Enter to record the first invoice number. Move the cell selector down one cell for the next entry.
3. Repeat step 2 for the remaining four invoice numbers, incrementing one cell downward each time. Type the following numbers: *2171, 2540, 2711,* and *2740.*

To enter the locations, follow these steps:

1. Move the cell selector to cell C7 to begin entering the locations.
2. Type *San Francisco* and press Enter to record the purchase location for the first invoice. Then, move the cell selector down one cell.
3. Repeat step 2 for the remaining four location labels, incrementing one cell downward each time. Type the following locations: *San Diego, Los Angeles, San Diego,* and *San Francisco.*

To enter the prices, follow these steps:

1. Move the cell selector to cell D7 to begin entering the price data.
2. Type *949.99* and press Enter to record the purchase price for the first invoice. Then, move the cell selector down one cell.
3. Repeat step 2 for the remaining four prices, incrementing one cell downward each time. Type the following prices: *1879.95, 1250, 199.99,* and *250.*

Your spreadsheet should look like figure 1.5.

Notice that the San Francisco and Los Angeles location labels shown in figure 1.5 do not display in full. Column C is not wide enough to accommodate them. The section "Changing Column Widths" covers this subject later.

PART I—USING QUATTRO PRO SPREADSHEETS

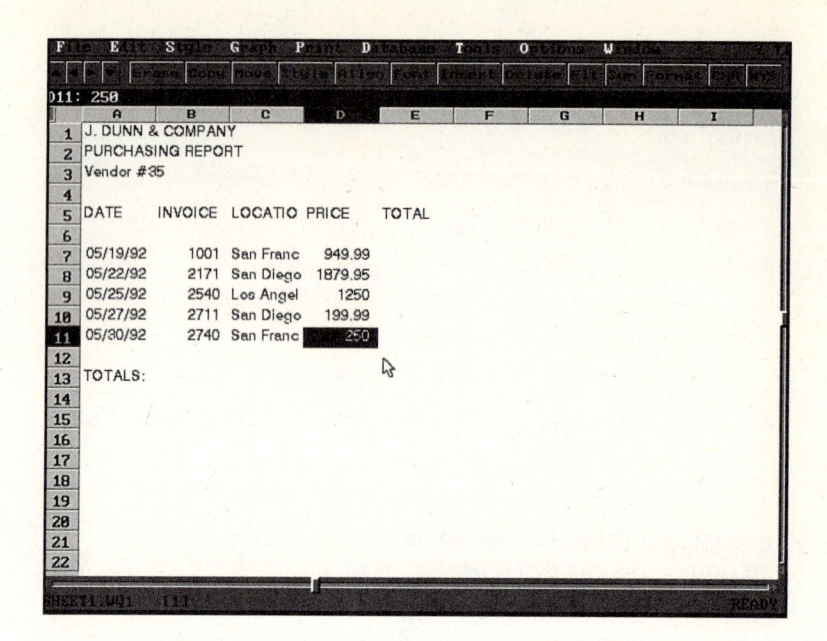

Fig. 1.5

The purchasing report with dates, invoice numbers, locations, and prices.

For now, turn your attention to creating formulas that complete the basic form of this spreadsheet report.

Entering Formulas

Quattro Pro evaluates spreadsheet formulas and returns answers in the cells in which the formulas reside. You can create simple arithmetic formulas to add a column of figures, to multiply values, and to return percentages.

To create a formula in cell E7 to add 7.25 percent sales tax to the value appearing in cell D7, follow these steps:

1. Move the cell selector to cell E7.

2. Type *+D7*1.0725*. Check the input line to ensure that you typed the correct formula.

TIP You also can press the plus sign (+), move the cell selector to cell D7, and then finish typing the rest of the formula beginning with the asterisk (*).

1 — QUICK START: USING QUATTRO PRO

3. Press Enter to record the formula.

Quattro Pro displays the value 1018.864 in cell E7. Notice that this value is not rounded properly. You learn how to format numbers in an upcoming section titled "Formatting Numbers."

For now, concentrate on copying this formula so that all the prices in column D display in column E with tax included.

Copying Formulas

Although you can repeat steps 2 and 3 to create the same formulas for cells E8..E11, you easily can copy the formula in cell E7 so that Quattro Pro calculates the tax-included totals for cells E8..E11. Follow these steps:

1. Move the cell selector to cell E7.
2. Type /EC to activate the **Copy** command on the **E**dit menu, or press the shortcut key, Ctrl-C.
3. Press Enter to choose cell E7 as the source cell.
4. Move the cell selector to cell E8, which becomes the destination cell on the input line.
5. Press Enter to copy the formula. Quattro Pro moves the cell selector back to cell E7.

    Now move the cell selector to cell E8. Look at the input line at the top of the spreadsheet to check that Quattro Pro has entered the formula +D8*1.0725.

6. Using cell E7 as the source cell, repeat steps 1 through 5 and copy the tax-included formula to cells E9, E10, and E11.

Your spreadsheet should look like figure 1.6.

> **TIP**
>
> You also can copy the formula to all the cells at once. When you select the destination cells, press the period key (.) to anchor the cell selector. Use the down-arrow key to highlight cells E8..E12 and press Enter to copy the formula.

PART I—USING QUATTRO PRO SPREADSHEETS

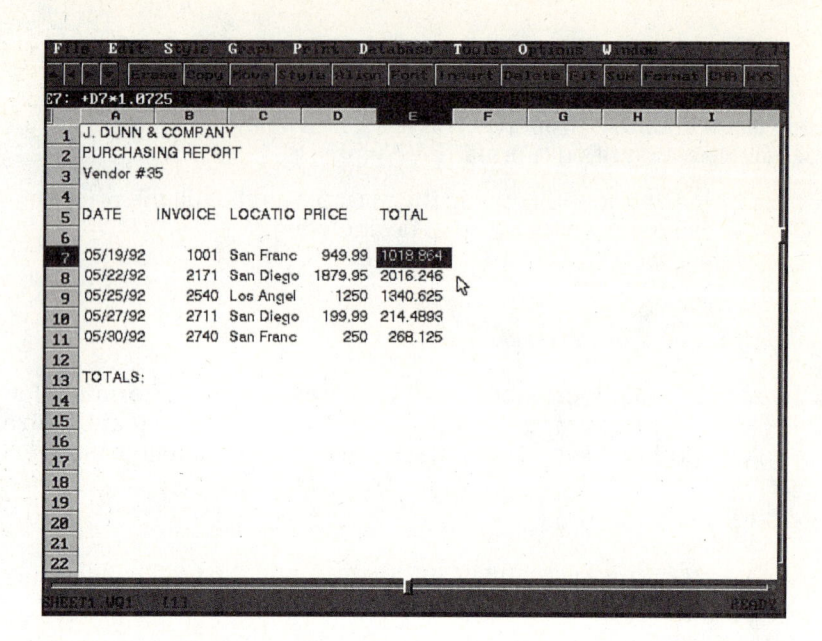

Fig. 1.6

The purchasing report with tax-included invoice totals.

Using @Functions

Quattro Pro's built-in formulas, called *@function commands*, perform basic and advanced mathematical operations. The formula +A1+A2+A3, for example, returns the same answer as the @function formula @SUM(A1..A3). The greatest benefit of @function commands is that when created in POINT mode, they greatly simplify the process of adding formulas to a spreadsheet.

When you are creating a formula in a cell and you move the cell selector away from that cell (using the keyboard or the mouse), Quattro Pro changes to POINT mode. Place the cell selector at the cell address you want to include in the formula, and then press an operator key or the closing parenthesis. The cell selector returns to the cell with the formula, the cell address automatically appears in the formula, and the mode returns to READY.

To display a list of the Quattro Pro @function commands, press Alt-F3 from anywhere on the spreadsheet.

To create a formula (while in POINT mode) that totals the column D data, follow these steps:

1. Move the cell selector to cell D13.

2. Type *@SUM(* and press the up-arrow key six times to make cell D7 the active cell. Quattro Pro enters POINT mode.

1 — QUICK START: USING QUATTRO PRO

3. Press the period key (.) to anchor cell D7 as the first cell in the range to be summed.

4. Press the down-arrow key four times to make cell D11 the active cell.

5. Press the closing parenthesis key ( )) and press Enter to record the formula.

To create a formula that adds the values in the TOTAL column, you can repeat steps 1 through 5 for the values in column E. Instead, copy the formula in cell D13 to cell E13 so that Quattro Pro totals the data appearing in column E. Follow these steps:

1. Move the cell selector to cell D13.

2. Type /EC to activate the Copy command on the Edit menu or press the shortcut key, Ctrl-C.

3. Press Enter to choose cell D13 as the source cell.

4. Move the cell selector to cell E13. This cell becomes the destination cell on the input line.

5. Press Enter to copy the formula. Quattro Pro moves the cell selector back to cell D13.

Now move the cell selector back to cell E13. Look at the input line at the top of the spreadsheet to be sure that Quattro Pro has entered the formula @SUM(E7..E11).

Your spreadsheet should look like figure 1.7.

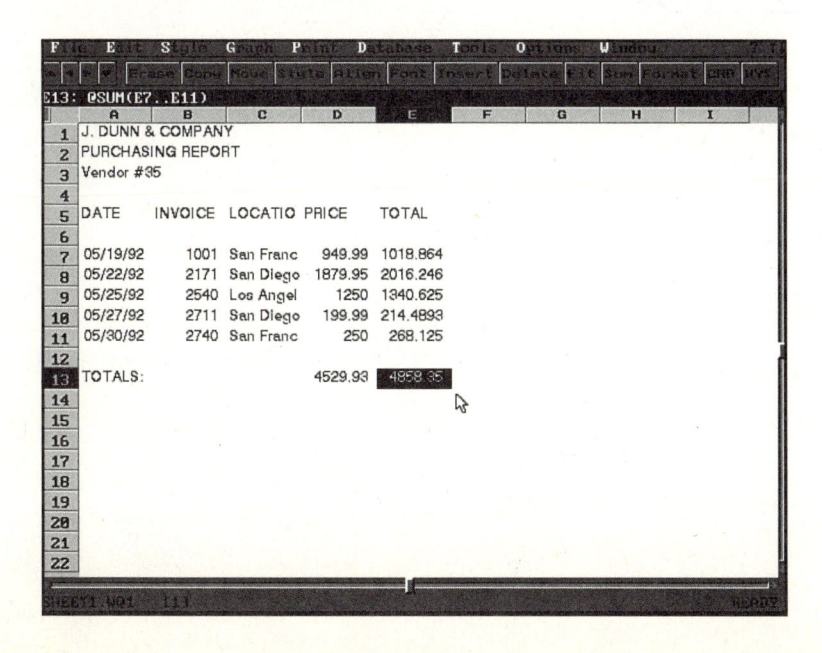

Fig. 1.7

The purchasing report with formulas that display total purchases for May, 1992.

Editing Data

Quattro Pro enables you to edit data as you enter the data on the input line or after you press Enter to place the text into a spreadsheet cell. You can reverse the effects of many menu-command operations by choosing the /Edit Undo command, which is discussed in one of the following sections.

Changing Data in EDIT Mode

To edit the contents of a spreadsheet cell, press F2 to enter EDIT mode. If you have a mouse, click the cell you want to edit and then click the input line just below the pull-down menu bar. Quattro Pro displays the unformatted cell data on the input line. When you finish editing, press Enter to record the changes.

To see how easy editing data is, change an invoice number appearing on the spreadsheet shown in figure 1.7. Follow these steps:

1. Place the cell selector in cell B7.
2. Press F2 to enter EDIT mode.
3. Press the left-arrow key three times to place the edit cursor on the first 0.
4. Press Del.
5. Enter *9* and then press Enter to record the new invoice number.

Using the Alt-F5 Undo Key

With the /Edit Undo command, you can undo the most recent edit performed or command executed. By default, the Undo key is disabled (turned off). To use this feature, you first must choose /Options Other Undo Enable. After you enable the Undo key, save this setting for future work sessions by choosing /Options Update.

To reverse the edit operation you just performed, follow these steps:

1. Type */EU* (or press Alt-F5) to activate the Undo command on the Edit menu.

    Quattro Pro displays the original invoice number, 1001, in cell B7.

2. Type */EU* again (or press Alt-F5) to reinstate the edited invoice number, 1901, in cell B7.

Your spreadsheet should look like figure 1.8. In this figure, the cell selector is in cell B7, showing that the edited invoice value has been reinstated.

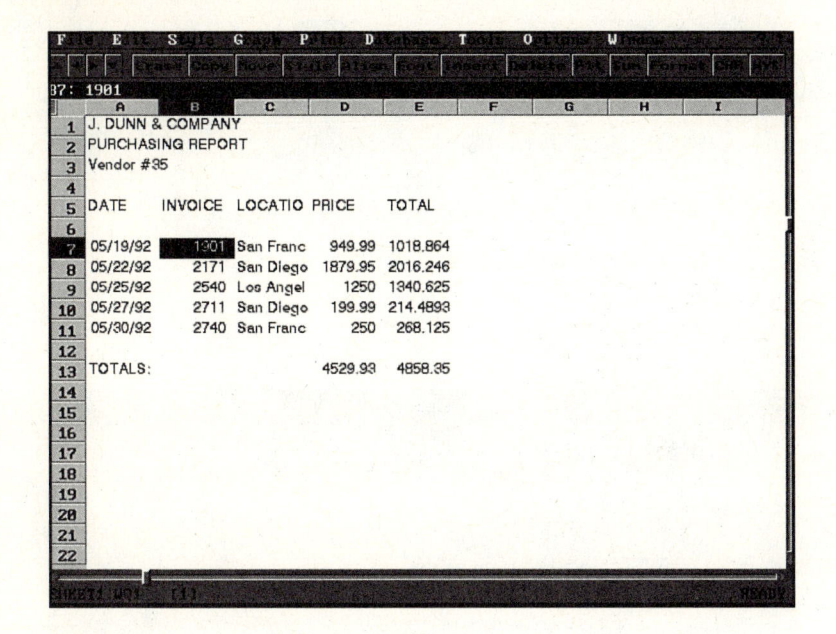

Fig. 1.8

The purchasing report spreadsheet, complete with formulas and cell edits.

Improving Spreadsheet Style

Another look at figure 1.8 reveals that although the data is complete, the format leaves much to be desired. The data in certain cells appears crowded and/or aligned improperly. The invoice amounts also do not have dollar symbols.

The following sections describe how to improve the appearance of your data.

Moving Data

You can relocate data from one area of the spreadsheet to another by choosing /**E**dit **M**ove. To move the report titles to a more central location on the J. Dunn & Company spreadsheet, for example, follow these steps:

1. Type /*EM* to execute the /**E**dit **M**ove command or press the shortcut key, Ctrl-M.

PART I—USING QUATTRO PRO SPREADSHEETS

2. When prompted, type *A1..A3* and press Enter to choose the source block.

> **TIP** Alternatively, you can press Esc to unanchor the cell, move to cell Al, press the period key (.) to reanchor the cell, move to cell A3, and press Enter.

3. When prompted for a destination block, type *C1*.
4. Press Enter to move the report titles to column C.

Your spreadsheet should look like figure 1.9. In this figure, the titles formerly in A1..A3 now appear in C1..C3.

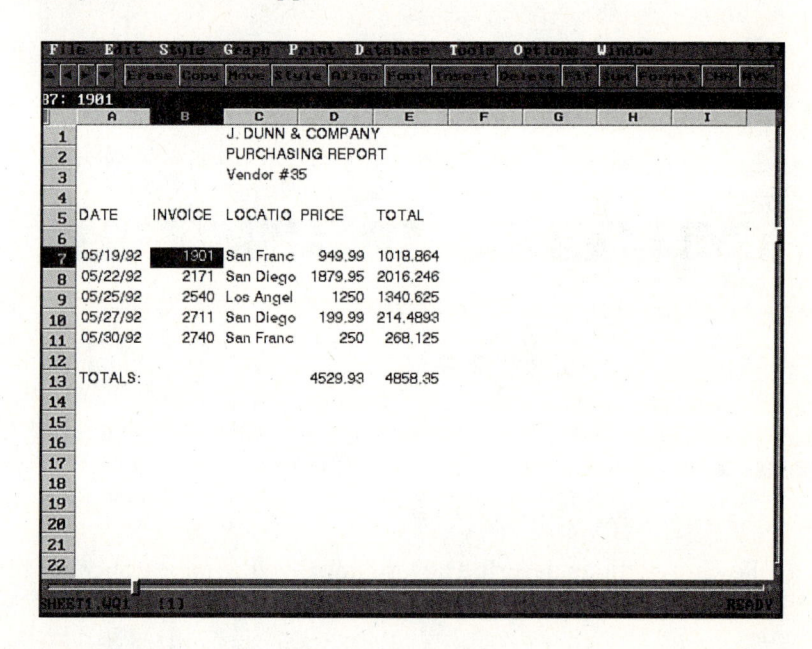

Fig. 1.9

Relocated titles on the purchasing report.

Changing Column Widths

By default, each spreadsheet column is nine characters wide. To enter data longer than nine characters, use the /**S**tyle **C**olumn Width command to change the width of the column.

After you change the column widths, the new entry on the input line is [W *column width*].

To change the widths of columns B, C, D, and E on the J. Dunn & Company spreadsheet, for example, try each of the following techniques:

Technique 1:

1. Place the cell selector in cell B1.
2. Type */SC* to execute the */Style Column Width* command.
3. Type *10* and press Enter to make column B 10 characters wide.
4. Place the cell selector in cell C1.
5. Type */SC* to execute the */Style Column Width* command.
6. Type *20* and press Enter to make column C 20 characters wide.

Technique 2:

1. Place the cell selector in cell D1.
2. Press Ctrl-W, the Ctrl-key shortcut for the */Style Column Width* command.
3. Press the right-arrow key 3 times and then press Enter to make column D 12 characters wide.

Technique 3:

1. Place the cell selector in cell E1.
2. Click and hold the mouse button on the column letter E and drag to the right until 12 appears next to the prompt display on the input line.
3. Release the mouse button to make column E 12 characters wide.

Your spreadsheet should look like figure 1.10. This figure reflects the new width settings for columns B, C, D, and E.

Aligning Data in Cells

Uniformly aligned headings make identifying the values that belong to a particular heading easier.

To center-align the report title on row 3, for example, follow these steps:

1. Place the cell selector in cell C3.
2. Type */SAC* to execute the */Style Alignment Center* command.
3. Press Enter to center-align the title label.

PART I—USING QUATTRO PRO SPREADSHEETS

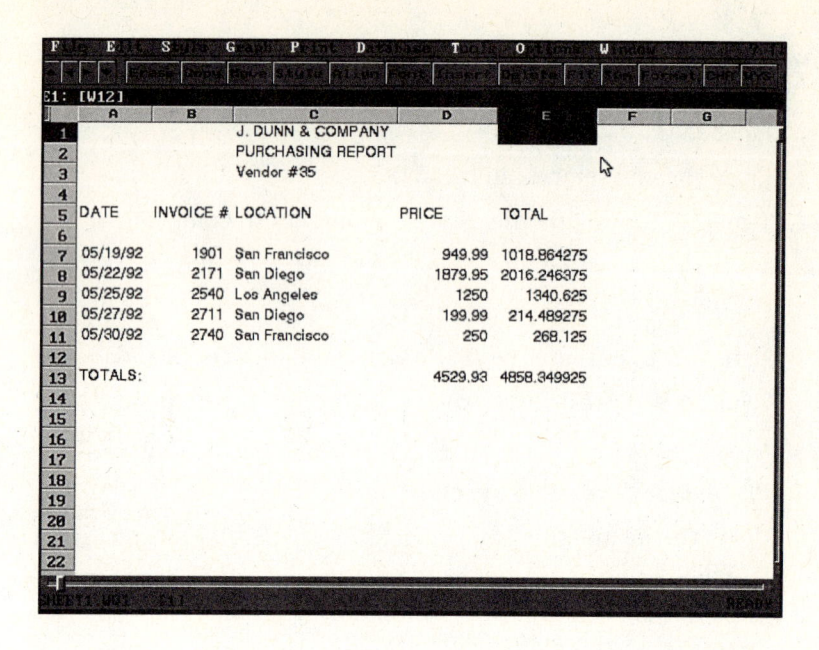

Fig. 1.10

Changed column widths on the purchasing report.

To center-align each of the column headings on row 5, use the following steps:

1. Place the cell selector in cell A5.
2. Press Ctrl-A, the Ctrl-key shortcut for this command.
3. Enter *C*, the boldface letter for the **C**enter option.
4. Press the End key to highlight a block of contiguous data quickly.
5. Press the right-arrow key to extend the highlighted block to cell E5.
6. Press Enter to center-align all labels on row 5.

    This input line displays a caret (^) rather than an apostrophe (') at the beginning of each label to indicate that the label is center-aligned.

To center-align the invoice numbers in column B, follow these steps:

1. Place the cell selector in cell B7.
2. Press Ctrl-A, the Ctrl-key shortcut for this command.
3. Enter *C*, the boldface letter for the **C**enter option.
4. Press End to enter END mode.

1 — QUICK START: USING QUATTRO PRO

5. Press the down-arrow key to extend the highlighted block to cell B11.
6. Press Enter to center-align all values in column B.

NOTE Values do not display the caret (^) to indicate center alignment—only labels.

Your spreadsheet should look like figure 1.11. This figure displays the new title, heading, and data alignments.

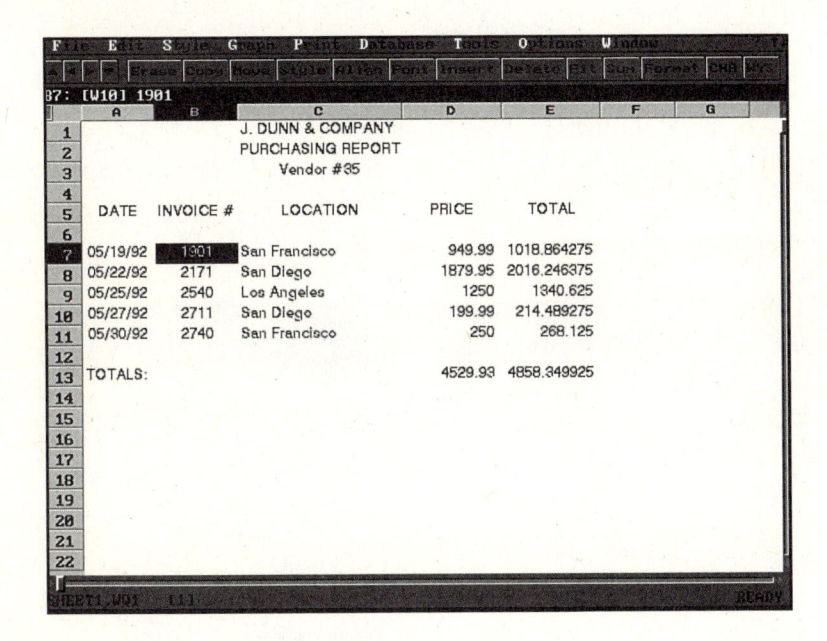

Fig. 1.11

Aligned data on the purchasing report.

Formatting Numbers

Properly formatted numbers tell more about the values on a spreadsheet and make it easier to read. Formatting a number only changes how the number displays, but does not change the number, itself: the underlying number appears on the input line, and the formatted number appears in the spreadsheet. Format the PRICE and TOTAL column numbers so that they display commas and two decimal places by following these steps:

1. Place the cell selector in cell D7.
2. Type /SN to execute the /Style Numeric Format command.
3. Press the comma key (,) to choose the comma format.

4. Press Enter to accept the default setting of two decimal places.

5. Press the right-arrow key, press End on the numeric keypad, and then press the down-arrow key to highlight cell block D7..E11.

6. Press Enter to format the numbers in the highlighted block.

Now format the numbers on the TOTALS row to display a dollar sign and commas with two decimal places. Follow these steps:

1. Place the cell selector in cell D13.

2. Press Ctrl-F, the Ctrl-key shortcut for this command.

3. Enter *C* to choose the **C**urrency format.

4. Press Enter to accept the default setting of two decimal places.

5. Press the right-arrow key to highlight cell block D13..E13.

6. Press Enter to format the numbers in the highlighted block.

Your spreadsheet should look like figure 1.12. This figure displays the numeric formats of the values appearing in the report.

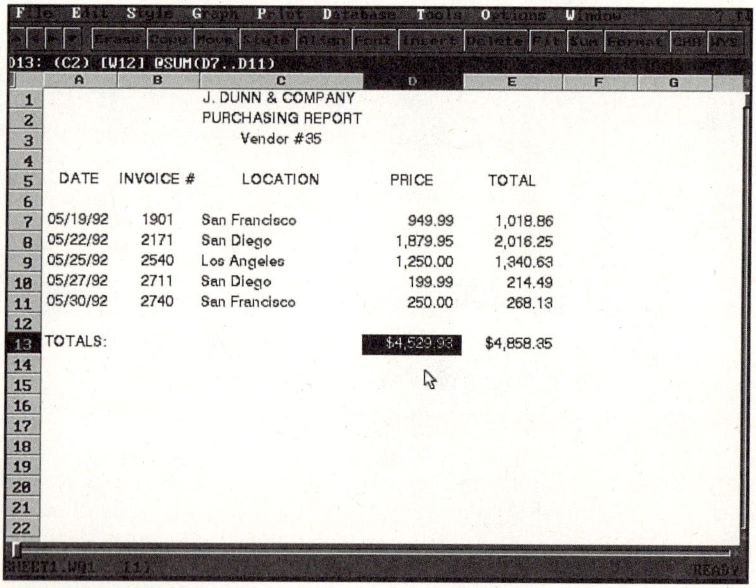

Fig. 1.12

Formatted numeric data on the purchasing report.

Drawing Lines

Drawing lines around your spreadsheet data transforms a basic spreadsheet document into a professional-looking report. You can add a few final stylistic touches to the J. Dunn & Company report.

1 — QUICK START: USING QUATTRO PRO

To draw a line around the data area, follow these steps:

1. Type **/SL** to execute the **/S**tyle **L**ine Drawing command.
2. When Quattro Pro prompts you for the block to draw lines, type **A5..E13** and press Enter to choose the source block.
3. When Quattro Pro displays the Placement menu, enter **O** to choose the **O**utside line option.
4. When Quattro Pro displays the Line Types menu, enter **S** to choose the **S**ingle line option.
5. Enter **Q** to choose the **Q**uit option and return to the spreadsheet.

Your spreadsheet should look like figure 1.13. This figure displays the addition of drawn lines around the purchasing report.

> **TIP**
>
> To remove the lines, type **/SL** and indicate the block from which you want to remove the lines. Choose the line type you want to remove from the block, or choose All to remove all lines and then choose None as the line type.

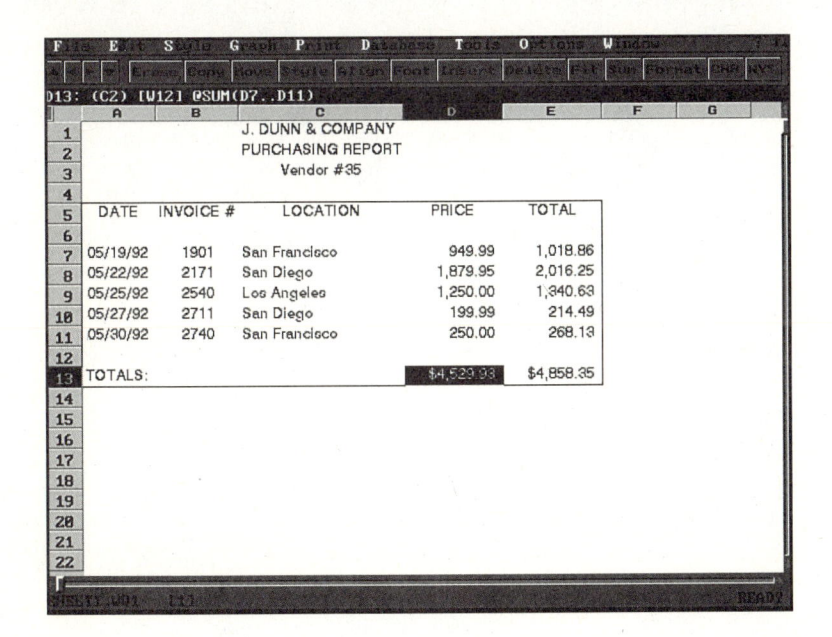

Fig. 1.13

Drawn lines around the purchasing report.

PART I—USING QUATTRO PRO SPREADSHEETS

Inserting Rows and Columns

To conclude this exercise, add some finishing touches to the J. Dunn & Company purchasing report. First, insert a column before column A to center the report on the spreadsheet, using the following steps:

1. Press the Home key to place the cell selector quickly in cell A1.
2. Press Ctrl-I, the Ctrl-key shortcut for the /Edit Insert command.
3. Enter *C* to insert **Columns**.
4. When Quattro Pro prompts you for a column insert block, press Enter to accept the single-column default, A1..A1.

To conclude, insert one row on top of the first title line in the report by following these steps:

1. Press Ctrl-I, the Ctrl-key shortcut for the /Edit Insert command.
2. Enter *R* to insert **Rows**.
3. When Quattro Pro prompts you for a source block, press Enter to accept the single-row default.

Figure 1.14 shows the finished form of the sample report for J. Dunn & Company.

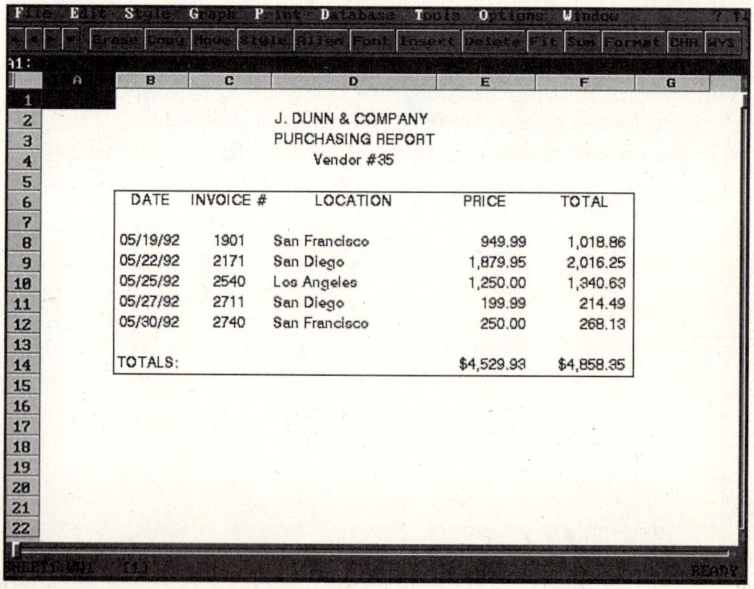

Fig. 1.14

A presentation-quality version of the J. Dunn & Company purchasing report.

Managing Documents

Managing documents is an important part of each Quattro Pro work session. Without the **S**ave, create (**N**ew), **R**etrieve, and **O**pen spreadsheet files capabilities, Quattro Pro is useless.

Saving a Spreadsheet to a Hard Drive

To save the J. Dunn & Company spreadsheet as VENDOR35, perform the following steps:

1. Type */FA* to execute the /**F**ile Save **A**s command.
2. When prompted to enter a save file name, type *vendor35*.
3. Press Enter to save the new file name to the current hard disk drive.

> **NOTE** If you use the /**F**ile **S**ave command to save this file every time, Quattro Pro automatically uses the same file name.

Saving a Spreadsheet to a Floppy Disk

If you want to save the J. Dunn & Company spreadsheet to a drive other than the default drive, include a drive designator in the file name. To save the file on a disk in drive A, for example, follow these steps:

1. Type */FA* to execute the /**F**ile Save **A**s command.
2. When prompted to enter a file name, press Esc twice to place the cursor at the beginning of the input line inside the file name prompt box.
3. Type *a:\vendor35*.
4. Press Enter to save the new file name to the disk in drive A.

Ending a Work Session

To end a Quattro Pro work session and save all files open in Quattro Pro's memory, follow these steps:

1. Type */FX* to execute the /**F**ile **E**xit command.

PART I—USING QUATTRO PRO SPREADSHEETS

Alternatively, if you have a mouse, click **File** (on the menu bar) to pull down the menu and then click the **Exit** command to exit Quattro Pro; or press Ctrl-X, the Shortcut key for ending a work session.

If you have not made any changes to the open spreadsheets since the last save operation, Quattro Pro clears the screen display and returns to the DOS command prompt.

If you have made changes, Quattro Pro displays the following prompt:

    Lose your changes and Exit?

2. To exit the program without saving open files, enter *Y* to choose **Y**es; to remain on the active spreadsheet, enter *N* to choose **N**o; enter *S* to choose **S**ave & Exit if you want to save all open spreadsheets before returning to DOS (see fig. 1.15).

If you choose **S**ave & Exit, one by one, Quattro Pro activates each open spreadsheet as it saves it and displays the following prompt:

    File already exists:

3. When prompted, enter *C* to **C**ancel and remain on the active spreadsheet; enter *R* to **R**eplace the active spreadsheet's file with the on-screen information, and then display the next spreadsheet; or enter *B* to **B**ackup an open file before exiting the program (see fig. 1.16).

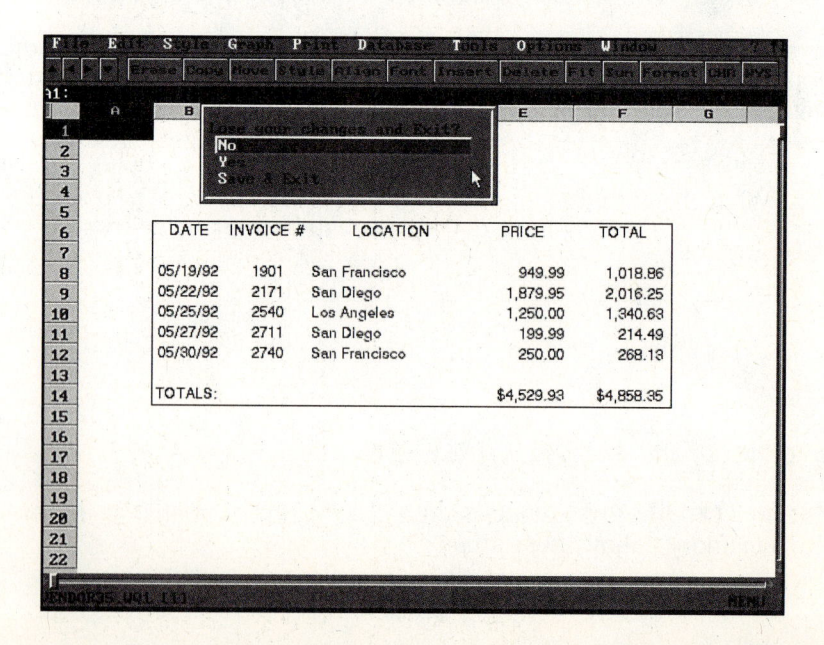

Fig. 1.15

The File Exit command prompt.

1 — QUICK START: USING QUATTRO PRO

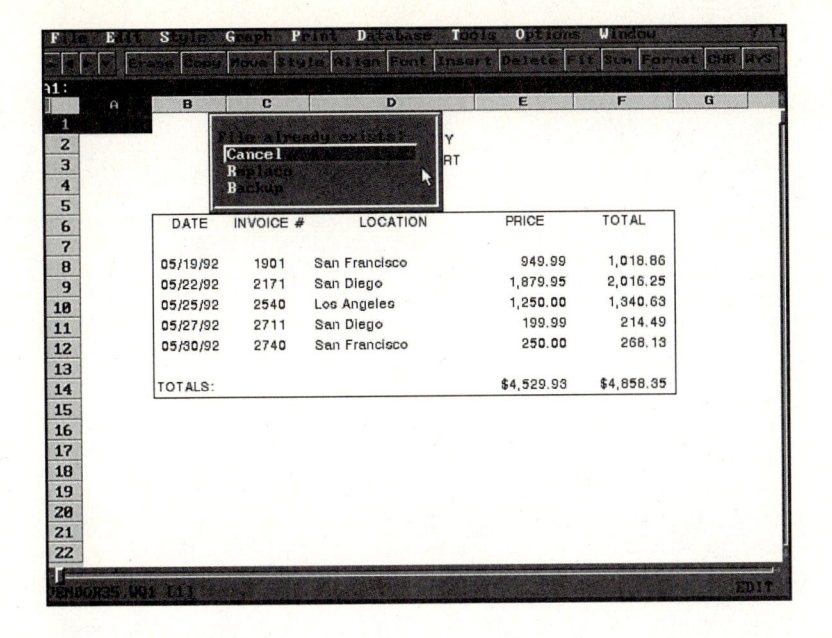

Fig. 1.16

The Save & Exit command prompt.

Summary

After completing this quick start, you should be familiar with the following concepts:

- Beginning and ending a work session
- Pulling down a menu and executing a command
- Entering values and labels into spreadsheet cells
- Editing, copying, and moving data and formulas on the spreadsheet
- Using the Undo feature to reverse operations
- Creating a basic spreadsheet report that contains a title, column heading, formatted data, and drawn lines
- Saving spreadsheet files to a hard and floppy disk

Chapter 2 expands on the information you became acquainted with in this quick start and broadens the scope of coverage to help you get started with Quattro Pro.

CHAPTER 2

Getting Started

This chapter helps you to envision how to use a spreadsheet for a wide range of simple tasks. Read this chapter carefully because the terminology and ideas in later chapters rely heavily on the concepts presented here.

For first-time spreadsheet users, this chapter discusses the basics of working with Quattro Pro. You see how a spreadsheet is more than just rows and columns of numbers and letters. You learn how to begin and end a work session. You also review how to use a keyboard and mouse. The chapter presents an in-depth, feature-by-feature review of the Quattro Pro WYSIWYG ("what-you-see-is-what-you-get") screen display. You learn how to switch between WYSIWYG and character (text) display modes.

The chapter concludes with a discussion of the Quattro Pro built-in help windows. This final section shows you how to get general and context-sensitive help from any location on a spreadsheet.

Chapter 2 is an important stepping stone to later chapters. If you master the basics outlined in this discussion, you can begin to tackle the Quattro Pro spreadsheet basics presented in Chapter 3, "Entering and Editing Data."

Learning about Spreadsheets

Basically, Quattro Pro is a large electronic worksheet with millions of cells of storage area. You can enter data into these cells and enter formulas that perform mathematical operations on a group, or *block*, of cells.

Whether you are adding 2 numbers or 2,000 numbers, Quattro Pro calculates an answer in seconds. If you change a number on a manual accounting worksheet, you must add the numbers over again. After you change a number in a Quattro Pro formula, however, the program recalculates the new answer in a few seconds.

Quattro Pro remembers all the cell relationships that you define on a spreadsheet. A formula that adds values appearing in two cells, such as +D8+D9, creates the most common type of cell relationship. If you design a spreadsheet to record your monthly business expenses, for example, you have to do the work only once. For subsequent months, you retrieve and modify the original spreadsheet file by entering new numbers into the cells storing the current month's expenses.

Understanding Columns and Rows

A typical spreadsheet program displays a two-dimensional worksheet made up of columns and rows. You can enter numbers, letters, and formulas into a spreadsheet *cell*, which is the intersection of any column and row.

The active cell on a Quattro Pro spreadsheet appears as a highlighted rectangle—the *cell selector* (see fig. 2.1). Notice that the row number on the left and column letter on top at this intersection also are highlighted.

Finally, observe the arrow pointer in the middle of the screen. This mouse pointer appears if you have a mouse attached to your computer. If you use a mouse in the character-based display mode, Quattro Pro displays a small, highlighted rectangle instead of the arrow pointer.

Each cell in a spreadsheet has a unique name. A *cell address* combines the column and row locations into one description. The cell in figure 2.1 is named D10, which describes the intersection of column D and row 10.

2 — GETTING STARTED

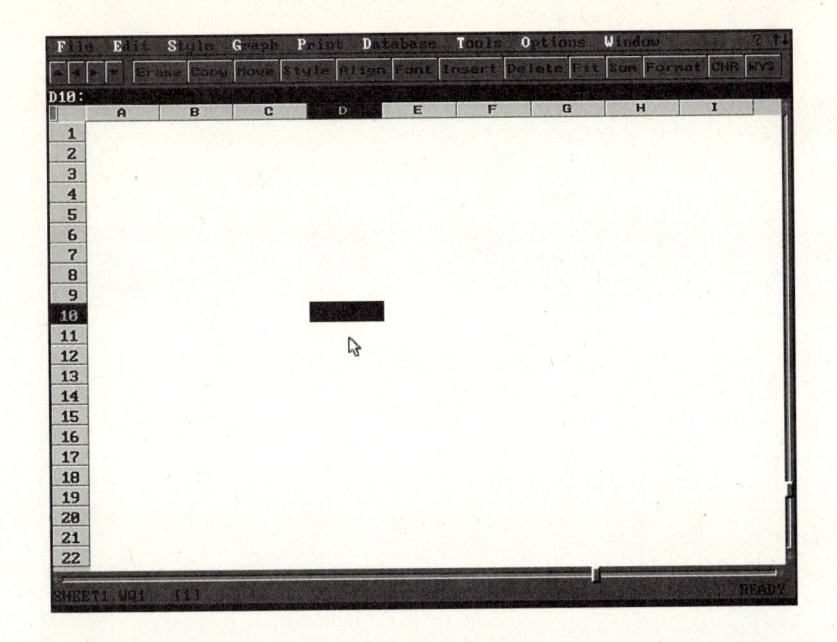

Fig. 2.1

The Quattro Pro spreadsheet, with the cell selector in D10.

> **T I P**
>
> Columns always use letter descriptions, and rows always use number descriptions. *Cell 10D*, then, has no meaning, although *cell D10* has a meaning.

A Quattro Pro spreadsheet contains 256 columns and 8,192 rows. One Quattro Pro spreadsheet, therefore, contains 2,097,152 unique cells.

The rows on a Quattro Pro spreadsheet are numbered from 1 to 8,192; the columns are labeled from A to IV. The first 26 spreadsheet columns are named using the alphabet. Columns 27 through 52 are named AA, AB, AC, AD, and so on. Columns 53 through 79 are named BA through BZ. This naming scheme continues through column 256, or column IV. Figure 2.2 shows the last cell on a Quattro Pro spreadsheet—cell IV8192.

Multiple windows is a powerful Quattro Pro feature that enables you to work with up to 32 spreadsheet windows simultaneously. The multiple windows feature, therefore, places up to 67,108,864 spreadsheet cells at your disposal. Imagine how many accounting ledger worksheets you need to equal that much calculation space.

Quattro Pro's real power, however, lies in its capability to remember the relationships that you define when you enter data into the spreadsheet cells. Think back to the formula (+D8+D9) defined in "Learning about Spreadsheets" as an example of a cell relationship. Because Quattro Pro can save a spreadsheet on a disk storage device, you have to type this formula only once. Every time you retrieve a saved spreadsheet from disk into Quattro Pro's memory, the formula and its calculated result reappear.

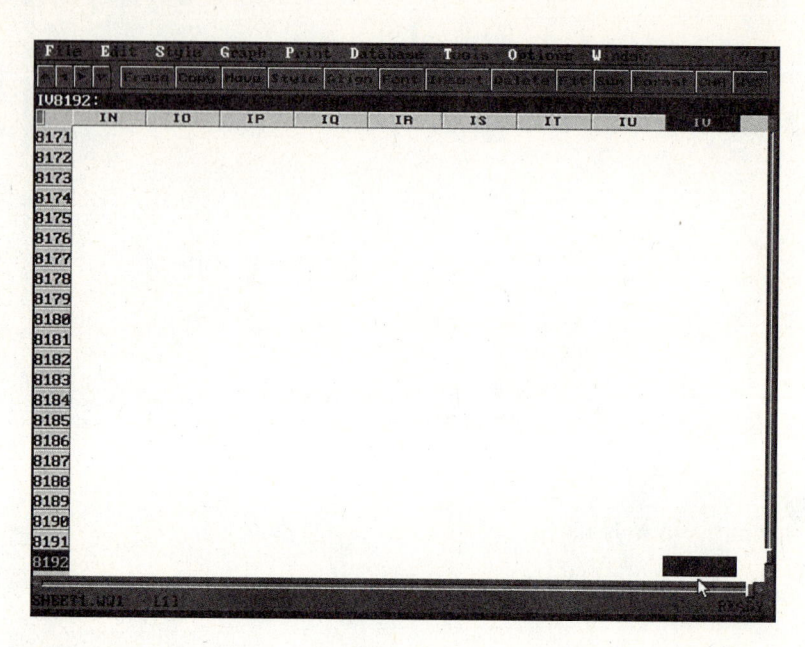

Fig. 2.2

The last cell on a spreadsheet.

Designing a Spreadsheet

When you design a spreadsheet, you must follow a few basic rules:

- Duplicate the organization and structure of the original document as closely as possible. You typically create spreadsheets to assume the duties of a written document or manually calculated report. Use this written document or report as a guide.

    To design a three-month income statement report, for example, you can place the ledger account titles in column B, the month descriptions in row 2, and the numbers in cells C3 through F10 (see fig. 2.3).

- Avoid mixing numbers and letters in the same cell until you are familiar with the rules for data entry (covered in Chapter 3, "Entering and Editing Data"). For now, remember that when you enter a number into a cell, Quattro Pro stores the number as a value. When you enter a word into a cell, Quattro Pro stores the word as a label by placing an apostrophe (') before the first letter.

2 — GETTING STARTED

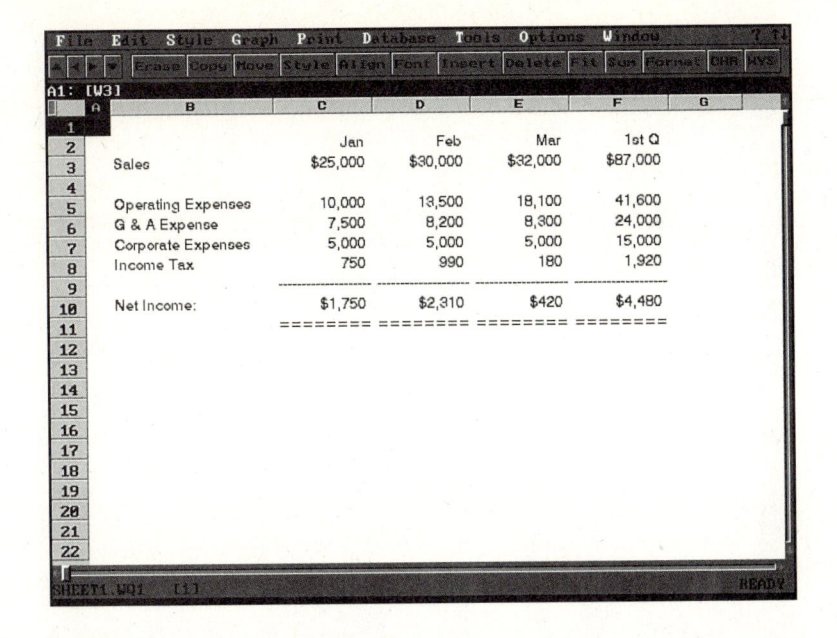

Fig. 2.3

A logically designed spreadsheet.

- Quattro Pro can perform mathematical operations only on numbers. If you try to add two text labels, for example, Quattro Pro returns the value 0.

In figure 2.3, you can perform mathematical operations on the data in cells C3 through F10. If you try to add or subtract the labels appearing in column B, Quattro Pro displays the value 0 because the program finds no numbers to add or subtract.

Asking What-If Questions

The real purpose of the electronic spreadsheet program is to ask questions and get acceptable answers. Examples of some typical what-if questions follow:

- What happens to profits if expenses rise by 10 percent?
- What happens to sales if a company loses three salespeople?
- What happens to the average height figure if Mark's height is removed from the sample?

Because Quattro Pro enables you to define and store numeric relationships, you can play out an infinite number of what-if scenarios with Quattro Pro spreadsheets. Figure 2.4 shows how easily you can turn the spreadsheet in figure 2.3 into a what-if analysis tool.

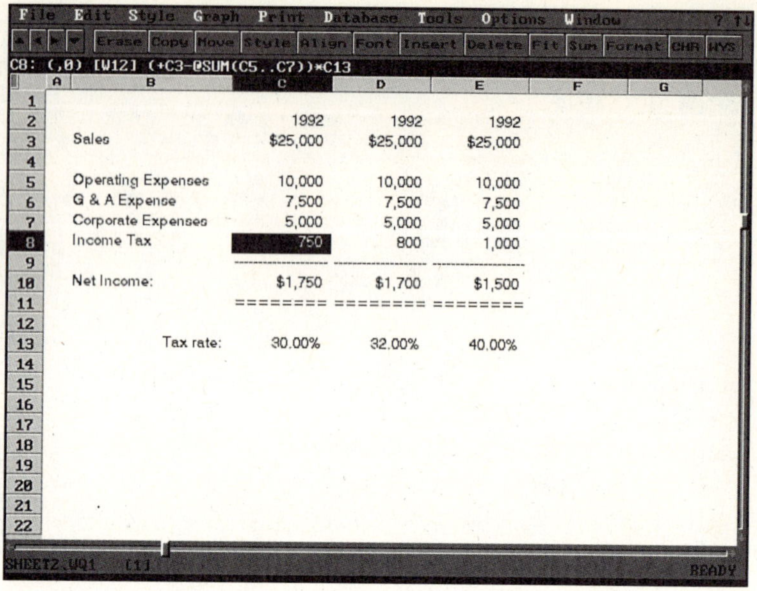

PART I — USING QUATTRO PRO SPREADSHEETS

Fig. 2.4

A report transformed into a financial analysis tool.

	B	C	D	E
2		1992	1992	1992
3	Sales	$25,000	$25,000	$25,000
5	Operating Expenses	10,000	10,000	10,000
6	G & A Expense	7,500	7,500	7,500
7	Corporate Expenses	5,000	5,000	5,000
8	Income Tax	750	800	1,000
10	Net Income:	$1,750	$1,700	$1,500
13	Tax rate:	30.00%	32.00%	40.00%

The spreadsheet in figure 2.4 follows a yearly format and shows only 1992 data. Except for the Income Tax row (row 8), columns D and E contain the same information as column C. The formula in cell C8 calculates income tax by multiplying pre-tax net income— C3_@SUM(C5..C7)—by the tax rate appearing in cell C13.

To perform a what-if analysis, alter the Tax Rate entry and watch how net income changes. Imagine that you want to see what net income would be under three different tax rate assumptions. By changing the tax rate values in cells C13, D13, and E13, you can create different scenarios in which net income rises and falls.

Quattro Pro goes one step further by supplying you with the **What-If** command on the **Tools** menu (see Chapter 7, "Analyzing Spreadsheets"). With this powerful command, you can create one-way and two-way sensitivity tables. A *sensitivity table* lists a wide range of possible solutions to a problem that you define. Rather than change cell values to test the effect on the results displayed in other cells, you create one table that lists all of the possible results.

This approach to asking what-if questions is more flexible and accurate and provides you with better information than ever before.

Reviewing the Uses of a Spreadsheet

The Quattro Pro spreadsheet is more than a collection of rows, columns, and cells. With a little imagination, you can turn a spreadsheet into a presentation-quality graph, a database application, or a macro program. In fact, the name *Quattro* (the number four in Italian) derives from these four main program features.

Constructing a Spreadsheet

The easiest way to design a Quattro Pro spreadsheet is to re-create the appearance of the original document.

Figure 2.5 illustrates how easily you can duplicate a simple multiplication exercise on a Quattro Pro spreadsheet. The formula in cell C7 multiplies the value in C4 by the value in C5. The formula in cell C7 appears on the input line below the menu bar.

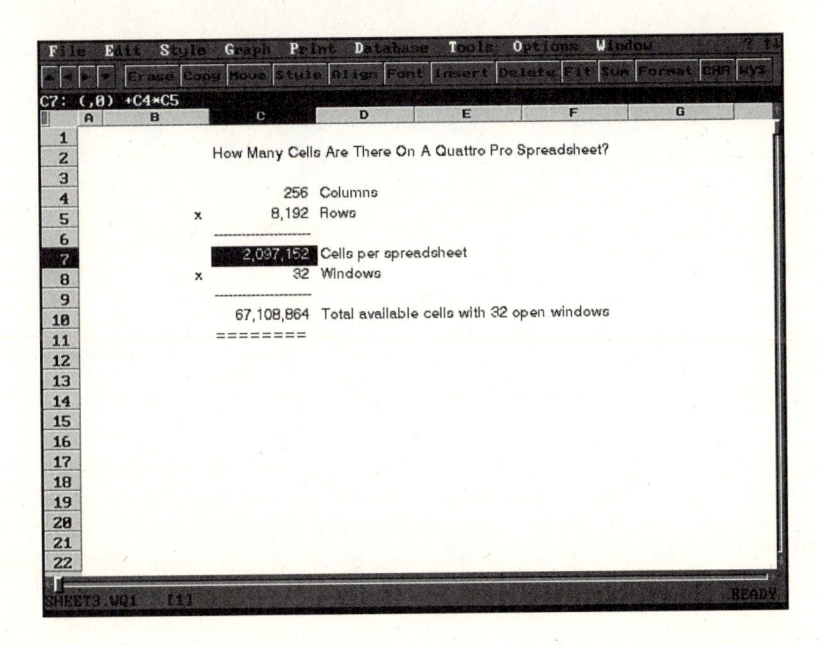

Fig. 2.5

A Quattro Pro spreadsheet.

Designing a Graph

With Quattro Pro, you easily can turn your spreadsheet data into an attractive, presentation-quality graph that you can view on-screen or print. Figure 2.6, for example, shows a pie graph of crop yields for a California orange grower.

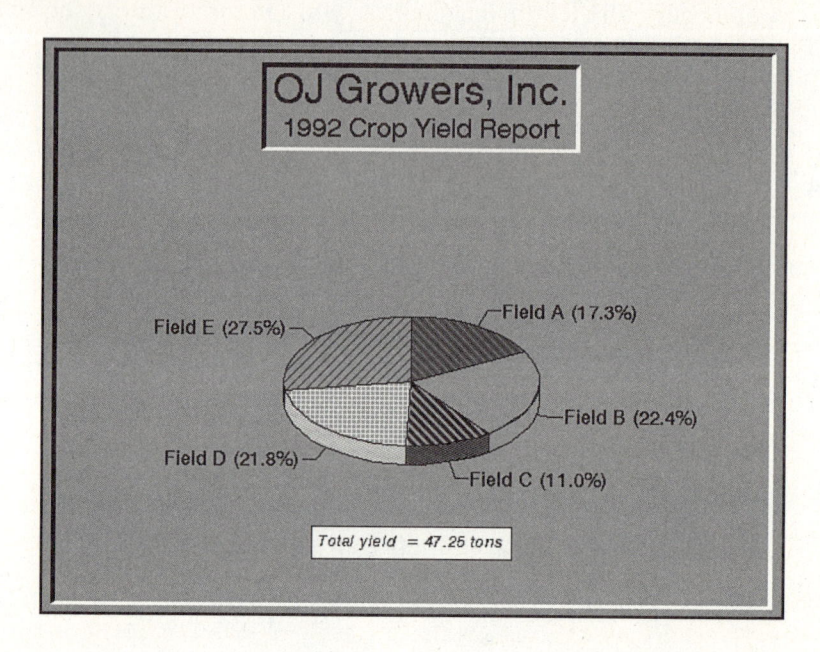

Fig. 2.6

A Quattro Pro pie graph.

Quattro Pro graphs are smart: each time you change numbers on the spreadsheet, the graph adjusts to reflect the new data. See Chapters 10, 11, and 12 for complete coverage of graphs.

Building a Database

You also can turn a Quattro Pro spreadsheet into a flat-file database using the commands found on the **D**atabase menu. After you enter your data records, you can sort them, extract records that meet specified criteria, and build new databases with the extracted data.

When you set up a database using Quattro Pro, you define rows as records and columns as fields. Figure 2.7 shows a database that inventories compact discs and cassette titles. See Chapter 13, "Managing Your Data," for complete coverage of database operations.

2 — GETTING STARTED

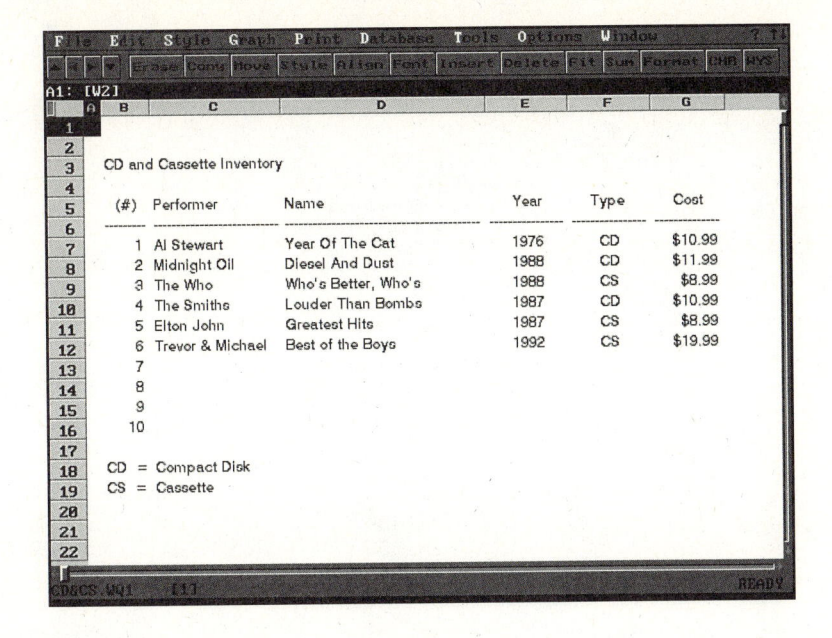

Fig. 2.7

A Quattro Pro database.

Creating a Macro Program

Certain spreadsheet operations are repetitive. Each time you create a spreadsheet, for example, you must format, name, enter data into, save, modify, and print the spreadsheet. A macro program can do many of these operations for you.

After you create a macro program, you give the program an Alt-key shortcut name. To run the macro program, press the Alt-key shortcut and then watch Quattro Pro duplicate each menu command that you want executed. Figure 2.8 shows a macro that opens a spreadsheet, changes the column width, and saves the spreadsheet under a new file name. See Chapter 15, "Creating Macros," for complete coverage of macro programming.

PART I — USING QUATTRO PRO SPREADSHEETS

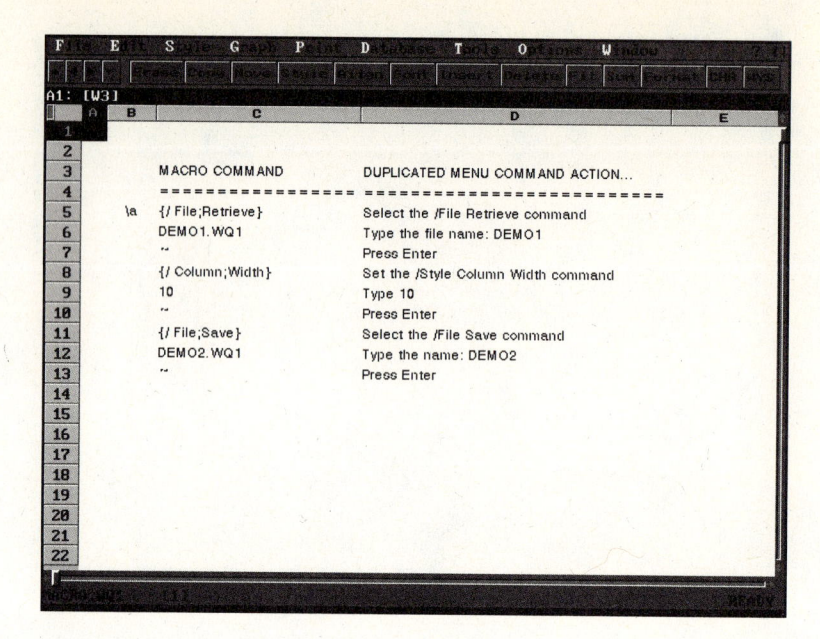

```
F  E   S  le  G aph  P int  D     a ase  T   o s  O   ons   W  ndow        2
                                                                            ?
A1: [W3]
   A     B           C                       D                         E
 1
 2
 3        MACRO COMMAND           DUPLICATED MENU COMMAND ACTION...
 4        ================        ===================================
 5    \a  {/ File;Retrieve}       Select the /File Retrieve command
 6        DEMO1.WQ1               Type the file name: DEMO1
 7        ~                       Press Enter
 8        {/ Column;Width}        Set the /Style Column Width command
 9        10                      Type 10
10        ~                       Press Enter
11        {/ File;Save}           Select the /File Save command
12        DEMO2.WQ1               Type the name: DEMO2
13        ~                       Press Enter
14
15
16
17
18
19
20
21
22
```

Fig. 2.8

A Quattro Pro macro.

Starting and Ending a Work Session

Q.EXE is the name of the program file that loads Quattro Pro into your computer's RAM memory. The Quattro Pro Installation Utility copies this file into the \QPRO directory on your hard disk drive. (See Appendix A, "Installing Quattro Pro," for a step-by-step look at the Quattro Pro installation process.) To start a new work session, first load Quattro Pro.

Starting Quattro Pro

To load Quattro Pro from the DOS command level, type *cd\qpro* and press Enter to move to the QPRO directory. Enter *q* and then press Enter to load Quattro Pro.

If you are operating in a Microsoft Windows operating environment, double-click the Quattro Pro icon to load the program.

When loaded, Quattro Pro displays a blank spreadsheet with the default file name SHEET1.WQ1. You now can enter data into the spreadsheet, load a different spreadsheet file, or end the current work session. To load an existing spreadsheet into Quattro Pro, choose /**File** **R**etrieve, type the name of the file you want to edit, and then press Enter.

Returning to the Operating System

You can conclude a successful Quattro Pro work session in many ways, some of which you may not want to use. The worst possible outcome of any computer work session is that you quit a program before saving your work.

Quattro Pro helps to ensure that you save your work before you exit the program. After you choose /**File** **E**xit, the program displays a dialog box that asks the following:

    Lose your changes and Exit?

Enter *N* to continue with the current work session, *Y* to exit without saving, or *S* to save your changes and exit the program.

> **TIP**
> Get in the habit of saving your spreadsheet several times during each work session to guard against the possibility of losing all your work if your system crashes or the power fails.

To save your spreadsheet and continue with your current work session, choose **S**ave from the **F**ile menu (type /*FS*, click **S**ave on the **F**ile menu, or press Ctrl-S).

Using Special Start-Up Parameters

You can load Quattro Pro with special start-up parameters that further clarify how the program should work with your hardware. The /X start-up parameter, for example, tells Quattro Pro to load with extended memory code-swapping enabled. This setting is recommended if you have a 286-based AT computer with 1M of RAM.

The /IM start-up parameter tells Quattro Pro to load with a monochrome palette rather than the default multicolored palette. To use the /IM start-up parameter, for example, type *q /im* at the DOS command prompt and then press Enter.

PART I — USING QUATTRO PRO SPREADSHEETS

> **TIP** For Microsoft Windows users, you can enter the Quattro Pro start-up parameters in the Optional Parameters field of your program information file (PIF). To load Quattro Pro with a monochrome palette for each new work session, for example, type /im in the Optional Parameters field.

For a complete discussion of start-up parameters, see the "Setting Start-Up Options" section in Chapter 16, "Customizing Quattro Pro."

Working with a Keyboard

You can use one of three accepted keyboard standards with your personal computer. Each keyboard has three sections in common: the function keypad, the alphanumeric keypad, and the numeric keypad (see figs. 2.9, 2.10, and 2.11). The extended keyboard in figure 2.11 also has two extra sections: a command keypad and an arrow-direction keypad.

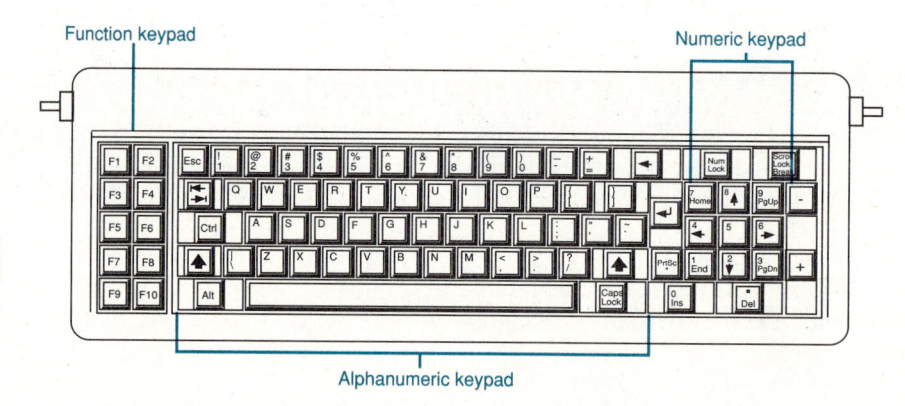

Fig. 2.9

The IBM PC keyboard.

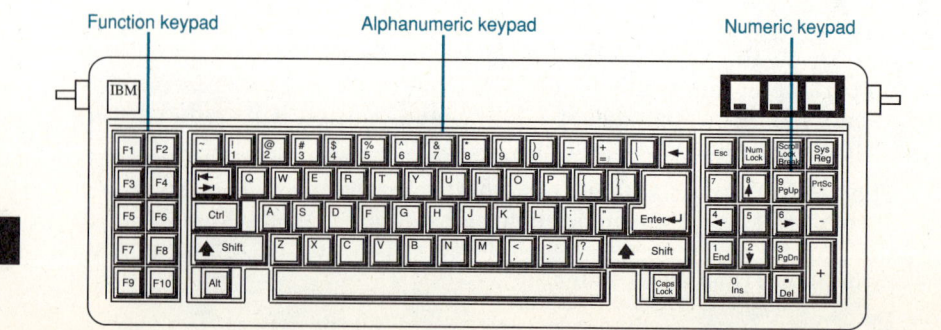

Fig. 2.10

The IBM AT keyboard.

2 — GETTING STARTED

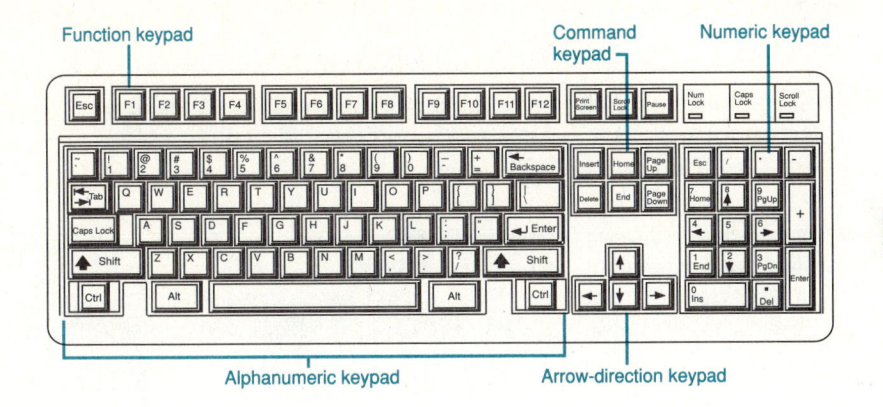

Fig. 2.11

The IBM AT extended keyboard.

(Keyboard diagram with labels: Function keypad, Command keypad, Numeric keypad, Alphanumeric keypad, Arrow-direction keypad)

Using the Alphanumeric Keyboard

The alphanumeric keyboard is located in the center of the keyboard. Except for the eight keys in table 2.1, the keys on the alphanumeric keyboard have the same functions as those on a typewriter.

Table 2.1 Special Keys on the Alphanumeric Keyboard

Key	Function
Tab	Moves cell selector one screen to the right; Shift-Tab moves cell selector one screen to the left
Alt	Invokes keyboard macros; when combined with one character, executes macro programs (see Chapter 15)
Shift	When pressed, enables you to use the numeric keypad to enter numbers, like a temporary Num Lock
Backspace	Deletes from right to left, one character at a time, while you are in EDIT mode
Slash (/)	Enters MENU mode so that you can choose a menu command; also is the divisor bar in a mathematical operation
Period (.)	Separates cell addresses like (A1..D10) and anchors cell addresses when in POINT mode; also is the decimal point in mathematical operations
Tilde (~)	Represents the action of pressing Enter once in macro programs
Ctrl	Executes menu commands quickly when combined with one character

Using the Numeric Keypad

You use the keys on the numeric keypad primarily to move the cell selector or the cursor. Ten keys, however, enable you to perform other actions when using Quattro Pro (see table 2.2).

Table 2.2 Special Action Keys on the Numeric Keypad

Key	Function
Esc	Cancels a menu or command selection; enables you to interrupt and cancel any sequence that ends with Enter by pressing Esc before Enter
Num Lock	Dedicates the numeric keypad to numeric entry only; when you press Num Lock again, reactivates the special-action keys
Scroll Lock/Break	Scroll locks the spreadsheet screen; the screen scrolls one row or column in the direction that you move the cursor; on certain keyboards, functions as the Break key; press Ctrl-Break to return to active spreadsheet from any location in Quattro Pro
PrtSc*	Shift-PrtSc* prints the contents of the active spreadsheet window; on Extended keyboards, prints with Print Screen key that does not require the Shift key
Home	Moves to the first item on an activated menu; with no active menu, relocates the cell selector to the home (cell A1) position
End	Moves to the last item on an activated menu; to enter END mode, make sure that no menus are active, press End, and press an arrow key to move to the last block of data in that direction, or press End and then Home to move the cursor to the lower right corner of the last data block on the spreadsheet
PgUp	Scrolls the spreadsheet up one full screen at a time
PgDn	Scrolls the spreadsheet down one full screen at a time
Ins	Toggles between the insert and typeover modes; in insert mode, each typed character moves the character under the cursor to the right one space
Del	Deletes the contents of the active cell; in EDIT mode, deletes the character at the current cursor position

Using the Arrow Keys

The four arrow keys enable you to move around the active spreadsheet in the directions that they point. You also can use these keys to position the cursor when you edit the contents of a cell in EDIT mode, to highlight commands on a menu, or to page through the help windows.

The End and Ctrl keys extend the power of the arrow keys by enabling you to take giant steps around the spreadsheet. Table 2.3 explains how to use the arrow keys.

Table 2.3 Extending the Power of the Arrow Keys

Key	Function
←	Moves the cell selector one cell to the left
→	Moves the cell selector one cell to the right
↑	Moves the cell selector up one cell
↓	Moves the cell selector down one cell
Ctrl-←	Moves the cell selector one screen to the left
Ctrl-→	Moves the cell selector one screen to the right
End-↑	Moves the cell selector up to the next nonblank cell below a blank one if the current cell contains an entry, or up to the next nonblank cell if the current cell is blank
End-↓	Moves the cell selector down to the next nonblank cell above an empty cell if the current cell contains an entry, or down to the next nonblank cell if the current cell is blank
End-→	Moves the cell selector right to the next nonblank cell followed by an empty cell if the current cell contains an entry, or right to the next nonblank cell if the current cell is blank
End-←	Moves the cell selector left to the next nonblank cell preceded by an empty one if the current cell contains an entry, or left to the next nonblank cell if the current cell is blank

TIP

When you type data into a cell and press Enter to record the data, the cell selector remains in the current cell. To move to another cell, press any arrow key, and Quattro Pro moves to the next cell in that direction. If you type data into cell A5 and then press the down-arrow key without first pressing Enter, for example, Quattro Pro enters the data into cell A5 and makes A6 the active cell.

PART I — USING QUATTRO PRO SPREADSHEETS

> **NOTE** If you want to use the cursor-movement keys on a nonextended keyboard, the Num Lock key must be toggled off. To dedicate the numeric keypad to only numerical entries, the Num Lock key must be on.

Using the Function Keys

Quattro Pro assigns 1 of 10 often-used spreadsheet commands to each function key found at the top or left of your keyboard. To invoke the Quattro Pro GoTo key, for example, and move the cell selector to a user-specified address, press F5.

You can access additional Quattro Pro commands by pressing Ctrl, Shift, or Alt and then pressing the appropriate function key. To display a menu of all of the open windows, for example, press Shift-F5, the Pick Window key.

When you use the File Manager or Graph Annotator, certain keys or key combinations have slightly different functions. The File Manager helps you to manage files on your hard disk; the Graph Annotator enables you to customize your graphs. Chapters 8 and 11 respectively discuss how to use these special secondary functions.

Table 2.4 lists the Quattro Pro function-key assignments available when you are using a spreadsheet.

Table 2.4 Quattro Pro Function-Key Assignments

Key	Function
F1 (Help)	Invokes a help window from anywhere on the spreadsheet or during any spreadsheet operation
F2 (Edit)	Enters EDIT mode so that you can make changes to a cell's contents
Shift-F2 (Debug)	Enters DEBUG mode so that you can execute a macro one command at a time
Alt-F2 (Macro Menu)	Displays the Macro menu
F3 (Choices)	Displays a list of block name choices when Quattro Pro prompts you for a block of cells; press again to enlarge the display of names; enlarges the display of file names when performing a function in the File menu
Shift-F3 (Macro List)	Displays a list of the macro commands for a spreadsheet

2 — GETTING STARTED

Key	Function
Alt-F3 (Functions)	Displays a list of the @function commands for a spreadsheet
F4 (Absolute)	Toggles through the four available cell reference formats; changes the format of the cell address to the left of or below the cursor on the input line
F5 (GoTo)	Moves the cell selector to a specified cell or block address
Shift-F5 (Pick Window)	Displays a list of open windows
Alt-F5 (Undo)	Undoes spreadsheet cell operations such as erasures, edits, deletions, and file retrievals
F6 (Pane)	Moves the cell selector between the active and inactive window panes when a spreadsheet window is split
Shift-F6 (Next Window)	Displays the next open window
Alt-F6 (Zoom)	When you are in text display mode, enlarges the active window so that it fills the screen; when the window is fully enlarged, shrinks the window back to its original size
F7 (Query)	Repeats the preceding /**D**atabase **Q**uery command
Shift-F7 (Select)	Enters EXT mode so that you can select a block of cells by pressing the arrow keys before performing a function on them; in the File Manager, selects and marks active the highlighted name in a list
Alt-F7 (All Select)	Selects and deselects active files in the active File Manager list
F8 (Table)	Repeats the last what-if command and recalculates a new sensitivity table
Shift-F8 (Move)	Removes files marked in the active File Manager list and stores them in temporary memory so that you can paste them in a new location
F9 (Calc)	Calculates formulas on the active spreadsheet if you are in READY mode; in VALUE or EDIT mode, converts the formula appearing in the input line to the end result

continues

Table 2.4 Continued

Key	Function
Shift-F9 (Copy)	Copies files marked in the active File Manager list into temporary memory so that you can paste them to a new location
F10 (Graph)	Displays a graph of selected data appearing on the current active spreadsheet; press Esc to return to the active spreadsheet
Shift-F10 (Paste)	Pastes files stored in temporary memory into the current directory displayed in the active File Manager file list
Ctrl-F10	Toggles between Paradox and Quattro Pro

Working with a Mouse

With a mouse you can duplicate any command or action that you can execute with a keyboard. A mouse actually simplifies many Quattro Pro spreadsheet operations. With one click, you can activate a menu; select a menu command; mimic the action of the Esc, Enter, and Del keys; invoke Quattro Pro help windows; select a cell or block of cells; scroll the active spreadsheet vertically or horizontally; resize the active spreadsheet; and so on.

Learning Basic Mouse-Movement Techniques

Many brands of mice are available. Some devices have one or two keys, and others have three or more. To accommodate as many types of mice as possible, Quattro Pro uses only the left and right mouse buttons.

Table 2.5 describes the five basic techniques that you must know to use a mouse with Quattro Pro.

Table 2.5 Basic Mouse-Movement Techniques

Technique	Action
Click	Press and release quickly the left or right button once
Double-click	Press and release the left or right button twice in quick succession
Drag	Drag the mouse pointer across the screen display—for example, from one cell to another
Point	Slide the mouse to relocate the pointer to different parts of the display
Release	Release a mouse button that you are holding down

Turbocharging Your Mouse

If your mouse's point-and-drag action seems sluggish, you need to adjust your mouse's tracking speed. The *tracking speed* determines how quickly the mouse pointer responds to your hand movement when you drag the mouse in any direction. A low tracking speed rating causes mouse action to appear sluggish; a high rating appears to turbocharge your mouse.

Many mouse manufacturers enable you to increase and decrease drag sensitivity when Quattro Pro is loaded, without requiring you to reinstall the driver program. For details, see the documentation that came with your mouse.

If you are running Quattro Pro under Microsoft Windows, you can click the Control Panel icon and then click the Mouse icon to alter your mouse's tracking speed.

Reviewing the Screen Display

The Quattro Pro screen display has five major areas: the pull-down menu bar, the SpeedBar, the input line, the spreadsheet area, and the status line.

By default, Quattro Pro displays in WYSIWYG display mode. This display mode is distinguished from other display modes by the presence of sculpted row and column borders and the horizontal SpeedBar at

PART I — USING QUATTRO PRO SPREADSHEETS

the top of the screen display. (In text display mode, the SpeedBar appears as a vertical bar along the right side of the spreadsheet area.) Figure 2.12 shows the Quattro Pro screen display.

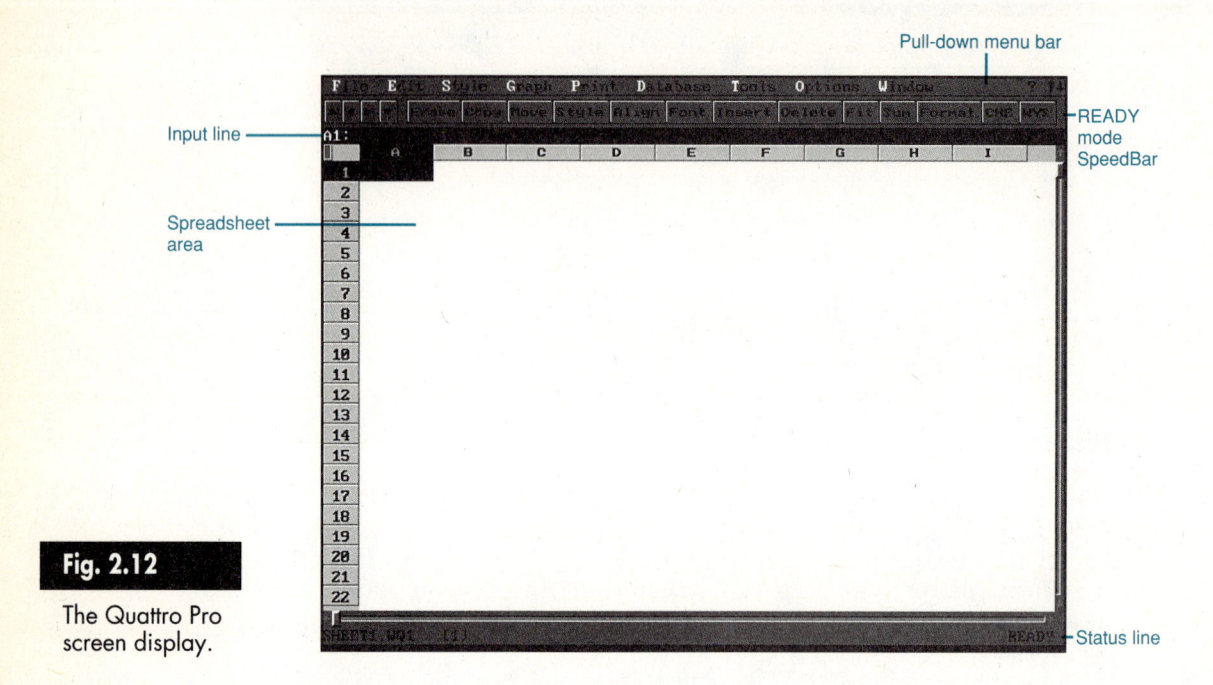

Fig. 2.12
The Quattro Pro screen display.

Pull-Down Menu Bar

Nine menus are available on the pull-down menu bar: **F**ile, **E**dit, **S**tyle, **G**raph, **P**rint, **D**atabase, **T**ools, **O**ptions, and **W**indow. Each menu has a different function. The **F**ile menu, for example, enables you to perform file operations. To create a file, retrieve an existing file, save and close a file, or do other file activities, you use the commands found on the **F**ile menu. For more information on choosing menu commands, see "Accessing Quattro Pro Menus" later in this chapter.

SpeedBars

Quattro Pro 4 has replaced the mouse palette on the right side of the spreadsheet with a new SpeedBar at the top of the spreadsheet. The

2 — GETTING STARTED

Speedbar contains sculpted buttons that enable you to reproduce commonly used keyboard keystrokes with one click of your mouse. The SpeedBar gives you instant access to many commands commonly used when creating, editing, and stylizing your spreadsheets.

After you load a mouse driver into memory, Quattro Pro detects its presence and displays the SpeedBar. If you disconnect the mouse, the palette does not appear the next time you load the program.

When you are in WYSIWYG display mode, the SpeedBar displays horizontally along the top of your screen. When you are in text mode, the SpeedBar displays on the right side of the screen.

In READY mode, Quattro Pro displays the READY mode SpeedBar. In EDIT mode, the EDIT mode SpeedBar appears. Both SpeedBars are fully customizable (see Chapter 16).

The READY Mode SpeedBar

The buttons on the READY mode SpeedBar duplicate many commands you frequently use when creating and customizing spreadsheets. If you don't see all these buttons on your SpeedBar, use the BAR button, located on the far right, to access more buttons. If the BAR button is not visible, all the buttons defined for your SpeedBar are visible.

Table 2.6 explains the function of each button on the READY mode SpeedBar, from left to right.

Table 2.6 READY Mode SpeedBar Buttons

Button	Function
Four triangles	Each duplicates the action of pressing the End key plus a cursor-movement key, enabling you to move quickly around your spreadsheet
Erase	Duplicates the action of choosing /Edit Erase Block
Copy	Duplicates the action of choosing /Edit Copy
Move	Duplicates the action of choosing /Edit Move
Style	Duplicates the action of choosing /Style Use Style
Align	Displays the /Style Alignment menu
Font	Displays the /Style Font menu
Insert	Duplicates the action of choosing /Edit Insert
Delete	Duplicates the action of choosing /Edit Delete
Fit	Duplicates the action of choosing /Style Block Size Auto Width

continues

Table 2.6 Continued

Button	Function
Sum	Uses @SUM to total rows, columns, or both
Format	Displays the /Style Numeric Format menu
CHR	Switches to character (text) display mode
WYS	Switches to WYSIWYG display mode
BAR	Displays more SpeedBar buttons when they are available

The EDIT Mode SpeedBar

The buttons on the EDIT mode SpeedBar give you instant access to many of the commands you use when editing spreadsheets (see fig. 2.13). With a click of your mouse, you can enter a named block, macro command, or @function on the input line. You also can construct and calculate formulas directly on the input line using your mouse.

Table 2.7 explains the function of each button on the EDIT mode SpeedBar, starting at the left. If you don't see all these buttons on your SpeedBar, click the BAR button located on the far right, to access more buttons.

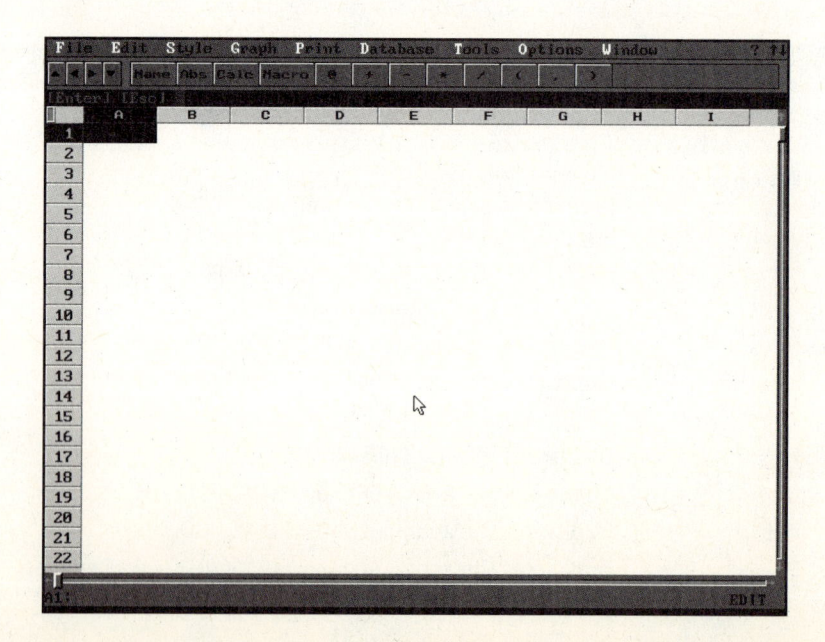

Fig. 2.13

The EDIT mode SpeedBar.

Table 2.7 The EDIT Mode SpeedBar

Button	Function
Four triangles	Each duplicates the action of pressing the End key plus a cursor-movement key, enabling you to move quickly around your spreadsheet
Name	Displays a list of named blocks; highlight a name and press Enter to enter it on the edit line (same as pressing F3)
Abs	Toggles cell coordinates between absolute and relative (same as pressing F4)
Calc	Calculates the formula on the input line (same as pressing F9)
Macro	Displays a list of menu-equivalent macro categories (similar to pressing Shift-F3); choose a main topic to reach a menu of specific actions, and then choose a specific action to place that menu-equivalent command on the edit line
@	Displays a list of @functions (similar to pressing Alt-F3); highlight one @function and press Enter to place it on the edit line at the current position
+	Enters a plus sign on the input line
–	Enters a minus sign on the input line
*	Enters a multiplication sign on the input line
/	Enters a division sign on the input line
(	Enters an open parenthesis on the input line
,	Enters a comma (argument separator) on the input line
)	Enters a close parenthesis on the input line
BAR	Displays more buttons when they are available

Input Line

The input line on the Quattro Pro screen contains seven data fields and presents two kinds of information (see fig. 2.14). The information displayed depends on whether you are in READY or EDIT mode.

PART I — USING QUATTRO PRO SPREADSHEETS

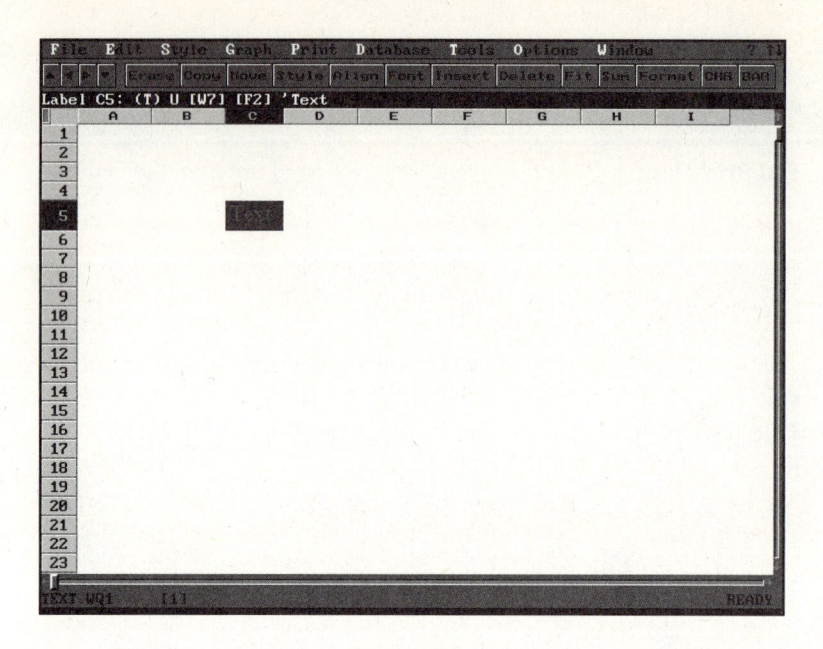

Fig. 2.14

The input line.

You are in READY mode when the active spreadsheet is ready to accept data into any cell. You are in EDIT mode when you press F2 to edit the data in a specific cell. You always can tell what mode you are in by looking at the status line at the bottom of the active spreadsheet. The mode indicator is located in the right corner of the status line.

When you are in READY mode, Quattro Pro displays format data for the active cell on the active spreadsheet. If the cell selector is in cell C5 and you are in READY mode, for example, the input line may show the format information displayed in figure 2.14. A brief description of each kind of field follows:

- The first field displays `Label`, `Date`, or `Graph`. The field displays `Graph` when the cell selector is on a graph. The field displays `Date` or `Label` when you use the /**D**atabase **D**ata Entry command to restrict acceptable cell entries to dates or labels.

- The second field displays the name of the active cell, such as C5.

- The third field displays a description of the numeric format and the number of decimal places, when applicable. The description (`T`) indicates that the cell is formatted to display text. Examples of other numeric formats include (`P2`) for percent with 2 decimals, (`C4`) for currency with 4 decimals, and (`,0`) for comma delimited with 0 decimals.

2 — GETTING STARTED

- The fourth field displays a description of the cell-protection status. A U indicates that a cell is unprotected. A P indicates that a cell is protected.

- The fifth field displays the width of the active column. Quattro Pro does not display this field when set to the default width. The description [W7] indicates that the active column is seven characters wide.

- The sixth field displays a description of the font used in the active cell. The description [F2] indicates that this cell is formatted by using font number 2.

- The last field displays the unformatted contents of the active cell. This field displays .15, for example, when the formatted cell displays 15.25% on the spreadsheet. In figure 2.14, cell C5 contains a label called Text.

Press F2 to place Quattro Pro in EDIT mode when you want to edit the contents of the active cell. Figure 2.15 shows how Quattro Pro displays the contents of cell C5 on the input line when in EDIT mode. Chapter 3 covers rules for editing the contents of a cell.

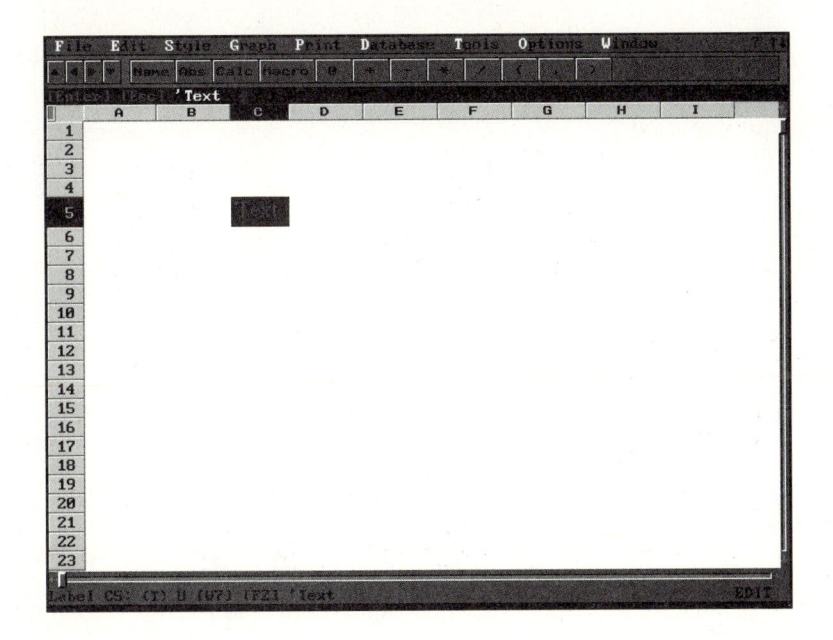

Fig. 2.15

The input line in EDIT mode.

PART I — USING QUATTRO PRO SPREADSHEETS

Spreadsheet Area

The spreadsheet area is the largest part of the Quattro Pro screen. The spreadsheet area is the part of the spreadsheet that you can see—the area where your cell selector is. Remember, a spreadsheet has 256 columns and 8,192 rows. The part you see on-screen represents just a fraction of the entire spreadsheet.

Figure 2.16 highlights the different elements of the spreadsheet window. The following sections describe each element.

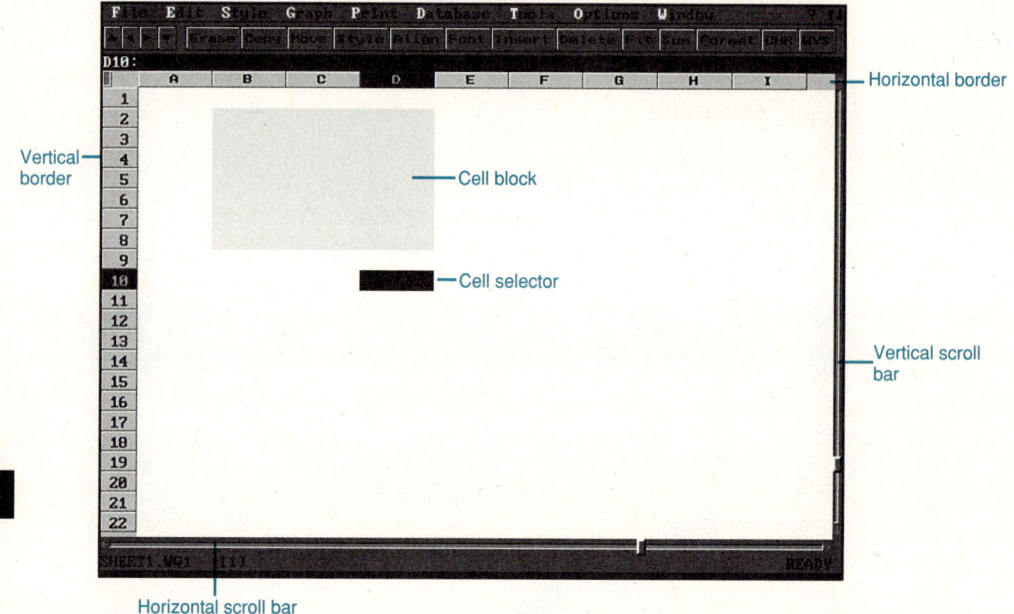

Fig. 2.16

The spreadsheet area.

Cell Selector

The cell selector is the rectangle you use to highlight a cell or a block of cells. You form a block of cells by clicking and holding down the left mouse button while in the active cell and then dragging the cell selector through the spreadsheet area. Alternatively, in READY mode, you can press Shift-F7 and identify the cell in the opposite corner of the block by clicking the cell or moving the cell selector to the cell using the arrow keys.

Quattro Pro names a block of cells as follows: the first element in the block name is the location of uppermost left cell in the block range; the second element in the block name is the location of the lowermost right cell in the block range. Quattro Pro separates the two cell locations with two decimal points, as in the cell block name (B2..D8). A *block name* is a set of cell coordinates that describes the far corners of the block.

> **TIP**
>
> Create cell blocks when you want to perform the same operation on multiple columns and rows. You can select the cell block range B2..D2, for example, to change the width of columns B, C, and D.

Scroll Bars

The horizontal and vertical scroll bars enable you to use your mouse to control the location of the cell selector on the active window. To move the cell selector around the active spreadsheet, point the mouse at a scroll box, click and hold down the left mouse button, and then drag the scroll box along the scroll bar or click anywhere on the scroll bar. The scroll box shows the position of the cell selector relative to the data on-screen.

Horizontal and Vertical Borders

The horizontal border contains the alphabetic name of each column, and the vertical border contains the numeric name of each row in the window. Both borders are highlighted or appear in reverse coloring so that they stand out from the rest of the spreadsheet area.

Status Line

The status line on the Quattro Pro screen contains four data fields and presents two kinds of information (see fig. 2.17). Like the input line, the type of information that the status line displays depends on whether you are in READY or EDIT mode.

When you are in READY mode, Quattro Pro displays information about the active spreadsheet file. If SHEET4.WQ1 is the active spreadsheet, and you are in READY mode, for example, the status line may display the information in figure 2.17. A brief description of each part of the status line follows.

PART I — USING QUATTRO PRO SPREADSHEETS

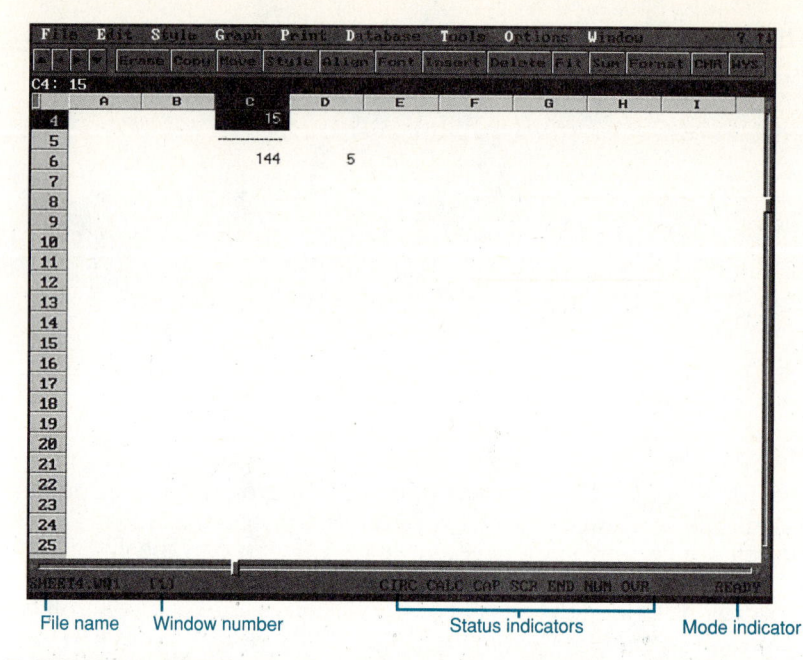

Fig. 2.17

The status line.

- *File Name.* The first field displays the name of the active spreadsheet file. Each time you load Quattro Pro, the default spreadsheet file name on the status line is SHEET1.WQ1 or the name of the file you have specified as the default file. During any work session, however, you may need to close one spreadsheet and create another. Quattro Pro names the files SHEET2.WQ1, SHEET3.WQ1, and so on. To change the default name of a spreadsheet, see Chapter 8, "Managing Files and Windows."

- *Window Number.* The second field displays the number of the current window. You can have up to 32 windows open at one time. In figure 2.17, [1] indicates the first window.

- *Status Indicator.* The status indicators to the right of the window number keep you informed of spreadsheet activity by displaying the current status of certain program features. This field displays NUM, for example, when the Num Lock key is on, CAP when the Caps Lock key is on, and so on. Table 2.8 defines the eight Quattro Pro status indicators.

- *Mode Indicator.* The mode indicator in the right corner of the status line tells you Quattro Pro's current program-execution mode. READY, for example, indicates that the current spreadsheet is ready to accept input. Table 2.9 defines the 15 mode indicators.

2 — GETTING STARTED

Table 2.8 Status Indicators

Status Code	Description
CALC	Current spreadsheet requires recalculation because a value referenced in a formula has been changed
CAP	Caps Lock key is on
CIRC	Formula on the current spreadsheet contains a circular reference, which occurs when a formula refers to itself or to a cell that refers back to the formula
END	End key is enabled; key is inoperative when in EXT mode
EXT	Shift-F7 has been pressed to extend a block; status is unavailable when End key is enabled
NUM	Num Lock key is on
OVR	Ins key has been pressed and can overwrite data on the input line
SCR	Scroll Lock key is on

Table 2.9 Mode Indicators

Status Code	Description
BKGD	Quattro Pro is recalculating spreadsheet formulas in the background, between presses of keystrokes on your keyboard
DEBUG	Quattro Pro invokes the macro debugger when a macro is started
EDIT	You are editing a cell on the current spreadsheet
ERROR	Quattro Pro encountered an operation error; press F1 to learn more about the error or Esc to cancel the ERROR code and return to the current spreadsheet
FIND	Quattro Pro is searching for a match to a search string specified in the Query command
FRMT	You are editing a format line during a parse operation
HELP	Quattro Pro is displaying a help window
LABEL	The entry you are about to make into a spreadsheet cell is a label
MACRO	Quattro Pro is executing a macro program

continues

Table 2.9 Continued

Status Code	Description
MENU	A menu is activated
POINT	You can choose a cell or block with the cell selector; press F3 to view a list of the block names on the current spreadsheet
READY	Quattro Pro is ready for you to make an entry or menu selection
REC	The macro recorder is turned on and is recording your keystrokes and mouse clicks
VALUE	The entry you are about to make into a spreadsheet cell is a value
WAIT	You must wait until Quattro Pro finishes with the current operation

Accessing Quattro Pro Menus

To use Quattro Pro properly, you must familiarize yourself with its menu-command language. Fortunately, Quattro Pro uses simple descriptive names for each menu command that you use to enter, edit, manipulate, and view your spreadsheet data. Each of the nine menus has a unique name, offers a unique set of command options, and requires a unique keystroke action to execute commands.

Activating a Menu

To execute a command, you first must activate a menu. To enter Quattro Pro's MENU mode, press the forward slash (/) key once. This action accesses the **F**ile menu. If you want to activate the **F**ile menu, press Enter. If you want to activate a different menu, use the arrow keys to highlight the menu name you want and then press Enter.

You can activate a menu using the boldface letter key assigned to the menu name. The letter E, for example, is the boldface letter key for the **E**dit menu. To activate the **E**dit menu, type /E. The screen shown in figure 2.18 appears.

2 — GETTING STARTED

You can use a mouse to simplify the process of activating and choosing Quattro Pro menu commands. To activate a menu, place the pointer on the menu name and click. Then choose a command by placing the pointer on a menu command and clicking.

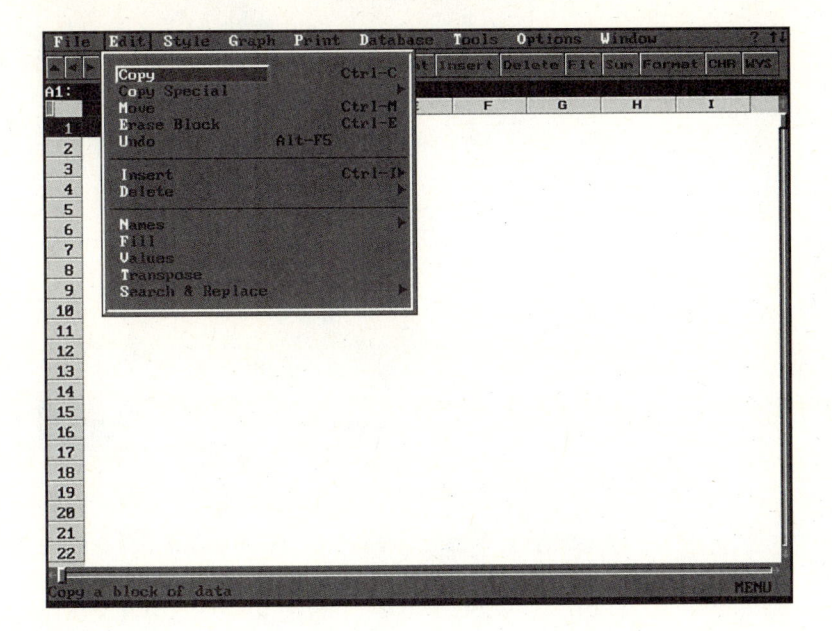

Fig. 2.18
The Edit menu.

Choosing a Command

When you activate (or pull down) a menu, Quattro Pro displays a list of menu commands. By default, Quattro Pro activates the first command on each menu. To choose this command, press Enter. If you want to choose a different command, use the arrow keys to highlight your choice and then press Enter.

> **NOTE** Press the forward slash (/) key plus the boldfaced letter key that appears in each menu name to activate a menu. From a pulled-down menu, press the boldface letter key in a command name to execute that command. Quattro Pro displays a brief description of a menu's or command's purpose on the status line when you activate, or highlight, the menu name or command name.

When you choose a menu command, Quattro Pro often displays a second submenu. To set the page orientation to **L**andscape for printing a graph, for example, you must travel through three "child" menus by choosing **/P**rint **G**raph Print **L**ayout **O**rientation (see fig. 2.19).

PART I — USING QUATTRO PRO SPREADSHEETS

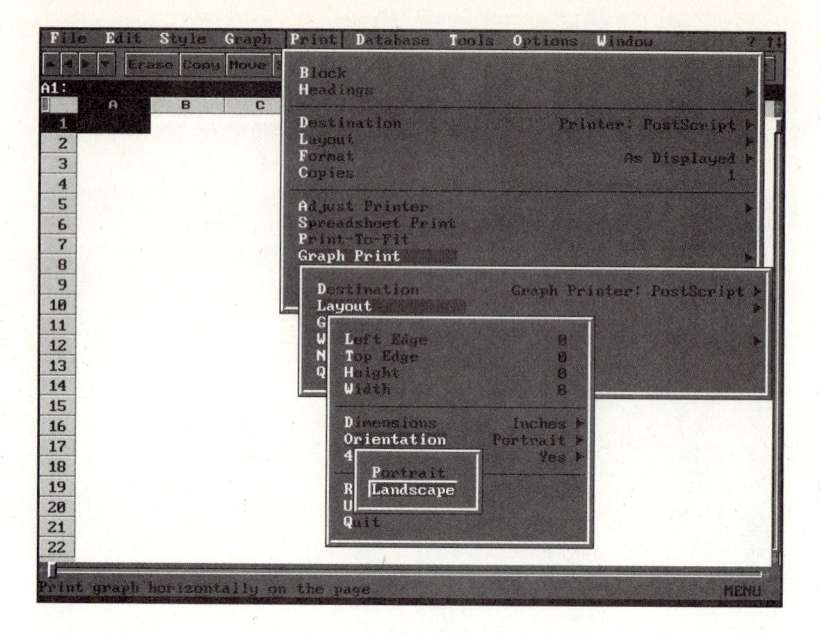

Fig. 2.19

The menu and three submenus to set the page orientation.

Quitting a Menu Selection

You can cancel a menu selection or command choice in three ways. Most menus have a Quit option, which you can select to return to the preceding menu. You also can press Esc to back up to the preceding menu. To close all menus and revert to the active spreadsheet, press Ctrl-Break. This key sequence is like pressing Esc several times to return to the active spreadsheet.

> **TIP** Although all extended keyboards have a Break key, many of the earlier keyboards (PC XT and some PC AT) do not have this key. If your keyboard does not have a Break key, try substituting the Scroll Lock key for the Break key when you use the Ctrl-Break sequence. If this substitution does not work, choose Quit or press Esc to return to the active spreadsheet.

If you use a mouse, you have several additional menu-management techniques at your disposal. Clicking a menu border makes that menu active and closes submenus. Clicking a spreadsheet while the menu is active closes all menus—like using Ctrl-Break.

2 — GETTING STARTED

Reviewing Data on a Quattro Pro Menu

Figure 2.20 shows the kinds of data you see on a pull-down menu. The menu command names appear at the left margin. Each command has a boldfaced letter key. Certain default settings—such as the default directory C:\QPRO4\—appear in the middle of the menu.

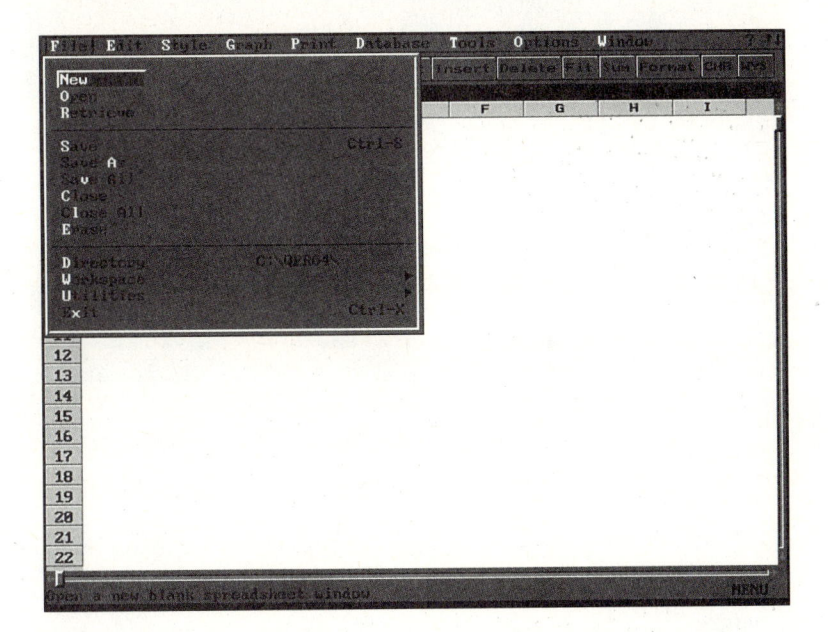

Fig. 2.20

The File pull-down menu.

The Ctrl-key shortcuts and submenu arrowheads appear on the right margin of a pull-down menu. A submenu arrowhead resembles a small triangle turned on its right side ▶. This symbol appears next to a menu command whenever the command has another submenu of commands. If you choose /**E**dit **I**nsert, Quattro Pro displays a submenu that asks you to specify what you want to insert—**R**ows, **C**olumns, Row **B**lock, or Column **B**lock (see fig. 2.21).

Because none of the commands on the submenu in figure 2.21 contains an arrowhead, choosing any option executes the **I**nsert command.

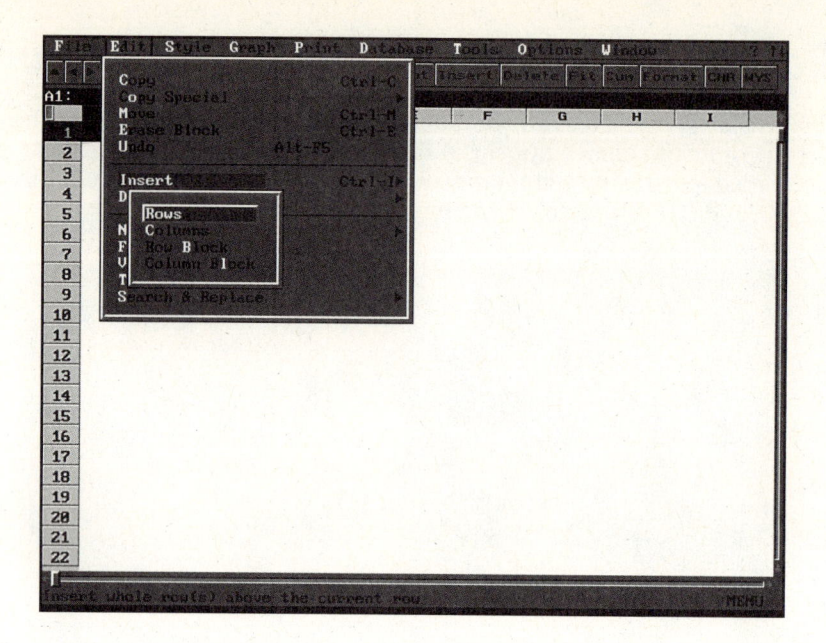

Fig. 2.21

The Insert submenu of the Edit menu.

Using Ctrl-Key Shortcuts

Most Quattro Pro menus offer Ctrl-key shortcuts with which you can execute a command quickly. The shortcuts are the next best thing to a mouse for saving you time because they replace all the steps required to execute a menu command. To exit Quattro Pro, for example, you must activate the **F**ile menu, scroll down to E**x**it, and press Enter. With the Ctrl-key shortcut, you can press Ctrl-X from the active spreadsheet and accomplish the same result more quickly.

Remember the following three factors when using Ctrl-key shortcuts:

- You must execute Ctrl-key shortcuts from the active spreadsheet. When you create a custom Ctrl-key shortcut (one that loads a file, for example), you can execute the shortcut only when no menus are active. (The next section describes how to create a custom shortcut.)

- You cannot assign the same Ctrl-key shortcut to two different commands.

- Ctrl-key shortcuts are menu-tree specific. Quattro Pro can display two menu-tree variations on its default menu structure. These trees are accessed with the /**O**ptions **S**tartup **M**enu Tree command. One variation displays all menu names and commands as they appear in the original version of Quattro, whereas the other variation reproduces the menu structure of Lotus 1-2-3. If you switch to the 1-2-3 menu tree, you must create Ctrl-key shortcuts that work with the menu names and command names for the 1-2-3 menu tree. (See Chapter 16 "Customizing Quattro Pro," for complete coverage of menu trees.)

Creating Custom Ctrl-Key Shortcuts

To create your own Ctrl-key shortcuts for frequently used menu commands, follow these steps:

1. Activate a menu and highlight the command you want.
2. Press Ctrl-Enter.
3. Press Ctrl and the letter you want to use as the shortcut key.

If another Ctrl-key shortcut already uses the letter, Quattro Pro displays an error message. When you perform this operation successfully, the Ctrl-key shortcut appears next to the command name on the menu.

Deleting Custom Ctrl-Key Shortcuts

To delete an existing Ctrl-key shortcut so that you can reassign its function, follow these steps:

1. Activate a menu and highlight the command you want.
2. Press Ctrl-Enter.
3. Press Del twice.

When you perform this operation successfully, the Ctrl-key shortcut next to the menu command disappears.

Table 2.10 lists Quattro Pro's Ctrl-key shortcuts. Except for Ctrl-D, you may reassign any of the shortcuts listed to suit your preferences.

> **TIP**
> You easily can remember most of these shortcuts because they use the boldfaced letter in the last command to start a spreadsheet operation.

Switching Display Modes

Thus far the figures in this chapter illustrate the look of Quattro Pro's WYSIWYG display mode. In WYSIWYG display mode, a horizontal SpeedBar—which displays if you have a mouse loaded—appears at the top of the spreadsheet. The WYSIWYG display mode setting is ideal for users who prefer to review presentation-quality spreadsheet settings such as custom fonts, drawn lines, and shaded cells as they use them. Quattro Pro users who are less concerned with the program's presentation-quality spreadsheet-building capabilities prefer text display mode.

Table 2.10 Ctrl-Key Shortcuts

Shortcut Key	Equivalent Menu Command
A	/Style Alignment
C	/Edit Copy
D	Date Prefix (cannot be reassigned)
E	/Edit Erase Block
F	/Style Numeric Format
G	/Graph Fast Graph
I	/Edit Insert
M	/Edit Move
N	/Edit Search & Replace Next
P	/Edit Search & Replace Previous
R	/Window Move/Size
S	/File Save
T	/Window Tile
W	/Style Column Width
X	/File Exit

Quattro Pro enables you to switch display modes to meet different viewing needs. If you previously used Quattro (Quattro Pro's predecessor) or 1-2-3, for example, you may want to display Quattro Pro in text display mode—the default display mode used by these other programs.

To switch to text display mode, choose the /Options Display Mode A: 80x25 command. Quattro Pro immediately switches to text display mode (see fig. 2.22).

2 — GETTING STARTED

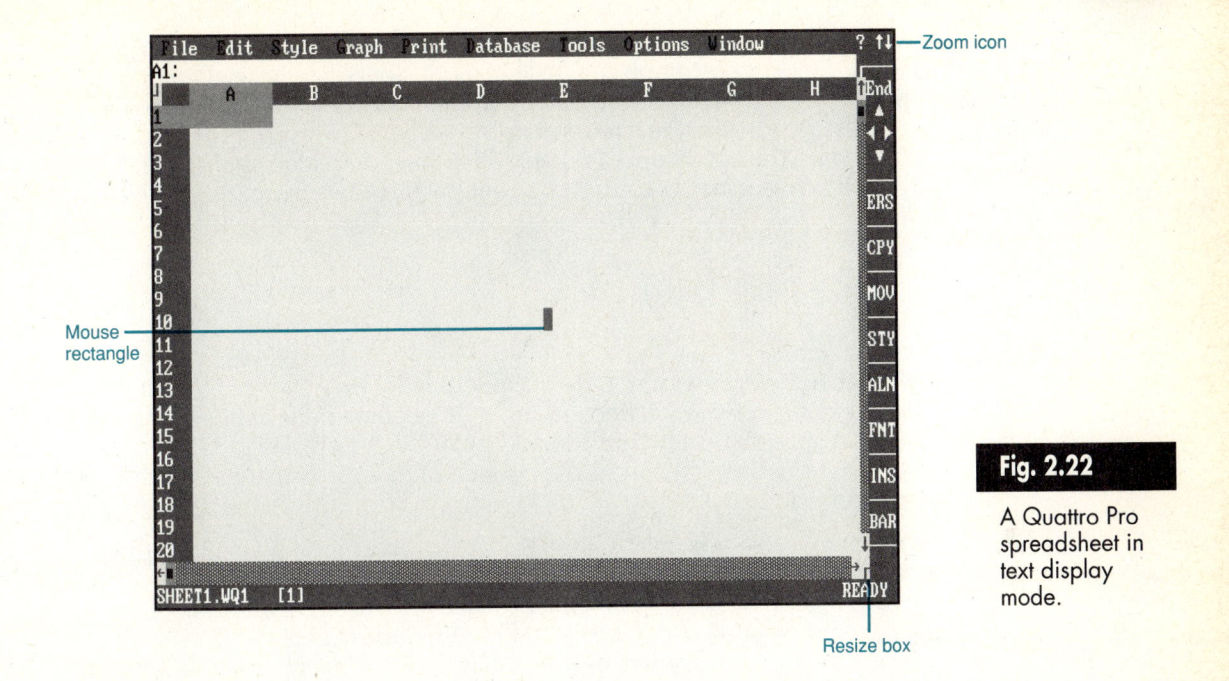

Fig. 2.22

A Quattro Pro spreadsheet in text display mode.

Notice that Quattro Pro's screen in text display mode is slightly different than in WYSIWYG display mode. The SpeedBar buttons lose their sculpted appearance, the SpeedBar itself becomes a vertical bar at the right edge of the spreadsheet, and the mouse arrow becomes a rectangle.

Quattro Pro offers two special features in text mode: the capability to zoom and resize a window and the capability to stack, or layer, windows on-screen so that they overlap each other. These features are not available in WYSIWYG mode.

If you own an EGA or VGA graphics display system, you also can access several extended text display modes. In general, Quattro Pro shows more rows and columns in extended text display mode than in the normal text or WYSIWYG display modes. For more information about extended text display modes, see the section titled "Setting Display Mode Options" in Chapter 16.

The Zoom Icon

The Zoom icon—located at the right end of the menu bar, above the SpeedBar—is a text-mode-specific tool that shrinks or enlarges the active window. In WYSIWYG display mode, the Zoom icon is inoperative even though it appears on-screen. Instead, use the /**O**ptions **W**YSIWYG Zoom % command to shrink and enlarge a spreadsheet.

To use the Zoom icon, you first must switch to text display mode by clicking the CHR button on the READY mode SpeedBar or using the /**O**ptions **D**isplay Mode **A**: Text 80x25 command. Click the Zoom icon once to shrink the active window and reveal other windows that are open behind the active spreadsheet. Click the Zoom icon again to enlarge the active window so that the window fills the screen.

The Resize Box

The Resize box—at the right edge of the horizontal scroll bar, above the mode indicator—is a text-mode-specific tool that changes the size of a spreadsheet window. Because no menu command is available for resizing a spreadsheet, when you are in WYSIWYG display mode you may wish to use the /**W**indow **T**ile command to approximate the same display effect.

To use the Resize box, first switch to text display mode by clicking the CHR button on the READY mode SpeedBar or using the /**O**ptions **D**isplay Mode **A**: Text 80x25 command. Click the Resize box and then drag the lower right edge of the spreadsheet. When the window is the correct size, release the mouse button. Quattro Pro draws the window to the specified proportions.

> **T I P** If you do not have a mouse and are operating in text display mode, use the /**W**indow **M**ove/Size command to shrink or enlarge a window. This command is inoperative when Quattro Pro is in WYSIWYG display mode.

Getting Help

If you have a question, encounter an error, or forget the purpose of a menu command, Quattro Pro's help window can provide the solution quickly. During most operations, you can press F1 to activate the help window from any location on the spreadsheet.

If you press F1 while in the active spreadsheet, Quattro Pro displays the help window shown in figure 2.23.

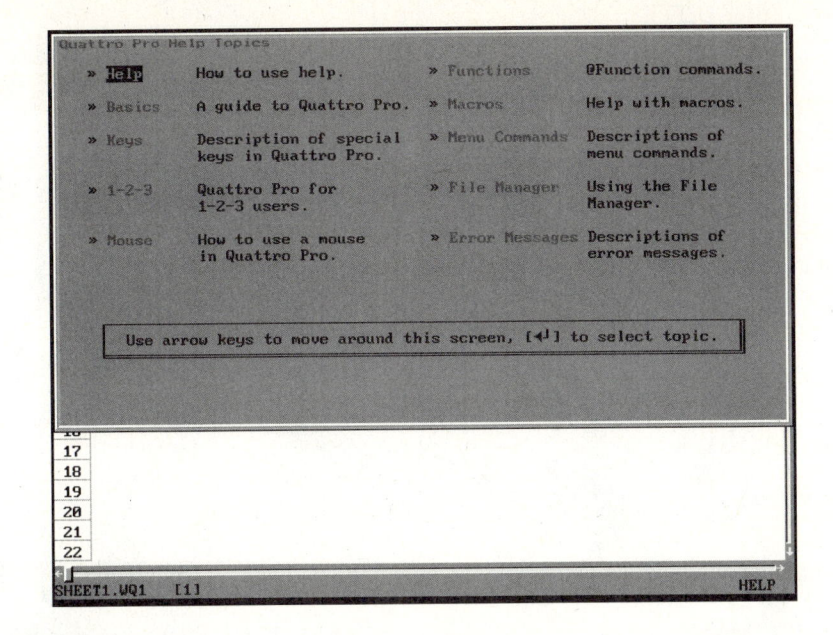

Fig. 2.23

Quattro Pro's main help window.

> **NOTE** Pressing F1 at any time invokes a Quattro Pro help window. You also can access the Help menu by clicking the ? on the far right of the pull-down menu bar when you are in READY mode.

Boldfaced names appearing in a help window are keywords. If you need more information about the topics covered in a help window, look for those keywords. To choose a topic, put the cursor on a keyword and then press Enter (or click the keyword).

After help is invoked, you quickly can access a specific help topic by typing the first few letters of the topic or command you want more information about. To use this feature, first press F1 and then press F3. Quattro Pro displays an alphabetical list of help topics.

If you want more information about shading cells, you can enter *S* to reach the first help topic beginning with S, or you can type the first few letters of the topic—*SHA* for example—to get even closer to your topic. After you reach the general area, use the arrow keys to scroll slowly or, if necessary, use the scroll bar to scroll quickly. A line at the top of the index displays the title of help screen to which the topic leads. To move to a help screen, highlight the topic and press Enter.

Quattro Pro help is context-sensitive. It displays data about the current operation taking place on your spreadsheet.

PART I — USING QUATTRO PRO SPREADSHEETS

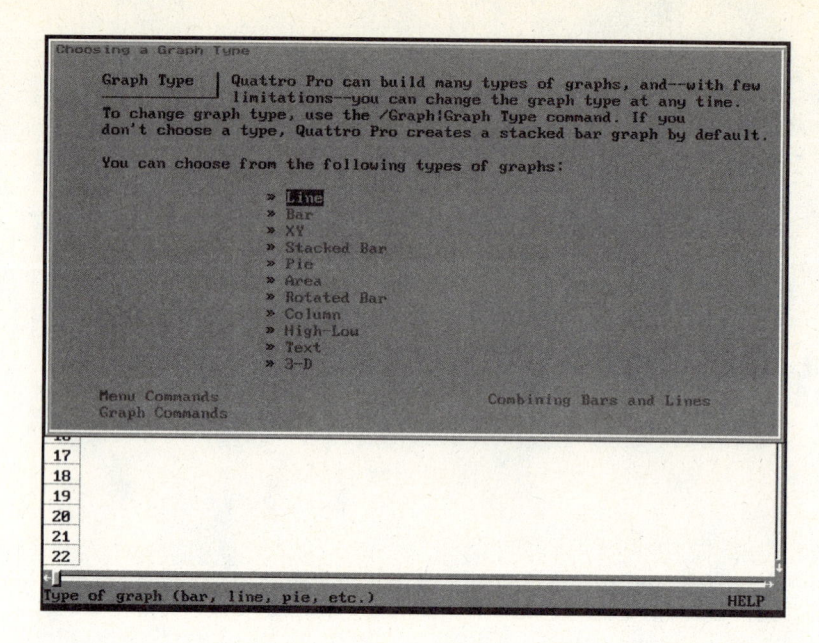

Fig. 2.24

The Graph menu's help windows.

Figure 2.24 shows the **G**raph menu's help window. To display this window, pull down the **G**raph menu and press F1. The screen displays the 12 graph types, and the four category names appearing at the bottom of the screen are the boldfaced keywords:

```
Menu Commands, Help Topics, Combining Bars and Lines,
Graph Commands
```

To exit a help window and return to the active spreadsheet, press Esc.

Using the help window saves time by preventing unnecessary interruptions of work sessions. Using Quattro Pro's help also can save you the time required to flip through reference manuals to find a solution.

You also can get on-line help using another method. When you scroll through a menu's commands, a short description of each command's purpose appears on the status line. Use this feature when you need help understanding the purpose of a menu command.

Questions & Answers

This chapter covers most of the basics you need to get started with Quattro Pro. If you have questions about any topic covered in this chapter and cannot find the right answer using the help windows, scan this section.

Loading Quattro Pro

Q: What do I do if Quattro Pro will not load onto my computer?

A: Make sure that you are logged on to the proper directory. By default, this directory is called C:\QPRO.

Quattro Pro may not recognize your display. Try reinstalling the program (see Appendix A). Alternatively, try using the various command-line options described in Chapter 16.

Q: What if the computer displays the message Not enough memory to run Quattro when I try to load the program?

A: Quattro Pro may not load because you have terminate-and-stay-resident (TSR) programs loaded into your computer.

To see whether the TSRs are causing the problem, temporarily disable the TSR statements in your CONFIG.SYS and AUTOEXEC.BAT files by typing *rem* before the TSR program name. Now reboot your computer.

If the TSR programs are not consuming too much memory, remove REM from the CONFIG.SYS and AUTOEXEC.BAT files and reboot your computer again. (To check whether the TSR programs are using too much memory, use the DOS CHKDSK.COM program to verify that you have at least 384K of free memory.)

Another possible answer is that your expanded memory may be incompatible with Quattro Pro. Disable the EMS driver in your CONFIG.SYS file. Reboot the system and try again (see Appendix A).

Q: What if I loaded Quattro Pro using the \IM monochrome start-up parameter, but Quattro Pro did not load the monochrome palette?

A: Precede any special start-up parameters with a forward slash. Type /im, for example, to load Quattro Pro with a monochrome palette. If you accidentally type \im, Quattro Pro loads without the proper palette. Press Ctrl-X to leave Quattro Pro. Restart the program using the /IM parameter. Choose /Options Update to save this palette setting for future work sessions.

Working with a Keyboard and Mouse

Q: Why can't I activate a menu when I press the forward slash key (/)?

A: The forward slash cannot activate a Quattro Pro menu unless the program is in READY mode. Check the mode indicator on the status line. If the indicator doesn't say READY, press Esc until you are in the correct mode and then try again.

Q: Why does pressing an arrow key cause my spreadsheet screen to shift up and down instead of moving the cell selector from cell to cell?

A: Press your Scroll Lock key to turn it off.

Q: Why doesn't my mouse work properly with Quattro Pro?

A: When installed, Quattro Pro tries to recognize and configure itself for use with your mouse. Check Appendix A to make sure that your mouse is compatible with Version 4.0.

You also can check the README text file included in your Quattro Pro package. To do so, type *readme* at the DOS command prompt, as in C:\QPRO\README.

Using SpeedBars

Q: I see only the READY mode SpeedBar on my screen. How can I get to the EDIT mode SpeedBar?

A: You must be in EDIT mode to access the EDIT mode SpeedBar. Press F2 to enter EDIT mode and display the EDIT mode SpeedBar.

Q: I selected a column of numbers, clicked the SUM button, and then got the error message Bottom cell/row must be blank for column totals. Why?

A: When selecting a column or row to sum, you also must select blank cells beneath or to the right of the block you want to sum. The blank cell indicates where Quattro Pro should display the total.

Accessing Quattro Pro Menus

Q: Why did Quattro Pro enter LABEL mode when I tried to activate a menu by pressing the forward slash key?

A: One of the common mistakes made when activating a menu is confusing the forward slash with the backslash key. The forward slash key (/) is located at the bottom of your alphanumeric keyboard and always is paired up with the question mark (?) key. If you type the backslash key, Quattro Pro enters LABEL mode and displays the \ on the input line.

The backslash key is used to enter repeating characters—for example, \– repeats the – across the width of the cell and adjusts as the width of the cell changes. The method of entering repeating characters also saves memory.

Q: Why did nothing happen when I pressed the first letter in a menu command?

A: Not all Quattro Pro commands use the first letter of the command name as the boldface letter key. On the **F**ile menu, for example, the **E**rase and E**x**it commands begin with the letter E, but they cannot both use E as a boldfaced letter key.

Q: Why did Quattro Pro beep when I tried to use a Ctrl-key shortcut to execute a menu command?

A: You must be on the active spreadsheet with no activated menus for Ctrl-key shortcuts to work.

The Ctrl-key shortcut you pressed may not exist. Pull down the menu on which the command resides and verify that you pressed the correct shortcut key.

Alternatively, you may have deleted the shortcut key you tried to use if you have tried creating and deleting your own shortcut keys.

Getting Help

Q: I pressed F1 for help, but nothing happened. What is wrong?

A: The program could not find the file called QUATTRO.HLP in the Quattro Pro directory (C:\QPRO by default). If you do not find the file in this directory, reinstall the program (see Appendix A).

Summary

This chapter introduces you to the electronic spreadsheet program. You learned how to get started using Quattro Pro. You now should understand the following basic Quattro Pro concepts:

- Using spreadsheet columns and rows
- Knowing how Quattro Pro deals with numbers and letters when you enter them into a spreadsheet cell
- Knowing the difference between spreadsheet, graph, database, and macro programs
- Beginning and ending a work session
- Using a keyboard and mouse
- Interpreting the information that appears in the various sections of the Version 4.0 screen
- Switching between WYSIWYG and character (text) display modes
- Getting on-line help during program operation

In Chapter 3, you take the next logical step toward learning how to enter, edit, move, and view data on the Quattro Pro Version 4.0 spreadsheet.

CHAPTER 3

Entering and Editing Data

In this chapter, you learn the skills you need to use Quattro Pro on a daily basis. The material presented in this chapter shows you how to enter, edit, and view data on the Quattro Pro spreadsheet. The chapter also defines some important Quattro Pro terminology used throughout the book.

Learning Spreadsheet Terminology

Before you begin creating spreadsheets, you should learn the following Quattro Pro terms: spreadsheet, cell address, block address, file name, file, window, and workspace.

This book uses the term *spreadsheet* to describe the area where data appears.

Chapter 2, "Getting Started," defines a *cell address* as the basic unit of a spreadsheet. The cell address also is part of a *block address*, which contains two coordinates (two cell addresses) that describe the upper left and lower right parts of a group of cells on a spreadsheet. D2 is one of two cell addresses, for example, appearing in block address D2..D10.

PART I — USING QUATTRO PRO SPREADSHEETS

All Quattro Pro menu commands that require you to enter a cell address also can work on a block address. Working with blocks of spreadsheet data is much more efficient than working with one cell at a time.

After you build a spreadsheet, you assign a *file name* to the spreadsheet and save the file on a disk. To accomplish both steps simultaneously, choose the /**F**ile **S**ave command. Doing so assigns a unique file name to the spreadsheet so that you easily can locate the spreadsheet the next time you want to review its data. To review the data, choose the /**F**ile **R**etrieve command and retrieve the file in which the Quattro Pro spreadsheet is stored.

Quattro Pro Version 4.0 enables you to open and view up to 32 windows at a time. A *window* is an area on-screen where you view a spreadsheet. When you have only one spreadsheet open during a work session, the spreadsheet window fills the entire screen display. When you open a second spreadsheet, Quattro Pro creates a second window. See "Viewing the Spreadsheet" later in this chapter for more details.

To display both spreadsheet windows at the same time, choose the /**W**indow **T**ile command. Now, each window occupies one half of the entire screen. The more spreadsheet windows you open, the smaller the program must make the windows so that they all can fit on-screen at the same time.

The term *workspace* describes all the spreadsheet files that you have loaded into your computer's memory at one time. Workspaces can be extremely useful when you link spreadsheets or work with several related spreadsheets during one work session.

To assign a file name to a workspace, choose /**F**ile **W**orkspace **S**ave. When you assign a workspace file name, you tell Quattro Pro to remember the names of all of the files currently in memory, and how they are arranged. The next time you need to work with this group of related spreadsheets, choose /**F**ile **W**orkspace **R**estore, type the name of the workspace file, and press Enter. Quattro Pro loads all of the spreadsheets originally saved as one workspace.

Entering Data

Quattro Pro accepts two types of data as valid entries: labels and values. A *label* is defined as a text entry; a *value* can be a number, a formula, or a date-and-time entry.

To enter data into a spreadsheet cell, follow these steps:

1. Select a cell by using the cursor-movement keys or by clicking with the mouse.

3 — ENTERING AND EDITING DATA

2. Type data using any of the keys on your keyboard.
3. Press Enter to tell Quattro Pro to store the data in the active cell.
4. Press a cursor-movement key to move to a new cell.

> **TIP**
>
> After typing data, instead of pressing Enter you can move to a second cell by pressing any cursor-movement key. Pressing a cursor-movement key enables you to store the data you typed and to move to the next cell with one keystroke.

Quattro Pro looks at the first character in an entry to decide whether the character is a label or a value (see fig. 3.1). When you enter a label into a cell, the mode indicator on the status line displays the word LABEL. When you enter a value into a spreadsheet cell, the mode indicator displays the word VALUE.

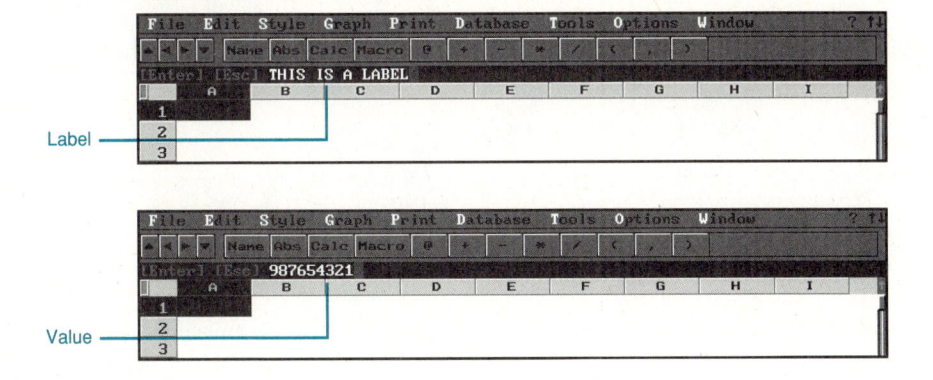

Fig. 3.1
A label and a value on the input line.

> **TIP**
>
> Always check the mode indicator to make sure that Quattro Pro interprets your data correctly. If you accidentally enter a number as text and the number is used in a spreadsheet formula, the formula cannot calculate an answer correctly.

If you try to enter a label when Quattro Pro is in VALUE mode, the program sounds an error tone beep. Press Esc, reenter the data correctly, and then press Enter.

Learning about Labels

The word *label* is just a formal description for text. Label also suggests that you can use text as column-heading labels and row-description labels to describe the data on a spreadsheet.

A text entry can be many things—the word *catch* as well as the words *catch22* or *22skidoo*. Remember, the first character you type tells Quattro Pro how to interpret the rest of the characters in the entry. If the first letter is a number but the entry is actually a label, you must enter a label prefix.

A label prefix has two functions. First, the prefix tells Quattro Pro that an entry is text, regardless of its composition of numbers and letters. Second, the prefix tells Quattro Pro how to align the text entry in a spreadsheet cell. Table 3.1 lists label prefixes.

Table 3.1 Label Prefixes

Label	Description
'	Left-justifies text in a cell
"	Right-justifies text in a cell
^	Centers text in a cell
\	Repeats a character or group of characters in a cell until the character fills the entire cell

By default, Quattro Pro places an apostrophe (the left-alignment prefix) in front of every entry initially recognized as text. If you want to change the alignment of text in a cell or enter a label that begins with a number, type one of the other label prefixes shown in table 3.1 before you type the first character of the entry. Figure 3.2 shows how each of these label prefixes aligns a text entry in a spreadsheet cell.

Quattro Pro enables you to enter up to 254 characters per label. When you enter a label longer than the width of the cell's column, Quattro Pro displays the entire label by extending the text into the next cell on the same row (see cell B4 in fig. 3.3). If the next cell contains data, Quattro Pro cuts off the initial entry, preventing the entry from overlapping onto the contents of the next cell (see cell B6 in fig. 3.3).

3 — ENTERING AND EDITING DATA

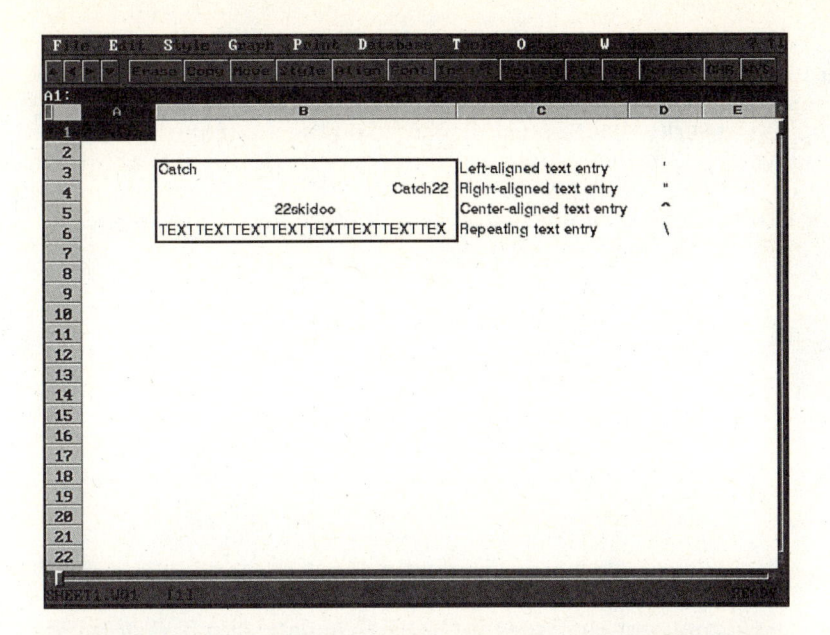

Fig. 3.2

The four label prefixes that change the alignment of your spreadsheet entry.

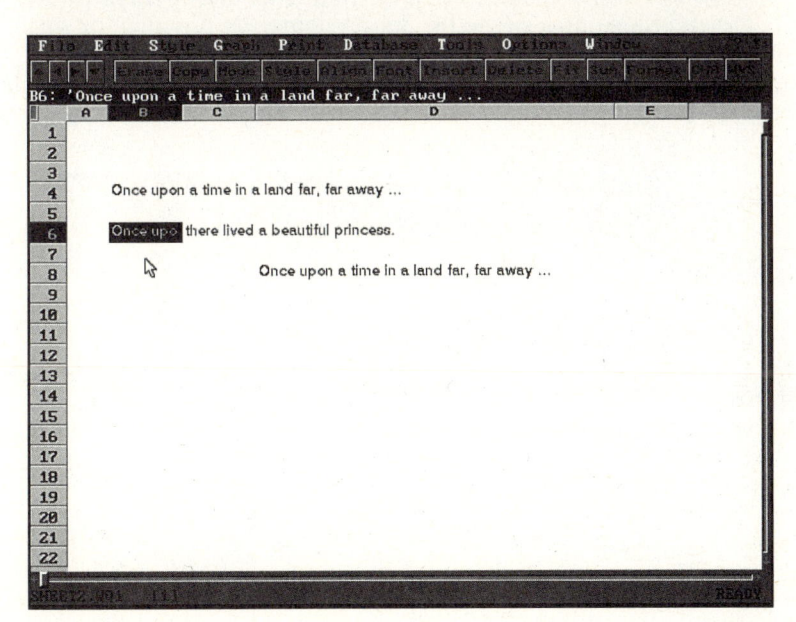

Fig. 3.3

An entry cut off when the next cell contains data.

PART I — USING QUATTRO PRO SPREADSHEETS

You can deal with the overlapping cell label in cell B6 shown in figure 3.3 in two ways. First, you can leave the entry as is. Although you cannot see the entire label entry, it is stored. Place the cell selector in the cell to verify that the text displayed on the input line is intact. Second, you can set the column width to equal the width of the entire label entry (like in cell D8). See "Setting the Width of a Column" in Chapter 5 for information about altering the width of a column. Figure 3.3 illustrates both alternatives.

> **T I P** Quattro Pro also cuts off an overlapping text entry when you surround the entry with a box by using the /Style Line Drawing Outside command (see "Drawing Lines and Boxes" in Chapter 5).

Learning about Values

The term *value* encompasses three types of data: numbers, formulas, and date-and-time entries (see fig. 3.4). A *number* is any digit or series of digits. A *formula* is an entry that performs a calculation on two or more digits or series of digits. A *date-and-time entry* enables you to use a spreadsheet cell to display commonly used date-and-time formats.

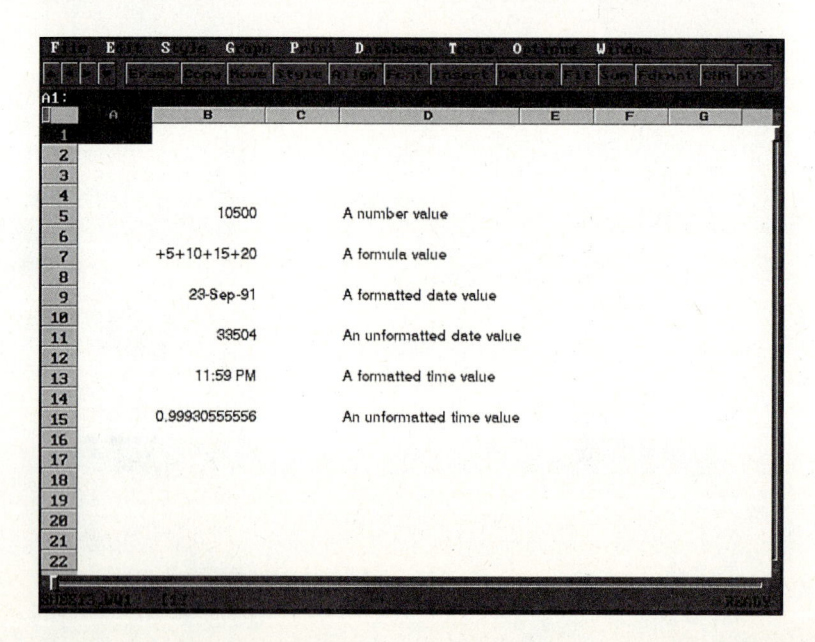

Fig. 3.4

A value as a number, a formula, or a date-and-time entry.

When you enter a value into a spreadsheet, Quattro Pro right-aligns the value in the cell. Unlike other spreadsheet programs, Quattro Pro enables you to change the alignment of numbers in a cell with the /**S**tyle **A**lignment command (see Chapter 5, "Formatting Data").

Entering Numbers

Although you can enter numbers and letters as text labels, a value entry must begin with a number (0 through 9) or one of the five value symbols listed in table 3.2. Quattro Pro also accepts a number entry if you follow the entry with a percent (%) sign, such as 10%.

Table 3.2 Value Symbols

Value Symbol	Description
+	Indicates a positive value
−	Indicates a negative value
(	Indicates a parenthetical calculation
$	Indicates a number entered with a currency symbol
.	Indicates a decimal value

> **TIP**
> Although Quattro Pro enables you to enter a currency symbol with a number, the program does not display the currency symbol in the cell until you choose the /**S**tyle **N**umeric Format **C**urrency command.

Quattro Pro assumes that all numbers are positive unless you specify otherwise. If you want to change a number's default value, precede the number with any of the value symbols shown in table 3.2.

When you enter a number longer than the width of the active cell's column, Quattro Pro does not overlap the entry into an adjacent blank cell (as the program does with labels). How Quattro Pro treats these "long" numbers depends on how you format the cell. Figure 3.5 shows how Quattro Pro treats a series of three numbers when the cell's numeric format is changed.

PART I — USING QUATTRO PRO SPREADSHEETS

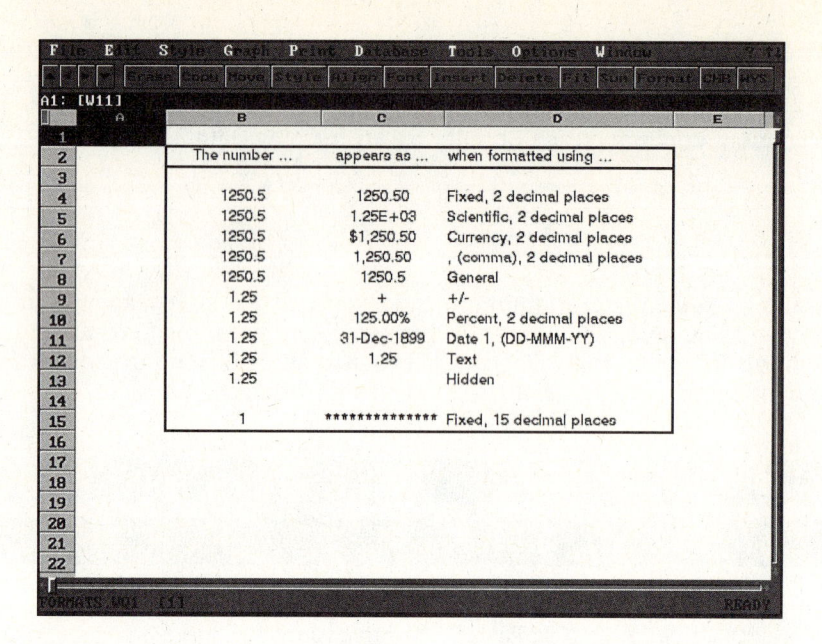

```
          A           B              C              D                    E
A1: [W11]
 1
 2              The number ...   appears as ...   when formatted using ...
 3
 4              1250.5           1250.50          Fixed, 2 decimal places
 5              1250.5           1.25E+03         Scientific, 2 decimal places
 6              1250.5           $1,250.50        Currency, 2 decimal places
 7              1250.5           1,250.50         , (comma), 2 decimal places
 8              1250.5           1250.5           General
 9              1.25             +                +/-
10              1.25             125.00%          Percent, 2 decimal places
11              1.25             31-Dec-1899      Date 1, (DD-MMM-YY)
12              1.25             1.25             Text
13              1.25                              Hidden
14
15              1                **************   Fixed, 15 decimal places
```

Fig. 3.5

The effect of the numeric format on the width of a number displayed in a spreadsheet cell.

To reveal the value pictured in cell C15, choose /**S**tyle **C**olumn Width (Ctrl-W) and press the right-arrow key until numbers appear in place of the asterisks.

Although entering numbers into a spreadsheet cell is simple, remember the following rules:

- Don't use parentheses to enter a negative number. Precede a negative number with a minus sign.

- Don't enter commas as part of a numerical entry. Format an entry so that it displays commas.

- Don't add spaces or nonnumerical characters between numbers. Mix numbers and characters only when you want to make a label entry.

- Be careful that you do not substitute a lowercase letter L for the number 1 or an uppercase letter O for the number 0.

- Use the /**S**tyle **N**umeric Format command to change the displayed and printed format of your spreadsheet numbers (see Chapter 5).

Entering Formulas

A Quattro Pro spreadsheet formula is a powerful tool. In its basic application, the spreadsheet formula adds, subtracts, multiplies, or divides two numbers on a spreadsheet, displaying the answer in a spreadsheet cell that you choose (see fig. 3.6).

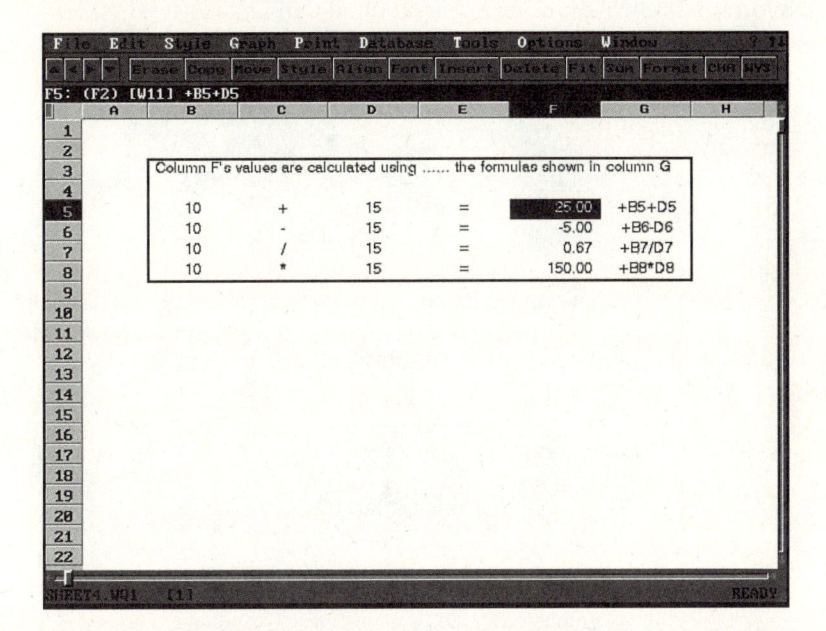

Fig. 3.6

Basic spreadsheet formulas add, subtract, divide, and multiply the data you enter.

Figure 3.6 illustrates how to use basic mathematical formulas in a spreadsheet. The formulas shown in this figure contain four parts: a value symbol, the address of a cell containing a number, a mathematical operator symbol, and another cell address.

The formulas in column F perform the mathematical operation indicated by the symbols shown in column C, using the numbers in columns B and D. To enter the formula appearing in cell F5, for example, follow these steps:

1. Place the cell selector in cell F5.
2. Press the plus sign (+) key to enter VALUE mode.
3. Type *B5*, the cell address of the first value to add.
4. Press + to choose an addition operation.
5. Type *D5*, the cell address of the second value to add.
6. Press Enter to record the formula in cell F5.

PART I — USING QUATTRO PRO SPREADSHEETS

After you store the formula in cell F5, Quattro Pro calculates the answer and displays 25.00.

You can produce this same answer by entering the following formula into cell F5:

+10+15

This formula, however, does not recalculate an answer if you later change the value appearing in cell B5 or D5.

TIP Use cell addresses instead of numbers when you build Quattro Pro formulas. When you change a cell value referenced by a formula, therefore, Quattro Pro recalculates the answer.

A Quattro Pro formula can be as complex as you need it to be. A more intricate formula may simultaneously perform mathematical operations on multiple sets of numbers and display an answer in a cell of your choosing (see fig. 3.7).

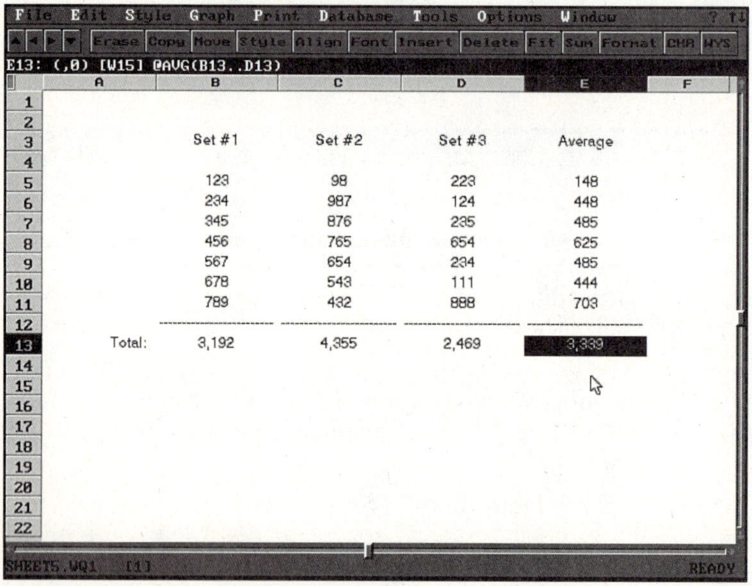

Fig. 3.7

A complex spreadsheet formula adds multiple sets of numbers, gives a total for each set, and averages a total for all sets combined.

3 — ENTERING AND EDITING DATA   93

Figure 3.7 illustrates how to use more advanced mathematical formulas in a spreadsheet. The formula shown in this figure contains three parts: the @ symbol, a function command name, and a description of a block of cells.

The formula in cell E13 averages the values appearing in cells B13, C13, and D13. To enter this formula, follow these steps:

1. Place the cell selector in cell E13.
2. Press the @ key to enter VALUE mode.
3. Type *avg* to use the built-in average function.
4. Type *(B13..D13)* to specify a block of cells to average.
5. Press Enter to record the formula in cell E13.

After you store the formula in cell E13, Quattro Pro calculates the answer and displays 3,339.

> **TIP**
>
> Quattro Pro has an extensive library of built-in @function commands (see Chapter 6, "Using Functions"). These commands reproduce many types of mathematical operations without requiring you to build long, complex formulas.

You can choose any of Quattro Pro's built-in formulas, known as *@function commands*, to perform specialized calculations for you. Chapter 6 shows you how to use @function commands in your Quattro Pro spreadsheets.

The electronic spreadsheet's capability to create custom formulas makes the program extremely valuable. Quattro Pro manipulates numbers and formulas electronically much more quickly than you can manually.

Valid formula entries can contain up to 254 characters and must begin with a number (0 through 9) or one of the following characters:

. + 1 (@ # $

When building a formula, you can use any of the five mathematical operators listed in table 3.3 to separate the parts of the formula. Version 4.0 arranges formulas in three groups: arithmetic, text, and logical.

Table 3.3 Basic Mathematical Operators

Operator	Description
+	Performs addition
−	Performs subtraction
*	Performs multiplication
/	Performs division
^	Raises a number to the power specified by the number following the operator (5^3, for example, raises 5 to the 3rd power)

Arithmetic Formulas

Arithmetic formulas perform calculations with numbers, cell addresses, and most of the @function commands using mathematical operators. An operator specifies to Quattro Pro which mathematical operation to perform.

The formulas in figures 3.6 and 3.7 are examples of arithmetic formulas. Arithmetic formulas can use the operators listed in table 3.3.

Quattro Pro makes every attempt to return a value when the program encounters an arithmetic formula. Evaluating formulas is usually a simple and straightforward task. Sometimes, however, Quattro Pro returns an unintended or nonsensical answer. When you enter the formula 10/2 into a cell, for example, Quattro Pro returns the value 5. If you want to display a date such as 9/23/62, and you enter this date as 09/23/62, Quattro Pro thinks it is looking at a two-step division formula—9 divided by 23 divided by 62. Quattro Pro returns the value 0.006. This value has no meaning when you want to display a date.

To enter a date directly into a cell so that Quattro Pro displays the value as a date, see the section, "Entering Dates or Times," later in this chapter.

Text Formulas

Text formulas enable you to perform specialized tasks that arithmetic and logical formulas cannot. Text formulas perform operations on strings of text enclosed in quotation marks, labels, and @function commands by using the ampersand (&).

3 — ENTERING AND EDITING DATA

Figure 3.8 illustrates a useful application for a text formula. In this figure, labels appear in three cells: B3, B5, and B7. Using the ampersand operator enables you to concatenate, or join, these labels in cell B9.

Briefly, a text formula is made up of three parts: the plus sign (+), the constant, and the variable.

The plus sign tells Quattro Pro to expect a formula.

In a text formula, quotation marks must surround the constant, which does not change. Figure 3.8 shows two constants in the formula. Each of these constants is one blank space surrounded by quotation marks. You use this type of constant to insert a space between labels when they are joined.

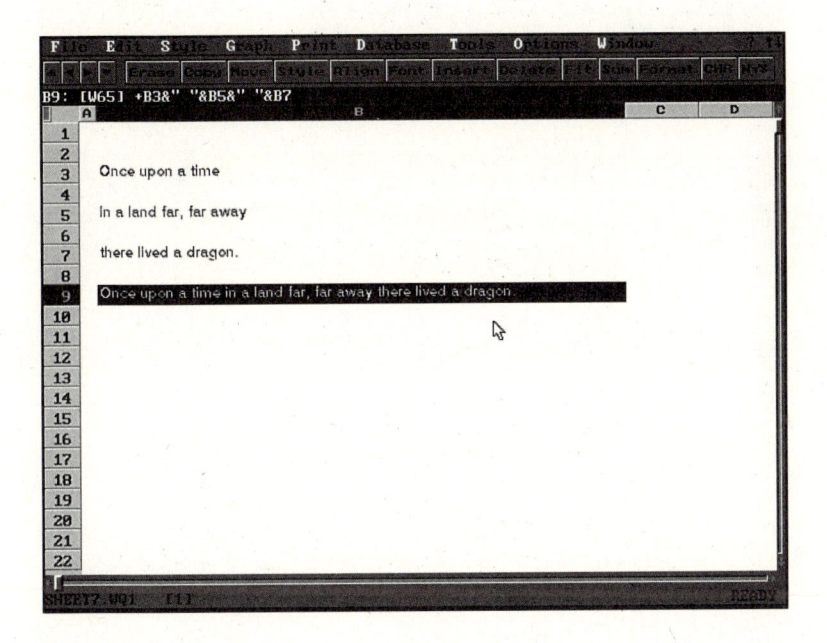

Fig. 3.8

A string formula using the ampersand to join two or more entries and quotation marks to enclose constants.

The formula also contains three variables: B3, B5, and B7. Text formula variables are much like the ones used in arithmetic formulas—as the cell values change, so do the displayed results.

Chapter 6 contains examples that illustrate how to use text formulas in spreadsheets to accomplish specific tasks.

Logical Formulas

A *logical formula* compares two or more pieces of data and gives the result in the form of true or false conditions (see fig. 3.9). If the result of the comparison is true, Quattro Pro returns the value 1; if the result is

PART I — USING QUATTRO PRO SPREADSHEETS

false, Quattro Pro returns the value 0. Logical formulas can use @function commands and the following operators: =, <, >, <=, >=, <>, #AND#, #OR#, and #NOT#.

In figure 3.9, cells D5 through D11 contain logical formulas. An expression of the logic that each formula tests appears in cells C5 through C11. Cells B2 and B3 contain the two variables referenced in each formula.

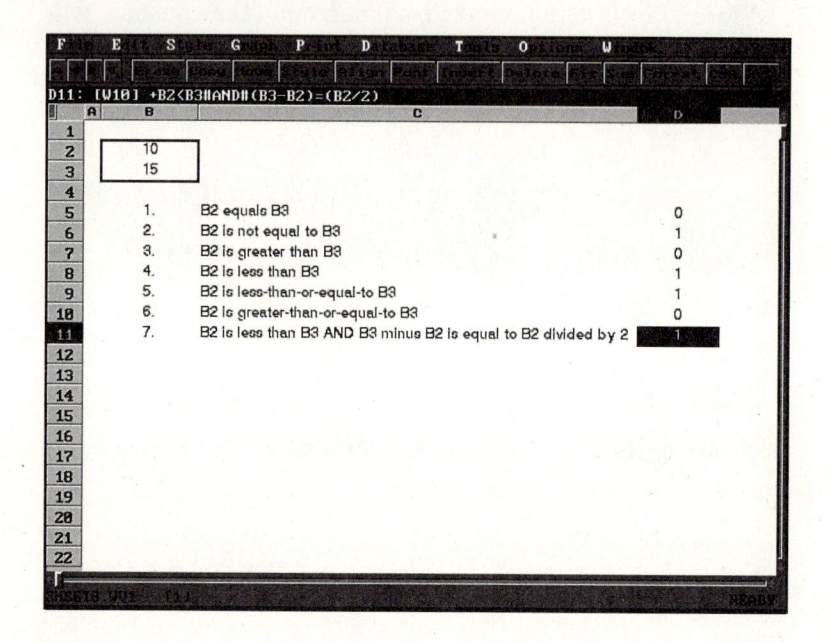

Fig. 3.9

Logical formulas evaluate true and false conditions.

The logical formula stored in cell D5, for example, is B2=B3. This formula determines whether the value in B2 is equal to the value in B3. Because this condition is false, Quattro Pro displays a 0.

The logical formula stored in cell D6 is B2<>B3. This formula determines whether the value in B2 is not equal to the value in B3. Because this condition is true, Quattro Pro displays a 1.

The formula in the highlighted cell in figure 3.9 appears on the input line at the top of the spreadsheet. This logical formula contains the #AND# operator. The #AND#, #OR#, and #NOT# operators have special significance when they appear in logical formulas.

The formula in cell D11 determines the following conditions:

- Is B2 less than B3?
- Is the difference between B2 and B3 equal to B2 divided by 2?
- Are expressions 1 and 2 both true?

Looking at the first logical expression, you can see that B2 is less than B3. The difference between B2 and B3 is equal to B2 divided by 2. Individually, both expressions are true, and Quattro Pro returns a 1.

Order of Precedence

When Quattro Pro first looks at a formula entry, the program determines which parts of the formula must be calculated first, second, third, and so on. The formulas 10+10 and 10+5+2, on the other hand, have no order of precedence because they perform only one mathematical operation: addition.

Because the formula 10+10/5^2 contains three mathematical operators, each with a different order of precedence, you may get more than one answer to this problem depending on how you perform the calculation. If you evaluate this formula from left to right, the answer is 16. If you calculate an answer using Quattro Pro's order of precedence, the answer is 10.40. Here, Quattro Pro performs the (5^2) operator first, divides that answer into 10, and then adds 10 to that result.

Table 3.4 shows the order of precedence that Quattro Pro uses when evaluating mathematical operators in your spreadsheet formulas.

Table 3.4 Quattro Pro's Order of Precedence

Operator	Operation	Order of Precedence
^	Exponent	1st
+, −	Positive and negative	2nd
*, /	Multiply and divide	3rd
+, −	Add and subtract	4th
= <>	Tests of equality	5th
<, >	Tests of relative value	5th
<=	Less-than-or-equal test	5th
>=	Greater-than-or-equal test	5th
#NOT#	Logical NOT test	6th
#AND#	Logical AND test	7th
#OR#	Logical OR test	7th
&	String union	7th

Formulas that contain more than one set of parentheses are said to contain *nested parentheses*. When you enter a formula with nested parentheses, Quattro Pro performs the operations enclosed in the innermost parentheses first. The order of precedence rule holds for multiple operations that appear within one set of parentheses.

To show how the order of precedence works, the following example uses nested parentheses to clarify the sample formula:

$$(10+(10/(5^2)))$$

(1) = 25.0

(2) = 0.4

(3) = 10.4

Quattro Pro evaluates this formula as follows: first the program raises 5 to the 2nd power, resulting in 25; then Quattro Pro divides 10 by 25, resulting in 0.4; finally, the program adds 10 to 0.4 and returns the final result of 10.4.

Nested parentheses clarify the way you want Quattro Pro to evaluate a formula and enable you to create complex formulas using all of the Quattro Pro operators.

Entering Dates and Times

Quattro Pro has several built-in @function commands that enable you to store date-and-time formats on a spreadsheet by setting the numeric format of a cell to Date or Time. Because date-and-time formats are considered formulas, you can add and subtract them just like numbers. This feature is helpful in applications that track progress over time.

Figure 3.10 shows a spreadsheet that lists 10 invoices. The formulas appearing in column E use the @NOW function in cell C2 to help you to determine the exact age of each invoice for credit collection purposes. The formula in cell E6, +$C$2-B6, for example, subtracts the invoice date from today's date to compute the "age" of the invoice.

The Quattro Pro shortcut key for entering a date or time is Ctrl-D. To use this shortcut, follow these steps:

1. Press Ctrl-D.

2. Type a date using one of the following date formats:

    DD-MMM-YY (31-Mar-92)

    DD-MMM (31-Mar, assumes the current year)

    MMM-YY (Mar-92, assumes the first day of the month)

3. Press Enter.

3 — ENTERING AND EDITING DATA

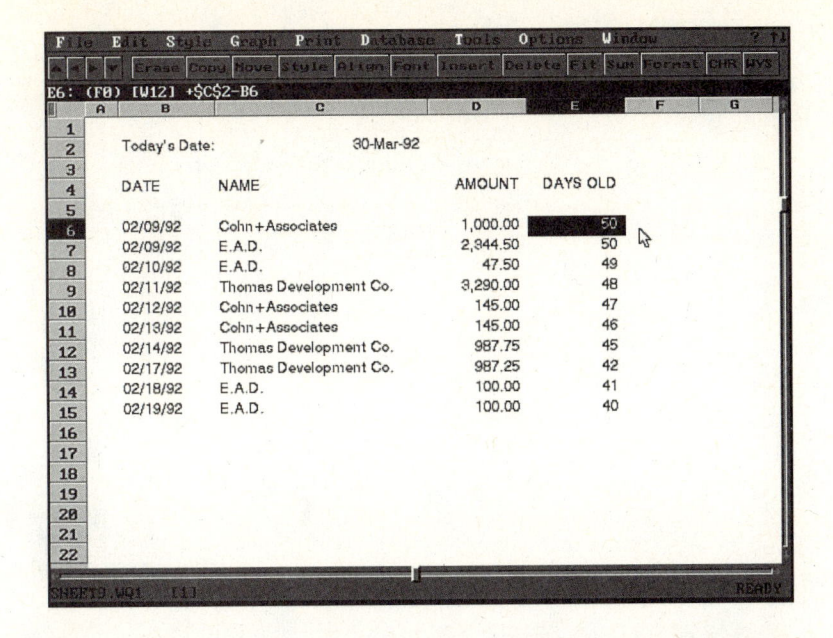

Fig. 3.10

Using date-and-time formats, the @NOW function determines the age of each invoice.

When you choose the appropriate format using the /**S**tyle Numeric Format **D**ate command, Quattro Pro enables you to use short (MM/DD) and long (DD/MM/YY) international dates. You also can enter a date using the international date formats; just supply the appropriate format in step 2.

Entering @Function Commands

The built-in Quattro Pro @function commands enable you to perform advanced mathematical operations and return values. You can use @functions by themselves or embed them inside other formulas (see fig. 3.11). Chapter 5 provides complete coverage of the @functions.

In figure 3.11, cells D3, D5, D7, and D9 contain @function commands. Each formula's syntax is listed in column E. The values that the formulas use in their calculations appear in cells B3 through B9.

The formula in cell D3, for example, sums the values appearing in B3 and B9; the formula in D5 averages the values; and the formula in D7 counts the values.

The formula in cell D9 is different than the others because this formula contains two @function commands. This formula counts the number of values in cells B3 through B9 and returns the square root of this number.

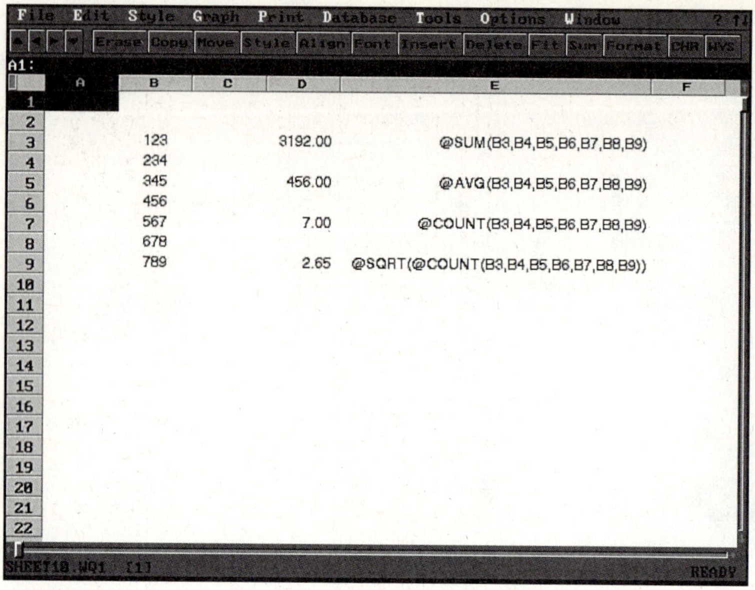

PART I — USING QUATTRO PRO SPREADSHEETS

[Screenshot of a Quattro Pro spreadsheet showing values in column B (123, 234, 345, 456, 567, 678, 789), results in column D (3192.00, 456.00, 7.00, 2.65), and the corresponding @function formulas in column E: @SUM(B3,B4,B5,B6,B7,B8,B9), @AVG(B3,B4,B5,B6,B7,B8,B9), @COUNT(B3,B4,B5,B6,B7,B8,B9), @SQRT(@COUNT(B3,B4,B5,B6,B7,B8,B9))]

Fig. 3.11

With @functions in a spreadsheet, you can perform advanced mathematical operations.

You can enter an @function onto a spreadsheet in two ways: manually enter the command or choose the command from the @function choice list.

Entering an @Function Manually

To enter an @function manually, press the @ key, type the function name, enter the appropriate arguments, and then press Enter.

An *argument* is a cell reference or a number on which Quattro performs the operation. The first three @function commands shown in figure 3.11, for example, use the same argument: the address of cells B3 through B9. The final @function command shown in figure 3.11 counts the number of values in cells B3 through B9 and passes this value along as the argument in the @SQRT command.

You can type an @function's name in upper- or lowercase text; Quattro Pro recognizes the @function either way. If you do not remember the name or purpose of a particular @function command, refer to Chapter 6.

Using the Choice List To Enter an @Function

If you press Alt-F3, Quattro Pro displays a list of @functions. Scroll through the list using the up- and down-arrow keys. When you locate the @function you want, press Enter, and Quattro Pro reproduces the @function on the input line, at the cursor position. To complete the @function, type the appropriate cell addresses and mathematical operators called for by the @function, type a right parenthesis, and then press Enter.

To enter an @function that sums cells B3, B4, and B5, for example, highlight the SUM function, press Enter, type *B3,B4,B5)* and press Enter to store the @function in the current cell.

You can use the @ button on the EDIT mode SpeedBar to display a list of @functions. To enter an @function onto the input line, press Alt-F3, highlight the function name in the list, and press Enter.

Working with Cell References and Blocks

The most common way to enter data is to type the data and press Enter. Quattro Pro, however, has several other data-entry techniques that help you build formulas using single cells and large blocks of cells. Before you learn these techniques, you need to understand the three types of Quattro Pro cell references and how to enter and modify the references for use in your spreadsheet formulas.

Quattro Pro has three types of cell reference formats: relative, absolute, and mixed. The cell reference format determines how Quattro Pro reproduces a formula when you copy the formula from one cell to another.

Defining Relative Reference Format

By default, Quattro Pro records new cell entries using the *relative reference format*. When you copy a relative reference formula, Quattro Pro changes the addresses to reflect the formula's new location on the spreadsheet. If you copy the formula in cell B7 to C7, Quattro Pro adjusts the formula in a relative fashion (see fig. 3.12). Initially, cell B7's formula references data appearing in column B. When you copy this formula to cell C7, Quattro Pro adjusts the cell addresses in the formula, creating a formula that references data in column C.

Fig. 3.12

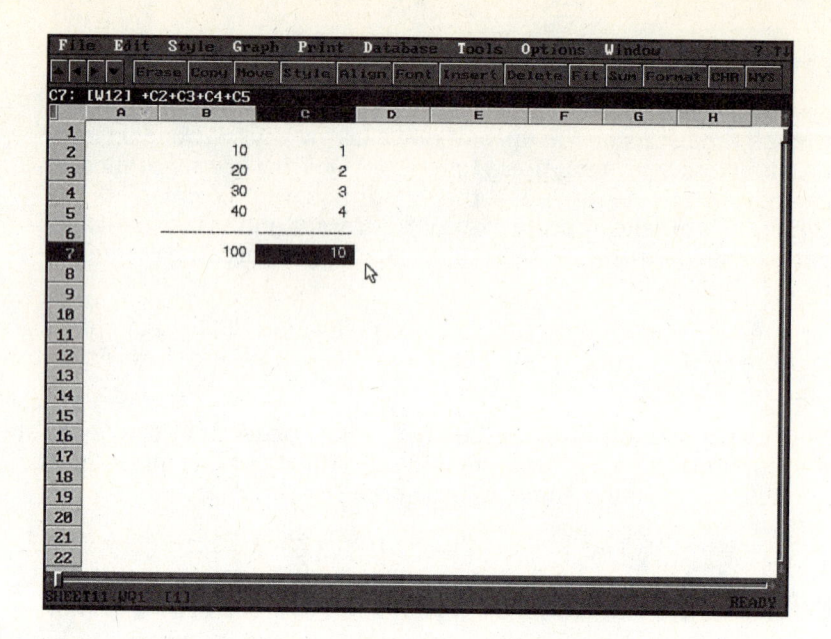

When you copy the formula used in cell B7 to cell C7, Quattro Pro adjusts the formula.

Defining Absolute Reference Format

You use the *absolute reference format* to anchor a cell address in a formula. If you *anchor* a cell address, the address does not change when you copy the formula to a different location on the spreadsheet. To format a cell address using an absolute reference format, place a dollar sign ($) in front of the cell address's row number and column letter.

You can copy the formula shown in figure 3.13 using the absolute reference format. If you copy the formula in cell C7 to cell E7, Quattro Pro does not adjust the formula (see fig. 3.13). The formula in cell E7 still sums data appearing in column C and does not sum the data in column E. You can copy this formula to cell IV8192, and the result remains 10. This operation is useful for displaying the result of a calculation in several locations on the same spreadsheet report.

Defining Mixed Reference Format

Formulas that have relative and absolute cell references are called *mixed references*. A mixed reference indicates that you are anchoring some mix of row numbers and column letters appearing in a formula (see fig. 3.14).

3 — ENTERING AND EDITING DATA

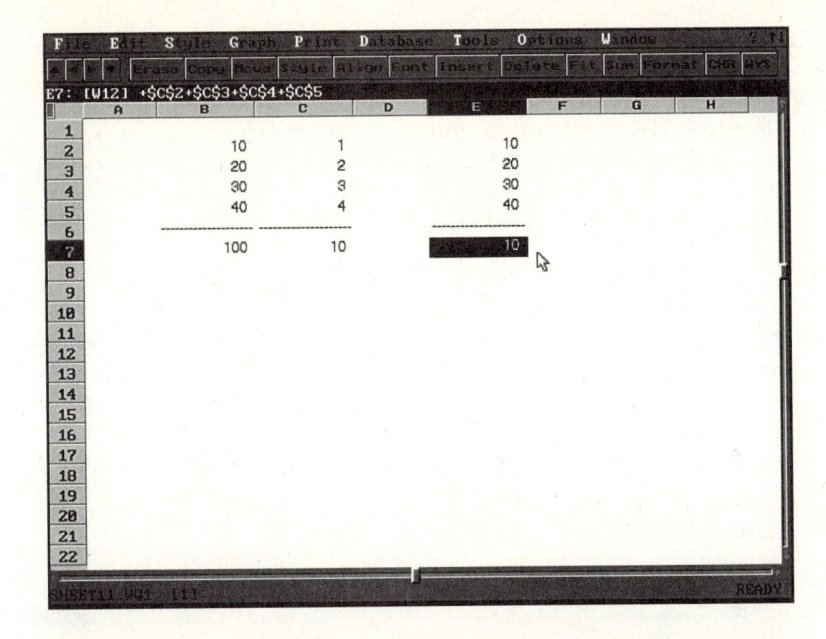

Fig. 3.13

Absolute reference formats do not change cell addresses when you copy a formula to a different cell.

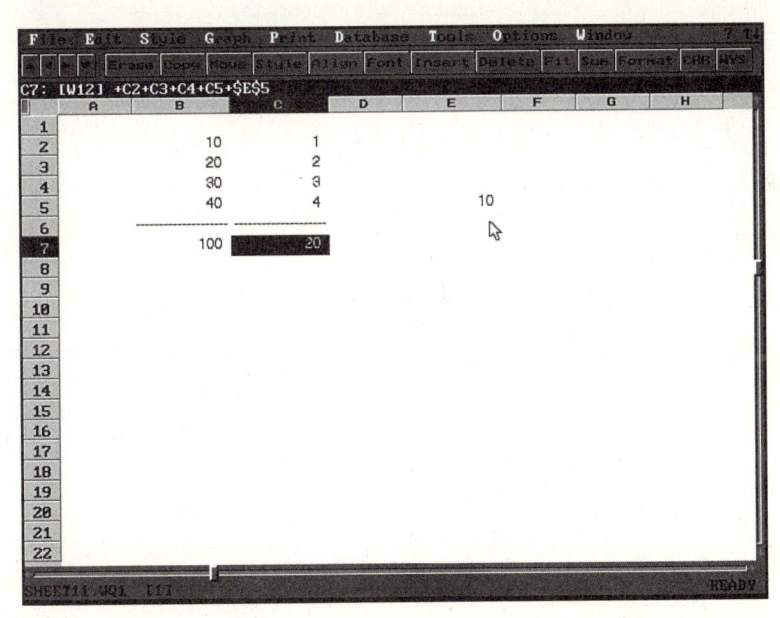

Fig. 3.14

The mixed reference format for absolute and relative references in a formula.

The formula shown in figure 3.14 is a mixed reference formula. The formula in cell C7 adds the value in cell E5 to the summed values in the range C2 through C5. The resulting answer is 20. The last cell address

($E$5) is an absolute reference. The first four cell addresses use the relative reference format. When you copy the formula in cell C7 back to cell B7, Quattro Pro adjusts the formula in a relative and absolute reference fashion. The following formula appears in B7:

+B2+B3+B4+B5+$E$5

Changing the Cell Reference Format

Quattro Pro enables you to change the reference format when you edit a formula on the input line. To change the reference format, place the cell selector on the target cell and press F2, the Edit key. Using the cursor-movement keys, place the edit cursor on or next to the cell name that you want to edit. Then, by pressing F4, the Abs key, you can view all the possible reference formats until you find the format you need.

The reference formats are as follows:

Reference Formats	Description
$A$1	Absolute column and absolute row
A$1	Relative column and absolute row
$A1	Absolute column and relative row
A1	Relative column and relative row

You can use the Abs button on the EDIT mode SpeedBar to change a cell's reference from relative to absolute, or vice versa. To change a cell's reference using the Abs button, press F2 to enter EDIT mode, select the cell coordinates, and then click the Abs button. Clicking the Abs button more than once toggles between absolute, relative, and mixed cell references.

Working with Cell References

Chapter 2 mentions using the Quattro Pro spreadsheet as a what-if analysis tool. This type of analysis involves changing the value in one cell and examining its effect on one or more other cells.

The formula in cell C15 in figure 3.15 relies on the data in cells C11 through C13 that shows the cost of goods sold. If you change the value of one or more of the cost accounts, the total cost of goods sold and gross margin values change.

3 — ENTERING AND EDITING DATA   105

```
F    E   S    G    P    D    T    O    W
C15: (,0) [W12] +C11+C12+C13
       A         B                C            D           E           F          G
  1
  2    BJP Manufacturing
  3                             Jan         Feb         Mar         1st Q
  4    REVENUES
  5      Wholesale            2,750       3,275       4,150       10,175
  6      Retail                1,050       1,000         775        2,825
  7                           -------     -------     -------     --------
  8    Total Revenues:        3,800       4,275       4,925       13,000
  9
 10    COST OF GOODS SOLD
 11      Materials              845       1,040       1,100        2,985
 12      Labor                  225         275         325          825
 13      Shipping               100         150         200          450
 14                           -------     -------     -------     --------
 15    Total COG Sold:        1,170       1,465       1,625        4,260
 16                           -------     -------     -------     --------
 17    GROSS MARGIN:          2,630       2,810       3,300        8,740
 18                           =======     =======     =======     ========
 19                            69.2%       65.7%       67.0%        67.2%
 20
 21
 22
```

Fig. 3.15

Changes made to the values in C11..C13 affect C15.

What-if analysis depends on cell referencing. To reference a cell in a formula, include the cell address (instead of a number) in the formula. January's gross margin, for example, equals the difference between total revenues (C8) and total cost of goods sold (the sum of the values in the range C11 through C13). If you replace the formula in cell C17 with the value 2,630, changing the value of any revenue or cost accounts does not affect gross margin because cell C17 no longer relies on these values (see figure 3.16).

What-if analysis requires spreadsheet variables that you can change to test different sets of assumptions.

You can include cell references in your formulas by using one of two techniques. The basic method used to add the contents of cells C11, C12, and C13 appears in figure 3.15. Follow these steps to create this formula in cell C15:

1. Make cell C15 the active cell by pressing the cursor-movement keys until the cell selector is in C15, or point your mouse arrow at C15 and click.

2. Enter the plus symbol (+) to tell Quattro Pro that you are entering a formula value.

3. Type *C11+C12+C13*.

4. Press Enter to record the formula.

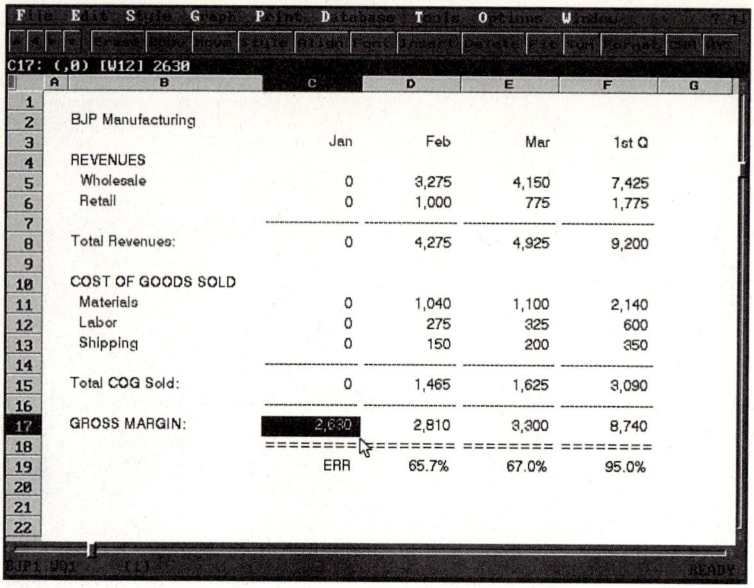

PART I — USING QUATTRO PRO SPREADSHEETS

Fig. 3.16

Changes made to the values in C5..C6 and C11..C13 do not affect C17.

	A	B	C	D	E	F
1						
2		BJP Manufacturing				
3			Jan	Feb	Mar	1st Q
4		REVENUES				
5		Wholesale	0	3,275	4,150	7,425
6		Retail	0	1,000	775	1,775
7						
8		Total Revenues:	0	4,275	4,925	9,200
9						
10		COST OF GOODS SOLD				
11		Materials	0	1,040	1,100	2,140
12		Labor	0	275	325	600
13		Shipping	0	150	200	350
14						
15		Total COG Sold:	0	1,465	1,625	3,090
16						
17		GROSS MARGIN:	2,630	2,810	3,300	8,740
18			========	========	========	========
19			ERR	65.7%	67.0%	95.0%

You can accomplish this same result by using a technique called *cell-selector pointing*. This method enables you to build a formula by pointing to the cell addresses on the spreadsheet that you want in the formula. To point to cell addresses to create a formula, follow these steps:

1. Make cell C15 the active cell by pressing the cursor-movement keys until the cell selector is in C15, or point your mouse arrow at C15 and click.

2. Enter the plus symbol (+) to tell Quattro Pro that you are entering a formula value.

3. Using the cursor-movement keys, make C11 the active cell. The cell address, C11, appears next to the plus sign on the input line.

4. Enter the plus sign (+) again to tell Quattro Pro that you are continuing to build the formula.

5. Repeat steps 3 and 4, using cell addresses C12 and C13 (instead of C11) to include them in the formula.

6. Press Enter to record the formula.

You also can click the cell references with a mouse, as in the following steps:

1. Make cell C15 the active cell by pointing your mouse arrow at C15 and clicking.

2. Enter the plus sign (+) to tell Quattro Pro that you are entering a formula value.
3. Click cell C11.
4. Enter the plus symbol (+) again to tell Quattro Pro that you are continuing to build the formula.
5. Repeat steps 3 and 4, using cell addresses C12 and C13 (instead of C11) to include them in the formula.
6. Press Enter to record the formula.

Working with Cell Blocks

If you want to sum the contents of the three cells in the cell block range C5 through E5, you can add each cell address by using the formula C5+D5+E5. Using a cell block range, however, is more efficient. The formula, @SUM(C5..E5), uses an @function to sum the values that appear in the cell block range C5..E5.

Pointing to the Block with the Keyboard

You can include a cell block in a formula in two ways. First, you can type the address of the first cell in the block, type two periods, and type the last cell address in the block. This basic data entry method is one with which you already are familiar.

The second method uses the cell selector and the cursor-movement keys to build formulas in POINT mode. In POINT mode, you use the cursor-movement keys to "point out" the cells that you want to reference in a formula. When you point to a cell, Quattro Pro writes the cell address on the input line next to the mathematical operator. To build a formula that adds the values in A1 and A2, for example, you press the plus sign (+), press a cursor-movement key to move the cell selector to cell A1, press the plus sign again, press the down-arrow key to move the cell selector to cell A2, then press Enter to store the formula.

> **TIP**
> The only time you can enter POINT mode while entering data is when you move the cell selector after a mathematical operator or an open parenthesis.

PART I — USING QUATTRO PRO SPREADSHEETS

You can use this pointing method to create the formulas that reside in cells F5, F6, F11, F12, and F13. The formula in cell F5, for example, sums the values appearing in block C5..E5.

To build the formula in cell F5, follow these steps:

1. Make cell F5 the active cell using the cursor-movement keys.
2. Type *@SUM(*.
3. Make cell C5 the active cell. Quattro Pro displays this cell address to the right of the parenthesis in the @SUM command from step 2.
4. Press the period (.) key or the Select key (Shift-F7) to anchor the first cell address and to enter POINT mode. (Check the mode indicator to be sure that you are in POINT mode.)
5. Press the right-arrow key twice to include cells D5 and E5 in the cell block range.
6. Press the closing parenthesis ( )) key.
7. Press Enter to record the formula.

Pointing to the Block with a Mouse

If you have a mouse, using the pointing technique is easier. To use a mouse to create the formula that sums the values in the range C5..E5, follow these steps:

1. Click cell F5.
2. Type *@SUM(*.
3. Click cell C5.
4. While holding down the left mouse button, drag the mouse pointer to cell E5 and release the button. Quattro Pro highlights each cell that you drag through in the cell block range.
5. Press the closing parenthesis ( )) key.
6. Press Enter to record the formula.

You also can use the following alternative mouse technique to highlight any cell block range on a spreadsheet:

1. Click the top left cell in the target cell block range.
2. Point the mouse pointer at the bottom right cell in the target cell block range.
3. Hold down the right mouse button and click the left button.

Editing Data

Editing cell data is an important function of using a spreadsheet program. Quattro Pro enables you to edit data as you type on the input line or after you press Enter to place data into a spreadsheet cell. Entering new cell data, changing characters or numbers in the active cell, and deleting the contents of a cell are all examples of editing data on the spreadsheet.

To edit the contents of a spreadsheet cell, press F2 to enter EDIT mode. If you have a mouse, click the cell you want to edit and then click anywhere on the input line. When you click the input line, Quattro Pro enters EDIT mode and displays the cell data on the input line in the data's unformatted form.

You also can toggle between EDIT, VALUE, POINT, DATE, and LABEL modes by pressing F2 (Edit) several times in succession. When you are in EDIT mode, you can use the editing keys listed in table 3.5 to edit the active spreadsheet cell.

Remember, when you are in EDIT mode, the program automatically displays the EDIT mode SpeedBar. The buttons on this SpeedBar give you immediate access to advanced editing features and enable you to move around the spreadsheet by block reference. (See Chapter 2, "Getting Started," for complete coverage of SpeedBars.)

When you finish editing the data in a cell, press Enter or click the Enter box on the input line to record the changes.

Table 3.5 Special Keys Available in EDIT Mode

Key	Description
Backspace	Deletes from right to left, one character at a time
Ctrl-Backspace	Erases everything on the input line
Ctrl-\	Deletes everything to the right of the cursor on the input line
Del	Deletes the character that the cursor is on
End	Relocates the cursor to the end of the input line
Enter	Stores data on the input line in the active spreadsheet cell; press Enter to exit EDIT mode and enter READY mode
Esc	Erases everything on the input line; press Esc to cancel EDIT mode and return to READY mode

continues

PART I — USING QUATTRO PRO SPREADSHEETS

Table 3.5 Continued

Key	Description
F2 (Edit)	Enters EDIT mode and displays the contents of the active cell on the input line
Home	Relocates the cursor to the first character on the input line
Ins	Toggles between INSERT (default) and OVERWRITE (OVR) modes
PgDn	Enters data into the active cell, exits EDIT mode, enters READY mode, and moves the cell selector down one screen
PgUp	Enters data into the active cell, exits EDIT mode, enters READY mode, and moves the cell selector up one screen
Shift-Tab or Ctrl-←	Moves the cursor five characters to the left on the input line
Tab or Ctrl-→	Moves the cursor five characters to the right on the input line
↑	Enters data into the active cell, exits EDIT mode, enters READY mode, and moves the cell selector up one cell
↓	Enters data into the active cell, exits EDIT mode, enters READY mode, and moves the cell selector down one cell
→	Enters data into the active cell, exits EDIT mode, enters READY mode, and moves the cell selector right one cell
←	Enters data into the active cell, exits EDIT mode, enters READY mode, and moves the cell selector left one cell

T I P When in LABEL or VALUE mode, press one of the four arrow keys, the PgUp key, or the PgDn key to enter data into the active cell, move to another cell, and enter READY mode. To enter POINT mode (to continue building a formula on the input line, for example), place a mathematical operator after the last character on the input line before you press one of these six keys.

Using the Alt-F5 Undo Key

Everyone has had accidents when working with a spreadsheet—accidentally erasing data, deleting the wrong row or column, or executing a command on the wrong spreadsheet cell. Quattro Pro has a built-in protection mechanism that enables you to reverse the most recent changes made to a cell or the most recent menu-command execution. To undo an operation, press Alt-F5, the Quattro Pro Undo key.

By default, the Undo key is deactivated. Activate the Undo key using the /Options Other Undo Enable command. To make this setting a default for future work sessions, choose /Options Update.

Recalculating Your Spreadsheet Formulas

Quattro Pro recalculates your spreadsheet formulas each time you edit or erase data referenced in a formula. This activity is called *background recalculation* because the operation takes place behind the scenes while you continue to work on your spreadsheet. For small- to medium-sized spreadsheets, background recalculation only takes a second or two. For large spreadsheet applications, background recalculation can take three or more seconds. When you see BKGD on the status line at the bottom of the spreadsheet, Quattro Pro is in the background recalculation mode.

You can control how Quattro Pro calculates and recalculates your spreadsheet formulas by choosing /Options Recalculation Mode. The submenu options for this command are Automatic, Manual, and Background. By default, this command is set to Background. If you want Quattro Pro to pause and recalculate your spreadsheet formulas, choose Automatic.

Choose Manual recalculation when you build large spreadsheet applications with formulas that require a great deal of time to recalculate. In this mode, Quattro Pro does nothing until you press F9, the calculation key. When you use cell referencing in a formula, such as @SUM(B1..B5) and then change a value appearing in the range B1..B5, Quattro Pro does not recalculate the formula until you press F9. Quattro Pro displays CALC on the status line when your spreadsheet formulas require recalculation.

PART I — USING QUATTRO PRO SPREADSHEETS

> **T I P** Regardless of the way you set the spreadsheet recalculation mode, Quattro Pro always calculates an answer to every new formula that you enter or edit on the spreadsheet.

Viewing the Spreadsheet

After you enter and edit data, you view the data. The **W**indow and **O**ptions menus contain several commands that enable you to control how Quattro Pro displays your spreadsheets on-screen. Using these commands, you can split a spreadsheet into two vertical panes, two horizontal panes, simultaneously display all open spreadsheets, or change the Quattro Pro display mode.

This section teaches you the basic ways to create the on-screen look that you need to enter, edit, and view your spreadsheet data successfully. The **W**indow and **O**ptions menus receive full coverage in Chapters 8 and 16.

Viewing the Basic Spreadsheet Window

Quattro Pro's screen display default setting is one full-screen window. One window displays a small portion of the spreadsheet with 9 columns and 22 rows (in WYSIWYG display mode). You often need more columns and rows than appear in one window. Except for the simplest applications, you want to use the rest of the spreadsheet that exists to the right and below of what you can see in one full-screen window.

Splitting the Screen Horizontally or Vertically

As your spreadsheets grow, you may need to look simultaneously at two cells in different parts of the spreadsheet. Quattro Pro enables you to split your spreadsheet into two vertical or horizontal panes. To create these panes, place the cell selector in a location you want to split and choose /**W**indow **O**ptions **H**orizontal (or **V**ertical).

If your application has more rows than columns, split the spreadsheet horizontally (see fig. 3.17). If your application has more columns than rows, split the spreadsheet vertically (see fig. 3.18).

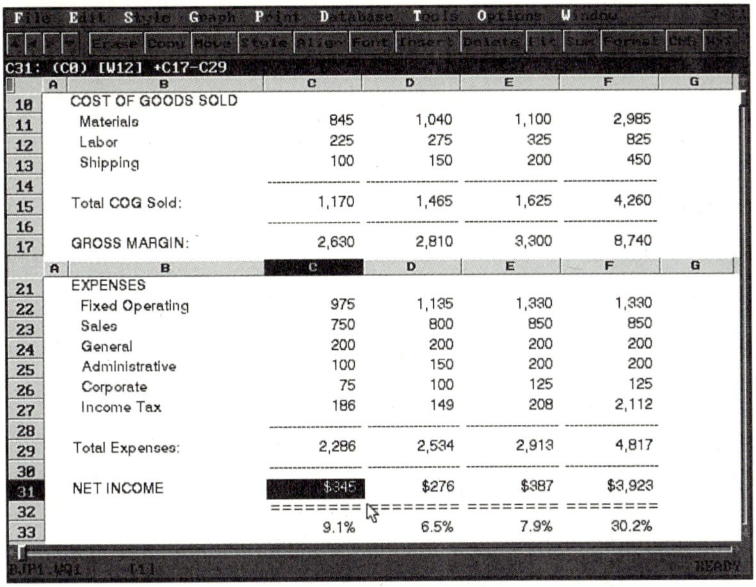

3 — ENTERING AND EDITING DATA

Fig. 3.17

A window split into two horizontal panes.

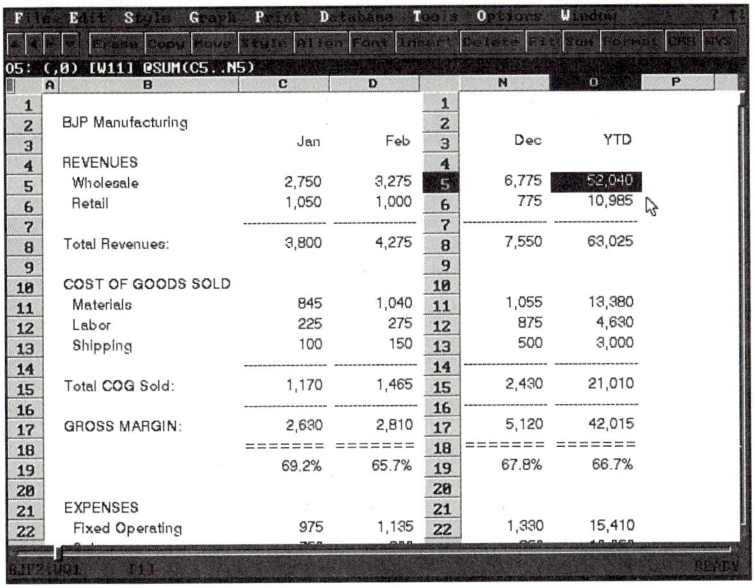

Fig. 3.18

A window split into two vertical panes.

You can arrange your window panes independently because the cursor movement on one pane does not affect the other pane. If you place your cell selector in the top pane shown in figure 3.17 and press PgDn,

PART I — USING QUATTRO PRO SPREADSHEETS

only the top pane scrolls down one screen. If you want to synchronize the scroll movement on both window panes, choose /**W**indow **O**ptions **S**ync. Press F6, the Window key, to move between window panes.

Displaying Tiled Spreadsheets

As you learn in Chapter 8, "Managing Files and Windows," Quattro Pro enables you to *tile* (display side-by-side) all open spreadsheets into one screen display when you select /**W**indow **T**ile (see fig. 3.19). This feature is useful if you have a large workspace application and you need to locate a particular spreadsheet in that workspace.

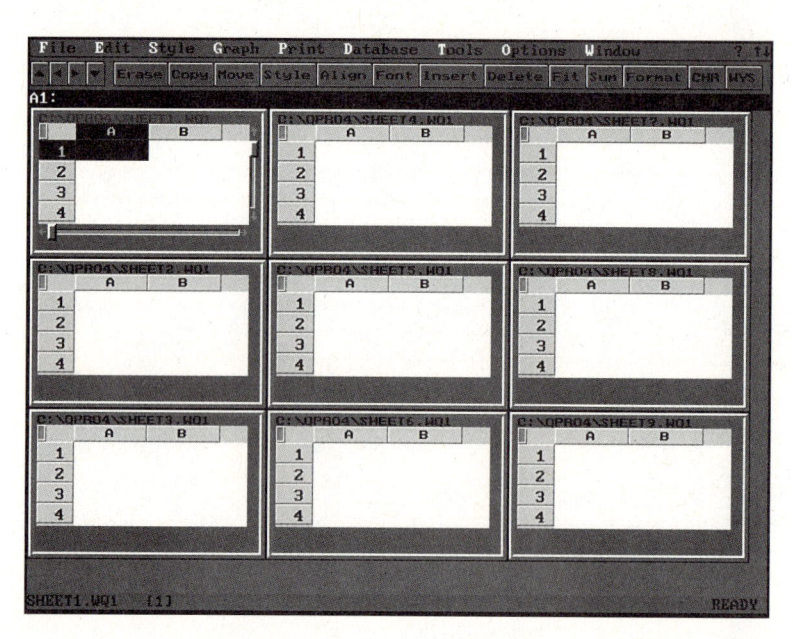

Fig. 3.19

Tiled spreadsheets.

Selecting the Screen Display Mode

Another way to change the basic look of your Quattro Pro screen display is to select a new display mode using the /**O**ptions **D**isplay Mode command (see fig. 3.20).

If you select the EGA: 80x43 display mode, for example, Quattro Pro can display the entire income statement that appears on the spreadsheets in figures 3.17 and 3.18.

3 — ENTERING AND EDITING DATA

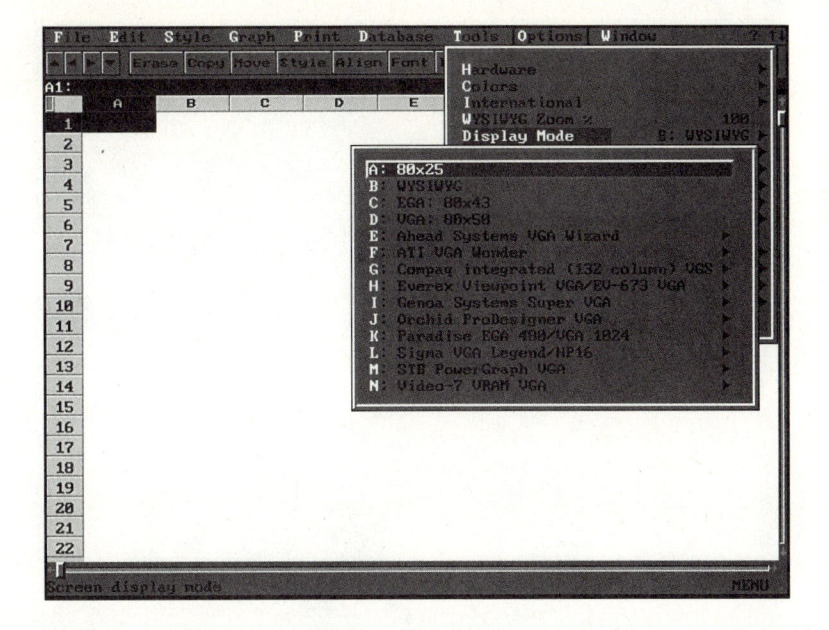

Fig. 3.20

Selecting a new screen display using the /**O**ptions **D**isplay Mode command.

Quattro Pro supports an extensive list of display mode settings that take full advantage of EGA and VGA graphics display cards. If your graphics card supports extended text mode, you can display up to 132 spreadsheet columns on-screen at the same time.

When you select display mode options E through N, Quattro Pro displays a submenu that lists the extended text modes supported by each graphics card. The number of available display options varies for each graphics display system. If you select option **H**: Everex Viewpoint VGA/EV-673 VGA, for example, Quattro Pro displays a submenu listing six extended text mode display settings (see fig. 3.21).

Questions & Answers

This chapter covers the basic procedures used to enter, edit, and view data on a Quattro Pro spreadsheet. If you have questions about any of the topics covered in this chapter and cannot find the answer by using Quattro's help windows, scan this section.

PART I — USING QUATTRO PRO SPREADSHEETS

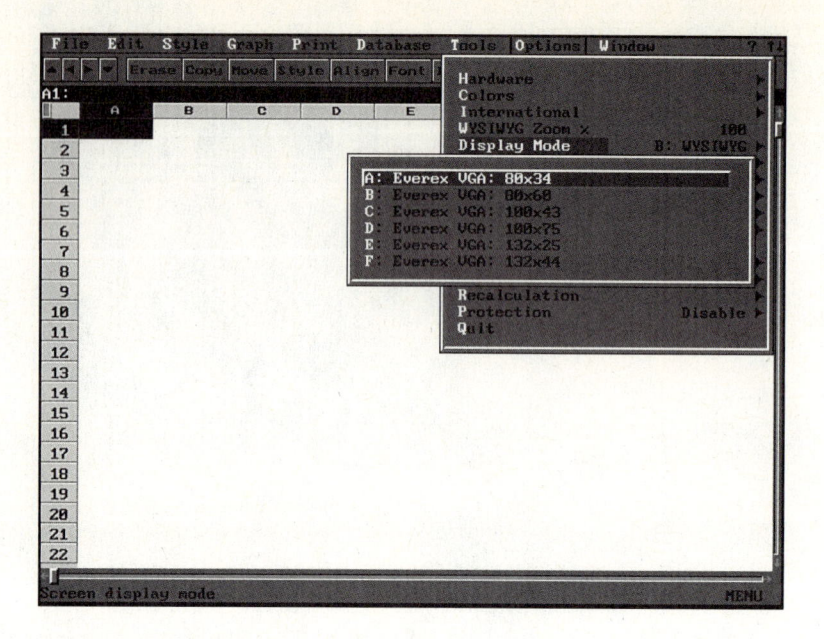

Fig. 3.21

A list of extended text mode display settings for the Everex Viewpoint graphics card.

Entering Labels

Q: Why doesn't Quattro Pro accept a label I am trying to enter?

A: You must adhere to the data-entry rules outlined in the section titled "Entering Data" at the beginning of this chapter. You must precede labels with a label prefix (', ", ^, or \), enter numbers without commas, press Ctrl-D before typing dates and times, precede formulas with a plus (+) or minus (–) sign, and enter an @function by first typing the @ symbol.

Q: Why did Quattro Pro display the ^ prefix with my label when I tried to center a label that I was entering?

A: When Quattro Pro sees a label character, the program adds the default label prefix (') to the front of the first character. To center a label, type the ^ prefix before you type the first character in the label.

Q: Why did Quattro Pro display a single hyphen (-) in a cell in which I entered a repeating hyphen label using the \ label prefix (such as \-)?

A: If you try to enter a repeating label into a cell that you previously formatted with the /**S**tyle **A**lignment (**C**enter, **R**ight, or **L**eft) command, Quattro Pro ignores the repeating label prefix. To

Entering Values

Q: Why doesn't Quattro Pro accept an @function that I am trying to enter?

A: When you enter an @function, do not place a space between the @ symbol and the command name, always follow the command name by parentheses, and make sure to use the correct syntax and all the appropriate arguments (see Chapter 6). Some @function commands require more information than the cell address or cell block range.

Q: Why is Quattro Pro displaying the formula I entered as a label?

A: You initially typed a character or accidentally typed a label prefix before entering the formula. Press F2 to enter EDIT mode, press Home to move to the beginning of the entry, delete the label prefix, and then press Enter to record the formula.

Q: Why didn't Quattro Pro display a new answer when I changed the value of a spreadsheet cell referenced by a formula?

A: Press F9 to recalculate the active spreadsheet. Choose the /Options Recalculation Mode command and set it to Background or Automatic. In these two modes, Quattro Pro recalculates spreadsheet formulas when you change cell data referenced by the formulas.

Q: Why is Quattro Pro displaying asterisks when I enter values into spreadsheet cells?

A: The values are longer than the width of the cell. To correct this problem, expand the width of the column using the /Style Column Width command.

Working with Cell References and Blocks

Q: Why did Quattro Pro enter a period on the input line when I pressed the period key to extend a cell block while in POINT mode?

A: The only time you can enter POINT mode while entering data is when you place the cell selector after an operator or an open parenthesis.

Editing Data

Q: Why did nothing appear on the input line when I pressed F2 to edit a cell?

A: You may be trying to edit overlapping data that actually is in a different cell. Press the left-arrow key a few times until you find the cell containing the label or press End-left arrow. The cell selector moves to the first cell to the left that contains data.

Viewing Data

Q: Why can't I split my screen display into two equal panes?

A: Quattro Pro splits a screen at the location of the cell selector. If you place the cell selector anywhere in column A and try to split the window vertically, Quattro Pro beeps. If you place the cell selector anywhere in row 1 and try to split the window horizontally, Quattro Pro beeps. Place the cell selector in the middle of the screen to split the screen into two equally sized horizontal or vertical panes.

Summary

This chapter introduces you to the basics of entering, editing, and viewing spreadsheet data. Having completed this chapter, you should understand the following Quattro Pro concepts:

- Entering labels and values into a spreadsheet
- Using and changing cell reference formats in formulas
- Using cell blocks and POINT mode to build formulas
- Editing data on the spreadsheet
- Viewing data on the spreadsheet

3 — ENTERING AND EDITING DATA

In Chapter 4, you learn how to build a fully functional spreadsheet application. Chapter 4 provides full coverage of the **File** and **Edit** menu commands. Although these commands represent only a small percentage of all Quattro Pro commands, you use these commands each time you create a spreadsheet. Chapter 4 encourages you to follow along in a spreadsheet-building exercise that demonstrates the best methods for using all the commands on the **File** and **Edit** menus.

CHAPTER 4

Manipulating Data

This chapter focuses on the commands found on Quattro Pro's Edit menu. Using the Edit menu commands and your knowledge of entering and editing data, you can manipulate the form and content of your spreadsheet applications.

In a typical spreadsheet-building work session, you load Quattro Pro, and a blank spreadsheet appears. Next, you enter and edit data on the spreadsheet. When you sit back and review the spreadsheet, however, you realize the data makes much more sense in another arrangement. You may need to switch row and column labels or delete one column of data from the spreadsheet.

Each time you must change data in your spreadsheet, you can do one of two things: erase the spreadsheet and start over or use the Edit menu commands to mold the existing spreadsheet into an organized, logical application.

The Edit menu commands enable you to change the organization, structure, and content of your spreadsheets. You can use these commands to do the following operations:

- Copy and move cell data and/or cell formatting
- Undo spreadsheet operations when you make a mistake

PART I — USING QUATTRO PRO SPREADSHEETS

- Perform copy, move, and erase operations on blocks of cell data
- Insert and delete columns and rows
- Assign unique names to cells and blocks
- Switch or transpose column and row data
- Search for and replace data on the spreadsheet

This chapter also introduces the Edit menu commands and single-operation topics, such as how to insert a row. Examples of spreadsheet applications built for a fictional company, Speedy Airlines, reinforce your understanding of the purpose and function of each Edit menu command.

Reviewing the Edit Menu

Quattro Pro's Edit menu commands make copying, moving, erasing, and manipulating cell data extremely easy. You use the 12 Edit menu commands to organize and manipulate data on a spreadsheet (see fig. 4.1).

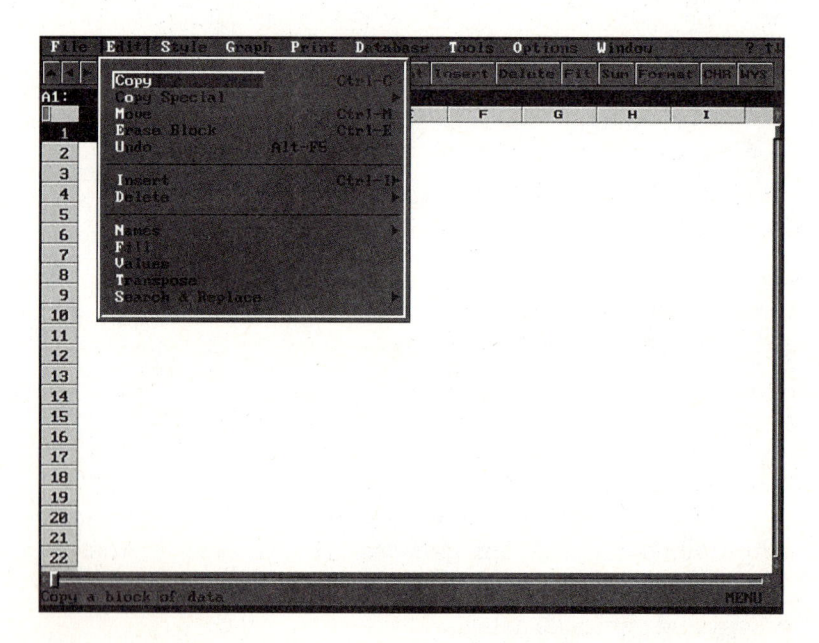

Fig. 4.1

Use the **E**dit menu commands to manipulate data.

Table 4.1 explains the purpose of the **E**dit menu commands. The command's name matches the command's function. You can use **C**opy, for example, to copy a value or a label to different parts of the spreadsheet.

> **TIP**
>
> Four commands on this menu have Ctrl-key shortcuts: **C**opy, **M**ove, **E**rase Block, and **I**nsert. The Ctrl-keys correspond to the boldfaced letters in each command name. When possible, Quattro Pro matches the Ctrl-key and the boldfaced letter key so that you don't have to remember two keys for one command.

Table 4.1 Edit Menu Commands

Command	Description
Copy	Copies the contents of one or more cells into another cell or a block of cells
Copy Special	Copies the contents or formatting from one cell or cell block into another
Move	Moves the contents of one or more cells to another location on the spreadsheet
Erase Block	Erases the contents of a block of cells
Undo	Reverses the most recent operation you performed using a Quattro Pro menu command
Insert	Inserts a blank row or column, or row or column block, on the spreadsheet
Delete	Deletes a row or column, or row or column block, from the active spreadsheet
Names	Assigns a unique name to a cell or block of cells; used in place of cell references in all Quattro Pro operations.
Fill	Enters a sequence of numbers into a user-specified block of cells on the spreadsheet
Values	Replaces all cell formulas on the active spreadsheet with their calculated values
Transpose	Switches the row and column organization of data appearing in a user-specified block of cells
Search & Replace	Searches for a user-specified label or value on the spreadsheet and replaces it with another user-specified label or value

The commands on the Edit menu perform operations on single cells and on blocks of cells. This section focuses on single-cell operations.

You can use the commands on the Edit menu in two ways: choose the command and then type the cell address, or highlight the cell and then choose the command.

Most Edit menu commands require two pieces of data to work: a source cell address and a destination cell address. By default, Quattro Pro uses the active cell as the source cell address. To use a different source cell, type the new address after you choose the command or click the cell with the mouse. When Quattro Pro prompts you, type the destination cell address and press Enter to complete the operation.

You can execute a menu command more quickly if you preselect the source cell and then choose the command. *Preselecting* a cell means making that cell active, or highlighting it, before executing a menu command. When you preselect a cell before choosing a command, Quattro Pro uses this cell address as the source cell address.

To preselect a block of cells, click the upper left cell in the block, drag the mouse pointer to the lower right cell and release the button.

When you preselect a cell or block, the item remains selected after the command is executed. You can perform several formatting operations on the same cell or block without having to reselect each time.

Copying, Moving, and Erasing Cell Data

Copy, Move, and Erase Block are good examples of intuitive Edit menu commands. These three commands are among the most heavily used Quattro Pro menu commands because they meet basic and essential spreadsheet-building needs.

The Copy command leaves the data in the source cell intact while copying the data to a new cell. This operation is useful for reproducing values and labels in several cells on the same spreadsheet.

The Move command deletes the data from the source cell and shifts the data to a new location. This operation enables you to shift data quickly around the spreadsheet until you create the design you seek.

The Erase Block command deletes the contents of one or more cells on the spreadsheet. This command is useful particularly when you must erase some—but not all—of the data from a spreadsheet.

To see how these commands work, start by reviewing the items shown in figure 4.2. This figure shows the four starting locations of a text label called HERE: cells C6, C8, C10, and C12.

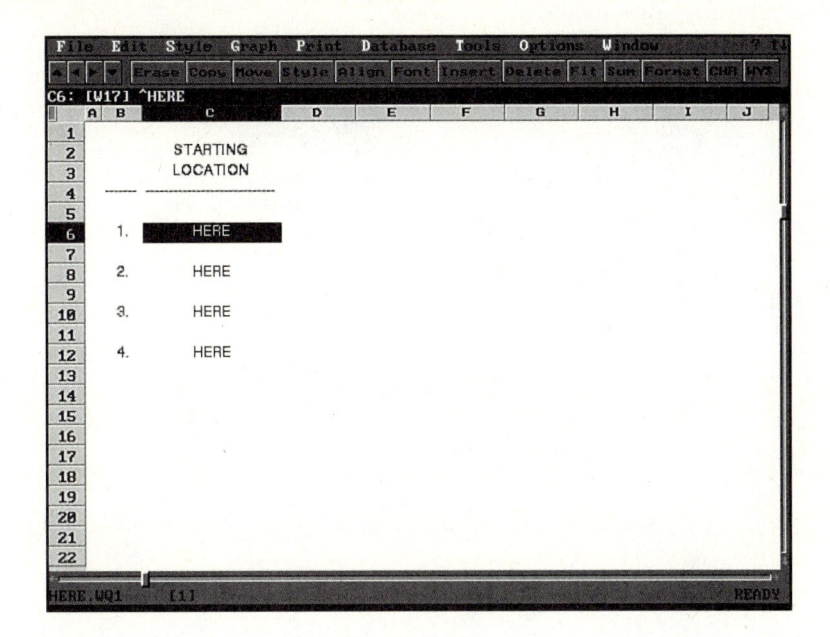

Fig. 4.2

The four starting locations of the label HERE.

You can copy or move the text label in four ways: copy one cell to another cell, copy one cell into a block of cells, move one cell to another cell, or move one cell into a block of cells. Each method gives you a different result (see fig. 4.3).

In example 1, when you copy the contents of cell C6, Quattro Pro duplicates the text label HERE in cell E6. In example 2, when you move the contents of cell C6, Quattro Pro relocates the text label HERE to cell E6.

Examples 3 and 4 use the **C**opy and **M**ove commands to perform more complex operations. In example 3, Quattro Pro copies the text label in cell C10 into all three cells in cell block E10..G10. In example 4, Quattro Pro moves the text label from cell C12 into the first address in cell block E12..G12. Quattro Pro relocates HERE only to the first address in the cell block because **M**ove is a relocating command and not a duplicating command.

Copying the Contents of a Cell

The **C**opy command saves you time when you build a spreadsheet. If you plan to use a value or a label many times on the same spreadsheet,

PART I — USING QUATTRO PRO SPREADSHEETS

enter the data once and copy it to other parts of the spreadsheet. You also can copy values and labels to other spreadsheets in Quattro Pro's memory. Chapter 8, "Managing Files and Windows," explains how to use multiple spreadsheets.

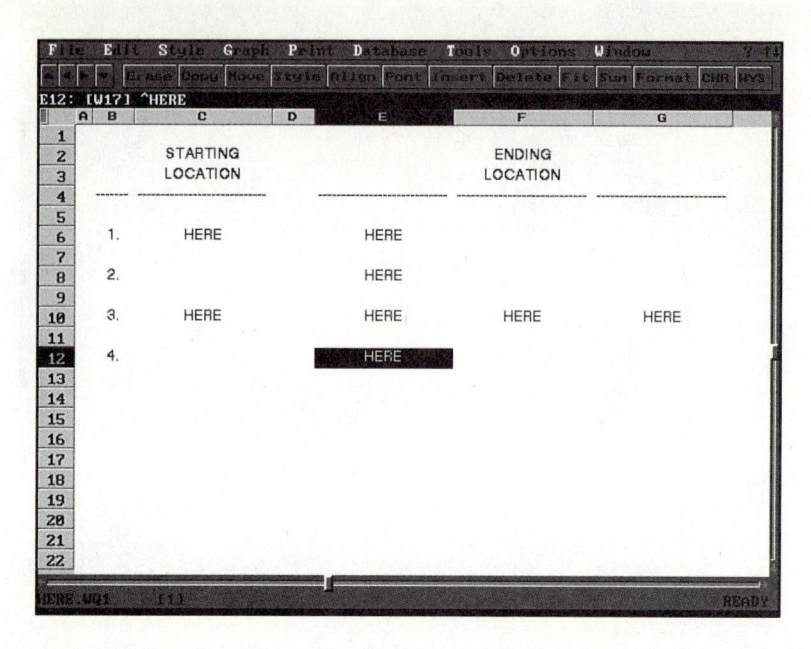

Fig. 4.3

Copy or move data four different ways.

You can execute a copy operation more quickly when you preselect the source cell and then choose the command. To copy the contents of cell A5 into cell Z5, for example, follow these steps:

1. Make A5, the cell you want to copy, the active cell, highlighting the cell using the mouse or the cursor-movement keys.

2. Choose **C**opy from the **E**dit menu. Press Enter when Quattro Pro displays A5..A5 as the source cell address.

3. When Quattro Pro prompts you for a destination, type the new cell location, *Z5*, and press Enter.

T I P Press Ctrl-C, the Ctrl-key shortcut for the **C**opy command, to execute a copy operation quickly.

You also can copy data using the Copy button on the READY mode SpeedBar. Highlight the cell or block you want to copy, click the Copy button, then click Enter. When Quattro Pro prompts you for a destination, click the new location and click Enter.

4 — MANIPULATING DATA

The **C**opy command is useful for duplicating formulas. When you copy a relative reference formula, Quattro Pro adjusts the cell addresses in the formula so that they refer to the row and column into which the formula was copied. In figure 4.4, the relative reference formula that sums data in column C is copied into adjacent cells in columns D, E, and F. Quattro Pro adjusts the formula to sum the data in these columns. When you copy an absolute reference formula, Quattro Pro does not adjust the cell addresses, which enables you to display a formula result in a different part of the spreadsheet.

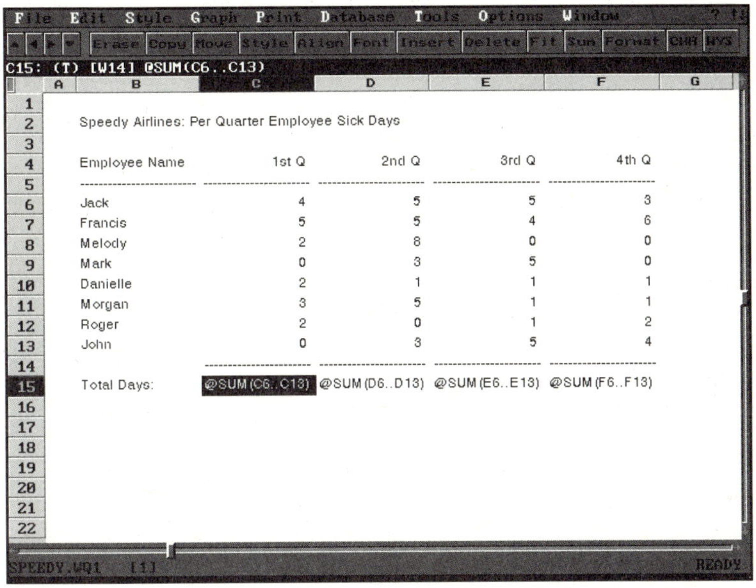

Fig. 4.4

When you copy a relative reference formula, Quattro Pro adjusts the cell addresses.

When you copy a cell, Quattro Pro copies the cell's format—alignment, display format, cell protection, and so on—into the destination cell. Cell C15 in figure 4.4, for example, is formatted to display a formula as text. When you copy the cell to the other columns, the formulas still display as text—you don't have to reformat copied cell data. See Chapter 5, "Formatting Data," for complete coverage of spreadsheet formatting.

Using Copy Special

The /**E**dit **C**opy Special, new in Version 4.0, command enables you to copy a cell block's contents without copying its formatting or copy a cell block's formatting without copying its contents. This feature is particularly helpful when you want to copy numeric data or formulas but don't want to copy the cell's style attributes, or when you want to reproduce cell formats elsewhere in the spreadsheet without copying the data.

To copy only the format or contents (value, label, or formula) of a cell, follow these steps:

1. Make the cell you want to copy the active cell.
2. Choose /Edit Copy Special.
3. Choose Contents or Format.
4. When Quattro Pro prompts you for a destination block, type the new cell location and press Enter.

If you chose Contents, the data in the source block now also appears in the destination block. If you have chosen Format, the destination block appears empty until you enter data or text into the cells. When you enter data into a cell, the data adopts the format attributes assigned with the Copy Special command.

> **T I P** When you copy data using the Format setting, Quattro Pro does not retain the alignment for labels, only for values.

Moving the Contents of a Cell

Like the Copy command, the Move command also saves time when you build a spreadsheet. You can move a label or a value to a different part of the spreadsheet or to other open spreadsheets in Quattro Pro's memory. You can execute a move operation more quickly when you preselect the source cell and then choose the command.

To move the contents of cell D15 to cell D17, for example, follow these steps:

1. Make D15 the active cell.
2. Choose Move from the Edit menu.
3. Press Enter after Quattro Pro displays D15 as the source cell address.
4. When Quattro Pro prompts you for a destination, type the new location, *D17*, and press Enter.

4 — MANIPULATING DATA

> **TIP**
> Press Ctrl-M, the Ctrl-key shortcut for the **M**ove command, to execute a move operation quickly.

You also can move data using the Move button on the READY mode SpeedBar. To execute a move operation with the Move button, highlight the cell or cells you want to move, click the Move button, then click Enter. When Quattro Pro prompts you for a destination, click the new location and click Enter.

When you relocate a formula with the **M**ove command, Quattro Pro does not adjust the cell reference formats (relative, absolute, mixed) appearing in the formula, as in a copy operation. This process enables you to display a formula result in a different spreadsheet location. In a move operation, however, Quattro Pro adjusts each formula containing a reference to the moved formula, reflecting the moved formula's new spreadsheet location.

In figure 4.5, the formula in cell D15 is moved into cell D17. The formula's original cell addresses and reference formats do not change.

> **TIP**
> Make sure that the destination cell is empty. Otherwise, Quattro Pro writes over the data.

When you use the **M**ove command to relocate a value whose cell address appears as part of a formula, several things can happen depending on the formula and where you move the value. The following example illustrates four possible scenarios.

Figure 4.6 displays an abbreviated version of the document appearing in figure 4.5. The formulas in cells C10 and D10 are equivalent to the formulas in cells E10 and F10.

Figure 4.7 shows the results of moving data referenced in spreadsheet formulas. Two types of formulas appear in this figure: individual cell addresses connected by mathematical operators (1st and 2nd Q) and @function commands (3rd and 4th Q). Quattro Pro moves each type of formula differently.

In the 1st Q column, the 3 in cell C7 is moved to cell C12. Quattro Pro adjusts the original cell reference (C7) in the formula to reflect the new location of the data in cell C12.

In the 2nd Q column, the 2 in cell D7 is moved to cell D8. Quattro Pro overwrites the data in cell D8, causing ERR to appear in the formula.

PART I — USING QUATTRO PRO SPREADSHEETS

Fig. 4.5

A formula remains unchanged when moved from one cell to another.

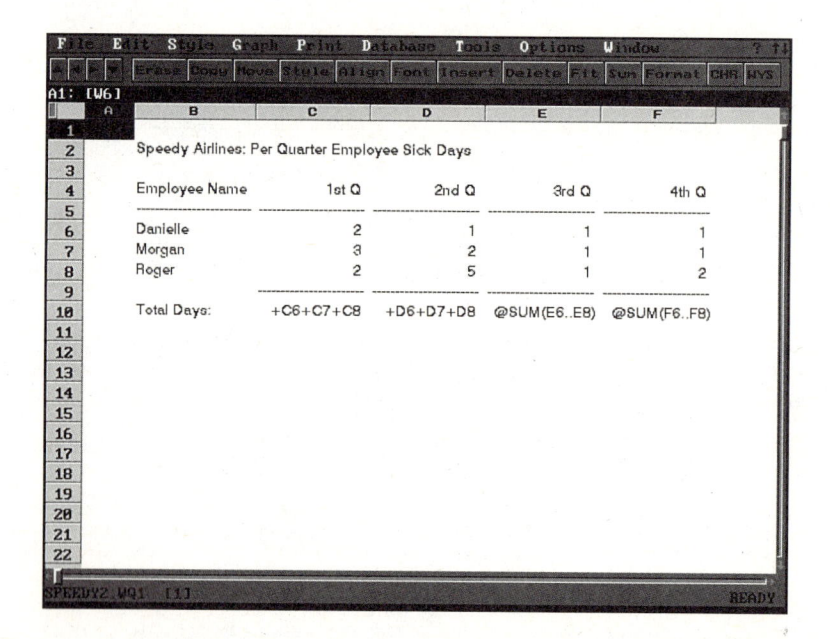

Fig. 4.6

The cell address before moving a cell referenced in a formula.

4 — MANIPULATING DATA

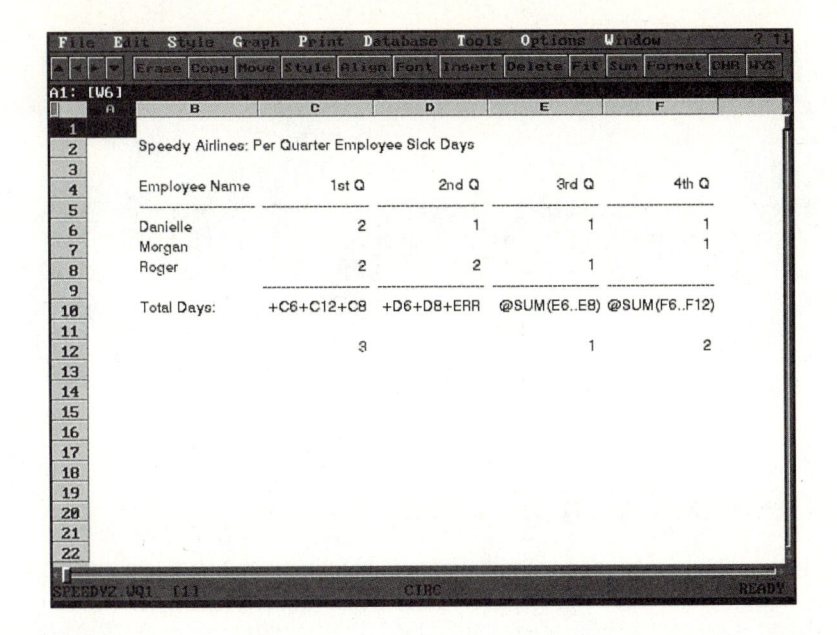

Fig. 4.7

Results of moving a cell referenced in a formula.

NOTE In any formula, when you overwrite a cell reference with another cell reference, Quattro Pro displays ERR, indicating an invalid formula. To correct the formula, reenter a valid address.

In the 3rd Q column, the 1 in cell E7 is moved to cell E12. Because cell E7 is not referenced specifically in the formula, Quattro Pro does not adjust this cell reference to reflect the data's new location. The program continues to add the numbers appearing in cell block E6..E8, but the formula result now equals 2 instead of 3.

In the 4th Q column, the 2 in cell F8 is moved to cell F12. Because F8 is one of the two coordinates in the cell block (F6 is the other coordinate), Quattro Pro adjusts the formula to include cell F12. If you move a cell listed in a formula as a coordinate in a cell block, Quattro Pro changes the formula to reflect the new coordinate location.

TIP Be careful when using the **Move** command on a cell address that also is a cell block coordinate in a formula. If you move the cell address in such a way that the adjusted cell block now includes the formula's cell address, you create a circular reference.

In a *circular reference*, the result changes each time you press F9 because the formula includes its own result in the calculation. Quattro Pro displays the CIRC indicator on the status line when the program encounters a circular reference in a formula. To correct this problem, reenter the formula so that the cells addressed in the formula do not include the address of the formula itself.

Erasing a Cell's Contents

The **Erase** Block command erases data from one cell, a group of cells, or every cell on the spreadsheet. Erasing data from a cell on a Quattro Pro spreadsheet is like pressing F2 and deleting the characters on the input line. When you erase a value from a formatted cell, Quattro Pro removes only the contents of the cell, not the cell format or alignment settings. If you do not need to save cell formats and want to erase the entire contents of a spreadsheet file, choosing the /**File Erase** command is easier.

NOTE You cannot erase cell data when spreadsheet protection is activated with the /**O**ptions **P**rotection command. See Chapter 8, "Managing Files and Windows," for details on how to enable and disable spreadsheet protection.

To erase the contents of a cell, follow these steps:

1. Make the cell you want to delete the active cell.
2. Choose **Erase** Block from the **E**dit menu.
3. When Quattro Pro displays the source cell address, press Enter.

TIP Press Ctrl-E, the Ctrl-key shortcut for the /**E**dit **E**rase Block command, to execute an erase block operation quickly.

You also can press Del to erase data from a cell. Make the cell you want to use the active cell, and then press Del. Use Del to erase one cell and the /**E**dit **E**rase Block command to erase multiple cells.

4 — MANIPULATING DATA

You also can erase data by using the Erase button on the READY mode SpeedBar. Highlight the cell or cells you want to erase and then click the button.

Working with Blocks

Besides working with single cells, the **C**opy, **M**ove, **E**rase Block, **I**nsert, and **D**elete commands also operate on blocks of cells. When you choose one of these commands, Quattro Pro displays the source cell as a cell block (A1..A1, for example). As you highlight cells, the program changes the display to reflect the new block (A1..D9, for example), giving you the flexibility to work with one, many, or all cells on the spreadsheet. You can move large chunks of data, copy an entire document onto a new spreadsheet, or delete large blocks of data from the active spreadsheet.

> **TIP**
>
> If you select a block before issuing a command, Quattro Pro uses the block as its source cell block. Remember that if you preselect a block, it remains selected after the command is executed, thus enabling you to perform several operations on the block without having to reselect it.

Copying a Block

When you copy a block of cells, highlight the cell block before choosing the command. To copy the contents of cell block A1..A5 into cell block D1..D5, for example, follow these steps:

1. Make cell A1 active, press Shift-F7 to enter EXT mode, and then use the cursor-movement keys to highlight cell A5. Alternatively, use the mouse to highlight the block.
2. Choose **C**opy from the **E**dit menu.
3. Type *D1..D5* as the destination cell block.
4. Press Enter.

Moving a Block

When you move a block of cells, preselect the cell block before choosing the **M**ove command. To move the contents of cell block A1..A5 into cell block D1..D5, for example, follow these steps:

1. Make cell A1 active, press Shift-F7 to enter EXT mode, and then use the cursor-movement keys to highlight cell A5. Alternatively, use the mouse to highlight the block.
2. Choose **M**ove from the **E**dit menu (or press Ctrl-M).
3. Type *D1..D5* as the destination cell block.
4. Press Enter.

> **T I P**   You can abbreviate the destination cell block used in Quattro Pro menu commands by typing the first coordinate in the cell block. You can type *D1*, for example, instead of *D1..D5* in step 3. When you abbreviate the destination cell block, Quattro Pro assumes that you want the destination cell block to have the same block dimensions as the source cell block.

Erasing a Block

When you erase a block of cells, highlight the cell block before you choose the command. To erase the contents of cell block D1..D5, for example, follow these steps:

1. Make cell D1 active, press Shift-F7 to enter EXT mode, and then use the cursor-movement keys to highlight cell D5. Alternatively, use the mouse to highlight the block.
2. Choose **E**rase Block from the **E**dit menu (or press Ctrl-E).

> **CAUTION:** In an **E**rase Block operation, you have no destination cell block. When you choose this command, Quattro Pro erases the source cell block.

Reversing Operations with Undo

If you forget to save a spreadsheet file after a Quattro Pro work session, all of your work goes down the drain. If you have experienced this

4 — MANIPULATING DATA

horror, then you probably accidentally have erased data on your spreadsheet, deleted the wrong row or column, or executed a command on the wrong spreadsheet cell.

Fortunately, Quattro Pro's **E**dit menu has a built-in protection mechanism that in many cases enables you to recall the most recent changes made to a cell or reverse the most recent menu command execution. When you must undo an operation, choose /**E**dit **U**ndo or press Alt-F5, the Quattro Pro Undo key.

By default, Quattro Pro's Undo key is disabled. Pressing Alt-F5 does not affect the active spreadsheet when the Undo key is disabled. To enable the Undo key, choose /**O**ptions **O**ther **U**ndo **E**nable. After the Undo key is enabled, choose /**O**ptions **U**pdate to keep the Undo key feature active for future work sessions.

The Undo key is useful for reversing Quattro Pro operations such as copying, moving, and erasing blocks of data. This feature, however, cannot undo every Quattro Pro operation. You cannot undo spreadsheet formats and presentation-quality enhancements added with many of the **S**tyle menu commands. You cannot use the Undo key, for example, to remove drawn lines or cell shading after you add them to a spreadsheet. See Chapter 5, "Formatting Data," for a complete list of the **S**tyle menu commands that are not reversible.

> **TIP**
>
> When you need to reverse more than the most recent change or menu command execution, use Quattro Pro's Transcript facility. The Transcript facility retains a history of all keystrokes and mouse clicks for the current work session. By "replaying" your transcript, you can reinstate the current spreadsheet to its condition at any point in its former status—even all the way back to when you first opened the spreadsheet as a new, blank file. See "Playing Back a Transcript Block" in Chapter 15 for further information.

Inserting and Deleting Rows and Columns

Use the /**E**dit **I**nsert and /**E**dit **D**elete commands to add and remove rows and columns, or row or column blocks, from a spreadsheet. When you delete a row or column, you delete all the data in the row or column. Before you use the /**E**dit **D**elete command, scan the target row or column for data you want to keep.

When you delete a row or column, the data in the next row or column moves up or left to fill in the blank row or column. Do not worry if you delete data used in your formulas—Quattro Pro automatically changes formulas to reflect the removed rows or columns.

You can use two ways to scan a row or column before executing the **D**elete command. The most direct way is to use the cursor-movement keys or Tab and PgDn to move around a row or column. This method works well when you don't have much territory to cover but becomes tedious when you must look at several screens.

The second method enables you to locate data in a row or column quickly in any part of a spreadsheet. To use this method, follow these steps:

1. Place the cell selector in row 1 of any column or in column A of any row.

2. Press End on your numeric keypad to enter END mode.

3. Press the right-arrow key to search a row or the down-arrow key to search a column. The cell selector moves to the first or last piece of data Quattro Pro locates before it encounters a blank cell. If you find yourself at column IV or in row 8,192, Quattro Pro did not find any data, and you can delete that row or column.

When you choose /**E**dit **I**nsert, a submenu appears, enabling you to select rows or columns for insertion into the spreadsheet. Quattro Pro inserts a row above the cell selector and inserts a column to the left of the cell selector.

When you choose /**E**dit **D**elete, a submenu also appears, enabling you to specify how many rows or columns to delete from the spreadsheet. Quattro Pro deletes a row or column at the cell selector.

Inserting a Row

To insert rows, Quattro Pro needs to know where to begin inserting and how many rows to insert. To insert one row, follow these steps:

1. Place the cell selector in the row below where you want to insert a row.

2. Choose /**E**dit **I**nsert **R**ows.

3. Press Enter.

4 — MANIPULATING DATA

> **TIP**
> Press Ctrl-I, the Ctrl-key shortcut for the /Edit Insert command, to execute an insert operation quickly.

To insert multiple rows, follow these steps:

1. Place the cell selector in the row below where you want multiple rows inserted.
2. Choose /**E**dit **I**nsert **R**ows.
3. Press the down-arrow key until you highlight the number of rows you want to insert, highlight the rows using the mouse, or type a valid cell block including all the row numbers you want to insert at the Enter row insert block: prompt.

   Type *D6..D8*, for example.

> **TIP**
> You can preselect an entire cell block quickly with a mouse. Select the first cell in the block and then click and hold down the left mouse button while you drag the pointer through the source range. When you reach the last cell in the block, release the left mouse button. Then, choose /**E**dit **I**nsert **R**ows and press Enter.

4. Press Enter. Quattro Pro inserts three rows.

You also can insert rows by using the Insert button on the READY mode SpeedBar. Place the cell selector in the row below where you want to insert a row, click the Insert button, and then click **R**ows. If you want to insert a single row, click Enter. If you want to insert multiple rows, highlight the number of the rows you want inserted and then click Enter.

Deleting a Row

To delete rows, Quattro Pro needs to know where to begin deleting and how many rows to delete. To delete one row, follow these steps:

1. Place the cell selector in the row you want to delete.
2. Choose /**E**dit **D**elete **R**ows.
3. Press Enter.

To delete multiple rows, follow these steps:

1. Place the cell selector in the first row you want deleted.
2. Choose /**E**dit **D**elete **R**ows.
3. Press the up- or down-arrow key until you highlight the number of rows you want deleted, use the mouse to highlight the rows, or type a valid cell block including the row numbers.

   Type *D6..D8*, for example.
4. Press Enter. Quattro Pro deletes three rows.

You also can delete rows by using the Delete button on the READY mode SpeedBar. To execute a delete operation this way, put the cell selector in the row you want to delete, click the Delete button, and then click **R**ows. If you want to delete a single row, click Enter. If you want to delete multiple rows, highlight the rows you want to delete and then click Enter.

Inserting a Column

To insert columns, Quattro Pro needs to know where to begin inserting and how many columns to insert. To insert one column, follow these steps:

1. Place the cell selector in the column left of where you want a column inserted.
2. Choose /**E**dit **I**nsert **C**olumns (or press Ctrl-I, and then press C).
3. Press Enter.

To insert multiple columns, follow these steps:

1. Place the cell selector in the column left of where you want columns inserted.
2. Choose /**E**dit **I**nsert **C**olumns (or press Ctrl-I, and then press C).
3. Press the left- or right-arrow key until you highlight the number of columns you want inserted, or type a valid cell block including the column letters.

   Type *D6..F6*, for example.
4. Press Enter. Quattro Pro inserts three columns.

You also can insert columns by using the Insert button on the READY mode SpeedBar. Place the cell selector in the column left of where you want to insert a row, click the Insert button, and then click **C**olumns. If you want to insert a single column, click Enter. If you want to insert multiple columns, highlight the number of columns you want to insert and then click Enter.

Deleting a Column

To delete columns, Quattro Pro needs to know where to begin deleting and how many columns to delete. To delete one column, follow these steps:

1. Place the cell selector in the column you want deleted.
2. Choose /**E**dit **D**elete **C**olumns.
3. Press Enter.

To delete multiple columns, follow these steps:

1. Place the cell selector in the first column you want deleted.
2. Choose /**E**dit **D**elete **C**olumns.
3. Press the right-arrow key until you highlight the number of columns you want deleted, use the mouse to highlight the columns, or type a valid cell block including the column letters.

   Type *D6..F6*, for example.
4. Press Enter. Quattro Pro deletes three columns.

You also can delete columns by using the Delete button on the READY mode SpeedBar. Place the cell selector in the column you want to delete, click the Delete button, and then click **C**olumns. If you want to delete a single column, click Enter. If you want to delete multiple columns, highlight the columns you want to delete and click Enter.

Inserting and Deleting Row Blocks and Column Blocks

With Quattro Pro 4, you can insert and delete blocks of cell data as well as whole rows and columns. Quattro Pro thinks of blocks of cell data as partial columns and rows. When you insert a block of rows, data previously in the block is pushed downward. When you insert a block of columns, data previously in the block is pushed to the right. Only data in the cells directly below or to the right of the inserted block shifts; data in the whole row or column does not shift.

PART I — USING QUATTRO PRO SPREADSHEETS

Inserting a Row Block

When you insert a row block of cells, highlight the cell block before choosing the command. To insert blank cells into row block B5..D5, for example, follow these steps:

1. Make cell B5 active, press Shift-F7 to enter EXT (extend block) mode, and then use the cursor-movement keys to highlight cell D5. Alternatively, use the mouse to highlight the block.

2. Choose /Edit Insert Row Block.

Quattro Pro inserts a single empty row into cell block B5..D5 and pushes existing labels and values downward.

You also can click the Insert button on the READY mode SpeedBar to reach the /Edit Insert menu and begin an insert row block operation.

Figures 4.8 and 4.9 show a spreadsheet before and after an insert row block operation. In figure 4.8, cell block C17..F17 is preselected and the /Edit Insert menu has been pulled down. The spreadsheet in figure 4.9 shows how Quattro Pro inserts multiple row blocks after you choose the Row Block command.

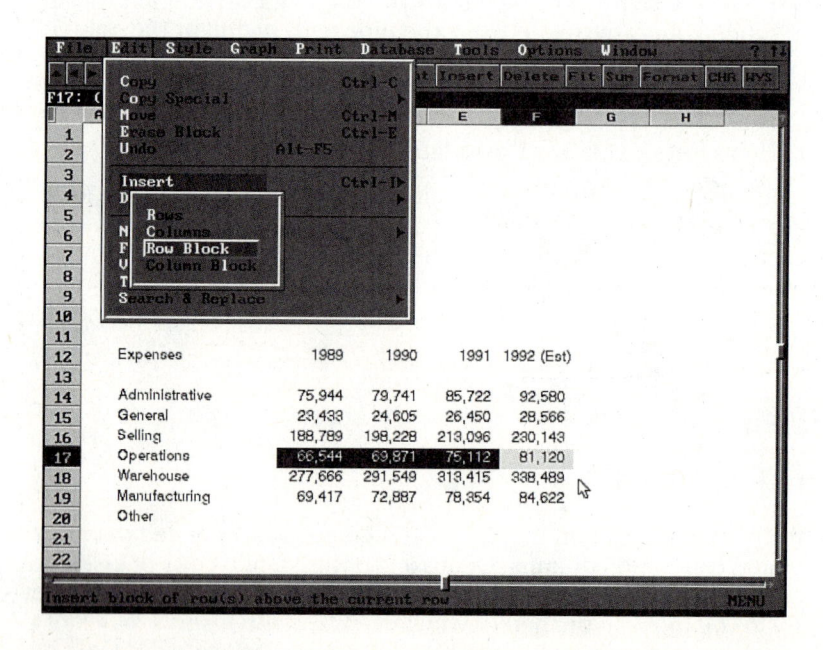

Fig. 4.8

A preselected block of rows on a spreadsheet.

4 — MANIPULATING DATA

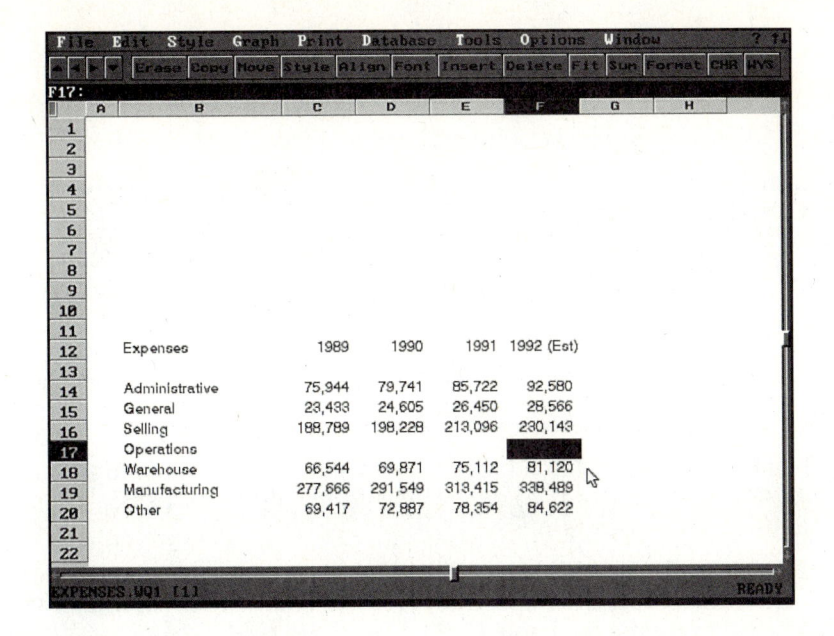

Fig. 4.9

The results of inserting multiple row blocks.

Deleting a Row Block

When you delete a row block of cells, highlight the cell block before choosing the command. To delete row block B5..D5, for example, follow these steps:

1. Make cell B5 active, press Shift-F7 to enter EXT mode, and then use the cursor-movement keys to highlight cell D5. Alternatively, use the mouse to highlight the block.
2. Choose /**E**dit **D**elete Row **B**lock.

Quattro Pro deletes row block B5..B9 and moves any data below the row block upward.

You also can click the Delete button on the READY mode SpeedBar to reach the /**E**dit **D**elete menu and begin a delete row block operation.

Inserting a Column Block

When you insert a column block of cells, highlight the cell block before choosing the command. To insert blank cells into column block B5..B10, for example, follow these steps:

PART I — USING QUATTRO PRO SPREADSHEETS

1. Make cell B5 active, press Shift-F7 to enter EXT mode, and then use the cursor-movement keys to highlight cell D5. Alternatively, use the mouse to highlight the block.

2. Choose /Edit Insert Column Block.

Quattro Pro inserts an empty column block in cell block B5..B10 and pushes existing data to the right.

You also can use the Insert button on the READY mode SpeedBar to reach the /Edit Insert menu and begin an insert column block operation.

Deleting a Column Block

When you delete a column block of cells, highlight the cell block before choosing the command. To delete cells from column block B5..B10, for example, follow these steps:

1. Make cell B5 active, press Shift-F7 to enter EXT mode, and then use the cursor-movement keys to highlight cell D5. Alternatively, use the mouse to highlight the block.

2. Choose /Edit Delete Column Block.

Quattro Pro deletes cell block B5..B10 and moves any data right of the row block to the left.

You also can use the Delete button on the READY mode SpeedBar to reach the /Edit Delete menu and begin a delete column block operation.

Naming a Block

Quattro Pro recognizes different areas of the spreadsheet in three ways. Two coordinates—a cell address and a cell block—enable you to figure out the addresses of all cells in a block.

The Names command assigns text names to cell addresses and cell blocks to create a third kind of spreadsheet area: *cell block names*. You can use cell block names instead of cell addresses in Quattro Pro menu commands and formulas. You can remember a cell block name more easily than you can remember a cell block's coordinates. You can create, delete, reset, and make tables of names using the commands found on the Names submenu (see fig. 4.10).

When in EDIT mode, you can click the Name button on the EDIT mode SpeedBar to display a list of named blocks (similar to pressing F3). If you click a named block, Quattro Pro enters it on the edit line.

Creating Names

When you create cell block names, you must remember five rules:

- A valid name can refer to a cell, a cell block, or the entire spreadsheet.

- Valid names can be up to 15 characters long.

- Cell block names can contain any character on your keyboard. You can use the punctuation characters and the mathematical symbols in a name, but you can remember names more easily if you stick to letters.

- You can combine names, cell addresses, and cell blocks in a formula; create two or more names for the same cell block; and create names for cell blocks with overlapping cell addresses. Figure 4.11 shows examples of valid spreadsheet names.

- Never name cells or blocks with a name that is the same as a cell address. If you create the name Q1 to represent Quarter 1 sales, for example, and then use the name in a formula, Quattro Pro uses the data in cell Q1.

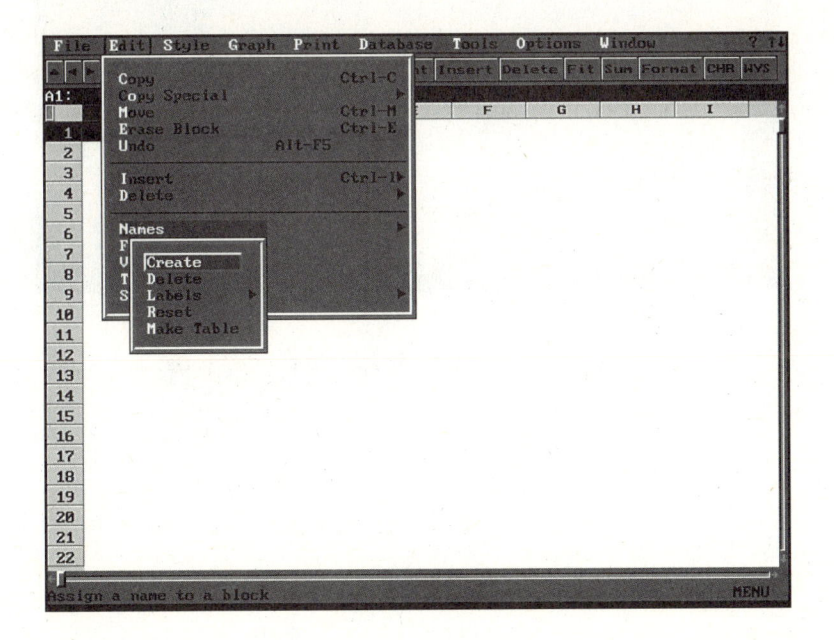

Fig. 4.10

You can create, delete, reset, and make tables of cell block names.

PART I — USING QUATTRO PRO SPREADSHEETS

> **TIP**
>
> Intermediate and advanced spreadsheet applications make frequent use of the **Create** command. You may want to assign a SpeedBar button to this operation. See Chapter 16, "Customizing Quattro Pro," for instructions about assigning menu command operations to a SpeedBar button.
>
> Alternatively, you can create a Ctrl-key shortcut for the command. Ctrl-N for NAMES works nicely.

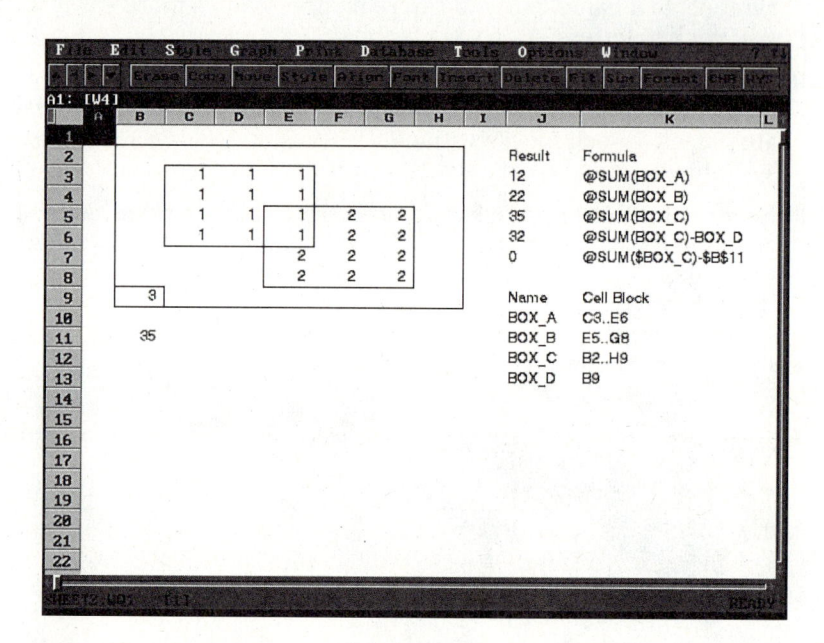

Fig. 4.11

Cell block names can refer to cells, cell blocks, or whole spreadsheets.

To create a name for cell block C3..E6, follow these steps:

1. Make cell C3 active, press Shift-F7 to enter EXT mode, and then use the cursor-movement keys to highlight cell E6. Alternatively, use the mouse to highlight the block.

2. Choose /**E**dit **N**ames **C**reate. Quattro Pro prompts you for a block name.

3. Type a valid name and then press Enter.

> **T I P**
>
> Quattro Pro updates a formula when you create a name to replace a cell address or cell block referenced in the formula (see fig. 4.12). If you create the name 1STQ for an existing formula reference such as C6..C8, for example, Quattro Pro substitutes 1STQ for C6..C8 in the formula. If you delete the name 1STQ later, Quattro Pro replaces 1STQ in the formula with the original cell block C6..C8.

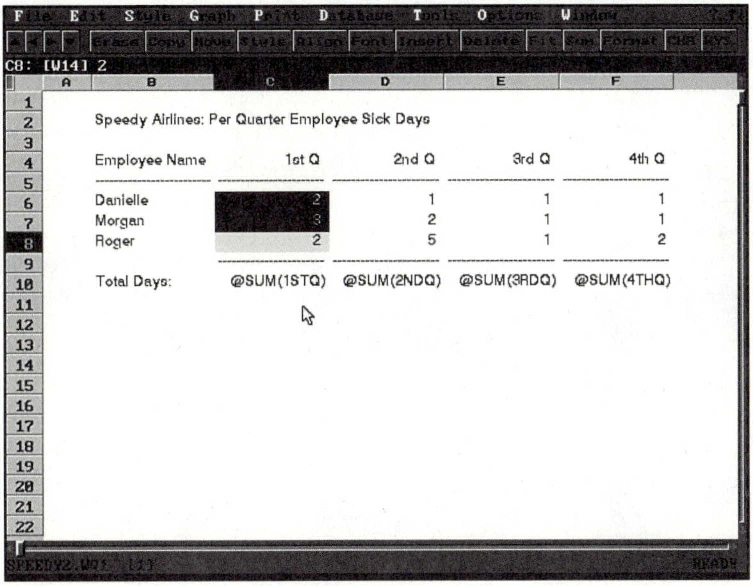

Fig. 4.12

Quattro Pro substitutes a name for a cell block address.

Each time you create a name, Quattro Pro stores the name with the active spreadsheet. After you create the first name on each spreadsheet or each time you modify an existing name, Quattro Pro displays a list of stored names for the active spreadsheet. Only the amount of memory your PC has limits the number of names you can create for a spreadsheet.

Deleting Names

When you modify and update spreadsheets, you sometimes must delete names. To remove a stored name from a spreadsheet, use the **De**lete command.

PART I — USING QUATTRO PRO SPREADSHEETS

If you delete a named cell block, Quattro Pro keeps the name but removes its cell block assignment when you delete the block. If you delete a name assigned to a cell block, Quattro Pro removes the name from the block names list and redisplays the block address in each formula that originally contained the name.

> **T I P**
>
> When you press F2 to edit a formula containing a name, Quattro Pro displays the cell addresses rather than the stored name on the input line so that you immediately know to which cells the name refers. In EDIT mode, the status line displays the formula with the block name.

To delete a cell block name, follow these steps:

1. Choose /**E**dit **N**ames **D**elete. Quattro Pro displays the block names list and prompts you for a block name (see fig. 4.13).

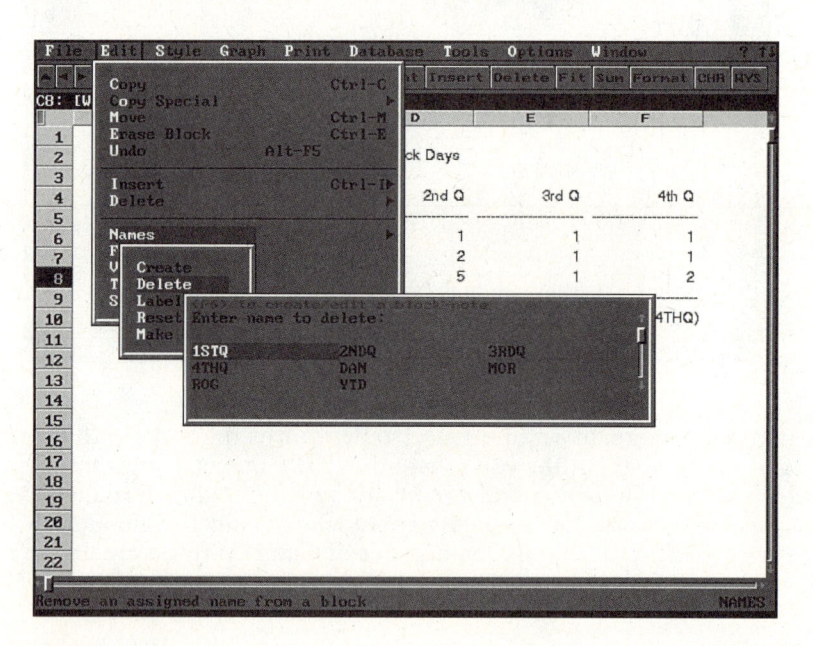

Fig. 4.13

Use the **D**elete command to remove a cell block name.

2. Type a valid name, use the mouse to highlight the block, or press the cursor-movement keys until you highlight the block you want to delete.

3. Press Enter.

> **TIP**
>
> When you create more block names than Quattro Pro can display on the block names list, you can press F2 and enter a search string. Quattro Pro displays a Search For * message on the status line at the bottom of your screen. Press as many letters as necessary to identify the block name. Press Enter to move the highlight bar to the first name on the list that matches the search string. You can press F3 to expand the block names list to a full-screen display and press the plus sign (+) to display the cell or block of cells for each name.

Adding Notes to Named Blocks

Quattro Pro 4.0 enables you to add notes to named blocks of data, besides adding notes to specified cells. After you name a block and create a corresponding note, the note appears above the list of block names when the block name list is displayed and the respective block name is highlighted. Remember that you must name a block before you can add a note to it.

Use block name notes to remind yourself and others about the information in your spreadsheets. Notes are helpful particularly for training new users about how macros in a spreadsheet application are designed to work (see fig. 4.14). See Chapter 15, "Creating Macros," for details on how to work with macros.

To add a note to a block name, follow these steps:

1. Choose /**E**dit **N**ames **C**reate.
2. Highlight the block name to which you want to add a note.
3. Press F6 to display a note entry box.

    Quattro Pro prompts you to enter the note you want attached to the name.
4. Type the note and press Enter.

Notes can be up to 72 characters long, but Quattro Pro displays only as many characters as can fit on the line containing the note.

You also can add notes to named blocks by clicking the Name button on the EDIT mode SpeedBar, highlighting the named block to which you want to add a note and then clicking F6.

PART I — USING QUATTRO PRO SPREADSHEETS

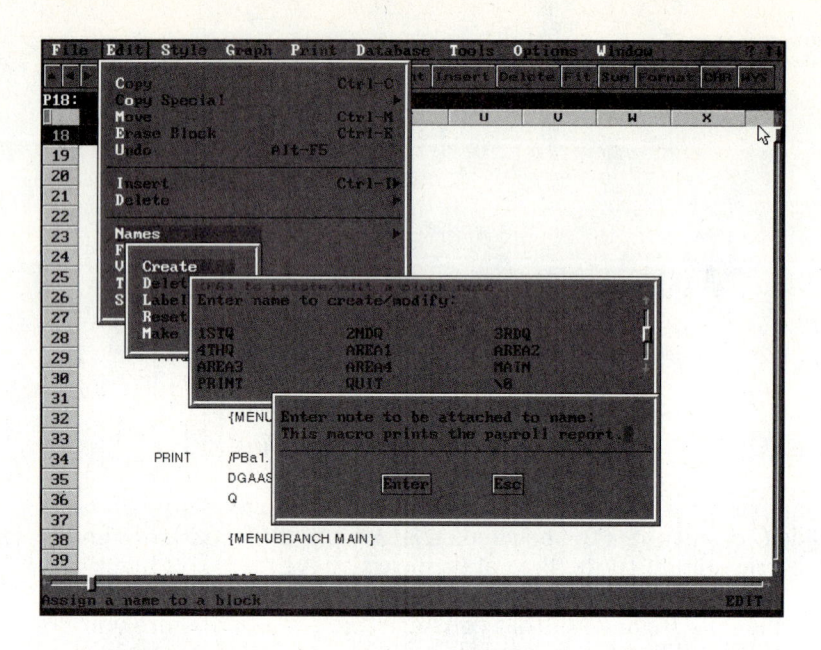

Fig. 4.14

A block name note.

To edit an existing block note, follow these steps:

1. Choose /**E**dit **N**ames **C**reate.

2. Highlight the block name for the notes you want to edit and then press F6.

   Quattro Pro displays your previously typed note.

3. Make any changes to the note and press Enter.

> **T I P** If you press F3 before pressing F6, you can view the entire note in the expanded block names list before you edit the note.

To delete a note from a block name but to keep the block name, follow these steps:

1. Choose /**E**dit **N**ames **C**reate.

2. Highlight the block name for the notes you want to delete and then press F6.

3. Press Ctrl-Backspace and then press Enter.

4 — MANIPULATING DATA   149

> **T I P**
>
> A Quattro Pro block name table lists all block names, cell addresses, and notes that you create for a spreadsheet. Block name tables are covered later in this chapter.

Using Labels To Create Names

The **L**abels command quickly creates names for rows and columns of data. This command is useful when you want to use labels on a spreadsheet as the names for a group of values appearing in adjacent cells.

The **L**abels command also is useful if you want to create names for the values in cell block G5..G9 by using the labels appearing in adjacent cell block F5..F9 (see fig. 4.15). Here, Quattro Pro assigns the name Sector 1 to cell G5, Sector 2 to cell G6, Sector 3 to cell G7, and so on.

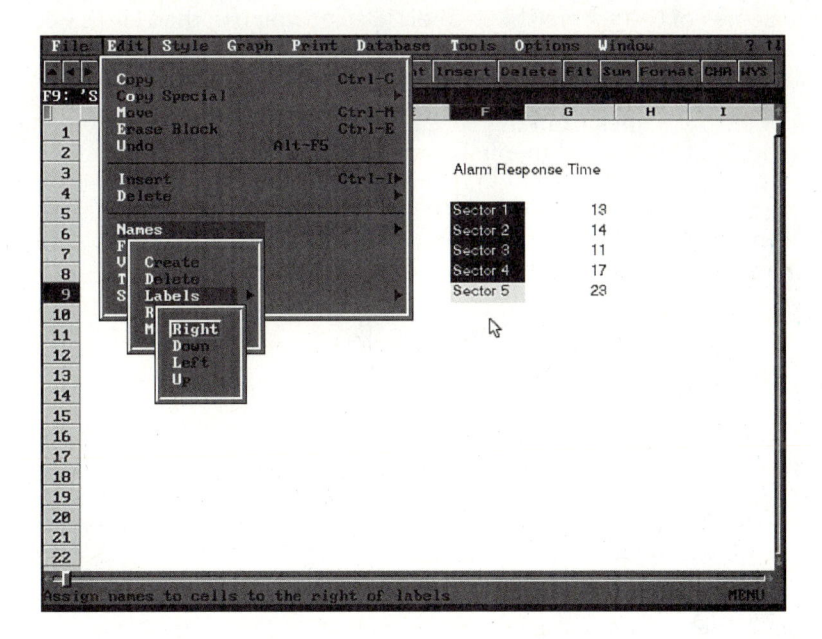

Fig. 4.15

Create names with the **L**abels command.

The **L**abels command is similar to the **C**reate command, except that **L**abels operates only on a group of cells appearing in two adjacent columns or rows.

To create names from the labels shown in figure 4.15, follow these steps:

1. Make cell F5 active, press Shift-F7 to enter EXT mode, and then use the cursor-movement keys to highlight cell F9. Alternatively, use the mouse to highlight the block.

2. Choose /**E**dit **N**ames **L**abels. Quattro Pro displays the **L**abel submenu.

3. Choose the **R**ight option, which describes the relative location of the cells to the labels.

Quattro Pro assigns each label name in column F to the corresponding value in column G.

Resetting Cell Block Names

Sometimes deleting all the names from the active spreadsheet is easier than creating names and then deleting the old ones. Suppose that you assign 20 names using the **L**abels command. Later you decide to change the names of the spreadsheet labels. Before you use the **L**abels command to assign new names to the spreadsheet, delete all of the old names and start with a clean slate.

To delete all names from the spreadsheet, choose the **R**eset command on the /**E**dit **N**ames submenu. **R**eset is like the **D**elete command except that **R**eset operates on all the names on the active spreadsheet. When you choose this command, Quattro Pro displays the prompt, `Delete all block names?` Press **N**o to cancel the operation or **Y**es to erase all names from the spreadsheet.

Making a Table of Names

As you build more sophisticated spreadsheets, using names instead of numbers makes creating and remembering formulas much easier. The formula @SUM(EXPENSE), for example, comes to mind more easily than the formula @SUM(F12..F15). If you frequently use names, you must know how to review all stored names quickly.

The **M**ake Table command copies a list of the current spreadsheet's names, their cell block assignments, and any notes you may have added onto the active spreadsheet in a location that you specify. Be careful not to overwrite data on the spreadsheet when you execute this command. When determining where to place the table, remember that Quattro Pro requires three columns—one for names, one for cell block assignments, one for block notes—and as many rows as names (see fig. 4.16).

4 — MANIPULATING DATA

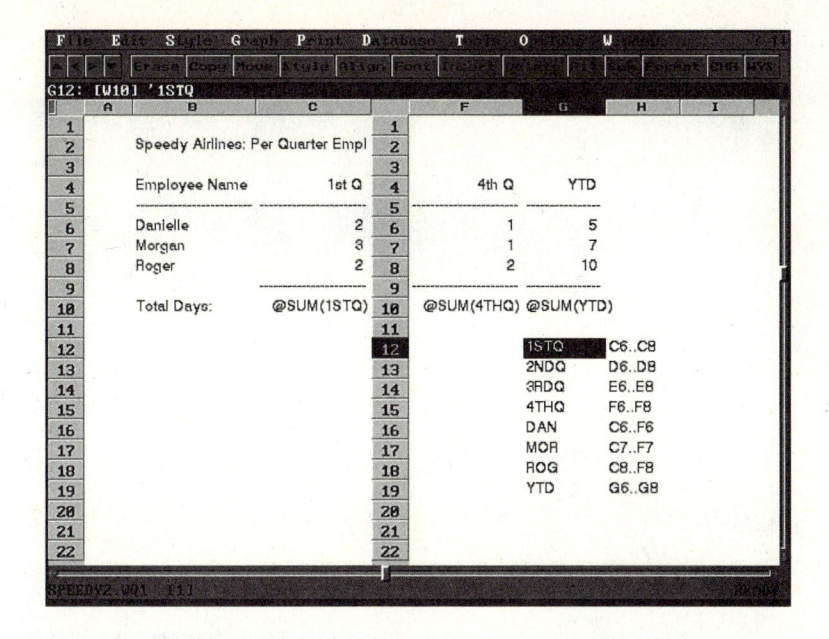

Fig. 4.16

The **M**ake Table command copies cell block names to a designated location.

To make the table of names shown in this figure, follow these steps:

1. Make cell G12 the active cell.
2. Choose /**E**dit **N**ames **M**ake Table.
3. Press Enter to copy the table into the active spreadsheet, beginning in cell G12.

Keep a table of cell block names somewhere on the spreadsheet. When you add or change a name, choose the **M**ake Table command to update your list because Quattro Pro does not perform automatic updates.

T I P

If you copy the names table into a block of columns with narrow widths, Quattro Pro may display asterisks in the cell block assignments column. In this event, you must widen the column. Press Ctrl-W (or choose /**S**tyle **C**olumn Width) and widen the column until the data reappears.

Quattro Pro also enables you to view stored names on-screen while you build or edit formulas. To view stored names, follow these steps:

1. In EDIT mode, place the edit cursor next to an open parenthesis, or simply press the plus sign (+) key to begin a formula.

PART I — USING QUATTRO PRO SPREADSHEETS

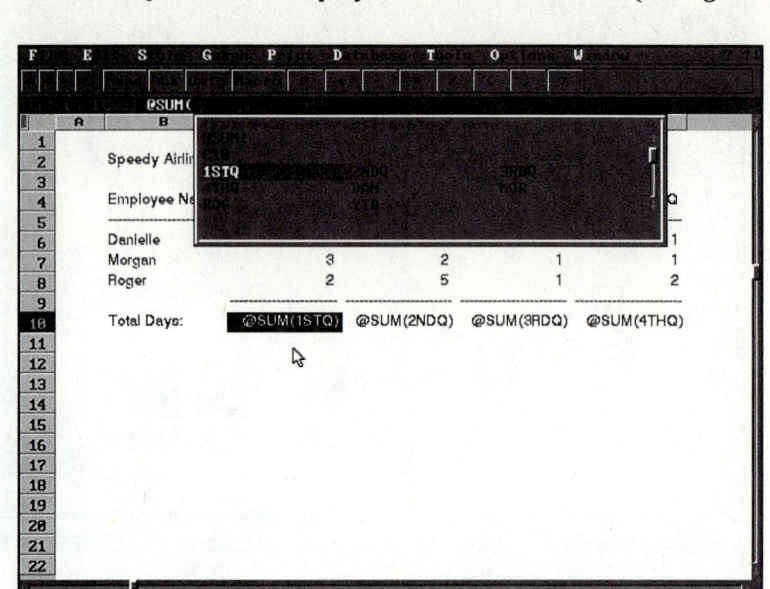

2. Press F3. Quattro Pro displays the block names list (see fig. 4.17).

Fig. 4.17

Press F3 to display a block names list.

3. Press the Expand key (+) to see the block coordinates for each cell.

4. Press the Contract key (–) to remove this display from your screen.

5. Press F3 again. Quattro Pro displays an expanded version of the stored names (see fig. 4.18).

6. Press Esc to return to the spreadsheet.

Using Names in Formulas

You know that you can substitute names for cell blocks in formulas. Figure 4.16 shows @function commands that contain names instead of cell block coordinates. To create the formula shown in cell C10, follow these steps:

1. Make cell C10 the active cell.

2. Type *@sum(* and press F3 to display the block names list.

3. Highlight 1STQ on the list.

4. Press Enter to copy the name to the right of the open parenthesis on the input line.

5. Type) and press Enter to store the formula in cell C10.

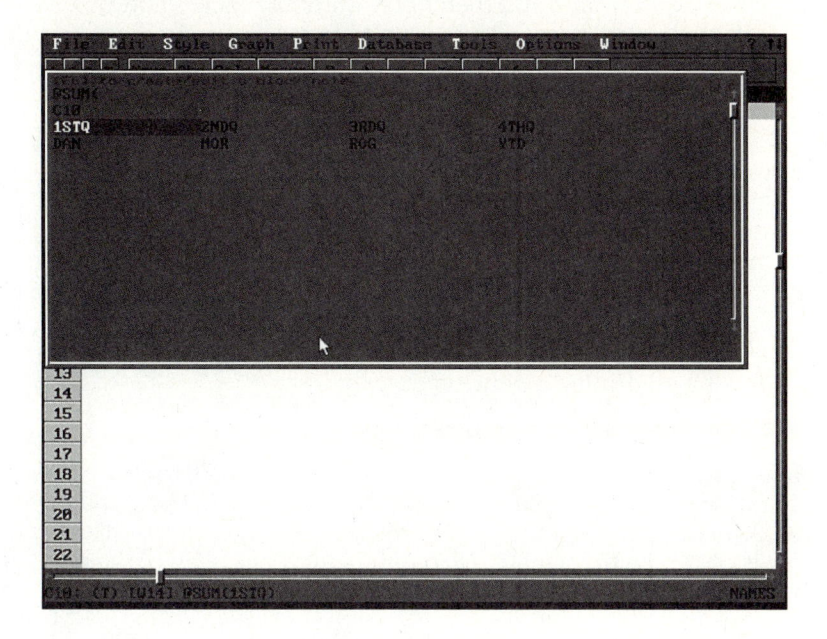

Fig. 4.18

Press F3 a second time to fill the window with the block names list.

You can use this method to build formulas as long as you define the block names first.

Filling a Block with Numbers

When you use a spreadsheet as a reporting tool, you probably order your data according to date, transaction number, or invoice number. To create a check register, for example, use the /**E**dit **F**ill command to assign a unique number to each transaction. You also can use the **F**ill command to create a series of incremental dates.

The /**E**dit **F**ill command simplifies the process of entering a large number of sequential values onto a spreadsheet. Using this command, you can enter numbers, formulas, and dates.

To fill numbers into a cell block, follow these steps:

1. Choose /**E**dit **F**ill. Quattro Pro highlights the active cell as the default destination cell block.

2. Enter a new destination cell block, use the mouse to highlight the cell block, or press the cursor-movement keys to extend the current block. Press Enter.

3. Enter a start value and then press Enter. If you are entering sequential dates, press Ctrl-D, type a start date (in the form MM/DD/YY), and then press Enter.

> **TIP**
>
> Because Quattro Pro stores dates in serial number form, you must keep two things in mind. First, choose a stop value that is greater than the date serial number (a value > 40,000 works well). Second, after you fill a group of cells with date serial numbers, choose /**S**tyle **N**umeric Format **D**ate and format the numbers to display as dates.

4. Enter a step value and press Enter.
5. Enter a stop value and press Enter.

In a fill operation, the *start value* is the value that Quattro Pro places in the first cell of the destination block. The *step value* is the amount by which Quattro Pro increases or decreases the series values. The *stop value* is the value that Quattro Pro places in the last cell of the destination block.

If you define a destination cell block with two or more columns, Quattro Pro fills in each row in the first column before entering data into the second column, and so on. You also can fill numbers in ascending and descending order by altering the step value (see fig. 4.19).

The data appearing in D3..D9 illustrates the results of filling a single column with sequentially increasing numbers. Here, the start value is 0, the step value is 1, and the stop value is 6.

The data appearing in C11..E17 shows the results of filling multiple columns with sequentially decreasing numbers. Here, the start value is 100, the step value is –1, and the stop value is 77. First, Quattro Pro fills values into C11..C18. Then, beginning in cell D11, the program fills values into D11..D18. Finally, Quattro Pro fills values into E11..E18.

Changing Formulas to Values

The /**E**dit **V**alues command converts a formula into the result, displays the result as a numerical value, and erases the original formula from the spreadsheet. Although the need for this kind of operation may not be obvious, the **V**alues command plays an important part in the process of maintaining and modifying your spreadsheet applications.

4 — MANIPULATING DATA

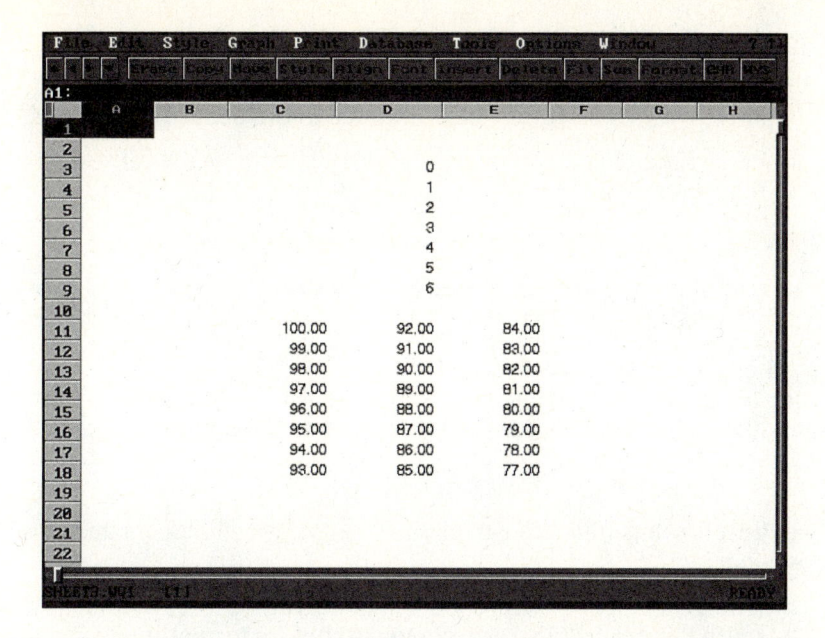

Fig. 4.19

Fill in cell blocks with ascending and descending numbers.

Spreadsheet formulas calculate answers to problems such as, "What is the value of cell C10 plus the value of cell C11?" If you create a formula that produces one answer, and the answer probably will not change, convert the formula to this value. If the value of C10 plus the value of C11 equals 10 and probably always will equal 10, for example, convert the formula C10+C11 to the value 10. This conversion frees memory for Quattro Pro to use for other areas of the spreadsheet in which you have ongoing calculations because it releases a cell's dependence on other cells. In this example, you can delete the contents of C10 or C11 without affecting the value "10."

Formulas also pinpoint important relationships among two or more variables such as, "What is the ratio of profits to sales for 1992?" You can use one spreadsheet to process your yearly financial data and another to record year-end historical data. The ratio information appears on a second historical report listing key financial ratios. Because last year's financial data is definitely not going to change this year, transfer the ratios as values to the second spreadsheet.

To change formulas to values, follow these steps:

1. Make the first cell in the target block active, press Shift-F7 to enter EXT mode, and then use the cursor-movement keys to highlight the last cell in the source block. Alternatively, use the mouse to highlight the block.

2. Choose /**E**dit **V**alues. Quattro Pro records the location of the source block.
3. Move the cell selector to the first cell in the destination block.
4. Press Enter to copy the formula results as values into the destination cell block.

Transposing Data in a Cell Block

Another way to manipulate data on a Quattro Pro spreadsheet is by using *transposition*. When you transpose spreadsheet data, you switch the organization of your column and row data. This command is useful after you create a spreadsheet application and decide that the data makes more sense if organized differently.

Use the following guidelines to ensure that your cell block data transposes correctly:

- When transposing formatted cell data, you generally should execute the /**E**dit **T**ranspose command before formatting your spreadsheet column width. If you already have formatted your spreadsheet's column width, your transposed data probably doesn't fit neatly into the current cell widths. Press Ctrl-W to change the column widths until all transposed data appears.

- Make sure to transpose a cell block to a different part of the spreadsheet. If you try to transpose a cell block onto itself, Quattro Pro loses the column and row organization and shows a block of garbled numbers. After executing the /**E**dit **T**ranspose command, you can move or copy the transposed block anywhere on the spreadsheet.

- If you try to transpose relative reference formulas, the formulas adjust incorrectly and do not refer to the right cell addresses. You have two options when you want to transpose blocks containing formulas: change all relative references into absolute references and edit them after transposition; or use the /**E**dit **V**alues command to convert cell block formulas to computed values.

- When you transpose a block of cells, preselect the cell block before choosing the command.

Suppose that you want to transpose the contents of cell block B4..G9 into cell B11. To do so, follow these steps:

1. Choose /**E**dit **T**ranspose. Quattro Pro prompts you for the source block of cells.

4 — MANIPULATING DATA

2. Type *B4..G9* and press Enter. Quattro Pro prompts you for the destination cell.
3. Type *B11*, or enter another destination cell block at least one column to the right or one row below the source cell block.
4. Press Enter to transpose information into the destination cell block.

Figure 4.20 displays an original and transposed cell block. Notice that the current column width does not accommodate the transposed data.

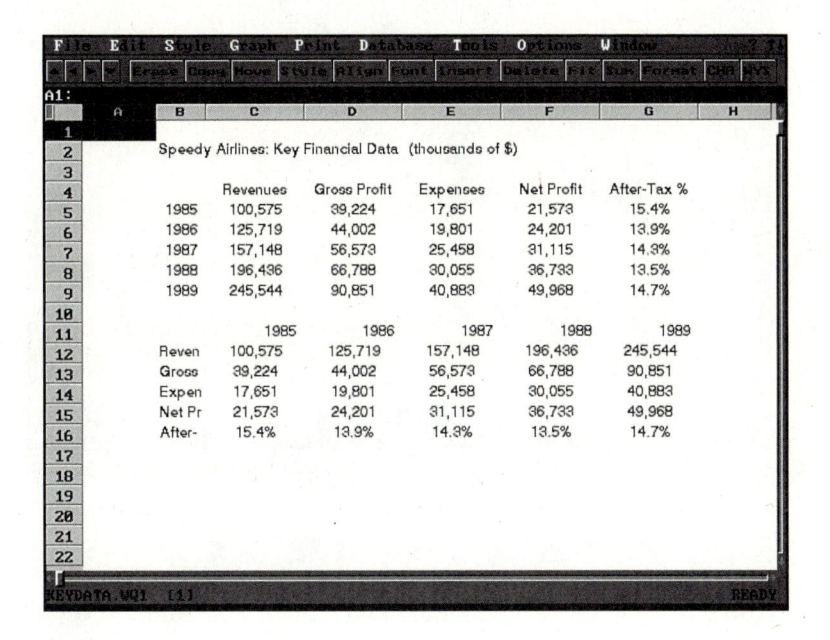

Fig. 4.20

Transpose cell blocks to switch the column and row organization.

Searching for and Replacing Data

After you enter, edit, display, reorganize, insert, delete, and transpose your spreadsheet data, you may need to search quickly through a large application, replacing letters and numbers with new or updated data. You need Quattro Pro's **S**earch & Replace command.

To use **S**earch & Replace, you must tell Quattro Pro what to look for, where to look, and with what to replace the searched-for item. If you need to create specialized search conditions, you can further refine the search operation by setting the commands found in the Options section of the **S**earch & Replace submenu.

PART I — USING QUATTRO PRO SPREADSHEETS

Figure 4.21 shows the mission statement for Speedy Airlines. A quick review of this document reveals that a few crucial phrases have been omitted. You can use the **S**earch & Replace command to insert the missing phrases.

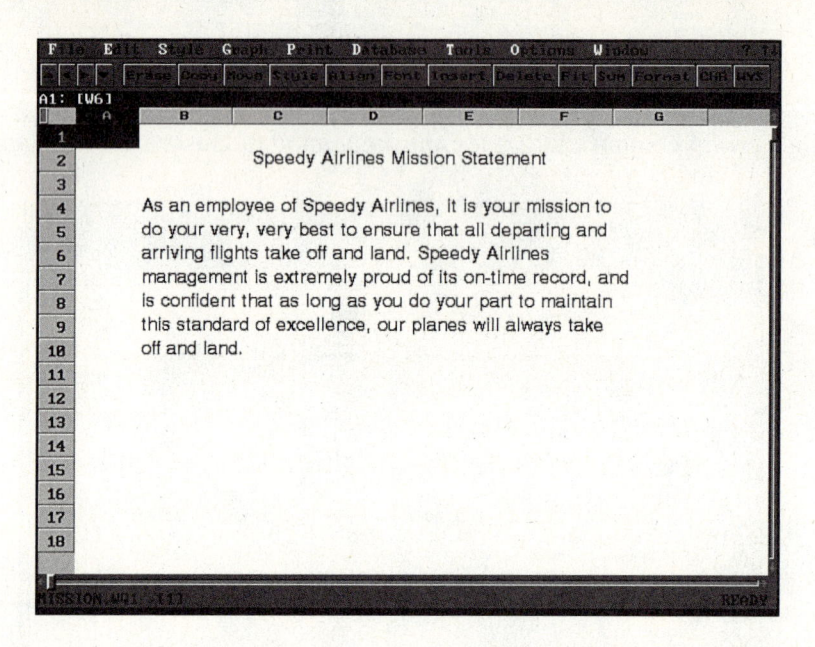

Fig. 4.21

Speedy Airlines' mission statement.

Setting the Search Parameters

With the **S**earch & Replace command, you quickly can update key label descriptions, revise out-of-date numbers, and alter the structure of your spreadsheet formulas. You have complete flexibility to devise the scope of a search-and-replace operation because Quattro Pro enables you to define the parameters explained in the following sections and found on the **S**earch & Replace menu shown in figure 4.22.

Choosing a Block

By default, Quattro Pro scans the entire spreadsheet for your search data. For large spreadsheet applications, you should restrict the search area to minimize the potential search time.

Suppose that you want to search the text appearing in cell block B4..B10. To do so, follow these steps:

4 — MANIPULATING DATA

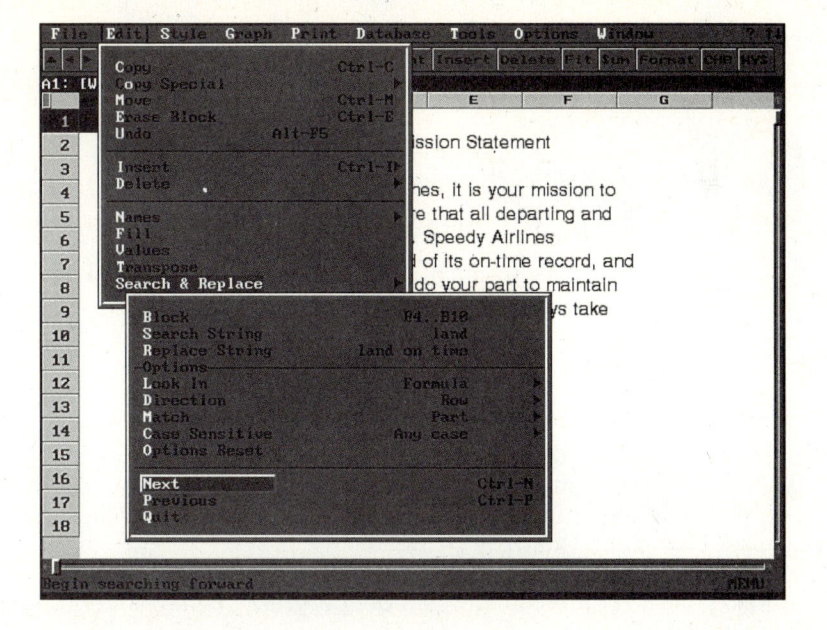

Fig. 4.22

Parameters set for Speedy Airlines' search-and-replace operation.

1. Choose /**E**dit **S**earch & Replace **B**lock.
2. Enter *B4..B10*.
3. Press Enter to store the cell block.
4. Quattro Pro returns to the **S**earch & Replace menu so that you can make other choices.

Entering a Search String

A crucial phrase, *on time*, is missing from two sentences in Speedy's mission statement. In both sentences, land is the last word before where *on time* should be added. *Land*, therefore, becomes the search string.

To enter *land* as the search string, follow these steps:

1. Choose **S**earch String.
2. Type *land*.
3. Press Enter to store the search string.
4. Quattro Pro returns to the **S**earch & Replace menu so that you can make other choices.

Entering a Replacement String

To enter *land on time* as the replacement string, follow these steps:

1. Choose **R**eplace String.
2. Enter *land on time*.
3. Press Enter to store the replacement string.
4. Quattro Pro returns to the **S**earch & Replace menu so that you can make other choices.

Executing the Search Operation

The minimum information needed to execute a search-and-replace operation is the search-and-replace string. With this data, Quattro Pro can begin scanning the spreadsheet. Choose **N**ext from the **S**earch & Replace submenu, and Quattro Pro locates the first occurrence of the string. When Quattro Pro locates a valid matching string, it highlights the string on the spreadsheet. Then the program displays the prompt shown in figure 4.23.

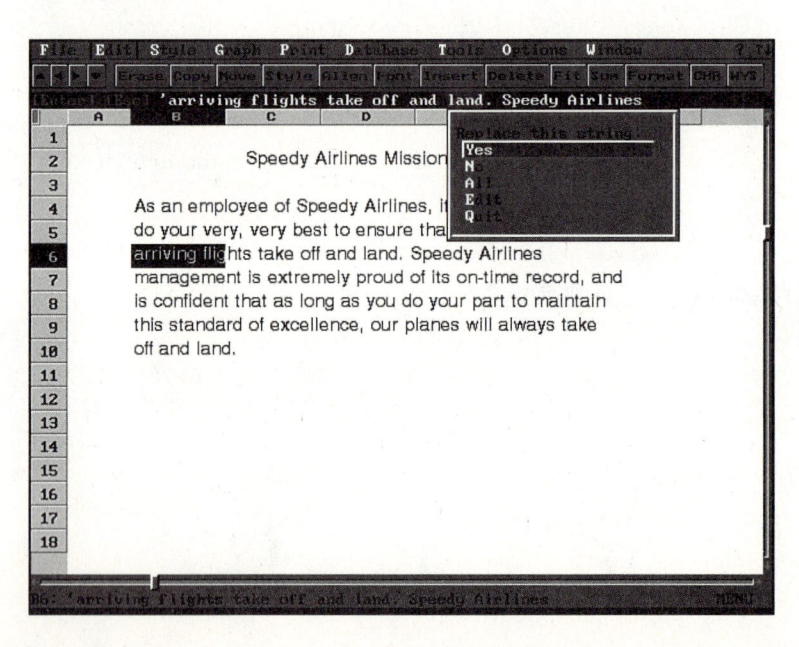

Fig. 4.23

Quattro Pro's prompt to replace the string.

Choose **Y**es to replace the string, **N**o to not replace the current string, **A**ll to replace the current string and all other matching strings without further prompting, **E**dit to edit the current string, or **Q**uit to cancel the operation without replacing the current string.

Choose **A**ll for the Speedy Airlines example to replace both occurrences of the string without further prompting.

> **T I P**
>
> Choose **E**dit to display the located text on the input line, where you can type a different replacement string. Press Enter to store the new data in the cell.

After Quattro Pro finishes the search-and-replace operation, the program returns to the active spreadsheet and makes the first cell address in the defined block (B4) the active cell (see fig. 4.24).

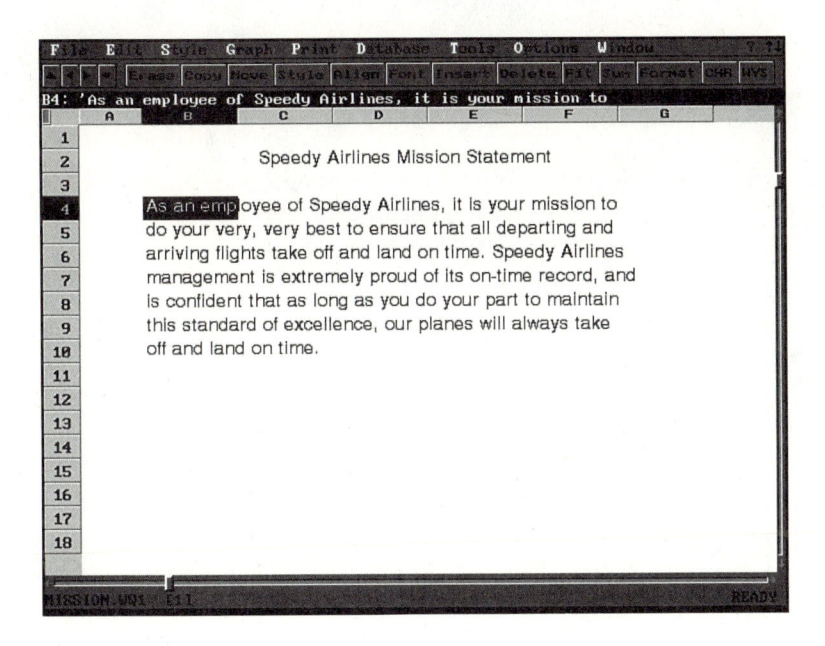

Fig. 4.24

The revised mission statement for Speedy Airlines.

Using Special Search Parameters

The Options area in the middle of the **S**earch & Replace menu contains the following five special parameters that you can use to delineate further how Quattro Pro evaluates your spreadsheet data in a search-and-replace operation (refer to fig. 4.22).

- Choose **Look In** to tell Quattro Pro to review each **F**ormula or **V**alue, or to set a search string **C**ondition, such as all cell values equal to 100 (?=100).

- Choose **D**irection to indicate that Quattro Pro should search by **R**ow or **C**olumn.

- Choose **M**atch to tell Quattro Pro whether to locate a search string as part of a **W**hole string or as **P**art of any string containing the search string.

- Choose **C**ase Sensitive to tell Quattro Pro whether to look for a string whose capitalization exactly matches the search string or to accept **A**ny Case.

- Choose **O**ptions Reset to erase all the settings that Quattro Pro stores on the right side of the **S**earch & Replace menu. Quattro Pro returns to the default search-and-replace settings.

Questions & Answers

This chapter has introduced you to the fundamental Quattro Pro cell block operations and spreadsheet sculpting techniques. If you have questions about any topics covered in this chapter, scan this section.

Copying, Moving, and Erasing Cell Data

Q: When do you preselect a cell block?

A: You may preselect cells before choosing any Quattro Pro menu command that performs an operation on a block. If you use a mouse, always preselect cells. If you execute commands from your keyboard, whether you preselect depends on how quickly you can extend a block in EXT mode.

Q: Why did a formula's result change when I copied it to a different part of the spreadsheet?

A: You used **C**opy instead of **M**ove. When you move a formula, Quattro Pro does not adjust the formula's cell references or change the result. When you copy a formula, Quattro Pro adjusts the cell references in the formula, unless you previously changed the formula to all absolute references.

If Undo is enabled, press Alt-F5 to undo the operation and choose /**E**dit **M**ove. If Undo is disabled, reenter the overwritten cell data. ERR then disappears, and your formulas display valid results again.

Q: Why did my formulas display ERR after I moved a cell on the spreadsheet?

A: You probably wrote over data in a cell referenced by other formulas on the active spreadsheet. If you cause one cell to display ERR and that cell's address appears in other spreadsheet formulas, the other formulas also display ERR.

Press Alt-F5 to undo the operation and choose a new destination cell for the **M**ove operation.

Q: When does using the Del key instead of the **E**rase Block command make sense?

A: To remove data from a cell and preserve its format and alignment settings, place the cell selector in the cell and press Del. To remove data from two or more cells and preserve their format and alignment settings, choose **E**rase Block.

Inserting and Deleting Columns and Rows

Q: Why can't I insert a column or row on my active spreadsheet?

A: Quattro Pro cannot insert a column or row when data is in the last column or row of the spreadsheet—the program has no room.

Q: What do I do if I deleted a column or row containing data I need, and my spreadsheet is displaying ERR everywhere?

A: You deleted a column or row containing a cell block coordinate being used in your spreadsheet formulas.

If Undo is enabled, press Alt-F5 to Undo the operation. If Undo is disabled, insert a column or row at the original point of deletion and reenter the lost data. ERR disappears, and your formulas redisplay valid results.

Naming Cell Blocks

Q: Why won't one of my spreadsheet formulas accept a block name that I created?

A: If you create a name for a block of cells and try to use that name in certain mathematical operations, Quattro Pro displays an error message saying that the block is invalid.

PART I — USING QUATTRO PRO SPREADSHEETS

If BLOCK is the name for C5..C10 and you attempt to enter the formula +*BLOCK+25*, Quattro Pro displays an error message. A cell block name describes an area but does not compute a value unless you tell the block name to do so. The same formula is valid when you include BLOCK in an @function command, such as @SUM(BLOCK)+25, for example.

Q: When I copied a named block on the spreadsheet, Quattro Pro did not copy the block name. Why?

A: Quattro Pro does not enable you to duplicate block names on the same spreadsheet. In a copy operation, when the source cell block is also a named block, Quattro Pro copies only the cell data to the destination cell block. The block name remains assigned to the source cell block. The only way to transfer a block name from one part of the spreadsheet to another is to use /Edit Move and relocate the cell block.

Q: I used /Edit Names Labels to create cell block names for a row of data, but when I used the name in a formula, the program did not return the correct answer. Why?

A: The Labels command assigns a name to only one adjacent cell in the direction you specify on the Labels submenu. Use the Create command to name a cell block.

Q: Why did nothing happen when I pressed F3 to display a list of stored names for the active spreadsheet?

A: You can display a block names list during two types of Quattro Pro operations: when you are in EDIT mode and the cursor is next to an open parenthesis, or when you are in POINT mode and Quattro Pro is prompting you for a cell block. When you press F5, the GoTo key, for example, Quattro Pro prompts you to type a cell block. Press F3 to view a list of all names assigned to cell blocks for the spreadsheet.

Filling, Transposing, Searching for, and Replacing Data

Q: Why does Quattro Pro display decimal or negative numbers when I try to fill a cell block with dates?

A: Quattro Pro is evaluating your start value (for example, 10/10/89 or 10-10-89) as a formula. To use this feature properly, press Ctrl-D after you enter the destination cell block and before you enter the start value.

Q: When I transposed a cell block on the spreadsheet, why did Quattro Pro display 0's and ERRs?

A: Your original cell block probably contains formulas. Quattro Pro cannot transpose relative reference formulas correctly. Change the references to an absolute format and edit them after the operation. You also can convert the formulas to their calculated values using /**E**dit **V**alues before choosing /**E**dit **T**ranspose.

Q: Why is Quattro Pro not finding a search string that I know exists on my spreadsheet?

A: Review your option settings on the **S**earch & Replace submenu. You may have specified the wrong **M**atch or **C**ase Sensitive option.

Summary

Chapter 4 explains how to copy, move, and erase cells and blocks of cells on the Quattro Pro spreadsheet. You also learned how to modify an application's organization by adding and deleting columns and rows. Special cell block operations, such as converting formulas to values, filling in cell blocks with sequential numbers, and searching for and replacing data on the spreadsheet also were discussed.

Having read this chapter, you should understand the following Quattro Pro concepts:

- Preselecting cell blocks on which to perform operations
- Copying one cell into another or into many cells
- Moving one cell or a block of cells to another part of the spreadsheet
- Erasing cells and cell blocks
- Reversing Quattro Pro operations with the Undo command
- Inserting and deleting multiple rows, columns, row blocks, and column blocks
- Creating text names for cell blocks
- Using cell block names in formulas
- Converting formulas to their values, filling a cell block with sequential numbers, and transposing column and row data
- Searching for and replacing data on a spreadsheet

PART I — USING QUATTRO PRO SPREADSHEETS

In Chapter 5, you learn how to add the finishing touches to your spreadsheet applications using Quattro Pro's **S**tyle menu commands. The commands on this menu help you to fine-tune your spreadsheet data. Choose options from Quattro Pro's **S**tyle menu when you need to display numbers as dollars or percentages, align data in a cell, draw a line around a cell, change fonts, and add shading so that you can create a final, presentation-quality report for an important meeting.

CHAPTER 5

Formatting Data

Although the discussion so far has centered on Quattro Pro's usefulness as a calculating tool, the inherent power of any electronic spreadsheet lies in its capability to store and remember numerical and formula relationships.

This chapter introduces techniques that enable you to expand the usefulness of a Quattro Pro spreadsheet by turning the spreadsheet into a presentation-quality reporting tool. Although much of the chapter talks about how to create reports that look good, you do not lose sight of the spreadsheet's important role as a mathematical tool.

This chapter introduces you to the 14 **S**tyle menu commands. The commands are organized into three groups: cell formatting commands, column- and row-adjustment commands, and presentation-quality commands.

The discussion also focuses on how to realign data in a cell; choose the appropriate format for values, labels, dates, and times; and protect important cell data.

The chapter continues by showing how to widen and narrow column widths, how to manage blocks of columns, how to enlarge and shrink row heights, and how to hide column data temporarily from prying eyes.

The final section in Chapter 5 examines how to turn a basic spreadsheet application into a presentation-quality report. You learn how to draw lines and boxes around cells to highlight critical data, add shading to cell blocks, use multiple fonts, and insert page breaks to control report printing. You also learn how to create customized styles, apply them to cell blocks on a spreadsheet, and save them in a file for future use.

As you read this chapter, keep in mind that preselecting cells simplifies the use of Quattro Pro menu commands. Preselect cells when you use the **S**tyle menu commands because this method is the most efficient for formatting and creating your reports.

Using Style Menu Commands

After you build the basic form of a spreadsheet application, you can use this form or enhance its appearance to call attention to and clarify important points. Quattro Pro's **S**tyle menu enables you to add stylistic effects to your spreadsheet applications. You can draw a box around text and values so that they stand out on-screen, for example, draw double lines under financial statement figures, and shade and protect important cell data.

Quattro Pro enables you to use different typefaces to give your reports and graphs a professional look. You may want to select a large Courier font for a report title; a medium-sized, boldfaced font for the secondary titles and headings; and a smaller, italicized font for account names or other descriptions. You can change the width of a column or a block of columns, or hide columns containing private data. You also can enlarge and shrink the height of a row or a block of rows to accommodate large-sized fonts or to create special effects.

Using the **S**tyle menu commands, you can mold basic spreadsheets into creative and informative reports and graphs. (See Chapters 10 and 11 for more information on creating and annotating graphs.)

You can use the 14 **S**tyle menu commands shown in figure 5.1 to fine-tune and enhance your spreadsheet's data display.

The **S**tyle menu commands are organized roughly in the order that you should use them during a work session. When you align and format cell data, you sometimes must change the column width so that the formatted data fits into a cell. You then add the final stylistic touches—such as lines, shading, and custom fonts—and even define and apply customized styles of grouped attributes. Table 5.1 explains the **S**tyle menu commands.

5 — FORMATTING DATA

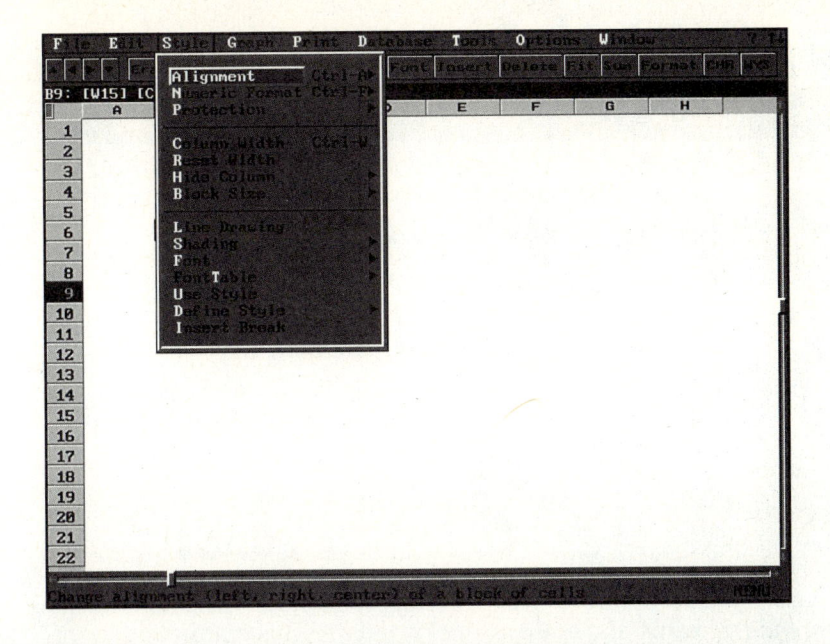

Fig. 5.1

The Style menu.

Table 5.1 Style Menu Commands

Command	Description
Alignment	Aligns data at the left edge, right edge, or in the center of a cell, or back to the default (General)
Numeric Format	Formats the spreadsheet display of values and text
Protection	Protects and unprotects cell data on the active spreadsheet
Column Width	Widens and narrows the width of the active column
Reset Width	Resets the width of the active column to the default column width setting
Hide Column	Hides columns on the active spreadsheet
Block Size	Widens, narrows, and resets the width and height of multiple columns and rows
Line Drawing	Draws and removes lines and boxes of various thicknesses around cells
Shading	Adds grey or black shading to spreadsheet cells and removes shading from cells

continues

Table 5.1 Continued

Command	Description
Font	Assigns different fonts and font styles to cells to enhance printouts
FontTable	Applies and modifies predefined fonts
Use Style	Applies a customized style to a cell block
Define Style	Creates, erases, and removes customized styles; saves and retrieves customized styles
Insert Break	Inserts a page break at the cell selector's location

Undoing Style Menu Commands

Pressing Alt-F5 reverses Quattro Pro spreadsheet operations such as copying, moving, and erasing blocks of data. This feature, however, cannot undo every Quattro Pro operation.

You cannot undo spreadsheet formats created with the following **S**tyle menu commands: **A**lignment, **N**umeric Format, **P**rotection, **C**olumn Width, **R**eset Width, **H**ide Column, and **B**lock Size. You also cannot undo presentation-quality enhancements achieved with the **L**ine Drawing, **F**ont, and **S**hading commands.

You can undo data alignments created manually or alter these alignments when in EDIT mode. You also can undo a page break inserted with the **I**nsert Break command.

Changing the Default Global Settings

Quattro Pro initially uses global format settings to format your data entries. Quattro Pro uses these format settings each time you load a spreadsheet. The program right-aligns values and left-aligns text in a cell, for example. Consider the income statement spreadsheet shown in figure 5.2. The labels in C3..E7 are aligned with the global default setting. The labels in C10..E14 are right-aligned with the /**S**tyle **A**lignment command.

5 — FORMATTING DATA

Fig. 5.2

Quattro Pro right-aligns values and left-aligns text in cells.

To change one of the global format settings, choose /**O**ptions **F**ormats and choose a command from the menu shown in figure 5.3. If you always want labels right-aligned in your spreadsheets, choose /**O**ptions **F**ormats **A**lign Labels **R**ight. Quattro Pro changes the global label alignment setting for the current work session.

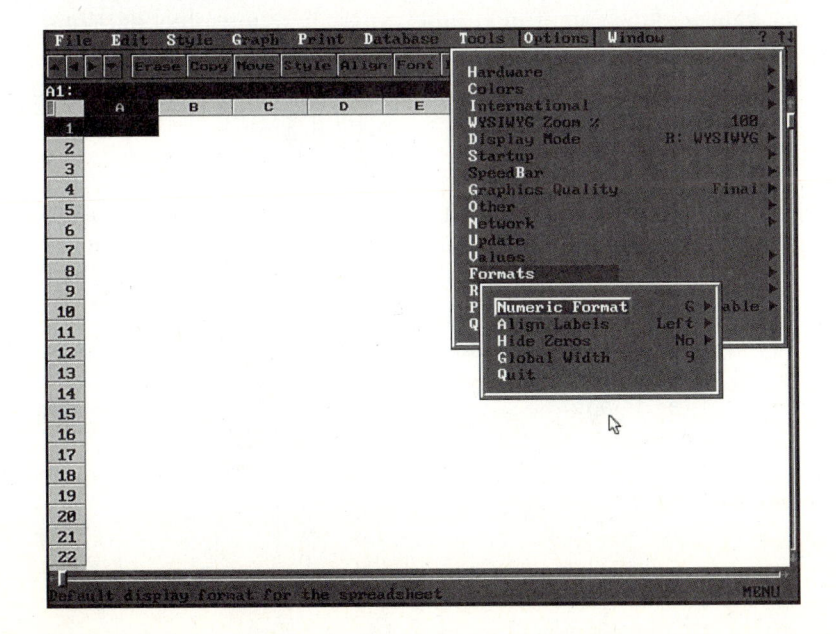

Fig. 5.3

The /**O**ptions **F**ormats default settings.

You can choose **N**umeric Format to change the global numeric format setting, **A**lign Labels to change the global label alignment setting, **H**ide Zeros to tell Quattro Pro whether or not to display zero values on the spreadsheet for the current work session, and **G**lobal Width to set the global column width to a new value.

To change the global currency symbol, punctuation method, or date-and-time settings to conform to international standards, choose /**O**ptions International.

When you change any of Quattro Pro's global format settings, choose **U**pdate before you end the current work session. The next time you load the program, the new default settings will be in effect. (See Chapter 16, "Customizing Quattro Pro," for complete coverage of the **O**ptions menu commands.)

> **NOTE** **H**ide Zeros is not a global default that can be saved with /**O**ptions **U**pdate; you must set the setting to **Y**es for each session (each time the program is loaded).

Controlling Data Display

The first three commands on the **S**tyle menu control the display of data within a spreadsheet cell and affect the appearance of data displayed in a printout. These commands enable you to realign data in a cell; format labels, values, dates, and times; and protect and unprotect data in a cell.

Aligning Data

Without the capability to align cell data, your Quattro Pro spreadsheets could look like a jumble of numbers and letters. The data shown in figure 5.4 appears disorganized, for example, because it has not been formatted.

When you write a report by hand, you intuitively know how to space numbers, letters, words, and paragraphs so that they make sense. When you enter data into a spreadsheet cell, Quattro Pro decides the type of data (value or label) and aligns that data according to predefined default global settings: labels are left-aligned in a cell; values, dates, and times are right-aligned.

5 — FORMATTING DATA

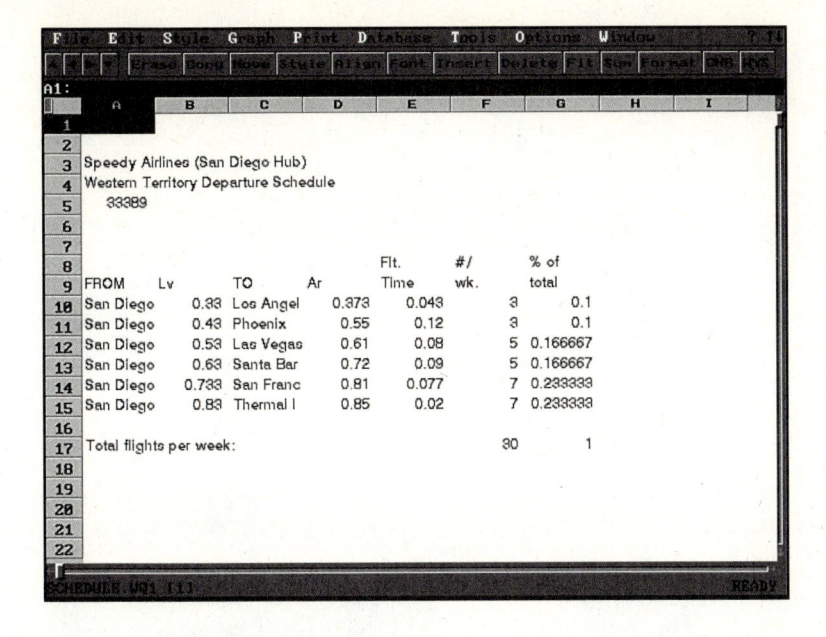

Fig. 5.4

An unformatted Quattro Pro spreadsheet.

Selecting a New Alignment

Use the /**S**tyle **A**lignment command to alter the alignment of values, labels, dates, and times in a cell block. Quattro Pro displays a submenu with four choices: **G**eneral, **L**eft, **R**ight, and **C**enter.

The **G**eneral format (the default alignment setting) right-aligns values and dates and aligns labels according to the /**O**ptions **F**ormats **A**lign **L**abels setting.

In a typical spreadsheet, report titles are center-aligned, column labels and data are right-aligned, and row headings usually are left-aligned.

To correct the confusing alignment of the data in figure 5.4, follow these steps:

1. Preselect cell block A3..G17.

2. Choose /**S**tyle **A**lignment.

3. Choose **L**eft from the submenu.

Quattro Pro aligns the data in the cell block. After your column data is aligned under a column heading, reviewing the report becomes easier. This operation is just the first of several that you perform in this chapter.

T I P Press Ctrl-A, the alignment shortcut key, to choose the /Style Alignment command.

You also can click the Align button on the READY mode SpeedBar to change a cell's alignment. When you click the button, Quattro Pro displays the /Style Alignment menu. Choose an alignment, highlight the block you want to align, and then click Enter. Remember, if you preselect the block you want to align before clicking the Align button, you need to select only the alignment to complete the operation.

Selecting an Alignment Manually

You can change the alignment of a label in two ways without using the **A**lignment command. You can align a label by preceding it with one of the following label prefix characters:

Prefix	Description
'	Left-justifies text in a cell
"	Right-justifies text in a cell
^	Centers text in a cell
\	Repeats a character or group of characters in a cell until the character fills the entire cell

To center-align the label in cell E8, for example, follow these steps:

1. Make cell E8 active.
2. Type ^ (the caret label prefix).
3. Type the label on the input line.
4. Press Enter to center-align the label.

You also can alter an existing label's alignment while in EDIT mode. To realign the label from the preceding example, follow these steps:

1. Press F2 to edit cell E8.
2. Press Home. Quattro Pro moves the cell selector to the label prefix at the beginning of the entry.
3. Press Del to delete the prefix.
4. Type a new label prefix and press Enter to realign the label.

> **TIP**
> Press Alt-F5 to undo either manual alignment operation.

You cannot adjust the alignment of a value manually because Quattro Pro does not store an alignment prefix with values. To align or realign a value, choose **A**lignment from the **S**tyle menu.

Formatting Values, Labels, Dates, and Times

Without the appropriate numeric format, you may not be able to tell whether a value is a percent, dollar, date, or time. Imagine receiving a bill from your credit card company and not knowing whether the bill is for $1,000 or $10.

With the /**S**tyle **N**umeric Format command, you can clarify the display of data on a spreadsheet. Using this command, you can create a monetary value by adding a dollar sign and decimal point, and commas to numbers greater than 999. You also can tell Quattro Pro to display a formula instead of a value, add a percent sign to a financial ratio, or display a date and time in several different formats.

The **N**umeric Format command affects the way Quattro Pro displays a value on-screen—not how the program stores the value in a cell. To check this setting, pick any formatted cell and look at its value on the input line. You also can press F2 and look at the value on the status line.

Even if you format the number 25.7565 to display as 26, Quattro Pro uses 25.7565 in all calculations. Quattro Pro performs mathematical operations using entire numbers—not their abbreviated, on-screen equivalents.

Another way to change the display of a value is to use the @ROUND function command. The cell entry @ROUND(25.7565,0) rounds the value 25.7565 to 0 decimal places, which displays the value 26. In this case, Quattro Pro performs mathematical operations using the rounded value 26—not the value 25.7565. (Chapter 6, "Using Functions," covers @ROUND and other mathematical @function commands.)

TIP Quattro Pro stores numbers with up to 16 significant digits. A *significant digit* is any integer except for a leading zero. Quattro Pro does not count decimals, commas, dollar signs, and percent signs as part of the total.

Selecting the Appropriate Numeric Format

To convey a point clearly, you must choose the most appropriate numeric format for your data. Otherwise, your data can be confusing or completely useless. If you format a percentage as a date, for example, the information is useless. If you format a monetary value with commas and a decimal point but without a dollar sign, the information is incomplete.

When you format a cell, Quattro Pro displays a format code on the input line when the cell is active. This code includes a character that identifies the format and a number that indicates the displayed decimal places. The format code (F2), for example, indicates a fixed format with two decimal places.

Because the date and time formats do not use decimal places, the number in a date or time code reflects the option number on the **D**ate or **T**ime submenu.

Table 5.2 describes each format option available on the **N**umeric Format submenu. Figure 5.5 displays numbers formatted with each format available on the **N**umeric Format submenu. Each cell's format code has been added to the right of the example.

Table 5.2 Numeric Formats

Format	Description
Fixed	Displays values with leading zeros and a user-specified number of decimal places
Scientific	Displays values in scientific notation form, such as 1.23E+03 for the number 1,23
Currency	Displays values with a currency symbol and commas to separate thousands; shows negative numbers in parentheses
, (comma)	Displays values with commas to separate thousands; shows negative numbers in parentheses

5 — FORMATTING DATA

Format	Description
General	Displays numbers as they are entered
+/−	Transforms values into a horizontal bar graph in which + represents a positive integer, − represents a negative integer, and the decimal point (.) represents zero
Percent	Displays values as percentages
Date	Displays values in user-specified date and time formats; you can use five standard date-and-time formats and several international formats
Text	Displays formulas as text rather than results
Hidden	Conceals the display of value and label entries; when the cell is selected, entries still appear on the input line
Reset	Returns the numeric format for this block to the default format (specified with the /Options Formats Numeric Format command); reveals entries hidden with the Hidden format

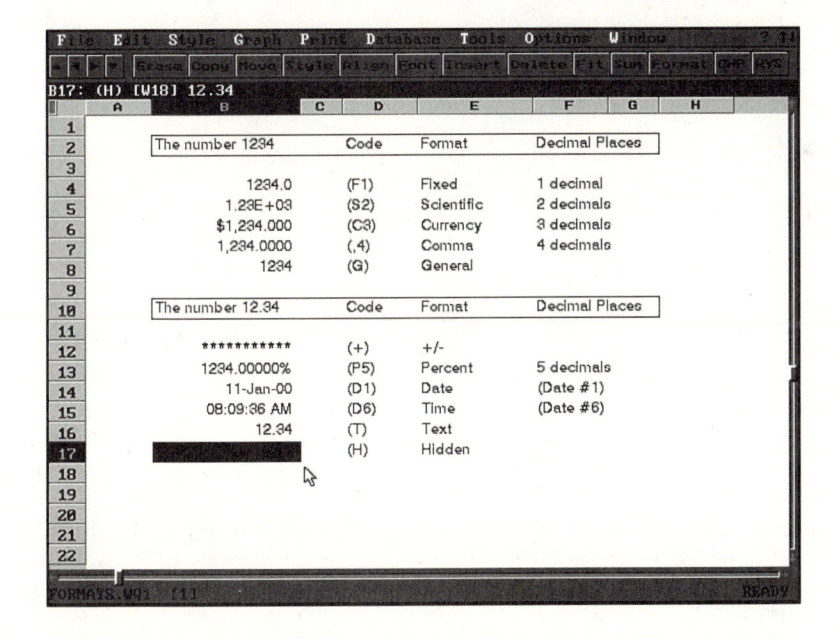

Fig. 5.5

Numeric formats in a spreadsheet.

Formatting Values

When you enter a number into a cell, Quattro Pro displays the number using the **G**eneral format, which displays most numbers in the form you entered. In some cases—for example, when a value is longer than the width of its cell—Quattro Pro displays a rounded value.

Quattro Pro always rounds a decimal value that has an equal or greater number of digits than the width of the column in which the value is positioned. The program begins rounding with the last digit in the value. If you enter the decimal value 0.399 into a cell that is 5 characters wide, for example, Quattro Pro displays 0.4. If you enter 0.309 into a cell of the same width, Quattro Pro displays 0.31 (see fig. 5.6).

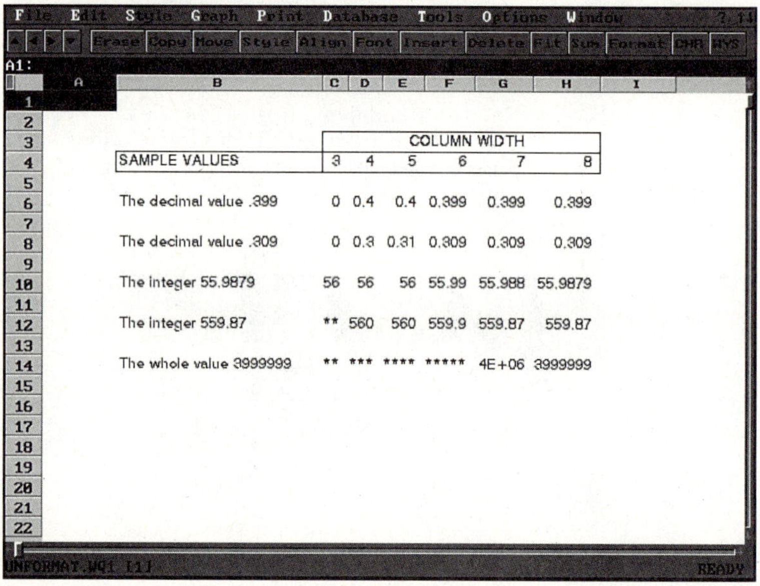

Fig. 5.6

Unformatted values in Quattro Pro.

Quattro Pro always displays a whole value in scientific notation when the number of digits in the value is greater than the character width of the active column less 1 character. If you enter a value that is 7 characters long into an 8-character-wide column, for example, the value is displayed as a whole value. If you enter the whole value 3999999 into a cell 7 characters wide, Quattro Pro displays 4E+06—the scientific notation form for this value. When you enter this same whole value into a column with a width of 6 characters or less, Quattro Pro displays asterisks.

5 — FORMATTING DATA

> **TIP**
>
> When you use text display mode, Quattro Pro's rule for displaying whole values versus scientific notation versus asterisks in a cell is slightly different when you draw lines around a cell with the /**S**tyle **L**ine Drawing command. A drawn line uses up a space equal to one character width. If you draw a line on the left or right edge of a cell, take this extra space into account when determining an appropriate column width.

To format values on a spreadsheet, follow these steps:

1. Preselect a cell block to format.
2. Choose /**S**tyle **N**umeric Format.
3. Choose a format option from the submenu.
4. If prompted, choose the number of decimal places to appear in numbers (from 0 to 15). (Only the **F**ixed, **S**cientific, **,** (comma), **C**urrency, and **P**ercent options display the decimal prompt.)
5. Press Enter. Quattro Pro redisplays the numbers in the cell block using the selected format option.

Now that this cell block has a numeric format, you can edit or delete the cell block data without erasing the cell format. When you copy the formatted contents of a cell to another location on the spreadsheet, Quattro Pro duplicates the cell format in the new location. If you move the formatted contents of a cell, Quattro Pro actually removes the cell format from the source cell and relocates it to the destination cell.

> **TIP**
>
> Press Ctrl-F, the format shortcut key, to choose the /**S**tyle **N**umeric Format command.

You also can click the Format button on the READY mode SpeedBar to display the **N**umeric Format menu.

The format option you choose may attempt to display data wider than the width of the current cell block. When this situation happens, Quattro Pro fills the cell block with asterisks. To correct this display problem, press Ctrl-W and widen the column until the data reappears.

Formatting Labels

The first nine **N**umeric Format options are intended to enhance the display of values, dates, and times. You can use the **H**idden option to remove the display of labels, values, dates, and times from your screen.

To hide cell data on a spreadsheet, use the **H**idden command. When you hide cell data, Quattro Pro removes the data from view—but you still can overwrite the contents of a hidden cell. To prevent the accidental erasure of a hidden cell, see the "Protecting Important Data" section later in this chapter.

Formatting a label with any other **N**umeric Format command has no effect on the label. If you format a label using **C**urrency and two decimal places, for example, Quattro Pro continues to display the label in its original form, even though the input line displays (C2). If you replace the label with a value, the currency format takes effect for the value.

When the cell selector is in a hidden cell, Quattro Pro displays the cell contents on the input line. To reveal a hidden label, choose /**S**tyle **N**umeric Format **R**eset.

Formatting Dates

To enter a date value onto a Quattro Pro spreadsheet, follow these steps:

1. Press Ctrl-D.
2. Enter a date using the exact form of date format 1, 2, or 3 (see table 5.3). You also can enter a date using formats 4 and 8, 5 and 9, 6 and 10, or 7 and 11 using the /**O**ptions **I**nternational **D**ate command to choose one pair as the global format.

Table 5.3 Date Command Formats

Format	Type
1. DD-MMM-YY	Day, month, year
2. DD-MMM	Day, month
3. MMM-YY	Month, year
4. MM/DD/YY	Long international #1
5. DD/MM/YY	Long international #2
6. DD.MM.YY	Long international #3

Format	Type
7. YY-MM-DD	Long international #4
8. MM/DD	Short international #1
9. DD/MM	Short international #2
10. DD.MM	Short international #3
11. MM-DD	Short international #4

Another way to enter a date is to use a date @function command and then reformat the cell using the **D**ate command. (Chapter 6 covers the @DATE, @DATEVALUE, @TODAY, and @NOW commands.)

You also can enter a date as a date serial number and then reformat the cell using the **D**ate command. A *date serial number* is an integer that is a unique code assigned by Quattro Pro to historical dates.

You easily can decipher a date serial number when you know how Quattro Pro creates the number. A date serial number equals the number of days between the date you enter and December 30, 1899. The serial number for December 30, 1899, is 0, for example, and the serial number for December 30, 1900, is 365—the number of days between the 2 dates. Figure 5.7 shows the decimal equivalents for several historical dates.

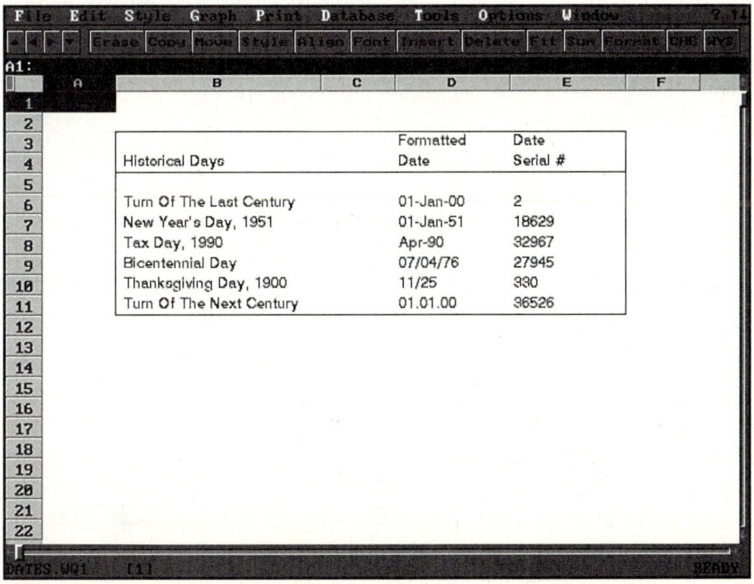
File Edit Style Graph Print Database Tools Options Window
Erase Copy Move Style Align Font Insert Delete Fit Sum Format CHR WYS
A1:
Historical Days
Formatted Date
Date Serial #
Turn Of The Last Century 01-Jan-00 2
New Year's Day, 1951 01-Jan-51 18629
Tax Day, 1990 Apr-90 32967
Bicentennial Day 07/04/76 27945
Thanksgiving Day, 1900 11/25 330
Turn Of The Next Century 01.01.00 36526
DATES.WQ1 [1] READY

Fig. 5.7

Date serial numbers.

PART I — USING QUATTRO PRO SPREADSHEETS

> **TIP** The date serial numbers for all dates before December 30, 1899, are negative. The date serial number for December 29, 1899, for example, is −1.

To enter and format a date serial number, follow these steps:

1. Enter a valid date serial number in a cell. (Valid serial numbers can be any integer in the range from −36463 for March 01, 1800, to 73050 for December 31, 2099.)
2. Choose **D**ate from the **N**umeric Format menu.
3. Choose a format option.

Whichever way you enter a date, Quattro Pro always stores a date in its serial number form so that you can use dates in spreadsheet calculations. When you enter a date serial number into a cell, you can edit the date as you can any other number. To add one day to the serial number 500, for example, change the number to 501.

If you press Ctrl-D and then enter a date using an acceptable date format, Quattro Pro displays the serial number as a date on the spreadsheet. If you press F2 and edit the serial number, the date reverts to a serial number display when you press Enter. The only way to affix a date format to a serial number is to format the date with the **/S**tyle **N**umeric Format **D**ate command.

Formatting Times

To enter a value in a time format, follow these steps:

1. Press Ctrl-D.
2. Enter a time using time format 1 or 2 (see table 5.4). You also can enter a time using the **/O**ptions **I**nternational **T**ime command to choose format pairs 3 and 7, 4 and 8, 5 and 9, or 6 and 10 as the global format.

Another way to enter a time is to use a time @function command and then reformat the cell using the **T**ime command. (Chapter 6 covers the @TIME, @TIMEVALUE, and @NOW commands.)

You also can enter a time as a time serial number and then reformat the cell using the **T**ime command. The code that Quattro Pro uses to represent a time is different from the code used for a date. Quattro Pro records time as a percentage of the 24-hour day. Quattro Pro assigns the decimal 0.5 to 12 noon, for example, because 12 noon occurs 50 percent of the way through a 24-hour day. Figure 5.8 shows the Quattro Pro decimal equivalents for each hour.

Table 5.4 Time Command Formats

Format	Type
1. HH:MM:SS AM/PM	Hour, minute, second
2. HH:MM AM/PM	Hour, minute
3. HH:MM:SS	Long international #1
4. HH.MM.SS	Long international #2
5. HH,MM,SS	Long international #3
6. HHh,MMm,SSs	Long international #4
7. HH:MM	Short international #1
8. HH.MM	Short international #2
9. HH,MM	Short international #3
10. HHhMMm	Short international #4

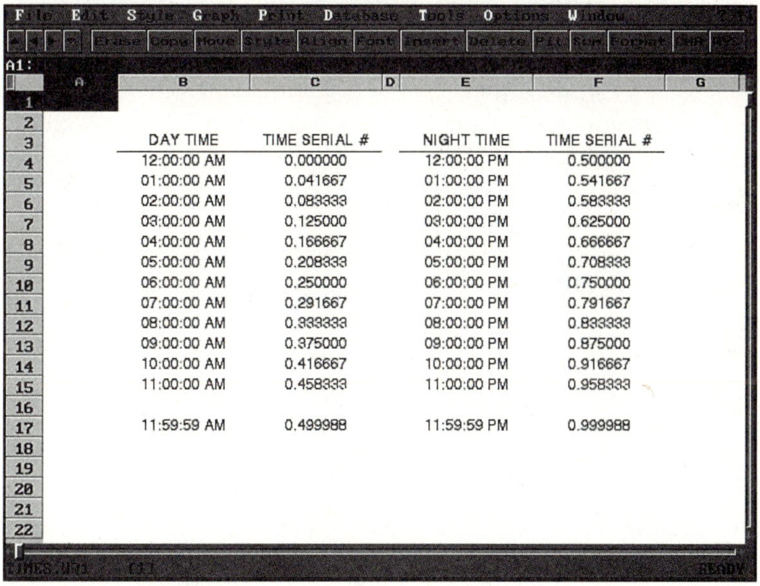

	DAY TIME	TIME SERIAL #	NIGHT TIME	TIME SERIAL #
	12:00:00 AM	0.000000	12:00:00 PM	0.500000
	01:00:00 AM	0.041667	01:00:00 PM	0.541667
	02:00:00 AM	0.083333	02:00:00 PM	0.583333
	03:00:00 AM	0.125000	03:00:00 PM	0.625000
	04:00:00 AM	0.166667	04:00:00 PM	0.666667
	05:00:00 AM	0.208333	05:00:00 PM	0.708333
	06:00:00 AM	0.250000	06:00:00 PM	0.750000
	07:00:00 AM	0.291667	07:00:00 PM	0.791667
	08:00:00 AM	0.333333	08:00:00 PM	0.833333
	09:00:00 AM	0.375000	09:00:00 PM	0.875000
	10:00:00 AM	0.416667	10:00:00 PM	0.916667
	11:00:00 AM	0.458333	11:00:00 PM	0.958333
	11:59:59 AM	0.499988	11:59:59 PM	0.999988

Fig. 5.8

Time serial numbers assigned by Quattro Pro.

To enter and then format a time serial number, follow these steps:

1. Enter a valid time serial number in a cell.
2. Choose **D**ate and then choose **T**ime from the **N**umeric Format menu.
3. Choose a format option.

PART I — USING QUATTRO PRO SPREADSHEETS

Quattro Pro always stores a time in its serial number form so that you can use times in spreadsheet calculations.

When you enter a time serial number into a cell, you can edit the time like you can any other number. To add 1 minute to the serial number 0.5, for example, add 0.000694 (the decimal value that equals 1 minute divided by 1440 minutes in a day).

> **TIP** Quattro Pro accepts 24-hour, or military, clock times. When you use Numeric Format, Quattro Pro converts 24-hour times into 12-hour clock time equivalents. For example, 23:00:00 displays as 11:00:00 PM.

If you press Ctrl-D and then enter a time using an acceptable time format, Quattro Pro displays the serial number as a time on the spreadsheet. If you press F2 and edit the serial number, the program reverts to a serial number display when you press Enter to record the editing changes. The only way to affix a time format to a serial number is to format the number with the /Style Numeric Format Date Time command.

Figure 5.9 shows a revised version of the spreadsheet from figure 5.4. This spreadsheet contains all of the appropriate numeric formats. Columns also have been widened where necessary to display all of the detail.

Changing Formats

Quattro Pro offers two ways to change cell formats. First, you can choose /Style Numeric Format Reset and cancel all format settings for a cell block that you define. Second, you can reformat a cell by choosing /Style Numeric Format and then selecting a new format option. When you reformat a cell, Quattro Pro overwrites and replaces the original format with the new format.

When you reformat a cell, Quattro Pro sometimes displays a value that doesn't make sense. When you format the value 50 using the Currency option with two decimal places, for example, Quattro Pro displays the value $50.00. If you reformat this value using the Percent option with 2 decimal places, Quattro Pro displays 5000%. You may have to edit the value to create the correct display.

5 — FORMATTING DATA

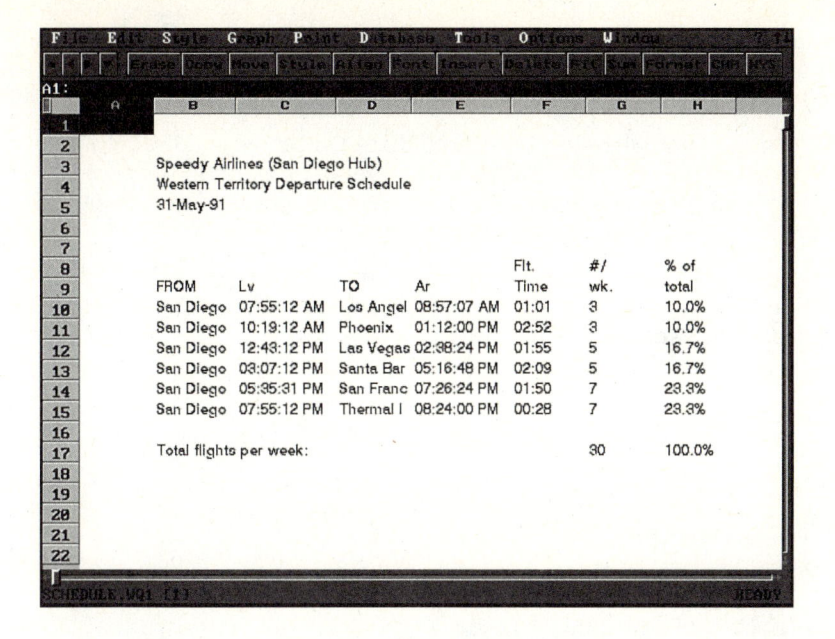

Fig. 5.9

A spreadsheet with numeric formats.

Protecting Important Data

The process of protecting a spreadsheet involves two operations: global spreadsheet protection and individual cell protection. To protect cells from change, the global protection and the individual cell protection settings must be on.

By default, all cells on a Quattro Pro spreadsheet are in protected mode, but the setting for spreadsheet protection is disabled. Use the /**O**ptions **P**rotection command to enable or disable global spreadsheet protection.

Protecting Spreadsheet Cells

Quattro Pro does not enable you to edit, replace, or delete entries from protected cells. You also cannot delete a column or row containing a protected cell. You can erase the entire spreadsheet, however, even if the spreadsheet contains protected cells.

To protect a block of cells, follow these steps:

1. Preselect the block of cells.
2. Choose /**S**tyle **P**rotection.
3. Choose **P**rotect.

Quattro Pro protects the preselected cell block. When you use /**O**ptions **P**rotection **E**nable to turn protection on, Quattro Pro displays PR on the input line for every protected cell that you make active.

Remember that when global spreadsheet protection is disabled using /**O**ptions **P**rotection **D**isable, you can overwrite data on the spreadsheet, regardless of the individual protection status of the spreadsheet cells.

Quattro Pro displays an error message if you attempt to alter the contents of a protected cell. Press Esc to cancel the error message and return to the active spreadsheet.

Unprotecting Spreadsheet Cells

To remove cell protection from a block of cells, follow these steps:

1. Preselect the block of cells.
2. Choose /**S**tyle **P**rotection.
3. Choose **U**nprotect.

Quattro Pro removes protection from the preselected cell block. When you use /**S**tyle **P**rotection to unprotect a cell, Quattro Pro displays U on the input line when you make that cell active.

> **TIP** Quattro Pro makes locating unprotected cells easy because the program always displays the contents of unprotected cells in a bright cyan color on a color monitor and in high intensity on a monochrome monitor. You may have to adjust the foreground and background intensity knobs on a monochrome monitor to see this display.

Using Global Formula Protection

You can protect important spreadsheet formulas from being altered by assigning a password to the spreadsheet. After you assign a password, the only way you can edit cells containing formulas is by reentering the password to remove the protection.

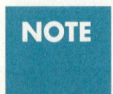

> **NOTE** When you password-protect spreadsheet formulas without enabling global spreadsheet protection, you can change labels or values on the spreadsheet.

To assign formula protection to your spreadsheet, follow these steps:

1. Choose /Options Protection Formulas Add.
2. Type a password.

   Remember this password because you will need it to remove formula protection so that you can edit cells containing formulas.
3. Press Enter.
4. When prompted to verify the password, retype it and press Enter. (If you type a different password the second time, you see the message Passwords do not match. Press Esc and repeat the entire procedure again.)

> **NOTE** Passwords are case-sensitive. You must reenter them exactly as you originally entered them. If you enter a password in all lowercase letters, reenter it the same way.

After you protect formulas in your spreadsheet, any user who tries to edit a formula will receive the message Formula protection is enabled. Formula protection also prevents users from performing other operations that can overwrite the cell, such as Copy, Move, or Insert.

To remove formula protection from the spreadsheet, follow these steps:

1. Choose /Options Protection Formulas Remove.
2. When prompted, type the password.

Quattro Pro removes the protection. If you close the file without saving it, however, formula protection is reinstated.

Working with Columns and Rows

The middle group of commands on the Style menu are column adjustment commands. You can use these commands to change the width of a column or a block of columns and to hide a group of columns on the active spreadsheet.

Four column-adjustment commands are on the Style menu: Column Width, Reset Width, Hide Column, and Block Size. Column Width widens and narrows the current column; Reset Width returns the active column back to the default column width; Hide Column removes a selected group of columns from display; and Block Size performs operations on a block of columns and rows.

PART I — USING QUATTRO PRO SPREADSHEETS

Setting the Width of a Column

Quattro Pro enables you to set the width of an individual column using the /Style Column Width command. Valid column widths range from 1 to 254 characters. To widen or narrow the width of a column, follow these steps:

1. Place the cell selector in a target column.

2. Choose /Style Column Width.

3. Type the number of the desired width (the default is 9) and then press Enter.

Quattro Pro adjusts the width of the active column to the number of characters you specify. After you change the width of a column, Quattro Pro displays the new width in brackets on the input line. [W12], for example, indicates a column width of 12.

> **TIP** Ctrl-W is the default shortcut for the /Style Column Width command.

Setting the Width with the Arrow Keys

Sometimes estimating the appropriate width for a column is difficult. If you are unsure about which width to use, you can use the following adjustment technique:

1. Place the cell selector in a target column.

2. Choose /Style Column Width.

3. Press the right-arrow key to widen or the left-arrow key to narrow the target column.

4. Press Enter when you create a visually acceptable width.

Setting the Width with a Mouse

If you have a mouse, you easily can change the width of a column by following these steps:

1. Click the target column's letter at the top of the spreadsheet.

2. Drag the column letter to the right to widen the column or left to narrow the column.

3. Release the mouse button when you attain the ideal width.

5 — FORMATTING DATA

If you click the Fit button on the READY mode SpeedBar, Quattro Pro widens or narrows the active column to accommodate the largest cell entry in that column. Clicking the Fit button duplicates the /Style Block Size Auto Width command.

Setting the Width in a Window Pane

The capability to split a spreadsheet into two window panes presents an interesting possibility for column widths, because with the /Style Column Width command, you can change column widths independently in either window pane.

If you split a window into two vertical or horizontal panes, for example, you can choose different widths for the same column in each pane. When you close a split window, however, Quattro Pro retains only those changes made to columns in the top (horizontal split) or left (vertical split) pane.

> **TIP**
> Press F6 to switch between panes in a split window.

Resetting a Column's Width

Use the /Style Reset Width command to reset the width of an adjusted column to its default setting. Follow these steps:

1. Place the cell selector in the target column.
2. Choose /Style Reset Width.

Quattro Pro resets the width of the active column to nine characters (unless you change the default width using /Options Formats Global Width, described in the "Changing the Default Global Settings" section). After you reset the width of a column, Quattro Pro erases from the input line the brackets containing the preceding width.

> **TIP**
> You can change the default global column width by choosing /Options Formats Global Width and typing a new width value.

Working with Multiple Columns

Use the /**S**tyle **B**lock Size command to set the width of multiple columns. When you choose this command, Quattro Pro displays four choices on the submenu; the first three operate on columns. Choose **S**et Width to assign a width to multiple columns or **R**eset Width to reset multiple columns to the default width.

The third command, **A**uto Width, performs a special block operation. Use this command to adjust the width of a block of columns according to the longest entry in each column. The fourth command, **H**eight, controls row height.

Setting the Width of a Block of Columns

Use the **S**et Width command to set the width of multiple columns in a block. Follow these steps:

1. Preselect the columns in the target block.
2. Choose /**S**tyle **B**lock Size **S**et Width.
3. Type any number from 1 to 254, or use the left- or right-arrow key to indicate the width on-screen.
4. Press Enter.

Quattro Pro adjusts each column included in the block to the specified width.

To reset the width of all columns in a block, follow these steps:

1. Choose /**S**tyle **B**lock Size **R**eset Width. Quattro Pro prompts you for the block to adjust.
2. Specify the block to adjust by highlighting the block or by typing the block address on the input line.

Quattro Pro resets the width of all columns in the block to the default value. Initially, the default column width is nine, but you can change this width using the /**O**ptions **F**ormats **G**lobal Width command.

Automatically Setting the Width of a Block of Columns

Figure 5.10 shows what the spreadsheet in figure 5.9 looks like before widening the column widths from 9 to 12 characters. Notice that asterisks appear in cell B5 and in columns C and E. The asterisks appear

5 — FORMATTING DATA   191

because the chosen numeric format creates a display wider than the width of the column. Look at the input line at the top of the spreadsheet to see that cell B5's data is intact.

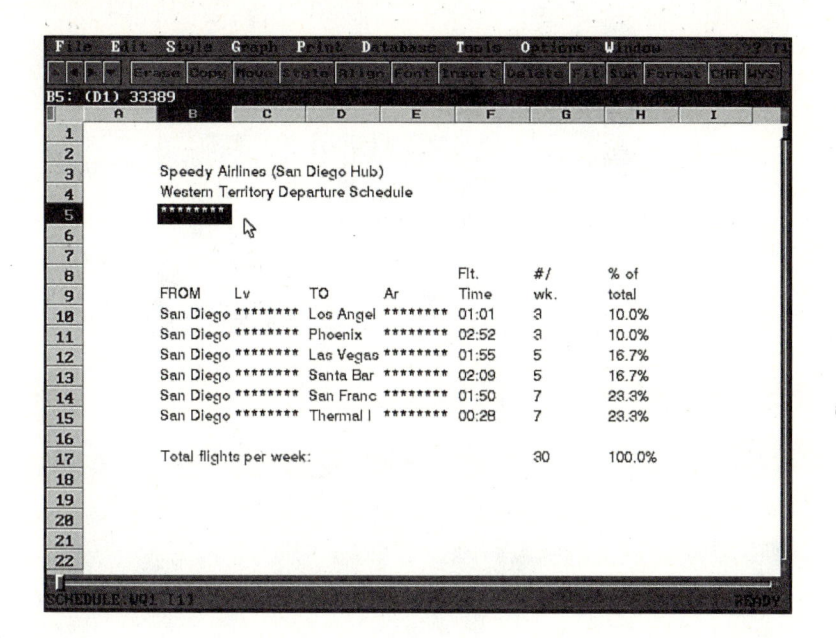

Fig. 5.10

A spreadsheet before column widths accommodate long numbers.

The **A**uto Width command provides yet another way to set your spreadsheet column widths. This command is particularly useful when the column data has a similar width—like a date or time serial number—because the command enables you to create a width quickly that accommodates the common length.

To use the **A**uto Width command to adjust column widths, follow these steps:

1. Preselect cell block B8..H17.

2. Choose /**S**tyle **B**lock Size **A**uto Width.

3. When prompted, press Enter to add an extra space to the longest entry in each column (see fig. 5.11).

You may specify from 0 to 40 extra spaces to add to the longest label or value when you choose this command. Normally, allowing 1 to 3 extra spaces creates enough distance between columns for you to see your data. Figure 5.12 shows the spreadsheet with auto-adjusted columns.

PART I — USING QUATTRO PRO SPREADSHEETS

Fig. 5.11

One space added to the longest entry in each column to determine column width.

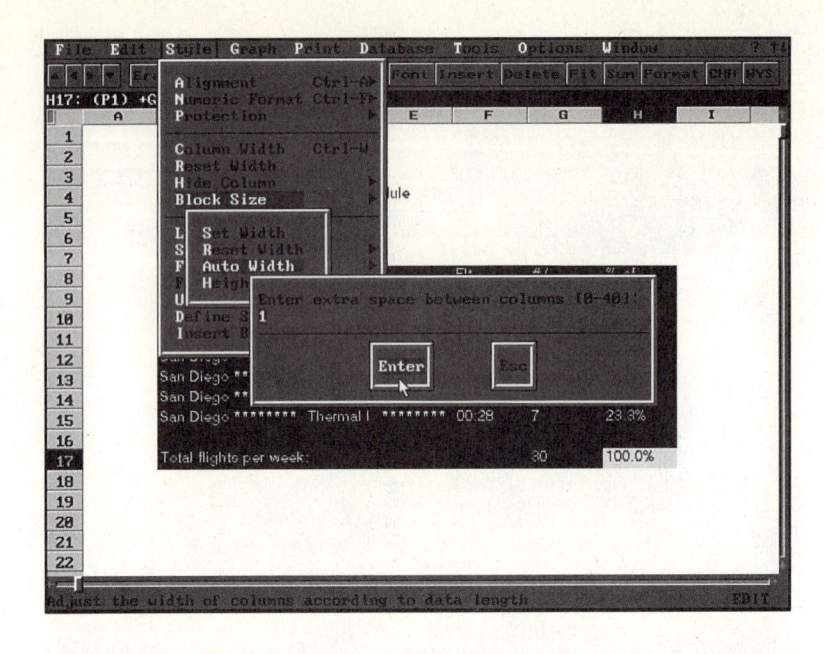

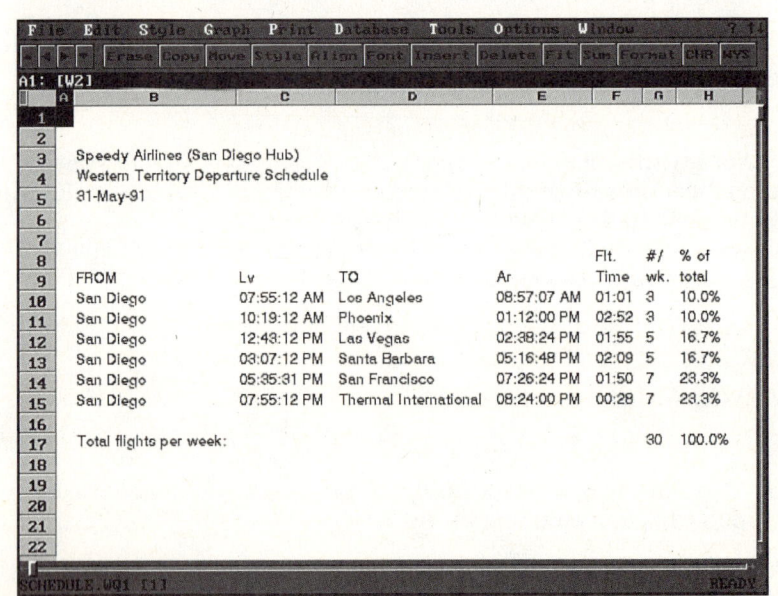

Fig. 5.12

The auto-adjusted spreadsheet.

When looking for the longest entry, Quattro Pro examines the first row and all cells following that row. The program then resets the widths of the columns according to the following formula: length of longest entry in the block + extra characters.

5 — FORMATTING DATA

If the longest entry is 10 characters long and you specified 2 extra spaces, for example, Quattro Pro sets the width of the column to 12.

If your spreadsheet contains an entry that is substantially longer than any other entry, preselect a cell block that does not include this entry. If you are working with the spreadsheet in figure 5.10, for example, you do not want to include the 37-character label in cell B4 in the cell block.

If the long entry appears in the middle of the spreadsheet, perform two auto-adjustment operations: one on the block above and one on the block below the long entry.

> **TIP**
>
> Sometimes using the **A**uto Width command pushes the right edge of the active spreadsheet out of view. If this happens, you can fine-tune the widths of individual columns using /**S**tyle **C**olumn Width until you achieve the appropriate display. To display the spreadsheet appearing in figure 5.12, for example, the width of column A is changed to 2.

Hiding a Column

Quattro Pro enables you to hide and reveal columns of data temporarily using the /**S**tyle **H**ide Column command. This command enables you to prevent unauthorized viewing of proprietary data. When you hide a column, Quattro Pro retains the column data in memory so that you can reveal the column.

Hiding Data in Columns

To hide columns from view, follow these steps:

1. Preselect the target column(s).
2. Choose /**S**tyle **H**ide Column.
3. Choose **H**ide from the submenu.
4. Press Enter to hide the target column(s).

When Quattro Pro hides columns, your spreadsheet looks as though the target columns are erased and the bordering columns are connected. In other words, Quattro Pro does not reletter the column names when you execute this command. Instead, the program joins the bordering columns to the right and left of the hidden columns so that no blank areas are on the spreadsheet.

PART I — USING QUATTRO PRO SPREADSHEETS

> **T I P**
>
> The **Hide Column** command creates an interesting screen effect similar to a vertical window split. Figure 5.13 illustrates how hiding columns F through P produces a split window effect without the annoying vertical border from the second pane.

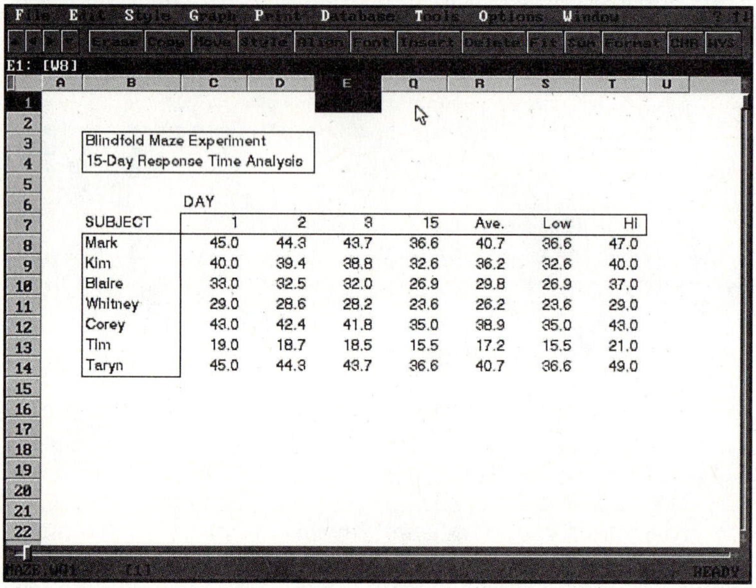

Fig. 5.13

The **H**ide Column command causes a split-window effect.

Quattro Pro keeps hidden only those columns initially hidden on the top and left panes when you clear the window. Quattro Pro does not include hidden columns on the printout of a spreadsheet.

Displaying Hidden Data in Columns

To display hidden columns, follow these steps:

1. Choose **/S**tyle **H**ide Column **E**xpose. Quattro Pro reveals hidden columns with asterisks (*) next to the column letters.

2. Type a cell address or cell block address that includes the columns you want to expose.

3. Press Enter to display the hidden columns.

Quattro Pro removes the asterisks and rehides columns that you choose not to expose when you execute this command.

The use of certain menu commands, such as /**E**dit **M**ove and /**E**dit **C**opy, causes Quattro Pro to display temporarily all hidden columns on the active spreadsheet. When you finish executing the command, Quattro Pro hides the columns again.

> **T I P**
>
> If you preselect a cell block that contains hidden columns before executing a **S**tyle menu command, Quattro Pro enhances the cells in the hidden columns. If you preselect cell block C7..T7 in figure 5.13 and then choose /**S**tyle **L**ine Drawing **O**utside, for example, Quattro Pro also draws lines around cell block F7..P7, the area hidden in this figure.

Setting the Height of a Row

You can set the height of an individual row with the /**S**tyle **B**lock Size **H**eight command. Quattro Pro rows are measured by point size, unlike columns, which are measured by character widths. In general, Quattro Pro makes the default height of a row slightly taller than the largest point size used on that row. Valid row heights range from a point size of 1 to 240, with a default setting of 15.

When you format a cell using a font with a large point size and then manually shorten the row height of that cell's row, Quattro Pro may truncate data that you enter into the cell. When this happens, you can adjust the height of the row containing truncated data.

To raise or lower the height of a row, follow these steps:

1. Place the cell selector in a target row.
2. Choose /**S**tyle **B**lock Size **H**eight **S**et Row Height.
3. Type the number of the desired height (the default is 15) and press Enter.

Quattro Pro adjusts the height of the active row to the point size you specify.

Setting the Row Height with the Arrow Keys

Sometimes estimating the appropriate height for a row is difficult. If you are unsure about a height setting, use the following adjustment technique:

1. Place the cell selector in a target row.
2. Choose /**S**tyle **B**lock Size **H**eight **S**et Row Height.
3. Press the up-arrow key to raise or the down-arrow key to lower the target row.
4. Press Enter when you find an acceptable height.

Setting the Row Height with a Mouse

If you have a mouse, you easily can change the height of a row by doing the following:

1. Click the target row's number at the left edge of the spreadsheet.
2. Drag the row number up to raise the row or down to lower the row.
3. Release the mouse button when you attain the ideal height.

Setting the Row Height in a Window Pane

Changing row height in a split window is like changing it with columns. With the /**S**tyle **B**lock Size **H**eight **S**et Row Height command, you can change column widths independently in either window pane.

If you split a window into two vertical or horizontal panes, for example, you can choose different heights for the same row in each pane. When you close a split window, however, Quattro Pro retains only those changes made to rows in the top (horizontal split) or left (vertical split) pane.

Resetting a Row's Height

You can use the /**S**tyle **B**lock Size **H**eight **R**eset Row Height command to reset the height of an adjusted row to its default setting. To do so, follow these steps:

1. Place the cell selector in the target row.
2. Choose /**S**tyle **B**lock Size **H**eight **R**eset Row Height.

Quattro Pro resets the height of the active row to a point size slightly larger than the tallest font in the row.

Although Quattro Pro has no command to change the default global row height, you can change the height by selecting a large point size for the default font (Font 1) using the /**S**tyle **F**ont **E**dit Fonts **1** **P**oint Size command.

Figure 5.14 shows that when you vary the point size of a font—Bitstream Swiss in this case—Quattro Pro adjusts the row height so that the font fits on that row.

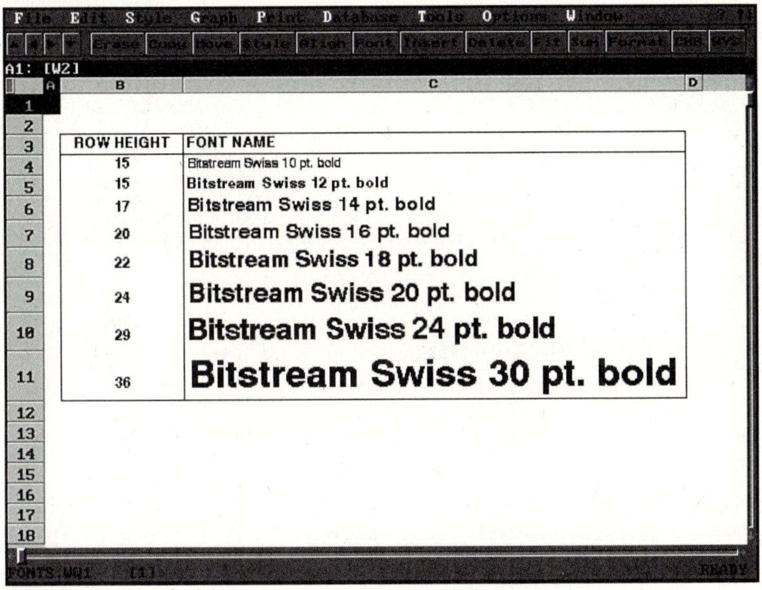

Fig. 5.14

Large point size fonts require correspondingly high row heights.

Make sure to choose /**S**tyle **F**ont**T**able **U**pdate so that Quattro Pro uses the new default font for all future spreadsheets.

Working with Multiple Rows

You also can use the /**S**tyle **B**lock **S**ize **H**eight command to set the height of multiple rows. Choose **S**et Row Height to assign a height to multiple rows or **R**eset Row Height to reset multiple rows to the default height.

Setting the Height of a Block of Rows

You can use the **S**et Row Height command to set the height of multiple rows in a block. To do so, follow these steps:

1. Preselect the rows in the target block.

2. Choose /**S**tyle **B**lock Size **H**eight **S**et Row Height.

3. Type any number from 1 to 240, or use the up- or down-arrow key to indicate the height on-screen.

4. Press Enter.

Quattro Pro adjusts each row included in the block to the specified height.

Recall that preselecting a cell block is just one of three ways to tell Quattro Pro about the spreadsheet area that you want to affect. Examples of using the two other methods—highlighting the cell block or typing the cell block address—appear next.

To reset the height of all rows in a block, follow these steps:

1. Choose /**S**tyle **B**lock Size **H**eight **R**eset Row Height. Quattro Pro prompts you for the block to adjust.

2. Specify the block to adjust by highlighting the block or by typing the block address on the input line.

Quattro Pro resets the height of all rows in the block to one slightly larger than the largest font in that row. If a font is too large to fit inside the default row height, increase the row height or reduce the font size with the /**S**tyle **F**ont **E**dit Fonts command.

Automatically Setting the Height of a Block of Rows

In WYSIWYG display mode, Quattro Pro automatically manages spreadsheet row height for you. When you add a font with a large point size to a spreadsheet, for example, Quattro Pro adjusts the height of the current row to accommodate the new font.

Unlike the default column width, the default height of a row is determined by the point size of the font on each row. As mentioned earlier, Quattro Pro makes the default height of a row slightly taller than the largest point size on that row. If row 2 uses a 14-point font, for example, Quattro Pro sets the default height of that row to at least 14 points. In some cases, Quattro Pro establishes a default row height that is a few points larger than the font point size so that you can see all text on a line.

NOTE You already know that Quattro Pro's default spreadsheet font (Bitstream Swiss-SC 12-point) requires a row height with a point size equal to 15. Because the program can use virtually hundreds of fonts—including the Bitstream and Bitstream-SC fonts that arrive with your Quattro Pro package and those available from third-party vendors—no cut-and-dried rule of thumb exists for determining the exact default row height point size that Quattro Pro requires for a particular font.

As with column widths, Quattro Pro saves all custom row heights with the spreadsheet when you choose the /File Save command. A word of caution: if you shrink the height of a row below the default height, Quattro Pro truncates the text on that row. Use the Set Row Height command to enlarge the row height and reveal the top portion of the truncated text.

Selecting Presentation-Quality Options

The last group of commands on the Style menu are the presentation-quality commands for adding stylistic enhancements to your spreadsheets. You can draw lines and boxes, add shading to cells, include multiple fonts, and add bullets. You also can assign style attributes directly to fonts, create and save customized spreadsheet styles, and insert page breaks to help control spreadsheet printing.

Previewing Enhancements

In WYSIWYG display mode, you can see on a spreadsheet all Style menu enhancements as soon as you add them to a cell. Quattro Pro immediately shows new data alignments, numeric formats, unprotected cells, column widths, hidden columns, drawn lines, and shading effects after you add them to a spreadsheet.

Spreadsheet enhancements such as custom font typefaces and cell bulleting also display immediately on a spreadsheet. If you are in text display mode, you do not have immediate "presentation-quality" display. In this case, Quattro Pro gives you an alternate feature to preview all of your spreadsheet enhancements before you print a spreadsheet.

PART I — USING QUATTRO PRO SPREADSHEETS

To use Quattro Pro's Screen Preview feature, follow these steps:

1. Preselect a cell block on the active spreadsheet that you want to preview.

2. Choose /**P**rint **B**lock. Quattro Pro displays the cell block address at the right margin of the **P**rint menu, next to the **B**lock command.

3. Choose **D**estination and then select the **S**creen Preview option. Quattro Pro returns you to the **P**rint menu.

4. Choose **S**preadsheet Print. Quattro Pro displays your spreadsheet on-screen, complete with its presentation-quality settings.

If your computer does not have a graphics display system, you cannot use the Screen Preview facility. You must print out a spreadsheet to review the look of your presentation-quality settings. (See Chapter 9, "Printing," for a complete discussion of printing in Quattro Pro.)

Drawing Lines and Boxes

You can add lines to a spreadsheet in the following three ways: enter a repeating hyphen into a cell so that the hyphens fill the cell, use the | symbol for vertical lines, or use the commands on Quattro Pro's Line Drawing menu.

Quattro Pro uses graphic imaging to form the lines and boxes on a spreadsheet. Instead of drawing lines in cells, therefore, the program actually adds the graphics image between cells on a spreadsheet.

To use the /**S**tyle **L**ine Drawing command to draw single, double, or thick lines and boxes around your spreadsheet cell data, follow these steps:

1. Preselect a block of cells.

2. Choose /**S**tyle **L**ine Drawing.

3. Choose a placement option from the Placement submenu (see table 5.5).

4. Choose a line type from the Line types submenu. (Your choices are **N**one, **S**ingle, **D**ouble, and **T**hick.)

5. Choose **Q**uit to exit the Placement submenu and return to the spreadsheet.

Table 5.5 Line Placement Options

Option	Description
All	Draws a box around the target cell block and adds vertical and horizontal lines between all cells
Outside	Draws a box around the target cell block
Top	Draws a horizontal line on top of the first row in the target cell block
Bottom	Draws a horizontal line below the last row in the target cell block
Left	Draws a vertical line along the left edge of the leftmost column in the target cell block
Right	Draws a vertical line along the right edge of the rightmost column of the target cell block
Inside	Draws vertical and horizontal lines between all cells in the target cell block
Horizontal	Draws lines between each row in the target cell block; does nothing if the target cell block contains only one row
Vertical	Draws lines between each column in the block; does nothing if the target cell block contains only one column
Quit	Returns to the spreadsheet without making any changes

Erasing Lines and Boxes

To remove all lines and boxes from a spreadsheet, follow these steps:

1. Preselect the cell block containing the lines or boxes (the cell block you originally selected as the target cell block).

2. Choose /**S**tyle **L**ine Drawing.

3. Choose the **A**ll placement option.

4. Choose the **N**one type option.

PART I — USING QUATTRO PRO SPREADSHEETS

T I P Quattro Pro enables you to partially remove lines from a spreadsheet. To remove the bottom line from a box, for example, highlight the target cell block and choose /**S**tyle Line Drawing **B**ottom None. To remove the top line, choose /**S**tyle Line Drawing **T**op and None.

Printing Lines and Boxes

You can print a spreadsheet containing lines and boxes in draft or graphics mode. In draft mode, Quattro Pro uses +, –, and the lowercase letter l to print lines and boxes. In graphics mode, Quattro Pro uses graphics characters to print smooth lines and boxes.

To print in graphics mode, set the /**P**rint Destination setting to **G**raphics Printer. (See Chapter 9 for information about printing.)

Figure 5.15 shows how adding lines to Speedy Airline's report highlights the arrival and departure data.

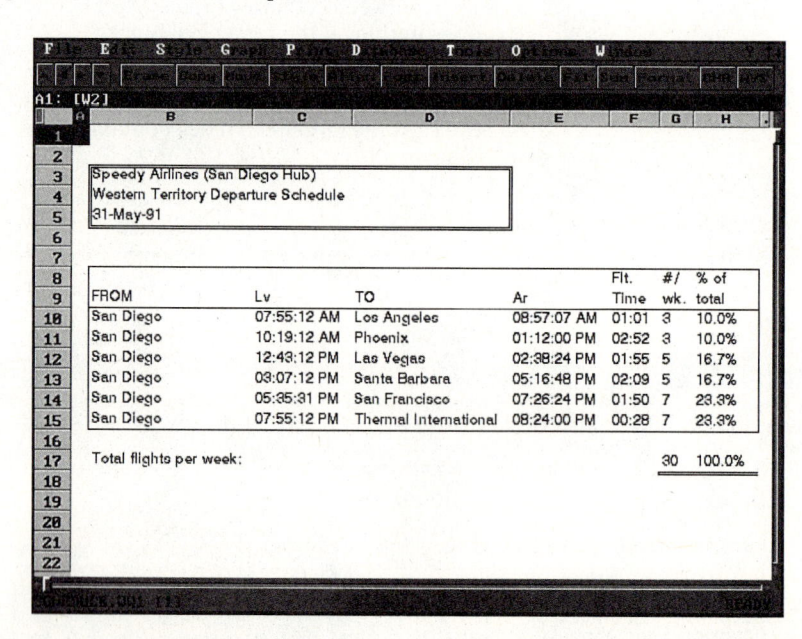

Fig. 5.15

Lines and boxes added to the Speedy Airlines report.

> **TIP**
>
> Drawn lines occasionally spill over off-screen when you add them to a row or column that is not entirely visible in the spreadsheet area. To create the spreadsheet display shown in figure 5.15, for example, you must reduce the width of columns A and I to 2. Quattro Pro attaches lines to the cell to the left for vertical and the cell below for horizontal; therefore, you may need to increase the print block if your bottom and/or right edge lines are not printing.

Shading Cell Data for Effect

Use the /**S**tyle **S**hading command to shade spreadsheet cells. With this command, you can shade in grey or black. The most common applications for cell shading are to indicate a data input area and to point out a block of protected cells.

To shade an area of a spreadsheet, follow these steps:

1. Preselect a block of cells to shade.
2. Choose /**S**tyle **S**hading.
3. Choose a shade option from the **S**hading submenu.

Quattro Pro displays the target cells with shading. When you use the **G**rey shading option, notice that the entire cell is colored grey rather than only the data. On a monochrome screen, black shading appears as boldface.

> **TIP**
>
> You can change the color of the shading with the /**O**ptions **C**olors **S**preadsheet **S**hading command. To change the color of text, use the /**S**tyle **F**ont **C**olor command.

To print shaded cells, you first must choose the /**P**rint **D**estination **G**raphics Printer command to tell Quattro Pro to print in graphics mode. If you don't choose this command, Quattro Pro does not print the shaded cells.

When you shade cells bordered by drawn lines, Quattro Pro sometimes overlaps the lines, but this is only an on-screen effect. When you print the spreadsheet, Quattro Pro properly encloses the shading in the lined cells.

PART I — USING QUATTRO PRO SPREADSHEETS

Figure 5.16 shows how adding cell shading to cell B5 and cell blocks C10..C15 and E10..E15 makes important data stand out on a report.

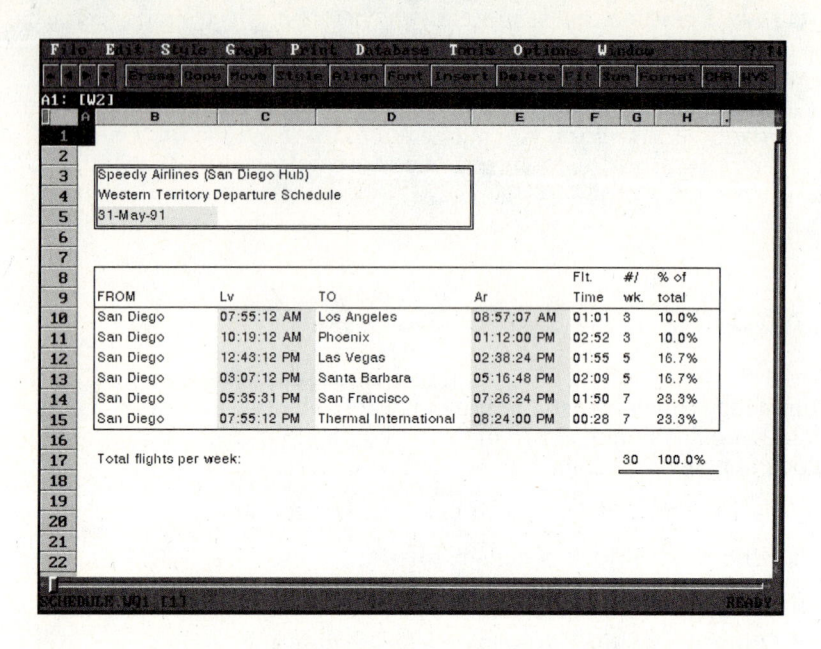

Fig. 5.16

Cell shading added to the Speedy Airlines report.

Selecting Fonts

Quattro Pro provides two methods for selecting fonts for your spreadsheets: you can select fonts and their display attributes "on the fly" (spontaneously) or choose from a list of eight predefined fonts.

Use the /**S**tyle **F**ont command to select a font typeface and its display attributes (point size, color, boldface, italics, and underline) and then apply the font to a spreadsheet. Selecting fonts "on the fly" enables you to experiment with an unlimited number of different fonts and font attributes in WYSIWYG display mode until you find the most appropriate look for a spreadsheet. Figure 5.17 shows examples of the built-in fonts that you can add to your Quattro Pro spreadsheets.

In WYSIWYG display mode, the /**S**tyle **F**ont command affects the fonts that Quattro Pro uses for printing and for screen display. Quattro Pro also displays a spreadsheet's custom font options when you use the **S**creen Preview command on the **P**rint menu. (See Chapter 9 for complete coverage of the **P**rint menu.)

5 — FORMATTING DATA

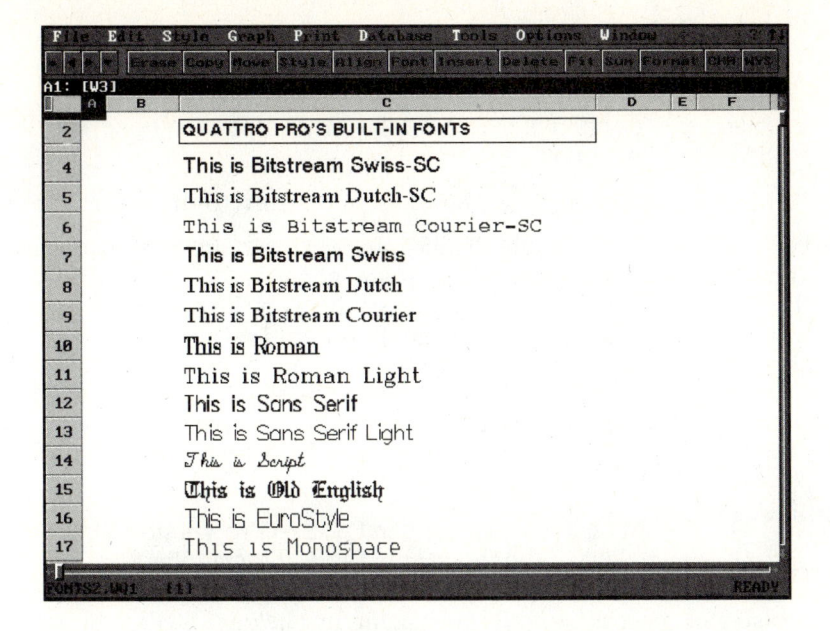

Fig. 5.17

Built-in fonts you can apply to spreadsheets.

Use the /**S**tyle Font**T**able command to add a predefined font to a spreadsheet. With Quattro Pro you can use up to eight predefined fonts in any one spreadsheet. (See "Customizing Predefined Fonts" later in this chapter for more information about using the /**S**tyle Font**T**able command.)

NOTE Periodically, Quattro Pro pauses to build fonts—for example, when you add a font that was not built during a recent work session. When Quattro Pro builds fonts, you must wait a few moments until the program is finished before you can continue with the current work session.

If you do not want Quattro Pro to build fonts and interrupt your work sessions, choose /**O**ptions **G**raphics Quality and then **D**raft from the submenu. If you want Quattro Pro to build fonts on an as-needed basis so that you can immediately display them in your spreadsheets, however, select the **F**inal option from the submenu.

Selecting a Different Font

To assign a new font to a cell block on a spreadsheet, follow these steps:

1. Preselect the target cell block.
2. Choose /**S**tyle Font.
3. Select the font typeface and display attributes from the options listed on the menu.
4. Choose **Q**uit to apply the new font and return to the spreadsheet.

When you apply fonts in text display mode, you do not see any changes in the spreadsheet. To verify the font you chose for a cell, make that cell active and review the font code displayed on the input line. If you see [F2], for example, you have customized this cell using font #2. Font codes correspond to the numbers displayed on the predefined fonts list, which Quattro Pro displays when you choose the /Style FontTable command. Quattro Pro does not display a font code on the input line for the default font or fonts added with the /Style Font command.

NOTE The /**S**tyle Font command in Quattro Pro Version 3.0 is equivalent to the /**S**tyle FontTable command in Version 4.0.

You also can access the /**S**tyle Font menu by clicking the Font button on the READY mode SpeedBar and then highlighting the block. Remember, if you highlight the block before clicking the Font button, you need to select only the font attributes to apply them.

Adding Bullets

Quattro Pro has a special stylistic feature called *bulleting* that enables you to add bullets and boxes to your spreadsheets. You cannot find this option anywhere on a Quattro Pro menu. To use this option, you must enter a special code into a spreadsheet cell.

To create a bullet, enter the following code into the cell in which you want the bullet to appear:

'\bullet #\ where # = the bullet style number (0-6)

To enter a bullet into a cell by itself, precede the bullet code with a label prefix ('). If you don't, Quattro Pro interprets the first \ as a repeating label prefix and repeats the entry in the cell. To specify a bullet style, choose one of the numbers that appears in table 5.6.

5 — FORMATTING DATA

Table 5.6 Bullet Character Code Designations

Number	Description
0	Box
1	Filled box
2	Checked box
3	Check
4	Shadowed box (3-D)
5	Shadowed, checked box (3-D)
6	Filled circle

When you are in WYSIWYG display mode, Quattro Pro instantly shows the bullet graphic on the spreadsheet. When in text display mode, however, you see only the bullet code in the spreadsheet cell. When you print a spreadsheet containing a bullet code, Quattro Pro reveals the bullet character instead of the code.

In text mode, you can review how the bullet character looks on-screen by choosing /**P**rint **B**lock and typing the address of a cell block to print. Next, set the /**P**rint **D**estination command to **S**creen Preview and choose **S**preadsheet Print.

You also can include bullet characters in a Quattro Pro graph using the graph annotator. (See Chapter 11, "Customizing Graphs," for complete coverage of graph annotation.)

> **TIP**
> You may press Alt-F5 to remove a bullet code immediately after you enter the code into a spreadsheet cell. If the bullet code does not appear when you print or preview the spreadsheet, widen that column until the code appears.

Figure 5.18 shows the final, presentation-quality version of the Speedy Airlines spreadsheet. Note the addition of custom fonts to the report title and to the data labels in rows 8 and 9. This spreadsheet also contains bullet graphics in column A.

208 PART I — USING QUATTRO PRO SPREADSHEETS

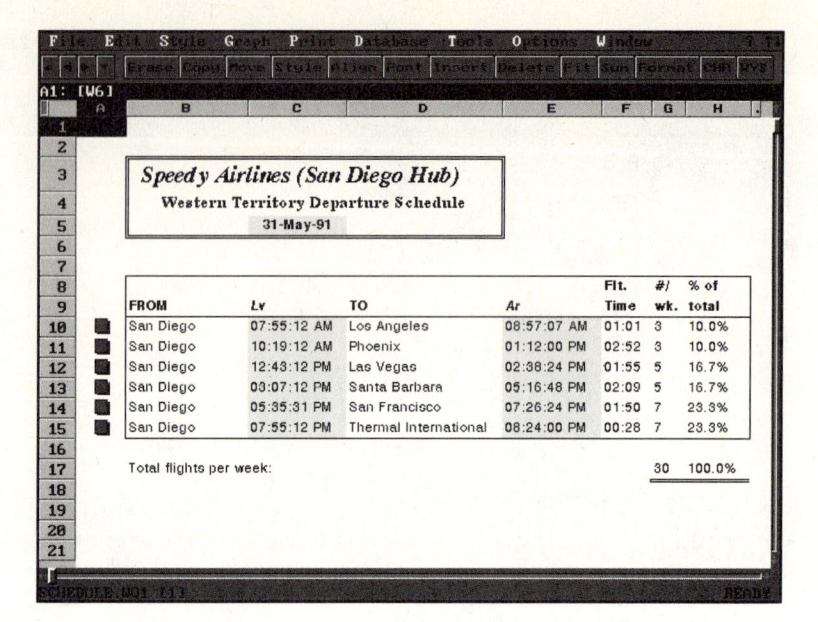

Fig. 5.18

The final presentation-quality version of the Speedy Airlines spreadsheet.

Using Custom Spreadsheet Styles

Quattro Pro Version 4.0 offers custom style management features to help you easily create top-notch presentations and business reports. As you know, you can apply font style attributes "on the fly" using the /**S**tyle **F**ont command. If you like the look of a particular combination of font style attributes, then you should name that combination as a custom style. You quickly can apply custom styles to other parts of the same spreadsheet or to other spreadsheet files that you open into memory. This process saves you the time of re-creating the font style by reselecting commands.

Custom styles can include other style attributes, though. You can create a custom style that includes drawn lines, a label alignment, cell shading, and numeric formats. You can create up to 120 unique custom styles per spreadsheet. When you have to produce several documents with similar style attributes, you will enjoy the easy-to-use, time-saving nature of custom styles.

Using Custom Styles

The /**S**tyle **D**efine Style command offers all the options necessary for creating and managing custom style definitions that you can use to format the current spreadsheet (see table 5.7). The **D**efine Style command options enable you to erase and remove custom styles from the current spreadsheet. One option enables you to create style files that can contain all of your favorite custom styles. Style files have a STY file name extension and can be retrieved for use in formatting any spreadsheet open in Quattro Pro's memory.

Table 5.7 Define Style Options

Option	Description
Create	Creates a new style or edits an existing one
Erase	Clears a custom style from a spreadsheet, leaving the character formatting intact (except font and data-entry attributes)
Remove	Deletes the custom style from the spreadsheet; blocks previously assigned this style retain their character formatting (except font and data-entry attributes)
File	Saves and retrieves custom style files

Creating a Custom Style

To assign a name to a group of style attributes that you have already applied to a spreadsheet, follow these steps:

1. Select the block containing the style attributes to be named.

2. Choose /**S**tyle **D**efine Style **C**reate.

3. When Quattro Pro prompts you to name the style, type a name of up to 15 characters, and then press Enter.

   Quattro Pro displays a menu of style attributes you can change.

4. Double-check that the currently selected attributes are acceptable.

5. Choose **Q**uit to save the newly named custom style and return to the **S**tyle menu.

PART I — USING QUATTRO PRO SPREADSHEETS

Figure 5.19 shows a list of the named custom styles for a sample spreadsheet.

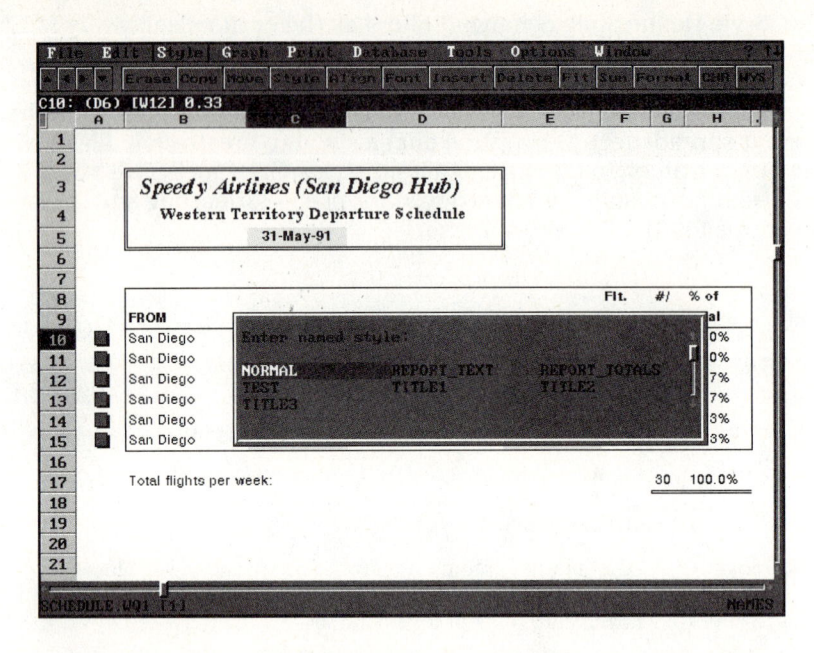

Fig. 5.19

The custom styles names for a sample spreadsheet.

If a particular combination of style attributes you want to use does not yet exist, you can create the custom style from the ground up. To do so, choose /**S**tyle **D**efine Style **C**reate. When Quattro Prompts you to name the style, type a name of up to 15 characters long and then press Enter. On the style attributes menu, select the attributes you want to appear in the new custom style. Choose **Q**uit to return to the **S**tyle menu, and then press Esc to return to the spreadsheet.

After you create a custom style, you can apply that style to the current spreadsheet using the /**S**tyle **U**se Style command.

Applying Custom Styles

To apply a custom style that you previously created, follow these steps:

1. Select the block you want to apply the style to.
2. Choose /**S**tyle **U**se Style.

    Quattro Pro displays a box listing all custom styles.

5 — FORMATTING DATA

3. Use the arrow keys to highlight the custom style you want to use, and then press Enter (or click the custom style).

Quattro Pro assigns the custom style to the block. When the cell selector is inside a block assigned a named style, the style name appears on the input line.

> **NOTE** When you apply a custom style, Quattro Pro overwrites any existing formatting in the block. If a cell is shaded and centered, for example, and you apply a style that makes the cell outlined, Quattro Pro removes the shading and alignment format prior to applying the new format.

You also can click the Style button on the READY mode SpeedBar to display a list of custom styles. To apply a style using the Style button, preselect the block you want to apply the style to, click the Style button, and then click the desired custom style.

Creating a Custom Numeric Format

In addition to the numeric formats offered on the /**S**tyle **N**umeric Format menu, Quattro Pro enables you to create custom numeric formats to further enhance the way numbers, dates, and times appear in your spreadsheets. Special codes, comprised of characters or symbols, are used to define Quattro Pro's custom numeric formats. Some examples of codes follow:

- The following code displays a number to four decimal places:

    N9.0000

    If you select this code, the number 104.8 displays as 104.8000 in your spreadsheet.

- The following code displays a date and time in the form of the day of the week the date falls on, and the time in hours, minutes, and seconds, separated by colons:

    TWeekday, H:M:S

    If you select this code, the date 1/15/92 at 5:25 and 10 seconds displays as Wednesday, 5:25.10.

To create a custom numeric format, follow these steps:

1. Choose /**S**tyle **D**efine Style **C**reate.

2. When prompted, type a name of up to 15 characters, and then press Enter.

3. Choose **N**umeric Format **U**ser Defined.

4. When prompted, enter the format code for the custom numeric format you want to display, using the symbols and syntax described in the preceding section.

5. Customize any other aspects of the style, such as **F**ont, **L**ine Drawing, **S**hading, **A**lignment, and **D**ata Entry by choosing the appropriate menu option.

6. Choose **Q**uit after you make all your desired changes.

Now, apply the custom numeric style using the /**S**tyle **U**se Style command, just as you would other custom styles.

Table 5.8 lists the special characters used to format codes. If you include any other characters as part of a defined numeric format, Quattro Pro displays them "as is" when you apply the style to a cell or block.

Table 5.8 Numeric Format Symbols

Symbol	Action
Number Format	
N	Tells Quattro Pro the code following N denotes a format for numbers, not dates or time
0	Displays the digit whether or not the number includes a digit in this position
9	Displays the digit unless the number doesn't include a digit in this position
%	Displays the number as a percentage
, (comma)	Inserts a comma for a thousands separator
. (period)	Inserts a period for a decimal separator
E+ or e+	Displays the number in scientific notation, preceding negative and positive exponents with a minus or plus sign, respectively; if the format includes at least one 0 or 9 following this symbol, Quattro Pro displays the number in scientific notation and inserts E or e; if the exponent contains more digits than 9's or 0's following this symbol, the extra digits are displayed
Date and Time Format	
T	Tells Quattro Pro the code following denotes a format for dates and times, not numbers
d or D	Displays the day of the month as a one- or two-digit number (1-31)

5 — FORMATTING DATA

Symbol	Action
dd or DD	Displays the day of the month as a two-digit number (01-31)
wday, Wday, WDAY	Displays the day of the week as a three-character abbreviation all lowercase, lowercase with the first letter capitalized, or all uppercase
weekday, Weekday, WEEKDAY	Displays the day of the week all lowercase, lowercase with the first letter capitalized, or all uppercase
m or M	Displays the month as a one- or two-digit number (1-12 for January through December), if not preceded by h, H, hh, or HH; otherwise, displays the minute as a one- or two-digit number (1-59)
mm or MM	Displays the month as a two-digit number (01-12), if not preceded by h, H, hh, or HH; otherwise, displays the minute as a two-digit number (01-59)
Mo	Displays the month as a one- or two-digit number (1-12)
MMo	Displays the month as a two-digit number (01-12)
mon, Mon, MON	Displays the month as a three-character abbreviation all lowercase, lowercase with the first letter capitalized, or all uppercase
month, Month, MONTH	Displays the name of the month all lowercase, lowercase with the first letter capitalized, or all uppercase
yy or YY	Displays the last two digits of the year (00-99)
yyyy or YYYY	Displays all four digits of the year (0001-2099)
h or H	Displays the hour as a one- or two-digit number; if the format includes ampm or AMPM, the number is between 1-12; if ampm or AMPM is not included, 24-hour format is used (0-23)
hh or HH	Displays the hour as a two-digit number; if the format includes ampm or AMPM, the number is between 01-12; if ampm or AMPM is not included, 24-hour format is used (00-23)
Mi	Displays the minute as a one- or two-digit number (1-59)
MMi	Displays the minute as a two-digit number (01-59)
s or S	Displays the second as a one- or two-digit number (1-59)

continues

Table 5.8 Continued

Symbol	Action
ss or SS	Displays the second as a two-digit number (01-59)
ampm or AMPM	Displays the time in 12-hour format with characters for morning (AM) or afternoon (PM)

Miscellaneous Format

\	Displays the next character in the format (to display a backslash, type \\)
*	Fills the column by repeating the character to the right of the asterisk, if the formatted entry is shorter than the column width
" "	Displays the characters inside the quotation marks as part or all of the cell contents

Figure 5.20 shows examples of user-defined numeric formats and the codes required to create them.

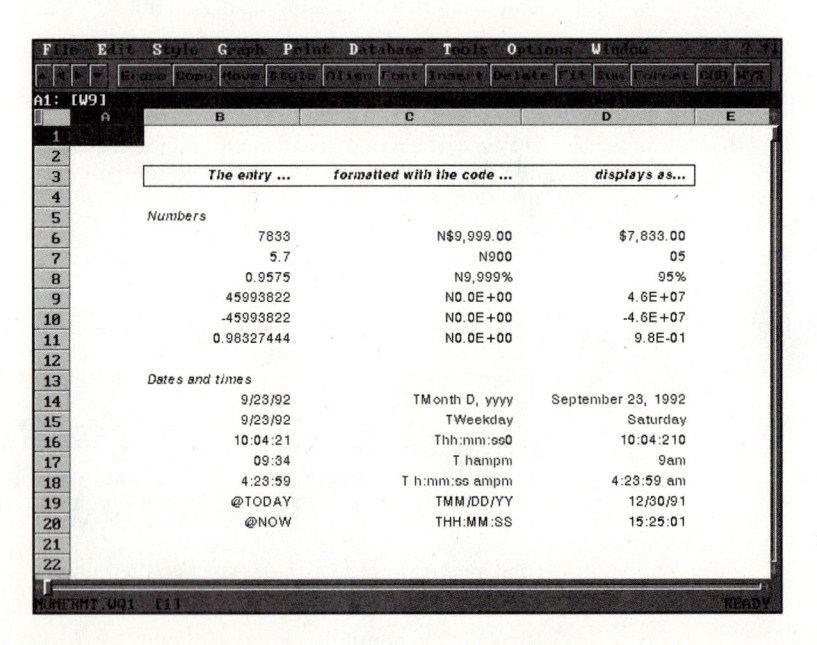

	The entry ...	formatted with the code ...	displays as...
Numbers	7833	N$9,999.00	$7,833.00
	5.7	N900	05
	0.9575	N9,999%	95%
	45993822	N0.0E+00	4.6E+07
	-45993822	N0.0E+00	-4.6E+07
	0.98327444	N0.0E+00	9.8E-01
Dates and times	9/23/92	TMonth D, yyyy	September 23, 1992
	9/23/92	TWeekday	Saturday
	10:04:21	Thh:mm:ss0	10:04:210
	09:34	T hampm	9am
	4:23:59	T h:mm:ss ampm	4:23:59 am
	@TODAY	TMM/DD/YY	12/30/91
	@NOW	THH:MM:SS	15:25:01

Fig. 5.20

Custom numeric format styles created for a sample spreadsheet.

Erasing Custom Styles from a Block

When you edit a custom style, Quattro Pro reflects those changes in all spreadsheet blocks that you previously have formatted with that custom style. To guard against this occurrence, you can erase a custom style from a spreadsheet without the block actually removing the character formatting.

To erase a custom style from a spreadsheet block, follow these steps:

1. Select the block you want to clear the custom style from.

2. Choose /**S**tyle **D**efine Style **E**rase.

Quattro Pro removes the name from the block. The style attributes remain, except for **F**ont and **D**ata Entry attributes.

Deleting Custom Styles from a Spreadsheet

You should delete custom styles that you no longer use to keep the /**S**tyle **U**se Style menu uncluttered. Deleting custom styles does not remove character formatting from your spreadsheets, but the style name no longer displays on the input line when the cell selector is in a cell formatted with the deleted custom style.

To remove a custom style name from a spreadsheet, follow these steps:

1. Choose /**S**tyle **D**efine Style **R**emove.

    Quattro Pro prompts you to select the name of the style you want to remove.

2. Highlight the style name.

    If the style is used elsewhere in the spreadsheet, Quattro Pro prompts you to confirm its deletion.

3. Choose **Y**es.

Quattro Pro deletes the custom style. Any blocks previously assigned that custom style retain their style attributes (except **F**ont and **D**ata Entry attributes), but the style name no longer appears in the list of custom styles or on the edit line when the cell selector is within the block.

Saving Custom Styles in Files

With Quattro Pro, you can save the custom styles you created for your current spreadsheet to a custom style file. You can retrieve and use these files to format other spreadsheets that you open into Quattro Pro's memory.

To save all custom styles in the current spreadsheet to a file, follow these steps:

1. Choose /**S**tyle **D**efine Style **F**ile **S**ave.

   Quattro Pro displays a list of existing style sheets and prompts you to enter a style sheet name.

2. Type the name of the style sheet—*STYLE1* for example—and then press Enter.

Quattro Pro saves the styles to a custom style sheet file with a STY file name extension. If you choose /**S**tyle **D**efine Style **F**ile **R**etrieve, STYLE1.STY appears as a custom style sheet. You now can retrieve this custom style sheet for use in formatting any spreadsheet in memory.

Retrieving a Style Sheet to the Active Spreadsheet

To retrieve a file of custom styles, follow these steps:

1. Choose /**S**tyle **D**efine Style **F**ile **R**etrieve.

   Quattro Pro prompts you to choose a style sheet.

2. Use the arrow keys to highlight the named style you want to retrieve and press Enter or click the name once with the mouse.

   Quattro Pro returns to the **D**efine Style menu.

3. Choose **Q**uit to return to the active spreadsheet.

Now you can apply any of the style sheet's named styles by selecting /**S**tyle **U**se Style, and then selecting the style's name.

Editing a Custom Style

A custom style is an ideal tool for automating the task of formatting spreadsheets with a specific group of style attributes. When your preferences in spreadsheet style change, Quattro Pro enables you to edit the style attributes for a custom style without having to re-create the style.

To change the attributes of an existing custom style, follow these steps:

1. Choose /**S**tyle **D**efine Style **C**reate.

   Quattro Pro displays a box listing all custom styles.

2. Use the cursor-movement keys to highlight the custom style you want to edit and then press Enter, or click the custom style.

   Quattro Pro displays a menu of style attributes you can change.

3. Edit the desired attributes using the same procedure that you followed for creating a custom style. Each time you change an attribute, Quattro Pro displays the main menu to show your current selections.

4. Choose **Q**uit to return to the **S**tyle menu.

When you edit a style, blocks previously assigned the style do not change. Changes to custom styles are saved with the spreadsheet.

Editing the Default Style

To customize the style Quattro Pro uses as its default style, follow these steps:

1. Choose /**S**tyle **D**efine Style **C**reate.

2. Choose NORMAL. (Because the option already is highlighted, you only need to press Enter.)

   Quattro Pro displays a menu of style attributes you can change.

3. Make any changes.

4. After you finish making changes to the style, highlight **Q**uit and then press Enter.

Quattro Pro returns to the **D**efine Style menu. Choose **Q**uit to return to the spreadsheet.

Customizing Predefined Fonts

Quattro Pro uses Bitstream Swiss-SC 12-point Black as the global default font. You can change this global setting by selecting **E**dit Fonts from the /**S**tyle Font**T**able menu. Quattro Pro uses the default font in every cell on a default spreadsheet (SHEET1.WQ1, for example).

A predefined font is much like a custom style for fonts—the predefined font groups in one location all of the font attributes you want to add to certain parts of your spreadsheets. When your preferences in font style change, Quattro Pro enables you to edit the font attributes for a pre-defined font without having to re-create the font.

To edit the typeface, point size, style, color, or other attributes for any of the fonts shown on the FontTable menu, follow these steps:

1. Choose /**S**tyle **F**ontTable.
2. Choose **E**dit Fonts.
3. Enter the number of the font you want to customize.
4. Choose **T**ypeface to change the font's typeface. Quattro Pro displays a list of 14 built-in fonts and any printer fonts that Quattro Pro includes for the printer defined with the /**O**ptions **H**ardware **P**rinters **D**efault Printer command.
5. Choose **P**oint Size to change the font's point size. Quattro Pro displays a list of 13 point sizes, ranging from 6 to 72.
6. Choose **S**tyle to change the font's style and then choose **B**old, **I**talic, **U**nderline, or **R**eset. (**R**eset returns the font to the default style.)
7. Choose **C**olor to change the font's printing color.
8. Choose **Q**uit after you finish customizing the font.

Quattro Pro displays the new custom settings for the font in the slot the original font occupied.

TIP

In WYSIWYG display mode, every change that you make to a font appears on-screen instantly. In text display mode, however, font changes do not appear on-screen, so changing the color of a font produces no visible change on your color display. Use the **C**olor option only if you own a color printer.

The printed size of the font also is not the same as on the spreadsheet. Therefore, you may need to change a column's width to accommodate all of the characters you want to print.

Certain Quattro Pro fonts support only some features available from the /**S**tyle **F**ontTable **E**dit Fonts submenu. The Bitstream Courier font, for example, does not support the **B**old option. Although Quattro Pro enables you to specify **B**old on the **E**dit Fonts submenu, the program does not boldface characters on your printouts.

5 — FORMATTING DATA   219

Choose /**S**tyle Font**T**able **R**eset to reset all fonts to Quattro Pro's default setting. Choose /**S**tyle Font**T**able **U**pdate to store all custom font definitions as the new defaults for the active spreadsheet. The next time you choose /**S**tyle Font**T**able while that spreadsheet is active, Quattro Pro displays the custom font definitions as the new defaults.

Using Page Breaks To Control Printing

Quattro Pro inserts soft page breaks in a spreadsheet according to the page length specified by the /**P**rint Layout **M**argins **P**age Length command. If you want to insert hard page breaks to further modify how a spreadsheet is printed, use the /**S**tyle Insert Break command.

Hard page breaks enable you to break one large print block into many smaller pieces. This technique is useful when you want to print a column of names and addresses on mailing labels, for example, or form-fed index cards.

Inserting a Page Break

You use the /**S**tyle Insert Break command to insert a hard page break on a spreadsheet at the location of the cell selector. To insert a hard page break, follow these steps:

1. Move the cell selector to the first cell in the row in which you want to begin a new page.
2. Choose /**S**tyle Insert Break.

Quattro Pro enters the symbol for a hard page break (¦ : :) at the specified location. Note that Quattro Pro has no soft page break symbol; the program uses the page length setting to determine normal page breaks.

> **TIP**
> To enter a page break manually, type |:: in the leftmost column of your print block. The manual page break symbol cannot be part of a left or top heading. Quattro Pro does not print data appearing on the same row as a page break.

Deleting a Page Break

To delete a page break when you want to enable Quattro Pro to manage the page break location, follow these steps:

1. Move the cell selector to the cell that contains the page break.
2. Press Del on the numeric keypad.

Quattro Pro deletes the hard page break but does not delete the inserted row.

> **TIP** Press Alt-F5 immediately after inserting a hard page break to remove it from a spreadsheet.

Questions & Answers

This chapter introduces you to Quattro Pro's cell formatting, column and row adjusting, and presentation-quality commands. If you have questions about any topic covered in this chapter, scan this section for solutions to common problems.

Controlling the Display of Your Data

Q: How do you manually edit the alignment of a number or a formula on a spreadsheet?

A: The only way to align values on a Quattro Pro spreadsheet is by using the /**S**tyle **A**lignment command. Because Quattro Pro values do not have alignment prefixes, you cannot edit their alignment while in EDIT mode.

Q: When I enter time serial numbers, why doesn't Quattro Pro display recognizable times?

A: Unless you first press Ctrl-D, Quattro Pro displays date and time serial numbers as integers. To display serial numbers as dates, choose **D**ate or **T**ime from the **N**umeric Format submenu.

Q: When I enter and then format dates, why does Quattro Pro display the wrong date?

5 — FORMATTING DATA

A: If you type a date into a cell (using hyphens or slashes) without first pressing Ctrl-D, Quattro Pro evaluates the entry as a formula. The date entry 10-09, for example, produces the value 1 when treated as a formula (10 minus 9 equals 1). When you format this cell using **D**ate, Quattro Pro sees the date serial number 1 and displays the date December 31, 1899.

Q: How do I perform mathematical operations on dates?

A: You can perform mathematical operations on dates and times just as you do on other numbers. Remember, dates and times are stored in cells as serial numbers—not as date labels.

Q: I protected cells on a spreadsheet, but Quattro Pro still enables me to write over the data in the cells. Why?

A: Turn global spreadsheet protection on with the /**O**ptions **P**rotection **E**nable command. With protection enabled, you cannot modify any cells unless they are explicitly unprotected.

Working with Columns and Rows

Q: Why does Quattro Pro display an error message when I try to delete columns and rows on my spreadsheets?

A: Turn global spreadsheet protection off with the /**O**ptions **P**rotection **D**isable command. Quattro Pro does not delete rows and columns when protected cells are on a spreadsheet and global protection is enabled.

Q: I used the /**S**tyle **B**lock Size **A**uto Width command to auto-set column widths on a spreadsheet. Now all of my columns are too wide. What can I do?

A: Your target cell block probably included a cell with a long label, such as a report title. Choose the same target block and use the **R**eset Width command to return the columns to their default width. Then try the **A**uto Width command again, excluding the cell containing the long label.

Q: I changed the global column width, but my spreadsheet columns are still the same width. Why?

A: Global column widths affect only new default spreadsheets.

Q: Why are some of my spreadsheet rows wider than others?

A: You chose a font point size that is larger than the point size Quattro Pro uses for its default row height (15). If you shrink the row height of a "wide" row, Quattro Pro may truncate the text on that row.

Selecting Presentation-Quality Options

Q: Why did nothing happen when I changed several font definitions on my spreadsheet?

A: Quattro Pro is in text display mode. In text display mode, you can review a spreadsheet cell's font setting in three ways: on-screen using /**P**rint **D**estination **S**creen Preview, on a printout using /**P**rint **D**estination **G**raphics Printer, or by making a cell active and reviewing the font code on the input line.

Although the first two methods enable you to inspect the look of a font, the third method does not. Even so, if you work with a particular font often, reviewing the font code on the input line at least enables you to verify that you used the correct font.

Q: How can I turn off spreadsheet grid lines and make that the global default for all new spreadsheets?

A: No menu command exists to set spreadsheet grid lines off and make it the global default setting, but you can do it nevertheless. Choose the /**O**ptions **C**olors **S**preadsheet **W**YSIWYG Colors **G**rid Lines command. When the coloring palette appears, highlight the color that matches the background color of your spreadsheet. (The background color is usually bright white.) Now choose /**O**ptions **U**pdate. The grid lines no longer appear on the current spreadsheet and on all future spreadsheets, because the lines are the same color as the background of your spreadsheet.

Q: Why don't my custom fonts, shading, and drawn lines look right on my spreadsheet printouts?

A: Choose /**P**rint **D**estination **G**raphics Printer to print custom fonts and shadings. For this option to work, you must have a printer that can print in graphics mode and /**O**ptions **G**raphics Quality must be set to **F**inal. (See your printer manual to determine whether your printer can print in graphics mode.)

Q: Why don't the font styles on my printouts correspond to the styles I specified in my spreadsheet cells?

A: Make sure that the /**O**ptions **G**raphics Quality command is set to **F**inal. When this command is set to **D**raft, Quattro Pro does not use any Bitstream fonts that haven't been built.

Q: When I edited the attributes for a custom style I created, Quattro Pro changed the appearance of formatted blocks in my spreadsheet. I really wanted to start with an existing style and add a few new attributes to the style without changing the rest of the spreadsheet. What did I do wrong?

A: You should have disassociated the original custom style from the formatted spreadsheet blocks using the /**S**tyle **D**efine Style **E**rase command. Using this command, you then can edit and apply the custom style to other blocks in the same spreadsheet without affecting any existing character formatting.

Q: I pressed Alt-F5 to remove a custom style I just added to a spreadsheet block, but nothing happened. Why?

A: Like with presentation-quality options that you add to your spreadsheets one at a time, you cannot reverse custom styles by using Alt-F5. Instead, choose the /**S**tyle **D**efine Style **E**rase command to remove a custom style from a spreadsheet block.

Summary

This chapter shows you how to align, format, and protect your spreadsheet data. You also learned how to widen and narrow columns and how to perform operations on blocks of columns. The chapter concluded with an in-depth review of drawing lines, shading cells, and using and modifying fonts on a spreadsheet.

Having completed this chapter, you should understand the following Quattro Pro concepts:

- Aligning values and labels manually with a **S**tyle menu command
- Selecting meaningful and appropriate numeric format values, labels, dates, and times
- Protecting and unprotecting cell data and enabling and disabling global spreadsheet protection
- Setting, resetting, and auto-setting the width of a column, a row, or a block of columns and rows
- Setting column widths in a window pane
- Hiding and unhiding column data
- Drawing, erasing, and printing lines and boxes
- Using, modifying, and printing shaded cells on a spreadsheet
- Selecting, changing, and customizing spreadsheet fonts to create presentation-quality reports
- Adding bullets to and inserting hard page breaks in a spreadsheet
- Changing default global format settings on the **O**ptions menu to create your own default spreadsheet formats

- Creating custom styles to associate character formatting options so that you easily can apply the styles to spreadsheet blocks
- Creating files that contain custom style names so that you can apply the customs styles to any spreadsheet open in memory

In Chapter 6, you learn how to incorporate Quattro Pro's powerful built-in @function commands into your spreadsheet applications. With these special commands, you can do complex mathematical, statistical, and database operations. These commands also enable you to manipulate data strings on a spreadsheet and extend the spreadsheet's capability to do what-if analyses with logical operators.

CHAPTER 6

Using Functions

In the preceding chapters, you learn how to build spreadsheets from the ground up and how to manage the form and content of your reports using Quattro Pro's menu tree of commands. You also learn how to create basic formula relationships so that you quickly can add, subtract, multiply, and divide data on a spreadsheet.

So far, you have created formulas primarily using mathematical operators. To add cells A5 and C9 and subtract cell D20, for example, enter *+A5+C9–D20* into a third cell.

What if you want to sum the contents of a large block of cells, compute an average, display the total number of values used in the calculations, and then display each piece of information in a separate cell? This type of analysis requires Quattro Pro's special built-in spreadsheet formulas, called *@function commands*.

@Function (pronounced "at function") commands perform a variety of special calculations and tasks that are too difficult or cumbersome for you to accomplish using simple spreadsheet formulas. These commands are the basic building blocks of all advanced spreadsheet applications. You can use these commands to average a group of numbers, to look up data in a block of cells, to create conditional formulas, and to perform calculations that help you determine the worth of an investment.

Other @function commands do tasks that are impossible to accomplish with basic mathematical formulas. Suppose that you want to generate a random number, convert a value to its hexadecimal equivalent, or determine how much system RAM is available for Quattro Pro. You easily can meet these and many other objectives by using Quattro Pro's @function commands.

Quattro Pro has 114 @function commands, divided into eight categories:

- Mathematical
- Statistical
- String
- Miscellaneous
- Logical
- Financial
- Date and Time
- Database Statistical

In this chapter, you learn how to use @functions in your own spreadsheets to solve unique, specific problems. In the first part of this chapter, you review the *structure*—or syntax—of the @function commands. When you understand the command syntax, go directly to the @function category that interests you most. The material in these sections reviews each command and often provides examples of how to use the command in a Quattro Pro spreadsheet.

Understanding Command Syntax

Each @function command has a three-part syntax: the @ symbol, the function name, and the argument(s). Table 6.1 describes these three parts.

Table 6.1 Components of the @Function Command Syntax

Syntax Element	Description
@	Indicates an "at function" command
FunctionName	Describes the type of operation to be performed
Argument(n)	Denotes the data to use; an argument can be a value or a cell address; the value n defines the order in which Quattro Pro evaluates an argument in an @function operation

A typical @function command looks like the following:

@AVG(C5..C8)

In this command, @ tells Quattro Pro to expect an @function. AVG is the name of the @function that averages numbers, and (C5..C8) is the argument that defines the cell block containing the four numbers to average.

Entering @Function Commands

Quattro Pro accepts three types of @function command arguments: numeric values, block values, and string values.

A *numeric value* can be a number, a cell that contains a number, or a reference to another spreadsheet cell that contains a number. Quattro Pro accepts as valid arguments block names and formulas that result in numeric values. You can create many different combinations of arguments, using all these types of numeric numbers.

@AVG(JAN,2500,A25..E30,(@ABS(G50))), for example, is a valid use of the @AVG command as long as the following conditions are true:

- JAN is the name of a block that contains numerical data.
- Block A25..E30 contains numerical data.
- @ABS does not return ERR as its result.

A *block value* can be a single cell, any two valid cell coordinates, a reference to data on another spreadsheet, a block name, or any combination of these items.

@AVG(JAN,A25..E30,(@ABS(G50))), for example, is a valid use of the @AVG command as long as the following conditions are true:

- JAN is the name of a valid block.
- Block A25..E30 contains data.
- @ABS does not return ERR as its result.

A *string value* can be a string enclosed in quotation marks, a cell that contains a label, a reference to a cell on another spreadsheet that contains a label, a block name that contains a label, or another @function command that returns a string value. You can create many different combinations using each type of argument.

@LENGTH(JAN,"Data Set #1",A25..E30,(@PROPER(G50))), for example, is a valid use of the @LENGTH and @PROPER commands as long as the following conditions are true:

PART I — USING QUATTRO PRO SPREADSHEETS

- JAN is the name of a block that contains a text string.
- Block A25..E30 contains text string data.
- @PROPER does not return ERR as its result.

When you enter @function commands into a spreadsheet, remember the following simple rules:

- Do not enter extra spaces between the @ symbol, the function name, and the argument; Quattro Pro cannot properly interpret an @function with extra spaces.
- You can use upper- or lowercase characters when entering an @function; Quattro Pro always displays the function in uppercase.
- The arguments in an @function must be enclosed in parentheses.
- The number and types of arguments used are different for each @function command.
- You can use one @function command as an argument in another @function command.

T I P Press Alt-F3 to display a list of Quattro Pro's @function commands. To select a command from the list, highlight the command name and press Enter. Quattro Pro displays the function with a left parenthesis on the input line. To complete the operation, enter the appropriate arguments, a right parenthesis, and then press Enter to calculate a result in the active cell.

You also can click the @ button on the EDIT mode SpeedBar to display the list of @function commands. Clicking an @function places it on the edit line at the current position. Remember, you must be in EDIT mode to access the EDIT mode SpeedBar.

The next section introduces Quattro Pro's mathematical @function commands.

Using Mathematical @Functions

The mathematical @functions fall into two categories: arithmetic and trigonometric. The mathematical @functions duplicate operations commonly found on scientific and financial calculators.

6 — USING FUNCTIONS

Using these commands, you can calculate natural and common logarithms; absolute values; cosine, sine, tangent, and their inverses; square roots and random numbers; and many other types of math functions.

Keep the following guidelines in mind when using mathematical @functions:

- Express @SIN, @COS, and @TAN angles in radians, not in degrees.
- The @ASIN, @ACOS, and @ATAN functions return angles in radian measure.
- To convert degrees to radians, use the @RADIANS function or multiply the degree value by @PI/180.
- To convert radians to degrees, use the @DEGREES function or multiply the radian value by 180/@PI.
- The base value of natural logarithms is *e*. The value *e*, as stored in Quattro Pro's memory, is 2.718281828459.

Using Arithmetic Commands in a Spreadsheet

Table 6.2 lists the arithmetic @function commands. The following definitions include examples of how you can use these commands in your own spreadsheets.

Table 6.2 Arithmetic Mathematical @Function Commands

@Function	Description
@ABS(*x*)	Returns the absolute value of *x*
@EXP(*x*)	Returns the constant *e*, raised to the *x*th power
@INT(*x*)	Drops the fractional portion of the number *x*
@LN(*x*)	Returns the natural logarithm of *x*
@LOG(*x*)	Returns the base 10 logarithm of *x*
@MOD(*x,y*)	Divides *x* by *y* and returns the remainder
@RAND	Supplies a random number between 0 and 1
@ROUND(*x,n*)	Rounds the value of *x* to *n* decimal places
@SQRT(*x*)	Returns the square root of *x*

@ABS(x)

@ABS returns the absolute or positive value of *x* when *x* is a numerical value.

    Examples: @ABS(–20) = 20
                             @ABS(0) = 0
                             @ABS(A1) = 0 (if A1 contains a label)

@EXP(x)

The @EXP function gives the mathematical constant *e*, raised to the *x*th power, where *x* is a numeric value less than or equal to 709. The @EXP function is the inverse of a natural logarithm function (@LN).

    Examples: @EXP(1) = 2.71828
                             @EXP(0) = 1.00000
                             @EXP(A1) =0 (if A1 contains a label)
                             @EXP(800) = ERR

@INT(x)

The @INT function drops the fractional portion of *x* when *x* is a numeric value and returns its integer value.

    Examples: @INT(1.9834) = 1
                             @INT(0.9921) = 0
                             @INT(A1) = 0 (if A1 contains a label)

@LN(x)

The @LN function returns the natural logarithm of *x* when *x* is a numeric value that is greater than 0. In any natural logarithm, the mathematical constant *e* is used as the base. You also can use @LN to return the inverse of @EXP.

    Examples: @LN(1.00000) = 0
                             @LN(2.71828) = 1
                             @LN(@EXP(10)) = 10
                             @LN(–1) = ERR
                             @LN(A1) = ERR (if A1 contains a label)

@LOG(x)

@LOG returns the base 10 logarithm of *x* when *x* is a numeric value that is greater than 0.

Examples:
@LOG(0) = ERR
@LOG(1) = 0
@LOG(10) = 1
@LOG(A1) = ERR (if A1 contains a label)

@MOD(x,y)

The @MOD function divides the *x* argument by *y* and returns any remainder. In this syntax, *x* must be a numeric value, and *y* must be a numeric value that is not equal to 0.

Examples:
@MOD(10,10) = 0
@MOD(10,3.5) = 3
@MOD(10,0) = ERR
@MOD(A1,1) = 0 (if A1 contains a label or is blank)
@MOD(3,A1) = ERR (if A1 contains a label)

@RAND

The @RAND function returns a fractional random number between 0 and 1. @RAND is useful when you must create a set of random numbers to use in statistical analysis.

To generate random numbers outside the 0 to 1 range, multiply the @RAND function by the difference between the high and low end of the new range, and then add the new low end number.

This formula is expressed as follows:

@RAND * (high number – low number) + low number.

Examples:
@RAND*6+1 = returns a random number between 1 and 7
@RAND+7 = returns a random number between 7 and 8

PART I — USING QUATTRO PRO SPREADSHEETS

> **T I P** Quattro Pro generates a new random number for each existing @RAND function on a spreadsheet every time you enter data into the spreadsheet or press F9 to recalculate.

@ROUND(x,Num)

The @ROUND function rounds the value of *x* to *Num* decimal places. In this syntax, *x* must be a numeric value, and *Num* must be a numeric value that falls in the range –15 to 15.

Examples:
@ROUND(4.53494,3) = 4.535
@ROUND(4.5,1) = 4.5
@ROUND(0.5994,16) = ERR
@ROUND(5.3,A1) = 5 (if A1 contains a label or is blank)
@ROUND(A1,3) = 0 (if A1 contains a label or is blank)
@ROUND(13.25,–1) = 10

@SQRT(x)

The @SQRT function supplies the square root of *x* when *x* is a numeric value that is greater than or equal to 0. Quattro Pro returns the value 0 when *x* is a label or a reference to a cell containing a label.

Examples:
@SQRT(16) = 4
@SQRT(–25) = ERR
@SQRT(A1) = 0 (if A1 contains a label or is blank)

Using Trigonometric Commands in a Spreadsheet

Table 6.3 lists the trigonometric @function commands. The following definitions include examples how to use these commands in your own spreadsheets.

Table 6.3 Trigonometric @Function Commands

@Function	Description
@ACOS(x)	Returns the arc cosine of radian angle x
@ASIN(x)	Returns the arc sine of radian angle x
@ATAN(x)	Returns the arc tangent of radian angle x
@ATAN2(x,y)	Returns the arc tangent of radian angle with coordinates x and y
@COS(x)	Returns the cosine of radian angle x
@DEGREES(x)	Converts x radians to degrees
@PI	Returns the value 3.1415926535898
@RADIANS(x)	Converts x degrees to radians
@SIN(x)	Returns the sine of radian angle x
@TAN(x)	Returns the tangent of radian angle x

@ACOS(x)

@ACOS returns the arc cosine of angle x when x is a numeric value between –1 and 1. The result is a radian angle with x as a cosine.

Examples: @ACOS(–1) = 3.1416
@ACOS(0) = 1.5708
@ACOS(1) = 0
@ACOS(2) = ERR

To convert radians to degrees, use @DEGREES.

Examples: @DEGREES(3.1416) = 180
@DEGREES(1.5708) = 90
@DEGREES(@ACOS(1)) = 0

@ASIN(x)

@ASIN returns the arc sine of angle x when x is a numeric value between –1 and 1. The result is a radian angle whose sine is x.

Examples: @ASIN(–1) = –1.5708
@ASIN(0) = 0
@ASIN(1) = 1.5708
@ASIN(2) = ERR

PART I — USING QUATTRO PRO SPREADSHEETS

To convert radians to degrees, use @DEGREES.

Examples: @DEGREES(–1.5708) = –90
@DEGREES(0) = 0
@DEGREES(@ASIN(1)) = 90

@ATAN(x)

@ATAN returns the arc tangent of angle x when x is a numeric value between –1 and 1. The result is a radian angle with the tangent x.

Examples: @ATAN(–1) = –0.7854
@ATAN(0) = 0
@ATAN(1) = 0.7854

To convert radians to degrees, use @DEGREES.

Examples: @DEGREES(–0.7854) = –45
@DEGREES(0) = 0
@DEGREES(@ATAN(1)) = 45

@ATAN2(x,y)

@ATAN2 returns the arc tangent of an angle with coordinates x and y when x and y are numeric values. The result is a radian angle with the tangent x/y.

Examples: @ATAN2(2,3) = 0.9828
@ATAN2(0,3) = 1.5708
@ATAN2(0,0) = ERR

To convert radians to degrees, use @DEGREES.

Example: @DEGREES(ATAN2(0,3)) = 90

@COS(x)

@COS returns the cosine of angle x, when x is a numeric value entered in radians.

Examples: @COS(–1) = –0.5403
@COS(0) = 1
@COS(1) = 0.5403

To convert degrees to radians, use @RADIANS.

    Example: @COS(@RADIANS(45)) = 0.707107

@DEGREES(x)

@DEGREES converts x radians to degrees when x is a numeric value. To convert x radians to degrees, you also can multiply x by (180/PI).

    Examples: @DEGREES(0.5236) = 30
                                      @DEGREES(1.0472) = 60
                                      @DEGREES(1.5708) = 90

@PI

@PI returns the value of pi as 3.1415926535898. *Pi* is the ratio of a circle's circumference to its diameter.

@RADIANS(x)

@RADIANS converts x degrees to radians when x is a numeric value. To convert x degrees to radians, you also can multiply x by (PI/180).

    Examples: @RADIANS(30) = 0.5236
                                      @RADIANS(60) = 1.0472
                                      @RADIANS(90) = 1.5708

@SIN(x)

The @SIN function returns the sine of the radian angle x when x is a numeric value entered in radians.

    Examples: @SIN(–1) = –0.8415
                                      @SIN(0) = 0
                                    @SIN(1) = 0.8415

To convert degrees into radians, use @RADIANS.

    Example: @SIN(RADIANS(30)) = 0.5

@TAN(x)

The @TAN function returns the tangent of the radian angle x when x is a numeric value entered in radians.

Examples: @TAN(–1) = –1.5574
                      @TAN(0) = 0
                      @TAN(1) = 1.5574

To convert degrees into radians, use @RADIANS.

Example: @TAN(@RADIANS(45)) = 1

Using Statistical @Functions

The statistical @function commands calculate common statistical measures using sample and population data sets. Table 6.4 describes the statistical @functions. Most of the statistical @functions use the *List* argument to define the location of the data set. In this syntax, *List* can be one or more numeric or block values. When you use more than one cell block in an argument, separate the blocks with commas.

Table 6.4 Statistical @Function Commands

@Function	Description
@AVG(*List*)	Calculates the average of the values in *List*
@COUNT(*List*)	Counts the number of nonblank cells in *List*
@MAX(*List*)	Returns the maximum numeric or date value in *List*
@MIN(*List*)	Returns the minimum numeric value in *List*
@STD(*List*)	Returns the population standard deviation of *List*
@STDS(*List*)	Returns the sample standard deviation of *List*
@SUM(*List*)	Sums all the numeric values in *List*
@SUMPRODUCT(*Block1,Block2*)	Returns the sum and product of *Block1* and *Block2*
@VAR(*List*)	Returns the population variance of *List*
@VARS(*List*)	Returns the sample variance of *List*

Figure 6.1 shows an application that uses the statistical @function commands to analyze automobile production statistics. In this example, *List* is the block C5..G8.

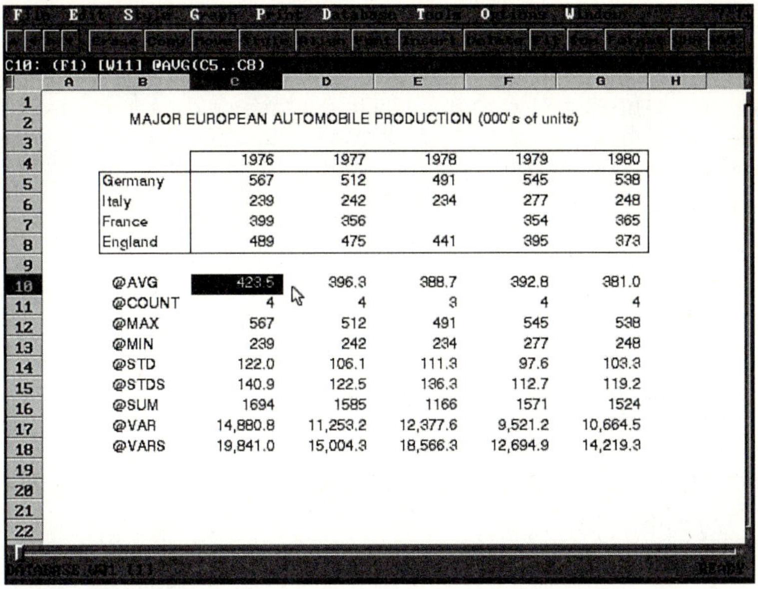

C10: (F1) [W11] @AVG(C5..C8)

MAJOR EUROPEAN AUTOMOBILE PRODUCTION (000's of units)

	1976	1977	1978	1979	1980
Germany	567	512	491	545	538
Italy	239	242	234	277	248
France	399	356		354	365
England	489	475	441	395	373
@AVG	423.5	396.3	388.7	392.8	381.0
@COUNT	4	4	3	4	4
@MAX	567	512	491	545	538
@MIN	239	242	234	277	248
@STD	122.0	106.1	111.3	97.6	103.3
@STDS	140.9	122.5	136.3	112.7	119.2
@SUM	1694	1585	1166	1571	1524
@VAR	14,880.8	11,253.2	12,377.6	9,521.2	10,664.5
@VARS	19,841.0	15,004.3	18,566.3	12,694.9	14,219.3

Fig. 6.1

A statistical @function application.

As you read through the following command definitions, refer to figure 6.1 to learn more about how to use a particular command in an application.

@AVG(List)

The @AVG function calculates the average of all values in *List*. Quattro Pro ignores blank cells and treats labels as 0 when calculating an average.

Examples:

@AVG(C5..C8) = 423.5
@AVG(D5..D8) = 396.3

@COUNT(List)

The @COUNT function counts the number of nonblank cells in *List*. This function can return the number of cells in *List* that contain data or locate the number of missing entries in a range of cells that always contains a fixed number of entries.

Examples:

@COUNT(C5..C8) = 4
@COUNT(C5..C8,D5..D8) = 8
@COUNT(E5..E8) = 3

@MAX(List)

The @MAX function returns the maximum numeric or date value in *List*. You can use this function to find the latest invoice date in a sales spreadsheet, pick the highest production figure from an analysis report, or locate the final transaction number in an accounting journal.

Examples: @MAX(D5..D8) = 512
@MAX(C5..C8,D5..D8) = 567

@MIN(List)

The @MIN function gives the minimum numeric or date value in *List*. You can use this function to find the first invoice date in a sales spreadsheet, pick the lowest production figure from an analysis report, or locate the first transaction number in an accounting journal.

Examples: @MIN(F5..F8) = 277
@MIN(E5..E8,F5..F8) = 234

@STD(List)

The @STD function calculates the standard deviation of the values in *List*, when *List* is the population data set. The square of this function—@STD(*List*)2—returns the population variance.

Standard deviation tells you how much each value in *List* differs from the average of all the values in *List*. One use of @STD is to determine the reliability of the average. The lower the standard deviation, the less each value in *List* varies from the average.

The @STD function ignores blank cells and treats labels as 0. When *List* contains only blank cells, @STD returns ERR.

Examples: @STD(G5..G8) = 103.3
@STD(B9..G9) = ERR

@STDS(List)

The @STDS function calculates the standard deviation of the values in *List* when *List* is a sample drawn from the population data set. The square of this function—@STDS(List)2—is the sample variance.

The @STDS function ignores any blank cells and treats labels as 0. When *List* contains only blank cells, @STDS returns ERR.

Example: @STDS(F5..F8) = 112.7

NOTE @STDS is not a 1-2-3 compatible @function command. If you must calculate standard deviation for data appearing on a 1-2-3 compatible spreadsheet, use the @STD function.

@SUM(List)

The @SUM function returns the sum total of all numeric values in *List*. This @function is used to add up data in cell blocks.

Examples: @SUM(C5..C8) = 1,694
@SUM(D5..D8) = 1,585
@SUM(C5..C8,D5..D8) = 3,279

@SUMPRODUCT(Block1,Block2)

The @SUMPRODUCT function returns the sum and the product of the two block arguments. In this syntax, Quattro Pro multiplies each corresponding cell value in *Block1* and *Block2* and then adds the results.

To use this command properly, the two blocks must have the same number of rows and columns. The blocks can be a one-dimensional row or column but must be equal in length. Quattro Pro returns ERR when the two blocks are unequal in length.

Suppose that the following cells contain the data shown:

D10 = 1 E10 = 1

D11 = 2 E11 = 2

D12 = 3 E12 = 3

D13 = 4 E13 = 4

The data in these cells yield the following results:

@SUMPRODUCT(D10..D11,E10..E11) = 5

@SUMPRODUCT(D12..D13,E12..E13) = 25

@SUMPRODUCT(D10..D13,E10..E13) = 30

NOTE @SUMPRODUCT is not a 1-2-3 compatible function. Do not use it in a spreadsheet that requires 1-2-3 compatibility.

@VAR(List)

The @VAR function calculates the variance of nonblank, numeric cells in *List* when *List* represents the population data set. The @VAR function uses the *n* method (biased), which divides the sum of components by *n* in determining population variance. In this syntax, Quattro Pro treats text as 0. Take the square root of this function to derive the population standard deviation.

Examples: @VAR(E5..E8) = 12,377.6
@VAR(G5..G8) = 10,664.5

@VARS(List)

The @VARS function supplies the variance of nonblank, numeric cells in *List* when *List* represents a sample drawn from the population data set. The @VARS function uses the *n–1* method (unbiased), which divides the sum of components by *n–1* in determining sample variance. In this syntax, Quattro Pro treats text as 0. Take the square root of this function to derive the sample standard deviation.

Examples: @VARS(E5..E8) = 18,566.3
@VARS(G5..G8) = 14,219.3

NOTE @VARS is not a 1-2-3 compatible function. Do not use it in a spreadsheet that requires 1-2-3 compatibility.

The next section introduces Quattro Pro's string @function commands.

Using String @Functions

The string @function commands give you the power to manipulate letters and numbers that appear in a label. These commands work only on labels, although they treat a number appearing in a label as though the number is text.

Manipulating strings is like doing mathematical operations on letters. Quattro Pro can manipulate strings because these @functions use special arguments. Table 6.5 describes these string @function arguments.

Table 6.5 String @Function Command Arguments

Argument	Description
Block	A block value
Code	A numeric value between 1 and 255
DecPlaces	A numeric value between 0 and 15
NewString	A string value that represents the characters to insert at position *Num*
Num	A numeric value >= 0
StartNumber	A numeric value, >= 0, that denotes the character position at which to begin the search
String	A string value; a hexadecimal number in quotation marks
String1	A valid string value
String2	A valid string value
SubString	A valid string value to search through
x	A numeric value

Among other things, these special functions enable you to add and subtract text strings, alter the upper- and lowercase settings for any character in a string and search through and replace data in labels. Table 6.6 describes the string @functions.

Table 6.6 String @Function Commands

@Function	Description
@CHAR(*Code*)	Returns the ASCII character corresponding to *Code*
@CLEAN(*String*)	Removes all non-ASCII characters from *String*
@CODE(*String*)	Changes the first character in *String* to ASCII
@EXACT(*String1*, *String2*)	Compares the value of *String1* to *String2*
@FIND(*SubString*, *String*,*StartNumber*)	Searches through *String* for *SubString*

continues

Table 6.6 Continued

@Function	Description
@HEXTONUM(*String*)	Converts the hexadecimal number in *String* to its equivalent decimal value
@LEFT(*String,Num*)	Displays the far-left *Num* characters in *String*
@LENGTH(*String*)	Returns the number of characters in *String*
@LOWER(*String*)	Converts *String* to lowercase characters
@MID(*String, StartNumber,Num*)	Returns the first *Num* characters in *String*, starting with character number *StartNumber*
@N(*Block*)	Returns the numeric value of the upper left cell in *Block*
@NUMTOHEX(*x*)	Converts *x* to its hexadecimal string value
@PROPER(*String*)	Converts the first letter of every word in *String* to uppercase
@REPEAT(*String,Num*)	Returns *Num* copies of *String* as one continuous label
@REPLACE(*String, StartNum,Num,NewString*)	Replaces characters in *String* with *NewString*
@RIGHT(*String,Num*)	Displays the last *Num* characters in *String*
@S(*Block*)	Returns the string value of the upper left cell in *Block*
@STRING(*x,DecPlaces*)	Converts *x* to a string, rounded to *DecPlaces*
@TRIM(*String*)	Removes extraneous spaces from *String*
@UPPER(*String*)	Returns *String* in uppercase characters
@VALUE(*String*)	Converts *String* into a numeric value

@CHAR(Code)

The @CHAR function displays the ASCII character equivalent of *Code*. The valid code range is 1-255. This function is the reverse of the @CODE function.

Examples: @CHAR(0) = ERR
@CHAR(60) = <
@CHAR(65) = A
@CHAR(94) = ^
@CHAR(256) = ERR
@CHAR(A1) = ERR when A1
contains the code 256

> **NOTE** Any time you use a cell address as an argument in a string function, the contents of the cell must be a string (preceded by one of the four label prefixes). When you use strings and cell addresses as arguments in a string function, remember this important difference: a string argument must be enclosed in double quotation marks, but a value or label in a referenced cell must be preceded by a label prefix.

@CLEAN(String)

The @CLEAN function erases all the non-ASCII characters encountered in *String*.

@CODE(String)

The @CODE function displays the ASCII code equivalent of the first character it encounters in *String*. This function is the reverse of the @CHAR function.

Examples: @CODE("<") = 60
@CODE("A") = 65
@CODE("^") = 94
@CODE(A1) = 94 when A1
contains the string ^

@EXACT(String1,String2)

The @EXACT function compares *String1* to *String2*. When the values are identical, Quattro Pro returns 1; otherwise it returns 0.

Enclose both compare strings in quotation marks except when the string is a block name. When Quattro Pro compares labels, it ignores numbers and label prefixes.

Examples: @EXACT("trust","Trust") = 0
@EXACT("Trust","Trust") = 1
@EXACT(50,"50") = ERR
@EXACT(A1,B1) = 1 when A1 contains the string Trust and B1 contains the string Trust

@FIND(SubString,String,StartNumber)

@FIND searches through *String* for *SubString*. If Quattro Pro finds *SubString*, it returns the character position of the first occurrence of *SubString*.

Quattro Pro begins the @FIND operation at position number *StartNumber* in *String*. The first character in *String* is designated as 0, the second as 1, and so on. *StartNumber* cannot be greater than the number of characters in *String*, minus 1.

Use the @FIND function with @REPLACE to perform a search-and-replace operation. When @FIND fails to find at least one occurrence of *SubString*, Quattro Pro returns ERR.

Examples: @FIND("i","girth",0) = 1
@FIND("h","girth",0) = 4
@FIND("G","girth",0) = ERR
@FIND(A1,B1,0) = 4 when A1 contains the string h and B1 contains the string girth

@HEXTONUM(String)

@HEXTONUM converts the hexadecimal number in *String* to its equivalent decimal value. In this syntax, *String* must be surrounded by quotation marks. This function is the reverse of the @NUMTOHEX function.

Examples: @HEXTONUM("f") = 15
@HEXTONUM("35") = 53
@HEXTONUM(A1) = 53 when A1 contains the string 35

@LEFT(String,Num)

The @LEFT function displays the number of characters specified (*Num*) that it finds in *String*. This function extracts characters from the left side of *String*.

Quattro Pro returns ERR when *String* is a numeric value, a date value, or a blank cell. Quattro Pro returns all of *String* if *Num* is longer than the length of *String*.

    Examples: @LEFT("John",2) = Jo
    @LEFT("John",10) = John
    @LEFT(45,2) = ERR
    @LEFT(A1,10) = John when A1 contains the string John

@LENGTH(String)

@LENGTH returns the character length of *String*, including spaces. Use the ampersand (&) to combine strings and cell addresses. Place quotation marks around *String* when it is a text string. Quattro Pro returns ERR if *String* references a blank cell or is not surrounded by quotation marks.

    Examples: @LENGTH("John") = 4
    @LENGTH("Hello"&"Greetings") = 14
    @LENGTH(123456) = ERR
    @LENGHT(A1) = 4 when A1 contains the string John

@LOWER(String)

@LOWER converts *String* to a lowercase character display. Quattro Pro does not alter numbers and symbols appearing in *String* but returns ERR when *String* is a blank cell or is a number or date value.

    Examples: @LOWER("STRING") = string
    @LOWER("Hello, John.") = hello, john.
    @LOWER("94 Carroll Canyon") = 94 carroll canyon
    @LOWER(32876) = ERR
    @LOWER(a1) = john when A1 contains the string JOHN

@MID(String,StartNumber,Num)

@MID extracts the first *Num* characters in *String*, beginning with character number *StartNumber*. In this syntax, *String* must be a text string surrounded by quotation marks or a reference to a cell containing a text string surrounded by quotation marks. Quattro Pro returns a blank cell when *StartNumber* is greater than the length of *String* and when *Num* is 0.

You cannot enter strings without quotation marks. If you try, the program beeps and displays an error message.

Examples:
@MID("John Donavan",5,7) = Donavan
@MID("Tim Atkins",20,5) = ""
@MID("Scott Matthews",6,4) = Matt
@MID(2519,1,2) = ERR
@MID(A1,5,7) = Donovan when A1 contains the string John Donovan

@N(Block)

The @N function returns the numeric value located in the upper left cell of *Block*. @N returns a 0 if the upper left cell in *Block* contains a label or is blank.

Examples:
@N(A1..A5) = 25 when A1 contains the value 25
@N(A1..A5) = 0 when A1 is blank
@N(A1..A5) = 0 when A1 contains the label "DATA"

Quattro Pro uses the @N function for compatibility with other spreadsheets. Other spreadsheets use this function to avoid ERR values resulting from attempts to do calculations using labels.

@NUMTOHEX(x)

The @NUMTOHEX function returns the hexadecimal equivalent of *x* as a string value. This function is the reverse of the @HEXTONUM function.

Examples:
@NUMTOHEX(106) = 6A
@NUMTOHEX(219) = DB
@NUMTOHEX(A1) = DB when A1 contains the value 219

@PROPER(String)

@PROPER modifies *String* so that the first letter of each word in *String* is uppercase and all other letters are lowercase. Blank spaces, punctuation marks, and numbers signify the end of a word.

Examples:
@PROPER("JOHN doNAVAN") = John Donavan
@PROPER("JAMES J. PARKER") = James J. Parker

@PROPER("1990's census") = 1990'S Census
@PROPER(A1) = James J. Parker when A1 contains the string JAMES J. PARKER

@REPEAT(String,Num)

The @REPEAT function returns *Num* copies of *String* as a single, continuous label. In this syntax, *Num* is a numeric value that is greater than or equal to 0. When repeating a text string, enclose *String* in double quotation marks.

Examples: @REPEAT("hello!",3) = hello!hello!hello!
@REPEAT("*",20) = ********************
@REPEAT(A1,3) = hi!hi!hi! when A1 contains the string hi!

@REPLACE(String,StartNum,Num,NewString)

The @REPLACE function enables you to replace *Num* characters in *String* with *NewString*, beginning at character *StartNum* in *String*. In this syntax, *Num* is a numeric value greater than or equal to 0 that identifies the number of characters to replace.

Examples: @REPLACE("O'Nickels",2,7,"Grady") = O'Grady
@REPLACE("Jenny L. Peters",6,3,"") = Jenny Peters
@REPLACE("Inventory Figures",10,0,"Control") = Inventory Control Figures

> **TIP**
> When you use this command to insert one string into another, leave a blank space after *NewString* and before the final quotation mark. This space ensures the proper number of spaces between words.

@RIGHT(String,Num)

The @RIGHT function displays the last *Num* characters in *String*. Use this function to extract characters from the right side of a label or string.

@RIGHT returns ERR when *String* is not a valid string. @RIGHT returns an empty string or "" when *Num* is 0. Quattro Pro returns the entire string when the character length of *Num* is greater than the number of characters in *String*.

Examples: @RIGHT("Jeff Turner",6) = Turner
@RIGHT("Jeff Turner",11) = Jeff Turner
@RIGHT("123",1) = 3
@RIGHT(567,1) = ERR
@RIGHT(A1,1) = 3 when A1 contains the string 123

@S(Block)

@S returns the string value located in the upper left cell of *Block*. Quattro Pro returns a blank cell if *Block* contains a numerical value, a date value, or a blank cell.

Examples: @S(A1..A5) = DATA when A1 contains the label "DATA"
@S(A1..A5) = " " when A1 is blank
@S(A1..A5) = " " when A1 contains the value 25

@STRING(x,DecPlaces)

The @STRING function converts *x* to a string rounded to *DecPlaces* decimal places. In this syntax, *x* is a numeric value, and *DecPlaces* must be a numeric value between 0 and 15.

After you convert a number or date to a label with the @STRING function, Quattro Pro does not enable you to format the display of the returned value.

Examples: @STRING(14.88,0) = 15
@STRING(78.7,2) = 78.70
@STRING("John",3) = 0.000
@STRING(A1,2) = 78.70 when A1 contains the value 78.7

@TRIM(String)

@TRIM removes extraneous spaces from *String*. This function deletes spaces after the last nonspace character or before the first nonspace character. @TRIM eliminates extra spaces between words. Quattro Pro returns ERR when *String* is empty or contains a numeric value.

6 — USING FUNCTIONS

Examples: @TRIM(" extra spaces ") = "extra spaces"
@TRIM("no extra spaces") ="no extra spaces"
@TRIM(456) = ERR
@TRIM(A1) = ERR when A1 contains the value 456

@UPPER(String)

@UPPER returns *String* in uppercase characters. Quattro Pro does not alter numbers and symbols and returns ERR when *String* is a numerical value, a date value, or a blank cell.

Examples: @UPPER("upper") = UPPER
@UPPER("Hello there") = HELLO THERE
@UPPER(1234) = ERR
@UPPER("94 Carroll Canyon") = 94 CARROLL CANYON
@UPPER(A1) = UPPER when A1 contains the string upper

@VALUE(String)

The @VALUE function converts *String* into a numeric value. *String* may contain arithmetic operators, but Quattro Pro ignores dollar signs, commas, and leading and trailing spaces. If Quattro Pro encounters an embedded space in *String*, this function returns ERR.

Examples: @VALUE(" 4.58") = 4.58
@VALUE(" 4.33 ") = 4.33
@VALUE("10. 25") = ERR
@VALUE(12/4) = 3
@VALUE("200,872") = 200872 (comma is omitted)
@VALUE(A1) = 1528 when A1 contains the label '1528

PART I — USING QUATTRO PRO SPREADSHEETS

Using Miscellaneous @Functions

The miscellaneous @function commands supply you with information about your spreadsheet and the current work session. These commands tell you the number of rows or columns in a block, for example, display the format attributes for a cell, and display the amount of extended or expanded memory now available to Quattro Pro.

When a command's syntax contains *Attribute* as an argument, you can use any attributes listed in table 6.7. *Attribute* must be enclosed in quotation marks or must be a reference to a cell that contains a valid attribute. (For a listing of possible formats, see tables 6.8, 6.9, and 6.10.)

Table 6.7 Valid Quattro Pro Attribute Codes

Code	Description
"address"	Specifies the address of the upper left cell in *Block*
"row"	Specifies the row number of the upper left cell in *Block*; the "row" code ranges from 1 to 8192
"col"	Specifies the column number of the upper left cell in *Block*; the "column" code ranges from 1 to 256
"contents"	Specifies the contents of the upper left cell in *Block*
"type"	Specifies the type of data in the upper left cell in *Block*, as follows: b is a blank cell 1 is a cell that contains a label v is a cell that contains a formula or number
"prefix"	Specifies the label-prefix character of the upper left cell in *Block*, as follows: \ is the repeating label prefix " is the right-aligned label prefix ^ is the centered label prefix ' is the left-aligned label prefix
"protect"	Specifies the protection status of the upper left cell in *Block*, as follows: 0 is an unprotected cell 1 is a protected cell

6 — USING FUNCTIONS

Code	Description
"width"	Specifies the width of the column containing the upper left cell in *Block*; the "width" code ranges from 1 to 254
"rwidth"	Specifies the width of *Block*
"format"	Specifies the current numeric format of the upper left cell in *Block*; table 6.8 shows the valid numeric formats

Table 6.8 Valid Numeric Formats

Code	Description
+ +/−	Bar graph
,*n*	Commas, where *n* = 0 to 15
C*n*	Currency, where *n* = 0 to 15
E*n*	Exponential, where *n* = 0 to 15
F*n*	Fixed, where *n* = 0 to 15
G	General
H	Hidden
P*n*	Percent, where *n* = 0 to 15
S*n*	Scientific, where *n* = 0 to 15
T	Formulas displayed as text

Table 6.9 Valid Date Formats

Code	Description
D1	DD-MMM-YY
D2	DD-MMM
D3	MMM-YY
D4	MM/DD/YY DD/MM/YY DD.MM.YY YY-MM-DD
D5	MM/DD DD/MM DD.MM MM-DD

You can choose one of four settings for codes D4 and D5 by choosing the /Options International command. When you choose a new default setting, that setting becomes the default long international date format when you choose /Style Numeric Format Date 1 (Long Intl.) or 2 (Short Intl.).

Table 6.10 Valid Time Formats

Code	Description
D6	HH:MM:SS AM/PM
D7	HH:MM AM/PM
D8	HH:MM:SS-24hr HH.MM.SS-24hr HH,MM,SS-24hr HHhMMmSSm
D9	HH:MM-24hr HH.MM-24hr HH,MM, HHhMMm

You can choose one of four settings for codes D8 and D9 by choosing the /Options International command. When you choose a new default setting, that setting becomes the default long international time format when you choose /Style Numeric Format Date Time 1 (Long Intl.) or 2 (Short Intl.).

Miscellaneous @function commands also enable you to look up entries in a data table. In a horizontal lookup table, Quattro Pro searches for values beginning in the top row, moving from left to right. In a vertical lookup table, Quattro Pro searches for values beginning in the left column, moving from top to bottom. Table 6.11 describes the miscellaneous @function commands.

Table 6.11 Miscellaneous @Function Commands

@Function	Description
@@(*Cell*)	Returns the contents of *Cell* as an address or cell block when *Cell* is a label
@CELL(*Attribute,Block*)	Returns attributes for a cell in *Block*
@CELLINDEX(*Attribute, Block,Column,Row*)	Returns attributes for a cell offset *Column* columns and *Row* rows
@CELLPOINTER (*Attribute*)	Returns attributes for the active cell
@CHOOSE(*Number,List*)	Returns the value from *List* located in the *Number* position

6 — USING FUNCTIONS

@Function	Description
@COLS(*Block*)	Returns the number of columns in *Block*
@CURVALUE(*GeneralAction, SpecificAction*)	Describes the most recent menu command execution
@ERR	Returns ERR in a cell
@HLOOKUP (*x,Block,Row*)	Searches for the first value <= to *x* and returns the value located *Row* rows below it in *Block*
@INDEX(*Block, Column,Row*)	Searches a data table for a value
@ISAAF(*"Addin.Function"*)	Tests whether a custom @function is defined in a loaded add-in
@ISAPPC(*"Addin"*)	Tests whether an add-in is loaded into memory
@MEMAVAIL	Returns the number of available bytes of conventional memory
@MEMEMSAVAIL	Returns the number of available bytes of expanded memory
@NA	Returns the special value NA (not available)
@ROWS(*Block*)	Returns the number of rows in a given block
@VERSION	Supplies the version number of Quattro Pro
@VLOOKUP(*x, Block,Column*)	Searches for the first value <= to *x* and returns the value located *Column* columns to the right of it in *Block*

Figure 6.2 illustrates how to use a table to analyze every possible attribute for three cells using the @CELL command. The attributes for the data appearing in D3, E3, and F3 appear in block D4..F13. As you read the next four command definitions, refer to figure 6.2 to learn more about how to use a particular command in an application.

@@(Cell)

The @@(*Cell*) function converts *Cell* into a single-cell address. In this syntax, *Cell* must be a single-cell address or block name in label form. The @@ function translates the label and then returns the contents of that cell.

Examples: @@("B6") = C (refer to fig. 6.2)
@@("E2") = Target Cells (Block) (refer to fig. 6.2)
@@("D4") = $D$3 (refer to fig. 6.2)

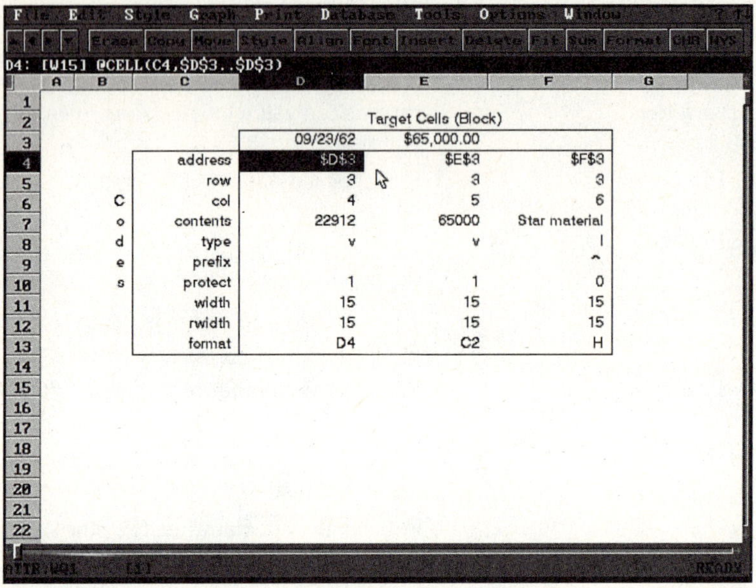

Fig. 6.2

Analyze attributes in a table.

@CELL(Attribute,Block)

The @CELL function evaluates *Block* and returns an attribute code specified by *Attribute*. In this syntax, *Attribute* must be one of the attribute codes from table 6.7, and *Block* must be a value or label.

You can enter *Attribute* in upper- or lowercase but must surround it by quotation marks. *Attribute* also can be the address of a cell that contains a value or label.

Examples: @CELL("address",D3) = $D$3 (refer to fig. 6.2)
@CELL("format",E3) = C2 (refer to fig. 6.2)
@CELL("protect",F3) = 0 (refer to fig. 6.2)

@CELLINDEX(Attribute,Block,Column,Row)

The @CELLINDEX function evaluates *Block* and returns an attribute code specified by *Attribute*. In this syntax, *Attribute* must be one of the attribute codes from table 6.7, and *Block* must be a value or label.

6 — USING FUNCTIONS

Examples: @CELLINDEX("type",D4..F13,2,4) = 1
(refer to fig. 6.2)
@CELLINDEX("width",D4..F13,2,1) = 19
(refer to fig. 6.2)

This function works like @CELL but returns the attribute for a cell offset *Column* columns and *Row* rows from the first coordinate in *Block* (refer to fig. 6.2).

@CELLPOINTER(Attribute)

The @CELLPOINTER function evaluates the active cell (where the cell selector is located) and returns an attribute code specified by *Attribute*. In this syntax, *Attribute* must be one of the attribute codes from table 6.7.

This function works like @CELL and @CELLINDEX but returns the specified *Attribute* code for the active cell. If you move the cell selector to a different cell, press F9 to calculate a new result for the @CELLPOINTER function (refer to fig. 6.2).

Examples: @CELLPOINTER("rwidth") = 19 when
F12 is the active cell
@CELLPOINTER("contents") = 65000
when E7 is the active cell

@CHOOSE(Number,List)

The @CHOOSE function returns the value from *List* located in the *Number* position. In this syntax, *Number* is a numeric value that is less than or equal to the number of items in *List* minus 1, and *List* is equal to a group of numeric or string values separated by commas.

The value of *Number* determines which *List* value is selected. For example, 0 selects the first value in *List*, 1 the second, 2 the third, and so on. *Number* may be a cell address, an integer, a string, or a mixture of the three. *List* must not exceed 254 characters.

Examples: @CHOOSE(0,"John","Pat","Craig") =
John
@CHOOSE(1,"John","Pat","Craig") = Pat
@CHOOSE(2,"John","Pat","Craig") =
Craig
@CHOOSE(5,"John","Pat","Craig") = ERR

@COLS(Block)

The @COLS function returns the number of columns in *Block*. In this syntax, *Block* may be a cell block or a block name.

Examples: @COLS(A1..IV1) = 256
@COLS(A1..A1) = 1

@CURVALUE(General Action,SpecificAction)

The @CURVALUE function returns a description of a menu command setting specified by *GeneralAction* and *SpecificAction*. In this syntax, *GeneralAction* is a general menu category such as File, and *SpecificAction* is a specific menu choice such as Save As. Both arguments must be surrounded by quotation marks.

Examples: @CURVALUE("file","save") = C:\QPRO\SALES.WQ1 (the name of the last file saved with the Save As command on the File menu)
@CURVALUE("file","directory") =C:\QPRO (the name of the current directory setting on the File menu)
@CURVALUE("graph","type")= Stacked Bar (the current Graph Type setting on the Graph menu)

@ERR

The @ERR function returns the value ERR. Use this function to return ERR in the active cell and in any other cells that reference the active cell.

The following @function commands do not return ERR when they reference a cell containing ERR: @COUNT, @DCOUNT, @ISERR, @ISNA, @ISNUMBER, @ISSTRING, and @CELL.

When used with the @IF function, @ERR is useful for calling attention to errors on the active spreadsheet. The returned value ERR is not a label but a unique number that Quattro Pro reserves to identify error conditions on a spreadsheet.

@HLOOKUP(x,Block,Row)

The @HLOOKUP function moves through *Block* horizontally, looking for the last value that is less than or equal to *x*. This function provides you with an effective way to access information stored in a data table.

In this syntax, *x* can be a character string, a number, a cell address, or block name that references a label or value. When *x* is a string, Quattro Pro searches for an exact match. @HLOOKUP returns the highest number in the row that is not more than *x* when Quattro Pro cannot find an equal number.

Block must be a cell block address that describes the location of the data table. *Block* can describe the whole table or part of the table to restrict the lookup operation.

Row tells Quattro Pro how many rows to look down through to find the value that the program returns. The *Row* argument cannot exceed the number of rows in the data table, or Quattro Pro returns ERR. When *Row* is 0, @HLOOKUP returns the *x* value itself.

Quattro Pro searches from left to right through the table rows, looking for a match to *x*. When the program finds an exact match, it stops at that column. When it does not find an exact match, the program stops at the column that contains the value closest to but not greater than *x*.

Figure 6.3 shows different ways to look through a data table using the @HLOOKUP command.

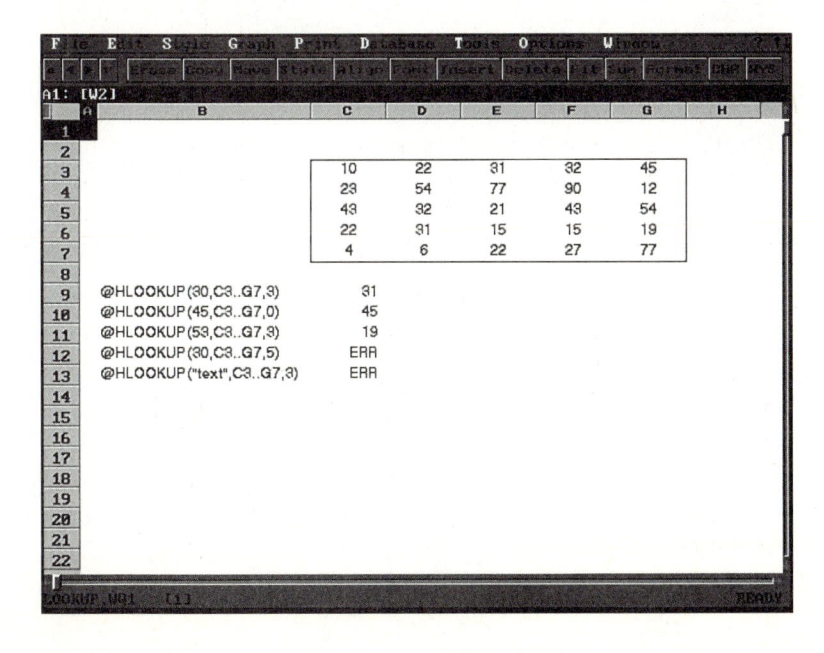

Fig. 6.3

A data table search with @HLOOKUP.

In the first example, Quattro Pro searches horizontally through the first row in block C3..G7. When the program locates the last value that is less than or equal to 30 before encountering a value that is greater than 30 (it stops at 22), Quattro Pro displays the cell value three rows down (the value 31).

In the second example, Quattro Pro searches horizontally through the first row in block C3..G7. When the program locates the last value that is less than or equal to 45 before encountering a value that is greater than 45 (it stops at 45), Quattro Pro displays the value in the cell 0 rows down (the value 45).

In the third example, Quattro Pro searches horizontally through the first row in block C3..G7. When the program locates the last value that is less than or equal to 53 before encountering a value that is greater than 53 (it stops at 45), Quattro Pro displays the cell value three rows down (the value 19).

In the fourth example, Quattro Pro searches horizontally through the first row in block C3..G7. When the program locates the last value that is less than or equal to 30 before encountering a value that is greater than 30 (it stops at 22), Quattro Pro tries to display the value in the cell five rows down. Because this cell falls outside of the defined *Block*, Quattro Pro displays ERR.

In the fifth example, Quattro Pro searches horizontally through the first row in block C3..G7. When the program encounters the illegal definition for the *x* argument ("text"), Quattro Pro displays ERR.

@INDEX(Block,Column,Row)

The @INDEX function uses the data table specified by *Block*. This function returns a value offset *Column* number of columns and *Row* number of rows.

In this syntax, *Column* and *Row* are not cell addresses, but offset values. In an @INDEX operation, Quattro Pro starts with the top left cell in *Block*, moves right *Column* number of columns, moves down *Row* number of rows, and then returns the value located in the active cell.

Column and *Row* must be values that are less than the number of rows or columns in the block and greater than or equal to zero. If a decimal is specified, Quattro Pro drops the fractional part of the decimal, rounding the value.

Figure 6.4 shows different ways to look through a data table using the @INDEX command.

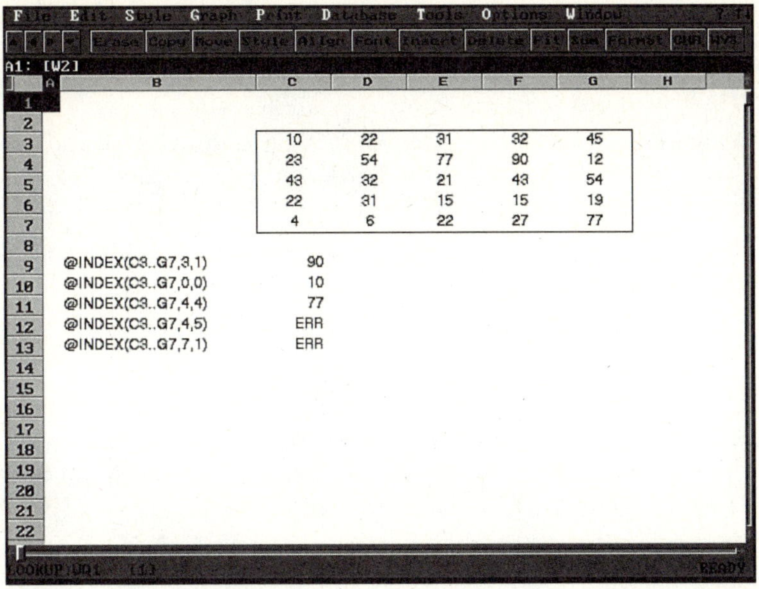

6 — USING FUNCTIONS

Fig. 6.4

A data table search with @INDEX.

In the first example, Quattro Pro begins at the first cell in block C3..G7. The program offsets 3 columns (to the 32 value) and 1 row (to the 90 value) and then displays 90.

In the second example, Quattro Pro begins at the first cell in block C3..G7. The program offsets 0 columns (to the 10 value) and 0 rows (to the 10 value) and then displays 10.

In the third example, Quattro Pro begins at the first cell in block C3..G7. The program offsets 4 columns (to the 45 value) and 4 rows (to the 77 value) and then displays 77.

In the fourth example, Quattro Pro begins at the first cell in block C3..G7. The program offsets 4 columns (to the 45 value) and 5 rows. Because this row offset falls outside the area defined in the *Block* argument, Quattro Pro displays ERR.

In the fifth example, Quattro Pro begins at the first cell in block C3..G7. The program offsets 7 columns. Because this column offset falls outside the area defined in the *Block* argument, Quattro Pro displays ERR.

@ISAAF("Addin.Function")

@ISAAF tells you if an @function is defined in an add-in module you have loaded into memory. This function returns the value 1 if *Addin* is loaded and *Function* is defined in the add-in; otherwise, the function returns the value 0. Refer to the documentation that came with your third-party add-in to determine the correct names for arguments *Addin* and *Function*.

Example: @ISAAF("SALES.FINANCE") = 1 when the SALES.QLL add-in is loaded into memory and @FINANCE is defined in that add-in

@ISAPP("Addin")

@ISAPP tells you if an add-in module is loaded into memory. This function returns the value 1 if *Addin* is loaded and returns the value 0 if the add-in is not loaded into memory. Refer to the documentation that came with your third-party add-in to determine the correct name for the argument *Addin*.

Example: @ISAPP("SALES") = 1 when the SALES.QLL add-in is loaded into memory

> **TIP** Choose /Tools Library Load to load a third-party add-in into memory.

@MEMAVAIL

@MEMAVAIL displays the number of bytes of conventional memory now available to Quattro Pro.

Example: @MEMAVAIL = 46923 (46,923 bytes of available memory)

@MEMEMSAVAIL

The @MEMEMSAVAIL function displays the number of bytes of expanded memory (EMS) now available to Quattro Pro. If your system does not contain expanded memory, Quattro Pro returns NA (not available).

Example: @MEMEMSAVAIL = 28000 (if your system contains 28K of free EMS)

@NA

The @NA function returns the value NA. Like ERR, NA is a unique number and not a label. When your spreadsheet contains formulas that reference a value entered as @NA, Quattro Pro returns NA.

@NA helps to prevent the trickle-down effect of displaying erroneous data in a spreadsheet, because Quattro Pro treats NA as a value and not as an ERR.

Figure 6.5, for example, shows the cell selector in cell F12. The formula in this cell uses data displayed in the range F7..F10. @NA is placed in cell F10 because this expense figure is not available. Quattro Pro displays NA as the result in all cells with formulas that depend on the data in block F7..F10. This is true for formulas that rely directly on the data, such as the formula in cell F12, or those that rely indirectly on the data, such as other formulas that use the F12 result in their own formula.

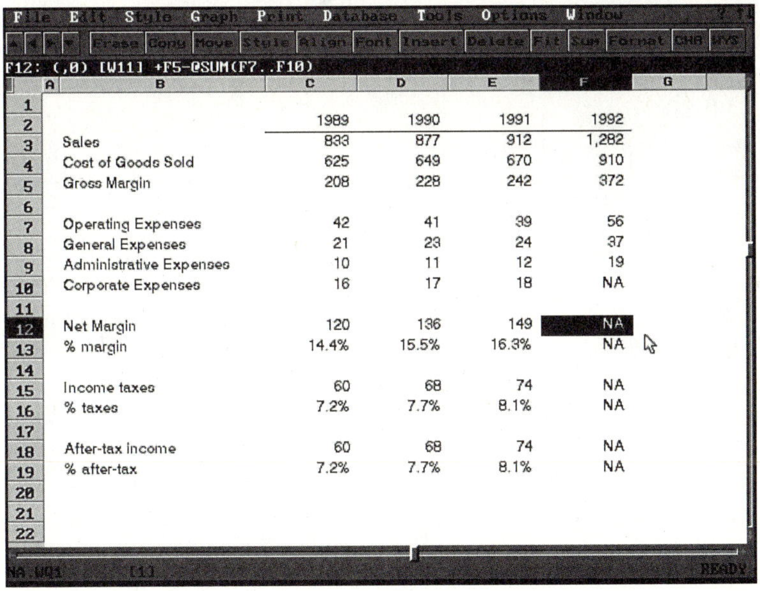

Fig. 6.5

Use @NA to indicate data not yet available.

@ROWS(Block)

The @ROWS function returns the number of rows in *Block*. In this syntax, *Block* may be a cell block or a block name.

Examples: @ROWS(A1..IV1) = 1
@ROWS(A1..A10) = 10
@ROWS(ADDRESS) = 50 (if ADDRESS = A1..A50, for example)

@VERSION

The @VERSION function displays Quattro Pro's version number in a user-specified cell.

@VLOOKUP(x,Block,Column)

The @VLOOKUP function works like @HLOOKUP, except that it searches through *Block* by columns instead of by rows.

The @VLOOKUP function moves through *Block* vertically, looking for the last value that is less than or equal to *x*. When the search succeeds, Quattro Pro returns the value located *Column* number of columns to the right. This function gives you an effective way to access information stored in a data table.

In this syntax, *x* can be a character string, a number, a cell address, or block name that references a label or value. When *x* is a string, Quattro Pro searches for an exact match. @VLOOKUP returns the highest number in the column not more than *x* when Quattro Pro cannot find an equal number.

Block must be a cell block address that describes the location of the data table. *Block* can describe the whole table or part of the table to restrict the lookup operation.

Column tells Quattro Pro how many columns to look through to find the value. If the *Column* argument exceeds the number of columns in the data table, Quattro Pro returns ERR. When *Column* is 0, @VLOOKUP returns the *x* value itself.

Quattro Pro searches from top to bottom through the table rows, looking for a match to *x*. When the program finds an exact match, it stops at that row. When Quattro Pro does not find an exact match, it stops at the row containing the value closest to but not greater than *x*.

Figure 6.6 shows different ways to look through a data table using the @VLOOKUP command.

In the first example, Quattro Pro searches vertically through the first column in block C3..G7. When the program locates the last value that is less than or equal to 30 before encountering one that is greater than 30 (it stops at 23), Quattro Pro displays the cell value three columns to the right (the value 90).

In the second example, Quattro Pro searches vertically through the first column in block C3..G7. When the program locates the last value that is less than or equal to 45 before encountering a value that is greater than 45 (it stops at 4), Quattro Pro displays the value in the cell 0 columns to the right (the value 4).

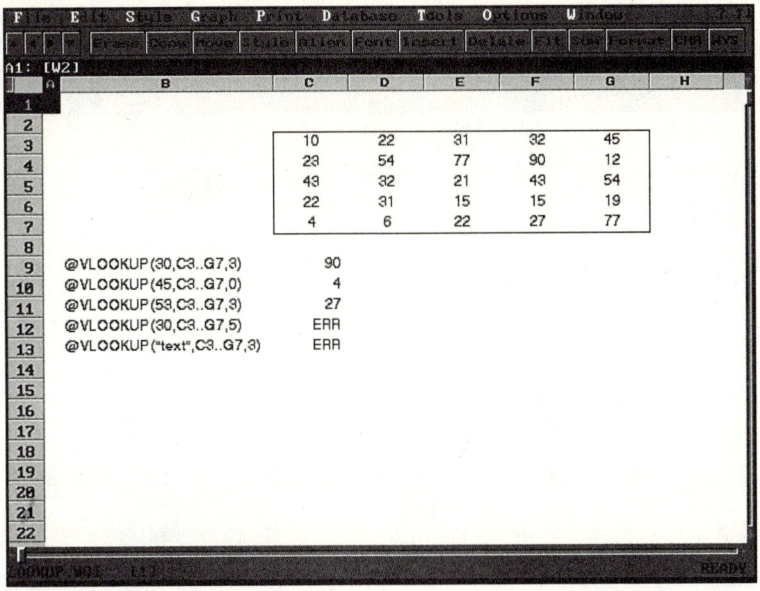

6 — USING FUNCTIONS

Fig. 6.6

A data table search with @VLOOKUP.

In the third example, Quattro Pro searches vertically through the first column in block C3..G7. When the program locates the last value that is less than or equal to 53 before encountering one that is greater than 53 (it stops at 4), Quattro Pro displays the cell value three columns to the right (the value 27).

In the fourth example, Quattro Pro searches vertically through the first column in block C3..G7. When the program locates the last value that is less than or equal to 30 before encountering a value that is greater than 30 (it stops at 23), Quattro Pro tries to display the value in the cell 5 columns to the right. Because this cell falls outside of the defined *Block*, Quattro Pro displays ERR.

In the fifth example, Quattro Pro searches vertically through the first column in block C3..G7. When the program encounters the illegal definition for the *x* argument ("text"), Quattro Pro displays ERR.

Using Logical @Functions

The logical @function commands test logical conditions (see table 6.12). Depending on the outcome of the tests, these @functions return different values and perform different actions.

Table 6.12 Logical @Function Commands

@Function	Description
@FALSE	Returns the logical value 0
@FILEEXISTS(*Filename*)	Returns the logical value 1 when *Filename* exists
@IF(*Cond,TrueExpr, FalseExpr*)	Evaluates a logical condition
@ISERR(*x*)	Checks the contents of a cell for errors
@ISNA(*x*)	Tests for the special value NA in a cell
@ISNUMBER(*x*)	Determines whether a cell contains a numeric value
@ISSTRING(*x*)	Determines whether a cell contains a label or text
@TRUE	Returns the logical value 1

Use these functions to control and validate the type of data entered into a cell; for example, you can make sure that cell B3 contains a value and not a label by entering the following function into cell B4:

@IF(@ISNUMBER(B3)=1," ","Needs a number")

This function says that if the data in B3 is a value (1 equals the TRUE condition), then display a blank, otherwise display the message Needs a number.

One of the most potent applications for logical @functions is the creation of spreadsheet error-trapping. Whenever a formula returns ERR, for example, every other cell that references the original cell also displays ERR. You can prevent this ripple effect using logical @function commands.

As you read through the following command definitions, refer to the examples to learn more about how to use a particular command in an application.

@FALSE

The @FALSE function displays the logical value 0 when Quattro Pro encounters a false condition. This function commonly is used in @IF formulas to test the validity of numerical calculations and text string comparisons.

Examples: @FALSE = 0
@IF(100=100,50,@FALSE) = 50
@IF(10=60,"Yes",@FALSE) = 0
@IF(A1="September",@TRUE,@FALSE) =
1 (when A1 = September)

@FILEEXISTS(Filename)

The @FILEEXISTS function returns the value 1 when Quattro Pro finds *Filename* in the current directory. When *Filename* does not exist in the current directory, Quattro Pro returns a 0. In this syntax, *Filename* must include the file-name extension and must appear in quotation marks.

To search for a file in a different directory, include the directory path as part of the *Filename* argument.

@IF(Cond,TrueExpr,FalseExpr)

The @IF function evaluates *Cond* and returns *TrueExpr* when *Cond* is true, and returns *FalseExpr* when *Cond* is false. In this syntax, *Cond* is a logical expression representing the condition to be tested, and *TrueExpr* and *FalseExpr* are numbers or string values surrounded by quotation marks. *Cond* must be some logical expression that Quattro Pro can evaluate as true or false.

Typically, *Cond* is a formula similar to the following function:

   @IF(B5=40,@TRUE,@FALSE)

You can create compound conditions by adding #AND#, #OR#, or #NOT# between the logical conditions. When you use #AND#, both expressions must be true for the entire condition to be true. When you use #OR#, at least one of the expressions must be true for the entire condition to be true. When you use #NOT#, the single expression must be false for the entire condition to be true.

Examples: @IF(10>1#AND#25=15,"TRUE","FALSE") = FALSE
@IF(10>1#OR#25=15,"TRUE","FALSE") = TRUE
@IF(#NOT#10>1,"TRUE","FALSE") = FALSE
@IF(#NOT#10<1,"TRUE","FALSE") = TRUE

The @IF function is most effective when you test multiple conditions from within one @IF function command by nesting other conditions. To nest conditions, include a second @IF function command as one of the expressions.

Example: @IF(A1="Larry",1,@IF(A1="Curly",2,@IF(A1="Moe",3,"No Stooges")))

This expression tells Quattro Pro to return a 1 if A1 contains the label Larry. If A1 does not contain the label Larry, Quattro Pro evaluates *FalseExpr*. This expression tells Quattro Pro to return a 2 if A1 contains the label Curly. If it does not contain the label Curly, Quattro Pro evaluates the *FalseExpr*. This expression tells Quattro Pro to return a 3 if A1 contains the label Moe. If it does not contain the label Moe, Quattro Pro evaluates the *FalseExpr* and displays the label No Stooges.

Valid nested @IF expressions cannot exceed 254 characters.

@ISERR(x)

The @ISERR function reviews the active cell for errors. When Quattro Pro finds ERR, it returns 1; otherwise it returns 0.

Use the @ISERR function with the @IF function to prevent the ripple effect of formula errors.

Example: @IF(@ISERR(A50),@NA,1.05*SALES)

@ISNA(x)

@ISNA tests to see whether *x* returns the value NA. When *x* equals NA, Quattro Pro returns a 1; otherwise it returns 0. In this syntax, *x* can be a cell address or an expression.

Quattro Pro does not interpret a label entered in the form NA as the special NA value. To create this value on a spreadsheet, you must use the @NA function.

Examples: @ISNA("NA") = 0
@ISNA(@NA) = 1

@ISNUMBER(x)

@ISNUMBER tests to see whether *x* contains a numeric value. When *x* contains a numeric value, ERR, NA, or is a blank cell, Quattro Pro returns a 1; otherwise the program returns 0. In this syntax, *x* can be a cell address or an expression.

Examples: @ISNUMBER(100) = 1
@ISNUMBER("100") = 0
@ISNUMBER(4/26/90) = 1
@ISNUMBER(@ERR) = 1
@ISNUMBER("ERR") = 0

@ISSTRING(x)

@ISSTRING tests to see whether *x* contains a label or a text string. When *x* contains either item, Quattro Pro returns 1. Quattro Pro returns 0 when *x* is a blank cell, a numeric value, or a date value. In this syntax, *x* can be a cell address or an expression.

Examples: @ISSTRING("STRING") = 1
@ISSTRING(12345) = 0
@ISSTRING(4/26/85) = 0
@ISSTRING("") = 1
@ISSTRING(@ERR) = 0

@TRUE

@TRUE returns the logical value 1 when Quattro Pro encounters a true condition. This function commonly is used in @IF formulas.

Examples: @IF(10=10,@TRUE,@FALSE) = 1
@IF(10=9,@TRUE,@FALSE) = 0

Using Financial @Functions

Quattro Pro's financial @functions provide you with powerful, real-world tools to help you manage your personal and business finances. You can use Quattro Pro's financial @function commands to aid in capital budgeting, predict results of various investments, compute payment schedules, and evaluate annuities.

@NPV(0.12,B5..B10), for example, tells you the net present value of a series of six future incoming cash flows at a 12 percent interest rate. Such information can help you to determine the desirability of an investment.

You also can calculate depreciation for assets using a variety of accepted methods; for example, @SLN(20000,3000,10) tells you that the yearly depreciation expense for a 10-year asset that costs $20,000 and has a $3,000 salvage value is $1,700.00.

You must follow these general rules when using financial @function commands:

- Use positive numbers to enter cash inflows and use negative numbers to enter cash outflows. The 1-2-3 compatible @functions described later in this section do not distinguish between positive and negative cash flows.

- You can enter interest rates as a percent (8%) or in decimal form (0.08). Quattro Pro converts percent entries to a decimal format.

- Make sure that the time units within an @function are standard for all arguments, a particularly important concern when using term and interest rate arguments. If you have an annual interest rate of 15% and a term of 36 months, for example, convert the annual interest rate to a monthly rate (15%/12) or express the months argument in terms of years (3).

Many financial @function commands use the same arguments, but in different order. Table 6.13 defines each argument that Quattro Pro requires for the financial @function commands.

Table 6.13 Financial @Function Command Arguments

Argument	Description
Rate	The fixed interest rate per compounding period
Fv	The value an investment will reach
Pv	The present value of an investment
Cost	The cost of an asset
Salvage	An asset's worth at the end of its useful life
Life	The expected useful life of an asset
Period	The depreciable period of an asset
Pmt	The amount of the period payment
Nper	The number of periods (an integer >= 2)
Type	0 denotes end-of-period payments; 1 denotes beginning-of-period payments
Per	The current payment period in *Nper*
Guess	An estimate of an internal rate of return
Block	A block containing the cash flow values

6 — USING FUNCTIONS

Five financial @function commands have two syntax forms so that you can save them on a spreadsheet in a Lotus-compatible format (see table 6.14). The Quattro Pro syntax, however, is more precise than its Lotus 1-2-3 equivalent.

Table 6.14 Financial @Function Command Syntax

Quattro Pro Syntax	Lotus 1-2-3 Syntax
@FVAL(*Rate,Nper,Pmt,<Pv>,<Type>*)	@FV
@IRATE(*Nper,Pmt,Pv,<Fv>,<Type>*)	@RATE
@NPER(*Rate,Pmt,Pv,<Fv>,<Type>*)	@CTERM
	@TERM
@PAYMT(*Rate,Nper,Pv,<Fv>,<Type>*)	@PMT
@PVAL(*Rate,Nper,Pmt,<Fv>,<Type>*)	@PV

The angle brackets indicate an optional argument. If one or both optional arguments are omitted, Quattro Pro assumes that the values for both optional arguments are 0.

Table 6.15 lists the financial @function commands.

Table 6.15 Investment Analysis @Function Commands

@Function	Description
@CTERM(*Rate,Fv,Pv*)	1-2-3-compatible form of the @NPER function when the investment is an ordinary annuity
@DDB(*Cost,Salvage,Life,Period*)	Calculates accelerated depreciation
@FV(*Pmt,Rate,Nper*)	1-2-3-compatible form of the @FVAL function
@FVAL(*Rate,Nper,Pmt,<Pv>,<Type>*)	Returns the future value of an ordinary annuity
@IPAYMT(*Rate,Per,Nper,Pv,<Fv>,<Type>*)	Returns the interest portion of a loan payment

continues

Table 6.15 Continued

@Function	Description
@IRATE(*Nper,Pmt,Pv,<Fv>,<Type>*)	Returns the periodic interest rate
@IRR(*Guess,Block*)	Returns an investment's internal rate of return
@NPER(*Rate,Pmt,Pv,<Fv>,<Type>*)	Returns the number of periods
@NPV(*Rate,Block,<Type>*)	Returns the net present value of discounted cash flows
@PAYMT(*Rate,Nper,Pv,<Fv>,<Type>*)	Returns the payment amount for a loan
@PMT(*Pv,Rate,Nper*)	1-2-3-compatible form of the @PPAYMT function
@PPAYMT(*Rate,Per,Nper, Pv,<Fv>,<Type>*)	Returns the principal portion of a loan payment
@PV(*Pmt,Rate,Nper*)	1-2-3-compatible form of the @PVAL function
@PVAL(*Rate,Nper,Pmt,<Fv>,<Type>*)	Returns the present value of an annuity
@RATE(*Fv,Pv,Nper*)	1-2-3-compatible form of the @IRATE function
@SLN(*Cost,Salvage,Life*)	Calculates straight-line depreciation
@SYD(*Cost,Salvage,Life,Period*)	Calculates sum-of-the-years'-digits' depreciation
@TERM(*Pmt,Rate,Fv*)	1-2-3-compatible form of the @NPER function, when the investment is an ordinary annuity

@CTERM(Rate,Fv,Pv)

The @CTERM function returns the number of time periods necessary for an investment of *Pv* to grow to *Fv*. In this syntax, the investment earns *Rate* interest per compounding period.

This function is based on the following formula:

$$\frac{\ln(Fv/Pv)}{\ln(1+Rate)}$$

The @CTERM function assumes that the investment is an ordinary annuity. In an ordinary annuity, the cash flows occur at the end of the period. For example, how long would it take a savings account deposit of $5,000 to grow to $10,000, when the annual interest rate is 8, 9, and 10 percent?

@CTERM(.08,10000,5000) = 9.01 (years)

@CTERM(.09,10000,5000) = 8.04 (years)

@CTERM(.10,10000,5000) = 7.27 (years)

@DDB(Cost,Salvage,Life,Period)

The @DDB function returns the periodic depreciation expense for an asset, using the double-declining balance method. For this function to work properly, the following conditions must be true:

- *Life* >= *Period* >= 1
- *Life* and *Period* must be integers
- *Cost* >= *Salvage* >= 0

The depreciation value (DDB) and book value are calculated as follows:

- Book Value = Cost
- DDB = (2*Book Value)/*Life*
- Book Value = Book Value - DDB

What are the first three annual depreciation expenses, for example, for an asset that costs $100,000, has a salvage value equal to $17,500, and has a useful life of 10 years?

@DDB(100000,17500,10,1) = 20,000 (refer to fig. 6.7)

@DDB(100000,17500,10,2) = 16,000

@DDB(100000,17500,10,3) = 12,800

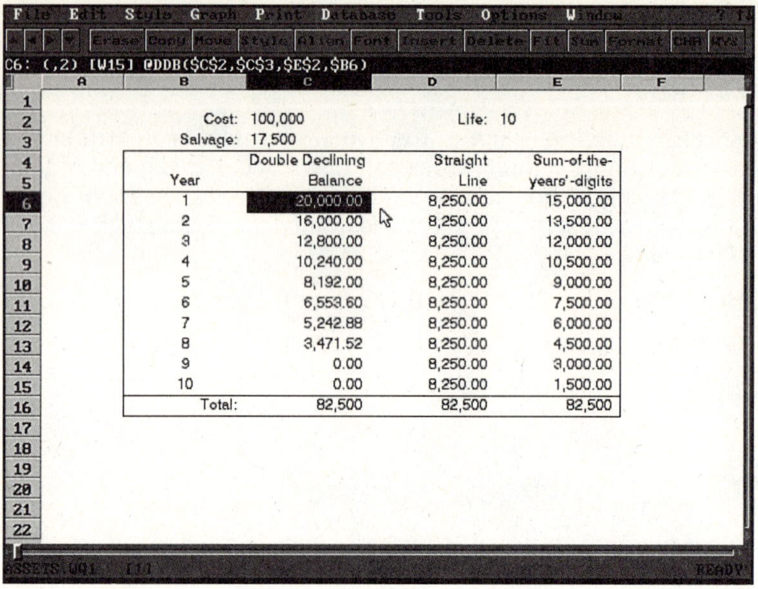

PART I — USING QUATTRO PRO SPREADSHEETS

Fig. 6.7

Cell C6 reveals the formula that calculates the first period depreciation expense under the double-declining balance method.

@FV(Pmt,Rate,Nper)

The @FV function calculates the future value of an investment when *Pmt* is invested for *Nper* periods at the rate of *Rate* per period. This function is based on the following formula:

$$\frac{(1+\text{Rate})^{\text{Nper}}-1}{\text{Pmt *Rate}}$$

What is the future value, for example, of making $1,000 deposits into a savings account that earns 8, 9, and 10 percent for periods of 5, 10, and 15 years respectively?

@FV(1000,.08,5) = $5,866.60

@FV(1000,.09,10) = $15,192.93

@FV(1000,.10,15) = $31,772.48

@FVAL(Rate,Nper,Pmt,<Pv>,<Type>)

The @FVAL function is a more precise version of the @FV function. In this syntax, the *Pv* and *Type* arguments are optional. Quattro Pro assumes that their values are zero if you omit *Type* or *Pv* and *Type*.

> **NOTE** This function is incompatible with Lotus 1-2-3. If you must save your spreadsheet in a Lotus-compatible format, use the @FV function. Remember, don't precede cash outflows with a negative sign when you use the @FV function.

What are the future values, for example, of making 5 annual end-of-year deposits versus 5 annual beginning-of-year deposits of $1,000 into a bank account earning 8 percent, whose current balance is $500?

@FVAL(.08,5,–1000,500,1) = $5,601.26

@FVAL(.08,5,–1000,500,0) = $5,131.94

What is the future value of making 15 annual deposits of $1,000 into a money market account that earns 10 percent interest?

@FVAL(.10,15,–1000) = $31,772.48

@IPAYMT(Rate,Per,Nper,Pv,<Fv>,<Type>)

The @IPAYMT function returns the value of the interest portion of a loan payment. In this syntax, *Fv* and *Type* are optional arguments. Quattro Pro assumes that their values are zero if you omit *Fv* or *Type*.

For example, what is the first year's interest deduction on a 15-year, 9.5 percent mortgage on a $300,000 loan? What is the fifth year's interest deduction?

@IPAYMT(.095/12,1*12,15*12,300000) = –$2,306.34

@IPAYMT(.095/12,5*12,15*12,300000) = –$1,926.15

@IRATE(Nper,Pmt,Pv,<Fv>,<Type>)

@IRATE returns the periodic interest rate earned (paid) on an investment (loan) equal to *Pv*. Here, *Nper* is the compounding term of the investment (loan); *Pmt* represents the per period interest payment earned (paid); and *Pv* is the current value of the investment.

The @IRATE function is a more precise version of the @RATE function. In this syntax, *Fv* and *Type* are optional. Quattro Pro assumes that their values are zero if you omit *Type* or *Fv* and *Type*.

For this function to work properly, the first and last cash flows must have opposite signs. If they do not, Quattro Pro assumes that the transaction may not have a meaningful rate, so it returns ERR.

Suppose that you want to finance the purchase of a $20,000 car and have the choice of paying $675.81 per month for three years or $538.54 per month for four years. Which is the better deal for you?

What annual interest rate do you need to earn to accumulate $20,000 at the end of three years if you make three annual deposits of $3,000, and your account balance is $5,000 today?

@IRATE(3,–3000,–5000,20000) = 21.37%

NOTE This function is incompatible with Lotus 1-2-3. If you must save your spreadsheet in a Lotus-compatible format, use the @RATE function. Remember, don't precede cash outflows with a negative sign when you use the @RATE function.

@IRR(Guess,Block)

The @IRR function calculates the internal rate of return on an investment. The @IRR function returns the interest rate that causes the net present value of an investment to be 0. Net present value (NPV) is the net worth today of investing a sum and receiving future cash flows. When the NPV of an investment is 0, the investment is considered to be a break-even venture.

When you calculate NPV, you discount future cash flows using an interest rate. This rate is equal to your opportunity interest rate—the maximum rate you can earn by investing elsewhere. In other words, if the best you can do is earn 12.5 percent in a bank account, your opportunity interest rate is 12.5 percent.

To evaluate the worth of potential investments, you must design a table that describes how the cash flows in and out of the investment. Figure 6.8 contains a 10-year cash flow table, which describes the same investment opportunity ($50,000) with differently timed cash flows.

In this syntax, *Block* contains the cash flows and *Guess* is a user-supplied estimate of the internal rate of return.

To use this function properly, you first must create a data table that contains each periodic cash flow. Negative signs must precede cash outflows.

The first cash flow must be negative to indicate that it is the initial investment. The ensuing cash flows can vary from period to period in size and sign.

6 — USING FUNCTIONS

Fig. 6.8

Cell C18 reveals the formula that calculates the internal rate of return for investment option 1.

What is the internal rate, for example, of return of investing $50,000 today, using the cash flow streams shown in figure 6.8?

Option 1 @IRR(.125,C4..C14) = 15.098%

Option 2 @IRR(.125,D4..D14) = 15.386%

Option 3 @IRR(.125,E4..E9) = 14.870%

Option 4 @IRR(.125,F4..F14) = 14.870%

@NPER(Rate,Pmt,Pv,<Fv>,<Type>)

The @NPER function determines the number of periods it takes for *Pv* to equal *Fv* when investing *Pmt* per period at a rate of *Rate*.

The @NPER function is a more precise version of the @CTERM and @TERM functions. In this syntax, *Fv* and *Type* are optional. Quattro Pro assumes their values are zero if you omit *Type* or *Fv* and *Type*.

NOTE This function is incompatible with Lotus 1-2-3. If you must save your spreadsheet in a Lotus-compatible format, use @CTERM or @TERM. Remember, don't precede cash outflows with a negative sign when you use the @CTERM or @TERM functions.

How long does accumulating $5,000 take, for example, if you deposit $1,000 annually into a bank account that pays 10 percent?

@NPER(.10,–1000,0,5000) = 4.25 (years)

How long does accumulating $5,000 take if you deposit $250 annually into a bank account that pays 10 percent and has a current balance of $2,500?

@NPER(.10,–250,–2500,5000) = 4.25 (years)

How long does accumulating $1 million take if you deposit $1,000 annually into a bank account that pays 10 percent?

@NPER(.10,–1000,0,1000000) = 48.42 (years)

@NPV(Rate,Block,<Type>)

The @NPV function calculates the net present value of the cash flows in *Block*, discounted at a periodic interest rate of *Rate*.

The @NPV function has one optional argument, *Type*. If the cash flows occur at the beginning of the period, set *Type* to 0. If they occur at the end of the period, enter 1.

NOTE The optional argument Type is not 1-2-3 compatible.

What is the net present value, for example, of an investment that requires you to invest $50,000 today and pays back dividends per the cash flow streams shown in figure 6.9?

Option 1 @NPV(.125,C4..C14) = $5,364

Option 2 @NPV(.125,D4..D14) = $7,004

Option 3 @NPV(.125,E4..E9) = $5,493

Option 4 @NPV(.125,F4..F14) = $11,589

@PAYMT(Rate,Nper,Pv,<Fv>,<Type>)

The @PAYMT function returns the fully amortized value of a loan payment. This function is a more precise version of the @PMT function. In this syntax, *Fv* and *Type* are optional arguments. Quattro Pro assumes that their values are zero if you omit *Type* or *Fv* and *Type*.

NOTE This function is incompatible with Lotus 1-2-3. If you must save your spreadsheet in a Lotus-compatible format, use @PMT. Remember, don't precede cash outflows with a negative sign when you use the @PMT function.

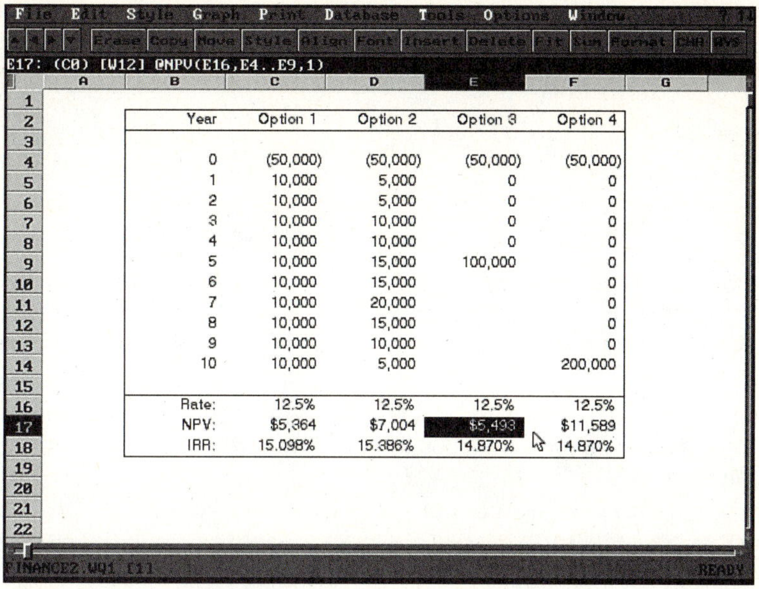

6 — USING FUNCTIONS

	A	B	C	D	E	F
2		Year	Option 1	Option 2	Option 3	Option 4
4		0	(50,000)	(50,000)	(50,000)	(50,000)
5		1	10,000	5,000	0	0
6		2	10,000	5,000	0	0
7		3	10,000	10,000	0	0
8		4	10,000	10,000	0	0
9		5	10,000	15,000	100,000	0
10		6	10,000	15,000		0
11		7	10,000	20,000		0
12		8	10,000	15,000		0
13		9	10,000	10,000		0
14		10	10,000	5,000		200,000
16		Rate:	12.5%	12.5%	12.5%	12.5%
17		NPV:	$5,364	$7,004	$5,493	$11,589
18		IRR:	15.098%	15.386%	14.870%	14.870%

E17: (C0) [W12] @NPV(E16,E4..E9,1)

Fig. 6.9

Cell E17 reveals the formula that calculates the net present value for investment option 3.

How much must you deposit, for example, in an account earning 25 percent to accumulate $10,000 in 5 years?

@PAYMT(.25,5,0,10000) = –$1,218.47

What is the monthly payment for a $225,000, 15-year, 12 percent fixed-interest mortgage? What if the loan term is stretched to 30 years?

@PAYMT(.01,180,225000) = –$2,700.38

@PAYMT(.01,360,225000) = –$2,314.38

@PMT(Pv,Rate,Nper)

@PMT returns the fully amortized payment when borrowing *Pv* dollars at *Rate* percent per period over *Nper* periods. In this syntax, interest is assumed to be paid at the end of each period.

The @PMT function assumes that the investment is an ordinary annuity. In an ordinary annuity, the cash flows occur at the end of the period.

What is the total annual payment, for example, on a $100,000, 30-year, 10 percent fixed-interest mortgage?

@PMT(100000,.10,30) = $10,607.92 (per year)

What is the monthly payment for a $225,000, 15-year, 12 percent fixed-interest mortgage? What if the loan term is stretched to 30 years?

@PMT(225000,.01,180) = $2,700.38

@PMT(225000,.01,360) = $2,314.38

@PPAYMT(Rate,Per,Nper,Pv,<Fv>,<Type>)

The @PPAYMT function returns the value of the principal portion of a loan payment. In this syntax, *Fv* and *Type* are optional arguments. Quattro Pro assumes their values are zero if you omit *Type* or *Fv* and *Type*.

What is the first year's principal payment, for example, on a 15-year, 9.5 percent mortgage on a $300,000 loan? What is the fifth year's principal payment?

@PPAYMT(.095/12,1*12,15*12,300000) = –$826.33

@PPAYMT(.095/12,5*12,15*12,300000) = –$1,206.52

@PV(Pmt,Rate,Nper)

The @PV function calculates the present value of an investment when *Pmt* is received for *Nper* periods and is discounted at *Rate* percent per period.

This function is based on the following formula:

$$\frac{1-(1+Rate)^{-Nper}}{Pmt * Rate}$$

The @PV function assumes that the investment is an ordinary annuity. In an ordinary annuity, the cash flows occur at the end of the period.

What is the most that you can pay today, for example, for an investment that provides you $500 per year for 10 years, if you can earn 7.5 percent on your money elsewhere? What if the investment provides you $750 per year? Or $1,000 per year?

@PV(500,.075,10) = $3,432.04

@PV(750,.075,10) = $5,148.06

@PV(1000,.075,10) = $6,864.08

@PVAL(Rate,Nper,Pmt,<Fv>,<Type>)

The @PVAL function is a more precise version of the @PV function. In this syntax, the *Fv* and *Type* arguments are optional. Quattro Pro assumes that they are zero if *Type* or both arguments are omitted.

> **NOTE** This function is incompatible with Lotus 1-2-3. If you must save your spreadsheet in a Lotus-compatible format, use @PV. Remember, don't precede cash outflows with a negative sign when you use the @PV function.

The local lottery official, for example, offers you 3 alternative annuities, all of which pay 10 percent. The first pays you $3,850 per year for 10 years, the second pays you $3,350 for 13 years, and the third pays you the lump sum of $100,000 after 15 years. Which annuity is the best alternative?

@PVAL(.10,10,–3850) = $23,656.58

@PVAL(.10,13,–3350) = $23,796.24

@PVAL(.10,15,0,–100000) = $23,939.20

@RATE(Fv,Pv,Nper)

The @RATE function calculates the interest rate needed for an investment of *Pv* to be worth *Fv* in *Nper* compounding periods. If you enter *Nper* in years, @RATE returns the annual interest rate; if you enter *Nper* in months, it returns the monthly interest rate.

This function is based on the following formula:

$$\left[\frac{Fv}{Pv}\right]^{1/Nper} - 1 \qquad \left[\frac{Fv}{Pv}\right]^{1/Nper} - 1$$

The @RATE function assumes that the investment is an ordinary annuity, in which the cash flows occur at the end of the period.

What interest rate, for example, must you earn for $100,000 to grow to $1,000,000 in 10 years?

@RATE(1000000,100000,10) = 25.89%

What interest rate must you earn for $1,000 to grow to $2,000 in 5 and 10 years?

@RATE(2000,1000,5) = 14.87%

@RATE(2000,1000,10) = 7.18%

@SLN(Cost,Salvage,Life)

The @SLN function returns one year's depreciation expense for an asset, using the straight-line method. This function is based on the following formula:

$$\frac{\text{Cost - Salvage}}{\text{Life}}$$

What is the annual depreciation expense, for example, for an asset that costs $100,000, has a salvage value equal to $17,500, and has a useful life of 10 years?

@SLN(100000,17500,10) = $8,250 (see fig. 6.10)

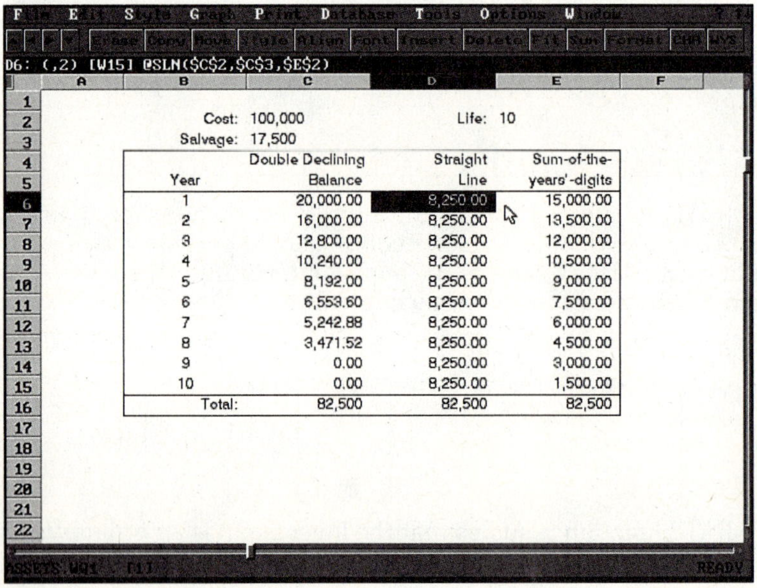

D6: (,2) [W15] @SLN($C$2,$C$3,$E$2)

Cost: 100,000 Life: 10

Salvage: 17,500

Year	Double Declining Balance	Straight Line	Sum-of-the-years'-digits
1	20,000.00	8,250.00	15,000.00
2	16,000.00	8,250.00	13,500.00
3	12,800.00	8,250.00	12,000.00
4	10,240.00	8,250.00	10,500.00
5	8,192.00	8,250.00	9,000.00
6	6,553.60	8,250.00	7,500.00
7	5,242.88	8,250.00	6,000.00
8	3,471.52	8,250.00	4,500.00
9	0.00	8,250.00	3,000.00
10	0.00	8,250.00	1,500.00
Total:	82,500	82,500	82,500

Fig. 6.10

Cell D6 reveals the formula that calculates the straight-line depreciation expense for year 1.

@SYD(Cost,Salvage,Life,Period)

The @SYD function returns the periodic depreciation allowance for an asset, using the accelerated depreciation method. This function offers higher depreciation in the earlier years of the asset's life. This function is based on the following formula:

$$\frac{(Cost-Salvage)*(Life-Period+1)}{Life*(Life+1)/2}$$

For this function to work properly, the following conditions must be true:

Cost >= Salvage >= 0

Life >= Period >= 1

What are the last three annual depreciation expenses, for example, for an asset that cost $100,000, has a salvage value equal to $17,500, and has a useful life of 10 years as in figure 6.11?

@SYD(100000,17500,10,8) = $4,500.00

@SYD(100000,17500,10,9) = $3,000.00

@SYD(100000,17500,10,10) = $1,500.00

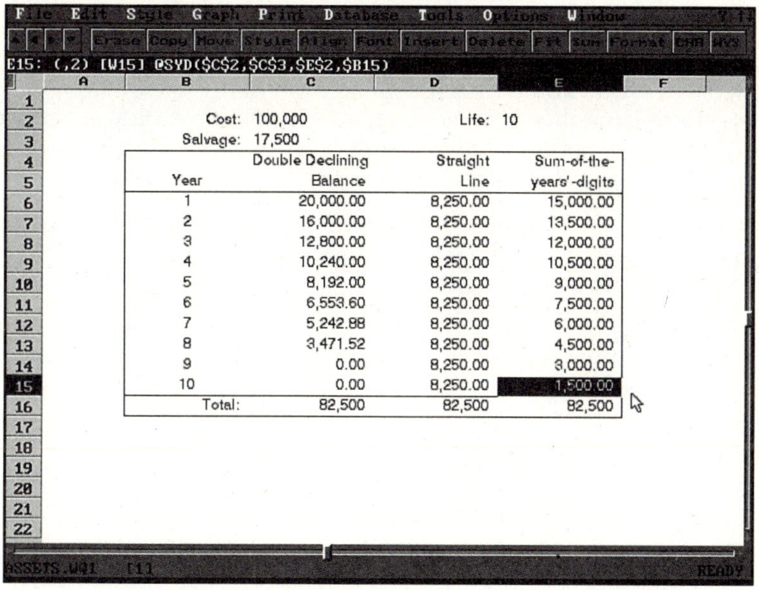

	Cost:	100,000	Life:	10
	Salvage:	17,500		
		Double Declining	Straight	Sum-of-the-
	Year	Balance	Line	years'-digits
	1	20,000.00	8,250.00	15,000.00
	2	16,000.00	8,250.00	13,500.00
	3	12,800.00	8,250.00	12,000.00
	4	10,240.00	8,250.00	10,500.00
	5	8,192.00	8,250.00	9,000.00
	6	6,553.60	8,250.00	7,500.00
	7	5,242.88	8,250.00	6,000.00
	8	3,471.52	8,250.00	4,500.00
	9	0.00	8,250.00	3,000.00
	10	0.00	8,250.00	1,500.00
	Total:	82,500	82,500	82,500

Fig. 6.11

Cell E15 reveals the formula that calculates the sum-of-the-years'-digits depreciation expense for the last year.

@TERM(Pmt,Rate,Fv)

The @TERM function calculates the number of payment periods required to accumulate holdings worth *Fv*. In this syntax, *Pmt* represents regular payments made while accruing interest at the rate of *Rate*. This function is based on the following formula:

$$\frac{\ln(1+Fv/Pmt*Rate)}{\ln(1+Rate)}$$

The @TERM function assumes that the investment is an ordinary annuity, in which the cash flows occur at the end of the period.

How long does accumulating $10,000 take, for example, if you make annual deposits of $1,000 into a bank account that pays 7.5 percent, 8.5 percent, or 9.5 percent?

@TERM(1000,.075,10000) = 7.74 (years)

@TERM(1000,.085,10000) = 7.54 (years)

@TERM(1000,.095,10000) = 7.36 (years)

Using Date and Time @Function Commands

Quattro Pro's date and time @functions have many uses. One popular use for these @functions is to determine elapsed time between two date or time entries. This type of operation is often a necessary part of business reporting, time management, project scheduling, and so forth.

Date and time @functions also are useful tools when you build spreadsheet applications. Put the @TODAY function, for example, at the top of your spreadsheet so that Quattro Pro displays the current date in that cell each time you load the spreadsheet.

Many date and time @function commands use the same arguments. Table 6.16 lists the commands. Table 6.17 defines each argument Quattro Pro requires for the date and time @function commands.

Table 6.16 Date and Time @Function Commands

@Function	Description
@DATE(*Yr,Mo,Day*)	Returns the date serial number of a date
@DATEVALUE(*DateString*)	Returns the date serial number that corresponds to *DateString*
@DAY(*DateTimeNumber*)	Converts a date or time serial number into the number associated with that day (1-31)
@HOUR(*DateTimeNumber*)	Returns the hour portion of the argument

@Function	Description
@MINUTE(*DateTimeNumber*)	Returns the minute portion of the argument
@MONTH(*DateTimeNumber*)	Returns the month portion of the argument
@NOW	Returns the serial number for the system's current time and date
@SECOND(*DateTimeNumber*)	Returns the second portion of the argument
@TIME(*Hr,Min,Sec*)	Returns the time serial number portion of the argument
@TIMEVALUE(*TimeString*)	Returns the time serial number for the argument
@TODAY	Returns the numeric value of the system's date
@YEAR(*DateTimeNumber*)	Returns the year portion of the argument

Table 6.17 Date and Time @Function Command Arguments

Argument	Description
Yr	A numeric value between 0 and 199
Mo	A numeric value between 1 and 12
Day	A numeric value between 1 and 31
DateString	A numeric or string value in any valid date format surrounded by quotation marks
DateTimeNumber	Any number under 73050.9999999
Hr	A number between 0 and 24, representing the hour
Mi	A number between 0 and 60, representing the minute
Sec	A number between 0 and 60, representing the second
TimeString	A numeric or string value in any valid time format, surrounded by quotation marks

As you read through the following command definitions, refer to the examples to learn more about how to use a particular command in an application.

@DATE(Yr,Mo,Day)

The @DATE function displays the date serial number specified by year, month, and day. A valid serial number ranges from 0 to 73,050, which represents the number of days between December 31, 1899, and the date referenced in the formula. December 31, 2099, is the highest date available. Quattro Pro returns ERR when it encounters an illegal date.

Examples: @DATE(87,2,29) = ERR (1987 was not a leap year)
@DATE(88,1,1) = 32143 (the serial date for January 1, 1988)

@DATEVALUE(DateString)

The @DATEVALUE function displays the date serial number that corresponds to *DateString*. Quattro Pro displays ERR when *DateString* is not in a valid date format or is not enclosed in quotation marks.

The five valid *DateString* formats follow:

- DD-MMM-YY ("02-Jan-90")
- DD-MMM ("02-Jan")
- MMM-YY ("Jan-90")
- The default Long International date format
- The default Short International date format

Examples: @DATEVALUE("02-Jan-90") = 32875
@DATEVALUE("02-Jan") = 32875
(Quattro Pro assumes the current year)
@DATEVALUE("Jan-90") = 32874
(Quattro Pro assumes the first day of the month)

@DAY(DateTimeNumber)

The @DAY function converts *DateTimeNumber* into the number associated with that day of the month (1-31). In this syntax, *DateTimeNumber* can be a day or time serial number.

Examples: @DAY(31779) = 2 (1/2/87)
@DAY(73055) = ERR (the number entered was larger than 73050.9999999)

@HOUR(DateTimeNumber)

The @HOUR function displays the hour portion of *DateTimeNumber*. In this syntax, *DateTimeNumber* is a numeric value between 1 and 73050.999999 (the combined date and time serial numbers).

The integer portion of the number is disregarded because only the decimal portion of a serial number pertains to time. The result is between 0 (midnight) and 23 (11 p.m.).

Examples: @HOUR(.25) = 6
@HOUR(.5) = 12
@HOUR(.75) = 18

@MINUTE(DateTimeNumber)

The @MINUTE function displays the minute portion of *DateTimeNumber*. The integer portion of the number is disregarded because only the decimal value in a serial number pertains to time. The result is between 0 and 59.

To extract the minute portion of strings in time format rather than serial format, use the @TIME within the @MINUTE function to translate the time into a serial number.

Examples: @MINUTE(.3655) = 46
@MINUTE(@TIME(3,15,22)) = 15

@MONTH(DateTimeNumber)

The @MONTH function displays the month portion of *DateTimeNumber*. The only portion used is the integer portion, and the result is between 1 (January) and 12 (December).

To extract the month portion of a string in date format rather than serial format, use the @DATEVALUE within the @MONTH function to translate the date into a serial number.

Examples: @MONTH(69858) = 4
@MONTH(@DATEVALUE("3/5/88")) = 3

@NOW

The @NOW function displays the serial number corresponding to the current date time (of your system's clock).

When you perform any function that re-evaluates the spreadsheet, the value generated by @NOW is updated to the current date and time each time you press the F9 (Calc) key.

The decimal portion pertains to time and the integer part of the date or time serial number pertains to the date.

> **Example:** @NOW = 31905.572338 or 5/8/87 or 1:45 PM (The value returned depends on the cell's format.)

@SECOND(DateTimeNumber)

The @SECOND function displays the second portion of *DateTimeNumber*. The integer portion of the number is disregarded because only the decimal portion of a serial number pertains to time. The result is between 0 and 59.

Use the @TIMEVALUE within the @SECOND function to translate the time into a serial number to extract the second portion of a string that is in time format instead of serial format.

> **Examples:** @SECOND(.3655445) = 23
> @SECOND(@TIMEVALUE ("10:08:45 am")) = 45

@TIME(Hr,Min,Sec)

The @TIME function displays the date or time serial number that is represented by *Hr,Min,Sec*. Each argument must be within the given range, and any fractional portions are omitted.

> **Examples:** @TIME(3,0,0) = 0.125 (3:00 am)
> @TIME(18,15,59) = 0.76109953704 (6:15:59 p.m.)

@TIMEVALUE(TimeString)

The @TIMEVALUE function displays the serial time value that corresponds to the value in *TimeString*. ERR results if the value in *TimeString* is not in the correct format or is not enclosed in quotation marks.

The four valid *TimeString* formats are as follows:

- HH:MM:SS AM/PM (03:45:30 PM)
- :MM AM/PM (03:45 PM)
- The default Long International time format
- The default Short International time format

Examples: @TIMEVALUE("03:30:15 AM")
=0.1460069444
@TIMEVALUE("18:15:59")
= 0.76109953704

@TODAY

The @TODAY function enters the numeric value of the system's date. This function is equal to the @INT(@NOW) expression.

Examples: @NOW = 33047.8687 (for June 23, 1990, at 08:50:57 p.m.)
@TODAY = 33047 (for June 23, 1990)
@INT(@NOW) = 33047 (for June 23, 1990)

@YEAR(DateTimeNumber)

The @YEAR function gives the year portion of the *DateTimeNumber*. The result is between 0 (1900) and 199 (2099). You can display the actual year by adding 1900 to the result of @YEAR. To extract the year portion of a string in date format, use @DATEVALUE within the @YEAR function to convert the string into a serial number.

Examples: @YEAR(22222) = 60 (1960)
@YEAR(@DATEVALUE("12-Oct-54") = 54

Using Database Statistical @Function Commands

The database statistical @function commands perform the same operations as the statistical @function commands. Here, though, the @functions operate on a specific field entry in the database instead of a block defined as *List*.

PART I — USING QUATTRO PRO SPREADSHEETS

Table 6.18 lists the functions. The database statistical @function commands have in common the arguments shown in table 6.19.

Table 6.18 Database Statistical @Function Commands

@Function	Description
@DAVG(*Block,Column,Criteria*)	Calculates the average of selected field entries in a database
@DCOUNT(*Block,Column,Criteria*)	Counts the number of selected field entries in a database
@DMAX(*Block,Column,Criteria*)	Returns the maximum value in a database
@DMIN(*Block,Column,Criteria*)	Returns the minimum value in a database
@DSTD(*Block,Column,Criteria*)	Returns the population standard deviation
@DSTDS(*Block,Column,Criteria*)	Returns the sample standard deviation
@DSUM(*Block,Column,Criteria*)	Returns the total of selected field entries in a database
@DVAR(*Block,Column,Criteria*)	Returns the population variance
@DVARS(*Block,Column,Criteria*)	Returns the sample variance

Table 6.19 Database Statistical @Function Command Arguments

Argument	Description
Block	The cell block containing the database, including field names
Column	The number of the column containing the field you want to evaluate; the first column in *Block* is 0, the second is 1, and so on
Criteria	A cell block containing search criteria; you can specify all or part of the database as *Block*, but you must include the field names for each field including *Block*; *Criteria* is defined as the coordinates of a block containing a criteria table; a criteria table specifies the search information

6 — USING FUNCTIONS

As you read through the following command definitions, refer to the examples in the statistical @function section to learn more about how to use a particular command in an application.

@DAVG(Block,Column,Criteria)

The @DAVG function averages selected field entries in a database. Only those entries in column number *Column* whose records meet the criteria specified in *Criteria* are included.

The field specified in the criteria and the field being averaged need not be the same. The field averaged is contained within the column you specified as *Column*.

@DCOUNT(Block,Column,Criteria)

The @DCOUNT function counts selected field entries in a database. Only those entries in column number *Column* whose records meet the criteria specified in block *Criteria* are included.

The field specified and the field being counted need not be the same. The field counted is contained within the column you specified as *Column*.

@DMAX(Block,Column,Criteria)

The @DMAX function finds the maximum value of selected field entries in a database. Only those entries in column number *Column* whose records meet the criteria specified in block *Criteria* are included.

The field specified in your criteria and the field whose maximum values you are finding need not be the same. The field for which you are finding the maximum values is that contained within the column you specify as *Column*.

@DMIN(Block,Column,Criteria)

The @DMIN function finds the minimum value of selected field entries in a database. Only those entries in column number *Column* whose records meet the criteria specified in block *Criteria* are included.

The field specified in your criteria and the field for which you are finding the minimum value need not be the same. The field for which you are finding the minimum value is that contained within the column specified as *Criteria*.

@DSTD(Block,Column,Criteria)

The @DSTD function finds the population standard deviation for selected field entries in a database.

Only those entries in column number *Column* whose records meet the criteria specified in block *Criteria* are included in @DSTD.

The field specified in your criteria and the field for which the standard deviation is being found need not be the same. The field for which you are finding the standard deviation is the field contained within the column you specify as *Column*.

@DSTDS(Block,Column,Criteria)

The @DSTDS function finds the sample standard deviation for the selected field in a database. @DSTDS computes the standard deviation of the population data.

NOTE This function is incompatible with Lotus 1-2-3. Use @DSTD if your spreadsheet requires 1-2-3 compatibility.

@DSUM(Block,Column,Criteria)

The @DSUM function adds up the selected entries in a database. Only those entries whose records meet the criteria specified in block *Criteria* are included in the column number *Column*.

The field specified in the criteria and the field whose sum is being found need not be the same. The field that is contained within the column you specified as *Column* is the field whose sum you are finding.

@DVAR(Block,Column,Criteria)

The @DVAR function calculates the population variance for the selected field in a database and computes the variance of the sample data.

Only those entries in column number *Column* whose records meet the criteria specified in block *Criteria* are included in @DVAR.

The field specified in the criteria and the field for which the variance is being calculated need not be the same. The field counted is contained within the column you specify as *Column*.

@DVARS(Block,Column,Criteria)

The @DVARS function calculates the sample variance for the selected field entries in a database and computes the variance of the population data.

NOTE This function is incompatible with 1-2-3. Use @DVAR if your spreadsheet requires 1-2-3 compatibility.

Questions & Answers

This chapter introduces you to @function commands. If you have any questions concerning particular situations that are not addressed in the examples given, look through this section—your questions may be answered here.

Q: Remembering the syntax for @function commands to use them on my spreadsheets is difficult. Is a quick and easy way to get this information available?

A: Press Alt-F3 to display a list of Quattro Pro's @function commands, then press F1 to display the Function Index window, a context-sensitive help window. Highlight the command that you want to use and press Enter. Quattro Pro displays a definition and the appropriate syntax for the highlighted @function command.

Q: When I use @AVG to calculate the average for a block of values, Quattro Pro returns an answer that I know is incorrect. What should I do?

A: Whenever an @function returns a result that you believe is incorrect, immediately examine the cell block containing the values used as arguments. In the case of the @AVG command, check to make sure that the cell block address you typed is valid, that all of the cells in the block contain values and not strings, and that the cells are not blank. Remember, Quattro Pro counts blanks cells as 0 when it calculates some @functions like @AVG.

Q: When I refer back to @functions at a later date, I have difficulty recalling the names and types of the arguments just by looking at them. I find that I must refer back to the original cell address on the spreadsheet to figure out what value the argument represents. Can I use an easier way to recall an argument's origin?

A: Quattro Pro offers two ways to help you to remember the origin of an argument used in an @function. First, assign a block name to an argument using the /**E**dit **N**ames **C**reate command. You can use cell block names instead of cell addresses in formulas and @function commands. (See the section titled, "Naming a Block" in Chapter 4, "Manipulating Data," for more information.)

Second, attach a comment to the @function command as you enter it into a cell. Comments serve to jog your memory about the purpose and origin of the arguments used in an @function. To attach the comment "Computes 1991 total sales" to @SUM(B10..B15), for example, type the following:

@SUM(B10..B15);Computes 1991 total sales

The length of such an entry (@function command plus the comment) cannot exceed 254 characters.

Q: I notice that several @function commands have two forms that seem to perform the same calculation. When do I use one and not the other?

A: Several @function commands have two forms: a Quattro Pro version and a 1-2-3 compatible version. If you do not require 1-2-3 compatibility for your Quattro Pro spreadsheets, you should use the Quattro Pro version of an @function command. The Quattro Pro versions are always more precise than their 1-2-3 counterparts.

Several financial @functions, for example, fall into this category: @FVAL and @FV, @IRATE and RATE, @NPER and CTERM, @PAYMT and @PMT, and @PVAL and @PV. Note that the Quattro Pro versions of these @function commands require additional arguments, which are what enable the Quattro Pro versions of the @function commands to return more precise results.

If you require 1-2-3 spreadsheet compatibility, do not use the Quattro Pro form of any @function command that has a 1-2-3 form. If you do, the @functions return incorrect results when retrieved into 1-2-3.

Q: The financial @function that I entered is displaying a negative value when it should be displaying a positive value. What's wrong?

A: A negative value indicates that you are paying out money, such as when you make an investment. A positive value indicates that you are receiving cash, such as when you earn interest in a bank account. To ensure that the @function result displays the correct sign, make sure to use the correct signs for the arguments appearing in the @function command.

Q: With respect to using the financial @function commands, how do I know whether an argument should be positive or negative?

A: Use a positive number to indicate an inflow of cash, such as when you receive an interest payment, withdraw money from a bank account, or cash out an investment. Use a negative number to indicate an outflow of cash, such as when you make a loan payment, deposit a sum in a bank, or invest in an annuity. If the value contained in the original cell is negative, and you want to supply a cell address as the argument, do not enter a negative argument (such as –C3).

Q: The result returned by a financial @function command is dramatically different than what I expected. What should I look for?

A: When a financial @function command returns a result that is much larger or smaller than you anticipated, the time periods used to express the arguments may be mismatched. For example,

@FVAL(.12,3,–1000)

returns $3,374.44—the value after 3 years of investing $1,000 in a bank account that earns 12% annually. If you instead enter

@FVAL(.12,36,–1000)

Quattro Pro returns the value $484,463.12. Here, the second argument is entered accidentally in months (36) instead of in years (3). Always make sure to match the time periods (all months, all years, and so on) for the arguments you enter into a financial @function.

Summary

Chapter 6 shows you how to use all Quattro Pro @function commands. Having completed this chapter, you should understand the following Quattro Pro concepts:

- Creating the correct syntax for an @function command
- Selecting and entering an @function command on a spreadsheet
- Using arithmetic and trigonometric @functions
- Using statistical @functions to return data about sample and population data sets
- Using string @functions to perform mathematical operations on text and string labels

PART I — USING QUATTRO PRO SPREADSHEETS

- Using miscellaneous @functions to monitor spreadsheet formulas and available system memory
- Using logical @functions to create test conditions that return values
- Using financial @functions to evaluate investments, amortize loans, and depreciate assets
- Using database statistical @functions to perform statistical analyses of data appearing in a database

Chapter 7 examines methods for analyzing @functions and other types of formulas. This chapter features two commands: the /Tools Solve For command and the /Tools Audit command. The Solve For command enables you to solve formulas backwards, and the Audit command monitors and troubleshoots spreadsheets that rely on accurate formulas.

CHAPTER 7

Analyzing Spreadsheets

In Chapter 3, "Entering and Editing Data," you learned how to enter numbers, formulas, and @function commands into a spreadsheet. You also learned how to correct obvious errors in formulas.

In Chapter 6, "Using Functions," you learned all about using @function commands in your spreadsheets. That chapter's topics ranged from basic mathematical operations to methods for using logical and string functions to tips about how to turn spreadsheets into statistical, scientific, and financial analysis tools.

Chapter 7 shows you how to analyze @functions and other spreadsheet formulas using two commands found on the **T**ools menu. The **S**olve For command enables you to solve formulas backwards. You supply the answer, and **S**olve For locates the variables that produce that answer. With the Au**d**it command, you can monitor and troubleshoot spreadsheet applications that depend on accurate formulas.

In this chapter you learn how to use the **S**olve For and Au**d**it commands to do the following activities:

- Solve the @SLN function backwards to locate an asset life that produces a certain straight-line depreciation expense
- Verify the accuracy of an investment return by solving the @IRR and @NPV functions backwards

PART I — USING QUATTRO PRO SPREADSHEETS

- Solve the @IPAYMT function backwards to locate a principal value that produces a certain annual interest expense
- Simultaneously run **What-If** analyses and **S**olve For operations
- Identify formula dependencies and locate circular, blank, label, and ERR references in spreadsheet formulas
- Monitor external formula links to other spreadsheet files

Using the Solve For Command

With the **S**olve For command, you can solve spreadsheet formulas backwards. You pick the answer and then tell Quattro Pro to build a formula that produces that answer. This technique for analyzing spreadsheet data is efficient because it eliminates the need for trial-by-error number crunching and enables you to concentrate on the more important details of the analysis at hand.

One of the most powerful uses for the **S**olve For command is in spreadsheets that use @functions. In a mortgage application, for example, the @PAYMT function determines the payment for a loan when the principal, rate, and term of the loan are known.

Suppose, however, that you also want to know the interest rate that produces a payment amount that is $250 less a month. Alternatively, suppose that you want to determine the loan term that produces a payment amount that is $500 less a month. You can use the @RATE and @TERM commands to locate these answers, but that method means entering two additional @functions and the appropriate arguments into the spreadsheet.

With the **S**olve For command, you can find answers to these types of questions all from one menu, with no additional spreadsheet entries required.

Reviewing the Solve For Menu

When you choose /**T**ools **S**olve For, Quattro Pro displays the **S**olve For menu. The six commands on this menu define each element in the formula that Quattro Pro is to solve (see table 7.1).

7 — ANALYZING SPREADSHEETS

Table 7.1 The Solve For Menu Commands

Command	Description
Formula Cell	Prompts you to identify the cell location of the mathematical formula you want to solve
Target Value	Prompts you for the value of the answer you seek
Variable Cell	Prompts you to identify the location of the cell that Quattro Pro varies in an attempt to reach the **T**arget Value
Parameters	Defines rules for Quattro Pro to follow when executing a **S**olve For operation
Go	Executes a **S**olve For operation
Reset	Clears all **S**olve For menu settings and returns them to their default values

NOTE The order in which you choose the **S**olve For options and identify values is not important as long as you supply a value or cell address for each before you choose **G**o.

Understanding the Rules for Using Solve For

You must know several rules before executing your first **S**olve For operation. The following rules cover what will and will not work when recording the settings on the **S**olve For menu:

- The **F**ormula Cell must contain a formula or a cell address that references a formula. The **F**ormula Cell cannot contain string values or text formulas.

- The **T**arget Value must be a value, a formula, or a cell address that references a value or formula. Any value that includes positive and negative numbers of up to eight significant digits is considered valid for this type of entry. The Target Value does not change if the referenced cell's contents change.

- The **V**ariable Cell is one that already is included in the **F**ormula Cell calculation and now contains an answer. Examples of invalid cells are protected cells or cells that contain formulas, dates, times, or text.

PART I — USING QUATTRO PRO SPREADSHEETS

- On the **Parameters** menu, choose **Max** Iterations to define the number of attempts Quattro Pro should make to solve the formula. By default, Quattro Pro makes 5 attempts to solve a formula; the program can make up to 99 attempts.

- On the **Parameters** menu, choose **Accuracy** to specify the accuracy for the computed **Target Value**. Enter a fractional number between 0 and 1. This feature enables you to control **Solve For**'s solutions up to 8 decimal places, resulting in answers that are within a certain number of decimal places of your **Target Value**. By default, Quattro Pro computes to an accuracy of 0.005.

T I P Decimal settings for files created with Quattro Pro Version 3.0 are converted to 0.0005, the new Version 4.0 default fractional setting.

In the next few sections you work with real-life examples that demonstrate the power of the **S**olve For command. Keep in mind that you can apply these same techniques to your own spreadsheets, even if they contain different formulas or @functions.

Solving for a Depreciation Expense

Figure 7.1 shows a spreadsheet that contains a typical Quattro Pro calculation using the @SLN command. In this example, you supply three numerical variables (Cost, Salvage, and Life). Quattro Pro computes the straight-line depreciation expense at $8,500 per year for a 10-year asset that originally cost $100,000 and is expected to be worth $15,000 at disposal.

Suppose, however, that you require at least $12,500 in write-offs on this asset each year. Because the Cost and Salvage values generally are assumed to be constant, you must vary the Life variable until the formula returns the value $12,500.

To solve this formula backwards, follow these steps:

1. Choose /**T**ools **S**olve For. Quattro Pro displays the **S**olve For menu.

2. Choose Formula Cell, type *C7*, and then press Enter to record the location of the cell containing the formula.

3. Choose Target Value, type *12500* (no commas), and press Enter to record the value of the answer you seek.

4. Choose **V**ariable Cell, type *C6*, and press Enter to record the location of the cell that you want Quattro Pro to vary.

5. Choose **G**o to execute the **S**olve For command and solve the formula.

6. Choose **Q**uit to return to the active spreadsheet.

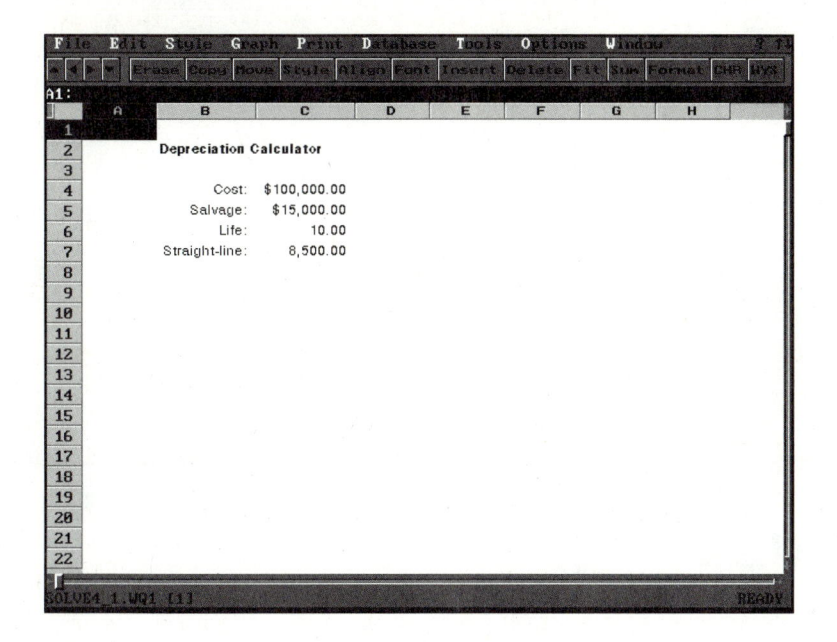

Fig. 7.1

A spreadsheet containing a formula to be solved.

Figure 7.2 shows the **S**olve For menu settings necessary to perform the operation.

Figure 7.3 shows the outcome of this **S**olve For operation.

Quattro Pro adjusts the value in C6, the variable cell, to 6.799961 years. Quattro Pro recalculates the @SLN command with this value, producing a yearly depreciation expense of $12,500.00—the exact target answer you seek. The value in C6 is not a whole number because the variables used in this calculation do not divide evenly into each other.

TIP

Return to the current spreadsheet and press Alt-F5, the Undo key, to reverse a **S**olve For operation and return the contents of the active spreadsheet to their original form.

PART I — USING QUATTRO PRO SPREADSHEETS

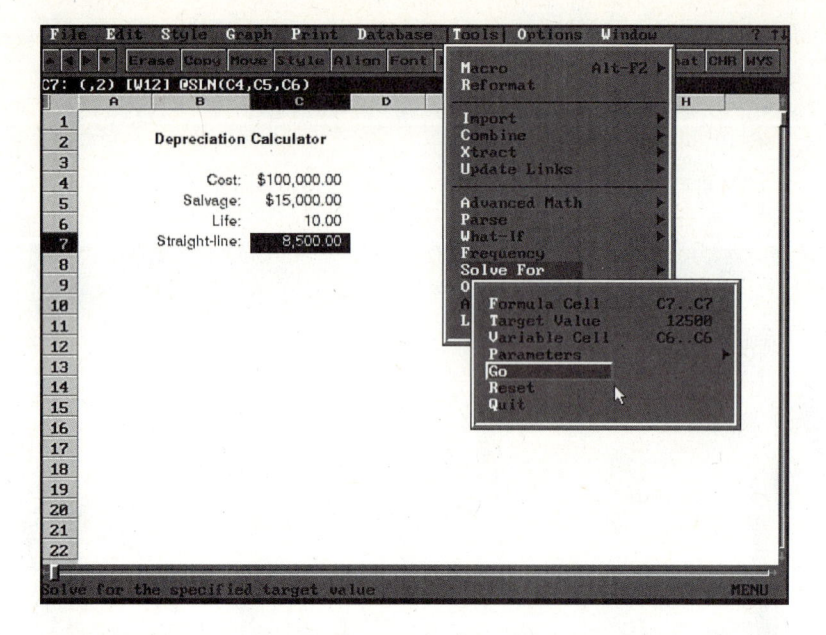

Fig. 7.2

Use the **S**olve For command to solve an @SLN command backwards.

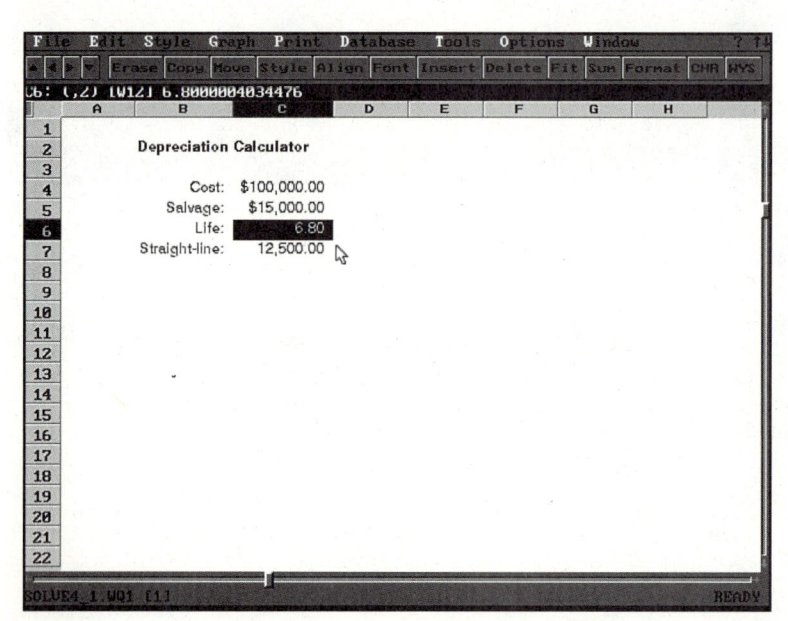

Fig. 7.3

Use **S**olve For to discover that when yearly depreciation is $12,500.00, Life equals 6.80.

Solving for an Investment Return

Figure 7.4 shows another way to use the **S**olve For command for investment calculations. This spreadsheet shows 10 years of cash flow data for an investment.

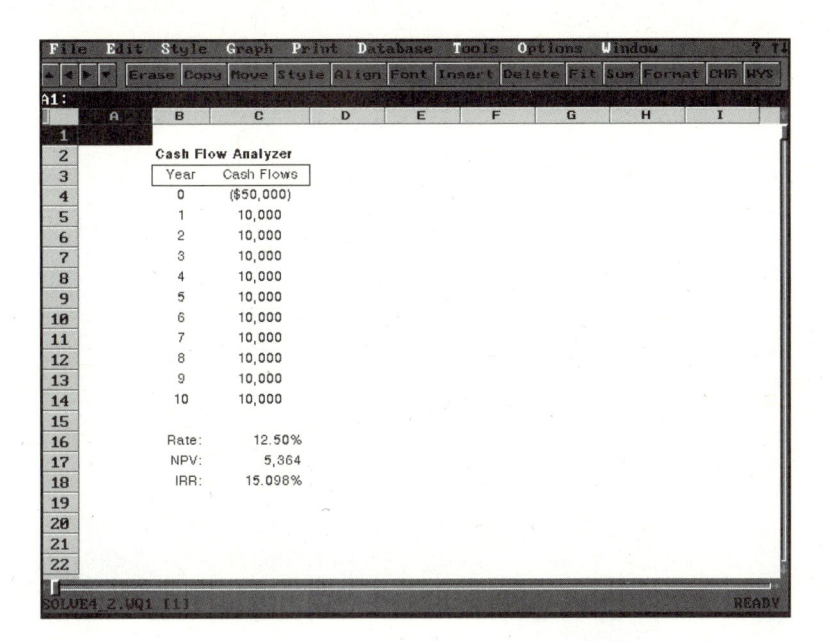

Fig. 7.4

Use the **S**olve For command to verify investment calculations.

Suppose that your investment counselor indicates that this investment offers a 15.098 percent internal rate of return (IRR). Given that your banker offers only a 12.5 percent return on similar investments, the first investment appears more profitable. When you calculate the net present value of this cash flow stream, as shown in cell C17, you discover that the investment's NPV is $5,364—so far so good.

To verify that your investment counselor's IRR calculation is correct, recall the relationship between IRR and NPV. The IRR provides the rate of return that causes an investment's NPV to equal 0.

Use the **S**olve For command to verify the IRR calculations by following these steps:

1. Choose /**T**ools **S**olve For. Quattro Pro displays the **S**olve For menu.

2. Choose **F**ormula Cell, type *C17*, and press Enter to record the location of the cell containing the formula.

PART I — USING QUATTRO PRO SPREADSHEETS

3. Choose **Target Value**, enter *0*, and press Enter to record the value of the answer you seek.

4. Choose **Variable Cell**, type *C16*, and press Enter to record the location of the cell that you want Quattro Pro to vary.

5. Choose **Go** to execute the **Solve For** command and solve the formula.

6. Choose **Quit** to return to the active spreadsheet.

Figure 7.5 shows the **Solve For** menu settings necessary to accomplish the objective.

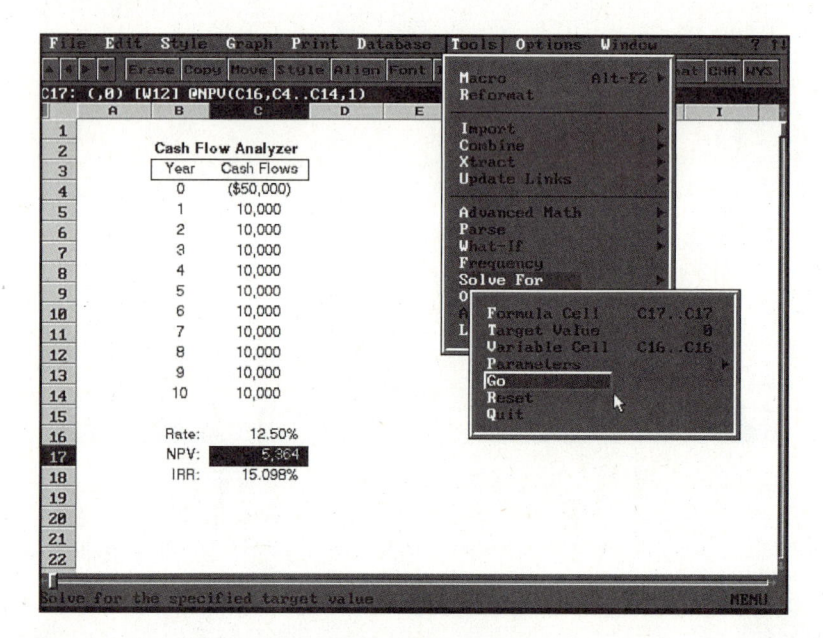

Fig. 7.5

Using the **Solve For** command to solve an @NPV command backwards.

Figure 7.6 shows the outcome of this **Solve For** operation.

As you can see, your investment counselor's calculation is correct within 0.001 decimal places. If you set **Parameters Accuracy** to .001 and rerun the **Solve For** operation, Quattro Pro returns the properly rounded value 15.098%.

Solving for a Mortgage Interest Payment

Figure 7.7 shows yet another application for the **Solve For** command. The @IPAYMT command shown in cell C9 uses four arguments to compute the total interest paid in the first year of a home loan: Interest Rate, Current Year, Total Years, and Principal.

7 — ANALYZING SPREADSHEETS

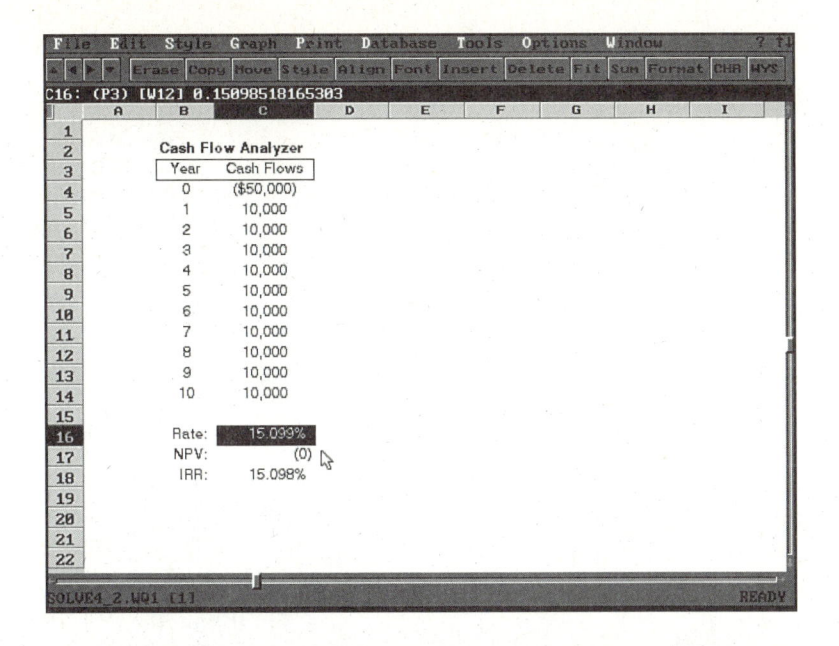

Fig. 7.6

Use **S**olve For to discover that when Net Present Value (NPV) equals 0, Rate equals 15.099 percent.

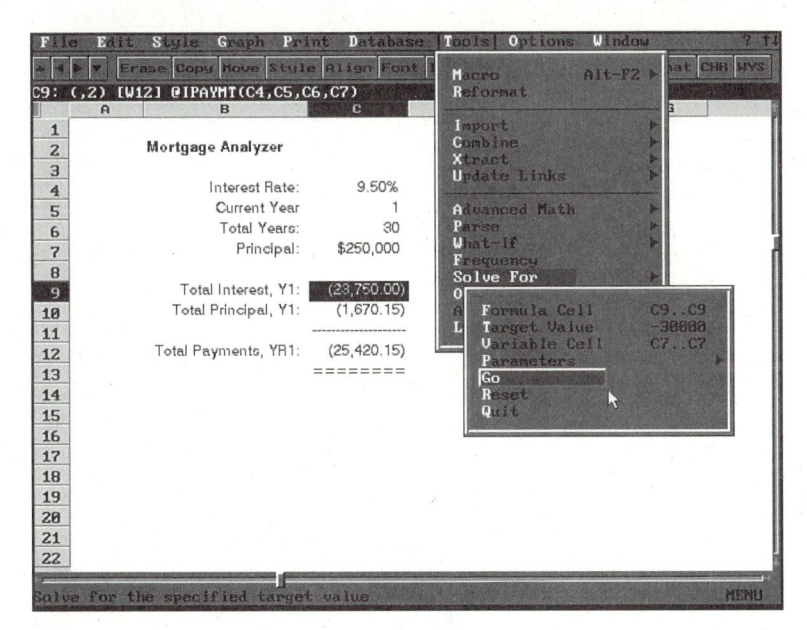

Fig. 7.7

Use the **S**olve For command to solve an @IPAYMT command backwards.

Suppose that your goal is to structure the terms of your home mortgage so that the first year's total interest payment equals $30,000.

You must pay special attention to **Solve For** menu definitions when using complex formulas and @functions. The @IPAYMT formula shown in figure 7.7, for example, uses four arguments to compute the value $23,750. At first glance, you may think that any of these arguments can work as the **Variable Cell**. Only the Interest Rate and Principal arguments work, however. If you define Current Year or Total Years as the **Variable Cell**, Quattro Pro displays the error message `Solve For is not converging on a solution`.

Quattro Pro may fail to execute a **Solve For** operation for several reasons. The most likely reason is that you defined an invalid parameter.

In the example, you should not define the Total Years value as the **Variable Cell** because large fluctuations of this value affect the interest payment only minimally. You should not define the Current Year value as the **Variable Cell** because this argument specifies the year for which the @IPAYMT command calculates the total interest paid. In most cases, you pay the highest amount of interest in year 1 (the current definition in cell C5). Because year 1 is the exact year for which you are running the analysis, cell C5 also is not a candidate as the **Variable Cell**.

When you define the **Target Value**, make sure that it has the same positive or negative sign as the formula's initial result. Notice, for example, that the **Target Value** field shown in the **Solve For** menu in figure 7.7 is negative. Quattro Pro's @IPAYMT command always returns a negative value to show how much interest you pay out of pocket.

> **T I P** As a rule, if a formula is expected to return a negative number, you must make the **Target Value** a negative number.

Figure 7.8 shows the outcome of this **Solve For** operation. The **Solve For** menu settings indicate that Total Interest, YI (in cell C9) is specified as the **Formula Cell**, and Principal (C7) is specified as the **Variable Cell**.

Now, after pressing Alt-F5 to undo the change to the principal, rerun this calculation by specifying cell C4, the Interest Rate value, as the **Variable Cell**. Quattro Pro returns an Interest Rate value equal to 12 percent.

Reflect on the significance of the solutions that Quattro Pro returns for these two **Solve For** operations. Remember, in this example your goal is to structure the terms of a home mortgage so that the first year's total interest payment equals $30,000. Which would you rather do: borrow $315,789 at 9.5 percent or borrow $250,000 at 12.0 percent?

7 — ANALYZING SPREADSHEETS

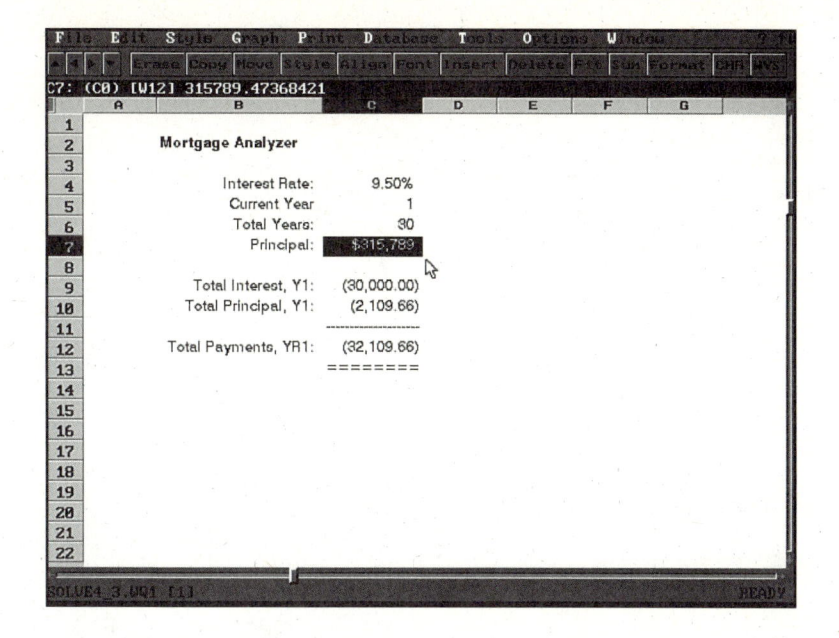

Fig. 7.8

Use **S**olve For to determine that when Total Interest equals ($30,000), Principal equals $315,789.

Solving for a What-If Analysis

The **S**olve For command also can perform what-if analyses with more sophisticated spreadsheet applications, such as the one shown in figure 7.9. This spreadsheet calculates royalties and total earnings for a moderately successful yet undeniably ambitious rock star.

The value in cell C4, 250,000, represents the total revenues to date for album revenues. The value, 100,000, in cell C6 represents a flat fee paid to the rock star for recording an album. The highlighted formula in cell C7 uses the @IF command to evaluate the total royalties to be paid to the rock star according to the royalty rate schedule shown in block B13..C14.

The formula in cell C7 is as follows:

@IF(C4>250000,(250000*C13)+((C4–250000)*C14),C4*C13)

This formula states that if album revenues are greater than $250,000 (C4>250000), multiply the first $250,000 by the initial royalty rate listed in cell C13 (250000*C13). For every revenue dollar over $250,000 the formula adds an additional royalty per the royalty rate listed in cell C14 ((C4–250000)*C14). If album revenues do not exceed $250,000, Quattro Pro uses the second condition listed in the formula, C4*13, which multiplies current album revenues by the initial royalty rate of 10 percent.

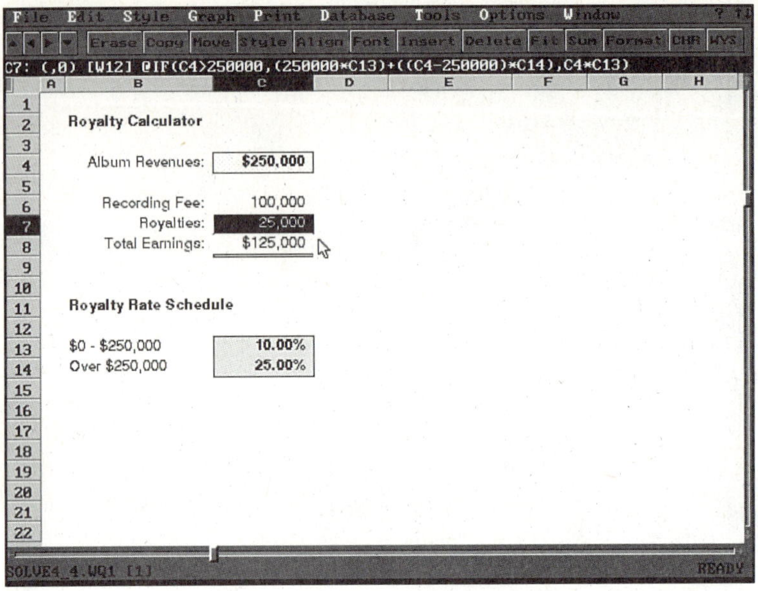

PART I — USING QUATTRO PRO SPREADSHEETS

Fig. 7.9

Use the **S**olve For command to perform a what-if analysis.

Based on this formula and current album revenues, the rock star has earned $125,000 to date ($100,000 plus 10 percent of $250,000).

Suppose now that the rock star is curious about how to increase his Total Earnings figure to $200,000. One way to increase that figure is to determine the level of album revenues necessary to increase Total Earnings to $200,000, given that the Recording Fee is a one-time payment. The spreadsheet in figure 7.10 shows the **S**olve For menu settings necessary to perform this what-if analysis.

In this operation, Quattro Pro evaluates the Royalties formula in cell C7 and varies the value of Album Revenues in cell C4 until the Royalties value equals 100,000. At this level of Royalties, Total Earnings equals $200,000 (see fig. 7.11).

An equally efficient way to accomplish the same objective is to choose the Total Earnings value in cell C8 as the **F**ormula Cell and change the **T**arget Value figure to 200000. This approach works because cell C8 also contains a formula, +C6+C7, which Quattro Pro can evaluate to determine the relationship between Album Revenues, the Recording Fee, the Royalties, and Total Earnings. Figure 7.12 shows the **S**olve For menu settings required for this analysis, and the final results after choosing **G**o.

7 — ANALYZING SPREADSHEETS

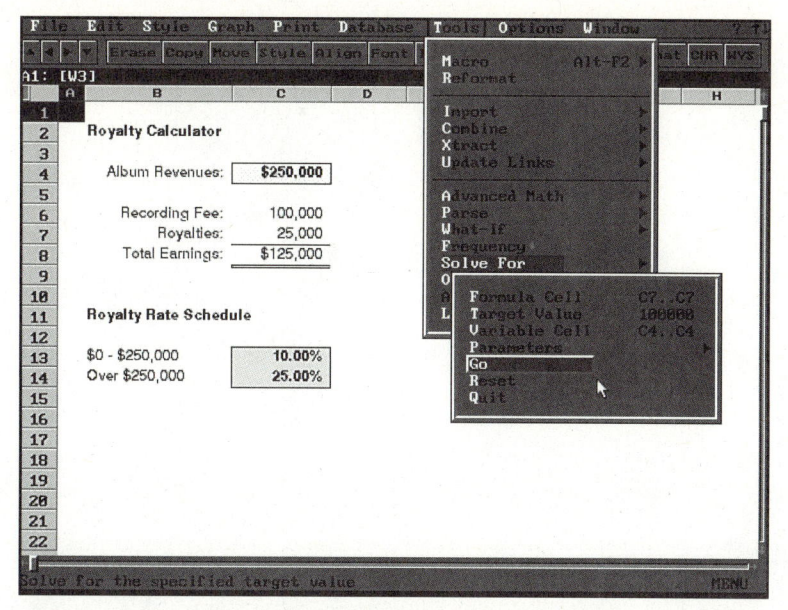

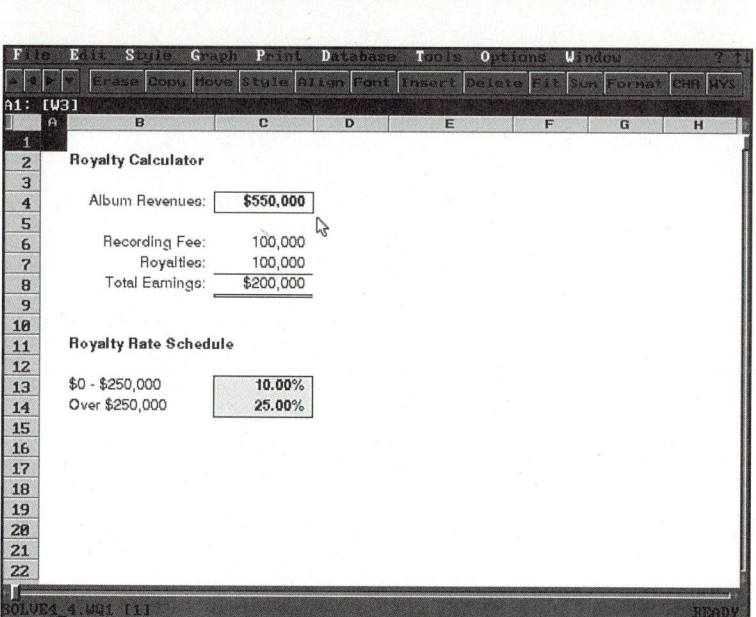

Fig. 7.10

Change the Album Revenues value to increase Total Earnings.

Fig. 7.11

Use **S**olve For to determine that when Royalties equal $100,000 and Total Earnings equal $200,000, Album Revenues equal $550,000.

PART I — USING QUATTRO PRO SPREADSHEETS

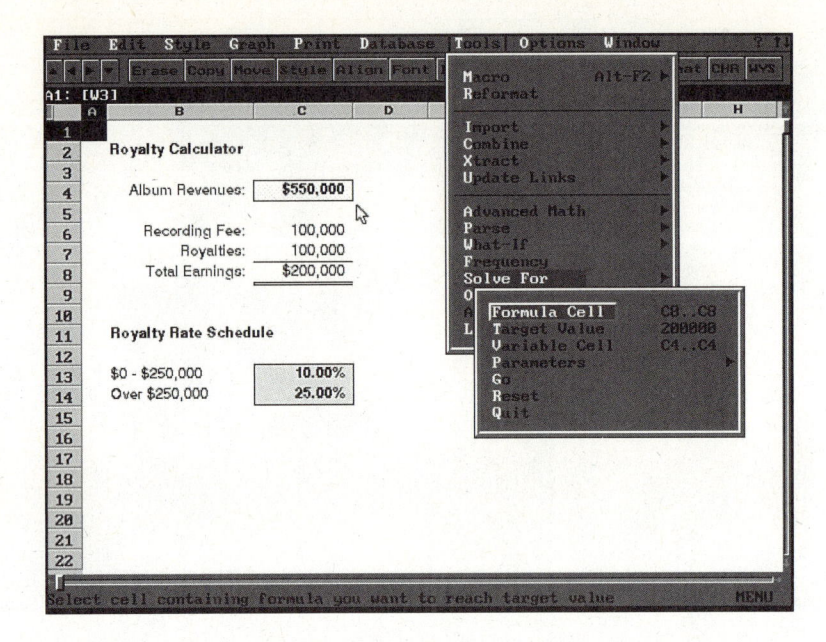

Fig. 7.12

Use the Total Earnings formula as the Formula Cell.

Because the rock star probably cannot influence album revenues after the record is cut, he may approach this problem from a different direction. Suppose that he wants to determine the initial Royalty Rate necessary to increase Total Earnings to $200,000. Figure 7.13 shows the **S**olve For menu settings required for this analysis and the final results after choosing **G**o.

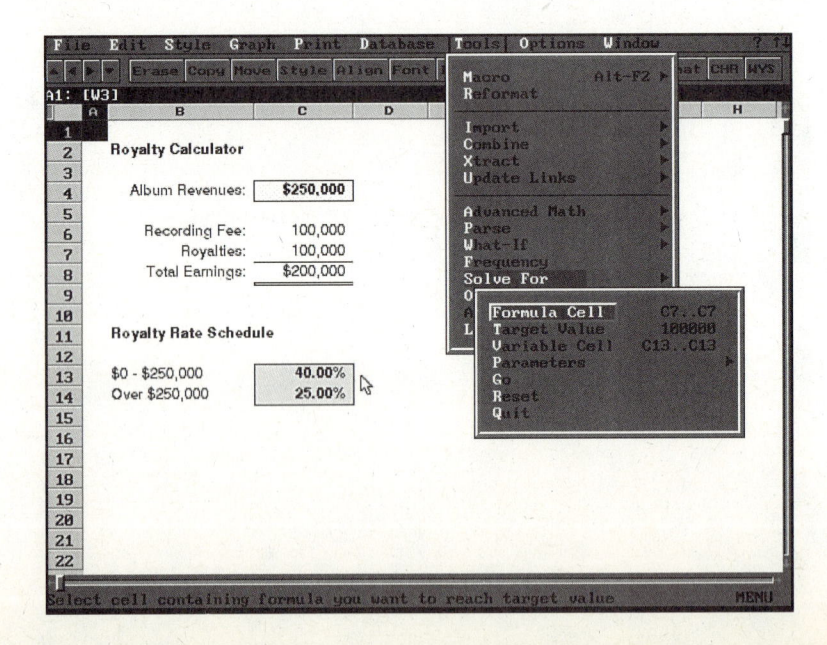

Fig. 7.13

Use **S**olve For to determine that when Total Earnings equal $200,000, the initial Royalty Rate equals 40 percent.

Reflect on the significance of the solutions that Quattro Pro returns for these **S**olve For operations. Remember, the rock star's goal is to increase his Total Earnings figure to $200,000. Which strategy, then, appears more likely: increasing album revenues to $550,000 or renegotiating the recording contract for a higher initial royalty rate?

Using the Audit Command

The /**T**ools Au**d**it command enables you to analyze spreadsheet formulas and provides you with useful information for the ongoing development and maintenance of your spreadsheet applications. If you are responsible for periodically updating spreadsheet applications, or if someone wants you to evaluate a complex spreadsheet that you have never seen before, you can use Quattro Pro's auditing tools to make your job easier.

The options on the Au**d**it menu can depict graphically specific details about formula relationships in a spreadsheet—information such as cell dependencies, circular references, and the presence of ERR values. The Au**d**it command performs detailed analyses of all formulas in a spreadsheet, one cell at a time.

Reviewing the Audit Menu

When you choose /**T**ools Au**d**it, Quattro Pro displays the Au**d**it menu. The first six commands on this menu direct Quattro Pro to perform formula audits, and the last command records the output location for an audit report (see table 7.2).

Table 7.2 The Audit Menu Commands

Command	Description
Dependency	Depicts a tree diagram of cells that are dependent on others for data
Circular	Depicts a tree diagram of cells that contain circular references
Label References	Displays addresses of cells that contain formulas referring to labels
ERR	Displays addresses of cells that contain formulas returning ERR as a result

continues

Table 7.2 Continued

Command	Description
Blank References	Displays addresses of cells that contain formulas referring to blank cells
External Links	Displays addresses of cells that contain formulas linking to other spreadsheets
De**s**tination	Determines whether Quattro Pro sends an audit report to the printer or to the screen

Auditing Spreadsheet Formulas

You follow the same sequence of steps to generate any of the audit options available on the Au**d**it menu. (Remember, you use the De**s**tination command only to identify where to send the audit report.)

To generate an audit report, use the following steps:

1. Choose /**T**ools Au**d**it. Quattro Pro displays the Au**d**it menu.

2. If you want to direct the audit report to a printer rather than the screen, choose De**s**tination **P**rinter.

3. Choose one of the six audit report options listed on the menu. To generate an audit report of ERR values in the current spreadsheet, for example, choose the **E**RR option.

4. When Quattro Pro prompts you for a spreadsheet block to audit, type a valid block address and press Enter.

Quattro Pro immediately begins evaluating formulas in the specified block on the current spreadsheet and then displays the audit report (or sends the report to the printer if you chose that as the destination). After you finish reviewing a displayed audit report, press Esc to return to the current spreadsheet with the Au**d**it menu displayed.

The next few sections describe each type of audit report available on the Au**d**it menu and discuss the circumstances under which you may want to view a particular type of report. The sample application that you audit in these sections appears in figure 7.14. With the exception of the value in cell D7 and those in ranges D12..F12 and D16..F16, every cell in range D7..I21 contains a formula, making this spreadsheet an ideal one for testing Quattro Pro's auditing capabilities.

7 — ANALYZING SPREADSHEETS

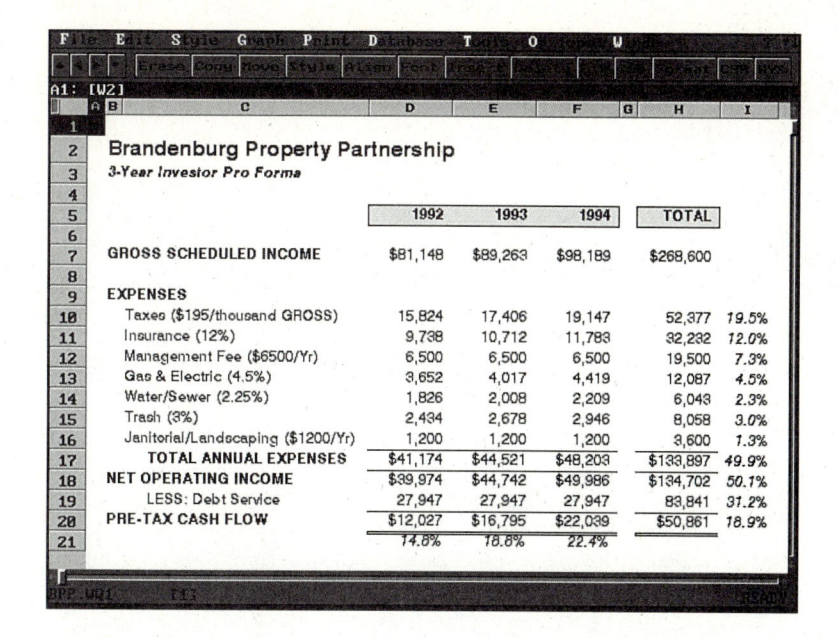

Fig. 7.14

The Brandenburg Property Partnership application to be audited.

Performing a Dependency Audit

A *dependency audit* graphically shows in a tree diagram the cell relationships for the current spreadsheet. You can use this type of report to learn about spreadsheet applications with which you are unfamiliar. You then don't have to search through a spreadsheet cell by cell to learn how the application works.

Printing out a dependency report before performing what-if analyses with a spreadsheet is useful. That way you can be sure of which values to change to test your theories.

To generate a dependency audit report, use the following steps:

1. Choose /**T**ools Au**d**it. Quattro Pro displays the Au**d**it menu.

2. Choose **D**ependency.

3. When Quattro Pro prompts you for a spreadsheet block to audit, type the block address—*D7..I21* for the example—and press Enter.

Quattro Pro immediately displays a graphical tree diagram on the audit screen, depicting the dependency relationships for cells in the spreadsheet.

PART I — USING QUATTRO PRO SPREADSHEETS

To see a list of the menu commands available on the audit screen, press the forward slash (/) key once. Figure 7.15 shows the dependency audit report for the Brandenburg Property Partnership application along with the menu commands available.

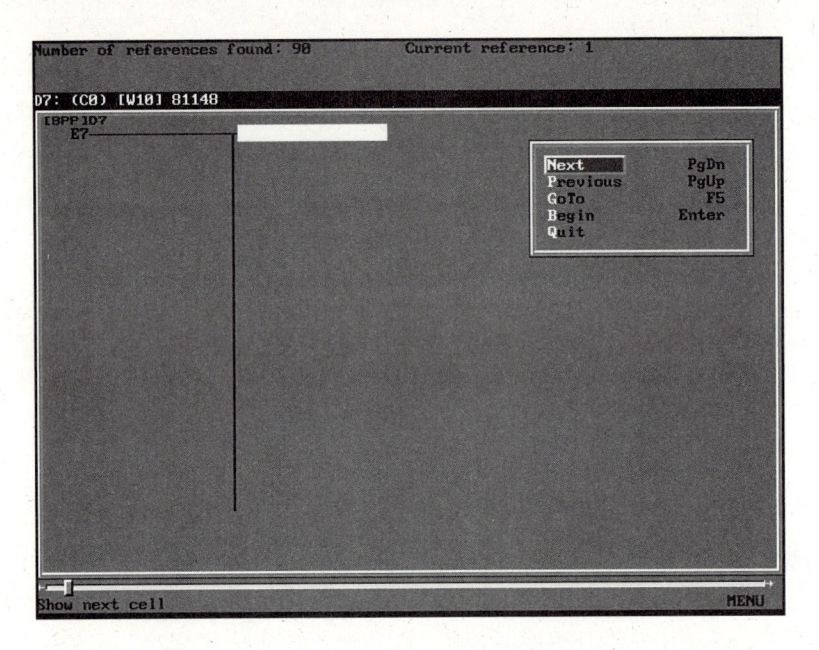

```
Number of references found: 90        Current reference: 1

D7: (C0) [W10] 81148
[BPP]D7
 E7
                                              ┌─────────────────────┐
                                              │ Next         PgDn   │
                                              │ Previous     PgUp   │
                                              │ GoTo         F5     │
                                              │ Begin        Enter  │
                                              │ Quit                │
                                              └─────────────────────┘




Show next cell                                                  MENU
```

Fig. 7.15

A dependency report on the audit screen.

The audit screen displays different types of information about the current audit operation. All the following elements apply to each report type:

DEPENDENCY:	Next, Previous, GoTo, Begin, Quit
CIRCULAR:	Next, Previous, GoTo, Begin, Quit
ERR:	Next, Previous, GoTo, Quit
LABEL REF:	Next, Previous, GoTo, Quit
BLANK REF:	Next, Previous, GoTo, Quit
EXTERNAL LINES:	Next, Previous, GoTo, Quit

The following list summarizes these elements:

■ The Number of references found prompt at the top of the screen displays the number of references located in a spreadsheet for the current audit. In the example shown in figure 7.15, the number of references is 90.

■ The Current reference prompt displays a number that represents the position number in the audit block for the currently highlighted cell—in the example, cell number 1.

7 — ANALYZING SPREADSHEETS

- The *input line* shows the cell address of the audited cell, all formatting information, and the contents of the cell.

- Just below the input line, the *audited cell* appears after the *audited file name*. These references are the cell and spreadsheet file whose dependencies now are depicted on the audit screen. In figure 7.15, D7 is the audited cell, and [BPP] is the audited spreadsheet file.

> **TIP**
>
> If an audited cell contains a formula link to a cell on another spreadsheet, Quattro Pro displays the linking reference directly to the right of the audited cell in the tree diagram. See Chapter 8, "Managing Files and Windows," for more information about file linking.

Table 7.3 contains a list of the menu commands and keys that you can use to maneuver around an audit screen. As you can see, each key corresponds to one of the commands listed in the audit screen menu, shown at the top of the audit screen in figure 7.15.

Table 7.3 The Audit Screen Menu Commands and Keys

Command and Key	Function
/Next (PgDn)	Displays the next cell in the audit block
/Previous (PgUp)	Displays the previous cell in the audit block and makes that cell the audited cell
/GoTo (F5)	Exits the audit screen and returns to the current spreadsheet at the location of the last audited cell
/Begin (Enter)	Audits the cell that currently is highlighted on the audit screen
/Quit (Esc)	Returns to the current spreadsheet with the Audit menu still active

On the audit screen, all dependencies fall to the left of the audited cell. Press the left-arrow key to move through the tree diagram of cell dependencies. In the sample spreadsheet, for example, pressing the left-arrow key four times moves you to cell I10, the last cell on that branch that depends on the audited cell (see fig. 7.16).

PART I — USING QUATTRO PRO SPREADSHEETS

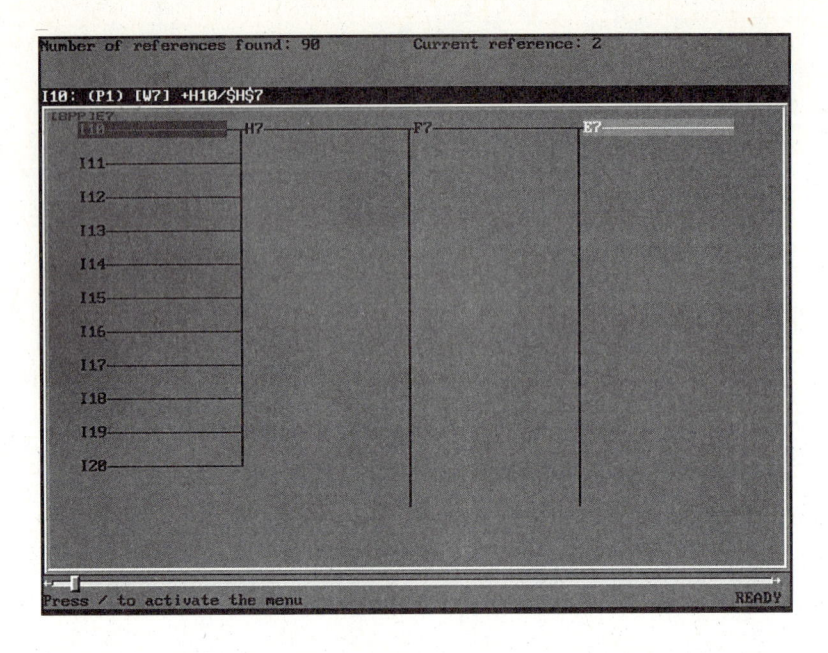

Fig. 7.16

The last cell on a branch for the audited cell.

If the first cell displayed on an audit screen has no dependents, pressing the arrow keys has no movement effect. In the example, choose /Next or press PgDn until a cell with branches appears. Then, press the arrow keys to trace the pathway of that cell's dependent cells.

No matter where you move the highlight, the audit screen displays information about the audited cell until you select another cell by choosing /Next or /Begin. To audit another cell that is displayed in a tree diagram, highlight the cell and choose /Begin, or choose /Next to audit the next cell in the audited block. To audit cell I10 in the sample spreadsheet, for example, highlight the cell and choose /Begin (see fig. 7.17).

T I P When you audit a cell that resides in the left half of the audit screen, Quattro Pro displays a tree diagram that is oriented from left to right rather than from right to left, as seen in previous figures.

Performing a Circular Audit

A *circular audit* graphically shows in a tree diagram all circular cells located in the current spreadsheet. A circular cell contains a formula that refers to itself, such as the formula @SUM(B5..B6) entered into cell B5.

Fig. 7.17

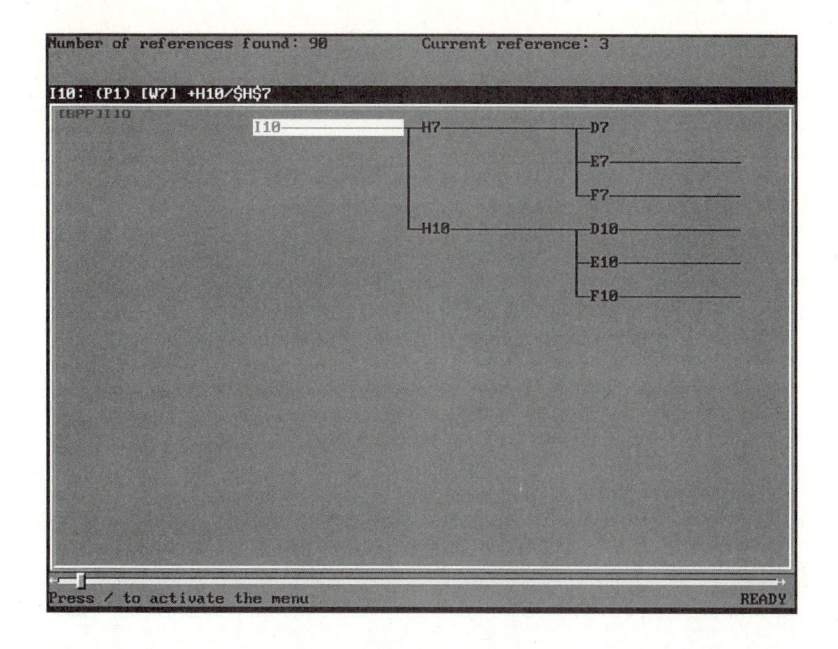

Select a different cell to audit.

Although Quattro Pro provides other means for locating circular cells (/**O**ptions **R**ecalculation and /**W**indow **O**ptions **M**ap View), this approach is the most efficient because it displays all other cells that are affected by the circular cell.

To generate a circular audit report, use the following steps:

1. Choose /**T**ools Au**d**it. Quattro Pro displays the Au**d**it menu.

2. Choose **C**ircular.

3. When Quattro Pro prompts you for a spreadsheet block to audit, type the block address—*D7..I21* for the example—and press Enter.

Quattro Pro immediately displays a graphical tree diagram depicting the circular relationships for cells in the spreadsheet. Figure 7.18 shows the circular audit report for the Brandenburg Property Partnership application.

When a spreadsheet contains more than one circular cell, Quattro Pro highlights the first cell it encounters when it displays the audit screen. In figure 7.18, Quattro Pro is highlighting cell E7 (a circular reference was created intentionally for this example). Because the formula in cell E7 contains a reference to cell F7, which in turn refers back to cell E7, Quattro Pro draws a branch between both cells. The `CIRC` indicator at the end of the branch identifies this relationship as a circular relationship.

PART I — USING QUATTRO PRO SPREADSHEETS

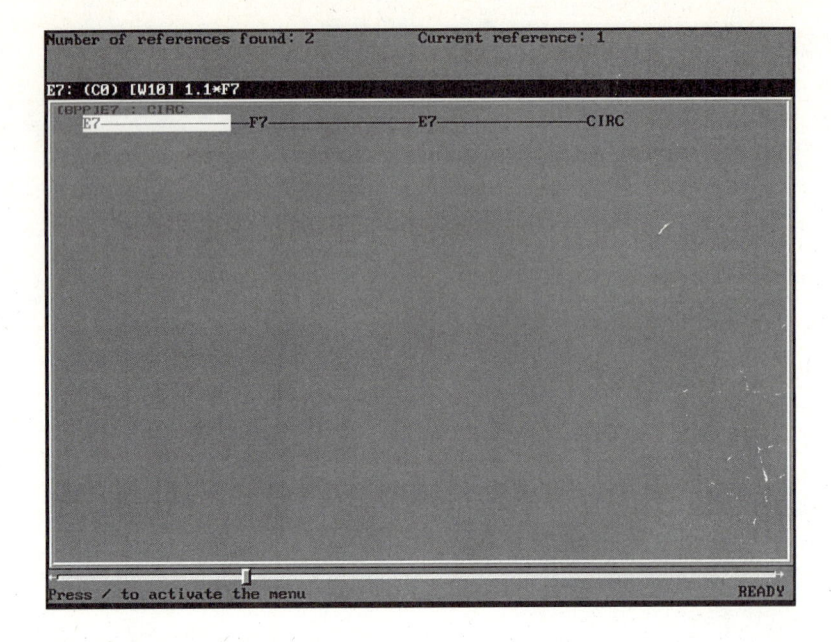

Fig. 7.18

Review a circular report on the audit screen.

You may have noticed that the circular cell audit screen looks much like the dependency audit screen. In fact, not only do they look alike, you can use many of the same keys and commands listed in table 7.3 to maneuver around the circular audit screen. Note that the /Begin command operates only from a dependency audit screen.

TIP Choose /GoTo from a circular audit screen to return to the spreadsheet at the exact cell location where the first circular cell was encountered. There, you can correct the cell referencing error quickly by changing the formula so that it doesn't refer to the cell in which it resides.

When no circular cells are found in the current spreadsheet, Quattro Pro displays the message No circular references found. Press Esc to return to the Audit menu.

Performing a Label Reference Audit

A *label reference audit* displays information about cells containing formulas that refer to labels rather than values. Because Quattro Pro treats labels as zeros when they appear in formulas, math calculations return incorrect answers. This auditing tool, therefore, is useful for verifying that your spreadsheet formula results are correct.

To generate a label reference audit report, use the following steps:

1. Choose /**T**ools Au**d**it. Quattro Pro displays the Au**d**it menu.

2. Choose **L**abel References.

3. When Quattro Pro prompts you for a spreadsheet block to audit, type the block address—*D7..I21* for the example—and press Enter.

Quattro Pro immediately displays the audit screen with information about the first spreadsheet formula encountered that refers to a label. Figure 7.19 shows the label reference audit report for the Brandenburg Property Partnership application.

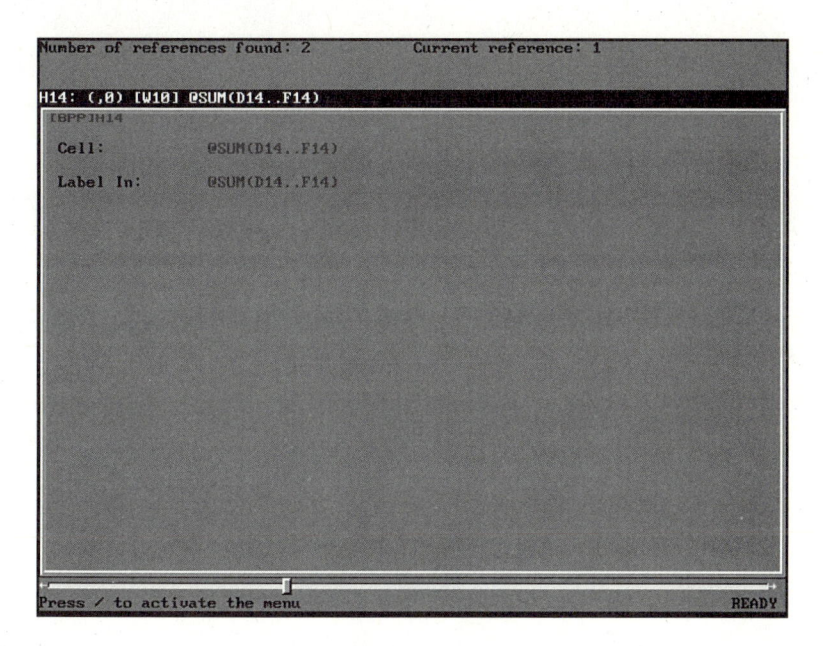

Fig. 7.19

Review a label reference report on the audit screen.

The information on the label reference audit screen helps you to locate what may be incorrect entries in your spreadsheets. When a spreadsheet contains more than one formula that refers to a label, press PgDn or choose /**N**ext to review the next occurrence.

In the sample spreadsheet, note that the audited cell, cell H14, contains the formula @SUM(D14..F14). This message tells you that the range address in the formula is incorrect or that a label rather than a value is included somewhere in range D14..F14.

PART I — USING QUATTRO PRO SPREADSHEETS

The easiest way to determine the cause of the problem is to choose /GoTo and return to the spreadsheet. Quattro Pro places the cell selector in the audited cell, cell H14 (see fig. 7.20). A quick glance at the data on row 14 reveals that the entry in cell F14 appears to be a label rather than a value.

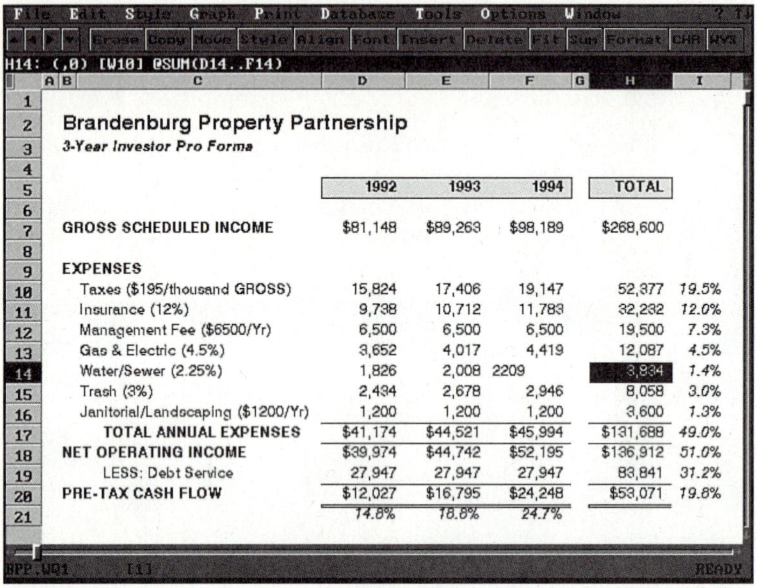

Fig. 7.20

Return to the spreadsheet to search for the cause of a label referencing problem.

On the label reference audit screen, you can use the same menu selections and shortcuts you use on other audit screens.

When no label references are included in the current spreadsheet, Quattro Pro displays the message No such references found. Press Esc to return to the Audit menu.

Performing an ERR Audit

An *ERR audit* displays information about cell formulas that return the value ERR as their result. Complex spreadsheets containing many formulas often pass their results along as input to other formulas. When one cell returns ERR, all cells that rely on that cell's data return ERR—this phenomenon is known as the ERR trickle-down effect. The ERR audit tool is useful for locating and correcting ERR values that appear in your spreadsheets.

To generate an ERR audit report, use the following steps:

1. Choose /**T**ools Au**d**it. Quattro Pro displays the Au**d**it menu.
2. Choose **ERR**.
3. When Quattro Pro prompts you for a spreadsheet block to audit, type the block address—*D7..I21* in the example—and press Enter.

Quattro Pro immediately displays the audit screen with information about the first spreadsheet formula encountered that returns the value ERR. Figure 7.21 shows the ERR audit report for the Brandenburg Property Partnership application.

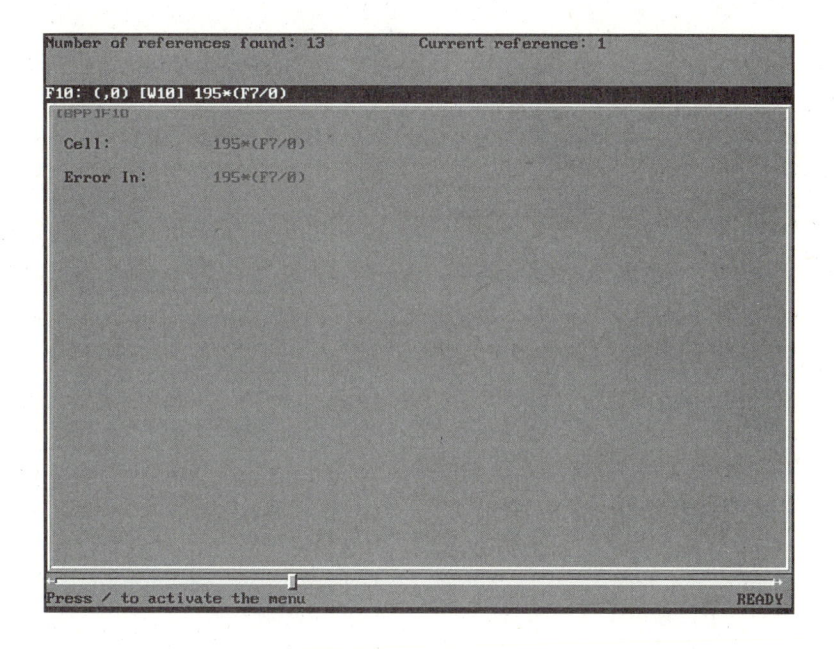

Fig. 7.21

An ERR report on the audit screen.

When a spreadsheet contains more than one formula that returns ERR, press PgDn or choose /**N**ext to review the next occurrence.

In the sample spreadsheet, note that the audited cell, cell F10, contains the formula 195*(F7/0). Any formula that tries to divide by 0 returns ERR as its result.

The easiest way to correct any ERR problems is to choose /**G**oTo and return to the spreadsheet. Quattro Pro places the cell selector in the audited cell—cell F10 in the example. Correct the formula, and Quattro Pro replaces all ERR values with the correct results.

When no ERR values are found in the current spreadsheet, Quattro Pro displays the message No such references found. Press Esc to return to the Au**d**it menu.

Performing a Blank Reference Audit

A *blank reference audit* displays information about cells containing formulas that refer to blank cells. Because Quattro Pro treats blanks as zeros when they appear in formulas, some math calculations return incorrect answers. This auditing tool therefore is useful for verifying that your spreadsheet formula results are correct.

To generate a blank reference audit report, use the following steps:

1. Choose /**T**ools Au**d**it. Quattro Pro displays the Au**d**it menu.

2. Choose **B**lank References.

3. When Quattro Pro prompts you for a spreadsheet block to audit, type the block address—*D7..I21* in the example—and press Enter.

Quattro Pro immediately displays the audit screen with information about the first spreadsheet formula encountered that refers to blank cells.

The information on the blank reference audit screen helps you to locate what may be missing entries in your spreadsheets. When a spreadsheet contains more than one formula that refers to a blank cell, press PgDn or choose /**N**ext to review the next occurrence.

When no blank references are found in the current spreadsheet, Quattro Pro displays the message `No such references found`. Press Esc to return to the Au**d**it menu.

Performing an External Links Audit

An *external links audit* displays information about cells containing formulas that link to other spreadsheets. Choose /**T**ools Au**d**it E**x**ternal Links to search through a spreadsheet for linking formulas before moving or erasing documents.

To generate an external links audit report, use the following steps:

1. Choose /**T**ools Au**d**it. Quattro Pro displays the Au**d**it menu.

2. Choose E**x**ternal Links.

3. When Quattro Pro prompts you for a spreadsheet block to audit, type the block address—*D7..I21* in the example—and press Enter.

Quattro Pro immediately displays the audit screen with information about the first spreadsheet formula encountered that links to another spreadsheet. Figure 7.22 shows the external links audit for the Brandenburg Property Partnership application. In the sample spreadsheet, Quattro Pro locates a single linking formula in cell D7, the audited cell. This formula links to cell B2 in a spreadsheet named FORECAST. If you want to delete FORECAST from your hard disk, change the linking reference in cell D7 in the current spreadsheet to a value before doing so.

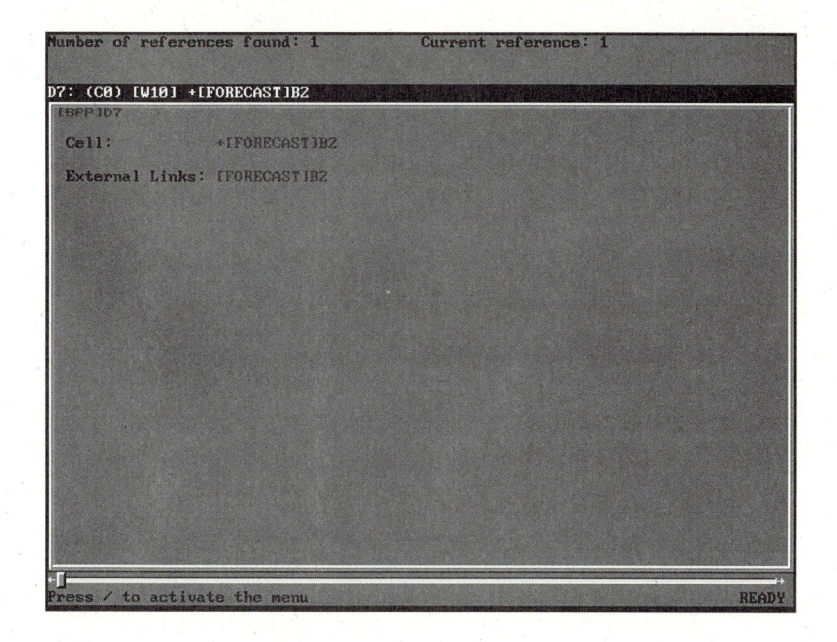

Fig. 7.22

An external links report on the audit screen.

When a spreadsheet contains more than one linking formula, press PgDn or choose /**N**ext to review the next occurrence.

> **TIP**
> Quattro Pro finds all linking formulas in a spreadsheet, regardless of whether the spreadsheets to which the audited spreadsheet is linked are open in memory at the time.

When no linking formulas are found in the current spreadsheet, Quattro Pro displays the message `No such references found`. Press Esc to return to the Au**d**it menu.

PART I — USING QUATTRO PRO SPREADSHEETS

Questions & Answers

This chapter introduces you to two of the analytical tools found on the **Tools** menu: **S**olve For and Au**d**it. If you have questions concerning particular situations that the examples in this chapter do not address, look through this section.

Solving Formulas

Q: I want to run multiple **S**olve For operations in a row, but I must exit the **S**olve For menu each time I want to review data in the spreadsheet that the menus are blocking. What can I do?

A: Press F6, the Window key, to toggle the display of the **S**olve For menu so that you can view data in the spreadsheet. Press F6 again to display the menus when you are ready to execute the next operation.

Q: Quattro Pro cannot locate an answer to a problem I defined—the program keeps displaying the message `No feasible solution is attainable`. I'm certain that the problem variables are realistic, so what went wrong?

A: Possibly Quattro Pro is not trying to solve the problem enough times, or perhaps the required **A**ccuracy setting is unrealistic.

Choose /**T**ools **S**olve For **P**arameters **M**ax Iterations and choose 99, the maximum number allowed. Also check the **A**ccuracy setting on the **P**arameters menu; you may have chosen an unrealistic setting (such as 0.0000000000001).

Q: I tried to use the **S**olve For command on criteria appearing in a database spreadsheet, but Quattro Pro keeps displaying the error message `Invalid value in Variable Cell`. My formula appears to be valid, so what else can be wrong?

A: Even though Quattro Pro accepts formulas for use in certain spreadsheet operations, the formulas may not be appropriate for use in **S**olve For operations. The formula +MONTH is an example of a valid criteria formula that you can use in database operations. You cannot define such a value, however, as the **V**ariable Cell in a **S**olve For operation. Just remember not to use formulas with the **S**olve For command that return dates, times, or strings.

Auditing Formulas

Q: When I generate a circular audit report, Quattro Pro displays the message `No circular references found`, even though the `CIRC` indicator appears on the status line. What's wrong?

A: Quattro Pro displays audit reports only for the selected block, even though, in this case, circular references exist elsewhere in the spreadsheet. Be sure to include the entire spreadsheet in the selected range before you run the audit report again.

Q: The current audit report has located so many references that I am having a difficult time getting an overall picture of the spreadsheet I am reviewing. Does Quattro Pro offer an easier way to do this process?

A: Choose /**W**indow **O**ptions **M**ap View to display general audit information for the current spreadsheet. In map view, Quattro Pro uses special characters to represent labels, formulas, circular references, and other types of spreadsheet entries. See Chapter 8, "Managing Files and Windows," for more information.

Q: I am having difficulty auditing a different cell in the current audit report. Each time I highlight the new cell, the audited cell reference displays the address of the cell Quattro Pro originally audited. What should I be doing?

A: Highlighting a cell appearing in an audit report does not cause Quattro Pro to audit that cell. To change the audited cell from within an audit screen, highlight the target cell and choose /**B**egin.

Q: How do I display the graphic tree diagram in a blank or label reference audit?

A: The audit screen that Quattro Pro displays for dependency and circular audits is different from the one it displays for `ERR`, blank and label reference, and external link audits. The main difference is that the audit screens for the latter group of audits do not display in a graphic tree diagram.

Summary

In this chapter, you learned how to analyze your data using two commands found on the **T**ools menu. These two commands, **S**olve For and Au**d**it, enable you to turn a Quattro Pro spreadsheet into an efficient environment for analyzing information.

PART I — USING QUATTRO PRO SPREADSHEETS

Having completed this chapter's material, you should understand the following concepts:

- Solving a formula backwards
- Auditing spreadsheet formulas for dependencies
- Auditing spreadsheet formulas for circular references
- Auditing spreadsheet formulas for blank and label references
- Auditing spreadsheet formulas for ERR results
- Auditing spreadsheet formulas for links to other spreadsheets
- Printing an Audit report to the screen or to a printer

In Chapter 8, you learn how to use one of Quattro Pro's most notable features: multiple spreadsheet operations. With these techniques, you learn how to link data on spreadsheets and pass information between applications. Chapter 8 also introduces you to the File Manager—Quattro Pro's built-in file-management utility. With the File Manager, you never again need to exit Quattro Pro to copy, move, or erase files.

CHAPTER 8

Managing Files and Windows

This chapter shows you how to create and use files, workspaces, and windows; oversee file operations with the File Manager; link multiple spreadsheets with special formulas; and combine and extract spreadsheet data. You can perform these operations using the commands from the **F**ile, **W**indow, and **T**ools menus.

In the first section of this chapter, you learn how to create, preserve, and recover spreadsheet files by choosing commands from the **F**ile menu. This section continues by explaining how to create a workspace file and save Quattro Pro spreadsheets in file formats that other programs can read.

The second section explains how to use the File Manager, with which you can perform DOS-like file-management operations without leaving Quattro Pro. You can copy, move, rename, and erase files from the File Manager, for example, and display a directory-tree graphic showing the organization of files on your hard disk drive.

Next, you learn about managing Quattro Pro windows. You learn how to display, move, resize, pick, and split windows. This section also shows you how to create special display effects for windows.

The chapter continues by introducing you to linked spreadsheets. By creating linked formulas, you can pass data between spreadsheet applications. Linked spreadsheets can improve your productivity and Quattro Pro's speed of execution.

The final section of this chapter introduces advanced file operations. Using commands found on the **Tools** menu, you learn how to import, combine, and extract data from multiple spreadsheet files.

Reviewing the File Menu Commands

You can use the 13 **F**ile menu commands to create, retrieve, and save files, and to manage the directories in which your files are stored (see fig. 8.1). After creating your own library of spreadsheet files, you can use the **F**ile menu to develop workspace applications that juggle several spreadsheets at the same time.

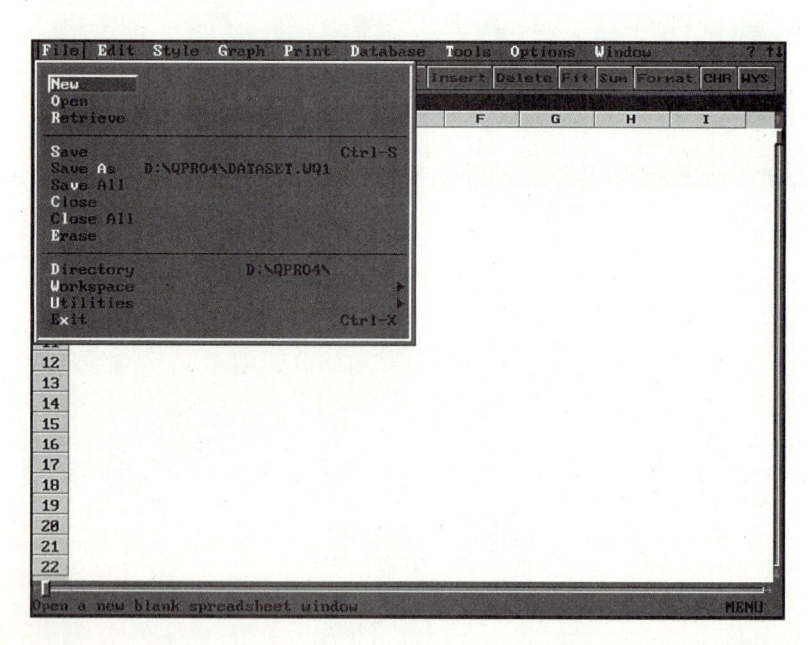

Fig. 8.1

The **F**ile menu commands.

You can use workspace applications to save nonlinked spreadsheets as one unit, save a File Manager window with a group of spreadsheets, and help to preserve the screen position and sequential order of a group of spreadsheets.

The **F**ile menu consists of three types of commands: file-access commands, file-management commands, and miscellaneous file commands. Quattro Pro displays the two Ctrl-key shortcuts and current command settings at the right margin of the **F**ile menu.

In figure 8.1, the active spreadsheet, DATASET.WQ1, is stored in the current directory named \QPRO4. Your screen always will show the active spreadsheet (unless the spreadsheet is SHEET1.WQ1, the default spreadsheet) and the current directory name for your computer.

The file-access commands control the flow of file data from your hard disk drive into Quattro Pro's operating environment. With these commands, you can create a spreadsheet file, load a saved file into its own window, and retrieve a previously saved file.

The file-management commands move file data from Quattro Pro's operating environment onto your hard disk drive. These commands save, rename, close, and erase spreadsheet files.

The miscellaneous commands perform operations such as setting the current directory, creating a workspace file, entering the DOS shell, and accessing file utilities.

Table 8.1 describes the purpose of each **F**ile menu command.

Table 8.1 File Menu Commands

Command	Description
New	Loads a new, blank spreadsheet into its own window
Open	Loads a previously saved spreadsheet file into its own window
Retrieve	Loads a previously saved spreadsheet file into the current window, closing the current spreadsheet
Save	Saves the current spreadsheet using a previously entered file name; prompts you to supply a file name if one has not been specified
Save **A**s	Prompts you for a file name and location; then saves the current spreadsheet using that name
Save All	Saves all currently open spreadsheets using a previously entered file name; prompts you to supply a file name if one has not been specified
Close	Closes the spreadsheet in the current window
Close All	Closes all spreadsheets in all open windows

continues

Table 8.1 Continued

Command	Description
Erase	Erases the current spreadsheet from RAM (but not from your hard disk or floppy disk) and displays a new, blank spreadsheet
Directory	Designates the default directory path name for storing files on the hard disk drive
Workspace	Saves the names of all open spreadsheets to a workspace file name or restores previously saved workspaces
Utilities	Exits to DOS, activates the File Manager window, or sets the SQZ! file compression options
Exit	Ends a work session by closing all open windows, exits Quattro Pro, and returns system control to DOS

Working with Files

This section reviews the processes that every user goes through in a Quattro Pro work session. Before reading the section, however, keep in mind a few basic terms.

Spreadsheet describes the physical area containing rows and columns into which you enter data. After you finish entering data, assign a unique file name to the spreadsheet so that you easily can locate and recall the spreadsheet the next time you want to use that data.

Quattro Pro enables you to open and view up to 32 windows at a time. A *window* is the area in which Quattro Pro displays the current spreadsheet. Each time you open a new spreadsheet, Quattro Pro assigns the spreadsheet a window number from 1 to 32 and displays the number in brackets on the status line to the right of the spreadsheet name.

Workspace describes a group of related spreadsheet files that are open in Quattro Pro's memory at the same time. When you restore a workspace file name, Quattro Pro loads each spreadsheet in the workspace into RAM.

Creating, Opening, and Retrieving Files

Each time you access Quattro Pro from your PC, the program displays a new, blank spreadsheet named SHEET1.WQ1 in the current window, unless you specify another file to be loaded automatically. With this spreadsheet, you can enter data, ignore the blank spreadsheet and open a saved spreadsheet, or close the blank spreadsheet by retrieving a saved spreadsheet.

The top three commands on the **F**ile menu give you access to new and saved spreadsheet files. To display another new, blank spreadsheet, choose /**F**ile **N**ew. You can load up to 32 spreadsheets into Quattro Pro's memory with this command.

To load a previously saved spreadsheet into the current window without affecting other spreadsheets that are open in memory, choose /**F**ile **O**pen. Quattro Pro displays the file list box, which lists the names of spreadsheet files saved in the current directory (see fig 8.2). While this box is on-screen, you can execute several keystrokes to display more information about your files. Table 8.2 describes the effect of the keystrokes you can use while the file list box is on-screen. You also can use the six buttons on the right side of the file list box to view lists of files, directories, and drives.

Table 8.2 Keys Affecting File List and File Name Prompt Boxes

Key	Description
Backspace	Displays a list of all files in the parent directory
Ctrl-Backspace	Removes the default prompt and file list
Enter	Accepts the file name highlighted on the list
Esc	Erases data on the line, one directory path name at a time
F2	Enters Search mode so that you can enter the first letter of the file you are searching for
F3	Expands the file list so that it fills the screen
+	Displays the file size and the last date altered for the files in the file list
–	Removes the file size and the last date altered from the file list display
Space bar	Highlights the next file name in the list

The six buttons on the right side of the file list box enable you to display details about files, directory paths, and disk drives on your PC. With one click, you can view a list of all available drives, directories, files opened in the current Quattro Pro work session, and more. If you don't have a mouse, you can access these buttons by pressing the slash (/) key, using the arrow keys to move between buttons, and pressing Enter to choose a button. To switch from the buttons back to the file list, press Esc. Table 8.3 describes the purpose of each button in the file list box.

Table 8.3 File-Name Prompt Box Buttons

Button	Action
..\	Lists the files in the parent directory
DRV	Lists all available drives
↑/↓	Expands or contracts the file-name prompt box
+/−	Reveals and hides the date-and-time stamp for each file
PRV	Lists all files previously opened during your current Quattro Pro work session so that you can open a file from that list
NET	Shows network drive mappings, if any exist

To load a spreadsheet into Quattro Pro's memory, highlight the file name in the file list box or the list of previously opened files and press Enter. Press the plus sign (+) key and F3 for a full-screen display of the file list box (see fig. 8.2).

To load a saved spreadsheet into the current window, choose /**F**ile **R**etrieve. If you have an unsaved spreadsheet in the current window when you issue this command, Quattro Pro asks whether you want to lose your changes. Choose **N**o to return to the spreadsheet so that you can save the file or **Y**es to erase the spreadsheet from memory. Like the **O**pen command, this command displays a file-name box. Highlight a file name and press Enter to retrieve that spreadsheet.

The major difference between these two commands is that Quattro Pro closes the current spreadsheet when you retrieve a saved spreadsheet file. After you choose /**F**ile **O**pen, Quattro Pro loads the spreadsheet file on top of all existing open spreadsheets.

You use the **O**pen command most when you link spreadsheets with formulas. The **O**pen command enables you to open and work simultaneously with several Quattro Pro spreadsheets.

8 — MANAGING FILES AND WINDOWS

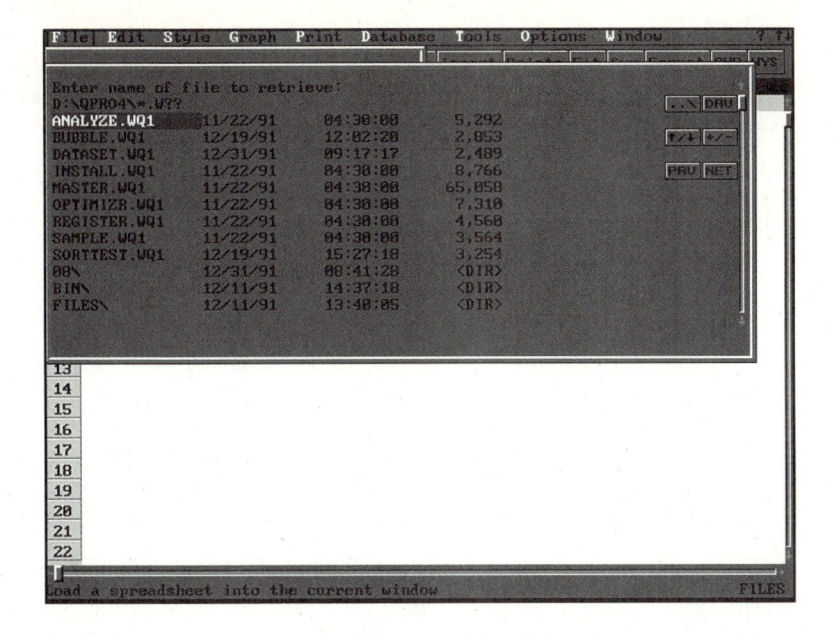

Fig. 8.2

The file list box in a fully enlarged format.

Quattro Pro assigns each open spreadsheet a window number according to the order in which you originally opened the spreadsheet in memory. Quattro Pro displays the window number in brackets on the status line.

Saving, Closing, and Erasing Files

The six commands in the middle of the File menu enable you to save spreadsheet files permanently, close previously saved files without saving changes, and erase the current spreadsheet from Quattro Pro's memory.

After you finish entering data, choose /File Save to assign a unique name to the spreadsheet. After you choose this command, Quattro Pro prompts you to enter a name. Type the name in the file name prompt box, and then press Enter to store the name permanently. When you choose /File Save in the future with the same spreadsheet, Quattro Pro displays a `File already exists` prompt if the file has been saved before and you opened or retrieved it. The program remembers the spreadsheet's name and asks you to specify whether you want to cancel the operation, replace the stored spreadsheet file with the current spreadsheet, or create a backup of the spreadsheet file. This last command also transfers a copy of the file onto your hard disk drive with the file extension BAK.

> **TIP** Press Ctrl-S, the Ctrl-key shortcut for the **S**ave command, to save a Quattro Pro spreadsheet file.

After a spreadsheet is saved to a file, you can recall the spreadsheet using the **O**pen or **R**etrieve command.

To give the current spreadsheet a new file name, choose /**F**ile **S**ave **A**s. When prompted, type a new file name and press Enter to copy the spreadsheet. You do not necessarily duplicate it; you can save a spreadsheet with changes to a new name and leave the original intact. When executed, Quattro Pro displays the new file name and window number on the status line.

To save all spreadsheets open in memory, choose /**F**ile **S**ave All. Quattro Pro first prompts you to save the active spreadsheet. If you previously saved the active spreadsheet, Quattro Pro asks you to specify whether you want to replace the stored spreadsheet file with the current spreadsheet, create a backup of the spreadsheet file, or cancel the operation. Quattro Pro activates the next spreadsheet open in memory and repeats this save operation. This process continues until the program saves all spreadsheets open in memory.

To close a spreadsheet and remove its window from the screen, choose /**F**ile **C**lose. To perform this operation for all open spreadsheet windows, use /**F**ile Close All.

To close a spreadsheet quickly, click the close box in the upper left portion of a spreadsheet. Quattro Pro treats a spreadsheet closed in this manner like one closed by choosing /**F**ile Close.

> **NOTE** When you click the close box, Quattro Pro prompts you to save changes before closing the spreadsheet.

You occasionally may want to erase a spreadsheet from Quattro Pro's memory without deleting the file from your hard disk drive. Choose /**F**ile **E**rase. Quattro Pro asks whether you really want to erase the spreadsheet. Choose **N**o to cancel the operation or **Y**es to blank the screen. If you have made changes to the file and you want to save those changes, you must save the changes before erasing the file from the workspace.

> **TIP**
>
> The difference between the /File Close and the /File Erase commands is subtle. When you close a spreadsheet, Quattro Pro closes the spreadsheet file and its window. This command is useful for freeing up additional memory when multiple spreadsheets are open in RAM.
>
> When you erase a spreadsheet, Quattro Pro discards changes made to the current spreadsheet since the last save operation, closes the current spreadsheet, and leaves a new, blank spreadsheet in its place. If the current spreadsheet is unnamed, Quattro Pro discards the entire spreadsheet. During a work session, you can use this command to erase the spreadsheet and start over again.

Password Protecting Your Files

Quattro Pro offers you the option of password protecting your files to prevent unauthorized viewing of confidential data. You can retrieve password-protected files only when you have the correct access code. Because Quattro Pro passwords are case-sensitive, you must supply the access code in the exact form (upper- and lowercase) in which you created the code.

To password protect a Quattro Pro file named NPV.WQ1, type the file name followed by a space and the letter *P*. Follow these steps:

1. Make NPV the active spreadsheet.

2. Choose /File Save As.

3. When prompted, type *npv p* and press Enter to invoke the password-protection facility.

4. Type a password consisting of up to 15 characters. (Quattro Pro does not display the characters as you type.)

5. Press Enter to assign the password to the NPV spreadsheet.

6. When prompted, reenter the password to verify it (see fig. 8.3). If you type the password incorrectly, Quattro Pro displays an error message. Press Esc and go back to step 3 to continue.

7. Press Enter to store the password.

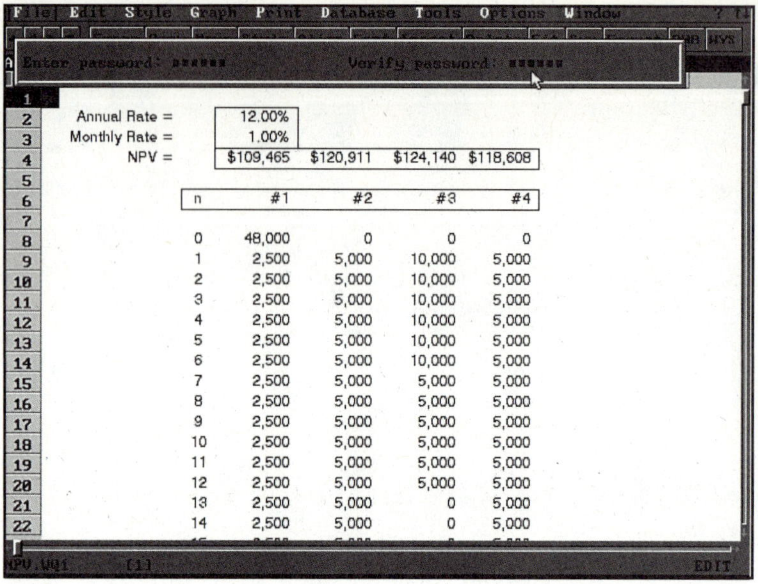

PART I — USING QUATTRO PRO SPREADSHEETS

Fig. 8.3

Password verification.

> **CAUTION:** After you assign a password to a file, you cannot access the file except by entering the correct sequence of characters. Quattro Pro has no facility for recovering a forgotten password. When a password is lost, so is the file.

You can rename or remove a spreadsheet password, but only when the spreadsheet is active. When a password-protected spreadsheet is active, the /File Save As file prompt box displays [Password Protected] next to the file name.

To remove password protection from the NPV spreadsheet, follow these steps:

1. Choose /File **R**etrieve.

2. Type *npv* and press Enter.

3. When prompted, type the password and press Enter to retrieve the file.

4. Choose /File Save **A**s.

5. When Quattro Pro displays the file prompt box, press the Backspace key once to delete [Password Protected] from the line.

6. Press Enter and choose **R**eplace to save NPV without a password.

To rename the password assigned to the NPV spreadsheet, follow these steps:

1. Choose /File Retrieve.

2. Type *npv* and press Enter.

3. When prompted, type the password and press Enter to retrieve the file.

4. Choose /File Save As.

5. When Quattro Pro displays the file prompt box, press the Backspace key once to delete [Password Protected] from the line.

6. Enter *P* after the file name (insert a space between the file name and the P) and then press Enter to invoke the password protection facility.

7. Type a new password.

8. Press Enter to assign the new password to the NPV spreadsheet.

9. When prompted, reenter the password to verify it.

Setting the Directory Path Name

The current directory setting determines where Quattro Pro looks just for files on your hard disk drive. The current setting appears at the right margin of the File menu next to the Directory command.

Choose /File Directory to create a current directory setting. When prompted, type a path name and press Enter to record the setting. When you choose this command and change the name of the current directory, the new setting remains in effect only for the current work session.

To change the current directory setting, choose /File Directory and press F2 to enter EDIT mode. Using the cursor-movement, Backspace, and Del keys, you can insert and delete information in the directory name prompt box. With this technique, you quickly can change the current directory setting—for example, adding a subdirectory name to the current directory setting—without having to retype the drive letter and directory path name.

You can change a Directory command setting permanently so that Quattro Pro recognizes the directory as the default directory each time you begin a new work session. Choose /Options Startup Directory and specify a new directory name. (See Chapter 16, "Customizing Quattro Pro," for complete coverage of Quattro Pro's start-up options.)

Creating a Workspace File

The **W**orkspace command is a spreadsheet file-organization tool. Whenever you design applications that use more than one open spreadsheet at a time, consider creating a workspace to group the associated spreadsheets under one file name. Grouping the spreadsheets makes reloading the files that you are using together much easier.

To save five spreadsheets now open in Quattro Pro's memory to a workspace file named SALES.WSP, for example, follow these steps:

1. Choose /**F**ile **W**orkspace **S**ave.

2. When prompted, type *sales* and press Enter to record the new workspace file name.

In the workspace file, Quattro Pro stores the name, the window number, and the position number for all the open spreadsheets (maximum of 32). This command does not save changes made to individual spreadsheets. After you finish with the current work session, you must save and replace each file before exiting Quattro Pro.

To reload the SALES.WSP workspace file, follow these steps:

1. Choose /**F**ile **W**orkspace **R**estore.

2. When prompted, highlight SALES.WSP on the displayed list and press Enter.

Quattro Pro loads all five spreadsheets into memory in their original order. To dismantle a workspace, just delete the .WSP file. Quattro Pro will not alter any of the spreadsheets in a deleted workspace. To move a spreadsheet from one workspace to another, open the spreadsheet and then the workspace, and resave the workspace using /**F**ile **W**orkspace **S**ave.

Translating Spreadsheets

Quattro Pro can save spreadsheet files in non-Quattro Pro file formats that several popular spreadsheet and database programs can retrieve. Table 8.4 presents a complete list of the file formats to which Quattro Pro can write. These file formats fall into four major categories: spreadsheet files, database files, compressed files, and graphics files.

To save a Quattro Pro spreadsheet in one of the file formats listed in table 8.4, append the appropriate extension to the file name. Choose /**F**ile Save **A**s, for example, and then press F2 to enter EDIT mode. Press the Backspace key three times to erase the WQ1 extension, type the appropriate extension from table 8.4, and then press Enter to save the spreadsheet in the new file format.

> **TIP**
>
> This operation is one of only two Quattro Pro operations that require you to supply a file-name extension (the other is SQZ!). In all other cases, the program appends the extension specified with the /**O**ptions **S**tartup **F**ile Extension command. With no extension specified, Quattro Pro appends WQ1, the default file extension.

Table 8.4 File Formats Quattro Pro Can Read and Write

File Extension	Program Name
Spreadsheet File Formats	
DIF	VisiCalc
SLK	Multiplan, Version 1 or 2
WKS	Lotus 1-2-3, Release 1A
WK1	Lotus 1-2-3, Releases 2.01, 2.2, 2.3
WK3	Lotus 1-2-3, Release 3.0
WKE	Lotus 1-2-3, Educational Release
FMT	Impress files
ALL	Allways files
WRK	Symphony, Version 1.2
WR1	Symphony, Version 2.0
WKQ	Quattro
WQ1	Quattro Pro (all versions)
WKP	Surpass
Database File Formats	
DB	Paradox
DB2	dBASE II
DBF	dBASE III, III Plus, and IV

continues

Table 8.4 Continued

File Extension	Program Name
RXD	Reflex, Version 1
R2D	Reflex, Version 2
Compressed File Formats (SQZ!)	
WK$	Lotus 1-2-3, Release 1A
WK!	Lotus 1-2-3, Release 2.01
WR$	Symphony, Version 1.2
WR!	Symphony, Version 2.0
WKZ	Quattro (earlier versions)
WQ!	Quattro Pro Squeeze
Graphics File Formats	
CHT	Harvard Graphics

Using dBASE File Formats

Translating Quattro Pro spreadsheets into dBASE file formats requires a slightly different approach. Although their file formats are different, dBASE II and III use the same file-name extension (DBF). To differentiate between the versions, Quattro Pro assigns a temporary extension (DB2) to spreadsheet files that you translate for use with dBASE II. Before you retrieve a translated file into dBASE II, rename the file so that the extension is DBF.

To save a Quattro Pro spreadsheet named DATA.WQ1 in a dBASE II file format, for example, follow these steps:

1. Make DATA.WQ1 the active spreadsheet.

2. Choose /**F**ile Save **A**s.

3. When prompted, type *data.db2* and press Enter.

4. When prompted, choose the **V**iew Structure option to examine the database structure information (Field-name, Type, Width, and Decimals) prior to saving the file as a database file.

5. Choose **W**rite to create the dBASE II file.

6. Press Ctrl-X to return to DOS. Type *ren data.db2 data.dbf* and press Enter to rename the file.

7. Load dBASE II and retrieve the file named DATA.DBF.

> **TIP**
> The **V**iew Structure and **W**rite options also are available for other database translations.

Using Lotus 1-2-3 2.X File Formats

Quattro Pro Version 4.0 is fully compatible with Lotus 1-2-3 Release 2.2 and 2.3 files. This enhancement is significant because 1-2-3 Releases 2.2 and 2.3 have file-linking capabilities similar to those available with Quattro Pro. When you retrieve a 1-2-3 Release 2.2 or 2.3 spreadsheet, Quattro Pro converts all 1-2-3 file-linking references into Quattro Pro's own linking syntax.

If you import a 1-2-3 spreadsheet containing a formula link such as +<<C:\123\DATASET.WK1>>A1, for example, Quattro Pro converts the formula link to +[C:\123\DATASET.WQ1]A1.

When you retrieve a 1-2-3 Release 2.2 or 2.3 file into Quattro Pro, you can save the file to one of three file formats: Quattro Pro, 1-2-3 Release 2.01, or 1-2-3 Release 2.2.

To save the file as a Quattro Pro spreadsheet, choose /**F**ile **S**ave **A**s. When Quattro Pro displays the file-name prompt box, press F2, erase the default extension; add the WQ1 extension to the file name.

To save the file as a 1-2-3 spreadsheet, choose /**F**ile **S**ave. After Quattro Pro displays the file-name prompt box, press Enter to accept the default file name (with the WK1 extension) and choose **R**eplace to replace the file. If the file was not retrieved from the Lotus format, choose /**F**ile **S**ave **A**s and then change the extension to WK1. Quattro Pro displays a new prompt box telling you that the program encountered a formula with a link translated to a value (see fig. 8.4).

Choose **N**o to cancel the save and erase the spreadsheet from your hard drive, **Y**es to convert all links to their end results for use with 1-2-3 Release 2.01 (Release 2.01 does not support linking), or **U**se 2.2 Syntax to keep all formula links intact for use with 1-2-3 Release 2.2.

PART I — USING QUATTRO PRO SPREADSHEETS

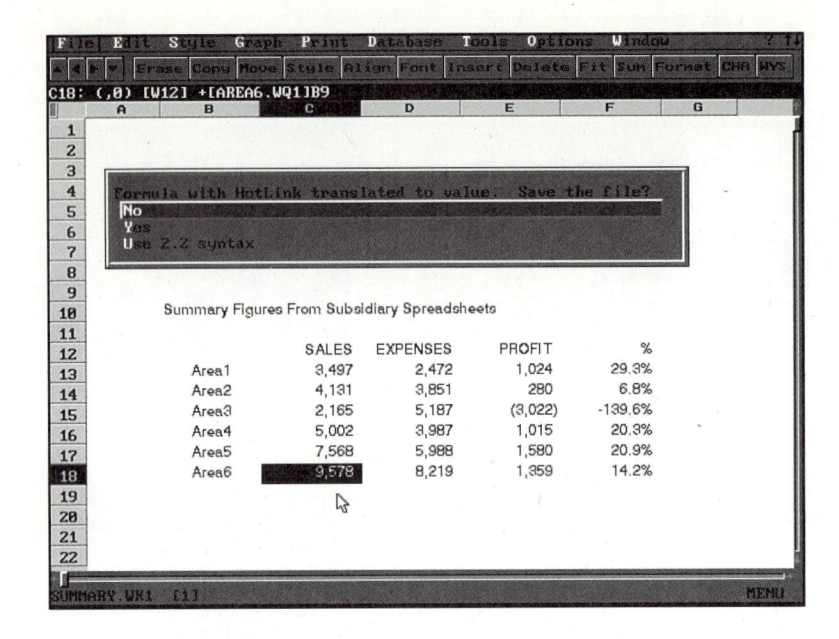

Fig. 8.4

The prompt box to save a 1-2-3 Release 2.2 file that contains a formula link.

> **T I P** 1-2-3 Releases 2.2 and 2.3 use the same linking syntax and the WK1 file-name extension. To save a 1-2-3 Release 2.3 worksheet and keep all formula links intact, treat the worksheet as though it is a Release 2.2 worksheet. Choose /**F**ile Save **A**s, press Enter, and choose the Use 2.2 Syntax option shown in figure 8.4.

If you choose **N**o or press Esc in response to the prompt, Quattro Pro erases the original spreadsheet from your hard disk drive and displays a warning message telling you so. If you want to keep a copy of the file, make sure you save the file before ending the current work session. Otherwise, you will lose the file permanently.

Using Lotus 1-2-3 3.X File Formats

Quattro Pro Version 4.0 is fully compatible with Lotus 1-2-3 Release 3.x files. You can import and export 1-2-3 Release 3.x files by specifying the WK3 extension when you open, retrieve, or save files. If the WK3 file contains no features unique to Release 3.x of 1-2-3, Quattro Pro opens and converts the file as though the file were a 1-2-3 Release 2.x file. If features in the spreadsheet are specific to Release 3.x, however, Quattro Pro makes some changes during conversion.

If the 3.x file contains multiple spreadsheets, Quattro Pro asks you whether you want the sheets saved as separate files. You can save up to 32 separate files. If the 1-2-3 file contains more than 32 sheets, you must break down the file in 1-2-3 before bringing the file into Quattro Pro.

Multiple 1-2-3 spreadsheets saved as separate files are named based on the original file name. To name spreadsheets, Quattro Pro uses the first six characters of the file name and then adds a letter, sequenced from A to Z, then AA to ZZ. The file named DIV.WK3, for example, which contains three spreadsheets, converts into Quattro Pro as DIVA.WQ1, DIVB.WQ1, and DIVC.WQ1.

3-D cell references in 3.x files containing multiple spreadsheets convert to linked references in Quattro Pro. If the formula +A:B25*1.15 is in DIV.WK3, for example, the reference changes to +[DIV0A.WQ1]B25*1.15 in Quattro Pro.

When converting 3.x files to Quattro Pro, labels longer than 256 characters are truncated and formulas longer than 256 characters are read but are truncated on the edit line. 1-2-3 @functions that do not exist in Quattro Pro convert to labels. @SHEETS, for example, converts to '@SHEETS. Similarly, references to 3-D blocks convert to labels. @SUM(A:A1..C:D25), for example, becomes '@SUM(A:A1..C:D25). References to external files convert to labels. Macro references, 3-D or otherwise, are not converted. Any WK3 graph feature not supported in Quattro Pro is lost.

Except for the first range, all multiple ranges in files with the WK3 extension are ignored. (This process applies only to 1-2-3 database and statistical @functions, and to the 1-2-3 /**P**rint **R**ange and /**D**ata **Q**uery **I**nput commands.)

Due to differences in the way Quattro Pro and Lotus 1-2-3 stores numbers, extremely large numbers (larger than 10^{308}) convert to ERR and extremely small numbers (smaller than 10^{-308}) convert to 0. 1-2-3 formula annotations are ignored. Numeric formatting of blank cells are not identical to the original cells after conversion.

After a WK3 file has been converted, Quattro Pro displays a message box showing how many labels have been truncated and how many 3-D blocks have been changed to labels. Press Esc to remove the message. To export a Quattro Pro file back to 1-2-3 Release 3.x format, save the file with the WK3 file extension.

Using Other File Formats

Version 4.0 also is compatible to several additional file formats, including Allways, Impress, and Harvard Graphics files. As with all import and export operations, you must specify the correct file extension.

Allways Files

If you have spreadsheets created with 1-2-3 Release 2.01 or 2.2 and designed with Allways, you can load these files directly into Quattro Pro. If Quattro Pro finds a file with the ALL extension and with the same name as the 1-2-3 file you're loading, the program asks whether you want to load the Allways file at the same time. If you answer yes, translation is automatic. Quattro Pro retrieves the WK1 file, reads the ALL file, and then applies the Allways formatting to the spreadsheet.

Quattro Pro does not import AFS, ALS, or ENC files. To import multiple saved formats or font sets, create a separate WK1 file for each saved format with a corresponding ALL file.

Quattro Pro does not support Allways inserted graphs. In Allways, you must store graphs in separate PIC files; in Quattro Pro, you can store named graphs right in the spreadsheet.

Quattro Pro imports format options such as font selection, line style, shading, boldface, underline, and font colors. Allways display (screen) colors do not import.

NOTE Quattro Pro converts up to 128 different combinations of font, color, boldface, underline, and italic. Any additional combinations convert to Normal style in Quattro Pro.

Some layout options import, including margins, titles, borders (top and left), and line weight; however, others do not, such as page-size, borders on the bottom, and grid on printing. Label alignment with spillover to the left, usually found in centered labels, also do not import.

Quattro Pro imports the print range option but not the printer type, orientation, print settings, and port bin print options.

For worksheet options, column width (rounded up to whole character widths) and row heights import, but page breaks, column page breaks, and display zoom options do not.

Impress Files

Quattro Pro 4.0 can import 1-2-3 files created with the Impress add-in or 1-2-3's WYSIWYG feature. When you retrieve a WK1, WKS, or WK3 file that has a corresponding FMT or FM3 file, Quattro Pro loads the 1-2-3 file and then asks whether you want to read the FMT or FM3 file and apply the Impress formatting. ENC files created by Impress are not imported. When retrieving a WK1 or WKS file, if corresponding ALL and FMT files are in the current directory, only FMT files are loaded; ALL files are ignored.

Quattro Pro retrieves and applies various graph formats. Not all graph formats are retained, however. Blank graphs and inserted graphs based on PIC or CGM files do not convert to Quattro Pro.

Quattro Pro retrieves many Impress formatting features, including assigned fonts, lines, shading, boldface, underline, italics, and font colors. Custom styles convert to /**S**tyle **U**se Style, but descriptions are not preserved. Quattro Pro does not retain line shadow settings and colors or formatting embedded in text.

Quattro Pro converts text alignment settings, except for label alignment with left-side spillover. Display option settings, however, including colors, mode, font directory, rows, and options do not convert. As for worksheet settings, row height and page break options convert, but column width and column page breaks do not.

Quattro Pro imports the following print settings: range, configuration/ orientation, settings, layout/compression (which converts to **P**rint-To-Fit and **P**ercent Scaling), layout margins, and layout titles. Quattro Pro cannot import the grid on printing, frame, and settings options, nor can it import print configuration commands and the Page-size and the Borders on Bottom print layout settings.

Harvard Graphics Files

To export a Quattro Pro file as a Harvard Graphics file, save the file with the CHT extension. Between the two products, however, are inherent differences that should cause users to exercise caution. First, Harvard Graphics doesn't support multiple graphs in one file. When you export a Quattro Pro graph to a Harvard Graphics file, only the current graph exports and named graphs are not transferred. Second, Harvard Graphics files can hold only graph information. Any nongraph data in the Quattro Pro file, such as spreadsheet formatting and macros, is not transferred.

To import Harvard Graphics Version 2.x graphs, use the CHT extension when you open or retrieve a file.

Quattro Pro converts a Harvard Graphics graph to the most similar Quattro Pro graph type. Occasionally, Quattro Pro cannot convert the graph, so the file opens as empty. Quattro Pro converts all Harvard Graphics graphs except for organization charts, multiple pie graphs (only the first pie is imported), and multiple graphs (combinations of graph types).

Some Harvard Graphics fill patterns and graph options do not have an exact match in Quattro Pro. In these cases, Quattro Pro applies the closest match available. Data series in Harvard Graphics appear as values in the spreadsheet in Quattro Pro.

After opening or retrieving the Harvard Graphics file, press F10 to see the graph. You can edit the graph in the Annotator like you can with any Quattro Pro graph.

Setting the SQZ! File Compression Options

Quattro Pro has a built-in file compression utility that helps you to conserve storage space on your hard disk drive. You also can use this facility when copying large spreadsheet files onto a floppy disk and before transmitting files over a modem line.

To compress a file, append the appropriate extension after typing a name at the file-name prompt (refer to table 8.4). To compress a file named DATELINE.WQ1, follow these steps:

1. Make DATELINE the active spreadsheet.

2. Choose /**F**ile Save **A**s.

3. When prompted, type *dateline.wq!* and press Enter to compress the file.

> **T I P** If you are using an earlier version of Quattro, you must specify the WKZ file-name extension to squeeze a file.

8 — MANAGING FILES AND WINDOWS

Figure 8.5 shows the menu options that Quattro Pro displays after you choose /**F**ile **U**tilities **S**QZ!. These options control how much data Quattro Pro eliminates from a spreadsheet file before squeezing the spreadsheet; thus, they must be specified before squeezing the spreadsheet. To save the options as a default, choose /**O**ptions **U**pdate.

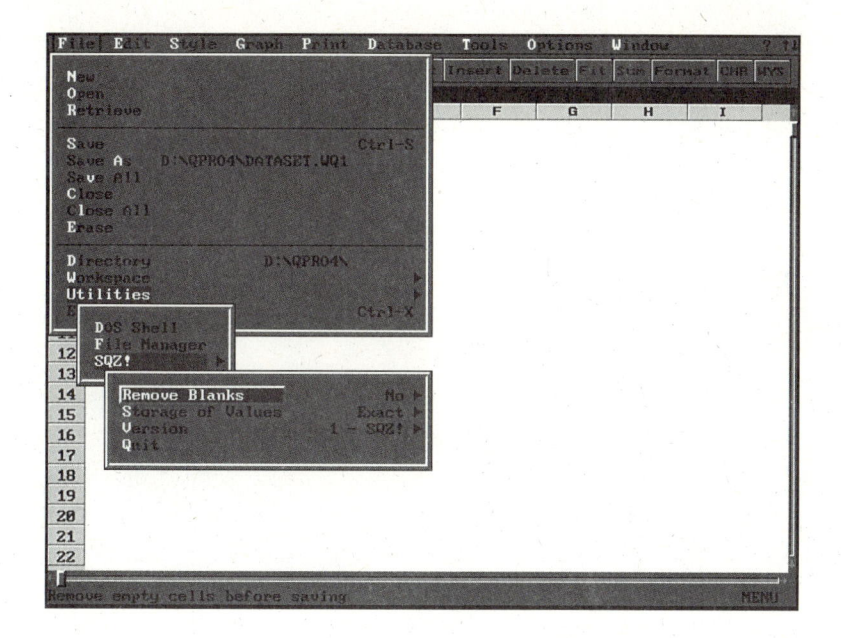

Fig. 8.5

The SQZ! menu options.

One way Quattro Pro can conserve space is by removing all the blank cells from a spreadsheet. To remove the blank cells, choose the **R**emove Blanks option and choose **Y**es.

Another way to conserve storage space is to have Quattro Pro remove spreadsheet values that result from formula calculations. Quattro Pro retains the formulas themselves but removes the cell results. After you retrieve the file, Quattro Pro recalculates all the formulas before displaying the spreadsheet.

To invoke this setting, choose the **S**torage of Values option and then choose **R**emove. You also can choose **A**pproximate so that Quattro Pro saves formula values using 7 (instead of 15) significant digits. The **E**xact option stores exact formula values up to 15 significant digits.

The third **S**QZ! menu option enables you to choose the SQZ! version to use. If you do not intend to use your compressed files in Symphony, choose the **S**QZ! Plus option. In any case, Quattro Pro expands the compressed file the next time you retrieve the file.

PART I — USING QUATTRO PRO SPREADSHEETS

Using the DOS Shell

The /**F**ile Utilities **D**OS Shell command enables you to execute DOS commands without first having to exit Quattro Pro. The DOS shell has two levels: partial and full.

The partial DOS shell enables you to execute a single DOS command and review the results of the command execution, and then returns to Quattro Pro. After choosing /**F**ile Utilities **D**OS Shell, type *dir* and press Enter to display a list of files for the current directory (see fig. 8.6). The command executes and you return to the active spreadsheet.

> **T I P**
> The file list may scroll by quickly, so be prepared to press Ctrl-S to pause the scrolling. Press any key to resume the scrolling.

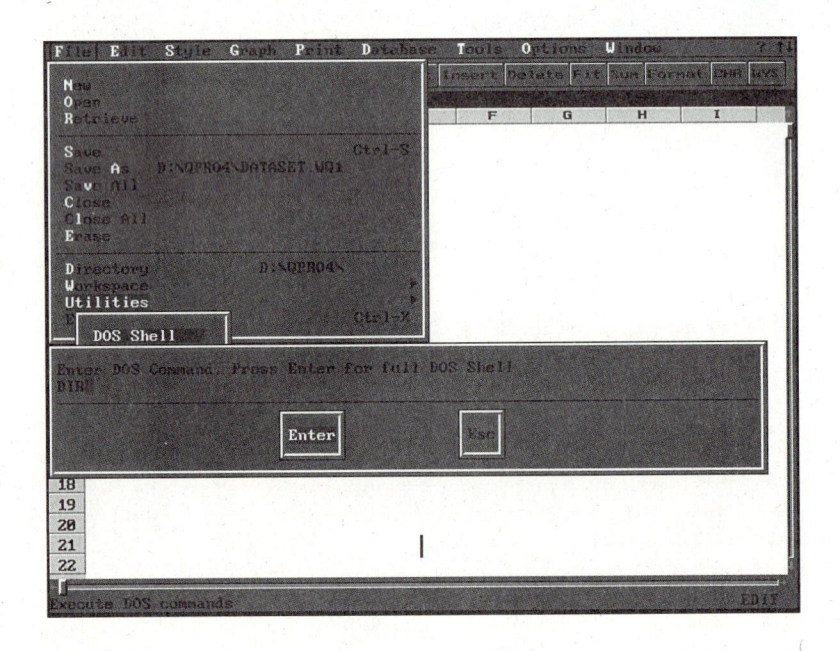

Fig. 8.6

The DOS DIR command in the partial DOS shell.

The full DOS shell returns temporarily to DOS command level, where you may execute as many DOS commands as you want. To use the full DOS shell, choose /**F**ile Utilities **D**OS Shell and press Enter. Quattro Pro disappears from the screen and displays the DOS command prompt. To return to Quattro Pro, type *exit* at the DOS command prompt and then press Enter.

> **TIP**
>
> If you are using Quattro Pro in the Microsoft Windows operating environment, you may receive an Out of Memory error message when you execute the **D**OS Shell command. The error occurs when Windows is unable to allocate enough memory to run the DOS shell. In this case, consider double-clicking the Windows DOS Prompt program with your mouse. This icon is located in the Main program group of the Program Manager.

While in the DOS shell, you can execute any valid DOS command. You probably should not delete Quattro Pro program files or load other application programs into memory from the shell because doing so may cause memory allocation problems that may lock up your PC. If this problem occurs, press Ctrl-Alt-Del to reboot your computer and clear its memory.

> **TIP**
>
> You should save any spreadsheet changes before using the DOS shell, just in case you make a mistake and need to reboot.

Using the File Manager

The File Manager enables you to link Quattro Pro directly to the DOS command environment. The File Manager can perform many useful file-management activities without requiring that you first exit Quattro Pro or use the DOS Shell feature.

Use the File Manager to list, move, copy, rename, and delete files, using the same wild-card designations that you use in DOS. This tool also can sort files by name, extension, size, and DOS order; show the time stamp on files; and display a tree graphic that shows the structure of the directory paths on the current disk.

Learning the File Manager Menus

When the File Manager is in the active window, Quattro Pro displays a slightly different set of menus at the top of the screen. You activate these menus and choose the menu commands as though a spreadsheet is in the active window.

Table 8.5 reviews the purpose and function of each menu.

Table 8.5 File Manager Menus

Menu Name	Description of Commands
File	Creates, opens, and closes windows; reads existing directories and creates directories; accesses DOS; exits the File Manager and Quattro Pro
Edit	Selects files for copy, move, erase, paste, duplicate, and rename operations
Sort	Sorts files using DOS wild-card characters
Tree	Opens, resizes, and closes the tree pane
Print	Prints a list of files in a directory
Options	Sets File Manager display options and standard spreadsheet options
Window	Resizes, reorganizes, and picks active windows

Maneuvering through the File Manager Window

To display the File Manager in the current window, choose /File Utilities File Manager (see fig. 8.7). Repeat this command to open a second File Manager window. To close the active File Manager, choose /File Close—the same command that closes a spreadsheet.

The File Manager window is divided into three sections: the control pane, the file list pane, and the tree pane. After you load this tool into the active window, Quattro Pro fills the entire screen.

All file-management operations that you perform with this tool are accomplished from inside one of the three panes. Before you can work in a pane, however, you must make that pane active. By default, Quattro Pro makes the control pane active each time you load the File Manager.

Table 8.6 lists all the key sequences you can use to navigate through the File Manager window.

8 — MANAGING FILES AND WINDOWS

Fig. 8.7

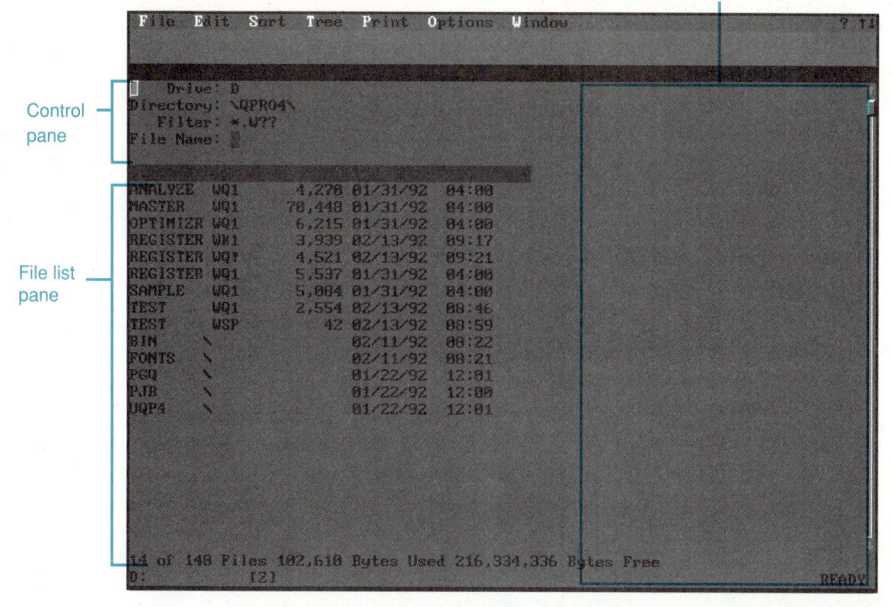

The File Manager window.

Table 8.6 File Manager Window Keys

Key	Key Name	Description
Shift-F5	Pick Window	Displays a list of all windows open in memory; also works by pressing Alt-0
F6	Pane	Activates the next pane in the File Manager window; also works by pressing Tab
Shift-F6	Next Window	Activates the next open File Manager window; activates a spreadsheet if no window is open
Alt-F6	Zoom Window	Enlarges and shrinks the active File Manager window if you are in text display mode
Alt-#		Press Alt plus a window number, and Quattro Pro makes that window active

Using the Control Pane

The *control pane* displays the current drive letter, the current directory path name, the filter prompt, and the file-name prompt. While in the control pane, you can change any of these settings to create a different type of directory display.

To display all files with a WQ1 extension in a directory called \FINANCE, for example, follow these steps:

1. Press the up-arrow key twice to highlight the current directory path name.
2. Press Esc to erase the entry.
3. Type *finance* and press Enter to record the new directory path name. Quattro Pro moves the cursor back to the file-name prompt.
4. Press the down-arrow key to move to the filter prompt setting.
5. Press Backspace twice to erase the question marks.
6. Type *wq1* and press Enter to store the new filter setting.

Quattro Pro displays all files in the \FINANCE directory that have a WQ1 file-name extension.

To create a negative filter, place the filter setting inside *square* brackets. Quattro Pro searches for all files that do not meet the bracketed condition. The filter setting [*.WQ1], for example, searches for all files that *do not* have a WQ1 file-name extension.

The file-name prompt is blank each time you load the File Manager. You can make any spreadsheet file active by typing a file name in this field. After you type the first letter of a file name, Quattro Pro moves the cursor to the first file in the current directory that begins with that letter. This search-and-highlight procedure continues as long as you continue to enter additional letters.

Table 8.7 lists all the keys that affect data displayed in the control pane.

Table 8.7 Control Pane Keys

Key	Key Name	Description
F2	Rename	Duplicates the action of choosing /**E**dit **R**ename while at the file-name prompt

Key	Key Name	Description
F5	GoTo	Moves the cursor to the file name specified at the file-name prompt
Esc		Erases the current setting at a control pane prompt
Enter		Moves the cursor to the blank file-name prompt or opens the file or subdirectory indicated next to the prompt settings
Del		Deletes the character at the cursor position
Home		Moves the cursor to the beginning of the prompt entry
End		Moves the cursor to the end of the prompt entry

Using the File Pane

The *file pane* shows the file names and directory path names that meet the conditions specified on the control pane. The file pane lists the full name, byte size, and the date last altered for each file.

Use the /**O**ptions **F**ile List command to specify a **F**ull View or a **W**ide View of the data displayed in the file pane.

Table 8.8 lists the key sequences that you can use when the file pane is active.

Table 8.8 File Pane Keys

Key	Key Name	Description
F2	Rename	Duplicates the action of choosing the /**E**dit **R**ename command
Shift-F7	Select	Selects and deselects a highlighted file name
Alt-F7	All Select	Selects all the file names in the displayed list or deselects those already selected with Shift-F7

continues

Table 8.8 Continued

Key	Key Name	Description
Shift-F8	Move	Transfers selected files to the paste buffer
Del		Deletes all highlighted or selected files
F9	Calc	Duplicates the action of choosing the /File Read Dir command
Shift-F9	Copy	Copies selected files into the paste buffer
Shift-F10	Paste	Moves all files from the paste buffer to the current directory
Esc		Cancels file selections and moves the cursor to the file-name prompt in the control pane
Enter		Opens the file or subdirectory indicated next to the prompt settings or moves to the directory or subdirectory indicated if it is highlighted when you press Enter
Home		Moves the highlight bar to the parent directory (..)
End		Moves the highlight bar to the end of the file list
PgUp		Moves the file list display up one screen
PgDn		Moves the file list display down one screen

You also can press any cursor-movement key on the keyboard to move around the file pane.

Using the Tree Pane

Choose /Tree Open to display the tree pane in the right side of the File Manager window. A tree pane initially displays the root directory drive letter, several application directory names, and two levels of application subdirectory names.

8 — MANAGING FILES AND WINDOWS

Use the /Tree Resize command to reveal additional subdirectory names in the tree pane. This command enables you to specify a value (from 10 to 100) that represents the percent of the File Manager window that the tree pane occupies. Figure 8.8, for example, shows a tree pane that occupies 40 percent of the File Manager window.

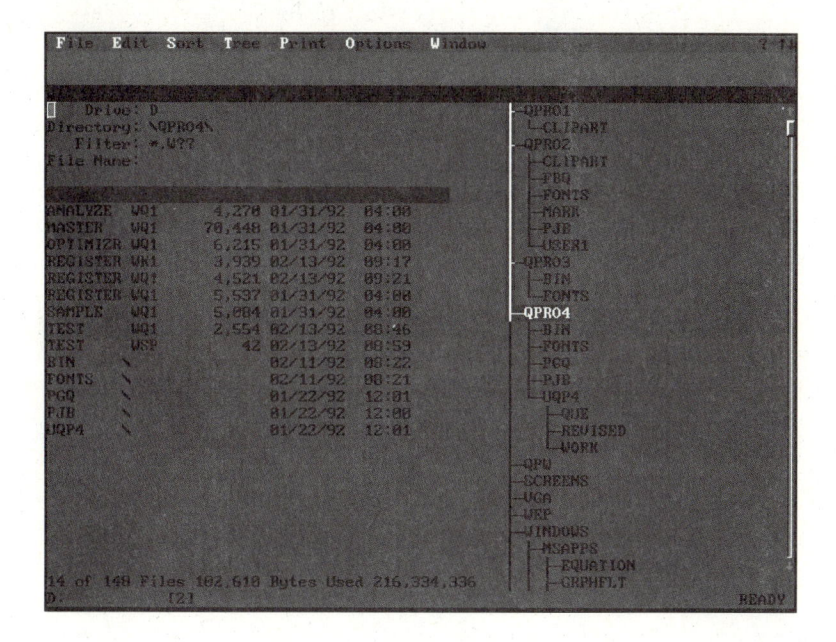

Fig. 8.8

A tree pane in the File Manager window.

In the tree pane, Quattro Pro highlights the application directory name that matches the directory path name appearing in the control pane. The files stored in the highlighted directory appear in the file pane. To display new files in the file pane again, press Tab until the tree pane is active and then highlight a different directory name. Quattro Pro immediately displays that directory's files in the file pane.

The tree pane enables you to copy and erase directories and to move large blocks of files from one directory into another. To learn how to scroll through a tree pane, review the keys defined in table 8.9.

PART I — USING QUATTRO PRO SPREADSHEETS

Table 8.9 Tree Pane Keys

Key	Key Name	Description
Esc		Cancels file selections and moves the cursor to the file-name prompt in the control pane
Del		Deletes all highlighted or selected files
F9	Calc	Duplicates the action of choosing the /File Read Dir command
PgUp		Scrolls the file list up
PgDn		Scrolls the file list down

To remove a tree pane from the active window, choose /Tree Close.

Manipulating Files with the File Manager

Many of the menu commands in the File Manager are the same commands you use to manipulate data in spreadsheet files. A few other commands also perform operations not available with spreadsheets. These special commands are covered in the next section.

Performing Multiple File Operations

The one characteristic shared by all the Edit menu commands in the File Manager is that each can perform an operation simultaneously on many files. You can copy, move, and erase all the files in the current directory. You also can rename a group of files simultaneously and then copy the files to another location on the same disk drive.

These maneuvers are possible due to the inclusion of two special menu commands: Select File and All Select. After you select a file, Quattro Pro displays the file name in reverse intensity or in a different color and places a check mark at the end of the cursor so that you can see clearly that the file is selected. Using the /Edit All Select command, you can select all the files displayed in the file pane. Quattro Pro does not highlight the names of subdirectories (see fig. 8.9).

TIP To choose a single file in the File Manager, highlight the desired file and press Esc.

8 — MANAGING FILES AND WINDOWS

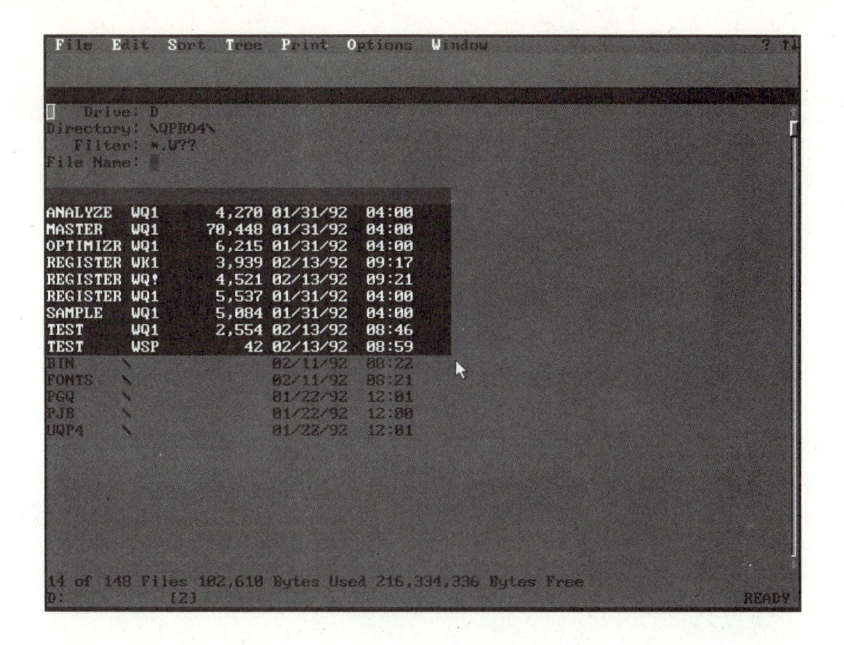

Fig. 8.9

Selecting all files in the file pane.

After the files are selected, you can perform any File Manager command on that block of files—an operation not available in other spreadsheet programs.

The following steps, for example, show how to erase all selected files from a hard disk:

1. Choose /**E**dit **A**ll Select or press Alt-F7 to highlight the names of all files displayed for the current directory.

2. Choose /**E**dit **E**rase. Quattro Pro displays the prompt, Are you sure you want to delete the marked files?

3. Choose **Y**es to begin erasing the selected files or **N**o to cancel the operation and return to the File Manager window.

Printing File Manager Data

The **P**rint menu in the File Manager is an abbreviated version of the **P**rint menu accessible when a spreadsheet is active. Using the commands on this menu, you can print lists of files in the displayed directory, a copy of the entire directory tree, or both (see fig. 8.10).

PART I — USING QUATTRO PRO SPREADSHEETS

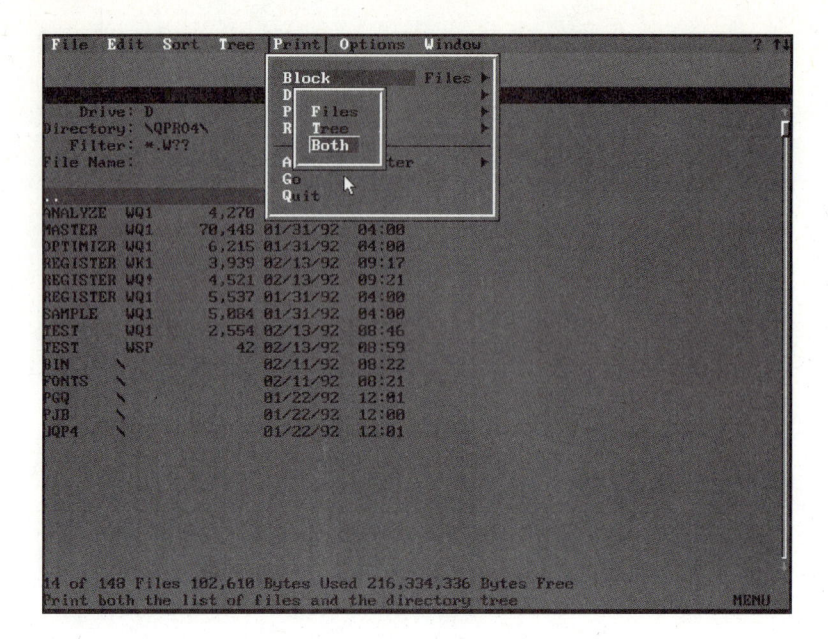

Fig. 8.10

Print a report that lists files and the directory tree graphic.

Working with Windows

You can have up to 32 windows open in Quattro Pro's memory at one time, but you can work in only one window at a time—the active window.

Even if you never create an application that uses 32 windows, you eventually may need at least 2, 3, or 4 windows open at the same time. Therefore, you must understand how to manage multiple windows, using the following options in the /Window menu.

Using the /Window menu commands, you can zoom in and out, tile and stack, and move and size windows that are open in Quattro Pro's memory. You also can create special displays for your spreadsheets by using the options on the Options submenu (see fig. 8.11).

The /Window Options command reveals a menu of window display options that enable you to work with large spreadsheets. You can split the active window into two panes, for example, or create a condensed map view of an entire spreadsheet.

Whenever you are unsure about the number of files open in memory, choose /Window Pick. Quattro Pro displays a complete list of all open windows and their file names. You also can press Alt-0 or Shift-F5, the Pick Window key, to produce the same display.

8 — MANAGING FILES AND WINDOWS

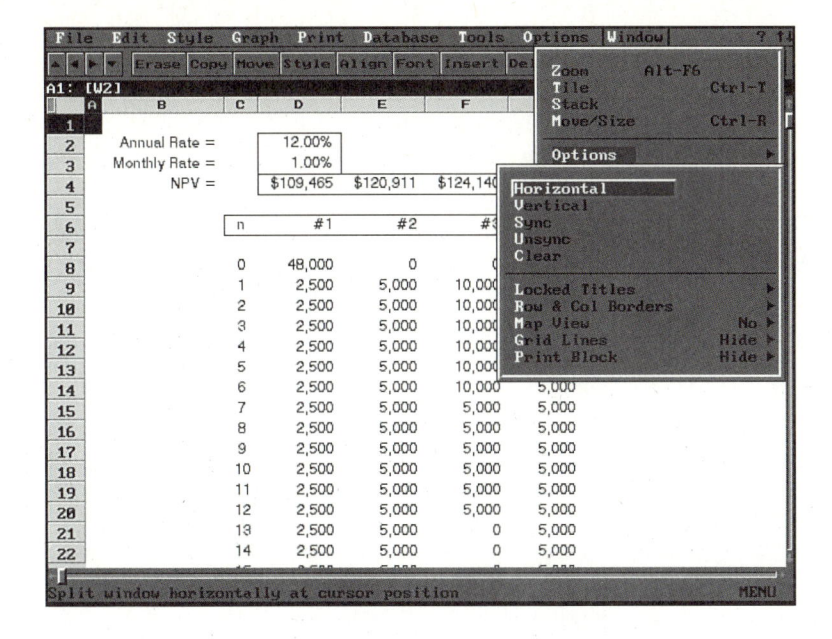

Fig. 8.11

The /Window Options menu commands.

To move from window to window, press Shift-F6, the Next Window key. If you already know the window number of the window you want to move to, press Alt and the window number to activate that window.

Organizing Windows On-Screen

Quattro Pro offers several alternatives for managing a window or for displaying all open windows. The following three sections teach you how to execute the **W**indow menu commands that organize windows on-screen.

> **T I P**
>
> The following /**W**indow menu commands have no effect when Quattro Pro is in WYSIWYG display mode: **Z**oom, **S**tack, and **M**ove/Size. To zoom a spreadsheet while in WYSIWYG display mode, use the /**O**ptions **W**YSIWYG Zoom % command. These commands are active when Quattro Pro is in text or extended text display mode.

Enlarging and Shrinking Windows

In text display mode, when you want the active window to fill your screen, choose /**W**indow **Z**oom or press Alt-F6, the Zoom key. Choosing this command twice in succession causes the active window to return to its original size.

Mouse users can perform this operation quickly by clicking the zoom icon located in the upper right corner of the screen (the two opposing arrows at the top of the SpeedBar).

You cannot enlarge or shrink a window in WYSIWYG display mode.

Tiling and Stacking Windows

Another useful way to display multiple windows involves processes called tiling and stacking. (Refer to figs. 8.19 and 8.20 later in this chapter for examples of spreadsheet tiling.)

Tiling reduces each window to a size that enables Quattro Pro to display the windows side-by-side. To tile all windows open in memory, choose /**W**indow **T**ile or press Ctrl-T, the Ctrl-key shortcut for this command.

Stacking shuffles the open windows into sequential order by window number and displays the windows in layers. In a stacked window display, the top of each window is revealed so that you can see the file name and window number. To stack all windows open in memory, choose /**W**indow **S**tack.

All Quattro Pro display modes support tiling, although only text and extended text display modes support spreadsheet window stacking.

Moving and Sizing Windows

The /**W**indow **M**ove/Size command enables you to fine-tune the size and position of a spreadsheet in the active window. You can use this technique when tiling and stacking do not create the display effect that you want. You cannot enlarge or shrink a window, however, that is in WYSIWYG display mode.

To change the size and position of a spreadsheet in a window, choose /**W**indow **M**ove/Size or press Ctrl-R, the Ctrl-key shortcut for this command.

Quattro Pro highlights the outside edges of the spreadsheet and displays MOVE in a box at the upper left corner of the spreadsheet. Initially,

8 — MANAGING FILES AND WINDOWS

you cannot move the spreadsheet because it already fills the display. You first must resize the spreadsheet.

To resize the spreadsheet by using your keyboard (mouse steps are covered later), follow these steps:

1. Press the Scroll Lock key until MOVE changes to SIZE.

2. Hold down the Shift key and press the cursor-movement keys until the spreadsheet is the correct size (see fig. 8.12).

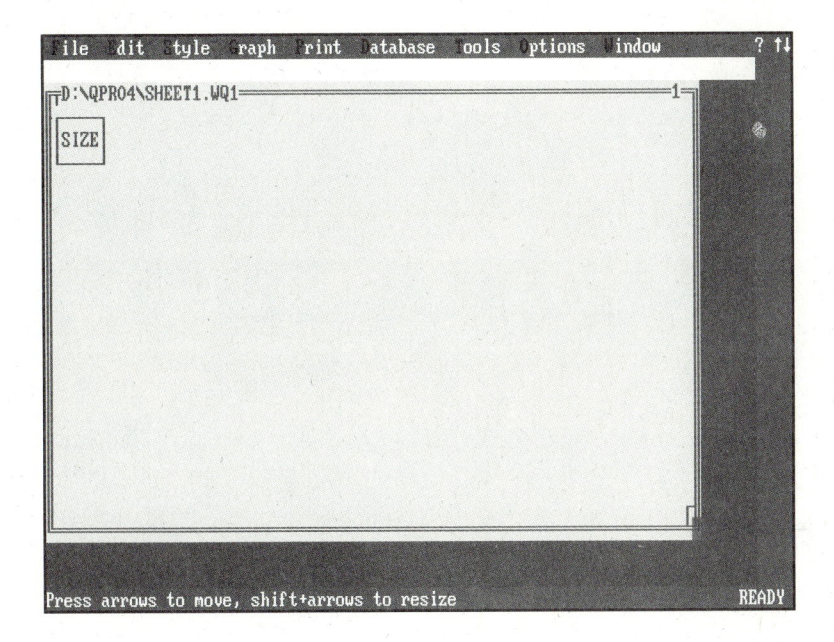

Fig. 8.12

Resize a spreadsheet in the current window.

3. Press Enter to store the new spreadsheet size.

Quattro Pro draws the resized spreadsheet in the current window (see fig. 8.13).

When a spreadsheet is smaller than the current window, you can move the spreadsheet around the screen display. To move a spreadsheet, follow these steps:

1. Choose /**W**indow **M**ove/Size. Quattro Pro highlights all four spreadsheet borders.

2. Press the cursor-movement keys to move the spreadsheet to another part of the current window.

3. Press Enter to store the new spreadsheet location.

PART I — USING QUATTRO PRO SPREADSHEETS

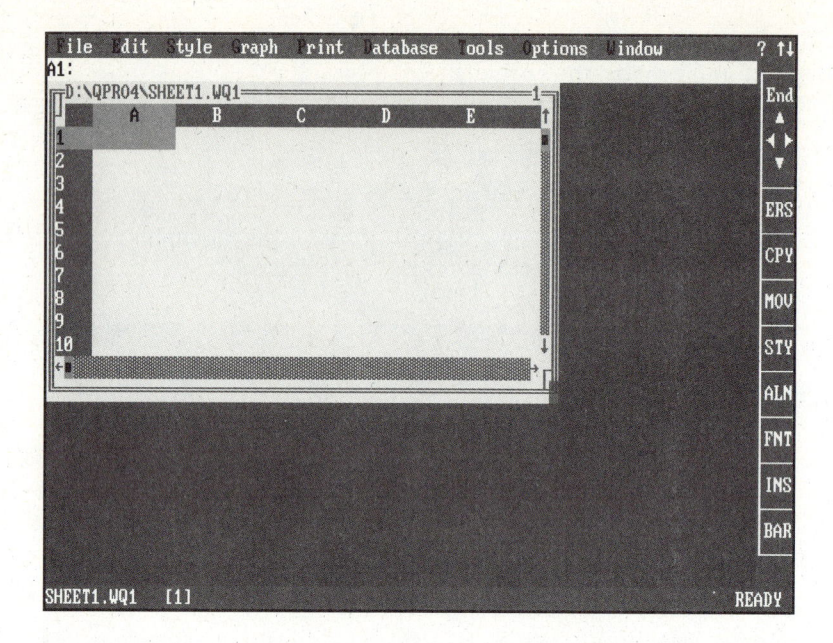

Fig. 8.13

Quattro Pro draws the resized spreadsheet in the current window.

Quattro Pro redraws the spreadsheet at that location.

If you have a mouse, you quickly can move and size a spreadsheet. The next sequence of steps describes the most efficient way to do both:

1. Put the mouse pointer on the resize box located at the bottom right portion of the spreadsheet and then click and hold down your mouse button. Quattro Pro highlights the spreadsheet borders, and displays SIZE in the upper left corner.

2. Drag the box to resize the spreadsheet.

3. Release the mouse button to retain a size. Quattro Pro draws the resized spreadsheet.

4. To move a resized spreadsheet, put the mouse pointer on any border and then drag the entire spreadsheet elsewhere in the current window (see fig. 8.14). The word MOVE appears in the upper left corner.

5. Release the mouse button. Quattro Pro draws the spreadsheet at that location.

T I P Press Alt-F6 to enlarge or shrink the active spreadsheet in the current window.

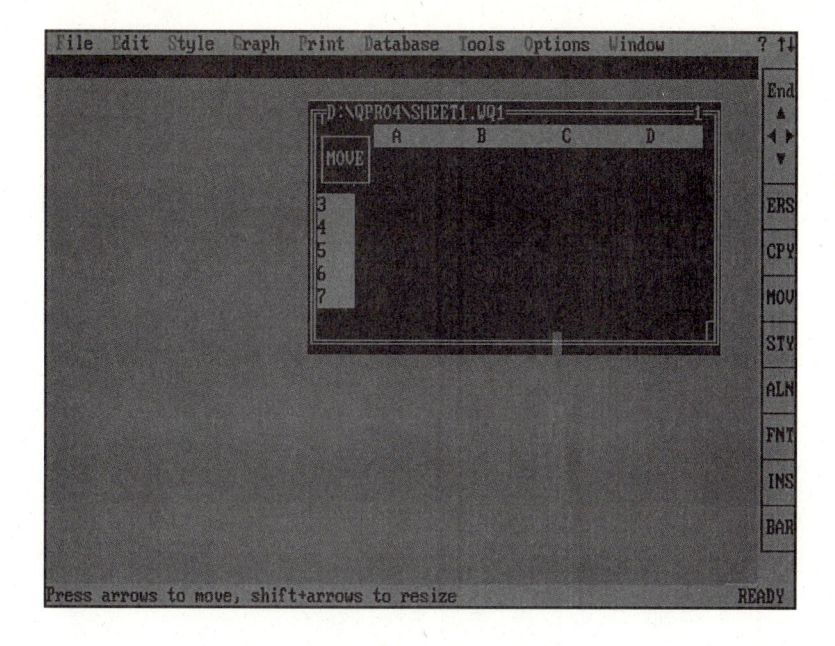

Fig. 8.14

Move a spreadsheet in the current window.

Creating Special Display Effects

The /**W**indow **O**ptions menu gives you access to commands that can create special window display effects. These effects are by no means strictly cosmetic. Each effect can help you to locate, organize, and manipulate spreadsheet data. These options work in both text and WYSIWYG display modes.

Splitting Windows into Panes

Choose the /**W**indow **O**ptions **H**orizontal command to split a window into two horizontal panes at the position of the cell selector, as long as the cell selector is not in row 1 or 8192 (see fig. 8.15). This effect is useful when a spreadsheet has more row data than column data. The **H**orizontal command also helps you to enter cell formulas that reference data in distant parts of the active spreadsheet.

Choose /**W**indow **O**ptions **V**ertical to split a window into two vertical panes at the position of the cell selector, as long as the cell selector is not in column A or IV. You can use this effect when a spreadsheet has more column data than row data. The **V**ertical command, like its counterpart, helps in the process of entering formulas into a spreadsheet.

To move between panes in a split window, press F6, the Pane key, or click in the desired pane with your mouse. To reset a split window to one pane, choose /**W**indow **O**ptions **C**lear.

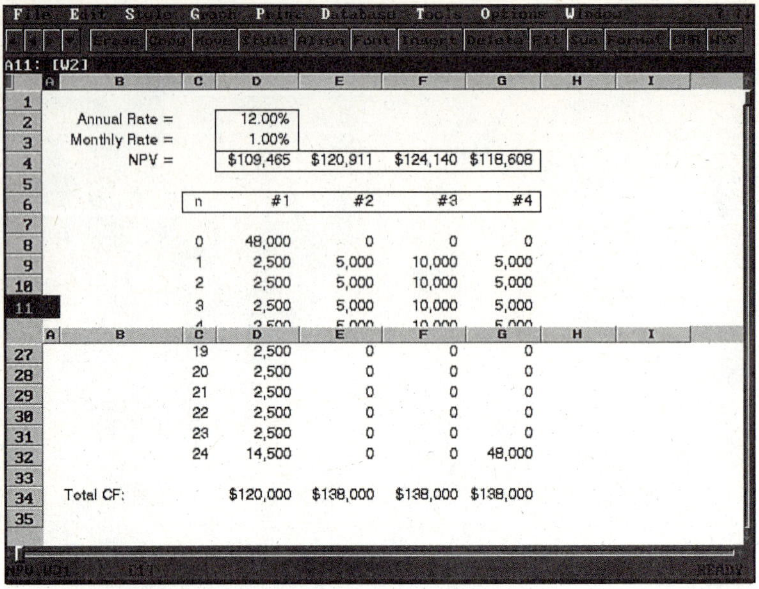

PART I — USING QUATTRO PRO SPREADSHEETS

Fig. 8.15

A spreadsheet window split into two horizontal panes.

Unsynchronizing Window Panes

By default, split window panes are synchronized so that any cell selector movement in one pane is duplicated in the second. To scroll window panes independently of each other, you must unsynchronize the panes by choosing /**W**indow **O**ptions **U**nsync, which enables you to scroll around one pane without affecting the other. To return the panes to synchronized scrolling, choose /**W**indow **O**ptions **S**ync.

Clearing Split Window Pane Settings

Choose /**W**indow **O**ptions **C**lear to return split windows to a single window display. When you issue this command, Quattro Pro retains the column width, locked title, and hidden column settings for only the top or left pane. Any of these changes made to the right or lower pane are discarded.

Locking Titles

Title locking is a useful display tool for a spreadsheet that contains numerous rows or columns of data. By anchoring a row (or column) of labels, you can scroll through the data under or to the right without moving the titles out of the spreadsheet area (see fig. 8.16). Quattro Pro shades the cell block containing locked title data in high-intensity colors so that you can identify clearly where the locking begins.

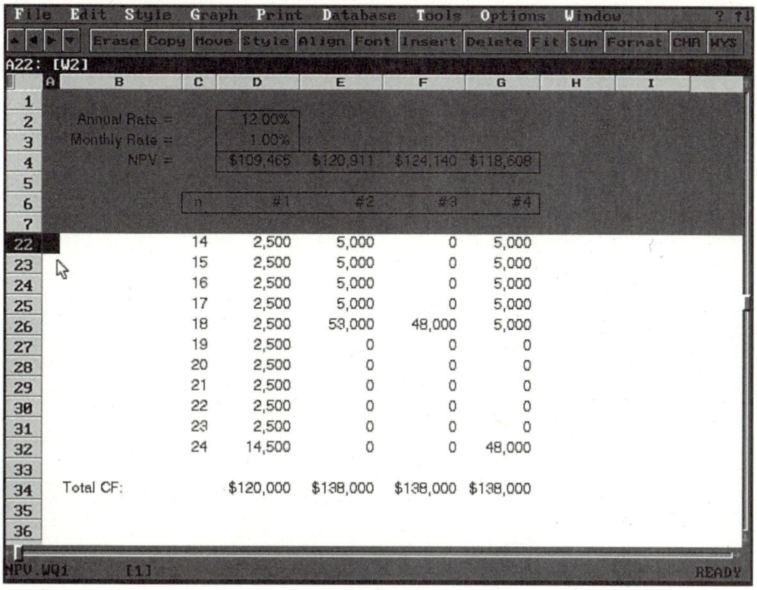

Fig. 8.16

Spreadsheet titles locked to restrict cursor movement to the data-entry area.

When in WYSIWYG display mode, to alter the color used to shade locked titles and locked titles text, use the /**O**ptions **C**olors **S**preadsheet **W**YSIWYG **C**olors **T**itles **B**ackground command. If you are in text display mode, use /**O**ptions **C**olors **S**preadsheet **T**itles to change these options.

To lock spreadsheet titles, place the cell selector in the row below or the column to the right of the titles you want to lock. Then, choose /**W**indow **O**ptions **L**ocked **T**itles. Quattro Pro displays a menu offering four options: **H**orizontal, **V**ertical, **B**oth, and **C**lear. Quattro Pro locks titles above or to the left of the cell selector, depending on which locked title option you choose.

When locked titles are in effect, Quattro Pro does not enable you to move the cell selector into the locked title area with the usual cursor-movement techniques. Only by using F5 (Goto) and specifying a cell or block can you go to a cell in the locked titles area.

PART I — USING QUATTRO PRO SPREADSHEETS

Removing Row and Column Borders

In some spreadsheet applications, removing the row and column borders can make a spreadsheet look more like a report. If you create an application that prompts a user to enter figures into a data-entry form, for example, displaying the row and column borders is not critical. Someone unfamiliar with the look of a spreadsheet may find the borders distracting. By eliminating the borders from your screen, you also can view more of the spreadsheet area at one time.

To remove column and row borders from your display, choose /**W**indow **O**ptions **R**ow & Col Borders. When prompted, choose the **H**ide option. Quattro Pro redraws the screen without row and column borders (see fig. 8.17).

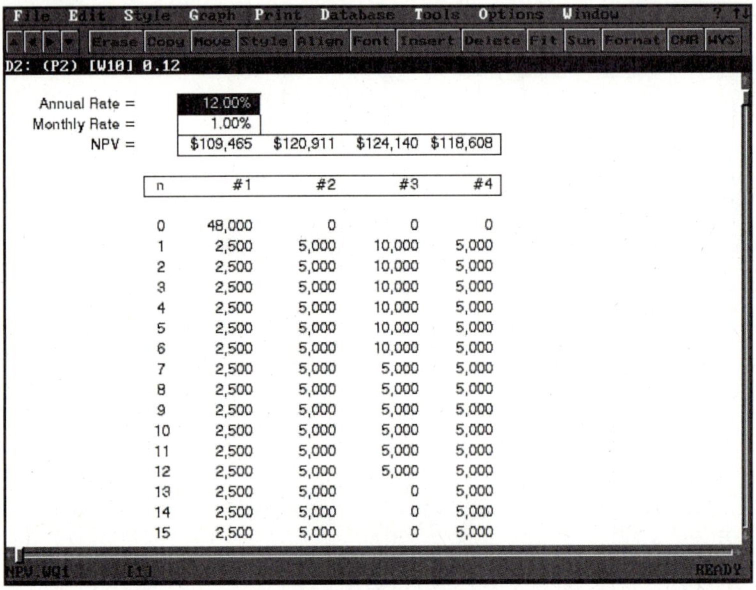

Fig. 8.17

Removing row and column borders.

To display the row and column borders again, choose the command again and then choose the **D**isplay option.

Note that the row and column border setting is spreadsheet dependent; when you choose /**F**ile **S**ave, Quattro Pro saves this display setting only with the current spreadsheet.

Creating Map View

The /**W**indow **O**ptions **M**ap View command creates a unique on-screen effect that can be described as a "bird's-eye view" of a spreadsheet (see fig. 8.18). In this mode, Quattro Pro compresses the column widths to one character space and then assigns and displays one character code that identifies the kind of data in each cell (see table 8.10).

While in Map mode, inserted graphs are virtually indistinguishable because the spreadsheet column widths are reduced to a single character.

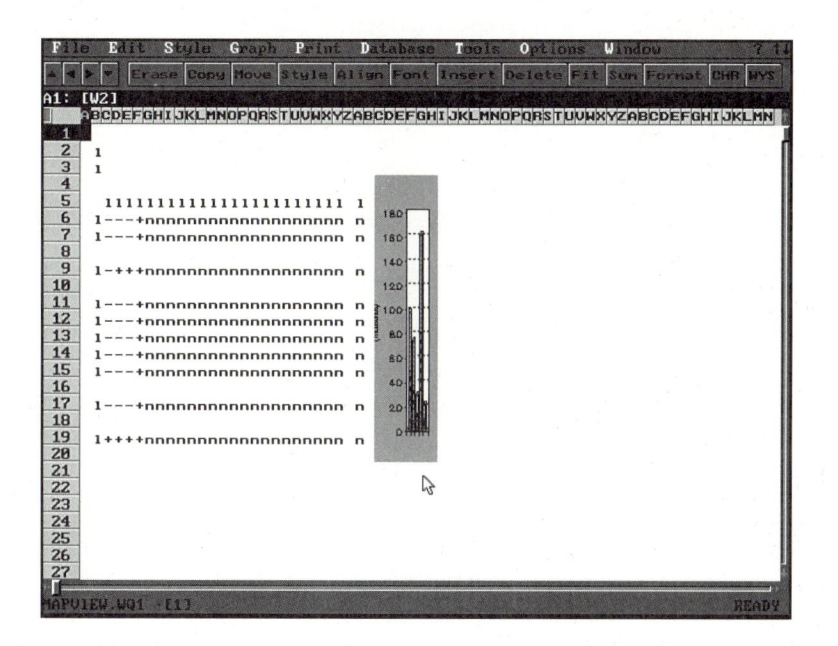

Fig. 8.18

A bird's-eye view of a spreadsheet.

Table 8.10 Map Mode Codes

Code	Type of Cell Data
l	Label
n	Number
+	Formula
−	Linked formula
c	Circular cell formula

You can use the /**E**dit **S**earch & Replace command to locate data quickly on a spreadsheet displayed in Map mode. Instead of specifying a label or number to search for, you can use any code listed in table 8.10. You can use the **S**earch & Replace command, for example, to locate the presence of a circular formula by specifying *c* as the text for which to search.

Displaying Spreadsheet Grid Lines

The /**W**indow **O**ptions **G**rid Lines command controls the display of grid lines on individual spreadsheets. By default, grid lines are turned off for any new spreadsheet you create in Quattro Pro. To add grid lines to a spreadsheet, use the **D**isplay option. To turn off spreadsheet grid lines so that you can see style enhancements such as drawn lines and shade cells better, choose the **H**ide option.

Note that a grid lines setting is spreadsheet dependent. When you choose /**F**ile **S**ave, Quattro Pro saves this display setting only with the current spreadsheet.

Linking Spreadsheets

Linked spreadsheets simplify complex relationships, help you to design more flexible applications, access information from a database, and enable Quattro Pro to be more memory-efficient. Like a group of related spreadsheets that you save to a workspace file, linked spreadsheets have something in common—they share data. Specifically, you can pass information between linked spreadsheets using live formula references.

An ordinary formula references data in cells on the current spreadsheet and displays the result in another cell on the same spreadsheet. A live formula references data in cells on supporting spreadsheets open in Quattro Pro's memory and displays the result in a cell on a primary spreadsheet, also open in memory. When you change data on a supporting spreadsheet, Quattro Pro updates the data displayed on the primary spreadsheet, as long as all the spreadsheets are open in memory at the same time.

Linked spreadsheets introduce a new set of possibilities for creating Quattro Pro applications. You can break down a large database spreadsheet into several smaller ones that are easier to access and update, for example. You also can create a small bookkeeping application that stores ledger transactions on supporting spreadsheets and transfers the end-of-period balances, using live formula references, to a group of primary financial statement spreadsheets.

After you learn how to create the links that tie spreadsheets together, you can begin to envision your own uses for this type of application.

Creating Linking Formulas

You can use several techniques to create linking formulas. You can type the formula directly on the input line; create three-dimensional consolidation formulas to link spreadsheets with common structures; and, if you have a mouse, use the familiar clicking method to create formulas as you go.

Before examining the process of building live formulas, review the linked spreadsheet application shown in figure 8.19. The active spreadsheet in figure 8.19, PARENT.WQ1, is the primary document in a linked spreadsheet application. The data that eventually appears on this spreadsheet comes from SUBSID_1.WQ1, SUBSID_2.WQ1, and SUBSID_3.WQ1 income statement spreadsheets for each of Auntie Deborah's three subsidiaries.

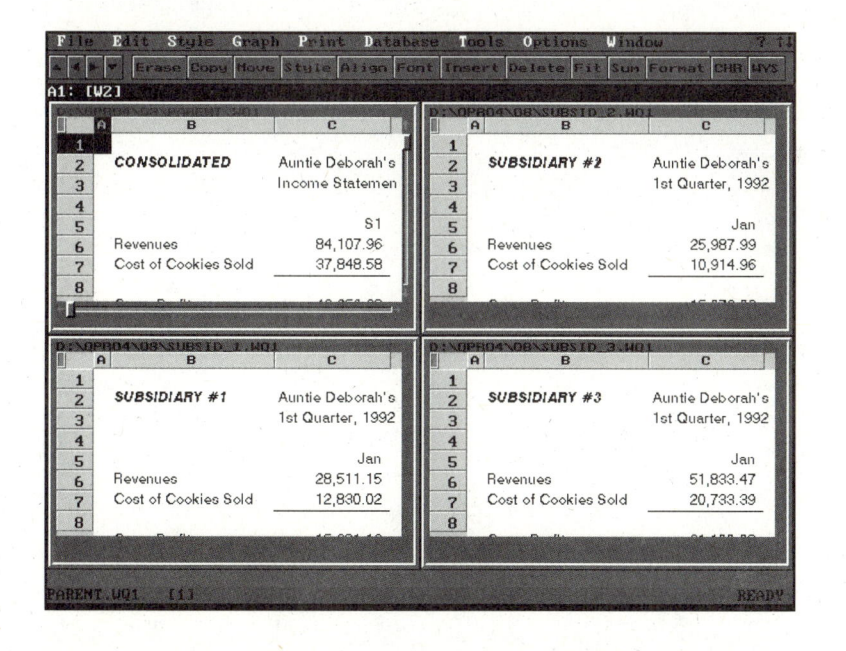

Fig. 8.19

A linking application that uses one primary and three supporting spreadsheets.

PART I — USING QUATTRO PRO SPREADSHEETS

Figure 8.19 shows that in linked spreadsheet applications, you must design and create two or more spreadsheets. In the sample application, the structure of each spreadsheet—except for a few label descriptions—is the same.

You can use one of three procedures to create formulas that link spreadsheets.

Typing a Linking Formula

A *linking formula* is a basic Quattro Pro formula that contains a reference to an external spreadsheet file name. In figure 8.20, the formula appearing in cell C6 on PARENT.WQ1 is created by doing the following:

1. Open all the spreadsheets to be linked into Quattro Pro's memory (in this case, just PARENT.WQ1).
2. Make cell C6 on PARENT.WQ1 active.
3. Type *+[subsid_1]f6* on the input line.
4. Press Enter to record the linking formula.

Quattro Pro evaluates cell F6 on SUBSID_1.WQ1 and displays the value 84,107.96 in the active cell on PARENT.WQ1 (see fig. 8.20).

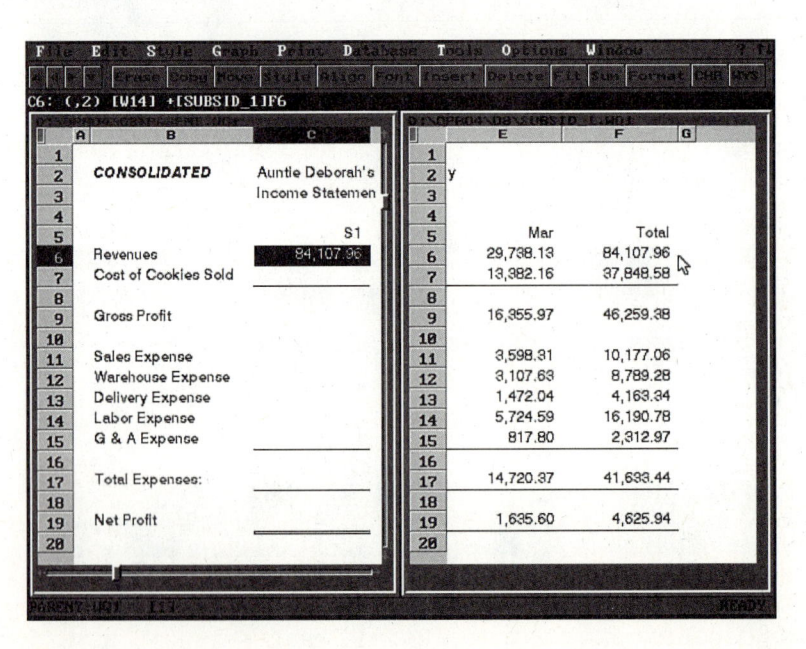

Fig. 8.20

Creating the initial linking formula.

Every linking formula contains three elements: the plus symbol (+), a bracketed file name, and an external cell (or block) reference from the file named in the brackets.

The + tells Quattro Pro that you are entering a formula. If you leave out this important symbol, the program thinks that you are entering a label.

When Quattro Pro encounters a file name in brackets, the program recognizes that it must look at another spreadsheet file open in memory. The description SUBSID_1 tells Quattro Pro the name of a specific supporting spreadsheet.

The third element in this syntax is the cell or block reference. Quattro Pro uses this reference to link to a specific cell address or block address on the spreadsheet file indicated in the brackets. In the example, the cell reference is C6—a cell address on SUBSID_1.

The syntax of this formula indicates that the primary and supporting spreadsheets reside in the same directory on the same disk drive. If the spreadsheets are not in the same directory, the formula may look something like the following:

+[A:\REPORT\SUBSID_1.WQ1]F6

This syntax says that the supporting spreadsheet is stored in a directory called \REPORT on a disk in drive A. Although you may link spreadsheets in different directories on different drives, you always should create and save the spreadsheets in the same directory on the same disk drive. When you then create linking formulas, you do not have to wonder whether you entered the correct drive name and path name, and you do not have to place a disk into a disk drive every time you want to work with the application.

This strategy also keeps the length of your linking formulas to an absolute minimum—an important point when you create longer, more complex formulas.

Creating 3-D Consolidation Formulas

Creating linking applications that use supporting spreadsheets with exactly the same structure has a great advantage: you have an additional formula-entry alternative at your disposal. This method, called *3-D formula consolidation*, uses wild-card designations in a linking formula to create live references to the same location on all spreadsheets open in Quattro Pro's memory.

> **TIP**
>
> This method references all spreadsheets open in Quattro Pro's memory. Before you begin, remember to close every spreadsheet file that will not be a part of the linking application.

Substituting the familiar wild-card code * (the asterisk) in place of a file name in a linking formula causes Quattro Pro to look at all open spreadsheets. To do more than look, you must include an @function command that performs a mathematical operation.

Every 3-D consolidation formula contains three elements: an @function command, a bracketed 3-D link code, and an external cell (or block) reference.

The @function command indicates a mathematical operation for Quattro Pro to perform. To average all the values appearing in the same cell on three supporting spreadsheets, for example, you use the @AVG function.

A properly constructed 3-D link code is critical to the success of this operation. The link code tells Quattro Pro which spreadsheets the program should look at when performing the mathematical operation indicated by the @function command. If you want Quattro Pro to perform a mathematical operation using data on all the supporting spreadsheets open in memory, for example, use the [*] link code. To look only at those spreadsheets with names that begin with the letter S, enter *[S*]*.

The third element in this syntax is the cell or block reference. Quattro Pro examines the value residing in this cell on each spreadsheet open in memory, according to the 3-D link code specification. To look at block A5..A10 on all open spreadsheets, for example, type *A5..A10* as the reference.

Suppose that you reenter the linking formula shown in figure 8.20 as @SUM([*]F6). This formula tells Quattro Pro to sum the F6 values from all open supporting spreadsheets and display the total in the active cell on the primary spreadsheet.

The formula displays total subsidiary revenues for the first quarter of 1992—a useful figure for this application, but one that does not belong in this particular cell. The viability of a consolidated formula depends mostly on its proper placement on a spreadsheet. In this example, the consolidated formula makes more sense appearing in a column that displays data for all subsidiaries.

With a little bit of forethought, you can streamline the process of building a linking application by duplicating your spreadsheet structures and then building formulas using 3-D consolidation. Be careful, however, to consolidate similar information in the correct location on the primary spreadsheet.

Creating Linking Formulas by Pointing and Clicking

Look at the formula displayed in cell C6 on PARENT.WQ1 in figure 8.20. The final method for building linking formulas is achieved when your screen looks like the one pictured in this figure.

To enter the same linking formula using a mouse, follow these steps:

1. Tile two spreadsheet windows so that the windows appear side by side.

2. Click the primary spreadsheet to make that spreadsheet active. Choose a cell as the destination cell and then click that cell to make it active.

3. Press the + key to enter VALUE mode.

4. Click the supporting spreadsheet to make that spreadsheet active. Locate the cell containing the value you want to use as the external reference if you did not click it the first time.

5. The cell reference—complete with the external file name—has been copied onto the input line.

6. Press Enter to record the linking formula. In the sample application, you first make cell C6 active on PARENT.WQ1. You then press the + key, point to cell F6 on SUBSID_1.WQ1, and then click to copy that cell reference onto the input line. Press Enter to store the formula.

Quattro Pro evaluates cell F6 on SUBSID_1.WQ1 and again displays the value 84,107.96 in the active cell on PARENT.WQ1.

You can use this technique in a way that does not require you to tile windows. With the primary spreadsheet displayed in a full-screen format, enter VALUE mode, press Alt-0, choose a window from the displayed menu, click the target cell, and then press Enter to record the linking formula. If you already know the number of the window, press Alt plus the window number to move directly there.

Moving and Copying Linking Formulas

Now that you are familiar with each method for creating and entering linking formulas, you can return to the sample application and complete PARENT.WQ1. After you create a linking formula, you can copy the formula to other cells on the primary spreadsheet (see fig. 8.21).

PART I — USING QUATTRO PRO SPREADSHEETS

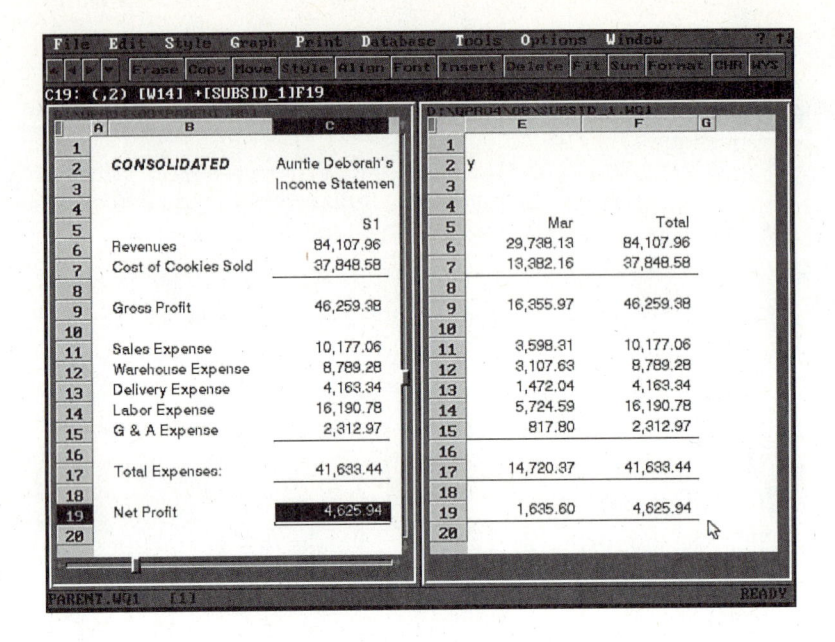

Fig. 8.21

Subsidiary 1's data linked to the primary document.

To duplicate the linking formula in cell C6, for example, make that cell active and follow these steps:

1. Choose /**E**dit **C**opy and press Enter to select C6 as the source block, or click the cell with your mouse.

2. Make cell C7 active, press Enter to select cell C7 as the destination block, press the period key to anchor the cell and then highlight other destination cells, or click cell C7 with your mouse.

Quattro Pro copies the formula into cell C7. Continue this operation, copying the linking formula into the appropriate cells, until you fill in all subsidiary data on the primary spreadsheet or the block you specify. After you finish, you have one final task: sum the values in each column to derive the parent company's totals. You can enter @SUM functions that total the subsidiary data or use the 3-D consolidation technique to create additional linking formulas.

Review the spreadsheet shown in figure 8.22. The formula displayed on the input line results when the 3-D consolidating formula @SUM([*]F6) is entered into cell F6 on PARENT.WQ1. Quattro Pro converts the consolidating formulas into results so that you later can edit the individual external references.

TIP

One easy way to make sure that you have open only those spreadsheet files that you want to consolidate is to use the workspace feature.

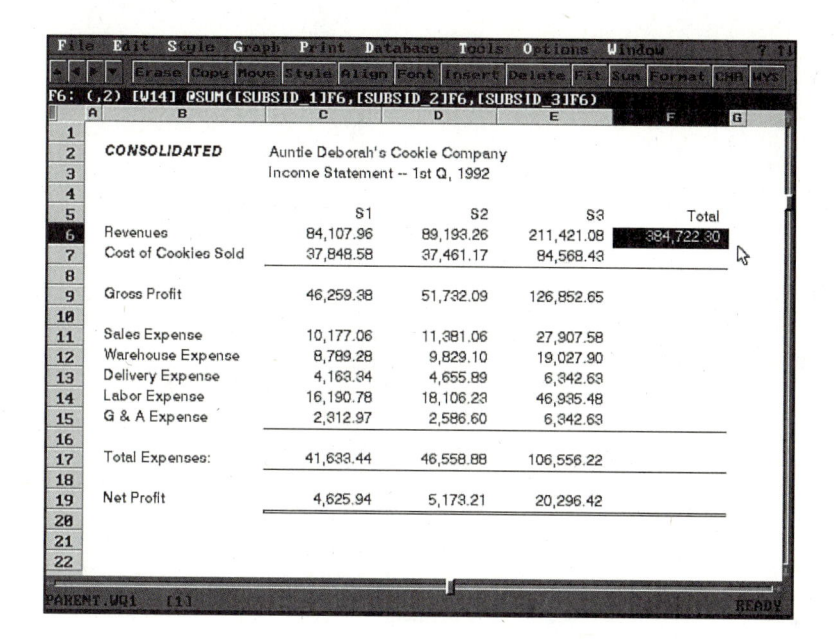

Fig. 8.22

A 3-D consolidation formula that sums values entered on the supporting spreadsheets.

You can copy this formula into the remaining cells in column F to complete the linking application.

When you apply **C**opy and **M**ove operations to linking formulas, Quattro Pro treats relative and absolute references the same as other formulas. If you move a linking formula into the spreadsheet that the formula references, however, Quattro Pro cancels and erases the link from the formula.

Opening and Updating Linked Spreadsheets

After you create the primary and supporting spreadsheets, you should save the spreadsheets to disk. You normally create a workspace file for multiple spreadsheets, which is helpful when you want to save and later load all the associated spreadsheets. Loading linked spreadsheet applications, however, requires special handling.

PART I — USING QUATTRO PRO SPREADSHEETS

Loading a Linked Spreadsheet Application

If you choose /**F**ile **R**etrieve to load the sample application, specify PARENT.WQ1 as the spreadsheet to retrieve. When you retrieve a primary file in a linked spreadsheet application, Quattro Pro displays the linking options menu shown in figure 8.23.

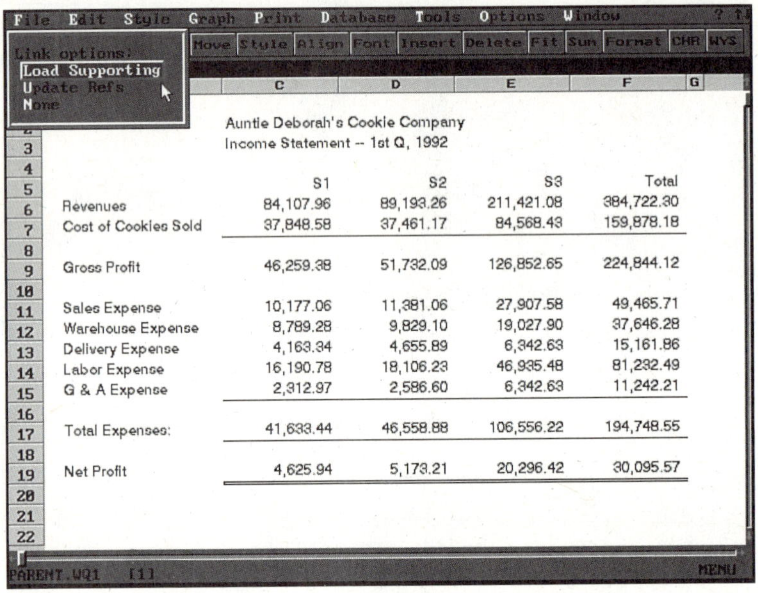

Fig. 8.23

Three options for retrieving a linked spreadsheet application.

To load each supporting spreadsheet, choose the **L**oad Supporting option. The **U**pdate Refs option causes Quattro Pro to update the linked formula results on the primary spreadsheet using data from the unopened supporting spreadsheets.

If you do not want to update the linking references on the primary spreadsheet, choose the **N**one option. This option causes Quattro Pro to display NA (not available) values in each cell on the primary spreadsheet that has a linking reference to an unopened, supporting document (see fig. 8.24).

This display of NA values enables you to review the structure of a primary document in a large linking application without first having to load each supporting document.

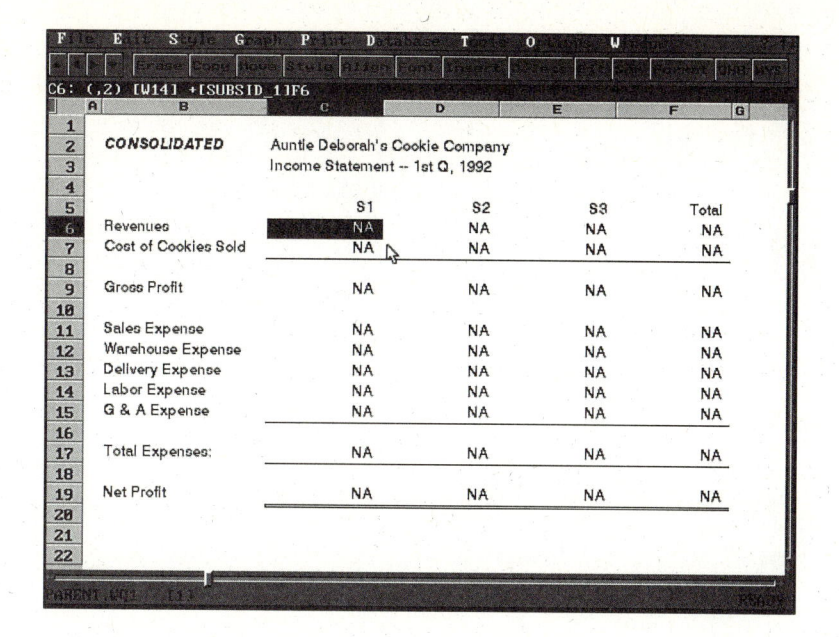

Fig. 8.24

NA values displayed on the primary spreadsheet.

Updating the Spreadsheet Links

Choose /Tools Update Links to display the Update Links menu. The four options on this menu enable you to control the interaction between primary and supporting documents in a linked spreadsheet application.

Choose the Open option to open individual supporting spreadsheets without reloading the entire linked application. When prompted, highlight the names of the spreadsheets you want to open and then press Enter to load those spreadsheets (see fig. 8.25). If you do not remember the names of the spreadsheets, press Esc to display a list of linked spreadsheet files for the current directory.

When no supporting spreadsheets are open in Quattro Pro's memory, choose the Refresh option to recalculate results for the linking formulas on a primary spreadsheet without opening that spreadsheet. When prompted, highlight the names of the supporting spreadsheets that contain cell values referenced by linking formulas on the primary spreadsheet. Press Enter to refresh the linking formula results on the primary spreadsheet.

Choose the Change option to unlink a supporting spreadsheet from the primary spreadsheet and relink it to a new spreadsheet (see fig. 8.26).

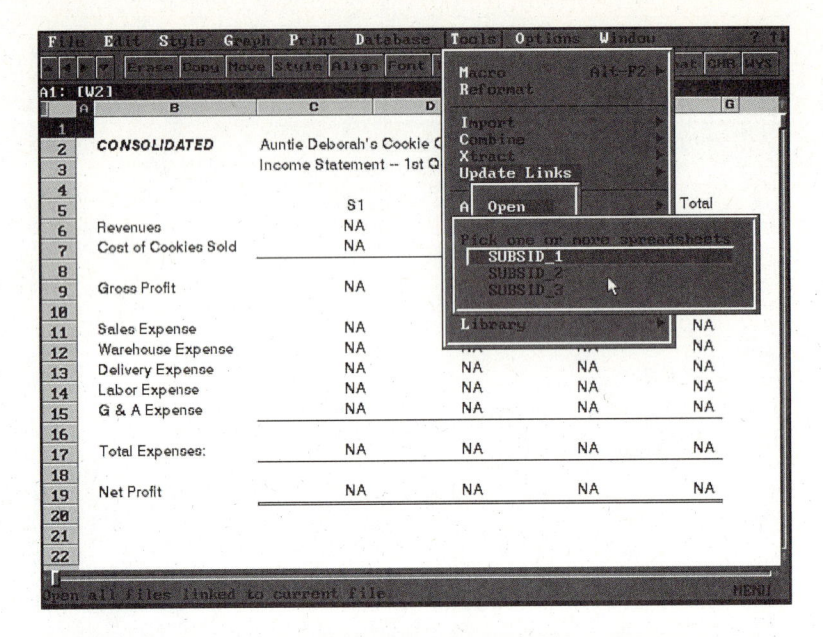

Fig. 8.25

Loading unopened supporting spreadsheets into Quattro Pro.

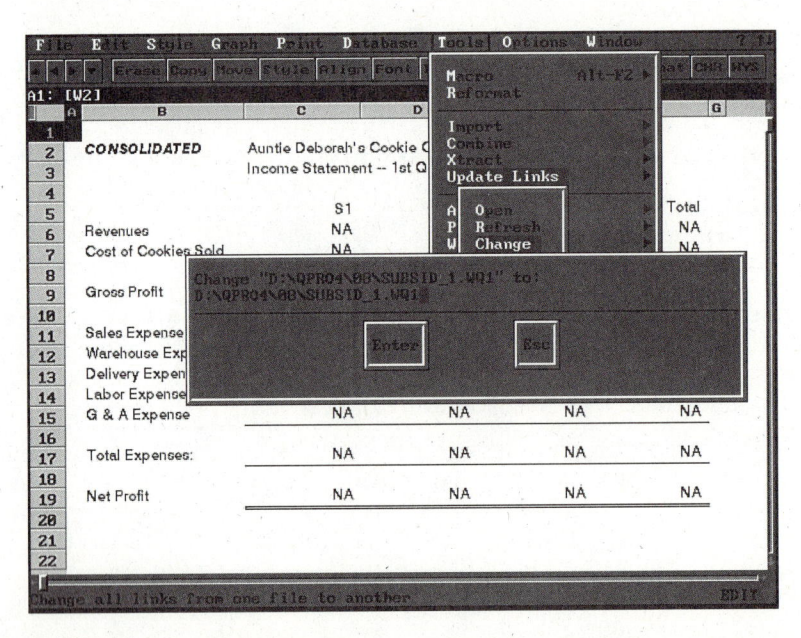

Fig. 8.26

The Quattro Pro prompts for the name of the spreadsheet to which you want to relink.

Choose the **D**elete option to erase links between the primary spreadsheet and one or more supporting spreadsheets. This technique is useful when you want to disassociate old or outdated supporting spreadsheets from the primary spreadsheet.

Using Advanced File Tools

The first three commands in the middle of the **Tools** menu provide you with the means to import, combine, and extract spreadsheet data. These commands can operate on spreadsheet data and data from other programs. By continuing with the sample application, you learn how to use each command to manipulate files in special ways.

Importing a File

The **Import** command enables you to load data from text files into a Quattro Pro spreadsheet. This operation is recommended for users who want to access data stored in file formats that Quattro Pro cannot translate. Importing text from a word processing file, for example, and financial data stored in a file used by an accounting software program is common.

The **Import** command can access data stored in three common file formats: ASCII text, comma- and quote-delimited, and comma-delimited. When you import data, Quattro Pro reads the foreign file format and copies the data into one column on the current spreadsheet.

To import text into a Quattro Pro spreadsheet, follow these steps:

1. Place the cell selector into the cell in which you want Quattro Pro to begin copying the imported data.

2. Choose **/Tools Import** and then choose **A**SCII Text File, **C**omma & "" Delimited File, or **O**nly Commas from the displayed list.

3. When prompted, type the name of the file to import and then press Enter to begin importing text from that file.

Review the data after Quattro Pro finishes importing the text. Depending on the source file format, Quattro Pro may have copied the imported data into one column without breaking up long labels. This situation occurs, for example, when you import data from an ASCII text file that does not delineate separate items that are grouped together on the same row. The item `Franklin Tracy E.`, for example, may end up as `FranklinTracyE`. To break up the long labels, you can use the **/Tools Parse** command. (See Chapter 14, "Analyzing Data," for comprehensive coverage of this command.)

Generally, Quattro Pro copies comma- and quote-delimited files into separate columns on the spreadsheet, based on the delimiters.

PART I — USING QUATTRO PRO SPREADSHEETS

Combining Two Files

The **C**ombine command enables you to copy, add, and subtract data on two spreadsheets. You can use this command for applications that are not formula linked yet require a certain level of data association. In most cases, linked formulas are easier to work with and provide you a greater degree of flexibility when designing and building spreadsheet applications.

Return to the sample application introduced in the preceding section. Start by assuming that the four spreadsheets are no longer linked by formulas. PARENT.WQ1 also contains no values. Using the **C**ombine command, you can create the same end result achieved with linked formulas.

> **TIP**
>
> Combined files do not update each other automatically like linked files do. To refresh the values in combined files, you must choose the command again and then recombine the data.

Before issuing this command, you must gather data about the two spreadsheets. First, jot down the exact block coordinates of the data from the source spreadsheet. Second, review the destination spreadsheet and then select an area to which you want to combine data.

> **CAUTION:** Before executing the command, note that Quattro Pro overwrites existing cell data (including protected cells) on the destination spreadsheet, unless you are performing an **A**dd or **S**ubtract combine operation.

Copying Data

To combine data from PARENT.WQ1 and SUBSID_1.WQ1, follow these steps:

1. Retrieve PARENT.WQ1 and place the cell selector in cell E6.

2. Choose /**T**ools **C**ombine **C**opy.

3. When prompted, choose the **B**lock option to copy only a block of data.

8 — MANAGING FILES AND WINDOWS

4. When prompted, type *C6..C19* and press Enter to record the source block.

5. After Quattro Pro displays the file list box, highlight SUBSID_1.WQ1 and press Enter.

Quattro Pro begins copying block C6..C19 from SUBSID_1.WQ1 to PARENT.WQ1, beginning at the location of the cell selector (cell E6). After you choose the **C**ombine **C**opy option, Quattro Pro reproduces the data exactly as the data appears in the source block, including cell formatting and presentation-quality display settings (see fig. 8.27).

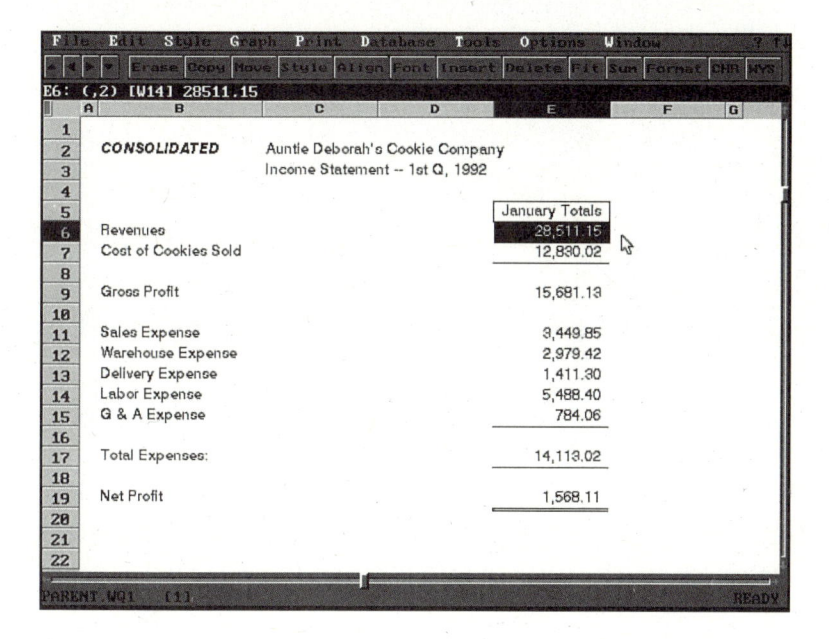

Fig. 8.27

Combining data by copying values.

Exercise extreme caution when using the /**T**ools **C**ombine **C**opy command to copy formulas. Quattro Pro may not display the answer you expect. Suppose that you copy the Total column data of column F from SUBSID_1.WQ1 to PARENT.WQ1. At first glance, this technique appears to be a good way to reproduce sales totals for Subsidiary #1 on PARENT.WQ1. If you had taken this approach, however, you would have created a circular reference.

Recall that in column F on SUBSID_1.WQ1, each formula sums data appearing in columns C, D, and E. When copied to PARENT.WQ1, these formulas now sum data appearing in columns C, D, and E on PARENT.WQ1. A circular formula results because the original copy destination on PARENT.WQ1 (column E) is included in the formula.

Be careful. Solving one problem sometimes reveals another. Suppose that you shift the copy destination to column F on PARENT.WQ1. This action eliminates the circular reference but exposes another problem. On PARENT.WQ1, a formula that sums data in columns C, D, and E returns a value of 0 because these columns are empty.

> **TIP**
>
> To copy formula results from one spreadsheet to another, convert formulas to their results using the /Edit Values command. Then, return to the spreadsheet containing the formulas and press Alt-F5 to reverse the /Edit Values operation. Quattro Pro displays the formulas again in their original form.

Adding and Subtracting Data

To add data to PARENT.WQ1, which is located on SUBSID_2.WQ1, follow these steps:

1. Retrieve PARENT.WQ1 and place the cell selector in cell E6.
2. Choose /Tools Combine Add.
3. When prompted, choose the Block option to add only a block of data.
4. When prompted, type *C6..C19* and press Enter to record the source block.
5. After Quattro Pro displays the file list box, highlight SUBSID_2.WQ1 again and press Enter.

Quattro Pro adds the values from the source block to the corresponding values on the active spreadsheet, beginning at the location of the cell selector. When you Add data, Quattro Pro does not alter any cell formatting or presentation-quality display settings in the target block (see fig. 8.28), whereas Copy brings the formatting in along with the data.

Repeat the Add operation again, except add the results from cell block C6..C19 on SUBSID_3.WQ1 to PARENT.WQ1. Your spreadsheet now contains the same values that appear in column C on PARENT.WQ1 in the linked spreadsheet application (refer to fig. 8.22).

The Subtract option on the Combine menu works like the Add option, except that the Subtract option subtracts the source-block values from the destination block values.

8 — MANAGING FILES AND WINDOWS

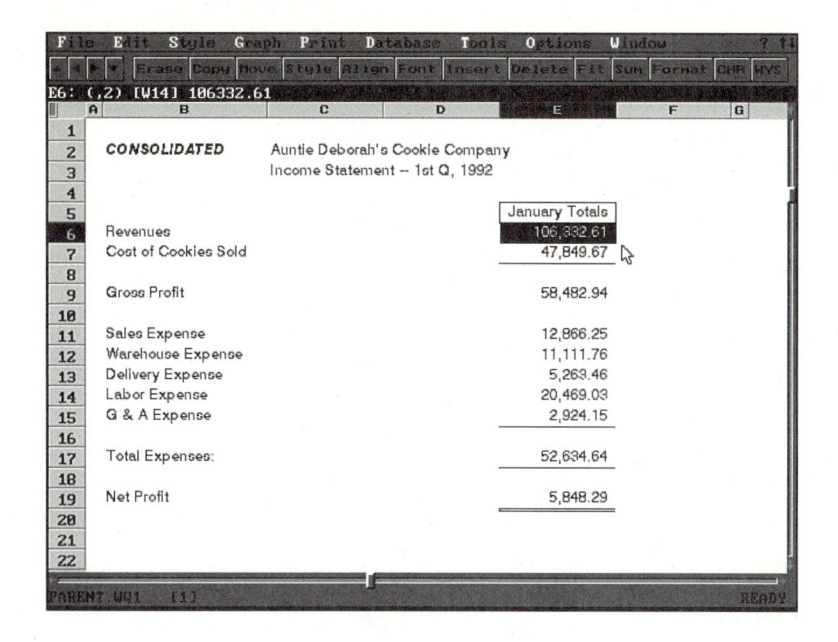

Fig. 8.28

Combine data by adding values.

> **NOTE** Labels and formulas are unaffected by adding and subtracting, but dates are affected.

Extracting Part of a File

The /**T**ools **X**tract command copies and saves part of a spreadsheet in a new spreadsheet file. This command is useful for breaking large spreadsheet applications into several smaller, more manageable spreadsheets.

When Quattro Pro performs an extraction operation, the program retains all block names, graph names, and format settings that applied to the source block before extraction. You also can extract **F**ormulas or **V**alues from the source spreadsheet. Choosing the **V**alues option is like choosing the /**E**dit **V**alues command.

To extract data from one spreadsheet and add the data to another, follow these steps:

1. Choose /**T**ools **X**tract.
2. Choose **F**ormulas or **V**alues.

3. When prompted, type a file name for the spreadsheet that will receive the extracted data.

4. When prompted, type the coordinates of the source block and press Enter to extract the data.

Questions & Answers

This chapter shows you how to create, use, and manage files, workspaces, and windows. If you have questions concerning situations not addressed in the examples given, look through this section.

Managing Files

Q: After I loaded two documents into Quattro Pro, I pressed Alt-0 to reveal the open **W**indow menu, but only one file name was displayed. What happened to my second spreadsheet?

A: You chose /**F**ile **R**etrieve to open the second document when you should have used /**F**ile **O**pen. The latter command overlays the current spreadsheet window with a saved spreadsheet, but the former command loads a saved spreadsheet into the current window, erasing the current spreadsheet from memory.

Q: Why doesn't Quattro Pro save my **D**irectory command setting for new work sessions?

A: You can save the settings, but not with the **D**irectory command. Choose /**O**ptions **S**tartup **D**irectory to choose a new default directory setting. You also can choose /**O**ptions **U**pdate to save the new setting. Quattro Pro writes the new default directory name on the **F**ile menu next to the **D**irectory command.

Q: Why don't my presentation-quality settings appear when I retrieve spreadsheet files saved in non-Quattro Pro file formats?

A: The file formats for many of the programs that Quattro Pro can read and write to do not support features such as line drawing, font selections, inserted graphs, and formula links. These features are Quattro Pro-specific and should be added only to spreadsheet files with the WQ1 extension.

If you try to save them in a format that doesn't support them, you get the error message `Desk top settings are removed. Save the file?` This gives you the option to save the file without the unsupported features.

Q: I cannot remember the password for a spreadsheet. How can I display a list of the current passwords?

A: You cannot. Quattro Pro does not enable you to access a password-protected file without the password. If you have forgotten the password, you must build the spreadsheet again.

Q: How do I rename a spreadsheet file without returning to DOS?

A: Choose /File Save As and type a new file name when prompted. This method copies the original spreadsheet. You also can highlight a name in the File Pane of the File Manager window and choose /Edit Rename or press F2. Quattro Pro prompts you for a new name. This method does not duplicate the file.

Displaying Windows

Q: Why is Quattro Pro sometimes unable to split a spreadsheet window into two panes?

A: Quattro Pro cannot execute the Vertical or Horizontal commands on the Window menu in the following cases: when the cell selector is in row 1, you cannot split a window into two horizontal panes; when the cell selector is in column A, you cannot split a window into two vertical panes; when a spreadsheet window already is split into two panes, you cannot select another split setting. To change the split pane style, choose /Window Options Clear before you select a new split pane setting.

Q: I cannot seem to scroll my split window panes together. Am I doing something wrong?

A: You have chosen /Window Options Unsync. Choose /Window Options Sync to return the inactive pane to the location of the active pane.

Linking Worksheets

Q: When I try to enter a linking formula, Quattro Pro beeps and displays an error message that says a drive is not ready. Then, the program displays NA in the cell. What is going on?

A: You created and tried to enter a linking formula containing a drive letter before the file-name reference. The drive you specified does not contain a disk now. Quattro Pro tries to read the drive for several seconds and then records the formula anyway; because the file-name reference is not valid, however, the program displays the NA value in the cell.

If you intend to include the drive letter, place the disk in the drive and then reenter the formula. This time, Quattro Pro finds the value and displays the correct formula result. If you do not intend to use the drive letter, delete the letter from the formula. In both cases, the NA value disappears.

Q: Why does Quattro Pro sometimes not display the link options prompt after I load a linking application?

A: Quattro Pro displays the link options prompt whenever you open a spreadsheet containing references to unopened spreadsheets. When you load the primary spreadsheet before the supporting spreadsheets, Quattro Pro always displays the link options prompt. When you load supporting document(s) first and then load the primary document, Quattro Pro does not need to display this prompt.

Q: I loaded the primary spreadsheet in a linking application, and Quattro Pro displayed a prompt box asking me to change a linking reference to a different file name. Why?

A: You deleted or renamed a spreadsheet file referenced by a primary spreadsheet in a linking application.

Press Esc until you cancel this prompt box, and Quattro Pro continues to load the rest of the linking application. When the application is completely loaded, Quattro Pro shows NA values in the cells that reference the unknown document. If you have renamed the spreadsheet, change the name back so that Quattro Pro displays the correct values. If you accidentally deleted the spreadsheet, you must edit the linking formulas and remove the references to this file name.

Q: I created a circular formula when I combined data from two spreadsheets in a linking application. What happened?

A: Don't use the /**Tools Combine** command to copy blocks containing formulas. If you use this command, you run the risk of creating circular formulas. Instead, choose /**Tools Xtract Values** so that Quattro Pro copies the formula results instead of the formulas.

Summary

Chapter 8 demonstrates some basic file-management skills and advanced file tools that you can use to link spreadsheets. This chapter reviews the **F**ile menu and **W**indow menu commands and introduces you to using the File Manager.

8 — MANAGING FILES AND WINDOWS

Having completed this chapter, you should understand the following Quattro Pro concepts:

- Creating, opening, and retrieving files
- Saving, closing, and erasing files
- Translating spreadsheets to and from non-Quattro Pro file formats
- Password protecting your files
- Using the File Manager to perform multiple file operations
- Enlarging, shrinking, tiling, stacking, moving, and sizing windows
- Splitting windows into panes
- Turning spreadsheet grid lines on and off
- Creating linking formulas in POINT mode
- Moving and copying linking formulas
- Importing and combining files

Chapter 9 introduces you to techniques for printing your Quattro Pro documents. You learn how to print draft-quality copies of documents, final-quality copies of documents, and how to print a large spreadsheet block so that it fits on a single page. You also learn about previewing the printed look of a document in the Screen Preview environment. Chapter 9 offers comprehensive coverage of the commands found on the /Print menu.

PART II

Printing and Graphing

OUTLINE

9. Printing
10. Creating Graphs
11. Customizing Graphs
12. Analyzing Graphs

CHAPTER 9

Printing

Quattro Pro provides you with the tools to format and print spreadsheet reports and graphs in several ways. You can print an unformatted snapshot of your screen's display, print a specific block of spreadsheet values, or print a presentation-quality version of a spreadsheet report. In this chapter, you learn the many printing techniques available on Quattro Pro's **P**rint menu.

This chapter introduces you to the **P**rint menu commands that enable you to select data on a spreadsheet, prepare the layout and format of a report, and then print the report.

In the next section, you look at each step in the process of printing a small spreadsheet report. You also learn a technique for generating a rough-draft screen preview of your spreadsheet data—a useful prelude to creating the final version of every printed report.

Next, you see how to access, understand, and set all of the options that control the appearance of a printed spreadsheet report. Specifically, you learn how to set layout options—such as footers, margins, and page orientation—that enable you to print larger spreadsheet reports successfully.

The chapter continues by explaining the two format styles that Quattro Pro can use when printing out a spreadsheet report.

The next section covers methods to help prepare for a printing session. You learn about aligning paper, issuing form feeds, and skipping lines to control the movement of paper in your printer.

PART II — PRINTING AND GRAPHING

The material continues by showing why and how to choose various destinations for your printed output. You can print to a printer, to a file, or to your screen, for example.

Next, this chapter reviews the procedures for printing a graph. As with a spreadsheet report, you can reproduce a graph on paper, print a graph to a file, and preview the finished form of a graph on-screen. An additional graph-printing option enables you to print to a file that can be used to produce 35mm slides.

The final section of this chapter looks at Quattro Pro's newest printing features: the Borland Print Spooler and the Print Manager. The Print Spooler enables you to continue working with the current spreadsheet while jobs are being printed, and the Print Manager displays vital information about the print jobs waiting in the printing queue.

Reviewing the Print Menu

You can use the 11 **P**rint menu commands to define a print block or a heading block, create a custom layout, control the movement of paper in a printer, and generate printouts of spreadsheet reports and graphs (see fig. 9.1).

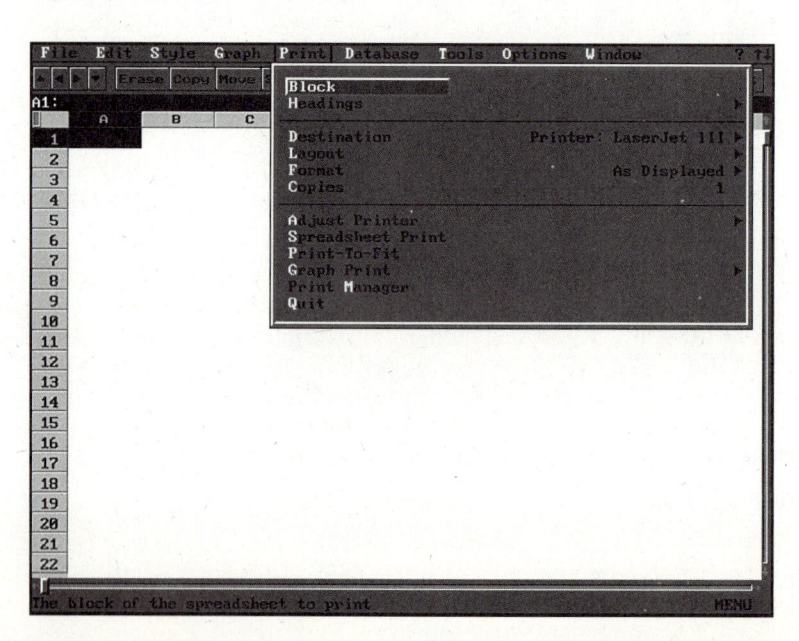

Fig. 9.1

The **P**rint menu commands.

The **P**rint menu consists of three types of commands: block definition, report formatting, and printer control. Quattro Pro displays the current system settings for certain commands at the right margin of the **P**rint menu.

The block definition commands tell Quattro Pro which block to print and which block to use as a heading at the top of each printed page.

The **D**estination command—found in the middle section of the **P**rint menu—enables you to choose where Quattro Pro prints a report: to a printer, to a file, or to the screen. (The name of the default printer appears next to the **D**estination command, when **D**estination is set to **P**rinter or **S**creen Preview but not **F**ile.)

The remaining commands in this section enable you to set print margins, set the page length, and alter the print orientation of a report. You can choose to print spreadsheet cell data as the data appears on-screen or in a report that lists each cell and its contents. You also can tell Quattro Pro to print multiple pages of any spreadsheet or graph.

The commands at the bottom section of the **P**rint menu control the printer. The first command enables you to advance the paper in the printer one line or one page at a time and align the printer to top of form. The second command tells Quattro Pro to print a spreadsheet using the print settings on the **L**ayout menu. The third command tells Quattro Pro to print a spreadsheet so that the spreadsheet fits onto your printer paper—regardless of the settings on the **L**ayout menu. The fourth command is for printing graphs. The fifth command opens a Print Manager window so you can view the status of your print jobs.

> **TIP**
>
> The important thing to remember about printing with Quattro Pro is that the program offers two different printing modes: draft and final quality. In draft mode, Quattro Pro sends only characters to your printer. Your printer controls items such as line spacing, font, character size, and characters per inch. When printing to a graphics printer in final mode, Quattro Pro controls everything.

Printing Small Spreadsheet Reports

Before learning how to use each print option, you should review two ways of obtaining a basic printout of a spreadsheet report.

First, you can obtain a draft-quality printout of a spreadsheet by using the **B**lock, **A**djust Printer, and **S**preadsheet Print commands. This method, which does not require you to alter any of Quattro Pro's default print settings, is accomplished by doing the following:

1. Choose /**F**ile **R**etrieve and retrieve a spreadsheet report.
2. Choose /**P**rint **B**lock.
3. When prompted, type the block coordinates of the area you want to print.
4. Turn the printer on, position the printer paper to the top of a page, and choose **A**djust Printer **A**lign to set Quattro Pro's line and page counters to top of form.
5. Choose **S**preadsheet Print. Quattro Pro begins to print the data on the printer.
6. Choose **A**djust Printer **F**orm Feed to advance the last page of the printout to the top of the form, so that the printer is ready for the next printout.

TIP Press Ctrl-Break to abort a print operation and return to the active spreadsheet.

This simple printing method works well for producing a working draft of a spreadsheet that is not more than 80 characters wide.

Second, you can print the portion of an on-screen spreadsheet by performing a screen dump operation. A *screen dump* sends an unformatted snapshot of the data displayed on your screen to a printer. This quick-print method is convenient for producing rough-draft versions of your printouts. With a rough draft, you can verify the look of the cell formats, the accuracy of data, and the spelling of labels and report headings before printing the final draft.

To execute a screen dump operation, Quattro Pro must be in text display mode; otherwise, the program prints a page full of unrecognizable graphic symbols. Before trying this operation, also be sure that your printer is on-line.

Follow these steps to produce a screen dump output:

1. Choose /**O**ptions Display Mode **A**:80x25.
2. Choose **Q**uit to quit the **O**ptions menu and return to the active spreadsheet.

3. Press Shift-PrtSc. (If you have an extended keyboard, press only the PrtSc key.)

Quattro Pro begins printing text. Because the output from a screen dump operation is "rough" in appearance (even in text mode), Quattro Pro offers other ways to produce higher quality versions of your printouts.

Printing larger spreadsheets and creating better printouts that display fonts, drawn lines, and shaded cells is fairly simple. The remainder of this chapter covers Quattro Pro's layout options and the procedures for generating higher quality spreadsheet and graph printouts.

Printing Large Spreadsheet Reports

The real benefit of using an electronic spreadsheet is that you can create complex reports made up of hundreds of rows and columns of data. When you print large reports, Quattro Pro occasionally wraps the text so that the text fits within the margins specified by the default print settings.

Text wrapping typically occurs when you define a right margin that is much wider than the width of your printer, or when you try to print more characters across a page than your printer is designed for. (Some dot-matrix printers, for example, can print only 80 characters across a page.) If you try to print a report, for example, that contains 30 columns of data, and each column is 15 characters wide, the printed report needs to be at least 450 characters wide.

When your spreadsheet report is wider than the width of a page, Quattro Pro prints as many columns as will fit onto the page and then prints the remaining columns on a new page (see fig. 9.2).

Fortunately, you have several alternatives for printing such a large spreadsheet so that it reproduces in a more readable form.

If you own a wide-carriage printer, you can print your report on wider paper; however, your printouts still are restricted to a width of approximately 132 standard characters. You also can use wider paper, change the default margins, and print in compressed mode, giving you a report width of up to 250 characters.

An alternative way of dealing with text wrapping involves using a header at the top of each printed page. This technique does not control text wrapping, but accepts the situation and helps to make the text more presentable in a printed report.

PART II — PRINTING AND GRAPHING

```
Business Decisions Consulting, Inc.
6-Month Cash Flow Report
                              +------------------------------------
                              |  Jan     Feb     Mar     Apr
                              +------------------------------------
                                 (a)     (a)     (a)     (a)
INFLOWS
  C.Ed. Software               8,629     846   4,476   3,559
  Definite Solutions, Inc.     8,187   8,430   8,596   6,051
  S.D. County School District  1,259   8,005   1,915   5,058
  Miscellaneous Consulting     4,000   8,809   5,380   5,381
                              ------------------------------------
  Total Cash Inflows          22,075  26,090  20,367  20,049
  Cumulative Inflows          22,075  48,165  68,532  88,581
OUTFLOWS
  Rent                         2,500   2,500   2,500   2,500
  Utilities                      425     415     395     387
  Supplies                     1,745   1,299     366     244
  Salaries                    10,000  10,000  10,000  10,000
  Debt Service                 2,500   2,500   2,500   2,500
  Subcontractor Payments           0       0       0       0
  Taxes and Legal                  0       0     575       0
  Other Expenses               1,273   2,633   1,225   1,274
                              ------------------------------------
  Total Cash Outflows         18,443  19,347  17,561  16,905
  Cumulative Outflows         18,443  37,790  55,351  72,256

NET CASH FLOW                  3,632   6,743   2,806   3,144
CUMULATIVE CF                  3,632  10,375  13,181  16,325

Beginning Cash:                1,199   4,831  11,574  14,380
    Ending Cash:               4,831  11,574  14,380  17,524
                              ------------------------------------
```

```
-------------------
   May       Jun
-------------------
   (a)       (pf)

  2,997         0
    540     6,220
  7,467     9,731
  6,519     9,902
-------------------

 17,523    25,853
106,104   131,957


  2,500     2,500
    490       425
  1,443       750
 10,000    10,000
  2,500     2,500
      0     1,000
      0       575
  1,419     1,225
-------------------

 18,352    18,975
 90,608   109,583

  (829)     6,878
 15,496    22,374

 17,524    16,695
 16,695    23,573
-------------------
```

Fig. 9.2

The spreadsheet report from Business Decisions Consulting, Inc.

You can create many different report styles by changing Quattro Pro's default print settings. The /**P**rint **H**eadings command, for example, enables you to print column and row headings on each page. When you choose /**P**rint **H**eadings, Quattro Pro displays a menu on which you specify whether to print a **L**eft Heading or a **T**op Heading. A left heading appears along the left border of each page, and a top heading prints at the top of each page.

To specify a block to be printed as a heading, follow these steps:

1. Choose /**P**rint **H**eadings.
2. Choose **L**eft Heading or **T**op Heading.
3. Type the coordinates of a block (on the active spreadsheet) that contains the heading you want to use.

Make sure that you exclude the heading block from the print block. If you specify a column or row of labels as a heading and then include the same column or row as part of the print block, Quattro Pro prints the heading twice on the first page—once as data and once as a heading.

Choosing Layout Options

Initially, Quattro Pro produces printouts using default print settings. For example, Quattro Pro assumes that you are using standard 8 1/2-by-11-inch printer paper, printing each page using a portrait orientation, and inserting margins around the entire printed document. Default settings can be changed for an individual spreadsheet or for all future spreadsheets.

The **L**ayout menu commands create report headers and footers; print reports without page breaks, footers, or headers; enable you to change the default margins, dimensions, and print orientation; and send special setup strings to your printer.

Quattro Pro stores the **L**ayout menu command settings with the current spreadsheet. If you open a new file or exit Quattro Pro and then return to the **L**ayout menu, each menu command displays its original default setting. To save custom settings as the new defaults, choose the /**P**rint **L**ayout **U**pdate command. To reinstate the preceding set of default settings, choose /**P**rint **L**ayout **R**eset.

Using the Print Layout Dialog Box

Quattro Pro Version 4.0 has redesigned the /**P**rint **L**ayout menu as a dialog box (see fig. 9.3). Using this dialog box, you quickly can scan and set all print layout options—such as header and footer text, margins, and orientation—all from one screen. The dialog box eliminates the need to move up and down layers of submenus to choose and verify print layout settings.

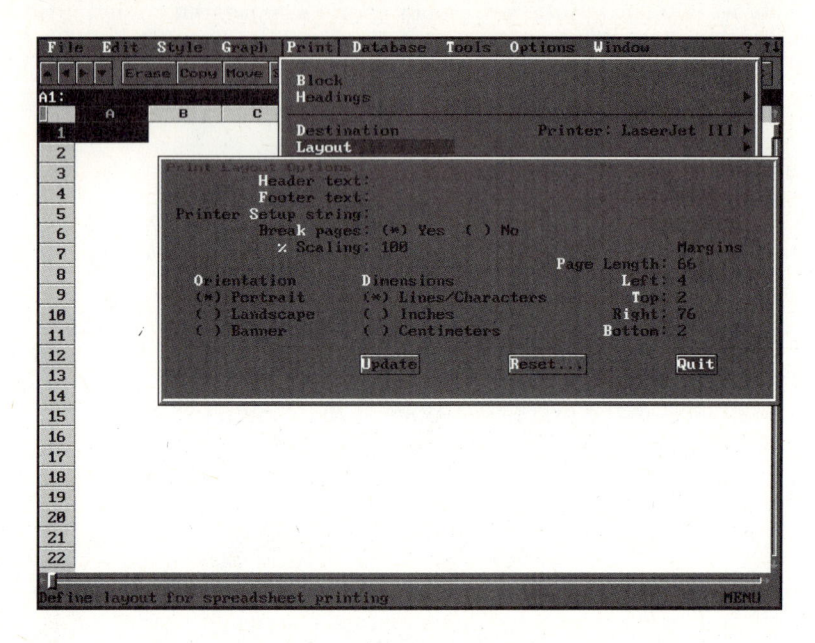

Fig. 9.3

The Print Layout dialog box.

In the Print Layout dialog box, Quattro Pro displays an asterisk next to the current setting, or a value for each option. To change a setting, type the highlighted letter in the option name, press the arrow keys to move the asterisk to the new setting, or type a new value; then, press Enter. If you have a mouse, click the option setting you want to use so that Quattro Pro moves the asterisk there. After you finish setting options, choose **Q**uit to return to the **P**rint menu.

To change the % Scaling setting to 80%, for example, press %. When prompted, type *80* and press Enter to return to the Print Layout dialog box. To change the Margins **T**op setting to 4, type *T*, and *1*, and then press Enter to return to the Print Layout dialog box. Choose **Q**uit to accept the current settings and return to the **P**rint menu. Choose **U**pdate to save all current settings as the new default, and **R**eset to return all settings to their original default setting.

The rest of this chapter features menus rather than dialog boxes. If you prefer to use dialog boxes, you can continue to follow the step-by-step instructions provided.

NOTE By default, Quattro Pro Version 4.0 displays dialog boxes rather than menus at start-up. If you are upgrading from a previous version of Quattro Pro and prefer to display the menus instead of the dialog boxes, choose /**O**ptions **S**tartup **U**se Dialog Boxes **N**o. Subsequently, each time you choose /**P**rint **L**ayout, you see the menu to which you are accustomed.

Reviewing Layout Menu Settings

Quattro Pro offers a convenient way to review all current **L**ayout menu settings. Choose /**P**rint **L**ayout **V**alues to display the settings screen shown in figure 9.4. The settings screen summarizes the current layout settings and current printer destination.

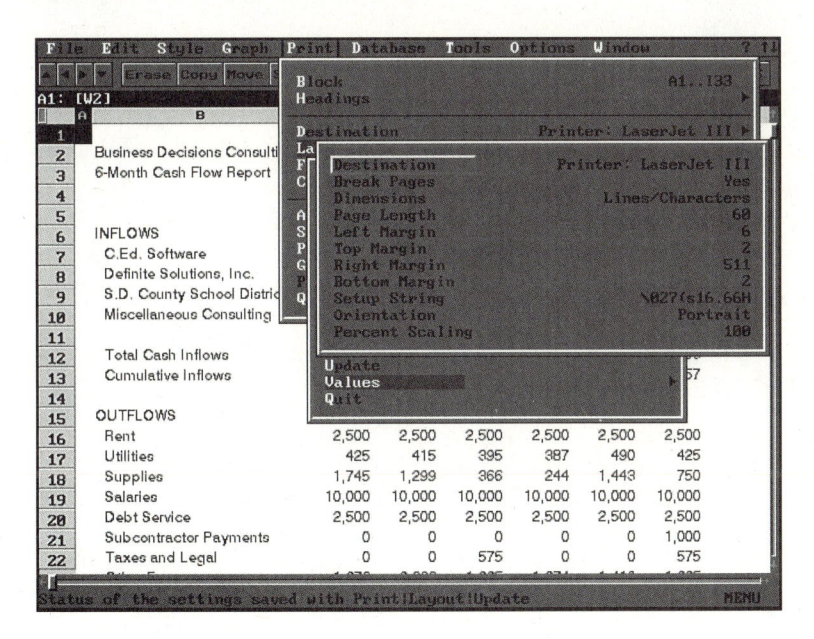

Fig. 9.4

The current page layout settings.

The screen shown in figure 9.4 is available only for review purposes. You cannot change print settings on this screen.

Adding Headers and Footers

Headers and footers are lines of text (up to 254 characters long) that may be added to the top or bottom of each page in a spreadsheet

PART II — PRINTING AND GRAPHING

printout. A header (/**P**rint **L**ayout **H**eader) is different from a heading (/**P**rint **H**eadings): a *header* is text that you type into a dialog box; a *heading* is a block of labels in the body of a spreadsheet.

Use headers and footers to append text to a printout. The advantage of using headers and footers is that you need to enter them only once for Quattro Pro to reproduce them on every page. If the header or footer data changes, you need to change the header or footer definition only once to update the text for all pages.

Commonly used header types include dates, file names, and titles. Commonly used footer types include comments, file names, and data legends. To add a footer to the sample spreadsheet report pictured in figure 9.2, for example, follow these steps:

1. Choose /**P**rint **L**ayout **F**ooter.

2. When prompted, type the text of the footer with any alignment prefixes. For example, type

   |(a) = actual; (pf) = pro forma

   and press Enter to record the footer text (see fig. 9.5). This text header centers the footer on the bottom of each page in the printout.

After you perform step 2, Quattro Pro displays the new setting at the right margin of the Layout menu, next to the footer command.

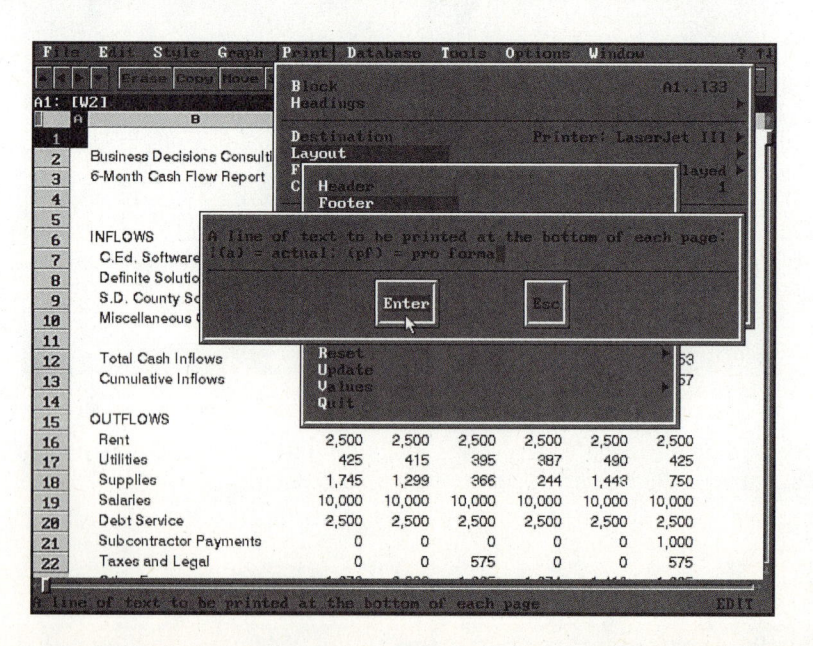

Fig. 9.5

Add a footer to a spreadsheet report.

To delete a header or footer entry, choose the command again and backspace over the existing text. To change an entry, modify the text.

You can use the vertical bar character (|) to justify headers and footers on a page. You also can use the pound (#) and at sign (@) characters to display information on the page. When you include one of these characters as part of the text entry, the following actions take place:

Character	Action
#	Displays the current page number
@	Displays the current date
|	Justifies text (right or center)

Actually, the | header and footer symbol is like a Tab key that has two justification settings: center and right. In a Quattro Pro printout, text is left-justified automatically. When you precede text with a | symbol, Quattro Pro centers the text on the page. When you precede text with two || symbols, Quattro Pro right-justifies the text.

For example, the header text

    @|Inventory Analysis Report|Page: #

may display the following header information:

    04/19/92   Inventory Analysis Report   Page: 5

Controlling Page Breaks

Quattro Pro observes hard and soft page breaks. Hard page breaks are inserted using the /Style Insert Break command or by placing the string |:: into a spreadsheet cell. Soft page breaks occur automatically between pages.

By default, soft page breaks occur every 56 spreadsheet rows. This row count assumes that your spreadsheet uses the default margin settings covered in the next section. When you change the default margin settings, you alter the amount of rows that Quattro Pro prints.

You can suppress the automatic placement of soft page breaks—a technique that results in data being printed in one continuous block. Quattro Pro continues to observe hard page breaks, however.

To suppress soft page breaks, follow these steps:

1. Choose /**P**rint **L**ayout **B**reak Pages.
2. When prompted, choose **N**o from the displayed menu.

> **NOTE** When you set **B**reak Pages to **N**o, headers and footers also do not print.

To undo this command so that Quattro Pro continues inserting soft page breaks, choose the **B**reak Pages command again and choose **Y**es.

Scaling a Spreadsheet Printout

Quattro Pro enables you to scale the printed size of spreadsheet text without first requiring you to adjust font point sizes (see Chapter 5, "Formatting Data"). The /**P**rint **L**ayout **P**ercent Scaling command is a spreadsheet printout-scaling tool. By default, Quattro Pro scales all printouts at 100 percent. To shrink the size of text on a printout, choose a scaling factor from 1 to 99 percent. To magnify the size of text, choose a scaling factor from 101 to 1000 percent.

The **P**ercent Scaling command operates only when the print destination is a graphics printer. Choose /**P**rint **D**estination **G**raphics Printer before you try to print a scaled spreadsheet. Quattro Pro ignores the scaling percentage setting when you generate a printout using the /**P**rint **P**rint-To-Fit command. Use the **S**preadsheet Print command to print a scaled spreadsheet.

You can use the Screen Preview tool to preview the look of a scaled spreadsheet before printing it. In the Screen Preview environment, you can verify that you have selected an appropriate scaling percentage setting.

> **T I P** Scaling percentages greater than 200 percent enlarge the size of a printout so much that in most cases Quattro Pro must print the spreadsheet on two or more sheets of paper.

Setting Margins

The **M**argins menu commands enable you to set margins and alter the number of lines that Quattro Pro prints on a page. By default, Quattro

9 — PRINTING

Pro places 1/2-inch margins on the top, bottom, left, and right of a document and prints 66 lines per page.

To change any of these settings, choose one of the commands described in the following sections.

To change the right margin of the sample spreadsheet, for example, perform the following steps:

1. Choose /**Print** Layout Margins.

2. Choose **Right**.

3. Type *511* and press Enter to record the new right margin setting (see fig. 9.6).

Quattro Pro displays the new setting at the right margin of the Margins menu, next to the command.

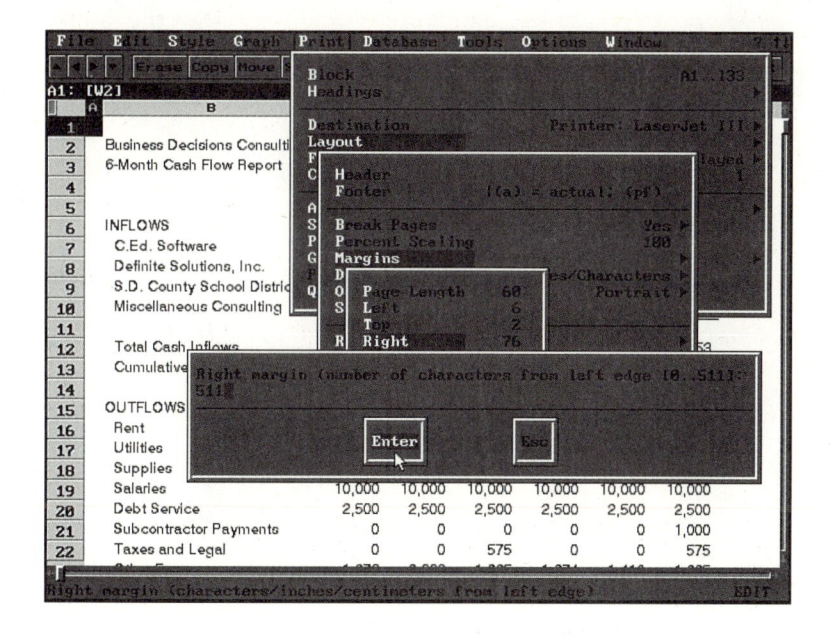

Fig. 9.6

Change the right margin of a spreadsheet report.

Page Length

The **P**age Length command determines how many lines are to be printed on each page. The default setting of 66 lines is the standard for most printers. Laser printer owners should try a setting of about 60 lines per page. If your pages do not seem to break in the correct place in your printouts, adjust the **P**age Length command until you achieve the effect that you want.

When calculating a page length, a good rule of thumb is that the length should equal the lines-per-inch value times the number of printable inches per page. Most dot-matrix printers print 6 lines per inch on a standard 8 1/2-by-11-inch page; therefore, page length equals 6 x 11, or 66 lines. The maximum page length setting for Quattro Pro is 100.

Top Margin

The **T**op margin command determines how much space is left between the top edge of the paper and the first row of data. The default setting is 2 rows, or approximately 1/2 inch. To change the default, choose **T**op margin and enter a new setting. The maximum setting is 32.

> **NOTE** Quattro Pro reserves three lines at the top and bottom of a page for headers and footers, whether or not the document has headers and footers when **B**reak Pages is set to **Y**es. The top and bottom margin settings are in addition to these three lines.

Bottom Margin

The **B**ottom margin command determines the number of blank lines to leave at the bottom of each page. The default setting is 2 rows, or approximately 1/2 inch. To change the default, choose **B**ottom margin and enter a new setting. The maximum setting is 32.

Left Margin

The **L**eft margin command determines how much space is left between the left edge of the paper and the first column of data. The default setting is 4 characters, or approximately 1/2 inch. Choose **L**eft margin and enter a new setting to change the left margin. The maximum left margin setting for Quattro Pro is 254.

Be careful that you do not choose a left margin that is to the right of the right margin (for example, left margin equal to 80 and right margin equal to 30). In this case, Quattro Pro cannot print your spreadsheet. The program displays an error message requesting that you change the margin settings.

Right Margin

The **R**ight margin command determines the space to leave between the *left* edge of the paper and the beginning of the right margin. The default setting is 76 characters, leaving approximately 1/2 inch at the right margin. To change the default, choose **R**ight margin and enter a new setting. The maximum setting is 511.

Defining Dimensions

By default, Quattro Pro specifies the page length and margin settings in terms of characters. The size of a character is 1/10 of an inch horizontally and 1/6 of an inch vertically. Rather than specify the margins and page length in terms of characters, you may want to use inches or centimeters. Choose /**P**rint **L**ayout **D**imensions and choose the measurement system you prefer.

The measurement system used by Quattro Pro is important because the layout settings control where text appears on a printout. Using the **I**nches measurement system, for example, shows **L**ayout menu command settings in terms of inches or fractions of inches. The top and bottom margins may be 0.5 inches, the page length setting may be 8.5 inches, and so on.

Settings that affect the top-to-bottom orientation of a printout—page length, top and bottom margins—generally are expressed in terms of lines. On the other hand, settings that shift printouts left or right on the paper—left and right margins—are expressed in terms of characters.

> **TIP**
>
> Defining margins in terms of lines and characters is easiest when **D**estination is set to **P**rinter. In inches, defining margins is easiest when **D**estination is set to **G**raphics Printer.

Choosing a Print Orientation

By default, Quattro Pro prints a spreadsheet using a portrait (vertical) orientation. By selecting the **O**rientation command, you can print a report using landscape (horizontal) orientation or banner.

To print a spreadsheet using landscape orientation, follow these steps:

1. Choose /**P**rint **L**ayout **O**rientation.
2. Choose **L**andscape.

The **D**estination command must be set to **G**raphics Printer, or Quattro Pro cannot print a spreadsheet with landscape orientation.

A third orientation option enables you to print sideways across several sheets of continuous feed paper. The **B**anner option performs landscape printing—minus the usual page breaks. Instead of ejecting the first page before printing on the second page, Quattro Pro prints a continuous stream of text. Banner style printing requires continuous-feed paper, so laser printer owners cannot use this orientation style.

Except for the right margin setting, Quattro Pro applies all header and margin settings in banner printing. Quattro Pro ignores the right margin setting because a banner's right margin is determined by the size of your print block. Quattro Pro prints sideways from left to right until the entire print block is printed.

> **T I P** When you save a spreadsheet, Quattro Pro automatically saves the **O**rientation setting. If you later want to print the spreadsheet, your original orientation setting is intact.

Using Setup Strings

All printers require codes to create nonstandard printing effects such as underlining, compressed and enhanced printing, and character strikethrough. Many manufacturers enable you to choose various printing modes directly from your printer's control panel. If you cannot achieve a certain printing effect from your panel, Quattro Pro enables you to send the control codes directly to your printer using the **S**etup String command.

Because each manufacturer uses a different set of printer codes, you need to refer to your printer manual for a list of the available printing effects and their corresponding codes. When you enter a printer code, you must supply the code in keyboard terms (the ASCII code equivalent) before entering the code as a setup string.

To print the sample spreadsheet in compressed mode, for example, follow these steps:

9 — PRINTING

1. Choose /**P**rint **L**ayout **S**etup String.
2. When prompted, type the appropriate setup string and press Enter. For the example, type *027(s16.66H* (the compressed printing code for an HP LaserJet) and then press Enter to accept the setup string (see fig. 9.7).

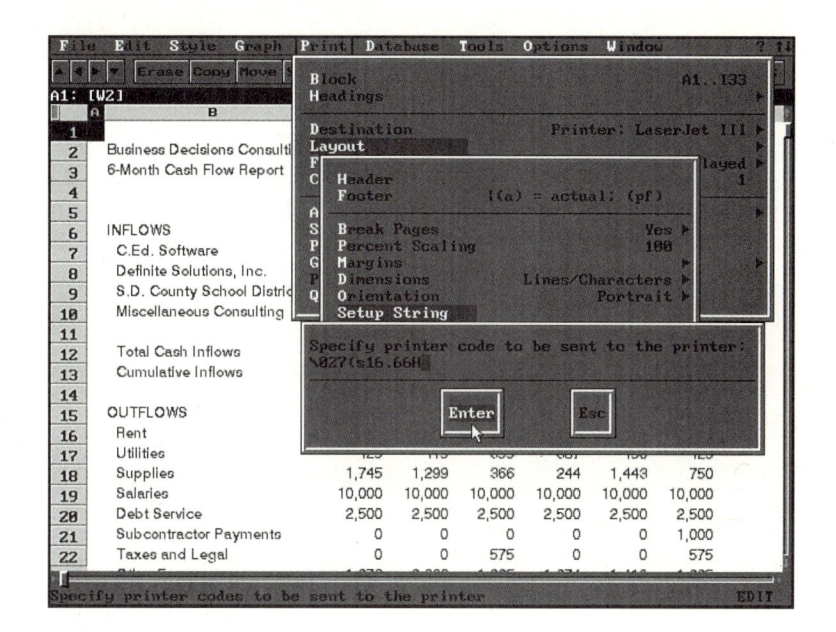

Fig. 9.7

Adding a setup string to a spreadsheet report.

> **T I P**
>
> You also can send a compressed print instruction to Quattro Pro when the /**P**rint **D**estination command is set to **G**raphics Printer. Choose /**S**tyle Font**T**able **E**dit Fonts and choose **1** Font 1. Then choose the **P**oint Size option and choose a 6- or 8-point font.

Setup strings are printer dependent. The \015 compressed mode printing string, for example, works for most IBM dot-matrix, Epson-compatible, and some Okidata printers. Other printers use different setup strings for compressed mode printing. If you own an Okidata Microline, for example, you must enter *029*; for the Toshiba P1350, enter *027\091*. Check your printer manual for the specific codes when you want to enter setup strings on your spreadsheets. (See Appendix D, "Using ASCII Characters," for examples of converting ASCII codes into printer setup strings.)

PART II — PRINTING AND GRAPHING

Quattro Pro displays the new setting at the right margin of the **Layout** menu, next to the command.

You may combine two or more printing effects by typing multiple setup strings, one after another. Valid setup strings may contain up to 39 characters but may not contain any spaces between multiple strings.

The **Setup String** command causes the printer to apply the printer codes to the entire printed spreadsheet. To create two printing effects for different parts of the same spreadsheet, you may embed extra printer codes in a spreadsheet.

To embed a setup string in a spreadsheet, enter the setup string into a blank cell just above the area where you want to create the second printing effect. This cell must be in the first column of the print block. Make sure that you precede the string with two vertical bar characters.

To embed the IBM setup string that cancels compressed mode printing on a dot-matrix printer and to print the remainder of a document in draft mode, follow these steps:

1. Select a blank cell directly above where you want to begin printing in draft mode and make that cell active.

2. Type | | \018.

3. Press Enter to embed the setup string.

Cells that follow this code now reflect this print setting.

Updating and Resetting the Layout Options

If you find that you use the same custom print settings for all of your printouts, you can store the values permanently by selecting the /**Print Layout Update** command.

To restore a spreadsheet to a preceding set of saved defaults, choose the /**Print Layout Reset** command (see fig. 9.8). Quattro Pro displays a menu of four choices. Choose **All** to reset all **Print** menu settings, **Print Block** to reset only the current print block setting, **Headings** to reset print headings, or **Layout** to reset all settings stored on the **Layout** menu.

9 — PRINTING 407

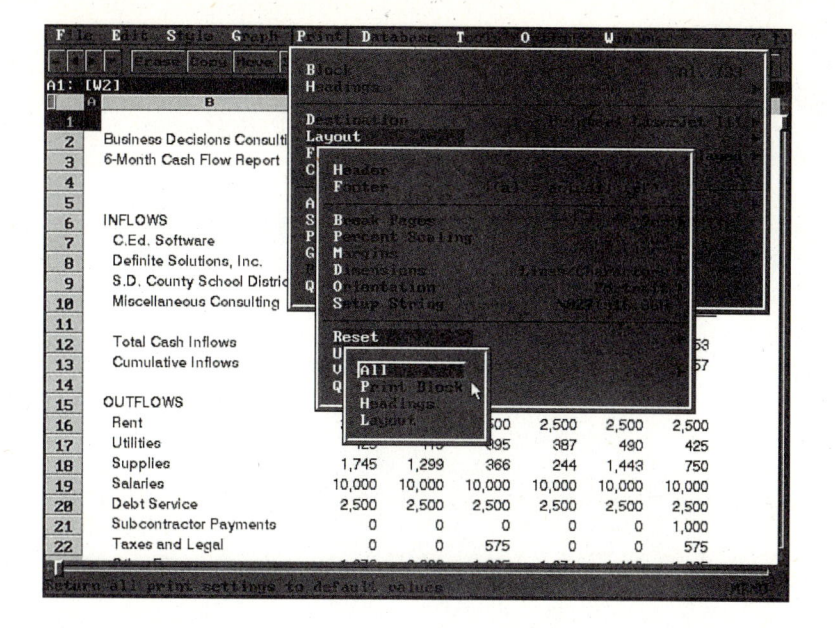

Fig. 9.8

The Reset command resets some or all print layout settings.

Using Other Print Commands

Next you learn how to use various other commands found on the **Print** menu to control the appearance of your printouts. These commands are useful for fine-tuning a print operation when changing the options on the /**P**rint **L**ayout menu just doesn't seem to address a situation.

In the next few sections, you learn how to change the display format that Quattro Pro normally uses to print a selected print block, print multiple copies of a document, adjust paper in your printer before printing, and force Quattro Pro to print a wide document onto a certain paper size without incurring the "text-wrapping" effect described earlier.

Choosing the Display Format

After you choose the /**P**rint **F**ormat command, Quattro Pro displays the Format menu. The **C**ell-Formulas format displays the address, the numeric format, the column width settings, and the contents of each cell in the print block. This display format provides you with a quick way to check that data was correctly entered into cells. Figure 9.9 shows the result of printing block B1..D13 on the sample spreadsheet using this format style.

```
B2: [W29] 'Business Decisions Consulting, Inc.
B3: [W29] '6-Month Cash Flow Report
C4: [W9] "Jan
D4: [W9] "Feb
C5: [W9] "(a)
D5: [W9] "(a)
B6: [W29] 'INFLOWS
B7: [W29] '   C.Ed. Software
C7: (,0) [W9] 8629
D7: (,0) [W9] 846
B8: [W29] '   Definite Solutions, Inc.
C8: (,0) [W9] 8187
D8: (,0) [W9] 8430
B9: [W29] '   S.D. County School District
C9: (,0) [W9] 1259
D9: (,0) [W9] 8005
B10: [W29] '   Miscellaneous Consulting
C10: (,0) [W9] 4000
D10: (,0) [W9] 8809
B12: [W29] '   Total Cash Inflows
C12: (,0) [W9] @SUM(C7..C10)
D12: (,0) [W9] @SUM(D7..D10)
B13: [W29] '   Cumulative Inflows
C13: (,0) [W9] +C12
D13: (,0) [W9] +C13+D12
```

Fig. 9.9

A spreadsheet printed using the Cell-Formulas format.

The printout in figure 9.9 does not list many of the cells that are part of the print block—such as cells B1, B4, B5, and B11—because when you use the **Cell-Formulas** format, Quattro Pro prints only cells that contain data. When you print a spreadsheet in the **Cell-Formulas** format, Quattro Pro also ignores formatting specifications such as page breaks, headers, and margins.

Specifying the Number of Copies

The **/Print Copies** command enables you to specify the number of copies to print of a particular spreadsheet. Valid numbers of copies range from 1 (the default) through 1000. If you choose a large number of copies, be sure that you have enough paper on hand to complete the operation.

Adjusting the Printer

Before sending data to a printer, make sure that your printer is on-line. Of course, the printer also must have a supply of paper.

The **Adjust Printer** menu commands help you to position paper properly in your printer. This menu offers three command choices. The **Skip Line** command moves the paper forward one line, the **Form Feed** command advances the paper to the top of the next page, and the **Align** command tells Quattro Pro that the paper in your printer is positioned at the top of the page.

9 — PRINTING

You always must align the paper in your printer before printing, whether you use a dot-matrix or laser printer. To align the paper for the sample spreadsheet report, perform the following steps:

1. Choose /**P**rint **A**djust Printer.
2. Highlight **A**lign on the menu and press Enter (see fig. 9.10).

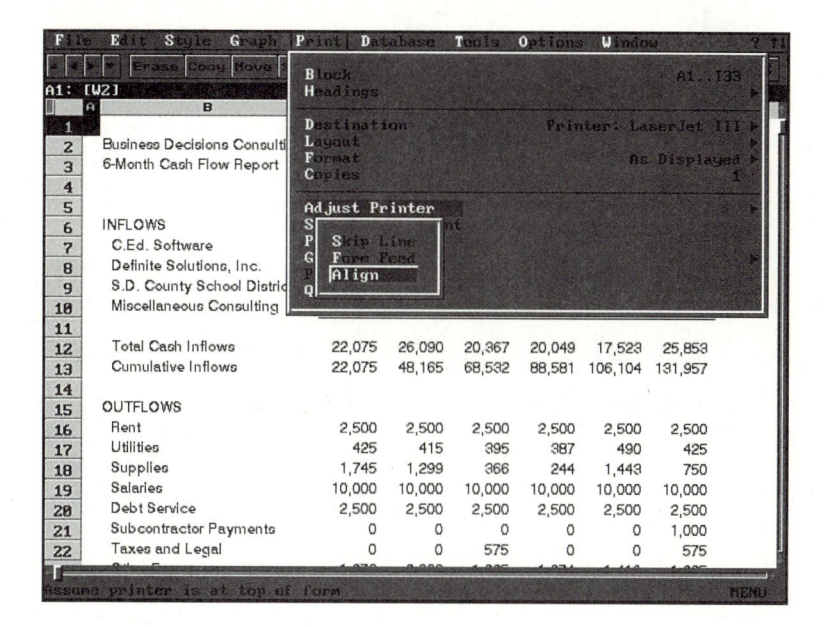

Fig. 9.10

The Adjust Printer menu.

> **TIP**
>
> When you execute the **A**lign command, nothing changes on-screen. The only way to check whether you correctly issued the command is by viewing a printout. When large blank areas appear on a printout, Quattro Pro is using the wrong top-of-page location. To fix this problem, reset the paper to the top-of-page and issue the **A**lign command before printing again.

Whenever the Form Feed lamp is lighted on your laser printer, a single page is waiting to be printed. You can eject the page manually by taking your printer off-line and then pressing the Form Feed button, or you can use the /**P**rint **A**djust Printer **F**orm Feed command to eject the final page in a printout or the first page when printing only one page.

If you own a daisywheel printer, you also can use the commands on the **A**djust Printer menu to prepare your printer for printing. Choose the

Skip Line and **F**orm Feed commands to move your paper so that the printing head is placed at the top of a page. Then use the **A**lign command to notify Quattro Pro that the paper is set to the top-of-form in your printer.

Printing a Spreadsheet That Fits

The /**P**rint **P**rint-To-Fit command is useful when your print block is too large to fit on a single page. When you choose **P**rint-To-Fit, Quattro Pro automatically adjusts the point size of the spreadsheet fonts so that the printout fits on a single page. If the print block is so large that it cannot fit on a single page, Quattro Pro prints the block on as few pages as possible.

The shrinking of font point sizes takes place behind the scenes—you do not see spreadsheet data shrinking on-screen. This command operates in both WYSIWYG and text (or extended text) display mode, but **G**raphics Printer must be the print destination.

You cannot use the /**P**rint **L**ayout **P**ercent Scaling command with the /**P**rint **P**rint-To-Fit command; you must use one command or the other. When you use the **P**rint-To-Fit command, Quattro Pro ignores the scaling setting for the **P**ercent Scaling command.

Choosing a Print Destination

The commands on the **D**estination menu enable you to specify where Quattro Pro sends a printout. You have two draft-mode and three final-quality destination choices (see fig. 9.11).

The first, most obvious destination choice is to print a document on a printer. The **P**rinter option is the default destination setting. Choosing this command sends an unformatted, basic printout to your default printer. Besides the default, you can choose other options, described in the following sections.

Printing to a Text File

If you want to import Quattro Pro spreadsheet data into other programs for additional processing, you can print a spreadsheet to a text file. A *text file* stores only the spreadsheet data and print format settings but does not retain presentation-quality options created with the **S**tyle menu commands.

9 — PRINTING

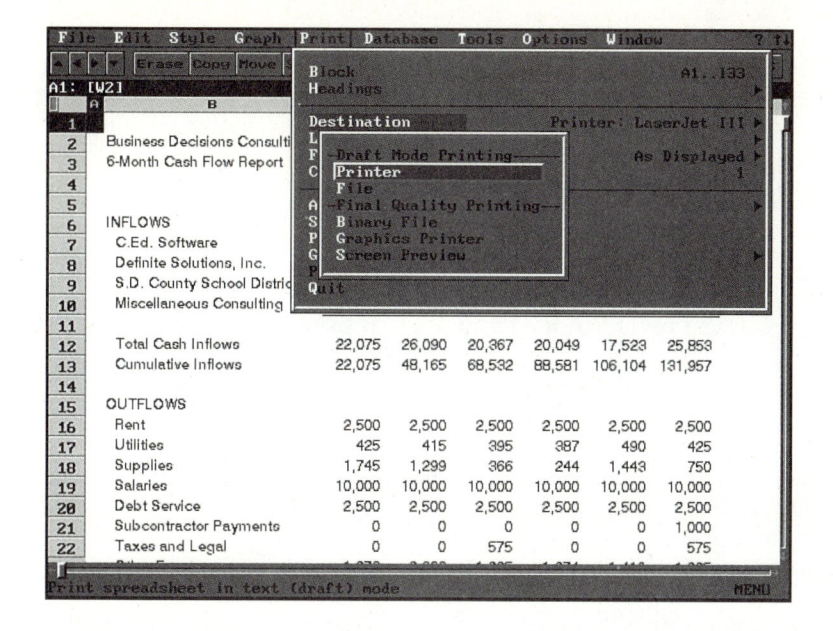

Fig. 9.11

The Destination menu.

You can import a text file into any program that can read DOS text file formats because this file format contains only ASCII characters. Most word processing programs, spreadsheets, and database programs read ASCII text file formats.

By loading a Quattro Pro text file into a word processor, you can include spreadsheet data in your reports. To tap the power of a dedicated database program, load a text file into the program and create a database using your spreadsheet data. (To save a Quattro Pro spreadsheet in a format used by other programs, see "Translating Spreadsheets" in Chapter 8.)

To print to a text file, perform the following steps:

1. Choose /**P**rint **D**estination **F**ile.
2. When prompted, type a file name and press Enter.
3. Return to the **P**rint menu and change the print layout and format settings as you want.
4. Choose **S**preadsheet Print. Quattro Pro writes the data to the file name you specified.
5. Choose **Q**uit to quit the **P**rint menu and close the text file.

Quattro Pro does not close the text file until you specify another text file, choose a new print destination, or press Q to exit the **P**rint menu.

PART II — PRINTING AND GRAPHING

As long as you continue to execute commands on the **P**rint menu, Quattro Pro continues to append data to the open text file. To print a second block and include it in the same text file, for example, specify the block and again choose **S**preadsheet Print. When you quit the **P**rint menu, Quattro Pro closes the text file and adds a PRN extension to the file name.

> **TIP** When you create a text file, be sure to use the **A**lign command before, and the **F**orm Feed command after, printing the document—just as though you are printing the spreadsheet on paper. Your document reproduces correctly when you print the text file on a printer.

To eliminate soft page breaks from the file, set /**P**rint Layout **B**reak Pages to **N**o. The file then will appear as a single, unformatted ASCII text block.

To print a text file on a printer, follow these steps:

1. Choose /**F**ile **E**xit and exit Quattro Pro.
2. At the DOS command prompt, type *copy <filename.PRN> prn*.
3. Press Enter to begin printing the data on your printer.

If you remembered to issue a **F**orm Feed command when you created the file, your printer is now reset to the top-of-form.

> **NOTE** You cannot write a text file if your default printer is a PostScript-type printer. Quattro Pro always writes PostScript code.

Printing to a Binary File

Unlike with the text file, when you print spreadsheet data to a binary file, Quattro Pro records all the presentation-quality settings created using the **S**tyle menu commands.

You can load a binary graphics file into any program that can convert the file into its own graphics file format. This conversion usually is accomplished from a conversion facility that comes with the software.

WordPerfect 5.1, for example, enables you to create and embed WPG graphics files in your word processing documents. The program also has a facility that converts a binary graphics file into a WPG graphics file. When you print your document in WordPerfect, the program reproduces a "near-presentation-quality" version of your graph in the word processing document.

To print a spreadsheet to a disk file in binary form, follow these steps:

1. Choose /**P**rint **D**estination **B**inary File.
2. When prompted, type a file name and press Enter.
3. Return to the **P**rint menu and change the print layout and format settings.
4. Choose **S**preadsheet Print. Quattro Pro writes the data to the file name you specified.
5. Choose **Q**uit to return to the **P**rint menu and close the text file.

Like a text file, Quattro Pro does not close a binary file until you specify another text file, choose a new print destination, or quit the **P**rint menu. Quattro Pro then closes the file and adds a PRN extension to the file name.

To print a binary file on a printer, follow these steps:

1. Choose /**F**ile **E**xit to exit Quattro Pro.
2. At the DOS command, type *copy <filename.PRN> /b lpt1*.
3. Press Enter to begin printing the data on your printer.

This command sequence sends the binary file to the LPT1 printer port. If your printer is connected to a different port, type that port address in place of LPT1 in step 2, or use PRN as the destination when you are not sure of the port designation for your printer.

Printing to a Graphics Printer

Graphics Printer is one of three final-version printing options available on the **D**estination menu. Actually, you can achieve two different results with this command, depending upon the current /**O**ptions **G**raphics Quality command setting.

When /**O**ptions **G**raphics Quality is set to **D**raft, the **G**raphics Printer command on the **D**estination menu produces "draft graphics quality" printouts.

This style of printout contains all of the presentation-quality graphics that you expect, such as drawn lines, shaded cells, and custom font selections. This printout is considered to be draft quality because if Quattro Pro encounters a Bitstream font that has not been built, the program substitutes a Hershey font rather than pausing to build the font.

PART II — PRINTING AND GRAPHING

When /**O**ptions **G**raphics Quality is set to **F**inal, the **G**raphics Printer command on the Destination menu produces "final graphics quality" printouts.

Like the draft graphics quality printouts, this style contains presentation-quality graphics. If Quattro Pro encounters a Bitstream font that has not been built, the program pauses to build the font before printing the final graphics version.

> **T I P** Quattro Pro must build a Bitstream font only once. The font then can be used immediately in other spreadsheets—Quattro Pro does not stop to rebuild the font.

To produce a final draft version of a report that contains presentation-quality settings, choose the **G**raphics Printer option from the **D**estination menu.

Previewing a Printout On-Screen

Before you print a spreadsheet, you can preview how the spreadsheet looks on a printed page with Quattro Pro's Screen Previewer. Specify **S**creen Preview on the **D**estination menu and then choose **S**preadsheet Print. Using **S**creen Preview as a destination, Quattro Pro displays the spreadsheet in the form the spreadsheet will take when printed (as though **D**estination were set to **G**raphics Printer), including all the special print settings and presentation-quality options (see fig. 9.12).

The Screen Previewer displays a group of commands at the top of the screen (see table 9.1).

Use any of the following methods to choose a command from the Screen Previewer menu bar:

- Press the boldface letter key in a command name.
- Click the command with a mouse.
- Press / to activate the menu bar, highlight the desired command, and then press Enter.

While in the Screen Previewer environment, you may use the keys in table 9.2 to navigate through a spreadsheet report.

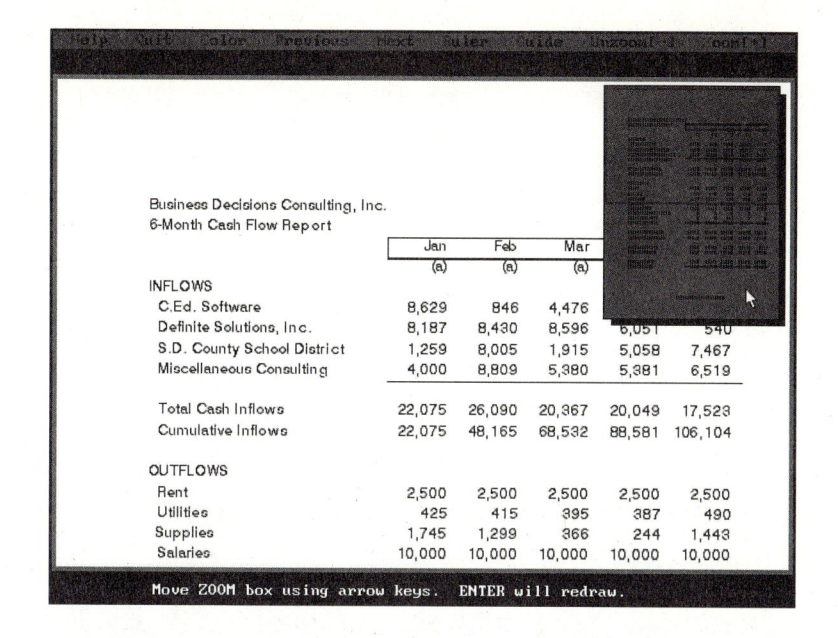

Fig. 9.12

The Screen Previewer.

Table 9.1 Screen Previewer Command Options

Command	Description
Help	Invokes a context-sensitive help window
Quit	Quits to the active spreadsheet
Color	Toggles between a black-and-white and color screen
Previous	Displays the preceding page of the print job
Next	Displays the next page of the print job
Ruler	Overlays a one-inch grid on-screen
Guide	Displays a miniature page in the upper right corner of the screen when in a zoomed view (press the cursor-movement keys to move the box around the miniature page; press Enter once to relocate the screen to that portion of the spreadsheet)
Unzoom [−]	Shrinks the display, moving down one zoom level
Zoom [+]	Enlarges the display by 100, 200, or 400 percent

PART II — PRINTING AND GRAPHING

Table 9.2 Screen Previewer Movement Keys

Key	Description
Esc	Exits the Screen Previewer
Arrow keys	Scrolls a zoomed display in four directions
PgUp	Moves to the preceding page
PgDn	Moves to the next page
Home	Displays the top of a zoomed page
End	Displays the bottom of a zoomed page
Del	Removes the page guide when a page is zoomed

In text display mode, you must preview spreadsheet printouts to see presentation-quality settings such as drawn lines, shaded cells, and custom font selections. Previewing a spreadsheet often reveals incorrect fonts, missing text, and so on. These mistakes happen because, in text display mode, Quattro Pro uses graphics characters to display some on-screen presentation-quality settings. Quattro Pro inserts extra spaces between rows and columns, for example, when you draw lines on a spreadsheet.

You sometimes do not know what effect the presentation-quality settings have until you preview your spreadsheet. When you insert a font with a large point size into a spreadsheet cell, for example, Quattro Pro does not display the font. Instead, the program assigns a font code to the cell; the code tells Quattro Pro which font to use for printing.

You must return to the spreadsheet and increase column widths to accommodate larger fonts and lopped off text or enlarge the print block setting on the **P**rint menu so that all drawn lines appear on the printout.

WYSIWYG display mode provides the most direct method for previewing the presentation-quality version of a spreadsheet or graph. Switch to WYSIWYG display mode with **/O**ptions **D**isplay Mode **B**: WYSIWYG so that Quattro Pro shows you exactly how your spreadsheet will look when printed.

Previewing Print Blocks

When you are in WYSIWYG display mode, you can tell Quattro Pro to display your print block and page breaks with dotted lines. You then can continue to edit the document and resize the print block accordingly before printing. Data you add to the document falls outside the print block when the print block is full.

This preview feature also enables you to see whether your page breaks are in the correct places. If not, you can insert them manually.

To display print blocks, make sure that you have completed the following steps:

1. Choose a printer, during installation or with /**O**ptions **H**ardware **P**rinters.
2. Set the /**P**rint **D**estination command to **G**raphics Printer or **S**creen Preview.
3. Make sure that your screen display is in WYSIWYG display mode.
4. Set /**W**indow **O**ptions **P**rint Block to **D**isplay.

The print block and page break lines remain visible until you choose /**W**indow **O**ptions **P**rint Block **H**ide or choose a print destination other than **G**raphics Printer, **S**creen Preview, or **B**inary File. Quattro Pro saves the current print block setting with a spreadsheet.

Printing Graphs

To print a Quattro Pro graph successfully, your printer must support a graphics character set. As a rule, most dot-matrix and all laser and thermal printers can print graphics images. Daisywheel printers cannot print Quattro Pro graphs because they are designed to produce text-only printouts.

When you choose the **G**raph **P**rint command, Quattro Pro displays the **G**raph **P**rint menu shown in figure 9.13. The commands on this menu are similar to those that you use to control the printing of spreadsheet reports—except that these commands control the printing of graphs.

The basic procedure for printing a graph follows:

1. Choose /**F**ile **R**etrieve and retrieve a spreadsheet file.
2. Choose /**P**rint **G**raph Print **N**ame and select a graph to print.
3. Make changes to the layout options on the **L**ayout menu as desired.
4. Choose **A**djust Printer **A**lign on the **P**rint menu to align your printer to the top of form.
5. Choose **G**raph Print **G**o.

PART II — PRINTING AND GRAPHING

After you execute the command, Quattro Pro begins printing the current graph.

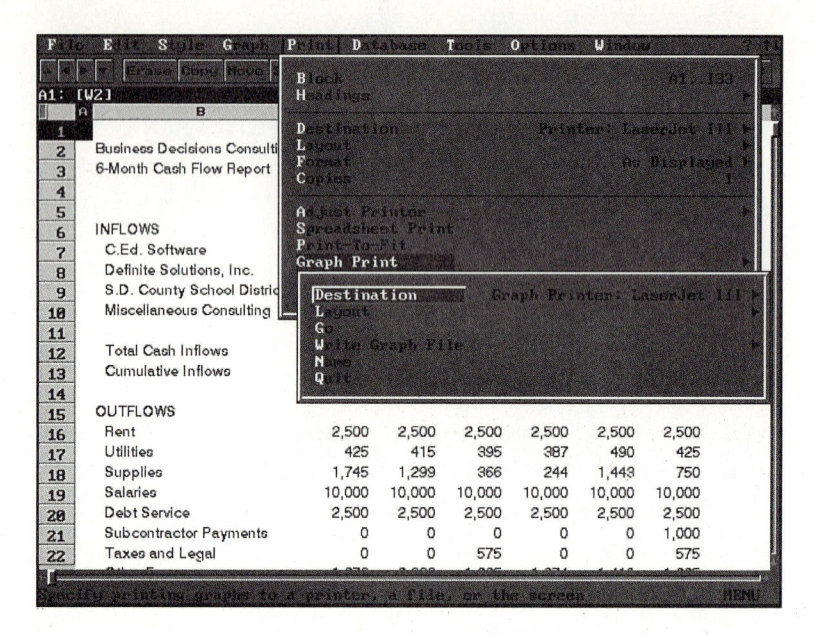

Fig. 9.13

The **G**raph Print menu.

Choosing a Destination

Three **D**estination options appear on the **G**raph Print menu: **F**ile, **G**raph Printer, and **S**creen Preview. The default setting is **G**raph Printer.

If you choose **F**ile, Quattro Pro prints the graph to a disk file. You print a graph to a file using the same procedure for saving a spreadsheet in binary file format.

The **S**creen Preview option instructs Quattro Pro to display the graph so that you can preview the graph's final print form. The preview facility functions exactly the same with a graph as with a spreadsheet (see fig. 9.14).

Creating the Layout of the Graph

Choose **L**ayout to access commands that enable you to alter the margins, size, page orientation, and aspect ratio of the printed graph. These options are described in the following sections.

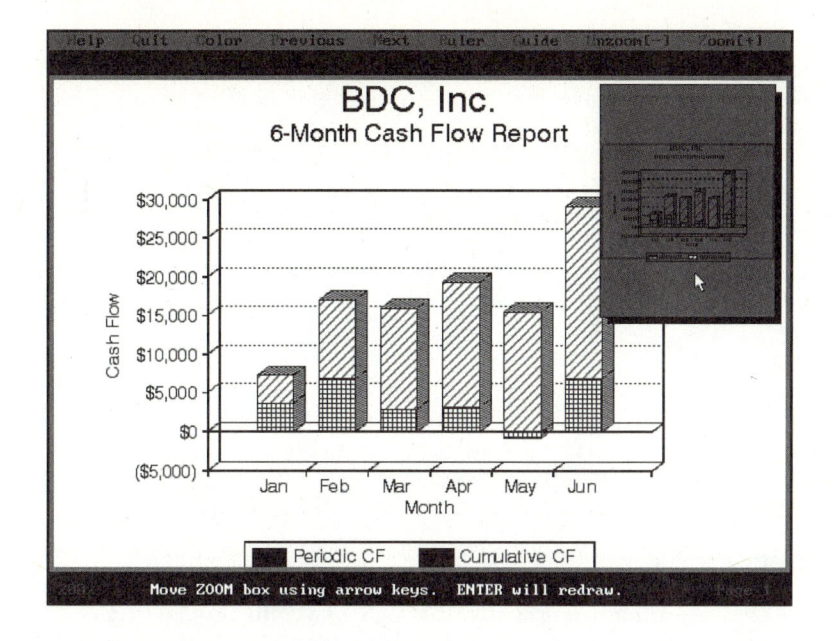

Fig. 9.14

Preview a graph on-screen before printing.

Setting the Graph Margins

The **Left Edge** option defines the distance between the left edge of the paper and the location where Quattro Pro prints a graph. The **Top Edge** option defines the distance between the top edge of the paper and the location where Quattro Pro prints a graph. The **Height** and **Width** options determine the height and width of the graph. By altering the margin settings on the **Layout** menu, you can create virtually any size graph to meet your reporting needs.

The **Dimensions** option specifies whether the edge and size settings are measured in inches or centimeters. This command is similar to the /**Print Layout Dimensions** command. The default setting for this command is **Inches**.

Positioning and Shaping the Graph

You can change the orientation of the graph on a printed page using the **Orientation** option. Just like with a spreadsheet, you can print a graph in **Portrait** or **Landscape** orientation.

The **4:3 Aspect** option determines whether Quattro Pro uses the default margin settings or prints a graph using your preferred settings. By default, this option is set to **Yes**. In the default condition, every Quattro

PART II — PRINTING AND GRAPHING

Pro graph has a size ratio of four to three. If you want Quattro Pro to print a graph to your own margin specifications, choose **No**. In this case, Quattro Pro scales a graph to fit precisely within the area you defined.

T I P In Chapter 10, "Creating Graphs," you learn how to insert a graph into a spreadsheet. When you want to insert a graph so that the graph completely fills any spreadsheet block that you highlight, set the **4**:3 Aspect option to **No**.

Figure 9.15 shows the **L**ayout menu with four custom command settings. The **L**eft Edge, **T**op Edge, **H**eight, and **W**idth commands are set to 0, 0, 6, and 4, respectively. To enable these commands to go into effect for printing, the **4**:3 Aspect command is set to **No**.

NOTE When all of the margin settings are 0, Quattro Pro sizes the graph automatically. Because changing any setting disables automatic sizing, try to set parameters for all the settings if you want to change one setting. If you set a top edge of 2 inches and leave the other settings at 0, for example, Quattro Pro may do strange things when printing the graph.

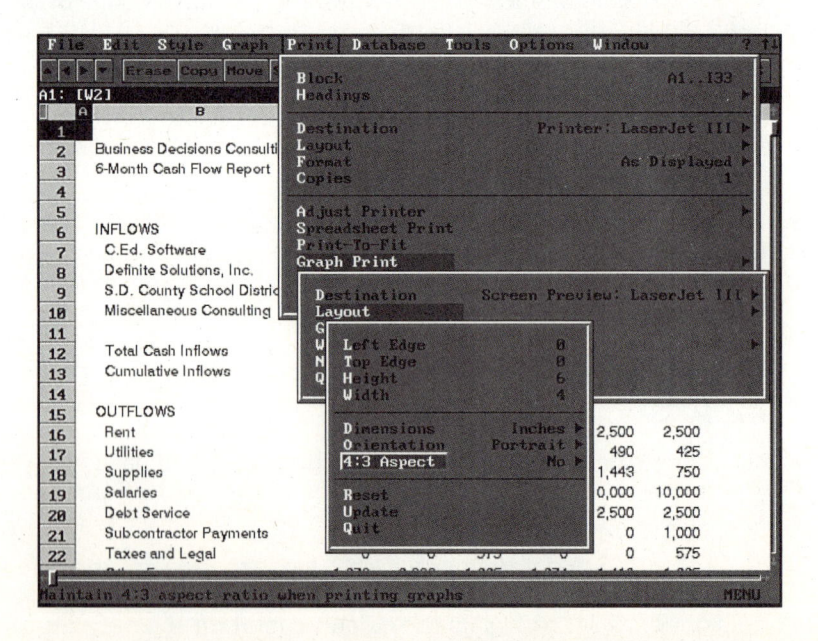

Fig. 9.15

The **/P**rint **G**raph Print **L**ayout menu.

Sometimes when you alter the shape of a graph, Quattro Pro pauses to build additional fonts. This hesitation occurs whenever the **L**ayout menu command settings are far enough from the default conditions that Quattro Pro requires different font sizes.

Updating and Resetting the Layout Options

Choose the **U**pdate option to replace the default graph layout settings with new settings that you have created. To restore the last saved set of defaults, choose the **R**eset option. Depending on the speed of your personal computer, Quattro Pro may take some time preparing a graph image for printing. If you need to halt the printing process, press Ctrl-Break. Quattro Pro returns you to the active spreadsheet.

Creating a Special Graph File

You can load a Quattro Pro graph into any graphics image editing program that can read EPS or PIC file formats. You can load EPS files into desktop publishing programs such as Ventura Publisher and Page-Maker, and word processors such as Borland's Sprint, WordPerfect 5.1, and Freelance. Some of these programs (like WordPerfect 5.1) have built-in conversion utilities that enable you to covert EPS or PIC files into formats that can be loaded and modified from within the program.

Choose the **W**rite Graph File command, and Quattro Pro displays the menu shown in figure 9.16.

Choose **E**PS to write a graph into an encapsulated PostScript file format. To print an EPS file, you must have a PostScript printer. Choose **P**IC to write a graph into a file format that can be accessed by Lotus 1-2-3.

The **S**lide EPS command creates an encapsulated PostScript file just like the **E**PS File command. Both commands convert Quattro Pro's Bitstream fonts into the closest PostScript font. The difference between the two is that the **S**lide EPS command creates a file that contains the exact specifications needed to create 35mm slides. With such a file, any graphics production company can reproduce your graph's color combinations, screen orientation, and height-to-width ratio in 35mm slide form.

After you load a PCX graph file into a graphics editor program, use the program tools to modify the graph. You cannot, however, modify a PCX graph file—or any graph file, for that matter—and then bring the file back into Quattro Pro. Likewise, any changes that you make to a PCX graph file with a graphics editor program do not affect the original Quattro Pro graph. To see these changes, retrieve the original Quattro Pro spreadsheet and press F10 to display the graph again.

PART II — PRINTING AND GRAPHING

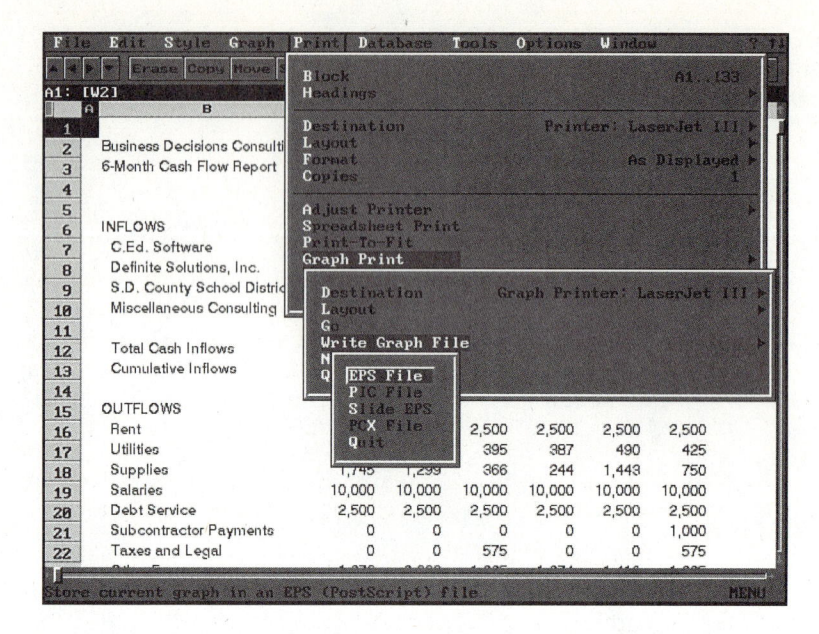

Fig. 9.16

The **W**rite Graph File menu options.

> **T I P** Although you can create 35mm slides from PCX and EPS graph files, the final display resolution that each file type offers varies. The crispness of an image produced from a PCX graph file depends on your screen display's resolution. Alternatively, because EPS graph file resolution is output device-dependent, devices that support higher resolution settings than your screen display can produce higher resolution output from an EPS graph file.

Managing Multiple Print Jobs

With Quattro Pro's Print Spooler feature, you can continue to work with your spreadsheets after sending multiple print jobs to the printer. The Borland Print Spooler program (BPS.COM) collects print jobs, temporarily saves them to your hard disk drive, and then releases control of Quattro Pro back to you. This process is known as *background printing*. While you continue to work with the current spreadsheet, the Print Spooler sends print data to the printer "in the background."

The Quattro Pro Print Manager enables you to keep track of and manipulate these multiple print jobs. You can view each job's status and delete or suspend selected print jobs.

Printing in the Background

To print jobs in the background with Quattro Pro, you must do two things: load the BPS.COM program into your PC's memory before loading Quattro Pro and enable background printing with the /**O**ptions **H**ardware **P**rinters **B**ackground command.

To load the BPS.COM program into your PC's memory, start from the DOS command prompt before you load Quattro Pro. Then, follow these steps:

1. At the DOS command prompt, type *bps* and press Enter.

> **NOTE** You can load the Borland Print Spooler program with command-line options that define how the program will operate with your PC. If you prefer, type these options on the command line after you type *bps*:
>
> S*n* Sets the transfer speed rate at which information is sent to the printer, where *n* is a number between 0 and 9, with 0 the lowest. The default setting is 3.
>
> C*n* Sets the asynchronous communication handshake, where *n* is one of the following: 0 = none; 1 = Xon/Xoff; 2 = DTR then CTS/DSR (the default); and 3 = CTS only.

2. Press Q to load Quattro Pro and press Enter.

After loading BPS.COM, make sure that the /**O**ptions **H**ardware **P**rinters **B**ackground command is set to **Y**es (the default setting). This command tells Quattro Pro that if BPS.COM is loaded into memory, Quattro Pro should send all print jobs to the Borland Print Spooler. Now when you print in Quattro Pro, the Print Spooler, not Quattro Pro, manages the print jobs.

The Borland Print Spooler program stores print jobs in temporary files that it creates and saves to your hard disk. Large, complex print jobs necessarily require large temporary files and can use a significant amount of disk space. If you have a limited amount of space available on your hard disk drive, you may want to free up additional space—at least 1M is a good rule—before trying to print large jobs in the background.

The Borland Print Spooler program remains in your PC's memory until you unload the program or turn off your PC. To remove the Print Spooler from memory without turning off your PC, follow these steps:

1. Choose /**F**ile E**x**it to exit Quattro Pro.

2. At the DOS command prompt, type *bps u* and press Enter.

PART II — PRINTING AND GRAPHING

If you unload the Print Spooler or turn off your PC while print jobs are in the queue, and then reload the Print Spooler and load Quattro Pro, the Print Spooler resumes its processing of print jobs previously left in the queue. If you don't want print jobs from former sessions to print, delete all files with an SPL file name extension from your hard disk drive before you load Quattro Pro.

> **CAUTION:** The Print Spooler does not replace—and may conflict with—a network print spooler. If you choose to use the Print Spooler on a network, load the program before you load the network shell. If you encounter problems, use the network spooler or the Borland Print Spooler—not both. (See Appendix E, "Using Quattro Pro on a Network," for more information.)

Monitoring Multiple Print Jobs

After you send multiple print jobs to the Print Spooler, you can view their status by choosing /**P**rint Print **M**anager. In the Print Manager window that appears, you can view, delete, and suspend print jobs. When the Print Spooler is not loaded, Quattro Pro displays the message `No queue selected` in the Print Manager window.

> **TIP** If the default printer's device is a network queue, the Print Manager window displays information about the network queue. This Print Manager window contains slightly different information from the BPS queue window. See Appendix E, "Installing Quattro Pro on a Network," for details on using the Print Manager on a network queue.

The Print Manager window includes six information fields that track the progress of all print jobs residing in the print queue (see fig. 9.17). These fields include the following:

- *Seq.* Displays the sequence in which your print jobs are printing.

- *File Name.* Displays the temporary file name that Quattro Pro has assigned to each print job in the queue. These names look like QPPRN1.SPL, QPPRN2.SPL, and so on.

- *Status.* Displays messages about the status of the current print job. The message `Active` indicates that the print job currently is printing; Ready indicates that the print job is ready to print and is waiting its turn in the queue; and Held indicates that the print job has been suspended.

- *Port.* Shows the location to which you are printing, as determined by the /**O**ptions **H**ardware **P**rinters **1**st (or **2**nd) Printer **D**evice setting.

- *File Size.* Displays the size in bytes of each temporary print job file.

- *Copies.* Shows the number of copies that will be printed for each print job, as determined by the /**P**rint **C**opies setting.

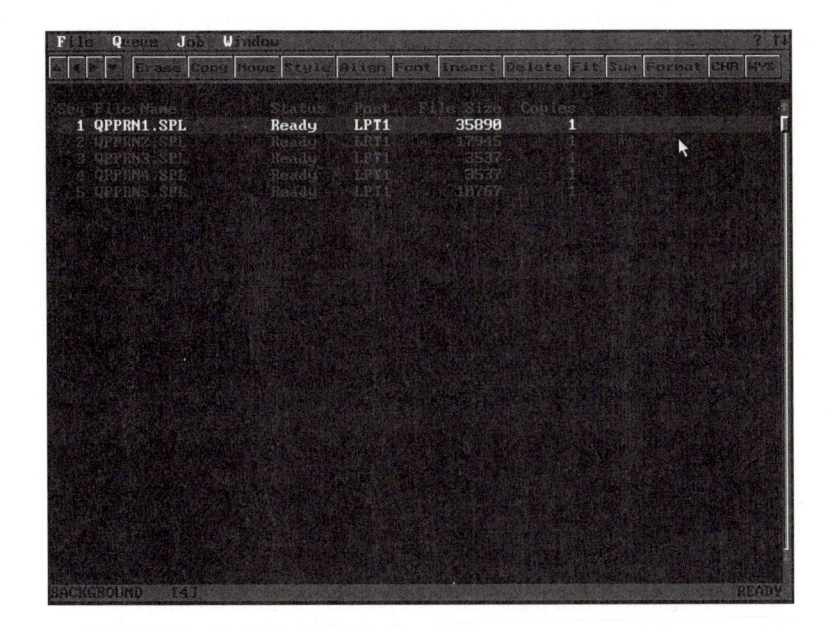

Fig. 9.17

The Print Manager window with five print jobs residing in the print queue

TIP

To change how frequently Quattro Pro updates the information in the Print Manager window, choose /**O**ptions **N**etwork **R**efresh Interval and enter a lower or higher refresh interval setting. The default setting is 30 (seconds).

Changing the Status of Print Jobs

When you are working in the Print Manager window, Quattro Pro displays a menu bar of commands that is unique to the Print Manager. You access these commands as you do any Quattro Pro command and use them to control the progress of a selected print job in the print queue. To select a print job, highlight it by using your arrow keys, click it, or use the Select (Shift-F7) or Select All (Alt-F7) keys. In figure 9.17, print job number 1 is the selected print job.

Table 9.3 lists the commands available on the Print Manager menu bar.

Table 9.3 The Print Manager Menu Bar

Command	Function
/File Close	Closes the Print Manager window
/File Close All	Closes all open windows
/Queue Background	Enables you to view the BPS (DOS) queue
/Queue Network	Enables you to choose a network print queue to display in the window
/Job Delete	Deletes a print job from the queue
/Job Hold	Holds a print job in the queue and keeps the job from printing
/Job Release	Releases a print job (that has been held in the queue) to resume printing

The commands on the Window menu in the Print Manager window are the same as those available in a spreadsheet window.

Figure 9.18 shows the menu that appears when you are about to delete a print job from the print queue. Choose Yes to delete the selected print job or No to cancel the current operation and return to the Print Manager window.

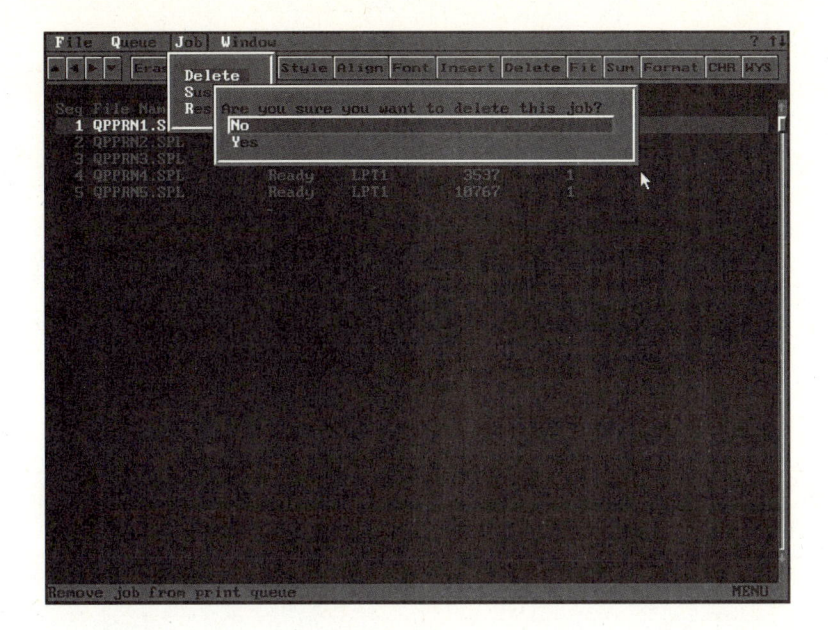

Fig. 9.18

Delete a print job from the Print Manager print queue.

Questions & Answers

This chapter introduces you to the **P**rint menu commands. If you have questions concerning particular situations that are not addressed in the examples given, look through this section.

Printing the Spreadsheet

Q: I want to generate a simple printout of a spreadsheet. I specified a print block and selected the **S**preadsheet Print command, but nothing happened. Why?

A: Make sure that your printer is on and in on-line mode.

Also, Quattro Pro may not be able to write to your printer because your printer may be configured incorrectly. Choose /**O**ptions **H**ardware **P**rinters and reconfigure the **D**efault Printer settings to match your printer's definition.

Q: I am trying to print on legal-size paper. Why isn't my **P**age Length definition creating the exact length I need?

A: Use the /**P**rint **L**ayout **D**imensions command to tell Quattro Pro to use **I**nch measurements. Then, specify your page length as 14 inches. Finally, set /**O**ptions **H**ardware **P**rinters **1**st Printer to a legal mode setting.

PART II — PRINTING AND GRAPHING

Q: Why do the drawn lines on my spreadsheet appear as dots and dashes instead of solid lines?

A: Before you can create a printout that reflects all of the presentation-quality options defined on a spreadsheet, specify the **G**raphics Printer options on the **D**estination menu.

Q: Quattro Pro is placing blank gaps in the middle of my printouts that do not exist on the spreadsheet I am printing. Why?

A: You forgot to issue the **A**djust Printer **A**lign command before printing. When the paper in your printer is not aligned properly, Quattro Pro cannot recognize where the top of the form is, and the program prints gaps in the printout.

Q: When I tried to print a binary file on my printer, why didn't the printer reproduce the presentation-quality settings I saved with the file?

A: Several things are possible. First, make sure that you saved the file using the **B**inary File command from the **D**estination menu—not the **F**ile command. In both cases, Quattro Pro appends a PRN extension to a print file. The only way to tell the difference between a text file and a binary file created from the same spreadsheet is that the binary file's size is much larger than the text file.

Second, when you print a binary file, you must use the following syntax: COPY *<filename.PRN>* /B LPT1. Don't forget to add the PRN extension to the file-name argument. To print a binary file named DATA.PRN, for example, type *copy data.prn /b lpt1*. To print a text file with the same name, type *copy data.prn prn*.

Q: Why isn't Quattro Pro printing the fonts that I specified on my spreadsheet?

A: Make sure that the /**O**ptions **G**raphics Quality command is set to **F**inal. If this command is set to **D**raft, Quattro Pro does not print any Bitstream fonts that are not built already.

Printing a Graph

Q: I am trying to print a graph. When I specify **G**raph Printer and then **S**preadsheet Print, my printer hangs up. Why?

A: This procedure is not correct for printing a graph. You must use the **G**raph Print command to print graphs and the **S**preadsheet Print command to print spreadsheets.

Q: I printed a graph using landscape orientation. Why are my margin alignments completely wrong?

A: When you print a graph horizontally, the orientation of the margin commands changes—for example, **H**eight becomes **W**idth and **W**idth becomes **H**eight. Return to the **G**raph Print **L**ayout menu and switch the definition for the margin settings.

Q: Why did Quattro Pro cut off the left and right portion of the graph's title text when I printed my graph?

A: Be very careful about choosing new margin, height, and width settings. When you enter a large left margin (say 6) and choose a large **W**idth setting, Quattro Pro may not have enough space to print an entire report title. In this case, you can alter the margin and aspect settings, shorten the title by selecting the /**G**raph **T**ext command, or do a combination of both.

Summary

This chapter discusses many different methods for printing spreadsheets and graphs in rough draft and final draft form. Having completed this chapter, you should be able to follow these steps:

- Print a screen dump of spreadsheet data
- Generate draft form, cell-listing form, and final-form printouts of a spreadsheet
- Add headings, headers, and footers to a printout
- Scale a printout so that it fits on one page
- Adjust the margins and page length of a printout
- Print in a portrait and landscape orientation
- Add special printing effects using setup strings
- Scale a printout so that it fits onto one page
- Properly control the movement of paper in your printer
- Print a spreadsheet to text and binary file formats
- Use the Screen Previewer to examine spreadsheets and graphs before printing them
- Cause a spreadsheet to print to fit
- Print a graph on a printer or to a file
- Adjust the margins and aspect settings to alter the shape of a printed graph

PART II — PRINTING AND GRAPHING

- Write a graph to PIC and EPS file formats
- Load the Borland Print Spooler program
- Open a Print Manager window and track the progress of jobs in the print queue.

CHAPTER 10

Creating Graphs

In previous chapters, you learned how to enter, edit, view, and print spreadsheet data. You also learned how to improve the style of your spreadsheets and manage multiple documents. Creating versatile, stylish-looking reports is important, yet sometimes getting an overall picture of the data by looking at numbers on a spreadsheet is difficult. In this chapter, you learn how to create, manage, and display Quattro Pro graphs as alternatives and complements to spreadsheets.

A Quattro Pro graph offers several advantages over a numerical report. Graphs call attention to variations in data. Graphs summarize data, enabling you to consider several different relationships at the same time. Most importantly, graphs disclose trends and pinpoint problem areas that otherwise may go unnoticed on a spreadsheet.

The first section of this chapter reviews the **G**raph menu commands and the system hardware that you need to display Quattro Pro graphs. The next section defines the utility and anatomy of a graph. You learn Quattro Pro's graph terminology, survey each element that makes up a graph, and study the 12 graph styles that Quattro Pro can display. The sample graphs shown in this section use real-world applications. After reviewing these sample graphs, you should understand better how to match your data with the most appropriate graph style.

The chapter continues by demonstrating two ways to create a basic Quattro Pro graph: from the ground up and by using the **F**ast Graph command. This command enables you to preview your spreadsheet data as a plain, unformatted graph—an important feature when you have 12 distinct styles from which to choose.

Next, you learn how to enhance the appearance of the basic graph by adding titles, legends, and customized fonts.

The final section in this chapter shows you how to manage graph files. When you save graph settings with a spreadsheet, a change on the spreadsheet is reflected on the graph. Finally, you learn two techniques for displaying your graphs: putting them in a slide show and inserting them as "live graphs" in the spreadsheet from which the graph was created.

The rules and techniques for printing Quattro Pro graphs appear in the last section of Chapter 9, "Printing."

Reviewing the Graph Menu

The **G**raph menu consists of three types of commands: graph building commands, graph customizing commands, and graph management commands. This chapter covers all of the graph building commands (except **A**nnotate) and all of the graph management commands. Chapter 11, "Customizing Graphs," offers complete coverage of the graph customizing commands and Quattro Pro's graph annotation tool. Chapter 12, "Analyzing Graphs," introduces you to analytical graphing, a new feature in Version 4.0.

You use the graph building commands, found at the top of the **G**raph menu, to choose a graph style, to record the location of the data to be graphed, and to add text to the basic graph (see fig. 10.1).

You use the graph customizing commands, found in the middle of the **G**raph menu, to customize an individual data series, to change the x- and y-axis scaling, and to format the background of the whole graph. (Graph customizing commands are covered in Chapter 11, "Customizing Graphs.")

The graph management commands, located at the bottom of the **G**raph menu, perform operations on a graph after the graph is created. With graph management commands, you can insert a graph onto a spreadsheet, assign a graph name to a particular graph, or view a graph on-screen. The final menu command, **A**nnotate, calls up a Quattro Pro editing tool for adding finishing touches to your graphs. (The **A**nnotate command is covered in Chapter 11.)

Table 10.1 explains the functions of the **G**raph menu commands. Like most other Quattro Pro commands, **G**raph menu commands are intuitive. To use a particular type of graph, for example, choose **G**raph

10 — CREATING GRAPHS

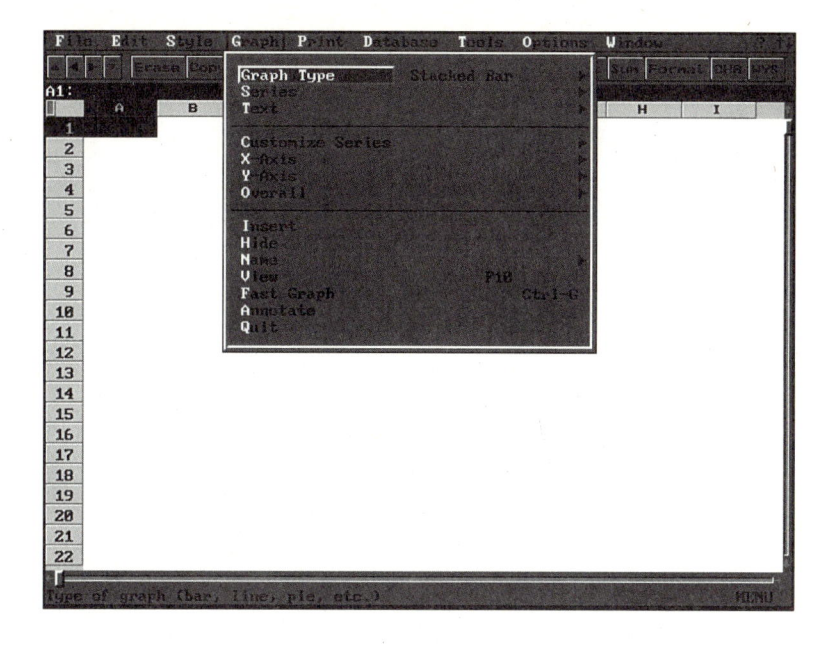

Fig. 10.1

The **G**raph menu commands.

Type; to add text to a graph, choose **T**ext; and to insert a graph into a spreadsheet, choose **I**nsert.

> **TIP**
> After you create the basic graph, press F10 to display the graph. As you add features to a graph, you can reexamine the new graph settings by pressing F10 at any time or choosing /**G**raph **V**iew.

Table 10.1 Graph Menu Commands

Command	Description
Graph Type	Chooses one of the 12 graph types
Series	Specifies the spreadsheet cell blocks to graph and performs analytical graphing operations
Text	Adds titles and a legend to a graph and changes the attributes of the text
Customize Series	Customizes the display of a data series

continues

PART II — PRINTING AND GRAPHING

Table 10.1 Continued

Command	Description
X-Axis	Adjusts the display and scaling of the x-axis
Y-Axis	Adjusts the display and scaling of the y-axis
Overall	Adds lines, patterns, colors, and 3-D effects to parts of a graph
Insert	Inserts a copy of a graph onto a spreadsheet
Hide	Removes a copy of a graph from a spreadsheet
Name	Creates, uses, and deletes named graphs
View	Displays a graph using the current graph settings
Fast Graph	Produces a rudimentary graph using a cell block
Annotate	Activates the Annotator, discussed in Chapter 11, "Customizing Graphs"

Reviewing Hardware Requirements

Quattro Pro enables anyone to create a graph, but to view a graph, your system must have the correct display hardware. Your screen and the display adapter card must be capable of displaying graphics. If your system does not have a graphics display adapter, you cannot view a created graph on-screen.

If you are using an older PC or XT system, you may not have a graphics display adapter. Although you cannot view graphs on-screen, you still can print them on a graphics printer.

Fortunately, most of today's PCs come equipped with at least a monochrome graphics display adapter. (See Appendix A, "Installing Quattro Pro," for a complete list of the display adapters that Quattro Pro supports.) To view Quattro Pro graphs, you must have one of the following types of display adapter systems or compatibles:

- Hercules monochrome graphics card (MGA or MCGA)
- Color Graphics Adapter (CGA)

- Enhanced Graphics Adapter (EGA)
- Video Graphics Array (VGA)

The monochrome and CGA graphics cards show Quattro Pro graphs in black and white, whereas the EGA and VGA cards show graphs in color. EGA and VGA adapter systems display graphics with a much sharper resolution than the monochrome or CGA systems.

> **TIP**
> Choose /**O**ptions **H**ardware **S**creen Resolution and pick the highest resolution that your display adapter supports. See Chapter 16, "Customizing Quattro Pro," for complete coverage of the **O**ptions menu commands that affect the display of graphs.

If your PC has none of the preceding graphics systems, you may view your graphs if you have the right printer or plotter. To view a graph, print the graph to the printer specified by the /**O**ptions **H**ardware **P**rinters **D**efault Printer command. If you use a dot-matrix or laser printer, your graph printouts contain various shades of gray.

Understanding Graphs

To explain how graphs can provide a clearer medium for analyzing your spreadsheet data, this section covers the benefits of graphing, the anatomy of a graph, and the types of graphs that Quattro Pro offers.

Utility of Graphs

Graphs help you to arrive at conclusions about spreadsheet data. Graphs also point out problem areas with a clarity often not available with even the most comprehensive spreadsheet reports. Figure 10.2 shows a Quarterly Revenue Analysis report for a hypothetical firm, Christensen Advertising.

The spreadsheet in figure 10.2 shows that Christensen's revenues nearly doubled over the course of the year (from $200,000 to $390,000). The report also shows that the firm's growth in revenues dipped between the first and second quarters (from $200,000 to $195,000).

Now look at the same report displayed as a stacked-bar graph (see fig. 10.3). Graphs sometimes display data trends that you didn't anticipate.

PART II — PRINTING AND GRAPHING

Fig. 10.2

The Christensen Advertising spreadsheet report.

(Screenshot of spreadsheet showing:)

Christensen Advertising
Quarterly Revenue Analysis
All figures in 000's of dollars

Client	1st Q	2nd Q	3rd Q	4th Q
Sluggo Soda	50	55	78	100
Timiteo's Tacos	40	50	100	200
Jefferson Cleaners	50	45	55	65
Basal-Seltzer	60	45	35	25
Total Revenues:	$200	$195	$268	$390

Take another look at figure 10.3 and see whether you can spot a third, less obvious trend. Notice that during the first and second quarters, revenues were divided evenly among all four clients. In the third and fourth quarters, however, Basal-Seltzer revenues declined, and Timiteo's Tacos revenues skyrocketed.

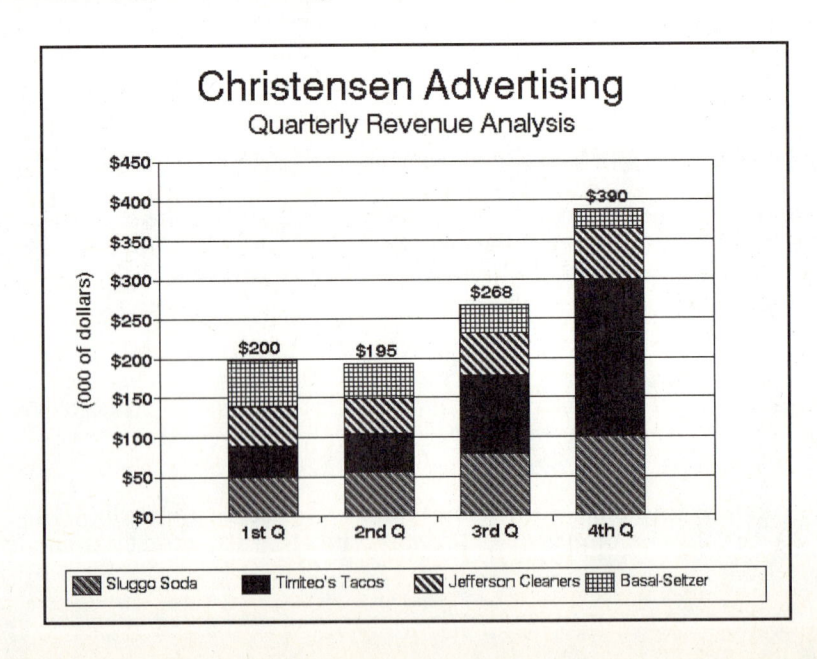

Fig. 10.3

A stacked-bar graph created from Christensen's spreadsheet report.

(Stacked bar graph titled "Christensen Advertising — Quarterly Revenue Analysis", y-axis in (000 of dollars) from $0 to $450, with bars for 1st Q = $200, 2nd Q = $195, 3rd Q = $268, 4th Q = $390. Legend: Sluggo Soda, Timiteo's Tacos, Jefferson Cleaners, Basal-Seltzer.)

The stacked-bar graph indicates that something is awry with the Basal-Seltzer account. Did Basal-Seltzer spend less with Christensen and more with other advertisers? Is Basal-Seltzer suffering fiscal difficulties? Should management now pay special attention to the Timiteo's Tacos account? These are the types of questions an analyst would consider when reviewing this graph.

Graphs can convey in a picture what sometimes is hard to articulate. Imagine the difficulty of evaluating revenue growth trends on a spreadsheet report if Christensen had 100 clients instead of only four.

Anatomy of Graphs

Just as a medical student learns about human anatomy, so must a Quattro Pro user learn about the elements that make up a graph. This section teaches you about the purpose and function of each part of a Quattro Pro graph and introduces the terminology that defines each part.

Line graphs show how data changes over time. In this type of graph, the *x-axis* (horizontal axis) represents time, whereas the *y-axis* (vertical axis) represents a data category. When you locate an intersection between the two axes, you have a *data point*.

Most graphs have several data points, each one representing a different intersection between the x- and y-axis. A collection of x-axis data points forms a *data series*, as does a collection of y-axis data points. On a spreadsheet, a data series appears in a cell block. Cell blocks can be vertical, as in block D5..D10, or horizontal, as in block D5..H5. You tell Quattro Pro which data to display on a graph by specifying the cell block.

Quattro Pro also can use spreadsheet labels when displaying a graph. A block of spreadsheet labels, for example, can appear on a graph to signify a time period (January, February, March, and so on), to identify the parts of a group (Client A, Client B, or Client C), or to display as a title. The range of data points associated with an axis form a *scale*.

Graphs also are used to show the relationship between two or more categories of data; one category is expressed as a function of another. *Function* implies that one of the categories is a dependent variable and the other is an independent variable; the value of one category depends on the value of the second. Business owners, for example, express profit as a function of revenue. When revenue increases, profit also is expected to increase. Profit is the dependent variable, and revenue is the independent variable.

PART II — PRINTING AND GRAPHING

Research psychologists graph intelligence as a function of age because the idea generally is accepted that people get smarter as they grow older. In this case, the dependent variable, intelligence, depends on the independent variable, age.

Family physicians plot approximate weight as a function of height to monitor a child's growth. Again, as children get taller (independent variable), they are expected to gain weight (dependent variable).

How do you know when a data category is an independent or a dependent variable? Common sense dictates this relationship much of the time. Consider the family physician example; children do not get taller just because they gain some weight.

Now consider the graph pictured in figure 10.4. This graph expresses the height-weight relationship. The range of height values appears on the x-axis and the range of weight values on the y-axis. Together, the x-axis data points form a data series, as do all of the y-axis data points.

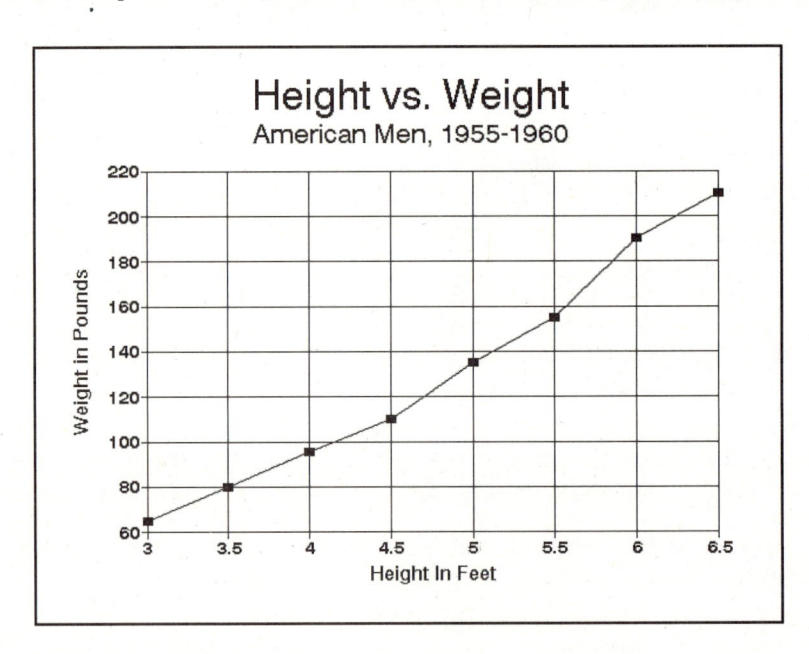

Fig. 10.4

A graph showing the relationship between height and weight for American males.

Tick marks—the hyphens that cross the axes beside each weight and height—are used to mark off regular intervals in the scale of those axes. Notice that the x-axis is scaled at intervals of 1/2 foot, and the y-axis scale is marked off in intervals of 20 pounds.

Each pair of values on a spreadsheet report corresponds to exactly one data point on a graph. In this example, therefore, each height on the

10 — CREATING GRAPHS

x-axis corresponds to a weight on the y-axis. Together these paired values can be found on the original spreadsheet report.

Quattro Pro can express data relationships using 12 styles of graphs. Many of these graphs share the same anatomy as the examples just described.

Basic Graphs

The first step in the process of creating a basic graph is choosing a graph style for your data. When you choose /**G**raph **G**raph Type in WYSIWYG mode, Quattro Pro displays a style options box (see fig. 10.5). In text mode, Quattro Pro displays a list of the 12 graph types. You often can use two or three graph styles to show the same data. You also can show data on a bar graph, for example, on a rotated bar graph or on a line graph. To change the graph type after you create a graph, again choose the /**G**raph **G**raph Type command and pick a new style.

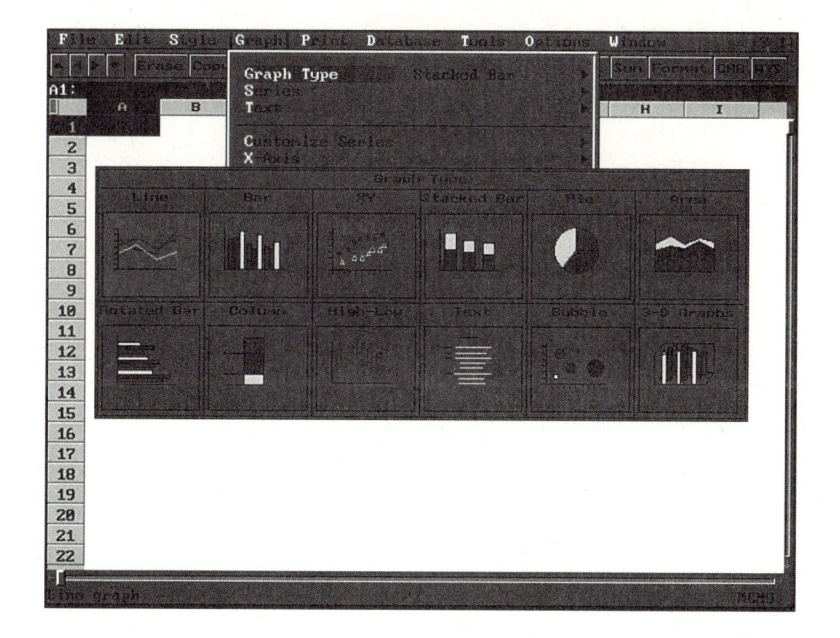

Fig. 10.5

Choose a graph style from the **T**ype menu in WYSIWYG.

At other times, the data is so specific that it makes sense only when viewed using a particular graph style. The high-low (open-close) graph type, for example, plots a range of prices for a firm's stock. This data makes little sense displayed on a pie or column graph.

PART II — PRINTING AND GRAPHING

Take a look at all 12 graph styles. As you examine each style, pay close attention to the types of data that work well with each graph type.

Line Graphs

The line graph is one of the most recognized graph types. The business and scientific communities use line graphs to show a progression of values over a period of time. A line graph, for example, is good for summarizing monthly sales data from an annual report or plotting the results of an IQ test taken over an 80-year period. In either case, because time is the independent variable, time is plotted on the x-axis.

Figure 10.6 shows that citizens from country A have higher tested IQ's than citizens from countries B and C. This graph reveals a second, more telling trend. Regardless of a country's percentile ranking versus the world, the tested IQ's for all three countries decline as their citizens grow older.

A line graph provides a useful way to track trends over time and to predict irregularities by using current data.

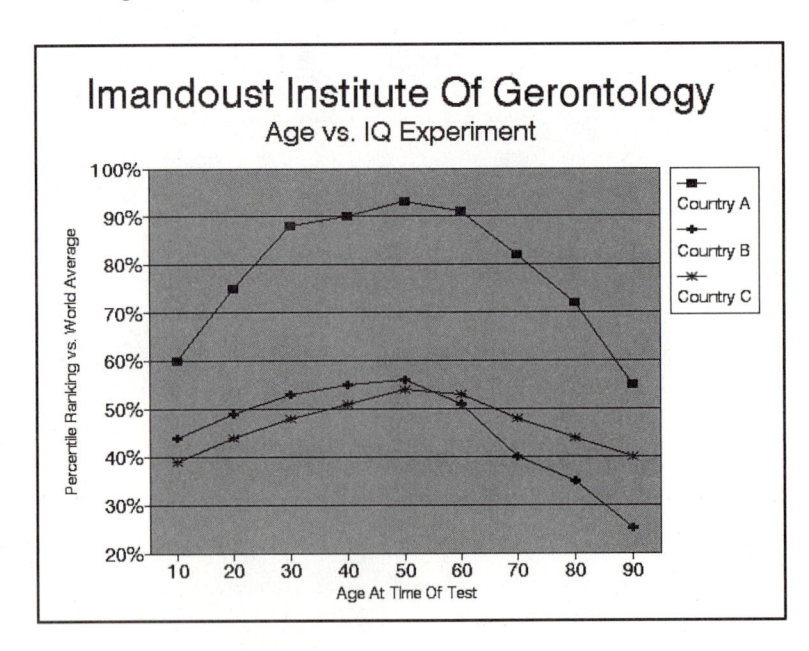

Fig. 10.6

A line graph showing the IQ test results for three countries over an 80-year period.

Bar Graphs

The bar graph is useful for comparing the values of different items at set periods in time. The primary advantage of a bar graph is that it clearly shows differences in the magnitude of the data: the higher the bar, the bigger or larger the value.

In figure 10.7, the bar graph is used to summarize the results of a six-month crop production report for two products: dates and nuts.

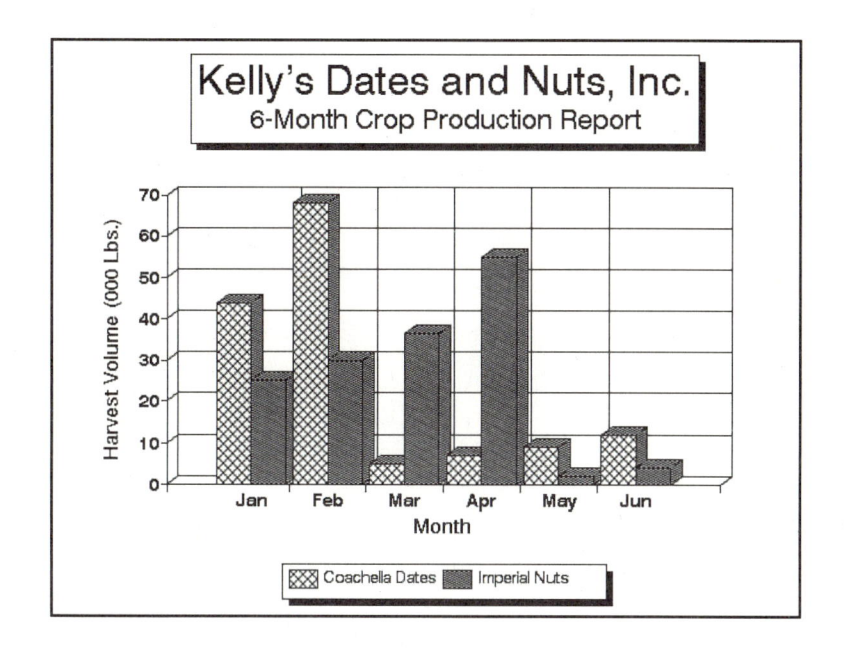

Fig. 10.7

A bar graph showing a six-month crop production report.

On the bar graph, you easily can spot the peak seasons for dates and nuts by examining the different bar heights. According to this report, date production peaks in February, and nut production peaks in April. Because those months are the peak for harvesting, the months immediately following the peak months have the lowest production.

XY Graphs

The XY graph, also called a scatter graph, is different from the graphs discussed so far. This graph type is used commonly in social science research to relate the value of one economic variable to another.

At first glance, an XY graph resembles a line graph. The x-axis and y-axis, however, are scaled with numeric data. In most of the graphs you have seen so far, the x-axis has represented a point in time—for example, a month or a quarter. Generally, XY graphs directly relate one set of data to one or more other sets of data without regard to time.

An XY graph, for example, is useful for showing the relationship between production volume, revenues, and costs for a manufacturing firm. The XY graph shown in figure 10.8 plots a range of production volumes on the x-axis. The x-axis measurement is not time, but production quantity. The associated costs and revenues at each production level appear on the y-axis. The bottom line is that on an XY graph, the x-axis must display numeric data—not labels or text.

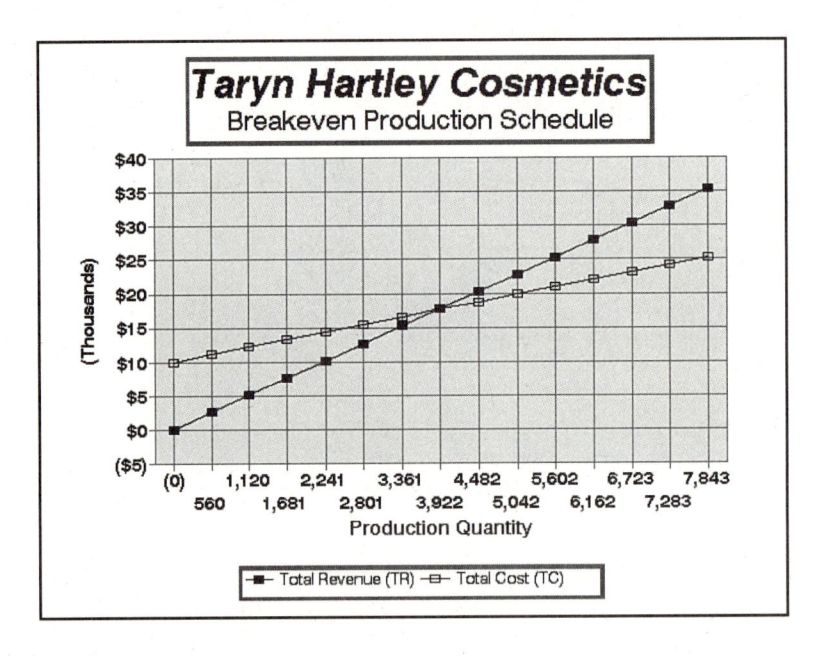

Fig. 10.8

An XY graph showing total revenue, total cost, and production quantity for a manufacturing firm.

Stacked-Bar Graphs

The stacked-bar graph resembles a bar graph at first glance. To create this type of graph, Quattro Pro first sums the value of each item in a data set. The program then plots the total value at a specific period in time, showing the contribution that each item makes to the total. This latter characteristic is shared by the area graph and the pie graph, covered later in this section.

The stacked-bar graph in figure 10.9 shows total sales per quarter and breaks down sales by territory for each quarter.

The stacked-bar graph is useful for looking at broader performance statistics (total sales) and for evaluating individual performance statistics (territory sales).

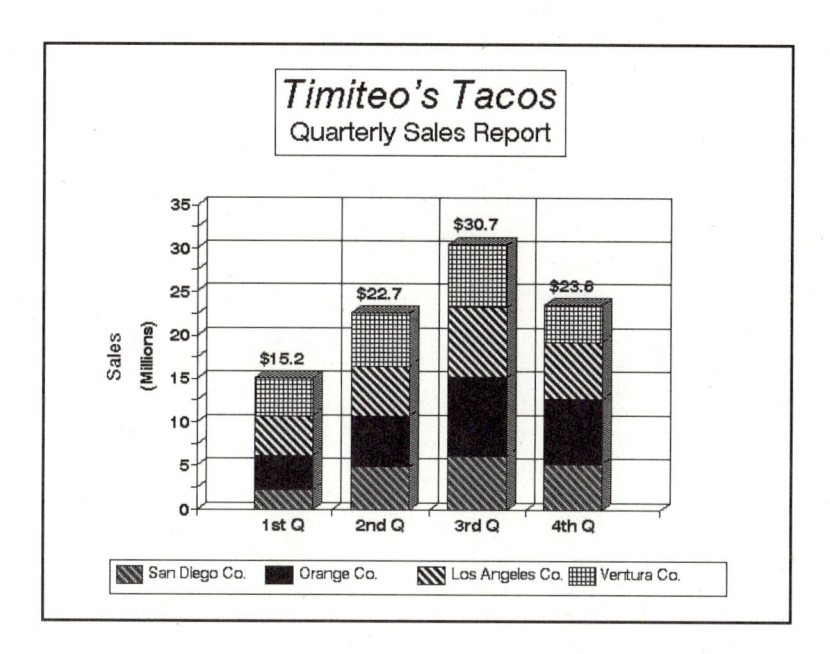

Fig. 10.9

A stacked-bar graph showing total quarterly sales by territory.

Pie Graphs

The pie graph shows the contribution of individual values to a whole. The individual values are called *slices*, and the whole value is called the *pie*. Figure 10.10 shows the percentage of total expenses allocated to each category in a sample household budget.

The two smallest pieces of this pie are set slightly out of the pie. This technique, called *exploding*, draws attention to key figures in the graph. Exploding also helps to improve the display of pie graph slices that are too small to fit well in the graph.

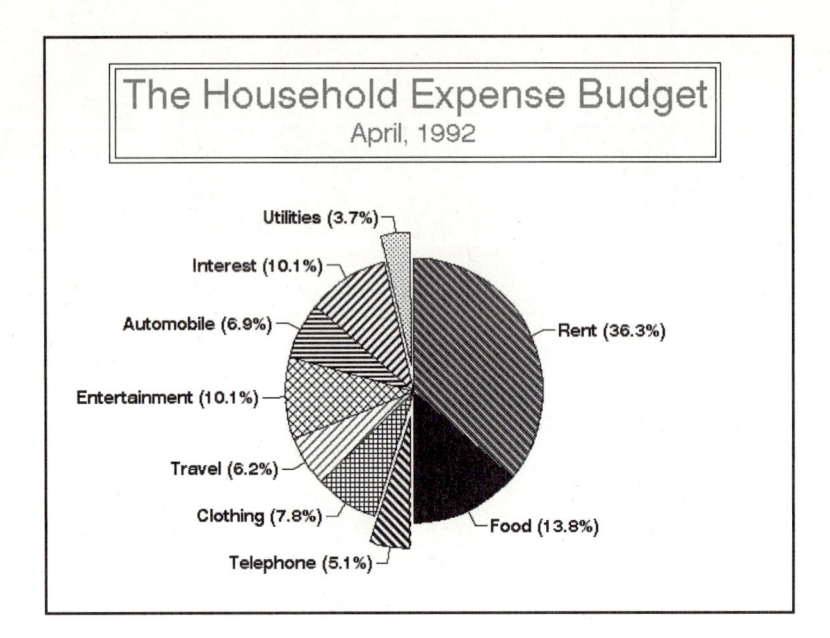

Fig. 10.10

A pie graph showing allocated expenses in a household budget.

[Pie graph: The Household Expense Budget, April, 1992 — Utilities (3.7%), Interest (10.1%), Automobile (6.9%), Entertainment (10.1%), Travel (6.2%), Clothing (7.8%), Telephone (5.1%), Food (13.8%), Rent (36.3%)]

Area Graphs

The area graph combines the line graph and bar graph. This graph type emphasizes changes in magnitude (like a bar graph) at a point in time and reveals trends over time (like a line graph). When plotting two or more data series, Quattro Pro stacks each data series on top of the other to convey a sense of "total area" for the graph. Figure 10.11, for example, is a graphic representation of Kelly's 12-month crop production report. A 6-month version of this report appeared in figure 10.7.

This report shows Kelly's total harvest volume for each month and the contribution made individually by dates and nuts. By looking at the entire graph, you also see how Kelly's total date and nut production volume fluctuates during the year.

Rotated Bar Graphs

The rotated bar graph basically is a bar graph turned on its side. Here, the x-axis and y-axis are reversed so that the graph bars extend horizontally. Using a rotated bar graph instead of a bar graph, or vice versa, is solely an aesthetic decision. Typically, you use rotated bar graphs to show the results of a competitive event such as a sales competition, a leg race, or a typing test. Often, this graph type is used to express data already displayed on a bar graph. Figure 10.12 shows the rotated bar graph form of the data displayed in figure 10.9.

10 — CREATING GRAPHS   445

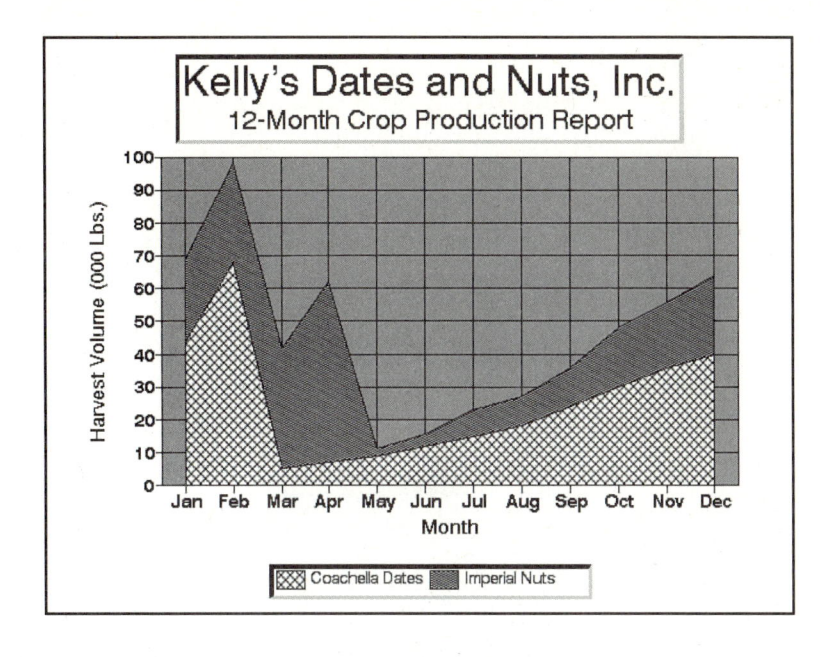

Fig. 10.11

An area graph showing a 12-month crop production report.

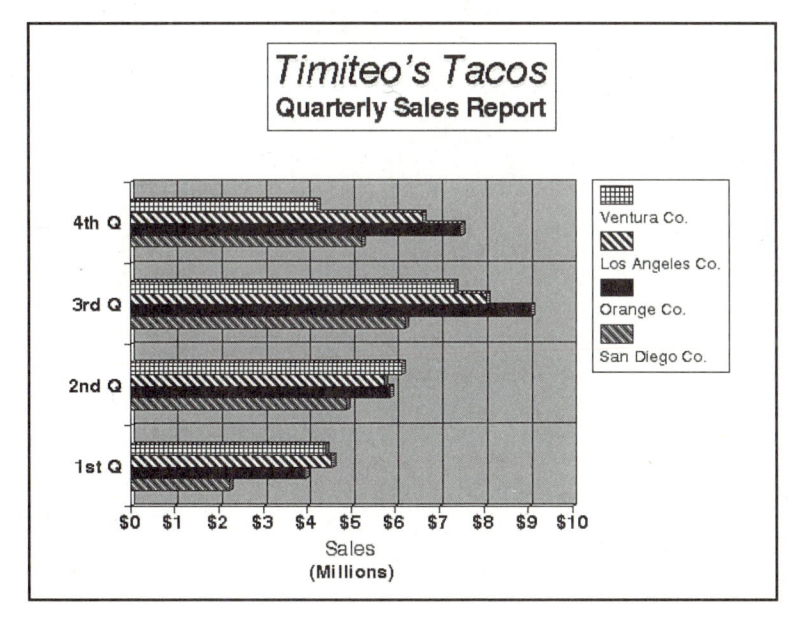

Fig. 10.12

A rotated bar graph showing quarterly sales totals by territory.

Column Graphs

The column graph, like the pie graph, shows the contribution of individual values to a whole. The individual values in a column graph also are called *slices*. Quattro Pro stacks the slices one on top of another to form the column. The column graph provides plenty of room for label descriptions next to each slice.

The column graph shown in figure 10.13 displays a typical college student's expense budget. The height of the bar is the expected annual expense, and the sections within the bar indicate the portion of the annual expense allocated to tuition, books, rent, and so on.

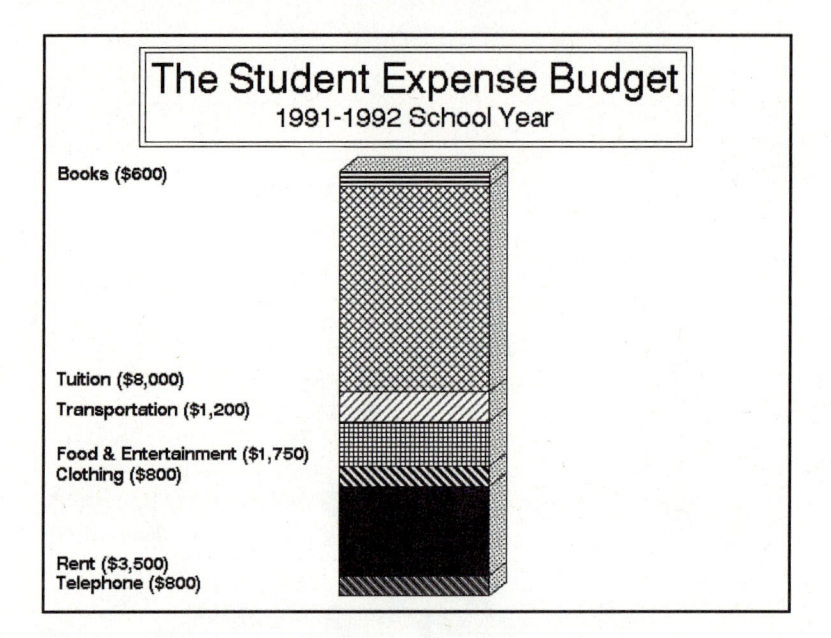

Fig. 10.13

A column graph showing allocated expenses in a student budget.

High-Low (Open-Close) Graphs

The high-low (open-close) graph is a data-specific graph. To use this graph properly, you need the high and low price of a stock at some point in time. You also may include the opening and closing prices to provide a complete assessment of a stock's performance (see fig. 10.14).

Although generally used to plot stock performance data, you can use a high-low graph to plot high, low, open, and close prices for other commodities, such as gold, silver, pork bellies. You also can plot any item in which you may want to track high and low numbers only, such as temperatures, prices of homes, or interest rates.

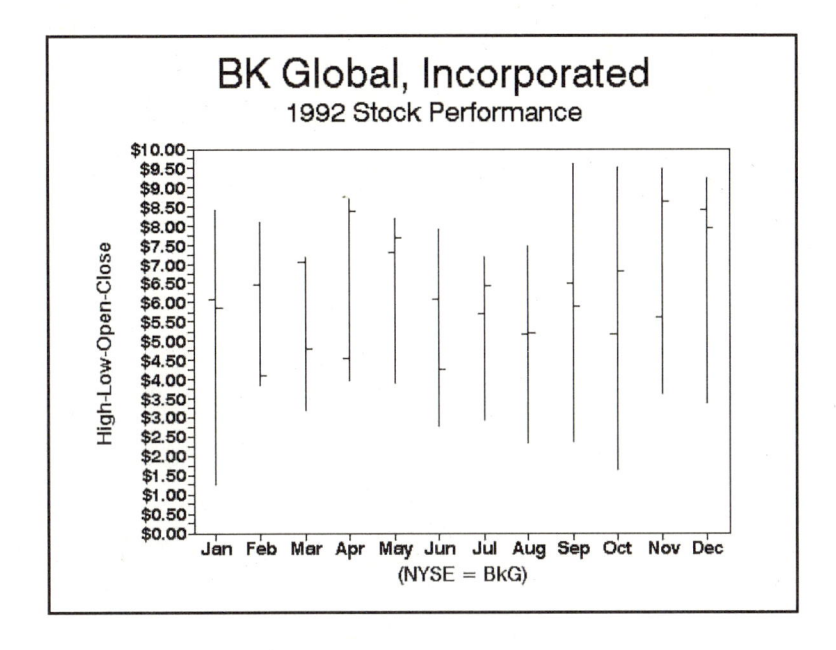

Fig. 10.14

A high-low (open-close) graph showing the one-year performance for BK Global, Incorporated stock.

The top of the vertical bar on this graph represents the high price, whereas the bottom of the bar represents the low price of the stock during each month. The small, vertical bar facing right indicates the opening price, and the bar facing left shows the closing price.

Text Graphs

A text graph is radically different from any graph covered so far. This type of graph has no x-axis, no y-axis, and no data series. Instead, a text graph consists of only text and special graphics available with the Annotator tool (covered in Chapter 11).

A popular use for the text graph is to draw an organizational chart showing the hierarchy of management in a firm. Another use for a text graph is to display two or three simple, enlarged words. Then, using Quattro Pro's "slide-show" capability, you can flash text graphs that say "Sales Up!" or "Increased Profits!" during a presentation.

Bubble Graphs

With a bubble graph, you can float bubbles of different sizes in an XY graph. Like an XY graph, both the x-axis and the y-axis in a bubble graph are scaled with numeric data. To determine how big the bubbles will be in relation to one another, you enter an additional data series that numbers the bubble sizes in order from smallest to largest.

A bubble graph is an excellent graph to use for comparing and relating data points. The bubble graph enables you to compare data not only by their position on the graph, as in an XY graph, but also by the relative size of each data point (see figure 10.15).

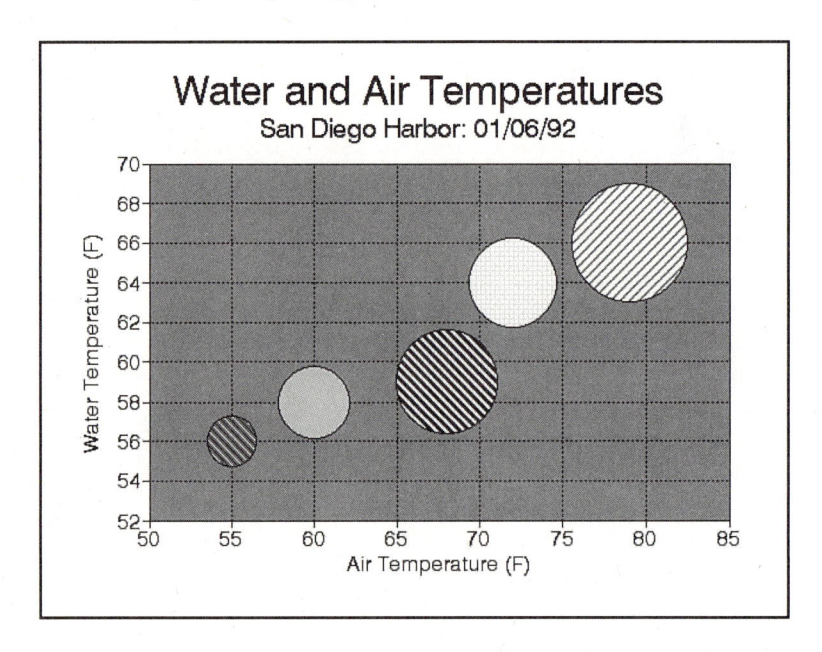

Fig. 10.15

A bubble graph showing water and air temperature readings for San Diego Harbor.

In a bubble graph, the largest bubble need not always reflect the data point with the highest value. For instance, you may be pitching a proposal to downsize the corporation's regional sales offices. In this case, you may want to use the largest bubble for the office carrying the lowest sales profits to draw attention to it as a poor performer and as a place to begin layoffs.

3-D Graphs

The 3-D graph displays spreadsheet data on a three-dimensional grid formed by the x-axis, the y-axis, and the z-axis. The *z-axis* begins at the *graph origin* (the intersection of the x-axis and y-axis) and projects outward, away from the viewer's perspective (see fig. 10.16). In this case, the more data series that appear on the graph, the longer the z-axis.

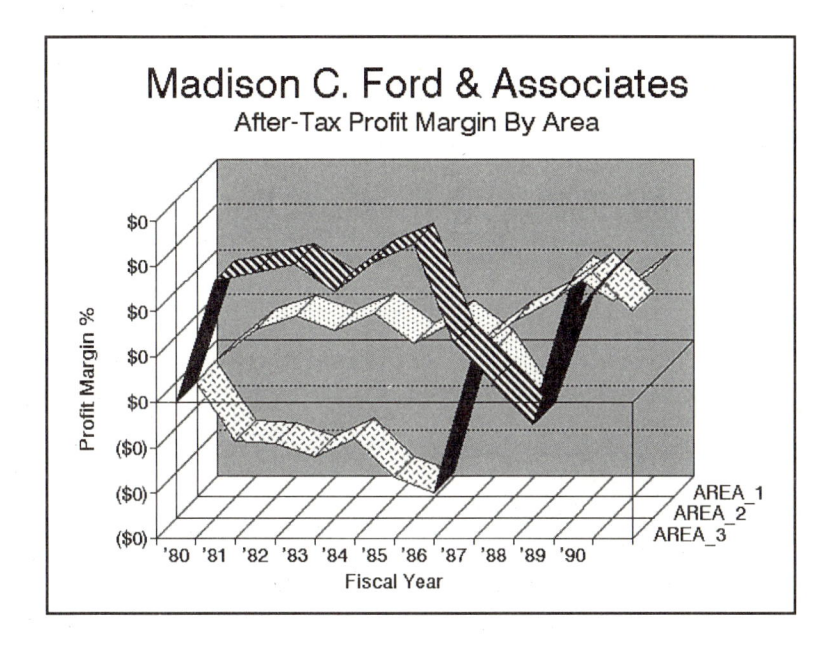

Fig. 10.16

A 3-D ribbon graph showing 10 years of after-tax margin data for Madison C. Ford & Associates.

3-D graphs offer several advantages over two-dimensional graphs. 3-D graphs more easily accommodate large numbers of data series, are ideal for summarizing data from several graphs in a slide show, and simply are more visually appealing.

In 3-D graphs, the data series appear in front of each other as opposed to under, above, or on top of each other as with the two-dimensional variety. When designing a 3-D graph, keep in mind that Quattro Pro places the first data series in the back of the graph, the second data series in front of that one, and so on. If at all possible, try to arrange your spreadsheet data so that the larger numbers are graphed before the smaller numbers. This strategy ensures that the bigger data series is graphed behind the smaller data series.

3-D graphs consist of four types: ribbon, bar, step, and area.

3-D Ribbon Graph

The 3-D ribbon graph is similar to the two-dimensional line graph. Like the regular line graph, the 3-D ribbon graph is useful for showing a progression of values over time (refer to fig. 10.16).

To create a combination 3-D ribbon and line graph, choose **/Graph Overall Three-D No**. Doing so forces the ribbons to display as lines but does not remove the z-axis from the graph. As a result, Quattro Pro displays two-dimensional lines floating in a three-dimensional grid. This type of graph is useful as a transition graph in a slide show that depicts both types of graphs.

3-D Bar Graph

The 3-D bar graph is similar to the two-dimensional bar graph. Like the regular bar graph, the 3-D bar graph is useful for comparing the values of different items at set periods in time (see fig. 10.17).

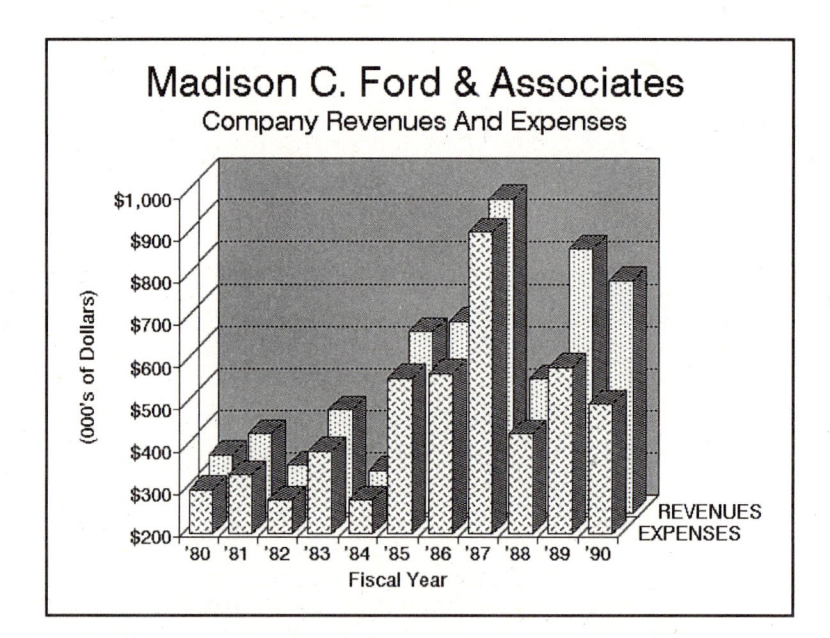

Fig. 10.17

A 3-D bar graph showing 10 years of revenue and expense data for Madison C. Ford & Associates.

The 3-D bar graph works best with sets of steadily increasing or decreasing numbers. If the numbers fluctuate, Quattro Pro may conceal the smaller bars (smaller values) behind the larger bars (larger values).

To create a combination graph, choose **/Graph Overall Three-D No**. Doing so forces the bars to display as flat bars, but does not remove the z-axis from the graph. As a result, Quattro Pro displays two-dimensional bars floating in a three-dimensional grid.

3-D Step Graph

The 3-D step graph resembles a 3-D bar graph. In a 3-D step graph, the bars for each data series are connected, forming a series of steps (see fig. 10.18).

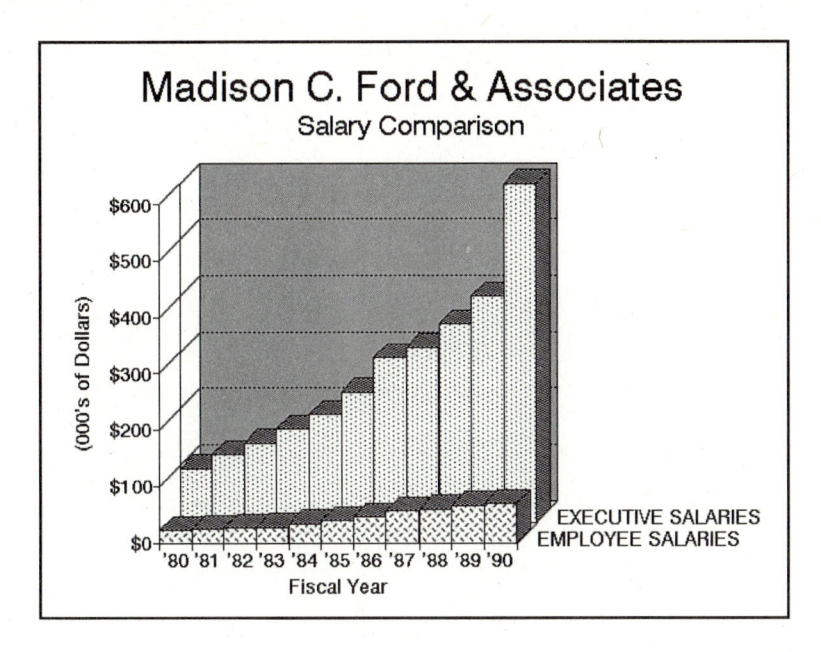

Fig. 10.18

A 3-D step graph showing 10 years of salary data for Madison C. Ford & Associates.

In a 3-D step graph, you should graph the larger numbers before the smaller numbers to keep the larger steps from concealing the smaller steps.

To create a combination 3-D step and bar graph, choose /**G**raph **O**verall **T**hree-D **N**o. Doing so forces the steps to display as flat bars but does not remove the z-axis from the graph. As a result, Quattro Pro displays two-dimensional bars floating in a three-dimensional grid.

3-D Area Graph

The 3-D area graph is a two-dimensional line graph with the area under the lines filled in. Like the regular line graph, the 3-D area graph helps you track trends by displaying a progression of values over a period of time (see fig. 10.19).

PART II — PRINTING AND GRAPHING

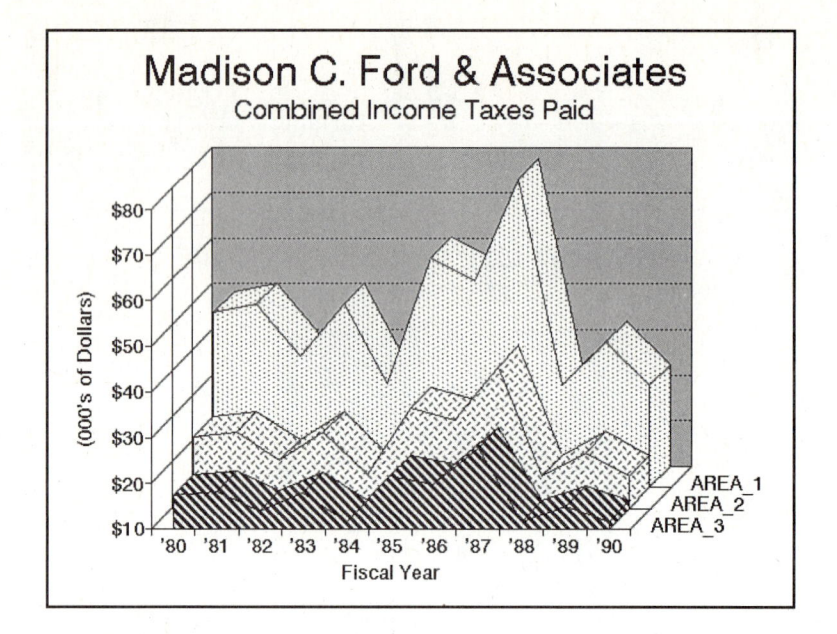

Fig. 10.19

A 3-D area graph showing 10 years of income tax data for Madison C. Ford & Associates.

The 3-D area graph differs from the two-dimensional area graph. A regular area graph stacks the data series areas on top of one another to review the cumulative effect of a trend. The 3-D area graph, however, displays the data series areas in front of one another, which clearly highlights differences in magnitude—a good way to analyze individual trends and the aggregate contribution to an overall trend.

To create a combination graph, choose /**G**raph **O**verall **T**hree-D **N**o. Doing so forces the areas to display flat but does not remove the z-axis from the graph. As a result, Quattro Pro displays two-dimensional areas floating in a three-dimensional grid.

Creating a Basic Graph

With Quattro Pro, you can create a basic graph in two ways: from the ground up or by using the **F**ast Graph command. Although both methods achieve roughly the same result, the **F**ast Graph command is much easier to use.

When you execute the **F**ast Graph command, Quattro Pro evaluates a selected block of data on the active spreadsheet and builds a graph from that block.

Preselecting a Block

Building Quattro Pro graphs with the **F**ast Graph command is easy when you know how to preselect a block to graph. This preselecting technique is discussed in Chapter 4, "Manipulating Data."

You can preselect a cell block in two ways:

- Place the cell selector in the uppermost left cell in the target block and press Shift-F7. Press the cursor-movement keys to highlight the target block, and then choose the command you want to execute.

- Point the mouse arrow at the uppermost left cell in the target block, drag to the last cell in the target cell block, and then release the button. Execute the command.

The following rules describe how Quattro Pro evaluates a preselected block when the block has more rows than columns:

- Each column is considered a single series.

- Labels appearing in the first column are designated as the x-axis labels.

- Labels appearing in the first row are designated as the graph legend labels.

- When the preselected block does not contain labels in the first column or row, Quattro Pro creates a graph without labels or legends.

The following rules describe how Quattro Pro evaluates a preselected block when the block has more columns than rows:

- Each row is considered a single series.

- Labels appearing in the first row are designated as the x-axis labels.

- Labels appearing in the first column are designated as the graph legend labels.

- When the preselected block does not contain labels in the first column or row, Quattro Pro creates a graph without labels or legends.

Creating a Fast Graph

When you preselect a block of data on the active spreadsheet and then choose **Fast Graph** from the **G**raph menu, Quattro Pro draws a barebones graph on-screen. A bare-bones graph shows only the basic graph elements: a scaled x-axis, a scaled y-axis, and the graphed data. When the preselected block contains labels in the first row and column, the graph also shows a legend and axes labels.

By default, Quattro Pro creates a stacked-bar graph when you choose **Fast Graph**.

Before you choose the **Fast Graph** command, make sure that the preselected block does not contain any blank rows or columns, because Quattro Pro will show the rows or columns as gaps within the graph.

> **TIP** To remove blank areas from a graph, return to the active spreadsheet and delete all blank rows and columns from the selected data block. Next, select the data block again and then choose **Fast Graph**. Quattro Pro displays the same graph without the gaps.

The preselected data block shown in figure 10.20 (B5..E9) is ready to be fast graphed. To create a bare-bones stacked-bar graph (the default graph type), follow these steps:

1. Highlight cell block B5..E9 on the active spreadsheet.
2. Choose **Fast Graph** from the **G**raph menu (or press Ctrl-G, the Ctrl-key shortcut for this command).

> **TIP** If you choose **Fast Graph** before preselecting a block, Quattro Pro returns you to the spreadsheet and asks you to enter the block address containing the data you want to fast graph.

After you choose the **Fast Graph** command, Quattro Pro builds a graph on-screen (see fig. 10.21). Notice that because the block had more columns than rows the labels in the first row are x-axis labels, and so on (see preceding rules). To return to the active spreadsheet, press any key except the /; the / activates the Annotator.

10 — CREATING GRAPHS   455

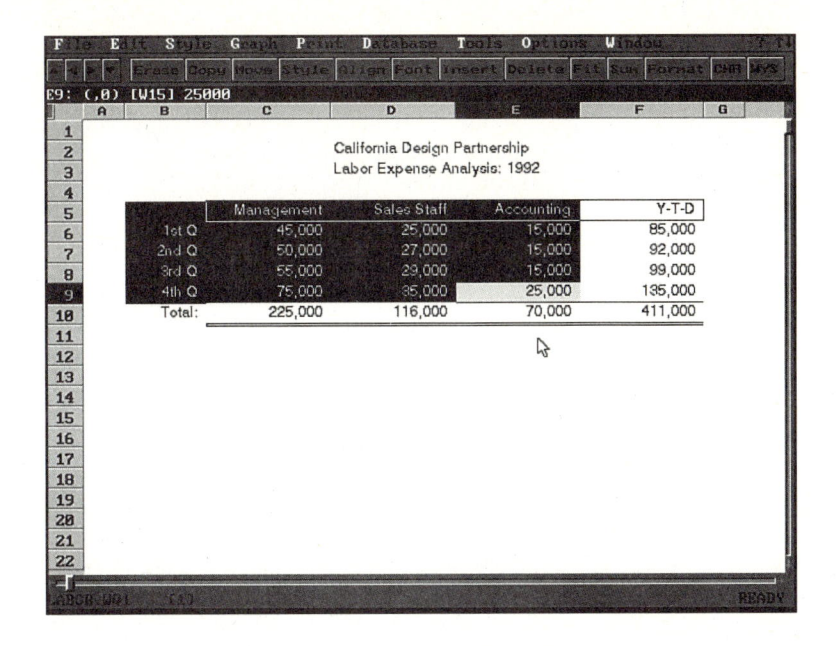

Fig. 10.20

A preselected cell block on a spreadsheet.

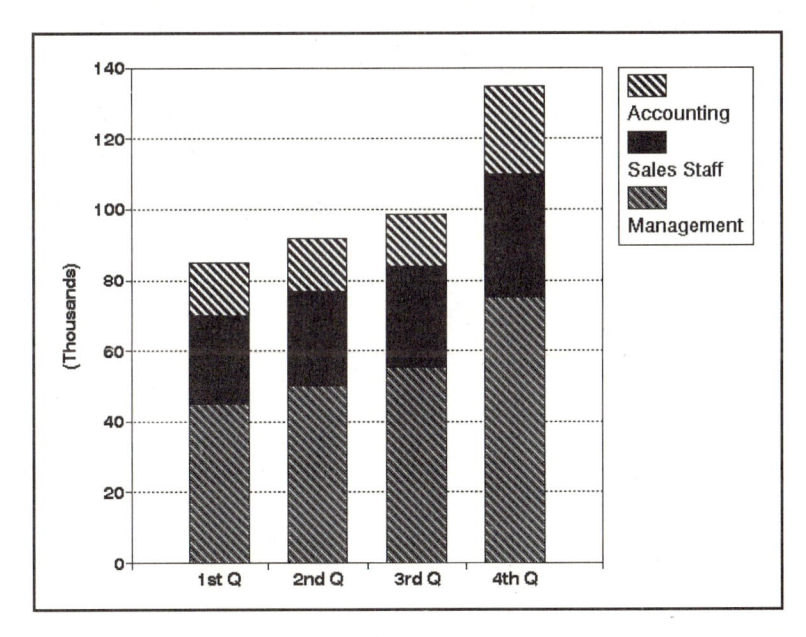

Fig. 10.21

A bare-bones stacked-bar graph created from the pre-selected data block.

A review of the four-step process that Quattro Pro used to create the fast graph follows:

1. If the selected block has more rows than columns, Quattro Pro follows the first set of rules outlined in the preceding section and uses the second set of rules when the selected block has more columns than rows.

2. Quattro Pro creates x-axis labels using the labels appearing in the first column of the block (B6..B9).

3. Quattro Pro creates a legend using the labels appearing in the first row of the block (C5..E5).

4. Quattro Pro uses the remaining row data (C6..E9) to create four unique series.

Because fast graphs are so easy to create, they are natural what-if analysis tools. After you make a fast graph, choose **Q**uit from the **G**raph menu to return to the active spreadsheet. Now modify any of the values in your graph block. When the data is edited to your satisfaction, press F10 (or Ctrl-G) to regenerate a new fast graph.

This approach to building graphs requires minimal effort on your part. The major drawback of using this method is that the **Fast Graph** command interprets only one block of data. When evaluating that block, Quattro Pro builds a graph based on one of only two possible conditions: the number of columns is greater than the number of rows, or the number of rows is greater than the number of columns. But what if the number of rows equals the number of columns? Or what if you want to use data from different locations on the same spreadsheet?

The **Fast Graph** command cannot meet all possible graph building needs. In fact, this command does not offer the flexibility that custom graph building provides. See Chapter 11, "Customizing Graphs," for further details.

Building a Customized Graph

The **S**eries menu commands enable you to choose up to six data series to graph. The primary advantage of using **S**eries menu commands instead of the **Fast Graph** command is that you can choose the data series that appears on the graph.

T I P You can edit the **S**eries menu settings that were created by using **Fast Graph** simply by reselecting each series option and specifying a different cell block.

10 — CREATING GRAPHS

In Quattro Pro, a valid series can be numbers in adjacent rows or columns or numbers from different parts of the same active spreadsheet. You even can use linked cells in your series—Quattro Pro uses the results of formulas and links the graph.

When you choose /**G**raph **S**eries, Quattro Pro displays the **S**eries menu. The commands found on this menu appear in table 10.2.

Table 10.2 Series Menu Commands

Command	Description
1st-6th Series	Defines up to six data series for Quattro Pro to graph
X-Axis Series	Defines a block containing labels to be used for the x-axis labels or values for an XY or bubble graph
Group	Defines a block of data to be graphed
Analyze	Accesses analytical graphing tools; see Chapter 12, "Analyzing Graphs," for complete coverage of this command

> **TIP**
> On an XY graph, the **X**-Axis Series command defines a data series rather than a block containing labels (as with all other graph types). With XY and bubble graphs, the x-axis must contain data.

When you choose the **G**roup command, Quattro Pro asks you to specify how to create a series from the block of data by **C**olumns or by **R**ows. If you choose the **C**olumns option, Quattro Pro assigns each column of values to a series; choosing the **R**ows option assigns each row of values to a series. The benefit of using the **G**roup command is that you can avoid specifying each individual series.

Now use the data from the spreadsheet pictured in figure 10.20 to create a basic graph by specifying the data series, one at a time.

Specifying Individual Series

You can specify individual data series, one at a time, and achieve the same result as with the **F**ast Graph command. When you build a graph

PART II — PRINTING AND GRAPHING

in this manner, you can choose data series from anywhere on the active spreadsheet. You even can link a graph to data in other spreadsheets open in Quattro Pro's memory or stored on disk. Also, the **Series** command is invaluable when you want to go back and append additional data series to an existing graph, even one that you created using **Fast Graph**.

To build a graph by specifying each individual data series, follow these steps:

1. Choose **1**st Series from the **S**eries menu.
2. Type or highlight the range containing the first series—*C6..C9*, for example—and then press Enter to record the first series.
3. Repeat step 2 for the second and third series.
4. Choose **X**-Axis Series from the **S**eries menu.
5. Type or highlight the range containing the labels—*B6..B9*, for example—and press Enter to record the x-axis labels.
6. Choose **Q**uit to return to the **G**raph menu.
7. Choose **V**iew to examine the graph.

Your displayed graph now should look like figure 10.21, which was created using **Fast Graph**.

> **TIP**
>
> When defining series for XY and bubble graphs, remember that your x-axis must display numeric data, not labels or text. Choose **S**eries **X**-Axis Series and enter the coordinates of your x-axis series. Then, choose **1**st Series to enter the y-axis. For bubble graphs, you also must use a **2**nd Series that defines the relative size of the bubbles.

Specifying a Group Series

The **G**roup command works like the **Fast Graph** command, except that you can choose how the data series are retrieved from the spreadsheet, by **C**olumn or **R**ow. The Fast Graph command does not give you this option because the command retrieves the data series according to the dimensions of the preselected data block and the two rules outlined earlier.

To build a graph by specifying a group data series, follow these steps:

1. Choose **G**roup from the **S**eries menu.

2. Choose **C**olumns from the **G**roup menu.
3. Type or highlight the range containing the data series—*C5..E9*, for example—and press Enter to record the data series.
4. Choose **X**-Axis Series from the **S**eries menu.
5. Type the range containing the labels—*B6..B9*, for example—and press Enter to record the x-axis labels.
6. Choose **Q**uit to return to the **G**raph menu.
7. Choose **V**iew to examine the graph.

Again, your displayed graph should look like figure 10.21.

Enhancing the Appearance of a Basic Graph

So far, you have learned how to build a basic, unadorned graph. Although some of the graphs you create with **F**ast Graph show axes labels or a legend, they often lack a finished quality common to most professional reports. In this section, you learn how to use the **T**ext command to turn a basic graph into a presentation-quality visual report.

The **T**ext menu commands add titles to a graph, append descriptive labels to the x-axis and y-axis, insert a legend, and control all of the fonts appearing on the graph. When you choose the **T**ext command, the **T**ext menu appears. The **T**ext menu commands are listed in table 10.3.

Table 10.3 Text Menu Commands

Command	Description
1st Line	Adds a main title above the graph
2nd Line	Adds a secondary title to a graph below the main title
X-Title	Adds a descriptive label below the x-axis
Y-Title	Adds a rotated vertical label to the left of the y-axis
Secondary Y-Axis	Adds a rotated vertical label to the right of the y-axis

continues

Table 10.3 Continued

Command	Description
Legends	Inserts and positions a graph legend
Font	Controls the typeface, point size, color, and style of the fonts appearing on the graph

Adding Titles

Use the first five commands on the Text menu to add titles to a basic graph. Titles add definition and lend clarity. The main title, for example, generally defines the name of a company or a report. The secondary title clarifies the main title by specifying a relevant time period (Fiscal Year 1992), the name of a department (Sales & Marketing Division), or the abbreviation style used for numbers appearing in the graph (All Values in 000's of Dollars).

You can create other titles to describe specific parts of the graph, such as the x-axis and y-axis data. *Legends* are a type of title that describe the data series appearing on a graph. You can create the graph shown in figure 10.22, for example, using the first five commands on the Text menu. The graph shown in figure 10.22 conveys more information to the viewer than does the original fast graph shown in figure 10.21.

To add a main title to the top of a graph, follow these steps:

1. Choose 1st Line from the Text menu.

2. Type the title when prompted.

3. Press Enter to record the title.

4. Press F10 or choose View from the Graph menu to see the new graph title.

You can perform the same operation for the remaining four title commands, because the commands work the same.

To remove a title from the graph, choose the command again, press Esc, and then press Enter to record a blank space in place of the old title.

Figure 10.23 shows the Text menu after all of the titles shown in figure 10.22 are entered. Figure 10.23 shows the two ways in which Quattro Pro can recognize title data. When you enter a graph title via the Text menu, Quattro Pro reproduces your keyboard entry at the right margin of the menu. The **X**-Title and **Y**-Title entries, for example, reflect the text titles "Fiscal Year Quarter" and "Dollars."

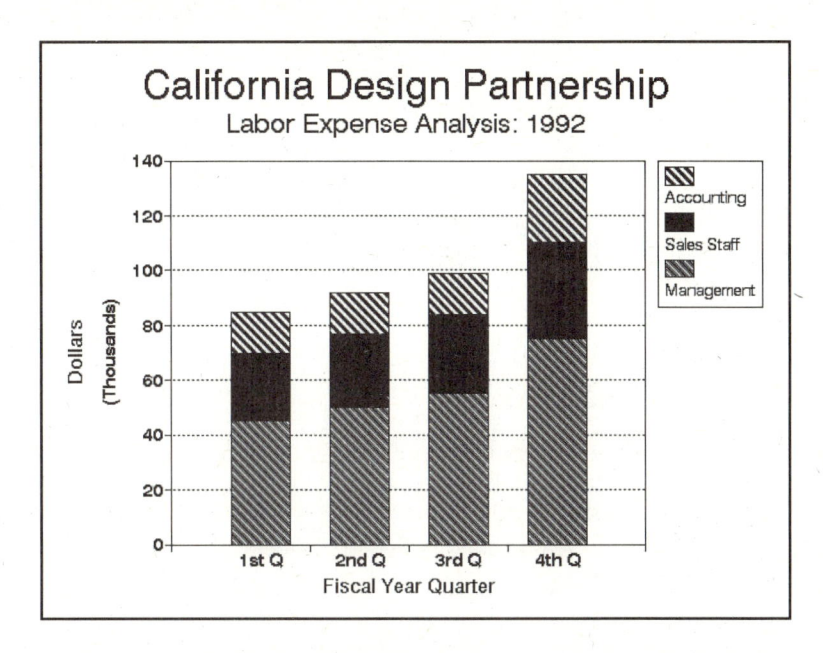

Fig. 10.22

Titles added to the basic graph.

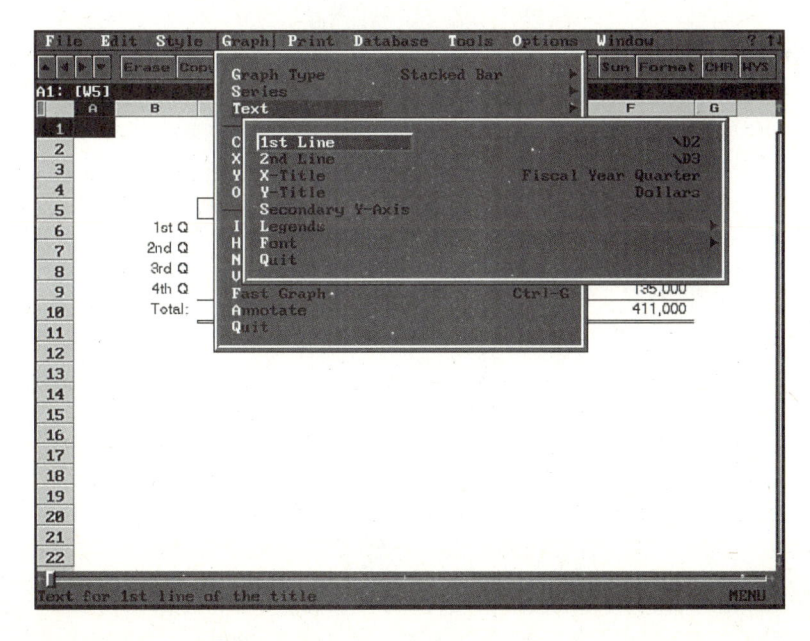

Fig. 10.23

The title entries on the Text menu.

PART II — PRINTING AND GRAPHING

Look at the title entries recorded with the **1**st Line and **2**nd Line commands. These entries are a combination of a backslash and a cell address. To use a label appearing on the active spreadsheet as a graph title, enter the label's cell address preceded by a backslash, or type the text to appear for that title.

> **TIP** You also may enter bullet characters as part of a graph title by preceding the title text with a backslash character followed by the bullet code. See Chapter 4, "Manipulating Data," for a review of the valid bullet codes.

Adding Legends

The Legends command adds a legend to a graph. A *legend* is a coding system that defines the individual parts that make up a data series on a graph. The legend shown at the right in figure 10.22 shows which section of each stacked bar represents management, sales, staff, and accounting labor expense.

To add and position a legend on a graph, follow these steps:

1. Choose **L**egends from the **T**ext menu.
2. Choose **1**st Series, type the text, and press Enter to record the first legend series.

   Repeat this step for each remaining legend series.
3. Choose **P**osition and choose a legend position from the **P**osition menu. Quattro Pro displays three choices: **B**ottom, **R**ight, and **N**one.

Figure 10.24 shows the **S**eries menu for the **L**egends command.

Like the title entries, the legend series entries can be a combination of a backslash and a cell address. To use a label appearing on the active spreadsheet as legend text, enter the label's cell address preceded by a backslash or type the text to appear in the legend box.

Changing the Font

With the **F**ont command, you can change the typeface, point size, style, and color of each text element on a graph. This command is powerful because **F**ont gives you the ability to alter the appearance of text on a graph like a typesetter can manipulate the appearance of a resume or a restaurant menu.

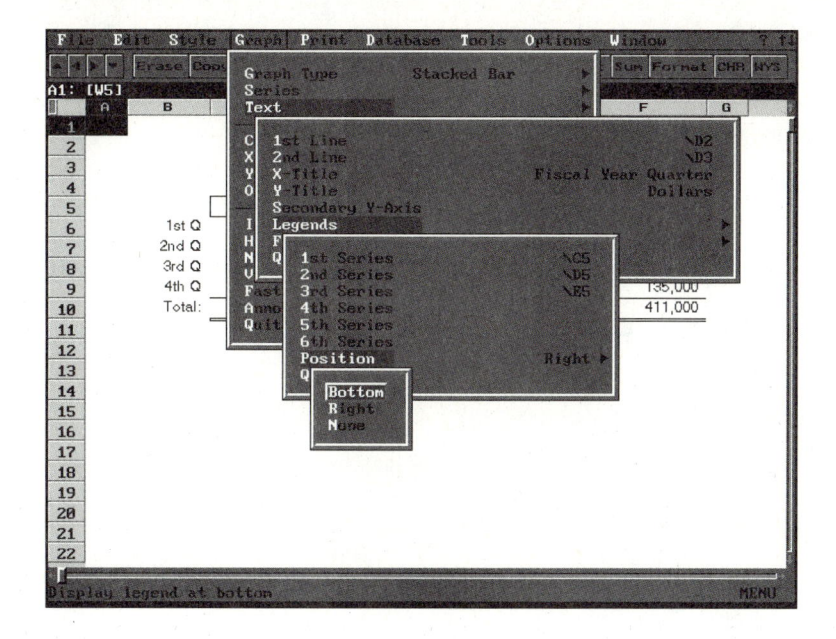

Fig. 10.24

The entries that define each series in the legend.

> **TIP**
>
> When you use **/G**raph **T**ext **F**ont **D**ata & Tick Labels to change the point size of labels, all markers and symbols automatically are scaled to the new size you selected.

To change the font used to display a legend's text, for example, choose **/G**raph **T**ext **F**ont **L**egends and then alter each available font characteristic. When you choose **/G**raph **T**ext **F**ont, the **F**ont menu appears. The commands found on this menu are listed in table 10.4.

Table 10.4 Font Menu Commands

Command	Description
1st Line	Changes the font display of the main title
2nd Line	Changes the font display of the secondary title

continues

PART II — PRINTING AND GRAPHING

Table 10.4 Continued

Command	Description
X-Title	Changes the font display of the x-axis title
Y-Title	Changes the font display of the y-axis title
Legends	Changes the font display of the legend text
Data & Tick Labels	Changes the font display of the tick labels and scaling data and 3-D graph legends

Changing the Typeface

Quattro Pro's default typeface is Bitstream Swiss-SC. To change the typeface used to display the main title on a graph, for example, follow these steps:

1. Choose /**G**raph **T**ext **F**ont **1**st Line.
2. Choose **T**ypeface.
3. Choose a new typeface from the menu (see fig. 10.25).

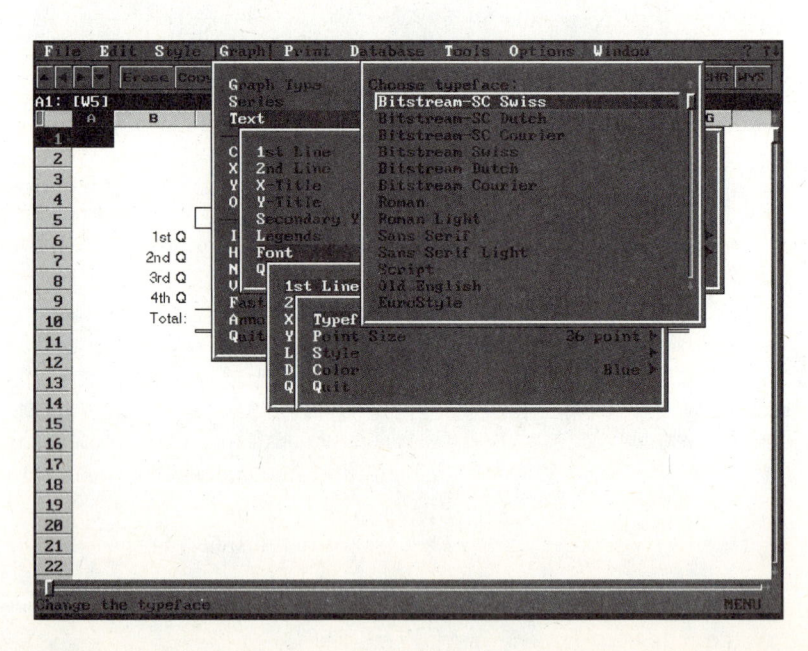

Fig. 10.25

The **T**ypeface menu selections.

10 — CREATING GRAPHS

4. Press F10 to review the new typeface on the graph.

If you choose a typeface that has not been built by Quattro Pro, the program displays a `Now building font` message. After a font is built, Quattro Pro does not need to build the font again.

> **TIP**
>
> If you have a laser printer, Quattro Pro displays additional fonts at the bottom of the **F**ont menu. These extra fonts are printer-specific fonts. If you install an HP LaserJet, for example, Quattro Pro displays fonts that work with LaserJet printers. Likewise, if you install a PostScript printer, Quattro Pro displays PostScript-specific fonts.

Changing the Point Size

Quattro Pro has different default point sizes for each text element on a graph. For example, the **1**st Line title appears in 36-point type, the **2**nd Line title appears in 24-point type, and all other text appears in 18-point type. Point size measures the height of letters; thus, the larger the point size, the larger the letters.

To change the point size used to display the secondary title on a graph, for example, follow these steps:

1. Choose /**G**raph **T**ext **F**ont **2**nd Line.
2. Choose **P**oint Size.
3. Choose a new point size from the menu (see fig. 10.26).
4. Press F10 to review the new point size on the graph.

> **TIP**
>
> Some LaserJet typefaces have fixed point sizes, so you may not be able to change point sizes using the **P**oint size menu commands. Check your printer manual. For these fonts you choose the point size in the **T**ypeface menu as well. If you try to change the point size on a typeface with a fixed point size, you get the message `Non-scalable font selected`. Choose size with the **T**ypeface menu.

PART II — PRINTING AND GRAPHING

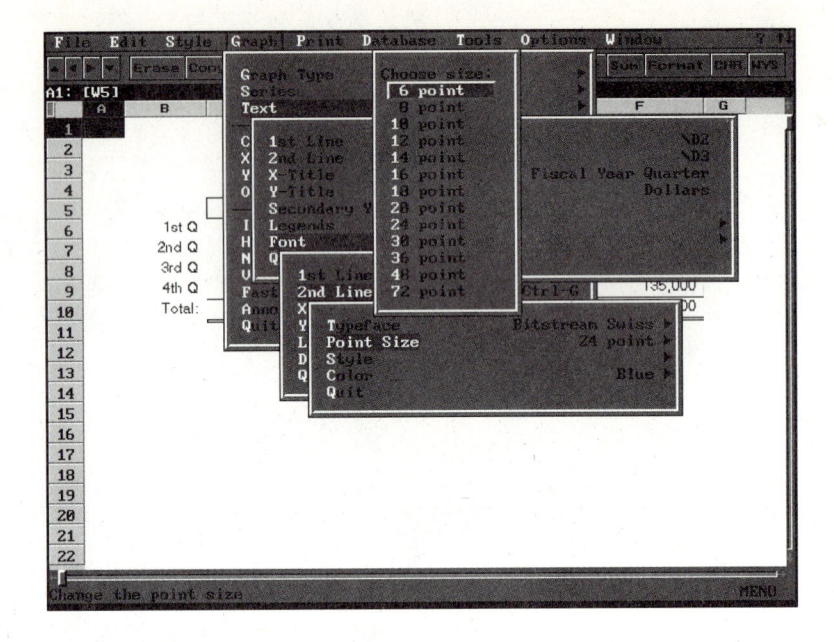

Fig. 10.26

The **P**oint Size menu selections.

Changing the Style

Quattro Pro has five font styles: regular (default), bold, italic, underlined, and drop shadow. To change the font style used to display the text in a legend, for example, follow these steps:

1. Choose **/G**raph **T**ext **F**ont **L**egends.

2. Choose **S**tyle.

3. Choose a new font style from the menu (see fig. 10.27).

4. Press F10 to view the new font style on the graph.

> **TIP** Because LaserJet typefaces have fixed styles as well as fixed point sizes, you cannot change style using the Font menu commands. Also, not all typefaces support all of the listed styles. If a style is unavailable, Quattro Pro uses the default (regular) style. To return a text element to its original font style display, choose **R**eset from the **S**tyle menu.

10 — CREATING GRAPHS

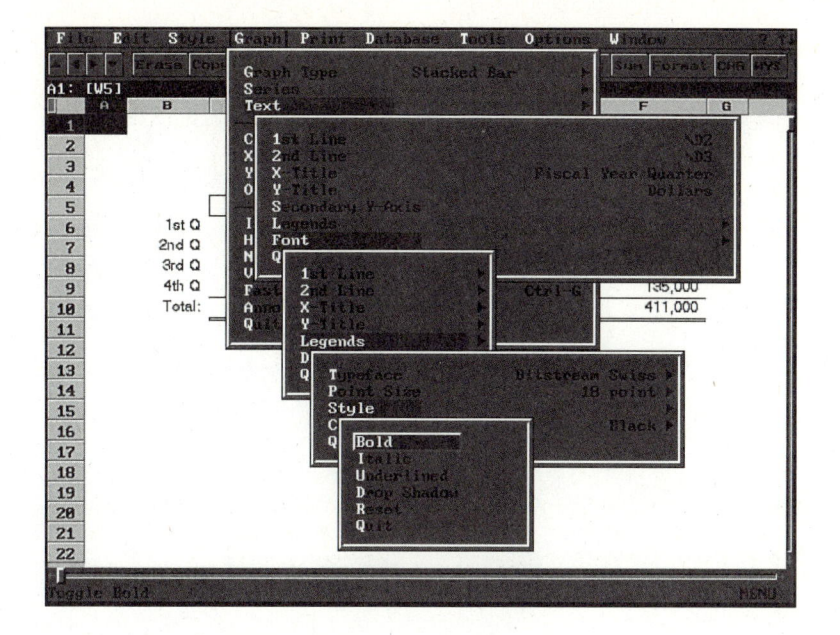

Fig. 10.27

The **S**tyle menu selections.

Changing the Colors

Quattro Pro enables you to change the colors used to display text on a graph with the **F**ont **C**olors command. If you do not own a color monitor, you still can use this command to control the color-coding scheme transmitted to color printers and plotters.

To change the colors used to display the data and tick labels, for example, follow these steps:

1. Choose /**G**raph **T**ext **F**ont **D**ata & Tick Labels.

2. Choose **C**olor.

3. Choose a new color from the color palette (see fig. 10.28). In text display mode, Quattro Pro displays a list of the color names instead of the palette.

4. Press F10 to view the new font color on the graph.

> **TIP**
> Use the cursor-movement keys to move around the color palette. If you have a mouse, click a color to select it, then press Enter to choose a color.

PART II — PRINTING AND GRAPHING

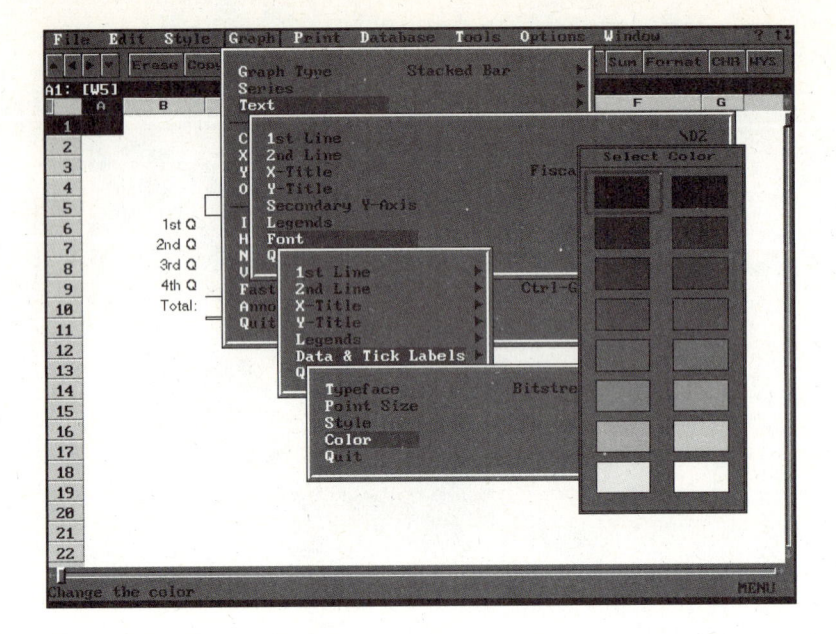

Fig. 10.28

The Color menu selections.

Managing Graph Files

Managing graph files is an important part of every graph building work session. When you build a graph, you must store that graph's settings with the active spreadsheet, or you lose the graph if you leave the current spreadsheet without saving the current changes. A graph's settings include the data series definitions, the title text, the legend, the font definitions, and so on—everything that makes the graph more than just a blank screen.

Fortunately, every time you save a spreadsheet, Quattro Pro also saves the current graph settings with the spreadsheet. The next time you retrieve the spreadsheet, you can press F10, and Quattro Pro will display the graph. This mechanism, however, works with only one graph per spreadsheet and does not actually name the graph.

Eventually, you may want to build more than one graph from a spreadsheet. Then, you need to use the **N**ame menu commands to help manage your graph files. Table 10.5 defines the **N**ame menu commands.

Table 10.5 Name Menu Commands

Command	Description
Display	Displays a graph that has been saved with a name
Create	Names a graph and saves it with a spreadsheet
Autosave Edits	Automatically saves edits to a graph when you switch to another graph
Erase	Erases a saved graph name from a spreadsheet
Reset	Erases all saved graph names from the current spreadsheet
Slide	Displays a named graph for a user-specified number of seconds or when any key is pressed
Graph Copy	Copies a graph from one spreadsheet to another

Naming and Saving a Graph

You must name a graph only when you want to create a second graph from the same spreadsheet. Save every graph under a unique name to ensure that you do not accidentally overwrite one graph's settings with another.

To name a graph and assign that graph's settings to the active spreadsheet, follow these steps:

1. Choose /**G**raph **N**ame **C**reate. Quattro Pro displays a list of graph names, if any exist.

2. If you are creating a graph, enter a name for the graph when prompted. (You may use up to 15 characters.) If you are saving an existing graph, highlight the name on the list.

> **CAUTION:** Quattro Pro will not warn you if you are overwriting an existing graph.

3. Press Enter to assign the graph name to the current spreadsheet.

Autosaving Edited Graphs

When you create two or more graphs from data on the same spreadsheet, use the **A**utosave Edits command to guard against overwriting one graph's settings with another graph's settings. This command has two settings: **Y**es (auto-save is on) and the default value, **N**o (auto-save is off).

With auto-save on, Quattro Pro saves the current graph's settings as soon as you make another graph's settings current. If the first graph has no name, Quattro Pro prompts you to name the graph before it makes the second graph current.

When **A**utosave Edits is set to **N**o, be careful if you are working with multiple graphs. Always remember to save the current graph's settings with the **S**ave command before you make another graph current with the **D**isplay command.

Displaying a Saved Graph

When you create two or more graphs from the same spreadsheet data, you need a way to choose which group of settings to display when you press F10.

To display a graph assigned to the active spreadsheet, follow these steps:

1. Choose /**G**raph **N**ame **D**isplay. Quattro Pro displays a list of graph names, if any exist.
2. Highlight a graph name on the list.
3. Press Enter to retrieve the graph settings assigned to that name.

> **TIP** Before you execute the /**G**raph **N**ame **D**isplay command, be sure that you have saved the current graph settings, because Quattro Pro replaces the current settings with those of the graph you specified in step 3.

When you execute /**G**raph **N**ame **D**isplay, Quattro Pro displays the graph. Press Enter to return to the active spreadsheet.

Erasing a Saved Graph

To erase a graph name from the active spreadsheet, follow these steps:

1. Choose /**G**raph **N**ame **E**rase. Quattro Pro displays a list of graph names, if any exist.
2. Highlight a graph name on the list.
3. Press Enter to erase the graph settings assigned to that name.

Resetting the Current Graph Settings

Finding a particular graph when you have 10 or 20 names to choose from can become tedious. Deleting the entire list of names and then saving the current settings under a new name often is easier.

To erase all of the saved graph names assigned to the active spreadsheet, follow these steps:

1. Choose /**G**raph **N**ame **R**eset. Quattro Pro displays a dialog box asking whether you want to delete all named graphs.
2. Choose **Y**es to erase all graph names or **N**o to cancel the operation.

Copying a Saved Graph

Quattro Pro enables you to copy saved graphs to other spreadsheets open in Quattro Pro's memory. This feature is particularly helpful when you want to use one spreadsheet's saved graph in another spreadsheet's slide show (covered in the next section).

Before you try to copy a graph to another spreadsheet, follow these steps:

1. Assign a unique name to the active graph with the /**G**raph **N**ame **C**reate command.

> **CAUTION:** Make sure that the name you choose does not exist for a graph in the destination spreadsheet. If you choose a duplicate name, Quattro Pro will overwrite that name (and graph settings) when you complete the operation, and the overwritten graph settings will be lost.

2. Open the destination spreadsheet into Quattro Pro's memory with the **/F**ile **O**pen command.

3. Press Alt-0 to display a list of the open windows. Highlight the name of the source spreadsheet—the one with the graph—and then press Enter to make that spreadsheet active.

To copy the saved graph from the source spreadsheet to the destination spreadsheet, follow these steps:

1. Choose **/G**raph **N**ame **G**raph **C**opy. Quattro Pro displays the names list.

2. Highlight the name of the graph you want to copy and press Enter.

    Quattro Pro prompts you to point to the destination spreadsheet.

3. Press Alt-0 to display a list of the open windows. Highlight the name of the source spreadsheet and press Enter to make that spreadsheet active.

> **T I P** You also can press Shift-F6, the Next Window key, to activate other windows open in Quattro Pro's memory.

4. Press Enter or click anywhere on the destination spreadsheet to copy the graph.

Keep the following three things in mind as you prepare to copy a graph from one spreadsheet to another:

- Copying a graph creates formula links between the source spreadsheet and the copied graph on the destination spreadsheet. If you change the numbers (on the source spreadsheet) upon which the graph is based, Quattro Pro redraws the graph on the destination spreadsheet.

- Copying text graphs does not create formula links.

- When you name the graph that is to be copied, be sure that the name does not already exist on the destination spreadsheet. If it does, the copied graph permanently replaces the existing graph settings on the destination spreadsheet.

Displaying a Graph

You already have learned two methods for displaying a graph: pressing F10 or choosing **/G**raph **V**iew. Three other techniques for viewing

10 — CREATING GRAPHS   473

graphs go beyond displaying them. You can zoom and pan a graph on-screen, create a slide show, and insert the graph into the spreadsheet.

Using Graph Zoom and Pan

If you have a mouse, you can use Quattro Pro's Graph Zoom and Pan feature to enlarge portions of a graph series, and can scroll left and right to examine areas of the graph in detail, one section at a time.

To use Zoom and Pan while viewing a graph, press the left and right mouse buttons at the same time. The Zoom and Pan palette appears in the upper left corner of the screen, and a position bar appears at the top of the graph. As you move around your graph, the position bar reflects your actions.

When you zoom, the position bar shrinks to indicate that a smaller percentage of the graph is displaying. When you pan, the position bar moves with you to indicate how far left or right you have scrolled. This feature reminds you where you are in the graph and is especially helpful when displaying a small, detailed section of a graph. Table 10.6 describes the functions of the buttons on the Graph Zoom and Pan palette.

Table 10.6 The Graph Zoom and Pan Palette

Button	Function
++	Zooms in on the left-most portion of the graph; each time you click this button, you see less of the graph, but in greater detail
—	Zooms out to show a larger percentage of the graph in less detail
==	Displays 100% of the graph
<<	Pans left, once you have engaged the zoom and are displaying a smaller percentage of the graph; click repeatedly to pan to the left-most portion of the graph
>>	Pans right, once you have engaged the zoom and are displaying a smaller percentage of the graph; click repeatedly to pan to the right-most portion of the graph
Right Mouse	Clears the Zoom and Pan palette but continues to display the graph

PART II — PRINTING AND GRAPHING

Creating a Slide Show

This chapter has shown you techniques to create presentation-quality graphics for use in important business meetings or at sales presentations. Quattro Pro's **S**lide command can help you to prepare for these meetings by creating an on-screen slide show of named graphs. Using the procedures outlined in Chapter 9, you can create special files that a slide production company can convert into 35mm slides for slide show presentations.

To use the slide show tool, you first must create a data table on the active spreadsheet that lists the name of the graph and the length of time you want the graph on-screen (see fig. 10.29).

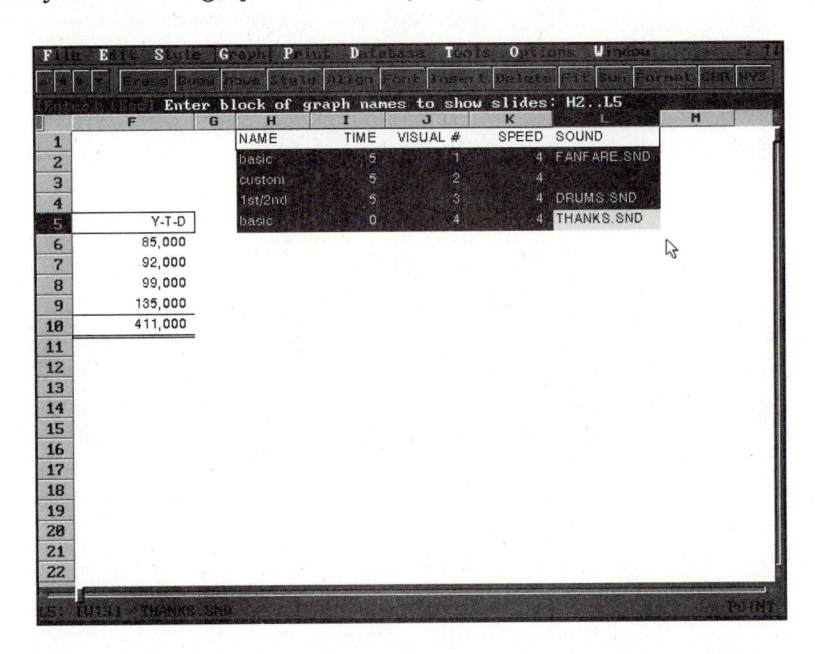

Fig. 10.29

Slide show instructions entered onto a spreadsheet.

The two columns of data shown in figure 10.29 tell Quattro Pro to display four named graphs in a slide show. Notice that each graph name is followed by an integer, which tells Quattro Pro the number of seconds to pause between each slide. To continue displaying a slide until you press a key, enter 0 (zero) next to the graph name.

To create this slide show, follow these steps:

1. Enter the data table (see fig. 10.29).

2. Preselect the range containing the data table.

3. Choose **/G**raph **N**ame **S**lide.

> **TIP**
>
> If you omit the column of data containing the slide display intervals, Quattro Pro assumes a value of 0 for each slide. To scroll forward through the slide show, you have to press a key after Quattro Pro shows each slide. Press the Backspace key or the right mouse button to scroll backward through the slide show.

When you execute /**G**raph **N**ame **S**lide, Quattro Pro begins the slide show. If a graph name does not exist, Quattro Pro skips that slide and moves down the list.

> **TIP**
>
> If you construct large slide shows that cause the program to become sluggish, you can tell Quattro Pro to store the slide show in expanded memory (if available). To use this technique, choose /**O**ptions **O**ther **E**xpanded **M**emory. When prompted, choose either **S**preadsheet Data or **B**oth.

Enhancing a Slide Show

You can enhance any Quattro Pro slide show with visual transitions and sound effects. These special effects can turn a predictable, ordinary slide show into a professional presentation that appeals to nearly all the senses.

Adding Visual Transitions

Visual transitions are special commands for creating slide-to-slide transitions like those a film editor creates between scenes in a movie. By default, Quattro Pro cuts from slide to slide, showing the next slide immediately after it removes the current slide from your screen. With visual transitions, you control the style of this transition. You can wipe from slide to slide, for example, scroll up or down, or even dissolve (fade-out) the current slide until the next slide appears.

Quattro Pro has 24 visual transitional effects, appropriately numbered 1 to 24. To use a transition, add the visual effect number to the third column in the slide show next to the column containing the slide pause times. In the fourth column, enter a number (for seconds) to specify the duration of the effect. During a slide show Quattro Pro looks into

PART II — PRINTING AND GRAPHING

columns 3 and 4 for visual effect numbers and duration numbers. If none are found, Quattro Pro immediately cuts to the next slide.

> **T I P**
>
> The best way to review all of the visual transition effects in one sitting is to create a 24-graph slide show, and apply one visual effect to each graph in the show. Highlight the **S**lide command on the **N**ame menu and press F1 for help, choose Slide, and then choose visual and sound effects to learn more about the individual transition effects.

Adding Sound Effects

To add *sound effects* to a slide show, create a fifth column in the slide show block. In this column, enter the name of a special digitized sound file. Sound effects can play through your computer's internal speaker (the default) or through an added sound card. If you install a sound card, Quattro Pro detects and uses it automatically. You can use any sound card compatible with Sound Blaster, including Sound Blaster, Sound Blaster Pro, and AdLib. Additional sounds are available from RealSound, Inc.

Your Quattro Pro package includes three sound effect files: FANFARE.SND (trumpets), DRUMS.SND (snare drum and cymbal), and THANKS.SND (voice saying "Thank you"). Also, the ProView Power Pack that arrives with Quattro Pro includes other sound effect files.

> **T I P**
>
> If you have trouble with the sound effect files, try unloading all non-essential TSR (terminate-and-stay-resident) programs from your computer's memory. If you are logged onto a network, try logging out and then running Quattro Pro again. Alternatively, if you are running Quattro Pro under Microsoft Windows in 386 Enhanced mode, try switching to Real mode.

Inserting a Graph onto a Spreadsheet

The Insert command offers another way to view a graph. Using this command, you can insert up to eight graphs onto a spreadsheet so that

10 — CREATING GRAPHS   477

you can view simultaneously the graph and the data that created the graph (see fig. 10.30).

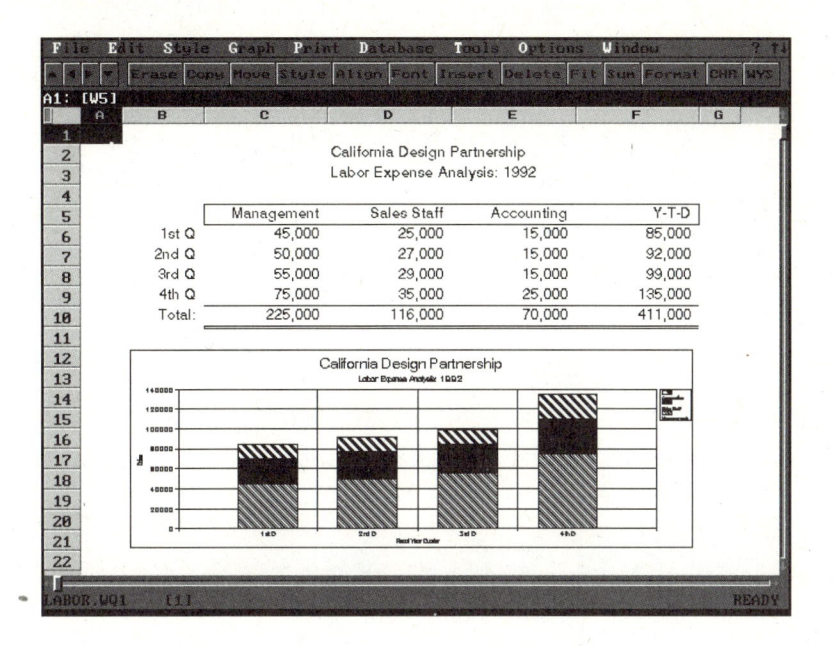

Fig. 10.30

A spreadsheet containing an inserted graph.

To view an inserted graph on a spreadsheet, you must have an EGA or VGA graphics adapter system. You also must invoke Quattro Pro's WYSIWYG display mode. When you insert a graph while in text display mode, Quattro Pro displays a blank, highlighted cell block. With any display mode you use, you can print a spreadsheet containing an inserted graph as long as you include the graph in the print range and choose /**P**rint **D**estination **G**raphics Printer.

To insert this graph onto the spreadsheet, follow these steps:

1. Choose /**O**ptions **D**isplay **M**ode **B**:WYSIWYG.
2. Preselect the target insert range—for example, B12..F23.

   NOTE The target range cannot be larger than 32 rows and 12 columns, no matter how small or large the rows and columns are.

3. Choose /**G**raph **I**nsert.
4. Highlight a graph name from the displayed names list.
5. Press Enter to insert the graph onto the spreadsheet.

When you insert a graph onto a spreadsheet, Quattro Pro floats the graph image in the target block that you specify. If this block is a cell, the inserted image is unreadable. In this situation, you have two choices.

First, you can place the cell selector in the target block and press F10 so that the graph fills your entire screen. This method is only a temporary fix because when you press Enter and return to the active spreadsheet, the inserted graph still appears in the cell. A second, better method for solving this problem is to select a larger target block and then choose /**G**raph **I**nsert again.

To remove the inserted graph from the spreadsheet, follow these steps:

1. Preselect the range—for example, B11..F20.
2. Choose /**G**raph **H**ide.
3. Highlight the graph's name on the displayed names list.
4. Press Enter to remove the inserted graph.

Questions & Answers

This chapter introduces you to the **G**raph menu commands. If you have questions concerning situations not addressed in the examples given, look through this section.

Creating a Graph

Q: When I press F10, why don't my graphs appear on my screen?

A: Remember that to display Quattro Pro graphs, you must have a graphics adapter system, and to display a graph inserted on a spreadsheet, you must set the /**O**ptions **D**isplay Mode command to **B**:WYSIWYG. Some graphics cards, such as the Hercules card, do not support the **B**:WYSIWYG display mode. You still can view a graph, just not one inserted onto a spreadsheet.

If you don't have at least a monographics display adapter system, you still can create and print graphs, but you cannot view them.

Q: Why can't I show a fast graph on my screen?

A: Assuming that you have the correct display adapter system, make sure that you have selected a valid block of data to fast graph. Quattro Pro does not make this selection for you.

The easiest way to create a fast graph is to preselect (highlight) a block of data on the active spreadsheet and then press Ctrl-G.

Q: Why doesn't my bubble graph show bubbles when I press F10 to display it?

A: Unlike XY graphs, bubble graphs require a second data series that describes the relative sizes of the bubbles. To define the relative sizes of five bubbles, for example, place the numbers 1 through 5 in a column or row next to the spreadsheet data being used as the first series data. Next, choose /**G**raph **S**eries **2**nd Series and define this data as the second series. Now press F10 to see your bubbles on the graph.

Enhancing the Appearance of a Basic Graph

Q: I created special fonts for a graph. Why aren't they showing when I press F10 to display the graph?

A: Some Bitstream font typefaces do not support bold and italic styles. Try choosing a different font typeface/style combination.

Q: How do I stop Quattro Pro from building so many fonts when I want to preview a graph?

A: Choose /**O**ptions **G**raphics Quality **D**raft to turn font-building off. Quattro Pro substitutes Hershey fonts for every Bitstream font that is not built already. While the on-screen difference between these two font styles is not dramatic, the differences on a graph printout are.

If you want to use Bitstream fonts for printing graphs, choose /**O**ptions **G**raphics Quality **F**inal before printing a graph. Quattro Pro then builds the necessary fonts for the printout.

Displaying Graphs

Q: Why do my pie graphs look like cigars?

A: Choose /**O**ptions **H**ardware **S**creen **A**spect Ratio and press the cursor-movement keys until the object on-screen becomes a perfect circle.

Q: I have a color graphics display system. Why does Quattro Pro show my graphs in black and white?

PART II — PRINTING AND GRAPHING

A: When your system has an EGA or VGA color graphics display, Quattro Pro can display graphs in black and white to give you an idea of how the graphs will appear in printed form. To do this, choose /**G**raph **O**verall **U**se Colors and choose **N**o.

If you have a color graphics adapter (CGA) card or a monochrome display, Quattro Pro can display graphs only in black and white.

Q: Why does the slide show I created display only some of the graphs I entered into the data table?

A: The slide show works only for graph names assigned to the active spreadsheet. If you included the names of graphs from other spreadsheets, Quattro Pro ignores them and continues reading down the column.

Be sure that the graph names match those created for the active spreadsheet. To check, choose /**G**raph **N**ame **D**isplay. Quattro Pro then shows a list of the valid graph names for the active spreadsheet.

You accidentally may have deleted all of the named graphs from the active spreadsheet by using the /**G**raph **N**ame **R**eset command. You have to re-create and save each graph again.

Q: Why is the graph I inserted onto a spreadsheet too small to see?

A: To increase the size of the inserted graph, select a larger target block and choose /**G**raph **I**nsert again.

Q: Why doesn't the graph I inserted onto a spreadsheet fill the target block that I preselected before executing the Insert command?

A: Choose /**P**rint **G**raph Print **L**ayout **4**:3 Aspect and choose **N**o. This command forces an inserted graph to fill the entire target cell block on the spreadsheet.

Q: I added sound effects to a slide show, but I hear nothing when I run the show. What's going on?

A: First, verify the correct spelling of the sound effect file. Next, check to make sure that you entered the file name into column five in the slide show data block. Then, verify that the name entered into the first column (the graph to which you are attaching the sound effect) is a valid graph name. Finally, be sure that the sound effect file exists and is in your /QPRO directory, or at least in a directory whose name appears in the PATH statement of your AUTOEXEC.BAT file.

Q: The sound effects that I added to a slide show are barely audible when I run the show. Is there anything I can do to amplify the sound?

A: If you're using Quattro Pro on a portable or laptop computer, you may have difficulty hearing sound effects because these systems tend to have small, low-volume output speakers. In this case, you can use a public address (PA) system to amplify the sound effects as needed.

Terminate-and-stay-resident (TSR) programs, network shell drivers, and Microsoft Windows may impede, distort, or otherwise interfere with the sound reproduction quality from your computer. If at all possible, remove these programs from memory before running the slide show.

Summary

In this chapter, you learned how to build and enhance the basic Quattro Pro graph and how to manage graph files. You also learned techniques for displaying a graph and inserting the graph onto a spreadsheet.

Having completed this chapter, you should understand the following Quattro Pro concepts:

- Understanding the anatomy and utility of a basic graph
- Choosing appropriate graph types for different data
- Creating a fast graph from a preselected block of data
- Creating a basic graph from the ground up
- Choosing individual or group series from which to create graphs
- Adding titles, legends, and customized fonts to a graph
- Creating, displaying, and erasing graph names
- Zooming and panning a graph on-screen
- Producing a slide show using graph names assigned to the active spreadsheet
- Using visual transition effects and digitized sound files to enhance a slide show
- Inserting a graph onto a spreadsheet
- Removing an inserted graph from a spreadsheet
- Copying graphs from one spreadsheet to another

PART II — PRINTING AND GRAPHING

Chapter 11 continues the discussion of building Quattro Pro graphs. In Chapter 11, you learn how to use the graph customizing commands, located in the middle of the **G**raph menu, and how to use Quattro Pro's graph editing tool to produce finished-quality, presentation-ready graphs.

CHAPTER 11

Customizing Graphs

In Chapter 10, you learned how to create and enhance the basic Quattro Pro graph. A basic graph is suitable for applications in which viewers can draw their own conclusions about the graph data. Basic graphs convey general ideas and impressions about spreadsheet data.

To leave a viewer with more than a general feeling, use the four commands located in the middle of the **G**raph menu to add impact to the graph. By using the **C**ustomize Series command, for example, you can customize the fill pattern in a bar graph, select unique marker symbols for a line graph, create unique color schemes for a pie graph, and turn basic graphs into three-dimensional displays.

You also can customize each element connected to the graph axes. If you don't like the default axis scale, design one that meets your own specifications. If you have trouble choosing between two graph types for a data set, you also can create a combination graph that uses both.

In this chapter's first section, you learn how to customize individual data series by changing colors, adding patterns, thickening lines, and using marker symbols. You also learn how to affect your data by changing bar widths and appending labels to each point in a data series.

PART II — PRINTING AND GRAPHING

The next section covers the process of creating combination graphs and teaches you how to plot a second y-axis. You also learn the differences in customizing pie and column graphs and the other Quattro Pro graph types.

The chapter continues with a presentation of the rules for customizing a graph's x-axis and y-axis. You learn how to scale an axis manually, format the values associated with tick marks, and switch between a normal and logarithmic display mode.

In the next section, you learn how to customize the overall appearance of a graph by displaying grid lines, designing special foreground and background color combinations, adding boxes around titles and legends, and displaying a graph in three dimensions.

This chapter concludes with an overview of Quattro Pro's built-in Graph Annotator tool.

Using the Graph Customize Dialog Box

Quattro Pro Version 4.0 enables you to display the /**G**raph **C**ustomize Series menu as a dialog box (see fig. 11.1). Using this dialog box, you quickly can scan and set graph customizing options such as colors, line styles, bar width, interior labels, and marker symbols. The Graph Customize dialog box eliminates the need to move up and down the layers of submenus on the **C**ustomize Series menu in order to choose and verify graph customizing options.

Notice that the graph data series appears along the top edge of the dialog box. You must select a series number before you can set the options for that series. For example, press S to select **S**eries, then press the right arrow to activate the second series, and press Enter or click 2 with your mouse. Then you can set all options for this series.

Quattro Pro displays an asterisk next to the current setting, or value, for each option in the Graph Customize dialog box. To change a setting, type the highlighted letter in the option name, press the arrow keys to move the asterisk to the new setting, or type a new value; then press Enter. To move between option categories, such as **S**eries to Color, press the Tab key. Alternatively, click the option setting you want to use and Quattro Pro immediately moves the asterisk there.

NOTE The options in the Graph Customize dialog box vary depending upon the graph type selected with the /**G**raph **G**raph Type command.

11 — CUSTOMIZING GRAPHS

Fig. 11.1

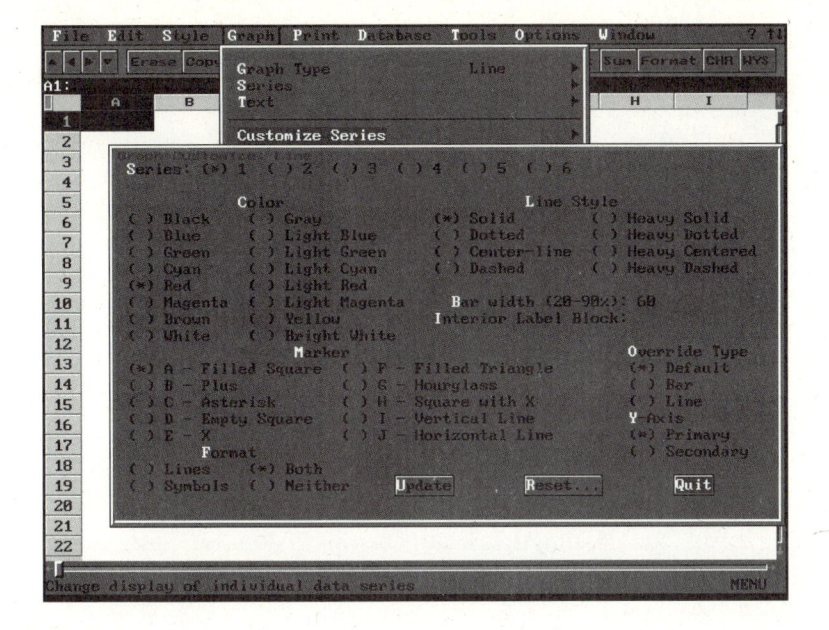

The **G**raph Customize dialog box for Line graphs.

After you finish setting options for a series, select another series or choose **Q**uit to return to the **G**raph menu. After you have set the options for all series, you can view them by selecting the series number. This feature is helpful when coordinating fill patterns or line styles and markers for multiple graph series (see fig. 11.2).

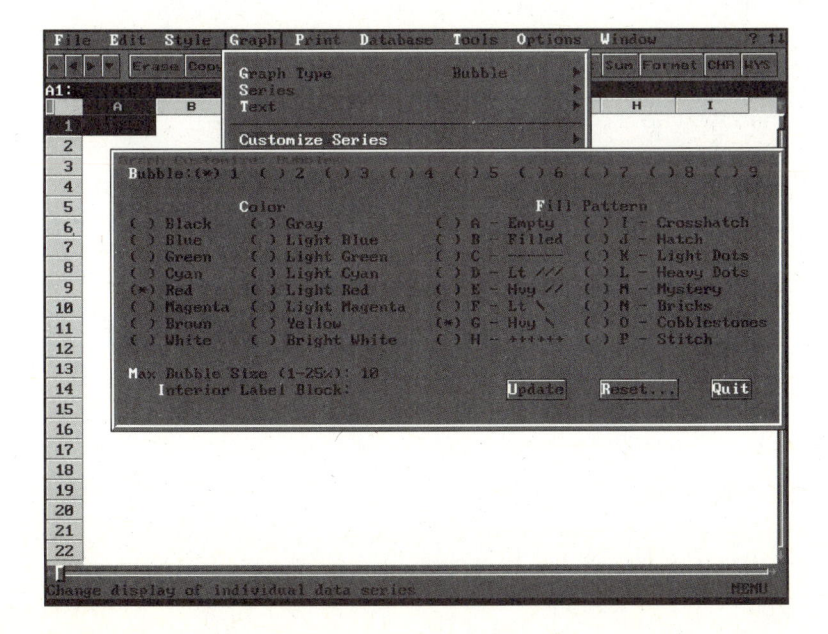

Fig. 11.2

The **G**raph Customize dialog box for Bubble graphs.

Choose **U**pdate to save all current settings as the new default, and **Re**set to return all settings to their original default setting.

The remainder of this chapter features menus instead of dialog boxes. If you prefer to use dialog boxes, you will have no trouble following the step-by-step menu instructions.

> **NOTE** By default, Quattro Pro Version 4.0 displays dialog boxes instead of menus at start-up. If you are upgrading from a previous version of Quattro Pro and prefer to display the menus instead of the dialog boxes, choose /**O**ptions Startup Use Dialog Boxes **N**o. Subsequently, each time you choose /**G**raph **C**ustomize Series, you see the menu to which you are accustomed.

For complete coverage of the other dialog boxes that are available on the **G**raph menu, see the sections titled, "Using the X-Axis and Y-Axis Dialog Boxes" and "Using the Graph Overall Dialog Box" later in this chapter.

Reviewing the Customize Series Menu Commands

The 11 commands found on the /**G**raph **C**ustomize Series menu enable you to fine-tune the appearance of a basic graph by customizing its individual parts (see fig. 11.3). Each command works on a specific part of a graph. To change the colors used to display a particular series, for example, choose the **C**olors command. To change the design of the patterns that fill the bars on a bar graph, use the **F**ill Patterns command.

Certain commands on the **C**ustomize Series menu require that you choose colors, fill patterns, line styles, and marker symbols. When you operate in text mode, Quattro Pro displays a menu of choices, listed as words. The **C**olors menu, for example, contains the names of each available color (see fig. 11.4). To make a selection, press the boldfaced letter key appearing in the option name, use the cursor-movement keys to move to a selection and press Enter, or click the name.

If you have a graphics screen display system and operate in WYSIWYG mode, Quattro Pro displays "graphic" menus, such as a palette or a gallery. The **C**olors command displays a coloring palette in WYSIWYG mode (see fig. 11.5). To make a selection, highlight the option and press Enter (or click the option) to record the new setting.

11 — CUSTOMIZING GRAPHS   487

Fig. 11.3

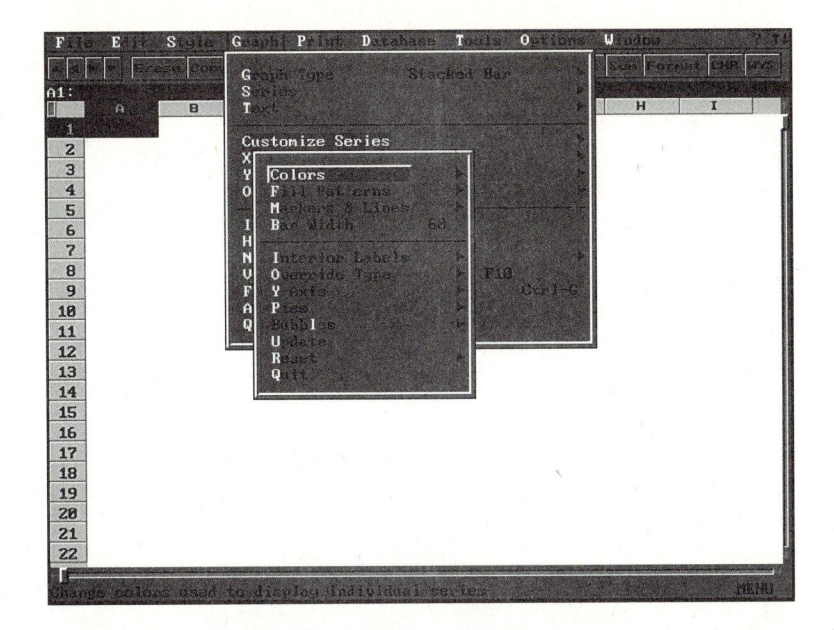

The **C**ustomize Series menu commands.

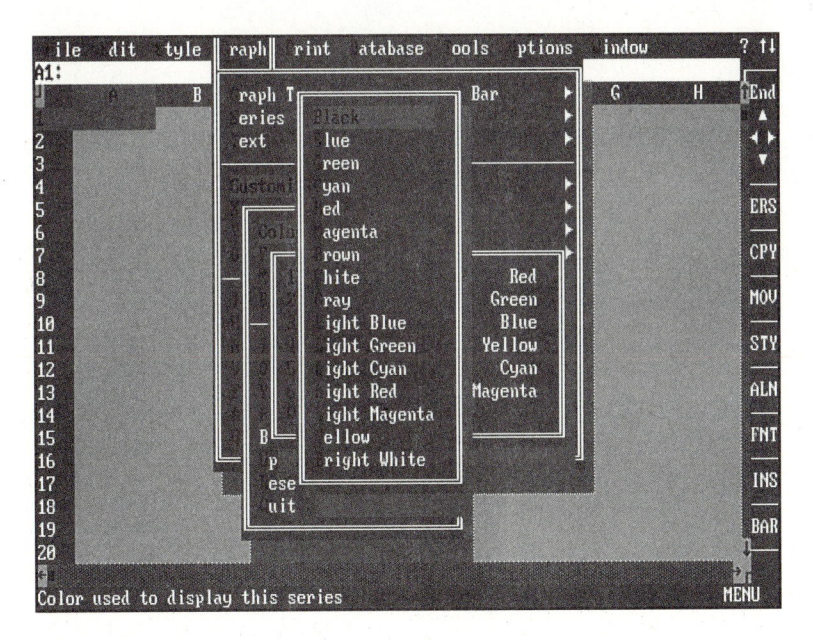

Fig. 11.4

A selection from the **C**olors menu.

All figures and instructions in this chapter assume that you are operating in WYSIWYG display mode. To see whether your system can support graphics display mode, choose /**O**ptions **D**isplay Mode. If the selection B: WYSIWYG appears, choose that option.

PART II — PRINTING AND GRAPHING

Fig. 11.5

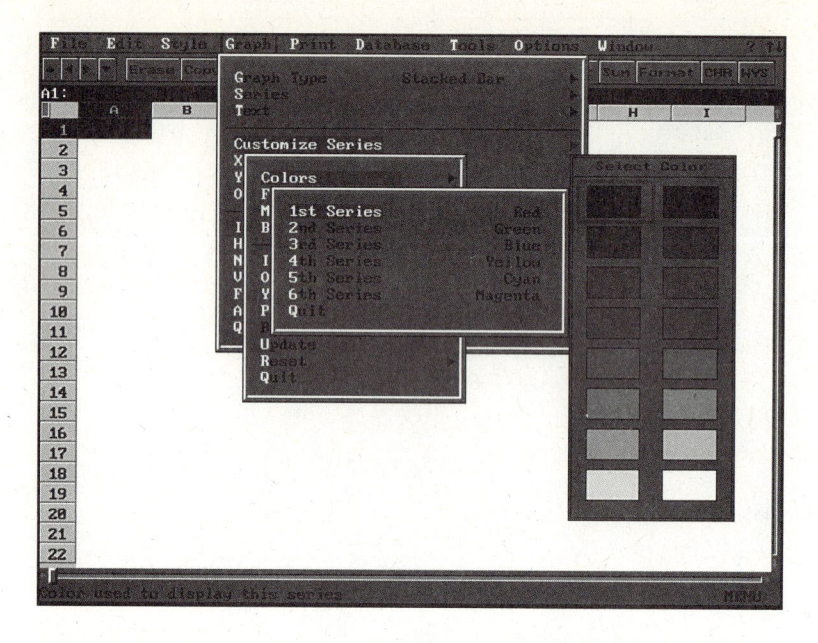

A selection from the coloring palette.

If you are using a monochrome screen display, Quattro Pro displays all data series in black. When you choose any other color on the palette, Quattro Pro displays that data series in white.

Press + (the Expand key) to display the current settings for any Customize Series command if the current settings do not display when you choose a particular command.

If you are using the same customizing commands repeatedly, consider choosing /Graph Customize Series Update to store those settings as the new default settings for use in other spreadsheets.

Customizing a Graph Data Series

When the default settings Quattro Pro uses to display a basic graph do not enhance your work, you can use any or all of the following commands to give your graphs "that extra something."

Take the time to learn how to use the customizing commands. After you are comfortable with their purpose and use, experiment with them on your own graphs. You eventually may find a use for each command during your graph-building sessions.

11 — CUSTOMIZING GRAPHS 489

A word of caution, however: you easily can go overboard when customizing a graph. With the hundreds of commands at your disposal, you may try to use too many of them on the same graph. Keep in mind that the purpose of customizing a graph is to enhance the graph data, not obscure it with unnecessary frills.

> **TIP**
>
> When you customize a graph, save the graph often with the /Graph Name Create command to ensure that you preserve the most immediate changes should your PC unexpectedly fail or lose power. When customizing several graphs during the same work session, use the /Graph Name Autosave Edits command to gain similar protection. (See "Saving Current Graph Settings" in Chapter 10 for detailed information on using the Autosave Edits command.)

Changing Colors

The Colors command stores the color settings for each data series on a graph. By default, Quattro Pro assigns a different color to each series so that you can distinguish one from the other. On a line graph in which the data series often parallel and intersect each other, for example, colored lines can help you follow the progression of a particular series.

To change the color assignment of a data series, follow these steps:

1. Choose /Graph Customize Series Colors. Quattro Pro displays a menu listing six data series and their current color assignments.

2. Choose the number of the series you want to change. Quattro Pro displays the coloring palette.

3. Highlight a color on the palette and then press Enter to record the new color assignment for that series.

   Quattro Pro returns to the Colors menu, where you can choose a new series to change.

4. Choose Quit to return to the Customize Series menu.

Changing Fill Patterns

The Fill Patterns command stores the pattern settings for each data series on a bar graph. Fill patterns help to distinguish one data series

PART II — PRINTING AND GRAPHING

from the next. Without fill patterns, to distinguish between each data series, a viewer has to match the height of each bar to a value on the spreadsheet.

To change the fill pattern assignment for a data series, follow these steps:

1. Choose /Graph Customize Series Fill Patterns. Quattro Pro displays a menu listing six data series and their current fill pattern assignments.

2. Choose the number of the series you want to change. Quattro Pro displays the Fill Patterns gallery (see fig. 11.6).

3. Highlight a pattern in the gallery and press Enter to record the new fill pattern assignment for that series.

   Quattro Pro returns to the Fill Patterns menu, where you can choose a new series to change.

4. Choose Quit to return to the Customize Series menu.

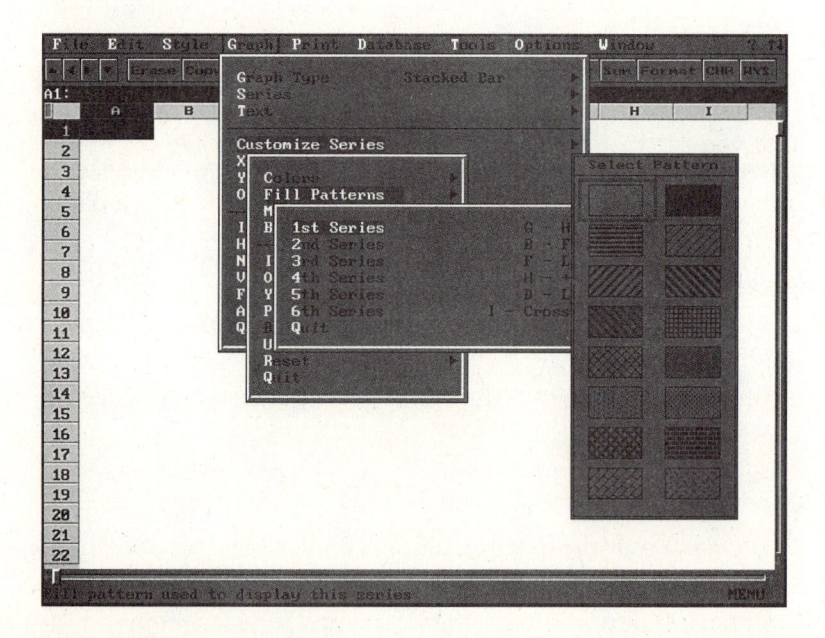

Fig. 11.6

Select a fill pattern from the gallery.

The Fill Patterns command affects only bar and area graphs. Altering the fill pattern assignments for data series that appear on a line graph or XY graph, or has no visible effect on the display of that graph. Figure 11.7 shows a graph that has custom fill patterns.

Fig. 11.7

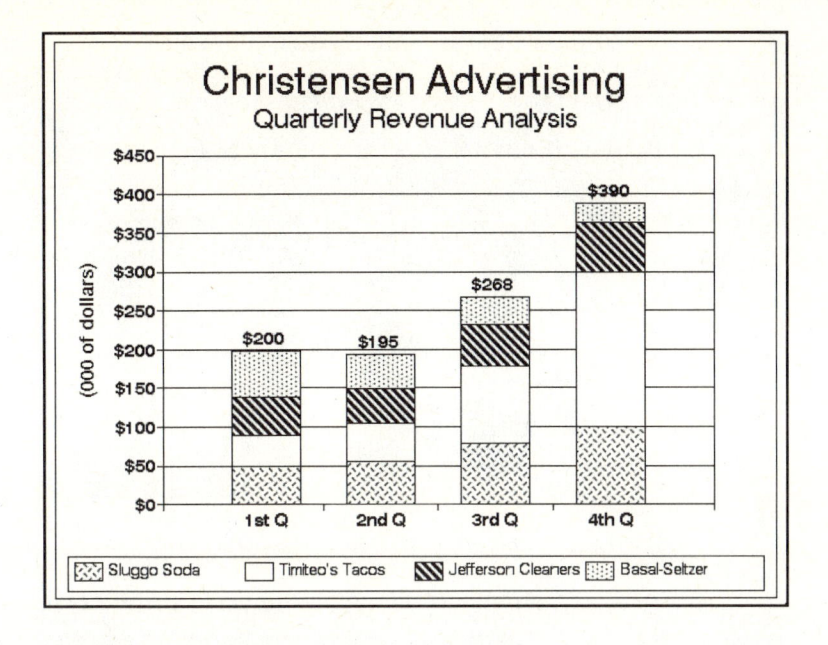

Create a custom look with fill patterns.

Changing Markers and Lines

The **M**arkers & Lines command stores the marker symbol and line style settings for each data series on a line and XY graph. This command also enables you to create your own display combinations for markers and lines.

Marker symbols indicate the location of each data point in a series. Without markers, line graphs lose much of their impact because they can describe only an overall trend rather than a series of intermediate trends. In cases in which showing an overall trend is the objective of the graph, you can eliminate the display of markers and lines.

To change the line style setting for a data series, follow these steps:

1. Choose **/G**raph **C**ustomize Series **M**arkers & Lines **L**ine Styles. Quattro Pro displays a menu listing six data series and their current line style assignments.

2. Choose the number of the series you want to change. Quattro Pro displays the line styles gallery (see fig. 11.8).

3. Highlight a line style and press Enter to record the new line style assignment for that series.

    Quattro Pro returns to the **L**ine Styles menu, where you can choose a new series to change.

PART II — PRINTING AND GRAPHING

4. Choose **Q**uit to return to the **Markers & Lines** menu.

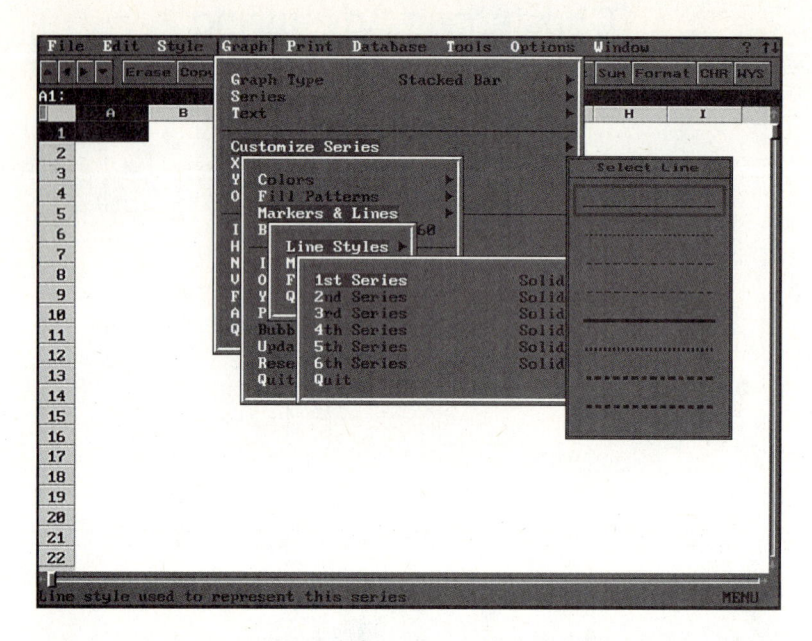

Fig. 11.8

Select a new line style from the gallery.

To change the marker symbol setting for a data series, follow these steps:

1. Choose **/G**raph **C**ustomize Series **M**arkers & Lines **M**arkers. Quattro Pro displays a menu listing six data series and their current symbol assignments.

2. Choose the number of the series you want to change. Quattro Pro displays the marker symbol gallery (see fig. 11.9).

3. Highlight a symbol in the gallery and press Enter to record the new symbol assignment for that data series.

   Quattro Pro returns to the **Markers** menu, where you can choose a new series to change.

4. Choose **Q**uit to return to the **Markers & Lines** menu.

When you want to create a custom display format for markers and lines, follow these steps:

1. Choose **/G**raph **C**ustomize Series **M**arkers & Lines **F**ormats. Quattro Pro displays a menu listing six individual data series command choices and one for the entire graph called **G**raph.

11 — CUSTOMIZING GRAPHS

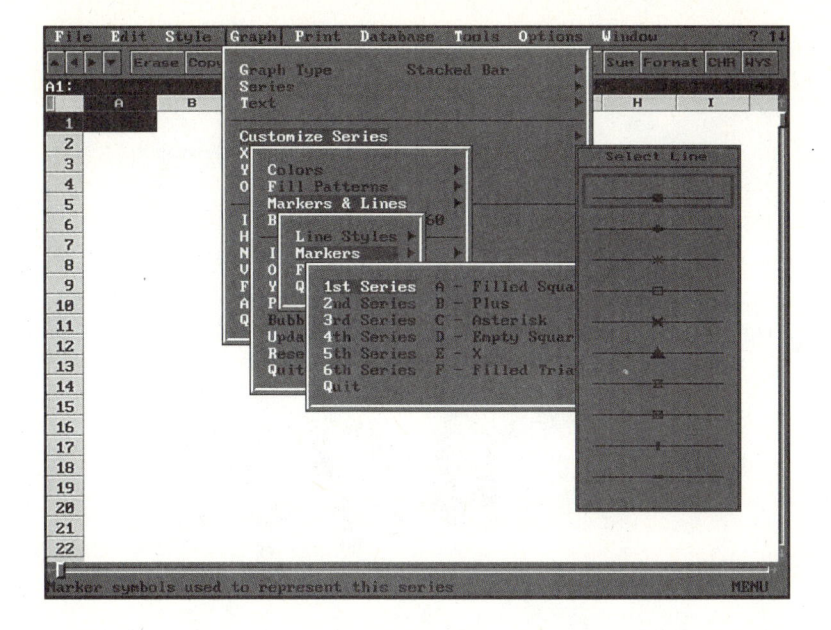

Fig. 11.9

Select a new marker symbol from the gallery.

2. Choose the number of the series you want to change or choose **G**raph to change all six data series. Quattro Pro displays a second menu listing four choices: **L**ines, **S**ymbols, **B**oth, and **N**either.

3. Press a letter to choose a display combination.

    Quattro Pro returns to the **F**ormats menu, where you can choose a new series to change.

4. Choose **Q**uit to return to the **M**arkers & Lines menu.

5. Choose **Q**uit again to return to the **C**ustomize Series menu.

Figure 11.10 shows a line graph that has customized line styles and marker symbols.

Changing the Width of Bars

The **B**ar Width command stores a value that Quattro Pro uses to determine the width of bars on a bar graph. By default, Quattro Pro creates bar widths that occupy 60 percent of the x-axis (bar) or y-axis (rotated bar) area. You can change this setting to any value in the range between 20 and 90 percent. The lower the value, the thinner the bar; the higher the value, the thicker the bar.

PART II — PRINTING AND GRAPHING

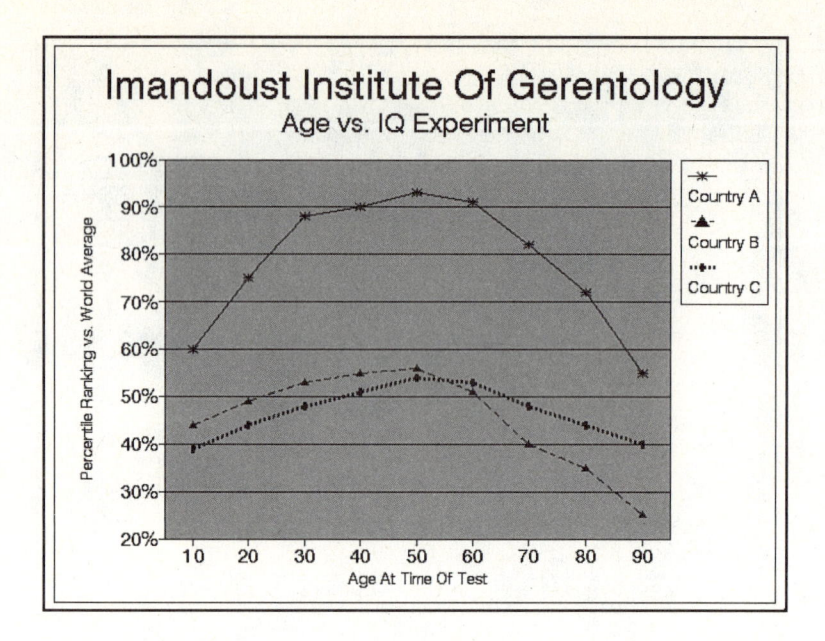

Imandoust Institute Of Gerentology
Age vs. IQ Experiment

[Line graph showing Country A, Country B, Country C — Percentile Ranking vs. World Average on Y-axis (20%–100%), Age At Time Of Test on X-axis (10–90)]

Fig. 11.10

A line graph enhanced with customized line styles and marker symbols.

To change the width value that Quattro Pro uses to build bars, follow these steps:

1. Choose /**G**raph **C**ustomize **S**eries **B**ar Width. Quattro Pro displays a dialog box listing the default width setting of 60 percent.

2. Type a number between 20 and 90 and press Enter to record that value.

When you execute this command, Quattro Pro stores the new bar width setting at the right margin of the **C**ustomize **S**eries menu, next to the **B**ar Width command.

Press F10 to view the new bar width on the current graph.

Adding Interior Labels

The **I**nterior Labels command places a value or a label from the active spreadsheet directly onto a particular data series on a graph. You can use this command to point out the exact magnitude of a data series when the axis scaling is too vague to permit accurate visual inspection. You also can add an **I**nterior label to a data series to function as an interior legend.

The **I**nterior Labels command has display restrictions dependent on the type of graph. This command, for example, has no effect on area,

11 — CUSTOMIZING GRAPHS

pie, and column graphs. Interior labels always appear above a data series on a bar graph and to the right of a data series on a rotated bar graph. On a stacked-bar graph, Quattro Pro can display interior labels for only the last, or top, data series. On a bubble graph, Quattro Pro always positions interior labels in relation to the center of the bubble.

To learn how to create and add custom annotations to any type of graph, see "Annotating Graphs" later in this chapter.

To add interior labels to a data series, follow these steps:

1. Choose /**G**raph **C**ustomize Series **I**nterior Labels. Quattro Pro displays a menu listing the six data series.

2. Choose the number of the series to which you want to add a label. Quattro Pro returns to the active spreadsheet.

3. Enter the cell address of a value or label to use.

4. Press Enter to record the address. Quattro Pro displays a second menu listing six placement choices.

5. Choose a placement choice from the menu. Quattro Pro returns to the **I**nterior Labels menu, where you can choose a new series to change.

6. Choose **Q**uit to return to the **C**ustomize Series menu.

Figure 11.11 shows a graph that has been customized by widening the bars and adding interior labels.

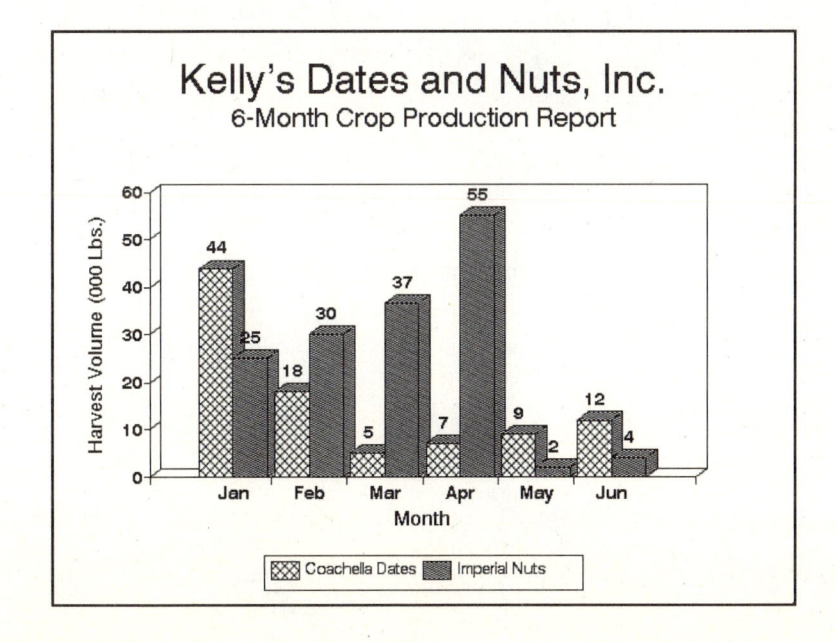

Fig. 11.11

A basic bar graph enhanced by altering the bar width and adding interior labels.

Creating Combination Graphs

If you have difficulty deciding which graph type to use for a particular set of data, consider the following novel approach to graph-building in Quattro Pro: the combination graph. This type of graph displays two graph types simultaneously on one graph.

To create this effect, use the **O**verride Type command on the **C**ustomize Series menu. Figure 11.12 shows a combination line and bar graph. This graph plots key financial data used in a firm's employee profit-sharing program. A line graph plots the firm's profits, and a bar graph plots the revenue dollars.

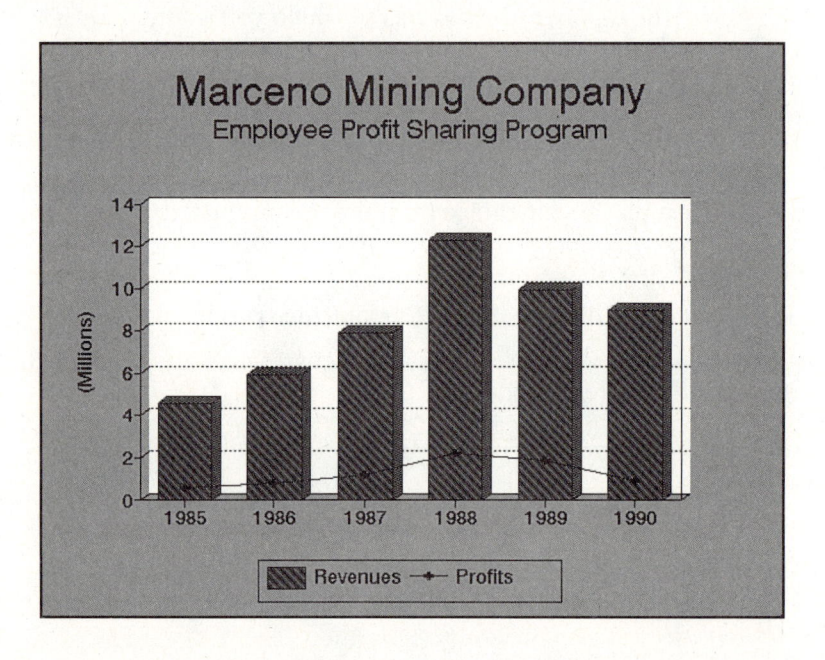

Fig. 11.12

A combination line and bar graph.

To create a combination graph using the current graph, follow these steps:

1. Choose /**G**raph **C**ustomize Series **O**verride Type. Quattro Pro displays a menu listing six data series.

2. Choose the number of the series you want to change.

3. When prompted, choose **D**efault, **B**ar, or **L**ine. Quattro Pro returns to the **O**verride Type menu.

4. Choose **Q**uit to return to the **C**ustomize Series menu.

5. Press F10 to review the combined graph on-screen.

If you choose not to override all the data series, Quattro Pro continues to use the default settings prescribed by the original **G**raph Type command selection.

Some graph types make little or no sense when united on a combination graph. Consider the difficulty you would have deciphering data appearing on a combination pie and line graph. Quattro Pro does not enable you to override area, stacked-bar, pie, column, bubble, and 3-D area graphs.

To return the current graph to its original look, choose **D**efault for each altered series on the **O**verride Type menu.

Plotting a Second Y-Axis

The **Y**-Axis command creates a second y-axis on the current graph. This technique is useful particularly for displaying data set values that have dramatically different magnitudes or use completely different systems of measurement.

Suppose that your manager has told you to create a bar graph depicting a subsidiary firm's total yearly postage expense versus the parent company's total revenues. Because the difference in the magnitudes of these two data sets is dramatic, consider creating the dual y-axis bar graph shown in figure 11.13.

Note that the word *Thousands* appears by the second y-axis to indicate that values have been scaled by a multiple of 1000. This notation helps you spot the bars that relate to this axis' scale—namely, the Revenues bars (the Postage Expense values are not likely to run into the hundreds of thousands of dollars).

To create a graph with a second y-axis, follow these steps:

1. Choose **/G**raph **C**ustomize Series **Y**-Axis. Quattro Pro displays a menu listing six data series.

2. Choose the number of the series you want to plot on the second y-axis.

3. When prompted, choose **S**econdary Y-Axis. Quattro Pro returns you to the **Y**-Axis menu.

4. Choose **Q**uit to return to the **C**ustomize Series menu.

5. Press F10 to review the graph with two y-axes.

You can move a data series to another axis by selecting that data series and then choosing **P**rimary Y-Axis or **S**econdary Y-Axis. You can continue adding data series to the secondary y-axis. Every time you add data series, Quattro Pro rescales the secondary y-axis to reflect the absolute-upper and absolute-lower range of values contained in both data series.

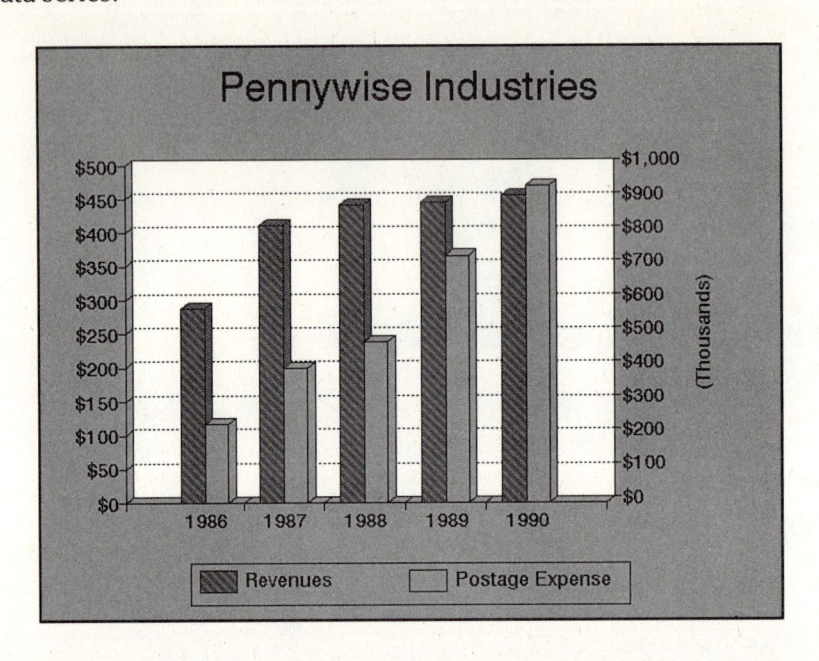

Fig. 11.13

A bar graph with two y-axes.

Now consider the graph shown in figure 11.14. This graph is a derivative of the graph shown in figure 11.12. In figure 11.12, the profits and revenues data series are measured in terms of dollars. The profit-sharing data series in figure 11.14 is expressed as a percentage of total revenues.

Customizing Pie Graphs and Column Graphs

Pie graphs and column graphs are so different from other Quattro Pro graph types that these graphs merit their own menu of customizing commands. To access this menu, choose /**G**raph **C**ustomize **S**eries **P**ies. Quattro Pro displays the menu shown in figure 11.15.

Changing the Label Format

Quattro Pro has four format options for labeling the slices of a pie graph and column graph: **V**alue; **%** (percent), **$** (dollar), and **N**one. Initially Quattro Pro displays the pie and column graphs using percent labels.

11 — CUSTOMIZING GRAPHS

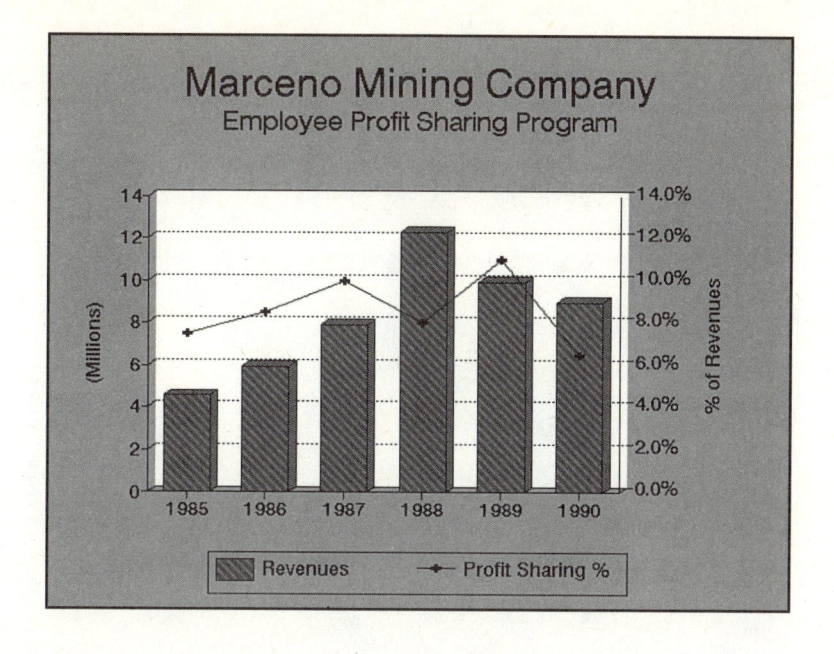

Fig. 11.14

A graph that uses data series with different systems of measurement.

To change the label format, follow these steps:

1. Choose /**G**raph **C**ustomize **S**eries **P**ies **L**abel Format.
2. When prompted, choose a label option from the displayed menu. Quattro Pro returns to the **P**ies menu, where you can choose a new item to change.
3. Press F10 to review the graph with the new label format.

The **L**abel Format command affects only the six data series elements on the **S**eries menu; the command does not affect any data series selected with the X-Axis command.

Exploding a Piece of the Pie

What pie graph is complete without at least one piece appearing exploded from the rest of the pie? Quattro Pro includes this recurrent feature in data graphing programs. To explode an element in a pie graph, follow these steps:

1. Choose /**G**raph **C**ustomize **S**eries **P**ies **E**xplode. Quattro Pro displays nine data series.
2. Choose the series you want to explode.
3. When prompted, choose **E**xplode. Quattro Pro returns to the **E**xplode menu, where you can choose a new pie slice to explode.

4. Choose **Q**uit to return to the **P**ies menu.

5. Press F10 to view the pie graph with an exploded slice.

Figure 11.16 shows a pie graph of the household budget report. The Entertainment category is exploded from the pie, and the percent symbol is added to the labels for effect.

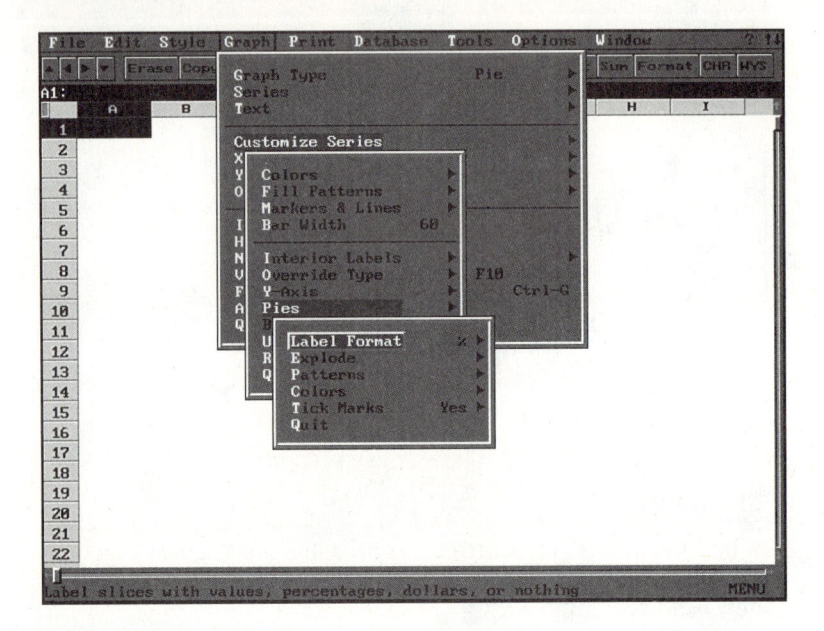

Fig. 11.15

The **P**ies menu commands.

If you want to unexplode a piece of the pie, choose the data series and then choose the **D**on't Explode option. If your data exceeds nine data series, the 10th will explode or not explode as the first slice option is specified.

Changing Fill Patterns

The **P**atterns command on the **P**ies menu stores the pattern settings for up to 9 slices of pie. Although 16 patterns are available on the fill patterns gallery, you can use only 9 at a time. When your data set exceeds 9 data series, Quattro Pro repeats the fill patterns beginning with slice 10. In other words, slice 10 and slice 1 share the same pattern setting, slice 11 and slice 2 share the same pattern setting, and so on.

Fill patterns help to distinguish one pie slice from another. Without fill patterns or labels, a viewer has difficulty distinguishing between the data series values.

11 — CUSTOMIZING GRAPHS

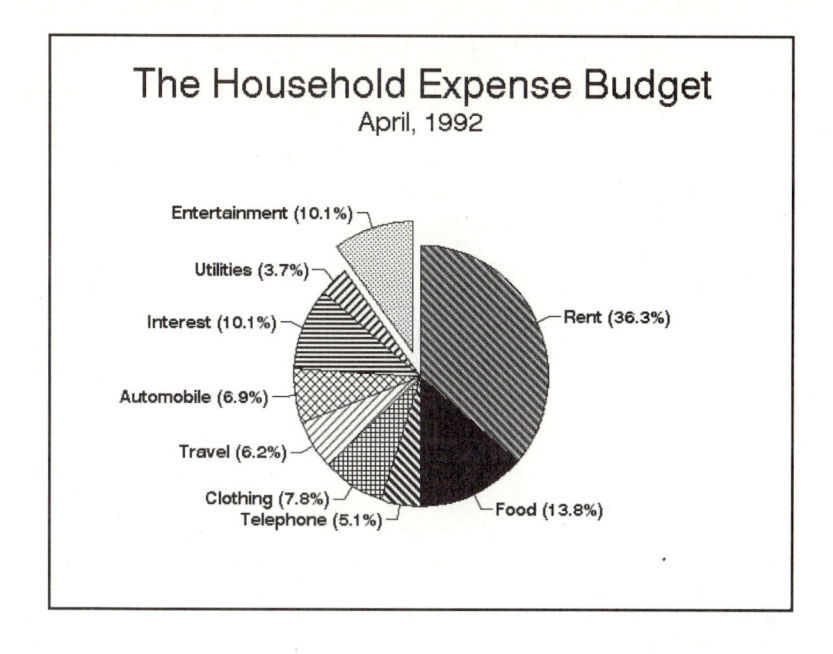

Fig. 11.16

A pie graph with an exploded pie slice, drawing attention to a data series.

To change the fill pattern assignment for a data series, follow these steps:

1. Choose /**G**raph **C**ustomize Series **P**ies **P**atterns. Quattro Pro displays nine pie slice series and their current fill pattern assignments.

2. Choose the series you want to change. Quattro Pro displays the fill pattern gallery.

3. Highlight a pattern in the gallery and press Enter to record the new fill pattern assignment for the selected series.

   Quattro Pro returns to the **P**atterns menu, where you can choose a new series to change.

4. Choose **Q**uit to return to the **P**ies menu.

Press F10 to view the new fill patterns in the graph.

Changing Colors

The **C**olors command stores the color settings for each pie slice or column section on a graph. By default, Quattro Pro assigns a different color to each series so that you can distinguish one from the other. When your data set exceeds 9 data series, Quattro Pro repeats the colors again, starting with slice 10. In other words, slice 10 and slice 1 share the same color setting, slice 11 and slice 2 share another color setting, and so on.

To change the color assignment of a data series, follow these steps:

1. Choose **C**olors from the **P**ies menu. Quattro Pro displays nine pie slice series and their current color assignments.
2. Choose the series you want to change. Quattro Pro displays the coloring palette.
3. Highlight a color on the palette and press Enter to record the new color assignment for the selected pie slice series.

   Quattro Pro returns to the **C**olors menu, where you can choose a new pie slice series to change.
4. Choose **Q**uit to return to the **P**ies menu.
5. Press F10 to view the new color selections on the graph.

Removing Tick Marks

A *tick mark* is the little line drawn from a data series label to the slice of the pie. Each time you create a column graph or pie graph, Quattro Pro draws tick marks.

To remove the tick marks from a graph, follow these steps:

1. Choose **T**ick Marks from the **P**ies menu. Quattro Pro displays an options menu.
2. Choose **N**o to remove the tick marks or **Y**es to return the tick marks to the graph.

Customizing Bubble Graphs

You customize bubbles in your bubble graph as you do slices in a pie graph. Fill patterns and colors are customized with the **P**atterns and **C**olors commands on the /**G**raph Customize Series Bubbles menu. Like a pie graph, when a bubble graph has more than nine bubbles Quattro Pro repeats the patterns and colors beginning with the tenth bubble.

Customizing the Color and Fill Patterns

To customize the fill patterns on a bubble graph, follow these steps:

1. Choose /**G**raph **C**ustomize **S**eries **B**ubbles **P**atterns.
2. Choose the bubble you want to change.
3. Choose the fill pattern.

11 — CUSTOMIZING GRAPHS

Repeat these steps for all bubbles in which you want to change fill patterns.

To customize the color of each bubble, follow these steps:

1. Choose /**Graph Customize Series Bubbles Colors**.
2. Choose the bubble you want to change.
3. Choose the color.

Repeat these steps for all bubbles whose colors you want to change.

Changing Bubble Sizes

Use the /**Graph Customize Series Bubbles Max Bubble Size** command to establish the radius of the largest bubble on a bubble graph. The radius is the distance from the center of the bubble to any point on the exterior of the bubble.

You can enter any number between 1 and 25 (see fig. 11.17). Quattro Pro views this number as a percentage of the x-axis. Therefore, if you enter 25%, the largest bubble will be one quarter the length of the x-axis; if you enter 10%, the largest bubble will occupy 10% of the x-axis, and so on. All other bubbles in the graph are sized relative to the largest bubble.

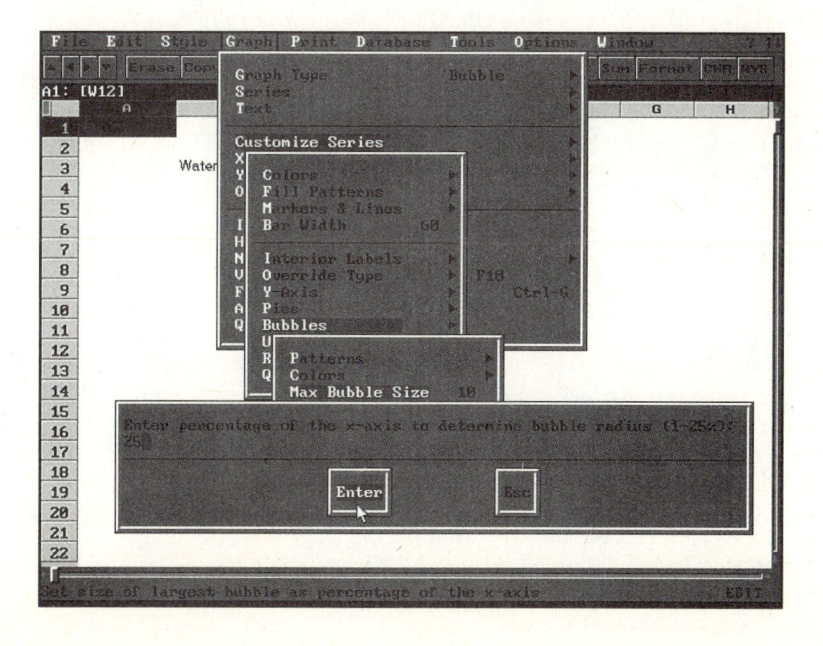

Fig. 11.17

Change the maximum bubble size for a bubble graph.

Updating and Resetting Default Settings

If you use many of the same custom graph settings for all your graphs, consider storing the values permanently by choosing the /Graph Customize Series Update command.

To erase the current graph settings and begin building a new set, choose /Graph Customize Series Reset Graph. To reset an individual series, choose the series name rather than Graph.

Customizing the X-Axis and Y-Axis

Another way you can enhance the basic graph is by altering the scale and format of a graph axis with the /Graph X-Axis and /Graph Y-Axis commands. When you create a graph, Quattro Pro scales it by looking at the range of values in each data series, recording the highest and lowest values, and then creating an axis value range encompassing these values.

A Quattro Pro graph can have up to four axes: an x-axis, a y-axis, a secondary y-axis, and a z-axis (which is reserved for 3-D graphs). Because the commands for adjusting the scales and formats of these axes are nearly identical, you generally can see how to adjust any axis by reviewing the /Graph Y-Axis command. When necessary, though, differences in the procedures or commands for adjusting an axis are pointed out in this chapter.

Using the X-Axis and Y-Axis Dialog Boxes

Quattro Pro Version 4.0 enables you to display the /Graph X-Axis and Y-Axis menus as dialog boxes. Figure 11.18 shows the dialog box that replaces the X-Axis menu. This dialog box is nearly identical to the Y-Axis dialog box; look for mention of the differences later in this section. Using these dialog boxes, you quickly can scan and set graph axis customizing options such as the axis scale, the low and high axis values, and the number of minor tick marks on an axis. The X-Axis and Y-Axis dialog boxes eliminate the need to move up and down the layers of submenus on the X-Axis and Y-Axis menus in order to choose and verify graph axis settings.

11 — CUSTOMIZING GRAPHS   505

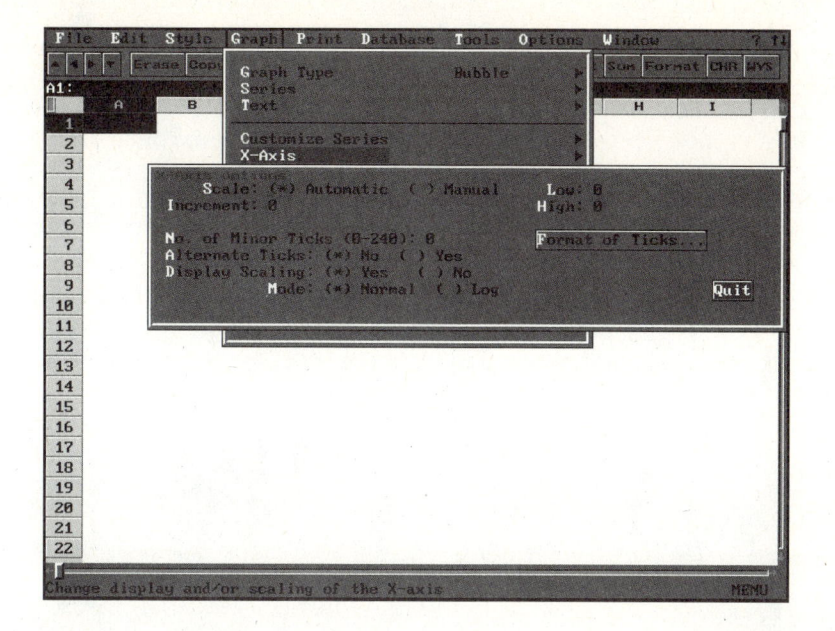

Fig. 11.18

The X-Axis dialog box.

Quattro Pro displays an asterisk next to the current setting, or a value for each option in the X-Axis and Y-Axis dialog box. To change a setting, type the highlighted letter in the option name, press the arrow keys to move the asterisk to the new setting, or type a new value, then press Enter. To move between option categories, such as **S**cale and **I**ncrement, press the Tab key. Alternatively, click the option setting you want to use and Quattro Pro immediately moves the asterisk there.

After you set options for an axis, choose **Q**uit to return to the **G**raph menu. Choose **F**ormat of Ticks to apply a numeric format to the values displayed along the current axis.

NOTE By default, Quattro Pro Version 4.0 displays dialog boxes rather than menus at start-up. If you are upgrading from a previous version of Quattro Pro and prefer to display the menus instead of the dialog boxes, choose /**O**ptions Startup **U**se Dialog Boxes **N**o. Subsequently, each time you choose /**G**raph **X**-Axis or /**G**raph **Y**-Axis, you see the menu to which you are accustomed.

For complete coverage of the other dialog boxes that are available on the **G**raph menu, see the sections titled, "Using the Graph Customize Dialog Box," and "Using the Graph Overall Dialog Box," in this chapter.

PART II — PRINTING AND GRAPHING

Adjusting the Scale of an Axis

Quattro Pro develops the scale of an axis using the highest and lowest values in the selected data series. By changing the scale of an axis, you can blow up a graph so that Quattro Pro compresses each data series to fit within a specified percentage of the graph area. You also can zoom in on a graph. Quattro Pro expands each data series so that portions of each data series may not appear on the graph.

Choose /**Graph Y-Axis** and review the **Y-Axis** menu commands. Use the **S**cale, **L**ow, **H**igh, and **I**ncrement commands to change the scale of the y- or x-axis on a graph. You can adjust the scale of the y-axis for the graph shown in figure 11.19, for example.

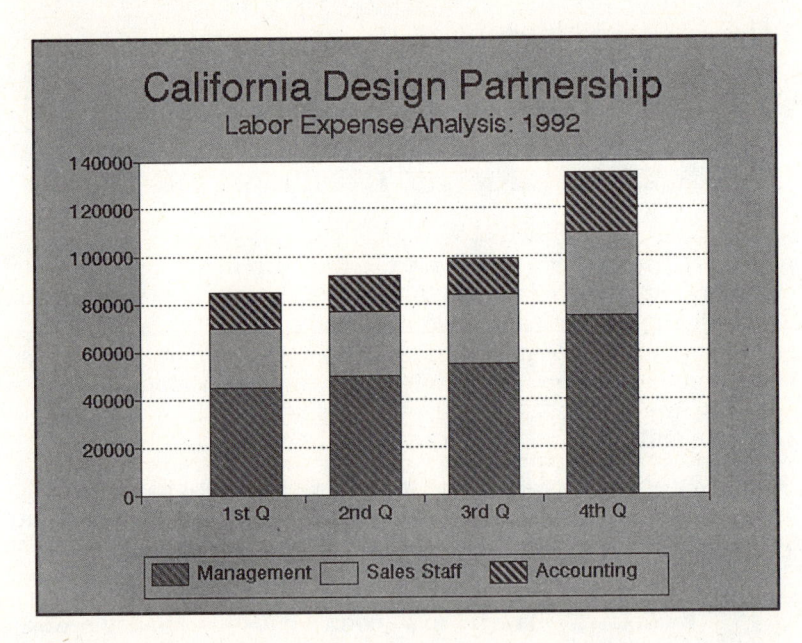

Fig. 11.19

Quattro Pro creates the scale for a graph using data series values from the spreadsheet.

Manually Scaling an Axis

The default setting for axis scaling is **A**utomatic. When you create a graph, Quattro Pro uses values from the data series to determine the scale.

To adjust the scale of the y-axis on a graph, follow these steps:

1. Choose /**Graph Y-Axis S**cale. Quattro Pro displays two **S**cale menu options.

2. Choose **M**anual. Quattro Pro returns to the **Y-Axis** menu.

When the **S**cale command is set to **M**anual, Quattro Pro uses the values stored on the **L**ow and **H**igh menus to determine how to scale an axis.

To enter high and low scaling values, follow these steps:

1. Choose **L**ow from the **Y**-Axis menu. Quattro Pro displays the **L**ow menu dialog box.

2. Type a number that you want to represent the smallest value on the y-axis. This number should be equal to or less than the smallest number in the data series. To zoom in, choose a number greater than the smallest number in the data series.

3. Press Enter to record that number. Quattro Pro returns to the **Y**-Axis menu.

4. Choose **H**igh from the **Y**-Axis menu. Quattro Pro displays the **H**igh menu dialog box.

5. Type a number that you want to represent the largest value on the y-axis. This number should be equal to or greater than the largest number in the data series. To zoom in, choose a number less than the largest number in the data series.

6. Press Enter to record that number. Quattro Pro returns to the **Y**-Axis menu.

Choosing a Scale Increment

Quattro Pro positions numbers on an axis using the **I**ncrement command setting's value. To scale an axis in increments of one thousand, for example, enter 1000.

To set an increment value, follow these steps:

1. Choose **I**ncrement on the **Y**-Axis menu. Quattro Pro displays the **I**ncrement dialog box. An increment of 0 enables Quattro Pro to increment automatically.

2. Type the number you want to use as the incremental axis scaling value.

3. Press Enter. Quattro Pro returns to the **Y**-Axis menu.

You can press F10 to view the newly scaled graph on-screen. If the scaling is unacceptable, press Enter to return to the **Y**-Axis menu and adjust each value accordingly.

Adjusting Axis Ticks

Axis ticks help you to match an axis label to its data point on a graph. Ticks also delineate regular scale intervals on an axis. In Quattro Pro, you can adjust the format and display of ticks on an axis.

Formatting Ticks

The **F**ormat of Ticks command enables you to choose a numeric display format for each value that corresponds to a tick on a graph axis. The numeric format menu that Quattro Pro displays when you choose this command is the same as the menu displayed when you choose /**S**tyle **N**umeric Format.

To format the ticks on the y-axis, follow these steps:

1. Choose /**G**raph **Y**-Axis **F**ormat of Ticks.

2. When Quattro Pro displays the **F**ormat of Ticks menu, highlight a format and press Enter to record the new format for the selected series.

3. Enter the number of decimal places, if required.

4. Press Enter. Quattro Pro returns to the **Y**-Axis menu.

> **T I P** To format the ticks on the x-axis of an XY graph, choose /**G**raph **X**-Axis **F**ormat of Ticks.

Adding Minor Ticks

When you add labels to a graph axis, Quattro Pro sometimes displays labels that overlap each other, because the width (or height) of the graph is not sufficient to accommodate the total combined width (or height) of the labels.

The **N**o. of Minor Ticks command can correct the problem of overlapping labels by replacing labels with a tick mark. This command works on all graph types except for pie and column graphs.

To skip labels on the y-axis, follow these steps:

1. Choose /**G**raph **Y**-Axis **N**o. of Minor Ticks.

2. When prompted, type a number of minor ticks to appear between each labeled tick.

3. Press Enter. Quattro Pro returns to the **Y**-Axis menu.

The default value for this command, which displays all graph labels, is 0. If you enter a number larger than the number of labels in the graph, only tick marks (and no labels) will appear.

Alternating the Display of Ticks

Setting the number of minor ticks is one way to correct the problem of overlapping labels. Another way to solve this problem is to use the **A**lternate Ticks command.

When you choose this x-axis-specific command, Quattro Pro reproduces every other tick label slightly below the x-axis labels so that long labels display in full.

To alternate labels on the x-axis, follow these steps:

1. Choose /**G**raph **X**-Axis **A**lternate Labels.

2. When prompted, choose **Y**es to alternate the labels. Quattro Pro returns to the **X**-Axis menu.

> **TIP**
> If your labels continue to overlap after you have tried both tick mark commands, shorten the label descriptions on the spreadsheet from which the graph was created.

The default setting for this command, which displays all graph labels next to each other on the x-axis, is **N**o. Figure 11.20 shows the **Y**-Axis menu after all the customizing values are entered.

You must set the **S**cale command to **M**anual, or Quattro Pro does not put the entered values into effect. Figure 11.21 shows the new form of this graph after Quattro Pro has redrawn the graph using all the new axis scaling settings.

Changing the Display of an Axis Scale

One final technique for adjusting the display of graph scales involves two commands. The **D**isplay Scaling command determines whether Quattro Pro truncates long values on an axis and then appends a scale label. The **M**ode command enables you to toggle the display of your graph between normal and logarithmic modes.

PART II — PRINTING AND GRAPHING

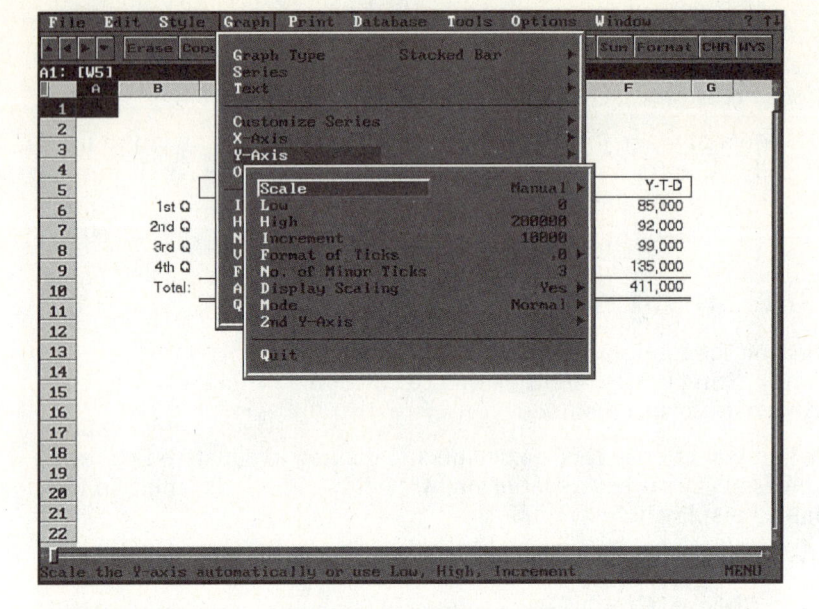

Fig. 11.20

The new scale settings stored at the right margin of the Y-Axis menu.

Fig. 11.21

An alternative display for the sample graph after manually setting the scaling values.

Adding and Removing Scaling Labels

When Quattro Pro encounters a data series that contains large numbers, the program reduces the numbers by a factor of 1,000 or 10,000 to save space on the graph area. Quattro Pro then appends a label by the axis, indicating that the numbers have been reduced.

By reducing the number 10,000,000 to 1,000, for example, Quattro Pro frees up space equal to 5 character widths—space that you can use for displaying the graph.

If you do not want Quattro Pro to scale large numerical data, follow these steps:

1. Choose /**G**raph **Y**-Axis **D**isplay Scaling.

2. When prompted, choose **N**o. Quattro Pro returns to the **Y**-Axis menu.

Press F10 to view the new form of your graph. If you decide that your graph looks better with scaled data, choose this command again and choose **Y**es on the **D**isplay Scaling menu.

Displaying Data on a Logarithmic Scale

A logarithmically scaled graph is different from the graphs covered to this point in the chapter. In normal scale mode, each data series value corresponds to a value on the graph. On a logarithmically scaled graph, each major axis division represents 10 times the value of the preceding division. You can use this scaling mode when the values in your data series have substantially different magnitudes.

Graphing zeros and negative numbers on a logarithmic scale is impossible. If you try to do so, Quattro Pro beeps and displays an error message. To scale a graph in logarithmic mode, use the following steps that include an extra step which the other scale customizing commands do not use:

1. If the lowest value on the axis to be scaled is zero or negative, rescale the axis using the **L**ow command and reset the value to 1.

2. Choose /**G**raph **Y**-Axis **M**ode. Quattro Pro displays the **M**ode menu.

3. Choose **L**og. Quattro Pro returns to the **Y**-Axis menu.

4. Press F10 to view the newly scaled graph. To return to a normal scale mode, choose the command again and choose **N**ormal from the **M**ode menu.

The final command on the **Y**-Axis menu is **2**nd Y-Axis. The menu that Quattro Pro displays after you choose /**G**raph **Y**-Axis **2**nd Y-Axis closely resembles the one shown in figure 11.20. The **2**nd Y-Axis command enables you to alter the display of any graph's second y-axis, such as the one shown in figure 11.14.

PART II — PRINTING AND GRAPHING

Customizing the Overall Graph

Consider the graph shown in figure 11.22. After you alter the individual parts of the graph, you can evaluate the overall look of the graph. Is the coloring OK? Have other customizing operations caused the graph titles and legend to lose their impact?

Using the **O**verall menu commands, you can enhance each part of this graph's overall display. You can add grid lines, draw outlines around the report titles, lighten the background colors, and even change the graph to a three-dimensional display.

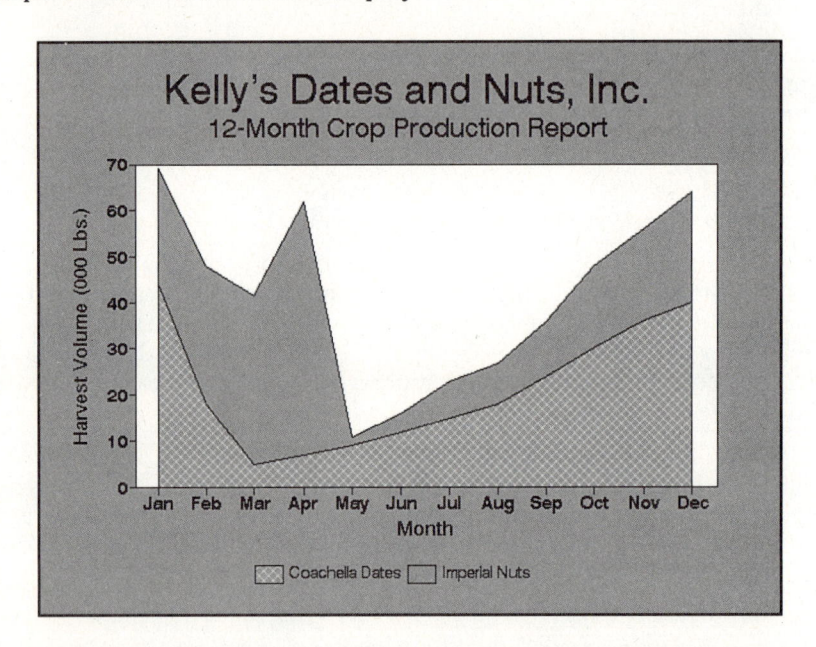

Fig. 11.22

A properly scaled graph ready for the finishing touches.

Using the Graph Overall Dialog Box

Quattro Pro Version 4.0 enables you to display the /**G**raph **O**verall menu as a dialog box. Figure 11.23 shows the dialog box that replaces the **O**verall menu. Using this dialog box, you quickly can scan and set overall graph customizing options such as outlines around titles, the legend, and the graph; the grid line style; and the colors displayed in the graph. The Graph Overall dialog box eliminates the need to move up and down the layers of submenus on the **O**verall menu to choose and verify the overall graph settings.

11 — CUSTOMIZING GRAPHS

Fig. 11.23

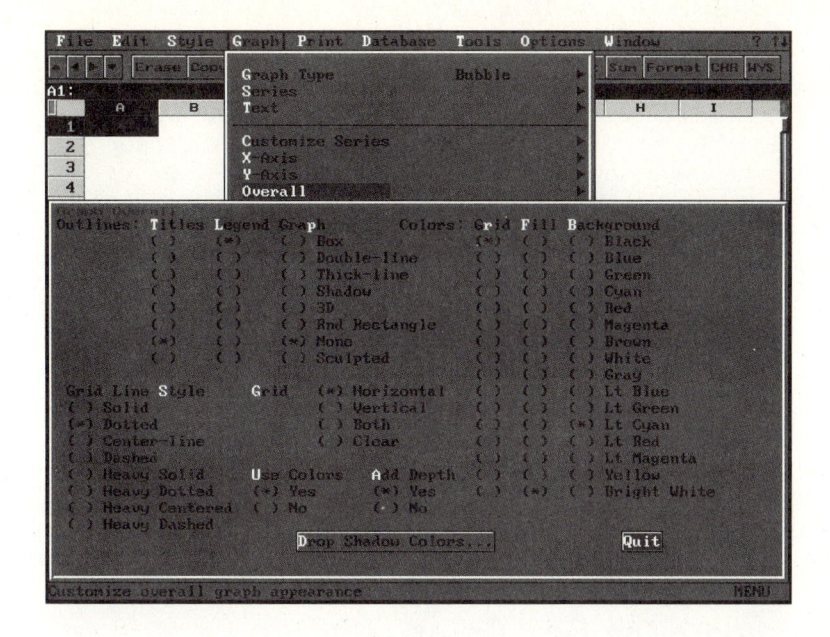

The Graph Overall dialog box.

Quattro Pro displays an asterisk next to the current setting, or a value for each option in the Graph Overall dialog box. To change a setting, type the highlighted letter in the option name, press the arrow keys to move the asterisk to the new setting, or type a new value; then press Enter. To move between option categories, such as **T**itles and **L**egend, press the Table key. Alternatively, click the option setting you want to use and Quattro Pro immediately moves the asterisk there.

After you set options for an axis, choose **Q**uit to return to the **G**raph menu. Choose **D**rop Shadow Colors to display a menu on which you can select the color pairings used to display drop shadows on a graph.

> **NOTE** By default, Quattro Pro Version 4.0 displays dialog boxes rather than menus at start-up. If you are upgrading from a previous version of Quattro Pro and prefer to display the menus instead of the dialog boxes, choose /**O**ptions Startup **U**se Dialog Boxes **N**o. Subsequently, each time you choose /**G**raph **O**verall, you see the menu to which you are accustomed.

For complete coverage of the other dialog boxes that are available on the **G**raph menu, see the sections titled, "Using the Graph Customize Dialog Box" and "Using the X-Axis and Y-Axis Dialog Boxes" earlier in this chapter.

Using Grid Lines on a Graph

Quattro Pro enables you to draw grid lines behind the data appearing in the graph area. Grid lines are like an on-screen ruler, enabling you to match data series points to corresponding axis values easily.

Adding Grid Lines

To add grid lines to a graph, follow these steps:

1. Choose /**G**raph **O**verall **G**rid. Quattro Pro displays the **G**rid menu of commands.
2. Choose **H**orizontal, **V**ertical, or **B**oth on the **G**rid menu.
3. Press F10 to view the grid lines on the current graph.

To remove grid lines from a graph, choose **C**lear on the **G**rid menu.

Changing the Grid Color

The **G**rid Color command determines the color used to display the lines surrounding the following items: the main title, legend, bars on a bar graph, pie and column slices, areas, and overall graph.

To change the color of the grid lines, follow these steps:

1. Choose /**G**raph **O**verall **G**rid **G**rid Color. Quattro Pro displays the familiar coloring palette.
2. Highlight a color on the palette and press Enter to record the new color assignment for the selected series. Quattro Pro returns to the **G**rid menu.

Changing the Line Style

You can change the line style used to display grid lines. To alter the line style, follow these steps:

1. Choose /**G**raph **O**verall **G**rid Line Style. Quattro Pro displays a menu of line styles.
2. Pick a new line style. Quattro Pro returns to the **G**rid menu.

Changing the Fill Color

You also can determine the color that Quattro Pro uses to display the graph area (the area behind the grid lines). When you change the colors used to display grid lines, you probably should change the graph area color setting. White grid lines, for example, are invisible on a graph whose fill color also is white.

To change the default color selection, follow these steps:

1. Choose /**G**raph **O**verall **G**rid **F**ill Color. Quattro Pro displays the coloring palette.

2. Choose a new color from the palette. Quattro Pro returns to the **G**rid menu.

Adjusting Outlines

When you create a graph, Quattro Pro draws a box around the legend but does not draw a box for any other part of the graph. To draw a box around other parts of the graph, use the **O**utlines command.

To draw boxes on a graph, follow these steps:

1. Choose /**G**raph **O**verall **O**utlines. Quattro Pro displays the **O**utlines menu.

2. Choose **T**itles, **L**egend, or **G**raph. Quattro Pro displays a menu of outline types.

3. Choose an outline from the menu. Quattro Pro immediately returns to the **O**utlines menu.

Quattro Pro offers eight outline styles, including the **N**one style that removes a drawn box from the graph for the selected item. These outline styles appear on the **O**utlines styles submenu shown in figure 11.24.

Changing the Background Color

You can change the portion of your screen outside the graph area (the area not affected by the /**G**raph **O**verall **G**rid **F**ill Color command). Like other color commands, when you begin to change one or more colors, you usually end up changing all the colors to maintain proper consistency.

PART II — PRINTING AND GRAPHING

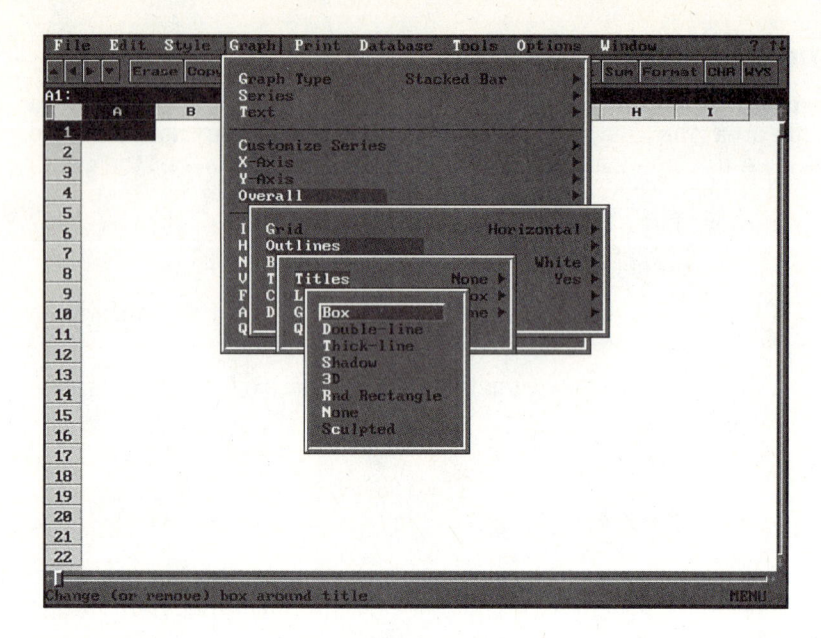

Fig. 11.24

The eight outline styles on the Outline menu.

To change the color outside the graph area, follow these steps:

1. Choose /**G**raph **O**verall **B**ackground **C**olor. Quattro Pro displays the coloring palette.

2. Highlight a new color on the palette and then press Enter to record the new color setting. Quattro Pro returns to the **G**raph menu.

3. Press F10 to view the new custom color setting.

Displaying a Graph in 3-D

Quattro Pro's capability to turn a flat graph into a three-dimensional display is one of the most impressive customizing tools on the **O**verall menu. Quattro Pro displays most graphs in this mode.

To turn a three-dimensional graph into a two-dimensional display, follow these steps:

1. Choose /**G**raph **O**verall **T**hree-D.

2. When prompted, choose **N**o.

3. Press F10 to view the new dimensional display setting.

To revert to the original three-dimensional display, choose the command again and choose **Y**es.

Toggling On-Screen Color Display

The **C**olor/B&W command on the **O**verall menu toggles the current graph between color and black and white. To use this command, choose /**G**raph **O**verall **C**olor/B&W and then choose an option from the menu.

Changing Drop Shadow Colors

In Chapter 10, "Creating Graphs," you learned that the /**G**raph **T**ext **F**ont **1**st Line **S**tyle menu offers several options for customizing the appearance of graph text. The **D**rop Shadow option adds background highlighting to title, legend, and axes text. In Quattro Pro, drop shadows are created by pairing dark colors with light colors. You can fully customize these color pairs. To change drop shadow color pairings, choose /**G**raph **O**verall **D**rop Shadow Color.

Figure 11.25 shows an example of a fully customized graph, created by using only a few of the available customizing tools. You are not obligated to use every customizing command on your graphs. The best way to learn which commands go well together is to experiment with your graphs.

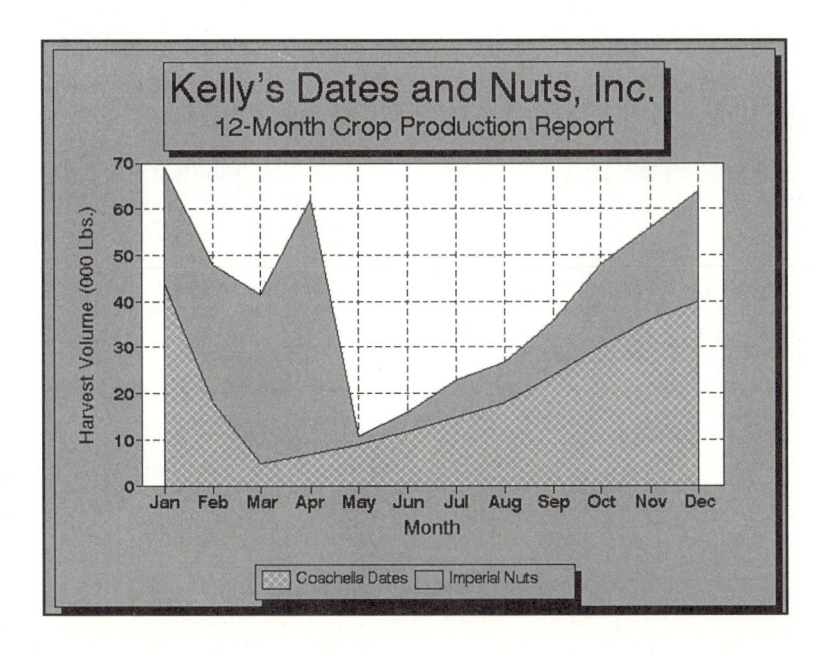

Fig. 11.25

The finished form of a customized graph.

Annotating Graphs

Using the **C**ustomize Series menu commands, you easily can turn a basic graph into a finished product. When your graph is missing that extra something, use Quattro Pro's Graph Annotator tool to finish the job.

The Graph Annotator is the final link in the graph-building process. This built-in graphics editor enables you to add descriptive text, boxes, lines, arrows, and other geometric shapes to your graphs. The easiest way to annotate a graph is by using a mouse, although you can annotate graphs from the keyboard. Without a mouse, however, you cannot use the graph buttons. For more details about graph buttons, see "Managing Graphs with Graph Buttons" later in this chapter.

To access this tool, choose /**G**raph **A**nnotate. Quattro Pro loads the current graph into the annotator environment. To load a different graph, choose **Q**uit to quit the annotator and return to the /**G**raph menu. Then, choose /**G**raph **N**ame **D**isplay, highlight the name of the graph you want to load, and then press Enter to display the graph. After the graph appears, press /. Quattro Pro loads the graph into the annotator environment.

To use the Graph Annotator, your graphics display system must meet the specifications outlined in Chapter 10.

Reviewing the Annotator Screen

A quick look at the Annotator screen reveals that this tool has many of the same features as stand-alone graphics editor programs (see fig. 11.26). In fact, finding a tool of this caliber in an electronic spreadsheet program is surprising.

A graphics editor is essentially a mouse-driven tool, but you can execute all the Graph Annotator commands directly from your keyboard.

The Annotator screen contains various icons, boxed areas, letters, and a few commands that you should find familiar.

Draw Area

Quattro Pro displays a graph in the draw area. In the draw area, you position, move, resize, delete, draw geometric elements, and paste clip art into the current graph.

11 — CUSTOMIZING GRAPHS

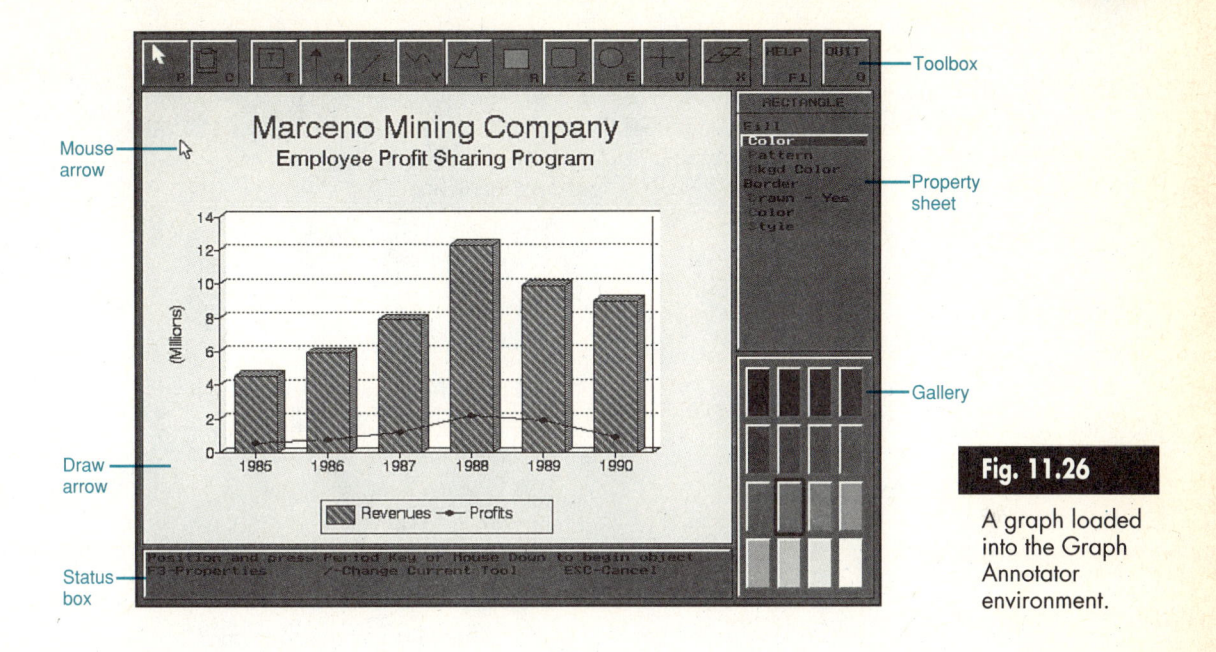

Fig. 11.26

A graph loaded into the Graph Annotator environment.

Toolbox

The toolbox is the long, rectangular row of symbols at the top of the screen. These icons describe actions that you can perform on a graph. You can add text boxes, draw arrows and lines, add geometric elements, link data series, invoke a Help window, and Quit the annotator from this facility (see table 11.1).

Press / to activate the toolbox and then press the capitalized letter beneath the icon. If you have a mouse, click any icon to activate that tool. You then can scroll through the toolbox by pressing the left- and right-arrow keys.

Property Sheet

The property sheet lists the command options available with each toolbox element. When you choose the rectangle tool, for example, the property sheet lists six command options: **C**olor, **P**attern, **B**kgd Color, **D**rawn, **C**olor, and **S**tyle (refer to fig. 11.26).

To activate the property sheet from elsewhere in the Annotator, press F3. Quattro Pro displays the command options for the active element.

PART II — PRINTING AND GRAPHING

Table 11.1 Graphics Design Elements in the Toolbox

Design Element	Description
White Arrow (/P)	Enters edit mode and enables you to change existing elements
Clipboard (/C)	Displays a list of commands in the property sheet to cut and paste existing elements
Boxed T (/T)	Adds boxed text
Arrow (/A)	Draws a line with an arrowhead at the end
Line (/L)	Draws a straight line anchored at each end
Polyline (/Y)	Draws a line anchored in two or more places, up to 1,000 points
Polygon (/F)	Draws a multisided figure with up to 1,000 points; same as Polyline, except its two ends are connected
Rectangle (/R)	Draws a rectangle with any dimensions
Rounded Rectangle (/Z)	Draws a rounded rectangle with any dimensions
Ellipse (/E)	Draws a circle using dimensions you specify
Vertical/Horizontal Line (/V)	Draws vertical and horizontal lines
Link icon (/X)	Links one or more elements to a specific point on a graph so that the elements move when the graph series change in size

Gallery

In the gallery, Quattro Pro displays special tools that are used with commands from the property sheet. When the rectangle tool is activated, for example, choose **C**olor to see the coloring palette in this area.

Status Box

The status box displays instructions, points out keyboard shortcuts, and describes menu commands when the commands are activated.

Learning Keyboard Assignments

Table 11.2 lists the Annotator-specific keys that you use to operate the feature.

Table 11.2 Graph Annotator Keys

Key	Description
F2	Enters EDIT mode when a text element is activated
F3	Activates the property sheet of the active element
F7	Resizes a group of selected elements
Shift-F7	Selects multiple elements in the draw area when used with the Tab key, with each Tab key adding an additional element to the group without unselecting the current selection
F10	Redraws the Annotator screen in full
Tab	Selects the next element in the draw area
Shift-Tab	Selects the preceding element in the draw area
Shift	Selects multiple elements in the draw area when used with a mouse; puts the mouse in a curve draw mode when drawing a polygon or polyline
Del	Erases a selected element from a group of selected elements
Period (.)	Anchors the selected element, alternating among the four corners as you press the period, so that you can resize it
Home, End, PgUp, PgDn	Move the corners of the active area diagonally
Arrows	Move or resize elements
Ctrl-Enter	Starts a new line when you are entering text or when you are in EDIT mode
Backspace	Deletes one character at a time to the left when you are in EDIT mode; connects a line with the line above it if you are at the beginning of the line
/	Activates the toolbox
Esc	Exits a menu selection and cancels an operation from the draw area
Enter	Accepts the results of an Annotation operation in the Draw area
Alt	When used with a mouse, selects multiple elements when in Proportional Resizing mode

You also may use the mouse and cursor-movement keys to move and resize a selected element or group of elements.

Annotating a Graph

When you understand how to operate the Graph Annotator, this tool is quite fun to use. To use the Graph Annotator, follow these steps:

1. Load a graph into the Graph Annotator.
2. Highlight an icon in the toolbox.
3. Position the pointer at the part of the graph you want to annotate.
4. Press Enter to move the pointer into the draw area, or click with the mouse in the Draw area.
5. Annotate symbols and text to the graph.
6. Type /Q to display the full-screen version of the graph.
7. Press any key except the / to return to the active spreadsheet.
8. Save the newly annotated graph with the /**G**raph **N**ame **C**reate command.

Figure 11.27 shows the results of annotating boxed text to a graph using these steps.

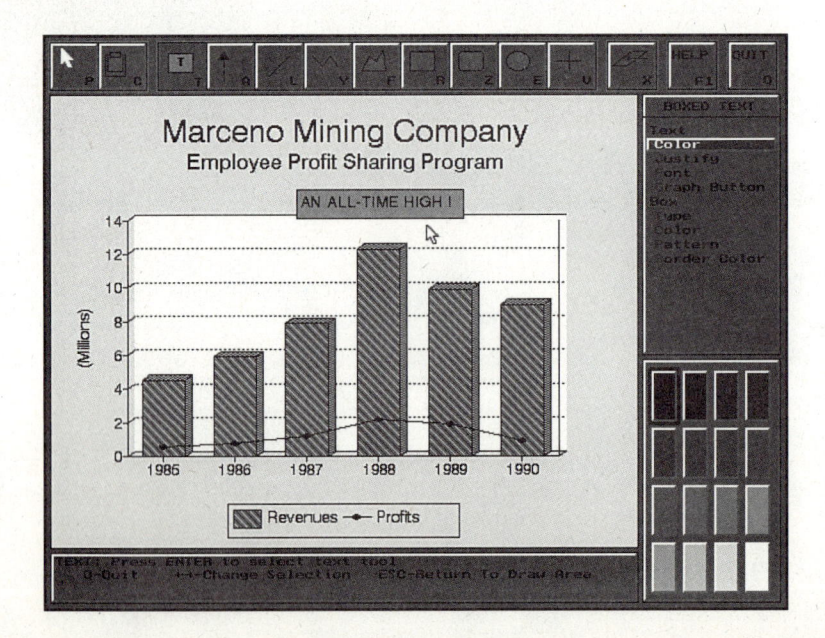

Fig. 11.27

Boxed up text added to a graph.

Selecting a Design Element

Selecting a design element is like selecting a cell on a spreadsheet. When a spreadsheet cell is active, the cell is highlighted; when a design element is selected, Quattro Pro places a ring of handles around the element (see fig. 11.28).

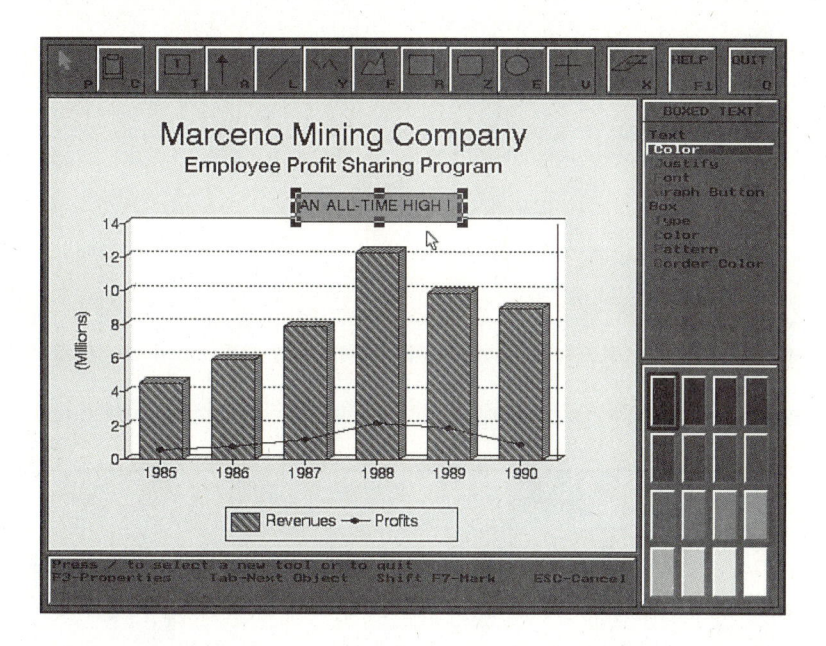

Fig. 11.28

A selected design element with handles on a graph.

Before you can perform operations on a design element, you must select that element. To select a design element using the keyboard, follow these steps:

1. Press Esc and move to the draw area.

2. Type /P to activate the arrow pointer.

3. Press Tab and Shift-Tab to relocate the arrow pointer to the target design element.

4. Press Shift-F7 to retain the current design element selection and continue selecting additional elements.

With a mouse, the process of selecting design elements is more direct. Click the design element. To select multiple elements, hold down the Shift key and click each element you want to select and add to the group.

PART II — PRINTING AND GRAPHING

Moving a Design Element

Moving a design element is like moving data from one cell into another. In the Annotator, you move a design element to reposition it on the graph.

To move a design element using the keyboard, follow these steps:

1. Press Esc and move to the draw area.
2. Select the design element you want to move.
3. Press the cursor-movement keys to relocate the element elsewhere on the graph.
4. Press Enter to anchor the design element to the new location.
5. Press Esc to unselect the design element.

To move a design element with a mouse, first select the design element. Click the element box anywhere except on the handles, drag the box to a new location on the graph, and release the button when you want to anchor the element. In figure 11.29, for example, the boxed text is moved from the top to the bottom of the graph using this procedure.

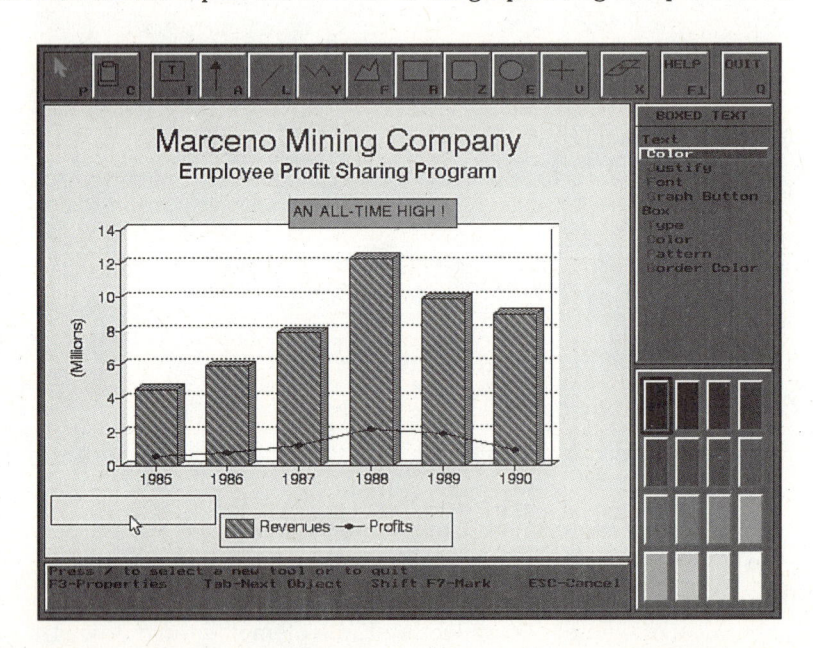

Fig. 11.29

Drag a design element to a new location on the graph.

Resizing a Design Element

Quattro Pro enables you to resize any element created in the Annotator environment. This capability gives you complete flexibility when you annotate a Quattro Pro graph. If you can change the typeface of a spreadsheet font, why not the size of a graph element?

To resize an element using the keyboard, follow these steps:

1. Press Esc and move to the draw area.
2. Select the design element you want to resize.
3. Press the period key (.) to enter Resize mode.
4. Continue pressing the period key until you highlight the corner of the element you want to resize (see fig. 11.30).

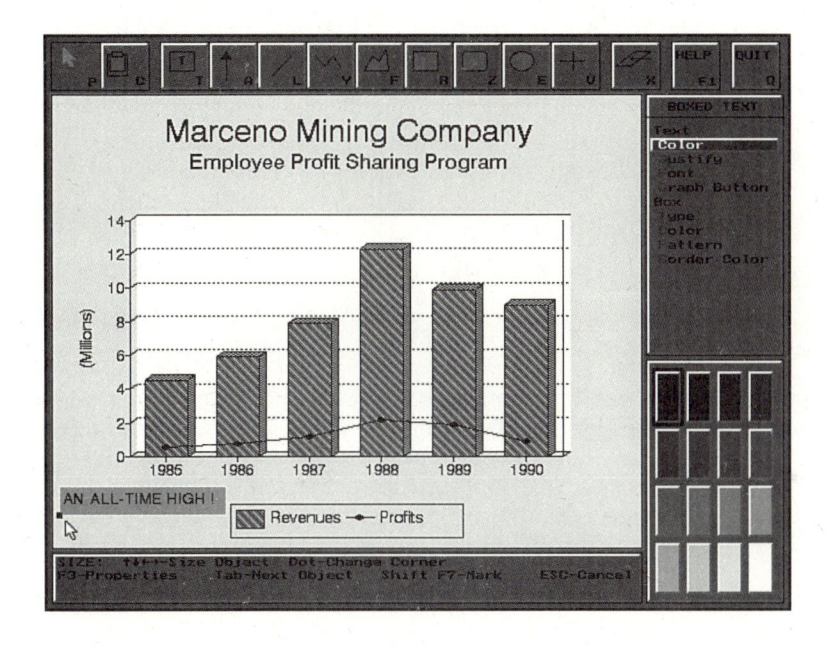

Fig. 11.30

A handle displayed in the corner of the element being resized.

5. Press the cursor-movement keys to resize the element or Home, End, PgUp, PgDn to resize it diagonally.
6. Press Enter to retain the new size.
7. Press Esc to unselect the element and not change the size.

To resize an element using a mouse, begin by selecting the element. Click any box appearing on the outline of the selected element and drag until the desired size is attained. Release the mouse button to retain the new size.

Editing a Text Design Element

To edit any text design element that originated in the Annotator environment, follow these steps:

1. Press Esc and move to the draw area.//
2. Select a text design element to edit.
3. Press F2 to enter EDIT mode.
4. Edit a design element's text using the same keys and procedures you use for editing spreadsheet cells.
5. When you finish editing the text, press Enter to reaffix the modified design element to the graph.

NOTE You also can perform **C**lipboard menu operations on a selected design element. To delete a group of selected elements, position the arrow pointer over the element and press Del.

Setting Design Element Properties

Each design element has a unique set of cosmetic properties that determines how Quattro Pro displays the element. If you annotate boxed text to a graph, for example, you can return later and change its color, justification, box style, text font, border color, and fill pattern. You also can set all the design element properties beforehand; later, when you annotate that element to a graph, the preset properties are in effect.

To preset the properties for a design element, follow these steps:

1. Select a design element icon from the toolbox.
2. Press F3 to display that element's property commands in the property sheet.
3. Press the boldfaced letter key in the command name to select the command.
4. Choose the desired property from the options displayed in the gallery area. Quattro Pro returns you to the property sheet.
5. Continue editing properties as desired.
6. Press Esc to return to the draw area.

The new properties will be in effect for the next time you select that element. In figure 11.31, for example, besides the text being edited, several of the boxed text properties are altered.

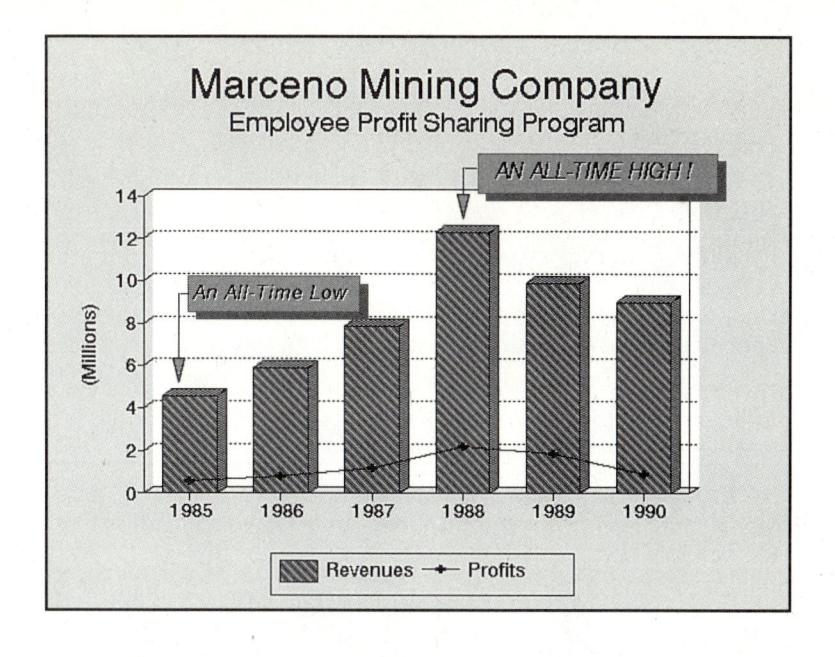

Fig. 11.31

Altered design element properties to add clarity and impact to a graph.

The new font is smaller to de-emphasize the "all-time low" data point, the text displays in an italic typeface with a grey drop shadow, and the box now appears with a shaded background. Finally, an arrow is added to connect the boxed text to a data series on the graph.

Using the Clipboard

Use the Clipboard icon commands to manage your annotation elements. When you activate this icon, Quattro Pro displays nine commands in the property sheet area.

These commands enable you to cut, copy, paste, and delete selected elements in the draw area. You also can create and paste clip art to and from other graphs using these commands. In fact, Quattro Pro comes with its own library of clip art that you may import into the Annotator for use with your graph files.

To copy a piece of clip art into the current graph, follow these steps:

1. Select an element in the draw area.
2. Activate the **C**lipboard icon by typing /C.
3. Select **C**opy to copy an element
4. Choose **Q**uit to quit the toolbox. Quattro Pro returns you to the current graph, or to the active spreadsheet if no graph is displayed.

PART II — PRINTING AND GRAPHING

5. Select **/G**raph **N**ame **D**isplay to display a different graph.
6. Press / to load the displayed graph into the Annotator.
7. Activate the **C**lipboard icon by typing /C.
8. Choose **P**aste From to copy the element from the **C**lipboard into the draw area.

Use this sample operation as a guideline for choosing and executing other **C**lipboard menu operations. In most cases, the sequence of steps is the same. Fortunately, you quickly can learn the **C**lipboard menu commands because their functions are fairly obvious from their names.

Use the final three commands on this menu to move elements in and out of clip art files for use with other Quattro Pro graphs or with applications that can read the CLP file format.

Quattro Pro can import clip art in the Computer Graphics Metafile (CGM) file format. To import a CGM file, follow the same rules to import Quattro Pro's CLP clip art.

If you want to export modified clip art to use in a different graphics editor program—PC Paintbrush, for example—follow these steps:

1. Activate the **C**lipboard icon by typing /C.
2. Choose **C**opy To to create a copy of the modified clip art file.
3. When prompted, type a file name and specify the CLP file-name extension. Press Enter to record the new clip art file name.

Linking an Element to a Graph Data Series

The Graph Annotator redraws itself periodically as you move in and out of the draw area. When redrawing happens, Quattro Pro retains the integrity of the selected elements with which you are working.

If later you recall an annotated graph into the Annotator, the Clipboard graph looks the same, as long as you have not modified any of the original graph settings. One way to guard against the possibility of ruining your annotation work, if you choose to alter a graph's settings, is to link an annotation element to a graph data series.

This technique maintains the original organization of the annotated graph as long as the original data series definition stays intact. When you do change series settings and remove the data point that you linked to, Quattro Pro moves the linked annotation element with the data series.

To link an annotation element to a data series on the current graph, follow these steps:

1. Select the element in the draw area.

2. Type /X to choose the **L**ink command.

3. When prompted, choose the number of the data series you want to link.

4. When prompted, type in the link index number (the relative position of the data series point to the whole data series).

5. Press Enter to create the link.

The link between the data series and the selected element remains intact until you reset a data series by choosing the /**G**raph **C**ustomize **S**eries **R**eset command or change the series to include fewer elements than the link index number.

Managing Graphs with Graph Buttons

Quattro Pro offers additional graph management capabilities with special action buttons called graph buttons. A *graph button* is boxed text that you place onto a graph. To distinguish a graph button from other boxed text, use the **G**raph Button command that appears in the property sheet area when you activate the Boxed **T**ext icon. This command enables you to assign special actions to the boxed text.

After you assign an action to boxed text, it becomes a graph button. When you click a graph button, Quattro Pro executes the action assigned to the button. Clicking a graph button may display another graph, for example, execute a macro, or even start a slide show. You decide what action the graph button takes.

> **NOTE** You must use a mouse if you want to execute a graph button on a graph. No keyboard method exists for executing a graph button. Even without a mouse, however, you can create and add graph buttons to a graph. This option is useful if you later want to test the graph buttons on a PC that has a mouse.

Figure 11.32 shows one way to use graph buttons. The six graph buttons (labeled 1985 through 1990) on the Marceno Mining Company graph perform six separate tasks. When you click graph button 1985, for example, Quattro Pro displays a graph containing detailed financial information for 1985. The boxed text containing the label `Detail?` is

PART II — PRINTING AND GRAPHING

just that—boxed text. No special operation is assigned to this element, so the boxed text serves as an introductory heading for the six graph buttons below it.

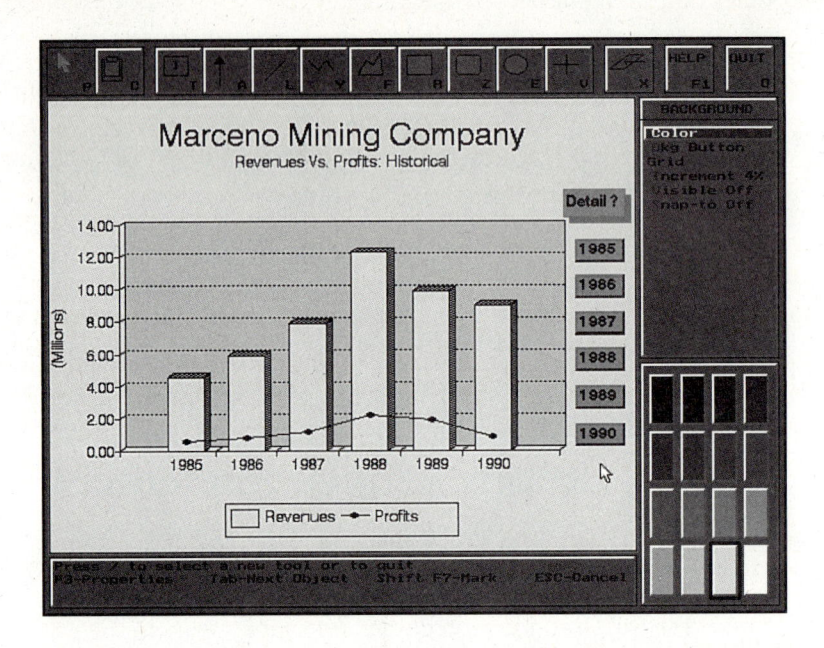

Fig. 11.32

A graph with graph buttons used to branch to other graphs.

To use graph buttons, you need to know the following rules:

- You must use the /Boxed **T**ext **G**raph Button command to activate a graph button.

- A graph button is "live" only when the graph displays in full-screen mode. To display the graph full screen, press F10 or choose /**G**raph **V**iew.

- You must have a mouse to use a graph button. When you display a graph that contains graph buttons, Quattro Pro also displays the mouse arrow pointer.

- Graph buttons appearing on graphs in a slide show can branch only to other graphs. Quattro Pro ignores macros assigned to graph buttons if you try to run them during a slide show.

Creating and Activating a Graph Button

Before you can use a graph button, you must draw and then activate the button with the **G**raph Button command. To create and activate a graph button, follow these steps:

11 — CUSTOMIZING GRAPHS

1. Load a graph into the Graph Annotator environment.

2. Draw a boxed text element on the graph. Include a word or two in the boxed text that describes the action you want the graph button to take.

3. Move and resize the boxed text so that you easily can see it. The text shouldn't interfere with data shown on the graph.

4. Highlight the boxed text and then type /T to activate the Boxed Text menu.

5. Choose the **G**raph Button command. Quattro prompts you to supply a name (see fig. 11.33).

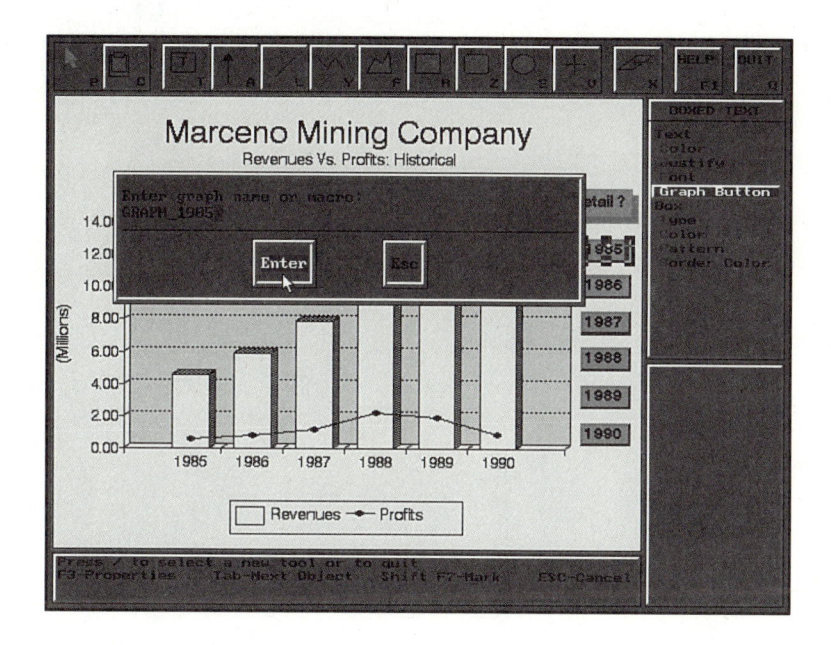

Fig. 11.33

Enter the name of a graph to activate the graph button.

6. If you want the button to branch to another graph, then type the name of a graph that is saved with the active spreadsheet.

7. If you want the button to execute an existing macro, type the name of the macro. If you want the button to execute a macro command, type any string of macro command(s) of up to 80 characters.

8. Choose **Q**uit to leave the Graph Annotator. Quattro Pro displays a full-screen version of the active graph.

9. Press Enter or Esc to return to the active spreadsheet.

PART II — PRINTING AND GRAPHING

10. Choose /**G**raph **N**ame **C**reate and save the current graph settings, including the new graph button settings, unless **A**utosave Edits is set to Yes.

A graph button does nothing until you execute the **G**raph Button command. If you draw boxed text elements on a graph and forget to activate them, the elements do not work when you click them.

> **TIP**
>
> Graph buttons are not active when the graph is in the Graph Annotator environment or when the graph is inserted onto a spreadsheet. To activate a graph button, you must display the graph so that it entirely fills your screen (see fig. 11.34). When you click a button on a fully displayed graph, Quattro Pro performs an action, such as displaying another graph or returning to the original graph.

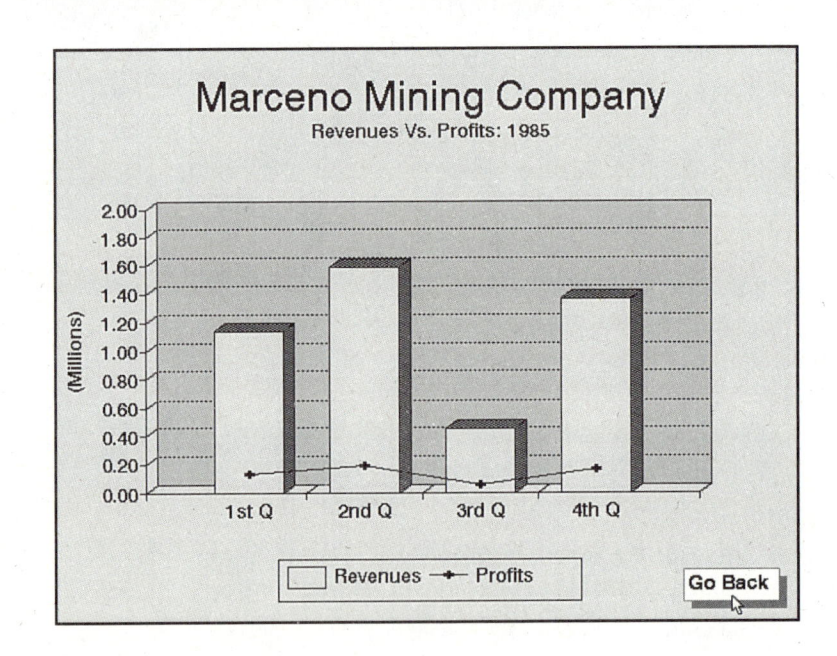

Fig. 11.34
A full-screen graph display.

Renaming and Deactivating a Graph Button

You can redefine a graph button's action by assigning a new graph or macro name to that button. Use the following steps:

1. Reload the graph into the Graph Annotator environment.

2. Highlight the graph button you want to edit, type /T to activate the Boxed **T**ext icon, and then choose the **G**raph Button command located in the property sheet area. Quattro Pro displays a dialog box with the current name.

3. Press the Backspace key until you entirely delete the name.

4. Type a new name and press Enter to rename the graph button.

To deactivate a graph button, use the following steps:

1. Reload the graph into the Graph Annotator environment.

2. Highlight the graph button you want to edit, type /T to activate the Boxed **T**ext menu, and then choose **G**raph Button. Quattro Pro displays a dialog box with the current name assignment.

3. Press the Backspace key until you entirely delete the name.

4. Press Enter to deactivate the graph button.

Turning a Graph Background into a Graph Button

By default, clicking a graph background while in full-screen display removes the graph from your screen and returns to the spreadsheet. With respect to graph buttons, this feature can be a nuisance. Suppose that in an attempt to execute a graph button, you inadvertently click just outside the boxed text area. Doing so causes Quattro Pro to cancel the graph and return to the spreadsheet. Because you did not intend this result, you must display the graph again and start over.

You can eliminate this nuisance with the **B**kgd Button command. This command enables you to assign a special operation to the background of a graph as though it is a graph button. To access this command, type /P or click the Edit icon. The command appears in the property sheet area. Now assign a special operation to the background of a graph so that clicking that area does not remove the graph from your display. The logical operation to assign, for example, is one that tells Quattro Pro to display the current graph every time you click the graph background. Do this by typing the name of the current graph.

> **T I P**
> When you click the background of a graph that has been defined as a graph button, the mouse pointer disappears from the display. The pointer disappears regardless of the operation you assign to the graph background. Slide the mouse in any direction to display the pointer again.

Annotating and Managing Multiple Graph Elements

The Graph Annotator has several commands that enable you to annotate and manage multiple graph elements more easily. The first set of commands simplify the process of aligning elements as you add them to a graph. These commands appear on the Background menu in the property sheet area when you activate the Edit icon. The second set of commands perform operations on groups of elements you have annotated to a graph. These commands appear on the Group menu in the property sheet area whenever you select more than one element.

Adding Multiple Elements to a Graph

A rudimentary but often used method for aligning elements on a graph involves moving and resizing the elements after they are annotated. This method relies on your visual inspection skills and usually requires you to spend extra time fine-tuning the placement of the element to get it just right.

The Annotator alignment grid is very useful when you have specific placement objectives for multiple elements that you are annotating to a graph. The Annotator alignment grid also enables you to align elements automatically as you annotate them to a graph.

To display the alignment grid, follow these steps:

1. Load a graph into the Graph Annotator environment.
2. Type /P to activate the Edit icon or click the Edit icon in the Toolbox.
3. If you are using a keyboard, press F3 to move to the property sheet, highlight the **Visible** command, and press Enter. With a mouse, click **Visible** in the property sheet area.

Quattro Pro displays the alignment grid at the top of the graph now displayed in the Annotator. To show the grid is active, Quattro Pro displays the word On next to the **Visible** command in the property sheet area.

Use the **Increment** command to fine-tune further the element placement process. This command alters the distance between the dots in the alignment grid. You can achieve very small placement differences between multiple elements on a graph, for example, by increasing the density of the dots in the alignment grid. This method is similar to using a measurement system based on millimeters rather than centimeters.

11 — CUSTOMIZING GRAPHS

To alter the density of the dots appearing in the alignment grid, use the following steps:

1. Load a graph into the Graph Annotator environment.
2. Type /P to activate the Edit icon or click the Edit icon in the Toolbox.
3. If you are using a keyboard, press F3 to move to the property sheet, highlight the Increment command, and press Enter. When using a mouse, click Increment in the property sheet area.

   Quattro Pro prompts you to enter an increment setting in the range from 1 to 25. A setting of 1 produces the highest density of dots, whereas a setting of 25 produces the lowest density. The percentage refers to % of an edge, with an edge consisting of 100 dots; therefore, 4% is 25 dots x 25 dots, 25% is 4 dots x 4 dots, 1% is 100 dots x 100 dots, and so on.

4. Type a number and press Enter.

Quattro Pro immediately redraws the alignment grid to reflect the new Increment command setting.

When the alignment grid is on, you can use the Snap-to command to align elements while you annotate them to a graph. When the Snap-to command is set to On, each object you add to a graph moves to the nearest grid line. To align multiple elements, place the elements near the same grid line as you annotate them to a graph. This command can save you valuable time when building a graph because it eliminates the need to "visually inspect" and fine-tune object placements after you annotate them to a graph.

Use the following steps to align elements while you annotate them to a graph:

1. Load a graph into the Graph Annotator environment.
2. Type /P to activate the Edit icon, or click the Edit icon in the Toolbox.
3. If you are using a keyboard, press F3 to move to the property sheet, highlight the Snap-to command, and press Enter. With a mouse, click Snap-to in the property sheet area. The word On appears next to the Snap-to command in the property sheet area.

TIP

With Snap-to set to On, the alignment grid aligns elements annotated to a graph whether the Visible command is set to On or Off.

Performing Operations on Groups of Elements

After you annotate several elements to a graph, you sometime may want to modify the alignments of those elements. Again, the rudimentary method for doing so involves a great deal of moving and resizing. Quattro Pro fortunately provides you with a much more efficient way to change the alignments of a group of elements.

Using the **A**lign command, you can realign simultaneously a group of selected elements. The alignment choices for this command are as follows: **L**eft Sides, **R**ight Sides, **V**ert (vertical) Centers, **T**ops, **B**ottoms, and **H**oriz (horizontal) Centers.

The following steps demonstrate how to modify the alignment for a group of selected elements:

1. Load a graph into the Graph Annotator environment.

2. Using the element selection procedure described earlier in this chapter, select a group of elements that you want to align. Quattro Pro displays the Group menu commands in the property sheet area.

3. If you are using a keyboard, press F3 to move to the property sheet, highlight the **A**lign command, and press Enter. With a mouse, click **A**lign in the property sheet area.

4. Choose an alignment option from the menu that Quattro Pro displays. Quattro Pro immediately realigns the group of selected elements.

> **TIP** You can modify other characteristics for a group of selected elements using the remaining commands on the **G**roup menu. You can change simultaneously the fill **C**olor, the fill **P**attern, or the **B**kgd (background) color, for example, for a group of selected elements.

Questions & Answers

This chapter introduces you to Quattro Pro's graph customizing commands. If you have questions concerning particular situations that are not addressed in the examples given, look through this section.

Q: When I press F10, why don't my graphs appear on-screen?

A: Remember, to display Quattro Pro graphs, you must have a graphics adapter system, and to display a graph inserted on a spreadsheet, the /**O**ptions **D**isplay Mode command must be set to **B**:WYSIWYG.

Q: Why do most of my color selections for the data series appear white?

A: You probably have a monochrome display system. With this type of system, you should change color selections with care. Remember that any color selection other than black always appears white when you display the graph.

Q: When I save a Quattro Pro spreadsheet in a Lotus 1-2-3-compatible format, why don't the spreadsheet's graphs display in color?

A: Quattro Pro does not store graph color information when you create 1-2-3-compatible spreadsheets from your Quattro Pro spreadsheets. If you retrieve the 1-2-3-compatible spreadsheet into Quattro Pro, however, the graph colors return to their default settings.

Q: Why doesn't Quattro Pro show the fill pattern selections I make for my pie graphs and column graphs?

A: You used the /**G**raph **C**ustomize Series **F**ill Patterns command to choose the new fill pattern. Instead, choose the /**G**raph **C**ustomize Series **P**ies **P**atterns command.

Q: Why is Quattro Pro showing the same marker symbol for all the text appearing in a legend box?

A: You selected the same marker symbol for every data series via the /**G**raph **C**ustomize Series **M**arkers & Lines **M**arkers command. Choose this command again and specify a different marker symbol for each data series. Quattro Pro updates the displayed symbol in the legend box.

Q: I cannot see any marker symbol assignments on the **M**arkers menu. Where are they?

A: Press the Expand key (+) on your numeric keypad to display a full view of the **M**arkers menu (or any menu for that matter) marker assignments.

Q: Quattro Pro keeps displaying a line graph when I want to display an area graph. How can this happen?

A: If you began by creating a combination graph, you must reset any overridden data series before selecting a new graph type. Choose /**G**raph **C**ustomize Series **O**verride Type **D**efault and reset all applicable data series.

Q: Does a quick way exist to erase a graph and begin all over again?

A: Yes. Choose /**G**raph **C**ustomize Series **R**eset **G**raph. Quattro Pro erases the current graph and returns to the default graph settings. Change the default settings to the current settings by choosing Update.

Q: I cannot seem to adjust the x-axis scale on a line graph. What's going on?

A: Quattro Pro enables x-axis scale adjustments only to XY graphs. To get around this restriction, you can add extra data series on your spreadsheet that define the upper and lower limits of the scale you want to create. Be sure to choose the /**G**raph **S**eries command again and define the new series so that Quattro Pro shows the series on a graph. Choose **N**either for **F**ormats under **C**ustomize Series if you don't want these numbers to show.

Q: I cannot seem to alter the numeric format of the x-axis values on an area graph by using the /**G**raph **X**-Axis **F**ormat of Ticks command. What's going on?

A: Quattro Pro enables x-axis numeric format adjustments only to XY graphs. To get around this restriction, return to the active spreadsheet, choose /**S**tyle **N**umeric Format, and format the cell data you want to alter. When you display the graph again, it reflects the new numeric formats.

Q: I thought that Quattro Pro displays most graphs in three-dimensional form. Why aren't any of my graphs displaying in 3-D?

A: The graphs you create may make three-dimensional display impossible for Quattro Pro. When a bar graph has numerous bars or when a pie graph has many slices, for example, the program may be incapable of displaying in three dimensions. To correct this situation, you can reduce the number of displayed data points in each series until the graph does display in 3-D or choose Bar Width and change it to 90%.

If you saved a set of graph defaults that included no 3-D display, Quattro Pro does not display graphs this way. To change this situation, choose /**G**raph **O**verall **T**hree-D **Y**es and then choose /**G**raph **C**ustomize **S**eries **U**pdate.

Alternatively, choose /**G**raph **G**raph Type **3**-D and choose one of the four new three-dimensional graphs styles available on this menu.

Q: Why does Quattro Pro superimpose a text graph on my current graph?

A: Anything you do in the Graph Annotator environment affects the current graph. To create a text graph by itself, save the current graph setting with the /**G**raph **N**ame **C**reate command and then reset the current graph settings. Choose /**G**raph **C**ustomize Series **R**eset **G**raph.

Summary

In this chapter, you learned how to turn a finished graph into a presentation-quality visual aid, using the commands found in the middle section of Quattro Pro's **G**raph menu. You also learned how to use the Graph Annotator tool, Quattro Pro's special built-in graphics editor facility.

Having completed this chapter, you should understand the following Quattro Pro concepts:

- Changing colors, fill patterns, markers and lines, and bar widths for individual data series
- Appending labels to individual points in a data series
- Creating combination bar and line graphs
- Plotting two y-axes on one graph
- Plotting two or more data series that use different systems of measurement
- Changing label formats, colors, fill patterns, and tick marks on pie and column graphs
- Changing colors, fill patterns, and bubble sizes on bubble graphs
- Updating and resetting the default **C**ustomize Series menu command settings for use with other spreadsheets
- Manually adjusting the default axis scale
- Adjusting, formatting, adding, and deleting axis tick marks
- Displaying a graph on a logarithmic scale
- Using grid lines, outlines, background colors, and special display settings to enhance the overall appearance of a graph

PART II — PRINTING AND GRAPHING

- Using the Graph Annotator to append boxed text, arrows, lines, and geometric figures to a graph
- Pasting clip art to and from the Annotator tool for use on graphs
- Using and managing graph buttons

Chapter 12 concludes the discussion of Quattro Pro graphs by introducing you to a feature that is completely new in Version 4.0: analytical graphing. In this chapter, you learn how to use the commands on the /Graph Series Analyze menu to combine a large data set into a smaller data set—making it easier to graph and interpret the data—without changing any information in your spreadsheet. The chapter also shows you how to analyze graphs using moving averages, linear fit lines, and exponential fit lines.

CHAPTER 12

Analyzing Graphs

In this chapter you learn another method for analyzing spreadsheet data that also involves graphs. This technique, called *analytical graphing*, is much different from the graphing techniques described in Chapters 10 and 11.

Analytical graphing enables you to graph the same data in several different ways without modifying the spreadsheet itself. With analytical graphing you can display custom groupings of data, moving averages, "best fit" linear lines, and more. You perform all of these operations using the commands on the /Graph Series Analyze menu.

In the first section of this chapter, you learn about the commands on the Analyze menu. This material provides you with all the specifics you need to apply analytical graphing techniques to your own spreadsheet data.

The second section explains an analytical graphing technique called *aggregation*. Aggregation, or the grouping of data, helps to convey general impressions about large sets of data. You may want to graph average quarterly stock performance using a spreadsheet that contains only daily totals, for example.

The next section introduces an analytical graphing technique based on the concept of moving averages. A *moving average graph* smooths widely fluctuating values by displaying progressive averages. When computer chip production totals vary widely, for example, a moving average graph may help to shed light on an overall production trend.

The chapter continues by showing how to use a third analytical graphing tool called *linear regression*. This tool enables you to graph a line that is representative of—or "best fits"—the data you are evaluating. Statisticians, economists, and forecasters use linear regression to predict future events (such as next year's sales) based on historical data.

The final analytical graphing technique is called *exponential graphing*. Like the linear fit line, data displayed in an exponential fit line often reveals general trends when trends exist. The exponential fit line, however, actually looks like a decreasing or increasing curve.

Defining Analytical Graphing

By now you realize that although designing and building complex, involved spreadsheet applications can be challenging and even fun, the real fruits of your labor should come in the form of healthier decision-making, improved reporting, and increased productivity. After all, you use Quattro Pro to aid you in the task of managing and presenting your data.

In other words, how you organize your spreadsheet data affects your ability to access and use that information efficiently. A spreadsheet that organizes total daily expense figures is overkill when management wants to analyze average weekly expenses. To correct the situation, should you start all over and build a new spreadsheet application?

Figure 12.1 shows a typical spreadsheet. In this application, the historical annual sales figures in column C are used in the formulas that appear in columns D through F. These formulas produce other values that are used to create a sales forecast for future years. The content of this spreadsheet isn't so important as is the notion that to evaluate sales information in terms of trends and historical performance, you must create formulas to manipulate the raw data.

12 — ANALYZING GRAPHS

Spreadsheet screenshot showing:

J. Testa Clothiers
Sales History: 1981 - 1991

Year	Sales ($000)	3-year moving ave.	5-year moving ave.	Growth in sales
1981	125			
1982	200	161.7		60.0%
1983	160	203.3	207.0	-20.0%
1984	250	236.7	232.0	56.3%
1985	300	266.7	257.0	20.0%
1986	250	291.7	285.0	-16.7%
1987	325	291.7	315.0	30.0%
1988	300	341.7	325.0	-7.7%
1989	400	350.0	350.0	33.3%
1990	350	375.0		-12.5%
1991	375			7.1%
1992	To be forecast			

Fig. 12.1

The J. Testa Sales History spreadsheet application.

If browsing through the numbers in this spreadsheet isn't sufficient to convey an impression about what's in store for J. Testa Clothiers in the future, then the next step may be to display all of the information in a graph (see fig. 12.2).

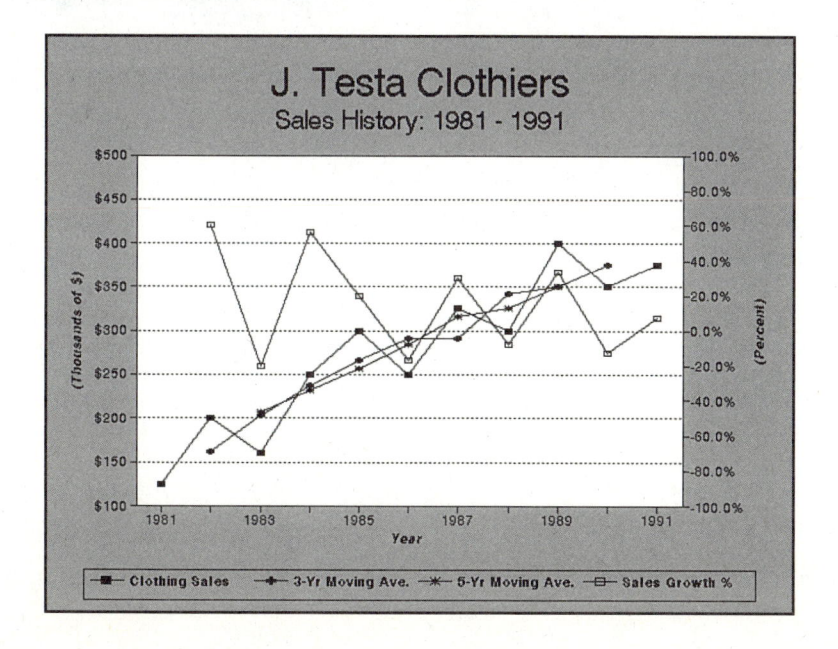

Fig. 12.2

The J. Testa Sales History graph.

PART II — PRINTING AND GRAPHING

You can use the graph customizing commands described in Chapter 11, "Customizing Graphs," to add a legend and custom axis formatting to the graph.

Instead of one, you now have two documents in hand, and the task of evaluating your information suddenly becomes twice as challenging. To streamline such efforts, Quattro Pro offers a powerful data evaluation tool called *analytical graphing*. In analytical graphing, you make menu selections (rather than build new spreadsheets) when you want to evaluate your data in a different light.

To use this tool, you start with a spreadsheet containing data and access the commands on the /**G**raph **S**eries **A**nalyze menu.

Reviewing the Analyze Menu Commands

You use the commands on the **A**nalyze menu to select a data series—including x-axis data that displays on an XY graph—for analysis. You must select at least one data series to do analytical graphing. To perform the same type of analysis for every data series defined on the /**G**raph **S**eries menu, choose the **A**ll option.

Table 12.1 describes the purpose of each **A**nalyze menu command.

Table 12.1 Analyze Menu Commands

Command	Description
1st Series	Selects the first data series for analysis
2nd Series	Selects the second data series for analysis
3rd Series	Selects the third data series for analysis
4th Series	Selects the fourth data series for analysis
5th Series	Selects the fifth data series for analysis
6th Series	Selects the sixth data series for analysis
X-Axis Series	Selects the x-axis data series for analysis
All	Selects all data series, including the x-axis data series, for analysis

You have complete freedom to choose which series you want to analyze. Quattro Pro enables you to analyze any data series, as long as the series has been defined on the /Graph Series menu. You can analyze the first and third series, for example; the first, second, and fourth series; the sixth series by itself; and so on.

Selecting the Analysis Option

Selecting a series for analysis always leads to the same submenu, on which you identify the type of analysis you want to perform on the selected series. When you choose **1**st Series, for instance, you see the same menu of choices as you do when you choose **2**nd Series, **3**rd Series, and so on.

Table 12.2 describes the purpose of each analysis option on the **A**nalyze *n*th Series menu.

Table 12.2 Analyze *n*th Series Menu Commands

Command	Description
Aggregation	Identifies the series time period, selects the aggregation time period, and chooses a method for transforming the data
Moving Average	Identifies a number of data points to average and chooses whether or not to create a weighted average
Linear Fit	Displays data on a "best fit" linear regression line
Exponential Fit	Displays data on an increasing or decreasing exponential curve
Reset	Clears the **A**nalyze menu settings in preparation for a new analysis
Table	Displays analytical graphing data in a table in the spreadsheet

TIP

To perform three different types of analysis on the same data series and to display the results of each analysis on the same graph, choose /**G**raph **S**eries **1**st Series through **3**rd Series and identify the same spreadsheet range each time. On the **A**nalyze menu, select a different analysis type for each data series to be analyzed.

The next few sections define the rules and outline the procedures for using the four analytical graphing tools: aggregation, moving average, linear fit, and exponential fit. In the following sections, examples are provided to explain the use of each tool and to help you to envision uses for analytical graphing in your own daily spreadsheet activities.

You also learn how to use the **R**eset and **T**able options to clear menu settings and copy the results of an analysis into the current spreadsheet.

> **NOTE** The examples throughout this chapter offer sufficient coverage of each analytical graphing tool to enable you to use all or most of the features available on each menu. You can consult an economics, mathematics, or sales forecasting text for more comprehensive presentations of the proofs and axioms on which these tools are based.

Using Aggregation Analysis

By using aggregation, you can group (or *transform*) two or more data points and plot them as a single point on a graph. The plotted point can represent the sum, average, standard deviation, minimum, or maximum of the data.

Plotting aggregated data is useful for making large, unwieldy data sets more manageable to work with. Displaying aggregated data on a graph also can reveal relationships that may not be obvious just from looking at the numbers in your spreadsheet.

Reviewing the Aggregation Options

The options on the **A**ggregation menu enable you to define the scope of a data transformation (see table 12.3). All you need to know is the time frame represented in a data series, the time frame you want to see in the aggregated data, and the method for transforming the data.

The **S**eries Period option tells Quattro Pro about the time frame represented in a data series. When identifying a series period for your data, you have five choices: **D**ays (the default), **W**eeks, **M**onths, **Q**uarters, and **Y**ears. If your data series contains daily values, for example, choose **D**ays on this menu. If the data series contains yearly data, and for your purposes a year represents 360 days, choose **Y**ears.

Table 12.3 Aggregation Menu Commands

Command	Description
Series Period	Defines the current time period of a data series
Aggregation Period	Selects the aggregation time period for a data series
Function	Selects the method for transforming the data series

Quattro Pro treats data identified with the **W**eeks, **M**onths, **Q**uarters, and **Y**ears settings as being equal to 7, 30, 90, and 360 days, respectively. Even though certain months have 31 days and a year consists of 365 days, this method for defining time periods has a negligible effect on the results from an analysis.

The **A**ggregation Period option tells Quattro Pro the time frame to use when grouping a data series. You always must choose an aggregation period that is larger than the series period. If you specify an aggregation period that is smaller than the series period, Quattro Pro displays the error message `Series period interval must be smaller than aggregation period interval` when you try to view the graph.

When identifying the aggregation period for your data, you have five choices: **W**eeks (the default), **M**onths, **Q**uarters, **Y**ears, and **A**rbitrary. If you want to aggregate weekly data into quarterly data, for example, choose the **Q**uarters option.

> **TIP**
>
> No daily aggregation period exists because daily is the smallest available series period. In other words, aggregating daily figures into daily figures does not make sense.

You use the **A**rbitrary setting to identify aggregation periods that are not available on this menu. When you select this option, Quattro Pro prompts you for an aggregation period value. Enter any value between 2 and 1000 that represents the number of days you want to use. If your data is organized by days and you choose an arbitrary aggregation setting of 3, for instance, Quattro Pro aggregates the data into groups of three days.

Although this rule may not make much sense to you now, it may become clearer to you after you learn how Quattro Pro transforms aggregated data. This process is discussed in the next section, "Performing a Basic Aggregation Analysis."

The **F**unction option tells Quattro Pro how to transform the data when the program aggregates the data. Quattro Pro offers six methods for transforming data values, each of which is based on one of the six following @function commands:

- The **S**UM setting uses the @SUM function to total the values appearing in a data series.

- The **A**VG setting uses the @AVG function to average the values appearing in a data series.

- The **S**TD setting uses the @STD function to calculate a population standard deviation for the values appearing in a data series.

- The **S**TDS setting uses the @STDS function to calculate a sample standard deviation for the values appearing in a data series.

- The **M**IN setting uses the @MIN function to locate the minimum value for the values appearing in a data series.

- The **M**AX setting uses the @MAX function to locate the maximum value for the values appearing in a data series.

Think of data aggregation as an expedient method for regrouping spreadsheet data without actually having to reenter numbers or create new formulas manually. During analytical graphing, Quattro Pro makes no changes to the raw data, so you can be sure that nothing has changed when you return to the spreadsheet.

In the next section you learn how to perform a typical aggregation analysis.

Performing a Basic Aggregation Analysis

The spreadsheet shown in figure 12.3 contains monthly sales data for J. Testa Clothiers. Suppose that you want to evaluate average quarterly sales performance for 1991. By using this spreadsheet, you can enter formulas to average three months' worth of data at a time. Then, you can display the information in a line graph.

12 — ANALYZING GRAPHS

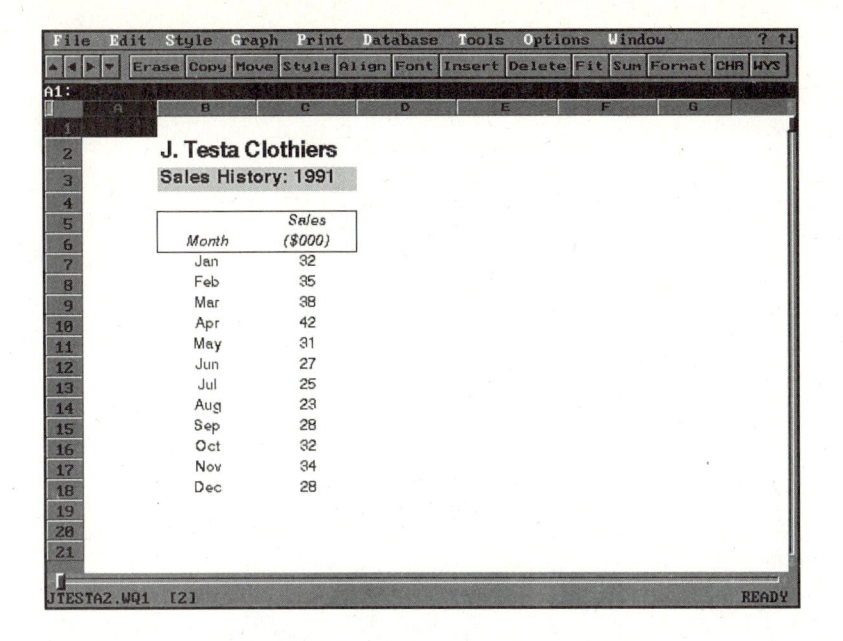

Fig. 12.3

The J. Testa Clothiers monthly sales report.

By using aggregation analysis, you can accomplish both objectives simultaneously in much less time. To perform this basic aggregation analysis using the data shown in figure 12.3, follow these steps:

1. Choose /**G**raph **G**raph Type and choose the **L**ine graph type.

2. Choose **S**eries **1**st Series. When prompted for the range to graph, type *C7..C18* and press Enter.

3. Choose **X**-Axis Series. When prompted for the x-axis range, type *B7..B18* and press Enter.

4. Choose **A**nalyze **1**st Series **A**ggregation.

5. To identify the time period represented in the **1**st Series values, choose **S**eries Period and then choose the **M**onths option.

6. To identify the time period you want to use for the aggregated data, choose **A**ggregation Period and then choose the **Q**uarters option.

7. To select a method for transforming the data, choose **F**unction and then choose the **A**VG option.

8. Press F10 to view the graph.

9. Press Enter and choose **Q**uit four times to return to the spreadsheet.

PART II — PRINTING AND GRAPHING

> **TIP** Remember to use /**G**raph **N**ame **C**reate to save the current graph settings in case you want to view or print the graph later.

Figure 12.4 shows all the menu settings required to perform this basic aggregation analysis. Note that the series selection on the **S**eries menu corresponds to the series selection on the **A**nalyze menu (both are **1**st Series). On the **A**ggregation menu, the **S**eries Period selection appropriately is smaller than the **A**ggregation Period selection.

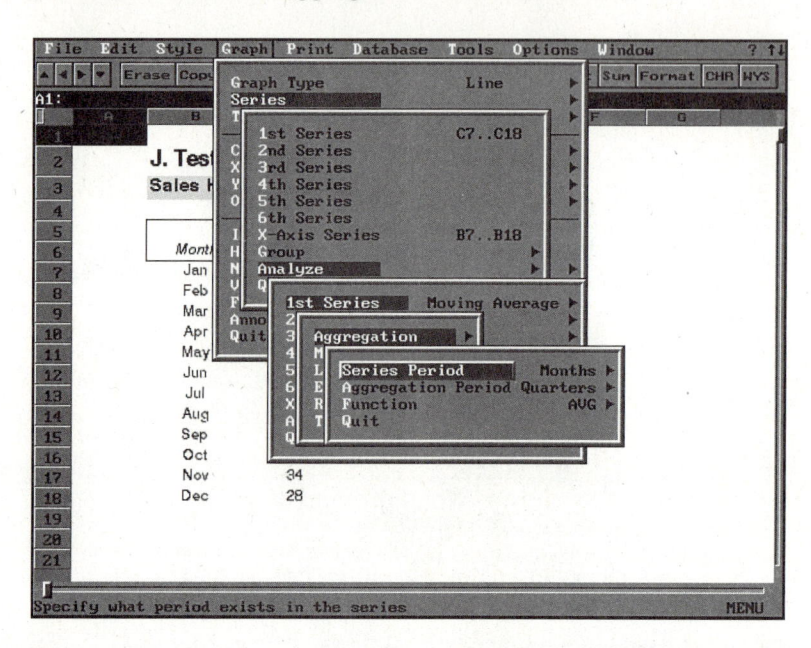

Fig. 12.4

The menu settings required for a basic aggregation analysis.

Figure 12.5 shows the final version of the graph that this analysis creates. The line graph type works well with aggregated data because the graph clearly shows a progression over time and reveals trends. You can use the graph customizing commands described in Chapter 11, "Customizing Graphs," to prepare fully formatted, presentation-quality graphs similar to the one shown in this figure.

12 — ANALYZING GRAPHS

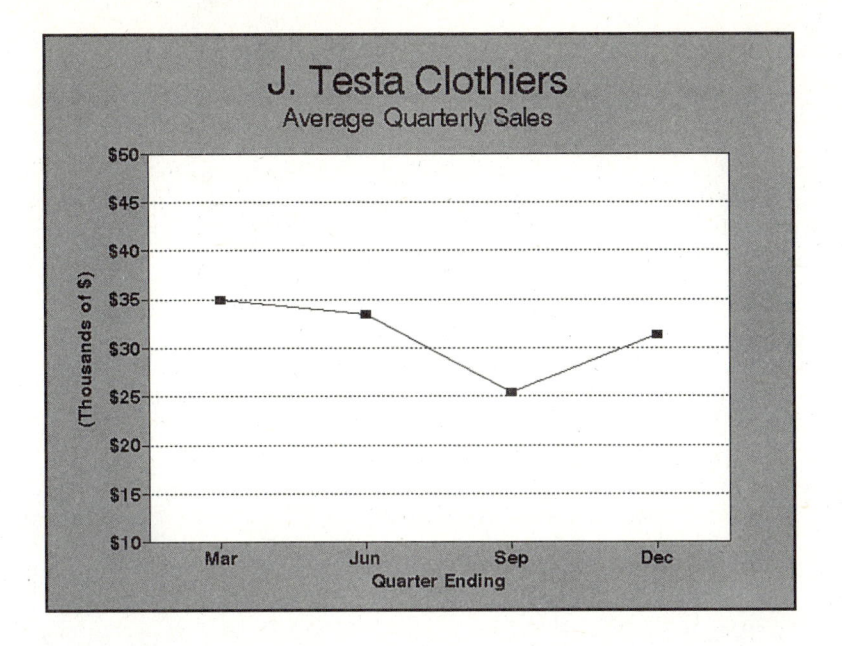

Fig. 12.5

The Average Quarterly Sales graph for J. Testa Clothiers.

Quattro Pro displays the correct x-axis labels for aggregated data as long as you first define an **X**-Axis Series range on the **S**eries menu. In this graph, for instance, Quattro Pro knows to display every third label from the range B7..B18 shown in figure 12.3 because the aggregation period selected is **Q**uarters.

> **NOTE** Quattro Pro does not aggregate numerical x-axis data on a line graph, even if you choose /**G**raph **S**eries **A**nalyze **X**-Axis Series **A**ggregation. Instead, the program treats the numbers as x-axis labels and displays the labels on the graph. To aggregate numerical data appearing on an x-axis, you first must display the data on an XY graph (choose /**G**raph **G**raph Type **X**Y).

To aggregate x-axis series data appearing on an XY graph, choose /**G**raph **S**eries **A**nalyze **X**-Axis Series Aggregation. Then, follow the procedure outlined for defining the **A**ggregation Period, **S**eries Period, and **F**unction settings.

Performing Aggregation Analysis with Multiple Series

You easily can enhance any analytical graphing operation by viewing the same data series on one graph and then choosing different aggregation methods. Examining total quarterly sales figures with the average quarterly sales figures from the preceding example may be interesting, for instance.

> **NOTE** You can use the /Graph Series and /Graph Series Analyze menu settings from the preceding exercise for the next exercise.

To add the same data series to the existing graph using a different aggregation method, follow these steps:

1. Choose /Graph Series 2nd Series. When prompted for the range to graph, type *C7..C18* and press Enter.

   (Because you are analyzing the same data series with a different aggregation method, be sure to specify the same range for the 1st Series and 2nd Series settings.)

2. Choose Analyze 2nd Series Aggregation.

3. To identify the time period represented in the 2nd Series values, choose Series Period and then choose the Months option.

4. To identify the time period you want to use for the aggregated data, choose Aggregation Period and then choose the Quarters option.

5. To select a new method for transforming the data, choose Function and then choose the SUM option.

6. Press F10 to view the graph.

7. Press Enter and choose Quit four times to return to the spreadsheet.

Figure 12.6 shows all the menu settings required to perform this multiple series aggregation analysis. Note that the series selection on the Series menu corresponds to the series selection on the Analyze menu (both show 1st Series and 2nd Series). On the Aggregation menu, however, the Function option for the 2nd Series displays the SUM setting.

12 — ANALYZING GRAPHS

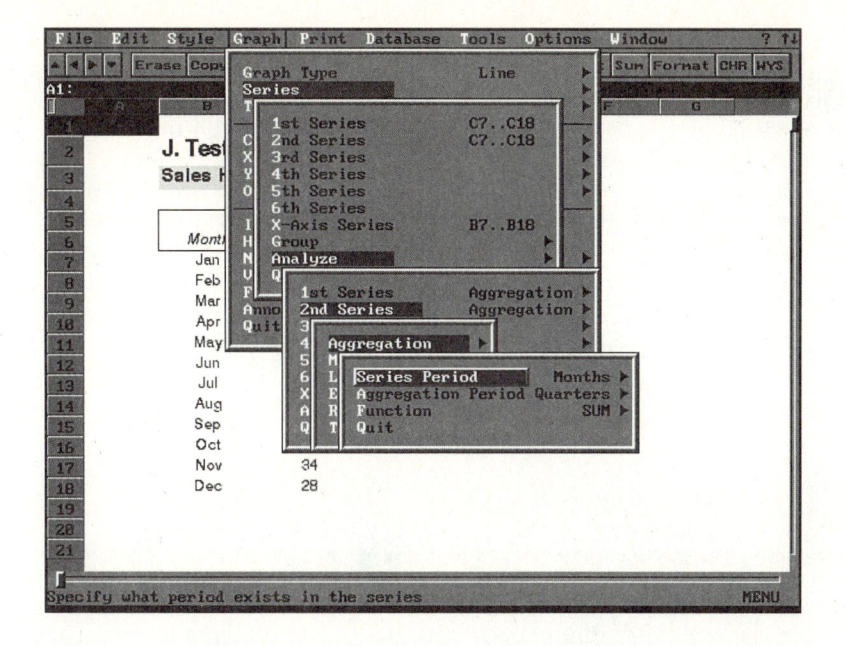

Fig. 12.6

The menu settings for a multiple series aggregation analysis.

Figure 12.7 shows the final version of the graph that this analysis creates. A legend has been added to the line graph to distinguish Average Sales data from Total Sales data. The graph title aptly reflects the addition of a new aggregated data grouping.

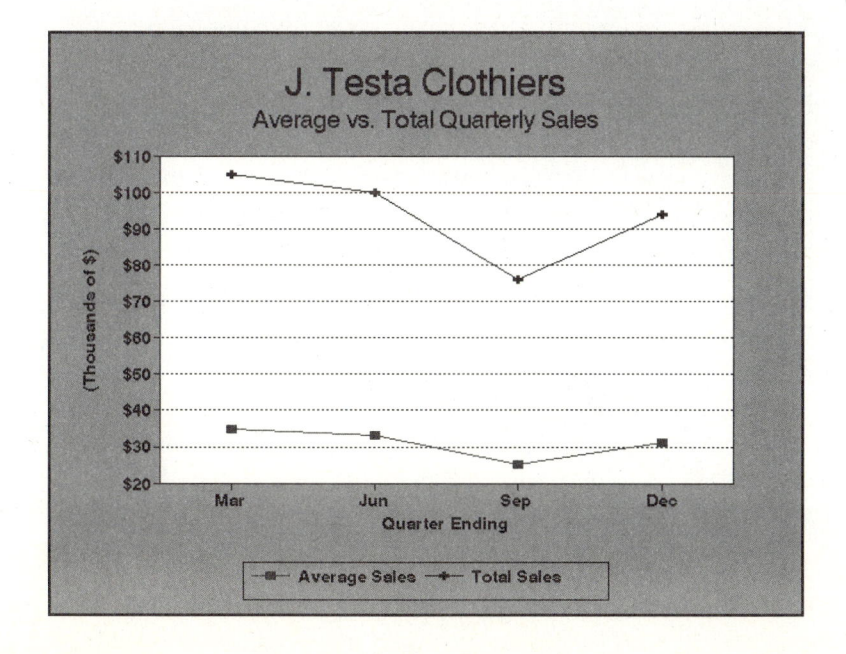

Fig. 12.7

The Average vs. Total Quarterly Sales graph for J. Testa Clothiers.

Quattro Pro continues to display the correct x-axis labels for this aggregated data because the **Aggregation Period** setting is the same: **Q**uarters. Trying to graph multiple series with different periods of aggregation can result in inaccurate plot points on the graph, even though the values of the transformed data always are correct in relation to the values appearing on the y-axis. Using the same **Aggregation Period** setting is better, therefore, when you evaluate multiple data series in a graph.

Quattro Pro also ignores the last aggregate grouping of data if the sum of the number of items in your spreadsheet is not a multiple of the aggregation period. If you choose the **Months** setting for your aggregation period and your spreadsheet contains 302 entries, for example, Quattro Pro plots 10 groups of 30 data points and ignores the remaining 2 data points.

Creating a Table of Aggregation Values

The **T**able command on the /**G**raph **S**eries **A**nalyze *n*th Series menu copies analytical graphing information into a spreadsheet range that you specify. Use this command to retain permanent records of the values that Quattro Pro calculates for each series analyzed during an aggregation analysis. You can use these numbers in reports and as input for other analytical commands such as those available on the /**T**ools menu.

Use the following steps to copy the aggregation values produced for the first series into the current spreadsheet:

1. Choose /**G**raph **S**eries **A**nalyze **1**st Series **T**able.

2. When Quattro Pro prompts you for a target table block, type the address of a cell that is well away from the spreadsheet area in which the raw data resides.

3. Press Enter to copy the data.

4. Choose **Q**uit three times to return to the spreadsheet.

You can supply an entire range address or just the first cell in the range as the target block. When you specify a single cell, Quattro Pro copies the data downward into the column specified.

When determining where to place the table, remember that Quattro Pro requires a single column and as many rows as necessary to accommodate the aggregated data. If you are aggregating 900 values by **M**onths, for example, then you need 30 rows for the table (900/30).

> **TIP**
>
> Use the /**G**raph **C**ustomize Series **I**nterior Labels command to label graph points with the values that Quattro Pro copies into a table. For further details see the section titled "Adding Interior Labels" in Chapter 11, "Customizing Graphs."

Resetting the Graph Series Analyze Settings

To reset the /**G**raph **S**eries **A**nalyze menu settings for a completely unique analytical graphing task, choose /**G**raph **S**eries **A**nalyze **A**ll **R**eset. To reset the settings for a single series (such as the **2**nd Series) on the **A**nalyze menu, choose **2**nd Series **R**eset.

> **TIP**
>
> To reset all /**G**raph menu settings, including those on the **A**nalyze menu, choose /**G**raph **C**ustomize Series **R**eset **G**raph.

Using Moving Average Analysis

Moving average analysis helps you to identify general trends in your data by *smoothing*, or averaging, the data set values. This type of analytical graphing also is known as *time-series analysis*.

With moving average analysis, you are more interested in conveying overall impressions about a data set than in providing precise information about individual values. Although comparing unemployment rates for Boston and San Diego may be interesting, for example, national unemployment figures give a more telling indication of the state of the nation.

The mechanics of moving average analysis are simple to grasp. Suppose that you want to create a three-period moving average for the following five numbers:

    6   2   4   9   104

To start, Quattro Pro plots the value 6. Next, the program averages the first 2 values and plots that value (4). Then, it averages the first 3 values and plots that value (4). For the fourth value (9), Quattro Pro drops the first value and calculates the average for the second, third, and fourth values (5). For the fifth and final value, Quattro Pro drops the second value and calculates the average for the last three (33)—a much lower value than the actual value of 104.

Moving average analysis smooths fluctuating data values because earlier values temper later values, thus providing you with a global impression of the direction that a data set is taking. In the preceding example, you can see how the average values 4, 9, 5, and 33 seem less wild than 6, 2, 4, 9, and 104.

Reviewing the Moving Average Options

The options on the **M**oving Average menu enable you to define the scope of a data transformation (see table 12.4). All you need to know is the number of data points you want to average and whether you want Quattro Pro to calculate a weighted moving average.

Table 12.4 Moving Average Menu Commands

Command	Description
Period	Specifies the number of points to average
Weighted	Selects whether or not to use a weighted moving average

The **P**eriod option defines the number of data values that Quattro Pro uses when calculating the moving average. High period values produce smoother curves but may mask the trends you are trying to disclose.

The **W**eighted option enables Quattro Pro numerically to place greater emphasis, or *weight*, on more recent data values and less weight on older values. This option helps to compensate for abnormally low or high values appearing in the latter part of a data set. By default, this option is set to **N**o. If you want to use weighted moving average analysis, set this option to **Y**es.

In the next section you learn the steps to follow to perform a typical moving average analysis.

Performing a Basic Moving Average Analysis

Before beginning this procedure, choose /**G**raph **C**ustomize Series **R**eset **G**raph to reset all graph settings. Then follow these general steps to calculate a moving average for a single data series and to display that average on a line graph:

1. Choose /**G**raph **G**raph Type **L**ine.
2. Choose **S**eries **1**st Series. When prompted, type a valid range for the current spreadsheet and then press Enter.
3. Choose **X**-Axis. When prompted, type the range that contains the labels you want to display on the x-axis and then press Enter.
4. Choose **A**nalyze **1**st Series **M**oving Average.
5. Choose **P**eriod, type a period value, and press Enter.
6. Press F10 to view the graph.
7. Press Enter and then choose **Q**uit four times to return to the **G**raph menu.

Moving average analysis is most revealing when you include different period scenarios for the same data series. The next section examines how to use this approach on your own data.

Performing Moving Average Analysis with Multiple Series

You easily can enhance any moving average analysis by viewing the same data series on one graph with different period intervals. If you suspect that daily sales totals are higher during the weekend than during the week and also are typically higher toward the middle and end of the month, for example, putting 7- and 14-day moving averages together on the same graph may reveal this trend.

The spreadsheet in figure 12.8 contains daily sales data for J. Testa Clothiers. Suppose that you want to create 7- and 14-day moving averages and display them on a line graph. Using moving average analysis, you can create both moving averages simultaneously in a short period of time.

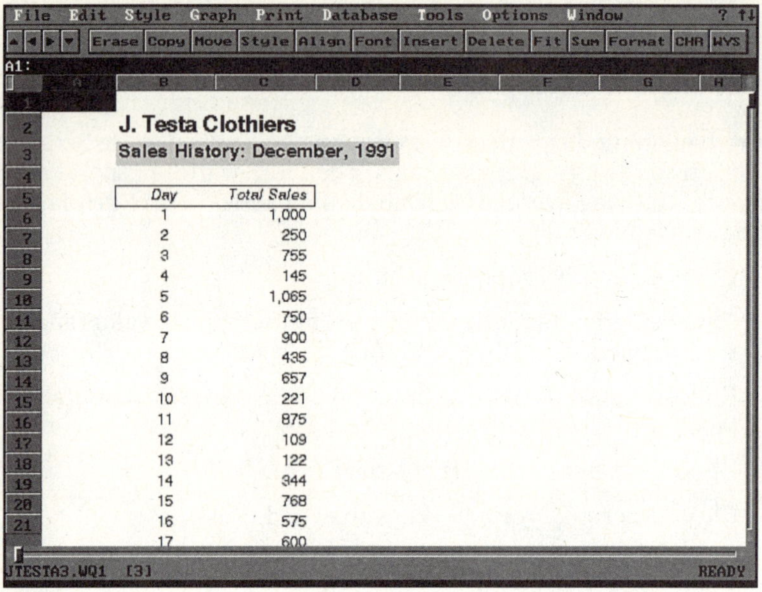

Fig. 12.8

The J. Testa Clothiers daily sales report.

To perform a moving average analysis with the data shown in figure 12.8, follow these steps:

1. Choose /**G**raph **G**raph Type and choose the **L**ine graph type.

2. Choose **S**eries **1**st Series. When prompted for the range to graph, type *C6..C36* and press Enter.

3. Choose **2**nd Series. When prompted for the range to graph, type *C6..C36* and press Enter. (Remember, you are analyzing the same data series with a different moving average period, so be sure to specify the same range for the **1**st Series and **2**nd Series settings.)

4. Choose **X**-Axis Series. When prompted for the x-axis range, type *B6..B36* and press Enter.

5. Choose **A**nalyze **1**st Series **M**oving Average.

6. To identify the time period for which you want to calculate the first moving average, choose **P**eriod, press 7, and then press Enter.

7. Choose **Q**uit to return to the **A**nalyze menu.

8. Choose **2**nd Series **M**oving Average.

9. To identify the time period for which you want to calculate the second moving average, choose **P**eriod, type *14*, and then press Enter.

12 — ANALYZING GRAPHS

10. Press F10 to view the graph.
11. Press Enter and choose **Q**uit four times to return to the spreadsheet.

> **TIP**
>
> Remember to use **/Graph Name Create** to save the current graph settings in case you want to view or print the graph later.

Figure 12.9 shows all the menu settings required to perform this moving average analysis. The final dialog box in this figure shows how to specify the number of periods to use for the second moving average (in this case, a 14-day period). Note that the series selections on the **S**eries menu correspond to the series selections on the **A**nalyze menu (both show **1**st Series and **2**nd Series).

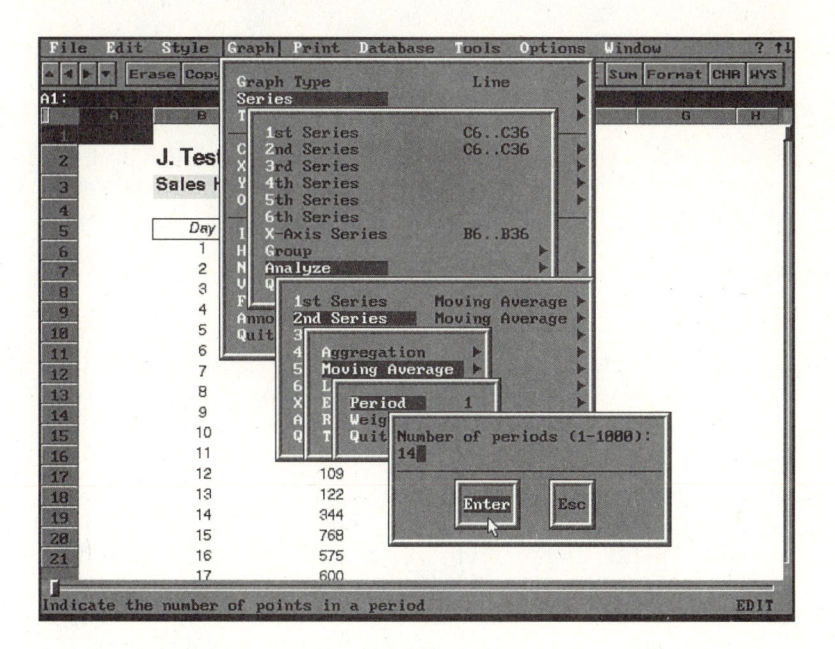

Fig. 12.9

The menu settings for a multiple series moving average analysis.

Figure 12.10 shows the final version of the graph that this analysis creates. The line graph type works well with moving average data because the graph clearly shows a progression over time and reveals trends.

PART II — PRINTING AND GRAPHING

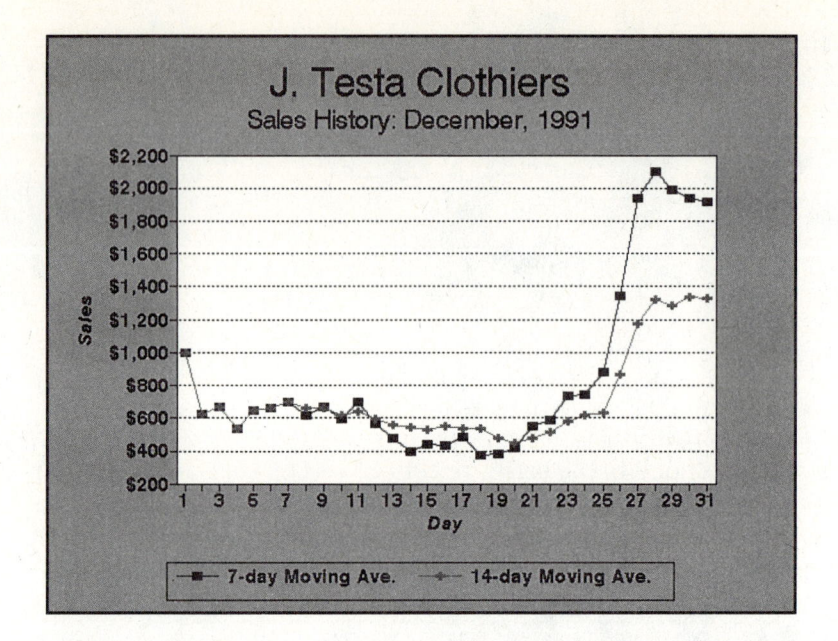

Fig. 12.10

The 7-day and 14-day moving average graph for J. Testa Clothiers.

Quattro Pro displays the correct x-axis labels for moving average data as long as you first define an **X**-Axis Series range on the **S**eries menu. In this graph, Quattro Pro displays every other label because the /**G**raph **X**-Axis **N**o. of Minor Ticks command is set to 1 (the default is 0). See the section titled "Adding Minor Ticks" in Chapter 11 for more details.

Creating a Table of Moving Average Values

The **T**able command on the /**G**raph **S**eries **A**nalyze *n*th Series menu copies analytical graphing information into a spreadsheet range that you specify. Use this command to retain permanent records of the values that Quattro Pro calculates for each series analyzed during a moving average analysis. You can use these numbers in reports and as input for other analytical commands, such as those available on the /**T**ools menu.

Use the following steps to copy the moving average values produced for the first series into the current spreadsheet:

1. Choose /**G**raph **S**eries **A**nalyze **1**st Series **T**able.

2. After Quattro Pro prompts you for a target table block, type the address of a cell that is well away from the spreadsheet area in which the raw data resides.

3. Press Enter to copy the data.
4. Choose **Quit** three times to return to the spreadsheet.

You can supply an entire range address or just the first cell in the range as the target block. When you specify a single cell, Quattro Pro copies the data downward into the column specified.

When determining where to place the table, remember that Quattro Pro requires a single column and as many rows as necessary to accommodate the moving average data. If you are calculating a moving average for 60 values, for example, you need 60 rows for the table.

> **TIP**
> Use the /**G**raph **C**ustomize Series **I**nterior Labels command to label graph points with the moving average values that Quattro Pro copies into a table. For further details, see the section titled "Adding Interior Labels" in Chapter 11.

Using Linear Fit Analysis

When you choose the /**G**raph **S**eries **A**nalyze *n*th Series **L**inear Fit command, Quattro Pro uses simple linear regression to generate a line that "best fits" the data you selected. You can use this type of analytical graphing to show a general trend among fluctuating points. Grasping regression information in graph form also is easier than in a table full of numbers.

Linear fit analysis requires no special advance understanding. You just identify the series for which you want to fit a linear line and choose **L**inear Fit from the **A**nalyze *n*th Series menu.

Performing a Basic Linear Fit Analysis

Using the same daily sales totals spreadsheet from figure 12.8 in the preceding section, you can create a linear fit line for J. Testa Clothiers and add the line to the moving averages graph. Before beginning this procedure, however, choose /**G**raph **C**ustomize Series **R**eset **G**raph to reset all graph settings.

PART II — PRINTING AND GRAPHING

To create a linear fit line, use the following steps:

> **NOTE** This exercise assumes that you already have created a moving average analysis for the first two data series.

1. Choose **/Graph Series 3rd Series**. When prompted, type *C6..C36* and then press Enter.

2. Choose **Analyze 3rd Series Linear Fit**.

3. Press F10 to view the graph.

4. Press Enter and choose **Quit** three times to return to the spreadsheet.

> **TIP** The Linear Fit command calculates and plots linear regression information in the spreadsheet even if your data has no obvious general trend.

Figure 12.11 shows all the menu settings required to perform this linear fit analysis. Note that the first two series are set for moving average analysis and the third series is set for linear fit analysis. Although displaying a linear fit in a graph by itself works fine, the linear fit leaves a greater impression when displayed next to the moving average lines from the previous example.

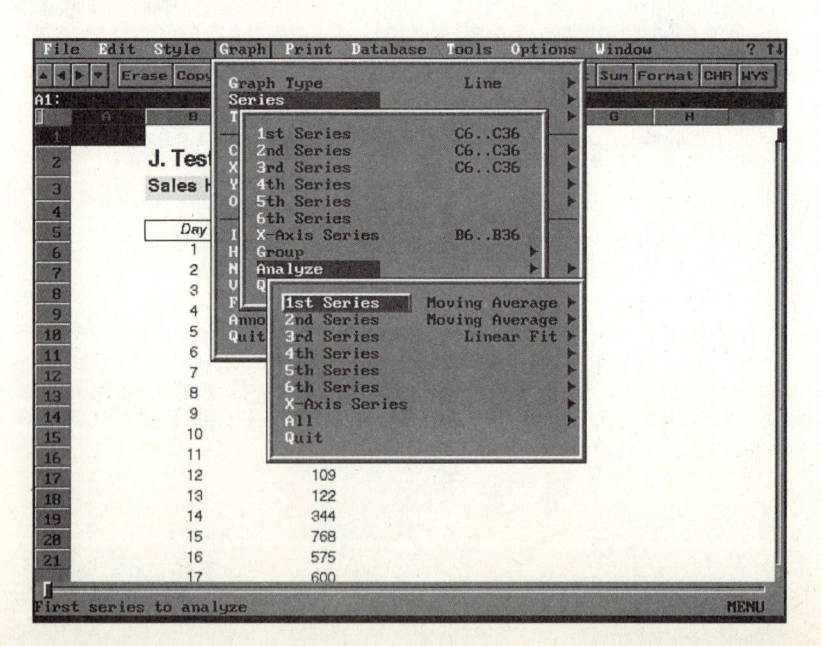

Fig. 12.11

The menu settings for a linear fit analysis.

Figure 12.12 shows the final version of the graph that this analysis creates.

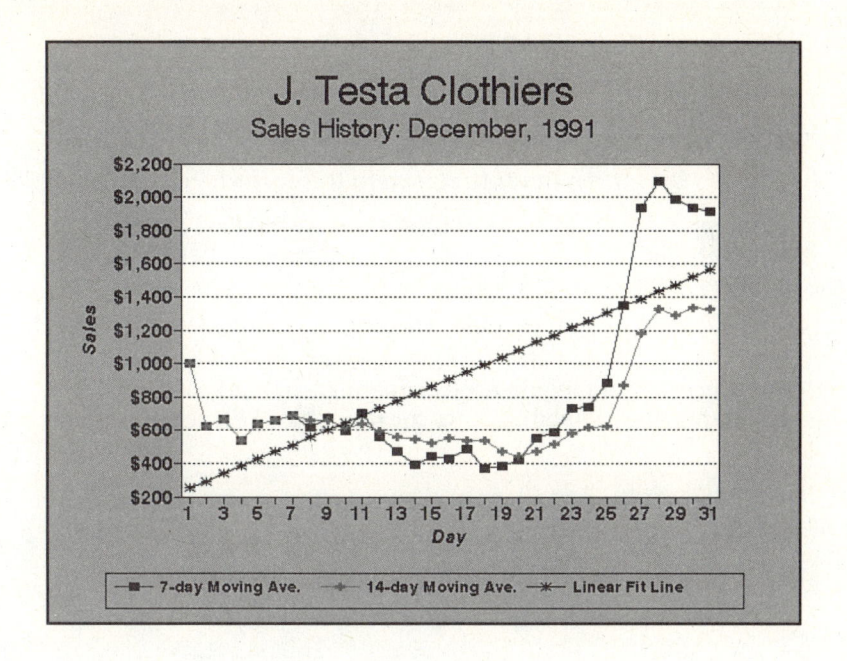

Fig. 12.12

The linear fit line on the moving average graph for J. Testa Clothiers.

Creating a Table of Linear Fit Regression Values

The **T**able command on the /**G**raph **S**eries **A**nalyze *n*th Series menu copies analytical graphing information into a spreadsheet range that you specify. Use this command to retain permanent records of the values that Quattro Pro calculates for each series analyzed during a linear fit operation. You can use these numbers in reports and as input for other analytical commands, such as those available on the /**T**ools menu.

Follow these steps to copy the linear fit and moving average values produced for the first three series into the current spreadsheet:

1. Choose /**G**raph **S**eries **A**nalyze **1**st Series **T**able.

2. When Quattro Pro prompts you for a target table block, type *E6*.

3. Press Enter to copy the data.

4. Choose **2**nd Series **T**able.

PART II — PRINTING AND GRAPHING

5. When Quattro Pro prompts you for a target table block, type *F6*.
6. Press Enter to copy the data.
7. Choose **3**rd Series **T**able.
8. When Quattro Pro prompts you for a target table block, type *G6*.
9. Press Enter to copy the data.
10. Choose **Q**uit three times to return to the spreadsheet.

You can supply an entire range address or just the first cell in the range as the target block. When you specify a single cell, Quattro Pro copies the data downward into the column specified.

When determining where to place the table, remember that Quattro Pro requires a single column and as many rows as necessary to accommodate the linear fit data. If you are calculating a linear fit line for 25 values, for example, you need 25 rows for the table.

> **TIP**
>
> Use the /**G**raph **C**ustomize Series **I**nterior **L**abels command to label graph points with the linear fit values that Quattro Pro copies into a table. For further details, see the section titled "Adding Interior Labels" in Chapter 11.

Figure 12.13 shows the results of copying the linear fit and moving average values into the daily sales totals spreadsheet. Column headings and lines have been added to the table to provide division and clarity.

Choose /**G**raph **C**ustomize Series **R**eset **G**raph to reset all settings in preparation for the final analytical graphing example.

Using Exponential Fit Analysis

Exponential Fit generates a curve to fit data that increases or decreases exponentially. For this feature to work, all values in the series must be nonzero and must have the same sign.

> **NOTE** For the purposes of exponential fit graphing, Quattro Pro treats all blank cells in a data series as zeros.

Fitting exponential data with a curve is as simple and direct as creating a linear fit line: select the series containing the data to be graphed and then choose /**G**raph **S**eries **A**nalyze *n*th Series **E**xponential Fit.

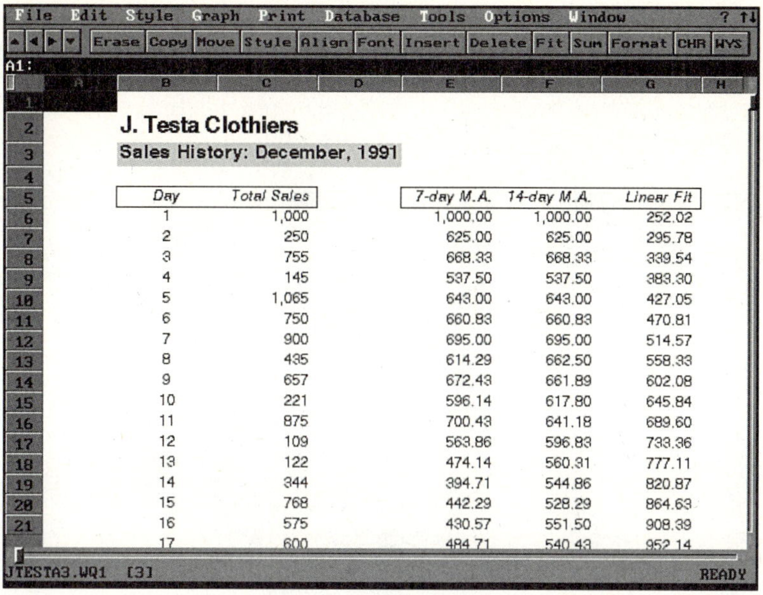

J. Testa Clothiers

Sales History: December, 1991

Day	Total Sales	7-day M.A.	14-day M.A.	Linear Fit
1	1,000	1,000.00	1,000.00	252.02
2	250	625.00	625.00	295.78
3	755	668.33	668.33	339.54
4	145	537.50	537.50	383.30
5	1,065	643.00	643.00	427.05
6	750	660.83	660.83	470.81
7	900	695.00	695.00	514.57
8	435	614.29	662.50	558.33
9	657	672.43	661.89	602.08
10	221	596.14	617.80	645.84
11	875	700.43	641.18	689.60
12	109	563.86	596.83	733.36
13	122	474.14	560.31	777.11
14	344	394.71	544.86	820.87
15	768	442.29	528.29	864.63
16	575	430.57	551.50	908.39
17	600	484.71	540.43	952.14

Fig. 12.13

A table of values in the J. Testa Clothiers spreadsheet.

Performing a Basic Exponential Fit Analysis

By using the same daily sales totals spreadsheet from the preceding section, you can create an exponential fit line for J. Testa Clothiers and add the line to a line graph that displays the actual daily sales figures.

To create an exponential fit line, follow these steps:

1. Choose /**G**raph **G**raph Type and then choose the **L**ine graph type.
2. Choose **S**eries **1**st Series. When prompted for the range to graph, type *C6..C36* and press Enter.
3. Choose **2**nd Series. When prompted for the range to graph, type *C6..C36* and press Enter. (Because you are analyzing the same data series using the exponential fit technique, be sure to specify the same range for the 1st **S**eries and **2**nd Series settings.)
4. Choose **X**-Axis Series. When prompted for the x-axis range, type *B6..B36* and press Enter.
5. Choose **A**nalyze **2**nd Series **E**xponential Fit.
6. Press F10 to view the graph.
7. Press Enter and choose **Q**uit four times to return to the spreadsheet.

PART II — PRINTING AND GRAPHING

Figure 12.14 shows all the menu settings required to perform this exponential fit analysis. Note that the first series has no analytical graphing setting and the second series is set for exponential fit analysis. The exponential fit line, like the linear fit line, leaves much more of an impression when displayed next to the data from which it was created.

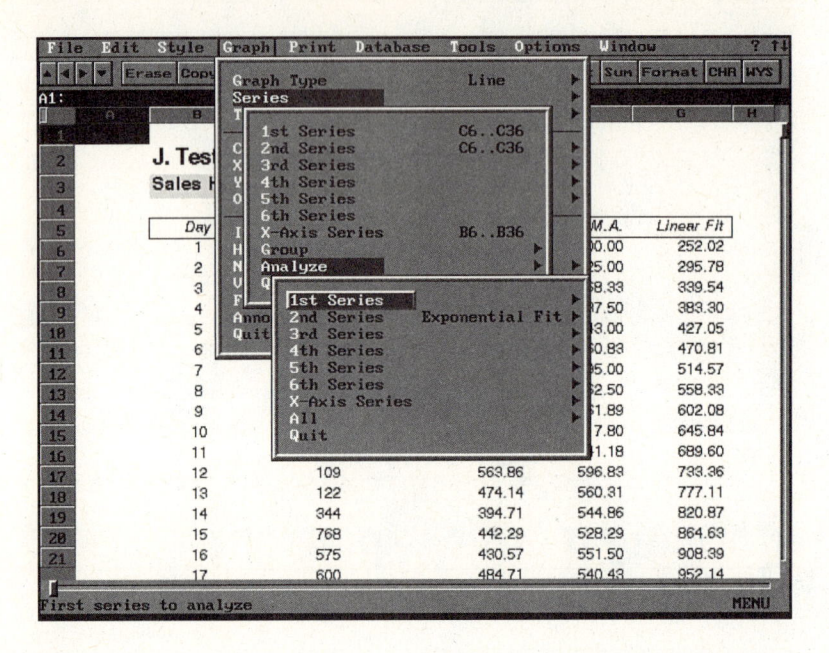

Fig. 12.14

The menu settings for an exponential fit analysis.

Figure 12.15 shows the final version of the graph that this analysis creates.

Creating a Table of Exponential Fit Regression Values

The **T**able command on the /**G**raph **S**eries **A**nalyze *n*th Series menu copies analytical graphing information into a spreadsheet range that you specify. Use this command to retain permanent records of the values that Quattro Pro calculates for each series analyzed during an exponential fit operation. You can use these numbers in reports and as input for other analytical commands, such as those available on the /**T**ools menu.

12 — ANALYZING GRAPHS

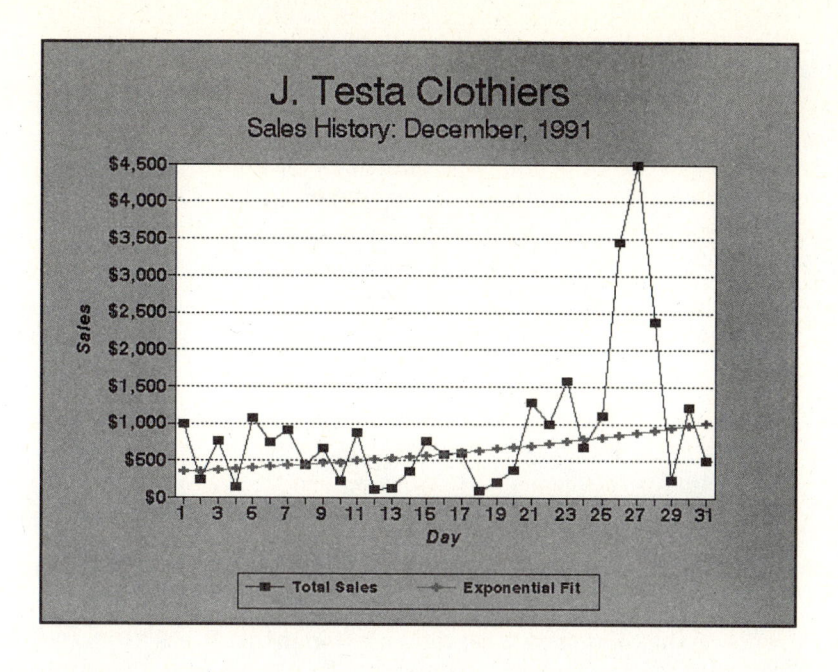

Fig. 12.15

The exponential fit line on the line graph for J. Testa Clothiers.

Use the following steps to copy the exponential fit values for the first data series into the current spreadsheet:

1. Choose /**G**raph **S**eries **A**nalyze **1**st Series **T**able.
2. After Quattro Pro prompts you for a target table block, type the address of a cell that is well away from the spreadsheet area in which the raw data resides.
3. Press Enter to copy the data.
4. Choose **Q**uit three times to return to the spreadsheet.

You can supply an entire range address or just the first cell in the range as the target block. When you specify a single cell, Quattro Pro copies the data downward into the column specified.

When determining where to place the table, remember that Quattro Pro requires a single column and as many rows as necessary to accommodate the exponential fit data. If you are calculating an exponential fit line for 25 values, for example, you need 25 rows for the table.

> **TIP**
>
> Use the /**G**raph **C**ustomize **S**eries **I**nterior **L**abels command to label graph points with the exponential fit values that Quattro Pro copies into a table. See the section titled "Adding Interior Labels" in Chapter 11 for further details.

Questions & Answers

This chapter introduces you to the four analytical tools found on the /Graph Analyze menu. If you have questions concerning particular situations that are not addressed in the examples given, look through this section.

Using Aggregation

Q: My spreadsheet contains daily data, and I want to evaluate the semimonthly totals without having to create new formulas and reorganize the data. Will one of the aggregation options enable me to do this?

A: Yes. Choose /Graph Series Analyze and select the data series you want to analyze. On the *n*th Series menu, choose Aggregation. Next, set the Series Period option to Days and the Aggregation Period option to Arbitrary; then, type *15* and press Enter. Finally, choose the SUM setting on the Function menu. Press F10 to view the graph.

Q: I added a second data series to a moving average graph, but the data does not appear on the graph. What's wrong?

A: Check the settings on the /Graph X-Axis and Y-Axis menus. If Scale is set to Manual, and the Low and High values fall outside the range of values for the data series you added, Quattro Pro does not display the new series on the graph. To correct this problem, set Scale to Automatic. If you still want to adjust the scale of either axis manually, be sure to choose Low and High values that include all values appearing in the data series.

Q: Quattro Pro displays the message Not enough data points to aggregate when I press F10 to display an aggregation graph. What did I do wrong?

A: Your graph series number does not match the series number selected for analysis. After you define a data series on the /Graph Series menu, you must select the matching option on the Analyze menu before you can aggregate data. To analyze the 3rd Series for a graph, for example, define the range on the Series menu and then choose the 3rd Series option on the Analyze menu.

Using Moving Averages

Q: I cannot read the x-axis labels on my moving average graph because the labels are grouped too closely together. Should I define a lower **P**eriod value to correct this problem?

A: No. To correct the display of x-axis labels that are bunched together, you should not decrease the **P**eriod setting. Although this approach decreases the number of points that appear on a graph, it also eliminates information that may be necessary for the analysis at hand.

Instead, choose /**G**raph **X**-Axis **N**o. of Minor Ticks and enter *1* to display every other label.

Q: When I created a table of values for the current moving average analysis, Quattro Pro failed to copy into the table all of the values that I expected. What happened?

A: When you create a table of values for a moving average analysis, Quattro Pro requires one row for each moving average value. If your data contains 50 values, you must specify a table block range that spans at least 50 rows.

Q: The moving average analysis I just performed has not smoothed out my data values as much as I anticipated. The older points in my data set appear to greatly influence the outcome of the analysis. Is there anything I can do?

A: By using the weighted average moving analysis method, you can cause Quattro Pro to place greater emphasis on more recent data points and less emphasis on older data points. To use this method, choose **W**eighted on the **M**oving Average menu, choose **Y**es, and then redisplay your graph.

Summary

In this chapter, you learned how to scrutinize your spreadsheet data closely by using the four analytical graphing commands found on the /**G**raph **S**eries **A**nalyze menu. You also learned how to add results tables to the current spreadsheet and how to reset the **A**nalyze menus settings for future analytical graphing operations. These six commands enable you to turn the Quattro Pro graphing environment into an efficient mechanism for analyzing spreadsheet information.

PART II — PRINTING AND GRAPHING

Having completed this chapter, you should understand the following concepts:

- Selecting the **A**nalyze menu option best suited to your analytical graphing needs
- Performing aggregation analyses using single and multiple data series
- Performing a moving average analysis using multiple data series
- Creating a linear line that "best fits" a series of data points
- Creating an exponential line to reflect a trend in erratic data
- Displaying the results of an analytical graphing operation in a spreadsheet table
- Resetting the settings on the **A**nalyze menu in preparation for a new analytical graphing operation

In Chapter 13 you learn how to manage your data using the commands found on the **D**atabase menu. These commands enable you to turn a Quattro Pro spreadsheet into an efficient environment for storing and accessing database information.

PART III

Advanced Spreadsheet Applications

OUTLINE

13. Managing Your Data
14. Analyzing Data
15. Creating Macros
16. Customizing Quattro Pro

CHAPTER 13

Managing Your Data

Besides being an electronic spreadsheet program, Quattro Pro can function as a flat-file database manager. This chapter focuses on this process and shows you how to use the commands on the **D**atabase menu to sort, extract, and delete records—operations basic to every good database software product.

The chapter begins by showing you how to turn a spreadsheet into a database. This material defines each part of a typical database, reviews the data management commands, and shows you how to prepare your data for processing into reports and documents.

The next section discusses different techniques you can use to sort database records, guidelines for maintaining the integrity of your database records, and instructions for returning an altered database to its original order. This section concludes with a brief review of how to modify Quattro Pro's default sort rules to meet special needs.

The chapter continues by discussing how to search a database and locate records that meet user-specified criteria. You learn how to locate, extract, and delete records—some of the most useful database operations.

The last section describes how to use a spreadsheet as a data-entry form and explains how to control record accuracy by restricting the types of permissible entries.

PART III — ADVANCED SPREADSHEET APPLICATIONS

Turning a Spreadsheet into a Database

The Quattro Pro database is a powerful information management and report creation tool. With this tool, you can manipulate large amounts of information that you can present in many different ways. Like a spreadsheet, a database helps you to organize names and numbers that appear on reports.

With a database, you can segregate information on a spreadsheet into sets of related data and then instantly reorganize the data to create different reports. To reorganize a spreadsheet report, you must execute several involved Copy and Move operations.

You can use a database to store all kinds of information. A phone book is a database, for example, that stores a set of related information: a name, an address, and a phone number. The uses for a database are literally endless and limited only by your imagination. You can build a database to catalog your favorite video tapes, to devise a business check register, or to create a statistical report for major league baseball players.

Often, the structure of an individual database is portable to other applications. If you create a database to catalog your video tapes, for example, you can use the same database structure to catalog your cassettes, CDs, and albums.

You easily can turn a spreadsheet into a database. Figure 13.1 shows the shell of a database that will be used to store performance statistics for the top 10 National League batters.

The *database shell* is the framework of the database: the field names row, the drawn lines (if any), and the database area where the records reside.

> **T I P** Drawing lines around the database shell is helpful when you build criteria tables and output blocks below the database shell.

Follow these steps to create a database shell like the one shown in figure 13.1:

1. Envision the database application. Do you want to manage employee names, business phone numbers, contact lists, baseball statistics? Begin by entering a report title at the top of a new, blank spreadsheet that describes the envisioned application.

13 — MANAGING YOUR DATA

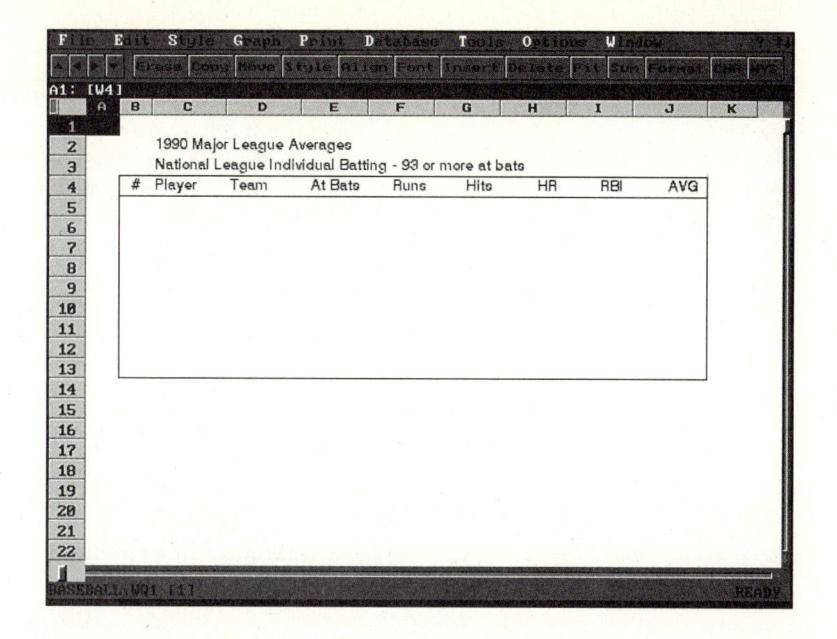

Fig. 13.1

The shell of a database.

2. Create field names and enter them on the row below the database title.

    Because each field name corresponds to an element in a database record, such as a phone number, the names should be descriptive of the field data. Create short, single-word names because many database operations enable you to use cell block names.

3. Set the widths of the columns in the database with the /**S**tyle **C**olumn Width command.

> **TIP**
> You should estimate the maximum number of records likely to appear in the database. Count down that number of rows from the field names row; the last row is the bottom of the database shell.

A database, like a spreadsheet report, uses label headings to define the type of information stored in a column or row. Each row in a database is a *record*, and each column is a *field*. The *database area* is the part of the spreadsheet in which you store your records.

The baseball database has nine field names that appear on row 4: #, Player, Team, At Bats, Runs, Hits, HR (home runs), RBI (runs batted in), and AVG (batting average). These fields identify the individual performance statistics collected for a group of baseball players.

PART III — ADVANCED SPREADSHEET APPLICATIONS

The shell pictured in figure 13.1 shows the commonly accepted way of creating the shell of a database. As with all good spreadsheet reports, you should create a database that looks like the document or report from which the database was created. To create a database using the names, addresses, and phone numbers of business associates, for example, design one that looks like a page out of your phone book.

When you build a database, follow these guidelines:

- The database area must be rectangular. Quattro Pro does not perform **D**atabase menu operations on unconnected blocks of data.

- Each column should contain only one type of data: numeric, alphabetic, or date and time serial numbers. (Don't mix dates with labels or labels with numbers.)

- Do not place an empty row (or column) between the field name row and the first record in the database.

- A Quattro Pro database can contain a maximum of 8,191 entries (8,192 total rows but one row contains field names).

TIP If you want to use a two-word field name, press Shift-hyphen to enter an underscore character between the words (for example, Sales_1991). Quattro Pro does not accept as valid any field name that contains blank spaces between words.

Reviewing the Database Menu

Use the first four **D**atabase menu commands to sort, search through, control movement, and enter data into a database (see table 13.1).

Use the fifth command, **P**aradox Access, to switch between Quattro Pro's and Paradox's operating environments so that you can access and share file data between these two programs. Paradox is a powerful database management program available from Borland International, publisher of Quattro Pro.

Except for the **R**estrict Input command, selecting a **D**atabase menu command displays a second menu. The following sections show how to use each command to build your own database applications.

13 — MANAGING YOUR DATA

Table 13.1 Database Menu Commands

Command	Description
Sort	Changes the order of database records
Query	Searches through a database
Restrict Input	Restricts movement of the cell selector to unprotected cells
Data Entry	Specifies the data type permitted in a block of cells
Paradox Access	Switches to the Paradox operating environment

Entering Data

To enter data into a database, apply the same techniques you use when you enter data into a spreadsheet. Like a spreadsheet, a database can contain several types of data: labels, numbers, and even formulas. Cell J5 in figure 13.2, for example, contains a formula that computes batting average by dividing the number of Hits by the number of At Bats.

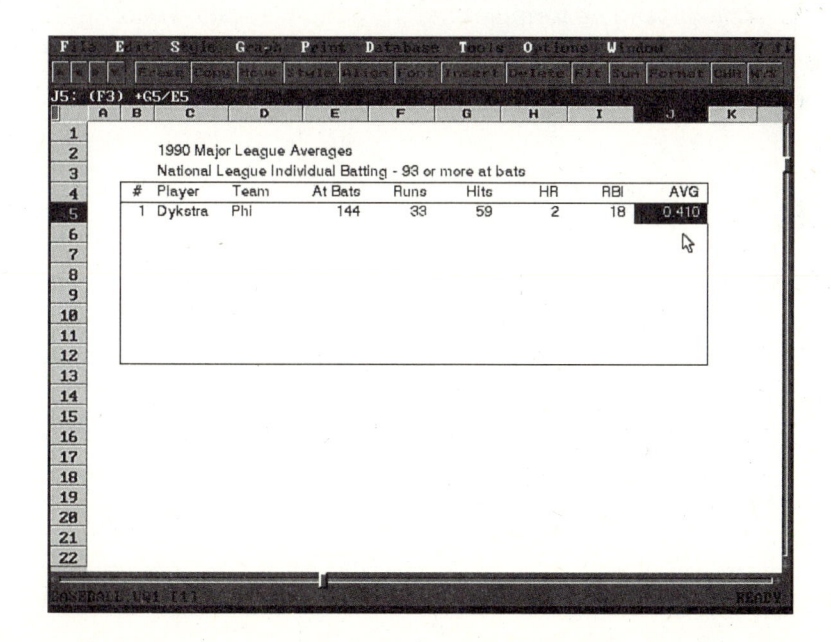

Fig. 13.2

The first record entered into the baseball database.

As you enter data into a database, remember the following three simple rules:

- Each category of data should have its own field. If you design a phone book database, for example, create one field for a person's first name and one for the last name. Entering the first and last names into one field offers you no flexibility when creating reports from sorted data.

  When you have two or more people with the same last name, you need to distinguish between them. You can place each person's first name, middle initial, or title into a field of its own.

- Do not enter different types of data into the same field. If you create a field for dates, for example, enter only dates into that field. When you enter a mixture of dates, labels, and numbers into a field, sorting and analyzing database reports becomes more difficult.

- Be careful about entering formulas into the database area. As long as the formulas are record-dependent, you can sort the formulas safely without generating bad data. A record-dependent formula references only values existing on that record's row (see the formula displayed on the input line for cell J5 in fig. 13.2).

In a sort operation, the order of the records is shifted around. If you create field-dependent formulas that rely on the location of one record in relation to another, shifting records can cause formulas to return different data, depending upon the order of the records in the database.

Sorting a Database

The **S**ort command is a powerful **D**atabase menu tool because it enables you to produce different combinations of the same data set without changing the value of any record in the database. You always should maintain the integrity of a database, because a database's integrity is integral to creating meaningful reports from one data set.

If you sort two fields out of sequence—for example, a first name field and a last name field—you destroy the integrity of a database. How useful is a database if a person's first name doesn't match the last?

After you finish entering data into a database, you are ready to manipulate the data to use in a report. Figure 13.3, for example, shows entries in the baseball database.

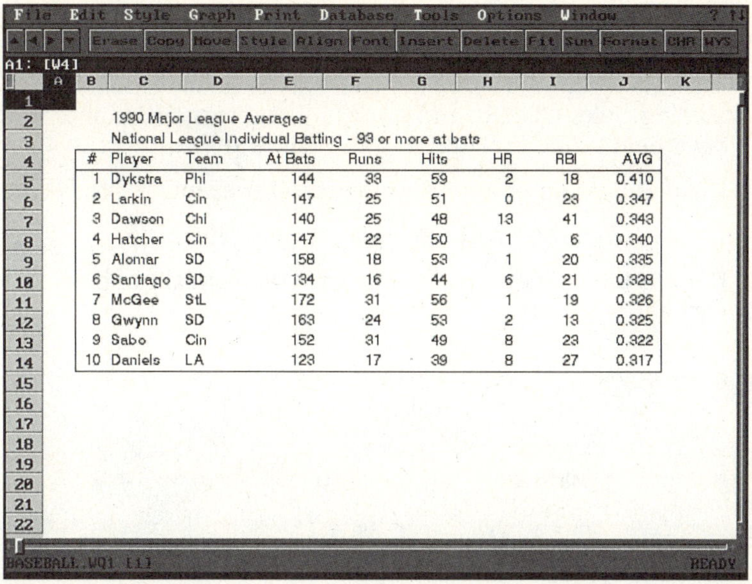

#	Player	Team	At Bats	Runs	Hits	HR	RBI	AVG
1	Dykstra	Phi	144	33	59	2	18	0.410
2	Larkin	Cin	147	25	51	0	23	0.347
3	Dawson	Chi	140	25	48	13	41	0.343
4	Hatcher	Cin	147	22	50	1	6	0.340
5	Alomar	SD	158	18	53	1	20	0.335
6	Santiago	SD	134	16	44	6	21	0.328
7	McGee	StL	172	31	56	1	19	0.326
8	Gwynn	SD	163	24	53	2	13	0.325
9	Sabo	Cin	152	31	49	8	23	0.322
10	Daniels	LA	123	17	39	8	27	0.317

Fig. 13.3

The baseball database complete with 10 records.

With nine available sort fields, you can create many different reports. You can create a report that lists the players sorted by team. Because the triple crown honor is awarded to a player who finishes the season with the highest batting average, the greatest number of RBIs, and the most home runs, for example, you also can sort the database three times to locate the best candidates for that honor.

You tell Quattro Pro how to sort your database by specifying sort criteria. You can sort a database alphabetically or numerically, in ascending and descending order.

The fields used to sort the records are called sort field keys, or *sort keys*. You can specify up to five sort keys per operation. Quattro Pro sorts a database according to each sort key's priority: the 1st Key has first priority, the 2nd Key has second priority, and so on.

Sort key priorities enable Quattro Pro to perform minisort operations. If five records with the same field value are specified by the 1st Key, for example, Quattro Pro re-sorts those records according to the 2nd Key. If two records remain with the same field value specified by the 2nd Key, Quattro Pro re-sorts the two records according to the 3rd Key.

Sorting a database is typically a three-step process: you define the block to be sorted, specify the sort key criteria, and then choose /**D**atabase **S**ort **G**o to begin the sort operation. To reset the sort criteria in preparation for a new operation, choose /**D**atabase **R**eset.

Using One Sort Key

Suppose that you want to sort the baseball database alphabetically and in ascending order (A, B, C, and so on) by each player's name. Specify the Player field as the first sort key and follow these steps:

1. Highlight the block you want to sort—for example, B5..J14.
2. Choose /Database Sort to display the Sort menu.
3. Choose Block. (Quattro Pro records the highlighted block as the sort block.)

> **T I P** Omit the field names row from the database block definition; otherwise, Quattro Pro sorts that row of labels into your database. If you do not omit the field names and Quattro Pro performs the sort, press Alt-F5 to undo the sort operation.

4. Choose 1st Key, type the column you want to use as the key C5 and press Enter.

> **T I P** You can enter any cell address or block that exists in the sort key column. The addresses C1, C5..C14, and C392, for example, all designate column C as the sort key column.

5. When prompted, choose Ascending and press Enter.
6. Choose Go.

Quattro Pro rearranges the records according to your sort criteria.

Figure 13.4 displays the result of this sort operation. Notice that Quattro Pro displays the sort block and sort key definition at the right margin of the Sort menu, next to the Block and 1st Key commands.

Using Multiple Sort Keys

You also can sort databases using two sort keys instead of one. You may want to organize the database alphabetically by Team in ascending order, for example; you also may want to sort members of the same team by the number of At Bats, in order from highest to lowest. You must specify the Team field as the 1st Key and the At Bats field as the 2nd Key.

13 — MANAGING YOUR DATA

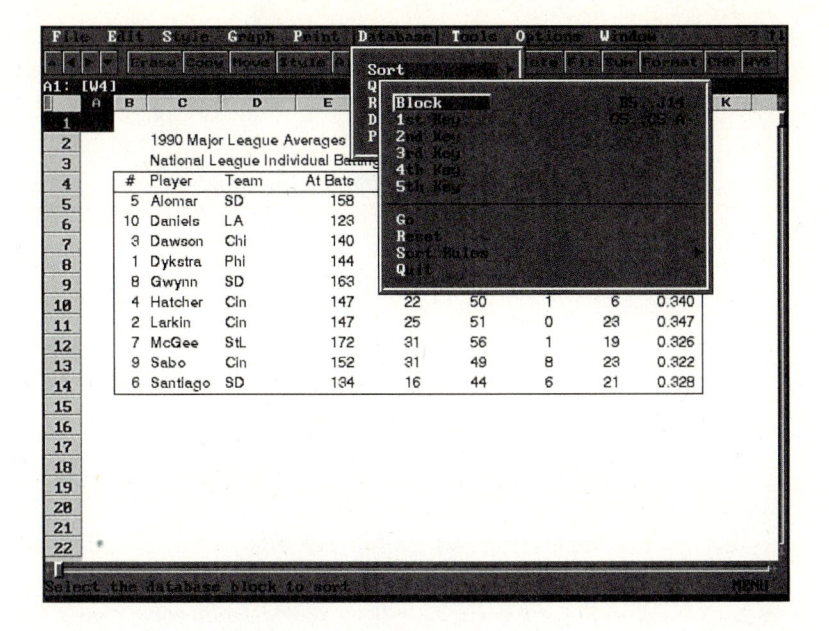

Fig. 13.4

The results of sorting the baseball database alphabetically by Player.

You always can substitute block names in place of cell addresses —a particularly useful technique for **D**atabase menu operations. To name a database area, select the block you want to name, choose /**E**dit **N**ames **C**reate, type a name, and then press Enter.

By naming the database area DATABASE, for example, you can type that name in place of the block address B5..J14. Likewise, when you name the fields, using the names on row 4, you can enter each name in place of a cell address when defining the sort keys. (See Chapter 4, "Manipulating Data," for more information about naming a cell block.)

To define the criteria for this sort operation, follow these steps:

1. Choose /**D**atabase **S**ort to display the **S**ort menu.

2. Choose **B**lock, type the coordinates or block name—*DATABASE*, for example—and press Enter.

TIP

After you specify a block or sort key address, Quattro Pro keeps the definition active as long as you are working with the same spreadsheet. When you later create names for your database, Quattro Pro replaces cell blocks and sort key addresses with their new names.

PART III — ADVANCED SPREADSHEET APPLICATIONS

3. Choose **1**st Key, type the key coordinates or name—*Team*, for example—and then press Enter.

4. When prompted, choose the sort order—**A**scending, for example—and press Enter.

5. Choose **2**nd Key, type the second key coordinates or name—*At Bats*, for example—and press Enter.

6. When prompted, choose the sort order and press Enter. (For the example, choose **D**escending and press Enter.)

7. Choose **G**o.

Quattro Pro rearranges the records according to your sort criteria (see fig. 13.5).

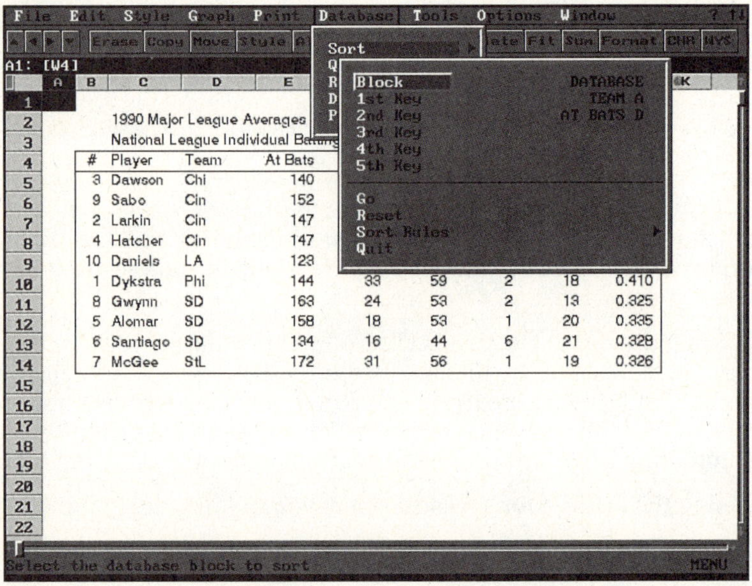

Fig. 13.5

The results of sorting alphabetically by Team and numerically by At Bats.

Figure 13.5 displays the result of this sort operation. Notice that Quattro Pro now displays each sort criterion definition at the right margin of the **S**ort menu, next to each command.

Experiment with this procedure by altering each sort key definition until you achieve the report style you want.

Returning the Database to Its Original Order

After you sort a database using several different sort keys, you sometimes need to return the database to its original order. Before you encounter this situation, consider the following three strategies for managing your database operations:

- Make a backup copy of the database file. When you need to recover the original database, choose /**F**ile **R**etrieve, type the name of the backup file, and press Enter to recover the original database.

- Copy the database records (the database area) to another part of the active spreadsheet. To guarantee the integrity of this data, do not perform any **D**atabase menu operations on the copied data.

- The most direct method is best understood by looking at the baseball database. Notice that the first field, #, identifies the numerical order of entry for each record. This technique, when used with all your databases, ensures that you always can return a sorted database to its original order. Choose # as the **1**st Key and sort the database in **A**scending order.

Fine-Tuning a Sort Operation

By default, Quattro Pro sorts data in the following order when **A**scending is chosen on a sort key menu:

1st	Blank cells
2nd	Labels starting with numbers (sorted in numerical order)
3rd	Labels beginning with letters and special characters (sorted in ASCII order)
4th	Values (sorted in numerical order)

When **D**escending order is chosen on a key menu, Quattro Pro sorts data in the opposite order (from 4th to 1st).

Figure 13.6 shows the three **S**ort Rules menu options: **N**umbers Before Labels, **S**ort Rows/Columns, and **L**abel Order. The default settings appear at the right margin of the menu, next to each command.

To change the default sorting order, choose /**D**atabase **S**ort **S**ort Rules **N**umbers Before Labels. When prompted, choose **Y**es to sort numbers before labels.

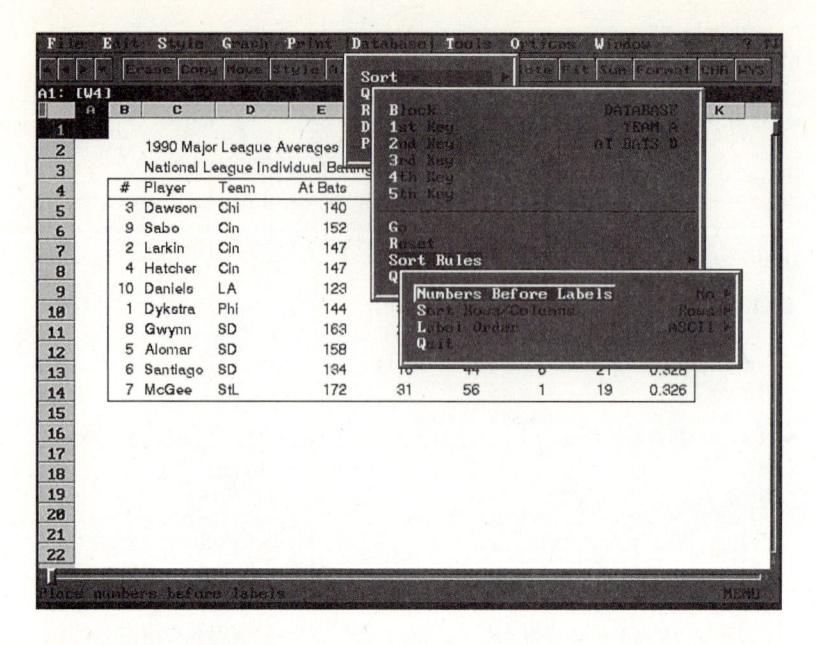

Fig. 13.6

The options on the **S**ort **R**ules menu.

To change how Quattro Pro sorts labels, choose /**D**atabase **S**ort **S**ort Rules **L**abel Order, and choose ASCII (the default) or **D**ictionary. The dictionary method disregards case in sorting labels so that the word *plaque* appears before *Plenty*.

The ASCII sort method considers case in sorting labels so that uppercase labels appear before lowercase labels—for example, *Plenty* before *plaque*, *Revere* before *plaque*, and so on. Labels beginning with special characters appear at the end.

> **TIP** After you change the sort rules, choose /**O**ptions Update to record those settings for future sort operations.

Sorting Columns

Quattro Pro enables you to sort data by columns and by rows. Sorting a database by columns is particularly helpful when you want to reorganize the order in which fields appear in a database, or when the field names appear in unique rows and the records are contained in unique columns. To sort a database by columns, choose /**D**atabase **S**ort **S**ort Rules **S**ort Rows/Columns **C**olumns before initiating the sort operation.

Figure 13.7 shows the baseball database after the database has been sorted by columns. In this sort operation, block B4..J14 has been specified as the sort **B**lock, cell B4 has been specified as the **1**st Key, the sort order is **A**scending, and the **S**ort Rows/Columns command has been set to **C**olumns.

```
File  Edit  Style  Graph  Print  Database  Tools  Options  Window    ?
      Erase Copy  Move   Style  Align  Font  Insert  Delete  Fit  Sum  Format  CHR  WYS
A1: [W4]
     A    B    C       D        E    F    G         H    I     J      K
 1
 2        1990 Major League Averages
 3        National League Individual Batting - 93 or more at bats
 4        #    AVG   At Bats   HR   Hits Player    RBI  Runs  Team
 5        3    ERR   140       13   48   Dawson    41   25    Chi
 6        9    ERR   152       8    49   Sabo      23   31    Cin
 7        2    ERR   147       0    51   Larkin    23   25    Cin
 8        4    ERR   147       1    50   Hatcher   6    22    Cin
 9       10    ERR   123       8    39   Daniels   27   17    LA
10        1    ERR   144       2    59   Dykstra   18   33    Phi
11        8    ERR   163       2    53   Gwynn     13   24    SD
12        5    ERR   158       1    53   Alomar    20   18    SD
13        6    ERR   134       6    44   Santiago  21   16    SD
14        7    ERR   172       1    56   McGee     19   31    StL
15
16
17
18
19
20
21
22
BASEBALL.WQ1 [1]                                              READY
```

Fig. 13.7

The results of sorting the baseball database alphabetically by the field name row labels, using the sort-by-column rule.

TIP

When you apply the sort-by-column rule to a database that contains record-dependent formulas (such as those in column C of fig. 13.7), Quattro Pro displays ERR values. To guard against this possibility, convert all record-dependent formulas to their values with /Edit Values before initiating a sort-by-column operation.

TIP

When you sort a database by column, you must include the field names row in the sort range when your database looks like the one pictured in figure 13.7. Including this row ensures that each row label remains paired with the data below the label after the sort operation. Don't include the field names in the sort block if the names are contained in unique rows; otherwise, Quattro Pro sorts the field names into the database area when you sort the database by column.

Searching a Database

You use the commands found on the **Q**uery menu to search a database, locate records that meet specific conditions, and then copy the records elsewhere on the same spreadsheet.

The records appearing in the baseball database, for example, come from a larger database containing statistics for all National League baseball players. To create the example database, you can search for the 10 players with the highest batting averages. You can extract the 10 lowest batting averages, the 10 highest averages with at least 120 hits, or all players whose last name begins with the letter Z.

Figure 13.8 shows a database containing inventory data for a sports car rental agency. In figure 13.8, the database shell is block B4..H10, and the database area is block B5..H10. Notice that the database area is a subset of the database shell.

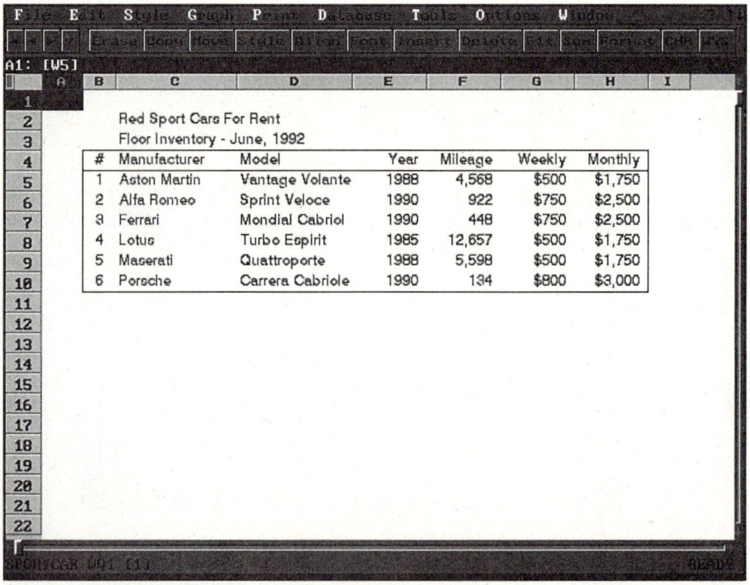

#	Manufacturer	Model	Year	Mileage	Weekly	Monthly
1	Aston Martin	Vantage Volante	1988	4,568	$500	$1,750
2	Alfa Romeo	Sprint Veloce	1990	922	$750	$2,500
3	Ferrari	Mondial Cabriol	1990	448	$750	$2,500
4	Lotus	Turbo Esprit	1985	12,657	$500	$1,750
5	Maserati	Quattroporte	1988	5,598	$500	$1,750
6	Porsche	Carrera Cabriole	1990	134	$800	$3,000

Fig. 13.8

The Red Sports Car rental agency database.

Remember, the database shell is the framework of the database: the field names row, the drawn lines (if any), and the database area where the records reside.

Defining the Search Block

The first step in every search operation is to define the search block. In most cases, the search block includes an entire database. Other valid search blocks include a portion of a database or even a database that resides on another spreadsheet in Quattro Pro's memory. Quattro Pro even can search databases not in memory, but stored on disk. Just supply the familiar linking syntax described in Chapter 8, "Managing Files and Windows."

You must follow one rule when you define a search block, however: the block must include the database field names that you want to search. Except for a few special cases, however, the search block and the database shell have the same coordinates.

This rule is the opposite of the rule applying to sort operations. In sort operations, you omit the field names when naming the database area. This action prevents Quattro Pro from sorting the field names into your database.

In a search operation, Quattro Pro does not shift the order of the records, because the program only looks at the records. When you define the search criteria, you must specify which field names the criteria apply to. After Quattro Pro knows what to search for, you need to indicate where in the search block to begin searching.

> **T I P**
>
> Choose /**E**dit **N**ames **C**reate and assign a unique name to the database shell. In this example, the name SHELL is assigned to block B4..H10.

To specify the search block, follow these steps:

1. Choose /**D**atabase **Q**uery **B**lock.

2. Type the name of the search block (*SHELL*, for the example) or type the block coordinates and press Enter.

Whether you choose to name your database shell or to supply block coordinates, be sure to include the field names row in the search block. If you don't, Quattro Pro does not search through your database correctly.

PART III — ADVANCED SPREADSHEET APPLICATIONS

Assigning Names to the Field Names Row

To assign names to the field names, choose /Database Query Assign Names. When you execute this command, Quattro Pro names the first entry in the first row below each field, using its field name label. In figure 13.8, for example, the name # is assigned to cell B5, Manufacturer to cell C5, Model to cell D5, and so on. This procedure enables Quattro Pro to begin the search operation at record #1 in the baseball database.

Assigning names to the field names row is optional but makes the process of creating and entering search criteria much easier. A name is easier to remember than a cell address.

Quattro Pro assigns the labels in the field names row to each field in the first record of the database. Quattro Pro knows which is the field names row and which is the first record in the database because when you specified the search block, you included the field names row as part of that block.

> **TIP** To execute a Query menu operation properly, Quattro Pro requires that your field names be no longer than 15 characters.

Defining the Search Criteria

The next step in the search process is to define the search criteria. You first must choose an area of the spreadsheet in which you can place the search conditions. In figure 13.9, a criteria table is entered into block B12..H13.

A *criteria table* contains field names and the criteria definitions that specify what to look for in a search block. A valid criteria table must include the name of at least one field and a condition (or conditions) to be met.

The first line of the criteria table in figure 13.9 is a duplicate of row 4 from the database shell. Although you need to include only one field name, this criteria table format enables you to define criteria selectively for one, some, or all the field names so that you can create an array of search conditions.

13 — MANAGING YOUR DATA

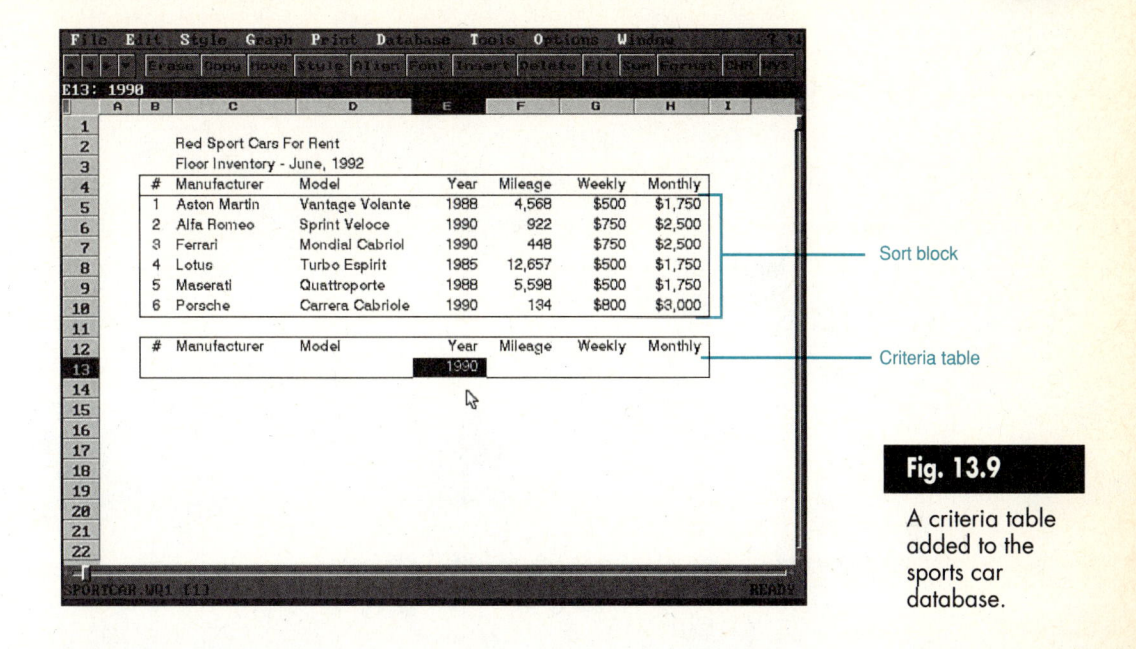

Fig. 13.9

A criteria table added to the sports car database.

> **TIP**
> Use the /Edit Copy command to copy the field names to the criteria tables, because names must match exactly.

Although the Year field in this criteria table contains only one definition, you easily can define additional criteria for the Year field. Enter the extra criteria definitions in the cells beneath the first one (for example, in cells E14, E15, and so on).

The following rules explain how Quattro Pro evaluates the search conditions appearing in a criteria table:

- When you enter more than one criterion definition on a row, Quattro Pro searches for records that satisfy all the search conditions. This operation is called an *AND search*.

- When fields have multiple criteria definitions, Quattro Pro searches for records that satisfy either condition. This operation is called an *OR search*.

The single criterion in figure 13.9 tells Quattro Pro to search for all records whose Year field contains the value 1990.

You can decide where on the spreadsheet to put the criteria table, although choosing an area just outside the database shell usually is most convenient.

To set up the criteria table, follow these steps:

1. Highlight block B4..H4.
2. Choose /**E**dit **C**opy.
3. Make cell B12 the active cell.
4. Press Enter to copy the field name labels to the criteria table.
5. Make cell E13 the active cell. Type *1990* and press Enter to record the criterion definition.

> **TIP**
>
> Choose /**E**dit **N**ames **C**reate and assign a unique name to the criteria table. In this example, the name CRITERIA is assigned to block B12..H13.

To define the criteria table, follow these steps:

1. Choose /**D**atabase **Q**uery **C**riteria Table.
2. Type *criteria* and press Enter to record the coordinates of the criteria table.

In step 2, you also can enter the block coordinates of the criterion definition, E12..E13. Both approaches return the same result. When a field in a criteria table has no definition, Quattro Pro ignores that field during a search operation.

Creating Search Formulas

The criterion definition in figure 13.9 is rather simple. To create more complex definitions, include formulas in your search criteria. You can search the rental car database for all cars whose model year is greater than or equal to 1988 (+YEAR>=1988), for example, or locate those cars whose monthly rental rate is less than four times the value of the weekly rate (+MONTHLY<+WEEKLY*4).

> **TIP**
>
> If you previously executed the **A**ssign Names command, use those names instead of cell addresses in your criteria formulas.

Criteria formulas must contain a cell reference, an operator, and a value. You can use any of the following mathematical and logical operators in a search formula:

13 — MANAGING YOUR DATA

Operator	Meaning
=	Equal
<	Less than
<=	Less than or equal
>	Greater than
>=	Greater than or equal
<>	Not equal
#AND#	AND logical operator
#NOT#	NOT logical operator
#OR#	OR logical operator

When you enter a formula as a search criterion, Quattro Pro displays a 1 or a 0 in the cell. A 0 value indicates that the first cell searched returned a FALSE value; a 1 indicates a TRUE value. These displayed values do not affect the search in any way. If you prefer to display a particular cell formula in text form, make that cell active, press Ctrl-F, and choose **Text**.

> **TIP**
> When creating the search formulas, press F3 to bring up a list of field names you can select rather than type those names.

Using Wild Cards

You also can use wild cards in your criteria table to delineate the conditions of a label search. Quattro Pro uses the following three different wild cards:

- ? A question mark replaces one character in a search label. When the search label is *p?t*, for example, Quattro Pro locates the labels *pat*, *pet*, *pit*, *pot*, and *put*, but not *spot* or *pate*.

- * An asterisk replaces any number of characters in a label. When the search label is *tre**, for example, Quattro Pro locates the labels *tree*, *tread*, and *treaty*, but not *retread* or *street*.

PART III — ADVANCED SPREADSHEET APPLICATIONS

■ ~ The tilde searches for all labels except those matching the label designation. When the search label is *~T**, for example, Quattro Pro finds all labels that do not begin with T. Quattro Pro can locate the labels *Fox*, *box*, and *CREATE*, but not *tiny* or *TREMENDOUS*.

NOTE If you leave the criteria definitions blank in the criteria block, Quattro Pro locates every record in the database.

Performing the Search

After you define the search block and the criteria table, Quattro Pro stores these definitions at the right margin of the **Query** menu, next to each command (see fig. 13.10). You now are ready to perform a search operation.

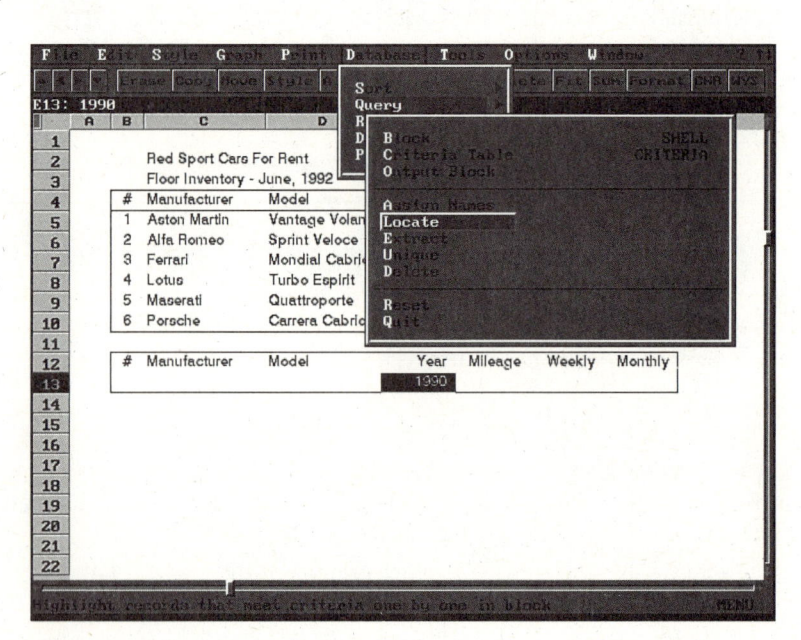

Fig. 13.10

The output block and criteria table definitions recorded on the Query menu.

Locating Records

To begin a search-and-locate operation, choose /**D**atabase **Q**uery **L**ocate. Figure 13.11 shows how Quattro Pro highlights the first field of the first record in the search block whose Year field contains the value 1990.

13 — MANAGING YOUR DATA

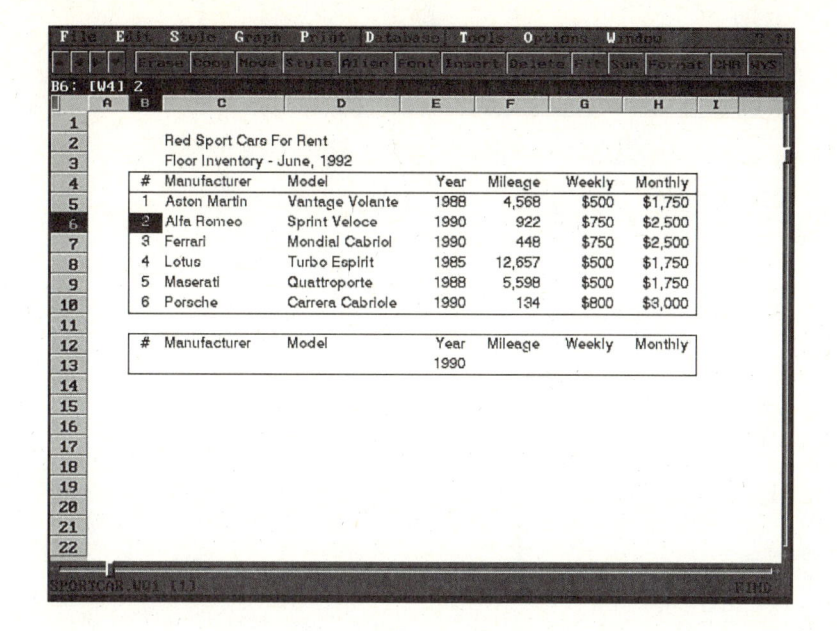

Fig. 13.11

Quattro Pro locates the first record in the database meeting the search criterion definition.

In the sports car database, the first match that Quattro Pro locates is record #2. To move to the next matching record (record #3), press the down-arrow key; to move to previous matches, press the up-arrow key. Press Home to move to the first matching record in the list and press End to move to the last matching record.

Occasionally, you may want to edit the contents of a highlighted record. Press the right-arrow or down-arrow key until the cell selector is in the field you want to edit, and then press F2 to enter EDIT mode. Make your changes on the input line and then press Enter to accept the new field data.

Figure 13.12 shows how to use a formula to narrow a search operation. The criterion formula in cell F13, +MILEAGE<400, adds an additional restriction that tells Quattro Pro to locate the records for all cars (built in 1990) that have mileage under 400 miles. Only one record, #6, meets this condition (see fig. 13.13).

Deleting Records

When you choose /**D**atabase **Q**uery **D**elete, Quattro Pro removes from the database all records that satisfy the defined criteria. Before deleting these records, Quattro Pro asks you to confirm your selection. Choose **D**elete to delete the records or **C**ancel to abort the operation.

PART III — ADVANCED SPREADSHEET APPLICATIONS

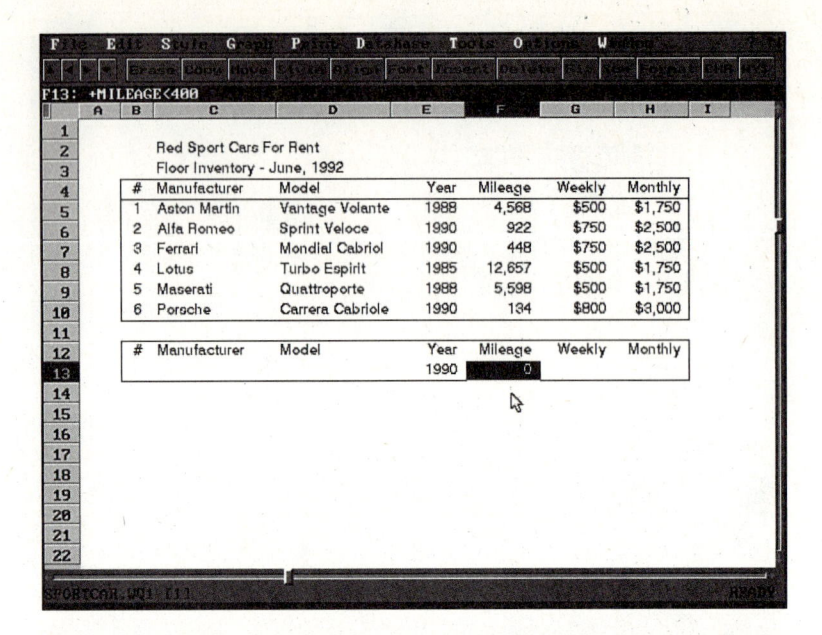

Fig. 13.12

Use a formula to narrow the search operation.

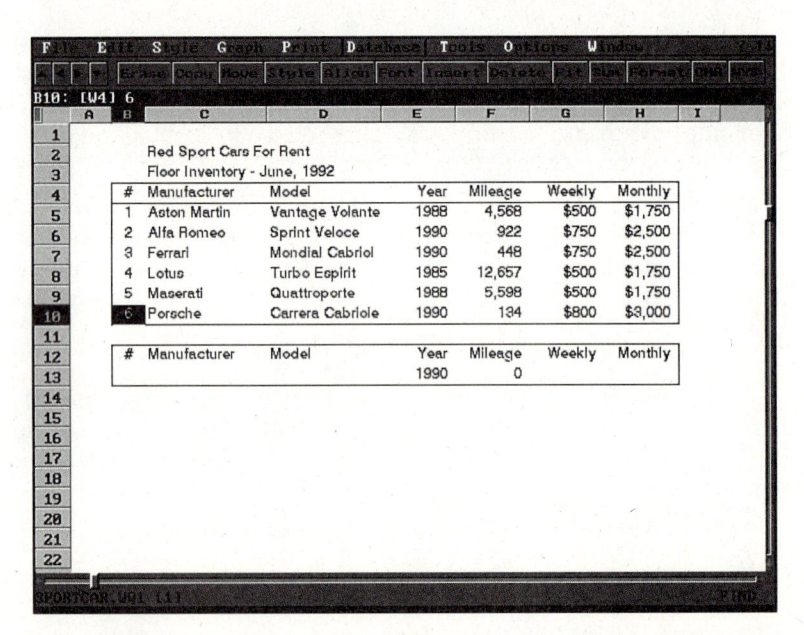

Fig. 13.13

Highlighted record #6, the only match in the database.

13 — MANAGING YOUR DATA

After Quattro Pro deletes all matching records from a database, all other records move up to fill the vacated spaces. If you accidentally delete records that you want to keep, press Alt-F5, the Undo key, to bring the records back.

Setting Up an Output Block

The **Extract** and **Unique** search commands find records that satisfy the criteria and then move the records to a different part of the spreadsheet for further processing. Before you use either search command, however, you must define an output block so that Quattro Pro knows where to store the extracted data.

These two commands are useful for extracting data from databases in several locations: spreadsheets open in memory, spreadsheets on disk, and other databases.

In figure 13.14, an output block appears in block B20..H20. When Quattro Pro locates records meeting the conditions specified in the criteria table, Quattro Pro copies the records to the output block beginning at the first line below the field names row.

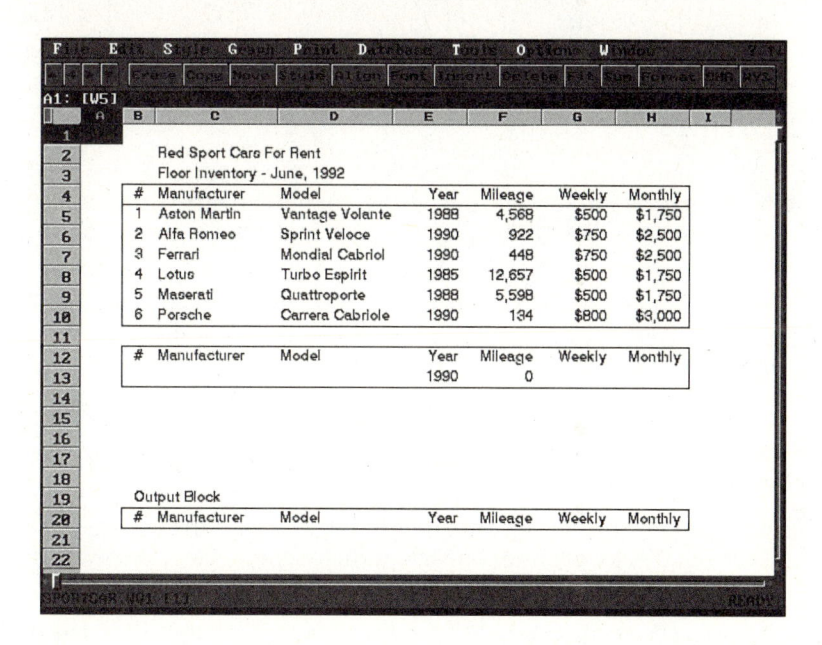

Fig. 13.14

An output block below the database and the criteria table.

To create this output block, follow these steps:

1. Highlight block B4..H4.
2. Choose /**E**dit **C**opy.
3. Make cell B20 the active cell.
4. Press Enter to copy the field name labels to the output block.

To define the output block, perform the following steps:

1. Highlight block B20..H20.
2. Choose /**E**dit **N**ames **C**reate.
3. Type *output* and press Enter to record this name.
4. Choose /**D**atabase **Q**uery **O**utput Block.
5. Type *output* and press Enter to record the name of the output block.

An output block, like a criteria table, does not need to contain every field name from the database—only the ones that currently are being searched. You should create an output block as you would create a criteria table, however, to ensure the greatest flexibility when you perform search operations.

Extracting Records

When you choose /**D**atabase **Q**uery **E**xtract, Quattro Pro copies all the matching records into the output block. Only the fields whose names appear on the first line of the output block are included in the copied records.

If you specify only the field names row when defining the output block, Quattro Pro uses as much space as necessary to copy the matching records. If you specify a limited number of rows below the field names row, Quattro Pro uses that space until that space is filled. When Quattro Pro runs out of space to copy to, the program displays a warning message explaining that all records cannot be extracted into the existing output block.

This problem is fairly easy to correct. First, erase all the records in the output block. Next, redefine the size of the output block. Finally, restart the search operation.

With the same criteria used in the search-and-locate operation from the preceding section, figure 13.15 shows the result of an extract operation. Instead of highlighting a matched record, Quattro Pro extracts a copy of the record and places the copy in the first row below the field names row in the output block.

13 — MANAGING YOUR DATA

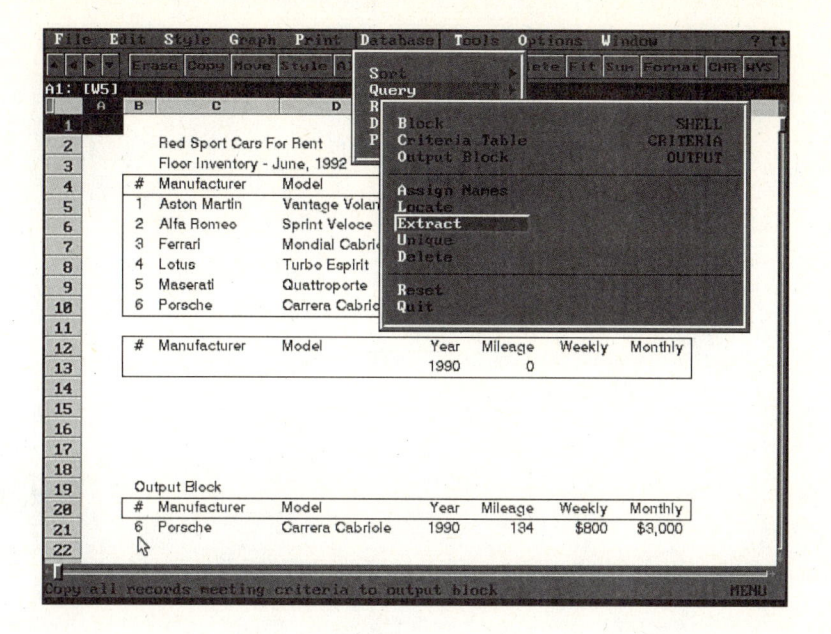

Fig. 13.15

Quattro Pro extracts and copies a matching record to the output block.

Identifying Unique Records

When you choose /**D**atabase **Q**uery **U**nique, Quattro Pro copies all unique records that meet the specified criteria into the output block. Unique works like Extract, except that Unique does not copy duplicate records into the output block.

Consider the revised sports car database shown in figure 13.16. Notice that record #5 appears twice in this version of the database. The larger the database, the greater the chances that you will encounter duplicated records.

The criteria table specifies all records whose # field equals 5 and whose Manufacturer field contains the label Maserati. In this situation, the **U**nique command copies the unique records that meet these conditions (see fig. 13.17).

Notice that the output block in this figure contains only one record. Because only two records met the search conditions in the criteria table, and these records are duplicates, Quattro Pro copies only one record into the output block.

Now look at the split window shown in figure 13.18. The results displayed in this output table were achieved by not specifying any criteria in the criteria table.

PART III — ADVANCED SPREADSHEET APPLICATIONS

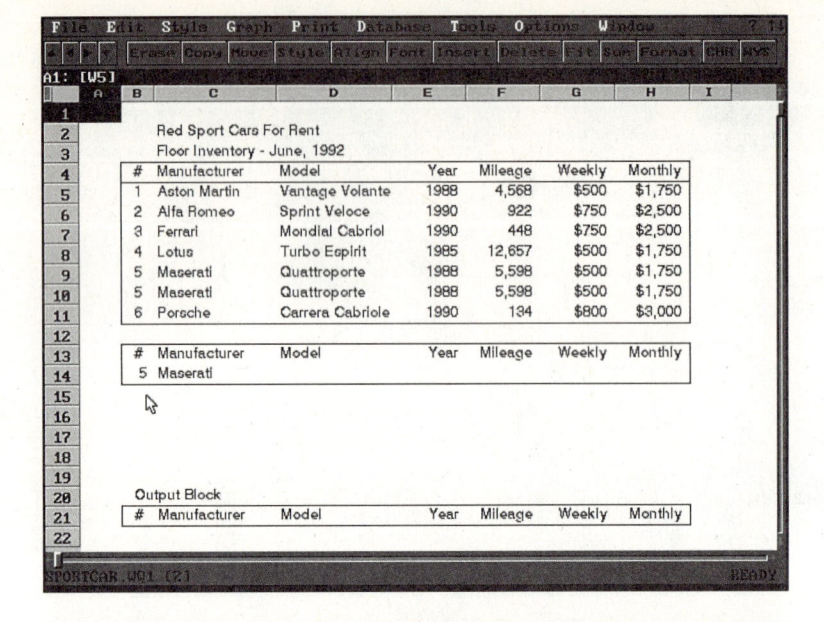

Fig. 13.16

Criteria entered to extract a list of unique records from the database.

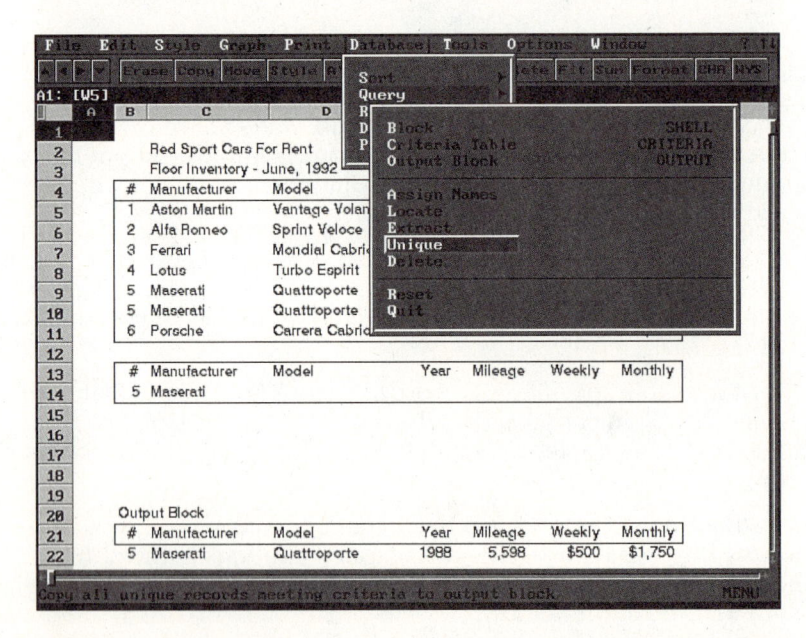

Fig. 13.17

All unique matching records are copied from the database into the output block.

13 — MANAGING YOUR DATA   599

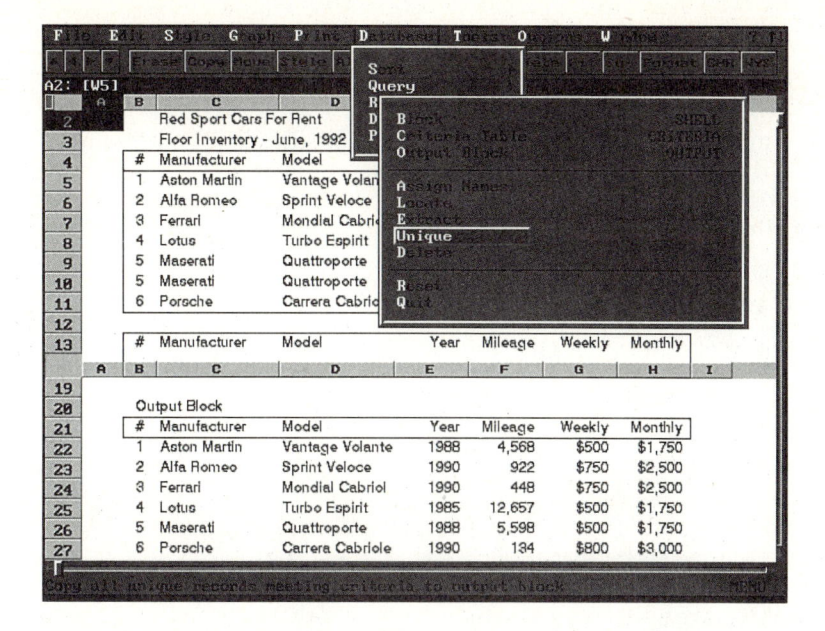

Fig. 13.18

The results of not specifying criteria.

Not specifying any criteria forces Quattro Pro to copy all unique records from the database into the output table. This procedure is a clever way to update a database when you suspect that duplicate records exist.

Using a Database as a Data-Entry Form

The /**D**atabase **R**estrict Input command enables you to set up your spreadsheet as a data-entry form. After executing this command, Quattro Pro limits movement of the cell selector only to unprotected cells.

To set up the sports car database for data entry, follow these steps:

1. Choose /**S**tyle **P**rotection **U**nprotect.

2. When prompted for a block to unprotect, type the block name (*database*, for the example) and press Enter.

3. Choose /**D**atabase **R**estrict Input.

4. Type the block to restrict—*database*—and press Enter.

PART III — ADVANCED SPREADSHEET APPLICATIONS

Quattro Pro immediately restricts movement of the cell selector to the database area for the sports car database.

When you execute **/D**atabase **R**estrict Input, however, Quattro Pro reframes the database in the window by positioning the first unprotected field in the database at the upper left portion of your screen. To prevent Quattro Pro from reframing your database, perform the following steps before selecting /**D**ata **R**estrict Input:

1. Place the cell selector in the first unprotected field in the database (cell B5).
2. Choose /**W**indow **O**ptions **L**ocked Titles.
3. When prompted, choose **B**oth.

When you perform these steps, your screen looks like the one shown in figure 13.19. On this screen, you cannot move your cell selector to any location above or to the left of the first cell in DATABASE (cell B5) or below or to the right of the active cell (cell H11). Quattro Pro shades locked titles to delineate cell blocks A1..A8192 and B1..IV4 from the rest of the spreadsheet. Now when you execute the **R**estrict Input command, Quattro Pro does not move your database.

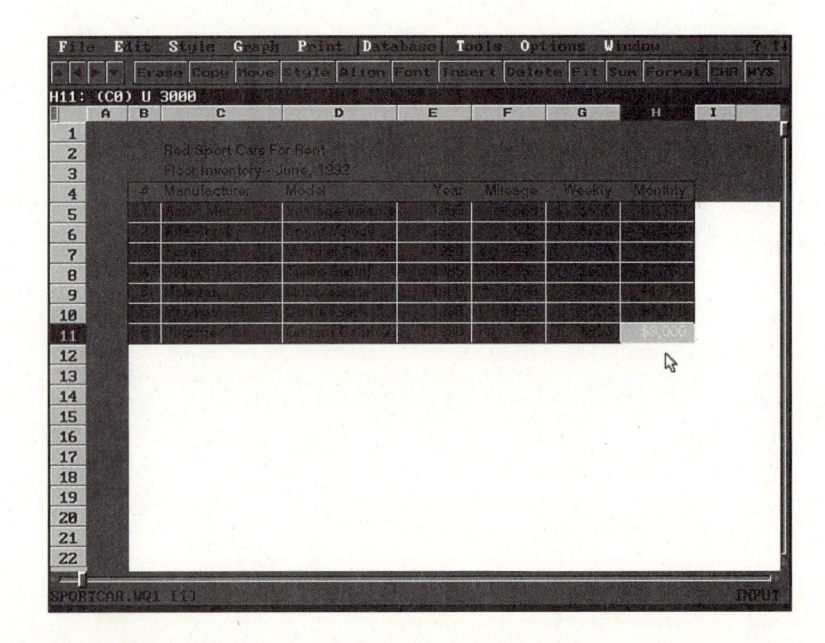

Fig. 13.19

Locked titles on a spreadsheet to control cell selector movement.

While in restricted entry mode, you cannot use the mouse. Use the cursor-movement keys to move about the database. To disable the restricted access, press Enter or Esc.

Controlling Data Entry

The /**D**atabase **D**ata Entry command controls the type of data that Quattro Pro accepts into a cell or a block. Use this command to increase the accuracy of data-entry activities. Suppose that a field (column) of data in a database is designated for only dates. By restricting the cells in this column to date-only entries, you can prevent data-entry errors.

To restrict the type of data acceptable in an entry, follow these steps:

1. Choose /**D**atabase **D**ata Entry.
2. When prompted, choose **L**abels Only to restrict all input to labels or choose **D**ates Only to restrict input to dates.

Choose /**D**atabase **D**ata Entry **G**eneral to enable a cell to accept any type of data.

Using Paradox Access

Users of Quattro Pro can read and write Paradox files that have a DB file-name extension. With this feature, you can load data from a Paradox database file into a Quattro Pro spreadsheet. Quattro Pro (Version 2.0 or later) also offers **P**aradox Access, a **D**atabase menu command that enables you to run Quattro Pro from within Paradox (Version 3.5 or later).

Quattro Pro's /**D**atabase **P**aradox Access command switches you into Paradox's operating environment. While in Paradox, you can switch back to Quattro Pro by pressing Ctrl-F10. This program-linking feature places the power of both program environments at your fingertips. You can use Quattro Pro's graph presentation and publishing capabilities to enhance your Paradox data, or use Paradox's sophisticated data management tools to manipulate Quattro Pro spreadsheet data.

Reviewing the Requirements for Using Paradox Access

Paradox and Quattro Pro have different minimum hardware needs. Quattro Pro usually uses expanded memory, whereas Paradox mostly uses extended memory. Although Quattro Pro can load and run on an IBM-PC with only 512K of RAM, Paradox's memory needs are somewhat

PART III — ADVANCED SPREADSHEET APPLICATIONS

greater. To use the **P**aradox Access command, you must have at least the following software and hardware:

- Quattro Pro (Version 2.0 or later)
- Paradox (Version 3.5 or later)
- 2M of extended RAM
- An 80286-AT personal computer

To achieve peak performance from the Quattro Pro-Paradox link, Borland recommends that you buy a separate product called Paradox SQL Link. This product enables you to access data stored on file servers running SQL (Structured Query Language). Many mainframes, minicomputers, and OS/2 servers support SQL software. Check with that system's administrator to verify that the file server supports Borland's Paradox SQL Link.

Preparing To Use Paradox Access

Before you use the **P**aradox Access command, you must alter the contents of three files: CONFIG.SYS, AUTOEXEC.BAT, and PXACCESS.BAT. The first two files reside in your root directory. Quattro Pro copies the third file into the /QPRO directory when you first install Quattro Pro.

> **NOTE** PXACCESS.BAT is a batch file that prepares Paradox for a program link and then loads Paradox into system memory.

Use the following procedure to prepare your computer for a Quattro Pro-Paradox link:

1. Set FILES=40 in your CONFIG.SYS file.

2. Add a line containing the word SHARE to your AUTOEXEC.BAT file. This terminate-and-stay-resident (TSR) program enables Quattro Pro and Paradox to share and lock files.

3. Verify that your AUTOEXEC.BAT file contains Quattro Pro and Paradox in the PATH statement.

4. Verify that Quattro Pro and Paradox are installed and reside in separate directories.

5. Verify that your Paradox working directory and private directory are different. If they are not different, enter Paradox's Custom Configuration Program and use the **D**efaults **S**et Directory command to change the location of the working directory.

13 — MANAGING YOUR DATA

6. Verify that the PXACCESS.BAT file contains the correct memory allocation arguments.

> **TIP**
> The last four of these changes are taken care of automatically during installation. Verifying these changes, however, is a good idea.

PXACCESS.BAT contains two command lines that serve to prepare your system's memory for the eventual program link. The first command line contains the DOS SHARE command (in case you forget to execute PXACCESS.BAT before establishing a program link). Executing the SHARE command twice causes no harm because DOS ignores the second attempt.

The second command line contains the following statement:

   PARADOX –qpro –leaveK 512 –emK 0

The function of each argument appearing on this command line is defined as follows:

Argument	Function
PARADOX	Loads Paradox into your computer's memory
–qpro	Establishes the Quattro Pro-Paradox link, enables Paradox to work in a multiuser environment, and allocates a minimum of 384K of conventional memory to Quattro Pro
–leaveK 512	Allocates the first 512K of memory to Quattro Pro
–emK 0	Allocates all expanded memory to Quattro Pro so that Paradox does not use the memory

You may need to edit the contents of PXACCESS.BAT depending on the type and amount of memory you have in your system. Consider the following scenarios:

- Your 80386 computer has 4M of expanded memory and uses the Quarterdeck QEMM-386 expanded memory manager. Edit your PXACCESS.BAT file as follows:

   PARADOX –qpro –leaveK 3000 –emK 0

   (Always set the –leaveK argument equal to 1M less than total system memory.)

PART III — ADVANCED SPREADSHEET APPLICATIONS

- Your 80286 computer has an AST RAMpage expanded memory card with 4M of memory. Edit your PXACCESS.BAT file as follows:

    PARADOX –qpro –leaveK 0 –emK 0

- Your 80286 computer has 4M of memory, which is configured as extended. Edit your PXACCESS.BAT file as follows:

    PARADOX –qpro –leaveK 2000 –emK 0

    (Set the –leaveK argument so that it is greater than 512 but less than the total amount of extended memory. Increase this setting if you have difficulty loading large Quattro Pro spreadsheets.)

- Your 80286 computer has 1M of extended memory. Your PXACCESS.BAT file uses the DOS SHARE file allocation table (FAT) distribution and requires the following modifications:

    PARADOX –qpro –leaveK 512 –emK 0 –share –prot

Finally, set /Options Other Expanded Memory to Both to ensure that memory is allocated in the most efficient manner.

> **TIP**
> When you establish a program link, Quattro Pro disables the /x start-up parameter (if you supply the parameter), which enables Quattro Pro to use 512K of extended memory.

After you edit the CONFIG.SYS, AUTOEXEC.BAT, and PXACCESS.BAT files, Quattro Pro and Paradox operate properly each time you load them into your system's memory.

Running Paradox Access

You can initiate the link between Quattro Pro and Paradox from within Paradox and from within Quattro Pro.

Initiating a Program Link from Paradox

The best method for initiating a Quattro Pro-Paradox link is to execute the PXACCESS.BAT file from DOS. This file initiates file locking and file sharing, properly allocates memory to Quattro Pro and Paradox, and then loads Paradox into system memory. To use this method, follow these steps:

13 — MANAGING YOUR DATA

1. If you are in Quattro Pro, choose /File Exit to return to DOS.
2. At the DOS command prompt, type *pxaccess* and press Enter to load Paradox into your computer's memory.
3. After you are inside Paradox, press Ctrl-F10 to switch to Quattro Pro.

You can load a Quattro Pro file the first time you switch to Quattro Pro from Paradox during a work session (as described in step 3). This feature helps you to manage shared file data between these two programs because initially, you always pass the data to the same Quattro Pro spreadsheet.

> **TIP**
>
> If you are not operating on a network and you get the error message `Cannot lock file for reading`, set the /Options Other Paradox Network Type command to Other. Choose /Options Update to save this setting.

To specify the spreadsheet that Quattro Pro should load, type the file name in brackets and place the file name after the –qpro argument in the second command line in the PXACCESS.BAT file. The syntax for using this feature is as follows:

   PARADOX –qpro [*filename macroname /options*]

If you want to load a Quattro Pro spreadsheet file named PXDATA.WK1 the first time you switch from Paradox to Quattro Pro during a work session, for example, use the following syntax:

   PARADOX –qpro [C:\QPRO\PXDATA.WK1]

Remember, this procedure works only once during each work session. If you switch back to Paradox and then return to Quattro Pro at a later time, Quattro Pro autoloads the spreadsheet file specified with the /Database Paradox Access Load File command. Quattro Pro workspace names and Paradox DB file names are valid substitutes for the *filename* argument in the syntax in the example.

If you want Quattro Pro to execute a macro named FORMAT that formats the autoloaded spreadsheet, for example, use the following syntax:

   PARADOX –qpro [C:\QPRO\PXDATA.WK1 FORMAT]

To autoload the spreadsheet named PXDATA.WK1, execute the macro named FORMAT, and initially load Quattro Pro with its monochrome display palette, supply the following statement in the PXACCESS.BAT file:

   PARADOX –qpro [C:\QPRO\PXDATA.WK1 FORMAT /IM]

Remember, Quattro Pro disables the /x parameter and instead uses the –leaveK and –emK commands in the PXACCESS.BAT file to manage system memory. See Chapter 16, "Customizing Quattro Pro," for a complete list of Quattro Pro's other start-up parameters.

Initiating a Program Link from Quattro Pro

To initiate a Quattro Pro-Paradox link from Quattro Pro, follow these steps:

1. Load Quattro Pro into your system's memory.
2. Choose /**D**atabase **P**aradox Access. Quattro Pro displays the **Pa**radox Access menu. Choose **G**o to switch to Paradox.

The commands on the **P**aradox Access menu enable you to control the operation and configuration of Paradox.

The **G**o command switches you from Quattro Pro to Paradox. This command is operable as long as you started the current work session by executing the PXACCESS.BAT file. The **G**o command now is active.

Use the **L**oad File command to specify the name of a file for Quattro Pro to load each time you switch back to Quattro Pro from Paradox. Remember, if you also specify a file-name argument to the –qpro command in PXACCESS.BAT, Quattro Pro loads that file the first time you switch from Paradox to Quattro Pro during the current work session. Every time thereafter, Quattro Pro loads the file specified by the Load File command.

The Autoload command enables and disables the **L**oad File command. If **A**utoload is set to **N**o, for example, Quattro Pro does not load the file specified by the Load File command. If you set /**D**atabase **P**aradox Access **A**utoload to **Y**es, Quattro Pro ignores the /**O**ptions **S**tartup Autoload File command setting.

Questions & Answers

This chapter introduces you to the **D**atabase menu commands. If you have questions concerning particular situations that are not addressed in the examples given, look through this section.

Sorting a Database

Q: I want to sort my database so that all clients from Oklahoma (having OK in the STATE field) are at the top of my database. Am I confined to ascending and descending orders?

A: Yes. Sort is confined to a few sorting orders. What you need to do is a search. If you really want to place all OK records on the top rows of your database, use /**D**atabase **Q**uery **E**xtract, then use /**D**atabase **Q**uery **D**elete, and finally copy the extracted records to the top lines of your database.

Q: On the **S**ort menu, can I specify **1**st Key as an ascending sort, with **2**nd Key as a descending sort?

A: Yes. Quattro Pro prompts you for sort direction after each key. The specified sort rules apply equally to all sort keys and operations, however.

Q: I am unable to decipher the results of a sort operation. Apparently my records have shifted by column but not by row. What should I check for?

A: When database records appear to have been sorted incorrectly, first try pressing Alt-F5 to undo the operation. (If the Undo feature is disabled, refer to Chapter 15's section on "Restoring Parts of the Transcript" to learn how to undo the operation.)

Next, choose /**D**atabase **S**ort **S**ort Rules and review the current setting for the **S**ort Rows/Columns command. If it is set to Columns (or **R**ows) when you want to sort by rows (or columns), choose the opposite setting and try the sort operation again.

Searching a Database

Q: When I enter a formula in my criteria table, I get the warning message Invalid cell or block address. What's wrong?

A: Quattro Pro doesn't recognize the field name you have used. First, make sure that the spelling matches that defined in the search block. Second, make sure that you have used the **A**ssign Names command following any changes you made to the field names. Third, supply the cell address in the formula.

Q: Can I possibly search for (and extract) all records in which any one field is zero?

A: Certainly. Set up a criteria table specifying that records in which field1=0, field2=0, and so on be selected.

PART III — ADVANCED SPREADSHEET APPLICATIONS

Accessing Paradox

Q: When I press Ctrl-F10 to switch from Paradox to Quattro Pro, I get a warning message that says Can't Load Quattro Pro. What's wrong?

A: The QPRO program directory is not included in the PATH statement found in the AUTOEXEC.BAT file. Edit the contents of the AUTOEXEC.BAT file to include QPRO in your PATH statement; then, rerun PXACCESS.BAT.

Q: When I press Ctrl-F10 to switch from Paradox to Quattro Pro, the program beeps at me. Now what's wrong?

A: You did not load Paradox with the PXACCESS.BAT file. Exit Paradox, type *pxaccess* at the DOS command prompt, press Enter to load Paradox, and configure your system for a Quattro Pro-Paradox link.

Q: Quattro Pro did not autoload the file that I typed next to the –qpro argument in the PXACCESS.BAT file. Why did this happen?

A: You forgot to place the file name in brackets, so Quattro Pro ignored your entry. You must place all –qpro arguments in brackets.

Q: I just switched to Paradox from Quattro Pro but forgot to save my spreadsheet. Did I lose all my data?

A: No. You need not choose **/F**ile **S**ave before switching to Paradox. When you return from the Paradox to the Quattro Pro environment, your spreadsheet appears just as you left it when you first switched. When you try to leave Paradox before saving an altered Quattro Pro spreadsheet, you are prompted to save the changes before quitting the program.

Q: I am having difficulty loading a Quattro Pro spreadsheet. Does this have something to do with the **P**aradox Access command?

A: In a way, yes. When you load Quattro Pro from within Paradox, presumably by executing PXACCESS.BAT, your memory is allocated differently than if you load Quattro Pro by itself. If your system has zero expanded memory available to Quattro Pro, for example, you likely can load only smaller spreadsheets. If Quattro Pro fails to load a spreadsheet in its entirety, increase the –leaveK setting in PXACCESS.BAT to free up more expanded memory.

Summary

In this chapter, you learned how to manipulate your data by using the commands found on the **D**atabase menu. These commands enable you to turn a Quattro Pro spreadsheet into an efficient environment for storing and accessing database information.

Having completed this chapter's material, you should understand the following concepts:

- Creating a database shell on a spreadsheet
- Entering data into a database
- Sorting records using field names as sort keys
- Sorting records by rows and by columns
- Searching a database for records that meet specific criteria definitions
- Using a spreadsheet as a data-entry form
- Using the **P**aradox Access command to link Quattro Pro to Paradox

Chapter 14 introduces you to the commands on the **T**ools menu that enable you to perform advanced data analysis. In Quattro Pro, advanced data analysis works on the principles of regression, data parsing, sensitivity analysis, and optimization modeling. The techniques described in this chapter can help you find answers to complex questions about data you have in your spreadsheets.

CHAPTER 14

Analyzing Data

Even the most complete and meticulously kept spreadsheet application can be ineffective if it does not yield simple and interpretable answers to specific questions. In a sales forecast application, for example, what is the effect on revenues of a 10 percent increase in advertising expenditures? In Southern California, what is the relationship between the average annual price of gasoline and the number of gallons consumed? How is a sporting goods store's gross profit affected by a 7 percent decline in the cost of goods sold and a simultaneous 4 percent increase in consumer demand?

This chapter starts by introducing you to the **Tools** menu commands that can produce answers to these types of questions, using data that you store in your spreadsheet applications.

In the next section, you learn how to do *regression analysis*, a technique in which you develop formulas to predict future results based on current and historical data. You then learn how to work with mathematical matrices—specifically, how to invert and multiply matrices.

Next, you learn how to reorganize data imported from other software. This technique is called *parsing*, which means breaking apart long lines of data into smaller, more manageable lines. Parsing is useful for preparing your data for further analysis in Quattro Pro.

The next section demonstrates how to perform *sensitivity analysis*, a technique that shows in one spreadsheet many different outcomes to the same formula or problem. You also learn how to create a frequency distribution to group similar elements from a large set of data.

PART III — ADVANCED SPREADSHEET APPLICATIONS

The chapter next covers the use of the Optimizer. This powerful tool enables you to identify optimal solutions to complex problems that contain many interrelated variables.

Finally, you learn how to load add-in @functions into Quattro Pro for use in your spreadsheets.

NOTE The examples in this chapter offer sufficient coverage of each command to enable you to use all or most of the features available for each tool. You can consult a statistics text for more comprehensive presentations of the mathematical proofs and axioms on which these tools are based.

Reviewing the Tools Menu

You can use the commands at the bottom of the **Tools** menu, shown in figure 14.1, to answer complex questions you have about data in your spreadsheets. With these commands, you can perform analyses that go well beyond the simple "what-is-the-average-of-these-three-numbers" type of questions that you have learned to answer by using arithmetic formulas and @functions.

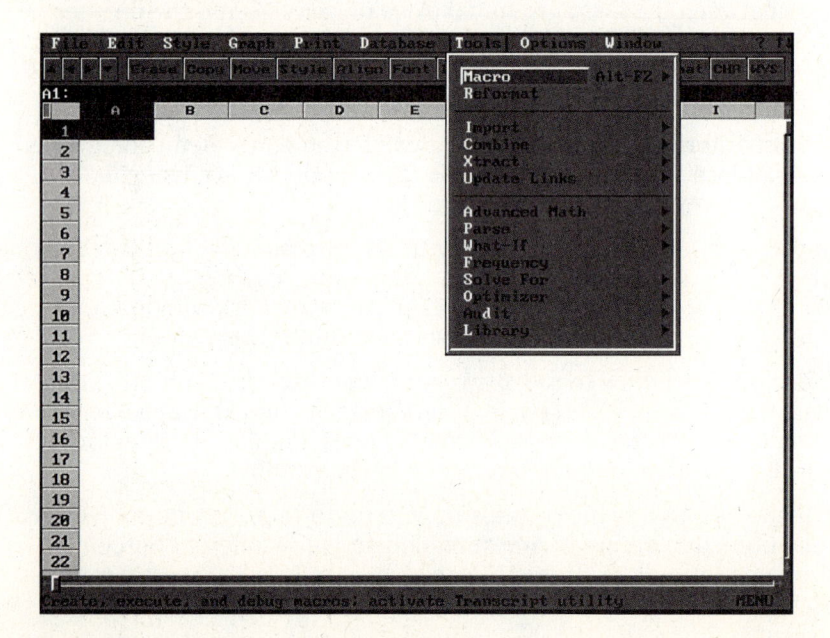

Fig. 14.1

The mathematical tools on the **Tools** menu.

NOTE See Chapter 7, "Analyzing Spreadsheets," to learn how to monitor the construction of spreadsheet formulas using the Au**d**it command and how to solve formulas backwards using the **S**olve For command.

The **A**dvanced Math tools use information from a spreadsheet to perform regression analysis and matrix operations. The **P**arse command breaks long labels from an imported data set and places the individual parts into separate cells. The **W**hat-If command performs one-way and two-way sensitivity analysis. The **F**requency command creates frequency distributions. The **O**ptimizer enables you to define and solve complex problems that encompass multiple variables and constraints. Finally, the **L**ibrary command enables you to load custom add-in @functions into Quattro Pro for use with your spreadsheets.

Using Advanced Math Tools

When you choose **A**dvanced Math from the **T**ools menu, you access another menu that offers three powerful statistical tools for analyzing different types of data. The **A**dvanced Math menu commands are listed in table 14.1.

Table 14.1 Advanced Math Menu Commands

Command	Description
Regression	Performs single-variable and multivariable data set regressions
Invert	Creates an inverted matrix from a matrix
Multiply	Multiplies one matrix by a second matrix

Performing Regression Analysis

Regression analysis attempts to devise an equation in which an independent variable predicts the value of a dependent variable. You can use more than one independent variable. Regression analysis, in fact, is one of the most effective methods for determining a linear relationship between a set of independent variables and a single dependent variable.

PART III — ADVANCED SPREADSHEET APPLICATIONS

Suppose that you want to determine the relationship between the average yearly price of gasoline and the quantity that you buy. The hypothesis is that your consumption (Cy) depends on the price (Px) of gasoline. Because only one independent variable exists (Px), this problem is a single-variable regression analysis.

The table in figure 14.2 contains data about average gasoline prices and consumption in gallons for a 10-year period. Notice also that the **Re**-**gression** menu displays the definitions for each variable (independent and dependent), the output block, and a y-axis intercept. You must enter these definitions before executing the **Regression** command.

Fig. 14.2

A data table containing yearly gasoline consumption and average yearly price per gallon.

Year	C(y)	P(x)
1978	154.46	$0.57
1979	154.11	$0.58
1980	150.30	$0.69
1981	143.72	$0.88
1982	138.18	$1.04
1983	128.99	$1.22
1984	118.33	$1.38
1985	101.67	$1.52
1986	100.09	$1.62
1987	104.40	$1.44
1988	107.76	$1.23

C(y) = Consumption in gallons
P(x) = Price per gallon

To do a regression analysis, perform the following steps:

1. Choose /**T**ools **A**dvanced Math **R**egression.

2. From the **R**egression menu, choose **I**ndependent, type the range that includes the independent variable—*F4..F14* in the example—and press Enter.

T I P To include other independent variables, enter additional data into the columns to the right of the first independent variable. Then, include these columns in the block you enter in step 2.

14 — ANALYZING DATA

3. Choose **D**ependent, type the range that includes the dependent variable—*D4..D14* in the example—and press Enter.

4. Choose **O**utput, type the cell that should be the upper left corner of the range to which you want to output the analysis—*H4* in the example—and press Enter.

> **TIP**
>
> Use the **Y** Intercept **C**ompute setting for most basic regression problems. To force the y-axis intercept value to 0, choose **Y** Intercept **Z**ero.

5. Choose **G**o to calculate the regression.

The **Regression** command appraises each pair of points supplied in your data table, which in turn enables you to derive an equation that minimizes each pair's distance from a "best fit" line. Quattro Pro calculates a formula constant and the coefficients for each independent value and then displays the results in a regression table (see fig. 14.3). Use the values in the regression table to create the equation with which you can predict a new dependent value based on a new independent value.

Dependent variables
Independent variables

Year	C(y)	P(x)			
1978	154.46	$0.57		Regression Output:	
1979	154.11	$0.58		Constant	188.4739
1980	150.30	$0.69		Std Err of Y Est	6.413204
1981	143.72	$0.88		R Squared	0.92223
1982	138.18	$1.04		No. of Observations	11
1983	128.99	$1.22		Degrees of Freedom	9
1984	118.33	$1.38			
1985	101.67	$1.52		X Coefficient(s)	-55.1529
1986	100.09	$1.62		Std Err of Coef.	5.338678
1987	104.40	$1.44			
1988	107.76	$1.23			

C(y) = Consumption in gallons
P(x) = Price per gallon

C(y) = 188.5 + -55.2 P(x) <======== Regression formula

Output block

Linear predictive formula (equation)

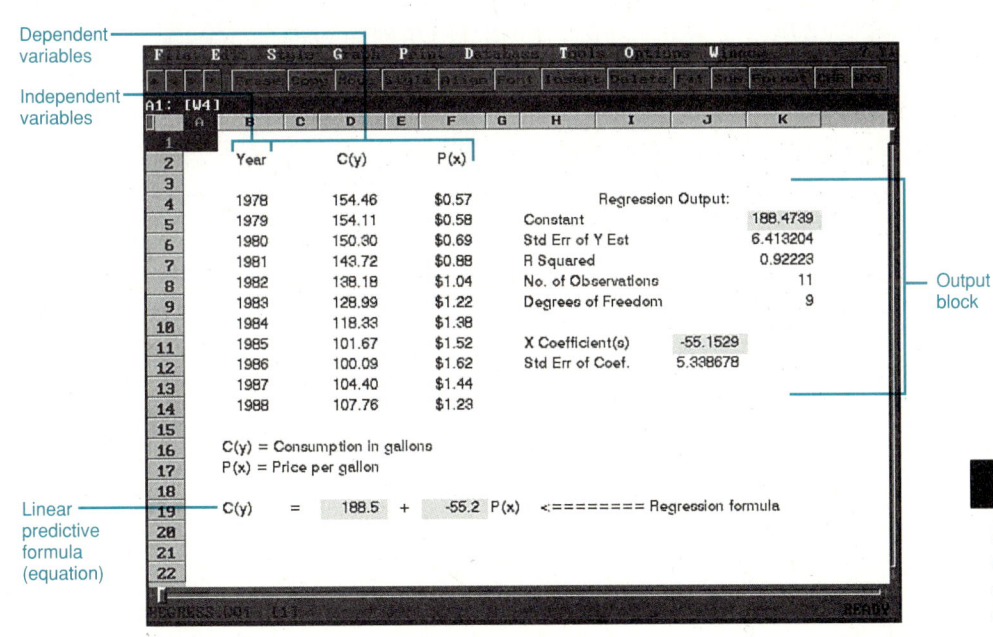

Fig. 14.3

A regression analysis table copied into the output block.

PART III — ADVANCED SPREADSHEET APPLICATIONS

The constant and the X coefficient are the key components of the equation. Each independent variable that you specify in your data table always has one constant and one coefficient. Use the following syntax to build a linear predictive formula from the data in this table:

Dependent Variable = Constant +

(1st X coefficient * 1st independent variable) +

(2nd X coefficient * 2nd independent variable) +

... + (nth X coefficient * nth independent variable)

Because the consumption versus price example contains only one independent variable, only one X coefficient exists.

The linear predictive formula appears at the bottom of figure 14.3. To create this formula, the value +K5 was placed in cell D19, and the value +J11 was placed in cell F19. This formula updates itself each time you rerun the regression with new data as long as you do not change the location of the output table. If you add independent variables to your data table, you must create additional cell references in the formula appearing on row 19 to accommodate the new X coefficients.

You can use this formula to test your theories about the relationship between the price of gasoline and the quantity of gasoline purchased by consumers. Suppose that a sudden oil crisis pushed the price of gasoline up to $3.00 per gallon. By substituting the value 3 into the linear predictive formula as follows:

$C(y) - 188.5 = -55.2(3.00)$

you can predict that average annual consumption will go to 22.9 gallons. Continue substituting values in for the $P(x)$ variable to test other theories you may have.

Performing Matrix Operations: Invert and Multiply

Using matrices, you can solve multivariable linear equations simultaneously. A *matrix* is a rectangular array of numbers that describes the coefficients for variables in a group of linear equations. If you have to solve linear equations using matrices, use Quattro Pro's **Invert** and **Multiply** commands to calculate the answers quickly.

Consider the matrices shown in figure 14.4. Each time you create an inverted matrix, you must go through the four-step process outlined in this figure. The values you are required to supply are highlighted.

14 — ANALYZING DATA

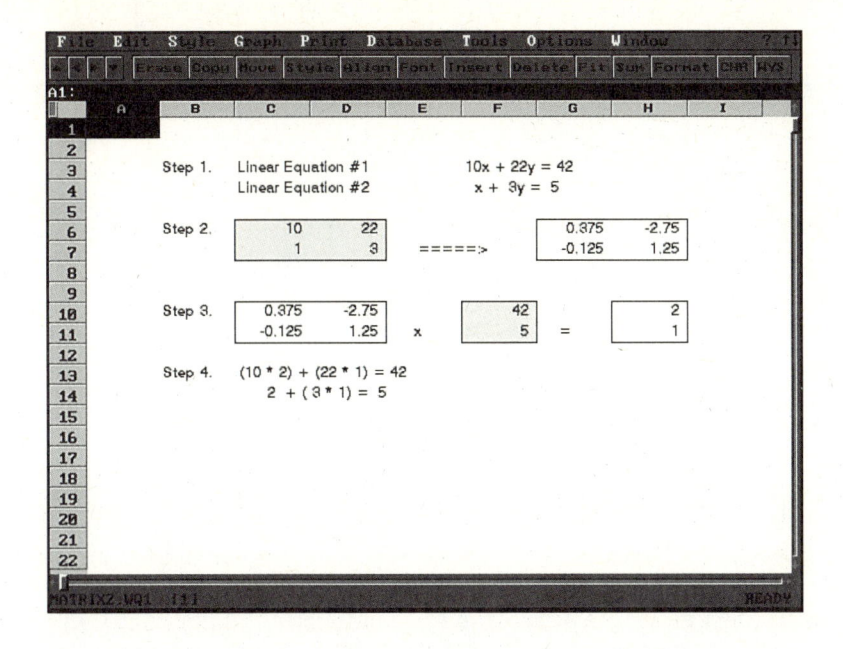

[Screenshot of spreadsheet showing matrix inversion example with Steps 1-4]

Fig. 14.4

Inverting a matrix to solve two linear equations simultaneously.

Suppose that you want to solve simultaneously the two linear equations pictured on rows 3 and 4 of figure 14.4. You can solve the equations using the **I**nvert and **M**ultiply commands.

To invert a matrix, perform the following steps:

1. Using the coefficients from each linear equation, create an input matrix and enter the matrix into a spreadsheet. The sample input matrix appears in cells C6..D7.

2. Choose /**T**ools **A**dvanced Math **I**nvert.

3. Type the range address for the input matrix—*C6..D7* in the example—and press Enter.

> **TIP**
>
> You can only invert a square matrix.

4. Type the number of the upper left cell of the block in which you want to place the inverted matrix—*G6* in the example—and press Enter.

5. Use the /**E**dit **C**opy command to copy the inverted matrix from G6..H7 to block C10..D11 to make it easier to work with this data in the next few steps.

To multiply matrices, perform the following steps:

1. Create a matrix using the constants from the original equations, and enter the matrix into the same spreadsheet. The sample constant matrix appears in cells F10..F11 of the spreadsheet shown in figure 14.4.

2. Choose /**T**ools **A**dvanced Math **M**ultiply.

3. Type the range address of the first matrix to multiply—*C10..D11* in the example—and press Enter.

4. Type the range address of the second matrix to multiply—*F10..F11* in the example—and press Enter.

5. Type the upper left cell of the block in which you want to place the solution matrix—*H10* in the example—and press Enter.

The solution matrix provides the two values that solve both linear equations. To prove that these values are correct, review step 4 in figure 14.4.

When you multiply two matrices, the number of columns in the first matrix must equal the number of rows in the second matrix. Otherwise, Quattro Pro does not perform this operation.

Another example is shown in figure 14.5. Matrix #1 contains the number of units produced for three products: X, Y, and Z. Matrix #2 contains the units of material (M) and labor (L) required to build a unit of X, Y, and Z. To produce one unit of X, for example, you need four units of material and one unit of labor.

To determine the total number of units of material and labor required to produce 20 units of X, 30 units of Y, and 50 units of Z, multiply matrix #1 by matrix #2. As you can see from the bottom of figure 14.5, you need 420 units of material and 230 units of labor.

Using the Parse Command

The **P**arse command on the **T**ools menu is used to break long labels into two or more smaller labels. Although this capability may not sound like an interesting or useful proposition, consider the **P**arse command in the more familiar context of database management.

In Chapter 8, you learned how to import outside data files into the Quattro Pro spreadsheet environment. When Quattro Pro imports a file, the program often places all the data into one column. This placement really isn't a problem; although the original formatting is lost, the imported file usually retains its general organization (see fig. 14.6).

14 — ANALYZING DATA

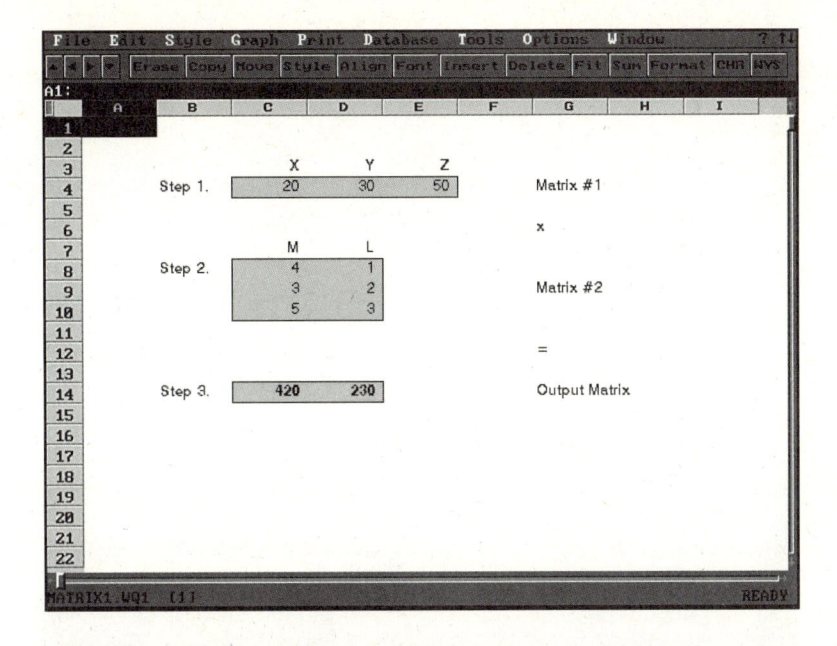

Fig. 14.5

Matrix multiplication used to determine input requirements for a production run.

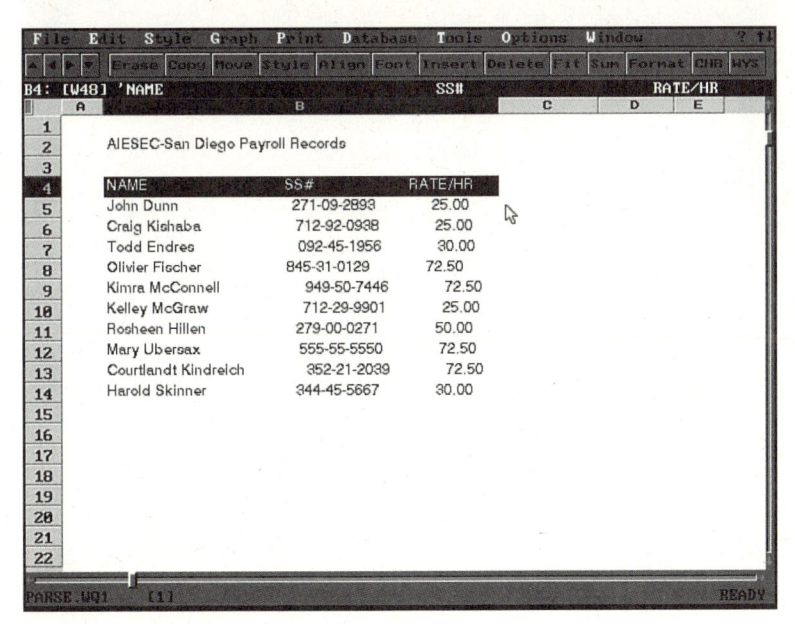

Fig. 14.6

An imported database in which each record appears in a cell in column B.

This database appears to have three individual fields: NAME, SS#, and RATE/HR. In fact, each record is contained in a cell within column B. Look at the input line at the top of the spreadsheet and review record #1.

PART III — ADVANCED SPREADSHEET APPLICATIONS

In WYSIWYG display mode, data from an imported file may appear to lose its column justification. In figure 14.6, for example, the SS# and RATE/HR data do not appear justified the same way as the NAME data. This display quirk has more to do with the default font selection in Quattro Pro than with the organization of the data. To check this situation, click the CHR button on the SpeedBar (or choose /**Options D**isplay **M**ode **A**:80x25) and review the same spreadsheet in text display mode (see fig. 14.7).

```
 File Edit Style Graph Print Database Tools Options Window    ? ↑↓
B4: [W48] 'NAME                        SS#                 RATE/HR
        A                         B                       C          End
1                                                                    ▲
2       AIESEC-San Diego Payroll Records
3
4       NAME                      SS#                     RATE/HR
5       John Dunn                 271-09-2893              25.00     ERS
6       Craig Kishaba             712-92-0938              25.00
7       Todd Endres               092-45-1956              30.00     CPY
8       Olivier Fischer           845-31-0129              72.50
9       Kimra McConnell           949-50-7446              72.50     MOV
10      Kelley McGraw             712-29-9901              25.00
11      Rosheen Hillen            279-00-0271              50.00     STY
12      Mary Ubersax              555-55-5550              72.50
13      Courtlandt Kindreich      352-21-2039              72.50     ALN
14      Harold Skinner            344-45-5667              30.00
15                                                                   FNT
16
17                                                                   INS
18
19                                                                   BAR
20
PARSE.WQ1    [1]                                             READY
```

Fig. 14.7

The imported file data when viewed in text display mode.

> **T I P** Although the LRate/Hr data appears to have shifted into column C in figure 14.7, it really hasn't—the Rate/Hr data in column LB is overlapping into C.

With the **P**arse command, you can re-create this database's original field structure without having to reenter any records or manually justify the data.

Executing a Parse Operation

A parse operation involves the following four steps:

1. Create a format line.
2. Define the input block.

14 — ANALYZING DATA

3. Define the output block.
4. Choose **Go** to parse the data.

You can use the **Parse** command to reformat the database shown in figure 14.6 by following these steps:

1. Place the cell selector in cell B4, the upper left corner of the block of imported data.

2. Choose **/Tools Parse Create**. Quattro Pro enters a format line in the row directly above the field names row (see fig. 14.8). The format line is Quattro Pro's "best guess" as to how the data should be divided.

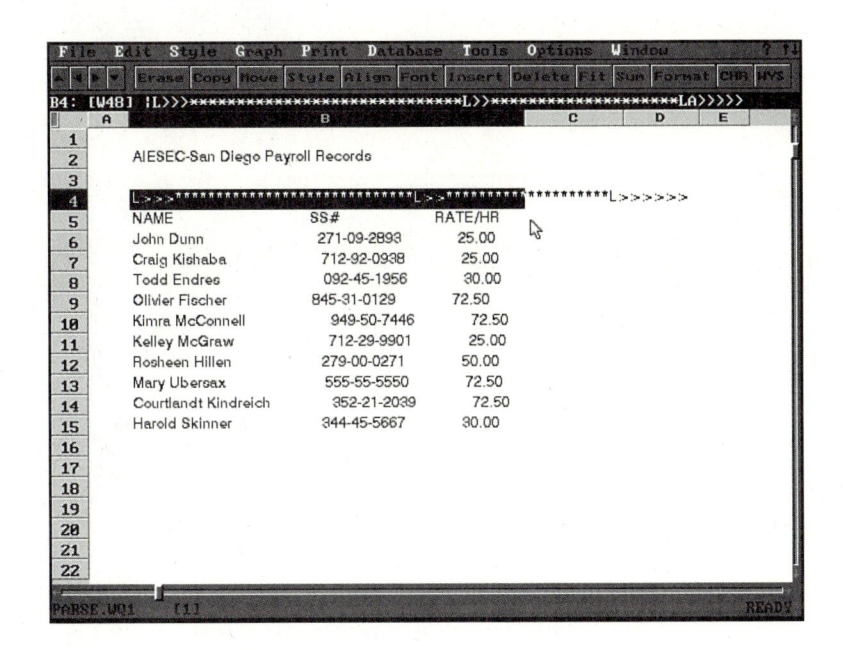

Fig. 14.8

A format line created for the database.

3. Choose **Input**, type *B4..B15*, and then press Enter to record the input block. The input block always must include the format line as the first row.

4. Choose **Output**, type *B28*, and then press Enter to record the output block (see fig. 14.9).

5. Choose **Go** to parse the database.

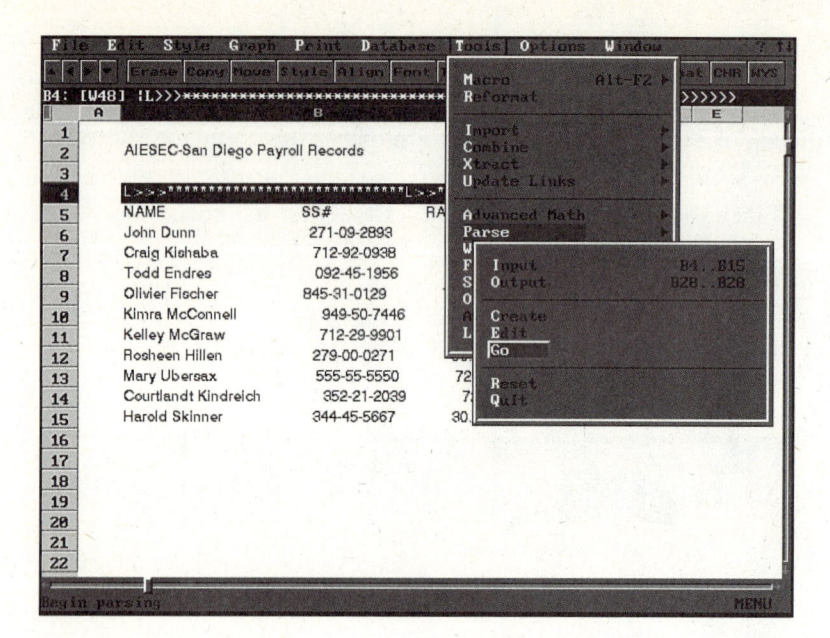

622 PART III — ADVANCED SPREADSHEET APPLICATIONS

Fig. 14.9

Each element's definition on the right side of the **P**arse menu.

If you have defined the input and output blocks correctly, the results of the operation should look like figure 14.10. Quattro Pro creates three columns of data, one for each field name that the program recognized.

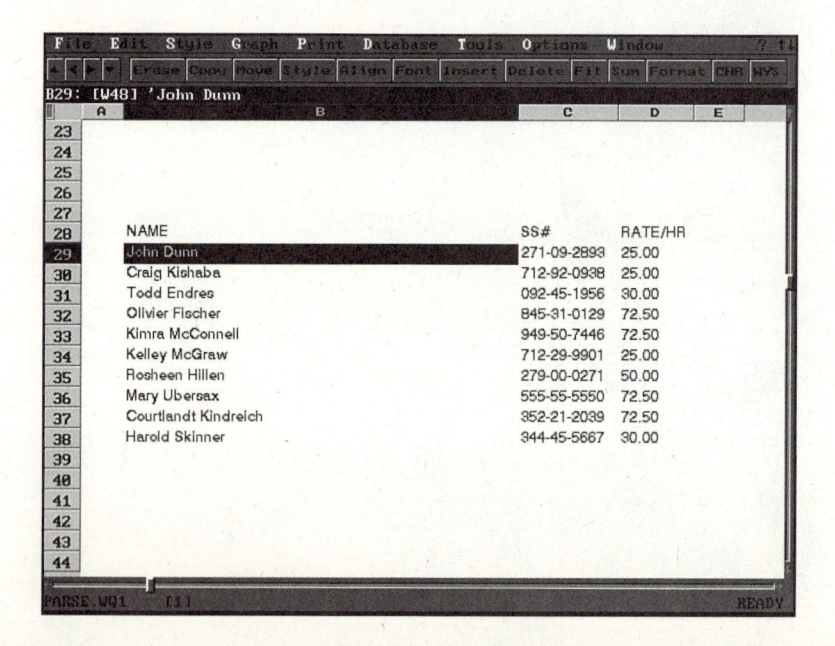

Fig. 14.10

The database restored to its original field name organization.

Performing Multiple Parse Operations

Quattro Pro has no rule restricting how many times you can parse a set of data. In the previous example, you also might want to parse the data in column B to separate the last name data from the first name data. You should parse data as long as parsing is easier than reentering all the records into a database.

Fortunately, you seldom need to parse a set of data more than a few times because the **E**dit command on the **P**arse menu enables you to create custom format lines. When the "best guess" format line created by the **C**reate command does not permit Quattro Pro to adequately parse your data, press Alt-F5 to reverse the most recent parse operations, then choose **E**dit and create a custom format line, using any of the characters shown in table 14.2.

Table 14.2 Format Line Symbols

Symbol	Description
|	Denotes the beginning of a format line
V	Precedes a value cell entry
L	Precedes a label cell entry
T	Precedes a time value entry
D	Precedes a date value entry
>	Indicates a continuing entry
*	Indicates blank spaces that Quattro Pro can fill in with longer entries
S	Tells Quattro Pro to skip (delete) the character in this position

Performing Advanced Parse Operations

In the preceding chapter, you were advised to create a unique field for each category of information in a database. The logic of creating separate fields for the two parts of a name—one field for the first name and one for the last—was discussed. When a field in your database fails to conform to this logic—such as in the NAME field of the sample database in the preceding section—the **P**arse command is limited.

Although the **P**arse command can create a format line and reorganize long labels into individual columns, the command generally cannot break apart two labels contained within one field.

To understand why, you first must understand how the **P**arse command functions. On the format line in figure 14.9, each L symbol tells Quattro Pro exactly where one field ends and another field begins. The data in each field is left-justified and far enough from the data in neighboring fields that Quattro Pro has no problem distinguishing between the fields.

Now take another look at the two elements in the NAME field. The last names are not left-justified, because the first names have different lengths. Quattro Pro does not know where to place the L symbols to distinguish between the two names.

You can use the **P**arse command to break apart multiple labels within a field but only when each label is left-justified and far enough from other labels in that field that Quattro Pro can distinguish between the labels.

With a little imagination and experimentation, however, you can sidestep these constraints by combining the capabilities of the **P**arse command with those of the **E**dit menu's **S**earch & Replace command. (See Chapter 4 for complete coverage of the **S**earch & Replace command.)

In the example, you need to place enough distance between the first and last names in the NAME field to enable Quattro Pro to distinguish between the names. Because the longest first name in the NAME field is 10 characters long (Courtlandt), you must left-justify all the last names somewhere past column 11.

Remember, you must leave column 11 blank so that Quattro Pro can distinguish between the two categories of data.

To allow enough space between first and last names, perform the following steps:

1. Highlight block B29..B38.

2. Choose /**E**dit **C**opy, type *B51*, and press Enter to copy the NAME field data to block B51..B60.

3. Choose /**E**dit **S**earch & Replace.

4. Choose **B**lock, type *B51..B60*, and then press Enter to record the location of the object block.

5. Choose **S**earch String, press the space bar once to enter a blank space, and press Enter.

6. Choose **R**eplace String, press the space bar 15 times to enter 15 blank spaces, and then press Enter. (You want Quattro Pro to replace each single space with 15 spaces.)

7. Choose **N**ext to begin the search-and-replace operation.

   After you complete step 7, Quattro Pro displays the menu shown in figure 14.11.

14 — ANALYZING DATA

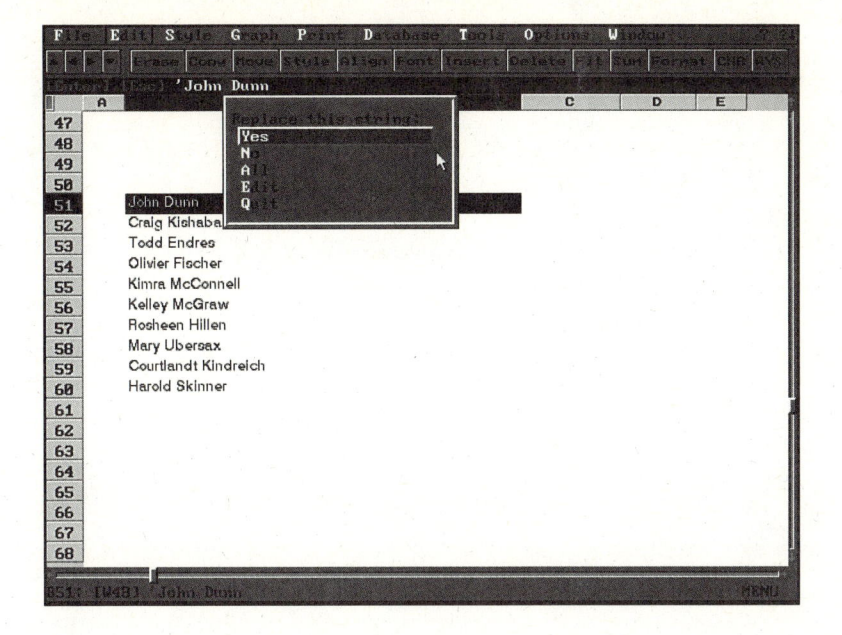

Fig. 14.11

The Replace This String menu appears when a match to the search condition is located in column B.

The first blank space that Quattro Pro locates is between John and Dunn in the first record. To check this result, look at the input line at the top of the spreadsheet.

8. Choose the **All** option to search and replace each record in the database.

Next, parse the data appearing in block B51..B60 and store the results beginning in cell B52. To do this operation properly, use the **/T**ools **P**arse **C**reate command to create a "best guess" format line. Then, use the **E**dit command to edit the format line so that the line looks like what appears in figure 14.12. (Add 10 > symbols to the end of the format line just to be sure that Quattro Pro correctly includes all the characters in each person's last name as part of the continuing entry. See table 14.2 for an explanation of the format line symbols.

To use the **S**earch & Replace command to left-justify the last name labels in column C, perform the following steps:

1. Choose **/E**dit **S**earch & Replace **O**ptions Reset to reset the search-and-replace conditions.

2. Choose **B**lock, type *C52..C61*, and then press Enter to record the location of the object block.

3. Choose **S**earch String, press the space bar once to enter a blank space, and then press Enter.

PART III — ADVANCED SPREADSHEET APPLICATIONS

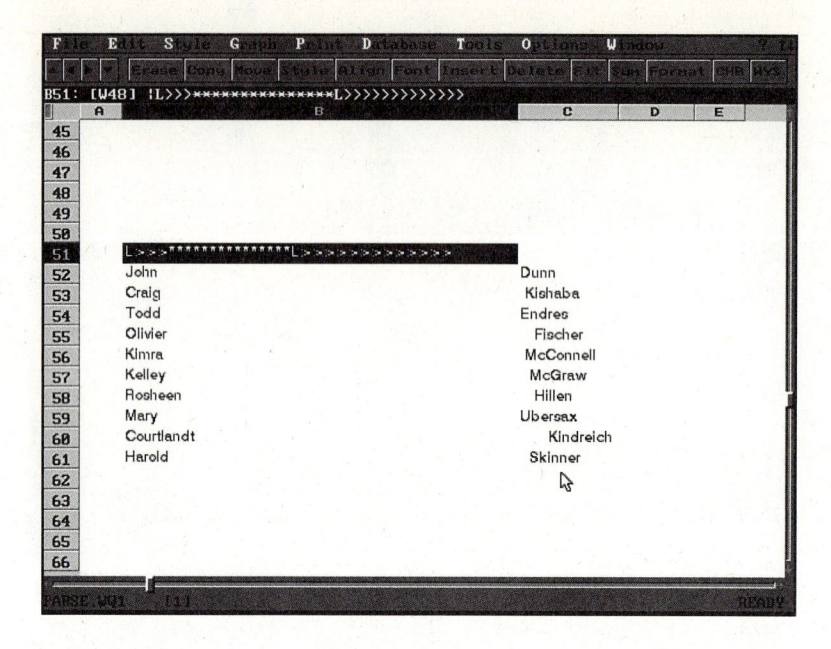

Fig. 14.12

Modify the format line.

4. Choose **N**ext to begin the search operation.

   You did not enter a replacement string this time. By entering nothing as the **R**eplace String condition, you tell Quattro Pro to search for blank spaces and replace the spaces with nothing.

   After completing the search operation, Quattro Pro displays the menu shown in figure 14.13.

   The first blank space that Quattro Pro locates is before Kishaba in the second record. To check this result, look at the input line at the top of the spreadsheet.

5. Choose the **A**ll option to search and replace each record in the database.

After step 5 is completed, Quattro Pro displays the results (see fig. 14.14).

To complete this exercise, enter the label *FIRST NAME* above the first name data on the field names row (in cell B51). Quattro Pro then deletes the format line from cell B51. Next, enter the label *LAST NAME* above the last name data on the field names row (in cell C51).

14 — ANALYZING DATA

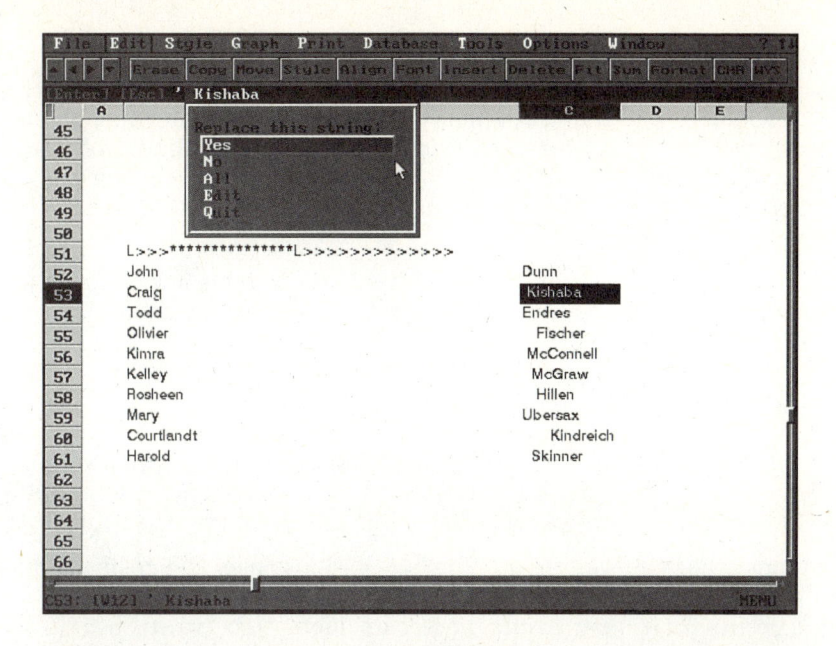

Fig. 14.13

Quattro Pro finds a match in column C to the search condition.

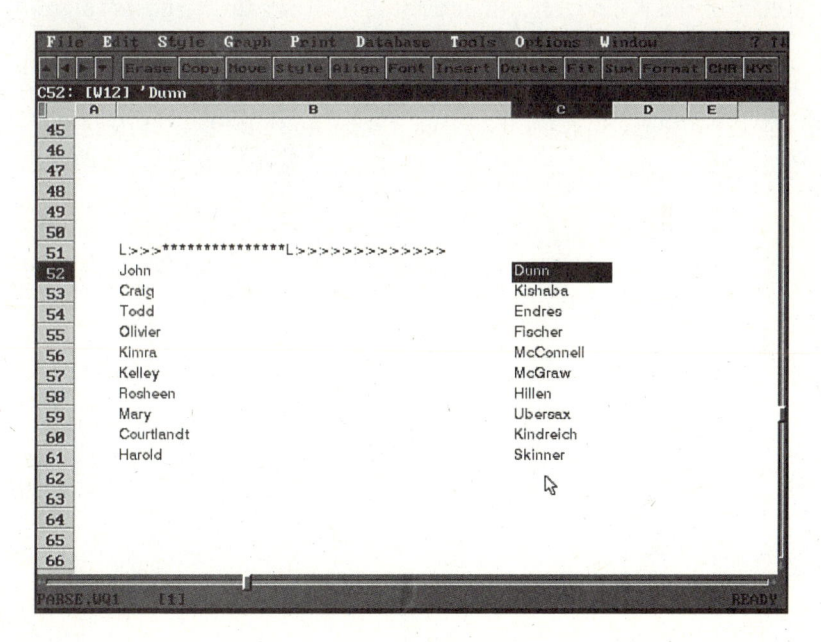

Fig. 14.14

The left-justified last names.

Using the What-If Function

The **T**ool menu's **W**hat-If command enables you to create one-way and two-way sensitivity tables. A *sensitivity table* contains a range of column values and row formulas that define the parameters of a problem. When executed, the **W**hat-If command returns one answer for each row and column intersection.

Using sensitivity analysis, you can review in one table a wide range of solutions for virtually any what-if questions you may encounter.

Performing a One-Way Sensitivity Analysis

A one-way sensitivity analysis table substitutes values into a variable appearing in one or more formulas. You set up a column of substitution values and then create a formula in which to substitute the values.

Suppose that you want to analyze how various sales and costs affect the gross profits for a business. In this business, sales range from $10,000 to $24,000 per month, and costs fluctuate between 55 and 75 percent of sales. The following formula relates sales to costs to gross profit:

> Gross Profit = Sales – Cost of Goods Sold

In this example, you want to create a sensitivity table that describes all possible gross profit values that can occur within a given range of sales values and cost percentages.

The first step is to enter the range of sales values into a column. The next step is to enter the formulas that calculate the gross profit values into a row. You enter five formulas, one for each likely cost percentage. You may want to change the format of this row to **T**ext so that you can see the formulas (see fig. 14.15).

TIP In figure 14.15, cell B2 is used to represent sales in the formulas on row 2. You can use any cell on the spreadsheet as long as it does not fall inside the block bounded by your row and column data (cell block C3..G17).

14 — ANALYZING DATA

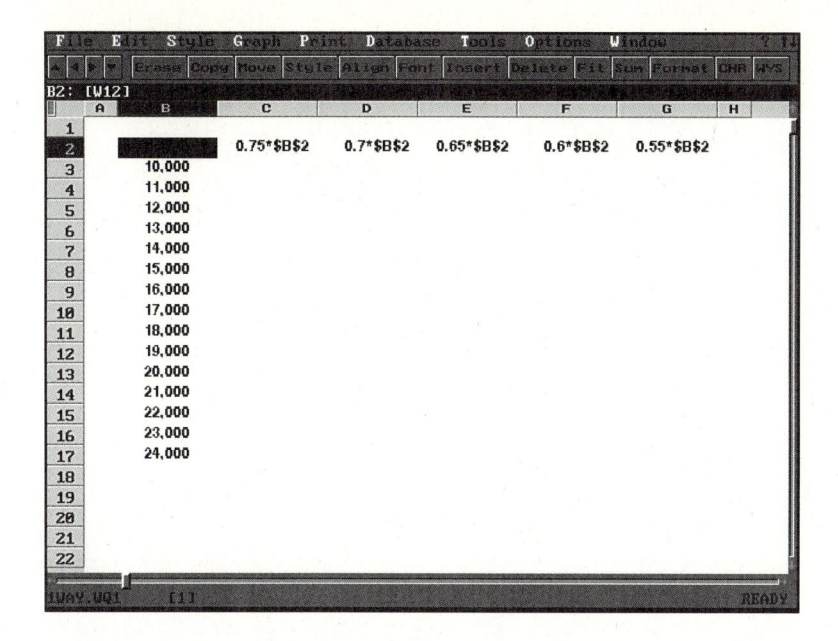

[Screenshot of Quattro Pro spreadsheet showing cell B2: [W12] selected, with row 2 containing formulas 0.75*$B$2, 0.7*$B$2, 0.65*$B$2, 0.6*$B$2, 0.55*$B$2 in columns C through G, and column B containing values 10,000 through 24,000 in rows 3 through 17.]

Fig. 14.15

Create a one-way sensitivity table.

After you enter all the appropriate values and formulas, you are ready to create the one-way sensitivity table by performing the following steps:

1. Choose /**T**ools **W**hat-If **1** Variable.

2. When prompted, type the data table block—*B2..G17* for the example—and press Enter.

3. When prompted, type the input cell—*B2* for the example—and press Enter.

In the example, Quattro Pro substitutes each sales value into cell B2, multiplies the substituted value by the percentage specified in each formula on row 2, and then places an answer in each intersection cell (see fig. 14.16).

Performing a Two-Way Sensitivity Analysis

A two-way sensitivity analysis uses a data table in a slightly different manner; you substitute two sets of values into a formula.

Consider a retail business that sells a particular product for $28 to $38, depending on the cost charged by the wholesale supplier. The following formula relates retail price to wholesale cost and the percent of profit on a sale:

Percent Profit = (Retail Price – Wholesale Cost) / Retail Price

PART III — ADVANCED SPREADSHEET APPLICATIONS

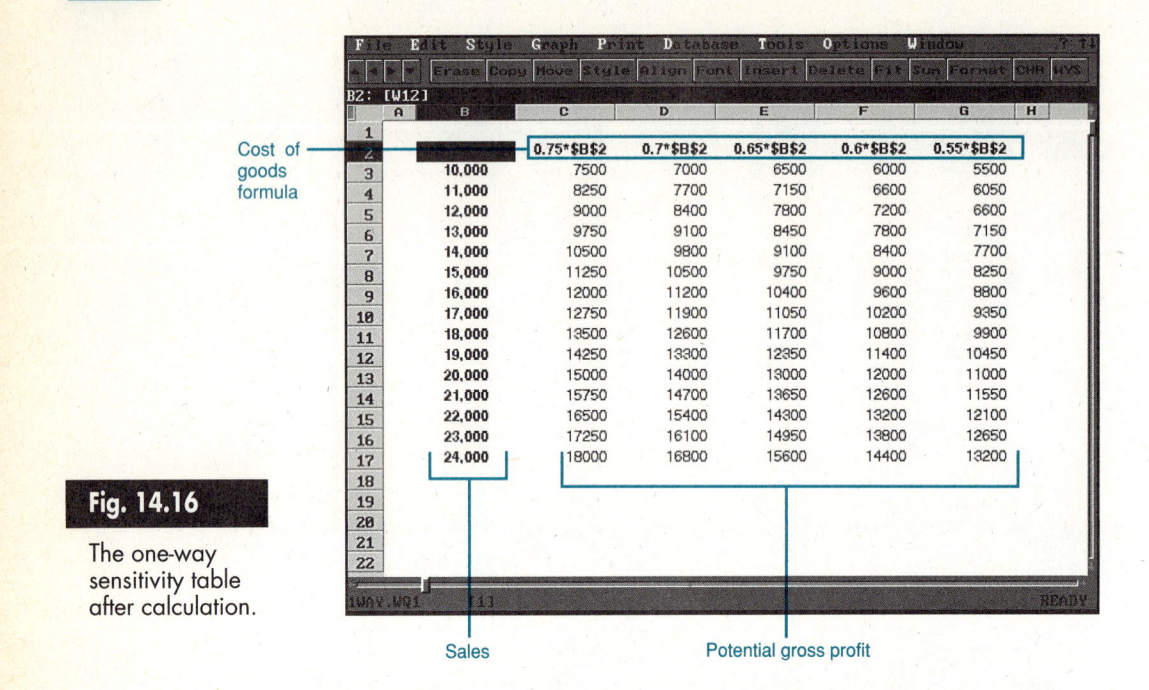

Fig. 14.16

The one-way sensitivity table after calculation.

(Screenshot shows a Quattro Pro spreadsheet with Cost of goods formula pointing to column B, Sales label under column B, and Potential gross profit bracket across columns C–G.)

	B	C	D	E	F	G
2		0.75*$B$2	0.7*$B$2	0.65*$B$2	0.6*$B$2	0.55*$B$2
3	10,000	7500	7000	6500	6000	5500
4	11,000	8250	7700	7150	6600	6050
5	12,000	9000	8400	7800	7200	6600
6	13,000	9750	9100	8450	7800	7150
7	14,000	10500	9800	9100	8400	7700
8	15,000	11250	10500	9750	9000	8250
9	16,000	12000	11200	10400	9600	8800
10	17,000	12750	11900	11050	10200	9350
11	18,000	13500	12600	11700	10800	9900
12	19,000	14250	13300	12350	11400	10450
13	20,000	15000	14000	13000	12000	11000
14	21,000	15750	14700	13650	12600	11550
15	22,000	16500	15400	14300	13200	12100
16	23,000	17250	16100	14950	13800	12650
17	24,000	18000	16800	15600	14400	13200

To determine the percent of profit that the business is earning, you can construct a two-way sensitivity table that analyzes various price/cost combinations and computes the corresponding profit percentage.

The first step is to enter the range of retail prices and wholesale costs into a row and a column (see fig. 14.17). The next step is to enter a formula (in cell B5, in this example), that calculates the percent of profit. The formula, (A6-A5)/A6, references two input cells that fall outside the sensitivity table, such as cells A5 and A6. You may enter the formula into any cell on the spreadsheet as long as it does not fall inside the block bounded by your row and column data (cell block C6..H19) and does not use either of the two input cells.

After you enter all the appropriate values and the formula, you are ready to create the two-way sensitivity table. Follow these steps:

1. Choose /**Tools What-If 2** Variables.

2. When prompted, type the data table block—*B5..H19* for the example—and press Enter.

> **TIP** Make sure that the data table block definition includes only the area bounded by the column and row—do not include the addresses for the blank input cells (A5 and A6).

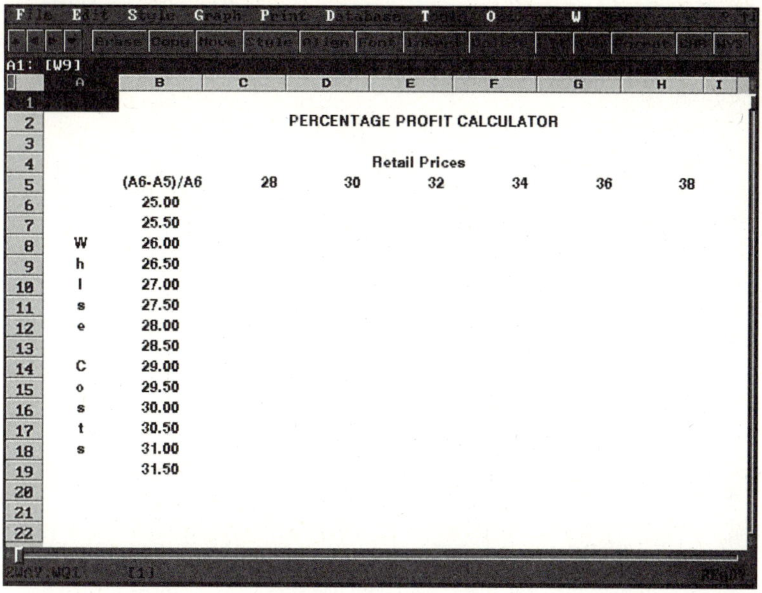

14 — ANALYZING DATA

Fig. 14.17

Create a two-way sensitivity table.

3. When prompted, type the input cell for the column of values—*A5* for the example—and press Enter.

4. When prompted, type the input cell for the row of values—*A6* for the example—and press Enter.

Quattro Pro substitutes each pair of retail and wholesale prices into the input cells, performs the operation indicated by the formula in cell B5, and then places an answer in each intersection cell (see fig. 14.18).

In figure 14.18, the calculated values are formatted to display in the percent format with one decimal place.

Creating Frequency Distributions

The **Frequency** command on the **Tools** menu counts the number of values that fall within specified ranges, groups the values into bins, and then produces a frequency distribution table using the bin data. A *frequency distribution table* provides a summary grouping of large data sets, enabling you to get a better picture of their distribution. After you create a table, you can display those values effectively in an XY graph.

Consider a commissioned study that analyzes the distribution of population among cities on Prince Edward Island (see fig. 14.19).

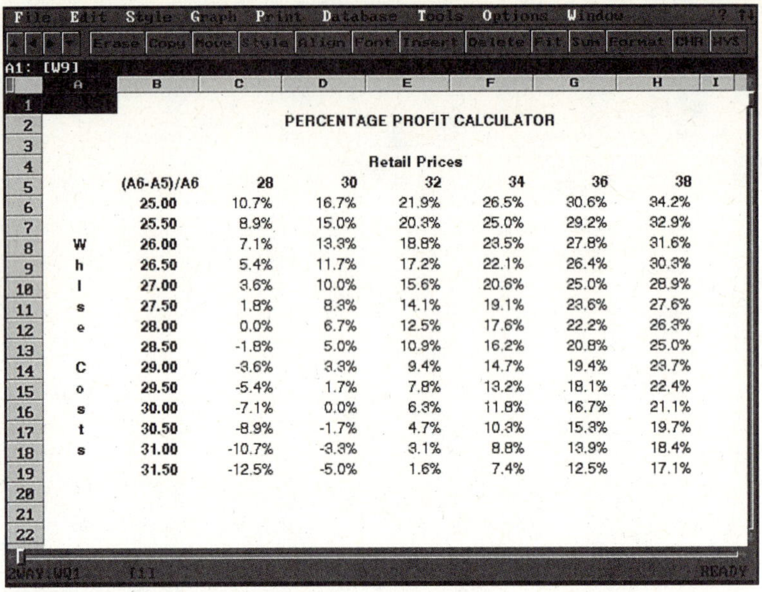

PART III — ADVANCED SPREADSHEET APPLICATIONS

```
                    PERCENTAGE PROFIT CALCULATOR

                              Retail Prices
         (A6-A5)/A6    28      30      32      34      36      38
           25.00      10.7%   16.7%   21.9%   26.5%   30.6%   34.2%
           25.50       8.9%   15.0%   20.3%   25.0%   29.2%   32.9%
      W    26.00       7.1%   13.3%   18.8%   23.5%   27.8%   31.6%
      h    26.50       5.4%   11.7%   17.2%   22.1%   26.4%   30.3%
      l    27.00       3.6%   10.0%   15.6%   20.6%   25.0%   28.9%
      s    27.50       1.8%    8.3%   14.1%   19.1%   23.6%   27.6%
      e    28.00       0.0%    6.7%   12.5%   17.6%   22.2%   26.3%
           28.50      -1.8%    5.0%   10.9%   16.2%   20.8%   25.0%
      C    29.00      -3.6%    3.3%    9.4%   14.7%   19.4%   23.7%
      o    29.50      -5.4%    1.7%    7.8%   13.2%   18.1%   22.4%
      s    30.00      -7.1%    0.0%    6.3%   11.8%   16.7%   21.1%
      t    30.50      -8.9%   -1.7%    4.7%   10.3%   15.3%   19.7%
      s    31.00     -10.7%   -3.3%    3.1%    8.8%   13.9%   18.4%
           31.50     -12.5%   -5.0%    1.6%    7.4%   12.5%   17.1%
```

Fig. 14.18

The two-way sensitivity table after calculation.

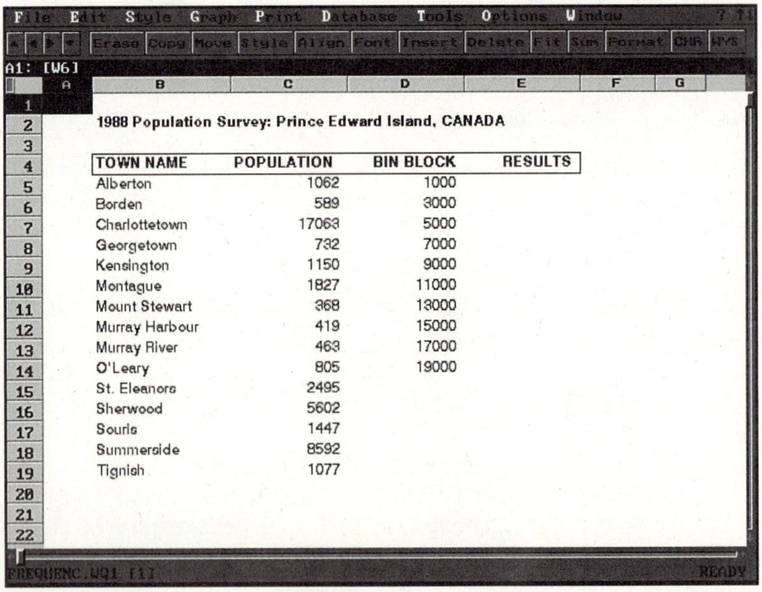

```
      1988 Population Survey: Prince Edward Island, CANADA

      TOWN NAME        POPULATION     BIN BLOCK      RESULTS
      Alberton            1062           1000
      Borden               589           3000
      Charlottetown      17063           5000
      Georgetown           732           7000
      Kensington          1150           9000
      Montague            1827          11000
      Mount Stewart        368          13000
      Murray Harbour       419          15000
      Murray River         463          17000
      O'Leary              805          19000
      St. Eleanors        2495
      Sherwood            5602
      Souris              1447
      Summerside          8592
      Tignish             1077
```

Fig. 14.19

Organize data to be used in frequency distribution analysis.

The name of each city appears in one column, the population in another, and the bin block definition in a third. To set up a frequency distribution table that counts the number of cities whose population falls into each bin block, follow these steps:

14 — ANALYZING DATA

1. Enter the names of each city into column B and enter each city's population into column C.
2. Define a bin block grouping that specifies the boundaries of the bins into which you want to put values. Generally, it is easiest to work with whole bin numbers that increment by a fixed amount.

> **TIP**
>
> Bin block numbers must appear in ascending order on the spreadsheet but do not necessarily require the same interval size.

3. Choose /Tools Frequency.
4. When prompted, type *C5..C19* and press Enter to define the values to include in the frequency analysis.
5. When prompted, type *D5..D14* to define the bin block.
6. When prompted, type *E5* to define the location where Quattro Pro is to copy the results. When you press Enter, the results display to the right of the bin block, overwriting any data stored there.

After you execute step 6, Quattro Pro copies the results of the frequency analysis into a block beginning at cell E5 (see fig. 14.20). Quattro Pro includes an extra result in cell E15 at the bottom of the results column. This result is 0 as long as Quattro Pro does not locate a value in the frequency table that is greater than the largest defined bin number.

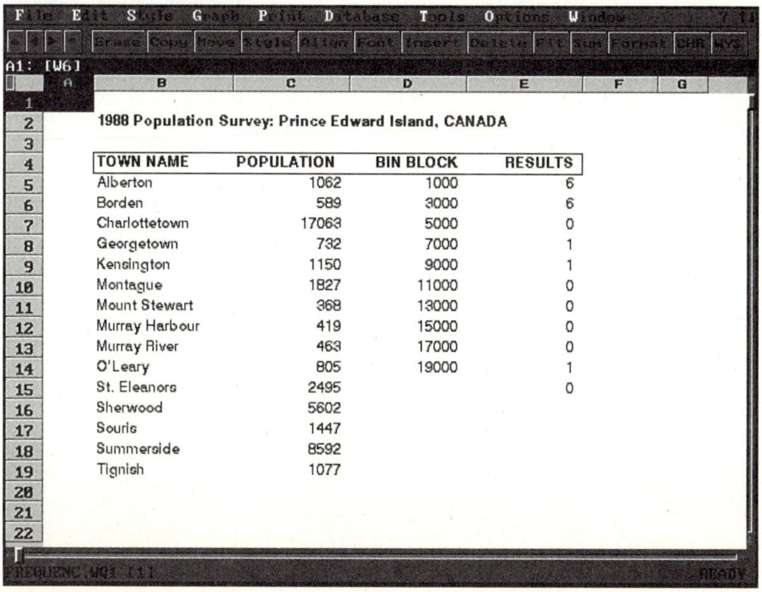

TOWN NAME	POPULATION	BIN BLOCK	RESULTS
Alberton	1062	1000	6
Borden	589	3000	6
Charlottetown	17063	5000	0
Georgetown	732	7000	1
Kensington	1150	9000	1
Montague	1827	11000	0
Mount Stewart	368	13000	0
Murray Harbour	419	15000	0
Murray River	463	17000	0
O'Leary	805	19000	1
St. Eleanors	2495		0
Sherwood	5602		
Souris	1447		
Summerside	8592		
Tignish	1077		

1988 Population Survey: Prince Edward Island, CANADA

Fig. 14.20

A completed frequency distribution analysis.

PART III — ADVANCED SPREADSHEET APPLICATIONS

Frequency distribution analyses lend themselves to XY graphing (see Chapter 10, "Creating Graphs," for more information about XY graphs). Figure 14.21 shows a graph constructed with the values appearing in the BIN BLOCK and RESULTS columns.

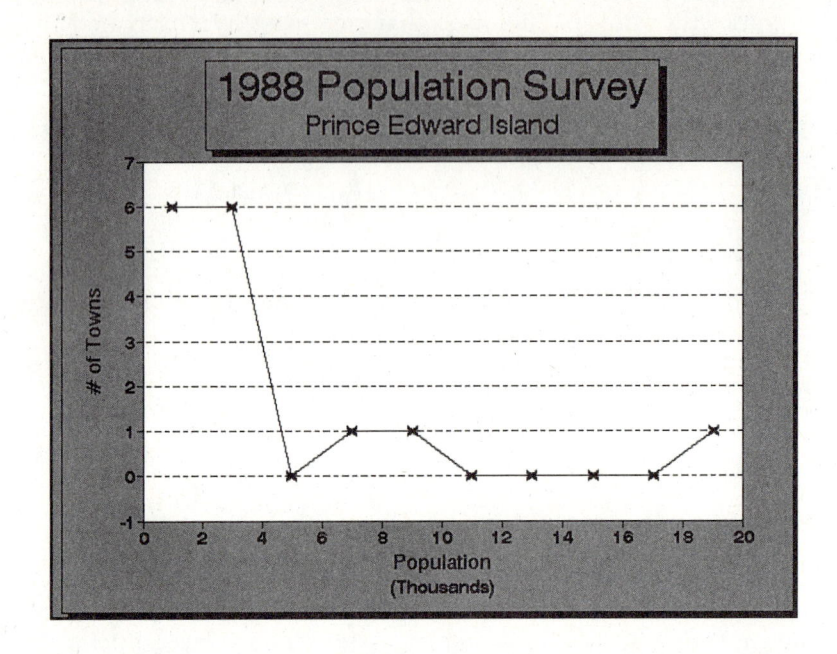

Fig. 14.21

An XY graph showing the distribution of the population on Prince Edward Island.

This graph was created by defining the BIN BLOCK column data as the x-axis and the RESULTS data as the y-axis. Because the final value in the RESULTS column is 0, this cell is not included in the x-axis series definition. This graph is often called a histogram.

Using the Optimizer

Quattro Pro's **O**ptimizer command, another command on the **T**ools menu, enables you to find the optimal solution to a problem that has more than one variable. Multivariable problems also are known as *nonlinear problems*; in many cases, nonlinear problems have more than one solution. When a problem has more than one solution, you can define a set of constraints for the problem so that Quattro Pro can locate the "best fit" answer.

The **O**ptimizer solves problems using a linear programming technique called *optimization analysis*—a tool commonly used in business management and social science research. You may use optimization analysis in any discipline, however, to juggle multiple considerations—for example, pollution levels versus job hazards versus company profits.

14 — ANALYZING DATA 635

> **TIP**
>
> The /Tools Optimizer command replaces the /Tools Advanced Math Optimization command in earlier versions of Quattro Pro. Macros from Versions 3.0 or earlier that use the /Tools Advanced Math Optimization command should execute correctly in Version 4.0 if they contain menu-equivalent commands rather than keystrokes.

For complete details about optimization modeling and linear programming, consult a statistics text. To gather ideas about how you can use optimization in your own field, review the journal studies and papers published by professionals in the discipline. In this discussion, you learn how to prepare an optimization model with known financial data for Magnus Manufacturing, a fictitious company that manufactures and sells sporting goods equipment.

Using the Optimizer to solve a problem involves the following four general steps:

1. Define the solution that you seek.
2. Identify the problem variables that the Optimizer can change in an attempt to reach the solution.
3. Define the problem constraints that the Optimizer must accommodate before a solution can be considered "optimal."
4. Execute the model.

You can use the 10 commands on the Optimizer menu to define the cell address for the solution, identify the cells containing variables that can be changed, define the problem constraints, set options that fine-tune an Optimizer operation, start solving the current problem, and review reports about the current solution. Other commands on this menu restore a previous Optimizer solution, load a predefined model, and reset the menu to the default settings.

Table 14.3 describes the purpose of each Optimizer menu command.

Setting Up the Optimizer

Figures 14.22 shows the 1993 production forecast for Magnus Manufacturing's water sporting goods line. This forecast provides information about each variable that influences management's decision to manufacture a particular amount of each product in the line.

Table 14.3 Optimizer Menu Commands

Command	Description
Solution Cell	Defines the cell containing a value to be maximized, minimized, or equaled (optional)
Variable Cells(s)	Defines the cells containing the variables to be adjusted; must not be protected, cannot contain labels, formulas, dates, or text
Constraints	Defines the cells containing the problem constraints
Options	Offers commands for fine-tuning an Optimizer operation
Answer Report	Displays in the spreadsheet a report containing information about the solution cell, variable cell(s), and constraint cell(s)
Detail Report	Displays in the spreadsheet a report containing the values of the solution cell and variable cell(s) at each iteration in the Optimizer operation
Go	Executes an Optimizer operation
Restore	Reinstates the value of all variable cells before the most recent Optimizer operation; press F9 if Recalculation is set to Manual
Model	Saves multiple scenarios for a problem with the current spreadsheet
Reset	Clears all Optimizer settings

The highlighted cell (C7) in figure 14.22 reveals the formula that Magnus' marketing staff has devised to forecast the number of units to produce for the first quarter. This formula

$$10*C10*(500+C16)^{.69}$$

and the others like it in row 7 relate two key components of the Magnus Manufacturing production forecast: the Seasonal Demand Factor values and the To-Dealer Rebates values.

The Seasonal Demand Factor values in row 10 reflect management's estimate of how consumers will demand their products during each quarter of the year. Because the production department requires at least a month or two lead time to manufacture and ship the water sporting products, management anticipates that the greatest demand for their products will occur in the two quarters preceding the warmest months of the year (Quarter 1 and Quarter 2). The values 1.32 (C10) and 1.09 (D10) reflect management's expectation that demand will be 132% and 109% of average yearly demand during these two quarters.

14 — ANALYZING DATA

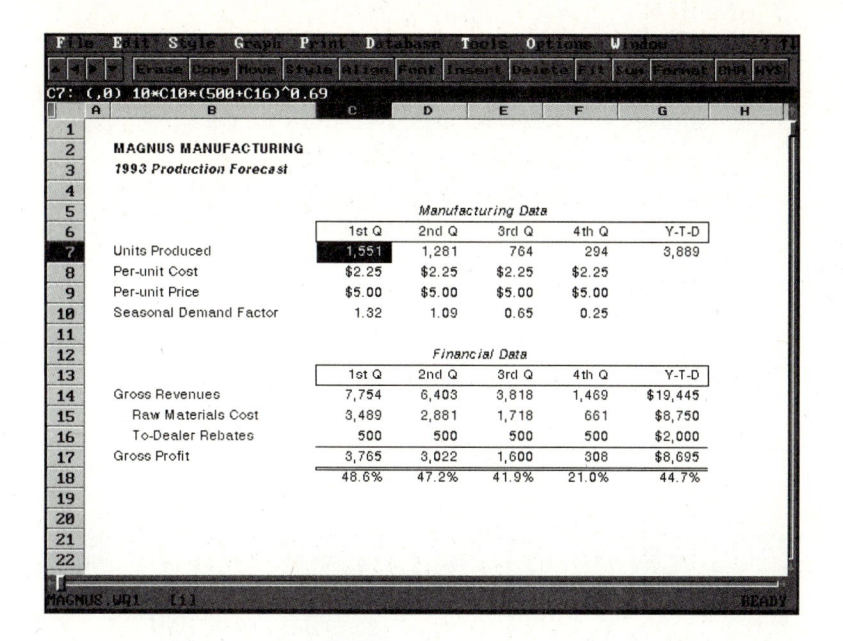

Fig. 14.22

The Magnus Manufacturing 1993 Production Forecast spreadsheet.

The To-Dealer Rebates values reflect management's long-standing policy of offering rebates to their wholesale sporting goods dealers to influence the level of orders placed.

In general, this formula says that more rebates equates to more gross revenues, but that at some point, each additional rebate dollar offered will produce less than a dollar in additional sales. This formula is based upon an economic principle known as diminishing marginal returns.

Solving a Basic Optimizer Problem

In this example, management wants to know the level of To-Deal Rebates required to push first quarter sales up to $10,000. Use the following steps:

1. Choose /Tools Optimizer. Quattro Pro displays the Optimizer menu.

2. Choose Solution Cell. Quattro Pro displays the Solution Cell submenu.

3. Choose the Cell option to specify the cell with the value for which you want to solve. When prompted, type a valid cell address and press Enter. In the example, to solve for cell C14, the Gross Revenues value for the 1st Q, type *C14* and press Enter.

PART III — ADVANCED SPREADSHEET APPLICATIONS

4. Choose the **Max,Min,Equal** option to specify the target value you want to reach. You have the following four options:

Maximize	Maximizes the resulting value for the formula in the solution cell
Minimize	Minimizes the resulting value for the formula in the solution cell
Equal	Attains a specific value for the formula in the solution cell
None	Searches for a value without considering the solution cell

In the example, to attain a Gross Revenues value of $10,000, select the **E**qual option. When prompted, type *10000* and press Enter (see fig. 14.23).

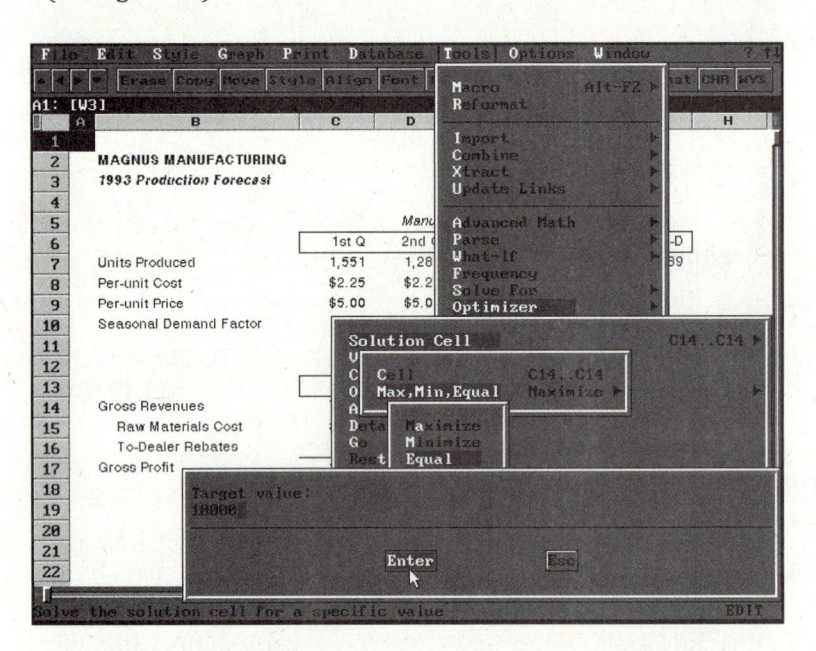

Fig. 14.23

The specified target value for the **O**ptimizer to attain.

5. Choose **V**ariable Cell(s) to specify the cell whose variables Quattro Pro can change to reach an optimal solution. To vary the To-Dealer Rebates value in the example, when prompted, type *C16*. Then press Enter.

6. Choose **G**o to begin the search for the optimal solution. After Quattro Pro locates a solution, the **T**ools menu reappears on-screen. Press Esc to return to the spreadsheet so that you can review the results.

14 — ANALYZING DATA

Figure 14.24 shows the results of solving this basic **O**ptimizer model. Quattro Pro locates the target Gross Revenues value of $10,000 by increasing the To-Dealer Rebates value to 946, which has the corresponding effect of raising Units Produced to 2,000.

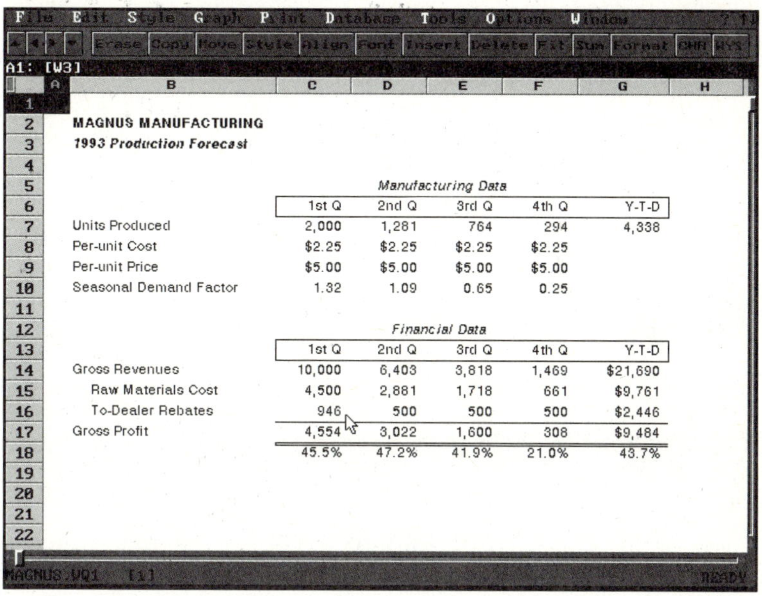

Fig. 14.24

The results of solving for a basic **O**ptimizer problem.

But what if Magnus Manufacturing has limits to the number of units it can produce in a year? In the last example, the Y-T-D Units Produced figure rose to 4,338. Suppose that production capacity is 4,000 units, invalidating the solution to the previous problem because the production capacity is unattainable.

In the next example, you learn how to define constraints in order to solve for more specific goals using the **O**ptimizer. Choose **/T**ools **O**ptimizer Restore to reverse the changes made to your spreadsheet during the most recent **O**ptimizer operation.

Using Constraints and Defining Multiple Variables

In this example, management wants to know the level of To-Dealer Rebates required to maximize the Y-T-D Gross Revenues value. Given a yearly production capacity of 4,000 units and a budget allocation of $4,000 for To-Deal Rebates, they want to identify the optimal production schedule. To accomplish this result, they must select a range of

PART III — ADVANCED SPREADSHEET APPLICATIONS

variable cells and then identify two constraints for this problem. Expressed in terms that Quattro Pro can understand, these constraints are as follows:

- Y-T-D Units Produced must be less than or equal to 4000
  G7<=4000

- Y-T-D To-Dealer Rebates must be less than or equal to $2,000
  G16<=2000

Additionally, to allow Quattro Pro to vary the To-Dealer Rebates values for all four quarters, specify cell block C16..F16 for the **Variable Cell(s)** option.

Use the following steps to solve this problem:

1. Choose **/T**ools **O**ptimizer. Quattro Pro displays the **O**ptimizer menu.

2. Choose **S**olution Cell. Quattro Pro displays the **S**olution Cell submenu.

3. Choose the **C**ell option to specify the cell with the value for which you want to solve. When prompted, type a valid cell address and press Enter. To solve for the Y-T-D Gross Revenues value in the example, type *G14* and press Enter.

4. Choose the **M**ax,Min,Equal option to specify the target value you want to reach. To maximize the Y-T-D Gross Revenues value in the example, select the **M**aximize option.

5. Choose **V**ariable Cell(s) to specify the cells with the variables Quattro Pro can change to reach an optimal solution. In the example, to enable Quattro Pro to vary all of four To-Dealer Rebates values on row 16, when prompted, type *C16..F16*, then press Enter.

6. Choose **C**onstraints to specify the limits you want to place on the variables' use in the problem. At the <Add New Constraints> prompt, press Enter and construct the constraint expression(s).

   In the example, to constrain the Y-T-D Units Produced and Y-T-D To-Dealer Rebates values, at the <Add New Constraints> prompt, press Enter. When prompted for the constraint cell, type *G7* and press Enter. From the **R**elation submenu, press Enter to choose the default relation operator, <=. When prompted for the constraint value, type *4000* and press Enter. Repeat this process and construct a second constraint that specifies that G16<=2000. The syntax for these two constraints appears on the **C**onstraints submenu shown in figure 14.25.

7. Choose **G**o to begin the search for the optimal solution.

14 — ANALYZING DATA

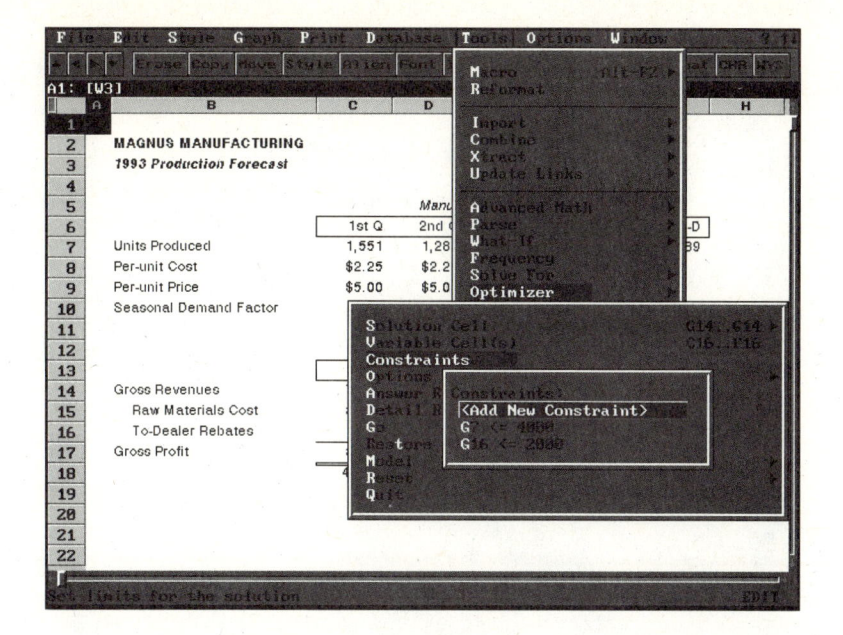

Fig. 14.25

Two constraints on the Constraints submenu.

Figure 14.26 shows the results of solving this more complex Optimizer model. As you can see, Quattro Pro has reallocated the To-Deal Rebates budget differently among the four quarters. Higher levels of rebates are offered in the first and second quarter simply because that is when the greatest demand for Magnus Manufacturing's products occur. In this solution, Magnus Manufacturing attains its production capacity of 4,000 units (G7), at which Gross Revenues will be maximized at $20,000 (G14).

Setting the Optimizer Options

The options on the Options submenu enable you to fine-tune an Optimizer model by adjusting the calculation rules that Quattro Pro uses when searching for solutions to a model. In almost all cases, the default settings on the Options submenu are sufficient to enable Quattro Pro to locate an acceptable solution. If Quattro Pro is unable to locate a solution to one of your problems, experiment with the various settings on the Options menu defined in table 14.4.

PART III — ADVANCED SPREADSHEET APPLICATIONS

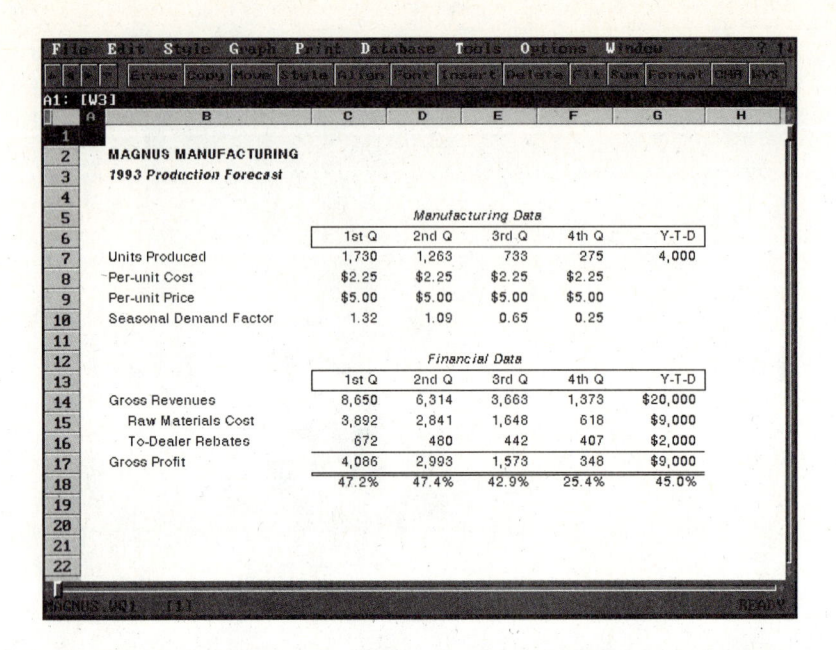

Fig. 14.26

The results of solving for a more complex **O**ptimizer model.

[Screenshot of Quattro Pro spreadsheet showing:]

MAGNUS MANUFACTURING
1993 Production Forecast

Manufacturing Data

	1st Q	2nd Q	3rd Q	4th Q	Y-T-D
Units Produced	1,730	1,263	733	275	4,000
Per-unit Cost	$2.25	$2.25	$2.25	$2.25	
Per-unit Price	$5.00	$5.00	$5.00	$5.00	
Seasonal Demand Factor	1.32	1.09	0.65	0.25	

Financial Data

	1st Q	2nd Q	3rd Q	4th Q	Y-T-D
Gross Revenues	8,650	6,314	3,663	1,373	$20,000
Raw Materials Cost	3,892	2,841	1,648	618	$9,000
To-Dealer Rebates	672	480	442	407	$2,000
Gross Profit	4,086	2,993	1,573	348	$9,000
	47.2%	47.4%	42.9%	25.4%	45.0%

Table 14.4 Option Submenu Options

Option	Description
Max Iterations	Specifies the number of times that Quattro Pro will attempt to find a best solution to the problem; enter a value between 1 and 1000; the default is 100
Precision	Describes the precision you want to observe in the answer that Quattro Pro finds; enter a value between 0 and 1; the default is 0.0005
Linear or Nonlinear	Sets this option to match the problem type: **L**inear or **N**onlinear (the default)
Show Iteration Results	Tells Quattro Pro whether or not to pause between iterations so that you can review the current solution; the default setting is **N**o
Estimates	Selects one of two approaches for obtaining initial estimates of basic variables in each iteration: **Q**uadratic or **T**angent (the default)
Derivatives	Selects one of two differencing methods for estimates of partial derivatives: **C**entral or **F**orward (the default)
Search	Selects the method for computing the search direction: **C**onjugate or **N**ewton (the default)

14 — ANALYZING DATA

Producing Optimizer Reports

In optimization modeling, you rarely will locate an acceptable solution to a problem on the first try. In many cases, successful optimization modeling involves identifying different groups of variables in a spreadsheet application in order to locate acceptable solutions. So that you do not have to create several copies of the same spreadsheet in order to test your different assumptions and theories, Quattro Pro offers two reports which display the results of the current **O**ptimizer session.

Choose the /**T**ools **O**ptimizer **A**nswer Report command to produce a report that lists the solution cell and variable cells with their original and final values and variable dual values (see fig 14.27). The Answer Report prints in the spreadsheet to a block that you specify and also contains information about the constraints you identified.

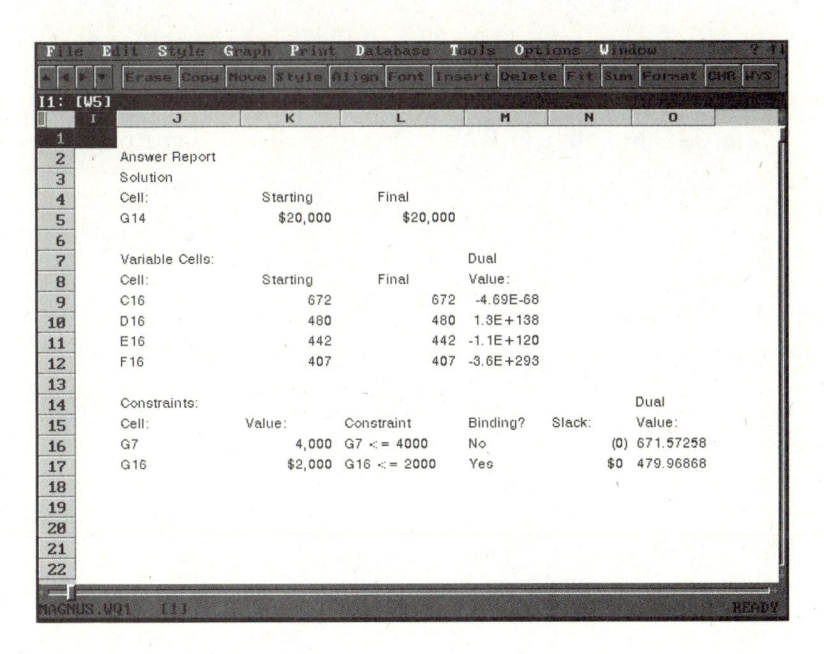

Fig. 14.27

An Answer Report displayed in a cell block on a spreadsheet.

Choose the /**T**ools **O**ptimizer **D**etail Report command to produce a report that lists, at each iteration, the variable cells and the solution cell.

Using Other Optimizer Commands

Choose the /**T**ools **O**ptimizer **Res**tore command to recover the previous variable cell values in the spreadsheet. However, if /**O**ptions **R**ecalculation is set to **M**anual, you must press F9 after choosing Restore to recalculate and display the previous values.

PART III — ADVANCED SPREADSHEET APPLICATIONS

Choose the /**T**ools **O**ptimizer **M**odel command to load and save multiple problem definitions, containing the **S**olution Cell, **V**ariable Cell(s), and **C**onstraint settings.

Choose the /**T**ools **O**ptimizer **R**eset command to clear Optimizer settings individually. Choose the **A**ll option to clear all settings on the **O**ptimizer menu.

Loading Add-In @Functions

You can load third-party add-in @functions into Quattro Pro with the /**T**ools **L**ibrary command. Then you can use the add-in @function with any of the spreadsheets you have in memory. All add-in @functions have a QLL file-name extension.

To load a third-party add-in @function, use the following steps:

1. Choose /**T**ools **L**ibrary **L**oad.

2. Choose a file with a QLL extension from the file-name prompt box.

3. Press Enter to load the add-in @function into memory.

You must use a special syntax to access an add-in @function after you load the @function into memory. This syntax consists of the @ sign, the module name, a period, the function name, and the arguments entered inside parentheses:

   @modulename.function_name(arguments)

The documentation that comes with your add-in @function provides you with the appropriate module name and complete instructions for using the add-in @function in a Quattro Pro spreadsheet.

After you finish using an add-in @function, you should remove it from memory. Follow these steps:

1. Choose /**T**ools **L**ibrary **U**nload.

2. Highlight the name of the module you want to unload.

3. Press Enter to remove the add-in @function from memory.

> **TIP**
>
> To test for the presence of an add-in @function in memory, use @ISAAF and @ISAPP. See Chapter 6, "Using Functions," for more information about using these two @functions.

Questions & Answers

This chapter introduces you to the analytical tools found on the **T**ools menu. If you have questions concerning particular situations that are not addressed in the examples given, look through this section.

Using Advanced Math Tools

Q: When I tried to invert a matrix in my spreadsheet Quattro Pro displayed the error message `Not a square matrix`. The matrix looks square to me, what could have happened?

A: In order to invert a matrix, Quattro Pro requires that matrix to contain the same number of rows as columns. Even though your matrix may look square (the currently defined column widths and row heights within your matrix can create the illusion that the data is in a square) it cannot be if you see this error message. Recreate the matrix so that the number of columns equals the number of rows.

Q: I changed several values in the column I defined as the **I**ndependent variable, but Quattro Pro did not reflect these changes in my results table. Have I accidentally deleted formulas or done something wrong?

A: No. Quattro Pro does not automatically update the results in a regression table if you change the values of your independent or dependent variables. To update the values in your regression table, choose /**T**ools **A**dvanced Math **R**egression **G**o to rerun the analysis.

Parsing Data

Q: The database information I imported into my Quattro Pro spreadsheet did not appear to be properly aligned, so I manually deleted and inserted spaces in each record in order to justify the data. When I parse the data, though, Quattro Pro occasionally lops off letters from the front of the field entries. What am I doing wrong?

A: When you import database information into a Quattro Pro spreadsheet while in WYSIWYG display mode, your data may not appear justified. This display quirk has to do with your default font selection, and often creates the impression that your data is not justified. To see if your imported data is properly justified, switch to text display mode with /**O**ptions **D**isplay Mode **A**: Text (80x25). If your data appears properly justified in text display mode, continue with your parsing operation.

When you manually delete and insert spaces into imported database records while in WYSIWYG display mode, Quattro Pro will create an incorrect format line when you choose /**T**ools **P**arse **C**reate command. With an incorrect format line, Quattro Pro may lop characters off the front of field entries when you parse the data. This occurs because Quattro Pro is using incorrect format line information as the basis for deciding where one database field ends and another begins. The best way to proceed if this situation occurs is to import the database records once more, then create a new format line using /**T**ools **P**arse **C**reate.

If working with data that "appears" unjustified annoys you, switch to text display mode when parsing database information.

Using Sensitivity Analysis

Q: I want to perform a two-way sensitivity analysis (using the **W**hat-If command). I made my column and row of values, entered my formula, and calculated the table. Unfortunately, each cell in the table was filled with a copy of my formula. Why?

A: You most likely changed the formula cell to display as text so that you could observe the formula. When you create the table, however, Quattro Pro must be capable of deciphering the formula in the cell. Change the cell format back to a general display format by selecting the /**S**tyle **N**umeric Format **G**eneral command.

Using the Optimizer

Q: Each time I attempt to define a **S**olution Cell value for my model, Quattro Pro displays the error message `Solution cell is not a formula`. What am I doing wrong?

A: The **S**olution Cell definition must be a reference to a cell that contains a formula. Quattro Pro must be able to adjust the formula variables in a solution cell formula in order for the **O**ptimizer to work.

Q: Each time I choose **G**o to solve an **O**ptimizer problem, Quattro Pro displays the error message `Objective function changing too slowly` or `No feasible solution can be found`. What can I do to correct this situation?

A: First, check your starting values and ask yourself the question "Are they realistic?" If it is apparent to you that your values are not realistic, adjust the starting values and choose **G**o again.

Second, consider constructing constraints for values in your model. If you know, for example, that total production can not exceed 50,000 units, construct a constraint that tells Quattro Pro this.

Third, try adjusting settings on the **O**ptions submenu. For example, try solving the model at a higher **M**ax Iterations value.

Q: When I selected the Re**s**tore command to recover the previous variables in my spreadsheet model, nothing happened. How can I recover my original spreadsheet values?

A: First, check to see if the /**O**ptions **R**ecalculation command is set to **M**anual. If it is, you'll see the `CALC` indicator displaying on the status line. In this case, press F9 and Quattro Pro immediately displays the original values in your spreadsheet.

If the `CALC` indicator is not displaying on the status line, you will have to discard the current spreadsheet, and retrieve the last saved copy of the spreadsheet in order to recover the original values.

Q: I wish to delete a constraint from my spreadsheet model, but the /**T**ools **O**ptimizer **R**eset **C**onstraints command deletes all constraints from the current spreadsheet. What can I do?

A: Choose the /**T**ools **O**ptimizer **C**onstraint(s) command. On the **C**onstraints submenu, highlight the constraint you want to delete, then press the Del key. Quattro Pro deletes the constraint without affecting other constraints defined for the current spreadsheet.

Summary

In this chapter, you learned how to manipulate and analyze your data using the commands found on the **Tools** menu. The commands on this menu enable you to turn a Quattro Pro spreadsheet into an efficient environment for storing, accessing, and analyzing database information.

Having completed this chapter's material, you should understand the following concepts:

- Performing regression analysis using one or more independent variables
- Multiplying and inverting matrices
- Parsing long labels into smaller parts and placing each part into a separate column
- Using the **P**arse and **S**earch & Replace commands together to meet special data-reorganization needs
- Creating one-way and two-way sensitivity tables
- Producing a frequency distribution and graphing the results
- Performing optimization modeling
- Loading and unloading add-in @functions

Chapter 15 introduces you to Quattro Pro macros—mini-programs that you create to reproduce often-used menu commands and to automate repetitive spreadsheet tasks. This chapter provides you with all of the fundamental basics that you will need to envision, create, name, test, debug, and then safely execute macros. This chapter also covers Quattro Pro's **T**ranscript command, a tool you use to review a history of all spreadsheet activities that have taken place during the current work session.

CHAPTER 15

Creating Macros

In this chapter, you learn about Quattro Pro's macro programming facility, which you access from the **T**ools menu. A *macro* is a productivity tool that enables users to store commonly used keystrokes and command selections in a file for future use. When a macro is executed, Quattro Pro reproduces exactly each keystroke action and menu command.

You can accomplish a wide variety of tasks with macros. Macros can automate tedious and repetitive actions that you perform during your work sessions. Macros also can be self-running miniprograms that solicit data input from a user and then manipulate and display the data on a report. You even can create macros to generate reports and graphs from your spreadsheet data.

In the first section of this chapter, you learn about creating a basic macro program. The commands on the /**T**ools **M**acro menu are defined, and then you review a step-by-step process for envisioning, planning, and writing a Quattro Pro macro.

The next section shows you how to create a macro automatically using the macro recorder. You learn how to paste a recorded macro into a spreadsheet, edit the macro instructions, and then replay the macro.

The chapter continues by showing you how to assign a name to a macro and how to create an autoload macro that executes each time you load a new, blank spreadsheet into Quattro Pro.

Managing spreadsheet macros is the topic of the next section. You learn how to document and create a macro library. This section concludes with a presentation of guidelines for editing and executing a macro and deleting an out-of-date macro.

The balance of this chapter is devoted to advanced macro topics. You learn how to enter macro instructions manually into an autorecorded macro, which is created with the /**T**ools **M**acro **R**ecord command. You are introduced to Quattro Pro's powerful macro debugger, a tool that enables you to locate and correct problems that cause macro execution errors.

This chapter concludes with an overview of the **T**ranscript facility. Using this tool, you can reproduce a command history of your work session efforts and monitor and protect these same efforts from power outages and system crashes.

Learning about Macros

A macro program (macro for short) is a collection of special instructions that Quattro Pro can execute. To create a macro, you enter each instruction into a column of cells on the active spreadsheet. When you execute a macro program—much like you execute any other program—Quattro Pro evaluates each cell and then performs the specific action called for by each instruction.

The actions performed by a macro depend entirely on you because you can make a macro duplicate any command action possible on a Quattro Pro menu. You can write a simple macro, for example, that alters the width of a column. You also can write a more involved macro that completely formats a new, blank spreadsheet and then prompts a user to enter data.

A Quattro Pro macro also contains instructions that mimic keystrokes, cursor movements, and other keyboard actions that you perform as you choose menu commands. Many Quattro Pro commands require you to supply block coordinates, type values, or press other keys as part of that command's execution, for example. In a macro program, you store all these keystrokes so that Quattro Pro performs each cell instruction exactly.

Quattro Pro macros also can include macro commands. Macro commands perform functions that menu commands cannot accomplish. You can use a macro command to request input from a user during the execution of a macro, for example, much as Quattro Pro requires you to supply data before executing a menu command. Other macro commands meet specific programming objectives, such as looping, branching, and passing program control to macro subroutines.

Reviewing the Macro Menu

You can use the 11 commands found on the /**T**ools **M**acro menu to create, execute, debug, and delete macros. This Quattro Pro feature has been assigned an Alt-key sequence that displays the **M**acro menu from anywhere on the active spreadsheet. To display the **M**acro menu, press Alt-F2 (see fig. 15.1).

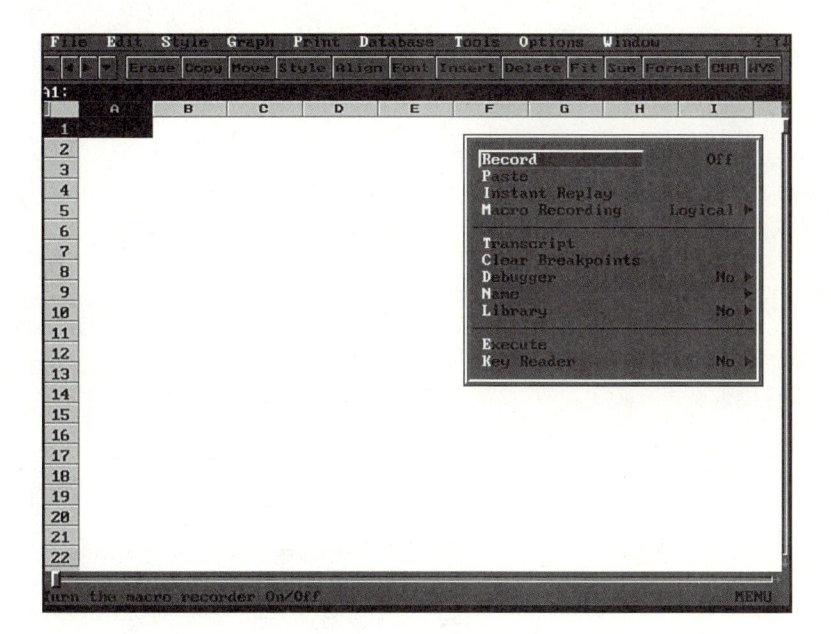

Fig. 15.1

The **M**acro menu commands.

The commands in the top third of this menu are macro-creation commands. Using these commands, you can record and store keystrokes into Quattro Pro's memory, paste a stored macro into a block on a spreadsheet, replay a macro that is stored in memory, and toggle the setting that controls how Quattro Pro interprets your keystrokes.

The commands in the middle third of the **M**acro menu are macro debugging commands. Using these commands, you can display a command history of recent Quattro Pro work sessions, debug your macro programs, and name and create libraries of macro programs for use in future work sessions.

The bottom menu division contains two commands: **E**xecute and **K**ey Reader. The **K**ey Reader command helps you to run Lotus 1-2-3 macros while using the Quattro Pro menu tree.

PART III — ADVANCED SPREADSHEET APPLICATIONS

Table 15.1 briefly defines each command on the **Macro** menu.

Table 15.1 Macro Menu Commands

Command	Description
Record	Toggles Quattro Pro's Macro Recorder on and off
Paste	Copies the last recorded macro into a spreadsheet block that you specify
Instant Replay	Replays the last recorded macro
Macro Recording	Toggles between **K**eystroke and **L**ogical macro recording modes
Transcript	Displays a command history of all recently executed keystrokes and menu command selections
Clear Breakpoints	Removes debugging breakpoints from a macro
Debugger	Toggles the Macro Debugger on and off
Name	Assigns a name to a macro
Library	Designates a spreadsheet as a macro library
Execute	Executes a macro specified by name
Key Reader	Helps Quattro Pro to execute 1-2-3 commands correctly

Creating a Basic Macro Program

The process of creating a basic macro program involves at least three steps:

1. Program the macro.
2. Paste and name the macro (optional).
3. Execute the macro.
4. Debug the macro (when a macro does not execute as planned).
5. Execute the macro (to test a debugged macro).

15 — CREATING MACROS

First, create the macro program. You must have a clear idea of which tasks you want the program to perform. Even though some people have the uncanny knack of programming as they go, for the rest of us, proper planning and development are essential to achieving success.

Naming a macro is no more complicated than, and very similar to, naming a spreadsheet block. You can create a library of commonly used macros that you can execute quickly on every spreadsheet in a new application.

When programmed, the macro is ready to be executed. If for some reason the macro fails to perform correctly, or if Quattro Pro encounters a macro program error, you need to debug the macro.

Debugging is the process of testing, editing, and retesting the integrity of your macro program. To help you to locate and correct errors, Quattro Pro offers many debugging tools. These tools help you transform even the most bug-infested program into a fully functional, streamlined, and efficient macro tool.

Using the Macro Recorder

The most frightening prospect about programming is the idea that you must learn a new, cryptic way of expressing yourself. Quattro Pro, however, offers you the capability to autorecord macro programs so that you do not have to become a multilingual programming genius.

Suppose that you want to create a macro that enters and aligns label headings in a new, blank spreadsheet. The spreadsheet is used to record high and low automobile repair quotes at an insurance company (see fig. 15.2).

To record a macro that reproduces this report, follow these steps:

1. Choose /**T**ools **M**acro **R**ecord. Quattro Pro displays the REC mode indicator on the status line.

> **TIP**
> Press Alt-F2 R to execute the **R**ecord command.

2. Type the headings on row 2, draw a single line under row 2, turn off spreadsheet grid lines, and then alter the column widths as desired.

PART III — ADVANCED SPREADSHEET APPLICATIONS

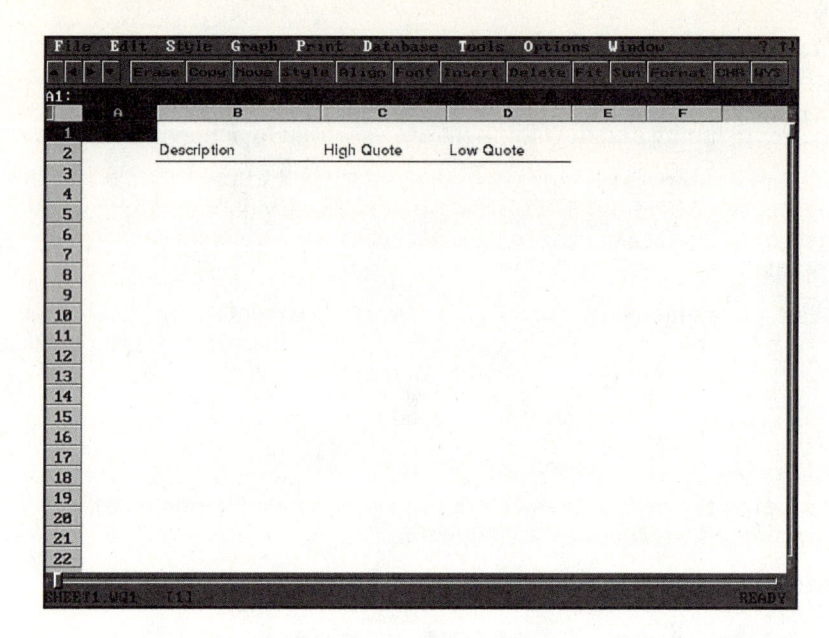

Fig. 15.2

Report headings for an automobile repair quote spreadsheet.

3. Choose /**T**ools **M**acro **R**ecord again to turn off the recorder and return to the active spreadsheet.

You can paste this recorded macro into a block on a spreadsheet to store the instructions permanently. In future work sessions, retrieve the spreadsheet, execute the macro, and watch as Quattro Pro reproduces the headings for this report.

Pasting the Recorded Macro into a Spreadsheet

When you record a macro, Quattro Pro retains the instructions in its memory until you choose **R**ecord and record a new macro. To save a macro so that you can recall and execute the macro later, choose the **P**aste option on the **M**acro menu. This command names and pastes the last recorded macro into a block on the active spreadsheet that you specify.

You can continue pasting the same recorded macro into other spreadsheets open in memory until the next time you record a macro with the **R**ecord command or until you end the current work session. After you record a new macro or end the current work session, Quattro Pro erases the old macro from memory.

15 — CREATING MACROS

To paste the recorded macro onto the active spreadsheet and to assign a unique name to the macro, follow these steps:

1. Choose /**T**ools **M**acro **P**aste. Quattro Pro prompts you for a macro name to create/modify (see fig. 15.3).

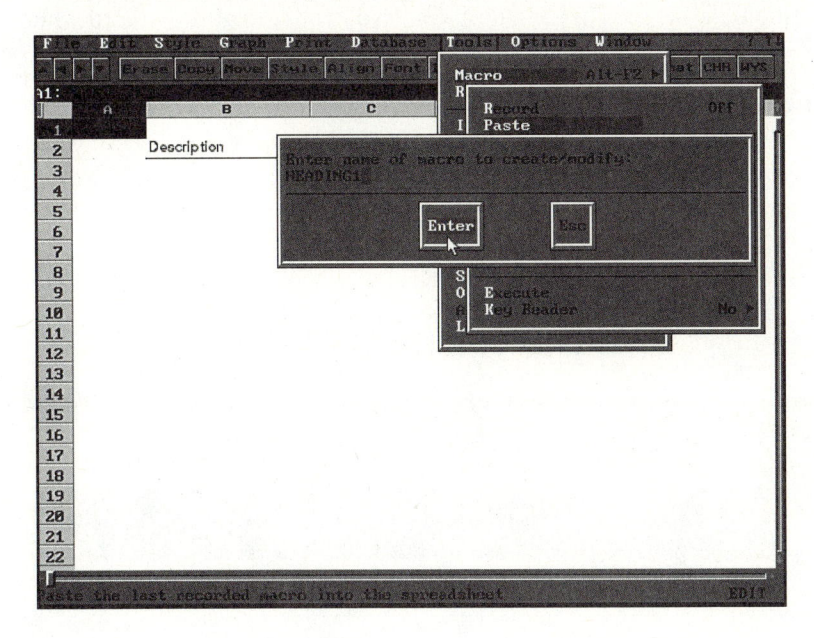

Fig. 15.3

Paste a recorded macro into a block on the active spreadsheet.

> **TIP**
> Press Alt-F2 P to execute the **P**aste command.

2. Type the name of the macro—*HEADING1* for the example—and press Enter to assign that name to the recorded macro.

3. When prompted for the block to paste to, type *B4* and press Enter to paste the macro.

Quattro Pro can paste a recorded macro into a block on the active spreadsheet or on another spreadsheet open in memory. To paste a recorded macro to another spreadsheet, supply the appropriate linking syntax (covered in Chapter 8, "Managing Files and Windows"). By typing +*[PROGRAM]A1*, for example, you can paste the macro onto a spreadsheet named PROGRAM.WQ1, beginning in cell A1.

In this syntax, PROGRAM is the name of a spreadsheet (the WQ1 extension is assumed). The brackets tell Quattro Pro that you are performing an operation on a spreadsheet other than the active one. A1 signifies

PART III — ADVANCED SPREADSHEET APPLICATIONS

the cell in PROGRAM.WQ1 into which Quattro Pro should copy the macro.

You also can specify a block address to paste to, instead of a single cell address. Specifying a block address prevents Quattro Pro from overwriting data on the spreadsheet. Quattro Pro truncates a macro when the macro is longer than the destination paste block. By specifying a block address, you confine the target paste area to an area bounded by the block coordinates.

When you specify a single-cell address, Quattro Pro pastes the macro beginning in that cell and continues pasting down the column until the entire macro is copied. Quattro Pro overwrites any data inside the paste destination.

Interpreting the Macro

Quattro Pro records macro instructions in one of two formats: keystroke-equivalent or menu-equivalent (see fig. 15.4).

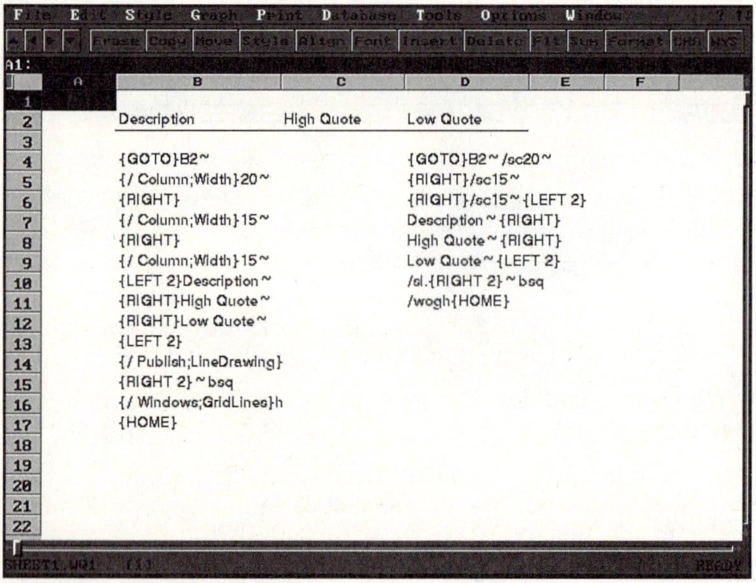

Fig. 15.4

The right macro uses keystroke-equivalent instructions; the left uses menu-equivalents.

The two macros shown in figure 15.4 perform the exact same operation. The macro on the right, however, contains keystroke-equivalent instructions; the macro on the left contains menu-equivalent instructions.

15 — CREATING MACROS

A *keystroke-equivalent instruction* records each menu and command execution that you make in a keystroke-by-keystroke fashion. Such instructions contain the forward slash, followed by each boldfaced letter key that you press to execute a menu command. Keystroke-equivalents often conclude with a ~ (tilde) to signify that Enter was pressed. Sometimes they conclude with a macro command that mimics the action of pressing a cursor-movement key, such as {HOME}.

The first row in the macro shown on the right of figure 15.4, for example, contains two instructions. The first of these instructions, {GOTO}B2~, is a keyboard macro. A *keyboard macro* reproduces the action of pressing a special Quattro Pro key. This instruction indicates that F5, the GoTo key, was pressed, the cell address B2 was typed, and Enter was pressed to move the cell selector to cell B2.

The second instruction is /sc20~, a keystroke-equivalent instruction indicating that the /**S**tyle **C**olumn Width command was selected, the number 20 was typed, and Enter was pressed to store the column width selection.

A *menu-equivalent instruction* looks different from a keystroke-equivalent instruction. This kind of instruction is embedded inside a pair of braces and consists of a forward slash, a space, and two descriptive words separated by a semicolon. When a menu-equivalent instruction requires additional information to perform its operation, that instruction generally concludes with the tilde character.

The instruction in cell B5 of the macro shown on the left of figure 15.4 is {/ Column;Width}20~, which also shows that the /**S**tyle **C**olumn Width command was selected, the number 20 was typed, and Enter was pressed.

Menu-equivalent instructions are easier to read than keystroke-equivalent instructions because, rather than single letters, they contain whole-word descriptions. Menu-equivalent instructions also are fully compatible with other menu trees, whereas the keystroke-equivalent instructions are not.

You can choose a menu command in two ways: by pressing the boldfaced letter key, or by highlighting the command and then pressing Enter. Quattro Pro records the same macro instructions when you press boldface letter keys as when you highlight a command and press Enter.

NOTE Quattro Pro does not have the capability to recognize your mouse clicks when recording a macro. Use only your keyboard when recording a macro.

PART III — ADVANCED SPREADSHEET APPLICATIONS

> **TIP** When the Caps Lock key is on, Quattro Pro records keystroke-equivalent instructions in uppercase instead of lowercase. This method does not affect the performance of the macro.

See Appendix C, "Menu-Equivalent Commands," for a complete list of the menu-equivalents.

Switching the Macro Recording Mode

By default, the **Macro Recording** command is set to **Logical**, which instructs Quattro Pro to record macro instructions as menu-equivalents. This default setting ensures that Quattro Pro macros work with all compatible menu trees. The **Logical** setting also tells Quattro Pro to disregard unintentional, extraneous keystrokes, such as cell selector movements between menu selections.

Quattro Pro macros that contain keystroke-equivalents do not work with every compatible menu tree. Each tree has its own menu names and command names and therefore has different boldfaced letter keys. In the Quattro Pro menu tree, for example, you choose the /**Edit Copy** command by typing /*EC*. In the 1-2-3-compatible menu tree, you type /*C* to choose the **Copy** command.

> **TIP** To ensure complete compatibility between your Quattro Pro macros and the various menu trees, set **Macro Recording** to **Logical**. To create a Quattro Pro macro under the 1-2-3-compatible menu tree and then execute the macro in Lotus 1-2-3, however, you must set this command to **Keystroke**.

To change the default recording setting, follow these steps:

1. Choose the /**Tools Macro Macro Recording** command.
2. When prompted, choose **Keystroke**.

Viewing an Instant Replay

Use the **Instant Replay** command to execute the last recorded macro in Quattro Pro's memory. This command is useful for testing a macro before pasting the macro into a block on a spreadsheet.

To show an instant replay of the last macro you recorded, choose the /**Tools** **M**acro **I**nstant **R**eplay command.

> **TIP**
>
> Press Alt-F2 I to execute the **I**nstant **R**eplay command.

Quattro Pro preserves the last recorded macro in memory as long as you are on the same active spreadsheet and have not recorded another macro. You can choose the **I**nstant **R**eplay command several times in succession as long as these two conditions hold.

Naming a Macro

To save a macro program for future use, you must paste the macro to the active spreadsheet and then save that spreadsheet in a file. When you use the **P**aste command, Quattro Pro requires you to name the macro.

To name a macro that you type into a spreadsheet or to assign a new name to a previously named macro, you must use the **N**ame command.

Using the Name Command

Naming a macro is like creating a block name. You can choose the /**E**dit **N**ames **C**reate command to name a macro when you are not on the **M**acro menu. Make sure that you do not assign an existing block name to a macro or vice versa. If you do, the block or the macro loses its name definition.

You can create autoexecute names that turn macros into instant macros. An *instant macro* has a special name that is comprised of the backslash (\) and a single letter—for example, \h. The backslash represents the action of pressing the Alt key.

You can execute an instant macro directly from your keyboard without having to choose **I**nstant **R**eplay or **E**xecute. Press Alt and the letter name, and Quattro Pro invokes that macro.

To assign the name \h to the sample macro program, for example, follow these steps:

1. Place the cell selector in cell B4.
2. Choose the /**T**ools **M**acro **N**ame command.

PART III — ADVANCED SPREADSHEET APPLICATIONS

3. When prompted, type \h and press Enter twice to assign that name to the macro starting in cell B4 (see fig. 15.5).

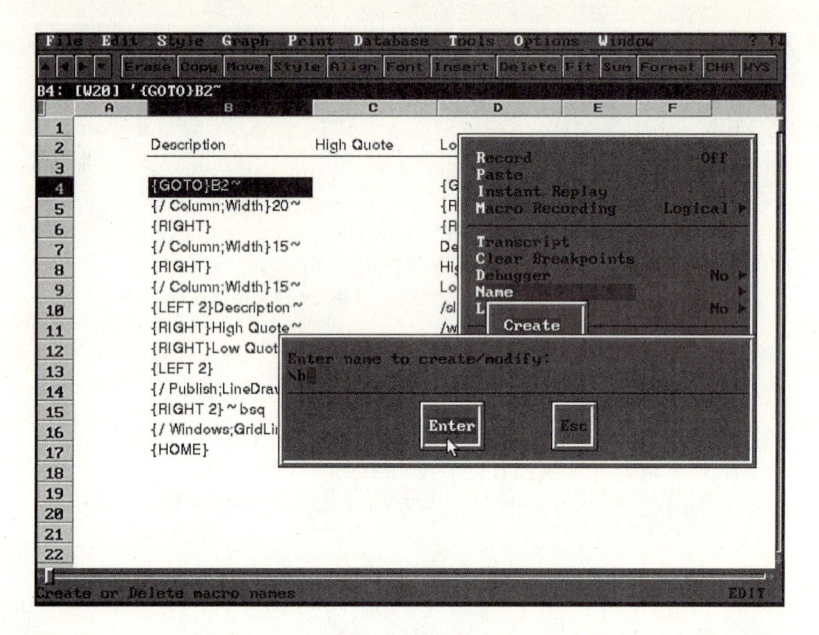

Fig. 15.5

Assign a name to an instant macro.

You can assign more than one unique name to a macro. The first name can describe the macro's purpose—HEADING2, for example—and the second name can be an autoexecute name that enables the name to be an instant macro—\h, for example.

> **TIP** Press F3 from the input line to display the block names choice list. This list shows all block and macro name assignments for the active spreadsheet.

Creating an Autoload Macro

In Chapter 16, "Customizing Quattro Pro," you learn how to specify an autoload macro name by choosing the /Options Startup Startup Macro command. By default, the setting for this command is \0.

Each time you load a spreadsheet, Quattro Pro checks for a macro named \0, unless you type /OSS and type a new name. If the macro exists, Quattro Pro executes it. The autoload macro feature is useful if you consistently perform the same formatting commands before entering data into a new spreadsheet.

Always begin a \0 macro with the {ESC} command. (Press Esc if you are recording the macro, or type the command in the first cell.) This step ensures that your autoload macros work with linked spreadsheets. (Remember that when you initially load a linked spreadsheet, Quattro Pro displays the Linking Options menu. Pressing Esc cancels this menu and enables Quattro Pro to continue executing the autoload macro.)

When you use linked spreadsheets and define an autoload macro in this manner, be sure to update links when the macro finishes executing. Choose /Tools Update Links and choose Open or Refresh. Remember, the Open option loads all linked spreadsheets into Quattro Pro's memory; the Refresh option updates only linked references appearing in the active spreadsheet.

> **TIP**
>
> You also can create and delete autoload macro names by choosing the /Tools Macro Name command and choosing Create or Delete.

Managing Quattro Pro Macros

You can store macros on the active spreadsheet or create a special spreadsheet called a *macro library* to hold the macros. A macro library enables you to choose and execute a macro from another spreadsheet that is open in Quattro Pro's memory. The only condition is that you must have the macro library also open in memory.

Another aspect of macro management concerns documentation. A properly documented macro can be a blessing in disguise. By including the name and adding brief comments to a macro, you guarantee that the user can understand what you are trying to accomplish with the code.

Storing Macros on a Spreadsheet

The execution of a macro is not affected by its location on the active spreadsheet. A macro stored in column IV executes as quickly as a macro stored in column A.

PART III — ADVANCED SPREADSHEET APPLICATIONS

Consider a few points before storing your macros, however. Depending on the instructions contained within a macro, its location on a spreadsheet relative to the spreadsheet data is significant. As a rule, you should store macros close to your spreadsheet data, but not so close that the macro accidentally overwrites itself.

Close proximity enables you to move quickly to the macro when you need to review its instructions. Also, the macro should be below and to the right of your data so that inserted or deleted rows and columns do not alter the macro.

Documenting Macros

You should document your macros so that others can understand what you are trying to accomplish. Documentation also helps you evaluate your program logic during debugging (described later). When you return to a macro that you created long ago, you can refresh your own memory. You may forget the purpose and logic behind a macro after you create 20 or 30 macros.

Macro documentation serves two specific needs: documentation displays the macro name (and autoexecute name, if one exists) and briefly describes the purpose of each instruction.

Figure 15.6 shows a typical macro library. The macro pictured here is the menu-equivalent version of the macro discussed earlier in this chapter.

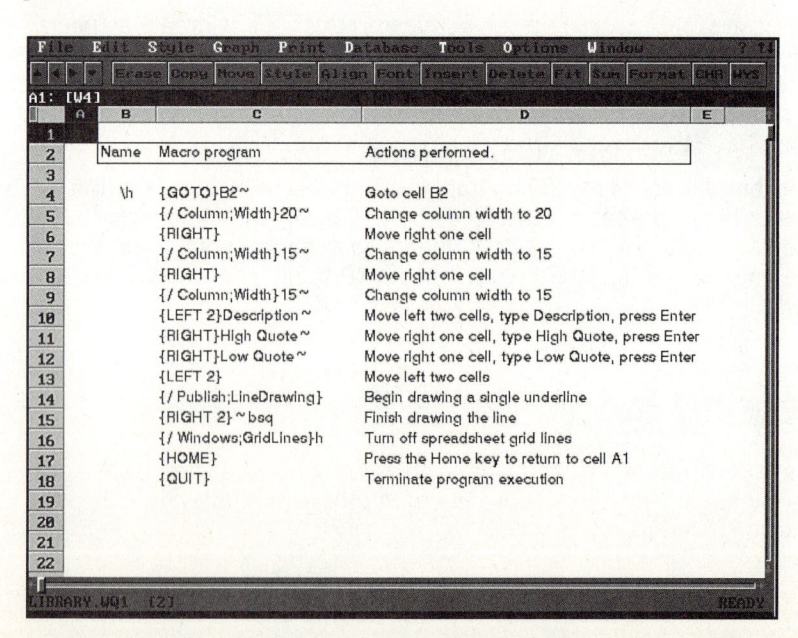

Fig. 15.6

Document a macro program that appears in a library.

Name	Macro program	Actions performed.
\h	{GOTO}B2~	Goto cell B2
	{/ Column;Width}20~	Change column width to 20
	{RIGHT}	Move right one cell
	{/ Column;Width}15~	Change column width to 15
	{RIGHT}	Move right one cell
	{/ Column;Width}15~	Change column width to 15
	{LEFT 2}Description~	Move left two cells, type Description, press Enter
	{RIGHT}High Quote~	Move right one cell, type High Quote, press Enter
	{RIGHT}Low Quote~	Move right one cell, type Low Quote, press Enter
	{LEFT 2}	Move left two cells
	{/ Publish;LineDrawing}	Begin drawing a single underline
	{RIGHT 2}~bsq	Finish drawing the line
	{/ Windows;GridLines}h	Turn off spreadsheet grid lines
	{HOME}	Press the Home key to return to cell A1
	{QUIT}	Terminate program execution

When Quattro Pro executes a macro, the program starts in the first cell and moves down the column until the program encounters the last instruction. By placing macro names in their own column, you can take advantage of Quattro Pro's quick-naming facility.

> **TIP**
>
> Choose the /**E**dit **N**ames **L**abels **R**ight command to quickly assign all names appearing in column B to the macros appearing in column C.

Placing the documentation comments in the column immediately to the right of the macro accomplishes two things. First, this location ensures that the comment labels are not assigned accidentally as names. Second, this placement prevents Quattro Pro from trying to execute the labels as macro instructions.

A final instruction has been added to the bottom of the \h macro shown in figure 15.6. The {QUIT} macro command signifies the end of a macro program. Be sure to add this command to the bottom of all your macros when you create a macro library. This command causes Quattro Pro to stop reading cells and returns control of the keyboard to the user. The next section introduces you to macro libraries.

Creating Macro Libraries

When creating a macro library, make sure that you follow the instructions outlined for documenting and stopping a macro. So that Quattro Pro does not execute a string of macros in the library, also be sure to leave a blank cell between macros and enter {QUIT} as the last macro command (see fig. 15.7).

The following advantages of storing macros in a macro library far outweigh those of storing macros on individual spreadsheets:

- When Quattro Pro cannot locate a macro that you want to execute on the active spreadsheet, the program searches through the macro libraries loaded in memory.

- You can eliminate any possibility of a macro's overwriting itself on the active spreadsheet.

- You conserve spreadsheet file sizes by not having to paste macros repeatedly onto new spreadsheets.

- A macro library is a permanent reference source, whereas spreadsheets often outlive their usefulness.

PART III — ADVANCED SPREADSHEET APPLICATIONS

	A	B	C	D	E
2		Name	Macro program	Actions performed.	
3					
4		\h	{GOTO}B2~	Goto cell B2	
5			{/ Column;Width}20~	Change column width to 20	
6			{RIGHT}	Move right one cell	
7			{/ Column;Width}15~	Change column width to 15	
8			{RIGHT}	Move right one cell	
9			{/ Column;Width}15~	Change column width to 15	
10			{LEFT 2}Description~	Move left two cells, type Description, press Enter	
11			{RIGHT}High Quote~	Move right one cell, type High Quote, press Enter	
12			{RIGHT}Low Quote~	Move right one cell, type Low Quote, press Enter	
13			{LEFT 2}	Move left two cells	
14			{/ Publish;LineDrawing}	Begin drawing a single underline	
15			{RIGHT 2}~bsq	Finish drawing the line	
16			{/ Windows;GridLines}h	Turn off spreadsheet grid lines	
17			{HOME}	Press the Home key to return to cell A1	
18			{QUIT}	Terminate program execution	
19					
20		\m	{GOTO}F30~	Goto cell F30	
21			{/ Math;Fill}F30..F53~	Fill numbers down column F.	
22			1~1~24~	Specify the start, step, and stop values	
23			{HOME}	Press the Home key to return to cell A1	
			{QUIT}	Terminate program execution	

Fig. 15.7

The first two macros stored on the LIBRARY.WQ1 spreadsheet.

To create the macro library pictured in figure 15.7, follow these steps:

1. Choose the /**F**ile **N**ew command to open a new spreadsheet into memory.

2. Copy any existing macros into the macro library or type macros directly onto the new spreadsheet.

3. Choose the /**T**ools **M**acro **L**ibrary command.

4. When prompted, choose the **Y**es option.

5. Choose /**F**ile **S**ave, type *LIBRARY*, and press Enter to save the macro library.

You can create as many macro libraries as you want. You can create separate macro libraries for business and personal spreadsheet applications, for example. To execute a macro stored in a library, press Alt-*key name* or choose /**T**ools **M**acro **E**xecute. The specific use of this command is discussed in the next section.

The rules that apply to one macro library apply to all. You may create as many unique macro names as you want, but you are limited to 26 Alt-key macro names per library. Also be careful about opening two or more macro libraries at the same time. If macro libraries contain duplicate macro names, you cannot predict which macro will execute, if at all.

15 — CREATING MACROS

The instructions in a macro executed from a macro library affect only the active spreadsheet, unless you specify otherwise. An instruction that tells Quattro Pro to choose /Style Line Drawing and draw a Single line around block A20..E25, for example, does so on the active spreadsheet, not on the macro library spreadsheet.

> **CAUTION:** Be careful not to execute library macros when the macro library spreadsheet is active. If you do, Quattro Pro executes the macro on the library spreadsheet. When the executed macro calls for Quattro Pro to delete rows and columns or write labels and values into cells, the macro overwrites itself. Keep backups of your macro library files in case you accidentally overwrite a macro.

An exception to the rule exists about executing a macro on the library in which it resides. Consider a macro that issues the same /Style Line Drawing Single command after a looping subroutine is executed five times. Storing the loop execution value in a cell may seem useful. Because this value pertains specifically to the operation of the macro, however, the value should be recorded in the library near the macro so that the subroutine can refer to it. In this case, the macro actually executes a command on itself before executing a command on the active spreadsheet.

Executing a Macro

To execute a macro that does not have an Alt-key name, follow these steps:

1. Choose the /Tools Macro Execute command.

> **TIP** Press Alt-F2 E to execute the /Tools Macro Execute command.

2. When prompted, type the name of the macro you want to execute.

Quattro Pro executes the macro program. During execution, Quattro Pro displays the MACRO mode indicator at the bottom of the spreadsheet on the status line.

If you do not know the name of the macro you want to execute, press F3. Quattro Pro displays the block names list. Highlight the name on the list and press Enter to execute the macro.

To execute the insurance macro stored on the CLAIMS.WQ1 spreadsheet after you load Quattro Pro into your PC, type *Q CLAIMS \H* and press Enter at the DOS command prompt.

Quattro Pro loads into your PC, retrieves the file named CLAIMS.WQ1, and then executes the \h macro. If the macro contains an error, Quattro Pro beeps and displays an error message. If the macro does not exist on CLAIMS.WQ1, Quattro Pro ignores the command.

To halt the execution of a macro, press Ctrl-Break and then press Esc to return to READY mode. You can use the {BREAKOFF} macro command to disable the effect of pressing Ctrl-Break to disrupt macro execution. When {BREAKOFF} is included in a macro you are trying to stop, Quattro Pro ignores the action of pressing Ctrl-Break. Place the {BREAKOFF} command at the beginning of a macro so that the command is active as soon as the macro begins executing. This technique is useful for preventing macro users from accessing and altering your macro instructions.

Editing a Macro

You have two options for editing a macro: manually or with the Macro Debugger. To edit a macro manually, apply the same editing tools you use with spreadsheet cells.

Tables 15.2 through 15.4, under "Entering a Macro Manually" later in this chapter, list each of the key-equivalent commands that you can use when writing or editing macros. Refer to Appendix B, "Macro Commands," for a comprehensive list of Quattro Pro's macro command language and Appendix C for a complete list of menu-equivalents.

To add a menu-equivalent instruction manually to a macro, follow these steps:

1. Press Shift-F3, the Macro List key, to display a list of the seven macro categories.

2. Highlight a category name and press Enter. Quattro Pro displays a list of all commands in that category.

3. To enter a command onto the input line, highlight the command and press Enter.

4. To store the command in the active cell, press Enter again.

15 — CREATING MACROS

667

You also can click the Macro button on the EDIT mode SpeedBar to reach the list of menu-equivalent macro categories. From there, choose a main topic to reach a menu of specific actions; then, click a menu-equivalent instruction to place it on the input line.

Deleting Macros and Macro Names

Deleting macros and macro names is another aspect of macro program management. By deleting out-of-date macros and macro names, you accomplish three things. First, you conserve spreadsheet space. Second, you reduce the number of names displayed on the block names list. Third, by eliminating instant macros, you free up a letter of the alphabet that you can use to create another, more useful instant macro.

> **TIP**
> Deleting a macro and deleting a macro name are two different procedures. If you delete a name but not the macro, you still can use the macro by renaming it. If you delete a macro but not the name, and then try to execute the macro, Quattro Pro does what it always does when encountering a blank cell—the program stops the execution.

Quattro Pro has two commands that meet this macro management objective. Choose /**E**dit **N**ames **D**elete or /**T**ools **M**acro **N**ame **D**elete to display the block names list. Choose a macro name from the list, or type a name, and press Enter to delete the macro name.

This command deletes only the macro name. To delete the macro from the spreadsheet, choose the /**E**dit **E**rase **B**lock command and type the block coordinates for the macro.

Interpreting Lotus 1-2-3 Macros

You occasionally may want to execute a 1-2-3 macro while running in Quattro Pro's menu tree. The /**T**ools **M**acro **K**ey Reader command helps you with this activity.

To turn on the macro key interpretation, choose /**T**ools **M**acro **K**ey Reader and choose **Y**es. The default setting is **N**o. To save the current setting for this command, choose /**O**ptions **U**pdate.

When Quattro Pro encounters a 1-2-3 macro instruction that begins with the forward slash key (/) or the macro command {MENU}, the key interpreter takes over. In 1-2-3 and Quattro Pro, you press the forward slash key (/) to enter MENU mode. The {MENU} command also causes 1-2-3 and Quattro Pro to enter MENU mode when this command is encountered in a macro program.

1-2-3 macros executed from Quattro Pro do not display all the menus you normally may see. When you type */FS* to choose the **/F**ile **S**ave command, Quattro Pro displays the **F**ile menu and then highlights and executes the **S**ave command (only for the first time you save a spreadsheet). When the same keystroke instruction appears in a 1-2-3 macro, Quattro Pro does not display the **F**ile menu but displays only the dialog box asking you to supply the file name.

If your 1-2-3 macro contains instructions that Quattro Pro cannot interpret, your computer beeps and displays an error message. Translate the instruction to a Quattro Pro-compatible instruction before you re-run the macro.

Using Advanced Macro Techniques

You now know how to record, paste, name, execute, and delete a basic macro. The remaining material in this chapter is devoted to reviewing macro programming techniques that assist you in managing longer, more sophisticated macros.

In the next sections, you learn how to type macros directly into a spreadsheet, link and debug macros, and enter macro commands directly onto the input line for inclusion in your programs.

Entering a Macro Manually

Consider the following approaches to creating a macro:

- Use the macro recorder exclusively.
- Create the macro from scratch by typing each instruction into a column of cells on the active spreadsheet.
- Use the macro recorder first; then, append additional instructions into the macro.

15 — CREATING MACROS

As an advanced macro user, you use the macro recorder for some tasks and enter instructions manually to do other tasks. This approach gives you the best of both worlds. First, you can rely on the macro recorder to duplicate commonly used menu commands. Second, you have the option of applying advanced programming logic to create loops, branches, and subroutines.

Entering a macro manually is no different from entering any other data manually. With a macro, however, you must be careful about the accuracy of your data entry; a single missing brace, disoriented bracket, or misspelled command can cause the macro to crash. When a macro crashes, it stops before executing all its commands, yielding minor or serious consequences.

If the macro that crashes performs spreadsheet operations such as copying data, aligning labels, and formatting numbers, the consequences of a crash are minor. At worst, Quattro Pro abandons the operation, leaving an unfinished or unformatted spreadsheet on-screen. If your macro contains instructions that perform external file operations such as opening a file on disk, writing data to the file, and saving the file, a macro crash may cause irreparable damage to the file.

When a macro crashes, Quattro Pro displays an error message that indicates the cell address at which the execution error occurred. You have only one option: press Esc and return to the active spreadsheet.

To enter instructions manually into a macro after using the macro recorder, follow these steps:

1. Envision the macro application. This planning stage helps you to divide tasks into two groups: tasks that can be accomplished with the recorder and tasks that must be entered manually.

2. Sketch out the structure of the macro on paper. For more complex applications, you may want to use the **/G**raph **A**nnotate command to create a flow chart.

3. Choose **/T**ools **M**acro **R**ecord and create the part of the macro that will contain menu command selections.

4. **P**aste the macro to a new, blank spreadsheet.

5. Move the cell selector to a blank area on the macro in which you want to enter instructions manually.

6. Press ' (the apostrophe label-prefix character) to enter LABEL mode, type an instruction, and press Enter to record that instruction.

7. Continue entering instructions until you finish. Then, follow normal procedures for naming and executing the macro.

You must enter macros into cells as labels, particularly if you are writing a keystroke-equivalent macro. If you try to enter the instruction /FS into a cell without using a label-prefix character, you find the task impossible. When you type the forward slash character (/), Quattro Pro enters MENU mode.

To include keyboard key-equivalent commands in your macros, use the special key-equivalent commands shown in table 15.2. To include function-key actions in your macros, use the special key-equivalent commands shown in table 15.3. To toggle status keys in your macros, use the special key-equivalent commands shown in table 15.4.

You can enter these commands in upper- or lowercase letters. Asterisks denote Quattro Pro-specific commands that are not included in other spreadsheet products.

Table 15.2 Keyboard Key-Equivalent Commands

Keyboard Key	Key-Equivalent Command
←	{LEFT} or {L}
→	{RIGHT} or {R}
↑	{UP} or {U}
↓	{DOWN} or {D}
Backspace	{BACKSPACE} {BS}
Ctrl-←	{BIGLEFT}
Ctrl-→	{BIGRIGHT}
Ctrl-Backspace	{CLEAR} *
Ctrl-Break	{BREAK} *
Ctrl-D	{DATE} *
Ctrl-|	{DELEOL} *
Del	{DEL} {DELETE}
End	{END}
Enter	{CR} or ~
Esc	{ESC} {ESCAPE}
Home	{HOME}
PgUp	{PGUP}
PgDn	{PGDN}
Shift-Tab	{BACKTAB}
Tab	{TAB}

Table 15.3 Function Key-Equivalent Commands

Function Key	Key-Equivalent Command
F2	{EDIT}
Shift-F2	{STEP} *
F3	{NAME} *
Shift-F3	{MACROS} *
Alt-F3	{FUNCTIONS} *
F4	{ABS}
F5	{GOTO}
Shift-F5	{CHOOSE} *
Alt-F5	{UNDO} *
F6	{WINDOW}
Shift-F6	{NEXTWIN} *
Alt-F6	{ZOOM} *
F7	{QUERY}
Shift-F7	{MARK} *
Alt-F7	{MARKALL} *
F8	{TABLE}
Shift-F8	{MOVE} *
F9	{CALC}
F9 (in a File Manager window)	{READDIR}
Shift-F9	{COPY} *
F10	{GRAPH}
Shift-F10	{PASTE} *

Table 15.4 Status Key-Equivalent Commands

Status Key	Key-Equivalent Command
Caps Lock off	{CAPOFF} *
Caps Lock on	{CAPON} *
Toggles Ins on or off	{INS} {INSERT} *
Ins off	{INSOFF} *
Ins on	{INSON} *
Forward Slash (/)	{MENU}
Num Lock off	{NUMOFF} *
Num Lock on	{NUMON} *
Scroll Lock off	{SCROLLOFF} *
Scroll Lock on	{SCROLLON} *

You also can repeat the action of pressing most of the status keys by specifying a repeat number with the code. To move the cell selector down 5 pages from its current position, for example, type *{PGDN 5}*, or type *{PGDN B10}* if cell B10 contains the value 5.

Entering Menu-Equivalent Instructions

The easiest and most accurate way to enter a menu-equivalent instruction into a macro is by pressing Shift-F3, the Macro List key. When you press this key, Quattro Pro displays a menu of seven categories.

Consider the Expenses macro shown in figure 15.8. This macro writes three expense values onto the spreadsheet and then sums their values. The menu-equivalent appearing in cell F12, for example, is entered by choosing from the menu displayed in the figure.

The first six items on the menu are the names of the six macro command categories. The last item, / Commands, enables you to enter menu-equivalent commands.

To enter the menu-equivalent of /**S**tyle **N**umeric Format into cell F12, follow these steps:

1. Make cell F12 the active cell.
2. Press Shift-F3 to display the Macro List menu.

15 — CREATING MACROS

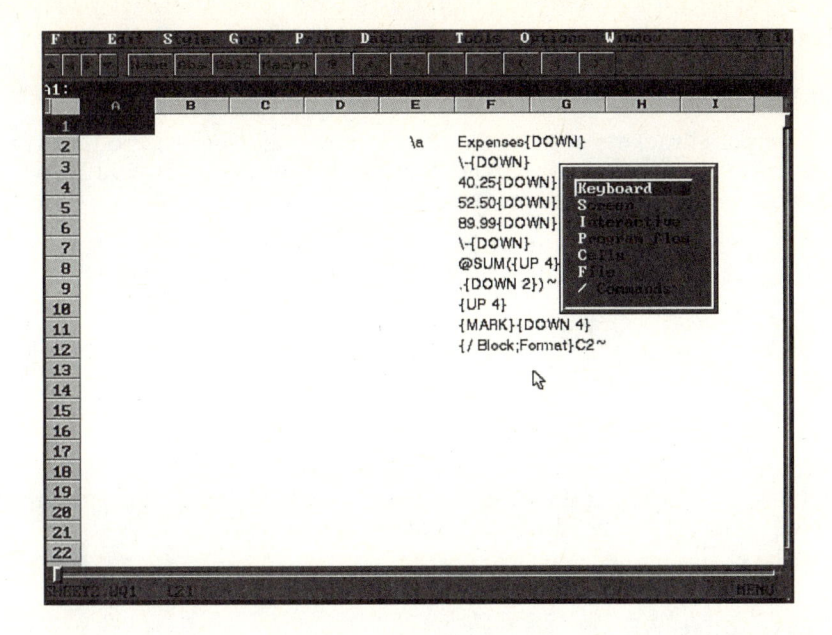

[Screenshot of Quattro Pro spreadsheet showing macro commands in column F with a Macro List menu displayed, containing options: Keyboard, Screen, Interactive, Program Flow, Cells, File, / Commands. Cell contents visible:]

```
              \a   Expenses{DOWN}
                   \-{DOWN}
                   40.25{DOWN}
                   52.50{DOWN}
                   89.99{DOWN}
                   \-{DOWN}
                   @SUM({UP 4}
                   .{DOWN 2})~
                   {UP 4}
                   {MARK}{DOWN 4}
                   {/ Block;Format}C2~
```

Fig. 15.8

Menu-equivalent instructions directly from the Macro List menu.

3. Press / to choose the / Commands option.
4. Highlight Block, the general-action category, and press Enter.
5. Highlight Format, the specific-action category, and press Enter.

   Quattro Pro writes onto the input line the menu-equivalent that you selected and places you in LABEL mode.

6. Type *C2* to choose **C**urrency with 2 decimal places, and press Enter to place the command in cell F12.

See Appendix C for a complete listing of the menu-equivalents.

Using Linking in Macros

Linking enables you to execute a macro in a different spreadsheet, use data from another file, or pass data back and forth between spreadsheet applications. The linking syntax in macro programs is exactly the same as for spreadsheets (see Chapter 8).

To link a macro to cell F15 on a spreadsheet named SALES that is stored in a directory named \ACCOUNTING on a disk in drive B, for example, type the following syntax:

   [B:\ACCOUNTING\SALES]F15

In this syntax, B: is the drive name, \ACCOUNTING is the path name, and \SALES is the file name. (Quattro Pro assumes that the extension is WQ1.)

The square brackets surrounding the formula tell Quattro Pro that you are linking to another spreadsheet. F15 indicates the cell in SALES.WQ1 to which Quattro Pro will link.

If you want to branch directly from a macro library to a cell on the active spreadsheet (in which, for example, another macro exists), use the standard linking syntax.

To branch a macro to cell B10 on the active spreadsheet, for example, type the following syntax:

{BRANCH [ ]B10}

The closed brackets in this syntax tell Quattro Pro to branch to the active spreadsheet. If the brackets are left out, Quattro Pro branches to cell B10 on the macro library spreadsheet.

Debugging a Macro

Quattro Pro's Macro Debugger helps you isolate problems that cause macro execution errors. To use this tool, you execute a macro while Quattro Pro is in DEBUG mode. In DEBUG mode, Quattro Pro executes each macro command one step at a time, pausing until you press any key to tell the program to continue.

You also can insert breakpoints and trace cells into a macro. Quattro Pro suspends execution when the program reaches a *breakpoint* (a cell that you define). Quattro Pro also suspends execution when a program *trace cell* (which contains a logical formula) returns a TRUE value. You also can edit the contents of a macro instruction while Quattro Pro is in DEBUG mode.

To enter DEBUG mode and then execute a macro, follow these steps:

1. Press Shift-F2 to place Quattro Pro in DEBUG mode.

2. Choose the /**T**ools **M**acro **E**xecute command to invoke the macro you want to debug, or press Alt plus the instant macro letter.

When the macro is executed, Quattro Pro displays the Debug window in the bottom half of your screen and positions the first cell of the macro program in the middle of the Debug window (see fig. 15.9).

15 — CREATING MACROS

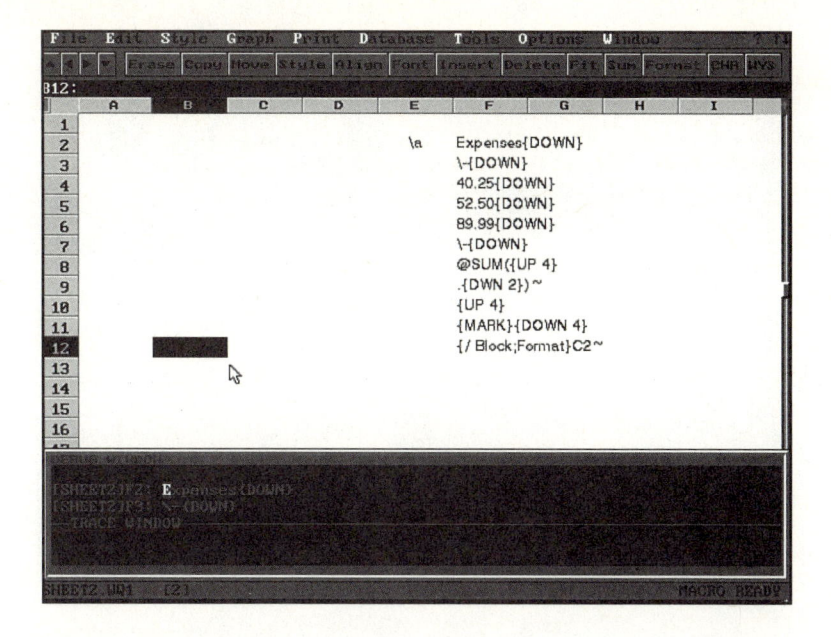

Fig. 15.9

The Debug window displayed when you execute a macro in DEBUG mode.

The active cell in this figure is B12, in which Quattro Pro begins executing the macro. Quattro Pro highlights the first letter in the first word in the first macro instruction appearing in the Debug window. When you press the space bar, Quattro Pro does two things. First, the program highlights the next character in the instruction displayed in the Debug window. Second, Quattro Pro types the character on the input line at the top of the screen.

> **TIP**
>
> Press Shift-F2 to place Quattro Pro in DEBUG mode and Alt-F2 E to execute the macro.

While in DEBUG mode, Quattro Pro stops when the program encounters an execution error. You can trace macro errors to many things: a missing tilde character, an illegal block name, or even an incorrectly spelled macro instruction.

Figure 15.10 shows how Quattro Pro reacts to locating a macro error. The displayed error message gives a specific reference to the spreadsheet name and the cell address in which the error was encountered. A review of the macro in this figure indicates that the cursor-movement instruction in cell F9 is misspelled.

PART III — ADVANCED SPREADSHEET APPLICATIONS

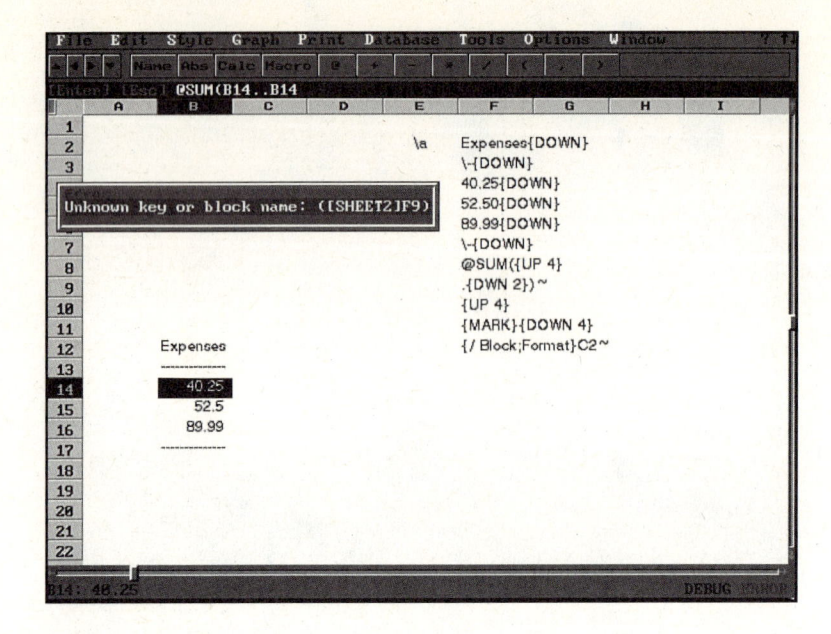

Fig. 15.10

An error encountered during the execution of a macro in DEBUG mode.

To display the Macro Debugger Commands menu, press the forward slash key (/) while the Debug window is active. Quattro Pro displays the Macro Debugger Commands menu. From this menu, you can fine-tune a DEBUG mode operation by specifying several conditions. You can insert and reset standard and conditional breakpoints, choose trace cells to monitor, and abort DEBUG mode. You also can edit individual cells in the macro (see table 15.5).

Table 15.5 Macro Debugger Commands Menu

Command	Description
Breakpoints	Specifies macro execution breakpoints
Conditional	Specifies logical conditions for evaluating breakpoints
Trace Cells	Tracks values in up to four cells during DEBUG
Abort	Halts macro execution and exits DEBUG mode
Edit a Cell	Enters EDIT mode from within DEBUG mode
Reset	Removes all breakpoint definitions
Quit	Exits DEBUG mode and executes the macro at full speed

15 — CREATING MACROS

Defining Standard Breakpoints

Executing a long macro in DEBUG mode can be time-consuming. By inserting breakpoints in a macro, you can specify which parts of the macro to debug step-by-step and which parts to execute at full speed.

When Quattro Pro encounters a breakpoint, the program pauses execution. Press the space bar to continue in DEBUG mode, or press Enter to resume macro execution until Quattro Pro encounters the next breakpoint. You can define up to four standard breakpoints per spreadsheet.

To see how breakpoints work, insert two into the sample Expenses macro by performing the following steps:

1. Press / (the slash key) from within the Debug window. Quattro Pro displays the Macro Debugger Commands menu (see fig. 15.11).

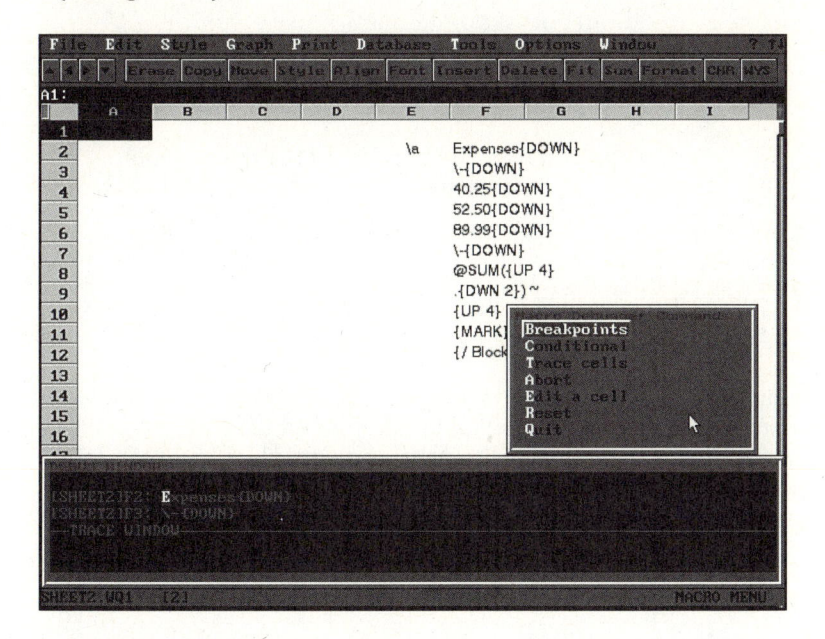

Fig. 15.11

The **B**reakpoints option on the Macro Debugger Commands menu.

2. Choose the **B**reakpoints option.

3. When prompted, choose *1* to insert the **1**st breakpoint.

4. When prompted, choose **B**lock, type *F9*, and press Enter to record the first breakpoint. Choose **Q** to **Q**uit the **1**st breakpoint menu.

5. Choose *2* to insert the **2**nd breakpoint.

6. When prompted, choose **B**lock, type *F12*, and press Enter to record the second breakpoint. Choose *Q* to **Q**uit the **2**nd breakpoint menu.

7. Choose **Q**uit twice to return to the Debug window.

Choose the **R**eset option on the Macro Debugger Commands menu to clear all standard breakpoints, conditional breakpoints, and trace cells. Alternatively, choose the **C**lear Breakpoints option on the /**T**ools **M**acro menu.

Defining Conditional Breakpoints

You also may define up to four *conditional breakpoints*. This type of breakpoint causes Quattro Pro to pause the execution of a macro when the value TRUE is returned by a cell condition that you define.

To define a conditional breakpoint, follow these steps:

1. Press / (the slash key) from within the Debug window.

2. Choose the **C**onditional option.

3. When prompted, choose the number of the conditional breakpoint you want to define.

4. When prompted, type the address of the cell containing the condition.

5. Set additional conditional breakpoints if you want.

6. Choose **Q**uit to return to the Debug window.

Conditional breakpoints are different from standard breakpoints. When you define a cell as a conditional breakpoint, you also must place some type of logical expression in the cell—for example, B25>=500. This logical expression forces Quattro Pro to wait until the value in B25 becomes greater than or equal to 500 before the program pauses the execution of the macro.

Defining Trace Cells

Trace cells are cells in a macro that contain values. You can trace the progress of calculations that affect the values in these cells. Advanced macro programs, for example, often use counters to keep track of values that the macro uses during execution. A *counter* is a formula that you enter into a cell which, for example, can store the number of passes that a macro makes in a looping operation. Advanced macro programs also store results from macro-generated calculations in results cells.

15 — CREATING MACROS

In either case, in a DEBUG mode operation, you can monitor the values stored in these cells to determine whether the execution error is somehow related. You may specify up to four trace cells per spreadsheet to monitor the values. During a DEBUG mode operation, Quattro Pro displays the contents of the trace cells in the Trace window pane at the bottom of the Debug window.

A trace cell can be a useful addition to the sample macro. Remember, this macro sums up three expense amounts and places the value in a results cell. By defining the results cell as the trace cell, you can monitor whether the macro program is performing this operation correctly.

To define a trace cell, follow these steps:

1. Press / (the slash key) from within the Debug window.
2. Choose the **Trace Cells** option.
3. When prompted, choose *1* to insert the **1**st Trace Cell.
4. When prompted, type *A7* and press Enter to define the trace cell.
5. Choose **Q**uit twice to return to the Debug window.

Editing a Cell in DEBUG Mode

When you locate the problem with a macro, use the **E**dit a cell command to edit the instruction in the problem cell. To review the use of this command, correct the spelling error uncovered in cell F9 during an earlier DEBUG mode operation.

To correct the spelling error in cell F9, follow these steps:

1. Press / (the slash key) from within the Debug window.
2. Choose the **E**dit a cell option.
3. When prompted, type *F9* and press Enter to enter EDIT mode so that you can edit the instruction.

   Quattro Pro displays the contents of cell F9 on the input line.

4. Correct the misspelling and press Enter to record the correct spelling.

   Quattro Pro displays the Debug window and the Macro Debugger Commands menu.

5. Choose **Q**uit to return to the Debug window.

Figure 15.12 shows the newly edited version of the Expenses macro. In this version of the DEBUG mode operation, Quattro Pro executes the macro commands on the cell selector location, which was in cell A1 initially.

PART III — ADVANCED SPREADSHEET APPLICATIONS

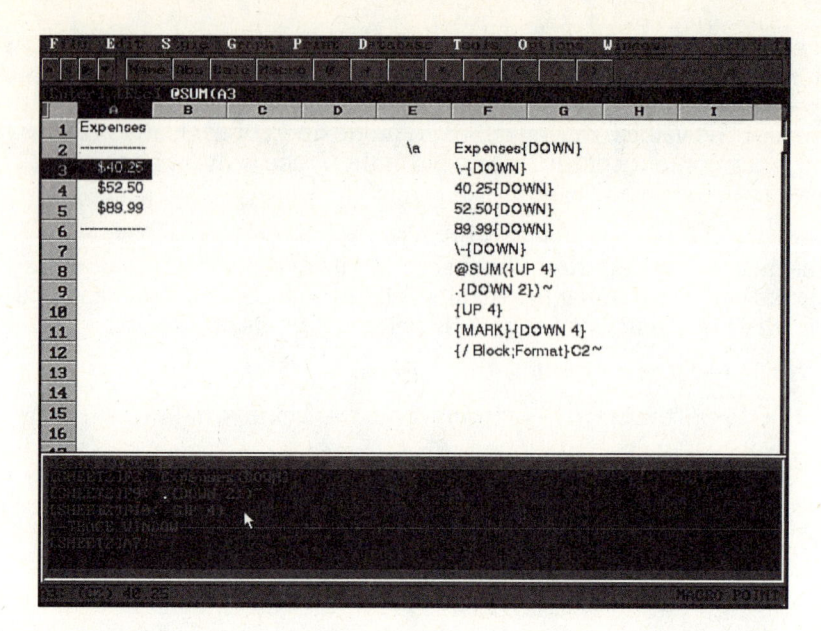

Fig. 15.12

Edit a macro instruction while in DEBUG mode.

The edited instruction from cell F9 now appears in the Debug window when Quattro Pro encounters the first breakpoint. Press Enter to continue executing the macro.

Quattro Pro halts again when the program reaches cell F12, the next breakpoint. Because this breakpoint occurs after the macro already has summed the three expense values, Quattro Pro displays the trace cell result in the Trace pane on the Debug window (see fig. 15.13).

Resetting Breakpoints and Trace Cells

Choose the **R**eset option on the Macro Debugger Commands menu to remove all breakpoints and trace cells set for the spreadsheet.

To reset all breakpoints and trace cells from within the spreadsheet instead of from the Debug window, choose the /**T**ools **M**acro **C**lear Breakpoints command.

Exiting DEBUG Mode

When a macro is finished executing in DEBUG mode, Quattro Pro removes the Debug window from your screen but leaves the DEBUG mode indicator on the status line at the bottom of the screen.

15 — CREATING MACROS   681

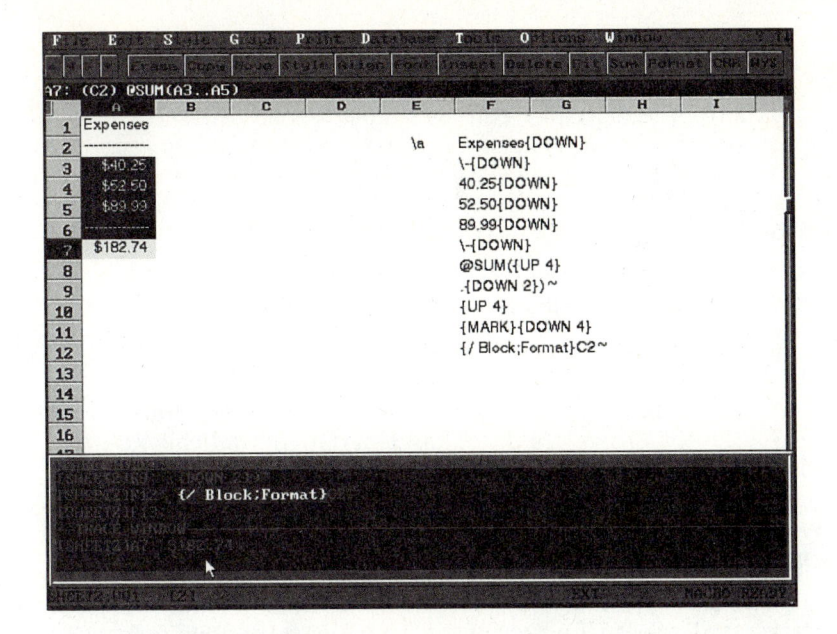

Fig. 15.13

A value displayed in the Trace pane on the Debug window.

You can exit DEBUG mode in the following three ways:

- Choose the /**T**ools **M**acro **D**ebugger **N**o command.
- Press Shift-F2, the Debug key (which toggles the DEBUG mode between on and off).
- Press Alt-F2, enter *D*, and then enter *N*.

To stop the execution of a macro before Quattro Pro finishes debugging it, press the forward slash key (/) and choose the **A**bort option displayed on the Macro Debugger Commands menu. Press Esc to return to the active spreadsheet. If Quattro Pro is in the middle of executing a menu command when you abort the execution, you may have to press Esc several times to return to the active spreadsheet.

> **TIP**
>
> When the Debug window is active, press Esc to return to the active spreadsheet so that you can view the current effects of the macro. Press Esc again to display the Debug window.

Using the Transcript Facility

Quattro Pro's Transcript facility is truly a "behind-the-scenes" tool. Each time you access Quattro Pro, the Transcript facility records each keystroke you make and every menu command you choose. Transcript recording is virtually undetectable; you cannot tell that the Transcript is working during your Quattro Pro work sessions.

The Transcript enables you to undo spreadsheet mistakes, protect valuable work against power failure and system crashes, audit the changes you make to a spreadsheet, and even create working macros out of pasted Transcripts.

This utility stores keystrokes and menu command selections in a Transcript. Quattro Pro writes the Transcript data periodically to a file called QUATTRO.LOG, which resides in the directory into which Quattro Pro was installed originally. Even during this updating operation, you barely can detect that the Transcript feature is working behind the scenes.

To restore lost work or to reverse mistakes made on the active spreadsheet, play back the Transcript. To print a copy of your Transcript, copy the Transcript to a spreadsheet and use the **P**rint menu commands.

Reviewing a Command History

To review the current entries in the Transcript log, choose the /**T**ools **M**acro **T**ranscript command so that Quattro Pro displays the Transcript window.

> **TIP** Press Alt-F2 T to execute the /**T**ools **M**acro **T**ranscript command.

The Transcript window reveals each keystroke and command selection that you have taken during recent work sessions. The last keystroke or command that you execute before invoking the Transcript window appears highlighted at the bottom of the Transcript window. In figure 15.14, a tilde (~) is highlighted at the bottom of the Transcript window, indicating that the Enter key was pressed just before executing the **T**ranscript command.

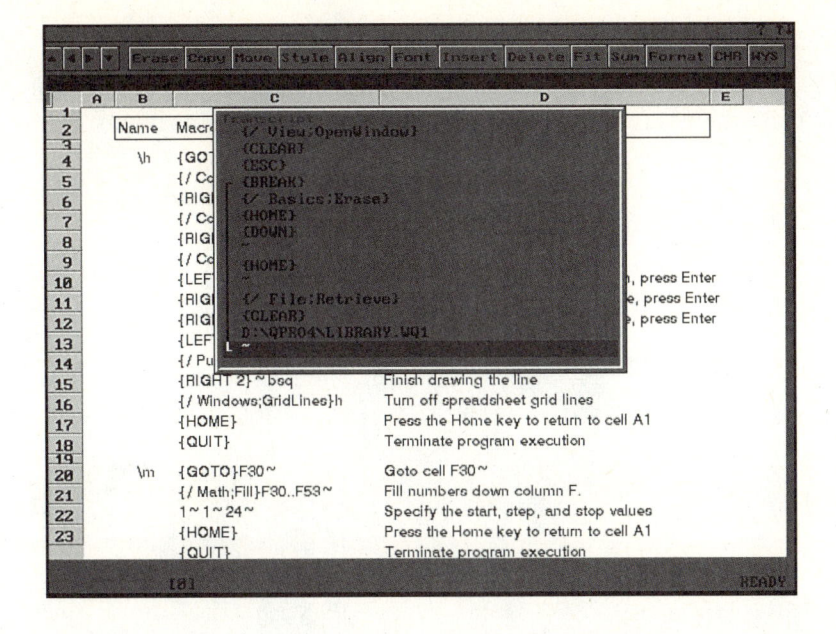

15 — CREATING MACROS

Fig. 15.14

The Transcript window.

Notice the long open square bracket at the left margin of the Transcript window. The commands appearing to the right of this line have not been written into the QUATTRO.LOG file but still reside in Quattro Pro's memory. These commands represent all the keystroke and menu command selections you have made since the last Transcript checkpoint.

Quattro Pro creates a checkpoint each time you choose /File **S**ave, /File **R**etrieve, or /File **E**rase and saves the Transcript to the log file. This action creates a new vertical line checkpoint in the Transcript window that indicates where Quattro Pro will record new keyboard actions until the next log update.

The commands in the Transcript are the same as the commands appearing in macros. To paste commands from the Transcript to the active spreadsheet, you can execute the commands just as you execute a macro. And like a macro, the commands in the Transcript can appear as menu-equivalent or keystroke-equivalent commands. Use the /**T**ools **M**acro **R**ecording options to create the display format that you prefer. (All of the pros and cons of these two formats still hold.)

Use the cursor-movement keys to scroll through the command lines in the Transcript. If any command appears to extend beyond the width of the Transcript window, highlight the command so that Quattro Pro displays the entire command on the input line at the top of your screen.

Manipulating a Command History

The Transcript menu contains the commands that enable you to manipulate the data stored in the Transcript. To access this menu, follow these steps:

1. Choose the /**T**ools **M**acro **T**ranscript command to activate the Transcript window.

2. Press / (the forward slash) to display the Transcript menu (see fig. 15.15).

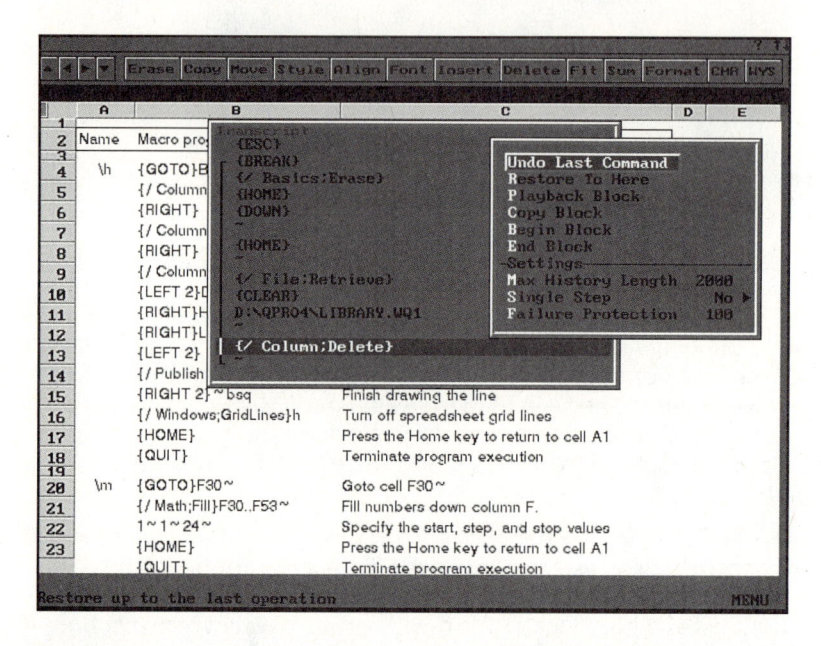

Fig. 15.15

The **T**ranscript menu.

Table 15.6 defines the commands on the Transcript menu.

Table 15.6 Transcript Window Commands

Command	Description
Undo Last Command	Restores the last recorded command
Restore to Here	Restores the command history from the last checkpoint to the end of the line highlighted in the Transcript window
Playback Block	Plays back a marked block of commands

Command	Description
Copy Block	Pastes a block of commands into a block on the active spreadsheet
Begin Block	Marks the beginning of a Transcript block
End Block	Marks the end of a Transcript block
Max History Length	Sets the maximum number of Transcript characters
Single Step	Replays commands one keystroke at a time
Failure Protection	Sets the maximum number of keystrokes before Quattro Pro writes the Transcript to disk

Undoing the Last Command

Suppose that you choose the /**E**dit **D**elete **C**olumns command and you delete columns A and B on the LIBRARY.WQ1 spreadsheet. Suddenly, you realize that you deleted the wrong columns.

If the **U**ndo command is enabled, you can choose the /**E**dit **U**ndo command, and Quattro Pro brings back columns A and B. If you opted against enabling the **U**ndo feature to conserve RAM memory, however, choosing the /**E**dit **U**ndo command has no effect on the deleted columns.

In this event, choose the **U**ndo Last Command on the Transcript menu to reverse the last operation you made. The **U**ndo Last Command does not actually reverse the last operation like /**E**dit **U**ndo does. Instead, Quattro Pro plays back all the commands in your Transcript, beginning at the last checkpoint and through the command preceding the one you want to undo ({/ Column;Delete}, highlighted in fig. 15.15).

When executed, Quattro Pro takes control of your spreadsheet, replaying all the keystrokes and menu command selections until your spreadsheet appears just as it did before issuing the /**E**dit **D**elete **C**olumns command.

To use this command properly, you must enter the Transcript menu immediately and choose **U**ndo Last Command. If you issue other keystrokes before doing so, you create a new "last command" in the

Transcript. To abort an **U**ndo Last Command operation, press Ctrl-Break; Quattro Pro stops the playback as soon as the current command finishes.

Restoring Parts of the Transcript

The **R**estore To Here command plays back portions of a Transcript. In this operation, Quattro Pro replays your command history beginning at the last checkpoint and concludes with the command that is highlighted in the Transcript window.

> **T I P** The **R**estore To Here command replays your Transcript only for the active spreadsheet. If you have multiple windows open in Quattro Pro's memory, this command does not replay the Transcripts for the other spreadsheets simultaneously.

The **R**estore To Here command provides the security and flexibility not available with the Undo Last Command option. Now suppose that you make the same delete column error described previously; this time, however, instead of choosing **U**ndo Last Command immediately, you continue to work with the active spreadsheet. Later, you realize your mistake.

To replay a portion of your Transcript and undelete the column, follow these steps:

1. Highlight the Transcript line containing the command immediately preceding the /**E**dit **D**elete **C**olumns command.
2. Select the Transcript menu and choose **R**estore To Here.

Quattro Pro replays your Transcript history up to the point before the delete operation.

Another benefit of the **R**estore To Here command is that this command can protect your spreadsheet data in the event you experience a system crash or power failure. Although the Restore To Here command cannot restore commands appearing before the last checkpoint, this command is extremely useful.

In either event, follow these steps:

1. Highlight the last command line in your Transcript.
2. Select the Transcript menu and choose **R**estore To Here.

Quattro Pro replays your Transcript history from the last checkpoint to the point of failure. To abort this command, press Ctrl-Break. Quattro Pro stops the replay operation at the end of the current command.

Playing Back a Transcript Block

The **P**layback Block command, like the **R**estore To Here command, plays back portions of a Transcript. This command replays all commands appearing inside a block in the Transcript that you specify.

To use this command, follow these steps:

1. Highlight the first command you want to play back, and then press / while in the Transcript window to activate the Transcript menu.

2. Choose **B**egin Block.

3. Highlight the last command line you want to play back, press / to activate the Transcript menu, and then choose End Block (see fig. 15.16).

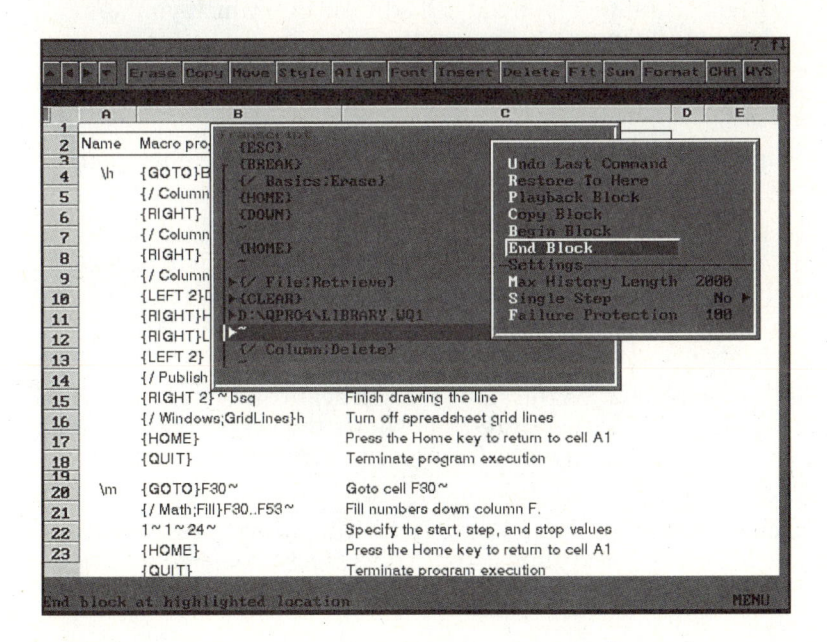

Fig. 15.16

Quattro Pro puts arrowheads next to each command line in the block.

4. Press / to activate the Transcript menu and choose **P**layback Block. Quattro Pro replays the commands marked in the block.

When you choose **P**layback Block, Quattro Pro plays back the marked command block. To abort this operation, press Ctrl-Break. Quattro Pro stops the playback at the end of the current command.

Copying a Transcript Block

The commands appearing in the Transcript are exactly the same as the instructions that appear in a macro. By copying commands from the Transcript into a spreadsheet, you can turn the commands into macro instructions.

A **C**opy Block operation is similar to a **P**layback Block operation—you specify the beginning and end blocks in the Transcript on which to perform an operation. To copy the block defined in the preceding section to a spreadsheet, for example, follow these steps:

1. Choose **C**opy Block. Quattro Pro prompts you to create/modify a macro name.

2. Type a name and press Enter to record the macro name.

3. When prompted, type the cell address into which you want to copy the Transcript commands.

4. Press Enter to copy the Transcript commands into the active spreadsheet.

To copy the block to another spreadsheet open in memory, you can use one of the following methods:

- When Quattro Pro prompts you for a destination block, press Alt-0, the Pick Window key, to display a list of open spreadsheets. Highlight a spreadsheet name and press Enter to load the spreadsheet into the active window. Position the cell selector on the spreadsheet and press Enter to copy the block to that location.

- You also can type the standard link syntax when prompted for a destination block. Figure 15.17 shows the syntax that was used to copy the block from the Transcript onto SHEET4.WQ1 beginning at cell D2.

You can choose the /**T**ools **M**acro **N**ame command to assign a macro name to the block and choose the /**T**ools **M**acro **P**aste command to copy the block into SHEET4.WQ1.

Fig. 15.17

Copy a Transcript command block onto another spreadsheet.

Defining the Maximum History Length

Transcript records your keystrokes and menu command selections in a file called QUATTRO.LOG. When you load Quattro Pro into your PC, the program opens this file and begins appending to it.

Quattro Pro enables you to establish the number of keystrokes the program stores in the QUATTRO.LOG file. By default, this setting is 2,000 keystrokes. When the QUATTRO.LOG file reaches this maximum, Quattro Pro renames the file QUATTRO.BAK and opens a new, empty QUATTRO.LOG file. When Quattro Pro updates QUATTRO.LOG, the program overwrites the QUATTRO.BAK file.

You can change the **M**aximum History Length setting, for example, to 7,500 keystrokes by performing the following steps:

1. Choose **M**aximum History Length from the Transcript menu.
2. When prompted, type *7500* (see fig. 15.18).
3. Press Enter to record the new setting.

The maximum value permitted for this setting is 25,000 keystrokes. Be careful of the value you enter here, however; if you enter *0* as the setting, Quattro Pro disables the Transcript facility altogether.

Fig. 15.18

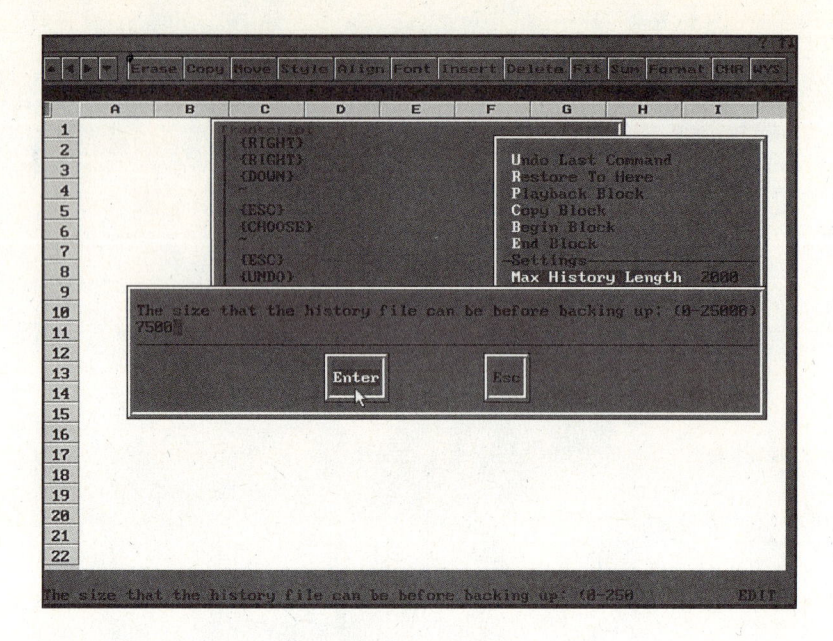

Choose a higher maximum history length setting.

Defining the Playback Mode

Choose the **S**ingle Step command to determine the speed with which Quattro Pro replays a Transcript command history when prompted.

By default, this command is set to **N**o. A **Y**es setting causes Quattro Pro to display the Transcript command history in DEBUG mode.

The **T**imed setting pauses the replay operation momentarily between each Transcript command line; the **Y**es setting pauses the replay until you press any key on the keyboard.

To replay a block of commands in timed fashion, follow these steps:

1. Choose **S**ingle Step from the Transcript menu.
2. Choose the **T**imed option (see fig. 15.19).

Now choose a replay operation. When executed, Quattro Pro replays the Transcript one command line at a time, pausing for a moment between commands.

Press Ctrl-Break during a replay operation to stop the operation.

Fig. 15.19

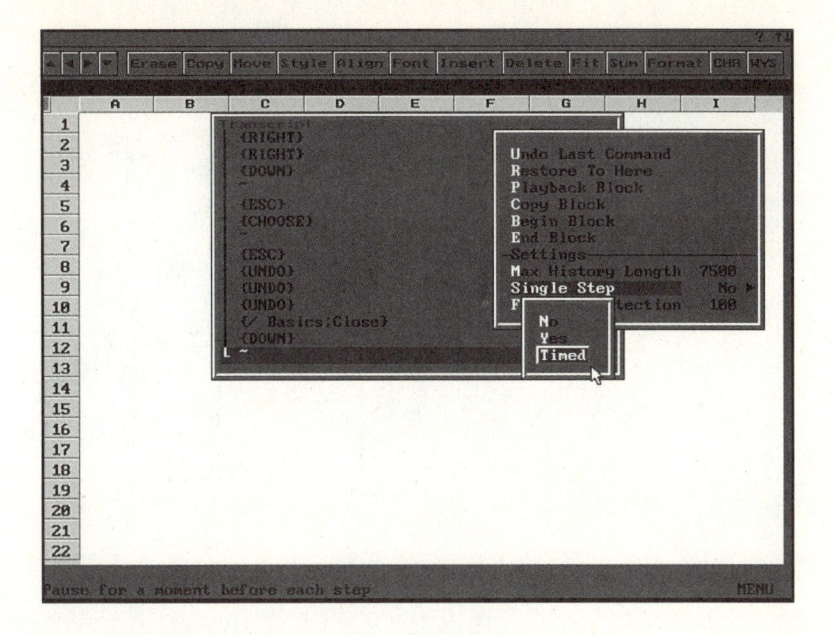

Pause the steps in a replay operation.

Defining Failure Protection

By default, Quattro Pro writes the Transcript to disk after every 100 keystrokes. The Failure Protection facility ensures that you can recover most or all of your work in the event of a power failure.

When you lower this setting, Quattro Pro writes to disk more often and increases the likelihood that the Transcript will slow down your work sessions. If you are comfortable with increasing the risk of data loss, choose the Failure Protection command and enter a higher setting.

To set this command to 500 keystrokes, for example, follow these steps:

1. Choose Failure Protection from the Transcript menu.
2. When prompted, type *500* (see fig. 15.20).
3. Press Enter to record the new setting.

At higher settings, Quattro Pro stores your keystrokes and menu command selections in a memory buffer and writes the keystrokes to disk at less frequent intervals.

PART III — ADVANCED SPREADSHEET APPLICATIONS

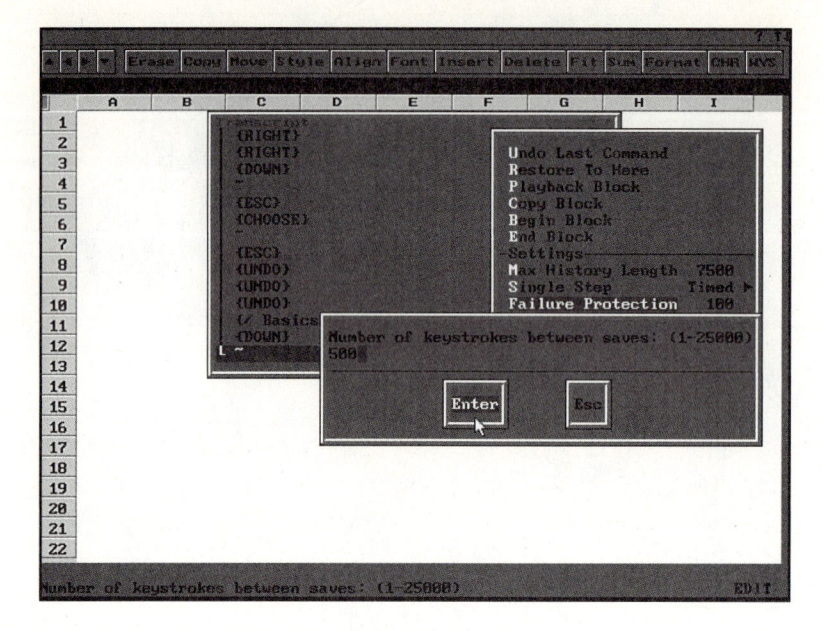

Fig. 15.20

Increase the number of keystrokes that Quattro Pro stores before writing the Transcript to disk.

Exiting Transcript

Press Esc to leave the Transcript menu and return to the Transcript window. To return to the active spreadsheet, press Esc again.

> **TIP** To disable the Transcript facility altogether and free RAM memory for use in other areas of Quattro Pro, set the **M**ax History Length setting to 0.

Questions & Answers

This chapter introduces you to the /**T**ools **M**acro menu of commands. If you have questions concerning particular situations that are not addressed in the examples given, look through this section.

Recording a Macro

Q: I pressed Alt-F2 R to begin recording a macro but nothing happened. Did I do something wrong?

A: When Quattro Pro is recording a macro, the program displays REC on the status line at the bottom of your screen. If this mode indicator does not appear, choose /**T**ools **M**acro **R**ecording **Y**es and try again. Note that Quattro Pro does nothing spectacular to indicate that it is recording a macro.

Q: Why doesn't Quattro Pro give me an instant replay of a macro I just recorded?

A: You may not have turned on the Macro Recorder, and Quattro Pro hasn't recorded anything. Make sure that the REC mode indicator is showing on the status line while you are recording.

You also may have exited the active spreadsheet before choosing the **I**nstant Replay command, and Quattro Pro erased the recorded macro from memory. To replay a macro properly, be sure to choose /**T**ools **M**acro **I**nstant Replay when you finish recording.

Also, be sure you didn't select your menu commands with your mouse.

Executing a Macro

Q: Why doesn't Quattro Pro execute my instant macro?

A: Remember, Quattro Pro accepts only letters as valid instant macro names. If you named your macro \5, for example, choose /**T**ools **M**acro **N**ame and rename the macro with a letter.

Q: Why doesn't Quattro Pro execute the instant macro I named /a?

A: When you name an instant macro, you must include the backslash (\) and not the forward slash (/). If your macro name contains the forward slash, Quattro Pro does nothing when you press Alt-a. Choose /**T**ools **M**acro **N**ame and rename the macro.

Q: Why doesn't my autoload macro work when I load a linked spreadsheet application?

A: Look at your macro. Is the first command in the macro {ESC}? If not, type {ESC} above the first command—this command is necessary to back Quattro Pro out of the linking options prompt. Choose /**T**ools **M**acro **N**ame and rename the macro, defining the cell that contains {ESC} as the first cell in the macro block.

Q: I don't want my autoload macro to affect every spreadsheet that I load. What should I do?

A: Choose /**O**ptions **S**tartup **S**tartup Macro, press Backspace until you delete the autoload name, and press Enter to record no autoload name. Choose /**O**ptions **U**pdate to save the new setting.

You must rename the macro if you originally named it \0 to correspond to the default setting for the **S**tartup Macro command.

Q: When I execute a macro, Quattro Pro modifies the spreadsheet that the macro is on and not the spreadsheet that I want modified. What's happening?

A: You did not define the first spreadsheet as a macro library. Choose /**T**ools **M**acro **L**ibrary **Y**es. Press Alt-0 and activate the target spreadsheet. Execute the macro again.

Q: Why doesn't Quattro Pro execute a macro that I created from the 1-2-3-compatible menu tree?

A: You can use such a macro only when the 1-2-3-compatible menu tree is active. If you switched menu trees since creating the macro, switch back by choosing /**O**ptions **S**tartup **M**enu Tree 123.MU.

Q: Why can I not execute a recorded macro in the 1-2-3-compatible menu tree?

A: Before you record macros from the Quattro Pro menu tree, you must choose /**T**ools **M**acro **M**acro Recording **L**ogical. In this setting, Quattro Pro records menu-equivalent commands that are compatible across menu trees.

In the **K**eystroke setting, Quattro Pro records keystroke commands that vary from menu tree to menu tree.

Using the Transcript

Q: Why is the Transcript window empty when plenty of command history should appear?

A: Quattro Pro disables the Transcript facility when the /**T**ools **M**acro **T**ranscript **M**ax History Length setting is 0. Enter a larger number if you want Quattro Pro to maintain a Transcript history of your work sessions.

Summary

In this chapter you learned how to create, debug, edit, and execute macro programs. You also were introduced to the Transcript facility, a tool that helps you to maintain the integrity of your Quattro Pro work sessions.

Having completed this chapter, you should understand the following Quattro Pro concepts:

- Recording, pasting, naming, editing, and executing basic macro programs
- Using the Macro Debugger to ferret out macro commands that cause execution errors
- Applying the commands on the Transcript menu to view your command history, replay Transcript blocks, and undo spreadsheet mistakes
- Copying a Transcript block to a spreadsheet, naming the block as a macro, and then replaying the block on-screen
- Defining parameters that determine the size of the Transcript, how often the Transcript is updated, and the Transcript's replay mode

In Chapter 16, you learn how to customize and streamline your Quattro Pro work sessions by creating default settings that are tailor-made to your specific needs.

Chapter 16 provides comprehensive coverage of Quattro Pro's Options menu. Using the commands on this menu, you can modify how Quattro Pro interacts with your system hardware, select complementary screen colors for your display, change the cell format default settings, and configure and then store start-up options for the next work session.

CHAPTER 16

Customizing Quattro Pro

This chapter introduces you to the **O**ptions menu commands, which enable you to fine-tune Quattro Pro's system and format settings. These two types of settings are important to your daily work sessions because they control how Quattro Pro interacts with your computer hardware and your active spreadsheet. If you don't change the options, Quattro Pro uses its default settings.

The **O**ptions menu commands are not so much operating commands as they are a set of rules that Quattro Pro follows each time it loads into your computer. Without these settings, Quattro Pro does not know whether to display in text or WYSIWYG mode, cannot properly use your computer's expanded memory, has no idea how to color the various parts of its screen display, and cannot send data to the correct printer port.

System options go into effect immediately, but others have an effect only when Quattro Pro loads into your computer. Format options affect only the active spreadsheet. In this chapter, you learn the domain of each type of option as it is discussed.

The first part of Chapter 16 is devoted to reviewing the commands on the **O**ptions menu. As in previous chapters, you come to understand the organization of the commands on this menu. A quick preview of Quattro Pro's coloring palette concludes this section.

PART III — ADVANCED SPREADSHEET APPLICATIONS

The next section shows you how to set and reset options that you use to define Quattro Pro's system settings. These settings remind Quattro Pro about your printer and screen, as well as which colors to use on-screen. You also learn how to create your own set of "start-up rules" for Quattro Pro to follow the next time it loads.

Then you review the Update command. Using the Update command saves your current system settings as defaults, which then go into effect the next time you start Quattro Pro.

The last part of the chapter teaches you about defining global format settings, selecting recalculation modes, and invoking global, spreadsheet, and formula protection. Remember, these final settings affect only individual spreadsheets. Update does not store the settings for each new spreadsheet you create.

Reviewing the Options Menu

Use the 15 Options menu commands to set, reset, and save the system and format defaults for using Quattro Pro. The Options menu contains two types of commands: system options and default format options (see fig. 16.1). Quattro Pro displays the current settings for certain commands on this menu at the right margin.

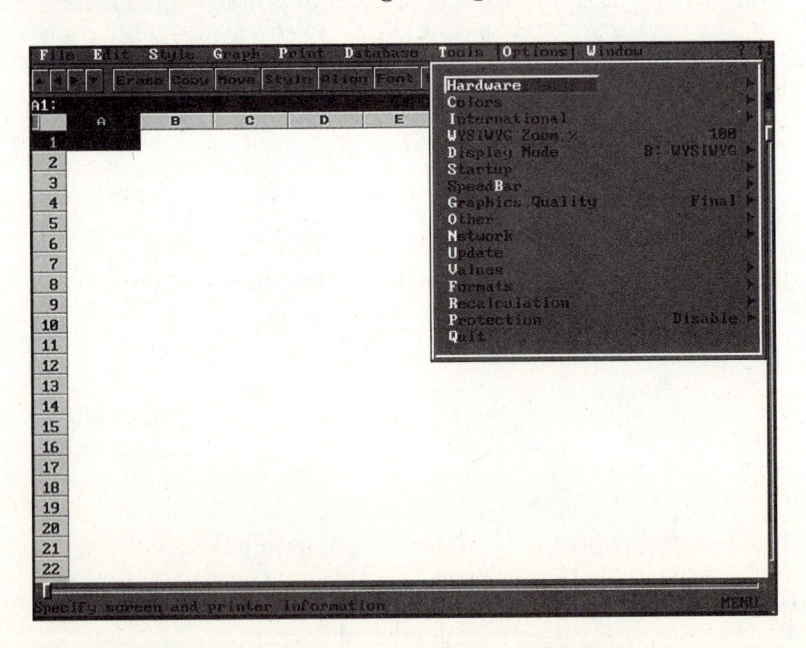

Fig. 16.1

The Options menu commands.

16 — CUSTOMIZING QUATTRO PRO

The first 10 commands are system options, which tell Quattro Pro how to interact with your screen display and printer, what colors to display, and where and how to store files. If Quattro Pro seems to perform well and you are comfortable with its on-screen appearance, you may not have to change many of the default system settings.

The **U**pdate command saves the current **O**ptions menu settings, which go into effect the next time you start another Quattro Pro work session. Quattro Pro stores the default menu settings in two files on your hard disk drive (RSC.RF and QUATTRO.MU). If you are using the 1-2-3 menu tree, Quattro Pro stores the menu settings in 123.MU. If you are on a network, you are using the QUATTRO.MP file, not the .MU file.

The **U**pdate command saves only system options—not any of the global options (Formats, Recalculation, and Protection)—for future work sessions. All other options are saved only with the active spreadsheet when you choose /**F**ile **S**ave, /**F**ile Save **A**s, or /**F**ile Sa**v**e All.

> **TIP**
> Choosing **U**pdate saves all system defaults that can be updated, including those defaults set on the **S**tyle, **G**raph, and **P**rint menus.

The /**O**ptions **V**alues command displays a settings window that summarizes all system defaults for the current work session. By using this command, you quickly can review all of Quattro Pro's current default settings. When you choose this command, Quattro Pro displays the status box shown in figure 16.2. Each time you choose /**O**ptions **U**pdate, Quattro Pro updates the settings information that appears in the status box.

The next three commands on the menu are default format options that affect only individual spreadsheets. The commands in this section store default numeric formats, enable you to choose the formula recalculation method, and turn global spreadsheet and formula protection on and off.

Table 16.1 explains the purpose of the **O**ptions menu commands. As with most other Quattro Pro commands, these commands are intuitive. Choose **C**olors to set color options, for example, **D**isplay Mode to change the display mode, or Speed**B**ar to reconfigure the SpeedBar.

PART III — ADVANCED SPREADSHEET APPLICATIONS

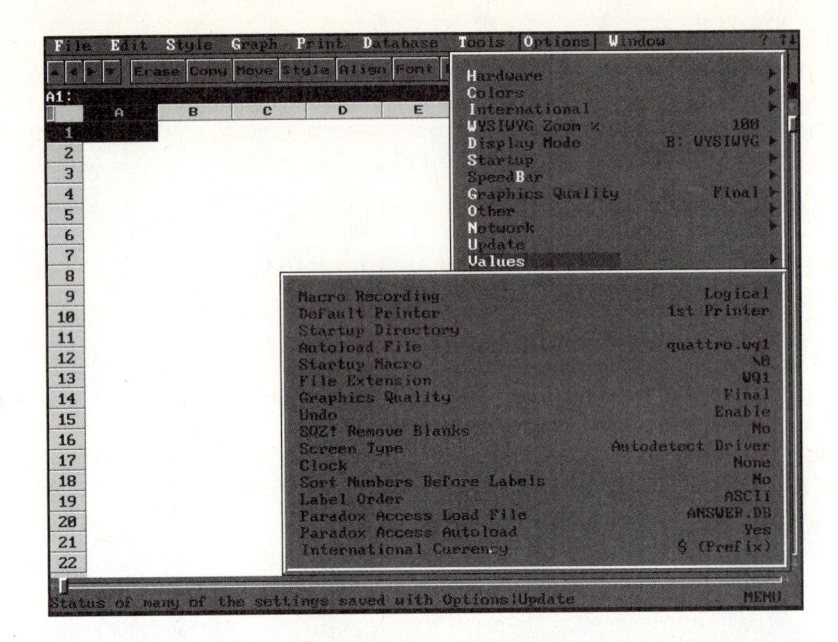

Fig. 16.2

Review the status of a Quattro Pro work session.

Table 16.1 The Options Menu Commands

Command	Description
Hardware	Shows screen, memory, and printer settings
Colors	Customizes colors for all Quattro Pro screens
International	Displays international standards for currency, date, and time
WYSIWYG Zoom %	Sets the percent zoom factor used to enlarge and reduce the spreadsheet area shown in one screen
Display Mode	Sets the display mode
Startup	Displays current start-up and default options
SpeedBar	Changes the macro key button assignments on the EDIT mode and READY mode SpeedBars
Graphics Quality	Toggles between final and draft graphics quality
Other	Sets **U**ndo, **M**acro, **E**xpanded Memory, **C**lock, and **P**aradox options
Network	Configures the network operating environment options, such as drive mappings

Command	Description
Update	Updates and saves all current default settings
Values	Displays a settings menu that summarizes all current defaults saved with the **U**pdate command
Formats	Sets the global display formats
Recalculation	Sets the recalculation mode
Protection	Enables and disables global spreadsheet protection and adds or removes formula password protection

Setting Hardware Options

When you choose /**O**ptions **H**ardware, Quattro Pro displays a submenu with three command options and three noninteractive fields that display only system data (see fig. 16.3). Table 16.2 describes the options available.

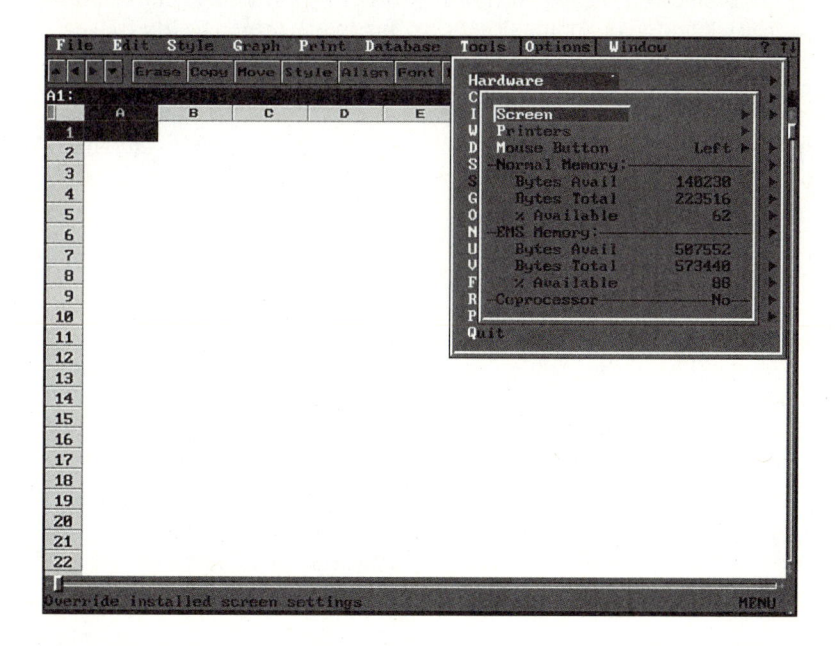

Fig. 16.3

The **H**ardware screen.

Table 16.2 Choosing Hardware Options

Command	Description
Screen	Sets characteristics for the screen display
Printers	Reconfigures and installs printers
Mouse Button	Determines which mouse button is used to choose commands
Normal Memory	Displays conventional memory statistics
EMS Memory	Displays expanded memory statistics
Coprocessor	Indicates whether a math coprocessor is installed

The **S**creen and **P**rinters commands enable you to change the system settings for your screen and printer. The **M**ouse Button command enables you to choose the mouse button (**L**eft or **R**ight) that is used to choose commands and highlight cells on a spreadsheet.

The final three commands, distinguished by a line through their names (and no available boldface letter shortcut key), display information about how Quattro Pro is using your hardware (refer to fig. 16.3). You cannot execute these commands. When you add memory or a coprocessor to your system, however, Quattro Pro updates the information in these three fields. (For more details, see the section titled "Reviewing Normal Memory, EMS, and Coprocessor Data" later in this chapter.)

Choosing a New Screen

During installation, Quattro Pro detects your screen display and installs the proper screen driver file. This file contains special codes that tell Quattro Pro how to display itself. Depending on your display model—and therefore the contents of this file—you may be able to modify certain display characteristics directly from the **O**ptions menu.

To change these stored specifications (without reinstalling the program), choose /**O**ptions **H**ardware **S**creen. Quattro Pro displays the menu shown in figure 16.4. These commands are described in the next sections.

16 — CUSTOMIZING QUATTRO PRO

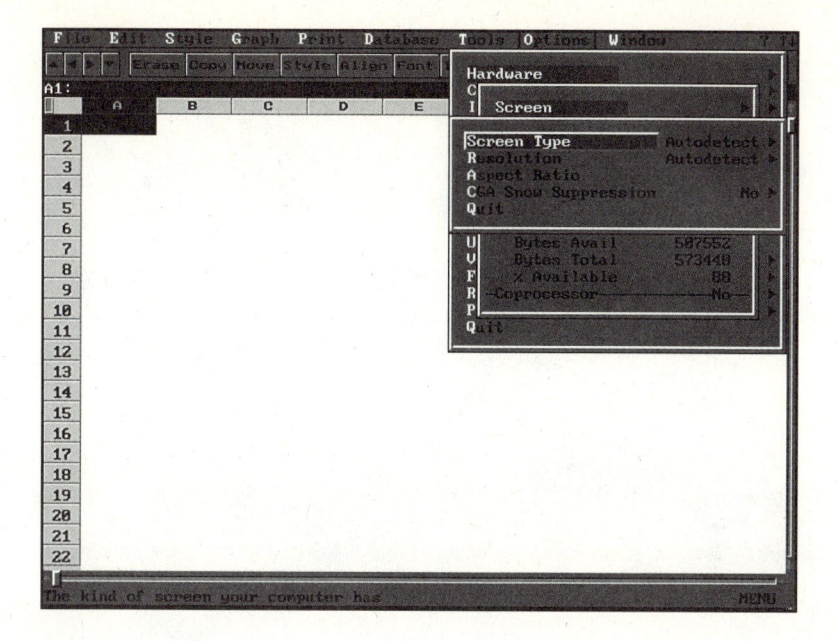

Fig. 16.4

The **S**creen submenu commands.

Screen Type

The **S**creen Type option enables you to choose a different screen driver for your display when you are not in WYSIWYG mode. The default setting, **A**utodetect, causes Quattro Pro to evaluate your screen type on its own.

> **T I P**
>
> During the installation of Quattro Pro, you may have selected WYSIWYG display mode, the default startup display mode that Quattro Pro suggested that you use. If you selected a non-WYSIWYG display mode and now want to switch to WYSIWYG, click the WYS button in the SpeedBar. To switch back to 80 x 25 text display mode, click the CHR button.

You should have Quattro Pro autodetect your screen type except in special cases, such as when you want to choose a special display setting like Monochrome EGA. If you choose a driver incompatible with your type of screen, Quattro Pro may not display correctly.

To choose a new screen type, choose **S**creen Type. Now choose a different driver from the list shown in figure 16.5.

Fig. 16.5

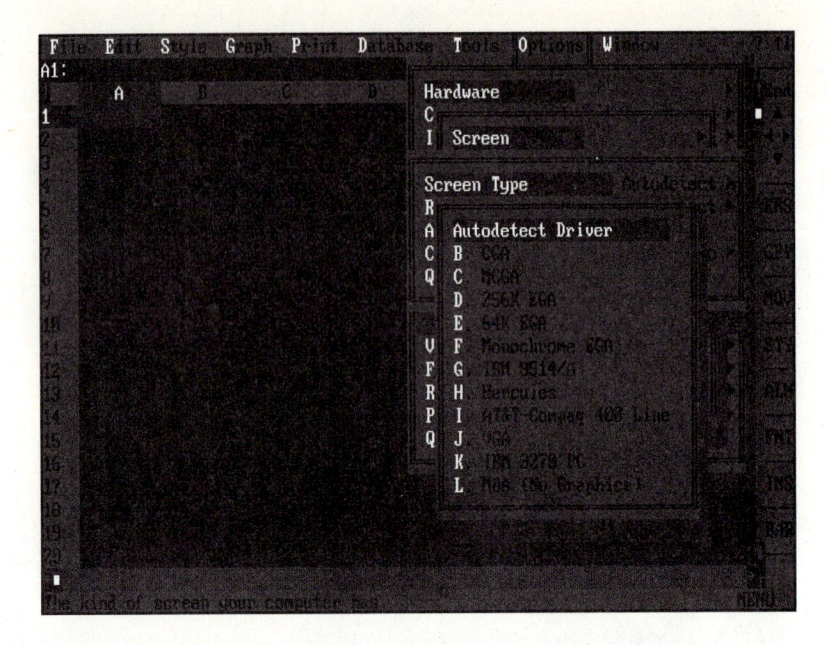

Select a new driver from the **S**creen Type list.

> **TIP** Quattro Pro doesn't execute the **S**creen Type or **R**esolution command when your display is in WYSIWYG display mode. To modify the display mode so that you can change the screen type, choose /**O**ptions **D**isplay Mode **A**: 80x25 before you execute either command.

Resolution

The number of pixels (or dots) your screen can display determines the clarity, or *resolution*, of a graphics image. A resolution of 640x480, for example, means that a screen can illuminate 640 dots horizontally and 480 dots vertically. The more dots a screen can display, the crisper the resolution of a graphics image. Some VGA screens are capable of displaying a resolution of 1280x1024—an ideal resolution for computer-aided design (CAD) applications.

Many display adapter cards support multiple resolution modes. In this case, you can choose one resolution mode for spreadsheet text and another for spreadsheet graphics. To choose a different screen resolution (if this option is available with your screen adapter card), choose **R**esolution and then choose a resolution setting from the list Quattro Pro displays. Quattro Pro supports resolution settings up to a maximum of 640x480.

> **T I P**
>
> Because Quattro Pro automatically chooses the highest resolution available for your display, you probably don't need to change this value.

Aspect Ratio

Each screen display has a height-to-width measurement called the *aspect ratio*. A properly adjusted aspect ratio ensures that the shape of a graph is correct so that a pie graph looks like a pie and not like an egg or a pancake.

To adjust the aspect ratio, choose the Aspect Ratio command from the Screen Type submenu. Quattro Pro displays a circle. Press the up- and down-arrow keys to mold the figure until it appears as a near-perfect circle. Press Enter to accept that height-to-width ratio or Esc to cancel the operation.

CGA Snow Suppression

If you have a Color Graphics Adapter (CGA) display, your screen may flicker when you scroll about the spreadsheet window. Use the CGA Snow Suppression command to eliminate this problem. To enable snow suppression, choose Yes on the submenu that appears when you choose this command.

Choosing Printers

During the initial program installation, you supplied Quattro Pro with your printer's brand name and model number. Quattro Pro used this information to create a driver file containing special codes that tell Quattro Pro how to print spreadsheets and graphs on your particular printer.

To make changes to the printer driver file without reinstalling the program, choose /Options Hardware Printers. Quattro Pro displays the submenu pictured in figure 16.6.

This submenu is divided into two sections. The top section contains commands for installing two printers and choosing one of them as the default printer. The bottom section of this menu contains printer setup commands that enable you to record plotter speed, choose printer

PART III — ADVANCED SPREADSHEET APPLICATIONS

fonts, adjust line feeds, toggle between continuous and single-sheet paper feeding, and invoke background printing.

Notice that the current settings for many of these commands appear in the right margin of the menu.

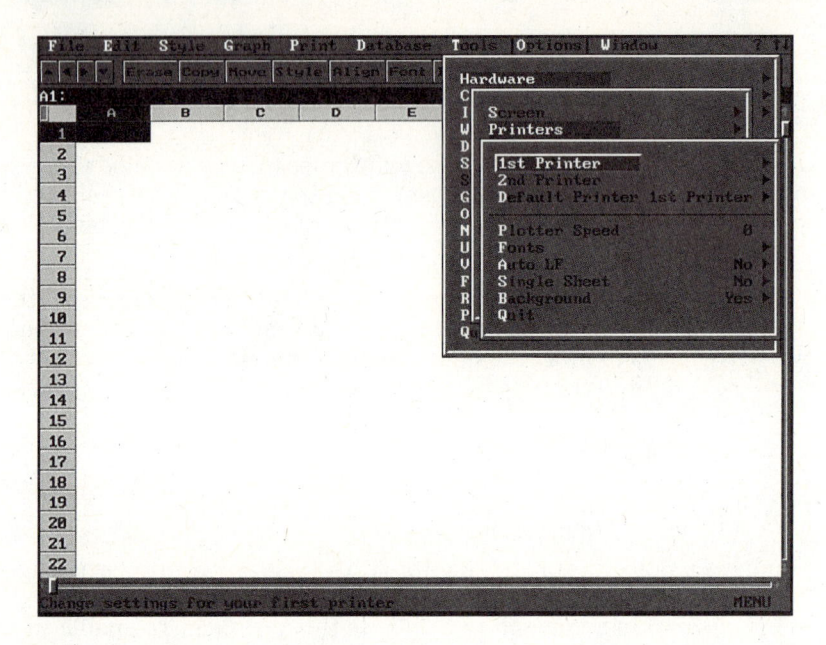

Fig. 16.6

The **P**rinters submenu commands.

Configuring a Second Printer

With the first three options on the **P**rinters menu, you can record configuration data for one or two printers. If you own only one printer, this printer must be the default. If you own two printers, you can configure both and toggle between them with the **D**efault Printer command.

> **T I P** If you own a printer that supports several print modes, you can configure up to two of those modes on the **P**rinters menu. If you own a Hewlett-Packard (HP) LaserJet III and a PostScript font cartridge, for example, you can set **1**st Printer to HP LaserJet III and **2**nd Printer to PostScript.

Follow these steps to configure a second printer:

1. Choose /**O**ptions **H**ardware **P**rinters **2**nd Printer.

16 — CUSTOMIZING QUATTRO PRO

2. Choose **T**ype of printer. Quattro Pro displays a scrollable list of printer manufacturers.

3. Choose the correct printer manufacturer from the list. Quattro Pro displays a scrollable list of printer models.

4. Choose the appropriate printer model from the list. Quattro Pro displays a list of possible print resolution settings.

5. Choose a resolution mode setting. Quattro Pro returns to the **2**nd Printer menu.

   The next two steps are necessary only when you own a serial printer or when you do not have a standard parallel printer connected to port LPT1, the default printer port for most PCs.

6. Choose **D**evice and specify the port to which the printer is connected.

> **TIP**
> If you are using Quattro Pro on a network with a shared printer, set **D**evice to **N** Network Queue.

7. If you own a serial printer, enter the appropriate data for **B**aud rate, **P**arity, and **S**top bits.

The **2**nd Printer menu now should reflect the new printer settings next to the Make, Model, and Mode headings (see fig. 16.7).

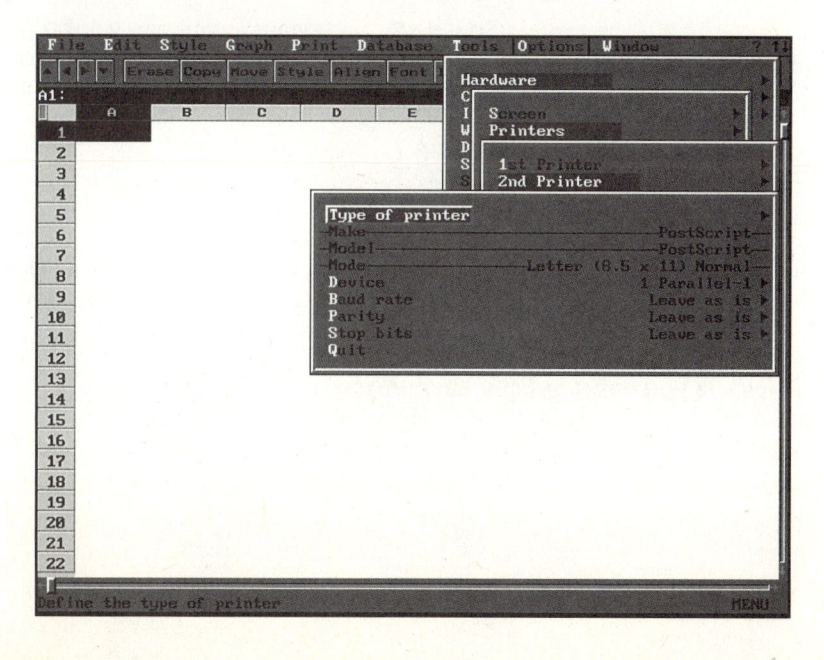

Fig. 16.7

Quattro Pro updates the **2**nd Printer menu.

To choose the new printer as the default printer, follow these steps:

1. Press Esc to return to the **P**rinters submenu.
2. Choose **D**efault Printer.
3. Choose the number of the printer you want to be the default printer. (This printer is the one Quattro Pro will print to unless otherwise instructed.)

> **TIP**
>
> Quattro Pro Versions 3.0 and 4.0 print faster on Hewlett-Packard (HP) laser printers than previous versions. If you prefer high-resolution printing, try the following two tricks for exploiting this speed improvement. First, configure your laser printer as a more recent model. (If you own a LaserJet model, for example, configure it as a LaserJet II.) Second, indicate that you have more printer memory than you actually do. If you get a memory error, switch back to the original setting.

Setting Plotter Speed

The **P**lotter Speed option enables you to specify the print speed for a color plotter. The fastest speed is 9, the slowest is 1. The default setting, 0, tells Quattro Pro to run at the plotter's fastest speed.

Experiment with the **P**lotter Speed setting because you may want to slow down the plotter speed intentionally when using older pens. Slowing down a plotter that uses old pens helps to improve the quality of your plotter's printouts.

Installing Fonts

You can install special printer fonts by using the **F**onts command. The first choice on this menu, **C**artridge Fonts, enables you to install font cartridges for a Hewlett-Packard LaserJet printer or Canon Laser Printer. After you choose this command, you need to tell Quattro Pro which fonts you have and in which port, or cartridge slot, on the printer (**R**ight Cartridge or **L**eft Cartridge) they are installed (see fig. 16.8).

16 — CUSTOMIZING QUATTRO PRO

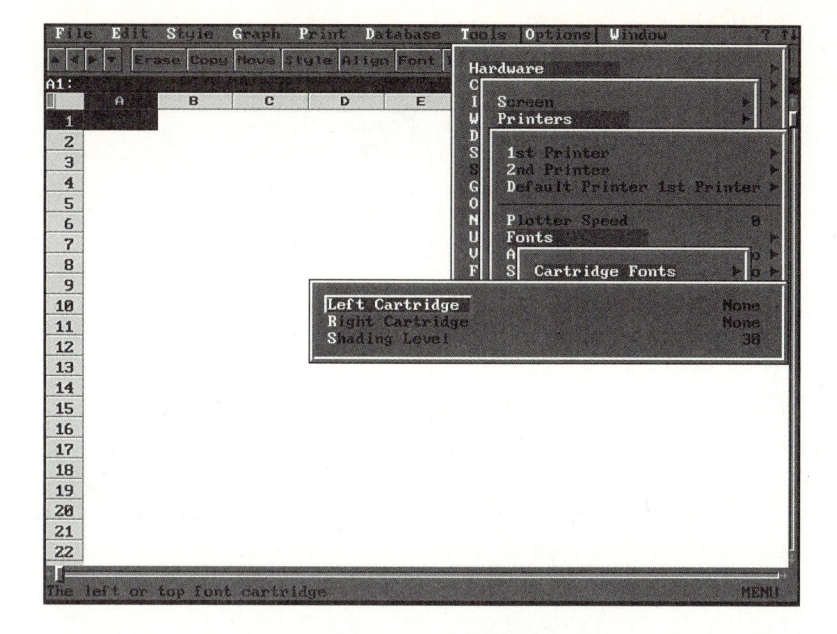

Fig. 16.8

Select the **F**onts command.

> **TIP**
>
> The /**O**ptions **H**ardware **P**rinters **F**onts **C**artridge Fonts command displays Canon or LaserJet cartridge fonts only when the /**O**ptions **H**ardware **P**rinters **D**efault Printer setting is a Canon or LaserJet printer.

The **S**hading Level command enables you to specify shading levels to use for cell shading. This command affects only the intensity of shaded cells on an HP LaserJet printout; it does not affect the appearance of shaded cells on the spreadsheet when you are in WYSIWYG display mode. (To change the colors that Quattro Pro uses to shade cells, choose the /**O**ptions **C**olors **S**preadsheet **S**hading command.)

When you choose the **S**hading level command, you specify a percent value, corresponding to one of the eight levels of shading available on an HP LaserJet printer (see table 16.3). The default shading level is 30%.

The second option on the **F**onts menu, **A**utoscale Fonts, enables you to decide how Quattro Pro scales fonts when printing graphs. The way in which Quattro Pro scales fonts normally depends on the size of the area in which you choose to display a graph. The less space Quattro Pro has to work in, the smaller is the actual font size. If you prefer that Quattro Pro not scale your fonts in this manner, choose **A**utoscale Fonts and choose **N**o.

PART III — ADVANCED SPREADSHEET APPLICATIONS

Table 16.3 HP LaserJet Shading Levels

Shading %	HP LaserJet Shading Level #	Shading Contrast
1-2%	1	Lightest
3-10%	2	
11-20%	3	
21-35%	4	Medium
36-55%	5	
56-80%	6	
81-99%	7	
100%	8	Darkest

Controlling Line Feeds

Using the **A**uto LF option tells Quattro Pro whether to issue a line-feed character after each carriage return. The default setting is **N**o. If your printouts are double-spaced, try choosing the **Y**es option. If the printer crams several lines of text onto one line, try choosing **N**o.

Printing on Single Sheets

Quattro Pro assumes that you are using continuous-feed (tractor-feed) paper to print your spreadsheets. When you choose /**O**ptions **P**rinters **S**ingle Sheet, the setting is **N**o, the normal setting for dot-matrix printers that use tractor feeding.

If you want to feed paper into your printer one sheet at a time, set the **S**ingle Sheet option to **Y**es. This technique is useful when your second printer is a letter-quality printer. Set the option to **N**o when printing to an ASCII file so that Quattro Pro doesn't ask you for the next sheet.

Printing in the Background

With Quattro Pro's print spooler feature, you can continue to work with your spreadsheets after sending multiple print jobs to the printer. The

Borland Print Spooler program (BPS.COM) collects print jobs, temporarily saves them to your hard disk drive, and then releases control of Quattro Pro back to you. While you continue to work with the current spreadsheet, the print spooler sends print data to the printer "in the background."

To print jobs in the background with Quattro Pro, you must do two things: type *bps* at the DOS prompt to load the BPS.COM program into your PC's memory, and enable background printing with the /**O**ptions **H**ardware **P**rinters **B**ackground **Y**es command. This command tells Quattro Pro that if the BPS.COM is loaded into memory, the program should send all print jobs to the Borland Print Spooler.

> **CAUTION:** The print spooler does not replace—and may conflict with—a network print spooler. If you choose to use the print spooler on a network, load the print spooler before loading the network shell. If you encounter problems, use the network spooler or the print spooler—not both. (See Appendix E, "Installing Quattro Pro on a Network," for more information.)

Reviewing Normal Memory, EMS, and Coprocessor Data

The **H**ardware submenu gives you access to some of Quattro Pro's knowledge of your computer system. The bottom three entries on this menu indicate the amount of memory in use and memory available to Quattro Pro (in bytes and as a percent of total available); the amount of expanded memory in use and available (in bytes and as a percent of total available); and whether a math coprocessor is installed. All three values are detected by Quattro Pro from DOS and displayed here for your convenience.

Figure 16.3 earlier in the chapter shows the current hardware status available on the **H**ardware submenu. Quattro Pro indicates that the computer has 140,230 bytes (or 62%) of free conventional memory, 223,516 bytes of total conventional memory, 507,552 bytes (or 88%) of free expanded memory, 573,440 bytes of total expanded memory, and no coprocessor available.

Using Quattro Pro's Coloring Palette

You can change the colors for each part of Quattro Pro's display by choosing the /**O**ptions **C**olors command. When you choose this command, you see a submenu listing areas of the program that you may color. Table 16.4 describes the choices that appear on this submenu.

Table 16.4 Changing Color Options

Command	Description
Menu	Changes colors on the pull-down menus
Desktop	Changes colors located behind a spreadsheet
Spreadsheet	Changes colors on a spreadsheet and those colors used in WYSIWYG display mode
Conditional	Sets colors for special numbers and formulas
Help	Changes colors on the help windows
File Manager	Sets colors for the File Manager
Palettes	Resets all default Quattro Pro colors

With the **C**olors command, you can choose the colors for Quattro Pro to use in all parts of its program display. Feel free to experiment with new combinations because you can reinstate the original scheme with the **P**alettes command.

After you choose a **C**olors menu command, Quattro Pro displays a special coloring tool called the *coloring palette* (see fig. 16.9). Look closely and notice the tiny bar positioned on one of the color pairs in this box. This bar indicates the current color combination setting for the Quattro Pro screen area selected. Figure 16.9, for example, shows this palette's setting when you choose /**O**ptions **C**olors **M**enu **K**ey Letter. Each time you want to alter one of Quattro Pro's display colors, this coloring tool appears. Use the arrow keys or click to choose a different color combination.

Note that a few screen elements require you to enter ASCII character codes (for example, the **S**hadow option). These ASCII codes enable Quattro Pro to display graphics characters in various parts of the screen when you are in text display mode. Consult the ASCII table in Appendix D, "Using ASCII Characters," for sensible values in these instances.

16 — CUSTOMIZING QUATTRO PRO   713

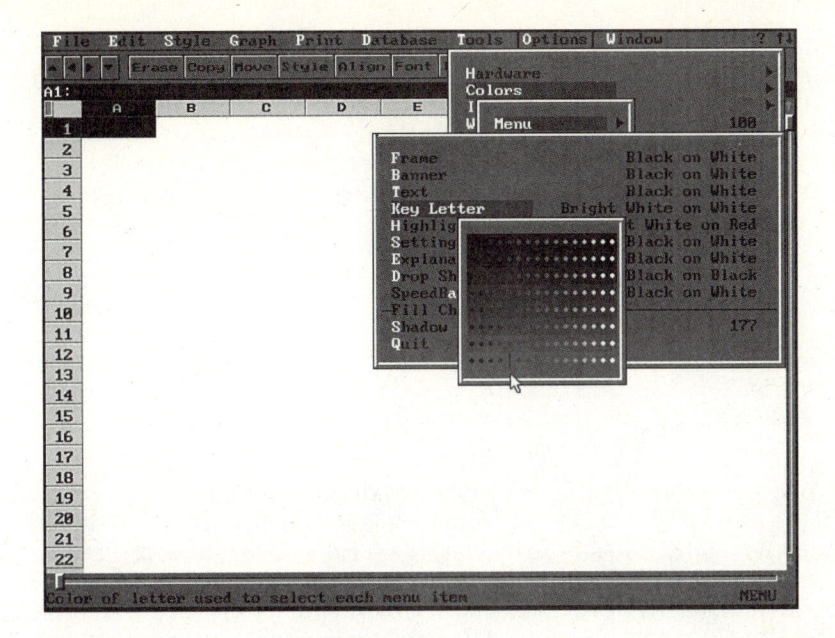

Fig. 16.9

Change Quattro Pro's colors.

Choosing Menu Colors

The **M**enu command enables you to choose new color combinations for Quattro Pro's pull-down menus (see fig. 16.10).

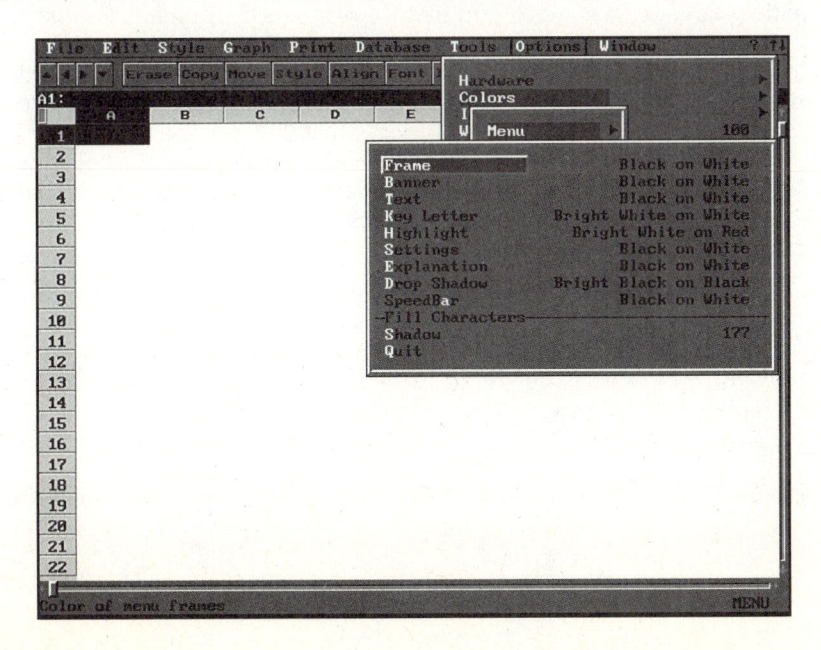

Fig. 16.10

The **M**enu submenu commands.

PART III — ADVANCED SPREADSHEET APPLICATIONS

After you choose /**O**ptions **C**olors **M**enu, Quattro Pro displays a list of the parts of a menu that may be colored. Choose a part to color, and Quattro Pro displays the coloring palette with the rotating bar. Choose a new color, and Quattro Pro immediately refreshes the screen display to show the new color combination. If you want to change the color of the SpeedBar, for example, choose /**O**ptions **C**olors **M**enu SpeedB**a**r.

Choosing Desktop Colors

By using the **D**esktop command, you can choose new color combinations for Quattro Pro's desktop. The desktop is the part of the display not filled with a spreadsheet window. Here, you also may specify ASCII characters for Quattro Pro to use as background shading.

When you choose /**O**ptions **C**olors **D**esktop, Quattro Pro displays a list of the parts of the desktop that may be colored, including the status line, the modes and status indicators on the status line, error messages, and the area below spreadsheet windows. Choose a part to color, and Quattro Pro displays the coloring palette with the rotating bar. Choose a new color, and Quattro Pro immediately refreshes the screen display to reflect the new color combination.

Choosing Spreadsheet Colors

The next command enables you to color various portions of a spreadsheet window, such as the frame around a spreadsheet window, locked titles text, unprotected cell data, drawn lines, and the WYSIWYG mode window. When you choose /**O**ptions **C**olors **S**preadsheet, Quattro Pro displays a list of the parts of the spreadsheet window that may be colored. Choose a part to color and Quattro Pro displays the coloring palette with the rotating bar. Choose a new color, and Quattro Pro immediately refreshes the screen display to reflect the new color combination.

To change the colors used to create Quattro Pro's WYSIWYG display mode, choose the **W**YSIWYG Colors option on the **S**preadsheet submenu. Quattro Pro displays a list of the parts of the WYSIWYG spreadsheet window that may be colored. Choose a part to color and Quattro Pro displays the coloring palette with the rotating bar. Choose a new color and Quattro Pro immediately reflects the new color combination.

Choosing Conditional Colors

The **/O**ptions **C**olors **C**onditional command displays the submenu pictured in figure 16.11. With the **C**onditional menu options, you can specify the color your data will have when certain conditions are met.

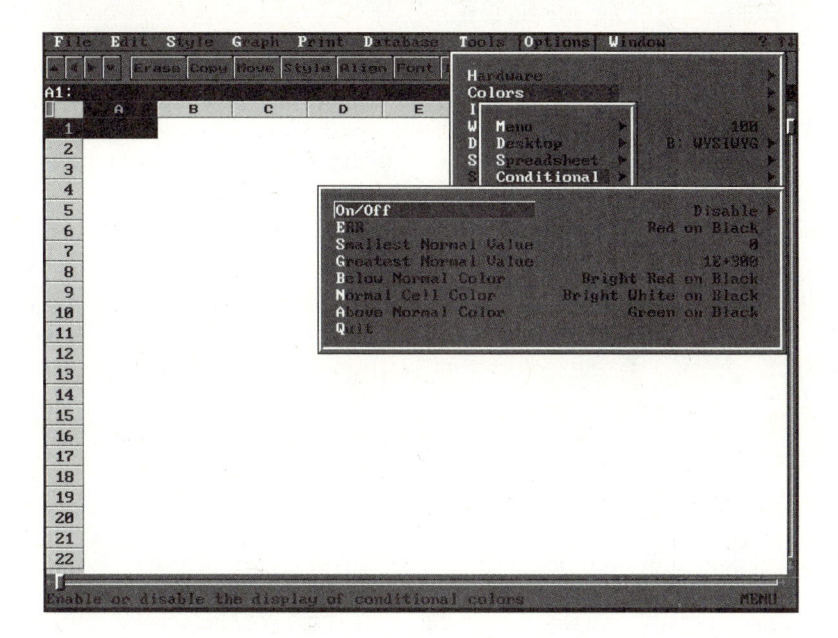

Fig. 16.11

The **C**onditional submenu commands.

The most common use for this option is to specify an acceptable range for a set of data and require Quattro Pro to show values outside that range in a different color. The **O**n/Off command tells Quattro Pro whether to display conditional colors, enabling the conditional coloring that you set up with commands on this menu.

ERR enables you to specify the color to use when ERR and NA values appear on a spreadsheet. **S**mallest Normal Value and **G**reatest Normal Value define the range of values that are considered "normal."

The next three command options enable you to define colors to be used when spreadsheet values fall below, equal, or are greater than a certain value. Define the colors using the **B**elow Normal Color, **N**ormal Cell Color, and **A**bove Normal Color options.

Remember, besides specifying the normal range and colors, you must enable the conditional color option by choosing the **O**n/Off command.

Another good use for the conditional command is to set negative numbers apart from positive numbers. In financial applications, for example, you may need to know whether a business is operating in the red or the black. By assigning the color red to negative numbers on a spreadsheet, you provide conclusive and easy-to-find evidence.

Choosing Help Colors

With the **H**elp command, you can choose different color combinations for Quattro Pro's Help windows. After you choose /**O**ptions **C**olors **H**elp, Quattro Pro displays a list of the parts of the Help window that may be colored. These parts include the frame around a help window, the text, and the highlighter in the window.

Choose a part to color and Quattro Pro displays the coloring palette with the rotating bar. Choose a new color and Quattro Pro immediately refreshes the screen display to reflect the new color combination.

Because Quattro Pro does not show Help windows as part of its normal display, press F1 to make sure that your color selection is acceptable before saving the changes.

Choosing File Manager Colors

The **F**ile Manager command enables you to change the color display of Quattro Pro's File Manager. When you choose /**O**ptions **C**olors **F**ile Manager, Quattro Pro displays a list of the parts of the screen that may be colored. These parts include the active cursor, inactive cursor, and marked text. Choose a part to color and Quattro Pro displays the coloring palette with the rotating bar. Choose a new color and Quattro Pro immediately refreshes the screen display to reflect the new color combination.

Because Quattro Pro does not show the File Manager as part of its normal display, type /FUF from the active spreadsheet to load the File Manager and make sure that your color selection is acceptable before saving the changes.

Choosing Palettes Colors

The **P**alettes command enables you to recall Quattro Pro's original color scheme, even if you previously saved custom color combinations with the **U**pdate command. To recall Quattro Pro's default color settings, follow these steps:

1. Choose /**O**ptions **C**olors **P**alettes.
2. Choose the **C**olor option.
3. Choose /**O**ptions **U**pdate to save the change.

Your other palette options include **M**onochrome, **B**lack & White, **G**ray Scale, and **V**ersion 3 Color.

Setting International Options

Quattro Pro offers excellent foreign-language compatibility. If you are using a non-English copy of the program, you can enter @function commands in your native language or in English. All other commands, including the menu-equivalent commands listed in Appendix C, "Menu-Equivalent Commands," must be entered in your local language.

When you retrieve Lotus 1-2-3 spreadsheets (or any other compatible spreadsheet) into Quattro Pro, the program translates the @function commands into your language.

Quattro Pro supports the LaserJet III printer and some printers that are more common in Europe. If you want to print text using Hershey or Bitstream characters from the international character set, Borland recommends that you contact Borland Technical Support at (408) 438-5300 (the number used at this writing) to obtain a special set of fonts containing additional international characters.

By default, Quattro Pro uses the United States conventions for the currency symbol, numerical punctuation, dates, and times. To change the default to international standards for displaying currency symbols, punctuation, dates, and times, choose /**O**ptions **I**nternational.

Businesses with an international clientele may find the **I**nternational command particularly helpful. You can create a contract bid containing the date format, punctuation style, and currency symbol of your client's country, for example.

Many international settings that you create with this command are accessed with the /**S**tyle **N**umeric Format command. If you enter a new currency symbol, for example, Quattro Pro attaches that symbol to monetary values on your spreadsheet when you format the values with the /**S**tyle **N**umeric Format **C**urrency command. The same holds true for international punctuation, dates, and times. Figure 16.12 and table 16.5 describe the commands on the **I**nternational submenu.

PART III — ADVANCED SPREADSHEET APPLICATIONS

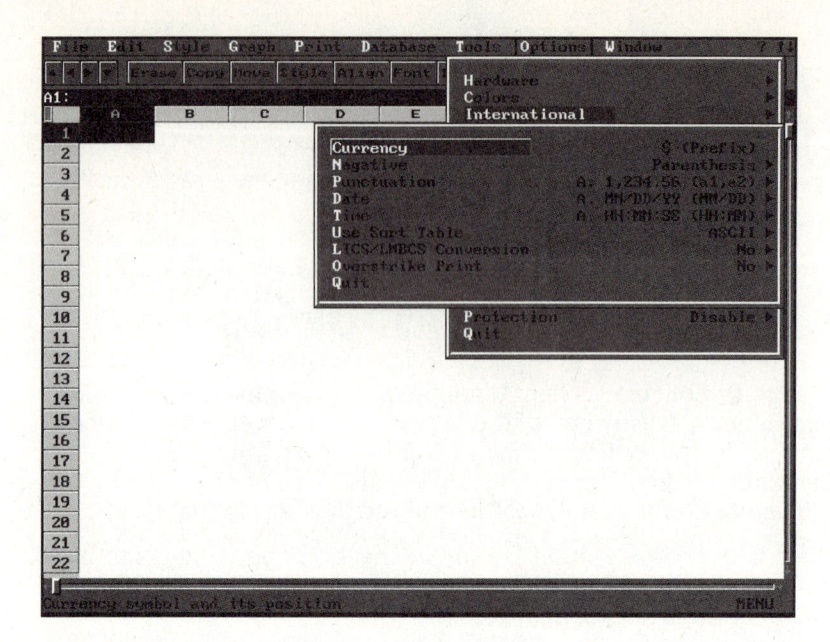

Fig. 16.12

The International default settings.

Table 16.5 The International Menu Commands

Command	Description
Currency	Assigns location and style of the currency symbol
Negative	Puts parentheses around or a negative sign in front of negative values
Punctuation	Assigns type of punctuation used in numbers
Date	Sets long and short international date formats
Time	Sets long and short international time formats
Use Sort Table	Specifies a set of sort rules to use
LICS Conversion	Converts LICS characters into uppercase ASCII characters
Overstrike Print	Allows for printing of accented characters

The International submenu commands enable you to specify the format in which values are displayed, as well as where in a cell the values are placed when you enter them. Figure 16.12 shows the current command settings in the right margin of the menu.

Choosing a Currency Symbol

With the **C**urrency command, you can choose the symbol that Quattro Pro attaches to monetary values on a spreadsheet. This symbol is the character that appears when you choose the /**S**tyle **N**umeric Format **C**urrency command. By default, Quattro Pro shows the dollar sign ($) symbol as a prefix to a number.

To choose a different currency and symbol setting, follow these steps:

1. Choose /**O**ptions **I**nternational **C**urrency.
2. Press the Backspace key until the current currency symbol is erased.
3. Enter the ASCII characters that correspond to the currency symbol. Press Enter to store them or Esc to cancel the operation.
4. Choose **S**uffix or **P**refix to set the orientation for the new currency symbol.

> **TIP**
>
> Entering an ASCII code to create a currency symbol is different from entering a code for a shadow on the **C**olors menu. In this case, you must press Alt-*Code*, in which *Code* is the ASCII code equivalent for the currency symbol. To enter the symbol for the Japanese yen, for example, hold down the Alt key and type *157* on the numeric keypad.

Attaching Symbols to Negative Values

Use the /**O**ptions **I**nternational **N**egative **P**arentheses command to put parentheses around all negative values in your spreadsheet. This style of displaying negative values is popular in financial and accounting applications.

Use the /**O**ptions **I**nternational **N**egative **S**igns command to place a negative sign in front of all negative values in your spreadsheet. This style of displaying negative values is popular in scientific and mathematical applications.

Choosing the Punctuation

The **P**unctuation command enables you to specify how Quattro Pro displays decimal points, separates arguments in @functions, and

PART III — ADVANCED SPREADSHEET APPLICATIONS

segregates zeros in numbers larger than 999. The default style is **A**. 1,234.56 (a1,a2).

To choose a new punctuation style, follow these steps:

1. Choose /**O**ptions **I**nternational **P**unctuation.

2. Choose a punctuation style from the menu shown in figure 16.13.

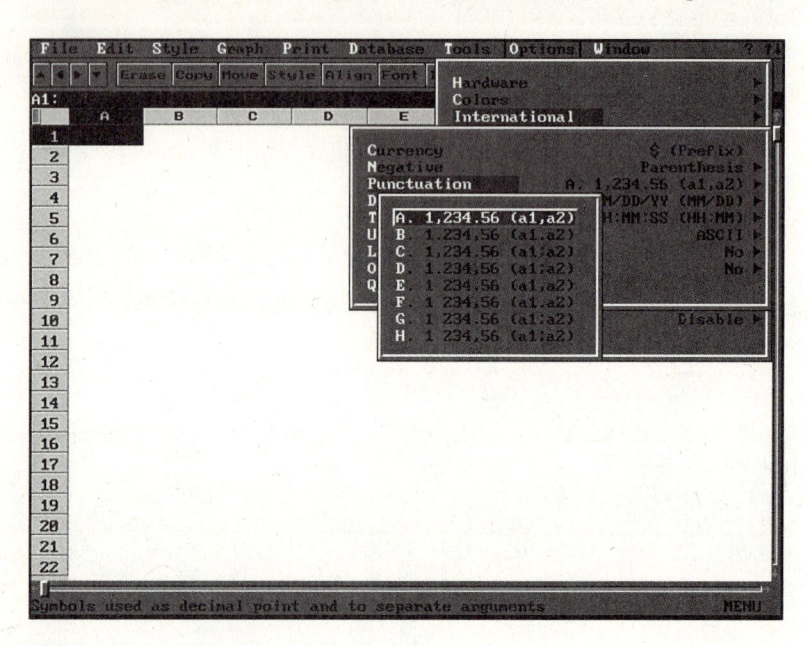

Fig. 16.13

Select an international punctuation setting.

Choosing Date Formats

The **D**ate command can display dates in several popular international formats. The date formats you choose with this command become available as the long and short international date formats when you choose /**O**ptions **F**ormats **N**umeric Format **D**ate. The default style is **A**. MM/DD/YY (MM/DD).

To choose a new international date format, follow these steps:

1. Choose /**O**ptions **I**nternational **D**ate.

2. Choose a date format from the menu displayed in figure 16.14.

If you now want to make that setting the default display format for the spreadsheet, choose /**O**ptions **F**ormats **N**umeric Format **D**ate and then choose either international date format.

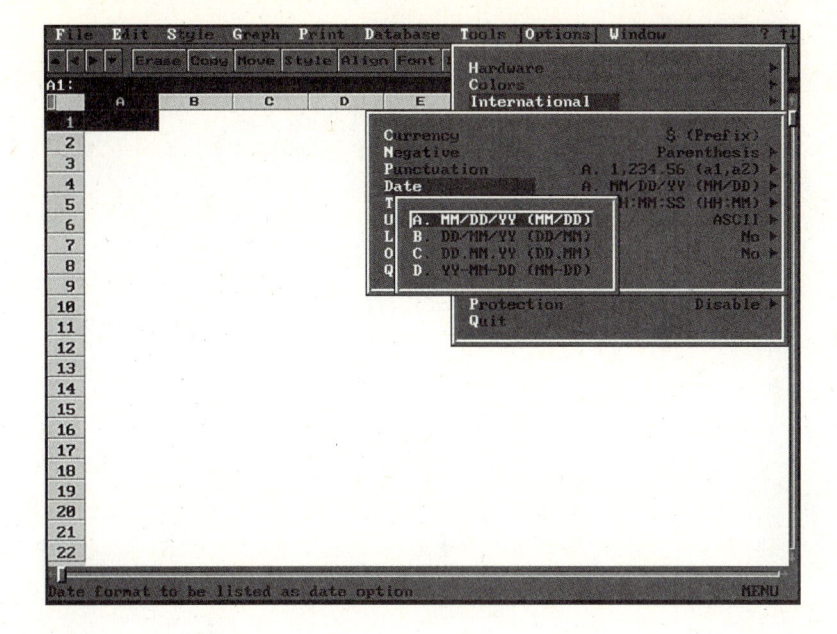

16 — CUSTOMIZING QUATTRO PRO   721

Fig. 16.14

Select an international date setting.

Choosing Time Formats

The time command can display times in several popular international formats. The time formats you choose with this command become available as the long and short international time formats when you choose /**O**ptions **F**ormats **N**umeric Format **T**ime. The default style is **A**. HH:MM:SS (HH:MM).

To choose a new international time format, follow these steps:

1. Choose /**O**ptions **I**nternational **T**ime.
2. Choose a time format from the menu shown in figure 16.15.

If you now want to make that setting the default display format for the spreadsheet, choose /**O**ptions **F**ormats **N**umeric Format **D**ate **T**ime and then choose one of the international time formats.

Choosing New Sort Rules

When you choose /**O**ptions **I**nternational **U**se Sort Table, Quattro Pro displays a menu offering four sort rule options: **A**SCII.SOR, **I**NTL.SOR, **N**ORDAN.SOR, and **S**WEDFIN.SOR.

PART III — ADVANCED SPREADSHEET APPLICATIONS

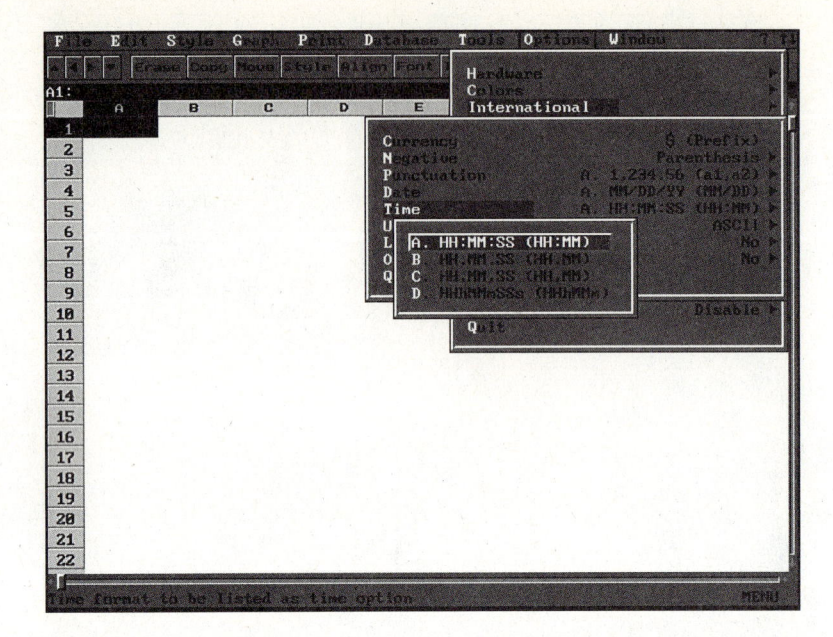

Fig. 16.15

Select an international time setting.

> **TIP**
>
> The **U**se Sort Table command names contain a SOR extension that identifies the name of the file that Quattro Pro uses to manage each type of sort operation. These files are standard Borland files and may be used with Paradox.

The ASCII sort rule option (**A**SCII.SOR) tells Quattro Pro to sort data so that uppercase letters appear before lowercase and accented letters appear after the letter z. See Appendix D for a complete list of ASCII characters.

The international sort rule option (**I**NTL.SOR) tells Quattro Pro to sort uppercase, lowercase, and accented characters according to the dictionary method (AaBbCc and so on). With this method, the diacritical character [135] appears with C and c; whereas in an ASCII sort, this character appears after the lowercase character grouping.

The Norwegian/Danish (**N**ORDAN.SOR) and Swedish/Finnish (**S**WEDFIN.SOR) sort rule options are like the international sort rule option, except that Quattro Pro sorts characters unique to these countries at the end of the regular alphabet.

16 — CUSTOMIZING QUATTRO PRO

> **T I P**
>
> Any file in the default Quattro Pro directory with an SOR extension appears on the Use Sort Table menu. If you have Russian and Japanese SOR files, for instance, the files appear on this menu.

Choosing LICS Conversion

Lotus 1-2-3 spreadsheets use a proprietary character set called the Lotus International Characters Set (LICS). This character set is the same as the ASCII character set until you reach character 128. The characters in positions 128 through 255 in the LICS table are not the standard IBM international and graphics characters that appear in Appendix D.

Before you load a 1-2-3 spreadsheet into Quattro Pro, choose the /Options International LICS Conversion Yes command to convert all LICS characters (128 through 255) to the normal ASCII characters. This procedure ensures that Quattro Pro's sort rules work properly on your 1-2-3 spreadsheets.

When you save a file in a 1-2-3 spreadsheet format, Quattro Pro converts characters to match the LICS character set specifications.

Choosing Overstrike Print

The **O**verstrike Print command ensures that Quattro Pro places the proper accent symbol over an international character when you own a 7-bit printer.

The Diablo 630, Qume Sprint, Epson FX-80, and Epson LQ-1500 are examples of common 7-bit printers.

Using WYSIWYG Zoom %

The **W**YSIWYG Zoom % command enables you to enlarge or shrink proportionately the active spreadsheet area—the area that Quattro Pro displays one screen at a time. This command is ideal for same-screen viewing of a large spreadsheet that has many rows and columns.

After you choose **W**YSIWYG Zoom %, Quattro Pro prompts you for a zoom percentage (%) factor. Enter any value between 25% and 200%

and press Enter. (The default setting is 100%.) Quattro Pro immediately resizes the spreadsheet area according to the zoom percentage.

To enlarge the displayed spreadsheet area, enter a percentage greater than 100%; to shrink the displayed spreadsheet area, enter a percent lower than 100%.

> **TIP**
>
> The **W**YSIWYG Zoom % command works only when Quattro Pro is displaying in WYSIWYG display mode. Changing the zoom percentage factor for this command from text display mode has no observable effect. If you switch back to WYSIWYG display mode, however, the spreadsheet reflects the change.

Setting Display Mode Options

The **D**isplay Mode command enables you to change the overall on-screen appearance of Quattro Pro. Normally, Quattro Pro displays in an 80 x 25 text mode. If you have the right display adapter card, however, you can display Quattro Pro in WYSIWYG mode or in several different extended text modes. Use WYSIWYG mode when you want to display an inserted graph on a spreadsheet.

When you choose /**O**ptions **D**isplay Mode, Quattro Pro presents you with display mode alternatives (listed in table 16.6). Choose the mode you want. After you choose a new display mode, Quattro Pro immediately refreshes the screen display to reflect the new mode. Experiment with each of the modes available for your screen type.

Table 16.6 Display Mode Options

Command	Description
A: 80x25	Sets display mode to 80 columns by 25 rows
B: WYSIWYG	Switches to WYSIWYG display mode
C: EGA: 80x43	Sets display mode to 80 columns by 43 rows
D: VGA: 80x50	Sets display mode to 80 columns by 50 rows

Version 4.0 also has an extensive list of extended text display modes. When you choose /**O**ptions **D**isplay Mode, Quattro Pro also shows a list of 10 extended text display mode settings (options **E** through **N** in fig. 16.16).

16 — CUSTOMIZING QUATTRO PRO

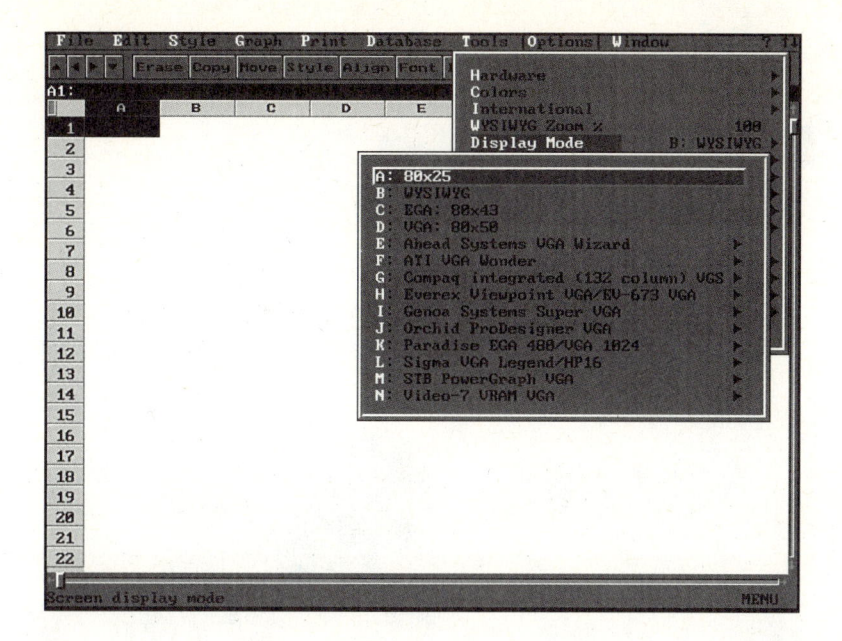

Fig. 16.16

Quattro Pro's 10 extended text mode settings.

Version 4.0 takes full advantage of EGA and VGA graphics cards that support extended text mode. (Most graphics cards do; check your owner's manual.) If your graphics card is not on the list, experiment with some of the others. If you have an EGA graphics display card, for example, try the Paradise EGA 480/VGA 1024 option. When you choose this option, Quattro Pro prompts you to choose a 132 x 25 or 132 x 43 (columns/rows) display mode.

> **TIP**
>
> If your screen blanks or displays garbled information, press Enter twice to reset your display mode to the default setting. This action chooses **D**isplay Mode on the **O**ptions menu and then chooses the first choice on the list, **A**: 80x25.

In extended text mode, you can view up to 132 columns and 75 rows per screen at the same time—ideal for reviewing large financial spreadsheets with many years of data. Note that these numbers refer to the total number of columns and rows displayed—not just those in the spreadsheet area. In the case of characters, Quattro Pro can display up to 132 characters from the left edge to the right edge of your screen display, and up to 75 characters from top to bottom.

PART III — ADVANCED SPREADSHEET APPLICATIONS

Setting Startup Options

When you choose /Options Startup, Quattro Pro displays the submenu shown in figure 16.17. The commands on this menu enable you to specify start-up information that Quattro Pro uses each time you load the program into your system or when you create a new spreadsheet file.

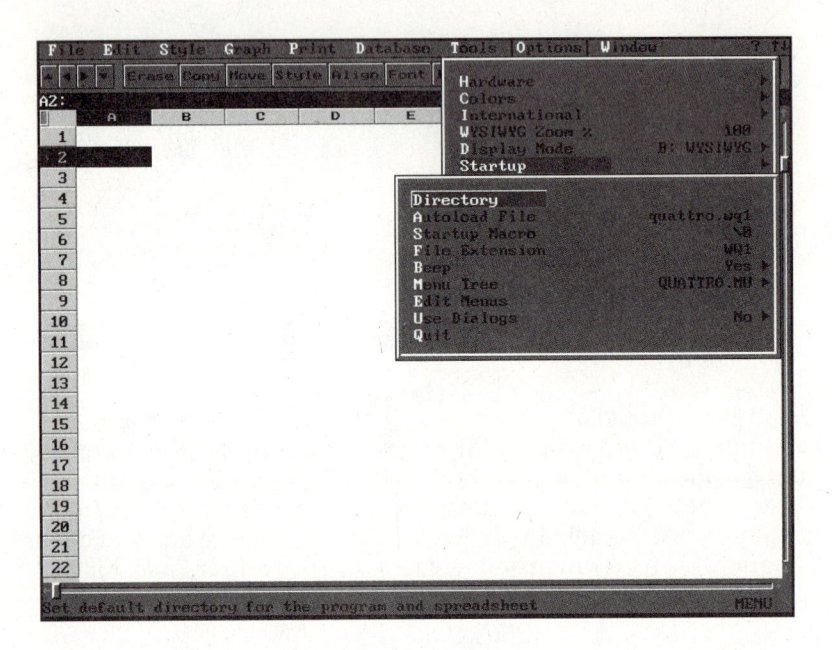

Fig. 16.17

The **S**tartup menu of commands.

Because the **S**tartup options are system options, you must execute /**O**ptions **U**pdate to store them permanently for the next work session. The default settings for these commands appear at the right margin of the menu.

Setting the Default Directory

With the **D**irectory command, you can choose the directory in which Quattro Pro will store spreadsheet files. The **S**ave and **R**etrieve commands on the **F**ile menu enable you to access a file on any drive and directory available to your system, not just the default directory. Even so, setting a default directory is useful when you find that you frequently use the same drive and directory.

Although you literally can store your spreadsheet files anywhere on your hard disk drive, you should create a special directory to hold all your Quattro Pro spreadsheets. If you want to store your files in a directory called C:\QPRO\FILES, for example, follow these steps:

1. Choose /Options Startup Directory.
2. Press the Backspace key until you erase the current directory name.
3. Type *C:\QPRO\FILES* (or another valid directory name).
4. Press Enter to record the new name or Esc to cancel the operation.

> **TIP**
>
> The directory name that you enter with the **Directory** command already must exist on your hard disk drive—Quattro Pro does not create it for you. When you specify a directory name that does not exist, Quattro Pro displays an error message. You can use the File Manager to make a directory. See Chapter 8, "Managing Files and Windows," for more details.

Using an Autoload File

With the Autoload File command, you can designate a spreadsheet file for Quattro Pro to open automatically each time you load the program. If the file is not in the directory named with the **Directory** option, be sure to enter the full path name here.

Initially, the default autoload file name is QUATTRO.WQ1. If you want to autoload a file named QUARTER1 that is in a directory named C:\SALES, follow these steps:

1. Choose /Options Startup Autoload File.
2. Press the Backspace key until you erase the current file name.
3. Type *C:\SALES\QUARTER1.WQ1* (or another valid autoload file).
4. Press Enter to record the new file name or Esc to cancel the operation.

A second method of autoloading a file does not require the use of this command. Type the file name on the DOS command line after Quattro Pro's program file name but before you press Enter to load the program. Type *q quarter2* at the DOS prompt, for example, and press Enter to load a spreadsheet file named QUARTER2.WQ1. Quattro Pro assumes that this file name's extension is WQ1; if not, type a different extension after the file name and before pressing Enter. The file must be in the default or program directory, or in the subdirectory from which you are loading Quattro Pro.

You can enter other command-line options—called *switches*—as you load the program. For these switches, use the following syntax and press Enter:

Q [*filename*][*macroname*][/*switches*]

These switches, shown in table 16.7, tell Quattro Pro how to configure certain parts of itself as it loads into your system.

Table 16.7 Command-Line Switches

Switch	Description
/D	Tells Quattro Pro to load a specific resource file with an RF extension; if the resource file is not in the current directory, you also must specify the directory and path name
/I	Tells Quattro Pro to autodetect the screen display and other hardware as it is loading
/IC	Tells Quattro Pro to load with a color palette
/IM	Tells Quattro Pro to load with a monochrome palette
/IB	Tells Quattro Pro to load with a black-and-white palette
/Ex	Tells Quattro Pro to load with LIM 4.0 Expanded Memory Specification (EMS); x specifies the numbers range from 0 (no EMS used) to 65355; each number represents one logical page, each page being 16,000 bytes
/X	Tells Quattro Pro to load with up to 512K extended-memory code-swapping enabled; recommended if you have a 286-based AT computer with 1M of RAM

Choosing a Startup Macro

The Startup Macro command enables you to run a macro automatically each time you retrieve a new spreadsheet. This command is useful if, for example, you normally use a macro to format your spreadsheets before entering data into them. (See Chapter 15, "Creating Macros," for complete coverage of macros.)

To execute a macro named \m each time you create a new spreadsheet, follow these steps:

1. Choose /Options Startup Startup Macro.
2. Press the Backspace key until you erase the current macro name.
3. Type \m (or another valid macro file name).
4. Press Enter to record the new name or Esc to cancel the operation.

Selecting a New Default File Extension

The File Extension command tells Quattro Pro the three-letter file-name extension that it should put on the end of each spreadsheet file name. By default, Quattro Pro uses the extension WQ1. If you want to change the extension to WQ5, for example, follow these steps:

1. Choose /Options Startup File Extension.
2. Press the Backspace key until the current extension is erased.
3. Type WQ5 (or another valid three-character extension).
4. Press Enter to record the new extension or Esc to cancel the operation.

The importance of this process is to enable the user to specify other applications for Quattro Pro, such as Paradox or 1-2-3, to which Quattro can write files. If you are in an office in which 1-2-3 and Quattro Pro are used, you probably want to change the extension to WK1.

Specifying Beep Tones

Use the Beep command to turn Quattro Pro's error tone on and off. This beep sounds each time you make an illegal entry or incorrectly execute a command. If you prefer not to hear the error tone, choose No. The default setting is Yes.

Choosing a Menu Tree

The **M**enu Tree command enables you to load one of Quattro Pro's compatible menu trees. When you choose this command, Quattro Pro displays a list of all available menu trees. By default, Quattro Pro shows two menu trees: **Q**UATTRO (the standard Quattro Pro tree) and **1**23 (the Lotus 1-2-3 tree). When you choose a new menu tree, Quattro Pro's menu bar immediately reflects the new menu tree structure.

To switch to the Lotus 1-2-3 menu tree, for example, follow these steps:

1. Choose /**O**ptions **S**tartup **M**enu Tree.
2. Choose **1**23.

Quattro Pro immediately displays the 1-2-3 menu tree but with full utilization of Quattro Pro features.

The **E**dit Menu's command accesses the Menu Editor tool. With this tool, you can reorganize and customize menu trees in the Menu Editor window.

Using Dialog Boxes

Version 4.0 has redesigned several menu commands as dialog boxes. A *dialog box* is a tool for setting options that normally appear on a command's submenu.

A dialog box makes viewing and setting options much easier because all the information needed to define a command appears on one screen. Quattro Pro dialog boxes eliminate the need to move up and down layers of menus and submenus in order to choose commands and options.

The following Quattro Pro commands now offer dialog boxes:

/**G**raph **C**ustomize Series

/**G**raph **O**verall

/**G**raph **X**-Axis

/**G**raph **Y**-Axis

/**P**rint **L**ayout

> **NOTE** For more details about how to use the dialog boxes associated with these commands, refer to the sections in Chapters 9 and 10, where these commands are covered.

Choose /**O**ptions **S**tartup **U**se Dialogs to define whether Quattro Pro displays dialog boxes rather than menus. The **Y**es option (the default) turns on the display of dialog boxes. To suppress the display of dialog boxes so that you can use the menus instead, choose /**O**ptions **S**tartup **U**se Dialogs **N**o.

Remember to choose **U**pdate if you want to save the current setting for this command for all future work sessions.

Customizing the SpeedBar

Note that the SpeedBar and the mouse arrow pointer appear on-screen only if you have a mouse attached to your system. Quattro Pro recognizes when a mouse is present. If you have a mouse but no SpeedBar appears, make sure that a mouse driver has been installed before running Quattro Pro.

The SpeedBar is the horizontal bar of sculpted buttons appearing at the top of Quattro Pro's display. You can customize any or all of the 15 buttons on the READY or EDIT mode SpeedBars. The four arrows at the left edge of the SpeedBar are not user-assignable.

Reassigning the SpeedBar buttons is useful if you find that you frequently execute a keystroke sequence. If you frequently press Ctrl-Break, for example, to cancel a menu command and return to the active spreadsheet, you can assign {BREAK} to one of the macro buttons. Afterwards, when you need to press Ctrl-Break, you can click the button assigned that task. Appendix B, "Macro Commands," contains a glossary of macro commands.

To assign a new function to one of the SpeedBar buttons, follow these steps:

1. Choose /**O**ptions Speed**B**ar.

2. Choose **R**EADY mode SpeedBar or **E**DIT mode SpeedBar.

3. Choose the button you want to customize (**A** Button, **B** Button, and so on).

4. Choose **S**hort name. Type in a name of up to three characters and then press Enter. The short name appears on a SpeedBar when you display Quattro Pro in text display mode.

5. Choose **L**ong name. Type in a name of up to 10 characters and then press Enter. The long name appears on a SpeedBar when you display Quattro Pro in WYSIWYG display mode.

PART III — ADVANCED SPREADSHEET APPLICATIONS

6. Choose **M**acro. Enter any valid macro command and press Enter.
7. Choose **Q**uit twice to return to the /**O**ptions Speed**B**ar menu.

Quattro Pro enables you to assign up to 15 button entries per SpeedBar (buttons A through O). When no more SpeedBar buttons can fit within the width of your screen display, Quattro Pro replaces the rightmost button on the SpeedBar with the BAR button. Click the BAR button to display additional button assignments for the current SpeedBar.

The SpeedBar shown in the upper half of figure 16.18 illustrates the appearance of a spreadsheet window when more buttons are defined than can fit onto the READY mode SpeedBar. Notice that the BAR button at the right end of the SpeedBar has replaced the WYS button that normally appears in that position.

Fig. 16.18

A SpeedBar when more buttons are defined than can fit in a spreadsheet window.

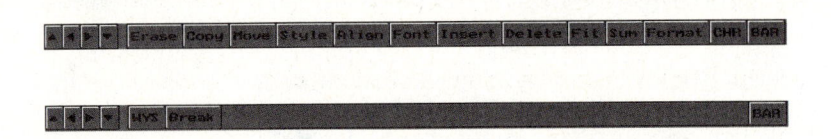

To reveal additional buttons for the READY mode SpeedBar, click the BAR button once; Quattro Pro shows the SpeedBar pictured in the lower half of this figure. On this SpeedBar, notice that the WYS button now appears in the first position and the Break button—the button responsible for extending the length of this SpeedBar—appears in the second position. To return to the READY mode SpeedBar shown in the upper half of this figure, click the BAR button again.

To remove a button from a SpeedBar, delete the button settings from the **R**EADY mode SpeedBar or **E**DIT mode SpeedBar submenus. For instance, if you choose /**O**ptions Speed**B**ar **R**EADY mode SpeedBar and then delete the definition for **N** Button (used to define the Break button), Quattro Pro updates the READY mode SpeedBar so that the WYS button displays in the position occupied by the BAR button in figure 16.18.

Figure 16.19 shows the **M**acro command entry for the first button on the READY mode SpeedBar. The {/ Block;Erase} command is the menu-equivalent of the /**E**dit **E**rase Block command, so clicking the Erase button has the effect of choosing the **E**rase Block command.

16 — CUSTOMIZING QUATTRO PRO

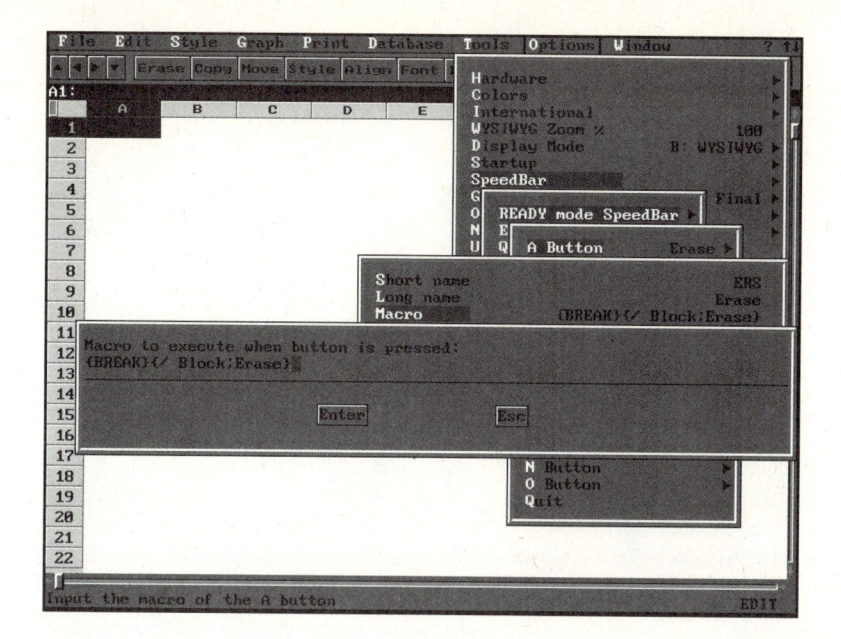

Fig. 16.19

Assign a macro command to a SpeedBar button.

> **T I P**
> Place the {BREAK} macro command in front of each SpeedBar button assignment. {BREAK} insures that Quattro Pro is in READY mode before executing the action called for by the **M**acro command entry.

Setting Graphics Quality Options

The **G**raphics Quality option enables you to choose the quality of Quattro Pro's printing graphics. Specify **D**raft or **F**inal quality.

Quattro Pro takes time to build the required font files before the program can display or print a font. Each time you choose a new font, Quattro Pro may pause to build these font files. After Quattro Pro creates a font file, the program can access that particular font the next time without making you wait.

To save time, you can choose **D**raft graphics quality to have Quattro Pro substitute Hershey fonts for Bitstream fonts. That way, Quattro Pro

PART III — ADVANCED SPREADSHEET APPLICATIONS

does not need to stop and build fonts. When you want to look in more detail at your file, return to **F**inal quality graphics.

To choose a different **G**raphics **Q**uality command setting, follow these steps:

1. Choose /**O**ptions **G**raphics **Q**uality.

   Quattro Pro displays the **D**raft and **F**inal options on the submenu.

2. Choose the quality you prefer.

Using Other Options

Choosing the **O**ther command from the **O**ptions menu option displays a submenu of miscellaneous system options (see fig. 16.20). Some of these options, such as the **U**ndo and **M**acro functions, become invaluable to you as you continue working with Quattro Pro. Notice that the current settings for some of the commands appear at the right margin of this menu.

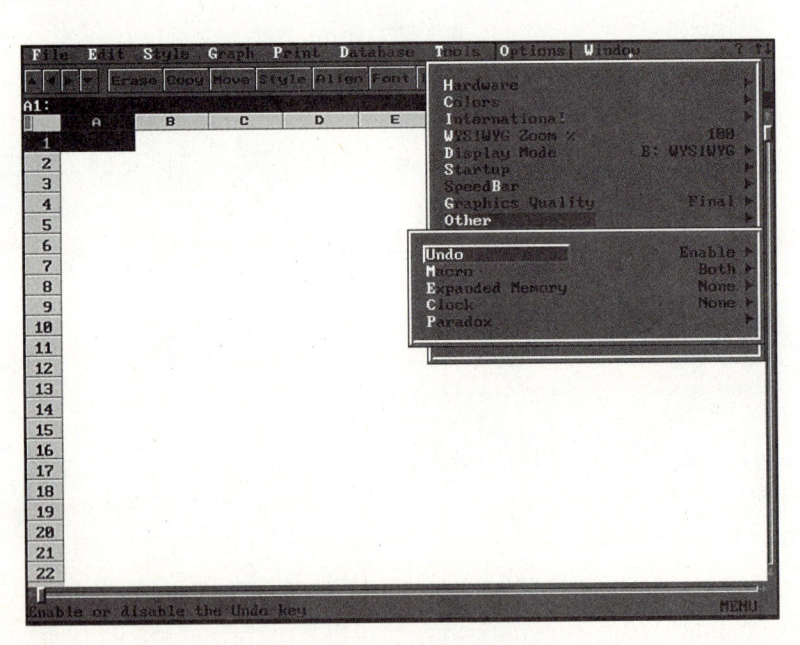

Fig. 16.20

The **O**ptions **O**ther submenu commands.

Undo

Choose **D**isable or **E**nable to control the status of the /Edit Undo command. Remember, this command can undo many—but not all—Quattro Pro operations. Disabling this function speeds up Quattro Pro's operation a bit. If you are at all prone to mistakes, however, leave the Undo command enabled—it is well worth the minor loss in operating speed.

Macro Redraw

The **M**acro option enables you to specify which parts of the screen to avoid redrawing during macro execution. The default setting, **B**oth, suppresses redrawing of menus and spreadsheet windows until macro execution is completed. This suppression speeds up the execution of macros. You can specify that Quattro Pro suppress redrawing of a spreadsheet **P**anel or **W**indow, or you can turn off redraw suppression altogether (**N**one).

> **TIP**
>
> Setting /Options **R**ecalculation **M**ode to **M**anual enables your macros to execute more quickly. If necessary, press F9 (Calc) to recalculate spreadsheet formulas after a macro finishes executing.

Expanded Memory

If your computer has Expanded Memory Specification (EMS), Quattro Pro detects and makes use of this memory area to store spreadsheet data. Although this memory enables you to work with more spreadsheets at a time or with larger spreadsheets, using expanded memory exclusively for spreadsheet information slows down performance.

Quattro Pro tries to balance speed and space considerations by storing only some of your spreadsheets in EMS. To influence this balance, you can specify the use of EMS with the Expanded Memory option (see fig. 16.21).

If you are working with large files and need more memory, you may want to have Quattro Pro store spreadsheet and format data in EMS by choosing the **B**oth option. If you need more speed from Quattro Pro, choose **S**preadsheet Data or **F**ormat. These two commands restrict EMS usage to formulas and labels, or just formats, respectively. Choose **N**one to ensure that Quattro Pro operates at the fastest possible speed.

PART III — ADVANCED SPREADSHEET APPLICATIONS

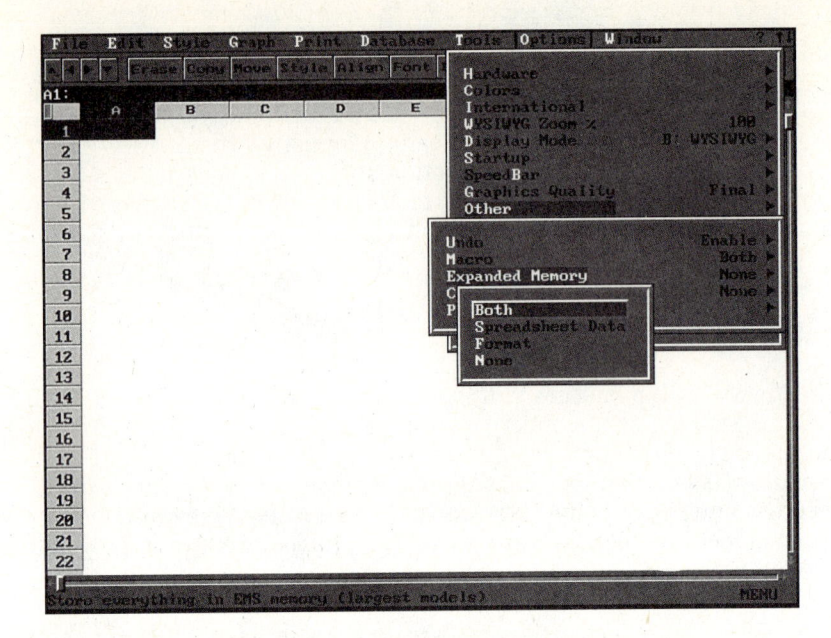

Fig. 16.21

The **E**xpanded Memory submenu.

To specify the use of expanded memory, follow these steps:

1. Choose /**O**ptions **O**ther **E**xpanded Memory.
2. Choose an option from the menu.

> **TIP**
>
> If you have trouble loading large spreadsheets when the **E**xpanded Memory command is set to **N**one, try using the **F**ormat setting. Format enables you to load parts of the spreadsheet into expanded memory while retaining much of the operation speed gains possible with the **N**one option.

Clock Display

The clock display option enables you to specify whether to display the time on the status line in Standard format, International format, or not at all (None, the default). To specify in detail the sort of international format you want, use the /**O**ptions **I**nternational **T**ime option.

To change the clock display, follow these steps:

1. Choose /**O**ptions **O**ther **C**lock.
2. Choose one of the three options on the clock menu: **S**tandard, **I**nternational, or **N**one.

Paradox

The **P**aradox command option enables you to set options for using Paradox files on a local area network (LAN). If you are working on a LAN, you need to specify further information: the type of area network you have, the directory where you have the PARADOX.NET file, and the amount of time that can pass between attempts to open a locked file. The **P**aradox menu provides these options via the **N**etwork Type, **D**irectory, and **R**etries options.

Setting Network Options

The /**O**ptions **N**etwork command enables you to configure options that control how Quattro Pro operates on a Novell network running NetWare Version 2.15c or later. These options include defining drive mappings, printing jobs with an identifying banner, setting a refresh interval, and monitoring the status of print jobs in the network queue.

> **CAUTION:** Before you try to modify any network options, consult with your network administrator to make sure that you have the appropriate access rights to make such changes on your network.

Drive Mappings

To create drive mappings for a network drive, choose /**O**ptions **N**etwork **D**rive mappings. Quattro Pro prompts you to supply several pieces of information about the network: the drive letter, the file server name, the volume name, the directory path name, and the user name. You may create up to eight drive mappings to drive letters G through Z with this command.

PART III — ADVANCED SPREADSHEET APPLICATIONS

Figure 16.22 shows two drive mappings created for user CATHY in the SYS volume on the B&A network drive.

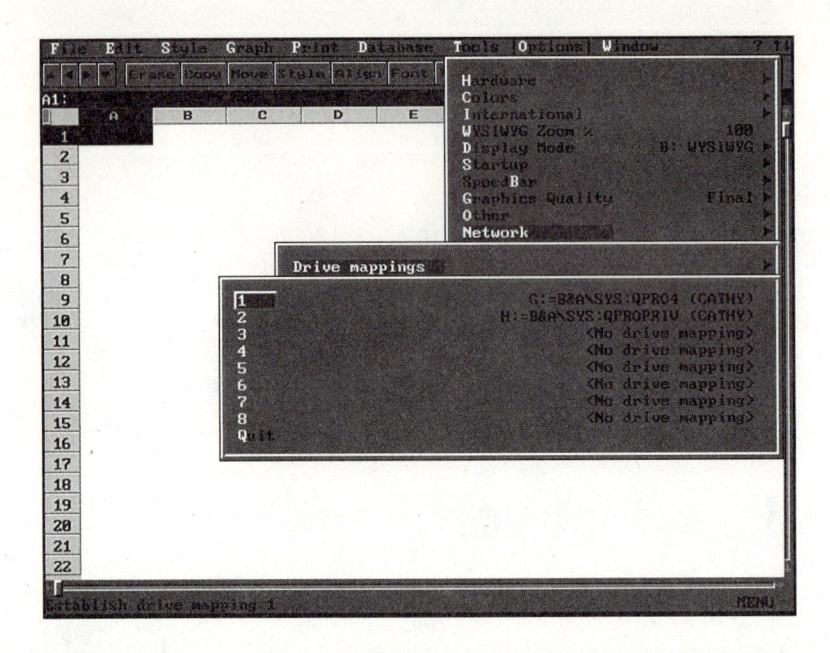

Fig. 16.22

Create drive mappings to a network drive.

> **T I P** Be sure to load the NetWare IPX shell before you try to create drive mappings for a network drive.

After you establish drive mappings to a network drive through Quattro Pro, you can use any of the File menu commands to read and write data to and from a network drive. To save a file named BUDGETS.WQ1 to the ACCTG directory on network drive H, for example, use the following steps:

1. Choose /File Save.

2. In the file-selection dialog box, click the DRV button to view a list of all local and mapped drives.

3. Click the H drive letter. Quattro Pro writes the drive letter and path (\ACCTG) on the input line and prompts you for a file name.

4. Type the file name *BUDGETS* and press Enter.

Print Job Banners

If you want to print an identifying banner before each print job, choose /**O**ptions **N**etwork **B**anner **Y**es. Choose the **N**o option to cancel network banner printing. This setting is the same as specifying the NB command line option to the NetWare CAPTURE command.

Refresh Interval

The /**O**ptions **N**etwork **R**efresh Interval command determines how often Quattro Pro updates queue information in the Print Manager window and on the status line while the Queue Monitor is engaged. Valid settings range from 1 to 300 seconds. You should choose a setting that does not burden the network workload; your network administrator can provide this information for you.

Queue Monitor

The Queue Monitor enables you to track the progress and status of print jobs that you send to the network print queue. Choose /**O**ptions **N**etwork **Q**ueue Monitor **Y**es to turn this feature on.

When engaged, the Queue Monitor displays three pieces of information on the status line: the number of print jobs you have sent from Quattro Pro not yet printed, the number of jobs ahead of the first job you sent, and the status of the first of your uncompleted print jobs. Queue Monitor information displays atop all other status line information for as long as your print jobs are in the network queue.

If your print job is ready to be printed, Quattro Pro displays `Actv` on the status line. If you have suspended your print job in the Print Manager, Quattro Pro displays `Held`. When your jobs are finished printing, Quattro Pro displays `Complete`.

User Name

To set the default user name for network access and logging on, choose /**O**ptions **N**etwork **U**ser Name. When Quattro Pro prompts you for a user name, type a name of up to 32 characters and press Enter.

Updating the Options

All the options discussed so far in this chapter are system options. If you make changes to your system settings but do not update Quattro Pro's resource file, you lose the new settings when you quit Quattro Pro. In this case, Quattro Pro reverts to the old default settings the next time you load the program into your computer.

To update new system settings so that they are active the next time you begin a Quattro Pro work session, type */OU* to choose **U**pdate.

Specifying Format Options

With the **F**ormats command, you can change how Quattro Pro displays formatted data on your spreadsheets (see fig. 16.23). Setting the **F**ormats command options affects the current spreadsheet window. These settings become the global stored settings for that spreadsheet. Notice that the current settings for these commands appear at the right margin on this menu. The following sections discuss each option in detail.

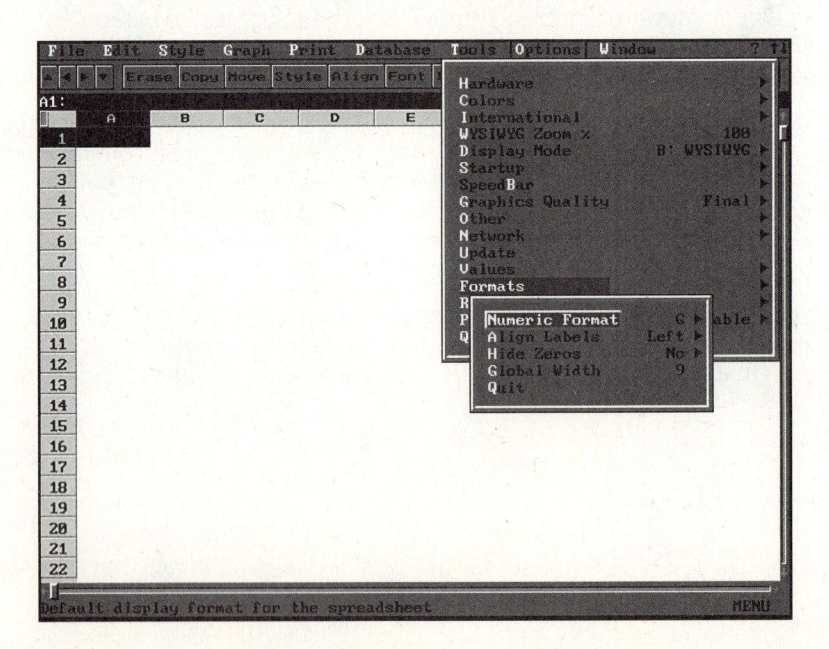

Fig. 16.23

The **F**ormats submenu of commands.

Numeric Format

The **N**umeric Format option enables you to specify the default format for displaying the values within your spreadsheet. All values are changed to the format you specify except those that have been specified with the /**S**tyle **N**umeric Format command as a block of values. Initially, the default format is **G**eneral, which right-aligns values and dates and aligns labels according to the /**O**ptions **F**ormats **A**lign **L**abels setting.

To change the global numeric format, follow these steps:

1. Choose /**O**ptions **F**ormats **N**umeric Format.
2. Choose a format from the submenu.

If you choose **D**ate or **T**ime, Quattro Pro presents a list of format choices for these options.

Align Labels

The **A**lign Labels option enables you to specify how Quattro Pro aligns labels in a spreadsheet cell. Initially, alignment is set to **L**eft, but you also may choose **C**enter or **R**ight alignment. Choose /**O**ptions **F**ormats **A**lign **L**abels to choose one of these three options.

Hide Zeros

With the **H**ide Zeros option, you can suppress the display of any cell whose value equals zero, whether the zero was entered directly or returned as the result of a formula calculation.

> **CAUTION:** When zero suppression is on, you easily can assume that a zero cell is empty and then accidentally write over cells that contain needed formulas.

Global Width

The **G**lobal Width option enables you to specify the width of all columns within a spreadsheet at one time. The initial default width is nine character spaces. To change the column width, choose /**O**ptions **F**ormats **G**lobal Width and type the value for the new default for the current spreadsheet.

Controlling Recalculation

The **R**ecalculation options enable you to specify how Quattro Pro updates formula results when you change cell values on which those formulas depend (see fig. 16.24). The following sections discuss each option in detail.

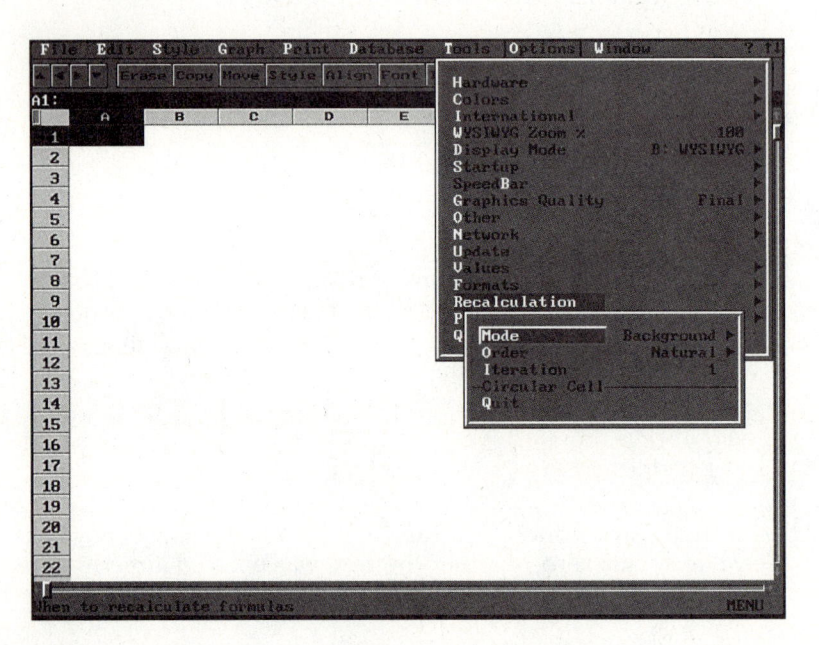

Fig. 16.24

The **R**ecalculation submenu.

Mode

The **M**ode option enables you to specify whether Quattro Pro calculates formulas behind the scenes (**B**ackground), while you wait (**A**utomatic), or on request (**M**anual). Choose /**O**ptions **R**ecalculation **M**ode and then choose the mode you want.

If you have chosen **M**anual, your spreadsheet occasionally may need to be recalculated. When a spreadsheet requires formula recalculation, Quattro Pro displays CALC on the status line at the bottom of the spreadsheet window. Press F9 (the Calc key) when you want to recalculate all the formulas on a spreadsheet.

Order of Recalculation

You can use the **O**rder option to specify the order in which the set of formulas is calculated. The order in which formulas update cells can affect the resulting values. In **N**atural order (the default), before a formula is calculated, all the cells the formula references first are recalculated.

The two other options are **C**olumn-wise and **R**ow-wise. In column-wise recalculation, Quattro Pro starts in cell A1 and proceeds down column A. When the formulas in column A are recalculated, Quattro Pro begins at the top of column B. **R**ow-wise calculation also starts at cell A1 but proceeds row by row.

To specify the order of formula recalculation, choose /**O**ptions **R**ecalculation **O**rder and then choose one of the three available orders.

Number of Iterations

Quattro Pro enables the specification of formulas that are circular in nature. A circular formula contains a cell or block address reference that includes the location of the formula. Each time you recalculate a circular formula, the formula adds itself to the resulting value.

The **I**teration option enables you to specify the number of cycles of recalculation Quattro Pro should perform each time the spreadsheet is recalculated. Only in the most complex of engineering or financial situations are circular references desirable.

To specify the number of recalculation iterations if circular references exist, follow these steps:

1. Choose /**O**ptions **R**ecalculation **I**teration.
2. Enter any number up to 255 iterations.

Circular Cell

Circular Cell is a noninteractive menu field. If your spreadsheet contains a formula with a circular reference, the address of the cell containing the formula is displayed in this field. After you correct a circular reference, this field again displays the heading Circular Cell.

Setting Protection Options

Use the **P**rotection option to **E**nable and **D**isable global spreadsheet protection. When enabled, this feature prevents cells that have not been protected otherwise (with /**S**tyle **P**rotection **U**nprotect) from being overwritten.

You also can assign a password to your spreadsheet to prevent formulas from being accidentally erased or overwritten. With formula protection in place, the only way to edit cells containing formulas is to enter a password and remove the protection.

To password-protect your formulas, follow these steps:

1. Choose /**O**ptions **P**rotection **F**ormulas **P**rotect (see fig. 16.25).

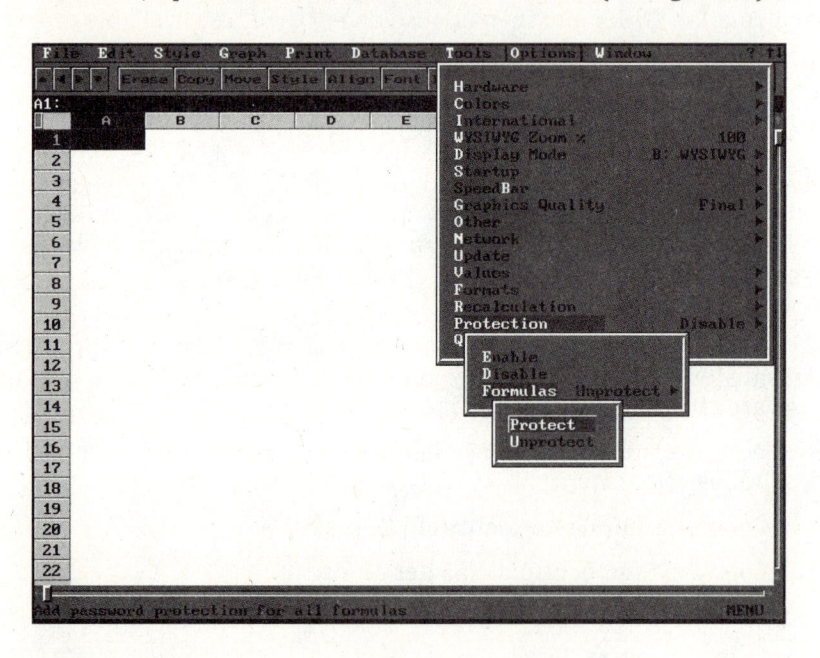

Fig. 16.25

Assign a password to protect spreadsheet formulas.

2. Type a password. This password is required to remove protection so that cells containing formulas can be edited.

3. Press Enter.

   Quattro Pro prompts you to verify the password you just entered.

4. Retype the password exactly, matching cases. Press Enter.

If you enter the password differently the second time, you see the message `Passwords do not match`. Press Enter to return to the **O**ptions menu.

Any user trying to edit a formula-protected cell receives the message Formula protection is enabled. To be able to edit the formula, the user must supply the appropriate password.

> **CAUTION:** Passwords are case-sensitive. If you type a word in all uppercase, all lowercase, or mixed format when you set your password, you must retype it exactly when you want to remove protection; otherwise, you have no way to regain access to the formulas.

As you invest time and energy into a spreadsheet, you may want to ensure that a simple error on your part does not result in the loss of valuable data. To avoid data loss, enable global spreadsheet protection and/or formula protection.

Questions & Answers

This chapter introduces you to the **O**ptions menu commands. If you have questions concerning particular situations not addressed in the examples given, the Q&A section may provide the answers.

Hardware Options

Q: Quattro Pro seems to run slower than it should, yet my spreadsheet applications are not all that big. What's going on?

A: In general, Quattro Pro slows down because you are running out of system memory. Limited hard disk space, however, also can affect Quattro Pro's speed. The VROOMM utility periodically writes part of the program onto your hard disk. If you have limited space on your hard disk, the VROOMM utility becomes less efficient.

See how much memory is available to Quattro Pro on the **H**ardware submenu and then check to see how much space is free on your hard disk drive. If you have free memory and disk space, consider making the following changes on the **O**ptions menu:

- Choose /**O**ptions **D**isplay Mode and choose a text display.

- Choose /**O**ptions **C**olors Co**n**ditional **O**n/Off **D**isable.

PART III — ADVANCED SPREADSHEET APPLICATIONS

- Choose /**O**ptions **O**ther **U**ndo and choose **D**isable.
- Choose /**O**ptions **O**ther **E**xpanded Memory and choose **N**one, if you do not have expanded memory in your computer.

Making some or all of these changes improves Quattro Pro's operating speed. You must weigh for yourself the loss of each feature, however, against a gain in operating speed.

Q: I installed a second printer on my computer system. I also have an AB switch box so that I can change quickly from one printer to the other. Do I need to tell Quattro Pro that I have two printers?

A: Using an AB switch box is not a substitute for configuring a second printer. Quattro Pro creates a printer driver file for each printer you configure. Not all printers use the same codes; therefore, using an AB switch box does not guarantee that one printer's driver file will work with a second printer.

To configure the second printer, choose /**O**ptions **H**ardware **P**rinters **2**nd Printer and specify the manufacturer, model, printing mode, and port connection. Next, choose /**U**pdate to store this information permanently. Finally, choose /**O**ptions **H**ardware **P**rinters **D**efault Printer to define this printer as the default printer.

Q: I'm getting garbled printer output. What should I check?

A: First, make sure that the definition file contains the correct configuration information. (Choose /**O**ptions **H**ardware **P**rinters and **1**st Printer or **2**nd Printer.)

Second, if you are using a serial printer, make sure that the parity, baud rate, and stop bits match those set on your printer's configuration panel. If you don't know these values, check your printer manual.

Third, choose /**O**ptions **H**ardware **P**rinters **A**uto LF and choose **N**o. Quattro Pro may be printing the data correctly but all on the same line.

Q: When I choose /**O**ptions **D**isplay Mode and choose an extended text display mode, why does Quattro Pro lock up? I cannot control the cell selector or input commands.

A: Make sure that you selected the correct screen driver with the /**O**ptions **H**ardware **S**creen **S**creen Type command. When in doubt, set this option to **A**utodetect and have Quattro Pro take over.

Q: Why does nothing happen when I choose **U**pdate?

A: You don't see the effects of your system settings changes immediately, although the settings no doubt have been saved. To see whether the new system specifications are in effect, choose /**O**ptions **V**alues. Alternately, you can exit and reload Quattro Pro to see if the changes you made are in effect.

Default Format Options

Q: When I choose /**O**ptions **F**ormats **H**ide Zeros, Quattro Pro does not remove the trailing zeros from a block of values I have marked. Why?

A: This option does not remove trailing zeros—it enables you to suppress only the display of entries with a numeric value that equals exactly zero.

To remove trailing zeros from a value, choose one of the formats on the /**S**tyle **N**umeric Format menu and reduce the number of displayed decimal places.

Q: Why isn't Quattro Pro recalculating my formulas when I enter new data into a spreadsheet?

A: Check the mode indicator on the status line at the bottom of your spreadsheet. If it says CALC, press F9, and Quattro Pro recalculates your formulas.

If you want Quattro Pro to recalculate formulas as the referenced data changes, choose /**O**ptions **R**ecalculation **M**ode **A**utomatic.

Summary

Chapter 16 shows you how to change many of the system settings Quattro Pro uses to interact with your computer and screen display. This chapter also discusses how Quattro Pro calculates values and sets global formats for the active spreadsheet.

You now should understand that you may store system settings permanently by choosing the **U**pdate command and that the global format settings apply only to the active spreadsheet.

Having completed this chapter, you should understand the following Quattro Pro concepts:

- Reconfiguring installed printers, displays, and your mouse
- Changing Quattro Pro's screen colors

PART III — ADVANCED SPREADSHEET APPLICATIONS

- Defining formats for displaying currency symbols, numerical punctuation, and dates and times
- Changing screen display modes
- Choosing your own "start-up rules"
- Setting the miscellaneous system settings
- Renaming and redefining the function of the SpeedBar buttons
- Choosing between slower but high-quality on-screen fonts, or faster but low-quality on-screen fonts
- Defining the network environment settings
- Storing the current system settings in Quattro Pro's resource files as the new defaults
- Reviewing all current system settings in the status box
- Changing the default global spreadsheet settings
- Specifying a recalculation mode and enabling global spreadsheet and formula protection

The next section contains the Command Reference. Refer to this section for in-depth coverage of Quattro Pro's menu commands.

The rest of *Using Quattro Pro 4*, Special Edition, is devoted to topics crucial to advancing your user skills. If you have not glanced through the appendixes, do so now.

Appendix A addresses installation and advanced user issues that help you to create the most efficient operating environment for Quattro Pro.

Appendix B is a glossary of macro command terms. The glossary includes descriptions and definitions of each command's syntax so that you know how to use the commands in your own macro programs.

Appendix C is a glossary of menu-equivalent commands. These commands are used in macros to duplicate commands on any of Quattro Pro's menus.

Appendix D contains an ASCII table. This appendix contains instructions for using ASCII characters and decimal-equivalent codes with three commands on the **O**ptions menu. Appendix D also discusses how to convert printer codes into setup strings using the ASCII table.

Appendix E shows you how to install and manage Quattro Pro on a local area network (LAN). Because Version 4.0 arrives "network-ready," the discussion concentrates on preparing your network for program installation.

Command Reference

The Command Reference is a comprehensive summary of Quattro Pro commands. Use the Command Reference when you are searching for a command to perform a specific operation, must learn quickly how to accomplish a task, or require hands-on information about a command.

The Quattro Pro Command Reference is organized so that you easily can find the command you need. The command categories in the Command Reference appear in the same order as those on Quattro Pro's command menu bar:

File **E**dit **S**tyle **G**raph **P**rint **D**atabase **T**ools **O**ptions **W**indow

The individual commands within each command group are listed alphabetically. To learn how to save a file, for example, turn to the File Commands section in the Command Reference. **S**ave is located alphabetically within the **F**ile Commands section between **F**ile **R**etrieve and **F**ile **S**ave All.

The command instructions contain the following five key elements of information:

Purpose	A description of the task(s) the command performs
Reminders	Information you must know before executing the command

Procedures	Step-by-step instructions on how to use the command
Important cues	Information about the benefits of the command and situations when you should use the command
Cautions	Warnings about possible adverse effects of the command

For more information about the individual Quattro Pro commands, refer to the appropriate discussion located in earlier chapters of this book.

File Commands /F

You use /File commands to save and retrieve spreadsheets, select the drive and directory for saving and retrieving files, exit Quattro Pro, and access DOS and the File Manager.

File Close /FC

Purpose

Removes the spreadsheet from the current window and closes the window.

Procedure

1. Type /FC.

   If you have not saved the latest changes to the spreadsheet, Quattro Pro warns you with a confirmation menu box.

2. Choose **Yes** to close the file and window without saving. Choose **No** to cancel the command.

3. To save the file, type /FS. Type /FC again.

Caution

■ Closing a window does not save changes to a spreadsheet. You must use /File **S**ave or /File Save **A**s before closing a window to save the most recent version of your spreadsheet.

FILE COMMANDS

For more information, see /File Close All, /File New, /File Open, /File Save, /File Save As, and /File Save All.

File Close All /FL

Purpose

Removes spreadsheets from all open windows and closes all windows.

Procedure

1. Type */FL*.

    If you have not saved the latest changes, Quattro Pro warns you with a confirmation menu box.

2. Choose **Yes** to close the files and windows without saving. Choose **No** to cancel the command.

3. Type */FS* or */FA* to save each file, or */FV* to save all files. Then, type */FL* again.

Caution

- Closing all windows does not save changes to the spreadsheets. You must use /File **S**ave or /File Save **A**s with each spreadsheet or /File Save All before closing all windows to use the most recent version of the spreadsheets in your next Quattro Pro session.

For more information, see /File Close, /File New, /File Open, /File Save, /File Save As, /File Save All, and /File Workspace Save.

File Directory /FD

Purpose

Changes the current disk drive or directory for the current work session.

Procedure

1. Type */FD*.
2. If the displayed drive and directory are correct, press Enter. If you want to change the settings, type a new drive letter and directory name and press Enter.

Important Cues

- Temporarily access another drive and directory by selecting /File **R**etrieve or /File Save **A**s and pressing Esc twice to clear the current drive and directory from the dialog box prompt. Next, type the drive designator and directory name, including a final backslash (\). You then can type a file name or press Enter to see a list box of file names on that drive or directory. Move the highlight bar and press Enter to select a name from the list or click with the mouse to select a file.

- You can change Quattro Pro's start-up drive and directory by using /**O**ptions **S**tartup **D**irectory to enter a new drive or directory. Make this change permanent by selecting /**O**ptions **U**pdate.

For more information, see **/File Utilities File Manager, /File Retrieve, /File Save, /File Save As, /File Save All,** *and* **/Options Startup**.

File Erase /FE

Purpose

Erases the entire spreadsheet from memory and resets all cell formats, label prefixes, and command settings to their original values so that you have a fresh work area.

Reminder

- Be sure to save active spreadsheet(s) before you use /**F**ile **E**rase.

Procedure

1. Type */FE*.

FILE COMMANDS

2. Choose **Yes** to erase the entire spreadsheet or **No** to cancel the operation and return to the active spreadsheet.

   If you have not saved the latest changes, Quattro Pro warns you by displaying a confirmation menu box.

3. Choose **Yes** to erase without saving. Choose **No** to cancel the command.

Important Cues

- Use /**F**ile **C**lose and /**F**ile **C**lose All to close and remove individual files and all open files, respectively, in memory.
- If you can use portions of a spreadsheet in the next spreadsheet, use /**E**dit **E**rase Block to erase only the unusable portions.
- /**F**ile **R**etrieve removes the current spreadsheet when you load the new spreadsheet.

Caution

- Files and spreadsheets erased from memory without first being saved are lost. Make sure that you save files and spreadsheets you want to use again.

For more information, see ***/File Save****,* ***/File Save As****,* ***/File Save All****,* ***/File Close****,* ***/File Close All****,* ***/File Retrieve****, and* ***/Edit Erase Block****.*

File Exit   /FX

Purpose

Leaves Quattro Pro for the current work session and returns to DOS.

Reminders

- Save the current spreadsheet before exiting Quattro Pro.
- You can use the Ctrl-X shortcut to invoke /**F**ile **E**xit.

Procedure

1. Type /*FX*.

   If you have not saved spreadsheet changes, Quattro Pro warns you by displaying a confirmation menu box.

2. Choose **N**o to cancel the command, **Y**es to exit the program without saving, or **S**ave & Exit to specify the type of save.

3. If you select **S**ave & Exit, choose an available option: **C**ancel cancels the save operation, **R**eplace replaces the existing file on disk with the active file that you are saving, and **B**ackup saves a copy of the original file.

   After you choose **R**eplace or **B**ackup, Quattro Pro saves your file and exits to DOS.

Caution

- Spreadsheets that are not saved with /File **S**ave, /File Save **A**s, /File Save A**l**l, or /Tools **X**tract are lost when you exit Quattro Pro. Changes to existing spreadsheets or graphs are not recorded unless the spreadsheet has been saved with one of the /File save commands.

For more information, see /File Save, /File Save As, /File Save All, and /Tools Xtract.

File New   /FN

Purpose

Creates a new, blank file on disk and covers up the current on-screen file with a new spreadsheet.

Reminders

- All current files remain in memory.
- Use the /**F**ile **O**pen command to open existing files without deleting files now in memory.

Procedure

Type /*FN*.

FILE COMMANDS

Important Cue

- After entering data in the spreadsheet, you must use /File Save, /File Save As, or /File Save All to save the spreadsheets to disk if you want to use the spreadsheet in another session.

For more information, see /File Open, /File Retrieve, /File Save, and /File Save All.

File Open   /FO

Purpose

Opens a previously saved file and places it in a new window in memory without removing currently open files.

Procedure

1. Type /FO.
2. Select the name of the file from the file-name box that you want to open. Press Enter.

Important Cues

- Files saved with a password require a password entered exactly as recorded originally.
- Use /File New to open a new, blank file in memory.
- If you make any changes to the open file, use /File Save, /File Save As, or /File Save All to update the file on disk.

For more information, see /File New, /File Retrieve, /File Save, /File Save As, /File Save All, and /Window Pick.

File Retrieve   /FR

Purpose

Loads a copy of a file from disk into memory.

Reminder

- Before you retrieve a new file, use /File **S**ave, /File Save **A**s, or /File Save All to save the active spreadsheet(s). A retrieved file replaces the file now in memory.

Procedure

1. Type */FR*.
2. Select the file name that you want to retrieve from the file-name box. Press Enter.

Important Cues

- Retrieve files from the DOS prompt when you first load Quattro Pro by typing *Q filename*, in which *filename* represents the name of the file that you want to retrieve.

- You can have the autoload file, QUATTRO.WQ1, load automatically each time you invoke Quattro Pro. Specify another name for the autoload file with the /**O**ptions Startup **A**utoload File command.

*For more information, see /**F**ile **D**irectory, /**F**ile **S**ave, /**F**ile Save **A**s, /**F**ile Save All, /**O**ptions **S**tartup, and /**T**ools **C**ombine.*

File Save /FS

Purpose

Saves the current file and settings under the current name.

Reminders

- Save frequently to guard against data loss.
- You can use the Ctrl-S shortcut key combination to invoke /**F**ile **S**ave.

Procedure

1. Place the cell selector in the home position in the active file that you want to save.

2. Type */FS*.

3. If you are prompted for a name, enter a name and press Enter.

4. If you have saved the file before, Quattro Pro displays the `File already exists:` prompt. Choose **C**ancel to cancel the save operation, **R**eplace to replace an existing file with the current file, or **B**ackup to save the active file and rename the existing file with a BAK extension.

   Choosing **R**eplace replaces the existing file on disk with the active file that you are saving. You cannot recover a file that you have replaced. Use **B**ackup to save a copy of the original file.

Important Cues

- Name files so that they are easy to remember and group together. If you give related files similar names (SALES_01, SALES_02, and SALES_03), you can use the wild cards * and ? to copy and erase files.

- Use up to eight characters when naming a file. You can use the letters A through Z, the numbers 0 through 9, and the underline character (_) or hyphen (-), but you cannot use spaces.

- Use password protection to prevent unauthorized access to Quattro Pro spreadsheets. See */File Save **As*** for password protection procedures.

- From the file list box, you can select a file name. When prompted for a name, press Esc to remove the default file name. Use the arrow keys to move to the file name you want to replace, and press Enter. Alternatively, use the mouse to click the file name you want to replace. You can press F3 (Choices) to display a full-screen list of file names.

- If a file is too large to save in its entirety, use */**T**ools **X**tract* to save portions of the file to disk as separate files.

Caution

- Saving a file under an existing file name replaces the old file.

For more information, see **/File Directory**, **/File Erase**, **/Tools Xtract**, **/File Save As**, *and* **/File Save All**.

File Save All /FV

Purpose

Saves all open files and settings, starting with the current window.

Reminder

- Save frequently to guard against data loss.

Procedure

1. Place the cell selector in home position in the active file that you want to save first.
2. Type */FV*.
3. If you are prompted for a file name, enter a file name and press Enter.
4. Choose an available option: **C**ancel cancels the save operation, **R**eplace replaces an existing file with the current file, and **B**ackup saves the active file and renames the existing file with a BAK extension.
5. Repeat steps 3 and 4 until you have saved all open files.

Caution

- Saving a file under an existing file name replaces the old file.

For more information, see /File Directory, /File Erase, /Tools Xtract, /File Save, and /File Save As.

File Save As /FA

Purpose

Saves the current file and settings under a new name.

Reminder

- Save frequently to guard against data loss.

Procedure

1. Place the cell selector in home position in the active file you want to save.

2. Type */FA*.

3. If the file has not been saved previously, Quattro Pro supplies a default name and extension (SHEET#.WQ1, for example). Highlight an existing name, type a new name, or enter a new drive designation, path name, and file name. Press Enter.

4. If a file already exists with the file name you have selected, Quattro Pro displays an Overwrite Warning menu. Choose Cancel to cancel the Save As operation, Replace to replace an existing file with the correct file, or Backup to save the active file and rename the existing file with a BAK extension.

Important Cue

- Password protection prevents unauthorized access to Quattro Pro spreadsheets. If you save spreadsheets with a password, you must enter the password before you can retrieve the file. To save a file with a password, follow these steps when you type the file name:

    1. Type the file name, press the space bar, and then enter *P*.

    2. Press Enter.

    3. Type a password of up to 15 characters (no spaces). A square appears in place of each letter. Press Enter.

    4. After the verification prompt appears, type the password again and press Enter.

    Remember that passwords are case-sensitive. When you retrieve the file, you must enter the password in exactly the same way.

Caution

- Saving a file under an existing file name replaces the old file.

For more information, see */File Directory*, */File Erase*, */File Save*, */File Save All*, *and* */Tools Xtract*.

File Utilities DOS Shell /FUD

Purpose

Leaves the current spreadsheet, exits from Quattro Pro temporarily so that you can run DOS commands, and enables you to return to Quattro Pro and the current spreadsheet. You also can issue a DOS command directly from Quattro Pro and then return to the current spreadsheet after executing the command.

Reminders

- Be certain that the programs you run from within Quattro Pro can fit in your computer's available memory. Do not load or run memory-resident programs from the DOS level.

- If you want to run an external DOS command, be sure that the command is available on your disk drive or is on the path for a hard disk system.

- You can perform certain DOS commands—such as copying, erasing, and renaming files—by using the File Manager and not leaving Quattro Pro.

Procedure

1. Type */FUD*.
2. Type the internal DOS commands or program names that you want to run.
3. If you are running a program, when you finish, return to DOS.
4. Return to Quattro Pro from the DOS prompt by typing *exit* and pressing Enter.

For more information, see **/File Utilities File Manager**.

File Utilities File Manager /FUF

Purpose

Displays all file names of a specific type that are stored on the current drive and directory. Displays the size of the file (in bytes) and the date and time that the file was created.

FILE COMMANDS

Procedure

1. Type */FUF*.
2. Select one of the following options:

Key(s)	Key Name	
Shift-F5 Alt-0	Pick Window	Displays a list of open windows and activates a different window
F6 or Tab	Pane	Activates the next File Manager window pane
Shift-Tab		Activates the control pane and moves the cursor to the `File Name` prompt
Shift-F6	Next Window	Activates the next open File Manager or spread sheet window
Alt-F6	Zoom Window	Enlarges an open window to full size and shrinks it back
Alt-#		Jumps to the specified window

3. If you want to change a drive, directory, filter prompt, or file name in the control pane, press F6 until the control pane is active.
4. Use the up- and down-arrow keys to move the cursor to the setting that you want to change.
5. Press Esc to erase the entry or press the Backspace key to erase one character at a time.
6. Type the drive, directory, or filter prompt or the file name.
7. Press Enter and the up- or down-arrow key.
8. To display files from different directories in the file list pane, type one of the following filters:

Filter	Function
.	Displays all files
*.WQ1	Displays spreadsheet files with WQ1 extensions
[*.WK?]	Displays all files except those with extensions beginning with WK

USING QUATTRO PRO 4, SPECIAL EDITION

9. Use the arrow keys to highlight individual file names and to display specific information.

10. Use **/F**ile **C**lose to return to the spreadsheet.

Caution

■ Any changes you make to the File Manager window become the default settings for future File Manager sessions. If you prefer to use the File Manager with its default settings intact, you must manually make the appropriate changes before exiting the File Manager window.

For more information, see **/File Directory**, **/File Utilities File Manager Edit**, **/File Utilities File Manager File**, **/File Utilities File Manager Print**, **/File Utilities File Manager Sort**, **/File Utilities File Manager Tree**, *and* **/File Utilities File Manager Window**.

File Utilities File Manager Edit   /FUF/E

Purpose

Copies, moves, renames, and duplicates files from the directory. Also erases Quattro Pro files from disk so that you have more available disk space.

Procedure

1. Type */FUF/E*.
2. Choose one of the following options:

Option	Function
Select File	Opens an individual file in a specified directory
All Select	Opens all the files in a specified directory
Copy	Copies selected files to temporary memory
Move	Moves selected files to temporary memory
Erase	Deletes a file from the file list
Paste	Copies or moves selected files to a different directory
Duplicate	Copies a file and renames the duplicate file
Rename	Changes the name of the file

3. If you choose **Copy**, move the cursor to the directory to which you want to copy the files; then, choose **E**dit **P**aste to copy the files.

   If you choose **M**ove, position the cursor in the directory to which you want to move the files. Then, choose **E**dit **P**aste to move the files.

   If you choose **E**rase, select **Y**es to delete the file. If you delete all the files from a directory, you can delete the directory name with **E**dit **E**rase.

   If you choose **D**uplicate, type the path and the new name for the file. Press Enter.

   If you choose **R**ename, type the path and the new name for the file and then press Enter.

4. Use /**F**ile **C**lose to return to the spreadsheet.

Caution

- You cannot restore an erased file. Make sure that you will not need a file before you erase it, or have a copy of the file on a floppy disk.

*For more information, see /**File Directory**.*

File Utilities File Manager File   /FUF/F

Purpose

Creates new windows, opens and closes active windows, and saves and retrieves workspaces for the same file options available within a spreadsheet window. Updates directory display, creates new directories, accesses DOS, and changes file-compression settings.

Procedure

1. Type */FUF/F*.

2. Select an available option as follows:

USING QUATTRO PRO 4, SPECIAL EDITION

Option	Function
New	Opens a new window and spreadsheet file
Open	Opens a new window and loads an existing file
Close	Closes the current file manager window
Close All	Closes all open files and windows
Read Dir	Updates the directory display
Make Dir	Adds a new directory
Workspace	Saves the current window setup and retrieves a workspace
Utilities	Accesses DOS, opens another File Manager window, and sets file-compression options
Exit	Exits Quattro Pro and returns to DOS

3. If you choose **Make Dir**, enter a directory name and press Enter.

   If you choose **Workspace**, choose **S**ave, enter a file name, and then press Enter to save the current window setup.

   If you choose **R**etrieve, enter a file name and press Enter to retrieve a workspace.

4. Use **/File Close** to return to the spreadsheet.

For more information, see **/File Directory**, **/File Utilities File Manager Edit**, **/File Utilities File Manager Print**, **/File Utilities File Manager Sort**, **/File Utilities File Manager Tree**, **/File Utilities File Manager Window**, and **/File Workspace**.

File Utilities File Manager Options /FUF/O

Purpose

Changes settings for the same options available within a spreadsheet window and two other options for the File Manager window.

FILE COMMANDS

Procedure

1. Type */FUF/O*.

2. Select an available option as follows:

Option	Function
Hardware	Changes printer and screen settings
Colors	Changes display colors
Beep	Sets the beep
Startup	Loads a new menu tree and displays the File Manager directory or the Quattro Pro directory
File List	Displays the File Manager file list
Display Mode	Displays screen in text or graphics mode
Update	Stores current option settings

3. If you choose **C**olors, you can change the display colors for the File Manager and other screen areas.

   If you choose **F**ile List, choose **F**ull View (the default) so that Quattro Pro displays the file names, file size, date, and time in several columns. Choose **W**ide View so that Quattro Pro displays only file names and extensions in a single column.

4. Use /**F**ile **C**lose to return to the spreadsheet.

*For more information, see /**Options Colors**, /**Options Display Mode**, /**Options Hardware**, /**Options Startup**, and /**Options Update**.*

File Utilities File Manager Print   /FUF/P

Purpose

Prints the File Manager windows.

Reminder

- Before initiating the /**F**ile **U**tilities **F**ile **P**rint command, make sure your printer is turned on and the paper is aligned properly.

Procedure

1. Type */FUF/P*.
2. Choose **B**lock.
3. Specify whether to print the **F**ile List, **D**irectory Tree, or **B**oth.
4. Choose **D**estination **P**rinter to send the specified block directly to the printer, or choose **D**estination **F**ile to send the specified block to a file.
5. Choose **P**age Layout if you want to change any print options.
6. Choose **A**djust Printer Align to set the top of the page on the printer.
7. Choose **G**o to print File Manager windows.
8. Choose **Q**uit to return to the File Manager window.

Important Cue

- Set */Print Layout Break Pages* to No to create an ASCII file.

*For more information, see */File Utilities File Manager* and */Print Layout*.

File Utilities File Manager Sort   /FUF/S

Purpose

Reorders files and subdirectories in the file list alphabetically, chronologically, and by size.

Procedure

1. Type */FUF/S*.
2. Choose one of the following options:

Option	Function
Name	Sorts file names and subdirectories in the file list alphabetically first by name, then by extension

FILE COMMANDS

Option	Function
Timestamp	Sorts file names and subdirectories chronologically by date and time from the oldest to the last file modified
Extension	Sorts the file list alphabetically first by extension, then by file name
Size	Sorts file names and subdirectories by DOS size in bytes, from the smallest to the largest file
DOS Order	Sorts file names in DOS DIR order, in the order of original creation

3. Select /File Close to return to the spreadsheet.

For more information, see /File Directory, /File Utilities File Manager, /File Utilities File Manager Edit, /File Utilities File Manager Options, and /File Utilities File Manager Tree.

File Utilities File Manager Tree   /FUF/T

Purpose

Displays directories and subdirectories in alphabetical order.

Procedure

1. Type */FUF/T*.
2. Choose an available option as follows:

Option	Function
Open	Displays the directory tree for the specified disk; Quattro Pro opens a tree pane below or to the right of the file list pane in the File Manager window
Resize	Changes the size of the tree pane; enter a percentage of the window that you want to use to display the tree, for example, type *80*, which stands for 80 percent; press Enter
Close	Removes the tree pane from the File Manager window; Quattro Pro removes the directory tree and expands the file list to fill the File Manager window

USING QUATTRO PRO 4, SPECIAL EDITION

3. Press an available key: Esc returns all selected files to normal, activates the control pane, selects the current file, and moves the cursor to the `File Name` prompt; PgUp scrolls the file list up; PgDn scrolls the file list down; Del deletes one or all selected files; and F9 (Calc) updates the directory tree display.

4. Use /File Close to return to the spreadsheet.

For more information, see /File Directory, /File Utilities File Manager, /File Utilities File Manager Edit, and /File Utilities File Manager File.

File Utilities File Manager Window /FUF/W

Purpose

Resizes, repositions, and expands the current window pane. Moves the cursor to a different window.

Reminders

- The **Z**oom, **S**tack, and **M**ove/Size options operate only in text display mode.
- If you **T**ile several windows, you can select **Z**oom to fully enlarge the active spreadsheet window.

Procedure

1. Type */FUF/W*.
2. Choose an available option as follows:

Option	Function
Zoom	Expands the active window to fill the screen
Tile	Displays all open windows simultaneously
Stack	Arranges open windows in layers and displays the top line of each window
Move/Size	Changes the size or position of the active window
Pick	Displays a list of open windows; activates a window

FILE COMMANDS

3. If you select **M**ove/Size to move a window, the MOVE indicator displays in the top left corner of the window. Use the arrow keys to move the window in the direction of the arrow.

   To move a window using the mouse, click and hold the mouse pointer on any double-edged window border and drag in the direction you want to move.

   If you select **M**ove/Size to change the size of a window, the MOVE indicator displays in the top left corner of the window. Press the Scroll Lock key to display the SIZE indicator in the top left corner of the window. Use the arrow keys to adjust the window's outline in the direction of the arrow and press Enter.

   To size a window using a mouse, click and hold the mouse pointer on the size box in the lower right corner of the window; drag in the direction you want to size.

4. Use /**F**ile **C**lose to return to the spreadsheet.

*For more information, see /**F**ile **D**irectory, /**F**ile **U**tilities **F**ile **M**anager, /**F**ile **U**tilities **F**ile **M**anager **E**dit, and /**F**ile **U**tilities **F**ile **M**anager **F**ile.*

/File Utilities SQZ! /FUS

Purpose

Selects the file compression options for the SQZ! feature.

Procedure

1. Type */FUS*.
2. Choose an available option as follows:

Option	Function
Remove Blanks	Deletes the formatting for empty cells and blank labels
Storage of **V**alues	Specifies whether cells with formulas contain formulas and values; values erased with the **R**emove Blanks option are restored upon file retrieval
Version	Specifies whether you want to use SQZ! or SQZ! Plus
Quit	Returns to the spreadsheet

USING QUATTRO PRO 4, SPECIAL EDITION

Important Cue

- If you or another user are using an earlier version of Quattro, you must use the WKZ version to compress files.

Cautions

- Do not use the **R**emove Blanks setting if you or someone else is planning to use your Quattro Pro spreadsheet with another software program. Other programs require formulas and their results to translate properly.

- Do not save workspace files with either SQZ! version or the information stored in the workspace will be lost. Only spreadsheet files can be compressed.

For more information, see **/File Retrieve**, **/File Save**, **/File Save As**, **/File Save All**, **/File New**, **/File Open**, **/File Close**, **/File Close All**, *and* **/File Workspace**.

File Workspace /FW

Purpose

Saves and retrieves the arrangement of multiple windows and files in memory to and from disk.

Reminders

- Retrieve workspace files from the DOS prompt when you first load Quattro Pro by entering *Q*, followed by the name of the workspace that you want to retrieve.

- You can save time using the **/F**ile **W**orkspace **R**estore command rather than using the **/F**ile **R**etrieve and **/F**ile **O**pen commands if your application uses multiple spreadsheets in memory.

- **/F**ile **W**orkspace **R**estore always retrieves the most current version of your spreadsheets from disk.

- When saving workspace files, Quattro Pro supplies the three-letter WSP file extension to workspace file names. You must furnish only a file name with up to eight valid characters.

Procedures

To save a workspace, follow these steps:

1. Place the cell selector in home position in any open file.
2. Type */FWS*.
3. Enter the file name for the workspace by typing a new name. Press Enter.

To retrieve a workspace, follow these steps:

1. Type */FWR*.
2. Select a workspace file name by using left-arrow or right-arrow key to highlight an existing name or by typing the name. Press Enter. To select a workspace file name using the mouse, click the name once.

Cautions

- Do not give workspace files the same name as spreadsheet files. Quattro Pro loads the spreadsheet file if a spreadsheet file and a workspace file have the same name.

- Saving a workspace file does not save spreadsheet files. You must save each individual spreadsheet file with the /**F**ile **S**ave or /File Save **A**s command, or all spreadsheets open in memory at one time with the /File Save All command. Otherwise, you lose all unsaved files or changes.

For more information, see **/File Close***,* **/File Close All***,* **/File Directory***, */File Open, /File New, /File Retrieve, /File Save, /File Save As, and /File Save All.*

Edit Commands /E

You use /Edit commands to copy, move, and erase cell contents; undo changes made to the spreadsheet; insert and delete rows and columns in the spreadsheet; create and delete block names; fill a block of cells with values; copy cells with formulas as values; rearrange columns of data into rows or rows of data into columns; and search and/or replace cell entries for values or strings.

Edit Copy /EC

Purpose

Copies formulas, values, labels, formats, and cell-protection attributes to new locations.

Reminders

- The copied data retains its format and cell-protection status.
- Make sure that the spreadsheets contain enough blank space to receive the cell or range of cells being copied. Multiple spreadsheets in memory must contain enough room in the destination block to hold the cells. The copied cells replace the original contents of the cells.
- You can use the Ctrl-C shortcut key combination to invoke /Edit Copy.

Procedure

1. Move the cell selector to the upper left corner of the block you want copied. If you are copying one cell, put the cell selector on that cell. If you are copying across multiple spreadsheets in memory, put the cell selector on the top spreadsheet.
2. Type /EC.
3. When prompted for the source block, highlight the block and then type the block name or address. Press Enter.
4. At the DESTINATION prompt, move the cell selector to the upper left corner of the block to specify that you want the duplicate to appear at that position. Press the period key (.) to anchor the first corner. Press Enter.

EDIT COMMANDS

Important Cue

- /**E**dit **C**opy creates copies of labels and values. Formulas that use relative cell references adjust to the new location; formulas that use absolute cell references remain fixed.

Cautions

- Overlapping source and destination blocks (original and duplicate) can cause formulas to yield incorrect results. To avoid producing incorrect results, move the cell selector off the original cell before anchoring the destination block with a period.

- If the spreadsheet lacks enough empty cells to receive a copied block, the contents of the existing cells are overwritten by the copied data. To fix this problem, use /**E**dit **I**nsert to insert blank columns or rows, and the use /**E**dit **M**ove to move existing data.

- Block names are copied with the cells if the entire named area is specified as the source block. If your formulas depend on block names, your spreadsheet may produce inaccurate results.

For more information, see **/Edit Move**, **/Edit Names**, **/Edit Values**, *and* **/Edit Insert**.

Edit Copy Special /EO

Purpose

Copies only the data or only the formatting of a cell block to new locations.

Reminders

- If you select **F**ormat, the destination block appears empty until you enter data.

- Make sure that the spreadsheets contain enough blank space to receive the cell or range of cells being copied. Multiple spreadsheets in memory must contain enough room in the destination block to hold the cells.

Procedure

1. Move the cell selector to the upper left corner of the block you want copied.

   If you are copying one cell, put the cell selector on that cell. If you are copying across multiple spreadsheets in memory, put the cell selector on the top spreadsheet.

2. Select **C**ontents to copy only the contents of the cell block, or select **F**ormat to copy only the block's formatting.

3. When prompted for the source block, highlight the block and then type the block name or address. Press Enter.

4. At the DESTINATION prompt, move the cell selector to the upper left corner of the block to specify that you want the copy to appear at that position. Press the period key (.) to anchor the first corner. Press Enter.

Important Cue

- When you copy only the contents, any formatting already existing in the destination block is preserved. When you copy only the formatting, any data already existing in the destination block is preserved.

Cautions

- Overlapping source and destination blocks (original and duplicate) can cause formulas to yield incorrect results. To avoid producing incorrect results, move the cell selector off the original cell before anchoring the destination block with a period.

- Block names are copied with the cells if the entire named area is specified as the source block. If your formulas depend on block names, your spreadsheet may produce inaccurate results.

For more information, see /Edit Copy, /Edit Move, /Edit Names, /Edit Values, and /Edit Insert.

Edit Delete /ED

Purpose

Deletes one or more columns or rows, or deletes a row block or column block from the spreadsheet, including data and formatting.

Reminders

- Before you delete a column, row, row block, or column block, move the cell selector using the End and arrow keys to ensure that the column or row does not contain necessary data or formulas.

- Before you delete a column, row, row block, or column block, save your spreadsheet to disk. If you make a mistake or change your mind, you have a copy of the old version. If you have enabled Undo, you also can press Alt-F5 (Undo) to reverse the effect of the deletion.

- Quattro Pro considers row and column blocks to be partial rows or columns. When you insert a row or column block, only the data in the cells directly below or to the right of the inserted blocks moves.

Procedure

1. Move the cell selector on the first column or row you want to delete.

2. Type */ED*.

3. Choose **R**ows, **C**olumns, Row **B**lock, or Column **B**lock.

   Rows deletes row(s) at the cell selector location. Remaining rows below the deleted rows move up. **C**olumns deletes column(s) at the cell selector location. Remaining columns to the right of the deleted columns move to the left.

   Row **B**lock deletes a row block at the cell selector location. Data directly below the Row Block moves up to fill the gap. Column **B**lock deletes a column block at the cell selector location. Data directly below the Column Block moves to the left to fill the gap.

4. Specify a block containing the columns or rows you want to delete.

Important Cues

- Formulas, named blocks, and blocks in command prompts automatically adjust to the new cell addresses after you delete a column or row, unless you delete either cell appearing in the block (for example, cell A1 in block A1..D5).
- Use /Edit Move when you must reposition part of the spreadsheet without deleting a column or row.

Cautions

- Formulas that refer to deleted cells have the value ERR.
- Deleting all cells belonging to a named block leaves the named block in formulas as an undefined name. You must redefine the name by using /Edit Names.
- Deleting a row that passes through an area containing macros can cause errors in the macros.

For more information, see **/Edit Erase Block**, **/Edit Insert**, **/Edit Move**, **/Edit Undo**, and **/Options Other Undo**.

Edit Erase Block   /EE

Purpose

Erases the contents of a single cell or block of cells, leaving the cell's format intact.

Reminders

- Before you erase a cell or block, save your spreadsheet to disk. If you make a mistake or change your mind, you have a copy of the old version of your spreadsheet. If you have Undo enabled, you also can press Alt-F5 (Undo) to reverse the effect of the deletion.
- You can use the Ctrl-E shortcut to invoke the /Edit Erase Block command.

Procedure

1. Move the cell selector to the first cell in the block with contents you want to erase.

2. Type */EE*.

 3. Specify the block to be erased and then press Enter.

Important Cues

- To erase protected cells, you first must remove spreadsheet protection if it is enabled by using the /Options **P**rotection **D**isable command. (Protected cells are indicated by a P displayed on the input line.)

- Erasing data or formulas may produce an ERR display in formulas that depend on the erased data or formulas.

Caution

- Be careful not to erase formulas or values hidden with /**S**tyle **N**umeric Format **H**idden or /**O**ptions **F**ormats **N**umeric Format **H**idden. Because you do not see hidden data on-screen, it is easy to delete the hidden data without knowing that you did so. By the time you realize what you did, it probably will be too late to recover the data with Alt-F5 (Undo).

For more information, see **/Edit Delete**, **/Options Formats**, **/Options Protection**, *and* **/Style Protection**.

Edit Fill   /EF

Purpose

Enters a series of equally incremented numbers, dates, times, or percentages in a specified block.

Procedure

 1. Move the cell selector to the upper left corner of the block you want to fill.

 2. Type */EF*.

 3. Specify the block to be filled.

 4. When a start value is requested, enter the start number, date, or time in the filled block and then press Enter. You also can reference a cell or block that results in a value. The default value is 0.

5. When you request a step value, type the positive or negative number by which you want the value to increment. Date or time step values can use special units, which are described in the Important Cues. The default value is 1.

6. Enter a stop value. You can use a date or time in any format except Short Intn'l. If the step is negative, make sure that the stop value is less than the start value.

The /Edit Fill command fills the cells in the block column by column from top to bottom and left to right until Quattro Pro encounters the stop value or the block is full. The default step value is 8191, which is one less than the maximum number of rows in Quattro Pro.

Important Cues

- If you do not supply a stop value, Quattro Pro uses the default, which may give results you don't want. Enter a stop value if you want Quattro Pro to stop at a particular value before the block is filled.

- You can use /Edit Fill to fill a block of numbers in descending order. Enter a positive or negative start value and enter a negative step value. The stop value must be less than the start value.

- Press Ctrl-D to enter the dates in the valid date format. Entering an MMM-YY combination results in the date for the first of that month.

- Enter date or time step values as date or time serial numbers.

Caution

- Numbers that you generate with /Edit Fill overwrite any existing cell entries.

For more information, see /Options Formats, /Style Numeric Format, /Tools Advanced Math Optimization, and /Tools What-If.

Edit Insert /EI

Purpose

Inserts one or more blank columns, rows, or insert a row block or column block in the spreadsheet.

Reminder

- You can use the Ctrl-I shortcut to invoke /Edit Insert.

Procedure

1. Place the cell selector in the column you want to move to the right when you insert column(s). Alternatively, you can place the cell selector in the row you want to move down when you insert row(s).

2. Type */EI*.

3. Choose **R**ows, **C**olumns, Row **B**lock, or Column **B**lock.

   Rows inserts row(s) at the cell selector and moves the current row down. **C**olumns inserts column(s) at the cell selector and moves the current column to the right.

   Row **B**lock inserts a block of rows at the cell selector and moves data downward. Column **B**lock inserts a block of columns at the cell selector and moves data to the right.

4. If you choose **R**ows, move the cell selector down to highlight one cell for each row that you want to insert and then press Enter. If you choose **C**olumns, move the cell selector right to highlight one cell for each column you want to insert and then press Enter. If you choose Row **B**lock or Column **B**lock, move the cell selector to highlight the block you want to insert and press Enter.

Important Cues

- Addresses and blocks adjust automatically to the new addresses created when columns or rows are inserted.

- The key difference between Row **B**lock and Column **B**lock is how each command moves existing data. Row **B**lock pushes data downward; Column **B**lock pushes data to the right.

Cautions

- Cell addresses in macros do not adjust automatically. Adjust cell addresses in macros to reflect the inserted column(s) or row(s). Block names in macros remain unchanged.

- Make certain that inserted columns and rows do not pass through databases, print blocks, or a column of macro code. Macros stop execution if they reach a blank cell. Database and data-entry macros may stop or malfunction if they encounter unexpected blank columns or rows in the database or data-entry areas.

For more information, see **/Edit Delete** and **/Edit Move**.

Edit Move /EM

Purpose

Moves blocks of labels, values, or formulas to different locations or spreadsheets.

Reminders

- Make sure that you have enough blank space in the receiving spreadsheet to receive the cell or block of cells being moved. The moved data replaces the original contents of the cell.

- You can use the Ctrl-M shortcut to invoke **/Edit Move**.

Procedure

1. Move the cell selector to the top left corner of the block to be moved.
2. Type */EM*.
3. Highlight the block, type the block name, or type the block address. Press Enter.
4. At the DESTINATION prompt, enter the address of the upper left corner of the block to which the cells will move. Press Enter.

EDIT COMMANDS

Important Cues

- /Edit Move does not change cell addresses. The block names and cell references in the formula remain the same. Formula results therefore don't change.

- Use /Edit Copy when you want to copy a block of cells to a new location, keeping the original block intact.

- Block names move with the moved cells if the entire named area is specified as the destination block.

- You can use /Edit Move to move data across files by specifying the file name and directory path in the destination block prompt.

Cautions

- The contents of moved cells replace the contents of existing cells. To make room for moved cells, use /Edit Move to move existing data; use /Edit Insert to insert rows or columns to provide additional room for copies.

- Moving cell contents over the top of a corner in a formula's block creates an error in the referencing formula. The formula's block is replaced by ERR, and dependent formulas show ERR.

- If a formula uses a named block, and cell contents are moved over a corner of the block, the name remains in the formula. The formula's results, however, display as ERR.

- Be careful when moving a named block that has the same upper left corner as another block. Moving one block changes the upper left corner of both named blocks.

For more information, see ***/Edit Copy*** *and* ***/Edit Names***.

Edit Names   /EN

Purpose

Assigns a name to a cell or a block of cells.

Reminder

■ Two types of block names exist: defined and undefined. A defined block name refers to a cell or block address and can be used in formulas or command prompts. An undefined block name has not been assigned an associated address or block and can be used only in formulas. Formulas that use undefined block names result in ERR.

Procedures

To create names, follow these steps:

1. Type */EN*.
2. Choose **C**reate.
3. Type a block name consisting of up to 15 characters. Avoid using symbols other than the underline (_) and backslash (\). Press Enter.
4. Specify the block to be named and press Enter.

To create block names from labels, follow these steps:

1. Type */EN*.
2. Choose **L**abels.
3. Choose **R**ight, **D**own, **L**eft, or **U**p. **R**ight uses the labels to name the cell to the right of each label. **D**own names the cell below each label. **L**eft names the cell to the left of each label. **U**p names the cell above each label.
4. Specify the block of labels to be used as block names for adjacent cells by entering the block address or highlighting the block. Press Enter.

To delete one or more block names, follow these steps:

1. Type */EN*.
2. Choose **D**elete to delete a single block name. Select **R**eset to delete all block names.
3. If you choose **D**elete, type or highlight the name that you want to delete and press Enter. Formulas that contain the block names now use cell and block addresses.

To display the cell address of existing block names, follow these steps:

1. Move the cell selector to a clear area of the spreadsheet. The table you create in these steps requires two columns and one more row than the number of block names.

2. Type */ENM*.
3. Press Enter to create a table of block names and associated addresses.

Important Cues

- Use a block name when you enter a function's argument. Instead of entering a function as *@sum(a1..a20)*, for example, type it as *@sum(expenses)*.

- Undefined block names remain in formulas, although the formulas result in ERR. Use the /**E**dit **N**ames **C**reate or **L**abels command to redefine the name.

- To move the cell selector rapidly to the upper left corner of any block, press F5 (GoTo) and then enter the block name, or press F3 (Choices) to display a full-screen list of block names. After you enter the block name or select a name from the list, press Enter.

- Macro names are block names. Therefore, you must name macros by using /**E**dit **N**ames **C**reate, /**E**dit **N**ames **L**abel, or /**T**ools **M**acro **N**ame **C**reate.

- The results of formulas are unchanged if you delete one or more block names. The formula references the block's cell address rather than the block name.

- Moving one or more corners of a block name can redefine the block name. To check the addresses that a block name applies to after a corner has been moved, use /**E**dit **N**ames **C**reate and select the name in question, or press the plus sign (+) key to display the block address next to the block name in the list. The name's block appears on-screen. Press Ctrl-Break or Esc to return to READY mode.

- When two named blocks have the same upper left corner, moving one of the corners moves the address location for both block names. To move a corner of overlapping named blocks, delete one block name, move the block, and re-create the deleted block name in its original location.

Cautions

- A block name can be alphanumeric (for example, SALES91), but avoid creating a block name that looks like a cell reference (for example, AD20). Block names that look like cell references do not function correctly in formulas or macros.

- If you have multiple spreadsheets in memory, make sure that you are in the correct file before deleting block names. Because you can create and use the same block name in different spreadsheets, you may accidentally delete the wrong name.

- Always delete existing block names before re-creating them in a new location. If you don't delete an original block name, formulas that used the original name may be wrong.

- Do not delete columns or rows that form the corner of a named block. Doing so produces an ERR in formulas.

- /**Edit Names Make** Table does not update itself automatically. If you move, copy, or change block names, you must re-create the block name table.

- /**Edit Names Make** Table overwrites existing cell entries. Select the location for your block names table before initiating the command.

For more information, see /**Edit Move**.

Edit Search & Replace   /ES

Purpose

Finds or replaces text within a block. You can limit searches and replaces to labels or formulas.

Reminder

- Use the Ctrl-N and Ctrl-P shortcuts to search for the next and preceding strings, respectively.

Procedure

1. Type /*ES*.

2. Choose **B**lock and specify the block that you want to search.

3. Choose **S**earch String and enter the search string that you want to find—a label, value, or formula. Text may be upper- or lowercase.

EDIT COMMANDS

4. Choose **R**eplace **S**tring and enter the string you want to replace—a label, value, or formula. Text may be upper- or lowercase.

5. Choose **L**ook **I**n and select one of the following options, if necessary:

Option	Function
Formula	Searches for string in the formulas
Value	Searches for string in the values of formulas
Condition	Searches for string as a conditional statement, such as B2<50

6. Choose **D**irection to search by **R**ow or **C**olumn, forward or backward.

7. Choose **M**atch to search for **P**art of or the **W**hole word.

8. Choose **C**ase Sensitive to search for **A**ny Case or **E**xact Case.

9. Choose **O**ptions Reset to remove entries in any of the **S**earch & Replace **S**tring options, and return Search & Replace commands to default settings.

10. Choose **N**ext to search forward; Quattro Pro stops at the first match. Select **N**ext to resume the search.

    Choose **P**revious to search backward; Quattro Pro stops at the first match that it finds.

11. If you enter a **R**eplace String, Quattro Pro finds and displays the cell containing the specified text. Then, choose **Y**es, **N**o, **A**ll, **E**dit, or **Q**uit. **Y**es replaces the string, **N**o leaves string as is, **A**ll replaces all occurrences of the string, **E**dit enables you to edit the current string, and **Q**uit quits the search process.

Important Cues

- Use spaces and label prefixes to prevent locating unwanted text. A search for *and*, for example, locates *and* and *sandwich*. A search for *'and* locates *and* as the first entry in a left-aligned text cell, but not *sandwich*. A search for *<space>and<space>* locates the phrase *this and that* but not *sandwich*.

- When no more matching text is found, an error message appears at the bottom of the screen. Press Enter or Esc to return to the spreadsheet.

Caution

- Be careful replacing with **All**. You easily can replace text or formulas you did not want to replace. Save your spreadsheet or enable Undo. Then, press Alt-F5 before initiating **All**.

For more information, see /Edit Undo.

Edit Transpose /ET

Purpose

Reorders columns of data into rows or rows of data into columns.

Reminders

- Transpose to a clear area. The transposed data overwrites existing cell entries.
- If CALC appears on the status line, press F9 (Calc) to recalculate the spreadsheet.

Procedure

1. Move the cell selector to the upper left corner to the block of cells you want to transpose.
2. Type */ET*.
3. Specify the block to be transposed and then press Enter.
4. When Quattro Pro displays the DESTINATION prompt, move the cell selector to the upper left of the destination cells and press Enter.

Important Cue

- Transposing copies the cell format and protection status from the original cell.

Cautions

- Using the same upper left corner for the original and transposed data can result in incorrect data.

EDIT COMMANDS

- Transposing overwrites existing data. Make sure that you transpose to an unused area of the spreadsheet.
- Transposing blocks with formulas creates inaccurate values. Use /Edit Move to rearrange columns and rows that contain formulas. Alternatively, use /Edit Values to change formulas into values.

For more information, see */Edit Move* and */Edit Values*.

Edit Undo /EU

Purpose

Reverses certain Quattro Pro spreadsheet operations.

Reminders

- You must enable Undo before you can use it with the /Options Other Undo Enable command.
- You can use Alt-F5 as a shortcut for invoking the /Edit Undo command.
- Quattro Pro must be in READY mode to undo block and graph name deletions.

Procedure

Type */EU*.

Important Cues

- Quattro Pro can reverse changes to cell entries, block and graph name deletions, file retrievals, and erased spreadsheets.
- By using Undo, you can see the result of a change to your spreadsheet and then return the spreadsheet to its original status.
- Quattro Pro always affects the last spreadsheet operation that can be undone.

Cautions

- Quattro Pro does not reverse line drawing, fonts, shading, command settings, and format settings.
- Enabling Undo has an adverse effect on the speed of spreadsheet operations.
- Quattro Pro displays an error message if you invoke Undo without enabling Undo first.

For more information, see /Options Other Undo and /Tools Macro Transcript.

Edit Values /EV

Purpose

Converts formulas in a block to their values so that you can copy only the values to a new location.

Reminders

- Check to see that the destination area is large enough to hold the copied values. The copied values replace existing cell contents.
- If CALC appears on the status line, press F9 (Calc) to recalculate the spreadsheet.

Procedure

1. Move the cell selector to the upper left of the block that contains the formulas.
2. Type */EV*.
3. Specify the source block and press Enter.
4. Specify the upper left cell of the destination block and then press Enter.

Important Cues

- The destination block values contain the same numeric formats that you used in the original formulas.

EDIT COMMANDS

- /Edit Values also copies labels and string formulas, and converts string (text) formulas to labels.

Cautions

- /Edit Values overwrites data in the destination block. Be sure that the destination block is unused.

- If you specify the destination block the same as the source block, formulas in the block are converted to their values. These values, however, overwrite the formulas from which they originated. The formulas are replaced permanently.

For more information, see */Edit Copy*.

Style Commands /S

The /Style commands align labels and values; format values; protect blocks; set the width and height of columns or rows, respectively; hide or expose columns; draw solid lines; apply shading and fonts to the spreadsheet; and insert page breaks into the spreadsheet.

Style Alignment /SA

Purpose

Enables you to select how you want to align labels and values.

Reminder

- You can use the Ctrl-A shortcut to invoke the /Style Alignment command.

Procedure

1. Move the cell selector to the first cell in the block that you want to align.
2. Type */SA*.
3. Select an available option as follows:

Option	Function
General	Aligns entries left and values and dates right
Left	Aligns entries with the left edge of a cell
Right	Aligns entries with the right edge of a cell
Center	Centers entries in the cell

4. Specify the block by entering the block address, highlighting the block, or using an assigned block name. Press Enter.

Important Cues

- The label prefix appears on the input line.

STYLE COMMANDS

- To align labels in a cell manually, enter one of the following label prefixes before typing the label:

Label	Name	Alignment/Function
'	Apostrophe	Left
"	Quotation mark	Right
^	Caret	Center
\	Backslash	Repeats character to fill a cell (cannot be selected from menu)

- The default alignment for new spreadsheets is left. Use /**O**ptions Formats Align Labels to set the label prefix used by text entries in areas not specified with /**S**tyle **A**lignment.

- Labels beginning with numbers or formula symbols require label prefixes. Enter the label prefix before entering the numbers or symbols. This process is necessary for such items as addresses, part numbers, Social Security numbers, and telephone numbers.

Caution

- Numbers or formulas preceded by label prefixes have a value of zero when evaluated by a numeric formula. In a database query, you must use text searches for these numbers that have label prefixes.

For more information, see **/Options Formats Align Labels** *and* **/Style Line Drawing**.

Style Block Size   /SB

Purpose

Adjusts the column width of a block of columns and inserts extra space between columns.

Procedure

1. Move the cell selector to the widest entry in the column.
2. Type */SB*.
3. Select an available option as follows:

Option	Function
Set Width	Sets the width of all columns in a specified block
Reset Width	Restores all columns in a specified block to the current default width
Auto Width	Inserts extra space between columns

4. If you choose **S**et Width, indicate the columns that you want to change and enter a number between 1 and 254. (Alternatively, press the left- or right-arrow key to shrink or expand the columns.) Press Enter.

   If you choose **R**eset Width, specify the columns that you want to change and then press Enter.

   If you choose Auto Width, enter a number between 0 and 40 to specify the amount of extra space between columns. Specify the block of columns that you want to change and press Enter.

Important Cue

- Column width settings from /Style **B**lock Size override settings from /Options Formats **G**lobal Width.

For more information, see /Options Formats Global Width, /Style Block Size Height, and /Style Column Width/Reset Width.

Style Block Size Height /SBH

Purpose

Enables you to adjust the height of one or more rows to display the entire font in that row in Screen Preview or WYSIWYG mode.

STYLE COMMANDS

Procedure

1. Move the cell selector to the largest font in the row.
2. Type */SB*.
3. Choose **S**et Row Height to set the height of all rows in a specified block. Select **R**eset Row Height to restore to the current default height all rows in a specified block.
4. If you choose **S**et Row Height, indicate the rows you want to change, enter a number between 1 and 254 or press the up- or down-arrow key to shrink or expand the rows. Press Enter.

   If you choose **R**eset Width, specify the rows you want to change and then press Enter.

Important Cue

- In Quattro Pro Version 4.0, row height is determined in each row individually by the point size of the largest font or the point size of Font 1—whichever is largest. In Version 2.0, however, row height is determined by the point size of the first font for the entire spreadsheet.

  If you read files in Version 4.0 that were created in Version 2.0, you may get a double-space effect. To eliminate this effect, you manually can override row height by using **/S**tyle **B**lock Size **H**eight **S**et Row Height, highlighting the entire block of rows, and then reducing row height. (See item 18 in the Quattro Pro README file for more information.)

*For more information, see */Style Block Size*.*

Style Column Width
/Reset Width /SC, /SR

Purpose

Adjusts columns wider than nine characters to display large numbers, display dates, and prevent text from being covered by adjacent cell entries. Also can be used to adjust columns narrower than nine characters.

Reminder

- You can use the Ctrl-W shortcut to invoke the /Style Column Width command.

Procedure

1. Move the cell selector to the widest entry in the column.
2. Type /SC.
3. Enter the new column width by typing the number of characters (1 to 254) or by pressing left- or right-arrow key to shrink or expand the column.
4. Press Enter.

Important Cues

- To change the column width to the default width, type /SR to select Style Reset Width.
- Asterisks appear in a cell whose column is too narrow to display numeric or date entries.
- Text or numeric entries in the cell to the right may partially cover text entries wider than the cell.
- Column width settings from /Style Column Width override settings from /Options Formats Global Width.

For more information, see /Options Formats Global Width and /Style Block Size.

Style Define Style /SD

Purpose

Enables you to create, edit, erase, and remove a custom style for a spreadsheet, and enables you to save and retrieve files of custom styles.

Reminder

- You can create a custom style by assigning a name to attributes you have previously applied to a cell block. You also can create a custom style by naming the style, and then building that custom style using the menu of style attributes.

STYLE COMMANDS

Procedure

1. Move the cell selector in the first cell of the block to which you want to apply a font.
2. Type **/SD**.
3. Select one of the available options as follows:

Option	Function
Create	Creates a new style or edits an existing one
Erase	Clears the custom style from the block but leaves the style attributes in the block, except font and data entry attributes
Remove	Deletes the custom style from the spreadsheet; all blocks in the spreadsheet that you assigned the custom style retain their attributes, except font and data entry attributes
File	Enables you to save and retrieve files of custom styles (select **S**ave or **R**etrieve)

4. If you choose **Create**, type a name for the style and press Enter. If you are creating a style for attributes that you have already assigned to a cell block, double-check your choices on the displayed menu, and then choose **Q**uit. If you haven't set your attributes, do so now, and then choose **Q**uit.

    If you choose **Erase**, highlight the custom style you want to erase and press Enter. Specify the block from which you want to clear the custom style.

    If you choose **Remove**, highlight the custom style you want to erase and press Enter. If the custom style is used anywhere else in the spreadsheet, Quattro Pro asks you to confirm its deletion. Choose **Y**es.

    If you choose **File** and then **Save**, type a name for the file to which you want Quattro Pro to save all the custom styles in your spreadsheet, and then press Enter. Quattro Pro appends a STY extension to files containing custom styles. If you choose **File** and then **Retrieve**, highlight the file name you want to retrieve and press Enter.

Important Cues

- One spreadsheet can hold up to 120 custom styles.
- After you retrieve a style file while in an active spreadsheet, Quattro Pro adds the custom styles to it. You do not have to retrieve the style file again when you reopen the spreadsheet.

For more information, see */Style Use Style*.

Style Define Style Create Numeric Format   /SDC, N

Purpose

Enables you to create your own numeric formats to customize the display of numbers, dates, and times.

Reminders

- To define custom formats, use the special codes defined in Chapter 5, "Manipulating Data."
- Apply custom numeric format styles with the */Style Use Style* command.

Procedure

1. Move the cell selector in the first cell of the block to which you want to apply a custom style.
2. Type */SDC*.
3. Type a name for the style (up to 15 character) and press Enter.
4. Select **N**umeric Format, and then select **U**ser Defined.
5. Enter the format code for your custom numeric format using the codes described in Chapter 5 and then press Enter. Use the attributes menu to customize any other aspects of your custom style.
6. Choose **Q**uit.

For more information, see */Style Define Style* and */Style Use Style*.

Style Font /SF

Purpose

Applies font attributes directly to spreadsheet fonts.

Reminder

- You can display fonts on-screen only in Screen Preview or WYSIWYG mode.

Procedure

To assign a font to a block, follow these steps:

1. Move the cell selector in the first cell of the block to which you want to apply a font.
2. Type */SF*.
3. Specify the cell or block of cells where you want to apply the font.
4. Select one or more of the available options as follows:

Option	Function
Typeface	Changes the typeface for the font
Point Size	Changes the font size
Color	Changes the color of the font
Bold	Boldfaces the font
Italic	Italicizes the font
Underlined	Underlines the font
Reset	Restores the font to the default style
Quit	Returns to the spreadsheet

5. Select **Quit**.

Important Cues

- Quattro Pro requires 125K of free memory to create a new Bitstream font file.

- To create a bullet character, position the cell selector where you want to add a bullet, type *'\bullet #*, in which *bullet #* is one of the bullet options. Press 0 for a box, 1 for a filled box, 2 for a checked box, 3 for a check, 4 for a shadowed box, 5 for a shadowed checked box, or 6 for a filled circle.

- The Version 3.0 /Style Font command is retained for compatibility in Version 4.0 as the /Style FontTable command.

For more information, see /Style FontTable, /Style Line Drawing, and /Style Shading.

Style FontTable /ST

Purpose

Applies one of eight fonts to a single cell or block of cells. Specifies the typeface, style, color, and point size for fonts.

Reminder

- You can display fonts only in Screen Preview or WYSIWYG mode.

Procedures

To change an existing font, do the following:

1. Move the cell selector in the first cell of the block to which you want to apply a font.
2. Type */ST*.
3. Select the font that you want to apply.
4. Specify the cell or block of cells where you want to apply the font.
5. Press Enter.

To edit an existing font, do the following:

1. Type */ST*.
2. Choose **E**dit Fonts.
3. Select the font slot that you want to change.

STYLE COMMANDS

4. Choose an available menu option as follows:

Option	Function
Typeface	Changes the typeface for the font
Point Size	Changes the font size
Style	Changes font style (select **B**old, **I**talic, **U**nderlined, or **R**eset; **R**eset restores the font to the default style)
Color	Changes the color of the font
Quit	Returns you to the **F**ont menu

5. Use **/S**tyle **F**ont **U**pdate to save the changes or **/S**tyle **F**ont **R**eset to restore the original default fonts.

Important Cues

- Quattro Pro requires 125K of free memory to create a new Bitstream font file.

- To create a bullet character, position the cell selector where you want to add a bullet, type '\bullet #\, in which *bullet #* is one of the bullet options. Press 0 for a box, 1 for a filled box, 2 for a checked box, 3 for a check, 4 for a shadowed box, 5 for a shadowed checked box, or 6 for a filled circle.

- To apply font attributes directly to a cell or block of cells, see **/S**tyle **F**ont.

For more information, see **/S**tyle **F**ont, **/S**tyle **L**ine **D**rawing, *and* **/S**tyle **S**hading.

Style Hide Column   /SH

Purpose

Hides an individual column or block of columns and exposes an individual hidden column or block of hidden columns.

Reminder

- Hidden columns appear temporarily in copy and move operations.

Procedure

1. Type */SH*.
2. Choose **Hide** to hide the column. Select **Expose** to unhide the column. Hidden columns have an asterisk (*) beside the column letter.
3. If you choose **Hide**, specify the column by pressing the left- or right-arrow key and then pressing Enter. To hide a block of adjacent columns, specify the block by typing the block address, entering a block name, or pressing the period key (.) to anchor the block. Then, move the cell selector to the opposite corner of the block.

   If you choose **Expose**, move the cell selector to the column that you want to expose and then press Enter. If you want to expose a block of columns, specify the block. After you press Enter, the specified columns display.

Caution

- When cells are hidden on an unprotected spreadsheet, blocks copied or moved to the hidden area overwrite existing data.

Style Insert Break /SI

Purpose

Inserts page breaks into spreadsheet printouts.

Reminders

- Quattro Pro automatically adjusts formulas after /Style Insert Break inserts a new row in the spreadsheet.
- You can insert a page break manually into your spreadsheet by typing pipe and a double colon (|::) in column A of the specified row.

Procedure

1. Move the cell selector in the leftmost column of the block and one row below where you want the page break.
2. Type */SI*.

Important Cue

- Use **/Edit Delete Rows** to delete the row containing the page break, or use **/Edit Erase Block (Ctrl-E)** to erase the page-break character (|::).

Caution

- Do not make entries in the row containing the page-break character (|::). Entries in this row do not print.

*For more information, see **/Edit Delete Rows** and **/Edit Erase Block**.*

Style Line Drawing /SL

Purpose

Adds horizontal and vertical lines to the spreadsheet.

Reminder

- You can use lines drawn with **/Style Line Drawing** as separator lines in your spreadsheets in text or WYSIWYG mode.

Procedure

1. Type */SL*.
2. Specify the cell or block around which you want to draw lines and press Enter.
3. Select one of the following menu items:

Option	Function
All	Draws lines between each cell of a block
Outside	Draws a line around a block of cells without creating a box around each cell
Top	Draws a line at the top of the block
Bottom	Draws a line at the bottom of the block
Left	Draws a line at the left side of the block

continues

Option	Function
Right	Draws a line at the right side of the block
Inside	Draws a line to enclose an entire block in a grid, with each cell in its own box
Horizontal	Draws lines horizontally within a block
Vertical	Draws lines vertically within a block

4. Choose an available option: **None** removes lines, **Single** draws a single line, **Double** draws a double line, and **Thick** draws a thick line.

5. Choose **Q**uit once to exit the **L**ine Drawing menu.

Important Cues

- You can change the display color of drawn lines with the /**O**ptions **C**olors **S**preadsheet **D**rawn Lines command.

- To print drawn lines solidly, use the /**P**rint **D**estination **G**raphics **P**rinter command.

- Specify an additional row and column in your print block if the block to be printed is outlined by drawn lines.

For more information, see /Style Shading, /Options Colors Spreadsheet Drawn Lines, and /Print Destination Graphics Printer.

Style Numeric Format /SN

Purpose

Enables cells containing values (numbers) and formula results to display a specific numeric format.

Reminders

- Use /**O**ptions **F**ormats **N**umeric Format to format most of the spreadsheet's cells that will contain numeric data. Use /**S**tyle **N**umeric Format **R**eset to reset formats for areas that will not contain numeric data.

STYLE COMMANDS

■ You can use the Ctrl-F shortcut to invoke the /Style Numeric Format command.

Procedure

1. Move the cell selector to the leftmost cell in the block you want to format.
2. Type */SN*.
3. Select a format from the following menu items:

Option	Function
Fixed	Sets the number of decimal places that display
Scientific	Displays large or small numbers, using scientific notation
Currency	Displays currency symbols ($, for example) and commas
, (comma)	Inserts commas to mark thousands and multiples of thousands
General	Displays values with no special formatting
+/–	Creates horizontal bar graphs, in which each symbol is equal to one whole number; positive numbers are displayed as plus (+) signs, whereas negative numbers are displayed as minus (–) signs
Percent	Displays a decimal number as a whole percentage number with a % sign
Date	Displays serial-date numbers in the following formats; select the corresponding number for each format: **1**: DD-MMM-YY (12-Jan-91) **2**: DD-MMM (12-Jan) **3**: MMM-YY (Jan-91) **4**: MM/DD/YY (01/12/91) **5**: MM/DD (01/12)
Time	Displays time fractions in the following formats: **1**: HH:MM:SS AM/PM (10:30:05 AM) **2**: HH:MM AM/PM (10:30 AM) **3**: Long intl. (10.30.05) **4**: Short intl. (10.30)

continues

Option	Function
Text	Continues to evaluate formulas as numbers, but displays formulas as text
Hidden	Hides contents from the display and does not print them; still evaluates contents
Reset	Returns numeric format to the default format

4. If Quattro Pro prompts you, enter the number of decimal places to display. A cell's full value is used for calculation, not for the displayed value.

5. Specify the block by entering the block address, highlighting the block, or using an assigned block name. Press Enter.

Important Cues

- Use /Style Protection Protect and /Options Protection Enable to protect cell contents hidden with /Style Numeric Format Hidden from being accidentally overwritten.

- /Style Numeric Format Hidden is the only format that affects labels. All other /Style Numeric Format commands operate on values and formula results.

- Dates and times entered with the @DATE and @TIME functions must be formatted with one of the Date and Time formats to display as a date and time, respectively.

- If you use a format other than General, asterisks fill the cell when a value is too large to fit the cell's current column width. (In General format, values that are too large are displayed in scientific notation.)

- Use /Options International to display non-USA formats.

- Block formats take precedence over /Options Formats formats.

Cautions

- /Style Numeric Format rounds only the appearance of the displayed number, not the underlying number used for calculation. This difference can cause displayed or printed numbers to be incorrect. In some spreadsheets, such as mortgage amortization tables, results may be significantly different than expected. Enclose numbers, formulas, or cell references using the @ROUND function to ensure that the values in calculation are truly rounded.

STYLE COMMANDS

- Preformatting large blocks of the spreadsheet uses a substantial amount of memory. Format cells containing only numeric data.

For more information, see ***/Options International***, ***/Style Alignment***, ***/Style Hide Column***, *and* ***/Style Protection***.

Style Protection /SP

Purpose

Changes the protection status of a block.

Procedure

1. Move the cell selector to the upper left corner of the block you want protected or unprotected.
2. Type */SP*.
3. Enter *U* to unprotect data. Enter *P* to protect data.
4. Specify the block by entering the block address, highlighting the block, or using an assigned block name. Press Enter.

Important Cues

- /**S**tyle **P**rotection **P**rotect and **U**nprotect affect data entry only when /**O**ption **P**rotection **E**nable is selected.
- Use /**D**atabase **R**estrict Input to limit cell selector movement to unprotected cells.
- Unprotected cells display U on the input line; protected cells display PR.

Caution

- Macros that make changes to cell contents do not work correctly if /**O**ptions **P**rotection **E**nable is selected and the macro tries to change protected cells. Prevent this situation by limiting cell selector movement to unprotected cells or by disabling spreadsheet protection when the macro starts. Macros should re-enable spreadsheet protection before they end.

For more information, see ***/Database Restrict Input*** *and* ***/Options Protection***.

Style Shading /SS

Purpose

Adds a gray or black shade to a specified block.

Reminders

- Shading displays best in Screen Preview or WYSIWYG mode.
- The intensity of gray shading can only be set on laser printers; you set the intensity by selecting **/O H P F C S**.

Procedure

1. Move the cell selector to the first cell of the block that you want to shade.
2. Type */SS*.
3. Choose a format: **N**one removes shade, **G**ray adds gray shade, and **B**lack adds black shade.
4. Specify the block that you want to shade by entering the block address, highlighting the block, or using an assigned block name.
5. Press Enter.

Caution

- Shaded cells print only when you use the **/P**rint Destination **G**raphics Printer command.

For more information, see /Style Line Drawing and /Print Destination Graphics Printer.

Style Use Style /SU

Purpose

Applies a custom style to a specified block.

Procedure

1. Move the cell selector to the first cell of the block that you want to set a custom style.
2. Type */SU*.
3. Choose the custom style from the displayed list.
4. Specify a cell or block of cells you want to apply the style to.

Important Cues

- When the cell selector is inside a block that has a custom style assigned to it, the style name appears in the input line.
- You also can reach the list of custom styles by clicking the Style button on the SpeedBar.

Caution

- When you apply a custom style, Quattro Pro overwrites any existing formatting in the cell block. Line drawing is not overwritten, however, because it is not part of custom styles.

*For more information, see */Style Define Style*.

Graph Commands /G

/Graph commands enable you to create and enhance the appearance of graphs from spreadsheet data.

Graph Annotate /GA

Purpose

Enables you to customize your graph with different shapes, text, color, patterns, size, and style.

Procedure

1. Type */GA*.
2. Select one of the following keys in the Graph Annotator:

Key	Function
F1	Accesses the on-line Help facility
F2	Activates Edit mode when you select a text element
F3	Activates the Property Sheet
F7	Enters Proportional Resize mode when you select a group of elements; adjusts the size of the elements and the space between them
Shift-F7	Retains the current element selection so that you can select additional elements
F10	Redraws the Annotator screen
Tab	Selects the next element in the Draw Area
Shift-Tab	Selects the previous element in the Draw Area
Shift	Selects multiple elements, if you have a mouse; press and hold the Shift key while clicking elements in the Draw Area
Del	Deletes a selected element or group of elements; if you have a mouse, click the element with the mouse and press Del to delete one element

GRAPH COMMANDS

Key	Function
. (period)	Anchors the selected area and resizes elements
Home, End PgUp, PgDn	Moves the corners of a selected area diagonally
Arrow keys	Moves or resizes selected elements
Ctrl-Enter	Starts a new line in Text or Edit mode
Backspace	Deletes the characters to the left of the cursor in Edit mode
/ (slash)	Activates the Toolbox
Esc	Cancels the current operation in the Draw area; in a menu, exits the menu; accesses the Draw area
Enter	Accepts and ends a Draw Area operation such as moving an element
Alt	Selects a group of elements in Proportional Resizing mode, if you have a mouse; press and hold the Alt key while pressing the left mouse button, drag to enclose a group of elements in a selection box, and then release the mouse button

For more information, see */Graph Annotate Clipboard*, */Graph Annotate Property Sheet*, and */Graph Annotate Toolbox*.

Graph Annotate Clipboard /GA/C

Purpose

Enables you to cut and paste annotation elements.

Procedure

1. Type */GA*.
2. Type */C* to display the Clipboard commands in the Property Sheet.
3. Select one of the following options:

Option	Function
Cut	Moves elements from the Draw area into temporary memory
Copy	Copies elements from the Draw area into temporary memory
Paste	Pastes elements into the Draw Area from temporary memory
Delete	Deletes selected elements from Draw area
To Top	Moves selected elements before any other elements
To Bottom	Moves selected elements behind any other elements
Cut To	Removes selected elements from the Draw area and stores them in a Clipboard file
Copy To	Copies selected elements from the Draw area and stores them in the specified Clipboard file
Paste From	Inserts elements that are stored as clip art in the specified Clipboard file into the current graph

4. If you select **Cut** or **Copy**, save the current graph with /**G**raph **N**ame **C**reate. Use /**G**raph **N**ame **D**isplay to load the graph in which you want to insert the element, or use /**F**ile **R**etrieve to load a different spreadsheet.

5. To insert the elements, type /*GA*, type /*C*, and choose **P**aste to insert the elements.

6. To store elements in a Clipboard file, select the elements and then select **C**ut **T**o or **C**opy **T**o. Enter the name for the Clipboard file and press Enter.

7. To paste elements stored in a Clipboard file into the current graph, select **P**aste From, enter the name of the Clipboard file, and press Enter.

For more information, see /**Graph Annotate** *and* /**Graph Annotate Property Sheet**.

GRAPH COMMANDS

Graph Annotate Property Sheet /GA

Purpose

Enables you to set design properties for each element.

Reminder

- Select an element or a group of elements before you use the Property Sheet commands.

Procedure

1. Type */GA*.
2. Press F3 to access the Property Sheet.
3. Use the up- and down-arrow keys to select a property and press Enter.
4. Use the up- and down-arrow keys to select the attribute and press Enter.
5. Press Esc to return to the Draw area.

Important Cue

- Group properties affect selected elements except graph titles, legends, and the graph itself.

For more information, see */Graph Annotate*, */Graph Annotate Clipboard*, and */Graph Annotate Toolbox*.

Graph Annotate Toolbox /GA/

Purpose

Enables you to add lines, boxes, rectangles, circles, polygons, polylines, text, and symbols to graphs.

Procedure

1. Type */GA*.
2. Press / to access the Toolbox.
3. Choose an available option as follows:

Option	Function
Pointer	Activates Edit mode (white arrow)
Clipboard	Displays Clipboard commands
Boxed Text	Adds text to graphs
Arrow	Draws a line with an arrowhead at the end
Line	Draws a straight line anywhere in the Draw Area
Y-Polyline	Draws a jointed line that is anchored in more than two places
F-Polygon	Draws a multisided shape
Rectangle	Draws a rectangle
Z-Round Rectangle	Draws a rectangle with rounded corners
Ellipse	Draws an elongated circle
Vertical/**H**orizontal	Draws a vertical or horizontal line Line
X-Link Icon	Connects one or more elements to a particular point in the graph
F1 (Help)	Accesses Quattro Pro's on-line help facility
Quit	Exits Graph Annotator and returns to zoomed graph or to the Graph menu

4. To link an element to a graph point, select the elements that you want to link, select **X**-Link, and then select the graph series that contains the value to which you want to link. Specify the value position.

*For more information, see /**Graph Annotate**, /**Graph Annotate Clipboard**, and /**Graph Annotate Property Sheet**.*

Graph Customize Series Bar Width /GCB

Purpose

Adjusts the percentage of space that Quattro Pro uses to calculate bar width.

Procedure

1. Type */GCB*.
2. Type a number between 20 and 90.
3. Press Enter.

Important Cue

- The Quattro Pro default is 60% space for bars and 40% space for blank space in the allotted axes area.

For more information, see **/Graph Graph Type Bar**, **/Graph Graph Type Stacked Bar**, *and* **/Graph Graph Type Rotated Bar**.

Graph Customize Series Bubbles /GCL

Purpose

Changes the color and fill patterns for each bubble in a bubble graph. Set the size of the bubbles by determining the radius of the largest bubble as a percentage of the X-axis. Other bubbles are sized relatively.

Procedure

1. Type */GCL*.
2. Choose one of the following options:

Option	Function
Patterns	Specifies the fill patterns for each bubble
Colors	Specifies the color for each bubble
Max Bubble Size	Sets the radius of the largest bubble as a percentage of the X-Axis (1-25%)
Quit	Returns to Customize Series menu

3. If you choose **Patterns**, choose the bubble for which you want to change the pattern (**1** through **9**) and choose the pattern with which you want to fill the bubble. Repeat this step to change the patterns of other bubbles.

    If you choose **Colors**, choose the bubble for which you want to change the color (**1** through **9**) and choose the color that you want to assign to the bubble. Repeat this step to change the colors of other bubbles.

    If you choose **Max Bubble Size**, enter a number between 1 and 25 to determine the size of the largest bubble. If you enter 10, the default, the largest bubble will be 10% of the x-axis.

4. Choose **Q**uit to return to the **/G**raph **C**ustomize Series menu.

Important Cues

- To make the new **P**atterns, **C**olors, or **M**ax Bubble Size the default Quattro Pro settings, use the **/G**raph **C**ustomize Series **U**pdate command.

- To return **P**atterns, **C**olors, or **M**ax Bubble Size to the default Quattro Pro settings, use the **/G**raph **C**ustomize Series **R**eset command.

- As with XY graphs, the x-axis must display numeric data, not labels or text.

Caution

- Remember to enter an additional data series to set the relative areas of the bubbles. Otherwise, Quattro Pro does not display them when you press F10 to view the graph.

*For more information, see **/Graph Graph Type Bubbles**, **/Graph Graph Type XY**, **/Graph Customize Series Update**, and **/Graph Customize Series Reset**.*

Graph Customize Series Colors   /GCC

Purpose

Selects the colors used by data series 1 through 6; also can hide a data series.

Reminders

- /Graph Customize Series Colors affects the displayed and printed graph.

- You do not have to use Customize Series Colors to create color graphs. Quattro Pro defaults to the following colors for the respective data series:

Data Series	Color
1	Red
2	Light Cyan
3	Blue
4	Yellow
5	Cyan
6	Magenta

Procedure

1. Type /GCC.
2. Specify the data series for which you want to change the color; you can select 1 through 6.
3. Choose a color from the list.

Important Cues

- The first color in a color series defines the color of the legend.

- Use /Graph Text Font to set text colors in a graph.
- Use /Graph Customize Series Update to make the new colors the default.

For more information, see /Graph Text Font and /Graph Customize Series Update.

Graph Customize Series Fill Patterns /GCF

Purpose

Changes the hatching (shading) for each data series in a bar graph.

Reminders

- /Graph Customize Series Fill Patterns affects the displayed and printed graph.
- Quattro Pro default fill patterns for the respective data series are as follows:

Data Series	Choice	Fill Pattern
1	G	Hvy \\\
2	B	Filled
3	F	Lt \\\
4	H	++++++
5	D	Lt ///
6	I	Crosshatch

Procedure

1. Type */GCF*.
2. Specify the series for which you want to change the fill pattern; you can choose series 1 through 6.
3. Choose the fill pattern.

Important Cues

- Use **/G**raph **C**ustomize Series **P**ies **P**atterns to change the patterns for slices in a pie graph.

- Use **/G**raph **C**ustomize Series **U**pdate to make the new colors the default.

- If you select a PostScript printer in Normal mode, you will not see patterns in screen preview or on the printout. To correct this problem, choose **/O**ptions **H**ardware **P**rinters **1**st Printer **T**ype of Printer and then select Use Patterns mode. If you want gray scale patterns, use Normal mode.

For more information, see **/Graph Customize Series Update** *and* **/Graph Customize Series Pies Patterns**.

Graph Customize Series Interior Labels   /GCI

Purpose

Labels graph points from data contained in cells.

Reminder

- Enter labels in an order corresponding to the order of the data-entry points they describe.

Procedure

1. Type */GCI*.

2. Choose the data series to which you want to assign labels. You can choose series 1 through 6.

3. Specify the block that contains the labels. This block should be the same size as the block that you selected when you defined series 1 through 6.

4. Choose the data label location that is relative to the corresponding data points, as follows:

Option	Function
Center	Centers a label on a data point
Left	Aligns a label left of a data point
Above	Aligns a label above a data point
Right	Aligns a label right of a data point
Below	Aligns a label below a data point
None	Removes labels from display

5. Choose **Quit** or return to step 2 to enter more data labels.

Important Cues

- Interior labels can be formulas, values, or labels.

- Interior labels always appear above the tops of the bars in bar graphs. Interior labels always appear to the right in rotated bar graphs. Interior labels appear for only the top data series in a stacked-bar graph.

- Interior labels do not appear on area, pie, or column graphs.

For more information, see **/Graph Text** and **/Graph X-Axis Scale**.

Graph Customize Series Markers & Lines   /GCM

Purpose

Selects the marker symbols and lines that identify and connect data points.

Reminders

- Time-related data usually is best represented by a continuous series of related data. Trends and slopes are more obvious when they are represented with lines rather than a cluster of data points.

- Quattro Pro default marker symbols for the respective data series are as follows:

GRAPH COMMANDS

Data Series	Symbol
1	Filled Square
2	Plus
3	Asterisk
4	Empty Square
5	X
6	Filled Triangle

Procedure

1. Type */GCM*.
2. Choose one of the following options:

Option	Function
Line Styles	Selects the line style on line and XY graphs
Markers	Selects the marker symbols for each data series
Formats	Selects how lines and markers display in a line or XY graph

3. Choose the series for which you want to specify a different line style, marker symbol, or format.
4. Choose an option from the **Formats** menu as follows:

Option	Function
Lines	Removes data point markers and connects data points with a line
Symbols	Encloses each data point in a marker symbol (different blocks have different symbols); used commonly with XY graphs
Both	Connects data points with a line and marks the data point
Neither	Selects neither lines nor marker symbols
Quit	Returns to **Customize Series** menu

Important Cue

■ Use the **/Graph Customize Series Colors** command to set the colors for lines in a set of data.

Caution

■ If your XY or line graphs are a confusing jumble of crossed lines, you must sort the data in x-axis order by arranging each x,y data pair in ascending or descending x-axis order within the spreadsheet block. Be sure to sort the y-axis data with the corresponding x-axis data.

For more information, see **/Graph Text**, **/Graph Customize Series Fill Patterns**, and **/Tools Advanced Math Regression**.

Graph Customize Series Override Type   /GCO

Purpose

Combines bars and lines in a graph. Relates trends in two distinct measurable quantities. Combined graphs can have up to three bars and three lines.

Reminder

■ Combined line and bar graphs are most effective when the data to be graphed represents more than one type of information and one data type is greater than the other.

Procedure

1. Type **/GG**.
2. Choose **B**ar or **L**ine.
3. Choose **C**ustomize Series **O**verride Type.
4. Choose the series that you want to assign to an overriding graph type.
5. Choose one of the following override types:

Option	Function
Default	Resets series to original graph type
Bar	Plots the series with a bar, if the overall graph type is line
Line	Plots the series with a line, if the overall graph type is bar

6. Repeat steps 4 and 5 to assign overriding graph types to other series.

Important Cues

- Display the data series with the lowest values as bars. In this manner, the bars don't cross over the lines, and your graph is easier to understand.

- If the scales for items vary significantly, you can add a second y-axis (2Y-Axis) with a different scale.

For more information, see */Graph Graph Type Bar*, */Graph Graph Type Line*, */Graph Y-Axis* and *Y-Axis*.

Graph Customize Series Pies   /GCP

Purpose

Changes the label format, fill patterns, and colors for each data series in a pie or column chart. Explodes slices of the pie. Removes tick marks from a pie or column chart.

Procedure

1. Type */GCP*.
2. Choose one of the following options:

Option	Function
Label Format	Changes the label format for the slices of the pie or column chart; **value** displays cell entries exactly as they appear in the spreadsheet, **%** displays the percentage of each value in relation to the whole pie or column, **$** displays spreadsheet values preceded by a dollar sign, and **None** removes all labels from the chart
Explode	Pulls out one or more slices of the pie
Patterns	Specifies the fill patterns for pie or column slices
Colors	Specifies the colors for pie or column slices
Tick Marks	Removes tick marks from a pie or column chart
Quit	Returns to **C**ustomize Series menu

3. If you choose **E**xplode, choose the number of the pie slice that you want to explode (**1** through **9**). The first slice (**1**) begins at 12:00 (straight up) and continues clockwise. Select **E**xplode to pull the slice away from the pie. Repeat this step to explode other pie slices. Use /**G**raph **C**ustomize Series **P**ies **E**xplode, choose the slice number, and choose **D**on't **E**xplode to return the slice to the pie.

   If you choose **P**atterns, choose the slice for which you want to change the pattern (**1** through **9**) and choose the pattern with which you want to fill the slice. Repeat this step to change the patterns of other slices.

   If you choose **C**olors, choose the slice for which you want to change the color (**1** through **9**) and choose the color that you want to assign to the slice. Repeat this step to change the colors of other slices.

   If you choose **T**ick Marks, choose **N**o to remove the lines connecting labels to slices. Choose **Y**es to return the tick marks to the chart.

Important Cues

- To make the new **P**atterns, **C**olors, or **T**ick Marks the default Quattro Pro settings, use the /**G**raph **C**ustomize Series **U**pdate command.

GRAPH COMMANDS

- To return **P**atterns, **C**olors, or **T**ick Marks to the default Quattro Pro settings, use the **/G**raph **C**ustomize **S**eries **R**eset command.

Caution

- Quattro Pro requires only the **1**st Series for data to create Pie and Column graphs. Specifying a **2**nd Series may affect the display of patterns and colors adversely, or unintentionally explode slices.

*For more information, see /**G**raph **G**raph **T**ype **P**ie, /**G**raph **G**raph **T**ype **C**olumn, /**G**raph **C**ustomize **S**eries **U**pdate, and /**G**raph **C**ustomize **S**eries **R**eset.*

Graph Customize Series Reset   /GCR

Purpose

Cancels all or some of a graph's settings so that you can create a new graph or exclude one or more data series from the old graph.

Procedure

1. Type */GCR*.
2. Choose one of the following options:

Option	Function
1-6	Resets a designated block and corresponding labels so that they are not displayed in the new graph
X-Axis	Resets the X block and removes the labels (except from XY graphs)
Graph	Resets all graph parameters, but does not alter a graph named with **/G**raph **N**ame **C**reate
Quit	Returns to the **C**ustomize **S**eries menu

Important Cues

- Use /**G**raph **C**ustomize **S**eries **R**eset **G**raph to remove the current graph and start over with Quattro Pro's default graph settings or a named graph.
- Use /**G**raph **G**raph **T**ype to change the type of graph.

For more information, see /**Graph Graph Type**, /**Graph Name Create**, *and* /**File Open**.

Graph Customize Series Update /GCU

Purpose

Saves current graph settings as the new defaults.

Procedure

Type /*GCU*.

Important Cue

- /**G**raph **C**ustomize **S**eries **U**pdate saves the background color, outline options, colors, and fill patterns as default graph settings. You can save these elements for data series 1 through 6 and pie or column chart slices 1 through 9, axis scaling options, markers and lines format, bar width, interior labels, override graph type, and three-dimensional graphs.

Caution

- /**G**raph **C**ustomize **S**eries **U**pdate makes the current graph settings the permanent default settings. The only way to return to the original default Quattro Pro graph settings is to make a note of each, change each one manually, and reissue /**G**raph **C**ustomize **S**eries **U**pdate, or reinstall Quattro Pro.

For more information, see /**Graph Customize Series Reset**.

GRAPH COMMANDS

Graph Customize Series Y-Axis /GCY

Purpose

Assigns a series to a second y-scale on the right side of the graph.

Procedure

1. Type */GCY*.
2. Choose the series that you want to plot on a second y-axis.
3. Choose **S**econdary Y-Axis to create a separate y-axis to the right of the graph.
4. Repeat steps 2 and 3 to plot other series on the second y-axis.

Important Cues

- Graphs with a second y-axis are appropriate when you want to display two or more sets of related data and a large difference exists between each data series' corresponding value.
- Line, bar, and XY graphs are the appropriate graph types for a second y-axis.

For more information, see /Graph Y-Axis 2nd Y-Axis, /Graph Graph Type Line, /Graph Graph Type Bar, /Graph Graph Type XY, and /Graph Customize Series Override Type.

Graph Fast Graph /GF

Purpose

Creates a graph instantly.

Reminder

- You can use the Ctrl-G shortcut to invoke the /**G**raph **F**ast Graph command.

Procedure

1. Type */GF*.
2. Specify the block of data to graph, including headings for the columns or rows of values.
3. After Quattro Pro displays the graph, press any key to return to the spreadsheet.

Important Cues

- **Fast Graph** creates a basic stacked-bar graph using Quattro Pro default graph settings. Enhance your graph with titles, colors, the Graph Annotator, and so on.
- You can preselect the block of data to be plotted with **Fast Graph** by pressing Shift-F7 and highlighting the block.

Caution

- Do not include any blank rows or columns in the block to be plotted with **Fast Graph**. The graph may display inaccurate results.

For more information, see /Graph Text, /Graph Annotator, /Graph Series Group, and /Graph X-Axis Series.

Graph Graph Type /GG

Purpose

Selects from among the Quattro Pro graph types according to which type of graph is best suited for displaying and analyzing specific types of data.

Reminders

- Before you can create a graph, you must create a spreadsheet that has the same number of cells in each x-axis and y-axis block. Each *y* data item must be in the same block position as the corresponding *x* value.

GRAPH COMMANDS

■ Except for pie graphs, graphs can have on the y-axis as many as six different series of data. The /Graph Series menu choices 1st through 6th Series are used to highlight the data series. The pie graph accepts data from only the 1st Series block.

Procedure

1. Type */GG*.
2. Choose from the following types of graphs:

Option	Function
Line	Usually depicts a continuous series of data; enter an x-axis label in the X-Axis series block from the /Graph Series menu
Bar	Usually displays distinctly separate data series; enter x-axis labels in the X-Axis series from the /Graph Series menu
XY	Graphs data sets of *x* and *y* data; XY graphs have data on both axes; enter x-axis data in the X-Axis series of the /Graph Series menu
Stacked Bar	Shows how proportions change within the whole; stacks bars on top of each other; enter x-axis labels in the X-Axis series from the /Graph Series menu; a bar can have as many as six portions
Pie	Shows how the whole is divided into component portions; use only the 1st Series block to contain the values of each portion; the X-Axis series block labels the pie wedges; Quattro Pro calculates each portion's percentage from the 1st Series values
Area	Shows individual series of data and the total over time; enter an x-axis label in the X-Axis series block from the /Graph Series menu
Rotated Bar	Usually displays distinctly separate data series; rotates the bar graph so that the y-axis is horizontal and the x-axis is vertical; enter x-axis labels in the X-Axis series from the /Graph Series menu

continues

Option	Function
Column	Shows how the whole is divided into component portions; stacks slices on top of each other as a percentage of the total; all stacks equal 100 percent; use only the 1st Series block to contain the values of each portion; use the X-Axis series block to label the column slices; Quattro Pro calculates each portion's percentage from the 1st Series values
High-Low	Tracks items that vary over time; good for plotting stock figures
Text	Usually conveys unified information using concise words
Bubble	Floats bubbles of relative sizes in an X-Y graph; enter x-axis data in the X-Axis series of the /Graph Series menu; enter y-axis data in the 1st Series of the /Graph Series menu; enter the relative bubble sizes in the 2nd Series of the /Graph Series menu
3-D Graphs	Displays three-dimensional bar, ribbon, step, and area graphs, in which data points and the grid show depth; shows data behind one another along a third axis, the z-axis

Important Cue

- When you save the spreadsheet to disk, you also save the most recently specified graph type and other graph settings.

For more information, see **/Graph Series**, **/Graph Customize Series Pies**, and **/Graph Customize Series Bubbles**.

Graph Hide /GH

Purpose

Removes a named graph or the current graph from a specified position of the spreadsheet.

Reminder

- You must have a graph currently displayed on the spreadsheet to use **/Graph Hide**.

Procedure

1. Type */GH*.

2. Select a graph from the list of graph names displayed or choose <Current Graph> to remove the current graph from a spreadsheet.

3. Press Enter. Quattro Pro removes the graph from the spreadsheet and blank cells appear on-screen.

For more information, see **/Graph Insert**.

Graph Insert /GI

Purpose

Adds a named graph or the current graph to a specified position on the spreadsheet.

Reminders

- To display graphs in a spreadsheet, your computer must have an EGA or VGA display and adapter, and Quattro Pro should be in WYSIWYG display mode. You can view the graph by moving the cell selector to the inserted graph block and pressing F10.

- An inserted graph is "live"—that is, as spreadsheet data changes, the graph is updated to reflect those changes.

Procedure

1. Type */GI*.

2. Choose a graph from the list of graph names displayed or choose <Current Graph> to insert the current graph into a spreadsheet.

3. Specify a block large enough to accommodate the size of the graph that you want to add to the spreadsheet.
4. Press Enter.

Important Cues

- Quattro Pro can display a maximum of eight graphs on one spreadsheet.
- A graph is scaled to require no more than one screen to display and generally displays horizontally. Make sure that you choose a block large enough to accommodate the size of your graph.
- The maximum size of an inserted graph is 12 columns by 31 rows.
- To print the spreadsheet and inserted graph, include the spreadsheet and graph in the specified print block and then use the **/P**rint **D**estination **G**raphics Printer command.

Cautions

- If Quattro Pro cannot fit a graph into the specified insert block, the program displays a `Graph too complex` error message.
- The current graph may not be necessarily the inserted graph. To make the inserted graph the current graph, move the cell selector to the block containing the inserted graph and use /**G**raph.

*For more information, see **/Graph Hide**, **/Print Graph Print Layout**, and **/Print Destination Graph Print**.*

Graph Name   /GN

Purpose

Stores graphs for later use with the same spreadsheet.

Reminders

- Before you name a graph, you should create one that you can view.
- If you want to name a graph, make sure that the graph is current.

Procedure

1. Type */GN*.
2. Choose one of the following options:

Option	Function
Display	Retrieves previous graph settings that have saved graph names
Create	Creates a graph name of up to 15 characters for the current graph
Autosave Edits	Updates automatically changes to the current graph that has been named
Erase	Removes the settings and name for the graph name that you select from the menu
Reset	Erases all graph names and settings
Slide	Creates a slide show; displays a named graph for a specified number of seconds
Graph Copy	Copies a named graph from one spreadsheet to another

3. If you are switching to a new graph, creating, erasing, or resetting names, specify the graph name.

   If you are creating a slide show, prepare two columns side by side in your spreadsheet, away from the main body of data. Enter the graph names that you want to display for a timed interval in the first column. Enter an integer that represents the duration of the interval in seconds for each graph in the second column. Use /**G**raph **N**ame **S**lide, specify the block for the two columns you prepared, and press Enter. Use the /**T**ext **G**raph **B**utton tool in the /**G**raph **A**nnotator's Property Sheet to enable your slide shows to be user-driven.

USING QUATTRO PRO 4, SPECIAL EDITION

If you are copying graphs, open the target spreadsheet to which you want to copy the graph. Move the cell selector to the source spreadsheet that contains the graph you want to copy. Use /**Graph** **N**ame **G**raph **C**opy and select the graph that you want to copy. Move the cell selector to the target spreadsheet and press Enter.

Important Cue

- Using /**Graph** **N**ame is the only way to store and recall graphs for later use with the same spreadsheet.

Cautions

- You can recall graphs in later Quattro Pro sessions only if you first saved the graph settings with /**Graph** **N**ame **C**reate and then saved the spreadsheet with /**File** **S**ave. Even in the same work session, you cannot return to a previous graph unless you have saved the graph settings with /**Graph** **N**ame **C**reate.

- Be careful when using /**Graph** **N**ame **R**eset. The command deletes all graph names and all graph parameters in the current spreadsheet.

For more information, see ***/Print Graph Print****,* ***/File Save****, and* ***/File Retrieve****.*

Graph Overall /GO

Purpose

Changes the features that affect the entire graph.

Reminders

- A horizontal grid is a default setting for appropriate graph types. You cannot use grid lines with pie graphs.

- If you have a monochrome display monitor, use /**Graph** **O**verall **C**olor/**B**&**W**. If you must print to a color printer, however, you must change to /**Graph** **O**verall **C**olor/**B**&**W** **C**olor. Color monitors set to /**Graph** **O**verall **C**olor/**B**&**W** **C**olor print black and white on printers that are capable of only black and white.

GRAPH COMMANDS

Procedure

1. Type */GO*.
2. Choose one of the following options:

Option	Function		
Grid	Overlays a grid on a graph to enhance readability; the grid lines can be horizontal, vertical, or both; select from the **Grid Overlays** options:		
	Horizontal	Draws horizontal grid lines over the current graph from each major y-axis division	
	Vertical	Draws vertical grid lines over the current graph from each major x-axis division	
	Both	Draws horizontal and vertical grid lines	
	Clear	Removes all grid lines	
	Grid Color	Changes the color of grid lines	
	Line Style	Changes the pattern that is used to create the grid lines	
	Fill Color	Changes the color that is used behind the grid lines	
	Quit	Returns to the **/G**raph **O**verall menu	
Outlines	Changes the outlines that are used to box Titles, Legends, and the overall Graph; select from **B**ox, **D**ouble-line, **T**hick-line, **S**hadow, **3**D, **R**nd Rectangle, **N**one, and **S**culpted		
Background Color	Changes the color behind the graph		

continues

Option	Function
Three-D	Toggles the three-dimensional effect on and off; choose **Yes** to give the data points and grid lines a three-dimensional effect and show depth; Three-D graph types display data behind one another, along a third z-axis; select **No** to return to a one-dimensional graph
Color/B&W	Switches displays between color and black and white; select **B&W** to see how your graph will print in black and white; select **C**olor to return the display to color
Drop Shadow Color	Specifies the color for the drop shadow for a specified text color

Important Cues

- Use /**G**raph **O**verall **T**hree-D to give your two-dimensional graphs a three-dimensional appearance. Use /**G**raph **G**raph Type **3**-D Graphs to create three-dimensional **B**ar, **R**ibbon, **S**top, and **A**rea graphs.

- Some data-point graphs are more accurate if you use data labels. Use /**G**raph **C**ustomize Series **I**nterior **L**abels to create data labels that display precise numbers next to the point on the graph.

Caution

- You must have a color printer to print color graphs properly.

For more information, see ***/Graph Customize Series Interior Labels***, ***/Graph Graph Type 3-D Graphs***, *and* ***/Graph X-Axis/Y-Axis***.

Graph Series /GS

Purpose

Specifies the spreadsheet blocks containing x-axis and y-axis data or labels.

Reminders

- The x-axis is the graph's horizontal (bottom) axis. The y-axis is the graph's vertical (left) axis. The labels or data assigned to the x-axis and the six possible sets of y-axis data (**1**st through **6**th Series) must have the same number of cells. To ensure that the x-axis and y-axis have an equal number of elements, place all the labels and data on adjacent rows.

- Pie and column graph blocks are different from those of other graph types. Pie and column graphs use only the **1**st Series for graphing.

Procedure

1. Type */GS*.
2. Choose the blocks for x- or y-axis data or labels to be entered from the following options:

Option	Function
1st Series	Enters first y-axis data block, which is the only one used by a pie and column graph
2nd Series	Enters second y-axis data block; enters pie graph shading values and extraction codes manually (optional)
3rd Series	Enters third y-axis data block; enters pie graph control over percentage labels manually (optional)
4th - 6th Series	Enters fourth through sixth data blocks
X-Axis Series	Enters x-axis label block; creates labels for pie graph wedges and line, bar, stacked-bar, area, and rotated bar graphs
Group	Selects quickly the data blocks for a graph, 1 through 6, when data in adjacent rows and columns is in consecutive order
Analyze	Enables you to analyze data in your spreadsheet and graph the results without changing the spreadsheet

3. Indicate the data block by entering the block address, using a block name, or highlighting the block.

4. Press Enter.

5. If you select **G**roup, choose **C**olumns if the data blocks are in columns or **R**ows if the data blocks are in rows. Specify the block containing **1** through **6** data values. The rows or columns must be adjacent and in the order 1, 2, 3, 4, 5, and 6. Quattro Pro ignores rows or columns that exceed six data blocks.

Important Cues

- If your graph data is in adjacent rows or columns, you may be able to save time by using /**G**raph **F**ast Graph or /**G**raph **S**eries **G**roup.

- You do not need to change the /**G**raph menu settings when you change or update the data in the series blocks; Quattro Pro remembers all the settings.

- Use /**G**raph **C**ustomize Series **R**eset **G**raph to clear all graph settings. Use /**G**raph **C**ustomize Series **R**eset (**1**st through **6**th) to clear individual blocks and their associated settings.

- Quattro Pro automatically updates graphs when you input new data in the spreadsheet (for new data or labels in the x-axis and y-axis blocks). After you create the graphs with the /**G**raph commands, you can view new graphs from the spreadsheet by pressing F10 (Graph). If the computer beeps and no graph appears, you have not defined that graph, or your computer does not have graphics capability.

- Pie and column graphs do not use the x-axis and y-axis title options, grids, or scales.

- /**G**raph **S**eries **G**roup assigns data blocks in the order X, 1st Series, 2nd Series, and so on. Rows or columns that exceed the six data blocks are ignored.

- Selecting a block for /**G**raph **S**eries **G**roup that contains blank rows or columns produces a graph containing blanks and may be inaccurate.

Caution

- If your graph has missing data or if the *y* values do not match the corresponding *x* positions, check to ensure that the x-axis and y-axis blocks have the same number of elements. The values in the *y* blocks (1st through 6th) graph the corresponding *x* block cells.

For more information, see /Graph Graph Type, /Graph Series Analyze.

Graph Series Analyze n Series Aggregation /GSAnA

Purpose

Groups two or more data points and plots them as a single point on a graph. The plotted point can represent the sum, average, standard deviation, minimum, or maximum of the data.

Reminders

- You aggregate data using series values that already have been specified with the /Graph Series command (*n* represents the 1st Series through 6th series and X-Axis series options).

- To aggregate data using all defined series, choose /Graph Series Analyze All.

- On the Aggregation menu, use the Series Period option to describe the time frame represented in a data series. Your choices are Days (the default), Weeks, Months, Quarters, and Years.

- On the Aggregation menu, use the Aggregation Period option to describe the time frame to use for grouping a data series. Your choices are Weeks (the default), Months, Quarters, Years, and Arbitrary. The Arbitrary setting identifies custom aggregation periods. Specify a number between 2 and 1000 that represents the number of days you wish to use.

- On the **A**ggregation menu, use the **F**unction option to describe how to transform the data when Quattro Pro aggregates it. Your choices are SUM, **A**VG, **S**TD, **S**TDS, **M**IN, and MAX.

- To aggregate x-axis series data appearing on an XY graph, select /**G**raph **S**eries **A**nalyze **X**-Axis Series Aggregation.

Procedure

1. Use /**G**raph **G**raph Type and /**G**raph **S**eries to select a graph type and one or more series to graph.
2. Type */GSAnA*.
3. To identify the time period represented in the *n Series* values, select **S**eries Period, then choose a period option.
4. To identify the time period you wish to use for the aggregated data, select **A**ggregation Period, then choose a period option.
5. To select a method for transforming the data, select **F**unction, then choose an @function option.
6. Press F10 to view the aggregation graph.
7. Press Enter and choose **Q**uit four times to return to the spreadsheet.

Important Cues

- To aggregate the same data series using two different aggregation methods, specify the same spreadsheet block for the **1**st Series and **2**nd Series options on the /**G**raph **S**eries menu. Then, select different **A**ggregation Period options on the **A**ggregation menu.

- Aggregate daily sales figures into monthly data or quarterly data to simplify the interpretation of the data.

- To reset the /**G**raph **S**eries **A**nalyze *n Series* menu settings in preparation for a completely unique analytical graphing task, select /**G**raph **S**eries **A**nalyze **A**ll **R**eset. To reset the settings for a single series (such as the **2**nd Series) on the **A**nalyze menu, select **2**nd Series **R**eset.

- Use /**G**raph **N**ame **C**reate to save the current graph settings should you wish to view or print the graph at a later time.

GRAPH COMMANDS

Cautions

- Always choose an **A**ggregation Period setting that is smaller than the series period. If you do not, Quattro Pro displays an error message.

- Always use the same **A**ggregation Period setting when aggregating two or more data series on the same graph. Graphing data series with different periods of aggregation will result in the inaccurate placement of plots points on a graph

- Quattro Pro ignores the last aggregate grouping of data if the sum of the number of items in your spreadsheet is not a multiple of the aggregation period. If you select the **M**onths setting for your aggregation period, and your spreadsheet contains 302 entries, Quattro Pro will plot 10 groups of 30 data points, and ignore the remaining 2 data points.

For more information, see **/Graph Graph Type**, **/Graph Name Create**, *and* **/Graph Series**.

Graph Series Analyze n Series Moving Average   /GSAnM

Purpose

Identifies general trends in data by smoothing, or averaging, the data series values.

Reminders

- You create a moving average graph using series values that already have been specified with the **/G**raph **S**eries command (*n* represents the **1**st Series through **6**th series and **X**-Axis series options).

- To create a moving average using all defined series, choose **/G**raph **S**eries **A**nalyze **A**ll.

- On the **M**oving Average menu, use the **P**eriod option to specify the number of points to use when creating the moving average.

- On the **M**oving Average menu, use the **W**eighted option to select whether or not to use a weighted moving average

Procedure

1. Use /**G**raph **G**raph Type and /**G**raph **S**eries to select a graph type and one or more series to graph.

2. Type /*GSAnM*.

3. To identify a period value, select **P**eriod, then enter a number between 1 and 1000.

4. To create a weighted moving average, select **W**eighted, then choose **Y**es.

5. Press F10 to view the moving average graph.

6. Press Enter and choose **Q**uit four times to return to the spreadsheet.

Important Cues

- High **P**eriod option values produce smoother curves, but may actually mask the trends you are attempting to disclose.

- Use the **W**eighted option to compensate for abnormally low or high values appearing in the latter part of a data set.

- To create a moving average using two different periods, specify the same spreadsheet block for the **1**st Series and **2**nd Series options on the /**G**raph **S**eries menu. Then, select different **P**eriod options on the **M**oving Average menu.

- To reset the /**G**raph **S**eries **A**nalyze *n Series* menu settings in preparation for a completely unique analytical graphing task, select /**G**raph **S**eries **A**nalyze **A**ll **R**eset. To reset the settings for a single series (such as the **2**nd Series) on the **A**nalyze menu, select **2**nd Series **R**eset.

- Use /**G**raph **N**ame **C**reate to save the current graph settings to view or print the graph at a later time.

For more information, see /Graph Graph Type, /Graph Name Create, and /Graph Series.

Graph Series Analyze n Series Linear Fit /GSAnL

Purpose

Uses simple linear regression to create a line that "best fits" the selected data.

Reminders

- You create a linear fit graph using series values that already have been specified with the /Graph Series command (*n* represents the **1**st Series through **6**th series and **X**-Axis series options).

- To create a linear fit line for all defined series, choose /Graph Series Analyze All.

Procedure

1. Use /Graph Graph Type and /Graph Series to select a graph type and one or more series to graph.
2. Type */GSAnL*.
3. Press F10 to view the graph.
4. Press Enter and select Quit three times to return to the spreadsheet.

Important Cues

- The **Linear Fit** command calculates and plots linear regression information in the spreadsheet, even if your data has no obvious general trend.

- Although it is fine to display a linear fit in a graph by itself, you create much more of an impression when you display it next to moving average or aggregation data on the same graph.

- To reset the /**Graph Series Analyze** *n Series* menu settings in preparation for a completely unique analytical graphing task, select /**Graph Series Analyze All Reset**. To reset the settings for a single series (such as the 2nd Series) on the **Analyze** menu, select **2**nd **Series Reset**.

- Use /**Graph Name Create** to save the current graph settings to view or print the graph at a later time.

For more information, see /**Graph Graph Type**, /**Graph Name Create**, and /**Graph Series**.

Graph Series Analyze n Series Exponential Fit /GSAnE

Purpose

Generates a curve to fit data that increases or decreases exponentially.

Reminders

- You create an exponential fit graph using series values that already have been specified with the /**Graph Series** command (*n* represents the **1**st Series through **6**th series and **X-Axis** series options).

- To create an exponential fit line for all defined series, choose /**Graph Series Analyze All**.

- All values in the selected data series must be nonzero, and they all must have the same sign.

- Quattro Pro treats all blank cells in a data series as zeros for the purposes of exponential graphing.

Procedure

1. Use /**Graph Graph Type** and /**Graph Series** to select a graph type and one or more series to graph.
2. Type /*GSAnE*.
3. Press F10 to view the graph.
4. Press Enter and select **Q**uit four three times to return to the spreadsheet.

Important Cues

- Although it is fine to display an exponential fit line in a graph by itself, you create a much more of an impression when you display it next to moving average or aggregation data on the same graph.

- To reset the /**Graph Series A**nalyze *n Series* menu settings in preparation for a completely unique analytical graphing task, select /**Graph Series A**nalyze **A**ll **R**eset. To reset the settings for a single series (such as the **2**nd Series) on the **A**nalyze menu, select **2**nd Series **R**eset.

- Use /**Graph N**ame **C**reate to save the current graph settings to view or print the graph at a later time.

For more information, see /Graph Graph Type, /Graph Name Create, and /Graph Series.

Graph Series Analyze n Series Table /GSAnT

Purpose

Copies analytical graphing data into a table in a spreadsheet range that you specify.

Reminders

- You must choose /**G**raph **G**raph Type, /**G**raph **S**eries, and /**G**raph **S**eries **A**nalyze *n Series* and perform an analytical graphing operation prior to creating a table of numbers.

- When creating a table, you can supply an entire range address as the block to copy to, or just the first cell in the range. When you specify a single cell, Quattro Pro copies the data downward into the column specified.

- When determining where to place the table, remember that Quattro Pro requires a single column for the data and as many rows as necessary to accommodate the data.

Procedure

1. Type */GSAnT*.
2. When Quattro Pro prompts you for a table block to copy to, type the address of a cell that is well away from the spreadsheet area in which the raw data resides.
3. Press Enter to copy the data.
4. Select **Q**uit three times to return to the spreadsheet.

Important Cues

- Use analytical tables to retain permanent records of the values that Quattro Pro calculates for each series analyzed during aggregation, moving average, linear fit, and exponential fit operations.
- Use the numbers in analytical tables in reports, and as input for other analytical commands, such as those available on the /**T**ools menu.
- Use the /**G**raph **C**ustomize **S**eries **I**nterior **L**abels command to label graph points with the values that Quattro Pro copies into a table.

For more information, see /Graph Customize Series Interior Labels, /Graph Graph Type, and /Graph Series.

Graph Text Font   /GTF

Purpose

Changes the typeface, size, color, and style for graph text.

Reminders

- /**G**raph **T**ext **F**ont affects the displayed and printed graph.
- You must use /**G**raph **O**verall **C**olor/**B**&W to set the graph display to color if you want to print color text on a color printer.
- Text colors vary among monitors. To see a sample of which printer colors are available, print a sample output by using /**P**rint **G**raph **P**rint.

Procedure

1. Type */GTF*.

2. Choose an available option as follows:

Option	Function
1st Line	Changes the font for the first title line of a graph
2nd Line	Changes the font for the second title line of a graph
X-Title	Changes the font for the x-axis title
Y-Title	Changes the font for the primary and secondary y-axis titles
Legends	Changes the font for legends
Data & Tick	Changes the font for labels, scaling information, and 3-D graph labels
Quit	Returns to /Graph Text menu

3. Choose an available font option as follows:

Option	Function
Typeface	Specifies the typeface that is used to display text
Point Size	Specifies the point size of the text
Style	Specifies boldface, italic, or underline for the specified typeface
Color	Specifies the color used to display text
Quit	Returns to Font menu

4. Choose the typeface, point size, style, or color for the text that you want to change.

Caution

■ Quattro Pro may reduce font sizes automatically to keep text on-screen. Text that cannot be reduced enough is cut off.

For more information, see /Graph Overall Color/B&W.

Graph Text Legends /GTL

Purpose

Indicates which line, bar, or point belongs to a specific y-axis data block.

Procedure

1. Type */GTL.*
2. Choose the series for which you want to create a legend for y-axis blocks 1 through 6.
3. Enter the text for the legend. Text can be up to 19 characters.
4. If you want to move a legend, choose **P**osition and choose one of the available options as follows:

Option	Function
Bottom	Moves legend to bottom of graph
Right	Moves legend to right of graph
None	Removes legend from graph

Important Cues

- Customize the appearance of your legends using /**G**raph **T**ext **F**ont **L**egends **T**ypeface, **P**oint Size, **S**tyle, and **C**olor.

- Legends in 3-D graphs are x-axis labels. Customize 3-D legends using /**G**raph **T**ext **F**ont **D**ata & **T**ick Labels.

- You can use cell contents for a legend by entering a backslash (\) followed by the cell address.

Cautions

- If you relocate data used by a graph using /**E**dit **M**ove, Quattro Pro does not adjust cell addresses used to create legends. Create your graphs by using block names to assign data and legends to prevent this problem.

GRAPH COMMANDS

- Quattro Pro may cut off legends if they exceed the graph's frame. If the legend is cut off, enter a shorter legend.

*For more information, see */Edit Names Create*, */Graph Series 1st-6th Series* and *X-Axis Series*, and */Graph Text Font Legends* and *Data & Tick Labels*.*

Graph Text Titles   /GT, 1, 2, X, Y, S

Purpose

Adds headings to the graph and to each axis.

Reminder

- Quattro Pro automatically scales graphs to fit accordingly and displays the scaling factor (for example, Thousands) along each axis.

Procedure

1. Type */GT*.
2. Choose the title to be entered from the available options as follows:

Option	Function
1st Line	Specifies the first title line of a graph
2nd Line	Specifies the second title line of a graph
X-Title	Specifies the title below the x-axis
Y-Title	Specifies the title to the left of the y-axis
Secondary Y-Axis	Specifies the title to the right of the second y-axis
Quit	Returns to **Graph** menu

3. Enter a title, cell address, or block name of a cell containing a title up to 39 characters.

Important Cue

- You can use cell contents for a title by entering a backslash (\) followed by the cell address.

Caution

- You can lose titles and headings contained in cell addresses if you move the cells with /**Edit M**ove. Using block names instead of cell addresses solves this problem.

*For more information, see /**Graph Customize Series Interior Labels** and /**Graph X- and Y-Axis**.*

Graph View /GV

Purpose

Displays a graph.

Reminder

- On a nongraphics computer screen, no graph is displayed. If your system has a graphics card and a monochrome display or a color monitor, you can see a graph instead of the spreadsheet after you select **V**iew. You must select /**G**raph **O**verall **C**olor/B&W to see the graph in color.

Procedure

1. Type /*GV*.
2. Press any key to return to the /**G**raph menu.
3. Choose **Q**uit to return to the spreadsheet and READY mode.

Important Cues

- You can use /**G**raph **V**iew to redraw the graph, but an easier way is to press F10 (Graph) while you are in READY mode.

- If you want to create a series of graphs and view the series, you must use /**G**raph **N**ame to name each graph.

GRAPH COMMANDS

849

- If the screen is blank after you select View, make certain that you have defined the graph adequately, that your system has graphics capability, and that Quattro Pro was installed for your particular graphics device(s).

For more information, see **/Graph Name** *and* **/Graph Overall Color /B&W**.

Graph X-Axis /Y-Axis /GX, /GY, or /GY2

Purpose

Varies the scale along either axes. You can vary the x-axis scale on XY-type graphs.

Reminder

- The **Alternate Ticks** option is not available on the **Y**-Axis or **Y**-Axis 2nd Y-Axis menus.

Procedure

1. Type */GX*, */GY*, or */GY2*.
2. Choose one of the following options:

Option	Function
Scale	Automatic scales the graph to fill the screen (default selection); **M**anual overrides automatic scaling with the scaling that you select
Low	Enters the lowest number for the axis; values are rounded
High	Enters the highest number for the axis; values are rounded
Increment	Specifies the distance between ticks along the axis

continues

Option	Function
Format of Ticks	Selects the formatting type and decimal display from these options: **F**ixed, **S**cientific, **C**urrency, comma (,), **G**eneral, +/–, **P**ercent (%), **D**ate, **T**ext, or **H**idden
No. of Minor Ticks	Changes the frequency of tick marks on an axis
Alternate Ticks	Displays labels on two alternating levels
Display Scaling	Displays or suppresses the scale measurement
Mode	Displays the scale using the linear or logarithmic scale
Quit	Returns to the /Graph menu

3. To adjust the axes scale, choose **S**cale **M**anual **L**ow and enter the first number that you want to appear on the axis. Be sure that this number is less than the lowest number assigned to the axis. Choose **H**igh and enter the last number that you want to appear on the axis. Be sure that this number is more than the highest number assigned to the axis. Choose **I**ncrement and enter the number of the interval that you want between tick marks on the axis.

4. If you choose **N**o. of Minor Ticks, enter a number to indicate the frequency intervals at which the x-axis scale tick marks will appear.

Important Cues

- Some blocks may be too large for the graph, whereas others may be too small. Scale down values on the y-axis by entering a larger exponent.

- You also can use /Graph **X**-Axis **A**lternate Ticks to correct overlapping x-axis labels on line, bar, XY, and area graphs. Every other label is displayed slightly below the next label. For pie and stacked-bar graphs, use the /Graph **T**ext **F**ont **D**ata & Tick Labels and **P**oint Size command to reduce the size of the labels.

For more information, see */Graph Overall Grid*.

Print Commands /P

The /Print commands print spreadsheet contents as values or formulas. Use /Print Destination Printer to send output to the printer; use /Print Destination File to send output as an ASCII file; use /Print Destination Binary File to send a spreadsheet in final quality to file; and use /Print Destination Screen Preview to display how the printout will look on paper.

Print Adjust Printer /PA

Purpose

When Printer is the Destination setting, controls paper movement by moving the paper to the bottom of the page for printing any footer and then advancing the paper farther until the print head is at the top of the next page. Aligns Quattro Pro's internal line counter to the top of a physical page in the printer. Resets the page number to 1.

Reminders

- Use /Style Insert Break to create a page break on the left margin of the print block (force a form feed) before printing a spreadsheet. When you print the spreadsheet, a new page begins at the page break.

- When Graphics Printer is the Destination setting, Quattro Pro handles form feeds automatically.

- Use /Print Adjust Printer Align only after you manually align the print head with the top of a sheet of printer paper. Use Align before printing for the first time, when printing to a printer that other individuals have used, or when using automatic page numbering.

- If you do not choose /Print Adjust Printer Align each time that you print, the printer may print a few lines and then leave blank lines sporadically throughout the page.

- The length of the printed page may not match the length of the paper. Check the paper-length settings with /Print Layout Margins Page Length. This problem also occurs when the page-length setting does not match the number-of-lines-per-inch setting.

- The paper in the printer can get out of alignment if you manually advance the paper to the top of the next page. This misalignment causes printing over the paper perforation and blanks in the middle of the page. To realign the paper and reset Quattro Pro, turn off the printer and roll the paper until the top of a page is aligned with the print head. Then, turn on the printer again and use /Print Adjust Printer Align to reset Quattro Pro.

Procedure

1. If necessary, manually position the printer paper so that the top of a page is aligned with the print head. (The *print head*, also called the *print element*, is the part of the printer that puts the image on paper.)
2. Type */PA*.
3. Choose one of the following options:

Option	Function
Skip Line	Advances printer paper by one line on dot-matrix and daisywheel printers; repeat the keystroke (or press Enter) as many times as necessary to advance the paper to the desired position
Form Feed	Advances the printer paper to the top of the next page; prints any footer at the bottom of the page
Align	Synchronizes Quattro Pro with the printer; resets the line counter and resets the page number to 1

For more information, see */Print Destination* and */Print Layout Margins*.

Print Block /PB

Purpose

Defines the area of the spreadsheet to be printed.

PRINT COMMANDS

Reminder

- Check the status line to determine whether the CALC indicator is displayed. If so, press F9 (Calc) and wait until the WAIT indicator stops flashing before you proceed with the /Print commands.

Procedure

1. Type /PB.
2. Specify the block to print by typing the block address, highlighting the block, or entering an assigned block name.
3. Press Enter.

Important Cues

- Because /Print Block "remembers" the last print block used, you can reprint the specified spreadsheet portion without reentering the block. You also can edit existing print blocks.

- Hidden columns within a print block do not print.

- Use /Print Headings to print headings at the top or side of every printed page. Use this technique, for example, when you want to print database field names at the top of every page.

- Use /Style Insert Break with the cell selector in column A to insert mandatory page breaks in a block beginning in column A.

- After a block has been printed, Quattro Pro does not advance the paper to the top of the next page if Destination is set to Printer. Instead, Quattro Pro waits for you to print another block. To advance the paper, use /Print Adjust Printer Form Feed.

- If the print block is wider than the distance between the left and right margins, the remaining characters are printed on the following page (if printed to paper) or in the rows below the data (if printed to disk).

Caution

- If you want long text labels to print, ensure that they are completely within the highlighted block. Highlighting only the cell containing text does not print text that extends beyond the cell.

For more information, see */Style Insert Break*.

Print Copies /PC

Purpose

Specifies the number of copies of your spreadsheet to print during a printing session.

Procedure

1. Type */PC*.
2. Enter the number of copies that you want to print and then press Enter.

Important Cue

- The default number of copies is 1. Values other than 1 are not saved. After printing, the number of copies returns to 1.

For more information, see */Print Block*.

Print Destination /PDP, /PDF, /PDB, /PDG

Purpose

Specifies where spreadsheets and graphs are to be printed.

Reminders

- All /**P**rint commands apply when output is printed directly to paper, but some do not apply when you use /**P**rint **D**estination **F**ile or **B**inary File.
- Before you print a file to disk, make sure that the columns are wide enough to display all the data. If a column is too narrow, values are changed to asterisks and labels are truncated.
- Check the /**P**rint menu to determine whether you have selected a default printer. If not, use /**O**ptions **H**ardware **P**rinters.

Procedure

1. Type */PD*.
2. Choose an available option as follows:

Option	Function
Printer	Prints data on the printer when you choose **S**preadsheet Print; does not print a graph, shading, or solid lines
File	Converts data to an ASCII text file and sends that file to disk so that you can import it into other programs or copy it to your printer
Binary File	Sends data with final-quality graphics to a binary file and then to disk so that you can import that file into other programs or copy it to your printer
Graphics Printer	Prints data on the graphics printer when you choose **S**preadsheet Print
Screen Preview	Displays spreadsheet (see /**P**rint **D**estination **S**creen Preview)

3. For /**P**rint **D**estination **F**ile or /**P**rint **D**estination **B**inary File, enter the print file name. With /PDF or /PDB, Quattro Pro gives the file name a PRN extension.
4. Use /**P**rint **B**lock and /**P**rint **S**preadsheet Print to print the spreadsheet. (See /**P**rint **B**lock and /**P**rint **S**preadsheet Print.)

Important Cues

- You can use Quattro Pro's **/P**rint commands to set formats for your reports. Use commands from **/P**rint **L**ayout to control formats for printing.

- Print an ASCII text file to disk by using **/P**rint **D**estination **F**ile. Most popular software programs, including word processing and database programs, can import ASCII text files. Don't have a PostScript printer selected as the default printer, however.

- **/P**rint **D**estination **B**inary File creates a file on disk that you later can send to a printer through the operating system's COPY command.

- Use **/P**rint **D**estination **G**raphics Printer to print fonts, cell shading, and inserted graphs.

- **/P**rint **D**estination **P**rinter prints faster than **G**raphics Printer.

- Different database programs accept data in different formats; check to see in what form dates are imported and whether the receiving program accepts blank cells. Make sure to prepare your Quattro Pro file accordingly before printing to an ASCII file.

- Because Quattro Pro can translate WQ1 files to many popular database file formats, check to see whether Quattro Pro can translate spreadsheet files to your database program.

For more information, see **/Print Spreadsheet Print**, **/Print Graph Print**, *and* **/File Save As**.

Print Destination Screen Preview   /PDS

Purpose

Displays your print block as it will appear when printed with **D**estination set to **G**raphics Printer, including graphics, fonts, page numbers, headers, and footers.

Reminder

- Your computer must have a graphics card to use **/P**rint **D**estination **S**creen Preview.

PRINT COMMANDS

Procedure

1. Choose /**P**rint **B**lock and specify the area to be printed.
2. Type */PDS*.
3. Choose **S**preadsheet Print.
4. Choose one of the following options:

Option	Function
Help	Accesses Preview on-line help screens
Quit	Quits and returns to the /**P**rint menu
Color	Switches to a color set for color screens with a monochrome printer and for color screens with a color printer; switches to black-on-white for monochrome monitors and to white-on-black for plasma and LCD displays
Previous	Displays the preceding page
Next	Displays the next page
Ruler	Displays a one-inch grid on the page for making precise modifications to the page layout; choose **R**uler again to turn off the grid
Guide	Displays a miniature version of the page in the upper right corner of the screen when zoomed; press + or – to toggle the display
Unzoom	Removes the enlargement that you added with **Z**oom
Zoom	Enlarges the preview display 200 or 400 percent

5. Choose **Q**uit or press Esc to return to the spreadsheet.

Caution

- Screen Preview displays how a printout will look if you use /**P**rint **D**estination **G**raphics Printer, not /**P**rint **D**estination **P**rinter.

For more information, see */Print Destination*.

Print Format /PF

Purpose

Selects the format in which to print cells.

Procedure

1. Type */PF*.
2. Choose an available option as follows:

Option	Function
As Displayed	Prints the block as displayed; default setting used for printing spreadsheets and graphs
Cell-Formulas	Prints the formula, label, or value contents of each cell on one line of the printout (contents match the information from the input line: cell address protection status, cell format, formula or value, and annotation)

Important Cues

- Use **/Print Format Cell-Formulas** to print documentation that shows the formulas and cell settings used to create the spreadsheet.

- In a **Cell-Formulas** listing, codes appear that indicate cell contents and formatting. P indicates a protected cell; U indicates an unprotected cell. Other codes, such as F2 for "fixed to 2 decimal places," are compatible with input line codes for different formats.

For more information, see */Print Layout*.

Print Graph Print /PG

Purpose

Prints a specified graph.

Reminders

- If you want more than one graph associated with a file, use /**G**raph **N**ame **C**reate to name each graph. You then can use these names when printing. Make sure to use /**F**ile **S**ave to save the graph names with the spreadsheet.
- If you have multiple files open in memory, make sure that the file containing the graph or graphs you want to print is in the active window on-screen.
- The current graph prints by default unless you specify another named graph.

Procedure

1. Type */PG*.
2. Choose one of the following options:

Option	Function
Destination	Specifies where to send your graph: **F**ile sends the graph to a file on disk so that you can print the graph later; **G**raphics Printer (the default) sends the graph to the graphics printer
Layout	Specifies layout options (see /**P**rint **G**raph **P**rint **L**ayout)
Go	Sends a graph to the specified destination
Write Graph File	Saves graph in a file on disk so that other programs can import the file: **E**PS stores a graph as a PostScript file to use with word processing and drawing programs; **P**IC stores a graph as a Lotus graph file; **S**lide EPS stores a graph in a file to use as a 35mm slide; and PC**X** stores a graph in a file to use with paint or presentation programs such as PC Paintbrush or SlideWrite Presenter

continues

Option	Function
Name	Specifies the name of the graph that you want to print
Quit	Returns to the /Print menu

3. If you choose **Name**, specify the name of the graph that you want to print. Otherwise, the current graph prints.

4. Choose **G**o to print the graph on your graphics printer.

5. If you choose **W**rite Graph File, enter the name of the graph file that you want to save and use with another program.

Important Cues

- Use /**P**rint **A**djust Printer **F**orm Feed to eject a graph from the printer. Do not manually roll the paper from the printer.

- Graphs are printed using settings that emulate graphs appearing on-screen.

- Printers that cannot print a graph print a blank space of equivalent size.

- A graph is not divided by a page break. The graph prints on the next page.

- You can print a graph in landscape orientation (horizontally) with /**P**rint **G**raph Print **L**ayout **O**rientation **L**andscape.

For more information, see */Print Graph Print Layout*.

Print Graph Print Layout /PGL

Purpose

Selects the quality, size, and orientation of printed graphs.

Procedure

1. Type */PGL*.

2. Choose one of the following options:

PRINT COMMANDS

Option	Function
Left Edge	Specifies the graph's left margin (default is 0)
Top Edge	Specifies the graph's top margin (default is 0)
Height	Specifies the graph's height (default is 0 inches)
Width	Specifies the graph's width (default is 0 inches)
Dimensions	Specifies the layout dimensions in Inches or Centimeters
Orientation	Sets Portrait (vertical) or Landscape (horizontal) print orientation (default is Portrait)
4:3 Aspect	Keeps the 4:3 aspect ratio of a graph to prevent distortion (a *4:3 aspect ratio* adjusts graph size to 4 units wide and 3 units high); default is Yes
Reset	Restores the graph layout settings that were saved last
Update	Saves the current graph layout settings as defaults
Quit	Returns to the Graph Print menu

Important Cue

■ Use /Print Graph Print Layout 4:3 Aspect No if you want your graph to fit the dimensions you entered. With 4:3 Aspect set to No, Quattro Pro changes the shape of the graph to fit the margins you have selected.

Caution

■ /Print Graph Print Layout Update makes the current layout settings the default settings. To restore the original settings, you must change each setting back to its default and issue /Print Graph Print Layout Update again or reinstall Quattro Pro.

For more information, see */Print Graph Print*.

Print Headings /PH

Purpose

Prints, on every page, the rows or columns that you selected from the spreadsheet.

Reminders

- Before you issue /**Print Headings**, move the cell pointer to the leftmost column of headings or to the top row of headings on the spreadsheet that you want repeated.

- /**Print Headings** does not print headings around blocks or graphs.

- You also can use /**Print Layout Header** and **Footer** to print information at the top and bottom, respectively, of each page.

Procedure

1. Type */PH*.
2. Choose an available option as follows:

Option	Function
Left Heading	Prints the selected columns at the left side of each page
Top Heading	Prints the selected rows at the top of each page

3. Press Esc to remove the current block. Specify the headings block. Press Enter.

Important Cues

- Including headings is useful when you want to print multiple pages. If you want to print sections of a wide spreadsheet, you can condense the columns further by using /**Style Hide Column Hide** to hide blank or unnecessary columns.

PRINT COMMANDS

- Use **/P**rint **H**eadings **T**op Heading to select spreadsheet rows that are printed above the data on each page. The **T**op Heading command is especially useful for printing database column headings above the data on each page.

Cautions

- If you include in the print block the rows or columns specified as headings, the rows or columns are printed twice.
- If your row heading is longer than the width of the spreadsheet according to the current margin settings, the heading will print on the following page.

For more information, see **/Print Layout**.

Print Layout /PL

Purpose

Enables you to use your printer's full printing capabilities to enhance printed spreadsheets.

Procedure

1. Type */PL*.
2. Choose one of the following options:

Option	Function
Header	Specifies text to print at the top of each page
Footer	Specifies text to print at the bottom of each page
Break Pages	Specifies whether to print with or without soft page breaks, headers, and footers; generally, use **Yes** to print to paper and **No** to print to disk
Percent Scaling	Enables you to select the percentage to shrink the print block to print on one page

continues

Option	Function
Margins	Specifies page length and margins: **P**age Length sets the number of lines printed on each page; **L**eft sets from 0 to 511 characters; **T**op sets from 0 to 32 lines; **R**ight sets from 0 to 511 characters; and **B**ottom sets from 0 to 32 lines
Dimensions	Specifies type of measurement used with **P**rint **L**ayout commands: Line/Characters (default setting) measures spreadsheet margins according to character size, **I**nches measures margins by inches, and **C**entimeters measures margins by centimeters
Orientation	Enables you to print the spreadsheet vertically or horizontally: **P**ortrait prints vertically; **L**andscape prints horizontally; and **B**anner prints lengthwise across continuous pages
Setup String	Sends special print codes to the printer when **D**estination is set to **P**rinter
Reset	Restores default settings for print block, headings, and layout commands: **A**ll clears all print options and resets all formats and setup strings to their defaults; **P**rint Block clears print blocks; **H**eadings clears the top and left headings; **L**ayout resets break pages, margins, dimensions, orientation, and setup string settings to the default setting
Update	Saves the current **P**rint **L**ayout settings to disk for printing all new files
Values	Displays print layout default settings
Quit	Returns to the /**P**rint menu

3. If you choose **H**eader or **F**ooter, type the header or footer. Press Enter.

   If you choose **M**argins, type the new margin settings. Press Enter.

   If you choose **P**ercent Scaling, type a percentage from 1% to 1000%. Press Enter.

If you choose **S**etup String, type the setup string. Each control code must begin with a backslash (\). You must type uppercase or lowercase letters as they appear in your printer's manual.

Important Cues

- To print the date and page number in the footer or header, enter an at sign (@) where you want the date to appear and a number sign (#) where you want the page number to appear.

- Use \ followed by a cell address to insert the contents of a cell into the header or footer. Separate the footer or header into as many as three centered segments by entering a vertical bar (|). To center the data, place one vertical bar to the left of the data. To left-justify the data, do not include vertical bars. To right-justify the data, insert two vertical bars to the left of the data.

- Headers and footers each occupy one line. Two blank lines are left between a header or a footer and the body of your report. Therefore, a header or a footer reduces the area available for printing by three lines each.

- Most printers print 6 lines per inch unless the ratio is changed with a setup string (printer control code). At 6 lines per inch, 11-inch paper has 66 lines and 14-inch paper has 84 lines.

- In Quattro Pro, print parameters remain in effect until you give different instructions. If you want to provide a new set of parameters, use **/P**rint **L**ayout **R**eset **A**ll to ensure that you are starting from the default parameters.

- Your printer manual contains lists of printer setup codes (also known as *printer control codes* or *escape codes*). These codes may be shown two ways: as a decimal ASCII number representing a keyboard character, or as the Esc key followed by a character.

- Quattro Pro setup strings include decimal number codes (entered as three-digit numbers), preceded by a backslash (\). Some codes start with the Esc character, followed by other characters. Because you cannot type the Esc character in the setup string, the ASCII decimal number for Esc (27) is used instead.

Cautions

- Do not combine setup strings with macro commands. The result can be unpredictable.

- If you get the same nonsense characters at the top of every printed page, you probably have those characters in your setup string.

*For more information, see **/Print Layout Header/Footer**, **/Print Layout Margins**, **/Print Layout Percent Scaling**, **/Print Layout Dimensions**, **/Print Layout Setup String**, and **/Print Layout Values**.*

Print Print Manager /PM

Purpose

Opens a Print Manager window. When the Borland Print Spooler is loaded, the Print Manager window enables you to monitor the status of jobs in the print queue.

Procedure

1. Type */PM*.

2. Quattro Pro opens a Print Manager window and displays six information fields which track the progress of all print jobs in the queue. The Seq field displays the sequence in which your print jobs are printing. The File Name field displays the temporary file name that Quattro Pro assigns to each print job in the queue. The Status field displays messages about the status of the current print job.

3. To select a print job, click it, use your arrow keys to highlight it, or use the Select (Shift-F7) or Select All (Alt-F7) keys.

Important Cues

- If the default printer's device is a network queue, the Print Manager window displays information about the network queue. The window contains different information from the BPS queue window. See Appendix E, "Installing Quattro Pro on a Network," for details on using the Print Manager on a network queue.

- To change how frequently Quattro Pro updates the information in the Print Manager window, choose /**O**ptions Network **R**efresh Interval and enter a lower refresh interval setting.

Caution

- Because BPS stores print jobs in temporary files, large, complex print jobs use much disk space. You may want to free up at least 1M of disk space before printing large jobs in the BPS queue.

For more information, see */Options Hardware Printers Background*.

Print Print Manager File /PM/F

Purpose

Closes the Print Manager window and returns to the spreadsheet or closes all open windows.

Procedure

1. Type */PM*. Quattro Pro opens a Print Manager window and displays information on the status of all print jobs in the queue.

2. Choose /**F**ile and choose one of the following options:

Option	Function
Close	Closes the Print Manager window
Close All	Closes all open windows

Important Cue

- You access the commands on the Print Manager menu bar like you do any Quattro Pro commands.

For more information, see */Print Print Manager*, */Print Print Manager Queue*, */Print Print Manager Job*, and */Print Print Manager Window*.

Print Print Manager Queue /PM/Q

Purpose

Enables you to view the BPS queue or the network print queue.

Procedure

1. Type */PM*. Quattro Pro opens a Print Manager window and displays information on the status of all print jobs in the queue.

2. Choose **/Q**ueue and choose one of the following options:

Option	Function
Background	Enables you to view the BPS queue
Network	Enables you to view a network queue

Important Cue

- You access the commands on the Print Manager menu bar like you do any Quattro Pro commands.

*For more information, see **/Print Print Manager**, **/Print Print Manager File**, **/Print Print Manager Job**, and **/Print Print Manager Window**.*

Print Print Manager Job /PM/J

Purpose

Enables you to control print jobs in the queue. You can delete, hold, or release a print job while it is in the queue.

Procedure

1. Type */PM*. Quattro Pro opens a Print Manager window and displays information on the status of all print jobs in the queue.

2. Choose **/Q**ueue and choose one of the following options:

Option	Function
Delete	Deletes a print job from the queue
Hold	Holds a print job in the queue to keep it from printing
Release	Releases a held print job and enables it to resume printing

Important Cue

■ You access the commands on the Print Manager menu bar like you do any Quattro Pro commands.

For more information, see /Print Print Manager, /Print Print Manager File, /Print Print Manager Queue, and /Print Print Manager Window.

Print Print Manager Window /PM/W

Purpose

Resizes, repositions, and expands the current window pane. Moves the cell selector to a different window.

Procedure

1. Type */PM*. Quattro Pro opens a Print Manager window and displays information on the status of all print jobs in the queue.

2. Choose /**W**indow and choose one of the following options:

Option	Function
Zoom	Increases the Print Manager window to full-screen
Tile	Tiles the Print Manager window with other Quattro Pro windows
Stack	Stacks the Print Manager window with other Quattro Pro windows

continues

Option	Function
Move/Size	Moves and/or resizes the Print Manager window
Pick	Displays the chosen window full-screen

Important Cue

- You access the commands on the Print Manager menu bar like you do any Quattro Pro commands.

For more information, see **/Print Print Manager**, **/Print Print Manager File**, **/Print Print Manager Queue**, *and* **/Print Print Manager Job**.

Print Print-To-Fit /PP

Purpose

Shrinks the specified print block so that it can print on one or as few pages as possible, and then prints.

Reminders

- **P**rint-To-Fit operates in character or WYSIWYG mode.
- Specify a block to print before initiating **/P**rint **P**rint-To-Fit.

Procedure

Type */PP*.

Important Cues

- Using **P**rint-To-Fit does not affect margins. Headers and footers and their corresponding margins, however, are scaled with spreadsheet data.
- **P**rint-To-Fit works best with blocks that are more wide than long.
- Change the **D**estination setting to **S**creen Preview to review the specified print block before invoking the **/P**rint **P**rint-To-Fit command.
- **/P**rint **P**rint-To-Fit sends the print block immediately to your printer if **D**estination is set to **G**raphics Printer. Make sure

PRINT COMMANDS

that your printer is turned on; otherwise, Quattro Pro displays an error message.

For more information, see ***/Print Spreadsheet Print***, ***/Print Layout Percent Scaling***, *and* ***/Print Block***.

Print Spreadsheet Print /PS

Purpose

Prints the specified block to the selected destination.

Reminders

- You must select a printer before printing during the Quattro Pro installation process or by using /**O**ptions **H**ardware **P**rinters.

- Before printing for the first time, align the top of the paper with the print head and choose the **A**lign command from /**P**rint **A**djust Printer.

- Use the /**P**rint **B**lock command to specify the block to print before selecting /**P**rint **S**preadsheet Print.

- Cancel a print job in process by pressing Ctrl-Break.

Procedure

Type */PS*.

Important Cues

- Printing to a disk file is not complete until you quit all print menus.

- Use the Screen Previewer to review the specified print block before invoking the /**P**rint **S**preadsheet Print command.

Caution

- Use the /**P**rint **A**djust Printer **F**orm Feed command to eject pages and keep the printer aligned. If you manually eject pages, realign the paper with the print head and choose /**P**rint **A**djust Printer **A**lign.

For more information, see ***/Print Block***, ***/Print Adjust Printer***, *and* ***/Print Graph Print***.

Database Commands /D

/Database commands work on data tables and enable you to perform three functions: database selection and maintenance, data analysis, and data manipulation. One of the most commonly used /Database commands is Query, which you use to find, update, extract, or delete information rapidly from within a large collection of data. You also use /Database commands to sort database records and access the Paradox relational database.

Database Data Entry /DD

Purpose

Restricts input to labels or dates.

Procedure

1. Type */DD*.
2. Choose **G**eneral to return to normal data entry, **L**abels Only to restrict all entries to labels, or **D**ates Only to restrict all entries to date-and-time data.
3. Specify the input block. Include a block that covers all cells in which you want to enter labels or dates.
4. Press Enter. Make label or date entries using normal data entry methods; numbers entered into a label cell are made into labels.

Important Cues

- You can enter time data using **D**ates Only.
- To return to normal data entry, use /**D**atabase **D**ata Entry **G**eneral and specify the previously restricted block.
- Use /**D**atabase **D**ata Entry, /**D**atabase **R**estrict Input, and /**S**tyle Line Drawing to create custom forms that increase the accuracy of data entry.

DATABASE COMMANDS

Caution

- Entering a label or value into a block specified as **D**ate Only causes Quattro Pro to beep and enter Edit mode.

For more information, see **/Database Restrict Input** *and* **/Style Line Drawing**.

Database Paradox Access   /DP

Purpose

Switches between Quattro Pro and Paradox.

Reminder

- The following hardware requirements and configurations are necessary to use **/D**atabase **P**aradox Access:

    Paradox 3.5

    2M random-access memory

    An IBM AT, PS/2, or compatible computer

    Quattro Pro and Paradox installed in separate directories

    Quattro Pro in your DOS path in your AUTOEXEC.BAT file

    The FILES setting in your CONFIG.SYS file set to FILES=40

Procedure

1. Type */DP*.
2. Choose one of the following options:

Option	Function
Go	Accesses Paradox
Load File	Retrieves a spreadsheet file or a Paradox table each time you switch from Paradox to Quattro Pro
Autoload	Specifies whether the default file named with **Load File** is retrieved into Quattro Pro each time you switch from Paradox to Quattro (default setting is **Yes**)
Quit	Returns to the **D**atabase menu

Important Cue

■ Review your Quattro Pro documentation to ensure your computer system and Quattro Pro are configured properly before invoking /**D**atabase **P**aradox Access.

*For more information, see /**Database Query Block** and /**Database Query Extract/Unique**.*

Database Query Assign Names   /DQA

Purpose

Assigns block names to field names.

Procedure

1. Type /*DQA*.
2. Specify the second row below the field names. Quattro Pro assigns a name to each cell in the second row according to the field name above it.
3. After you specify all the field names, press Enter.

Important Cues

■ A field name should be one word and can be up to 15 characters long.

DATABASE COMMANDS

- **/Database Query Assign Names** is useful for entering search criteria, using field names to refer to columns.

For more information, see **/Edit Names** and **/Database Query Criteria Table**.

Database Query Block /DQB

Purpose

Specifies a block of data records to be searched.

Reminders

- You must indicate a block before you use the **L**ocate, **E**xtract, **U**nique, or **D**elete command from the /**D**atabase **Q**uery menu.

- The block can consist of the entire database or part of the database. The block *must include the field names*.

Procedure

1. Type */DQB*.
2. Specify the block of data records you want to search. Make sure to include in the block the field names at the top of the block and portions of the records that may not be on-screen.
3. Press Enter.

Caution

- Redefine the block if you add one or more rows to the bottom of the block, add one or more columns before or after the block, or delete the first column or the last row or column of the block. A defined block is adjusted automatically if you insert or delete rows or columns within the block.

For more information, see **/Database Query Output Block** and **/Database Query Criteria Table**.

Database Query Criteria Table   /DQC

Purpose

Specifies the spreadsheet block containing the criteria that defines the records you want to find.

Reminders

- You must indicate a criteria block before you use the **L**ocate, **E**xtract, **U**nique, or **D**elete options of the /**D**atabase **Q**uery command.

- You do not need to include in the criteria table and output blocks all the field names in the database. If you include all the field names, however, you don't have to alter the criteria block to apply a criterion to a new field.

- The first row of the criteria table must contain field names that exactly match the field names of the database. Use the /**E**dit **C**opy command to copy field names from the database block to ensure that criteria table and database block field names match exactly.

- The row below the first row of the criteria table contains the search criteria.

- You can use more than one criteria for a search.

- More than one row can contain criteria.

- Criteria can be numbers, labels, or formulas. Criteria can contain logical operators (<, <=, >, >=, <>). You must position numbers and labels directly below the field name to which they correspond.

- Criteria labels can contain wild-card characters. An asterisk (*) stands for any group of characters; a question mark (?) represents a single character.

- A tilde (~) before a label excludes that label from a search.

- You can use #AND#, #NOT#, or #OR# to create compound logical formulas as criteria.

- Criteria on the same row of the criteria table are treated as though they are linked by #AND# for every condition to be met. Criteria on separate rows are treated as though they are linked by #OR# for any condition to be met.

Procedure

1. Type */DQC*.
2. Specify or highlight the block that will contain field names and criteria.

   The block must contain at least two rows: the first row includes the field names from the top row of the database that you want to search, and the second row includes the criteria that you specify.

3. Press Enter.

Important Cues

- Use wild cards in the criteria if you are unsure of spelling or want to find data that may have been misspelled. Quattro Pro searches only for exact matches for the characters in the criteria block.

- Including a blank row as the last row in the criteria block causes all records to be found, retrieved, or deleted with **Q**uery commands.

Caution

- If you alter the number of rows in a defined criteria block, you must redefine the block to reflect the change. Otherwise, Quattro Pro may not search through the entire criteria table.

*For more information, see **/Database Query Output Block** and **/Database Query Criteria Table**.*

Database Query Delete   /DQD

Purpose

Removes from the database any records that meet conditions in the criteria table.

Reminders

- You must define a Quattro Pro database complete with a database block and a criteria table before using **/D**atabase **Q**uery **D**elete.

- Create a backup file on disk before using /**D**atabase **Q**uery **D**elete. If data is deleted incorrectly, a copy of the original spreadsheet is intact.
- Before deleting, use the /**D**atabase **Q**uery **L**ocate command to test that your criteria is accurate.
- Another method of checking the records marked for deletion is to use /**D**atabase **Q**uery **E**xtract to make a copy of the records. Check this copy against the records you want to delete.

Procedure

1. Type /*DQD*.
2. Choose **C**ancel if you want to stop the command from deleting your records. Choose **D**elete if you want to remove the records.

Important Cues

- Use /**D**atabase **Q**uery **D**elete to "clean up" your database. You can remove records that are not current or that have been extracted to another spreadsheet.
- Create a "rolling" database that stores only current records and removes old records to archive files. Use /**D**atabase **Q**uery **E**xtract to extract old records from the file; save them to another spreadsheet by using /**T**ools **X**tract. Then, use /**D**atabase **Q**uery **D**elete to remove the old records from the database file.

Cautions

- As with other /**D**atabase **Q**uery commands, the field labels in the criteria table must match the field labels in the database. The labels can appear in a different order, but the spelling and cases must match. The easiest and safest method of creating criteria labels is to use /**E**dit **C**opy.
- You inadvertently can delete more than you want with /**D**atabase **Q**uery **D**elete, particularly if a row in the criteria table is empty when you execute /**D**atabase **Q**uery **D**elete. Make sure that your criteria block is set up correctly before you use this command.

For more information, see /**D**atabase **Q**uery **E**xtract/**U**nique, /**D**atabase **Q**uery **L**ocate, /**T**ools **X**tract, *and* /**F**ile **S**ave.

DATABASE COMMANDS

Database Query Extract/Unique   /DQE or /DQU

Purpose

Copies unique records to the output block that meet conditions set in the criteria.

Reminders

- You must define a Quattro Pro database complete with database block, output block, and a criteria table before using **/D**atabase **Q**uery **E**xtract and **U**nique. The output block must have field names entered exactly as they appear at the top of each database column.

- Choose an output block in a blank area of the spreadsheet. You can limit the output block to a specified number of rows or give the output block an unlimited number of rows.

Procedure

1. Type */DQ*.
2. Choose one of the following options:

Option	Function
Extract	Copies all records to the output block that meet the conditions set in the criteria table
Unique	Copies uncopied records that meet conditions set in the criteria table to the output block and sorts the copied records

Important Cues

- Records that match the criteria table are copied to the output block. If the output block does not have enough room, Quattro Pro beeps and an error message appears.

- To include duplicate records in the extract block, use **/D**ata **Q**uery **E**xtract.

- /Database Query Unique works the same way as Extract, but /Database Query Unique extracts only unique records that meet the criteria.

- /Database Query Unique uses only field names in the output block to test whether a record has a duplicate. A single copy of all duplicates appears in the output block.

- /Database Query Extract and Unique remember the last input, criteria, and output blocks used from the /Database Query menu. You do not have to enter the blocks if they are the same as the previous blocks. Check the current blocks by selecting Block, Criteria Table, or Output Block; then, press Enter to accept the blocks or Esc to clear the old block so that you can specify a new one. Choose Reset to clear all block settings.

Cautions

- As with other /Database Query commands, the field names in the criteria table must match the field names in the database.

- If you select only the field names as the output block, you are given an unlimited number of rows for the extracted report. Existing contents below the output field names, however, are erased.

*For more information, see **/Database Paradox Access**, **/Database Query Locate**, and **/Database Query Block**.*

Database Query Locate /DQL

Purpose

Finds records in the database that meet conditions you set in the criteria table.

Reminder

- You must define the database block and criteria table before using /Database Query Locate. Enter a criterion that specifies the type of records you want in the criteria table.

Procedure

1. Type /DQL.
2. Press the up-arrow or down-arrow key to move to the next record that meets the criteria. Press Home or End to find the first or last record in the database that meets the criteria.
3. To edit contents within a record, press F2 (Edit) when the cell selector highlights the cell you want to edit. Edit the cell contents and press Enter.

Important Cues

- After you enter the /Database Query commands and blocks, you can repeat the operation by changing the criteria and pressing the F7 (Query) key.
- /Database Query Locate remembers the database block and criteria table used from the /Database Query menu. You do not have to enter the database block and criteria table if they are the same as those used by the previous database command. Check the current blocks by selecting Block or Criteria Table; then, press Enter to accept the block. To clear the current setting in order to specify a new block, choose Reset.
- Using /Database Query Locate can be the best way to access a record in a database quickly.
- Use wild cards (* or ?) in the criteria table if you are unsure of the spelling or if you want to find data that may have been misspelled. Quattro Pro finds only exact matches for the characters in the criteria table.
- Before you delete records with /Database Query Delete, use /Database Query Locate to display the records to be deleted.

Cautions

- If /Database Query Locate does not find a record, use /Edit Erase Block to erase old criteria from the criteria table. A space character may have been used to "erase" a field in the criteria table. If so, /Database Query Locate looks for a space in the database, a process that can result in no found records.
- If /Database Query Locate finds all records, use the /Database Query Criteria command to check the size of the criteria table. Do not include blank rows in the criteria table; if you do, these commands find all records.

For more information, see ***/Database Query Criteria Table***.

Database Query Output Block   /DQO

Purpose

Assigns a location for the displayed records that are found in a search.

Reminders

- You must indicate an output block before you use the **Ex**tract and **U**nique options of the **/D**atabase **Q**uery command. The **L**ocate and **D**elete options do not use an output block.

- Locate the output block so that nothing is below it and so that it does not overlap the database block or criteria table.

- You can limit the output block by specifying the size of the (multiple-row) block. Alternatively, you can ensure that the output block is unlimited in size if you specify the block as the single row of field names. The results of the search, therefore, can be listed in the unlimited area below the field names.

- The first row of the output block must contain field names that match the field names of the input and criteria blocks, but the field names in the output block can be in any order, and the label prefixes and the case of the letters can be different.

Procedure

1. Type */DQO*.
2. Specify the output field names. If you want a limited number of extracted records, the number of rows in the output block should equal the number of extracted rows that you want.
3. If the block specification is acceptable, press Enter. If you want to change the block specification, choose **O**utput Block again, press Esc to clear the current block selection, highlight a new block, and then press Enter.

Caution

- If you specify the row of field names as a single-row output block and use /**D**atabase **Q**uery **E**xtract, matching records are listed below the output block. Those records, however, overwrite any information in the cells directly below the output block to the bottom of the spreadsheet. If you want to preserve any information in those cells, specify the output block as a multiple-row block. Cells below the last row of the output block therefore are not affected by any results of a search.

For more information, see ***/Database Query Block*** *and* ***/Database Query Criteria Table***.

Database Query Reset /DQR

Purpose

Clears the block specifications for **/D**atabase **Q**uery **B**lock, **C**riteria Table, and **O**utput Block.

Reminder

■ **/D**atabase **Q**uery **R**eset does not erase the database block, criteria table, or output block from the spreadsheet, only the specification now on the **/D**atabase **Q**uery menu.

Procedure

Type */DQR*.

For more information, see ***/Database Query Block***, ***/Database Query Criteria Table***, *and* ***/Database Query Output Block***.

Database Restrict Input /DR

Purpose

Restricts cell-pointer movement to unprotected cells.

Reminders

■ When you choose **R**estrict Input, the input line prompts you for a cell address.

- To use **R**estrict Input effectively, organize your spreadsheet so that the data-entry cells are together. Include text and examples that show the user the format and type of data to enter.
- Before using **R**estrict Input, use /**S**tyle **P**rotect **U**nprotect to identify unprotected data-entry cells. /**O**ptions **P**rotection does not need to be enabled.
- When you use **R**estrict Input, you cannot access any Quattro Pro commands. You also can use only the following function keys: F1 (Help), F2 (Edit), and F4 (Abs).
- When **R**estrict Input is active, you can move the cell selector only to those cells you specified as the restricted input block.

Procedure

1. Type /*DR*.
2. Specify the input block. Include a block that covers all cells in which you want to display or enter data.
3. Press Enter.
4. Make data entries, using normal methods. Press Esc or Enter to exit /**D**atabase **R**estrict Input and return to normal cell-selector movement.

Important Cues

- If you want to set up an entry form, select the entire block, not just the blank cells, when you issue the /**D**atabase **R**estrict Input command. In this manner, the entire form appears on-screen.
- If you select a block to use in **R**estrict Input, the cell selector moves to each cell or block in the unprotected cells in the order of your restricted cells.
- Pressing Esc or Enter is the only way to leave **R**estrict Input.
- Use /**D**atabase **D**ata Entry, /**D**atabase **R**estrict Input, and /**S**tyle **L**ine Drawing to create custom forms that increase the accuracy of data entry.

For more information, see /*Database Data Entry*, /*Style Protect*, /*Style Line Drawing*, and /*Options Protect*.

Database Sort   /DS

Purpose

Sorts the database in ascending or descending order.

Reminders

- You can sort one or more fields (columns). The first sort field is called the **1**st Key; the second is the **2**nd Key. Additional sorting is available using the **3**rd through **5**th keys. You can sort all keys in ascending or descending order.

- Save a copy of the spreadsheet to disk with /**F**ile Save **A**s before sorting. Save to a different name to preserve your original file.

- If you want the records (rows) returned to their original order after sorting, insert a column to the far left (or right) of the database block before you sort and use /**E**dit **F**ill to fill the block with index numbers. Re-sort the database records on the index numbers to return to the original order.

- Quattro Pro sorts in the following order during an ascending sort:

    Blank cells

    Labels beginning with numbers, in numerical order

    Labels beginning with letters and special characters in ASCII order

    Values in numerical order

  Quattro Pro sorts in the following order during a descending sort:

    Values in reverse numerical order

    Labels beginning with letters and special characters in reverse ASCII order

    Labels beginning with numbers in reverse numerical order

    Blank cells

Procedure

1. Type */DS*.
2. Choose **B**lock and highlight the data block to be sorted. You must include every field (column) in the database. Do not include the field labels at the top of the database, however, or Quattro Pro sorts the labels with the data.
3. Press Enter.
4. Move the cell selector to the column of the database that will be the **1**st Key and press Enter.
5. Specify **A**scending or **D**escending order.
6. Choose the **2**nd Key if you want to sort copies of the **1**st Key.
7. Specify **A**scending or **D**escending order.
8. Choose **3**rd Key, **4**th Key, and **5**th Key if you want to sort on additional keys. In the column, enter a cell address on which this key will sort.
9. Specify **A**scending or **D**escending order for these additional keys.
10. Choose **G**o.

Important Cues

- Choose **Q**uit to return to READY mode at any time. Choose **R**eset to clear previous settings.
- Sort settings are saved with the spreadsheet.
- Enable Undo with the /**O**ptions **O**ther **U**ndo **E**nable command and press Alt-F5 if the results of the sort operation are not what you expected.
- To sort columns instead of rows, use /**D**atabase **S**ort **S**ort **R**ules **S**ort Rows/Columns Column. Choose **Q**uit to return to the **S**ort menu. Follow the procedure for sorting rows. Remember to use rows when specifying sort keys.
- To sort numbers before labels, use /**D**atabase **S**ort **S**ort **R**ules **N**umbers before Labels **Y**es.
- To change the way Quattro Pro sorts labels, use /**D**atabase **S**ort **S**ort **R**ules **L**abel Order, and then choose an option as follows:

DATABASE COMMANDS

Option	Function
Dictionary	Sorts labels similar to entries in a dictionary; case is ignored
ASCII	Labels sorted alphabetically; uppercase before lowercase; special characters at the end of the sort

■ Use /**O**ptions **U**pdate to make the new sort settings permanent.

Cautions

■ If you sort a database without including the full width of records, the sorted portion is split from the unsorted portion. Putting the records back together may be nearly impossible. If you saved the spreadsheet to disk before sorting, you can retrieve the original file. You also can use Alt-F5 (Undo) if the command is enabled.

■ Do not include blank rows or the data labels at the top of the database when you highlight the data block. Blank rows sort to the top or bottom of the database in ascending or descending order, and the data labels are sorted into the body of the database.

■ Formulas in a sorted database may not be accurate because sorting switches rows to new locations. If the addresses do not use absolute and relative addressing correctly, the formulas in sorted records change. As a rule, use a relative address in a formula when the address refers to a cell in the same row. If the address refers to a cell outside the database, use an absolute address.

*For more information, see **/Edit Fill** and **/Options Update**.*

Tools Commands /T

The /Tools commands enable you to record, name, invoke, and debug macros; reformat text entries; import ASCII files; combine blocks or files into the current file; restore lost work saved in "keystroke" form (transcript); save a block or the entire file in memory to disk; update links to spreadsheets; perform advanced math operations, including frequency distributions, regression analysis, matrix multiplication, and optimizations; parse ASCII data; perform sensitivity analysis; and find the variable that produces a desired result.

Tools Advanced Math Invert /TAI

Purpose

Inverts columns and rows in square matrices.

Procedure

1. Type */TAI*.
2. Enter the address or name of the block you want to invert.
3. Type or highlight an output block to hold the inverted solution matrix.
4. Press Enter.

Important Cue

- Quattro Pro's maximum matrix that can be inverted is 90 rows by 90 columns.

Caution

- Any existing entries in the output block are overwritten.

For more information, see **/Tools Advanced Math Multiply**.

Tools Advanced Math Multiply /TAM

Purpose

Multiplies column-and-row matrices of cells. Use to solve simultaneous linear equations or to do array math or array manipulations.

Procedure

1. Type */TAM*.
2. Highlight the first block to multiply and press Enter.
3. Highlight the second block and press Enter.
4. Move the cell selector to the upper left corner of the cell that you want to contain the resulting output block, or click the cell with your mouse.
5. Press Enter.

Caution

- The output matrix overwrites any existing entries in the output block.

*For more information, see */Tools Advanced Math Invert*.*

Tools Combine /TC

Purpose

Combines values or formulas from a block or entire file on disk into the spreadsheet in memory.

Reminders

- You can use /Tools Combine three different ways: to copy the contents from the file on disk to the current file; to add values from the file on disk to the current file; and to subtract incoming values from the numeric values in the current file.

- Before starting the /Tools Combine operation, you must know the cell references or blocks you want from the disk and the name of the file on the disk.

- Using the /Tools Combine operation is easiest if the files on disk contain named blocks for the blocks to be combined with the current file in memory.

- Use /Tools Import and Parse to bring ASCII files into the current spreadsheet and organize them. To send your file to an ASCII text file, use /Print Destination File to print the file to disk.

- The format of the cells coming in from disk takes priority over the formats in the current file. Global formats, block names, and column widths do not change.

- /Tools Combine Copy combines values, labels, and formulas. All cell references, relative and absolute, are adjusted to reflect their new locations on the spreadsheet. Cell references are adjusted according to the upper left corner of the combined data block (the cell selector location). Combined formulas adjust for the difference between the cell selector and cell A1 on the current spreadsheet.

Procedure

1. Type */TC*.

2. Choose an available option as follows:

Option	Function
Copy	Copies incoming cell contents over the cells in the current spreadsheet
Add	Adds values from cells in the file spreadsheet to cells containing blanks or values in the current spreadsheet
Subtract	Subtracts values from cells in the file spreadsheet from the corresponding blanks or values in the current spreadsheet

3. Select how much of the saved spreadsheet file you want to use. File combines the entire file on disk with the file in memory, starting at your cell selector location. Block combines cell entries from a named block or block address on the disk-based file with the file in memory.

4. If you choose **File**, choose a file name. Press Enter. If you choose **B**lock, Quattro Pro asks you to enter the block name or the block address.

5. Press Enter.

Important Cues

- If you frequently combine a small portion from a file, first give that portion a block name. Use /**E**dit **N**ames **C**reate to name the portion on the file and save the file back to disk. You then can use /**T**ools **C**ombine and enter the block name as the part you want to combine.

- When creating spreadsheets, you can save time by using /**T**ools **X**tract and **C**ombine to merge parts of existing spreadsheets to form the new one.

- When you use /**T**ools **C**ombine **A**dd, cells in the incoming file that contain labels or string formulas are not added.

Cautions

- Data copied into the current spreadsheet replaces existing data. Blank cells in the incoming spreadsheet take on the value of the cells in the current spreadsheet.

- Block names are not brought to the new spreadsheet when a file is combined. This arrangement prevents possible conflicts with block names in the current spreadsheet. After combining files, you must re-create block names with /**E**dit **N**ames **C**reate or /**E**dit **N**ames **L**abels.

For more information, see /**Edit Names**, /**Tools Import**, /**Tools Parse**, *and* /**Tools Update Links**.

Tools Audit /TD

Purpose

Graphically displays cell dependencies, circular references, label references, cells that return ERR, blank references, and external links.

Procedure

1. Type */TD*.
2. Choose an available option as follows:

Option	Function
Dependency	Displays cell dependencies in a specified block
Circular	Finds all cells containing circular references
Label References	Finds all numeric formulas that refer to labels
ERR	Finds all formulas that return ERR
Blank References	Finds all formulas that refer to blank cells
E**x**ternal Links	Finds all cells containing external links
Destination	Specifies on-screen or printed output; choose **S**creen or **P**rint

3. An audit menu appears. Use the arrow keys to move around and then press the / key to activate the audit screen menu.

Important Cues

- Dependency screens display cell relationships in a tree diagram. Use the arrow keys to trace dependencies and move to other cells. Press the / key activate the menu. Choose **N**ext to audit the next cell in the specified block; choose **P**revious to audit the preceding cell. Choose **G**o**T**o to exit the audit screen and return to the active spreadsheet at the cell that was highlighted in the audit screen. To audit any cell, highlight and choose **B**egin. Choose **Q**uit to return to the active spreadsheet with the audit menu still active.

- Quattro Pro can detect a cell that contains a circular reference to a cell in another spreadsheet only if both spreadsheets are open.

- When checking a block for numeric formulas that refer to blank and label references, check the audit status line to determine the number of references found. If more than one is found, choose /**N**ext to view the next reference. The message `Last reference found` appears after you reach the last reference.

Caution

- Before you delete or rename a spreadsheet, you may want to make sure they do not contain formulas that are linked to other spreadsheets.

For more information, see ***/Options Recalculation*** *and* ***/Windows Options Map View***.

Tools Frequency /TF

Purpose

Creates a frequency distribution displaying how often specific data occurs in a database.

Reminders

- /Tools Frequency works only on numeric values.
- Data must be arranged in a value range: a column, row, or rectangular block.
- You must move the cell selector to a spreadsheet portion that has two adjacent blank columns. In the left column, enter the highest value for each entry in the bin range. Enter bin values in ascending order.

Procedure

1. Type */TF*.
2. Enter the value block, which contains the data being analyzed. Press Enter.
3. Enter the bin block, which contains likely values listed in ascending order in columnar form. Press Enter.

    The frequency distribution appears in the column to the right of the bin block. The frequency column extends one row beyond the bin block.

Important Cues

- Use /**E**dit **F**ill to create a bin range with evenly distributed values.

USING QUATTRO PRO 4, SPECIAL EDITION

- You can find distribution patterns of subgroups in your database by first using /Database Query Extract to create a select database. Use /Tools Frequency to find the distribution in the subgroup.

- Use @DCOUNT if you want to count items that match more than one criterion. (/Tools Frequency uses the bin as the only criterion.) Insert criteria in the criteria block by using /Tools What-If **1** Variable or **2** Variables.

Cautions

- Labels and blank cells are evaluated as zero in the value's range.

- /Tools Frequency overwrites any cell contents that previously existed in the frequency column.

For more information, see /Tools What-If 1 Variable, /Tools What-If 2 Variables, /Edit Fill, and /Database Query Extract.

Tools Import   /TI

Purpose

Brings ASCII text files created from other programs stored on disk into a Quattro Pro file in memory.

Reminders

- You can use the three Tools Import options to transfer data into a Quattro Pro spreadsheet. The first option reads each row of ASCII characters as left-aligned labels in a column; the second option reads into separate cells text enclosed in commas and quotation marks; and the third option reads text surrounded by only commas.

- Make sure that you have enough room on the spreadsheet to receive the imported data, because incoming characters replace the current cell contents. One row in an ASCII file equals one row on the spreadsheet. The number of columns depends on whether the incoming ASCII data is pure text (a single column) or delimited text (multiple columns).

■ ASCII files must have the extension PRN. If you want to import a text file without the PRN extension, use the DOS RENAME command to change the extension.

Procedure

1. Place the cell selector in the upper left corner of the block in which you want to import data.
2. Type */TI*.
3. Select the method of importing the ASCII file from the following options:

Option	Function
ASCII Text File	Makes each row of characters in the ASCII file a left-aligned label in the spreadsheet; labels are in a single column from the cell selector down
Comma & ""	Enters each row of characters in the ASCII Delimited File file into a row in the spreadsheet; characters within quotation marks are assigned to a cell as a label, whereas each group of numbers without quotation marks is assigned to a cell as a value and other characters are ignored
Only Commas	Enters each row of characters in the ASCII file into a row in the spreadsheet; characters within quotation marks are assigned to a cell as a label, whereas each group of numbers without quotation marks is assigned to a cell as a value and text that includes a comma is assigned to a cell as a label

4. Select or type the name of the ASCII file. Do not type the PRN file extension.
5. Press Enter.

Important Cues

■ Quattro Pro cannot import ASCII files with more than 8,192 rows. Lines longer than 254 characters wrap to the next spreadsheet row. If necessary, you can use a word processor to read, modify, and divide the ASCII files into smaller files before saving them to disk as ASCII files. Make sure that you save the files only as ASCII.

- You can separate ASCII text files that are not delimited by quotation marks or commas. Use /Tools Import ASCII Text File to bring the file into the spreadsheet. Use /Tools Parse to separate the resulting long label into separate cells of data.

Cautions

- Like /File Retrieve, /Tools Import does not replace the file in memory; incoming data replaces existing cell contents. Use a new spreadsheet or blank area of the current spreadsheet when importing PRN files. If you are unsure of the size of the file you are importing, use the DOS TYPE command to review the ASCII file.

- Word processing files contain special control codes that Quattro Pro cannot translate properly. Save your word processing document as an ASCII file before you try to import the document into Quattro Pro.

For more information, see **/Tools Parse** and **/File Retrieve**.

Tools Library /TL

Purpose

Enables you to load or unload add-in functions.

Procedure

1. Type */TLL*.
2. Choose an add-in file. (Add-in files have a QLL extension.)
3. You can test for the existence of add-in functions using two new @functions: @ISAAF and @ISAPP. Use @ISAAF to test for the existence of a specific @function in loaded add-ins; use @ISAPP to test whether a particular add-in file is loaded.
4. When using an add-in @function, you must append the add-in module name in front of the @function name, the two names must be separated by a period, and the string must be surrounded by quotation marks—for example, @ISAAF("BUDGETS.ROLLUP") or @ISAPP("BUDGETS").

TOOLS COMMANDS

Important Cues

- An add-in is loaded until you unload it by using the **/Tools Library Unload** command.
- For more information on @function arguments, refer to your add-in instructions.

Tools Macro   /TM

Purpose

Enables you to name, create, execute, and debug macros.

Reminders

- You can use Alt-F2 to invoke the **/Tools Macro** command menu.
- Record mode records keystroke-equivalent commands you initiate in Quattro Pro, not the keystrokes used to initiate the commands.
- To exit Record mode, choose **/Tools Record** (Alt-F2 **R**) again.

Procedure

1. Type */TM*.
2. Choose one of the following options:

Option	Function
Record	Places Quattro Pro in Record mode and records in memory your spreadsheet activity
Paste	Copies the keystrokes in memory to a specified block in the current file
Instant Replay	Executes the last macro recorded
Macro Recording	Specifies keystrokes recorded as menu-equivalent commands (Logical) or literal keystrokes (Keystroke)

continues

Option	Function
Transcript	Stores the exact keystrokes during your Quattro Pro session on file
Clear Breakpoints	Clears macro debugging breakpoints
Debugger	Activates Quattro Pro's macro debugger
Name	Names a macro
Library	Enables you to specify a spreadsheet as a macro library
Execute	Executes a selected macro
Key Reader	Enables Quattro Pro to translate 1-2-3 macros

Important Cues

- You also can exit Record mode by choosing **Paste**. When you choose **P**aste, Quattro Pro prompts you for a macro name and a block to place the macro from memory into the current spreadsheet.

- Use Instant Replay to execute and test a macro before copying the macro into the spreadsheet with **P**aste.

- You also can name macros with /**E**dit **N**ames **C**reate and **L**abels.

Caution

- Be careful if you use Instant Replay and your macro includes /**F**ile **S**ave. You may overwrite the original file accidentally with a file that has unwanted changes.

For more information, see /**E**dit **N**ames **C**reate and **L**abels and /**F**ile **S**ave.

Tools Optimizer /TO

Purpose

Defines and solves complex nonlinear problems that can involve multiple variables and constraints.

TOOLS COMMANDS

Reminders

- This command replaces the /Tools Advanced Math Optimization command in earlier versions.

- Macros from versions 3.0 or earlier that use the /Tools Advanced Math Optimization command should execute correctly in Version 4.0 if they contain menu-equivalent commands rather than keystrokes.

Procedure

1. Type */TO*.

2. Choose Solution Cell Cell to specify the cell whose value you want to maximize, minimize, or equate with another value.

3. Choose Solution Cell Max, Min, Equal. Choose one of the following options:

Option	Function
Maximize	Maximizes the formula's resulting value in the solution cell
Minimize	Minimizes the formula's resulting value in the solution cell
Equal	Makes the formula in the solution cell a specific value
None	Searches for a solution without considering the solution cell

4. Choose Variable Cell(s) to specify the cell or cells whose variables Quattro Pro can change to reach an optimal solution.

5. Choose Constraints to specify the limits you want to place on the Variable Cell(s) and the Solution Cell. At the Add New Constraints prompt, press Enter and type the constraint expression(s).

6. Choose Options to adjust settings that can improve the accuracy of an Optimizer operation. Your choices are as follows:

Option	Function
Max Iterations	Specifies the number of times that Quattro Pro must try to find a best solution to the problem; enter a value between 1 and 1000 (the default is 100)
Precision	Enter a value between 0 and 1 to describe the precision you want to observe in the answer that Quattro Pro finds (default is 0.0005)
Linear or Nonlinear	Set this option to match the problem type: Linear or Nonlinear (the default)
Show Iteration	Tells Quattro Pro whether to pause between Results iterations so that you can review the current solution; default setting is No
Estimates	Chooses one of two approaches for obtaining initial estimates of basic variables in each iteration: Quadratic or Tangent (the default)
Derivatives	Chooses one of two differencing methods for estimates of partial derivatives: Central or Forward (the default)
Search	Chooses the method for computing the search direction: Conjugate or Newton (the default)

7. Choose Go to begin the search for the optimal solution.

Important Cues

- The default settings on the Options menu usually are sufficient to enable Quattro Pro to locate an acceptable solution. If Quattro Pro cannot locate a solution, experiment with the various settings on the Options menu.

- Choose /Tools Optimizer Answer Report to produce a report that lists the solution cell and variable cells with their original and final values and variable dual values. The Answer Report prints in the spreadsheet to a block that you specify and contains information about the constraints you identified.

- Choose /Tools Optimizer Detail Report to produce a report that lists, at each iteration, the variable cells and the solution cell.

TOOLS COMMANDS

- Use the /Tools Optimizer Restore command to recover the previous variable cell values in the spreadsheet. If /Options Recalculation is set to Manual, however, you must press F9 after choosing Restore to recalculate and display the previous values.

- Use the /Tools Optimizer Model command to load and save multiple problem definitions containing the Solution Cell, Variable Cell(s), and Constraint settings.

- Use the /Tools Optimizer Reset command to clear Optimizer settings individually. Choose the All option to clear all settings on the Optimizer menu.

Tools Parse /TP

Purpose

Separates ASCII file's long labels into distinct text and numeric cell entries.

Reminders

- Import the PRN file with /Tools Import ASCII Text File. Each row of text from the file appears in a single cell. Rows of text appear down a single column.

- The long label resulting from /Tools Import ASCII Text File may appear to be entries in more than one cell; however, the long label is located in the single cell at the far left of the spreadsheet.

- If the file you are importing includes numbers surrounded by spaces and text within quotation marks, use /Tools Import Comma & "" Delimited File or Only Commas. These commands separate numbers and text into separate cells.

- Find in the spreadsheet a clear area to which you can copy the parsed data, and then note the cell addresses of the corners. Move the cell selector to the first cell in the column you want to parse. You also can copy the parsed data on top of itself, thereby erasing the original data.

- /Tools Parse separates the long label by using the rules displayed in the format line. You can edit the format line if you want the data to be separated in a different way.

Procedure

1. Type /*TP*.
2. Choose **C**reate. Quattro Pro inserts above the current cell selector a format line that shows its "best guess" at how Quattro Pro should separate the data in the cell selector.
3. If you want to change the rules that Quattro Pro displays, choose **E**dit from the /**T**ools **P**arse menu. Change the format line to include or exclude data and press Enter. To change the format line, type over the existing symbols with different symbols.
4. If the imported data is in different formats, you must create additional format lines. Enter these new format lines at the row where the data format is different. Create additional format lines by selecting **C**reate and repeating the procedure. Then, change that format line by selecting **E**dit.
5. Choose **I**nput.
6. Highlight the column that contains the data and the format lines. Press Enter.
7. Choose **O**utput.
8. Move the cell selector to the upper left corner of the block to receive the parsed data and press Enter.
9. Choose **G**o.

Important Cues

- Use symbols to indicate the first character of a label (L), value (V), date , or time (T). You also can choose to skip a character (S), specify additional characters of the same type (>), or add a blank space (*) if the data is longer than the > symbols indicate.

- You can use editing keys on the format line to change the parsing rules. You also can use the up- and down-arrow keys and the PgDn and PgUp keys to scroll the information on-screen. Use this method to see whether the format line has assigned enough space for each piece of data being parsed.

Caution

- In most cases, the output block should be blank. Parsed data overwrites any cell entries in the output block.

For more information, see /**Tools Import**.

Tools Reformat /TR

Purpose

Fits text within a desired block by wrapping words to form complete paragraphs. Redistributes words so that text lines are approximately the same length.

Reminders

- **/Tools R**eformat does not format labels to be flush right as most word processors do. This command fits labels as closely as possible into a given block.

- **/Tools R**eformat affects only one column of long labels. The command does not justify other columns of labels in the same row.

- If you are uncertain about the results of **/Tools R**eformat, save your spreadsheet to disk with **F**ile Save **A**s. If you have Undo enabled, press Alt-F5 before using **/Tools R**eformat.

- Other cells are moved to reflect the reformat unless you specify a block for **/Tools R**eformat.

Procedure

1. Place the cell selector at the top of the columns of text that you want to justify.
2. Type */TR*.
3. Highlight the block in which you want the text justified. If you choose not to specify a block for the justification, highlight only the first row of the text column.
4. Press Enter.

Important Cues

- **/Tools R**eformat reformats all text in a column until Quattro Pro reaches a blank cell or number.

- If the specified block is not large enough to hold the justified text, Quattro Pro displays an error message. To solve this problem, enlarge the block or move the text to a new location. If you enlarge the block, you may need to move other cell contents.

Cautions

- If you reformat a block that includes a text formula, the formula is no longer valid.

- If the data below the justified labels includes formulas, and Quattro Pro moves data below the justified labels, formulas may miscalculate without warning. Quattro Pro adjusts formulas with relative cell references when they are moved; consequently, the formulas may refer to different cells and result in different answers. Formulas do not necessarily result in ERR.

For more information, see */Tools Import*, */File Save As*, */Tools Import*, */Style Protect*, and */Options Protection*.

Tools Solve For /TS

Purpose

Recalculates a formula backwards, starting with the desired result and solving for a variable that produces the result.

Procedure

1. Type */TS*.
2. Choose **F**ormula Cell and specify the cell that contains the formula.
3. Choose **T**arget Value and specify the result that you want from the formula.
4. Choose **V**ariable Cell and specify the cell that Quattro Pro can vary to achieve the result that you want.
5. Choose **G**o to solve the formula.

Important Cues

- The **T**arget Value must be a single value, not a conditional statement.

- The **T**arget Value can reference a cell or a formula's result.

- You can change the number of iterations. The */Tools Solve For Parameters Max Iterations* default is 5. The maximum iteration amount is 99.

TOOLS COMMANDS

- The **/T**ools **S**olve For **P**arameters **A**ccuracy default is 0.0005.
- Use **/T**ools **S**olve For **R**eset to remove variables and return **P**arameters settings to Quattro Pro defaults.

Caution

- **S**olve For calculates only values, not dates.

Tools Update Links   /TU

Purpose

Updates linked spreadsheets. Recalculates formulas in the linked spreadsheet to ensure that your spreadsheet is using current data when users share files, such as on a network; changes the link from one supporting spreadsheet to another; and cancels the link between spreadsheets.

Procedure

1. Type */TU*.
2. Choose one of the following options:

Option	Function
Open	Opens one or more supporting spreadsheets that are linked to the current spreadsheet
Refresh	Recalculates in the current spreadsheet formulas that depend on data in other unopened files on disk; ensures that your spreadsheet is using current data when users share files, such as on a network
Change	Unlinks your spreadsheet from one supporting spreadsheet and links it to another
Delete	Cancels the link between your primary spreadsheet and one or more supporting spreadsheets

3. Press Shift-F7 (Select) to select each spreadsheet. To deselect a spreadsheet, press Shift-F7 (Select) again. To select or deselect all spreadsheets, press Alt-F7 (All Select).
4. Press Enter.

Important Cues

- Use /**T**ools **U**pdate Links **R**efresh if you use Quattro Pro on a network to access the most current data or if the current spreadsheet contains links to unopened spreadsheets.

- Structure your linked spreadsheet applications in a hierarchical fashion so that you can update links quickly.

Tools What-If /TW

Purpose

Generates a table composed of one or two various input values and the result from single or multiple formulas.

Reminders

- Formulas in /Tools What-If tables can include @functions.

- Use /Tools What-If **1** Variable to show how changes in one variable affect the output from one or more formulas. Use /Tools What-If **2** Variables to show how changes in two variables affect the output in a single formula.

- Before executing /Tools What-If **1** Variable, enter data and formulas as though you are solving for a single solution.

- Before executing /Tools What-If **2** Variables, enter data and formulas as though you are solving for a single solution.

- In the leftmost column of the /Tools What-If **1** Variable table, enter the numbers or text to be used as the replacement for the first variable (Input 1). In the second blank cell in the top row of the what-if table, type the address of the cell containing the formula. Enter additional formulas to the right on the same row. The upper left corner of the /Tools What-If **1** Variable area remains blank.

- In the leftmost column of the /Tools What-If 2 Variables table, enter the numbers or text to be used by the first variable, Input 1. In the top row of the table, enter the numbers or text to be used by the second variable, Input 2. In the blank cell in the upper left corner of the table, type the address of the cell containing the formula.

- Use /Style Numeric Format Text to display the cell addresses of the formulas at the top of the /Tools What-If 1 Variable table. You may need to widen the columns if you want to see entire formulas.

- To update the table after spreadsheet changes are made, press F8 (Table) to repeat the most recent /Tools What-If operation.

Procedure

1. Type */TW1* or */TW2*.

2. For /TW1, enter the table block so that it includes the Input 1 values or text in the extreme left column and the formulas in the top row.

   For /TW2, enter the table block so that it includes the Input 1 values in the extreme left column and the Input 2 values in the top row.

3. Enter the address for Input 1 formula cell. For /TW2, enter the address for the formula cell for Input 2.

Important Cues

- Make the formulas in the top row of the data table area easier to understand by using /Edit Names Create to change address locations into descriptive text. /Style Numeric Format Text displays formulas as text, although the formulas still execute as though cell addresses are displayed.

- After you designate block and input values, you can enter new variables in the table and recalculate a new table by pressing F8 (Table). You cannot recalculate a what-if table the same way you recalculate a spreadsheet by setting /Options Recalculation Mode to Automatic, by pressing F9 (Calc), or by placing {CALC} in a macro.

- If input values vary by a constant amount, create the input values by using /Edit Fill.

- **/Tools What-If** tables, combined with @D functions, is useful for cross-tabulating information from a what-if table.

- **/Tools A**dvanced Math **O**ptimization may find the solution to a problem more efficiently than /Tools What-If tables.

Caution

- The what-if table overwrites any existing cell entries.

For more information, see /Edit Fill, /Style Numeric Format, and /Tools Advanced Math Optimization.

Tools Xtract   /TX

Purpose

Saves a copy of a portion of the current spreadsheet to another file on disk. You can save the block as it appears on the spreadsheet (with formulas) or save only the results of the formulas.

Reminders

- Extracted blocks that include formulas should include the cells the formulas refer to; otherwise, the formulas will not be accurate.

- If the CALC indicator appears at the bottom of the screen, calculate the file before extracting values. Press F9 (Calc) to calculate the file.

Procedure

1. Type */TX*.

2. Choose an available option. **Formulas** saves formulas and cell contents from the current spreadsheet as a new spreadsheet. **Values** saves only formula results.

3. Type a file name other than the current spreadsheet name. If you want to overwrite the data in a particular file, select that file name from the menu.

4. Highlight the block of the spreadsheet that you want to extract as a separate file. Press Enter.

5. If the file name you selected in step 3 already exists, choose **C**ancel to cancel the Xtract operation, **R**eplace to replace the existing file with the **X**tract block you specified, or **B**ackup to create a backup file (extension BAK) of the existing file. The Xtract block is saved with the file name you indicated in step 3.

Important Cues

- If you use **/T**ools **X**tract **F**ormulas to save a portion of a spreadsheet, the extracted file can function as a normal spreadsheet.

- To freeze a spreadsheet so that formulas and results don't change, extract a file with **/T**ools **X**tract **V**alues. Values replace the formulas.

- Use **/T**ools **X**tract to save memory when a spreadsheet becomes too large. Separate the spreadsheet into smaller spreadsheets that require less memory.

- Increase spreadsheet execution speed and save memory by breaking large spreadsheets into smaller ones with **/F**ile **X**tract **F**ormulas. Link the extracted spreadsheets so that they still pass data between them.

- You easily can extract a block or entire file by using **/F**ile **N**ew and copy cell entries to the new spreadsheet with **/E**dit **C**opy.

Caution

- Make sure that the extracted spreadsheet does not use values or formulas outside the extract block.

For more information, see **/Tools Combine**, **/Tools Update Links**, **/File Save**, **/File New**, *and* **/Edit Copy**.

Options Commands /O

/**O**ptions commands control the display formats, protection, and start-up settings of Quattro Pro. If you want to change these settings for only part of the spreadsheet, use the /**S**tyle commands. To change settings that affect the entire spreadsheet or file, however, use the /**O**ptions commands.

Options SpeedBar /OB

Purpose

Assigns a new function to any of the Speedbar buttons on the READY or EDIT mode SpeedBars.

Reminder

- The /**O**ptions Speed**B**ar command replaces the /**O**ptions **M**ouse Palette command of earlier versions.

Procedure

1. Type */OB*.
2. Select the READY mode or EDIT mode SpeedBar.
3. Choose the button you want to customize.
4. Choose **S**hort Name. Type a name of up to 3 characters and press Enter. The short name appears on the button when you are in text display mode.
5. Choose **L**ong Name. Type a name of up to 10 characters and then press Enter. The long name appears on the button when you are in WYSIWYG mode.
6. Choose **M**acro. Enter any valid macro command and press Enter.
7. Choose **Q**uit to return to the /**O**ptions Speed**B**ar menu.

OPTIONS COMMANDS

911

Important Cues

- Quattro Pro enables you to customize all 15 buttons on each SpeedBar. When the number of SpeedBar buttons is unable to fit into the width of your screen display, Quattro Pro replaces the rightmost button with the Bar button. Click the bar button to display additional button assignments for the current SpeedBar.

- To change the color of a SpeedBar button, choose /**O**ptions **C**olors **M**enu Speed**B**ar.

- You cannot assign text or macros to the help icon (?) or to the arrow keys in conjunction with the End key.

- Quattro Pro uses the changes to the SpeedBar buttons for only the current session of Quattro Pro. If you want to use the SpeedBar button changes in future Quattro Pro sessions, initiate the changes and then choose /**O**ptions **U**pdate.

For more information, see /**Options Colors** and /**Options Update**.

Options Colors /OC

Purpose

Specifies display colors for each part of the Quattro Pro program.

Procedure

1. Type /*OC*.
2. Choose an available option as follows:

Option	Function
Menu	Changes the display colors of the command menus
Desktop	Sets the colors for on-screen error and status messages and for the area outside of windows
Spreadsheet	Sets the colors in spreadsheet windows; in WYSIWYG mode, this option changes the colors for various screen elements

continues

Option	Function
Conditional	Changes the colors for spreadsheet values that meet certain conditions
Help	Specifies the display colors of the help system
File Manager	Changes the colors in a File Manager window
Palettes	Restores the default colors for a display in color, monochrome, or black and white with a CGA video adapter
Quit	Returns to the /Options menu

3. Select the part of the program area for which you want to change the color, choose a color or option, and then press Enter.

Important Cue

■ Quattro Pro displays the colors you select for the current session of Quattro Pro. If you want to set the display colors permanently, specify the colors and then choose /Options Update.

For more information, see /Options Update.

Options Display Mode /OD

Purpose

Sets the screen display mode for text and graphics modes.

Procedure

1. Type */OD*.
2. Choose one of the following options:

OPTIONS COMMANDS

Option	Function
A: 80x25	Displays regular text, 80 columns and 25 lines; graphs inserted in the spreadsheet are indicated by highlighting; if you have a mouse installed, the pointer appears as a block
B: WYSIWYG	Displays spreadsheets with font types and sizes; shows the mouse buttons, SpeedBar, and scroll boxes with a sculpted three-dimensional look; displays the mouse pointer as an arrowhead rather than a block; Graph Annotator displays a pictorial gallery of colors and other menu choices
C: EGA:80x43	Displays 80 columns and 43 lines if you have an EGA card
D: VGA:80x50	Displays 80 columns and 50 lines if you have a VGA card
E through **N**	Displays up to 132 columns in extended text mode

3. Press Enter.
4. If your monitor and graphics card support extended text, choose an option (from E through N) and then choose an extended display mode from the list that Quattro Pro displays.

Important Cues

■ You cannot stack windows in WYSIWYG mode.

■ Quattro Pro uses the display mode you choose for the current session of Quattro Pro. If you want to set the display mode permanently, specify the mode and then choose **/O**ptions **U**pdate.

*For more information, see **/Options Hardware**.*

Options Formats Align Labels /OFA

Purpose

Specifies default label alignment for the entire spreadsheet.

Reminders

- Before you build the spreadsheet, decide how to align the labels. Use /Options Formats Align Labels to select left alignment (the default setting), right alignment, or center alignment.

- Using /Options Formats Align Labels after you begin to build the spreadsheet does not affect existing labels. Alignment previously set with /Style Alignment is not altered by /Options Formats Align Labels.

Procedure

1. Type */OFA*.
2. Choose one of the following options:

Option	Function
Right	Aligns label with cell's right edge
Left	Aligns label with cell's left edge (the default)
Center	Centers label in a cell

For more information, see */Options Formats Numeric Format*, */Style Alignment*, and */Style Numeric Format*.

Options Formats Global Width /OFG

Purpose

Sets column width for the entire spreadsheet.

Reminder

- Before you use /**O**ptions **F**ormats **G**lobal Width, decide on the column widths you need for the spreadsheet and position the cell pointer so that an average column width is displayed.

Procedure

1. Type */OFG*.
2. Enter the number for the column width that you use most frequently. Alternatively, you can press the right-arrow key to increase column width or the left-arrow key to decrease column width. Press Enter.

Important Cues

- Use /**S**tyle **C**olumn Width to set individual columns so that numbers and labels display correctly. When the column width is too narrow for the value entered, asterisks display in the cell.

- Column widths previously set with /**S**tyle **C**olumn Width or /**S**tyle **B**lock Widths **S**et Width keep their original settings.

- The default column width is 9 characters in text mode. Column width settings can range from 1 to 254 characters.

Caution

- If you use a spreadsheet with two panes and change the column width in one or both panes, settings in the bottom and right panes in a horizontally and vertically split window, respectively, are lost when the panes are cleared. Quattro Pro retains the column widths used in the top pane of a horizontal split or the left pane of a vertical split.

For more information, see ***/Style Block Size*** *and* ***/Style Column Width/Reset Width***.

Options Formats Hide Zeros　　　　　　/OFH

Purpose

Suppresses the display of zeros on-screen and on printed reports.

Procedure

1. Type */OFH*.
2. Choose **Yes** or **No**. **Y**es suppresses the display of cells containing zero or a result of zero. **N**o (the default) displays a zero in cells containing zero, or a result of zero.

Important Cues

- Zeros that display despite the /**O**ptions **F**ormats **H**ide Zeros command are actually values greater than zero. The values look like zero because their format displays them rounded to zero.

- Suppressed zeros in formulas and typed entries still are evaluated as zeros by other formulas.

- Use one of the following as a start-up macro to suppress the display of zeros in your spreadsheet each time you retrieve the spreadsheet:

    {/ Defaults;Zero}y

    /ofhy

Caution

- If zeros are suppressed, you accidentally may erase or overwrite parts of the spreadsheet that appear blank but contain suppressed zeros. To prevent accidental erasures and typeovers, use /**O**ptions **P**rotection **E**nable and /**S**tyle **P**rotect **U**nprotect.

For more information, see */Options Protection* and */Style Protection*.

Options Formats Numeric Format   /OFN

Purpose

Defines the default display format for numeric values and formulas in the spreadsheet.

Reminders

- Before you use /**O**ptions **F**ormats **N**umeric Format, determine the appropriate format for the spreadsheet application.

- To format only part of the spreadsheet, use /**S**tyle **N**umeric Format rather than /**O**ptions **F**ormats **N**umeric Format.

Procedure

1. Type */OFN*.
2. Choose one of the following options:

Option	Function
Fixed	Determines the number of decimal places that display
Scientific	Displays large or small numbers using scientific notation
Currency	Displays currency symbols ($, for example) and commas
, (comma)	Inserts commas to mark thousands and multiples of thousands
General	Displays values with no special formatting
+/−	Creates horizontal bar graphs; each symbol equals one whole number, in which positive numbers display as plus (+) symbols and negative numbers display as minus (−) symbols
Percent	Displays a decimal number as a whole percentage number with a % sign

continues

Option	Function
Date	Displays serial-date numbers in the following formats: DD-MMM-YY 12-Jan-91 DD-MMM 12-Jan MMM-YY Jan-91 MM/DD/YY 01/12/91 MM/DD 01/12
Text	Evaluates formulas as numbers but displays formulas as text
Hidden	Hides contents from the display and does not print them; however, still evaluates cell contents

3. If you choose **F**ixed, **S**cientific, **C**urrency, comma (,), or **P**ercent, enter the number of decimal places. Press Enter.

Important Cues

■ If you enter a number too large for the formatted cell, the cell displays asterisks. To remove the asterisks, move the cell pointer to the cell, choose /**S**tyle **C**olumn Width, and press the right-arrow key until the column is wide enough to display the entire number.

■ To display non-USA formats with commands, use /**O**ptions **I**nternational.

■ /**O**ptions **F**ormats **N**umeric Format does not affect formats that you entered previously with /**S**tyle **N**umeric Format.

Cautions

■ /**O**ptions **F**ormats **N**umeric Format rounds displayed numbers to the specified decimal setting, but Quattro Pro always calculates to 15-decimal precision. To keep Quattro Pro from displaying apparently wrong values, use @ROUND to round formula results so that calculated results match displayed values.

■ Other users may enter percentage values incorrectly if you use the **P**ercent format. Consider entering a screen prompt into the spreadsheet to remind users to place a percent sign (%) after percentages.

For more information, see /**Style Numeric Format**.

Options Graphics Quality /OG

Purpose

Selects the quality of the printed font for text in a spreadsheet or graph.

Reminder

- **/Options Graphics Quality** affects how your printouts appear when you use **/Print Destination Graphics Printer**.

Procedure

1. Type */OG*.
2. Choose **D**raft or **F**inal font quality.

Important Cues

- **D**raft suppresses building new Bitstream font files until you finish working, substituting Hershey fonts for Bitstream fonts Quattro Pro has not built already.
- **F**inal builds separate Bitstream font files when you access the Screen Previewer, access the Graph Annotator, display a graph, or begin printing.

For more information, see **/Print Destination** and **/Graph Text Font**.

Options Hardware /OH

Purpose

Specifies display formats and start-up settings for your computer system. Controls how Quattro Pro works with the screen, printers, mouse buttons, conventional memory, expanded memory (EMS), and a coprocessor.

Procedure

1. Type */OH*.
2. Choose the setting that you want to change from the following options:

Option	Function
Screen	Specifies screen settings: **Screen Type** selects a different screen driver for displaying graphs, **Resolution** changes the resolution to attain a better-looking screen, **Aspect Ratio** adjusts the screen so that it displays a perfect circle, **CGA Snow Suppression** prevents CGA screens from flickering when you scroll, and **Quit** returns to the /Options menu
Printers	Specifies printer settings and connections: **1**st Printer and **2**nd Printer specify the make, model, mode, device baud rate, parity, and stop bits for the primary and secondary printer, respectively; **Default Printer** specifies the primary or secondary printer as the default printer; **Plotter Speed** sets the speed for running a color plotter; **Fonts** specifies the LaserJet or Canon font cartridges that you are using in your HP LaserJet printer, turning off automatic scaling for fonts in graphs; **Auto-LF** instructs Quattro Pro to insert a line feed after each printer line; **Single Sheet Yes** or **No** specifies single sheets of paper or continuous-feed paper, respectively; and **Background Yes** or **No** specifies whether background printing is to be used if the BPS is loaded
Mouse Button	Specifies the **Left** or **Right** mouse button for selecting commands and highlighting cell blocks
Normal Memory	Displays the number of bytes available in system memory (RAM), total bytes available, and the percentage of memory available
EMS	Displays the number of bytes available in expanded memory, total bytes available, and the percentage of memory available
Coprocessor	Displays whether your PC is using a math coprocessor

Important Cues

- The **/O**ptions **H**ardware **P**rinters **P**lotter **S**peed default value is 0, the fastest speed allowed by your plotter. The speed 1 is the slowest and 9 is the fastest that Quattro Pro permits.

- **L**eft is the default setting for **/O**ptions **H**ardware **M**ouse **B**utton.

- Quattro Pro uses the hardware settings you select for only the current session. If you want to set the hardware settings permanently, specify the settings and then choose **/O**ptions **U**pdate.

- If you are working on a network, set your printer device to Network Queue by selecting **/O**ptions **H**ardware **P**rinters **1**st (or **2**nd) **P**rinter **D**evice **N**etwork **Q**ueue.

For more information, see ***/Options Network Queue Monitor****.*

Options International /OI

Purpose

Specifies international display formats and start-up settings for currency, punctuation, dates, time, and overstrike print. Controls how Quattro Pro works with sort rules and the Lotus International Character Set (LICS).

Procedure

1. Type */OI*.
2. Select the setting that you want to change from the following options:

Option	Function
Currency	Specifies display settings for currency. Enter a character, character combination, or a special ASCII character; **P**refix specifies the position of the character before the currency value, **S**uffix specifies the position of the character after the currency value

continues

Option	Function
Punctuation	Specifies display settings for punctuation; designates a decimal point in numbers, separates arguments in @functions and macro commands, and separates thousands in numbers
Date	Displays the long and short international date formats; choose from the following options: **A**: MM/DD/YY (01/12/91) **B**: DD/MM/YY (12/01/91) **C**: DD.MM.YY (12.01.91) **D**: YY-MM-DD (91-01-12)
Time	Displays the long and short international time formats; choose from the following options: **A**: HH:MM:SS (10:25:30) **B**: HH.MM.SS (10.25.30) **C**: HH,MM,SS (10,25,30) **D**: HHhMMmSSs (10h25m30s)
Use Sort Table	Changes the sort rules used with /**D**atabase **S**ort; choose from the following options: **A**SCII.SOR sorts uppercase before lowercase, and accented letters appear after Z's; **I**NTL.SOR sorts uppercase, lowercase, and international accented letters; **N**ORDAN.SOR sorts uppercase, lowercase, Norwegian, and Danish characters; **S**WEDFIN.SOR sorts uppercase, lowercase, Swedish, and Finnish characters
LICS	During file retrieval, converts Lotus International Conversion Character Set characters in your Lotus 1-2-3 WK1 spreadsheets into ASCII characters
Overstrike	Prints accented letters if you have a 7-bit Print printer
Quit	Returns to READY mode

Important Cue

- Quattro Pro uses the international settings you choose for only the current session of Quattro Pro. If you want to use the international settings in future Quattro Pro sessions, specify the settings and then choose /**O**ptions **U**pdate. When you choose /**O**ptions **U**pdate, Quattro Pro changes the settings for all entries in your spreadsheet.

For more information, see /*Options Update*.

Options Network /ON

Purpose

Configures options that control how Quattro Pro operates on a Novell network running NetWare 2.15c or later.

Reminder

- Make sure that you load the NetWare IPX shell before you create drive mappings for a network drive.

Procedure

1. Type /*ON*.

2. Choose **D**rive Mappings to create drive mappings for a network drive. When prompted, enter the drive letter, the file server name, the volume name, the directory path name, and the user name.

3. Choose **B**anner **Y**es if you want to create an identifying banner before each print job. Choose **B**anner **N**o to cancel network banner printing.

4. To specify how often Quattro Pro updates queue information in the Print Manager window and on the status line while the Queue Monitor is engaged, choose **R**efresh Interval and enter a number between 1 and 300. Check with your network administrator to determine a **R**efresh setting that will not overburden the network.

5. To track the progress of print jobs in the network print queue, choose **Q**ueue Monitor **Y**es. The Queue Monitor displays on the status line the number of print jobs you have sent, the number of jobs ahead of you in the queue, and the status of your first uncompleted job.

6. To set the default user name for network access, choose **U**ser Name. Type in a name of up to 32 characters and then press Enter.

Important Cue

- After you establish drive mappings for a network drive through Quattro Pro, you can use any of the **F**ile menu commands to read and write data to and from a network drive.

Caution

- Before you change any network options, consult with your network administrator to make sure you have the appropriate access rights to make changes to your network.

For more information, see **/Print Print Manager**.

Options Other   /OO

Purpose

Enables or disables the Undo feature. Also specifies start-up settings for redrawing the screen during macro execution, selecting the clock display, and working with Paradox files on a network.

Procedure

1. Type */OO*.
2. Choose one of the following options:

Option	Function
Undo	Activates or deactivates Undo: choose **E**nable to activate Undo or **D**isable to deactivate Undo; **Q**uit returns to the /**O**ptions **O**ther menu

OPTIONS COMMANDS

Option	Function
Macro	Specifies which parts of the screen (if any) to redraw during macro execution
Expanded Memory	Specifies how Quattro Pro uses expanded memory (EMS): **B**oth stores spreadsheet data and formats, **S**preadsheet Data stores only cell data, **F**ormat stores only spreadsheet formatting data, and **N**one tells Quattro Pro not to use expanded memory
Clock	Displays **S**tandard or **I**nternational date and time formats; choose **N**one to not display the date and time
Paradox	Specifies the network type, sets the directory in which PARADOX.NET is stored, and specifies the time interval that Quattro Pro waits between trying to open locked files on a network

Important Cue

- Quattro Pro uses the /**O**ptions **O**ther settings for only the current session of Quattro Pro. If you want to use the /**O**ptions **O**ther settings in future Quattro Pro sessions, make the changes and then choose /**O**ptions **U**pdate.

For more information see /Edit Undo, /Options Update, and /Tools Macro Transcript.

Options Protection /OP

Purpose

Enables or disables spreadsheet protection.

Reminder

- Before you enable spreadsheet protection, save time by making sure that your spreadsheet is complete. After the spreadsheet is protected, you must disable protection or unprotect a block before you can modify the spreadsheet.

Procedure

1. Type */OP*.
2. Choose **E**nable to protect the spreadsheet. Choose **D**isable to remove protection from the spreadsheet.

Important Cues

- Before or after you protect the entire spreadsheet, you can use /**S**tyle **P**rotection **U**nprotect to specify cells that can be changed.

- Protected cells display PR in the input line. Unprotected cells display U in the input line.

- While /**O**ptions **P**rotection is enabled, the /**D**atabase **R**estrict Input command restricts the cell pointer to cells left unprotected by the /**S**tyle **P**rotection **U**nprotect command. This arrangement makes movement between data-entry cells easier.

Cautions

- Macros that change cell contents can change only unprotected cells. When you create a macro, include a command to enable or disable protection.

- /**F**ile **E**rase is one of the few commands that you can use when /**O**ption **P**rotection is enabled.

For more information, see */Style Protection* and */Database Restrict Input*.

Options Recalculation   /OR

Purpose

Defines the method and number of iterations for recalculation of the spreadsheet.

Reminders

- If you change the recalculation order to **C**olumn-wise or **R**ow-wise, enter formulas in a specific order so that they are calculated correctly. Quattro Pro's default settings are **N**atural and **B**ackground recalculation. In nearly all cases, you should leave recalculation in **N**atural mode.

- **M**anual recalculates only formulas you enter or edit. **M**anual does not recalculate formulas that depend on cell references that have changed. To recalculate, you must press F9 (Calc), or Quattro Pro must encounter {CALC} in a macro. The CALC indicator appears at the bottom of the screen when recalculation is needed for the spreadsheet to display current values. If updating your spreadsheet takes a long time every time you enter something, use **M**anual.

Procedure

1. Type /OR.
2. Choose one of the following options:

Option	Function
Mode	Specifies the recalculation method: **B**ackground recalculates formulas between keystrokes in the background, **A**utomatic recalculates when cell contents change, and **M**anual recalculates formulas when you press F9 (Calc)
Order	Specifies the sequence in which Quattro Pro calculates formulas: **N**atural calculates each cell referenced in a formula and then calculates the formula; **C**olumn-wise begins recalculation at the top of column A, recalculates downward, moves to column B, recalculates downward, and so on; and **R**ow-wise begins recalculation at the beginning of row 1 and recalculates to the end of the row before continuing through the following rows
Iteration	Recalculates the spreadsheet a specified number of times
Circular	Displays the first occurrence, if any, of the cell Cell address containing a formula that refers to itself
Quit	Returns to the /**O**ptions menu

3. If you choose **Iteration**, enter a number from 1 to 255. The default setting is 1. **Iteration** works with **Column-wise** and **Row-wise** recalculations or with **Natural** recalculation when the spreadsheet contains a circular reference.

Important Cues

- Use **B**ackground or **M**anual recalculation to increase data-entry speed on large spreadsheets or databases.

- **C**olumn-wise or **R**ow-wise recalculation often requires multiple recalculations. Set the number of automatic recalculations by choosing /**O**ptions **R**ecalculation **I**teration.

- Quattro Pro uses the /**O**ptions **R**ecalculation settings for only the current session of Quattro Pro. If you want to use the /**O**ptions **R**ecalculation settings in future Quattro Pro sessions, make the changes and then choose /**O**ptions **U**pdate.

- To locate all circular references quickly in a spreadsheet, use the /**W**indow **O**ptions **M**ap View **Y**es command.

Caution

- When you use **M**anual recalculation, the screen display does not display current values when the CALC indicator appears at the bottom of the screen. This indicator means that changes have been made to the spreadsheet. You must press F9 (Calc) to recalculate the spreadsheet to reflect the changes.

For more information, see **/Options Update** *and* **/Window Options**.

Options Startup   /OS

Purpose

Specifies the start-up settings that Quattro Pro uses each time you invoke the program.

Procedure

1. Type */OS*.
2. Choose one of the following options:

OPTIONS COMMANDS

Option	Function
Directory	Specifies the automatically accessed disk and directory; specifies the directory for read or write operations; type the new directory and press Enter
Autoload File	Specifies the spreadsheet file that is retrieved automatically each time you start Quattro Pro
Startup Macro	Specifies the macro that executes automatically each time you retrieve a spreadsheet
File Extension	Changes the file extensions with which files are saved and are displayed by File commands; type the new extension and press Enter
Beep	Toggles on and off the beep that Quattro Pro sounds when you make an error (default is Yes); choose No to turn off the beep
Menu Tree	Specifies the command menu; choose one of the following options: QUATTRO is the Quattro Pro menu tree, and 123 is the Lotus 1-2-3 menu tree
Edit Menus	Customizes a menu tree
Quit	Returns to the /Options menu

Important Cue

■ Quattro Pro uses the /Options Startup settings for only the current session of Quattro Pro. If you want to use the /Options Startup settings in future Quattro Pro sessions, make the changes and then choose /Options Update.

For more information, see /Options Update.

Options Update /OU

Purpose

Saves the current option settings to disk for use during the next Quattro Pro session.

Procedure

Type */OU*.

Important Cue

- Use /**O**ptions **U**pdate to save the option settings for hardware, colors, international formats, display modes, start-up options, graphics quality, other options, formats, and recalculation.

Options Values /OV

Purpose

Displays the current default option settings for use during the next start-up. Choose **U**pdate to save these settings if any of them have changed since you last saved them.

Procedure

Type */OV*.

Important Cue

- Choose /**O**ptions **V**alues to display the default option settings for Macro Recording, Default Printer, Startup Directory, Autoload File, Startup Macro, File Extension, Graphics Quality, Undo, SQZ! Remove Blanks, Screen Type, Clock, Sort Numbers Before Labels, Label Order, Paradox Access, Load File, Paradox Access Autoload File, and International Currency.

Options WYSIWYG Zoom %   /OW

Purpose

Reduces or enlarges the spreadsheet display when Quattro Pro is in WYSIWYG mode.

Reminder

- /Options WYSIWYG Zoom % is applicable only if Quattro Pro is in WYSIWYG mode.

Procedure

1. Type */OW*.
2. Type a scaling percentage between 25 and 200 and then press Enter.

Important Cue

- A scaling percentage of 200 percent enlarges the size of text on-screen to twice the actual printing size, whereas 25 percent reduces the text to a quarter of the actual printing size.

*For more information, see */Options Display Mode WYSIWYG*.

Window Commands /W

The /Window commands control how Quattro Pro displays your spreadsheets. You can display a single spreadsheet with two panes (horizontally or vertically); stack or tile the display of multiple spreadsheets in memory; lock column and/or row labels so that they don't scroll off the screen; display a map view of your spreadsheet; and choose whether to display grid lines in WYSIWYG mode.

Window /W

Purpose

Specifies the way Quattro Pro displays windows.

Reminders

- You can use Alt-F6 to invoke /Window Zoom.
- You can use the Ctrl-R shortcut key combination to invoke the /Window Move/Size command.
- You can use Shift-F5 or Alt-0 to invoke the /Window Pick command.
- You can use the Ctrl-T shortcut key combination to invoke the /Window Tile command.

Procedure

1. Type /W.
2. Choose an available option as follows:

Option	Function
Zoom	Expands the active window to fill the screen
Tile	Displays all open windows simultaneously in text display mode
Stack	Arranges open windows in layers and displays the top line of each window

WINDOW COMMANDS

933

Option	Function
Move/Size	Changes the size or position of the active window in text display mode
Pick	Displays a list of open windows and activates a window

Important Cue

- If you choose /**W**indow **M**ove/Size to change the size of a window, the MOVE indicator displays in the top left corner of the window. Press the Scroll Lock key. The SIZE indicator displays in the top left corner of the window. Use the arrow keys to adjust the window's outline in the direction of the arrow and press Enter.

For more information, see **/File Open**, **/Window Options**, *and* **/Window Options Locked Titles**.

Window Options /WO

Purpose

Specifies the spreadsheet areas displayed.

Reminders

- If you want to see two views of the same spreadsheet, decide whether you want the spreadsheet split horizontally or vertically. If you want two horizontal windows, move the cell selector to the top row of what is to be the lower window. To produce two vertical windows, move the cell selector to the column that is to be the left edge of the right window. Position the screen so that the cell selector is at midscreen.

- If you want to lock titles, move the cell selector so that the column headings occupy the top row of the spreadsheet. Place the cell selector on the leftmost row heading so that it freezes at the left edge of the screen.

- Grid lines are visible only in WYSIWYG mode.

Procedure

1. Type */WO*.
2. Choose the desired option(s) as follows:

Option	Function
Horizontal	Splits the spreadsheet into two horizontal panes at the cell selector
Vertical	Splits the spreadsheet into two vertical panes at the cell selector
Sync	Synchronizes two panes so that they move together
Unsync	Unsynchronizes two panes so that you can view different rows and columns simultaneously
Clear	Removes the bottom or right window
Locked Titles	Freezes specified rows and/or columns: **H**orizontal creates titles from the rows above the cell selector; **V**ertical creates titles from the columns to the left of the cell selector; **B**oth creates titles from the rows above the cell selector and from the columns to the left of the cell selector; **C**lear removes all frozen title areas so that all spreadsheet areas scroll and are accessible
Row & Col Borders	Hides or displays the column letters and row numbers: **H**ide removes the borders, **D**isplay displays the borders
Map View	Displays a map view of the spreadsheet: **Y**es turns on the map; **N**o turns off the map
Grid Lines	In WYSIWYG mode, removes or displays the grid lines in a spreadsheet: **H**ide removes the grid lines; **D**isplay displays the grid lines
Print Block	Outlines the print block in WYSIWYG mode; choose **H**ide if you do not want page breaks to display or **D**isplay to display page breaks

Important Cues

- Panes are synchronized when you first display them. Choose /**W**indow **O**ptions **U**nsync if you want the two panes to move independently of each other.

- Press F6 (Pane) to move the cell selector to the other window. Move the cell selector to the cell address in the second window as needed.

- Each pane can have different column widths. When /**W**indow **O**ptions **C**lear is selected, the setting used in the top or left window determines the column width for the rest of the spreadsheet.

- Horizontal panes are useful when you work with databases. The criteria table and database column labels can appear in the upper window while the data or extracted data appears in the lower window.

- If you split the spreadsheet into two windows with /**W**indow **V**ertical or /**W**indow **H**orizontal, each window can have its own title.

- The map view displays labels as 1, values as n, formulas as plus signs (+), link formulas as minus signs (-), circular cells as c, and an inserted graph as g.

- To return the spreadsheet to the normal Quattro Pro display, choose the /**W**indow **O**ptions **C**lear command.

- You can use /**W**indow **O**ptions **L**ocked **T**itles to display protected screen areas when /**D**atabase **R**estrict Input is active. Position titles so that they display labels and instructions adjacent to the unprotected input block.

- /**W**indow **O**ptions **L**ocked **T**itles **H**orizontal is especially useful for freezing column headings over a database or an accounting spreadsheet. You also can freeze rows of text that describe figures in adjacent cells.

- You can change the color of the grid lines with the /**O**ptions **C**olors **S**preadsheet **W**YSIWYG **G**rid **L**ines command.

APPENDIX A

Installing Quattro Pro

Creating an ideal hardware and operating system environment is critical to installing and using Quattro Pro. Many possible hardware and operating system combinations exist for Quattro Pro because the program can run on an IBM PC, an 80486 system, and everything in between.

Appendix A begins by discussing how to create the ideal operating environment. Issues covered include obtaining peak performance from your computer's microprocessor, managing random-access memory (RAM), managing your disk effectively, selecting an appropriate video display and printer, and using peripherals.

Throughout the discussion, you can take stock of your computer equipment. You may discover a need for additional hardware. Because Quattro Pro can effectively use your equipment, however, you may find that your computer system is sufficient to install Quattro Pro.

The next section offers step-by-step instructions for installing your copy of Quattro Pro.

> **CAUTION:** If you currently use an earlier version of Quattro Pro, read "Upgrading a Previous Version of Quattro Pro to 4.0" in this appendix before you install Version 4.0 on your computer.

After Quattro Pro is installed, you can reconfigure many hardware settings from the **O**ptions menu. The commands on this menu enable you to fine-tune your copy of Quattro Pro until you attain the most productive operating environment.

This chapter also includes a step-by-step explanation of the procedure to follow if you need to upgrade from a previous version of Quattro Pro.

This appendix concludes with a look at some common questions and answers about installing the program. Scan this section for quick solutions to questions concerning system configuration or program installation.

Setting Up the Ideal System Configuration

The ideal system configuration depends on your computer equipment. Unless you can afford to purchase a fully loaded AT 80386 or 80486 system with a great deal of RAM, a math coprocessor chip, a VGA display, and so on, you are in the same boat as most Quattro Pro users. Most users can benefit from knowing several tricks for getting the best performance from their computer equipment.

Program Requirements

To operate Quattro Pro, you must have at least the following hardware and operating system software available:

Hardware

- IBM XT, AT compatible, or PS/2
- 512K of RAM (640K recommended)
- 6M of free space on your hard disk drive
- A monochrome graphics display system

Operating system

- DOS 2.0 or later

The following configuration is an example of an ideal operating environment for using Quattro Pro.

A — INSTALLING QUATTRO PRO

Hardware

- 80386-based computer
- 2M of RAM
- 10M of free space on your hard disk drive
- Super-VGA graphics display system

Operating system

- Microsoft- or Logitech-compatible mouse
- DOS 5.0

Other

- Microsoft Windows

Quattro Pro's performance improves noticeably when you can improve the recommended minimum hardware configuration. Not all users have access to 80386- or 80486-based computers and have to make the best of what they have. Fortunately, even with the minimum recommended configuration, Quattro Pro performs well.

Microprocessor Clock Speed and Math Coprocessor Chip

Your computer's microprocessor clock speed determines how fast Quattro Pro processes commands. The original IBM PC and XT systems use the 8086 or 8088 chip, running at 4.77 MHz (megahertz). A *hertz* is a unit of frequency equal to one cycle per second. A *megahertz* equals 1 million cycles per second.

The AT systems use an 80286 chip with clock speeds ranging from 6 to 25 MHz. The 80386 chips process data from 16 to 33 MHz, and the new 80486 chips process data from 25 to 50 MHz. The processing speed difference between the first PC and today's powerful 80486 AT is truly remarkable. In some instances, the processing speed of an 80486 is 40 times faster than the speed of the original IBM PC.

Unless you want to upgrade your microprocessor chip—which may mean purchasing a new computer system—only two methods exist for speeding up Quattro Pro execution with the microprocessor. First, if your current chip has an adjustable clock speed, make sure that the clock speed is on the highest setting.

Second, you can purchase a math coprocessor chip. These add-on chips decrease your microprocessor's workload by assuming many of the number-crunching responsibilities. Best of all, math chips are relatively inexpensive ($200-$400 in most cases). Quattro Pro detects the presence of a math coprocessor chip—no special installation is necessary.

Random-Access Memory Management

To use Quattro Pro, your personal computer must have a minimum of 512K of random-access memory (RAM). Quattro Pro can operate more efficiently with more RAM. Gains in efficiency come in two forms: the capability to create bigger spreadsheets with more complex formulas, and increased program execution speed.

Most personal computer systems come with a minimum of 640K of RAM. This first 640K of RAM—otherwise known as *conventional memory*—is used by DOS to store program code and other data while your computer is on. When your computer has 640K of RAM, DOS uses what memory is available to store Quattro Pro program code; the rest is available for building and temporarily storing spreadsheets.

When you have other software programs running on your system, they also require some of the 640K. Terminate-and-stay-resident (TSR) programs like SideKick, Superkey, RAM drives, print spoolers, and mouse drivers, for example, load into your system's RAM and remain there during Quattro Pro work sessions. The RAM that your computer allocates to these programs decreases the memory available to Quattro Pro for building spreadsheets.

You can add two types of memory beyond the 640K of RAM: *extended memory* and *expanded memory*. The first extra 384K of RAM that you add to the basic 640K is *high memory*, which is used primarily to store CPU instructions and video display data. Neither DOS nor Quattro Pro can use this memory as is to store program code or spreadsheet data.

Memory beyond 1M is *extended memory*, which is used by RAM disks, printer spoolers, and Microsoft Windows applications. DOS and Quattro Pro cannot access and use extended memory for spreadsheet data. Fortunately, however, memory drivers enable you to configure extended memory as expanded memory.

Quattro Pro can use expanded memory to store spreadsheet labels, values, and formatting. This memory usually comes on a card that you plug into an expansion slot inside your computer. Expanded-memory cards are sold with software driver programs that enable you to install the cards for use with your computer (the names of four cards that Quattro Pro supports appear later in this section). You add the driver name to your CONFIG.SYS file.

A — INSTALLING QUATTRO PRO

Regardless of how your memory is configured, recognize that all RAM has the same purpose—to store data while your computer is on. What differentiates one type of memory from the other is that DOS can recognize and use only the first 640K of RAM. Although Quattro Pro recognizes and uses expanded memory, the program cannot use extended memory. Remember the following rule of thumb: if your computer has more than 640K of RAM, configure the added memory as expanded memory so that Quattro Pro can use it.

One of Quattro Pro's most unique features is the *Virtual Real-Time Object-Oriented Memory Manager (VROOMM)*. Borland created this RAM-management utility to enable Quattro Pro to work on a wide range of personal computers. VROOMM technology takes into account the different memory allocation schemes used by different systems. With VROOMM, you can better manage your memory by allocating as much RAM as possible to spreadsheet operations. VROOMM accomplishes this allocation by loading small portions of program code on an as-needed basis.

VROOMM works no matter what memory configuration your computer has. If your computer system has less than 1M of RAM, and all memory above 640K is configured as extended memory, you can invoke a special start-up parameter to tell Quattro Pro to set up a cache for VROOMM objects in extended memory.

To use VROOMM in this way, type *q/x* at the DOS prompt and press Enter to load Quattro Pro. If you have a windows application manager such as Microsoft Windows, enter */x* as the loading parameter. Similarly, you can enter *q/x* as the final line in the AUTOEXEC.BAT file. Each time you boot your system, Quattro Pro loads with VROOMM objects caching in place.

This start-up parameter is not recommended for systems with more than 1M of RAM. Remember, always configure memory above 1M as expanded memory. Quattro Pro operates with any LIM 3.2 or 4.0 card and supports the following expanded memory cards:

 Intel Above Board

 AST RAMpage!

 Quadram Liberty

 STB Memory Champion

External features such as operating systems, memory-resident utilities, and application drivers affect the amount of RAM available to Quattro Pro. You can maximize the memory available to Quattro Pro by removing unused peripheral driver programs and terminate-and-stay-resident (TSR) applications from your system's memory. These programs consume RAM that Quattro Pro otherwise can use for storing spreadsheet data. To free up RAM used by a TSR application or set aside for peripheral driver programs, remove the program name from the CONFIG.SYS or AUTOEXEC.BAT file and reboot your system.

The simplest way to remove a program name from a CONFIG.SYS file or from an AUTOEXEC.BAT file is to create a new, streamlined CONFIG.SYS or AUTOEXEC.BAT file.

> **TIP** You should make a copy of your original CONFIG.SYS file before creating a new file, in case you later want to revert back to the original file. To make a copy, rename CONFIG.SYS to CONFIG.OLD before you proceed with these steps.

To create a new, streamlined CONFIG.SYS file, for example, follow these steps:

1. At the DOS command prompt, type the following and press Enter:

    copy con config.sys

2. Now type the following to close the file and save it on your hard disk:

files=20	(press Enter)
buffers=20	(press Enter)
^z	(press Ctrl-Z)

3. Reboot the system to place the new CONFIG.SYS file into effect.

Entering data into a spreadsheet, building a graph, and opening multiple spreadsheets are examples of internal activities that consume your computer's RAM. You can maximize the memory available to Quattro Pro by building efficient spreadsheets. Quattro Pro activities such as cell formatting, using the Undo feature, and opening multiple spreadsheets consume system memory. To minimize this memory loss, follow these rules:

- *Regain unused memory blocks.* Quattro Pro uses system memory in blocks. The larger the active area of a spreadsheet, the more memory Quattro Pro needs. When you erase areas of your spreadsheet, memory remains allocated but unused. First, save your spreadsheet. Then, erase the spreadsheet from memory and recall the spreadsheet. Quattro Pro recalls the spreadsheet into a smaller memory block.

- *Review the number of open spreadsheet files.* Keep open only those spreadsheet files that must be open for the Quattro Pro session at hand. Close unneeded documents to recover system memory.

A — INSTALLING QUATTRO PRO

- *Recover memory by erasing unneeded data and cell formats from the current spreadsheet.* Quattro Pro uses memory to retain the data and cell formats for the current spreadsheet(s).

- *Build streamlined spreadsheets.* Instead of creating huge spreadsheets to assimilate large volumes of data, try using several smaller linked spreadsheets. You can recall and update several smaller spreadsheets faster—and with less memory used—than struggling with large spreadsheets. If, however, you are using several spreadsheets, each containing a small amount of data, combine them into one larger spreadsheet. The idea is to find the happy medium between using one large, memory-intensive spreadsheet and several small spreadsheets, which, when loaded into memory at the same time, can be equally memory-intensive.

Hard Disk Drive Management

Borland recommends a minimum of 6M of free space on your hard disk drive for Quattro Pro. This figure is based on the total disk storage space necessary for the program files, the font files, and several spreadsheet and graph files.

If you do not have this much free space on your hard disk drive, you must delete files until you do have enough free space before you can install Quattro Pro.

Video Displays and Printers

Quattro Pro supports all the video display types available in today's market and the following graphics cards:

- IBM Color/Graphics Adapter
- Hercules Graphics Card (monochrome)
- IBM Enhanced Graphics Adapter (monochrome or color)
- IBM Video Graphics Array (monochrome or color)
- IBM 3270/PC and 3270/AT with APA
- AT&T 6300 640 x 640
- MCGA (IBM Model 30)
- IBM 8514 Graphics Adapter

Quattro Pro also supports most dot-matrix, daisywheel, laser, inkjet, and PostScript printers.

The super-VGA graphics display system is the current state-of-the-art in video displays. This display type offers superior color graphics and unsurpassed resolution. If you can afford one, a super-VGA display system is the ideal way to display Quattro Pro graphs on-screen.

Fortunately, Quattro Pro enables you to build and annotate graphs with just a graphics card and a monochrome display capable of high-resolution graphics. If you do not have a graphics card, you can build and print graphs, but you cannot see them on-screen. You also can display Quattro Pro in text or graphics display modes. You can toggle between the two modes from the Quattro Pro Options menu, or by clicking the CHR and WYS buttons on the SpeedBar.

Mice

If you never have used a mouse, you are missing out on a great productivity tool. Building Quattro Pro spreadsheets is easier and more efficient when you use a mouse and a keyboard together. Quattro Pro supports all mice compatible with the Microsoft mouse interface, including the Microsoft serial and bus mice, the Mouse Systems mouse (with the MSMOUSE driver), and the Logitech mouse.

Installing the Program

Quattro Pro's installation utility is self-explanatory and mostly self-running. Before you begin installing Quattro Pro, review the following checklist to ensure that you have the correct system configuration for using Quattro Pro:

- IBM-XT, IBM-AT, or PS/2-compatible computer with at least 512K of RAM
- PC DOS or MS-DOS Version 2.0 or later
- Hard disk drive with at least 6M of available storage space
- RAM exceeding 1M defined as expanded memory

> **TIP** The Quattro Pro installation utility changes your CONFIG.SYS and AUTOEXEC.BAT files if you enable the program to do so. The installation utility is the easiest way to change those files. To change the files yourself—for example, to add an expanded memory card—use a word processing program in nondocument or DOS text file mode.

A — INSTALLING QUATTRO PRO

The CONFIG.SYS file must contain the following statements:

BUFFERS=20

FILES=20

The AUTOEXEC.BAT file path statement should contain QPRO, the name of the directory in which Quattro Pro resides.

Copying Files

During the first part of the installation process, Quattro Pro copies program files to the default directory. To start the installation, place installation disk 1 into drive A. From your DOS C:\ prompt, type *a:\install* and press Enter. After a moment or two, the screen shown in figure A.1 appears.

> **TIP**
> You cannot use a mouse at any time during the installation of Quattro Pro.

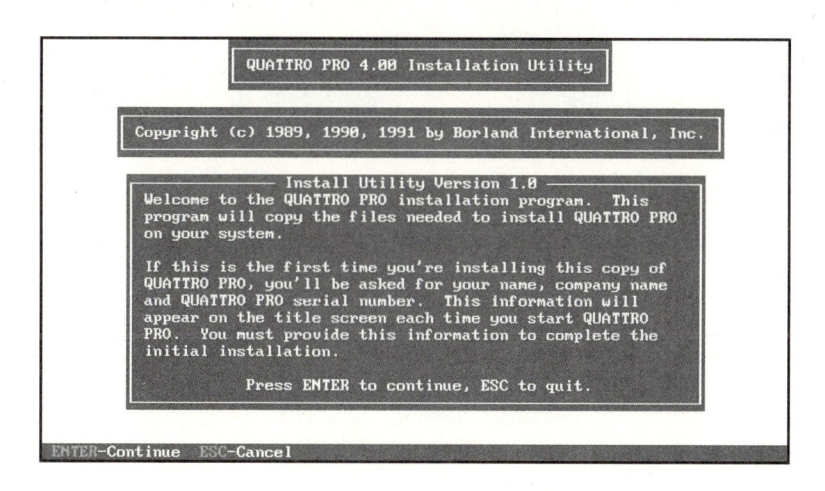

Fig. A.1

The initial installation screen.

Figure A.1 shows that Quattro Pro first requires your name, company name, and disk serial number. Because you cannot complete the installation without this information, gather it before continuing. Press Enter to begin the installation or Esc to quit.

Quattro Pro can install itself from any drive you specify. Generally, drive A is the source drive from which you copy the Quattro Pro files. If you copy the Quattro Pro files onto your hard disk drive prior to installing the program, enter that drive's letter (for example, C or D) as the source drive. You can specify B as the source drive if the Quattro Pro installation disks fit only in your B drive (see fig. A.2).

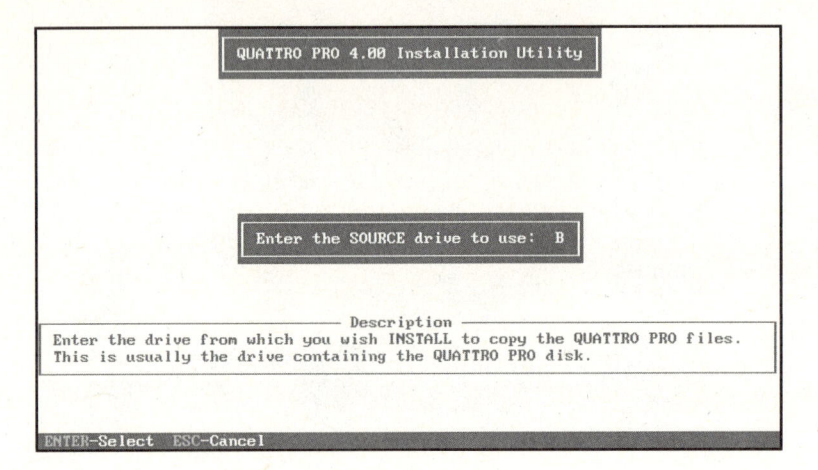

Fig. A.2

Select the source drive from which to install Quattro Pro.

The installation utility ensures that you have enough free storage space on your computer's hard disk drive and displays the directory to which files are copied (see fig. A.3). To install Quattro Pro into a different path on your hard disk drive, press F2 to change the default selection, use the cursor-movement keys to move to your selection, and press Enter. When finished, press Enter to continue or press Esc to quit.

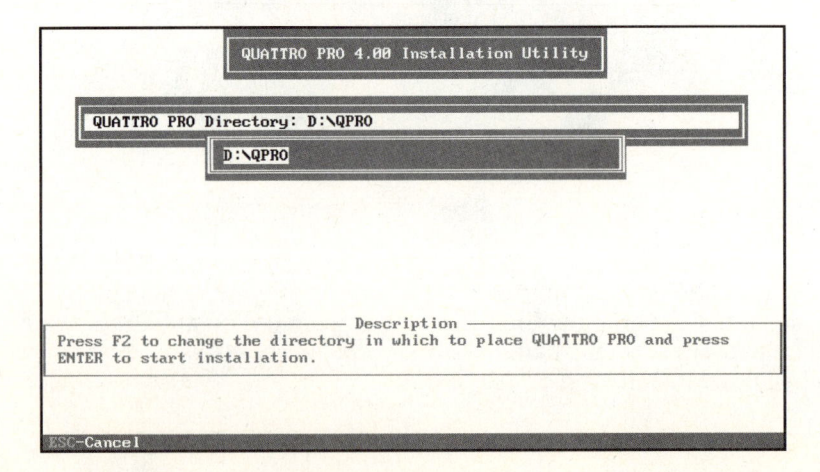

Fig. A.3

Choose the destination drive and Quattro Pro directory name.

A — INSTALLING QUATTRO PRO

If you do not have at least 6M of free storage space, Quattro Pro displays an error message telling you so. If you see this error message, exit the installation program and delete files from your hard disk drive until you free up at least 6M of storage space.

The installation utility copies the Quattro Pro files to the default path, \QPRO (or to the path you specified in the preceding section). During this process, Quattro Pro prompts you to change disks and press a key until the files are copied from all disks (see fig. A.4).

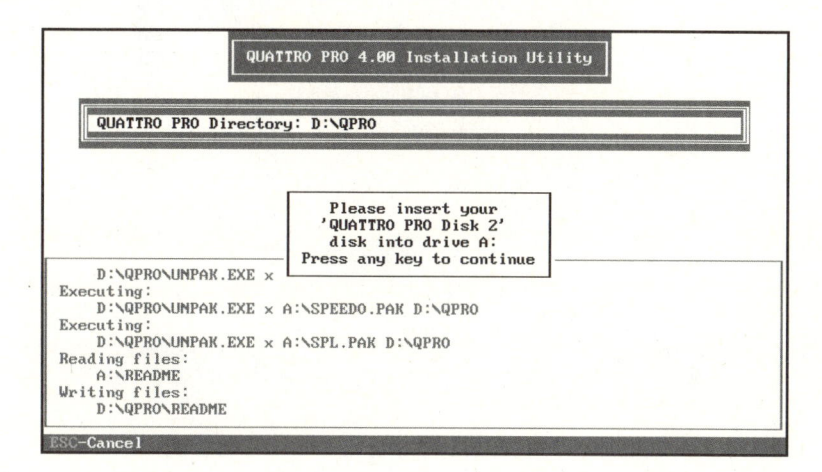

Fig. A.4

Copy Quattro Pro files.

You see the progress of the installation on-screen as the installation utility reads and writes files. When all the files are transferred, Quattro Pro displays the message shown in figure A.5.

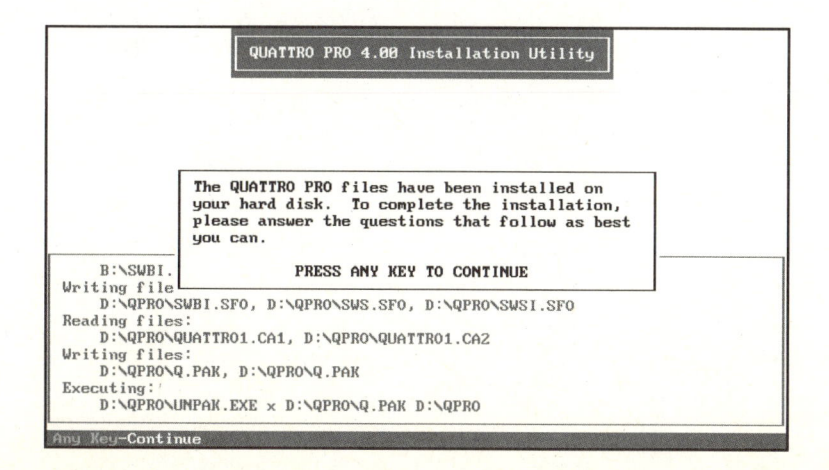

Fig. A.5

A successful file transfer.

USING QUATTRO PRO 4, SPECIAL EDITION

This completes phase one of the installation process. If your screen does not look like the one shown in figure A.5, you must start the installation again. As long as you swapped disks correctly when prompted by Quattro Pro, you are ready to move on to phase two of the installation procedure.

Selecting Your Equipment

You must tell Quattro Pro about your equipment. In the second phase of installation, you select a monitor type, determine whether you will operate Quattro Pro on a network, choose a menu tree interface, and define how Quattro Pro will display spreadsheets, printouts, and graphs.

Selecting a Monitor Type

The installation utility detects whether you have a color graphics display card installed in your computer. You must tell Quattro Pro, however, whether your monitor is color, monochrome, or gray scale (see fig. A.6).

To change the default selection, press F2, use the cursor-movement keys to move to your selection, and press Enter. When finished, press Enter to continue or press Esc to quit.

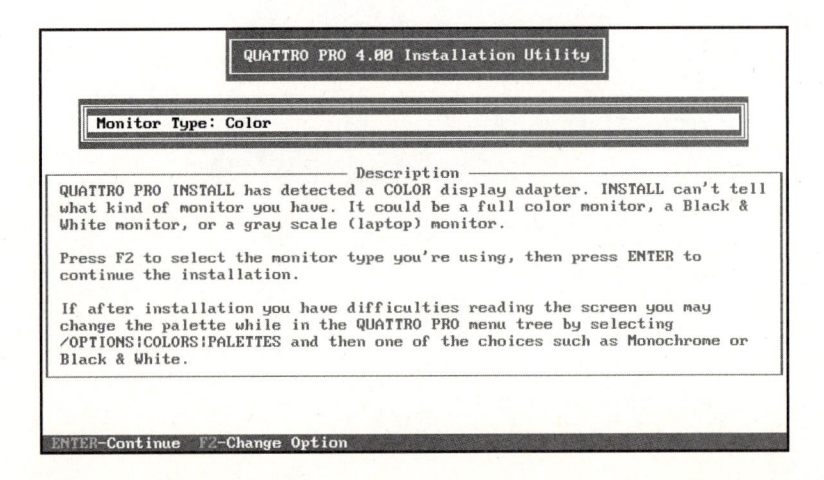

Fig. A.6

Specify a color or monochrome monitor.

```
                QUATTRO PRO 4.00 Installation Utility

   ┌─────────────────────────────────────────────────────────────┐
   │ Monitor Type: Color                                         │
   └─────────────────────────────────────────────────────────────┘
   ──────────────────────── Description ──────────────────────────
   QUATTRO PRO INSTALL has detected a COLOR display adapter. INSTALL can't tell
   what kind of monitor you have. It could be a full color monitor, a Black &
   White monitor, or a gray scale (laptop) monitor.

   Press F2 to select the monitor type you're using, then press ENTER to
   continue the installation.

   If after installation you have difficulties reading the screen you may
   change the palette while in the QUATTRO PRO menu tree by selecting
   /OPTIONS|COLORS|PALETTES and then one of the choices such as Monochrome or
   Black & White.

   ENTER-Continue   F2-Change Option
```

Entering Your Name and Serial Number

Version 4.0 next displays a screen prompting you to enter your company name, name, and the serial number that appears on Disk 1. You must supply this information to complete the installation.

Version 4.0 then asks whether you want to install Quattro Pro on a network server. The default setting is No. To install Quattro Pro Version 4.0 on a network server, press F2, choose Yes, and press Enter. (Refer to Appendix E, "Installing Quattro Pro on a Network," for instructions.) After you finish, press Enter to continue or press Esc to quit.

Selecting a Printer

Select a printer manufacturer and model from the Printer Manufacturer screen (see fig. A.7). Press F2, use the cursor-movement keys to highlight the appropriate manufacturer, and then press Enter. If your printer manufacturer is not on this screen, check your printer manual for information on the types of printers your printer can emulate. Many printers emulate Epson and IBM printers.

After you select a printer manufacturer, Quattro Pro displays the Printer Model screen (see fig. A.8). To choose a printer model, highlight the appropriate name on the list and press Enter. Press Enter once more to continue.

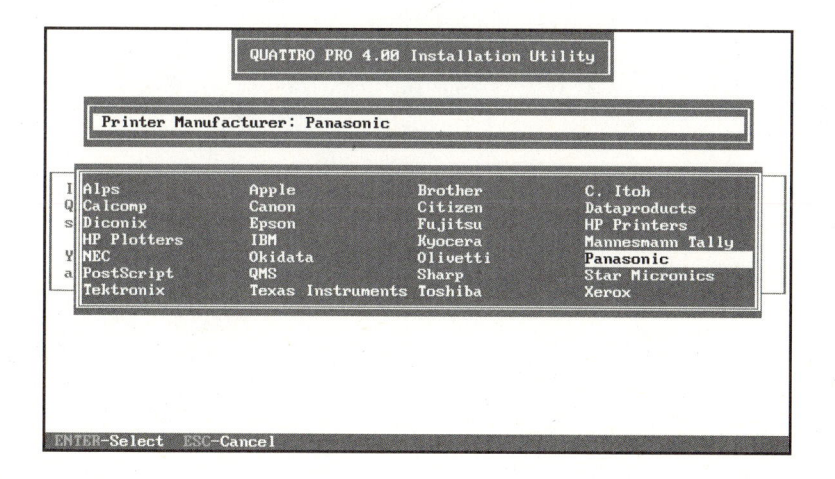

Fig. A.7

Select a printer manufacturer.

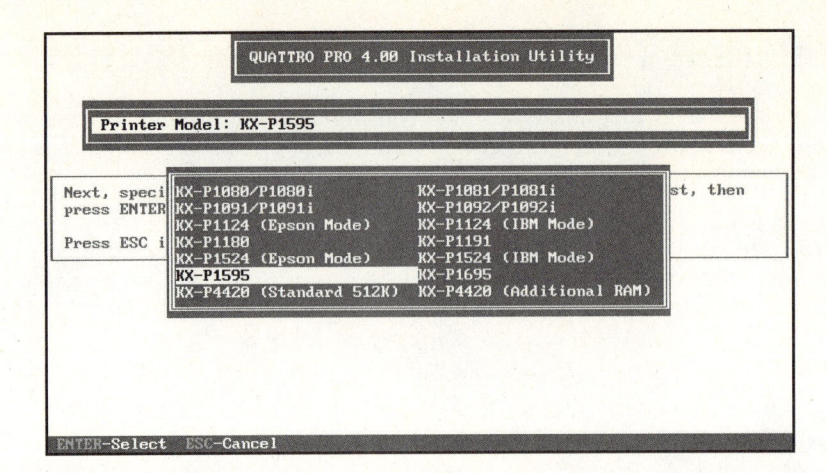

Fig. A.8

Select a printer model.

After you select a printer model, Quattro Pro asks you to choose an initial mode at which to print spreadsheets and graphs. Figure A.9 displays a high-resolution mode in which the dots per inch (dpi) setting is 240 x 216, and the paper size setting is 14 by 11 inches.

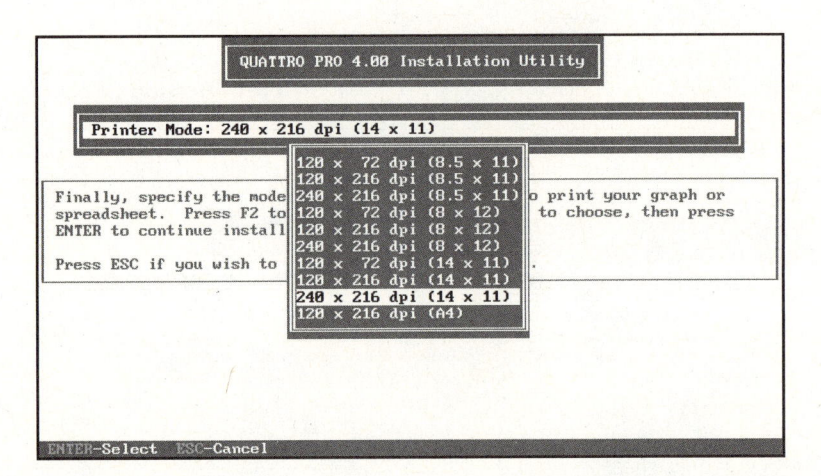

Fig. A.9

Select a default printer mode.

By default, Quattro Pro highlights the first mode setting on the Printer Mode screen. The first setting always selects the lowest resolution supported by your printer. You can select a medium or high mode by pressing F2 and selecting a different option. The actual dpi ratings available on this menu depend on the individual printer. If you select an Epson LQ-2500 printer, for example, the dpi rating in high mode is 360 x 180.

A — INSTALLING QUATTRO PRO

Selecting the Default Display Mode

You next decide whether or not to use WYSIWYG as the default display mode. WYSIWYG display mode offers the highest resolution and crispest display of all available Quattro Pro display modes. To use this mode, you must have an EGA or VGA graphics display card installed in your PC that supports at least 640 x 350 resolution.

> **T I P**
>
> WYSIWYG, "What You See Is What You Get," is a common computer term that describes a state-of-the-art spreadsheet design capability.

If you choose Yes (see fig. A.10), Quattro Pro uses WYSIWYG as the default display mode each time you begin a work session.

```
          QUATTRO PRO 4.00 Installation Utility

   WYSIWYG Mode: Yes

                      Description
   Do you want WYSIWYG mode as your default display mode?
   You must have an EGA or VGA card that supports at least 640x350 resolution
   to use WYSIWYG mode.




 ENTER-Continue   F2-Change Option   Ctrl-X-Quit
```

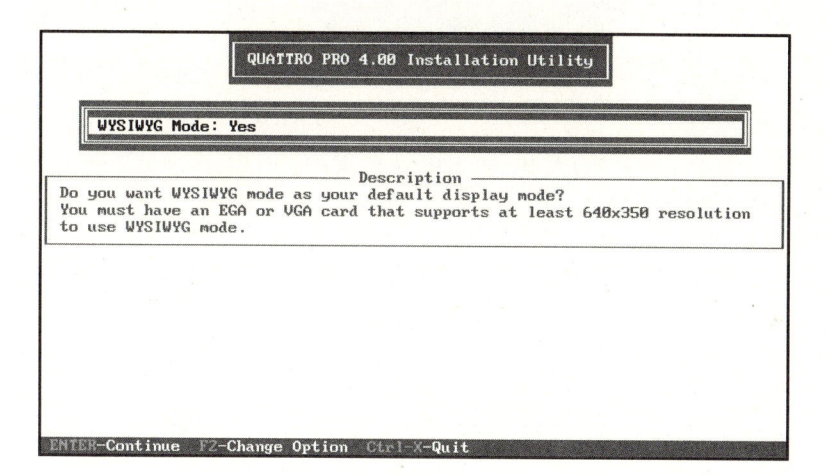

Fig. A.10

Choose WYSIWYG as the default display mode.

Installing for Use with Microsoft Windows

Quattro Pro asks whether you want to install Quattro Pro to work with Microsoft Windows. If you own a copy of Windows, press F2, highlight Yes, and then press Enter (see fig A.11). Press Enter once more to continue.

Quattro Pro then asks you for the path to the Windows directory. Press F2, type the drive letter and path name, and press Enter. Press Enter to continue. The next time you load Windows, Quattro Pro installs and stores a special icon inside a group window called QPRO (see fig. A.12). To start the Quattro Pro program, double-click the icon.

Selecting the Character Set

Next, you choose the character set used by Quattro Pro. Quattro Pro uses the character set definition when displaying the default Bitstream-SC fonts. The choices on this menu are Standard U.S. (the default) and Standard European (see fig. A.13).

If you want to display any special characters or diacritical marks that are part of the international character set, press F2, choose Standard European, and press Enter. When finished, press Enter to continue.

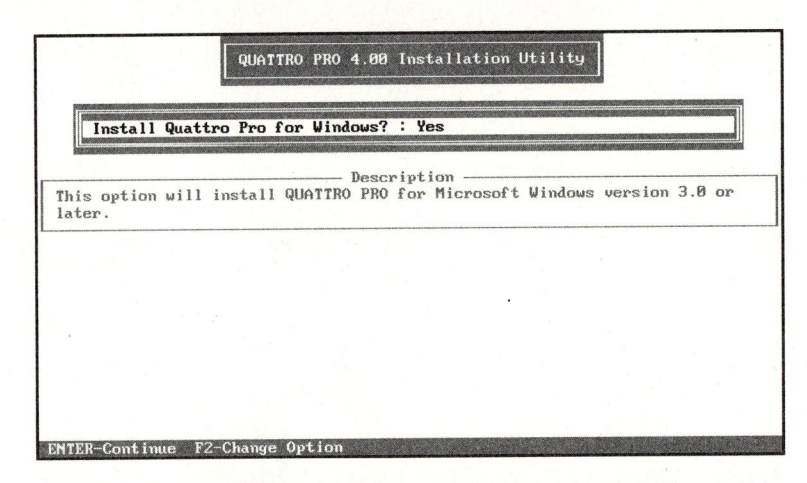

Fig. A.11

Install Quattro Pro for use with Microsoft Windows.

Fig. A.12

The Windows program icon for Quattro Pro 4.0.

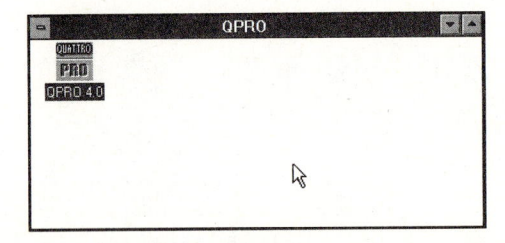

A — INSTALLING QUATTRO PRO

953

Completing the Installation

When the installation utility successfully installs Quattro Pro, the screen shown in figure A.14 is displayed. Press Enter to leave the Installation utility and return to DOS. Next, press Ctrl-Alt-Del to reboot your machine to place all changes made to your AUTOEXEC.BAT and CONFIG.SYS files into effect.

If Quattro Pro fails to transfer all configuration files successfully, you must begin the process again. Installation can fail for a number of reasons. The most common reason for failure is because the hard disk drive is full. Make sure that you have 6M of space on your hard disk before attempting to install Quattro Pro.

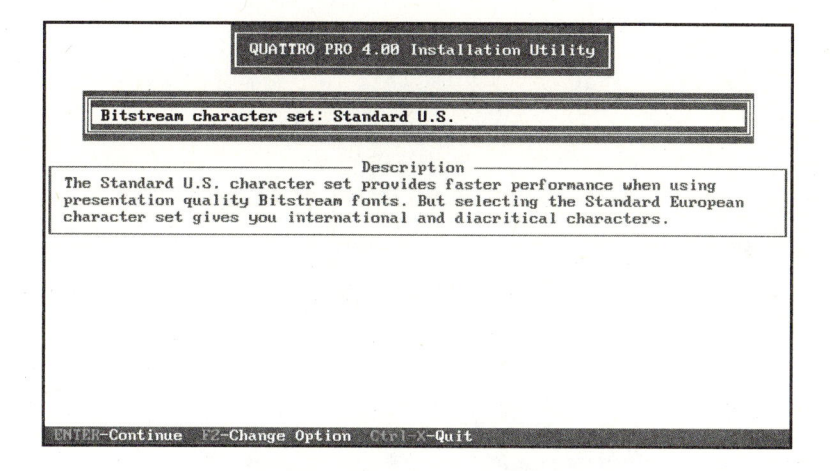

Fig. A.13

Select the character set to use with Quattro Pro.

Fig. A.14

The Installation Successful screen.

After Installing Quattro Pro

In the next section of this appendix, you learn how to load Quattro Pro into your PC's memory and review two important post-installation topics. The first of these topics shows you how to reconfigure and enhance your copy of Quattro Pro. The second topic discusses issues that users who are upgrading from a previous version of Quattro Pro will find helpful.

Loading and Quitting Quattro Pro

To load Quattro Pro, type *q* at the DOS prompt and then press Enter.

To quit the program, choose **F**ile **E**xit (type */FX*) or press Ctrl-X, and Quattro Pro returns to the operating system.

Reconfiguring and Enhancing Quattro Pro

You never should have to install Quattro Pro again. Many software companies require you to reinstall their programs when you want to alter the way your computer equipment interacts with the software.

You easily can reconfigure your copy of Quattro Pro. You can add new printers, customize the SpeedBar buttons, and switch to the Lotus 1-2-3 menu tree directly from Quattro Pro's **O**ptions menu (see Chapter 16, "Customizing Quattro Pro").

Upgrading a Previous Version of Quattro Pro to 4.0

Upgrading from Version 1.0, 2.0, or 3.0 to Quattro Pro Version 4.0 is simple. Be careful, however, when you perform the steps outlined in this section, because you will delete many Quattro Pro files from at least two directories on your hard disk drive.

The Quattro Pro Version 4.0 Installation Facility does not upgrade your Version 1.0, 2.0, or 3.0 files automatically. The only files that you may use with Version 4.0 are spreadsheet files (W*), workspace files (WSP), clip art files (CLP), and custom menu tree files (MU). Copy these files to

A — INSTALLING QUATTRO PRO

another directory (outside of the \QPRO directory) before you install Version 4.0.

> **TIP**
>
> If you are upgrading from Version 3.0, you have the option to continue using your Version 3.0 Bitstream fonts with Version 4.0, even though Version 4.0 uses faster Bitstream-SC fonts. To do so, skip steps 1 and 2 in the next set of steps. After you load Quattro Pro, your 3.0 fonts appear beside the 4.0 fonts on the Typeface menu when you choose the /Style Font and /Style FontTable commands.

The following procedure shows you how to prepare a hard disk drive for Version 4.0 installation. You should have two Quattro Pro directories: \QPRO, in which files from previous versions reside; and \QPRO\FONTS, the subdirectory in which all previous versions of the font files reside.

> **CAUTION:** Make sure that you don't have any of your spreadsheet files in the QPRO directory.

To prepare a hard disk drive for installation, follow these steps:

1. At the DOS command prompt, type *cd\qpro\fonts* and press Enter to go to the FONTS subdirectory.

2. Type *del *.** and press Enter to delete all Version 1.0, 2.0, or 3.0 font files from the FONTS subdirectory.

3. Type *cd\qpro* and press Enter to go to the QPRO directory.

4. Type *del *.** and press Enter to delete all Version 1.0, 2.0, or 3.0 program files from the QPRO directory.

You must remove all Version 1.0, 2.0, or 3.0 program files and font files from your hard disk drive prior to installing Version 4.0. Do not intermingle program and font files from the versions because you may get unpredictable results during your work sessions.

> **TIP**
>
> The DOS DEL command deletes only files that have read-write status. If you originally changed the attributes of your program files to read-only, then you must make your files read-write before you attempt to delete them. If you do not, the installation procedure fails when Quattro Pro attempts to install the new program files.

If you used the BSINST.EXE program to convert third-party Bitstream fonts for use with Version 1.0, 2.0, or 3.0, you must rebuild those fonts after you complete the installation of Version 4.0.

To rebuild those fonts, place the disk containing the third-party Bitstream typefaces (files with a BCO extension) in drive A. Go to your QPRO directory, type *spdinst a:, name* and then press Enter. NAME is the name of the desired symbol set: your choices are ROMAN8 or ASCII. The ROMAN8 symbol set provides access to extended characters, such as an international character set. The ASCII symbol set provides access only to the first 128 characters. After you complete these steps, load Quattro Pro. The Bitstream fonts you installed are available on the **T**ypeface menu when you choose the /**S**tyle Font**T**able **E**dit Fonts command.

> **TIP** Use the SPDINST.EXE program to install third-party Bitstream-SC fonts—the new default fonts in Quattro Pro Version 4.0.

Copy your custom menu tree files back to the newly installed \QPRO directory. Run the NEWMU.BAT batch file to convert all custom menu tree files into Version 4.0 menu tree files. To convert a custom Version 3.0 menu tree named CUSTOM3.MU into a Version 4.0 menu tree, for example, type the following:

   newmu d:\qpro\custom3 d:\qpro\custom4

You must supply a different name for the converted menu tree. Quattro Pro does not convert a menu tree using the same name.

Questions & Answers

This section deals with commonly asked questions and start-up problems and solves glitches encountered when creating the ideal system configuration and installing Quattro Pro.

Ideal System Configuration

Q: Why does Quattro Pro operate slowly on my system?

A: If you have expanded memory, make sure that the EMS driver is included in the CONFIG.SYS file.

If your system has between 640K and 1024K bytes of RAM, load Quattro Pro by using the Q /X option. The X option enables Borland's VROOMM memory manager to use extended memory for object caching.

Q: Why doesn't my mouse work properly when I use Quattro Pro's graphics display mode?

A: Older mouse drivers support only 80 x 24 screen displays. Quattro Pro supports EGA 80 x 43, VGA 80 x 50 and EGA/VGA graphics modes. To display Quattro Pro in a mode other than 80 x 24, your mouse driver version must conform to the following specifications:

Brand	Version
Microsoft Mouse	6.11 or higher
Mouse Systems	6.01 or higher
Logitech	4.0 or higher
PC Mouse	6.01 or higher

Installation Utility

Q: The text of the installation utility is difficult to read. What can I do?

A: Exit INSTALL. Then type *a:install /b* and press Enter to force Quattro Pro to display in a black-and-white mode or type */m* for monochrome.

Q: The computer displays the message `Not enough disk space to install Quattro Pro` when I try to install the program. What can I do?

A: Exit the installation utility. Erase nonessential files from your hard disk drive until you have at least 6M of free storage space on your hard disk drive.

Q: I am upgrading from a previous version of Quattro Pro and noticed that during installation, I was not prompted to install any fonts. Did I do something wrong?

A: No. Quattro Pro Version 4.0 uses faster Bitstream-SC fonts in place of the Bitstream fonts that came in Version 3.0.

In previous versions of the program it was necessary to prebuild a single bit-map font file (FON) for each point size within a particular typeface file (SFO); in Version 4.0, the Bitstream-SC fonts use a single typeface file (SPO) and a single bit-map font file (FN2). This improvement in Quattro Pro's font management technology has eliminated the need for building fonts in advance during installation.

Q: When I try to load the program, the computer displays the message Not enough memory to run Quattro Pro. What can I do?

A: Erase all TSR programs from your CONFIG.SYS and AUTOEXEC.BAT files. Reboot your system and try again.

If your computer has expanded memory that conforms to the LIM 3.2 or 4.0 standard, the memory card may not be Quattro Pro-compatible. Contact the manufacturer. Try loading Quattro Pro without loading the EMS driver via the CONFIG.SYS file.

Load CONFIG.SYS into a word processing program as a DOS text file. Delete the name of the driver program, save the file, and then reboot your computer so that the new CONFIG.SYS settings take effect.

Create alternate, streamlined AUTOEXEC.BAT and CONFIG.SYS files by following these steps:

1. Rename AUTOEXEC.BAT to AUTOEXEC.OLD.

2. Rename CONFIG.SYS to CONFIG.OLD.

3. Use COPY CON CONFIG.SYS to create a file with the following entries:

   FILES=20
   BUFFERS=20
   ^Z

4. Press Ctrl-Alt-Del to reboot your system.

APPENDIX B

Macro Commands

Appendix B—a guide to Quattro Pro's macro commands—begins with general guidelines for using macro commands within macro programs. The second half of Appendix B is a glossary of Quattro Pro's macro commands, organized alphabetically so that you easily can reference each command.

Using Macro Commands in a Macro Program

Quattro Pro offers an extensive set of commands that you use in macro programs to accomplish specific tasks and perform unique functions.

Macro commands enable you to access functions and accomplish tasks that you generally cannot do by pressing keys. The {BEEP} macro command, for example, causes your computer to emit a beep tone. The {GETLABEL} macro command prompts the macro user to type a label on the input line. Also, macro commands such as {BRANCH} and {DISPATCH} help you to control the execution flow of a macro program—as with other programming languages.

You can use Quattro Pro's macro commands with menu-equivalent commands to create advanced macros. The macro shown in figure B.1, for example, uses the {GETNUMBER} and {GETLABEL} commands to prompt a user for an account name and three account values. Quattro Pro stores each response in a specific cell, creates an @function command that sums the three values, and then executes the menu-equivalent command that displays the numbers in currency format with no decimal places.

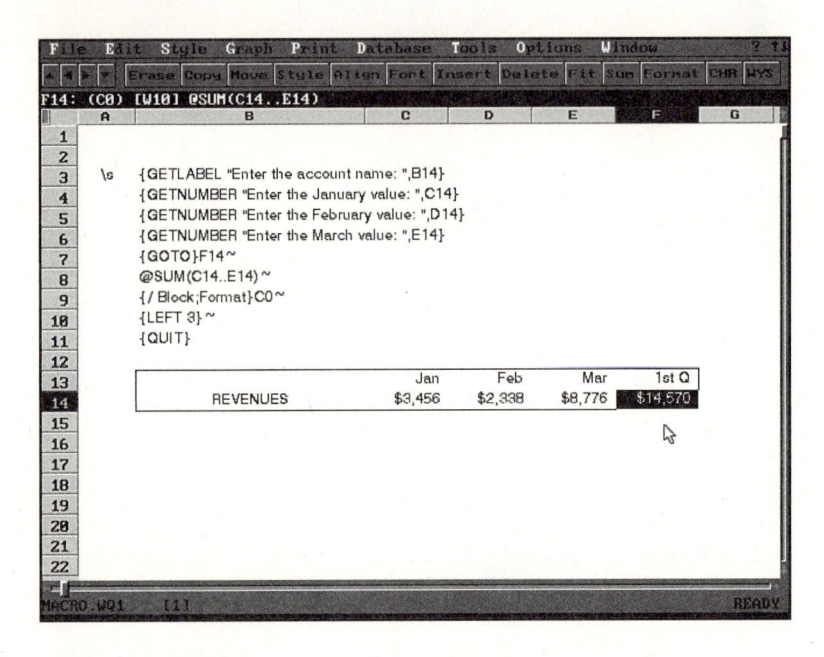

Fig. B.1

Use macro commands with menu-equivalent and keystroke commands to build advanced macros.

As you build advanced macro programs, notice that each command has its own distinctive syntax. The general syntax for Quattro Pro macro commands is as follows:

{*MACRO_COMMAND_NAME Argument1,Argument2,Argument3...*}

MACRO_COMMAND_NAME is the exact name of the command.

Argument#, where # denotes the argument's order of appearance in the macro command, is additional data needed by the macro command. Typically, an argument specifies the data or cell address that the macro operates on.

The four types of arguments are as follows:

- A valid *Number* argument can be an actual number (a number not enclosed in quotation marks), a formula that returns a number, or the address of a cell containing a number.

- A valid *String* argument can be a text string or the address of a cell that references another cell containing a text string.

- A valid *Location* string can be a cell address that contains a reference to a cell or cell block. The reference can be a block name or the cell coordinates for a block containing one or more cells.

- A valid *Condition* argument must be a logical expression that contains a cell reference, a number, a string, or a string-valued formula that Quattro Pro can evaluate as TRUE or FALSE.

When you use string values in a macro, you don't always need to enclose the string in quotation marks. If a string value contains a comma or a semicolon, however, you must enclose strings and block names in quotation marks.

You must enclose in quotation marks a formula that appears as a label and any string value identical to a block name.

In macro programs, Quattro Pro does not update block references when you change the block coordinates. If you move a cell or insert or delete a row or column, for example, the macro no longer references the correct block.

You should create block names whenever possible. If you move a named block referenced in a macro program, Quattro Pro updates the cell addresses associated with the block, and the macro program continues to reference the correct block.

When you use macro commands in your macro programs, use the following rules to create the correct syntax:

- Always begin and end a macro command with braces ({}).

- Place a space between the command name and the argument(s).

- Separate multiple arguments with commas.

- Always enter the type of argument specified by the macro command definition. If an argument requires a string, enter a string; if the argument requires a number, enter only a number.

- Do not enter extra spaces or punctuation, except within quoted strings. You can use {GETLABEL "Enter the account name",A4}, for example, but not {GETLABEL 'Enter the account name; A4}.

- Enter each expression into one cell.

- Macro commands can appear in upper- and lowercase letters.

- When you enter more than one command per line, type each command before typing the next one.

Note that some macro commands—such as {QUIT}—do not require arguments.

Using Subroutines in a Macro Program

As you develop more advanced programming skills, you may find yourself re-creating certain sequences of macro commands repeatedly in your applications. You may develop your own techniques for controlling the input and output of data, for example. All of your macro programs also may use the same print routine such as the same margin settings, setup strings, and graphics quality. You also may have retyped a sequence of commands repeatedly in the same macro program.

You can reduce the effort and time required to re-create these commands by designing mini-macros, or *subroutines*. A subroutine assumes responsibility for repetitive operations in a macro program. By referencing the subroutine many times, you then can execute the operation repeatedly without having to retype the commands.

When you reference a subroutine, you can instruct Quattro Pro to "pass along" arguments to the subroutine. These arguments are stored in cells referenced by the subroutine.

The subroutine {DATA1 D5,D6}, for example, sends control of the macro to a subroutine named DATA1 and passes two arguments (D5 and D6) along. Using the {DEFINE} command, you instruct the subroutine to perform an operation on the passed arguments. The {DEFINE} command tells Quattro Pro where to store the arguments and whether they are values or labels.

> **CAUTION:** Don't give a subroutine the same name as a macro command name (such as {DEFINE}). Doing so invali dates the macro command for the active spreadsheet until you delete the name or assign a new name in the subroutine.

Using /x Commands

Quattro Pro also uses */x commands* in macro programs. The /x commands are abbreviated versions for eight commonly used macro commands (see table B.1). The advantage of using /x commands is that you can enter them from your keyboard while recording a macro. You also can enter /x commands from the macro list that Quattro Pro displays when you press Shift-F3.

Table B.1 /x Commands

/x Command	Macro Command Equivalent
/xc	{SUBROUTINE}
/xl	{GETLABEL}
/xn	{GETNUMBER}
/xg	{BRANCH}
/xi	{IF}
/xm	{MENUBRANCH}
/xq	{QUIT}
/xr	{RETURN} and {RET}

When you use an /x command in a macro, place the argument directly after the command—just like with its macro command equivalent. To pass control of a macro program to a subroutine named SUB5, for example, enter the following:

/xcSUB5~

Suppose that you write a macro that solicits a sales value from a user and then enters the value into cell E5 on the active spreadsheet. The /x command syntax may look like the following:

/xnSales?~E5~

When Quattro Pro reaches the line containing this syntax, the program displays Sales? as a prompt at the top of the screen. When you enter a value and press Enter, Quattro Pro copies the value into cell E5.

You must place a ~ (tilde) after each argument used in an /x command. The /xl and /xn commands do not require a location parameter as do their macro command equivalents. When you do not specify a location argument, Quattro Pro uses the active cell.

Appendix C, "Menu-Equivalent Commands," offers a menu tree list of Quattro Pro's menu-equivalent macro commands. For examples of how to use the macro commands defined in this appendix, see Chapter 15, "Creating Macros."

Macro Command Glossary

Quattro Pro macro commands fall into seven categories. In this appendix, each category name follows the command name, making cross-referencing the commands easy. Table B.2 lists the categories.

Table B.2 Macro Command Categories

Command Category	Command Function
Keyboard	Reproduces the action of the keyboard keys
Screen	Affects the display of items
Interactive	Pauses a macro's execution and prompts a user to enter data from the keyboard
Program Flow	Controls the flow of data in a macro program
Cell	Affects the contents of cells
File	Manipulates data stored in nonspreadsheet files and files other than your current spreadsheet file
Miscellaneous	Performs miscellaneous actions on a macro program

NOTE All arguments appearing inside angle brackets (<>) are optional. The macro command functions with or without that argument.

{}

Command category: Miscellaneous

The {} command inserts a blank line in a macro. This command does not affect the execution of a macro because Quattro Pro skips over the command and executes the next macro command in the program.

The {} command is useful for segregating blocks of commands in a macro program that performs different functions.

{;String}

Command category: Miscellaneous

The {;} macro command enters side remarks into a macro program without affecting the execution of the program. In this syntax, *String* can be any combination of alphanumeric characters that does not exceed a length of 237.

The {;} command is useful for documenting a macro program. You can place {;Sum all sales values}, for example, above the first command in a group of commands that sum sales values.

{?}

Command category: Interactive

The {?} macro command pauses the execution of a macro program so that a user can enter data from the keyboard. Press Enter to continue the program execution.

This command is not available for use with graph buttons.

{ABS}

Command category: Keyboard

The {ABS} macro command is equivalent to pressing F4, the Abs key.

{BACKSPACE} and {BS}

Command category: Keyboard

These macro commands are equivalent to pressing the Backspace key.

{BACKTAB}

Command category: Keyboard

The {BACKTAB} macro command is equivalent to pressing Ctrl-← or Shift-Tab. This command functions like the {BIGLEFT} macro command.

{BEEP <Number>}

Command category: Screen

The {BEEP} macro command sounds a beeping tone from the computer's built-in speaker. The argument *Number* determines the frequency of the tone. If *Number* is omitted, Quattro Pro defaults to the low tone.

In this syntax, *Number* can be any number from 1 to 4, which uses the following frequencies:

    {BEEP1} sounds a low tone

    {BEEP2} sounds a standard tone

    {BEEP3} sounds a medium tone

    {BEEP4} sounds a high tone

You can use the {BEEP} command to call attention to a screen prompt, to indicate that the user did not enter the correct type of data, and to signify the end of a macro program.

{BIGLEFT}

Command category: Keyboard

The {BIGLEFT} macro command is equivalent to pressing Ctrl-← or Shift-Tab. This command functions like the {BACKTAB} macro command.

{BIGRIGHT}

Command category: Keyboard

The {BIGRIGHT} macro command is equivalent to pressing Ctrl-→ or Tab. This command functions like the {TAB} macro command.

{BLANK Location}

Command category: Cell

The {BLANK} macro command is equivalent to choosing /Edit Erase Block. Because this macro command does not access Quattro Pro's Edit menu directly, you can execute the command while another menu is on-screen.

In this syntax, *Location* designates a cell or block to erase.

{BRANCH Location}

Command category: Program flow

The {BRANCH} macro command exits the current macro and branches to another macro.

In this syntax, *Location* is the location or name of another macro.

Think of a macro named SALES, for example, that prompts a user to input 10 sales values. When all 10 values are entered, the user presses Q to quit.

The macro shown here tests the value entered into a cell named INPUT. If this value is not Q, the macro branches to a macro called SALES; if the value is Q, the macro branches to RATIOS.

{IF INPUT<>"Q"}{BRANCH SALES}{BRANCH RATIOS}

{BREAK}

Command category: Keyboard

The {BREAK} macro command is equivalent to pressing Ctrl-Break.

{BREAKOFF}

Command category: Interactive

The {BREAKOFF} macro command prevents a user from stopping the execution of a macro program by pressing Ctrl-Break.

{BREAKON}

Command category: Interactive

The {BREAKON} macro command cancels the {BREAKOFF} command, enabling a user to stop the execution of a macro program by pressing Ctrl-Break.

{CALC}

Command category: Keyboard

The {CALC} macro command is equivalent to pressing F9, the Calc key.

{CAPOFF} and {CAPON}

Command category: Keyboard

These macro commands are equivalent to pressing Caps Lock, which toggles between upper- and lowercase letters.

{CHOOSE}

Command category: Keyboard

The {CHOOSE} macro command is equivalent to pressing Alt-0 or Shift-F5, the Pick Window key.

{CLEAR}

Command category: Keyboard

The {CLEAR} macro command is equivalent to pressing Ctrl-Backspace. This command erases any preceding entry on a prompt line.

{CLOSE}

Command category: File

The {CLOSE} macro command saves and closes an open file. Quattro Pro enables only one file to be open at a time.

{CONTENTS Dest,Source,<Width>,<Format>}

Command category: Cell

The {CONTENTS} macro command copies data from one cell into another. Optional arguments enable the user to choose a column width and format for the copied data.

In this syntax, *Dest* is a cell that you want to write data to, and *Source* is a cell containing the data to be copied. The *Width* and *Format* arguments, which specify a column width and format code, are optional. (*Width* is optional unless you are specifying a *Format*.) Valid *Width* arguments range from 1 to 72. Valid *Format* arguments appear in table B.3.

{COPY}

Command category: Keyboard

The {COPY} macro command is equivalent to pressing Shift-F9, the Copy key.

Table B.3 Valid Format Arguments

Argument	Format description
0-15	Fixed, displaying 0 to 15 decimals
16-31	Scientific, displaying 0 to 15 decimals
32-47	Currency, displaying 0 to 15 decimals
48-63	Percent (%), displaying 0 to 15 decimals
64-79	Comma (,), displaying 0 to 15 decimals
112	+/− bar graph
113	General
114	Date format 1 (DD-MMM-YY)
115	Date format 2 (DD-MMM)
116	Date format 3 (MMM-YY)
117	Text
118	Hidden
119	Time format 1 (HH:MM:SS AM/PM)
120	Time format 2 (HH:MM AM/PM)
121	Date format 4 (Long Int'l)
122	Date format 5 (Short Int'l)
123	Time format 3 (Long Int'l)
124	Time format 4 (Short Int'l)
127	Default (specified by choosing /**O**ptions **F**ormats **N**umeric Format)

{CR} and ~ (Tilde)

Command category: Keyboard

These macro commands are equivalent to pressing Enter.

{DATE}

Command category: Keyboard

The {DATE} macro command is equivalent to pressing Ctrl-D, the Date-entry key.

{DEFINE Location1:<Type1>,Location2:<Type2>,...}

Command category: Program Flow

The {DEFINE} macro command passes sequentially ordered arguments for use in a subroutine.

In this syntax, *Location* is the cell in which you want to store a passed argument. The optional argument *Type* defines the type of argument being passed to *Location*.

Type can be a string or value, as shown in the following macro:

    {DEFINE K1:string,K2:value}

{DEL}, {DELEOL}, and {DELETE}

Command category: Keyboard

The {DEL} and {DELETE} macro commands are equivalent to pressing Del, the Delete key. The {DELEOL} macro command is equivalent to pressing Ctrl-\, which deletes every character from the cursor to the end of a line in EDIT mode.

{DISPATCH Location}

Command category: Program Flow

The {DISPATCH} macro command continues the execution of a macro at a different location in the program.

In this syntax, *Location* defines a cell containing a block name or address of another macro.

Like the {BRANCH} command, {DISPATCH} branches to other locations in the same macro program. The main difference between the two is that the *Location* argument in {DISPATCH} can specify a cell containing the address or name of a macro to branch to. If the macro program can place different addresses or names in *Location* depending upon a set of conditions specified in the macro, {DISPATCH} reroutes the macro execution.

{DOWN <Number>} and {D <Number>}

Command category: Keyboard

These macro commands are equivalent to pressing ↓, the down-arrow key. The optional *Number* argument specifies the number of times to press the ↓ key.

{EDIT}

Command category: Keyboard

The {EDIT} macro command is equivalent to pressing F2, the Edit key.

{END}

Command category: Keyboard

The {END} macro command is equivalent to pressing End on the numeric keypad.

{ESC} and {ESCAPE}

Command category: Keyboard

These macro commands are equivalent to pressing Esc on the keyboard.

{FILESIZE Location}

Command category: File

The {FILESIZE} macro command calculates the size of an open file and copies the result (in bytes) to *Location*.

In this syntax, *Location* indicates a cell address or block name.

{FOR CounterLoc,Start#,Stop#,Step#,StartLoc}

Command category: Program Flow

The {FOR} macro command repeatedly executes a macro subroutine, creating a macro loop.

In this syntax, *CounterLoc* is a cell that keeps track of the number of macro iterations, and *Start#* is the first value placed in cell *CounterLoc*. The *Stop#* argument indicates the maximum value that can appear in cell *CounterLoc*. The value of *Step#* is added to the value in cell *CounterLoc* after each iteration. The *StartLoc* argument indicates a cell containing the subroutine to be executed.

{FORBREAK}

Command category: Program Flow

The {FORBREAK} macro command cancels the execution of a subroutine and stops the processing of the {FOR} macro command.

{FUNCTIONS}

Command category: Keyboard

The {FUNCTIONS} macro command is equivalent to pressing Alt-F3, the Functions key.

{GET Location}

Command category: Interactive

The {GET} macro command pauses the execution of a macro, accepts a keystroke from the user, and stores that keystroke in the form of a left-aligned label in cell *Location*.

In this syntax, *Location* is a cell in which Quattro Pro stores the keystroke entered by the user.

{GETLABEL Prompt,Location}

Command category: Interactive

The {GETLABEL} macro command pauses the execution of a macro, displays *Prompt*, and accepts keystrokes entered by the user. Press Enter to resume macro execution.

In this syntax, *Prompt* is a string that displays as a prompt, and *Location* is a cell in which Quattro Pro stores the user's response to *Prompt*.

{GETNUMBER Prompt,Location}

Command category: Interactive

The {GETNUMBER} macro command pauses the execution of a macro, displays *Prompt*, and accepts a number entered by the user. Press Enter to resume macro execution. The {GETNUMBER} command accepts only numbers, a formula resulting in a number, or a cell address or block name returning a value as valid entries.

In this syntax, *Prompt* is a string that displays as a prompt, and *Location* is a cell in which Quattro Pro stores the user's response to *Prompt*.

{GETPOS Location}

Command category: File

The {GETPOS} macro command evaluates an open file and enters the value-equivalent position of the file pointer into *Location*. (A *file pointer* is a number that defines the location in a file where new data is written.)

In this syntax, *Location* is a cell in which Quattro Pro stores a retrieved value.

{GOTO}

Command category: Keyboard

The {GOTO} macro command is equivalent to pressing F5, the GoTo key.

{GRAPH}

Command category: Keyboard

The {GRAPH} macro command is equivalent to pressing F10, the Graph key.

{GRAPHCHAR Location}

Command category: Interactive

The {GRAPHCHAR} macro command stores in *Location* the character pressed to exit a displayed graph or to remove a message box.

You can use the stored character to branch to other parts of the macro. When an input prompt asks you to press Y for yes or N for no, for example, {GRAPHCHAR} can store and use the response to branch to other parts of the macro.

In this syntax, *Location* is a cell address or block name in which Quattro Pro stores a returned character.

{HOME}

Command category: Keyboard

The {HOME} macro command is equivalent to pressing Home.

{IF Condition}

Command category: Program Flow

The {IF} macro command is an "@IF function" for macros. {IF} evaluates *Condition* and returns the value TRUE or FALSE.

When Quattro Pro returns the value TRUE, the macro continues to execute in the same row; when the program returns FALSE, the macro skips to the next row and continues to execute in the first cell.

In this syntax, *Condition* is a logical expression or a cell address containing a label, a value, or another logical expression.

{IFKEY String}

Command category: Interactive

The {IFKEY} macro command returns TRUE when the macro name of a valid key is encountered.

In this syntax, *String* is a valid macro name for a key (such as HOME or PGUP) and is not surrounded by braces. *String* also can be a string that returns a key macro name without braces.

{INDICATE String}

Command category: Screen

The {INDICATE} macro command displays *String* as a mode indicator on the status line at the bottom right of a spreadsheet.

In this syntax, *String* is a character string consisting of five characters or less.

{INS},{INSERT},{INSOFF}, and {INSON}

Command category: Keyboard

The macro commands {INS} and {INSERT} are equivalent to pressing Ins to turn INSERT mode on and off. The {INSOFF} macro turns the INSERT mode off; {INSON} turns INSERT mode on.

{LEFT <Number>} and {L <Number>}

Command category: Keyboard

These macro commands are equivalent to pressing ←, the left-arrow key. The optional *Number* argument specifies the number of times to press the ← key.

{LET Location,Value:Type}

Command category: Cell

The {LET} macro command enters a value into a cell while a macro is running, without first moving the cell selector to that cell.

In this syntax, Quattro Pro stores *Value* in *Location*. Use the *Type* argument to specify whether *Value* should be stored as a string or as a value.

{LOOK Location}

Command category: Interactive

The {LOOK} macro command ensures that if any keystrokes are stored in Quattro Pro's type ahead buffer, the first one is executed after the current macro program execution stops. (A *type ahead buffer* is an internal storage facility where Quattro Pro records the keys you press after a macro begins executing.)

In this syntax, Quattro Pro stores a typed character in cell *Location*.

{MACROS}

Command category: Keyboard

The {MACROS} macro command is equivalent to pressing Shift-F3, the Macros key.

{MARK}

Command category: Keyboard

The {MARK} macro command is equivalent to pressing Shift-F7, the Select key.

{MARKALL}

Command category: Keyboard

The {MARKALL} macro command is equivalent to pressing Alt-F7, the Select All key.

{MENU}

Command category: Keyboard

The {MENU} macro command is equivalent to pressing the slash key (/).

{MENUBRANCH Location}

Command category: Interactive

The {MENUBRANCH} macro command displays a custom menu. When the user selects a choice from the custom menu, Quattro Pro continues executing the macro directly below the description of that choice in the macro program.

In this syntax, *Location* is a cell containing the definition for a custom Quattro Pro menu.

{MENUCALL Location}

Command category: Interactive

The {MENUCALL} macro command displays a custom menu. When the user selects a choice from the custom menu, Quattro Pro continues executing the macro directly below the cell containing the {MENUCALL} macro command.

In this syntax, *Location* is a cell containing the definition for a custom Quattro Pro menu.

{MESSAGE Block,Left,Top,Time}

Command category: Interactive

The {MESSAGE} macro command displays a message box during the execution of a macro program.

In this syntax, *Block* is a block name or cell address containing message text. The *Left* and *Top* arguments indicate the screen column number and line number, respectively, where the top left corner of the message box should appear.

The *Time* argument is an @ function expression that tells Quattro Pro how long to display the message. Enter *0* as the *Time* argument to keep the message box on-screen until the user presses a key.

{MOVE}

Command category: Keyboard

The {MOVE} macro command is equivalent to pressing Shift-F8, the Move key.

{NAME}

Command category: Keyboard

The {NAME} macro command is equivalent to pressing F3, the Choices key.

{NEXTWIN}

Command category: Keyboard

The {NEXTWIN} macro command is equivalent to pressing Shift-F6, the Next Window key.

{NUMOFF} and {NUMON}

Command category: Keyboard

These macro commands are equivalent to pressing Num Lock to toggle between numbers and other key functions on the numeric keypad.

{ONERROR BranchLocation,<MessageLocation>,<ErrorLocation>}

Command category: Program Flow

The {ONERROR} macro command prevents Quattro Pro from stopping a macro program when encountering an error. Use this command to trap errors that occur when the user enters commands from the keyboard.

In this syntax, *BranchLocation* is the first cell of the macro that Quattro Pro should execute when an error is encountered. *MessageLocation* tells Quattro Pro the cell in which the error message is stored, and *ErrorLocation* identifies the address of the cell containing the error.

{OPEN Filename,AccessMode}

Command category: File

The {OPEN} macro command opens a file so that Quattro Pro can use other file-access macro commands with the file.

In this syntax, *Filename* is the name of an open file. You can use four valid *AccessMode* arguments: R (read-only), M (modify), W (write), and A (append).

{PANELOFF}

Command category: Screen

The {PANELOFF} macro command disables the normal display of menus and prompts during the execution of a macro. Use this macro command to speed up the execution of macro programs that rely on keystrokes to select commands from Quattro Pro's menus.

{PANELON}

Command category: Screen

The {PANELON} macro command enables Quattro Pro to display all of the menus and prompts that previously were disabled with the {PANELOFF} command.

{PASTE}

Command category: Keyboard

The {PASTE} macro command is equivalent to pressing Shift-F10, the Paste key.

{PGDN <Number>} and {PGUP <Number>}

Command category: Keyboard

These macro commands are equivalent to pressing PgDn and PgUp on the keyboard. The optional *Number* argument specifies the number of times to press the PgUp or PgDn keys.

{PDXGO}

Command category: Keyboard

The {PDXGO} macro command is equivalent to pressing Ctrl-F10, the shortcut key to execute the /**D**atabase **P**aradox Access **G**o command.

{PLAY Filename}

Command category: File

The {PLAY} macro command reads the digitized sound file specified by *Filename* and plays that sound file on the internal speaker. The *Filename* argument may contain a drive letter and directory path, or may reference a spreadsheet cell containing that information.

{PUT Location,Column#,Row#,Value:<Type>}

Command category: Cell

The {PUT} macro command copies a value into a cell. The copied value is offset by a user-specified number of columns and rows.

In this syntax, Quattro Pro stores *Value* in the block specified by *Location*. The optional *Type* argument specifies whether *Value* should be stored as a string or as a label. The *Column#* and *Row#* arguments indicate how many columns and rows into the specified block Quattro Pro should offset before storing *Value* (0 is the first row or column, 1 the second, and so forth).

This command is similar to the {LET} macro command.

{QUERY}

Command category: Keyboard

The {QUERY} macro command is equivalent to pressing F7, the Query key.

{QUIT}

Command category: Program Flow

The {QUIT} macro command stops the execution of a macro and returns Quattro Pro to READY mode.

{READ #Bytes,Location}

Command category: File

The {READ} macro command reads a certain number of bytes worth of characters from an open file and stores these characters in a cell on the spreadsheet.

In this syntax, *#Bytes* is the number of bytes of characters to read, and *Location* is the cell in which Quattro Pro stores the characters.

{READDIR}

Command category: Keyboard

The {READDIR} macro command is equivalent to pressing F9 when Quattro Pro's File Manager is open.

{READLN Location}

Command category: File

The {READLN} macro command is similar to the {READ} command. The only difference is that {READLN} automatically reads forward from the current file pointer location, up to and including the carriage-return (or line-feed) command at the end of the line. (A *file pointer* is a number that defines the location in a file where new data is written.)

In this syntax, *Location* is the cell in which Quattro Pro stores the characters.

{RECALC Location,<Condition>,<Iteration#>}

Command category: Cell

The {RECALC} macro command forces Quattro Pro to recalculate a specific part of the active spreadsheet in row-by-row order.

In this syntax, *Location* indicates the cell block to recalculate. The optional argument *Condition* must be met before Quattro Pro halts the recalculation. The optional argument *Iteration#* sets the maximum number of recalculations that Quattro Pro should execute.

Set /**O**ptions **R**ecalculation **M**ode to **M**anual before using {RECALC} in a macro.

{RECALCCOL Location,<Condition>,<Iteration#>}

Command category: Cell

The {RECALCCOL} macro command forces Quattro Pro to recalculate a specific part of the active spreadsheet in column-by-column order.

In this syntax, *Location* indicates the cell block to recalculate. The optional argument *Condition* must be met before Quattro Pro halts the recalculation. The optional argument *Iteration#* sets the maximum number of recalculations that Quattro Pro should execute.

{RESTART}

Command category: Program Flow

The {RESTART} macro command changes the current subroutine to the starting routine. Quattro Pro accomplishes this change by removing all preceding FOR loops and subroutine calls.

{RETURN}

Command category: Program Flow

The {RETURN} macro command halts execution of the current subroutine and passes control back to the original macro.

{RIGHT <Number>} or {R <Number>}

Command category: Keyboard

These macro commands are equivalent to pressing →, the right-arrow key. The optional *Number* argument specifies the number of times to press the → key.

{SCROLLOFF} and {SCROLLON}

Command category: Keyboard

These macro commands are equivalent to pressing Scroll Lock to toggle the scroll-locking feature on and off.

{SETPOS FilePosition}

Command category: File

The {SETPOS} macro command moves the file pointer for an open file to the value *FilePosition*. (A *file pointer* is a number that defines the location in a file where new data is written.)

In this syntax, *FilePosition* indicates the number of bytes to which Quattro Pro should set the file pointer.

{STEP}

Command category: Keyboard

The {STEP} macro command is equivalent to pressing Shift-F2, the Debug key.

{STEPOFF}

Command category: Interactive

The {STEPOFF} macro command exits Quattro Pro's DEBUG mode, returning macro execution to normal operation.

{STEPON}

The {STEPON} macro command enters Quattro Pro's DEBUG mode, causing the macro to execute one step at a time.

{SUBROUTINE <ArgumentList>}

Command category: Program Flow

The {*SUBROUTINE*} macro command passes arguments to a called subroutine.

In this syntax, *SUBROUTINE* is the name of the subroutine being called. *ArgumentList* is a list containing one or more arguments to be passed to the subroutine. You can call, or *nest*, up to 32 levels of subroutines as defined using the {DEFINE} command.

{TAB}

Command category: Keyboard

The {TAB} macro command is equivalent to pressing Ctrl-→ or Tab.

{TABLE}

Command category: Keyboard

The {TABLE} macro command is equivalent to pressing F8, the Table key.

{UNDO}

Command category: Keyboard

The {UNDO} macro command is equivalent to pressing Alt-F5, the Undo key. Set /**O**ptions **O**ther **U**ndo to **E**nable before using {UNDO} in a macro.

{UP <Number>} and {U <Number>}

Command category: Keyboard

These macro commands are equivalent to pressing ↑, the up-arrow key. The optional *Number* argument specifies the number of times to press the ↑ key.

{WAIT DateTimeNumber}

Command category: Interactive

The {WAIT} macro command pauses the execution of a macro until a user-specified time.

In this syntax, *DateTimeNumber* indicates the date and time when Quattro Pro resumes macro execution.

{WINDOW<Number>}

Command category: Keyboard

The {WINDOW} macro command is equivalent to pressing F6, the Pane key. With the optional *Number* argument, the macro switches to the specified open spreadsheet window number.

{WINDOWSOFF}

Command category: Screen

The {WINDOWSOFF} macro command prevents Quattro Pro from displaying any screen changes that normally occur during the execution of a macro program.

{WINDOWSON}

Command category: Screen

The {WINDOWSON} macro command cancels a {WINDOWSOFF} command, enabling Quattro Pro to display any screen changes that normally occur during the execution of a macro program.

{WRITE String}

Command category: File

The {WRITE} macro command copies a string of characters into an open file, beginning at the location of the file pointer. (A *file pointer* is a number that defines the location in a file where new data is written.)

In this syntax, *String* is a string of characters that Quattro Pro writes into the open file.

{WRITELN String}

Command category: File

The {WRITELN} macro command copies a string of characters into an open file, starting at the location of the file pointer. The command adds a carriage return and line-feed command to the end of the written string.

In this syntax, *String* is a string of characters that Quattro Pro writes as a line into the open file.

{ZOOM}

Command category: Keyboard

The {ZOOM} macro command is equivalent to pressing Alt-F6, the Zoom Window key.

APPENDIX C

Menu-Equivalent Commands

Appendix C is a comprehensive reference source for Quattro Pro's menu-equivalent commands.

Quattro Pro uses menu-equivalent commands in macro programs to represent keystroke actions. When you record a logical macro (rather than a keystroke macro), Quattro Pro converts each of your keystrokes into a menu-equivalent command.

See Appendix B, "Macro Commands," for a comprehensive glossary of Quattro Pro's macro commands. See Chapter 15, "Creating Macros," for more information about creating macro programs.

To understand how Quattro Pro uses menu-equivalent commands in a macro program, suppose that you want to create a macro that opens a file called SALES.WQ1, moves the cell selector down five rows, inserts a line, and then saves the edited file. To create this program using Quattro Pro's macro recorder, perform the following steps:

1. Select **/T**ools **M**acro **M**acro **R**ecording **L**ogical so that Quattro Pro stores your keystrokes as macro-equivalent commands.
2. Select **/T**ools **M**acro **R**ecord to turn on the recorder.
3. Select **/F**ile **R**etrieve, type *sales*, and press Enter.
4. Press the down arrow key five times.
5. Select **/E**dit Insert **R**ows and press Enter.
6. Select **/F**ile **S**ave **R**eplace.
7. Select **/T**ools **M**acro **R**ecord to turn off the recorder.

Quattro Pro converts these keystrokes into the following macro program:

{/ File;Retrieve}	(menu-equivalent command)
{CLEAR}	(keyboard command)
C:\QPRO\SALES.WQ1~	{DOWN 5}
{/ Row;Insert}~	(menu-equivalent command)
{/ File;SaveNow}r	(menu-equivalent command)

Use menu-equivalent commands in your macro programs to instruct Quattro Pro to perform operations such as saving a file, erasing a block, switching display modes, and so on.

The following tables show each Quattro Pro menu and menu-equivalent commands.

Table C.1 File Menu Commands

Command	Menu-Equivalent Command
New	{/ View;NewWindow}
Open	{/ View;OpenWindow}
Retrieve	{/ File;Retrieve}
Save	{/ File;SaveNow}
Save As	{/ File;Save}
Save All	{/ File;SaveAll}
Close	{/ Basics;Close}
Close All	{/ System;TidyUp}
Erase	{/ Basics;Erase}

C — MENU-EQUIVALENT COMMANDS

Command	Menu-Equivalent Command
Directory	{/ File;Directory}
Workspace	
Save	{/ System;SaveWorkspace}
Restore	{/ System;RestoreWorkspace}
Utilities	
DOS Shell	{/ Basics;Shell}[1]
	{/ Basics;OS}[2]
File Manager	{/ View;NewFileMgr}
SQZ!	
Remove Blanks	{/ SQZ;Blanks}
Storage of Values	{/ SQZ;Values}
Version	{/ SQZ;Version}
Exit	{/ System;Exit}

[1] *Returns to Quattro after executing the command.*
[2] *Must type* exit *to return to Quattro.*

Table C.2 Edit Menu Commands

Command	Menu-Equivalent Command
Copy	{/ Block;Copy}
Copy Special	{/ Block;CopyPartial}
Contents	{/ Block;CopyContents}
Format	{/ Block;CopyFormat}
Move {/ Block;Move}	
Erase Block	{/ Block;Erase}
Undo	{/ Basics;Undo}
Insert	
Rows	{/ Row;Insert}
Columns	{/ Column;Insert}

continues

Table C.2 Continued

Command	Menu-Equivalent Command
Row Block	{/ Row;InsertBlock}
Column Block	{/ Column;InsertBlock}
Delete	
Rows	{/ Row;Delete}
Columns	{/ Column;Delete}
Row Block	{/ Row;DeleteBlock}
Column Block	{/ Column;InsertBlock}
Names	
Create	{/ Name;Create}
Delete	{/ Name;Delete}
Labels	
Right	{/ Name;RightCreate}
Down	{/ Name;UnderCreate}
Left	{/ Name;LeftCreate}
Up	{/ Name;AboveCreate}
Reset	{/ Name;Reset}
Make Table	{/ Name;Table}
Fill	{/ Math;Fill}
Values	{/ Block;Values}
Transpose	{/ Block;Transpose}
Search & Replace	
Block	{/ Audit;ReplaceRange}
Search String	{/ Audit;SearchString}
Replace String	{/ Audit;ReplaceString}
Options	
LookIn	{/ Audit;SearchLookIn}
Formula	{/ Audit;SearchFormula}
Value	{/ Audit;SearchValue}
Condition	{/ Audit;SearchCondition}

Command	Menu-Equivalent Command
Direction	{/ Audit;SearchDirection}
Row	{/ Audit;SearchByRow}
Column	{/ Audit;SearchByCol}
Match	{/ Audit;SearchMatch}
Part	{/ Audit;SearchForPart}
Whole	{/ Audit;SearchForWhole}
Case Sensitive	{/ Audit;SearchCase}
Any Case	{/ Audit;SearchAnyCase}
Exact Case	{/ Audit;SearchExactCase}
Options Reset	{/ Audit;SearchReset}
Next	{/ Audit;Replace}
Previous	{/ Audit;SearchPrev}

Table C.3 Style Menu Commands

Command	Menu-Equivalent Command
Alignment	
General	{/ Publish;AlignDefault}
Left	{/ Publish;AlignLeft}
Right	{/ Publish;AlignRight}
Center	{/ Publish;AlignCenter}
Numeric Format	{/ Block;Format}
Protection	
Protect	{/ Block;Protect}
Unprotect	{/ Block;Unprotect}
Column Width	{/ Column;Width}
Reset Width	{/ Column;Reset}
Hide Column	
Hide	{/ Column;Hide}
Expose	{/ Column;Display}

continues

Table C.3 Continued

Command	Menu-Equivalent Command
Block Size	
Set Width	{/ Block;SetWidth}
Reset Width	{/ Block;ResetWidth}
Auto Width	{/ Block;AdjustWidth}
Height	
Set Row Height	{/ Block;SetHeight}
Reset Row Height	{/ Block;ResetHeight}
Line Drawing	{/ Publish;LineDrawing}
Shading	
None	{/ Publish;ShadingNone}
Grey	{/ Publish;ShadingGrey}
Black	{/ Publish;ShadingBlack}
Font	{/ Publish;ApplyAnonymousStyle}
FontTable	{/ Publish;Font}
Edit Fonts	{/ Publish;Font}E
Reset	{/ Publish;Font}R
Update	{/ Publish;Font}U
Use Style	{/ Publish;UseNamedStyle}
Define Style	
Create	{/ Publish;EditNamedStyle}
Erase	{/ Publish;EraseNamedStyle}
Remove	{/ Publish;DeleteNamedStyle}
File	
Retrieve	{/ Publish;LoadStyleSheet}
Save	{/ Publish;SaveStyleSheet}
Insert Break	{/ Print;CreatePageBreak}

C — MENU-EQUIVALENT COMMANDS

Table C.4 Graph Menu Commands

Command	Menu-Equivalent Command
Graph Type	{/ Graph;Type}
Series	
1st Series	{/ 1Series;Block}
2nd Series	{/ 2Series;Block}
3rd Series	{/ 3Series;Block}
4th Series	{/ 4Series;Block}
5th Series	{/ 5Series;Block}
6th Series	{/ 6Series;Block}
X-Axis Series	{/ XAxis;Labels}
Group	
Columns	{/ Graph;ColumnSeries}
Rows	{/ Graph;RowSeries}
Analyze	
*N*Series	{/ Graph Analyze*n*;ShowKind}
Aggregation	{/ GraphAnalyze*n*;Aggregation}
Series Period *period*	{/ GraphAnalyze*n*;AgSeries*period*}
Aggregation Period *period*	{/ GraphAnalyze*n*;A*period*}
Function *function*	{/ GraphAnalyze*n*;AgFunction*function*}
Moving Average	{/ GraphAnalyze*n*;MovingAvg}
Period	{/ GraphAnalyze*n*;MovingAvgPeriods}
Weighted	{/ GraphAnalyze*n*;MovingAvgWeighted}
Linear Fit	{/ GraphAnalyze*n*;LinearFit}
Exponential Fit	{/ GraphAnalyze*n*;ExponFit}
Reset	{/ GraphAnalyze*n*;Reset}
Table	{/ GraphAnalyze*n*;Table}
All	
Aggregation	{/ GraphAnalyzeAll;Aggregation}
Series Period *period*	{/ GraphAnalyzeAll;AgSeries*period*}

continues

Table C.4 Continued

Command	Menu-Equivalent Command
Aggregation Period *period*	{/ GraphAnalyzeAll;Ag*period*}
Function *function*	{/ GraphAnalyzeAll;AgFunction*function*}
Moving Average	{/ GraphAnalyzeAll;MovingAvg}
Period	{/ GraphAnalyzeAll;MovingAvgPeriods}
Weighted	{/ GraphAnalyzeAll;MovingAvgWeighted}
Linear Fit	{/ GraphAnalyzeAll;LinearFit}
Exponential Fit	{/ GraphAnalyzeAll;ExponFit}
Reset	{/ GraphAnalyzeAll;Reset}
Text	
1st Line	{/ Graph;MainTitle}
2nd Line	{/ Graph;SubTitle}
X-Title	{/ XAxis;Title}
Y-Title	{/ YAxis;Title}
Secondary Y-Axis	{/ Y2Axis;Title}
Legends	
1st Series	{/ 1Series;Legend}
2nd Series	{/ 2Series;Legend}
3rd Series	{/ 3Series;Legend}
4th Series	{/ 4Series;Legend}
5th Series	{/ 5Series;Legend}
6th Series	{/ 6Series;Legend}
Position	{/ Graph;LegendPos}
Font	{/ GraphPrint;Fonts}
Customize Series (dialog box)	{/ Dialog;GraphCustomize}
Colors	
1st Series	{/ 1Series;Color}
2nd Series	{/ 2Series;Color}
3rd Series	{/ 3Series;Color}
4th Series	{/ 4Series;Color}

C — MENU-EQUIVALENT COMMANDS

Command	Menu-Equivalent Command
5th Series	{/ 5Series;Color}
6th Series	{/ 6Series;Color}
Fill Patterns	
1st Series	{/ 1Series;Pattern}
2nd Series	{/ 2Series;Pattern}
3rd Series	{/ 3Series;Pattern}
4th Series	{/ 4Series;Pattern}
5th Series	{/ 5Series;Pattern}
6th Series	{/ 6Series;Pattern}
Markers & Lines	
Line Styles	
1st Series	{/ 1Series;LineStyle}
2nd Series	{/ 2Series;LineStyle}
3rd Series	{/ 3Series;LineStyle}
4th Series	{/ 4Series;LineStyle}
5th Series	{/ 5Series;LineStyle}
6th Series	{/ 6Series;LineStyle}
Markers	
1st Series	{/ 1Series;Markers}
2nd Series	{/ 2Series;Markers}
3rd Series	{/ 3Series;Markers}
4th Series	{/ 4Series;Markers}
5th Series	{/ 5Series;Markers}
6th Series	{/ 6Series;Markers}
Formats	
1st Series	{/ CompGraph;AFormat}
2nd Series	{/ CompGraph;BFormat}
3rd Series	{/ CompGraph;CFormat}
4th Series	{/ CompGraph;DFormat}
5th Series	{/ CompGraph;EFormat}
6th Series	{/ CompGraph;FFormat}

continues

Table C.4 Continued

Command	Menu-Equivalent Command
Graph	{/ CompGraph;GraphFormat}
Bar Width	{/ Graph;BarWidth}
Interior Labels	
1st Series	{/ CompGraph;ALabels}
2nd Series	{/ CompGraph;BLabels}
3rd Series	{/ CompGraph;CLabels}
4th Series	{/ CompGraph;DLabels}
5th Series	{/ CompGraph;ELabels}
6th Series	{/ CompGraph;FLabels}
Override Type	
1st Series	{/ 1Series;Type}
2nd Series	{/ 2Series;Type}
3rd Series	{/ 3Series;Type}
4th Series	{/ 4Series;Type}
5th Series	{/ 5Series;Type}
6th Series	{/ 6Series;Type}
Y-Axis	
1st Series	{/ 1Series;YAxis}
2nd Series	{/ 2Series;YAxis}
3rd Series	{/ 3Series;YAxis}
4th Series	{/ 4Series;YAxis}
5th Series	{/ 5Series;YAxis}
6th Series	{/ 6Series;YAxis}
Pies	
Label Format	{/ Pie;ValueFormat}
Explode	
1st Slice	{/ PieExploded;1}
2nd Slice	{/ PieExploded;2}
3rd Slice	{/ PieExploded;3}

C — MENU-EQUIVALENT COMMANDS

Command	Menu-Equivalent Command
4th Slice	{/ PieExploded;4}
5th Slice	{/ PieExploded;5}
6th Slice	{/ PieExploded;6}
7th Slice	{/ PieExploded;7}
8th Slice	{/ PieExploded;8}
9th Slice	{/ PieExploded;9}
Patterns	
1st Slice	{/ PiePattern;1}
2nd Slice	{/ PiePattern;2}
3rd Slice	{/ PiePattern;3}
4th Slice	{/ PiePattern;4}
5th Slice	{/ PiePattern;5}
6th Slice	{/ PiePattern;6}
7th Slice	{/ PiePattern;7}
8th Slice	{/ PiePattern;8}
9th Slice	{/ PiePattern;9}
Colors	
1st Slice	{/ PieColor;1}
2nd Slice	{/ PieColor;2}
3rd Slice	{/ PieColor;3}
4th Slice	{/ PieColor;4}
5th Slice	{/ PieColor;5}
6th Slice	{/ PieColor;6}
7th Slice	{/ PieColor;7}
8th Slice	{/ PieColor;8}
9th Slice	{/ PieColor;9}
Tick Marks	{/ Pie;TickMarks}
Bubbles	
Patterns	
1st Bubble	{/ BubblePattern;1}

continues

Table C.4 Continued

Command	Menu-Equivalent Command
2nd Bubble	{/ BubblePattern;2}
3rd Bubble	{/ BubblePattern;3}
4th Bubble	{/ BubblePattern;4}
5th Bubble	{/ BubblePattern;5}
6th Bubble	{/ BubblePattern;6}
7th Bubble	{/ BubblePattern;7}
8th Bubble	{/ BubblePattern;8}
9th Bubble	{/ BubblePattern;9}
Colors	
1st Bubble	{/ BubbleColor;1}
2nd Bubble	{/ BubbleColor;2}
3rd Bubble	{/ BubbleColor;3}
4th Bubble	{/ BubbleColor;4}
5th Bubble	{/ BubbleColor;5}
6th Bubble	{/ BubbleColor;6}
7th Bubble	{/ BubbleColor;7}
8th Bubble	{/ BubbleColor;8}
9th Bubble	{/ BubbleColor;9}
Max Bubble Size	{/ BubbleSize;All}
Update	{/ Graph;UpdateGraph}
Reset	
1st Series	{/ Graph;Reset1}
2nd Series	{/ Graph;Reset2}
3rd Series	{/ Graph;Reset3}
4th Series	{/ Graph;Reset4}
5th Series	{/ Graph;Reset5}
6th Series	{/ Graph;Reset6}
X-axis Series	{/ XAxis;Reset}
Graph	{/ Graph;ResetAll}

C — MENU-EQUIVALENT COMMANDS

Command	Menu-Equivalent Command
X-Axis (dialog box)	{/ Dialog;GraphXaxis}
Scale	{/ XAxis;ScaleMode}
Low	{/ XAxis;Min}
High	{/ XAxis;Max}
Increment	{/ XAxis;Step}
Format of Ticks	{/ XAxis;Format}
No. of Minor Ticks	{/ XAxis;Skip}
Alternate Ticks	{/ XAxis;Alternate}
Display Scaling	{/ XAxis;ShowScale}
Mode	{/ XAxis;ScaleType}
Y-Axis (dialog box)	{/ Dialog;GraphYaxis}
Scale	{/ YAxis;ScaleMode}
Low	{/ YAxis;Min}
High	{/ YAxis;Max}
Increment	{/ YAxis;Step}
Format of Ticks	{/ YAxis;Format}
No. of Minor Ticks	{/ YAxis;Skip}
Display Ticks	{/ YAxis;ShowScale}
Mode	{/ YAxis;ScaleType}
2nd Y-Axis	
Scale	{/ Y2Axis;ScaleMode}
Low	{/ Y2Axis;Min}
High	{/ Y2Axis;Max}
Increment	{/ Y2Axis;Step}
Format of Ticks	{/ Y2Axis;Format}
No. of Minor Ticks	{/ Y2Axis;Skip}
Display Scaling	{/ Y2Axis;ShowScale}
Mode	{/ Y2Axis;ScaleType}
Overall (dialog box)	{/ Dialog;GraphOverall}
Grid	{/ Graph;GridStatus}

continues

Table C.4 Continued

Command	Menu-Equivalent Command
Horizontal	{/ CompGraph;GridHorz}
Vertical	{/ CompGraph;GridVert}
Both	{/ CompGraph;GridBoth}
Clear	{/ CompGraph;GridClear}
Grid Color	{/ Graph;GridColor}
Line Style	{/ Graph;GridLines}
Fill Color	{/ Graph;GridFill}
Outlines	
Titles	{/ Graph;TitleOtl}
Legend	{/ Graph;LegendOtl}
Graph	{/ Graph;GraphOtl}
Background Color	{/ Graph;BackColor}
Three-D	{/ Graph;3D}
Color/B&W	
Color	{/ Graph;Color}
B&W	{/ Graph;BW}
Drop Shadow Color *color name*	{/ Graph;DS*colorname*}
Insert	{/ Graph;NameInsert}
Hide	{/ Graph;NameHide}
Name	
Display	{/ Graph;NameUse}
Create	{/ Graph;NameCreate}
Autosave Edits	{/ Graph;NameAutosave}
Erase	{/ Graph;NameDelete}
Reset	{/ Graph;NameReset}
Slide	{/ Graph;NameSlide}
Graph Copy	{/ Graph;NameCopy}
View	{/ Graph;View}
Fast Graph	{/ Graph;FastGraph}
Annotate	{/ Graph;Annotate}

Table C.5 Print Menu Commands

Command	Menu-Equivalent Command
Block	{/ Print;Block}
Headings	
Left Heading	{/ Print;LeftBorder}
Top Heading	{/ Print;TopBorder}
Destination	{/ Print;Destination}
DraftMode Printing	
Printer	{/ Print;OutputPrinter}
File	{/ Print;OutputFile}
FinalQuality Printing	
Binary File	{/ Print;OutputHQFile}
Graphics Printer	{/ Print;OutputHQ}
Screen Preview	{/ Print;OutputPreview}
Layout (dialog box)	{/ Dialog;PrintLayout}
Header	{/ Print;Header}
Footer	{/ Print;Footer}
Break Pages	{/ Print;Breaks}
Percent Scaling	{/ Print;PercentScaling}
Margins	
Page Length	{/ Print;PageLength}
Left	{/ Print;LeftMargin}
Top	{/ Print;TopMargin}
Right	{/ Print;RightMargin}
Bottom	{/ Print;BottomMargin}
Dimensions	{/ Print;Dimensions}
Orientation	{/ Print;Rotated}
Setup String	{/ Print;Setup}
Reset	
All	{/ Print;ResetAll}
Print Block	{/ Print;ResetBlock}
Headings	{/ Print;ResetBorders}

continues

Table C.5 Continued

Command	Menu-Equivalent Command
Layout	{/ Print;ResetDefaults}
Update	{/ Print;Update}
Format	{/ Print;Format}
Copies	{/ Print;Copies}
Adjust Printer	
Skip Line	{/ Print;SkipLine}
Form Feed	{/ Print;FormFeed}
Align	{/ Print;Align}
Spreadsheet Print	{/ Print;Go}
Print-To-Fit	{/ Print;PrintToFit}
Graph Print	
Destination	{/ GraphPrint;Destination}
File	{/ GraphPrint;DestIsFile}
Graph Printer	{/ GraphPrint;DestIsPtr}
Screen Preview	{/ GraphPrint;DestIsPreview}
Layout	
Left Edge	{/ GraphPrint;Left}
Top Edge	{/ GraphPrint;Top}
Height	{/ GraphPrint;Height}
Width	{/ GraphPrint;Width}
Dimensions	{/ GraphPrint;Dimensions}
Orientation	{/ GraphPrint;Rotated}
4:3 Aspect	{/ Hardware;Aspect43}
Reset	{/ Print;ResetAll}
Update	{/ Print;Update}
Go	{/ GraphPrint;Go}
Write Graph File	
EPS File	{/ GraphFile;PostScript}
PIC File	{/ GraphFile;PIC}

Command	Menu-Equivalent Command
Slide EPS	{/ GraphFile;SlideEPS}
PCX File	{/ GraphFile;PCX}
Name	{/ GraphPrint;Use}
Print Manager	{/ View;NewPrintMgr}

Table C.6 Database Menu Commands

Command	Menu-Equivalent Command
Sort	
Block	{/ Sort;Block}
1st Key	{/ Sort;Key1}
2nd Key	{/ Sort;Key2}
3rd Key	{/ Sort;Key3}
4th Key	{/ Sort;Key4}
5th Key	{/ Sort;Key5}
Go	{/ Sort;Go}
Reset	{/ Sort;Reset}
Sort Rules	
Numbers Before Labels	{/ Startup;CellOrder}
Sort Rows/Columns	{/ Startup;SortOrder}
Label Order	{/ Startup;LabelOrder}
Query	
Block	{/ Query;Block}
Criteria Table	{/ Query;CriteriaBlock}
Output Block	{/ Query;Output}
Assign Names	{/ Query;AssignNames}
Locate	{/ Query;Locate}
Extract	{/ Query;Extract}
Unique	{/ Query;Unique}
Delete	{/ Query;Delete}

continues

Table C.6 Continued

Command	Menu-Equivalent Command
Reset	{/ Query;Reset}
Restrict Input	{/ Block;Input}
Data Entry	
General	{/ Publish;DataEntryFormula}
Labels Only	{/ Publish;DataEntryLabel}
Dates Only	{/ Publish;DataEntryDate}
Paradox Access	
Go	{/ Paradox;SwitchGo}
Load File	{/ Paradox;SwitchFile}
Autoload	{/ Paradox;SwitchAutoLoad}

Table C.7 Tools Menu Commands

Command	Menu-Equivalent Command
Macro	{/ Macro;Menu}
Record	{/ Macro;Record}
Paste	{/ Macro;Paste}
Instant Replay	{/ Macro;Replay}
Macro Recording	{/ Startup;Record}
Transcript	{/ Macro;Transcript}
Clear Breakpoints	{/ Name;BkptReset}
Debugger	{/ Macro;Debug}
Name	
Create	{/ Name;Create}
Delete	{/ Name;Delete}
Library	{/ Macro;Library}
Execute	{/ Name;Execute}
Key Reader	{/ Macro;Reader}
Reformat	{/ Block;Justify}

C — MENU-EQUIVALENT COMMANDS

Command	Menu-Equivalent Command
Import	
ASCII Text File	{/ File;ImportText}
Comma & "" Delimited File	{/ File;ImportNumbers}
Only Commas	{/ File;ImportComma}
Combine	
Copy	
File	{/ File;CopyFile}
Block	{/ File;CopyRange}
Add	
File	{/ File;AddFile}
Block	{/ File;AddRange}
Subtract	
File	{/ File;SubtractFile}
Block	{/ File;SubtractRange}
Xtract	
Formulas	{/ File;ExtractFormulas}
Values	{/ File;ExtractValues}
Update Links	
Open	{/ HotLink;Open}
Refresh	{/ HotLink;Update}
Change	{/ HotLink;Change}
Delete	{/ HotLink;Delete}
Advanced Math	
Regression	
Independent	{/ Regression;Independent}
Dependent	{/ Regression;Dependent}
Output	{/ Regression;Output}
Y Intercept	{/ Regression;Intercept}
Go	{/ Regression;Go}
Reset	{/ Regression;Reset}

continues

Table C.7 Continued

Command	Menu-Equivalent Command
Invert	{/ Math;InvertMatrix}
Multiply	{/ Math;MultiplyMatrix}
Parse	
Input	{/ Parse;Input}
Output	{/ Parse;Output}
Create	{/ Parse;CreateLine}
Edit	{/ Parse;EditLine}
Go	{/ Parse;Go}
Reset	{/ Parse;Reset}
What-If	
1 Variable	{/ Math;1CellWhat-If}
2 Variables	{/ Math;2CellWhat-If}
Reset	{/ Math;ResetWhat-If}
Frequency	{/ Math;Distribution}
Solve For	
Formula Cell	{/ Math;SolveFormula}
Target Value	{/ Math;SolveTarget}
Variable Cell	{/ Math;SolveVariable}
Parameters	
Max Iterations	{/ Math;SolveMaxIt}
Accuracy	{/ Math;SolveAccuracy}
Go	{/ Math;SolveGo}
Reset	{/ Math;SolveReset}
Optimizer	
Solution Cell	
Cell	{/ Solution;GoalCell}
Max,Min,Equal	
Maximum	{/ Solution;Maximum}
Minimum	{/ Solution;Minimum}

C — MENU-EQUIVALENT COMMANDS

Command	Menu-Equivalent Command
Equal	{/ Solution;Equal}
None	{/ Solution;NoGoal}
Variable Cell(s)	{/ Solution;Variable}
Constraints	{/ Solution;Constraints}
Options	
Max Time	{/ Solution;MaxTime}
Max Iterations	{/ Solution;MaxIterations}
Precision	{/ Solution;Precision}
Linear or Nonlinear	
Linear	{/ Solution;SetLinear}
Nonlinear	{/ Solution;SetNonlinear}
Show Iteration Results	{/ Solution;Show}
Estimates	
Tangent	{/ Solution;Tangent}
Quadratic	{/ Solution;Quad}
Derivatives	
Forward	{/ Solution;Forward}
Central	{/ Solution;Central}
Search	
Newton	{/ Solution;Newton}
Conjugate	{/ Solution;Conjugate}
Answer Report	{/ Solution;Answer}
Detail Report	{/ Solution;Detail}
Go	{/ Solution;Go}
Restore	{/ Solution;Restore}
Model	
Load	{/ Solution;Load}
Save	{/ Solution;Save}
Reset	
Solution Cell	{/ Solution;ResetSol}

continues

Table C.7 Continued

Command	Menu-Equivalent Command
Variable Cell(s)	{/ Solution;ResetVar}
Constraints	{/ Solution;ResetCon}
Options	{/ Solution;ResetOpt}
Answer Report	{/ Solution;ResetLine}
Detail Report	{/ Solution;ResetDet}
All	{/ Solution;Reset}
Audit	
Dependency	{/ Auditor;TypeDependency}
Circular	{/ Auditor;TypeCIRC}
Label References	{/ Auditor;TypeLabelReference}
ERR	{/ Auditor;TypeERR}
Blank References	{/ Auditor;TypeBlankReference}
External Links	{/ Auditor;TypeExternalReference}
Destination	{/ Auditor;Destination}
Library	
Load	{/ Library;Load}
Unload	{/ Library;Unload}

Table C.8 Options Menu Commands

Command	Menu-Equivalent Command
Hardware	
Screen	
Screen Type	{/ ScreenHardware;GraphScreenType}
Resolution	{/ Graph;ScreenMode}
Aspect Ratio	{/ ScreenHardware;AspectRatio}
CGA Snow Suppression	{/ ScreenHardware;Retrace}
Printers	

C — MENU-EQUIVALENT COMMANDS

Command	Menu-Equivalent Command
1st Printer	
Type of printer	{/ GPrinter1;Type}
Make	{/ GPrinter1;ShowMake}
Model	{/ GPrinter1;ShowModel}
Mode	{/ GPrinter1;ShowMode}
Device	{/ GPrinter1;Device}
Baud Rate	{/ GPrinter1;Baud}
Parity	{/ GPrinter1;Parity}
Stop Bits	{/ GPrinter1;Stop}
2nd Printer	
Type of printer	{/ GPrinter2;Type}
Make	{/ GPrinter2;ShowMake}
Model	{/ GPrinter2;ShowModel}
Mode	{/ GPrinter2;ShowMode}
Device	{/ GPrinter2;Device}
Baud Rate	{/ GPrinter2;Baud}
Parity	{/ GPrinter2;Parity}
Stop Bits	{/ GPrinter2;Stop}
Default Printer	{/ Defaults;PrinterName}
Plotter Speed	{/ GraphPrint;PlotSpeed}
Fonts	
Cartridge Fonts	
Left Cartridge	{/ Hardware;LJetLeft}
Right Cartridge	{/ Hardware;LJetRight}
Shading Level	{/ Hardware;LJShadeLevel}
Autoscale Fonts	{/ Hardware;AutoFonts}
Auto LF	{/ Hardware;AutoLF}
Single Sheet	{/ Hardware;SingleSheet}
Background	{/ Hardware;BackgroundPrint}
Mouse Button	{/ Hardware;MouseButton}

continues

Table C.8 Continued

Command	Menu-Equivalent Command
Normal Memory	
Bytes Available	{/ Basics;ShowMem}
Bytes Total	{/ Basics;ShowMemTotal}
% Available	{/ Basics;ShowMemPct}
EMS	
Bytes Available	{/ Basics;ShowEMS}
Bytes Total	{/ Basics;ShowEMSTotal}
% Available	{/ Basics;ShowEMSPct}
Coprocessor	{/ Basics;ShowCoProc}
Colors	
Menu	
Frame	{/ MenuColors;Frame}
Banner	{/ MenuColors;Banner}
Text	{/ MenuColors;Text}
Key Letter	{/ MenuColors;FirstLetter}
Highlight	{/ MenuColors;MenuBar}
Settings	{/ MenuColors;Settings}
Explanation	{/ MenuColors;Explanation}
Drop Shadow	{/ Startup;Shadow}
SpeedBar	{/ Startup;PaletteCol}
Shadow	{/ Startup;ShadowChar}
Desktop	
Status	{/ Color;Status}
Highlight (Status)	{/ Color;Indicators}
Errors	{/ ErrorColor;SetErrorColor}
Background	{/ Startup;DesktopColor}
Desktop	{/ Startup;DesktopChar}
Spreadsheet	
Frame	{/ Color;Frame}

C — MENU-EQUIVALENT COMMANDS

Command	Menu-Equivalent Command
Banner	{/ Color;Banner}
Cells	{/ Color;Cells}
Borders	{/ Color;Border}
Titles	{/ Color;Titles}
Highlight	{/ Color;Cursor}
Graph Frames	{/ Color;GraphFrame}
Input Line	{/ Color;Edit}
Unprotected	{/ Color;Unprotect}
Labels	{/ ValueColors;Labels}
Shading	{/ Color;Shading}
Drawn Lines	{/ Color;LineDrawing}
WYSIWYG Colors	
Background	{/ WYSIWYG;Cells}
Cursor	{/ WYSIWYG;Cursor}
Grid Lines	{/ WYSIWYG;Grid}
Unprotected	{/ WYSIWYG;Unprotected}
Drawn Lines	{/ WYSIWYG;Lines}
Shaded Cells	{/ WYSIWYG;Shading}
Locked Titles Text	{/ WYSIWYG;TitlesF}
Titles Background	{/ WYSIWYG;TitlesB}
Row and Column Labels	
Highlight	{/ WYSIWYG;BezelTop}
Shadow	{/ WYSIWYG;BezelBottom}
Face	{/ WYSIWYG;BezelFront}
Text	{/ WYSIWYG;BezelText}
Conditional	
On/Off	{/ ValueColors;Enable}
ERR	{/ ValueColors;Err}
Smallest Normal Value	{/ ValueColors;Min}
Greatest Normal Value	{/ ValueColors;Max}

continues

Table C.8 Continued

Command	Menu-Equivalent Command
Below Normal Color	{/ ValueColors;Low}
Normal Cell Color	{/ ValueColors;Normal}
Above Normal Color	{/ ValueColors;High}
Help	
Frame	{/ HelpColors;Frame}
Banner	{/ HelpColors;Banner}
Text	{/ HelpColors;Text}
Keywords	{/ HelpColors;Keyword}
Highlight	{/ HelpColors;Highlight}
File Manager	
Frame	{/ FileMgrColors;Frame}
Banner	{/ FileMgrColors;Banner}
Text	{/ FileMgrColors;Text}
Active Cursor	{/ FileMgrColors;ActiveCursor}
Inactive Cursor	{/ FileMgrColors;InactiveCursor}
Marked	{/ FileMgrColors;Marked}
Cut	{/ FileMgrColors;Cut}
Copy	{/ FileMgrColors;Copy}
Palettes	
Color	{/ Color;ColorPalette}
Monochrome	{/ Color;BWPalette}
Black & White	{/ Color;BWCGAPalette}
Gray Scale	{/ Color;GSPalette}
Version 3 Color	{/ Color;Version3Palette}
International	
Currency	{/ Intnl;CurrencyLocation}
Negative	{/ Intnl; Negative}
Punctuation	{/ Intnl;Punctuation}
Date	{/ FormatChanges;IntlDate}

C — MENU-EQUIVALENT COMMANDS

Command	Menu-Equivalent Command
Time	{/ FormatChanges;IntlTime}
Use Sort Table	{/ Intnl;UseSortTable}
LICS Conversion	{/ Intnl;LICS}
Overstrike Print	{/ Intnl;PrintComposed}
WYSIWYG Zoom %	{/ WYSIWYG;Zoom}
Display Mode	{/ ScreenHardware;TextScreenMode}
Startup	
Directory	{/ Defaults;Directory}
Autoload File	{/ Startup;File}
Startup Macro	{/ Startup;Macro}
File Extension	{/ Startup;Extension}
Beep	{/ Startup;Beep}
Menu Tree	{/ Startup;Menus}
Edit Menus	{/ MenuBuilder;Run}
Use Dialogs	{/ Dialog;Enable}
SpeedBar	
READY mode SpeedBar	
nth Button	
Short Name	{/ Buttons1;SmlText*n*}
Long Name	{/ Buttons1;LrgText*n*}
Macro	{/ Buttons1;Macro*n*}
EDIT mode SpeedBar	
nth Button	
Short Name	{/ Buttons2;SmlText*n*}
Long Name	{/ Buttons2;LrgText*n*}
Macro	{/ Buttons2;Macro*n*}
Graphics Quality	{/ Defaults;GraphicsQuality}
Other	
Undo	{/ Defaults;Undo}
Macro	{/ Defaults;Suppress}

continues

Table C.8 Continued

Command	Menu-Equivalent Command
Expanded Memory	{/ Defaults;ExpMem}
Clock	{/ Defaults;ClockFormat}
Paradox	
Network Type	{/ Paradox;NetType}
Directory	{/ Paradox;NetDir}
Version 3.5 or earlier	{/ Paradox;V35}
Version 4.0	{/ Paradox;V40}
Network	
Drive Mappings	{/ Network;DriveMaps}
Banner	{/ Network;Banner}
Refresh Interval	{/ Network;Interval}
Queue Monitor	{/ Network;MonitorQueue}
User Name	{/ Network;UserName}
Update	{/ Defaults;Update}
Formats	
Numeric Format	{/ Defaults;Format}
Align Labels	{/ Defaults;Alignment}
Hide Zeros	{/ Defaults;Zero}
Global Width	{/ Defaults;ColWidth}
Recalculation	
Mode	{/ Defaults;RecalcMode}
Automatic	{/ CompCalc;Automatic}
Manual	{/ CompCalc;Manual}
Background	{/ CompCalc;Background}
Order	{/ Defaults;RecalcOrder}
Natural	{/ CompCalc;Natural}
Columnwise	{/ CompCalc;ColWise}
Rowwise	{/ CompCalc;RowWise}
Iteration	{/ Defaults;RecalcIteration}

C — MENU-EQUIVALENT COMMANDS

Command	Menu-Equivalent Command
Circular Cell	{/ Audit;ShowCirc}
Protection	{/ Protection;Status}
Enable	{/ Protection;Enable}
Disable	{/ Protection;Disable}
Formulas	
Add	{/ Protection;FormProtect}
Remove	{/ Protection;FormUnprotect}

Table C.9 Window Menu Commands

Command	Menu-Equivalent Command
Zoom	{/ View;Zoom}
Tile	{/ View;Arrange}
Stack	{/ View;Cascade}
Move/Size	{/ View;Size}
Options	
Horizontal	{/ Windows;Horizontal}
Vertical	{/ Windows;Vertical}
Sync	{/ Windows;Synch}
Unsync	{/ Windows;Unsynch}
Clear	{/ Windows;Clear}
Locked Titles	
Horizontal	{/ Titles;Horizontal}
Vertical	{/ Titles;Vertical}
Both	{/ Titles;Both}
Clear	{/ Titles;Clear}
Row & Col Borders	
Display	{/ Windows;RowColDisplay}
Hide	{/ Windows;RowColHide}
Map View	{/ Windows;MapView}

continues

Table C.9 Continued

Command	Menu-Equivalent Command
Grid Lines	{/ Windows;GridLines}
Print Block	
Hide	{/ Windows;PrintBlock}H
Display	{/ Windows;PrintBlock}D
Pick	{/ View;Choose}

Table C.10 File Manager File Menu Commands

Command	Menu-Equivalent Command
New	{/ View;NewWindow}
Open	{/ View;OpenWindow}
Close	{/ Basics;Close}
Close All	{/ System;TidyUp}
Read Dir	{/ FileMgr;ReadDir}
Make Dir	{/ FileMgr;MakeDir}
Workspace	
Save	{/ System;SaveWorkspace}
Restore	{/ System;RestoreWorkspace}
Utilities	
DOS Shell	{/ Basics;Shell}
File Manager	{/ View;NewFileMgr}
SQZ!	
Remove Blanks	{/ SQZ;Blanks}
Storage of Values	{/ SQZ;Values}
Version	{/ SQZ;Version}
Exit	{/ System;Exit}

Table C.11 File Manager Edit Menu Commands

Command	Menu-Equivalent Command
Select File	{/ FileMgr;Mark}
All Select	{/ FileMgr;AllMark}
Copy	{/ FileMgr;Copy}
Move	{/ FileMgr;Cut}
Erase	{/ FileMgr;Erase}
Paste	{/ FileMgr;Paste}
Duplicate	{/ FileMgr;Duplicate}
Rename	{/ FileMgr;Rename}

Table C.12 File Manager Sort Menu Commands

Command	Menu-Equivalent Command
Name	{/ FileMgr;SortName}
Timestamp	{/ FileMgr;SortDate}
Extension	{/ FileMgr;SortExt}
Size	{/ FileMgr;SortSize}
DOS Order	{/ FileMgr;SortNone}

Table C.13 File Manager Tree Menu Commands

Command	Menu-Equivalent Command
Open	{/ FileMgr;TreeShow}
Resize	{/ FileMgr;TreeSize}
Close	{/ FileMgr;TreeClear}

Table C.14 File Manager Print Menu Commands

Command	Menu-Equivalent Command
Block	{/ FileMgrPrint;Block}
Destination	
Printer	{/ FileMgrPrint;OutputPrinter}
File	{/ FileMgrPrint;OutputFile}
Page Layout	
Header	{/ FileMgrPrint;Header}
Footer	{/ FileMgrPrint;Footer}
Break Pages	{/ FileMgrPrint;Breaks}
Margins & Length	
Page Length	{/ FileMgrPrint;PageLength}
Left	{/ FileMgrPrint;LeftMargin}
Top	{/ FileMgrPrint;TopMargin}
Right	{/ FileMgrPrint;RightMargin}
Bottom	{/ FileMgrPrint;BottomMargin}
Setup String	{/ FileMgrPrint;Setup}
Reset	
All	{/ FileMgrPrint;ResetAll}
Print Block	{/ FileMgrPrint;ResetBlock}
Layout	{/ FileMgrPrint;ResetDefaults}
Adjust Printer	
Skip Line	{/ FileMgrPrint;SkipLine}
Form Feed	{/ FileMgrPrint;FormFeed}
Align	{/ FileMgrPrint;Align}
Go	{/ FileMgrPrint;Go}

Table C.15 File Manager Options Menu Commands

Command	Menu-Equivalent Command
Hardware	(See the Hardware command in Table C.8)
Colors	(See the Colors command in Table C.8)
Beep	{/ Startup;Beep}
Startup	
Menu Tree	{/ Startup;Menus}
Edit Menus	{/ MenuBuilder;Run}
Directory	
Previous	{/ FileMgr;SameDir}
Current	{/ FileMgr;CurrDir}
File List	
Wide View	{/ FileMgr;Wide}
Full View	{/ FileMgr;Narrow}
Display Mode	{/ ScreenHardware;TextScreenMode}
Update	{/ Defaults;Update}

Table C.16 File Manager Window Menu Commands

Command	Menu-Equivalent Command
Zoom	{/ View;Zoom}
Tile	{/ View;Tile}
Stack	{/ View;Cascade}
Move/Size	{/ View;Size}
Pick	{/ View;Choose}

Table C.17 Print Manager Window Menu Commands

Command	Menu-Equivalent Command
File	
Close	{/ Basics;Close}
Close All	{/ System;TidyUp}
Queue	
Background	{/ Queue;Background}
Network	{/ Queue;Network}
Job	
Delete	{/ Queue;DeleteJob}
Suspend	{/ Queue;SuspendJob}
Resume	{/ Queue;ResumeJob}
Window	
Zoom	{/ View;Zoom}
Tile	{/ View;Arrange}
Stack	{/ View;Cascade}
Move/Size	{/ View;Size}
Pick	{/ View;Choose}

APPENDIX D

Using ASCII Characters

Table D.1 lists the American Standard Code for Information Interchange (ASCII) character table. The table lists 255 characters and their decimal and hexadecimal equivalents.

Entering ASCII Characters in Spreadsheet Cells

Quattro Pro accepts all ASCII characters in spreadsheet cells. When you create a graph from a spreadsheet containing ASCII characters, some of the characters display as text in the graph.

The ASCII characters of particular importance are the international characters (for example, é, £, and ˜), mathematical characters (for example, π and √), and border characters.

To enter an ASCII character into a spreadsheet cell, press and hold down the Alt key as you type the decimal code equivalent on your numeric keypad. When you release the Alt key, the character appears on the input line.

USING QUATTRO PRO 4, SPECIAL EDITION

To enter the mathematical symbol for a square root into a spreadsheet cell, for example, do the following:

1. Press and hold down the Alt key.
2. Type the decimal code *251*.
3. Release the Alt key. Quattro Pro reproduces the square root symbol on the input line at the top of your screen.
4. Press Enter to store the symbol in the cell.

Table D.1 ASCII Codes

Decimal	Hex	Graphic Character	Decimal	Hex	Graphic Character
0	0		24	18	↑
1	1	☺	25	19	↓
2	2	☻	26	1A	→
3	3	♥	27	1B	←
4	4	♦	28	1C	∟
5	5	♣	29	1D	↔
6	6	♠	30	1E	▲
7	7	•	31	1F	▼
8	8	◘	32	20	
9	9	○	33	21	!
10	A	◙	34	22	"
11	B	♂	35	23	#
12	C	♀	36	24	$
13	D	♪	37	25	%
14	E	♫	38	26	&
15	F	☼	39	27	'
16	10	►	40	28	(
17	11	◄	41	29	)
18	12	↕	42	2A	*
19	13	‼	43	2B	+
20	14	¶	44	2C	,
21	15	§	45	2D	-
22	16	▬	46	2E	.
23	17	↨	47	2F	/

D — USING ASCII CHARACTERS

Decimal	Hex	Graphic Character	Decimal	Hex	Graphic Character
48	30	0	96	60	`
49	31	1	97	61	a
50	32	2	98	62	b
51	33	3	99	63	c
52	34	4	100	64	d
53	35	5	101	65	e
54	36	6	102	66	f
55	37	7	103	67	g
56	38	8	104	68	h
57	39	9	105	69	i
58	3A	:	106	6A	j
59	3B	;	107	6B	k
60	3C	<	108	6C	l
61	3D	=	109	6D	m
62	3E	>	110	6E	n
63	3F	?	111	6F	o
64	40	@	112	70	p
65	41	A	113	71	q
66	42	B	114	72	r
67	43	C	115	73	s
68	44	D	116	74	t
69	45	E	117	75	u
70	46	F	118	76	v
71	47	G	119	77	w
72	48	H	120	78	x
73	49	I	121	79	y
74	4A	J	122	7A	z
75	4B	K	123	7B	{
76	4C	L	124	7C	|
77	4D	M	125	7D	}
78	4E	N	126	7E	~
79	4F	O	127	7F	Δ
80	50	P	128	80	Ç
81	51	Q	129	81	ü
82	52	R	130	82	é
83	53	S	131	83	â
84	54	T	132	84	ä
85	55	U	133	85	à
86	56	V	134	86	å
87	57	W	135	87	ç
88	58	X	136	88	ê
89	59	Y	137	89	ë
90	5A	Z	138	8A	è
91	5B	[	139	8B	ï
92	5C	\	140	8C	î
93	5D	]	141	8D	ì
94	5E	^	142	8E	Ä
95	5F	_	143	8F	Å

continues

Table D.1 Continued

Decimal	Hex	Graphic Character	Decimal	Hex	Graphic Character
144	90	É	192	C0	└
145	91	æ	193	C1	┴
146	92	Æ	194	C2	┬
147	93	ô	195	C3	├
148	94	ö	196	C4	─
149	95	ò	197	C5	┼
150	96	û	198	C6	╞
151	97	ù	199	C7	╟
152	98	ÿ	200	C8	╚
153	99	Ö	201	C9	╔
154	9A	Ü	202	CA	╩
155	9B	¢	203	CB	╦
156	9C	£	204	CC	╠
157	9D	¥	205	CD	═
158	9E	₧	206	CE	╬
159	9F	ƒ	207	CF	╧
160	A0	á	208	D0	╨
161	A1	í	209	D1	╤
162	A2	ó	210	D2	╥
163	A3	ú	211	D3	╙
164	A4	ñ	212	D4	╘
165	A5	Ñ	213	D5	╒
166	A6	ª	214	D6	╓
167	A7	º	215	D7	╫
168	A8	¿	216	D8	╪
169	A9	⌐	217	D9	┘
170	AA	¬	218	DA	┌
171	AB	½	219	DB	█
172	AC	¼	220	DC	▄
173	AD	¡	221	DD	▌
174	AE	«	222	DE	▐
175	AF	»	223	DF	▀
176	B0	░	224	E0	α
177	B1	▒	225	E1	β
178	B2	▓	226	E2	Γ
179	B3	│	227	E3	π
180	B4	┤	228	E4	Σ
181	B5	╡	229	E5	σ
182	B6	╢	230	E6	µ
183	B7	╖	231	E7	τ
184	B8	╕	232	E8	Φ
185	B9	╣	233	E9	θ
186	BA	║	234	EA	Ω
187	BB	╗	235	EB	δ
188	BC	╝	236	EC	∞
189	BD	╜	237	ED	φ
190	BE	╛	238	EE	∈
191	BF	┐	239	EF	∩

Decimal	Hex	Graphic Character	Decimal	Hex	Graphic Character
240	F0	≡	248	F8	°
241	F1	±	249	F9	∙
242	F2	≥	250	FA	·
243	F3	≤	251	FB	√
244	F4	⌠	252	FC	ⁿ
245	F5	⌡	253	FD	²
246	F6	÷	254	FE	■
247	F7	≈	255	FF	

Entering ASCII Characters in Dialog Boxes

You also enter ASCII characters into Quattro Pro dialog boxes. When you choose /**O**ptions **I**nternational **C**urrency, Quattro Pro displays a dialog box and prompts you to enter a new currency symbol. To enter the British pound currency symbol, do the following:

1. Press the Backspace key to delete the dollar sign (the default currency symbol).
2. Press and hold down the Alt key.
3. Type the decimal code *156* on the numeric keypad.
4. Release the Alt key. Quattro Pro reproduces the pound symbol in the dialog box.
5. Press Enter to store the pound symbol setting.

When you choose /**S**tyle **N**umeric Format **C**urrency and format a value, the pound symbol appears instead of the dollar sign. To keep the pound symbol as the global default, choose /**O**ptions **U**pdate.

> **TIP**
> Some terminate-and-stay-resident (TSR) programs like SuperKey assign special operations to the Alt key. If you have such programs on your PC, pressing Alt plus a decimal code does not display the ASCII character. Instead, press Shift-Alt and then type the decimal code.

Other special characters can be used with Quattro Pro. The /Options Colors Menu Shadow command, for example, prompts you to enter the decimal code equivalent for the ASCII character that Quattro Pro uses to create menu shadows. ASCII decimal code 2 displays smiling faces in the menu shadows.

The /Options Colors Desktop command prompts you to enter the decimal code equivalent for the ASCII character that Quattro Pro uses to create fill characters when no windows are displayed. ASCII decimal code 14 displays musical note symbols in the background area.

Notice that these two commands require you to enter the decimal code equivalents for the ASCII character. Do not enter the actual symbols by pressing Alt plus the decimal code. If you do, Quattro Pro does not interpret the command settings correctly.

> **TIP** These last two techniques for displaying special symbols on-screen are operable only when you are in text display mode.

Converting ASCII Codes into Printer Setup Strings

Another use for the ASCII table is to create printer setup strings that you supply at the /Printer Layout Setup String command prompt.

As discussed in Chapter 9, "Printing," the control panel on a printer enables you to invoke various print modes such as draft printing, bold printing, and compressed printing. Other print modes that your printer supports often do not appear as hardware options on the control panel (italic mode is a good example).

You can create and issue software commands that invoke special print modes. You first must review your printer manual. In the manual, you find a table of software commands. These software commands look like CTRL+F or ESC+4.

Printing modes generally are set through the use of control codes, which consist of one or more ASCII characters. These control codes, which vary from printer to printer, fall into two categories: control sequences and escape sequences.

In a *control sequence*, each code begins with the control key and is followed by a hexadecimal character. CTRL+F, for example, invokes the compressed printing mode for a Panasonic printer. To use this software command, convert the command to a code that your printer understands. The printer code that signifies a CTRL sequence is \0. The decimal equivalent for the hexadecimal F is 15.

To invoke compressed mode, do the following:

1. Choose /**P**rinter **L**ayout **S**etup String.
2. When prompted, type *\015* and press Enter.

The next time you print a spreadsheet, the text prints in compressed type.

In an *escape sequence*, each code begins with the ASCII code for the ESCAPE character (ESC). Do not confuse this character with the Escape (Esc) key on your keyboard—the character and the key are not the same thing. For example, ESC+4 invokes the italic printing mode for a standard IBM printer. To use this software command, convert the command to a code that your printer understands. The code that signifies an ESC sequence is \027.

To invoke the italic printing mode, do the following:

1. Choose /**P**rinter **L**ayout **S**etup String.
2. When prompted, type *\0274* and press Enter.

The next time you print a spreadsheet, the text appears in italic. Consult your printer manual for the appropriate control and escape sequences. Some printer manuals even list setup strings that can be used with several popular software products.

After Quattro Pro sends a setup string to your printer, that printing mode remains the default until you issue a setup string that cancels it.

You also can turn your printer off and then back on to clear the setup string settings from the printer's memory. If you use this technique, you must delete the setup string entered at the /**P**rinter **L**ayout **S**etup String prompt before you print another spreadsheet.

APPENDIX E

Installing Quattro Pro on a Network

With a few notable exceptions, installing Quattro Pro on a network is similar to installing the program on a single PC. (Appendix A covers single PC installation.) This appendix contains information that shows a network administrator how to install Quattro Pro successfully on a local area network (LAN).

Appendix E begins by discussing the hardware and software required to install and operate Quattro Pro on a network server. The second section shows how to prepare a network server for installation. To prepare the network server, you create special directories to store program files, shared data files, and each user's private files. The third section contains step-by-step instructions for installing Quattro Pro on a network server.

After installing Quattro Pro on the network server, you prepare each workstation to use Quattro Pro. A section of the appendix shows how to prepare each workstation, update custom menu trees, and create start-up defaults for each user. Then you learn how to add additional users after you install Quattro Pro on a network server. For each Quattro Pro user you want to add to the network, you must purchase a Quattro Pro LAN Pack from Borland.

This appendix also includes a step-by-step explanation of the procedure to follow if you need to upgrade a Quattro Pro Version 3.0 network configuration to Version 4.0.

> **CAUTION:** If you currently use Quattro Pro Version 3.0 on a network, read the "Upgrading a Network from Version 3.0 to Version 4.0" section later in this appendix before you install Version 4.0 on your computer.

One section of the appendix discusses the difference between using Quattro Pro on a single PC and concurrently on multiple network workstations.

This appendix concludes with a look at some common questions and answers about installing and managing the program on a network. Scan through this section if you need a quick solution to questions concerning system configuration or program installation issues.

What You Need To Run Quattro Pro on a Network

To install and operate Quattro Pro on a network server, you must have at least the following hardware and operating system software available:

Hardware

- A network server (preferably a dedicated server) with at least 6M (megabytes) of free hard disk space
- One or more 100% IBM-PC compatible workstations, each with at least 640K (kilobytes) of RAM
- A monochrome or color graphics display system

E — INSTALLING QUATTRO PRO ON A NETWORK

Operating systems

- Novell Advanced NetWare Version 2.0A or higher
- 3Com 3+ Version 1.0 or higher
- Banyon Vines network
- A network that is 100% compatible with Novell, 3Com, or Banyon Vines
- DOS 3.1 or higher

The performance of Quattro Pro improves noticeably when you can improve the recommended minimum hardware configuration. For suggestions about how to achieve optimum performance from Quattro Pro (whether you are using the program on a single PC or on multiple workstations), see the section "Setting Up the Ideal System Configuration" in Appendix A.

Preinstallation Preparation

The network administrator is the person best qualified to install Quattro Pro on a network server. The network administrator has the network rights necessary to copy files, create directories, and modify each workstation's operating environment. If you do not have the appropriate rights for your network, consult with the person who does.

Before installing Quattro Pro, prepare the network server by creating special directories to store program files, shared data files, and each user's private files. As outlined in the following steps, you must create a minimum of four directories to complete the preinstallation preparation:

1. Create a system file directory named QPRO. This directory stores the Quattro Pro program files.

2. Create a subdirectory named FONTS under the system file directory. This directory stores the font files that Quattro Pro creates.

3. Create a shared directory named QPRODATA. This directory stores all spreadsheet files that can be shared among users.

4. Create a private directory named QPROPRIV. Under this directory, create private subdirectories for each user (/QPROPRIV/JEAN, for example, for a user named Jean). Each user's private subdirectory stores the user's unique Quattro Pro defaults and private data files.

USING QUATTRO PRO 4, SPECIAL EDITION

> **TIP**
> You may place the private directories on any drive that users can access from their workstations. A user may want to store all private files, for example, on the workstation's hard disk drive.

The directory names QPRO, QPRODATA, and QPROPRIV are only suggested directory names—you may call them anything you want. Quattro Pro creates a subdirectory named FONTS, however, which appears under the system file directory (generally QPRO).

> **NOTE**
> Do not restrict access rights to the directories before installing the program. The directories all must have full read-write network rights so that Quattro Pro can copy files into the directories.

Installing the Program

Quattro Pro's installation utility is self-explanatory and mostly self-running. Before you begin, review the following checklist to ensure that you have prepared the network server correctly for installation:

- Created a system file directory called QPRO
- Created a private directory called QPROPRIV
- Created one or more private subdirectories under the private directory (such as \QPROPRIV\JEAN for user Jean)
- Assured that all aforementioned directories have read-write network rights

To begin the installation, log onto the network server from any workstation that has at least one floppy drive. Place installation Disk 1 into drive A at that workstation. Type *a:\install* and then press Enter to begin the installation.

Choosing the Source Drive and Destination Directory

When prompted for the source drive, press Enter to accept the default setting (drive A).

E — INSTALLING QUATTRO PRO ON A NETWORK

When prompted for the Quattro Pro directory, verify that the default setting includes the correct network drive letter and system file directory name. If the default setting is not correct, press F2 to display an edit box. Type in the correct drive letter and directory path name and then press Enter to store that setting. To install Quattro Pro in a system file directory named QPRO on network drive F, for example, type *f:\qpro* (see fig. E.1).

```
┌─────────────────────────────────────────────────────────┐
│            QUATTRO PRO 4.00 Installation Utility        │
│                                                         │
│  QUATTRO PRO Directory: F:\QPRO                         │
│                                                         │
│              F:\QPRO                                    │
│                                                         │
│                                                         │
│                                                         │
│              ─────── Description ───────                │
│  Press F2 to change the directory in which to place     │
│  QUATTRO PRO and press ENTER to start installation.     │
│                                                         │
│  ESC-Cancel                                             │
└─────────────────────────────────────────────────────────┘
```

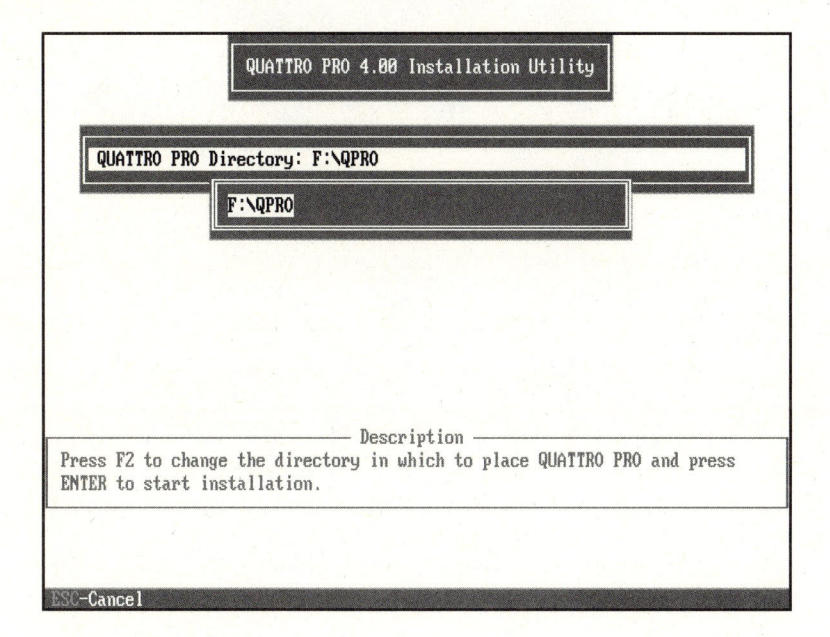

Fig. E.1

Choose the network drive and system file directory where Quattro Pro copies its program files.

Copying Files

Press Enter to begin copying the program files. Quattro Pro prompts you to swap disks until all files are copied into the system file directory on your network server.

Entering the Personal Signature Data

Quattro Pro next prompts you to identify your monitor type so that the program can correctly display the remaining installation screens. The program also asks you to enter information about yourself: your company name, your name, and the serial number stamped on Disk 1. You must supply this personal signature data to continue the installation.

Each time you start Quattro Pro, the program displays your personal signature data on the start-up screen.

Specifying a Network Installation

Quattro Pro asks `Are you installing Quattro Pro on a network server?` The default setting is No for single PC installations. Press F2 and choose the Yes option (see fig. E.2).

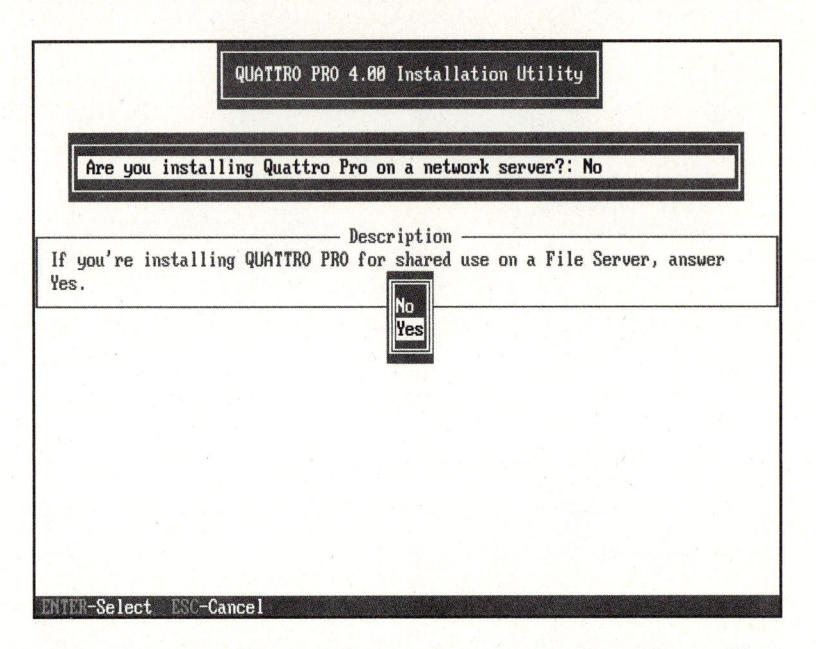

Fig. E.2

Specify that installation is taking place on a network server.

Quattro Pro then asks you to enter the directory location of the QPRO.NET file. The QPRO.NET file controls the Quattro Pro user count on the network and must reside in a directory that has read-write network rights (use the FONTS or the QPRODATA directory, for example). Press F2 and type *f:\qprodata* (see fig. E.3). Press Enter twice to continue the installation.

Selecting Your Equipment

Quattro Pro asks questions about the hardware you are using. Answer for the workstation from which you are installing Quattro Pro. You later can customize the hardware settings for other workstations connected to the network.

NOTE Refer to Appendix A for comprehensive coverage of this part of the installation process.

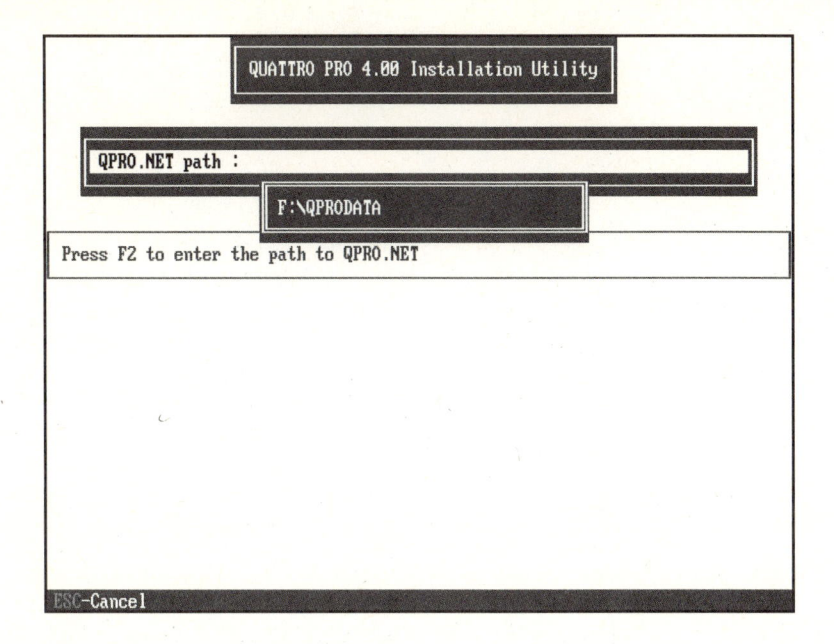

E — INSTALLING QUATTRO PRO ON A NETWORK

```
         QUATTRO PRO 4.00 Installation Utility

 QPRO.NET path :
                     F:\QPRODATA

 Press F2 to enter the path to QPRO.NET




ESC-Cancel
```

Fig. E.3
Select the location for the QPRO.NET file.

Recording Serial Numbers

After you select your equipment, you must perform one final step to conclude the installation of Quattro Pro on the network server. Execute the QPUPDATE.EXE program to store the Quattro Pro serial numbers you want to dedicate to network use in a file called QPRO.SOM. The serial number on Disk #1 enables you to install one user. To provide for additional users (to be able to record other serial numbers), you must purchase an appropriate number of Quattro Pro LAN Packs from Borland.

Quattro Pro copies the QPUPDATE.EXE program and the QPRO.SOM file into your system file directory (QPRO) during installation. Change to this directory now, and then execute the QPUPDATE.EXE program. Type *cd\qpro*, for example, and then press Enter.

Next, type *qpupdate* and press Enter.

The first screen that appears verifies that the QPRO.SOM file exists in your system file directory. Press Enter to continue.

The second screen displays the personal signature data you entered during the installation. You cannot change this information (see fig. E.4). Press F2 to continue.

```
                    ┌─────────────────────────────────────────────────┐
                    │          Quattro Pro Personal Signature         │
                    │                                                 │
                    │  Please enter the following information:        │
                    │    Network Administrator Name: Patrick J. Burns │
                    │              Company Name: Burns & Associates   │
                    │                                                 │
                    │                                                 │
                    │                                                 │
                    │  ┌───────────────────────────────────────────┐  │
                    │  │ [F2]     = Save Network Administrator     │  │
                    │  │            Name and CONTINUE              │  │
                    │  │ [Ctrl←-] = Change Network Administrator   │  │
                    │  │            Name                           │  │
                    │  └───────────────────────────────────────────┘  │
                    │ Press Esc to exit                               │
                    └─────────────────────────────────────────────────┘
```

Fig. E.4

Personal signature data.

The third screen displays the serial number that you entered during the installation (see fig. E.5). To enter additional serial numbers so that more than one person at a time may use Quattro Pro, press the down-arrow key and type in the second serial number. Repeat this process until all serial numbers are entered. Press F2 to save the serial numbers and continue the installation.

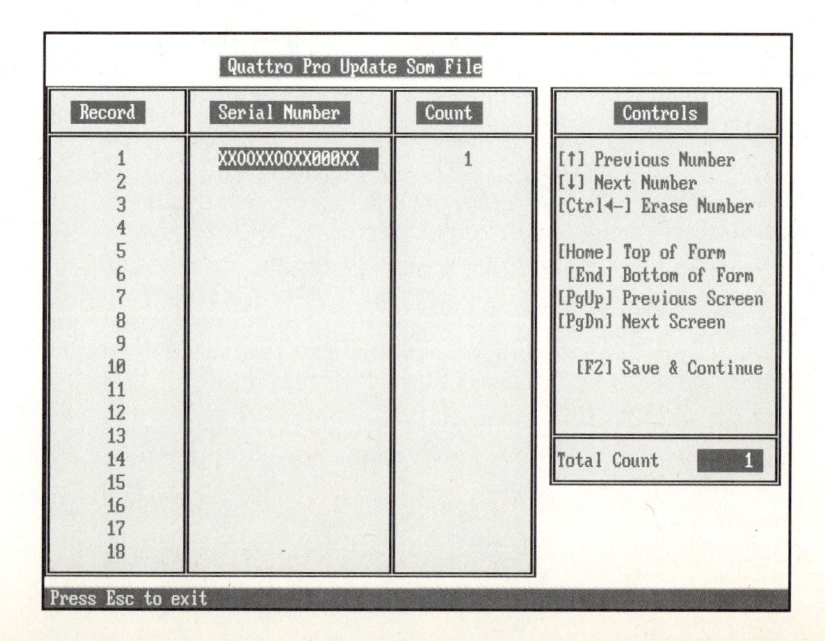

```
              ┌─────────────────Quattro Pro Update Som File─────────────────┐
              │  Record  │  Serial Number  │  Count  │      Controls        │
              │     1    │  XX00XX00XX000XX│    1    │ [↑] Previous Number  │
              │     2    │                 │         │ [↓] Next Number      │
              │     3    │                 │         │ [Ctrl←-] Erase Number│
              │     4    │                 │         │                      │
              │     5    │                 │         │ [Home] Top of Form   │
              │     6    │                 │         │ [End]  Bottom of Form│
              │     7    │                 │         │ [PgUp] Previous Screen│
              │     8    │                 │         │ [PgDn] Next Screen   │
              │     9    │                 │         │                      │
              │    10    │                 │         │ [F2] Save & Continue │
              │    11    │                 │         │                      │
              │    12    │                 │         │                      │
              │    13    │                 │         │                      │
              │    14    │                 │         │ Total Count    1     │
              │    15    │                 │         │                      │
              │    16    │                 │         │                      │
              │    17    │                 │         │                      │
              │    18    │                 │         │                      │
              │ Press Esc to exit                                            │
              └──────────────────────────────────────────────────────────────┘
```

Fig. E.5

The QPRO.SOM file stores the serial numbers dedicated for network use.

E — INSTALLING QUATTRO PRO ON A NETWORK

NOTE: Quattro Pro does not enable you to enter invalid or nonexistent serial numbers. If you try to enter an invalid serial number, the error message `Invalid serial number - please reenter` appears.

The fourth and final screen enables you to specify the type of network and verify the directory location for the QPRO.NET file (see fig. E.6). To specify a Novell network, for example, press 1. Then, press F3 to save all information in the QPRO.SOM file and exit.

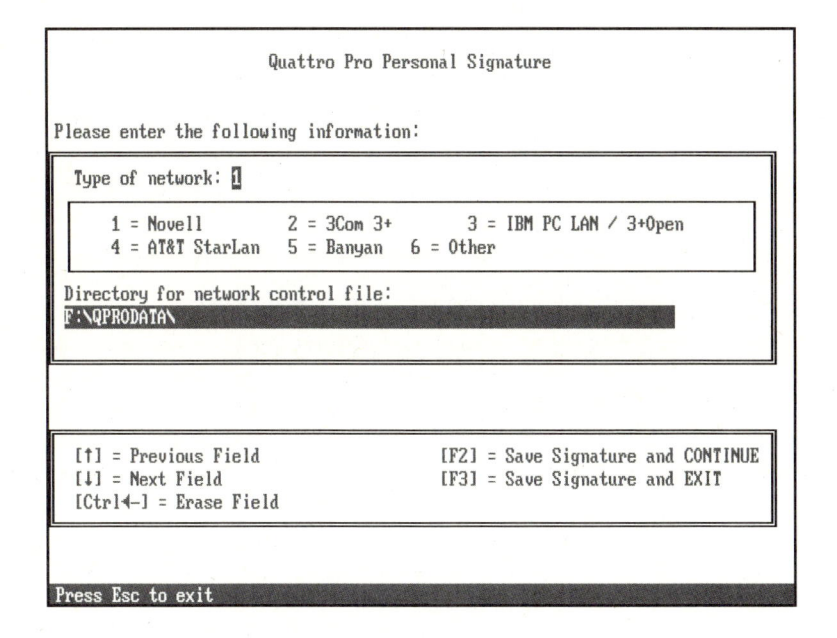

```
                    Quattro Pro Personal Signature

   Please enter the following information:

    Type of network: 1

         1 = Novell       2 = 3Com 3+       3 = IBM PC LAN / 3+Open
         4 = AT&T StarLan 5 = Banyan        6 = Other

    Directory for network control file:
    F:\QPRODATA\




     [↑] = Previous Field            [F2] = Save Signature and CONTINUE
     [↓] = Next Field                [F3] = Save Signature and EXIT
     [Ctrl←] = Erase Field



   Press Esc to exit
```

Fig. E.6
Specify the network type.

You now are ready to prepare individual workstations to operate Quattro Pro from the network server.

Preparing the Workstations

Before you operate Quattro Pro on a network server, you must prepare each workstation connected to the network server. This process involves modifying the AUTOEXEC.BAT and CONFIG.SYS files, establishing menu tree and program defaults for each user, assigning network access rights to all Quattro Pro directories, and updating each user's log-on script.

Before you begin, review the following checklist to ensure that each workstation is ready for preparation:

- One private directory has been created as a subdirectory of QPROPRIV for each Quattro Pro network user. Each private directory has full read-write-create rights.
- Each workstation has AUTOEXEC.BAT and CONFIG.SYS files.
- Each workstation has a copy of DOS 3.1 or later (with the DOS SHARE.EXE program) available.

> **TIP** Each user's private directory can reside on the workstation hard disk. For diskless workstations, however, the private directory must reside on the network server.

Creating a Menu Preference File

During installation, Quattro Pro copies the default user interface file—called a *menu tree*—that the program displays when loaded. In a network configuration, users need their own menu preference (MP) file. Users who created a custom menu tree with a previous version of Quattro Pro can continue to use those menu preference (MP) files by adding them to their private directories. Menu preference files belong in a user's private directory; do not store MP files in the QPRO directory.

To create a menu preference file for each user, change to the system file (QPRO) directory. Type *cd\qpro*, for example, and press Enter.

Execute the MPMAKE.EXE program using the following syntax:

    MPMAKE name.mu dirname\

Here, *name.mu* is the name of the menu file to create, and *dirname* is the name of the directory in which Quattro Pro copies the MP file. Supply a drive letter and a full directory path name for both of these arguments. Valid MP files include the following:

QUATTRO.MP	The standard Quattro Pro menu tree
123.MP	The Lotus 1-2-3 menu tree

To create an MP file for user Jean that displays the standard Quattro Pro menu tree, for example, type the following and press Enter:

mpmake f:\qpro\quattro.mu f:\qpropriv\jean

Repeat this process for each network user who will use Quattro Pro.

E — INSTALLING QUATTRO PRO ON A NETWORK

> **T I P**
>
> Only the menu trees for which you create MP files appear on the users' menu pick list when the users choose the /Options Startup Menu Tree command.

Creating a Default File

Each user also needs one default file (RF) in his/her private directory. This file stores information about each user's preferred Quattro Pro defaults—items that users may change using the /Options menu. This file includes screen and printer configurations, screen colors, start-up directory, default file-name extension, and so on. To use the 1-2-3 menu tree, for example, each user needs a copy of the 123.RF file.

To create a default file for each user, change to the system file (QPRO) directory. Type *cd\qpro* and press Enter.

Copy the RSC.RF file into each user's private directory using the DOS COPY command. To copy the RSC.RF file into user Jean's private directory, for example, type the following and then press Enter:

   copy rsc.rf f:\qpropriv\jean

After a copy of the RSC.RF file exists in each user's private directory, delete the RSC.RF file from the system file directory (QPRO).

> **CAUTION:** If you forget to delete the RSC.RF file from the QPRO directory, Quattro Pro uses that as the default file for the first user who loads Quattro Pro at a workstation. Subsequent users will be unable to load Quattro Pro from their workstations.

Modifying the AUTOEXEC.BAT and CONFIG.SYS Files

The AUTOEXEC.BAT and CONFIG.SYS files at each workstation also require some modification. The CONFIG.SYS file should contain at least the following statement:

   FILES=20

TIP Set FILES=40 if you intend to access Paradox database files using Quattro Pro's /**D**atabase **P**aradox Access command.

Modify the DOS PATH statement at each workstation to reflect, in the order shown, the following information:

- The name of a user's private directory
- The name of the system file directory (QPRO)
- The DOS SHARE command

The AUTOEXEC.BAT file for user Jean, for example, may look like the following:

    PATH F:\QPROPRIV\JEAN;F:\QPRO
    SHARE

> **CAUTION:** Don't forget to include the DOS SHARE command in each user's AUTOEXEC.BAT file. You need the SHARE.EXE program to be able to use Quattro Pro spreadsheet files concurrently.

If you want to add a log-on command to an AUTOEXEC.BAT file—a command that automatically logs a user onto the network server—place the command before the DOS PATH statement. This statement will determine which directories are part of the search path and not the path specified in the network login script. See your network documentation for details about coordinating search paths using the DOS PATH statement and the network login script.

The AUTOEXEC.BAT file for a user on a Novell network, for example, may look like the following:

    IPX
    NET3
    F:
    LOGIN JEAN
    PATH F:\QPROPRIV\JEAN;F:\QPRO
    SHARE

In this file, the IPX command loads a network card driver, the NET3 command loads the Novell Workstation Shell, and F: switches the user to drive F. The line LOGIN JEAN is a Novell-specific command that logs in user Jean to the network. Now that the network-workstation connection is complete, the PATH statement containing references to the network server drive (such as F:\QPRO) is valid.

E — INSTALLING QUATTRO PRO ON A NETWORK

> **T I P**
> When the PATH statement appears after the LOGIN line, your network login script may supersede the DOS PATH statement. See your network documentation for details.

The DOS SHARE command is critical to the use of Quattro Pro on a network. This command loads a memory-resident DOS module that enables file sharing and file locking on a network. To use the SHARE.EXE program, first verify that it exists in the DOS directory on the network server. If the program does not exist, copy it into the DOS directory from a master DOS floppy disk. Add the name of the DOS directory (probably \DOS) to the PATH statement in each user's AUTOEXEC.BAT file.

Assigning Access Rights to the Quattro Pro Directories

Table E.1 contains a list of the suggested directory names and suggested access rights. Use the information in this table as a guide for setting up user access rights on your network. (See your network manuals for information about assigning access rights on your network.) You may want to assign different levels of access rights to different users on your network. Table E.1 indicates the required network rights for each directory when applicable.

Table E.1 Network Directories and Their Access Rights

Directory	Suggested Name	Suggested Rights
System files	QPRO	Read-Open-Search
Fonts	FONTS (\QPRO\FONTS)	Read-Write-Create-Modify (required)
Shared data	QPRODATA	Read-Write-Create-Modify
Private data	QPROPRIV\username	Full rights except Supervisor and Parental

After you assign network rights, each workstation is ready to operate Quattro Pro. Now, you should reboot each workstation to place into effect all changes made to the workstation start-up files.

Starting Quattro Pro from a Workstation

Start Quattro Pro at each workstation. If you have dedicated four serial numbers for network use, you may operate Quattro Pro concurrently at four workstations. To start Quattro Pro from DOS, switch to the user's private directory, press Q, and then press Enter.

After the program loads into each workstation, users may want to further modify the default settings for their own workstations. This process may involve selecting a different menu tree or modifying any of the Quattro Pro environment defaults using the commands found on the /Options menu. After finishing this customization process, each user must choose /Options Update to save those settings (in the RSC.RF file located in his/her private directory) for all future work sessions.

Adding Users to the Network

To increase the number of concurrent Quattro Pro users permitted on a network, purchase additional Quattro Pro LAN packs from Borland. Each Quattro Pro LAN Pack provides you with one serial number.

To add the new serial number to the network, execute the QPUPDATE.EXE program, enter the new serial number, and press F3 to save the new number in the QPRO.SOM file. (See "Recording Serial Numbers" earlier in this appendix for full instructions.)

Next, prepare the new workstation to operate Quattro Pro as described in the preceding section. Remember, because each Quattro Pro user must have a private directory, be sure to create a new private directory for a new user. To add user Sara to the network, for example, create a subdirectory of the QPROPRIV directory called SARA, for example, QPROPRIV\SARA, and copy a set of MP and RF files to this directory.

Finally, check that the new users' /Options menu settings match the network hardware and the hardware in use at that particular workstation. The following checklist suggests those items you should check before starting Quattro Pro on a new workstation:

- Check the printer definition setting by choosing the /Options Hardware Printers 1st Printer Type of Printer command.

- Verify that the user's printer device setting matches the port connection on the network using the /Options Hardware Printers 1st (or 2nd) Printer Device command. The appropriate setting for this command is N Network Queue if the user will be printing on a shared network printer.

E — INSTALLING QUATTRO PRO ON A NETWORK

- Select a screen type setting that matches the user's display system using the /**O**ptions **H**ardware **S**creen **S**creen Type command.
- Change the Quattro Pro default directory setting to the user's private data directory with /**O**ptions **S**tartup **D**irectory command.
- Choose /**O**ptions Update to save all changes.

Upgrading a Network from Version 3.0 to Version 4.0

Upgrading from a Version 3.0 to a Version 4.0 network configuration is simple. Be careful when you perform the steps outlined in this section, however; you will be deleting many Quattro Pro files from your system file (QPRO) and Font file (FONTS) directories. If these directories contain any spreadsheet files (W*), workspace files (WSP), or clip-art files (CLP) you want to keep, copy those files to another directory before proceeding.

> **TIP**
>
> If you are upgrading from Version 3.0, you may continue using your Version 3.0 Bitstream fonts with Version 4.0, even though Version 4.0 uses faster Bitstream-SC fonts. To do so, skip steps 1 and 2 in the following procedure. Then, after you load Quattro Pro, your 3.0 fonts appear beside the 4.0 fonts on the Typeface menu when you choose the /**S**tyle **F**ont and /**S**tyle **F**ont**T**able commands.

> **NOTE** The QPRO and FONTS directories must have read-write-delete network rights before you can upgrade the Quattro Pro files.

To use custom menu trees (MU) created under Quattro Pro 1.0 or 2.0 you first must translate them into a Version 4.0 format using the NEWMU.BAT program. Quattro Pro copies this program into your system file directory during installation.

To translate custom menu tree files, use the following steps:

1. To log onto the system file directory (QPRO), type *cd\qpro* and press Enter.

2. Use the following syntax to translate a Version 3.0 (or Version 2.0 or 1.0) menu tree named CUSTOM3.MU to one called CUSTOM4.MU and then press Enter:

   newmu custom3 custom4

Supply the drive letter and full directory path name if the menu tree file is in a different directory.

After a menu tree file is translated into a Version 4.0 format, the file name displays on the menu pick list when a user chooses the /**O**ptions **S**tartup **M**enu Tree command.

To upgrade to Version 4.0, follow these steps:

1. At the DOS command prompt, type *cd\qpro\fonts* and press Enter to log onto the FONTS subdirectory.

2. Type *del *.** and press Enter to delete all Version 3.0 font files from the FONTS subdirectory.

3. Type *cd\qpro* and then press Enter to log onto the QPRO directory.

4. Type *del *.** and press Enter to delete all Version 3.0 program files from the QPRO directory.

5. Run the INSTALL.EXE program on Disk 1 as described in "Installing the Program" earlier in this appendix.

6. Copy a set of Version 4.0 MP and RF files to each user's private directory.

What's Different about Using Quattro Pro on a Network?

One significant difference exists between using Quattro Pro on a single PC and on a network. On a single PC, a user has full, unrestricted access rights to all files on the PC hard disk. On a network, the network administrator assigns access rights to each user and to each directory. (For a list of suggested directory rights, see table E.1 earlier in this appendix.) Some users may be permitted free rein to copy, modify, delete, and create files on the network; others may have these rights only in shared data and private directories.

On a network, when several users want to modify Quattro Pro spreadsheet files simultaneously, access-priority rules govern this activity. Basically, the first user to open a Quattro Pro data file from a shared

E — INSTALLING QUATTRO PRO ON A NETWORK

network directory has full read-write network rights to that file. A second user may open the same file, but Quattro Pro prevents that user from saving the file under the same name in the same directory—as long as the first user continues to work with the file. As soon as the first user closes the spreadsheet file, the second user is given full read-write network rights to that file. If a third user wants to save the same file, that user must wait for the second user to close the spreadsheet file before saving.

In Quattro Pro, attempts to retrieve an open file cause the program to display a message asking if the user wants to open the file in read-only status. Respond **Y**es to open the file. A user can read and edit the file but cannot save it under the same name in the same directory. If the user tries to do so, Quattro Pro displays a prompt asking the user to rename the file or save it in a different directory. Choose /**F**ile Save **A**s and enter the new file name or new directory name.

> **TIP**
> Quattro Pro displays a sharing violation message when a user tries to save a read-only file without first changing the file name or the directory. Press Esc or Enter to remove the message and then save the file under a different name or in a different directory.

Quattro Pro Version 4.0 provides better support for network installations than previous versions of the program do. Table E.2 summarizes the Version 4.0 network features and references the chapter where you can locate more specific information about a feature.

Table E.2 Quattro Pro Version 4.0 Network Features

Feature	Command	Chapter
Create/edit a drive mapping	/**O**ptions Network **D**rive Mappings	16
Show a drive mapping	/**F**ile **O**pen and click the NET button	8
Set up a user name	/**O**ptions Network User Name	16
Control banner printing	/**O**ptions Network **B**anner	16
Set up a network printer	/**O**ptions Hardware **1**st Printer **D**evice **N** Network Queue	16

continues

Table E.2 Continued

Feature	Command	Chapter
Access a network drive	/**F**ile **O**pen and click the DRV button	8
View jobs in a network queue	/**P**rint **P**rint Manager then **Q**ueue **N**etwork	9
Monitor progress of network queue	/**O**ptions **N**etwork **Q**ueue **M**onitor **Y**es	16

Questions & Answers

This section deals with commonly asked questions and start-up problems. Here you learn how to solve glitches encountered when installing and using Quattro Pro on a network server.

Installing the Program

Q: When I attempted to install the program onto my network server drive, Quattro Pro displayed an error message saying that the drive is invalid. Why?

A: The workstation from which Quattro Pro is being installed must be physically wired to the network server and must be logged onto the network drive before you start installation. Return to DOS and use the appropriate network log-on procedure to connect to the network server. Restart the installation.

Q: After I installed Quattro Pro and attempted to read the program, I received the error message `Cannot open QPRO.NET file`. What do I do?

A: Quattro Pro couldn't find the QPRO.NET file. Make sure that QPRO.NET is located on the path specified in QPRO.SOM and that you have read-write access to that directory.

Q: I am upgrading from Quattro Pro Version 3.0 to Version 4.0 on my network. I have a system file directory named QPRO but do not have a private directory named QPROPRIV or QPRODATA. Will the installation work?

E — INSTALLING QUATTRO PRO ON A NETWORK

A: Yes. The only directory name that Quattro Pro requires for a successful installation is FONTS, a subdirectory it automatically creates under the system file directory. You may choose different names for the other directories or accept Quattro Pro's defaults.

Q: I accidentally installed QPRO.NET in the QPRO directory when I meant to specify QPRODATA. If I just copy the QPRO.NET file into the QPRODATA directory, will Quattro Pro load?

A: No. After you specify the path for the QPRO.NET file, you cannot change it except by updating the directory path field in the QPUPDATE.EXE program (refer to fig. E.6). Remember that the QPRO.NET file must reside in a directory with read-write network rights (hence the suggestion to use QPRODATA). If you accidentally install the file in a different directory and want to use that directory, to load Quattro Pro you must rerun QPUPDATE.EXE, specify that directory, and then assign read-write rights to that directory.

Using Quattro Pro on a Network

Q: One user on our network created a custom menu tree that we want to adopt for the entire Quattro Pro user base on our network. Is there an easy way to adopt this customized menu tree?

A: The user who created the custom menu tree has an MU and an MP (menu preference) file in a private directory. Move the MU file to the Quattro Pro system file directory (QPRO), and then copy the MP file into each user's private directory. After each user restarts Quattro Pro, the user must choose /Options Startup Menu Tree and choose the custom menu from the list. Choose /Option Update to use the custom menu tree as the default for future work sessions.

Printing on a Network Printer

Q: When I print a spreadsheet to a shared network printer, Quattro Pro first prints a title, then prints the spreadsheet, and then feeds a blank page out of the printer. Is there a way that I can control this problem?

A: Each network has its own methods for managing print jobs. On a Novell network, the CAPTURE command is useful for controlling your print jobs. Borland recommends that you use the following syntax when printing to a shared printer on a Novell network:

CAPTURE /TI=50 /NB /NT /NFF /P=0 /NA

In this syntax, /TI=50 sets the timeout option to 50 seconds, /NB tells the network to omit the banner page, /NT and /NFF tells the network to leave all tabs and form feeds unchanged, /P=0 indicates that the name of the shared network printer is 0, and /NA disables the Autoendcap feature. See your network manuals for more specific information about controlling print jobs on a shared network printer.

Q: When I choose the /**P**rint **S**preadsheet Print command to print a spreadsheet, nothing happens. What should I check for?

A: Choose the /**O**ptions **H**ardware **P**rinters **1**st (or **2**nd) Printer **De**vice command, which should be set to **N** Network Queue. If this setting does not solve the problem, try using one of the LPT settings or the Parallel setting. Experiment with each setting until you find one that works.

INDEX

Symbols

, (comma) numeric format, 176
(/) slash key, 68, 80
   activating Annotator, 454
(~) tilde
   key, 51
   macro command, 971
+ (Expand) key, 488
+/- numeric format, 177
\0 macros, 661
; macro command, 966
< (less than) operator, 591
<= (less than or equal) operator, 591
= (equal) operator, 591
> (greater than) operator, 591
>= (greater than or equal) operator, 591
? macro command, 967
@ button (EDIT mode SpeedBar), 101, 228
@@ miscellaneous function, 252-253
{} macro command, 966
↓ (down arrow)
   {DOWN} macro instruction, 670
   key, 53, 110
→ (right arrow)
   {RIGHT} macro instruction, 670
   key, 53, 110
← (left arrow)
   {LEFT} macro instruction, 670
   key, 53, 110
↑ (up arrow)
   {UP} macro instruction, 670
   key, 53, 110
3-D
   formula consolidation, 369-373
   graphs, 448
      3-D area graph, 451
      3-D bar graph, 450
      3-D ribbon graph, 449
      3-D step graph, 451
   z-axis, 448

A

ABS (F4) macro function instruction, 671
@ABS arithmetic function, 229-230
Abs button (EDIT mode SpeedBar), 104
ABS macro command, 967
Absolute (F4) function key, 55
absolute reference format, 102
access rights, assigning to directories, 1043
accessing Paradox
   menus, 81
   troubleshooting tips, 608

@ACOS arithmetic function, 233
activating menus, 17, 68-69
active columns, adjusting, 189
add-in @functions, 644
AdLib, 476
aggregation, 541, 546-551
    multiple series, 552-554
    table of values, 554
    troubleshooting tips, 568
Align button (READY mode SpeedBar), 174
All Select (Alt-F7) function key, 55
Allways file formats, 342
alphanumeric keyboard, 51
Alt key, 51
Alt-0 (Pick Window) key, 688
Alt-F2 (/Tools Macro Instant Replay) function key, 659
Alt-F2 E (/Tools Macro Execute) function key, 665
Alt-F2 T (/Tools Macro Transcript) function key, 682
Alt-F3 (displaying @function commands) key, 24
Alt-F3 (Functions) function key, 291
Alt-F3 {FUNCTIONS} macro function instruction, 671
Alt-F5 (Undo) function key, 170
Alt-F5 {UNDO} macro function instruction, 27, 671
Alt-F6 (/Window Zoom) shortcut key, 358
Alt-F6 {ZOOM} macro function instruction, 671
Alt-F7 {MARKALL} macro function instruction, 671
Alt-key name (executing macros stored in library), 664
analytical graphing, 541-544
    aggregation, 541, 546-554, 568
    exponential graphing, 542, 564-567
    linear fit analysis, 561-563
    moving average graphs, 542, 555-561, 569

Analyze command, 4
analyzing data
    add-in @functions, 644
    frequency distributions, 631, 634
    Optimizer, 634-635
        reports, 643
        setting constraints/defining multiple variables, 640-641
        setting options, 641-642
        setting up, 635-637
        solving basic problems, 637-639
    parsing, 618-620
        advanced parse operations, 623-626
        multiple parse operations, 623
    performing matrix operations, 616-618
    regression analysis, 613-616
    sensitivity analysis, 628
        one-way analysis, 628
        two-way analysis, 629-631
#AND# logical operator, 591
annotating graphs, 518, 522
    activating Annotator with / key, 454
    Annotator screen, 518-520
    editing text design elements, 526
    linking elements to graph data series, 528
    managing elements with Clipboard, 527-528
    moving design elements, 524
    multiple, 534-536
    resizing design elements, 525
    selecting design elements, 523
    setting design element properties, 526
appearance of graphs, enhancing, 459
    legends, 462
    titles, 460-462

INDEX

changing fonts, 463-464
  colors, 467
  point size, 465
  styles, 466
  typeface, 465
  troubleshooting tips, 479
area graphs, 444
arguments, 100
  financial @function
    commands, 268
arithmetic formulas, 94
arithmetic @function
  commands, 230-236
arrow keys, 53
ASCII
  characters
    converting codes into
      printer setup strings,
      1028-1029
    entering into dialog boxes,
      1027
    entering into spreadsheet
      cells, 1023
  codes, 1024-1027
@ASIN arithmetic function, 233
aspect ratio, 705
asterisk (*) wild-card code, 370
@ATAN arithmetic function,
  233-234
@ATAN2 arithmetic function,
  233-234
Attributes (function
  @commands), 250-251
Audit command, 5
audits
  blank reference, 320
  circular, 314-316
  dependency, 311-314
  ERR, 318-319
  external links, 320-321
  label reference, 317-318
AUTOEXEC.BAT file, modifying
  during Quattro Pro
  installation, 1039-1043
@AVG statistical function,
  236-237

B

background
  printing, 422-424, 711
  recalculation, 111
Backspace {BS} macro
  instruction, 670
Backspace key, 51, 109
BACKSPACE macro command,
  670, 967
BACKTAB (Shift-Tab) macro
  instruction, 670
BACKTAB macro command, 967
bar graphs, 441
BEEP macro command, 961, 967
beep, specifying tone, 729
BIGLEFT (Ctrl-←) macro
  instruction, 670
BIGRIGHT (Ctrl-→) macro
  instruction, 670
BIGLEFT macro command, 968
BIGRIGHT macro command, 968
binary files, printing
  spreadsheet reports to, 413
BKGD mode, 67
blank reference audit, 320
block name, 65
block value (@function
  command argument), 227
BRANCH macro command, 961,
  968
BREAK (Ctrl-Break) macro
  instruction, 670
BREAK macro command, 969
BREAKOFF macro command,
  666, 969
BREAKON macro command, 969
breakpoints, 674
  defining conditional
    breakpoints, 678
  defining standard
    breakpoints, 677
  resetting, 680
BS (Backspace) macro
  instruction, 670

bubble graphs, 448
   customizing
      bubble sizes, 503
      color/fill patterns, 502
bulleting, 206-208

C

Calc (F9) function key, 55
CALC (F9) macro function instruction, 671
CALC macro command, 969
CALC status indicator, 67
CAP status indicator, 67
CAPOFF (Caps Lock off) status key macro instruction, 672
CAPOFF macro command, 969
CAPON (Caps Lock on) status key macro instruction, 672
CAPON macro command, 969
Caps Lock off {CAPOFF} status key macro instruction, 672
Caps Lock on {CAPON} status key macro instruction, 672
categories, macro commands, 966
   cell, 968-970, 977, 981-983
   file, 970, 975, 980-984, 987
   interactive, 967-969, 974-978, 984-986
   keyboard, 967-987
   miscellaneous, 966
   program flow, 968, 972-973, 976, 980-985
   screen, 967, 976, 980, 986
cautions, 11
cell blocks, 107-108, 117
   copying, 133
   erasing, 134
   filling with numbers, 153-154
   moving, 133
   names, 142
      adding notes, 147-149
      creating, 143-145
      creating with labels, 149
      deleting, 146-147
      in formulas, 153
      making table of names, 151-152
      resetting names, 150
   naming, 163-164
cell macro command category, 968-970, 977, 981-983
@CELL miscellaneous function, 252-254
cell references, 104-107, 117
cell selector, 40, 65
@CELLINDEX miscellaneous function, 252-254
@CELLPOINTER miscellaneous function, 252, 255
cells, 40
   addresses, 40, 83
   aligning
      data in, 29-31
      labels in spreadsheets, 741
   alignment, changing, 174
   anchoring with absolute reference format, 102
   breakpoints, 674
      defining standard breakpoints, 677-678
   Circular Cell, 743
   circular references, 132
   data
      copying, 124-128, 162
      erasing, 124, 132, 162
      moving, 124, 128-129, 132, 162
   editing in DEBUG mode, 679-680
   entering ASCII characters into, 1023
   mixed references, 102
   new, defining with relative reference format, 101
   preselecting, 124
      cell blocks, 453
   references
      relative to absolute, 104
      troubleshooting tips, 117

INDEX

trace, 674
    defining, 678-679
    resetting, 680
  with zero values, 741
    troubleshooting tips, 747
@CHAR string function, 241-242
character set, selecting during Quattro Pro install, 952
Choices (F3) function key, 54
CHOOSE (Shift-F5) macro function instruction, 671
CHOOSE macro command, 970
@CHOOSE miscellaneous function, 252, 255
CHR button (SpeedBar), 76, 620
CIRC status indicator, 67
circular
  audits, 314-316
  references, 132
Circular Cell, 743
@CLEAN string function, 241-243
CLEAR (Ctrl-Backspace) macro instruction, 670
CLEAR macro command, 970
clicking, 57
clock display, changing, 737
CLOSE macro command, 970
closing files, 332
@CODE string function, 241-243
coloring palette, 712
  choosing
    desktop colors, 714
    File Manager colors, 716-717
    help colors, 716
    menu colors, 713
    spreadsheet colors, 714
  specifying data color when meeting conditions, 715
@COLS miscellaneous function, 253, 256
Column Block command, 4
column graphs, 446
columns, 40, 221
  adjusting
    active, 189
    widths, 28

blocks
  deleting, 142
  inserting, 142
deleting, 135, 139, 163
  Delete button on READY mode SpeedBar, 139
entering headings in spreadsheets, 19
hiding/revealing, 193-195
inserting, 135, 138-139, 163
  Insert button on READY mode SpeedBar, 138
  into spreadsheets, 34
removing column borders from windows, 364
setting width, 188-189
  of multiple columns, 190-193
sorting databases by, 584
specifying width, 741
combining files, 378
  adding/subtracting data, 380
  copying data, 378-380
command-line switches, 728
commands
  Analyze, 4
  Audit, 5
  choosing, 69
  Column Block, 4
  Copy Special, 4
  /Data Query Input, 341
  /Database Data Entry, 62, 601, 872-873
  /Database Data Entry General, 601
  /Database Paradox Access, 601-606, 873-874, 1042
  /Database Paradox Access Load File, 605
  /Database Query Assign Names, 588, 874-875
  /Database Query Block, 587, 875
  /Database Query Criteria Table, 590, 876-877
  /Database Query Delete, 593, 607, 877-878

/Database Query Extract, 596, 607
/Database Query Extract/Unique, 879-880
/Database Query Locate, 592, 880-881
/Database Query Output Block, 596, 882-883
/Database Query Reset, 883
/Database Query Unique, 597
/Database Reset, 579
/Database Restrict Input, 599, 883-884
/Database Sort, 578-581, 885-887
/Database Sort Go, 579
/Database Sort Sort Rules, 607
/Database Sort Sort Rules Label Order, 584
/Database Sort Sort Rules Numbers Before Labels, 583
/Database Sort Sort Rules Sort Rows/Columns Column, 584
DOS SHARE, 1043
/Edit Copy, 124-127, 133, 372, 589-590, 596, 617, 624, 658, 772-773
/Edit Copy Special, 128, 773-774
/Edit Delete, 135, 775-776
/Edit Delete Column Block, 142
/Edit Delete Columns, 139, 685-686
/Edit Delete Row Block, 141
/Edit Delete Rows, 137
/Edit Erase Block, 124, 132-134, 667, 776-777
/Edit Fill, 153-154, 777-778
/Edit Insert, 34, 135, 779
/Edit Insert Column Block, 142
/Edit Insert Columns, 138-139
/Edit Insert Row Block, 140
/Edit Insert Rows, 136-137
/Edit Move, 27, 124, 128-129, 132-133, 162, 780-781
/Edit Names, 781-784
/Edit Names Create, 147-148, 292, 581, 587, 590, 596, 659
/Edit Names Delete, 146, 667
/Edit Names Label, 149, 164
/Edit Names Labels Right, 663
/Edit Names Make Table, 151
/Edit Names Reset, 150
/Edit Rename, 350-351, 383
/Edit Search & Replace, 366, 624, 784-786
/Edit Search & Replace Block, 159-162
/Edit Search & Replace Options Reset, 625
/Edit Select File, 354
/Edit Transpose, 156-157, 165, 786-787
/Edit Undo, 26, 135, 685, 735, 787-788
/Edit Values, 154, 380-381, 585, 788-789
executing, 17
/File All Select, 354
/File Close, 332, 750
/File Close All, 332, 751
/File Directory, 335, 751-752
/File Erase, 332-333, 683, 752-753
/File Exit, 35, 49, 605, 753-754
/File New, 329, 664, 754-755
/File Open, 329-330, 472, 755
/File Read Dir, 352-354
/File Retrieve, 49, 84, 330, 374, 382, 583, 683, 755-756
/File Save, 84, 331, 608, 664, 668, 683, 756-757
/File Save All, 758
/File Save As, 35, 332, 758-759
/File Utilities DOS Shell, 346, 760
/File Utilities File Manager, 348, 760-762

INDEX

/File Utilities File Manager Edit, 762-763
/File Utilities File Manager File, 763-764
/File Utilities File Manager Options, 764-765
/File Utilities File Manager Print, 765-766
/File Utilities File Manager Sort, 766-767
/File Utilities File Manager Tree, 767-768
/File Utilities File Manager Window, 768-769
/File Utilities SQZ!, 345, 769-770
/File Workspace, 770-771
/File Workspace Restore, 84, 336
/File Workspace Save, 84, 336
@function, *see* @function commands
/Graph Annotate, 518, 669, 808-809
/Graph Annotate Clipboard, 809-810
/Graph Annotate Property Sheet, 811
/Graph Annotate Toolbox, 811-812
/Graph Customize Series, 483, 486
/Graph Customize Series Bar Width, 494, 813
/Graph Customize Series Bubbles, 813-814
/Graph Customize Series Bubbles Colors, 503
/Graph Customize Series Bubbles Max Bubble Size, 503
/Graph Customize Series Bubbles Patterns, 502
/Graph Customize Series Colors, 489, 815-816
/Graph Customize Series Fill Patterns, 490, 537, 540, 816-817
/Graph Customize Series Interior Labels, 495, 555, 561, 564, 567, 817-818
/Graph Customize Series Markers & Lines, 818-820
/Graph Customize Series Markers & Lines Line Styles, 491-493
/Graph Customize Series Markers & Lines Markers, 537, 540
/Graph Customize Series Override Type, 496, 820-821
/Graph Customize Series Override Type Default, 537, 540
/Graph Customize Series Pies, 498, 821-823
/Graph Customize Series Pies Colors, 502
/Graph Customize Series Pies Explode, 499
/Graph Customize Series Pies Label Format, 499
/Graph Customize Series Pies Patterns, 501
/Graph Customize Series Pies Tick Marks, 502
/Graph Customize Series Reset, 823-824
/Graph Customize Series Reset Graph, 504, 538-540, 555, 561, 564
/Graph Customize Series Update, 488, 504, 824
/Graph Customize Series Y-Axis, 497, 825
/Graph Fast Graph, 452-454, 825-826
/Graph Graph Type, 439, 484, 549, 565, 826-828
/Graph Graph Type Line, 557
/Graph Hide, 478, 828-829
/Graph Insert, 477-480, 829-830
/Graph Name, 830-832

/Graph Name Autosave Edits, 489
/Graph Name Create, 469-471, 489, 522, 550
/Graph Name Display, 470, 480, 518, 528
/Graph Name Erase, 471
/Graph Name Graph Copy, 472
/Graph Name Reset, 471, 480
/Graph Name Slide, 475
/Graph Overall, 832-834
/Graph Overall Background Color, 516
/Graph Overall Color/B&W, 517
/Graph Overall Drop Shadow Color, 517
/Graph Overall Grid, 514
/Graph Overall Grid Fill Color, 515
/Graph Overall Grid Grid Color, 514
/Graph Overall Grid Line Style, 514
/Graph Overall Outlines, 515
/Graph Overall Three-D, 450-452, 516
/Graph Overall Use Colors, 480
/Graph Series, 457, 834-837
/Graph Series 2nd Series, 479, 552
/Graph Series 3rd Series, 562
/Graph Series Analyze, 541, 544-546, 554-555, 568
/Graph Series Analyze 1st Series Table, 554, 560, 563, 567
/Graph Series Analyze All Reset, 555
/Graph Series Analyze n Series Aggregation, 837-839
/Graph Series Analyze n Series Exponential Fit, 842-843
/Graph Series Analyze n Series Linear Fit, 841-842
/Graph Series Analyze n Series Moving Average, 839-840
/Graph Series Analyze n Series Table, 843-844
/Graph Series Analyze nth, 566
/Graph Series Analyze nth Series Exponential Fit, 564
/Graph Series Analyze nth Series Linear Fit, 561
/Graph Text 1st Line, 460
/Graph Text Font, 463, 844-845
/Graph Text Font 1st Line, 464
/Graph Text Font 2nd Line, 465
/Graph Text Font Data & Tick Labels, 463, 467
/Graph Text Font Legends, 463, 466
/Graph Text Legends, 462, 846-847
/Graph Text Titles, 847-848
/Graph View, 472, 848-849
/Graph X-Axis, 504-505, 849-850
/Graph X-Axis Alternate Labels, 509
/Graph X-Axis Format of Ticks, 508, 538
/Graph X-Axis No. of Minor Ticks, 569
/Graph Y-Axis, 504-506, 849-850
/Graph Y-Axis 2nd Y-Axis, 511
/Graph Y-Axis Display Scaling, 511
/Graph Y-Axis Format of Ticks, 508
/Graph Y-Axis Mode, 511
/Graph Y-Axis No. of Minor Ticks, 508

INDEX

/Graph Y-Axis Scale, 506
@IPAYMT, 304
menu-equivalent, 990
   Database menu, 1005-1006
   Edit menu, 991-993
   File Manager Edit menu, 1019
   File Manager File menu, 1018
   File Manager Options menu, 1021
   File Manager Print menu, 1020
   File Manager Sort menu, 1019
   File Manager Window menu, 1022
   File menu, 990-991
   Graph menu, 995-1002
   Options menu, 1010-1018
   Print menu, 1003-1005
   Style menu, 993-994
   Tools menu, 1006-1010
Optimizer, 5
/Options Colors, 712, 911-912
/Options Colors Conditional, 715
/Options Colors Conditional On/Off Disable, 745
/Options Colors Desktop, 714, 1028
/Options Colors File, 716
/Options Colors Help, 716
/Options Colors Menu, 714
/Options Colors Menu Key Letter, 712
/Options Colors Menu Shadow, 1028
/Options Colors Menu SpeedBar, 714
/Options Colors Palettes, 717
/Options Colors Spreadsheet, 714
/Options Colors Spreadsheet Shading, 203, 709
/Options Colors Spreadsheet WYSIWYG Colors Grid Lines, 222
/Options Colors Spreadsheet WYSIWYG Colors Titles Background, 363
/Options Display Mode, 114, 392, 478, 487, 537, 540, 704, 724-725, 745, 912-913
/Options Display Mode A: Text (80x25), 646
/Options Display Mode B:WYSIWYG, 477
/Options File List, 351
/Options Formats Align Labels, 741, 914
/Options Formats Global Width, 189, 742, 914-915
/Options Formats Hide Zeros, 741, 747, 916
/Options Formats Numeric Format, 741, 917-918
/Options Formats Numeric Format Date, 720
/Options Graphics Quality, 413, 734, 919
/Options Graphics Quality Draft, 479
/Options Hardware, 701, 919-921
/Options Hardware Printers, 417, 705
/Options Hardware Printers 1st Printer Type of Printer, 1044
/Options Hardware Printers 2nd Printer, 706, 746
/Options Hardware Printers Background, 423, 711
/Options Hardware Printers Default Printer, 435, 746
/Options Hardware Printers Fonts Cartridge Fonts, 709
/Options Hardware Screen, 702

/Options Hardware Screen Aspect Ratio, 479
/Options Hardware Screen Resolution, 435
/Options Hardware Screen Screen Type, 746, 1045
/Options International, 172, 717, 921-923
/Options International Currency, 719, 1027
/Options International Date, 180, 720
/Options International LICS Conversion, 723
/Options International Negative Parentheses, 719
/Options International Negative Signs, 719
/Options International Punctuation, 720
/Options International Time, 182, 721, 736
/Options International Use Sort Table, 721
/Options Network, 737, 923-924
/Options Network Banner, 739
/Options Network Drive mappings, 737
/Options Network Queue Monitor, 739
/Options Network Refresh Interval, 425, 739
/Options Network User Name, 739
/Options Other, 924-925
/Options Other Clock, 737
/Options Other Expanded Memory, 736, 746
/Options Other Expanded Memory Both, 604
/Options Other Paradox Network Type to Other, 605
/Options Other Undo, 746
/Options Other Undo Enable, 26, 111, 135
/Options Protection, 925-926
/Options Protection Enable, 186
/Options Protection Formulas Add, 187
/Options Protection Formulas Protect, 744
/Options Protection Formulas Remove, 187
/Options Recalculation, 315, 643, 647, 926-928
/Options Recalculation Iteration, 743
/Options Recalculation Mode, 111, 117, 742
/Options Recalculation Mode Automatic, 747
/Options Recalculation Mode Manual, 735
/Options Recalculation Order, 743
/Options SpeedBar, 731, 910-911
/Options Startup, 726, 928-929
/Options Startup Autoload File, 606, 727-728
/Options Startup Directory, 335, 382, 727, 1045
/Options Startup File Extension, 337, 729
/Options Startup Menu Tree, 730, 1041, 1046
/Options Startup Menu Tree 123.MU, 695
/Options Startup Startup Macro, 660, 694, 729
/Options Startup Use Dialog Boxes, 397, 486, 505, 513, 731
/Options Update, 111, 345, 382, 584, 605, 667, 694, 717, 726, 929-930, 1027
/Options Values, 699, 930

INDEX

/Options WYSIWYG Zoom %, 357, 931
/Print Adjust Printer, 409-410, 851-852
/Print Block, 392, 852-854
/Print Copies, 408, 854
/Print Destination, 391, 405, 417, 854-855
/Print Destination Binary File, 413
/Print Destination File, 411
/Print Destination Graphics Printer, 203, 400, 477
/Print Destination Screen Preview, 856-857
/Print Format, 407, 858
/Print Graph Print, 859-860
/Print Graph Print Layout, 480, 860-861
/Print Graph Print Name, 417
/Print Headings, 395, 398, 862-863
/Print Layout, 863-866
/Print Layout Break Page, 400
/Print Layout Dimensions, 403
/Print Layout Footer, 398
/Print Layout Header, 398
/Print Layout Margins, 401
/Print Layout Margins Page Length, 219
/Print Layout Orientation, 404
/Print Layout Percent Scaling, 400
/Print Layout Reset, 395, 406
/Print Layout Setup String, 405
/Print Layout Update, 395, 406
/Print Layout Values, 397
/Print Print Manager, 424, 866-867
/Print Print Manager File, 867
/Print Print Manager Job, 868-869
/Print Print Manager Queue, 868
/Print Print Manager Window, 869-870
/Print Print-To-Fit, 400, 410, 870-871
/Print Range, 341
/Print Spreadsheet Print, 871
/Printer Layout Setup String, 1028-1029
@SLN, 298
/Style Alignment, 89, 116, 169-170, 173, 220, 790-791
/Style Alignment Center, 29
/Style Block Size, 169, 190, 791-792
/Style Block Size Auto Width, 189
/Style Block Size Height, 792-793
/Style Block Size Height Set Row Height, 195-196
/Style Block Size Set Width, 190
/Style Column Width, 28, 90, 169, 188, 575, 657
/Style Column Width/Reset Width, 793-794
/Style Define Style, 170, 209, 794-796
/Style Define Style Create, 211, 217
/Style Define Style Create Numeric Format, 796
/Style Define Style File Retrieve, 216
/Style Define Style File Save, 216
/Style Font, 170, 204-208, 797-798, 956, 1045
/Style Font Color, 203
/Style FontTable, 170, 205-206, 218, 798-799, 956, 1045
/Style FontTable Edit Fonts, 405, 957

/Style FontTable Update, 197, 219
/Style Hide Column, 169, 193, 799-801
/Style Hide Column Expose, 194
/Style Insert Break, 170, 219, 800-801
/Style Line Drawing, 33, 169, 179, 200, 665, 801-802
/Style Line Drawing Outside, 88, 195
/Style Numeric Format, 31, 90, 169, 175, 179, 508, 672, 717, 741, 802-805
/Style Numeric Format Currency, 89, 717, 1027
/Style Numeric Format Date, 182
/Style Numeric Format Date Time, 184
/Style Numeric Format General, 646
/Style Numeric Format Reset, 180, 184
/Style Protection, 169, 185, 805
/Style Protection Unprotect, 599
/Style Reset Width, 169, 189
/Style Shading, 169, 203, 806
/Style Use Style, 170, 210-212, 343, 806-807
/Tools Advanced Math Invert, 617, 888
/Tools Advanced Math Multiply, 618, 889
/Tools Advanced Math Optimization, 635
/Tools Advanced Math Regression, 614
/Tools Audit, 309-310, 891-893
  auditing spreadsheet formulas, 310-321
  tips for auditing formulas, 323
/Tools Combine, 378, 889-891
/Tools Combine Add, 380
/Tools Combine Copy, 378-379
/Tools Frequency, 633, 893-894
/Tools Import, 377, 894-896
/Tools Library, 644, 896-897
/Tools Library Load, 644
/Tools Library Unload, 644
/Tools Macro, 897-898
/Tools Macro Clear Breakpoints, 680
/Tools Macro Debugger, 681
/Tools Macro Execute, 664-665, 674
/Tools Macro Instant Replay, 659, 693
/Tools Macro Key Reader, 667
/Tools Macro Library, 664, 694
/Tools Macro Macro Recording, 658
/Tools Macro Macro Recording Logical, 695, 990
/Tools Macro Name, 659-661, 688, 693-694
/Tools Macro Name Delete, 667
/Tools Macro Paste, 655, 688
/Tools Macro Record, 650, 653, 669
/Tools Macro Recording, 683, 693
/Tools Macro Transcript, 682-684
/Tools Macro Transcript Failure Protection, 691
/Tools Macro Transcript Max History Length, 689, 692-694
/Tools Macro Transcript Playblock Block, 687-688
/Tools Macro Transcript Restore To Here, 686
/Tools Macro Transcript Single Step, 690

INDEX

/Tools Optimizer, 635-637, 640, 898-901
/Tools Optimizer Answer Report, 643
/Tools Optimizer Constraint(s), 647
/Tools Optimizer Detail Report, 643
/Tools Optimizer Model, 644
/Tools Optimizer Reset, 644
/Tools Optimizer Reset Constraints, 647
/Tools Optimizer Restore To Here, 639, 643
/Tools Parse, 377, 618-620, 901-902
/Tools Parse Create, 621, 625, 646
/Tools Reformat, 903-904
/Tools Solve For, 296-297, 904-905
   rules for using, 297-298
   solving for depreciation expenses, 298-299
   solving for investment returns, 301-302
   solving for mortgage interest payments, 302-304
   solving for what-if analysis, 305, 309
   tips for solving formulas, 322
/Tools Update Links, 375, 661, 905-906
/Tools What-If, 906-908
/Tools What-If 1 Variable, 629
/Tools What-If 2 Variables, 630
/Tools Xtract, 381, 908-909
/Tree Close, 354
/Tree Open, 352
/Tree Resize, 353
What-If, 44
/Window, 932-933
/Window Move/Size, 76, 358-359
/Window Options, 356, 933-935
/Window Options Clear, 361-362, 383
/Window Options Grid Lines, 366
/Window Options Horizontal, 361
/Window Options Locked Titles, 600
/Window Options Map View, 315, 323, 365
/Window Options Print Block Display, 417
/Window Options Row & Col Borders, 364
/Window Options Sync, 114, 362, 383
/Window Options Unsync, 362, 383
/Window Options Vertical, 361
/Window Pick, 356
/Window Stack, 358
/Window Tile, 84, 114, 358
WYSIWYG Zoom %, 724
compressing files, 344-345
conditional breakpoints, 678
CONFIG.SYS file, modifying during Quattro Pro installation, 1039-1043
CONTENTS macro command, 970
control pane (File Manager), 350-351
control sequences, 1029
conventional memory, 940
Copy (Shift-F9) function key, 56
COPY (Shift-F9) macro function instruction, 671
Copy button (READY mode SpeedBar), 126
COPY macro command, 970-971

copying
- cell blocks, 133
- cell data, 124-128, 162
- data
  - combining files, 378-380
  - READY mode SpeedBar, 126
- files during installation, 945, 948, 1035
- formulas in spreadsheets, 23
- linking formulas, 372-373
- part block of Transcript facility, 688
- saved graphs, 471-472

@COS arithmetic function, 233-234
@COUNT statistical function, 236-237
CR (Enter) macro instruction, 670
CR macro command, 971
crashed macros, 669
creating
- basic macros, 652-653
- combination graphs, 496
- drive mappings for network drive, 738
- files, 329
  - workspace, 336
- graphs, 452
  - customized, 457-458
  - preselecting cell blocks, 453
- macro libraries, 663-665
- macros, 668-670
- map views of windows, 365
- search formulas for defining search criteria, 590

criteria table, 588-590
@CTERM financial function, 269-271
Ctrl key, 51
Ctrl-\ key, 109
Ctrl-| {DELEOL} macro instruction, 670
Ctrl-← {BIGLEFT} macro instruction, 670
Ctrl-← key, 53
Ctrl-→ {BIGRIGHT} macro instruction, 670
Ctrl-→ key, 53, 110
Ctrl-A (Style Alignment) shortcut key, 74, 174
Ctrl-Backspace {CLEAR} macro instruction, 670
Ctrl-Backspace key, 109
Ctrl-Break {BREAK} macro instruction, 670
Ctrl-Break key combination, 690
Ctrl-C (Edit Copy) shortcut key, 74, 126-127
Ctrl-D (Date Prefix) shortcut key, 74
Ctrl-D {DATE} macro instruction, 670
Ctrl-E (Edit Erase Block) shortcut key, 74, 132
Ctrl-F (Style Numeric Format) shortcut key, 74
Ctrl-G (Graph Fast Graph) shortcut key, 74, 454
Ctrl-I (Edit Insert) shortcut key, 74
Ctrl-key shortcuts, 72-73
Ctrl-M (Edit Move) shortcut key, 27, 74, 128-129, 132
Ctrl-N (Edit Search & Replace Next) shortcut key, 74
Ctrl-P (Edit Search & Replace Previous) shortcut key, 74
Ctrl-R (Window Move/Size) shortcut key, 74, 358
Ctrl-S (File Save) shortcut key, 49, 74, 332, 346
Ctrl-T (Window Tile) shortcut key, 74, 358
Ctrl-W (Style Column Width) shortcut key, 74, 90, 188
Ctrl-X (File Exit) shortcut key, 74
@CURVALUE miscellaneous function, 253

customizing
- graphs, 457, 484
  - bubble graphs, 502-503
  - data series, 488-495
    - adding interior labels to data series, 495
    - adding second y-axis, 497
    - changing colors, 489
    - changing fill patterns, 490
    - changing line style settings, 491-493
    - changing marker symbol, 491-493
    - changing width value for building bars, 494
    - creating combination graphs, 496
  - Graph Customize dialog box, 484
  - overall, 512-517
    - adding grid lines, 514
    - changing color of grid lines, 514
    - changing drop shadow color pairings, 517
    - changing from 3-D to 2-D, 516
    - changing line style of grid lines, 514
    - determining background color, 516
    - determining fill color, 515
    - drawing boxes on graphs, 515
    - toggling between color and black and white, 517
  - pie graphs, 498-502
    - changing colors, 502
    - changing fill patterns, 501
    - changing label formats, 499
    - exploding pieces of, 499
    - removing tick marks, 502
  - specifying each data series, 458
  - specifying group data series, 458
  - troubleshooting tips, 536-539
- menu tree files, translating, 1045
- SpeedBar, 731-733
- styles, creating for spreadsheets, 209-215
  - applying styles, 210-211
  - deleting from spreadsheets, 215
  - editing custom styles, 217
  - retrieving style sheet to active spreadsheet, 216
  - saving styles in files, 216
- x-axis, 504
  - adjusting axis ticks, 508-509
  - adjusting scale of, 506-507
  - changing display, 509-511
- y-axis, 504
  - adjusting ticks, 508-509
  - adjusting scale, 506-507
  - changing display, 509-511

D

/D command-line switch, 728
data
- adding when combining files, 380
- aligning
  - in cells, 29-31
  - in spreadsheets, 172-175
- copying
  - READY mode SpeedBar, 126
  - when combining files, 378-380
- editing within spreadsheets, 26, 109-110, 118
  - Alt-F5 (Undo) key, 27, 111

EDIT mode, 26
   recalculating formulas,
    111-112
entering into databases, 577
entering into spreadsheets,
  18-22, 84-85
   @function commands,
    99-101
   column/row headings, 19
   labels, 86-88
   report titles, 19
   values, 89-98
entries, global format
  settings, 170-172
erasing with Erase button on
  READY mode, 133
filling, 164
formatting in spreadsheets,
  175, 220
   changing formats, 184
   dates, 180-182
   labels, 180
   numeric formats, 176-177
   times, 182-184
   values, 178-179
moving
   READY mode SpeedBar, 129
   within spreadsheets, 27
on menus, 71
parsing, troubleshooting tips,
  645
points, 437
protecting spreadsheet data,
  185
   globally, 186-187
restricting data entered into
  databases, 601
searching and replacing,
  159-164
series, 437
shading cell data in
  spreadsheets, 203-204
specifying color when
  meeting certain conditions,
  715

   stored in Transcript facility,
    manipulating, 684-685
   subtracting when combining
    files, 380
   transposing, 156-157, 164
   unprotecting spreadsheet
    data, 186
   viewing, 118
data analysis
  add-in @functions, 644
  frequency distributions, 631,
   634
  Optimizer, 634-635
   producing reports, 643
   setting constraints/
    defining multiple
    variables, 640-641
   setting options, 641-642
   setting up, 635-637
   solving basic problems,
    637-639
  parsing, 618-620
   advanced operations,
    623-626
   matrix operations, 616-618
   multiple operations, 623
  regression analysis, 613-616
  sensitivity analysis, 628
   one-way analysis, 628
   two-way analysis, 629-631
/Data Query Input command,
  341
data-entry forms, databases as,
  599
database
  area, 575
  shell, 574
/Database Data Entry command,
  62, 601, 872-873
/Database Data Entry General
  command, 601
Database menu, 576-577
  menu-equivalent commands,
   1005-1006

INDEX

/Database Paradox Access command, 601-606, 873-874, 1042
/Database Paradox Access Load File command, 605
/Database Query Assign Names command, 588, 874, 875
/Database Query Block command, 587, 875
/Database Query Criteria Table command, 590, 876-877
/Database Query Delete command, 593, 607, 877-878
/Database Query Extract command, 596, 607
/Database Query Extract/Unique commands, 879-880
/Database Query Locate command, 592, 880-881
/Database Query Output Block command, 596, 882-883
/Database Query Reset command, 883
/Database Query Unique command, 597
/Database Reset command, 579
/Database Restrict Input command, 599, 883-884
/Database Sort command, 578-581, 885-887
/Database Sort Go command, 579
/Database Sort Sort Rules command, 607
/Database Sort Sort Rules Label Order command, 584
/Database Sort Sort Rules Numbers Before Labels command, 583
/Database Sort Sort Rules Sort Rows/Columns Column, 584
database statistical @function commands, 287-291
databases
    as data-entry forms, 599
    entering data into, 577
    fields, 575
    records, 575
    restricting data entries, 601
    running Quattro Pro from within Paradox, 601-606
    searching, 586, 592
        assigning names to field names rows, 588
        defining search block, 587
        defining search criteria, 588-592
        deleting records, 593
        locating records, 592-593
        setting up output blocks, 595-596, 599
        troubleshooting tips, 607
    sorting, 578, 583-584
        by columns, 584
        returning to original sort order, 583
        troubleshooting tips, 607
        with multiple sort keys, 581-582
        with one sort key, 580
    turning spreadsheets into, 574-576
DATE (Ctrl-D) macro instruction, 670
date and time @function commands, 282-287
date and time formats, symbols, 212-214
date command formats, 180
@DATE date and time function, 282-284
date formats, 251
DATE macro command, 971
Date numeric format, 177
date-and-time entries (values), 88, 98
dates, formatting, 180-182
@DATEVALUE date and time function, 282-284
@DAVG database statistical function, 288-289

@DAY date and time function, 282-284
dBASE file formats, 338-339
@DCOUNT database statistical function, 288-289
@DDB financial function, 269-271
Debug (Shift-F2) function key, 54
DEBUG mode, 67, 674-676
   editing cells in, 679-680
   exiting, 680
debugging, 653
   macros, 674-676
      DEBUG mode, 679-680
      defining breakpoints, 677-678
      defining trace cells, 678-679
      resetting breakpoints, 680
      resetting trace cells, 680
default
   directory, setting, 727
   display mode, selecting, 951
   files, 1041
   settings, 171
   style, editing, 217
   default user name, 739
DEFINE macro command, 972
defining
   search block in database searches, 587
   search criteria in searching databases, 588-592
@DEGREES arithmetic function, 233-235
Del {DELETE} macro instruction, 670
Del key, 52, 109
DEL macro command, 972
DELEOL (Ctrl-\) macro instruction, 670
DELEOL macro command, 972
DELETE (Del) macro instruction, 670
Delete button (READY mode SpeedBar), 138-139

DELETE macro command, 972
deleting
   cell block names, 146-147
   columns, 135, 139, 163
      blocks, 142
      Delete button on READY mode SpeedBar, 139
   custom
      Ctrl-key shortcuts, 73
      styles from spreadsheets, 215
   macros, 667
   page breaks, 220
   records when searching databases, 593
   row/column borders, 364
   rows, 135-137, 163
      blocks, 141
      Delete button on READY mode SpeedBar, 138
dependency audits, 311-314
depreciation expenses, solving for, 298-299
desktop, choosing desktop colors, 714
dialog boxes, 730
   entering ASCII characters into, 1027
   Graph Customize, 484
   Graph Overall, 512
   Print Layout, 396
directories
   assigning access rights, 1043
   default, setting, 727
   \QPRO, 48
   path name, 335
DISPATCH macro command, 961, 972
display modes
   setting options, 724-725
   WYSIWYG, 199
displaying
   @function commands, 228
   custom styles, 211

INDEX

graphs, 473
    inserting onto
      spreadsheets, 477-478
    panning, 473
    slide show, 474-476
    troubleshooting tips,
      479-481
    zooming, 473
Numeric Format menu, 179
syntax information for
  @function commands, 291
values in spreadsheets, 741
windows, 383
    special effects, 361-364
@DMAX database statistical function, 288-289
@DMIN database statistical function, 288-289
documenting macros, 662-663
DOS SHARE command, 1043
DOS shell, 346
DOWN (↓) macro instruction, 670
DOWN macro command, 973
draw area (Graph Annotator screen), 518
@DSTD database statistical function, 288-290
@DSTDS database statistical function, 288-290
@DSUM database statistical function, 288-290
@DVAR statistical function, 288-290
@DVARS statistical function, 288, 291

E

Edit (F2) function key, 54, 110
EDIT (F2) macro function instruction, 671
/Edit Copy command, 124-127, 133, 372, 589-590, 596, 617, 624, 658, 772-773
/Edit Copy Special command, 128, 773-774
/Edit Delete command, 135, 775-776
/Edit Delete Column Block command, 142
/Edit Delete Columns command, 139, 685-686
/Edit Delete Row Block command, 141
/Edit Delete Rows command, 137
/Edit Erase Block command, 124, 132-134, 667, 776-777
/Edit Fill command, 153-154, 777-778
/Edit Insert command, 34, 135, 779-780
/Edit Insert Column Block command, 142
/Edit Insert Columns command, 138-139
/Edit Insert Row Block command, 140
/Edit Insert Rows command, 136-137
EDIT macro command, 973
Edit menu, 123-124
    menu-equivalent commands, 991-993
EDIT mode, 26, 61, 67
    input line, 62
    special keys, 109
    SpeedBar, 60-61
/Edit Move command, 27, 124, 128-129, 132-133, 162, 780-781
/Edit Names Delete command, 146, 667
/Edit Names command, 781-784
/Edit Names Create command, 147-148, 292, 581, 587, 590, 596, 659
/Edit Names Labels command, 149, 164
/Edit Names Labels Right command, 663

/Edit Names Make Table
  command, 151
/Edit Names Reset command,
  150
/Edit Rename command,
  350-351, 383
/Edit Search & Replace
  command, 366, 624, 784-786
/Edit Search & Replace Block
  command, 159-162
/Edit Search & Replace Options
  Reset command, 625
/Edit Select File command, 354
/Edit Transpose command,
  156-157, 165, 786-787
/Edit Undo command, 26, 135,
  685, 735, 787-788
/Edit Values command, 154,
  380-381, 585, 788-789
editing
  cells in DEBUG mode, 679-680
  custom styles, 217
  data in spreadsheets, 26-27,
    109-110, 118
    recalculating formulas,
      111-112
    with Alt-F5 (Undo) key, 111
  default style, 217
  macros, 666
END (End) macro instruction,
  670
End key, 52, 109
END macro command, 973
END status indicator, 67
End-← key, 53
End-↑ key, 53
End-→ key, 53
End-↓ key, 53
enlarging windows, 358
Enter {CR} macro instruction,
  670
Enter key, 109
entering
  data into databases, 577
  special status key-equivalent
    macro commands, 672-673

equal (=) operator, 591
Erase button (READY mode
  SpeedBar), 133
erasing
  cell blocks, 134
  cell data, 124, 132, 162
  data with Erase button on
    READY mode, 133
  files, 332
  saved graphs, 471
ERR audit, 318-319
@ERR miscellaneous function,
  253
ERROR mode, 67
ESC (Esc) macro instruction, 670
Esc key, 52, 109
ESC macro command, 661, 973
/Ex command-line switch, 728
@EXACT string function, 241-243
executing
  commands, 17
  macros, 665
    troubleshooting tips,
      693-695
exiting
  DEBUG mode, 680
  Transcript facility, 692
@EXP arithmetic function,
  229-230
expanded memory, 940
  specifying use of, 736
Expanded Memory Specification
  (EMS), 735
exploding (pie graphs), 443, 499
exponential graphing, 542,
  564-566
    creating table of exponential
      fit regression value, 566-567
EXT status indicator, 67
extended memory, 940
external links audit, 320-321
extracting
  parts of files, 381
  records when searching
    databases, 596

F

F2 {EDIT} macro function instruction, 671
F3 {NAME} macro function instruction, 671
F4 {ABS} macro function instruction, 671
F5 {GOTO} macro function instruction, 671
F6 {WINDOW} macro function instruction, 671
F7 {QUERY} macro function instruction, 671
F8 {TABLE} macro function instruction, 671
F9 {CALC} macro function instruction, 671
F9 {READDIR} macro function instruction, 671
F10 (Graph View) function key, 433
F10 {GRAPH} macro function instruction, 671
Failure Protection facility, 691
@FALSE logical function, 264
fields, 575
   assigning names to, for database searches, 588
/File All Select command, 354-354
/File Close command, 332, 750
/File Close All command, 332, 751
/File Directory command, 335, 751-752
/File Erase command, 332-333, 683, 752-753
/File Exit command, 35, 49, 605, 753-754
file formats
   Allways, 342
   compressed files, 336-338
   database files, 336-338
   dBASE, 338-339
   graphics files, 336-338
   Harvard Graphics, 344
   Impress, 343
   Lotus 1-2-3, 339-341
   spreadsheet files, 336-337
file macro command category, 970, 975, 980-984, 987
File Manager, 347
   choosing File Manager colors, 716-717
   control pane, 350-351
   Edit menu, menu-equivalent commands, 1019
   File menu, menu-equivalent commands, 1018
   file pane, 351-352
   moving through File Manager window, 348
   Options menu, menu-equivalent commands, 1021
   performing multiple file operations simultaneously, 354
   Print menu, 356
      menu-equivalent commands, 1020
   Sort menu, menu-equivalent commands, 1019
   tree pane, 353
   Window menu, menu-equivalent commands, 1022
File menu, 326-328
   menu-equivalent commands, 990-991
file names, 84
/File New command, 329, 664, 754-755
/File Open command, 329-330, 472, 755
file pane (File Manager), 351-352
/File Read Dir command, 352-354
/File Retrieve command, 49, 84, 330, 374, 382, 583, 683, 755-756
/File Save command, 84, 331, 608, 664, 668, 683, 756-757

/File Save All command, 758
/File Save As command, 35, 332, 758-759
/File Utilities DOS Shell command, 346, 760
/File Utilities File Manager command, 348, 760-762
/File Utilities File Manager /Edit command, 762-763
/File Utilities File Manager /File command, 763-764
/File Utilities File Manager /Options command, 764-765
/File Utilities File Manager /Print command, 765-766
/File Utilities File Manager /Sort command, 766-767
/File Utilities File Manager /Tree command, 767-768
/File Utilities File Manager /Window command, 768-769
/File Utilities SQZ! command, 345, 769-770
/File Workspace command, 770-771
/File Workspace Restore command, 84, 336
/File Workspace Save command, 84, 336
@FILEEXISTS logical function, 264-265
files, 328
   AUTOEXEC.BAT, modifying during installation, 1039-1043
   automatically opening at start-up, 727-728
   binary, printing spreadsheet reports to, 413
   closing, 332
   combining two files, 378
      adding/subtracting data, 380
      copying data, 378-380
   compressing, 344-345

   CONFIG.SYS, modifying during Quattro Pro installation, 1039-1043
   copying during Quattro Pro installation, 945, 948
   creating, 329
   custom menu tree, translating, 1045
   default (RF), 1041
   erasing, 332
   extensions, selecting new, 729
   extracting part, 381
   graphs, managing, 468-469
      autosaving edited graphs, 470
      copying saved graphs, 471-472
      erasing saved graphs, 471
      naming, 469
      resetting current graph settings, 471
      saving, 469
   importing, 377
   managing, 382
   menu preference, 1040-1041
   multiple operations, performing simultaneously, 354
   opening, 329-330
      cell selector within/saving with macro, 989
   password-protecting, 333-335
   QPRO.SOM, 1037
   QUATTRO.LOG, 682, 689
   resource, saving startup options to, 740
   retrieving, 330
   saving, 331-332
   text, printing spreadsheet reports to, 411-412
   workspace, creating, 336
FILESIZE macro command, 973
financial @function commands, 267-281
   negative values, 292

INDEX

FIND mode, 67
@FIND string function, 241, 244
Fit button (READY mode SpeedBar), 189
Font button (READY mode SpeedBar), 206
fonts, 222
   changing in graphs, 463-464
      colors, 467
      point size, 465
      styles, 466
      typeface, 465
   installing on printer, 708-710
   predefined, customizing, 218-219
   selecting for spreadsheets, 204-205
footers, 398-399
FOR macro command, 973
FORBREAK macro command, 974
Format button (READY mode SpeedBar), 179
formats
   changing cell formats, 184
   choosing format for printing spreadsheet reports, 407
   date, 251
      command, 180
   date and time symbols, 212-214
   file
      Allways, 342
      compressed, 336-338
      database, 336-338
      dBASE, 338-339
      graphics, 336-338
      Harvard Graphics, 344
      Impress, 343
      Lotus 1-2-3, 339-341
      spreadsheet, 336-337
   numeric, 176, 251
      creating custom numeric formats, 211-215
      symbols, 212
   time, 252
      command, 183

formatting
   data in spreadsheets, 175
      changing formats, 184
      dates, 180-182
      labels, 180
      numeric formats, 176-177
      times, 182-184
      values, 178-179
   numbers within spreadsheets, 31-32
formulas
   changing to values, 154
   copying, 23
   entering into spreadsheets, 22-23
   in spreadsheets, recalculating, 111-112
   using cell block names in, 153
   value formulas, 88, 91-94
      arithmetic, 94
      logical, 96
      order of precedence, 97-98
      text, 95
Forward Slash (/) {MENU} status key macro instruction, 672
frequency distribution tables, 631, 634
FRMT mode, 67
@function commands, 24, 93, 99-101, 225-226
   database statistical, 287-289
      @DAVG, 288-289
      @DCOUNT, 288-289
      @DMAX, 288-289
      @DMIN, 288-289
      @DSTD, 288-290
      @DSTDS, 288-290
      @DSUM, 288-290
      @DVAR, 288-290
      @DVARS, 288, 291
   date and time, 282-284
      @DATE, 282-284
      @DATEVALUE, 282-284
      @DAY, 282-284
      @HOUR, 282, 285
      @MINUTE, 283, 285

@MONTH, 283, 285
@NOW, 283, 286
@SECOND, 283, 286
@TIME, 283, 286
@TIMEVALUE, 283, 286
@TODAY, 283, 287
@YEAR, 283, 287
displaying
  list of, 101, 228
  syntax information, 291
entering, 227-228
financial, 267-269
  @CTERM, 269-271
  @DDB, 269-271
  @FV, 269, 272
  @FVAL, 269, 273
  @IPAYMT, 269, 273
  @IRATE, 269-270, 273
  @IRR, 270, 274
  negative values, 292
  @NPER, 269-270, 275
  @NPV, 270, 276
  @PAYMT, 269-270, 276
  @PMT, 270, 277
  @PPAYMT, 270, 278
  @PV, 270, 278
  @PVAL, 269-270, 279
  @RATE, 270, 279
  @SLN, 270, 280
  @SYD, 270, 280
  @TERM, 270, 281
forms, 292
logical, 263
  @FALSE, 264
  @FILEEXISTS, 264-265
  @IF, 264-265
  @ISERR, 264-266
  @ISNA, 264-266
  @ISNUMBER, 264-266
  @ISSTRING, 264, 267
  @TRUE, 264, 267
mathematical, 228-229
  arithmetic, 229-233
    @ABS, 230
    @EXP, 230
    @INT, 230

@LN, 230
@LOG, 231
@MOD, 231
@RAND, 231
@ROUND, 232
@SQRT, 232
trigonometric, 233-236
  @ACOS, 233
  @ASIN, 233
  @ATAN, 233-234
  @ATAN2, 233-234
  @COS, 233-234
  @DEGREES, 233-235
  @PI, 233-235
  @RADIANS, 233-235
  @SIN, 233, 235
  @TAN, 233, 236
miscellaneous, 250-253
  @@, 252-253
  @CELL, 252-254
  @CELLINDEX, 252-254
  @CELLPOINTER, 252, 255
  @CHOOSE, 252, 255
  @COLS, 253, 256
  @CURVALUE, 253
  @ERR, 253
  @HLOOKUP, 253, 257-258
  @INDEX, 253, 258
  @ISAAF, 259
  @ISAPP, 260
  @MEMAVAIL, 253, 260
  @MEMEMSAVAIL, 253, 260
  @NA, 253, 261
  @ROWS, 253, 261
  @VERSION, 253, 262
  @VLOOKUP, 253, 262-263
remembering origin of
  arguments used in, 292
statistical, 236
  @AVG, 236, 237
  @COUNT, 236-237
  @MAX, 236-238
  @MIN, 236-238
  @STD, 236-238
  @STDS, 236-238
  @SUM, 236, 239

INDEX

@SUMPRODUCT, 236, 239
@VAR, 236, 240
@VARS, 236, 240
string, 240-241
  @CHAR, 241-242
  @CLEAN, 241-243
  @CODE, 241-243
  @EXACT, 241-243
  @FIND, 241, 244
  @HEXTONUM, 242-244
  @LEFT, 242-244
  @LENGTH, 242, 245
  @LOWER, 242, 245
  @MID, 242, 245
  @N, 242, 246
  @NUMTOHEX, 242, 246
  @PROPER, 242, 246
  @REPEAT, 242, 247
  @REPLACE, 242, 247
  @RIGHT, 242, 247
  @S, 242, 248
  @STRING, 242, 248
  @TRIM, 242, 248
  @UPPER, 242, 249
  @VALUE, 242, 249
syntax, 226
function keys, 54-56
  Alt-0 (Pick Windows), 688
  Alt-F2 (Macro Menu), 54
  Alt-F2E (/Tools Macro Execute), 665
  Alt-F2I (/Tools Macro Instant Replay), 659
  Alt-F2T (/Tools Macro Transcript), 682
  Alt-F3 (Functions), 24, 55, 291
  Alt-F5 (Undo), 27, 55, 111, 170
  Alt-F6 (Zoom), 55, 358
  Alt-F7 (All Select), 55, 426
  Ctrl-F10, 56
  F1 (Help), 54
  F2 (Edit), 54, 110
  F3 (Choices), 54
  F4 (Absolute), 55
  F5 (GoTo), 55
  F6 (Pane), 55, 114
  F7 (Query), 55
  F8 (Table), 55
  F9 (Calc), 55
  F10 (Graph), 56, 433
  Shift-F2 (Debug), 54
  Shift-F3 (Macro List), 54, 666
  Shift-F5 (Pick Window), 54-55
  Shift-F6 (Next Window), 55, 357
  Shift-F7 (Select), 55, 426
  Shift-F8 (Move), 55
  Shift-F9 (Copy), 56
  Shift-F10 (Paste), 56
Functions (Alt-F3) function key, 55
FUNCTIONS (Alt-F3) macro function instruction, 671
functions (graphs), 437
FUNCTIONS macro command, 974
@FV financial function, 269, 272
@FVAL financial function, 269, 273

G

gallery (Graph Annotator screen), 520
GET macro command, 974
GETLABEL macro command, 961, 974
GETNUMBER macro command, 962, 975
GETPOS macro command, 975
GoTo (F5) function key, 55
GOTO (F5) macro function instruction, 671
GOTO macro command, 975
Graph (F10) function key, 56
GRAPH (F10) macro function instruction, 671
/Graph Annotate command, 669, 518, 808-809
/Graph Annotate Clipboard command, 809-810

/Graph Annotate Property Sheet
command, 811
/Graph Annotate Toolbox
command, 811-812
Graph Annotator
  annotating graphs, 518, 522
    Annotator screen, 518-520
    editing text design
      elements, 526
    linking elements to graph
      data series, 528
    managing elements with
      Clipboard, 527-528
    moving design elements,
      524
    resizing design elements,
      525
    selecting design elements,
      523
    setting design element
      properties, 526
  keys, 521
  managing
    and annotating multiple
      graphs, 534-536
    graphs with graph buttons,
      529-533
graph buttons, 529-533
Graph Customize dialog box,
  484
/Graph Customize Series
  command, 483, 486
/Graph Customize Series Bar
  Width command, 494, 813
/Graph Customize Series
  Bubbles Colors command, 503
/Graph Customize Series
  Bubbles command, 813-814
/Graph Customize Series
  Bubbles Max Bubble Size
  command, 503
/Graph Customize Series
  Bubbles Patterns command,
  502
/Graph Customize Series Colors
  command, 489, 815-816

/Graph Customize Series Fill
  Patterns command, 490, 537,
  540, 816-817
/Graph Customize Series
  Interior Labels command, 495,
  555, 561, 564, 567, 817-818
/Graph Customize Series
  Markers & Lines command,
  818-820
/Graph Customize Series
  Markers & Lines Line Styles
  command, 491-493
/Graph Customize Series
  Markers & Lines Markers
  command, 537, 540
/Graph Customize Series
  Override Type command, 496,
  820-821
/Graph Customize Series
  Override Type Default
  command, 537, 540
/Graph Customize Series Pies
  command, 498, 821-823
/Graph Customize Series Pies
  Label Format command, 499
/Graph Customize Series Pies
  Colors command, 502
/Graph Customize Series Pies
  Explode command, 499
/Graph Customize Series Pies
  Patterns command, 501
/Graph Customize Series Pies
  Tick Marks command, 502
/Graph Customize Series Reset
  command, 823-824
/Graph Customize Series Reset
  Graph command, 504, 538-540,
  555, 561, 564
/Graph Customize Series Update
  command, 488, 504, 824
/Graph Customize Series Y-Axis
  command, 497, 825
/Graph Fast Graph command,
  452-454, 825-826
/Graph Graph Type command,
  439, 484, 549, 565, 826-828

INDEX

/Graph Graph Type Line command, 557
/Graph Hide command, 478, 828-829
/Graph Insert command, 477-480, 829-830
GRAPH macro command, 975
Graph menu, 432-434
    menu-equivalent commands, 995-1002
/Graph Name command, 830-832
/Graph Name Autosave Edits command, 489
/Graph Name Create command, 469-471, 489, 522, 550
/Graph Name Display command, 470, 480, 518, 528
/Graph Name Erase command, 471
/Graph Name Graph Copy command, 472
/Graph Name Reset command, 471, 480
/Graph Name Slide command, 475
graph origin, 449
/Graph Overall Background Color command, 516
/Graph Overall Color/B&W command, 517
/Graph Overall command, 832-834
Graph Overall dialog box, 512
/Graph Overall Drop Shadow Color command, 517
/Graph Overall Grid command, 514
/Graph Overall Grid Grid Color command, 514
/Graph Overall Grid Fill Color command, 515
/Graph Overall Grid Line Style command, 514
/Graph Overall Outlines command, 515

/Graph Overall Three-D command, 450-452, 516
/Graph Overall Use Colors command, 480
/Graph Series command, 457, 834-837
/Graph Series 2nd Series command, 479, 552
/Graph Series 3rd Series command, 562
/Graph Series Analyze command, 541, 544-546, 554-555, 568
/Graph Series Analyze 1st Series Table command, 554, 560, 563, 567
/Graph Series Analyze All Reset command, 555
/Graph Series Analyze n Series Aggregation command, 837-839
/Graph Series Analyze n Series Exponential Fit command, 842-843
/Graph Series Analyze n Series Linear Fit command, 841-842
/Graph Series Analyze n Series Moving Average command, 839-840
/Graph Series Analyze n Series Table command, 843-844
/Graph Series Analyze nth command, 566
/Graph Series Analyze nth Series Exponential Fit command, 564
/Graph Series Analyze nth Series Linear Fit command, 561
/Graph Text 1st Line command, 460
/Graph Text Font command, 463, 844-845
/Graph Text Font 1st Line command, 464
/Graph Text Font 2nd Line command, 465
/Graph Text Font Data & Tick Labels command, 463, 467

/Graph Text Font Legends
  command, 463, 466
/Graph Text Legends command,
  462, 846-847
/Graph Text Titles command,
  847-848
/Graph View command, 472,
  848-849
/Graph X-Axis command,
  504-505, 849-850
/Graph X-Axis Alternate Labels
  command, 509
/Graph X-Axis Format of Ticks
  command, 508, 538-540
/Graph X-Axis No. of Minor
  Ticks command, 569
/Graph Y-Axis command,
  504-506, 849-850
/Graph Y-Axis 2nd Y-Axis
  command, 511
/Graph Y-Axis Display Scaling
  command, 511
/Graph Y-Axis Format of Ticks
  command, 508
/Graph Y-Axis Mode command,
  511
/Graph Y-Axis No. of Minor
  Ticks command, 508
/Graph Y-Axis Scale command,
  506
GRAPHCHAR macro command,
  975
graphical user interface (GUI), 3
graphics printing
  graphics printers, 413
  quality options, 734
graphs, 431
  3-D, 448
    area graph, 451
    bar graph, 450
    ribbon graph, 449
    step graph, 451
    z-axis, 448
  annotating, 522
    editing text design
      elements, 526
    Graph Annotator screen,
      518-521
    linking elements to graph
      data series, 528
    managing elements with
      Clipboard, 527-528
    moving design elements,
      524
    resizing design elements,
      525
    selecting design elements,
      523
    setting design element
      properties, 526
  area, 444
  bar, 441
  bubble, 448
  column, 446
  creating, 452
    /Graph Fast Graph
      command, 454-456
    customized, 457
    preselecting cell blocks,
      453
    troubleshooting tips,
      478-479
  customizing, 484
    bubble graphs
      changing bubble size,
        503
      customizing color/fill
        patterns, 502
    data series, 488
      adding interior labels to
        data series, 495
      adding second y-axis,
        497
      changing colors, 489
      creating combination
        graphs, 496
      fill patterns, 490
      line style settings,
        491-493
      marker symbol, 491
      specifying, 458

INDEX

width value for building bars, 494
Graph Customize dialog box, 484
marker symbol, 493
overall graphs, 512
   determining fill color, 515
   adding grid lines, 514
   changing color of grid lines, 514
   changing drop shadow color pairing, 517
   changing from 3-D to 2-D, 516
   changing line style of grid lines, 514
   determining background color, 516
   drawing boxes on graphs, 515
   toggling between color and black and white, 517
pie graphs
   changing colors, 502
   changing fill patterns, 501
   changing label formats, 499
   exploding pieces of, 499
   removing tick marks, 502
troubleshooting tips, 536-539
displaying, 473
   in slide show, 474-476
   inserting onto spreadsheets, 477-478
   panning, 473
   troubleshooting tips, 479-481
   zooming, 473
enhancing appearance, 459
   adding legends, 462
   adding titles, 460-462
   changing fonts, 463-464

      colors, 467
      point size, 465
      styles, 466
      typeface, 465
   troubleshooting tips, 479
files, managing, 468-469
   autosaving edited graphs, 470
   copying saved graphs, 471-472
   erasing saved graphs, 471
   naming, 469
   resetting current graph settings, 471
   saving, 469
grid lines, adding, 514
high-low (open-close), 446
line, 440
   data points, 437
   x-axis, 437
   y-axis, 437
managing
   and annotating multiple graphs, 534-536
   with graph buttons, 529-533
pie, 443
   exploding, 443
   slices, 443
printing, 417, 428-429
   choosing destination, 418
   positioning/shaping, 420-421
   setting graph margins, 419
   special graph files for, 421
rotated bar, 444
stacked-bar, 442
text, 447
viewing, hardware requirements, 434
XY, 441
greater than (>) operator, 591
greater than or equal (>=) operator, 591
grid lines, adding to graphs, 514

H

hard drive
  managing during Quattro Pro installation, 943
  saving spreadsheets to, 35
hardware requirements
  for installing Quattro Pro, 938-939
  for viewing graphs, 434
Harvard Graphics file formats, 344
headers, 398-399
help
  accessing, 76-78, 81
  choosing help colors, 716
Help (F1) function key, 54
HELP mode, 67
hertz, 939
@HEXTONUM string function, 242-244
high memory, 940
high-low (open-close) graph, 446
@HLOOKUP miscellaneous function, 253, 257-258
HOME (Home) macro instruction, 670
Home key, 52, 110
HOME macro command, 976
horizontal/vertical borders, 65
@HOUR date and time function, 282, 285

I

/I command-line switch, 728
/IB command-line switch, 728
/IC command-line switch, 728
@IF logical function, 264-265
IF macro command, 976
IFKEY macro command, 976
/IM command-line switch, 728
importing files, 377
Impress file formats, 343
@INDEX miscellaneous function, 253, 258
INDICATE macro command, 976
input line, 62
INS (Toggles Ins) status key macro instruction, 672
Ins key, 52, 110
INS macro command, 977
Ins off {INSOFF} status key macro instruction, 672
Ins on {INSON} status key macro instruction, 672
Insert button (READY mode SpeedBar), 137-138
inserting
  columns, 135, 138-139, 163
    blocks, 142
    into spreadsheets, 34
    with Insert button on READY mode SpeedBar, 138
  page breaks, 219
  rows, 135-137, 163
    blocks, 140
    into spreadsheets, 34
    READY mode SpeedBar, 137
INSOFF (Ins off) status key macro instruction, 672
INSOFF macro command, 977
INSON (Ins on) status key macro instruction, 672
INSON macro command, 977
Installation Utility, 48, 958-959
installing
  fonts on printers, 708-710
  Quattro Pro, 944, 953
    choosing printers, 702-711
    choosing screens, 705
    copying files, 945, 948
    for use with Microsoft Windows, 952
    hardware/software requirements, 938-939
    managing hard disk drives, 943

INDEX

managing random-access memory (RAM), 940-943
math coprocessor chip, 939
microprocessor clock speed, 939
on networks, 1031, 1034-1037, 1040-1048
on networks:
    hardware/software requirements, 1032-1033
    preinstallation procedures, 1033-1034
selecting character set, 952
selecting default display mode, 951
selecting monitor type, 948
selecting printers, 950
video displays/printers supported, 943
instant macros, 659
@INT arithmetic function, 229-230
interactive macro command category, 967-969, 974-978, 984-986
international options, 717-718
    attaching symbols to negative values, 719
    setting
        different currency and symbol, 719
        LICS conversion, 723
        new date formats, 720
        new punctuation style, 720
        new sort rules, 721
        new time formats, 721
        overstrike print, 723
inverting matrices, 617
investment returns, solving for, 301-302
@IPAYMT command, 304
@IPAYMT financial function, 269, 273

@IRATE financial function, 269-270, 273
@IRR financial function, 270, 274
@ISAAF miscellaneous function, 259
@ISAPP miscellaneous function, 260
@ISERR logical function, 264-266
@ISNA logical function, 264-266
@ISNUMBER logical function, 264-266
@ISSTRING logical function, 264, 267

K

keyboard, 50, 80
    alphanumeric, 51
    arrow keys, 53
    macro command category, 967-987
    macros, 657
    numeric keypad, 52
keys
    + (Expand), 488
    affecting File List/file name prompt boxes, 329
    arrow, 53
    available in EDIT mode, 109
    control pane (File Manager), 350
    Ctrl-key shortcuts, 72
        creating custom Ctrl-key shortcuts, 73
        Ctrl-A (Style Alignment), 74, 174
        Ctrl-Break key combination, 690
        Ctrl-C (Edit Copy), 74, 126-127
        Ctrl-D (Data Prefix), 74
        Ctrl-E (Edit Erase Block), 74, 132
        Ctrl-F (Style Numeric Format), 74

Ctrl-G (Graph Fast Graph), 74, 454
Ctrl-I (Edit Insert), 74
Ctrl-M (Edit Move), 27, 74, 128-129, 132
Ctrl-N (Edit Search & Replace Next), 74
Ctrl-P (Edit Search & Replace Previous), 74
Ctrl-R (Window Move/Size), 74, 358
Ctrl-S (File Save), 49, 74, 332, 346
Ctrl-T (Window Tile), 74, 358
Ctrl-W (Style Column Width), 74, 90, 188
Ctrl-X (File Exit), 74
deleting custom Ctrl-key shortcuts, 73
file pane (File Manager), 351-352
function, *see* function keys
Graph Annotator, 521
macro function keys
  see, macros, keystroke-equivalent commands: functions
  see, macros, keystroke-equivalent commands: keyboard
  see, macros, keystroke-equivalent commands: status
slash (/), 68, 80
sort, 579-582
tree pane (File Manager), 354
keystroke-equivalent instructions, 657

L

LABEL mode, 18, 67
label reference audits, 317-318
labels, 18, 84
  aligning in spreadsheets, 741
  entering, 116
    troubleshooting tips, 115-117
  formatting, 180
  label prefixes, 86-88
LEFT (←) macro instruction, 670
LEFT macro command, 977
@LEFT string function, 242-244
legends, 460-462
@LENGTH string function, 242, 245
less than (<) operator, 591
less than or equal (<=) operator, 591
LET macro command, 977
line feeds, controlling, 710
line graphs, 440
  data points, 437
  x-axis, 437
  y-axis, 437
linear fit analytical graphing, 561-562
  creating table of linear fit regression value, 563
lines
  adding to spreadsheets, 200-201
  drawing around spreadsheets, 32
  erasing from spreadsheets, 201-202
  printing within spreadsheets, 202
linking
  formulas
    creating for linking spreadsheets, 368, 371
    moving/copying, 372-373
    typing, 368-369
  macros, 673-674
  spreadsheets, 367
    creating 3-D consolidation formulas, 369-372

INDEX

creating linking formulas, 368, 371
moving/copying linking formulas, 372-373
typing linking formulas, 368-369
worksheets, 383
@LN arithmetic function, 229-230
loading
  add-in @functions, 644
  linked spreadsheet applications, 374-375
  Quattro Pro, 79, 955
local area networks (LANs) *see* networks
locking titles (windows), 362-363
@LOG arithmetic function, 229-231
logical @function commands, 263-267
logical
  formulas, 96
  macros, 989
  operators, 591
LOOK macro command, 977
Lotus 1-2-3
  file formats, 339-341
  macros, interpreting, 667-668
Lotus International Characters Set (LICS), 723
@LOWER string function, 242, 245

M

Macro button (EDIT mode SpeedBar), 667
Macro Debugger, 676
macro libraries, 661-662
  creating, 663-665
Macro List (Shift-F3) function key, 54
Macro Menu (Alt-F2) function key, 54

MACRO mode, 67
macros, 649-650
  categories, 966
  commands
    {?}, 967
    {~}, 971
    {;}, 966
    {}, 966
    {ABS}, 967
    {BACKSPACE}, 967
    {BACKTAB}, 967
    {BEEP}, 961, 967
    {BIGLEFT}, 968
    {BIGRIGHT}, 968
    {BLANK}, 968
    {BRANCH}, 961, 968
    {BREAK}, 969
    {BREAKOFF}, 666, 969
    {BREAKON}, 969
    {BS}, 670
    {CALC}, 969
    {CAPOFF}, 969
    {CAPON}, 969
    {CHOOSE}, 970
    {CLEAR}, 970
    {CLOSE}, 970
    {CONTENTS}, 970
    {COPY}, 970-971
    {CR}, 971
    {DATE}, 971
    {DEFINE}, 972
    {DEL}, 972
    {DELEOL}, 972
    {DELETE}, 972
    {DISPATCH}, 961, 972
    {DOWN}, 973
    {EDIT}, 973
    {END}, 973
    {ESC}, 661, 973
    {FILESIZE}, 973
    {FOR}, 973
    {FORBREAK}, 974
    {FUNCTIONS}, 974
    {GET}, 974
    {GETLABEL}, 961, 974
    {GETNUMBER}, 962, 975

{GETPOS}, 975
{GOTO}, 975
{GRAPH}, 975
{GRAPHCHAR}, 975
{HOME}, 976
{IF}, 976
{IFKEY}, 976
{INDICATE}, 976
{INS}, 977
{INSOFF}, 977
{INSON}, 977
{LEFT}, 977
{LET}, 977
{LOOK}, 977
{MACROS}, 977
{MARK}, 978
{MARKALL}, 978
{MENU}, 978
{MENUBRANCH}, 978
{MENUCALL}, 978
{MESSAGE}, 979
{MOVE}, 979
{NAME}, 979
{NEXTWIN}, 979
{NUMOFF}, 979
{NUMON}, 979
{ONERROR}, 980
{OPEN}, 980
{PANELOFF}, 980
{PANELON}, 980
{PASTE}, 981
{PDXGO}, 981
{PGDN}, 981
{PGUP}, 981
{PLAY}, 981
{PUT}, 981
{QUERY}, 982
{QUIT}, 663, 982
{READ}, 982
{READDIR}, 982
{READLN}, 982
{RECALC}, 983
{RECALCCOL}, 983
{RESTART}, 983
{RETURN}, 983
{RIGHT}, 984
{SCROLLOFF}, 984
{SCROLLON}, 984
{SETPOS}, 984
{STEP}, 984
{STEPOFF}, 984
{STEPON}, 984
{SUBROUTINE}, 985
{TAB}, 985
{TABLE}, 985
{UNDO}, 985
{UP}, 985
{WAIT}, 986
{WINDOW}, 986
{WINDOWSOFF}, 986
{WINDOWSON}, 986
{WRITE}, 986
{WRITELN}, 987
{ZOOM}, 987
crashing, 669
creating
  basic macros, 652-653
  entering instructions into
    manually, 668-670
  macro programs, 47
debugging, 653, 674-676
  defining breakpoints,
    677-678
  defining trace cells,
    678-679
  in DEBUG mode, 679-680
  resetting breakpoints, 680
  resetting trace cells, 680
deleting, 667
documenting, 662-663
editing, 666
executing, 665
  troubleshooting tips,
    693-695
instant, 659
keyboard, 657
keystroke-equivalent
  instructions, 657
  commands: function
    F2 {EDIT}, 671
    F3 {NAME}, 671

INDEX

F4 {ABS}, 671
F5 {GOTO}, 671
F6 {WINDOW}, 671
F7 {QUERY}, 671
F8 {TABLE}, 671
F9 {CALC}, 671
F9 {READDIR} in File Manager Window, 671
F10 {GRAPH}, 671
Shift-F2 {STEP}, 671
Shift-F3 {Macro List}, 54, 666, 671
Shift-F5 {CHOOSE}, 671
Shift-F6 {NEXTWIN}, 671
Shift-F7 {MARK}, 671
Shift-F8 {MOVE}, 671
Shift-F9 {COPY}, 671
Shift-F10 {PASTE}, 671
keystroke-equivalent commands: keyboard
  ↑ {UP}, 670
  ↓ {DOWN}, 670
  → {RIGHT}, 670
  ← {LEFT}, 670
  Backspace {BS}, 670
  Ctrl-| {DELEOL}, 670
  Ctrl-← {BIGLEFT}, 670
  Ctrl-→ {BIGRIGHT}, 670
  Ctrl-Backspace {CLEAR}, 670
  Ctrl-Break {BREAK}, 670
  Ctrl-D {DATE}, 670
  Del, {DELTE}, 670
  End {END}, 670
  Enter {CR}, 670
  Esc {ESC}, 670
  Home {HOME}, 670
  PgDn {PGDN}, 670
  PgUp {PGUP}, 670
  Shift-Tab {BACKTAB}, 670
  Tab {TAB}, 670
keystroke-equivalent commands: status
  Cpas Lock Off {CAPOFF}, 672
  Caps Lock on {CAPON}, 672
  Forward Slash (/) {MENU}, 672
  Ins Off {INSOFF}, 672
  Ins On {INSON}, 672
  Num Lock off {NUMOFF}, 672
  Num Lock on {NUMON}, 672
  Scroll Lock off {SCROLLOFF}, 672
  Scroll Lock on {SCROLLON}, 672
  Toggle Ins on or off {INSERT}, 672
linking, 673-674
logical, 989
Lotus 1-2-3 macros, interpreting, 667-668
menu-equivalent instructions, 657
naming, 659-661
  deleting names, 667
programs, 11
  /x commands, 964-965
  creating, 47
  macro commands in, 961-963
  subroutines in, 964
recording, 653
  executing last recorded macro, 658
  pasting into spreadsheets, 654-656
  switching macro recording mode, 658
  troubleshooting tips, 693
special
  function key-equivalent commands, 671
  key-equivalent commands, 670
  status key-equivalent commands, 672-673

storing
  in macro library, 661, 663-665
  in spreadsheets, 661
MACROS (Shift-F3) macro function instruction, 671
MACROS macro command, 977
managing
  and annotating multiple graphs, 534-536
  files, 382
  graph files, 468-469
    autosaving edited graphs, 470
    copying saved graphs, 471-472
    erasing saved graphs, 471
    naming, 469
    resetting current graph settings, 471
    saving, 469
  graphs with graph buttons, 529-533
margins, setting, 401-403
  for graphs, 419
MARK (Shift-F7) macro function instruction, 671
MARK macro command, 978
MARKALL (Alt-F7) macro function instruction, 671
MARKALL macro command, 978
mathematical @function commands, 228-236
matrices, 616-618
  inverting, 617
  multiplying, 618
  troubleshooting tips, 645
@MAX statistical function, 236-238
megahertz, 939
@MEMAVAIL miscellaneous function, 253, 260
@MEMEMSAVAIL miscellaneous function, 253, 260

memory
  conventional, 940
  expanded, 940
    specifying use of, 736
  Expanded Memory Specification (EMS), 735
  extended, 940
  high, 940
  random-access (RAM), 940-943
  reviewing memory available, 711
  troubleshooting tips, 745
MENU (Forward Slash (/)) status key macro instruction, 672
MENU macro command, 978
MENU mode, 17, 68
menu preference file, 1040-1041
menu trees, 730, 1040
menu-equivalent instructions, 657
MENUBRANCH macro command, 978
MENUCALL macro command, 978
menus
  activating, 17, 68-69, 81
  choosing menu colors, 713
  Database, 576-577
    menu-equivalent commands, 1005-1006
  Edit, 123-124
    menu-equivalent commands, 991-993
  File, 326-328
    menu-equivalent commands, 990-991
  File Manager menus
    Edit, menu-equivalent commands, 348, 354, 1017
    File, menu-equivalent commands, 348, 1016
    Options, menu-equivalent commands, 348, 1019
    Print, menu-equivalent commands, 348, 355, 1018

INDEX

Sort, menu-equivalent commands, 348, 1017
Tree, menu-equivalent commands, 348, 1017
Window, menu-equivalent commands, 348, 356-360, 1019-1020
Graph, 432-434
  menu-equivalent commands, 995-1002
menu bar, 58
Options, 698-701
  menu-equivalent commands, 1010-1018
Print, 390
  menu-equivalent commands, 1003-1005
quitting menu selections, 70
Style enhancement capabilities, 199
Print Manager menus,
  File, 867
  Queue, 868
  Job, 868-869
  Window, 869-870
Style enhancement capabilities, 168-170, 199
  menu-equivalent commands, 993-994
  undoing commands, 170
Tools, 612-613
  menu-equivalent commands, 1006-1010
/Tools Macro, 651-652
Window, 323, 356-366, 383, 932-935
MESSAGES macro command, 979
microprocessor, 939
Microsoft Windows, installing Quattro Pro for use with, 952
@MID string function, 242, 245
@MIN statistical function, 236-238
@MINUTE date and time function, 283-285

miscellaneous @function commands, 250-253
  @@, 252-253
  @CELL, 252-254
  @CELLINDEX, 252-254
  @CELLPOINTER, 252, 255
  @CHOOSE, 252, 255
  @COLS, 253, 256
  @CURVALUE, 253
  @ERR, 253
  @HLOOKUP, 253, 257-258
  @INDEX, 253, 258
  @ISAAF, 259
  @ISAPP, 260
  @MEMAVAIL, 253, 260
  @MEMEMSAVAIL, 253, 260
  @NA, 253, 261
  @ROWS, 253, 261
  @VERSION, 253, 262
  @VLOOKUP, 253, 262-263
macro command category, 966
@MOD arithmetic function, 229-231
modes
  default display, selecting during installation, 951
  display, setting options, 724-725
  indicators, 67-68
  indicators, 66-67
    BKGD, 66
    DEBUG, 67, 674-676, 679-680
    EDIT, 21, 60-62, 67, 109
    ERROR, 67
    FIND, 67
    FRMT, 67
    HELP, 67
    LABEL, 18, 67
    MACRO, 67
    MENU, 17, 68
    POINT, 68
    READY, 59-62, 65, 68
    REC, 68

VALUE, 18, 68
WAIT, 68
screen display mode, 114
switching, 74-75
WYSIWYG, 74
monitors, selecting during installation, 948
@MONTH date and time function, 283-285
mortgage interest payments, solving for, 302-304
mouse, 56-57, 80, 944
Move (Shift-F8) function key, 55
MOVE (Shift-F8) macro function instruction, 671
Move button (READY mode SpeedBar), 129
MOVE macro command, 979
moving
  cell
    blocks, 133
    data, 124, 128-129, 132, 162
  data
    with Move button on READY mode SpeedBar, 129
    within spreadsheets, 27
  design elements when annotating graphs, 524
  linking formulas, 372-373
  through File Manager window, 348
  windows, 358-360
moving average graphs, 542, 555-557
  creating table of moving average values, 560-561
  performing with multiple series, 558-560
  troubleshooting tips, 569
multiple print jobs, monitoring, 424-425
multiplying matrices, 618
multivariable
  linear equations, solving, 616

problems, *see* nonlinear problems

N

@N string function, 242, 246
@NA miscellaneous function, 253, 261
NAME (F3) macro function instruction, 671
NAME macro command, 979
naming
  cell blocks, 163-164
  graph files, 469
  macros, 659-661
    deleting names, 667
networks
  adding users, 1044-1046
  drive mappings, 738
  installing Quattro Pro on, 1031, 1034, 1037, 1040-1046, 1048
    choosing source drive/destination directory, 1034
    copying program files, 1035
    hardware/software requirements, 1032-1033
    preinstallation procedures, 1033-1034
  printing, 1049
    identifying jobs with banners, 739
    setting default user name, 739
    setting options, 737
  using Quattro Pro on, 1047-1049
Next Window (Shift-F6) function key, 55
NEXTWIN (Shift-F6) macro function instruction, 671
NEXTWIN macro command, 979

INDEX

nonlinear problems, 634
not equal (<>) operator, 591
#NOT# logical operator, 591
@NOW date and time function, 283, 286
@NPER financial function, 269-270, 275
@NPV financial function, 270, 276
Num Lock key, 52
Num Lock off {NUMOFF} status key macro instruction, 672
Num Lock on {NUMON} status key macro instruction, 672
NUM status indicator, 67
numbers (values), 88-90
Numeric Format menu, displaying, 179
numeric
    formats, 176, 251
        custom, 211-215
        symbols, 212
    keypad, 52
    value (@function command argument), 227
NUMOFF (Num Lock off) status key macro instruction, 672
NUMOFF macro command, 979
NUMON (Num Lock on) status key macro instruction, 672
NUMON macro command, 979
@NUMTOHEX string function, 242, 246

O

ONERROR macro command, 980
OPEN macro command, 980
opening
    files, 17, 329-330
        automatically at startup, 727-728
    linked spreadsheets, 373
operators in search formulas, 591

optimization analysis, 634
Optimizer, 5, 634-635
    producing reports, 643
    setting
        constraints/defining multiple variables, 640-641
        options, 641-642
    solving basic problems, 637-639
    troubleshooting tips, 646
/Options Colors command, 712, 911-912
/Options Colors Conditional command, 715
/Options Colors Conditional On/Off Disable command, 745
/Options Colors Desktop command, 714, 1028
/Options Colors File command, 716
/Options Colors Help command, 716
/Options Colors Menu command, 714
/Options Colors Menu Key Letter command, 712
/Options Colors Menu Shadow command, 1028
/Options Colors Menu SpeedBar command, 714
/Options Colors Palettes command, 717
/Options Colors Spreadsheet command, 714
/Options Colors Spreadsheet Shading command, 203, 709
/Options Colors Spreadsheet WYSIWYG Colors Grid Lines command, 222
/Options Colors Spreadsheet WYSIWYG Colors Titles Background command, 363
/Options Display Mode command, 114, 392, 478, 487,

537, 540, 724-725, 745, 912-913
/Options Display Mode A: 80x25 command, 646, 704
/Options Display Mode B:WYSIWYG command, 477
/Options File List command, 351
/Options Formats Numeric Format command, 917-918
/Options Formats Align Labels command, 741, 914
/Options Formats default settings, 171
/Options Formats Global Width command, 189, 742, 914-915
/Options Formats Hide Zeros command, 741, 747, 916
/Options Formats Numeric Format command, 741
/Options Formats Numeric Format Date command, 720
/Options Graphics Quality command, 413, 734, 919
/Options Graphics Quality Draft command, 479
/Options Hardware command, 701, 919-921
/Options Hardware Printers command, 417, 705
/Options Hardware Printers 1st Printer Type of Printer command, 1044
/Options Hardware Printers 2nd Printer command, 706, 746
/Options Hardware Printers Background command, 423, 711
/Options Hardware Printers Default Printer command, 435, 746
/Options Hardware Printers Fonts Cartridge Fonts command, 709
/Options Hardware Screen command, 702
/Options Hardware Screen Aspect Ratio command, 479
/Options Hardware Screen Resolution command, 435
/Options Hardware Screen Screen Type command, 746, 1045
/Options International command, 172, 717, 921-923
/Options International Currency command, 719, 1027
/Options International Date command, 180, 720
/Options International LICS Conversion command, 723
/Options International Negative Parentheses command, 719
/Options International Negative Signs command, 719
/Options International Punctuation command, 720
/Options International Time command, 182, 721, 736
/Options International Use Sort Table command, 721
Options menu, 698-701
    menu-equivalent commands, 1010-1018
/Options Network command, 737, 739, 923-924
/Options Network Drive Mappings command, 737
/Options Network Queue Monitor command, 739
/Options Network Refresh Interval command, 425, 739
/Options Network User Name command, 739
/Options Other Clock command, 737
/Options Other command, 924-925
/Options Other Expanded Memory command, 736, 746
/Options Other Expanded Memory Both command, 604

INDEX

/Options Other Paradox Network Type Other command, 605
/Options Other Undo command, 746
/Options Other Undo Enable command, 26, 111, 135
/Options Protection command, 925-926
/Options Protection Enable command, 186
/Options Protection Formulas Add command, 187
/Options Protection Formulas Protect command, 744
/Options Protection Formulas Remove command, 187
/Options Recalculation command, 315, 643, 647, 926-928
/Options Recalculation Iteration command, 743
/Options Recalculation Mode command, 111, 117, 742
/Options Recalculation Mode Automatic command, 747
/Options Recalculation Order command, 743
/Options Recalculation Mode Manual command, 735
/Options SpeedBar command, 731, 910-911
/Options Startup command, 726, 928-929
/Options Startup Autoload File command, 606, 727-728
/Options Startup Directory command, 335, 382, 727, 1045
/Options Startup File Extension command, 337, 729
/Options Startup Menu Tree command, 730, 1041, 1046
/Options Startup Menu Tree 123.MU command, 695
/Options Startup Startup Macro command, 660, 694, 729
/Options Startup Use Dialog Boxes command, 486, 505, 513, 731
/Options Update command, 111, 345, 382, 584, 605, 667, 694, 717, 726, 929-930, 1027
/Options Values command, 699, 930
/Options WYSIWYG Zoom % command, 357, 931
#OR# logical operator, 591
order of precedence (formulas), 97-98
organizing windows on-screen, 357
   enlarging/shrinking, 358
   moving/sizing, 358-360
   tiling/stacking, 358
output blocks, during database searches, 595-596, 599
OVR status indicator, 67

P

page
   breaks
      controlling printing, 219
      deleting, 220
      inserting, 219
      soft, suppressing, 400
   dimensions, defining, 403
   orientation, printing, 403-404
Pane (F6) function key, 55
PANELOFF macro command, 980
PANELON macro command, 980
panning graphs, 473
Paradox
   accessing, troubleshooting tips, 608
   running Quattro Pro databases, 601-606
parameters, Quattro Pro special start-up parameters, 49
parsing, 611, 618-620

advanced operations, 623-626
  multiple operations, 623
  troubleshooting tips, 645
password-protecting files, 333-335
Paste (Shift-F10) function key, 56
PASTE (Shift-F10) macro function instruction, 671
PASTE macro command, 981
pasting macros into spreadsheets, 654-656
path names for directories, setting, 335
@PAYMT financial function, 269-270, 276
PDXGO macro command, 981
Period (.) key, 51
personal signature data, 1035
PgDn {PGDN} macro instruction, 670
PgDn key, 52, 110
PGDN macro command, 981
PgUp {PGUP} macro instruction, 670
PgUp key, 52, 110
PGUP macro command, 981
@PI arithmetic function, 233-235
Pick Window (Shift-F5) function key, 55
pie graphs, 443
  customizing, 499-502
  exploding, 443
  slices, 443
pixels, 704
PLAY macro command, 981
plotter speed, setting, 708
@PMT financial function, 270, 277
POINT mode, 68
@PPAYMT financial function, 270, 278
predefined fonts, customizing, 218-219
preselecting cell blocks, 453
preselecting cells, 124
/Print Adjust Printer command, 409-410, 851-852
/Print Block command, 392, 852-854
/Print Copies command, 408, 854
/Print Destination command, 391, 405, 417, 854-856
/Print Destination Binary File command, 413
/Print Destination File command, 411
/Print Destination Graphics Printer command, 203, 400, 477
/Print Destination Screen Preview command, 856-857
/Print Format command, 407, 858
/Print Graph Print command, 859-860
/Print Graph Print Layout command, 480, 860-861
/Print Graph Print Name command, 417
/Print Headings command, 395, 398, 862-863
/Print Layout command, 863-866
/Print Layout Break Pages command, 400
/Print Layout dialog box, 396
/Print Layout Dimensions command, 403
/Print Layout Footer command, 398
/Print Layout Header command, 398
/Print Layout Margins command, 401
/Print Layout Margins Page Length command, 219
/Print Layout Orientation command, 404
/Print Layout Percent Scaling command, 400

INDEX

/Print Layout Reset command, 395, 406
/Print Layout Setup String command, 405
/Print Layout Update command, 395, 406
/Print Layout Values command, 397
Print Manager window, 424-426
Print menu, 390
    File Manager, 356
        menu-equivalent commands, 1003-1005
/Print Print Manager command, 424, 866-867
/Print Print Manager /File command, 867
/Print Print Manager /Job command, 868-869
/Print Print Manager /Queue command, 868
/Print Print Manager /Window command, 869-870
/Print Print-To-Fit command, 400, 410, 870-871
/Print Range command, 341
/Print Spreadsheet Print command, 871
/Printer Layout Setup String command, 1028-1029
printers
    choosing during installation, 705-711
    graphics, printing spreadsheet reports to, 413
    selecting during installation, 950
    setup strings, converting ASCII codes into, 1028-1029
    supported by Quattro Pro, 943
    troubleshooting tips, 746
printing
    background, 422-424, 711
    controlling with page breaks, 219
    copies of Transcript, 682
    graphics, setting quality options, 734
    graphs, 417, 428-429
        choosing destination, 418
        positioning/shaping, 420-421
        setting graph margins, 419
        special graph files, 421
    identifying jobs with banners, 739
    lines within spreadsheets, 202
    multiple jobs, monitoring, 424-425
    on network printers, 1049
    single sheets, 710
    spreadsheet reports, 392-395, 427-428
        adding headers/footers, 398-399
        adjusting printer, 409-410
        choosing display format, 407
        choosing print settings, 395-397, 400
        controlling page breaks, 399
        defining page dimensions, 403
        fitting into single page, 410
        previewing printout on-screen, 414-417
        print settings, updating/resetting, 406
        selecting print orientation, 403-404
        setting margins, 401-403
        specifying number of copies, 408
        to binary files, 413
        to graphics printers, 413
        to text files, 411-412
        using setup strings, 404-406
    status of print jobs, changing, 426

1092 USING QUATTRO PRO 4, SPECIAL EDITION

program flow macro command
  category, 968, 972-973, 976,
  980-985
@PROPER string function, 242,
  246
property sheet (Graph
  Annotator screen), 519
protecting spreadsheet
  formulas, 744-745
  data, 185-187
PrtSc* key, 52
pull-down menu bar, 58
PUT macro command, 981
@PV financial function, 270, 278
@PVAL financial function,
  269-270, 279

Q

\QPRO directory, 48
QPRO.SOM file, 1037
QPUPDATE.EXE program, 1037
Quattro Pro
  ending work sessions, 49
  features, 3-5
  installing, 944, 953
    character set, selecting,
      952
    copying files, 945, 948
    default display mode,
      selecting, 951
    for use with Microsoft
      Windows, 952
    hard disk drives,
      managing, 943
    hardware/software
      requirements, 938-939
    math coprocessor chip,
      939
    microprocessor clock
      speed, 939-940
    monitor type, selecting,
      948
    on networks, 1031-1037,
      1040-1048

    printers, 950
    random-access memory
      (RAM), managing, 940-943
    video displays/printers
      supported, 943
  loading, 79, 955
  menus and menu-equivalent
    commands, 990
    Database menu, 1005-1006
    Edit menu, 991-993
    File Manager Edit menu,
      1019
    File Manager File menu,
      1018
    File Manager Options
      menu, 1021
    File Manager Print menu,
      1020
    File Manager Sort menu,
      1019
    File Manager Window
      menu, 1022
    File menu, 990-991
    Graph menu, 995-1002
    Options menu, 1010-1018
    Print menu, 1003-1005
    Style menu, 993-994
    Tools menu, 1006-1010
  quitting, 955
  reconfiguring, 955
  running databases from
    within Paradox, 601-606
  starting, 49
    from workstations, 1044
  upgrading to Version 4.0,
    956-957, 1046
  using on a network, 1047-1049
QUATTRO.LOG file, 682, 689
Query (F7) function key, 55
QUERY (F7) macro function
  instruction, 671
QUERY macro command, 982
Queue Monitor, 739
QUIT macro command, 663, 982

INDEX

quitting
   menu selections, 70
   Quattro Pro, 955

R

@RADIANS arithmetic function, 233, 235
@RAND arithmetic function, 229-231
random-access memory (RAM), managing, 940-943
@RATE financial function, 270, 279
READ macro command, 982
READDIR (F9) macro function instruction, 671
READDIR macro command, 982
READLN macro command, 982
READY mode, 59-60, 68
   input line, 62
   SpeedBar, 59-60
   status line, 65
REC mode, 68
RECALC macro command, 983
RECALCCOL macro command, 983
recalculating spreadsheets, 742-743
   troubleshooting tips, 747
reconfiguring
   Quattro Pro, 955
   SpeedBar, 699
recording macros, 653
   executing last recorded macro, 658
   pasting into spreadsheets, 654-656
   switching macro recording mode, 658
   troubleshooting tips, 693
records, 575
   deleting when searching databases, 593

extracting when searching databases, 596
locating when searching databases, 592-593
regression analysis, 611-616
relative reference format, 101
@REPEAT string function, 242, 247
@REPLACE string function, 242, 247
Resize box, 76
resolution, 704
resource file, saving startup options to, 740
RESTART macro command, 983
retrieving files, 330
RETURN macro command, 983
RIGHT (→) macro instruction, 670
RIGHT macro command, 984
@RIGHT string function, 242, 247
rotated bar graphs, 444
@ROUND arithmetic function, 229, 232
rows, 40, 221
   deleting, 135-137, 163
      blocks, 141
      with Delete button on READY mode SpeedBar, 138
   entering row headings in spreadsheets, 19
   inserting, 135-137, 163
      blocks, 140
      into spreadsheets, 34
      with Insert button on READY mode SpeedBar, 137
   removing row borders from windows, 364
   setting height, 195-196
      automatically, 198-199
      for multiple rows, 198
@ROWS miscellaneous function, 253, 261

S

@S string function, 242, 248
saving
   custom styles, 216
   files, 331-332
   graph files, 469
   spreadsheets
      dBASE file format, 338-339
      Lotus 1-2-3 file format, 339
   to hard drive, 35
SCR status indicator, 67
screen display, 57
   input line, 62
   pull-down menu bar, 58
   SpeedBar, 58
      EDIT mode, 61
      READY mode, 59-60
   spreadsheet area, 64-65
   status line, 65-67
screen dumps, 392
screen macro command category, 967, 976, 980, 986
Screen Preview feature, 200, 414-416
screens
   choosing new screens, 702-705
   Graph Annotator, 518-520
   organizing windows, 357
      enlarging/shrinking, 358
      moving/sizing, 358-360
      tiling/stacking, 358
   pixels, 704
   resolution, 704
   selecting display mode, 114
scroll bars, 65
Scroll Lock off {SCROLLOFF} status key macro instruction, 672
Scroll Lock on {SCROLLON} status key macro instruction, 672
Scroll Lock/Break key, 52
SCROLLOFF (Scroll Lock off) status key macro instruction, 672
SCROLLOFF macro command, 984
SCROLLON (Scroll Lock on) status key macro instruction, 672
SCROLLON macro command, 984
search formulas, 590
searching
   databases, 586, 592
      assigning names to field names rows, 588
      defining search block, 587
      defining search criteria, 588-592
      deleting records, 593
      locating records, 592-593
      setting up output blocks, 595-596, 599
      troubleshooting tips, 607
@SECOND date and time function, 283, 286
Select (Shift-F7) function key, 55, 426
Select All (Alt-F7) shortcut key, 426
sensitivity
   analysis, 611, 628-631
      one-way analysis, 628
      two-way analysis, 629-631
      troubleshooting tips, 646
   tables, 44, 628
serial number, recording when installing Quattro Pro, 1037
SETPOS macro command, 984
setup strings, 404-406
shading data in spreadsheets, 203-204
Shift key keys, 51
   Shift-F2 {STEP} macro function instruction, 671

INDEX

Shift-F3 (Macro List), 666
Shift-F3 {MACROS} macro function instruction, 671
Shift-F5 (Pick Window), 54
Shift-F5 {CHOOSE} macro function instruction, 671
Shift-F6 (Next Window), 357
Shift-F6 {NEXTWIN} macro function instruction, 671
Shift-F7 {MARK} macro function instruction, 671
Shift-F8 {MOVE} macro function instruction, 671
Shift-F9 {COPY} macro function instruction, 671
Shift-F10 {PASTE} macro function instruction, 671
Shift-Tab {BACKTAB} macro instruction, 670
Shift-Tab, 110
shrinking windows, 358
SideKick, 940
@SIN arithmetic function, 233-235
sizing windows, 358-360
slash (/) key, 51, 68, 80
slices
   column graphs, 446
   pie graphs, 443
slide show, displaying graphs in, 474-475
   sound effects, 476
   visual transitions, 475
@SLN command, 298
@SLN financial function, 270, 280
smoothing, 555
soft page breaks, suppressing, 400
software requirements, for installing Quattro Pro, 938-939
sort keys, 579-582
sorting
   databases, 578, 583-584
      by columns, 584
         returning to original sort order, 583

   troubleshooting tips, 607
   with multiple sort keys, 581-582
   with one sort key, 580
Sound Blaster Pro, 476
sound effects, adding to graph slide shows, 476
SpeedBar, 2-4, 58-59, 74, 80
   accessing
      list of custom styles, 807
      /Style Font menu, 206
      Zoom icon, 76
   adding
      menu-equivalent instructions to macros, 667
      notes to named blocks, 147
   adjusting active column, 189
   assigning new functions to SpeedBar buttons, 910
   Bar button, 911
   beginning
      delete column block operation, 142
      delete row block operation, 141
      insert column block operation, 142
      insert row block operation, 140
   changing
      cell's alignment, 174
      cell's reference from relative to absolute, 104
      color of SpeedBar buttons, 911
   checking column justification, 620
   copying data, 126
   customizing, 731-733
   deleting
      cell block names, 146-147
      columns, 139
      rows, 138

displaying
    list of @function
        commands, 101, 228
    list of custom styles, 211
    list of named blocks, 142
EDIT mode, 60-61
erasing data, 133
inserting
    columns, 138
    rows, 137
moving data, 129
naming cell blocks, 143-145
    adding notes to names,
        147-149
    making table of names,
        151-152
    resetting names, 150
    using names in formulas,
        153
    with labels, 149
READY mode, 59-60
reconfiguring, 699
switching to text display
    mode, 76
troubleshooting tips, 80-81
Zoom icon, 76
splitting windows into panes, 361
spreadsheet area, 64-65
spreadsheets, 83, 328
    adding
        bullets, 206-208
        lines, 200-201
    aligning labels in cells, 741
    building databases, 46
    cells, 40
        aligning data within, 29-31
        alignment, changing, 174
        entering ASCII characters
            into, 1023
    choosing spreadsheet colors,
        714
    columns, 40, 221
        adjusting widths, 28
        deleting with Delete button
            on READY mode
            SpeedBar, 139
        hiding/revealing, 193-195
        inserting, 34
            with Insert button on
                READY mode
                SpeedBar, 138
        setting width, 188-189
            of multiple columns,
                190-193
        specifying width, 741
    constructing, 45
    copying formulas, 23
    creating graphs, 46
    data
        aligning, 172-175
        formatting, 175, 184, 220
            dates, 180-182
            labels, 180
            numeric formats,
                176-177
            times, 182-184
            values, 178-179
        protecting blocks of cells,
            185
        ptotecting globally, 186-187
        searching and replacing,
            159-162
        shading cell data, 203-204
        unprotecting, 186
    deleting
        columns, 135, 139
        rows, 135-137
    designing, 42
    displaying
        list of @function
            commands, 24
        values in, 741
    drawing lines around, 32
    editing data within, 26,
        109-110, 118
        in EDIT mode, 26
        recalculating formulas,
            111-112
        with Alt-F5 (Undo) key, 27,
            111
    entering data into, 18-22,
        84-85

INDEX

@function commands, 99-101
  entering column/row headings, 19
  entering report titles, 19
  labels, 86-88
  values, 89-98
entering formulas into, 22-23
erasing lines from, 201-202
filling data, 164
formatting numbers, 31-32
formatting with custom styles, 209-210
  creating custom numeric formats, 211-215
  deleting custom styles, 215
  editing custom styles, 217
  retrieving style sheet to active spreadsheet, 216
  saving styles in files, 216
formulas, auditing, 310
  blank reference audit, 320
  circular audits, 314-316
  dependency audits, 311-314
  ERR audit, 318-319
  external links, 320-321
  label reference audits, 317-318
global format settings for data entries, 170-172
inserting
  columns, 135, 138-139
  graphs onto, 477-478
  rows, 135-137
labels, entering, 116
linked, 367
  creating 3-D consolidation formulas, 369-372
  creating linking formulas, 368, 371
  loading, 374-375
  moving/copying linking formulas, 372-373
  opening/updating, 373
  typing linking formulas, 368-369

  updating links, 375-376
moving data within, 27
pasting macros into, 654-656
previewing Style menu enhancements, 199
printing, 392-395, 427-428
  adding headers/footers, 398-399
  adjusting printer, 409-410
  choosing display format, 407
  choosing print settings, 395-397, 400
  controlling page breaks, 399
  defining page dimensions, 403
  fitting into single page, 410
  lines, 202
  previewing printout on-screen, 414-417
  print settings, updating/resetting, 406
  selecting print orientation, 403-404
  setting margins, 401-403
  specifying number of copies, 408
  to binary files, 413
  to graphics printers, 413
  to text files, 411-412
  using setup strings, 404-406
protecting formulas, 744-745
recalculating, 742-743
  troubleshooting tips, 747
rows, 40, 221
  deleting with Delete button on READY mode SpeedBar, 138
  inserting, 34
    with Insert button on READY mode SpeedBar, 137
  setting height, 195-196
    automatically, 198-199

      for multiple rows, 198
saving
   in dBASE file format,
     338-339
   in Lotus 1-2-3 file format,
     339
   to hard drive, 35
searching and replacing data, 164
selecting fonts for, 204-205
storing macros in, 661
translating, 336
   into Allways file formats, 342
   into dBASE file formats, 338
   into Harvard Graphics file formats, 344
   into Impress file formats, 343
   into Lotus 1-2-3 file formats, 339-341
transposing data, 156-157, 164
turning into databases, 574-576
values, entering, 117
viewing, 112
   data, 118
   data in graph form, 435
what-if analysis on, 43
@SQRT arithmetic function, 229, 232
stacked-bar graphs, 442
stacking windows, 358
start values, 154
starting
   Quattro Pro, 49
     from workstations, 1044
     special start-up parameters, 49
startup options, setting, 726
   automatically opening file at startup, 727-728
   choosing menu tree displayed, 730
   default directory, 727

running macros automatically when retrieving spreadsheets, 729
saving to resource file, 740
selecting new default file extensions, 729
specifying beep tones, 729
statistical @function commands, 236-240
status
   box (Graph Annotator screen), 520
   indicators, 67
     CALC, 67
     CAP, 67
     CIRC, 67
     END, 67
     EXT, 67
     NUM, 67
     OVR, 67
     SCR, 67
   line, 65-67
@STD statistical function, 236-238
@STDS statistical function, 236-238
STEP (Shift-F2) macro function instruction, 671
STEP macro command, 984
STEPOFF macro command, 984
STEPON macro command, 984
storing macros
   in macro library, 661, 663-665
   in spreadsheets, 661
string @function commands, 240-249
@STRING string function, 242, 248
string value (@function command argument), 227
/Style Alignment command, 89, 116, 169-170, 173, 220, 790-791
/Style Alignment Center command, 29
/Style Block Size command, 169, 190, 791-792

/Style Block Size Auto Width command, 189
/Style Block Size Height command, 792-793
/Style Block Size Height Set Row Height command, 195-196
/Style Block Size Set Width command, 190
Style button
 READY mode SpeedBar, 211
 SpeedBar, 807
/Style Column Width command, 28, 90, 169, 188, 575, 657
/Style Column Width/Reset Width command, 793-794
/Style Define Style command, 170, 209, 794-796
/Style Define Style Create command, 211, 217
/Style Define Style Create Numeric Format command, 796
/Style Define Style File Retrieve command, 216
/Style Define Style File Save command, 216
/Style Font command, 170, 204-208, 797-798, 956, 1045
/Style Font Color command, 203
/Style Font menu, accessing, 206
/Style FontTable command, 170, 218, 205-206, 798-799, 956, 1045
/Style FontTable Edit Fonts command, 405, 957
/Style FontTable Update command, 197, 219
/Style Hide Column command, 169, 193, 799-801
/Style Hide Column Expose command, 194
/Style Insert Break command, 170, 219, 800-801
/Style Line Drawing command, 33, 169, 179, 200, 665, 801-802
/Style Line Drawing Outside command, 88, 195
Style menu, 168-170
 enhancement capabilities, 199
 menu-equivalent commands, 993-994
 undoing commands, 170
/Style Numeric Format command, 31, 90, 169, 175, 179, 508, 672, 717, 741, 802-805
/Style Numeric Format Currency command, 89, 717, 1027
/Style Numeric Format Date command, 182
/Style Numeric Format Date Time command, 184
/Style Numeric Format General command, 646
/Style Numeric Format Reset command, 180, 184
/Style Protection command, 169, 185, 805
/Style Protection Unprotect command, 599
/Style Reset Width command, 169, 189
/Style Shading command, 169, 203, 806
/Style Use Style command, 170, 210-212, 343, 806-807
SUBROUTINE macro command, 985
subroutines in macro programs, 964
subtracting data when combining files, 380
@SUM statistical function, 236, 239
@SUMPRODUCT statistical function, 236, 239
SuperKey program, 940, 1027
switches, 728
switching modes, 74-75
@SYD financial function, 270, 280
syntax, displaying syntax information for @function commands, 291

system configuration, 957-958
   setting up, 938

T

Tab {TAB} macro instruction, 670
Tab key, 51, 110
TAB macro command, 985
Table (F8) function key, 55
TABLE (F8) macro function instruction, 671
TABLE macro command, 985
@TAN arithmetic function, 233, 236
@TERM financial function, 270, 281
text
   files, printing spreadsheet reports to, 411-412
   formulas, 95
   graphs, 447
tick marks, 438, 502
tilde (~), 11
tiling windows, 358
@TIME date and time function, 283, 286
time formats, 182-184, 252
time-series analysis, *see* moving average graphs
@TIMEVALUE date and time function, 283, 286
@TODAY date and time function, 283, 287
Toggles Ins {INS} status key macro instruction, 672
/Tool Import command, 377
toolbox (Graph Annotator screen), 519
/Tools Advanced Math Invert command, 617, 888
/Tools Advanced Math Multiply command, 618, 889
/Tools Advanced Math Optimization command, 635
/Tools Advanced Math Regression command, 614
/Tools Audit command
   auditing spreadsheet formulas, 310
      blank reference audit, 320
      circular audits, 314-316
      dependency audits, 311-314
      ERR audit, 318-319
      external links, 320-321
      label reference audits, 317-318, 891-893
   tips for auditing formulas, 323, 309-310
/Tools Combine command, 378, 889-891
/Tools Combine Add command, 380
/Tools Combine Copy command, 378-379
/Tools Frequency command, 633, 893-894
/Tools Import command, 894-896
/Tools Library command, 644, 896-897
/Tools Library Load command, 644
/Tools Library Unload command, 644
/Tools Macro command, 897-898
/Tools Macro Clear Breakpoints command, 680
/Tools Macro Debugger command, 681
/Tools Macro Execute command, 664-665, 674
/Tools Macro Instant Replay command, 659, 693
/Tools Macro Key Reader command, 667
/Tools Macro Library command, 664, 694
/Tools Macro Macro Recording command, 658

/Tools Macro Macro Recording
   Logical command, 695
/Tools Macro menu, 651-652
/Tools Macro Name command,
   659-661, 688, 693-694
/Tools Macro Name Delete
   command, 667
/Tools Macro Paste command,
   655, 688
/Tools Macro Record command,
   650, 653, 669
/Tools Macro Macro Recording
   Logical command, 683, 693,
   990
/Tools Macro Transcript
   command, 682-684
/Tools Macro Transcript Failure
   Protection command, 691
/Tools Macro Transcript Max
   History Length command,
   689, 692-694
/Tools Macro Transcript
   Playback Block command,
   687-688
/Tools Macro Transcript
   Restore command, 686
/Tools Macro Transcript Single
   Step command, 690
Tools menu, 612-613
   menu-equivalent commands,
      1006-1010
/Tools Optimizer command,
   635-637, 640, 898-901
/Tools Optimizer Answer Report
   command, 643
/Tools Optimizer Constraint(s)
   command, 647
/Tools Optimizer Detail Report
   command, 643
/Tools Optimizer Model
   command, 644
/Tools Optimizer Reset
   command, 644
/Tools Optimizer Reset
   Constraints command, 647
/Tools Optimizer Restore
   command, 639, 643
/Tools Parse command, 377,
   618-620, 901-902
/Tools Parse Create command,
   621, 625, 646
/Tools Reformat command,
   903-904
/Tools Solve For command,
   296-297
   rules for using, 297-298
   solving for depreciation
      expenses, 298-299
   solving for investment
      returns, 301-302
   solving for mortgage interest
      payments, 302-304
   solving for what-if analysis,
      305, 309
   tips for solving formulas, 322,
      904-905
/Tools Update Links command,
   375, 661, 905-906
/Tools What-If command,
   906-908
/Tools What-If 1 Variable
   command, 629
/Tools What-If 2 Variables
   command, 630
/Tools Xtract command, 381,
   908-909
trace cells, 674
   defining, 678-679
   resetting, 680
tracking speed, 57
Transcript facility, 650, 682
   copying part of, 688
   determining speed of replay,
      690
   establishing number of
      keystrokes stored, 689
   exiting, 692
   Failure Protection facility, 691
   manipulating data stored in,
      684-685

playing back part of, 687
restoring part of, 686-687
reviewing current entries in
  log, 682-683
troubleshooting tips, 694
undoing last command, 685
translating
  spreadsheets, 336
    into Allways file formats,
      342
    into dBASE file formats, 338
    into Harvard Graphics file
      formats, 344
    into Impress file formats,
      343
    into Lotus 1-2-3 file
      formats, 339-341
transposing spreadsheet data,
  156-157, 164-165
/Tree Close command, 354
/Tree Open command, 352
tree pane (File Manager), 353
/Tree Resize command, 353
@TRIM string function, 242, 248
troubleshooting tips
  accessing Paradox, 608
  aggregation analysis, 568
  auditing formulas, 323
  cell referencing, 117
  columns
    deleting, 163
    inserting, 163
    working with, 221
  controlling display of data,
    220-221
  copying data, 162-163
  displaying windows, 383
  entering
    labels, 115-117
    values, 117
  erasing data, 162-163
  executing macros, 693-695
  filling data, 164-165
  @function commands
    displaying syntax
      information, 291

    forms, 292
    negative values in financial
      functions, 292
    remembering origin of
      arguments used in, 292
  graphs
    creating, 478-479
    customizing, 536-539
    displaying, 479-481
    enhancing appearance, 479
  installing Quattro Pro
    ideal system configuration,
      957-958
    problems with installation
      utility, 958-959
  linking worksheets, 383
  managing files, 382
  matrices, working with, 645
  memory shortages, 745
  moving
    averages analysis, 569
    data, 162-163
  naming cell blocks, 163-164
  Optimizer, working with, 646
  parsing data, 645
  presentation quality options,
    222-223
  printers, 746
  printing
    graphs, 428-429
    spreadsheet, 427-428
  recalculating spreadsheets,
    747
  recording macros, 693
  replacing data, 164-165
  rows
    deleting, 163
    inserting, 163
    working with, 221
  searching
    databases, 607
    for data, 164-165
  sensitivity analysis, 646
  solving formulas with /Tools
    Solve For command, 322

INDEX

sorting databases, 607
SpeedBar, 80-81
Transcript window, 694
transposing data, 164-165
viewing data, 118
zero value cells, 747
@TRUE logical function, 264, 267

U

UNDO macro command, 985
Undo (Alt-F5) function key, 55, 111
UNDO (Alt-F5) macro function instruction, 671
unsynchronizing window panes, 362
UP (↑) macro instruction, 670
UP macro command, 985
updating
    linked spreadsheets, 373
    spreadsheet links, 375-376
upgrading to Version 4.0, 956-957, 1046
@UPPER string function, 242, 249
user name, setting default, 739
users, adding to networks, 1044-1046

V

VALUE mode, 18, 68
@VALUE string function, 242, 249
values, 18, 84, 89
    changing formulas to, 154
    date-and-time entries, 88, 98
    entering, 117
    formatting, 178-179
    formulas, 88, 91-94
        arithmetic, 94
        logical, 96
        order of precedence, 97-98
    text, 95
    numbers, 88-90
@VAR statistical function, 236, 240
@VARS statistical function, 236, 240
@VERSION miscellaneous function, 253, 262
video displays supported by Quattro Pro, 943
viewing
    data within spreadsheets, 118
    spreadsheets, 112
Virtual Real-Time Object-Oriented Memory Manager (VROOMM), 941
visual transitions, adding to graph slide shows, 475
@VLOOKUP miscellaneous function, 253, 262-263

W

WAIT macro command, 986
WAIT mode, 68
what-if analysis
    on spreadsheets, 43
    solving for, 305, 309
wild cards, utilizing in defining search criteria, 591
Window (F6) function key, 114
/Window command, 932-933
WINDOW macro command, 986
/Window Move/Size command, 76, 358-359
/Window Options command, 356, 933-935
/Window Options Clear command, 361-362, 383
/Window Options Grid Lines command, 366
/Window Options Horizontal command, 361
/Window Options Locked Titles command, 600

/Window Options Map View command, 315, 323, 365
/Window Options Print Block to Display command, 417
/Window Options Row & Col Borders command, 364
/Window Options Sync command, 114, 362, 383
/Window Options Unsync command, 362, 383
/Window Options Vertical command, 361
/Window Pick command, 356
/Window Stack command, 358
/Window Tile command, 84, 114, 358
windows, 84, 328
   creating special display effects, 361
      clearing split window pane settings, 362
      locking titles, 362-363
      map view, 365
      removing row/column borders, 364
      splitting windows into panes, 361
      unsynchronizing window panes, 362
   displaying, 383
   File Manager, moving through, 348
   organizing on-screen, 357
      enlarging/shrinking, 358
      moving/sizing, 358-360
      tiling/stacking, 358
   Print Manager, 424-426
   Transcript, 694
WINDOWS (F6) macro function instruction, 671
WINDOWSOFF macro command, 986
WINDOWSON macro command, 986
work sessions
   ending sessions, 35, 49
   starting new sessions, 16
workspace, 84, 328
   files, creating, 336
workstations, preparing for Quattro Pro installation, 1039
WRITE macro command, 986
WRITELN macro command, 987
WYSIWYG, 2
   display mode, 74, 199
   Zoom % command, 724

X

/X command-line switch, 728
/x commands, 964-965
x-axis, 437
   customizing, 504
      adjusting axis ticks, 508-509
      adjusting scale of, 506-507
      changing display of, 509-511
XY graphs, 441

Y

y-axis, 437
   adding second y-axis to graphs, 497
   customizing, 504
      adjusting axis ticks, 508-509
      adjusting scale of, 506-507
      changing display of, 509-511
@YEAR date and time function, 283, 287

Z

z-axis, 448
zero value cells, 741
   troubleshooting tips, 747

INDEX

Zoom (Alt-F6) function key, 55
ZOOM (Alt-F6) macro function
  instruction, 671
Zoom icon, 76
ZOOM macro command, 987
zooming graphs, 473

Computer Books from Que Mean PC Performance!

Spreadsheets

1-2-3 Beyond the Basics	$24.95
1-2-3 Database Techniques	$29.95
1-2-3 for DOS Release 2.3 Quick Reference	$ 9.95
1-2-3 for DOS Release 2.3 QuickStart	$19.95
1-2-3 for Windows Quick Reference	$ 9.95
1-2-3 for Windows QuickStart	$19.95
1-2-3 Graphics Techniques	$24.95
1-2-3 Macro Library, 3rd Edition	$39.95
1-2-3 Release 2.2 PC Tutor	$39.95
1-2-3 Release 2.2 QueCards	$19.95
1-2-3 Release 2.2 Workbook and Disk	$29.95
1-2-3 Release 3 Workbook and Disk	$29.95
1-2-3 Release 3.1 Quick Reference	$ 8.95
1-2-3 Release 3.1 + QuickStart, 2nd Edition	$19.95
Excel for Windows Quick Reference	$ 9.95
Quattro Pro Quick Reference	$ 8.95
Quattro Pro 3 QuickStart	$19.95
Using 1-2-3/G	$29.95
Using 1-2-3 for DOS Release 2.3, Special Edition	$29.95
Using 1-2-3 for Windows	$29.95
Using 1-2-3 Release 3.1, + 2nd Edition	$29.95
Using Excel 3 for Windows, Special Edition	$29.95
Using Quattro Pro 3, Special Edition	$24.95
Using SuperCalc 5, 2nd Edition	$29.95

Databases

dBASE III Plus Handbook, 2nd Edition	$24.95
dBASE IV PC Tutor	$29.95
dBASE IV Programming Techniques	$29.95
dBASE IV Quick Reference	$ 8.95
dBASE IV 1.1 QuickStart	$19.95
dBASE IV Workbook and Disk	$29.95
Que's Using FoxPro	$29.95
Using Clipper, 2nd Edition	$29.95
Using DataEase	$24.95
Using dBASE IV	$29.95
Using ORACLE	$29.95
Using Paradox 3	$24.95
Using PC-File	$24.95
Using R:BASE	$29.95

Business Applications

Allways Quick Reference	$ 8.95
Introduction to Business Software	$14.95
Introduction to Personal Computers	$19.95
Norton Utilities Quick Reference	$ 8.95
PC Tools Quick Reference, 2nd Edition	$ 8.95
Q&A Quick Reference	$ 8.95
Que's Computer User's Dictionary, 2nd Edition	$10.95
Que's Using Enable	$29.95
Que's Wizard Book	$12.95
Quicken Quick Reference	$ 8.95
SmartWare Tips, Tricks, and Traps, 2nd Edition	$26.95
Using DacEasy, 2nd Edition	$24.95
Using Managing Your Money, 2nd Edition	$19.95
Using Microsoft Works: IBM Version	$22.95
Using Norton Utilities	$24.95
Using PC Tools Deluxe	$24.95
Using Peachtree	$27.95
Using PROCOMM PLUS, 2nd Edition	$24.95
Using Q&A 4	$27.95
Using Quicken: IBM Version, 2nd Edition	$19.95
Using SmartWare II	$29.95
Using Symphony, Special Edition	$29.95
Using TimeLine	$24.95
Using TimeSlips	$24.95

CAD

AutoCAD Quick Reference	$ 8.95
Que's Using Generic CADD	$29.95
Using AutoCAD, 3rd Edition	$29.95
Using Generic CADD	$24.95

Word Processing

Microsoft Word Quick Reference	$ 9.95
Using LetterPerfect	$22.95
Using Microsoft Word 5.5: IBM Version, 2nd Edition	$24.95
Using MultiMate	$24.95
Using PC-Write	$22.95
Using Professional Write	$22.95
Using Word for Windows	$24.95
Using WordPerfect 5	$27.95
Using WordPerfect 5.1, Special Edition	$27.95
Using WordStar, 3rd Edition	$27.95
WordPerfect PC Tutor	$39.95
WordPerfect Power Pack	$39.95
WordPerfect 5 Workbook and Disk	$29.95
WordPerfect 5.1 QueCards	$19.95
WordPerfect 5.1 Quick Reference	$ 8.95
WordPerfect 5.1 QuickStart	$19.95
WordPerfect 5.1 Tips, Tricks, and Traps	$24.95
WordPerfect 5.1 Workbook and Disk	$29.95

Hardware/Systems

DOS Tips, Tricks, and Traps	$24.95
DOS Workbook and Disk, 2nd Edition	$29.95
Fastback Quick Reference	$ 8.95
Hard Disk Quick Reference	$ 8.95
MS-DOS PC Tutor	$39.95
MS-DOS 5 Quick Reference	$ 9.95
MS-DOS 5 QuickStart, 2nd Edition	$19.95
MS-DOS 5 User's Guide, Special Edition	$29.95
Networking Personal Computers, 3rd Edition	$24.95
Understanding UNIX: A Conceptual Guide, 2nd Edition	$21.95
Upgrading and Repairing PCs	$29.95
Using Microsoft Windows 3, 2nd Edition	$24.95
Using MS-DOS 5	$24.95
Using Novell NetWare	$29.95
Using OS/2	$29.95
Using PC DOS, 3rd Edition	$27.95
Using Prodigy	$19.95
Using UNIX	$29.95
Using Your Hard Disk	$29.95
Windows 3 Quick Reference	$ 8.95

Desktop Publishing/Graphics

CorelDRAW! Quick Reference	$ 8.95
Harvard Graphics Quick Reference	$ 8.95
Que's Using Ventura Publisher	$29.95
Using Animator	$24.95
Using DrawPerfect	$24.95
Using Harvard Graphics, 2nd Edition	$24.95
Using Freelance Plus	$24.95
Using PageMaker 4 for Windows	$29.95
Using PFS: First Publisher, 2nd Edition	$24.95
Using PowerPoint	$24.95
Using Publish It!	$24.95

Macintosh/Apple II

The Big Mac Book, 2nd Edition	$29.95
The Little Mac Book	$12.95
Que's Macintosh Multimedia Handbook	$24.95
Using AppleWorks, 3rd Edition	$24.95
Using Excel 3 for the Macintosh	$24.95
Using FileMaker	$24.95
Using MacDraw	$24.95
Using MacroMind Director	$29.95
Using MacWrite	$24.95
Using Microsoft Word 4: Macintosh Version	$24.95
Using Microsoft Works: Macintosh Version, 2nd Edition	$24.95
Using PageMaker: Macintosh Version, 2nd Edition	$24.95

Programming/Technical

C Programmer's Toolkit	$39.95
DOS Programmer's Reference, 2nd Edition	$29.95
Network Programming in C	$49.95
Oracle Programmer's Guide	$29.95
QuickC Programmer's Guide	$29.95
UNIX Programmer's Quick Reference	$ 8.95
UNIX Programmer's Reference	$29.95
UNIX Shell Commands Quick Reference	$ 8.95
Using Assembly Language, 2nd Edition	$29.95
Using BASIC	$24.95
Using Borland C++	$29.95
Using C	$29.95
Using QuickBASIC 4	$24.95
Using Turbo Pascal	$29.95

For More Information, Call Toll Free!
1-800-428-5331

*All prices and titles subject to change without notice.
Non-U.S. prices may be higher. Printed in the U.S.A.*

Que—The Leader In Spreadsheet Information!

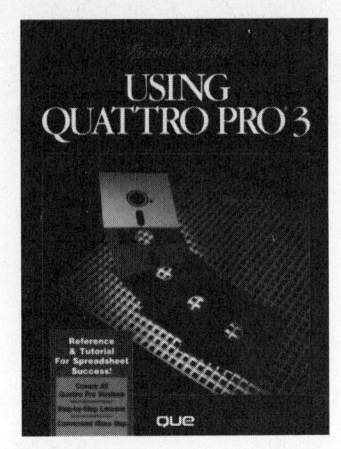

Using Quattro Pro 3, Special Edition

Patrick Burns

This complete, easy-to-follow introduction to Quattro Pro includes in-depth tutorials, tips, and a tear-out Menu Map.

Through Version 3

Order #1348 $27.95 USA
0-88022-721-4, 750 pp., 7 3/8 x 9 1/4

Using Excel 3 for Windows, Special Edition

Ron Person

This introduction to Excel includes **Quick Start** tutorials plus tips and tricks to help improve efficiency and trouble-shoot problems. It also provides advanced techniques for using Windows 3.

Version 3

Order #1297 $29.95 USA
0-88022-685-4, 984 pp., 7 3/8 x 9 1/4

More Spreadsheet Titles From Que

Excel 3 for Windows Quick Reference
Version 2.1
$9.95 USA
0-88022-722-2, 160 pp., 4 3/4 x 8

Quattro Pro Quick Reference
Through Version 3
$8.95 USA
0-88022-692-7, 160 pp., 4 3/4 x 8

Quattro Pro 3 QuickStart
Through Version 3
$19.95 USA
0-88022-693-5, 450 pp., 7 3/8 x 9 1/4

Excel 3 for Windows QuickStart
Version 3 for Windows
$19.95 USA
0-88022-762-1, 500 pp., 7 3/8 x 9 1/4

Using SuperCalc5, 2nd Edition
SuperCalc4 & SuperCalc5
$29.95 USA
0-88022-404-5, 575 pp., 7 3/8 x 9 1/4

To Order, Call:
(800) 428-5331 OR (317) 573-2500

Find It Fast With Que's Quick References!

Que's Quick References are the compact, easy-to-use guides to essential application information. Written for all users, Quick References include vital command information under easy-to-find alphabetical listings. Quick References are a must for anyone who needs command information fast!

1-2-3 for DOS Release 2.3 Quick Reference
Release 2.3
$9.95 USA
0-88022-725-7, 160 pp., 4 3/4 x 8

1-2-3 Release 3.1 Quick Reference
Releases 3 & 3.1
$8.95 USA
0-88022-656-0, 160 pp., 4 3/4 x 8

Allways Quick Reference
Version 1.0
$8.95 USA
0-88022-605-6, 160 pp., 4 3/4 x 8

AutoCAD Quick Reference, 2nd Edition
Releases 10 & 11
$8.95 USA
0-88022-622-6, 160 pp., 4 3/4 x 8

Batch File and Macros Quick Reference
Through DOS 5
$9.95 USA
0-88022-699-4, 160 pp., 4 3/4 x 8

CorelDRAW! Quick Reference
Through Version 2
$8.95 USA
0-88022-597-1, 160 pp., 4 3/4 x 8

dBASE IV Quick Reference
Version 1
$8.95 USA
0-88022-371-5, 160 pp., 4 3/4 x 8

Excel for Windows Quick Reference
Excel 3 for Windows
$9.95 USA
0-88022-722-2, 160 pp., 4 3/4 x 8

Fastback Quick Reference
Version 2.1
$8.95 USA
0-88022-650-1, 160 pp., 4 3/4 x 8

Hard Disk Quick Reference
Through DOS 4.01
$8.95 USA
0-88022-443-6, 160 pp., 4 3/4 x 8

Harvard Graphics Quick Reference
Version 2.3
$8.95 USA
0-88022-538-6, 160 pp., 4 3/4 x 8

Laplink Quick Reference
Laplink III
$9.95 USA
0-88022-702-8, 160 pp., 4 3/4 x 8

Microsoft Word Quick Reference
Through Version 5.5
$9.95 USA
0-88022-720-6, 160 pp., 4 3/4 x 8

Microsoft Works Quick Reference
Through IBM Version 2.0
$9.95 USA
0-88022-694-3, 160 pp., 4 3/4 x 8

MS-DOS 5 Quick Reference
Version 5
$9.95 USA
0-88022-646-3, 160 pp., 4 3/4 x 8

MS-DOS Quick Reference
Through Version 3.3
$8.95 USA
0-88022-369-3, 160 pp., 4 3/4 x 8

Norton Utilities Quick Reference
Norton Utilities 5 & Norton Commander 3
$8.95 USA
0-88022-508-4, 160 pp., 4 3/4 x 8

PC Tools 7 Quick Reference
Through Version 7
$9.95 USA
0-88022-829-6, 160 pp., 4 3/4 x 8

Q&A 4 Quick Reference
Versions 2, 3, & 4
$9.95 USA
0-88022-828-8, 160 pp., 4 3/4 x 8

Quattro Pro Quick Reference
Through Version 3
$8.95 USA
0-88022-692-7, 160 pp., 4 3/4 x 8

Quicken Quick Reference
IBM Through Version 4
$8.95 USA
0-88022-598-X, 160 pp., 4 3/4 x 8

UNIX Programmer's Quick Reference
AT&T System V, Release 3
$8.95 USA
0-88022-535-1, 160 pp., 4 3/4 x 8

UNIX Shell Commands Quick Reference
AT&T System V, Releases 3 & 4
$8.95 USA
0-88022-572-6, 160 pp., 4 3/4 x 8

Windows 3 Quick Reference
Version 3
$8.95 USA
0-88022-631-5, 160 pp., 4 3/4 x 8

WordPerfect 5.1 Quick Reference
WordPerfect 5.1
$8.95 USA
0-88022-576-9, 160 pp., 4 3/4 x 8

WordPerfect Quick Reference
WordPerfect 5
$8.95 USA
0-88022-370-7, 160 pp., 4 3/4 x 8

To Order, Call:
(800) 428-5331 OR (317) 573-2500

Teach Yourself
With QuickStarts From Que!

The ideal tutorials for beginners, Que's QuickStart books use graphic illustrations and step-by-step instructions to get you up and running fast. Packed with examples, QuickStarts are the perfect beginner's guides to your favorite software applications.

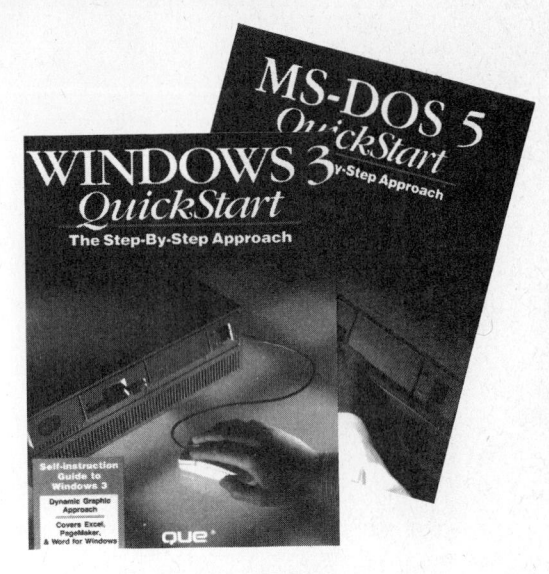

1-2-3 for DOS Release 2.3 QuickStart
Release 2.3
$19.95 USA
0-88022-716-8, 500 pp., 7 3/8 x 9 1/4

1-2-3 for Windows QuickStart
1-2-3 for Windows
$19.95 USA
0-88022-723-0, 500 pp., 7 3/8 x 9 1/4

1-2-3 Release 3.1 + QuickStart, 2nd Edition
Releases 3 & 3.1
$19.95 USA
0-88022-613-7, 569 pp., 7 3/8 x 9 1/4

dBASE IV 1.1 QuickStart,
Through Version 1.1
$19.95 USA
0-88022-614-5, 400 pp., 7 3/8 x 9 1/4

Excel 3 for Windows QuickStart
Version 3 fo rWindows
$19.95 USA
0-88022-762-1, 500 pp., 7 3/8 x 9 1/4

MS-DOS QuickStart, 2nd Edition
Version 3.X & 4.X
$19.95 USA
0-88022-611-0, 420 pp., 7 3/8 x 9 1/4

Q&A 4 QuickStart
Versions 3 & 4
$19.95 USA
0-88022-653-6, 400 pp., 7 3/8 x 9 1/4

Quattro Pro 3 QuickStart
Through Version 3.0
$19.95 USA
0-88022-693-5, 450 pp., 7 3/8 x 9 1/4

WordPerfect 5.1 QuickStart
WordPerfect 5.1
$19.95 USA
0-88022-558-0, 427 pp., 7 3/8 x 9 1/4

Windows 3 QuickStart
Ron Person & Karen Rose

This graphics-based text teaches Windows beginners how to use the feature-packed Windows environment. Emphasizes such software applications as Excel, Word, and PageMaker and shows how to master Windows' mouse, menus, and screen elements.

Version 3
$19.95 USA
0-88022-610-2, 440 pp., 7 3/8 x 9 1/4

MS-DOS 5 QuickStart
Que Development Group

This is the easy-to-use graphic approach to learning MS-DOS 5. The combination of step-by-step instruction, examples, and graphics make this book ideal for all DOS beginners.

DOS 5
$19.95 USA
0-88022-681-1, 420 pp., 7 3/8 x 9 1/4

To Order, Call:
(800) 428-5331 OR (317) 573-2500

Complete Computer Coverage From A To Z!

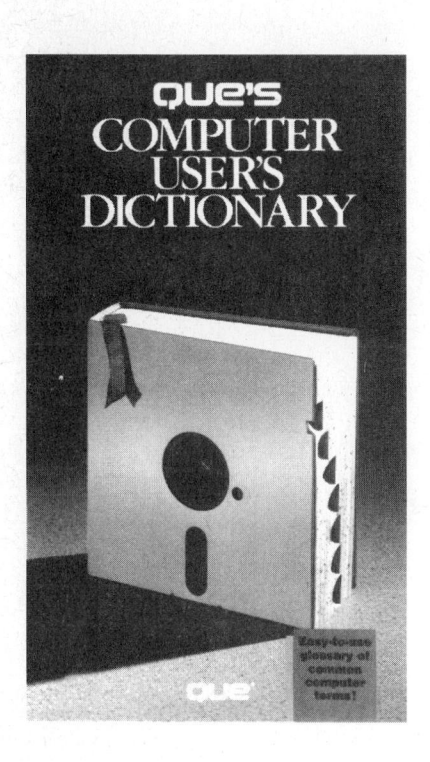

Que's Computer User's Dictionary, 2nd Edition

Que Development Group

This compact, practical reference contains hundreds of definitions, explanations, examples, and illustrations on topics from programming to desktop publishing. You can master the "language" of computers and learn how to make your personal computers more efficient and more powerful. Filled with tips and cautions, *Que's Computer User's Dictionary* is the perfect resource for anyone who uses a computer.

IBM, Macintosh, Apple, & Programming

$10.95 USA

0-88022-697-8, 550 pp., 4 3/4 x 8

The Ultimate Glossary Of Computer Terms— Over 200,000 In Print!

"Dictionary indeed. This whammer is a mini-encyclopedia...an absolute joy to use...a must for your computer library...."

Southwest Computer & Business Equipment Review

**To Order, Call:
(800) 428-5331 OR (317) 573-2500**

Learning is Easy with Easy Books from Que!

Easy WordPerfect
Shelley O'Hara

The ideal coverage of WordPerfect for beginners! 4-color illustrations and text as well as before-and-after screen shots illustrate each task. The book also includes a command summary and a glossary.

Version 5.1
$19.95 USA
0-88022-797-4, 200 pp., 8 x 10

Que's Easy Series offers a revolutionary concept in computer training. The friendly, 4-color interior, easy format, and simple explaniations guarantee success for even the most intimidated computer user!

Easy Lotus 1-2-3
Shelley O'Hara

Releases 2.01 & 2.2
$19.95 USA
0-88022-799-0, 200 pp., 8 x 10

Easy Quattro Pro
Shelley O'Hara

Versions 3.X, 4.X, & 5
$19.95 USA
0-88022-798-2, 200 pp., 8 x 10

Easy Windows
Shelley O'Hara

Versions 3 & 4
$19.95 USA
0-88022-800-8, 200 pp., 8 x 10

To Order, Call: (800) 428-5331 OR (317) 573-2500

Free Catalog!

Mail us this registration form today, and we'll send you a free catalog featuring Que's complete line of best-selling books.

Name of Book _____

Name _____

Title _____

Phone ( ) _____

Company _____

Address _____

City _____

State _____ ZIP _____

Please check the appropriate answers:

1. Where did you buy your Que book?
   - [ ] Bookstore (name: _____)
   - [ ] Computer store (name: _____)
   - [ ] Catalog (name: _____)
   - [ ] Direct from Que
   - [ ] Other: _____

2. How many computer books do you buy a year?
   - [ ] 1 or less
   - [ ] 2-5
   - [ ] 6-10
   - [ ] More than 10

3. How many Que books do you own?
   - [ ] 1
   - [ ] 2-5
   - [ ] 6-10
   - [ ] More than 10

4. How long have you been using this software?
   - [ ] Less than 6 months
   - [ ] 6 months to 1 year
   - [ ] 1-3 years
   - [ ] More than 3 years

5. What influenced your purchase of this Que book?
   - [ ] Personal recommendation
   - [ ] Advertisement
   - [ ] In-store display
   - [ ] Price
   - [ ] Que catalog
   - [ ] Que mailing
   - [ ] Que's reputation
   - [ ] Other: _____

6. How would you rate the overall content of the book?
   - [ ] Very good
   - [ ] Good
   - [ ] Satisfactory
   - [ ] Poor

7. What do you like *best* about this Que book?
   _____
   _____

8. What do you like *least* about this Que book?
   _____
   _____

9. Did you buy this book with your personal funds?
   - [ ] Yes   [ ] No

10. Please feel free to list any other comments you may have about this Que book.
    _____
    _____

Order Your Que Books Today!

Name _____

Title _____

Company _____

City _____

State _____ ZIP _____

Phone No. ( ) _____

Method of Payment:

Check [ ]   (Please enclose in envelope.)

Charge My: VISA [ ]   MasterCard [ ]

American Express [ ]

Charge # _____

Expiration Date _____

Order No.	Title	Qty.	Price	Total

You can **FAX** your order to **1-317-573-2583**. Or call **1-800-428-5331, ext. ORDR** to order direct.
Please add $2.50 per title for shipping and handling.

Subtotal _____

Shipping & Handling _____

Total _____

NO POSTAGE
NECESSARY
IF MAILED
IN THE
UNITED STATES

BUSINESS REPLY MAIL
First Class Permit No. 9918   Indianapolis, IN

Postage will be paid by addressee

que®

11711 N. College
Carmel, IN 46032

NO POSTAGE
NECESSARY
IF MAILED
IN THE
UNITED STATES

BUSINESS REPLY MAIL
First Class Permit No. 9918   Indianapolis, IN

Postage will be paid by addressee

que®

11711 N. College
Carmel, IN 46032

Quattro Pro Cursor-Movement Keys

Key	Function
←	Moves the cell selector one cell to the left
→	Moves the cell selector one cell to the right
↑	Moves the cell selector up one cell
↓	Moves the cell selector down one cell
Ctrl-←	Moves the cell selector one screen to the left
Ctrl-→	Moves the cell selector one screen to the right
End-↑	Moves the cell selector up to the next nonblank cell beneath an empty cell if the current cell contains an entry
End-↓	Moves the cell selector down to the next nonblank cell above an empty cell if the current cell contains an entry
End-→	Moves the cell selector right to the next nonblank cell followed by an empty cell if the current cell contains an entry
End-←	Moves the cell selector left to the next nonblank cell preceded by an empty cell if the current cell contains an entry.

TIP: When you type data into a cell and press Enter to record the data, the cell selector remains in the current cell. To move to another cell, press any cursor-movement key except Enter, and Quattro Pro moves to the next cell in that direction. If you type data into cell A5 and then press the down-arrow key, for example, Quattro Pro enters the data into cell A5 and makes A6 the active cell.

NOTE: If you want to use the cursor-movement keys, the Num Lock key must be toggled off. To dedicate the numeric keypad to numeric entries only, the Num Lock key must be on unless you have an extended keyboard.

Using Quattro Pro 4
Special Edition

Using Quattro Pro 4
Special Edition

Quattro Pro Function-Key Assignments

Key	Function
F1 (Help)	Invokes a help window from anywhere on the spreadsheet or during any spreadsheet operation
F2 (Edit)	Enters EDIT mode so that you can make changes to the contents of a cell
Shift-F2 (Debug)	Enters the DEBUG mode so that you can execute a macro one command at a time
Alt-F2 (Macro Menu)	Displays the Macro menu
F3 (Choices)	Displays a list of block name choices when Quattro Pro prompts you for a block of cells or moves you to the Property sheet in the Annotator
Shift-F3 (Macro List)	Displays a list of the macro commands for a spreadsheet
Alt-F3 (Functions)	Displays a list of the @function commands for a spreadsheet
F4 (Absolute)	Toggles through the four available cell reference formats; changes the format of the cell address to the left of the cursor on the input line
F5 (GoTo)	Moves the cell selector to a specified cell address
Shift-F5 (Pick Window)	Displays a list of the open windows
Alt-F5 (Undo)	Undoes spreadsheet cell operations such as erasures, edits, deletions, and file retrievals
F6 (Pane)	Moves the cell selector between the active and inactive window panes in a split spreadsheet window
Shift-F6 (Next Window)	Displays the next open window
Alt-F6 (Zoom)	Enlarges the active window so that it fills one full screen; when window is fully enlarged, shrinks the window back to its original size (in text mode)

Key	Function
F7 (Query)	Repeats the preceding Query command; selects a group of objects in the Annotator for Proportional Resize mode
Shift-F7 (Select)	Enters EXT mode, which enables you to select a block of cells by pressing the arrow keys; in the File Manager, marks the highlighted name in a list
Alt-F7 (All Select)	Selects and deselects active files in the active File Manager list
F8 (Table)	Repeats the last what-if command
Shift-F8 (Move)	Removes files marked in the active File Manager list and stores them in temporary memory, enabling you to paste them in a new location
F9 (Calc)	Calculates formulas on the active spreadsheet in READY mode; in VALUE or EDIT mode, converts the formula appearing in the input line to the end result; in graphics display mode, reprints the screen
Shift-F9 (Copy)	Copies files marked in the active File Manager list into temporary memory so that you can paste them to a new location
F10 (Graph)	Displays the current graph of selected data appearing on the current active spreadsheet; press Esc to return to the active spreadsheet
Shift-F10 (Paste)	Pastes files stored in temporary memory into the current directory displayed in the active File Manager file list
Ctrl-F10	Switches from Paradox to Quattro Pro while in Paradox Access